EDITION
3

⌈ w

Management

Principles and P~~ractices~~
for Tomorrow's Leaders

GARY DESSLER

Florida International University

PEARSON
Prentice
Hall

Pearson Educational International

Senior Acquisitions Editor: Jennifer Simon
Editor-in-Chief: Jeff Shelstad
Managing Editor (Editorial): Jessica Sabloff
Editorial Assistant: Kelly Wendrychowicz
Senior Developmental Editor: Jeannine Ciliotta
Media Project Manager: Michele Faranda
Executive Marketing Manager: Shannon Moore
Marketing Assistant: Christine Genneken
Managing Editor (Production): Judy Leale
Production Editor: Cindy Spreder
Production Assistant: Joe DeProspero
Permissions Supervisor: Suzanne Grappi
Manufacturing Buyer: Diane Peirano
Design Manager: Maria Lange
Art Director: Janet Slowik
Interior Design: Wanda España/Wee Design Group
Cover Design: Janet Slowik
Cover Illustration/Photo: PhotoDisc
Illustrator (Interior): Matrix Art Services
Photo Researcher: Melinda Alexander
Image Permission Coordinator: Carolyn Gaunt
Manager, Print Production: Christy Mahon
Composition: UG/GGS Information Services
Full-Service Project Management: Heidi Allgair-UG/GGS Information Services
Printer/Binder: RR Donnelley/Willard

Pearson Education LTD.
Pearson Education Australia PTY, Limited
Pearson Education Singapore, Pte. Ltd
Pearson Education North Asia Ltd
Pearson Education, Canada, Ltd
Pearson Educación de Mexico, S.A. de C.V.
Pearson Education–Japan
Pearson Education Malaysia, Pte. Ltd
Pearson Education, Upper Saddle River, New Jersey

10 9 8 7 6 5 4 3 2 1
ISBN 0-13-120972-8

To the Management, 3 *team:*
Jeff, Jeannine, Judy, Jennifer, Cindy,
Janet, Shannon, Jessica, and Melissa.

BRIEF CONTENTS

CONTENTS

ABOUT THE AUTHOR

GARY DESSLER (Ph.D., business administration, Bernard Baruch School of Business) is Professor of Business at Florida International University. In addition to *Management: Principles and Practices for Tomorrow's Leaders*, he is the author of a number of other books including, most recently, *Human Resource Management*, 9th edition (Prentice Hall), *Framework for Human Resource Management* (Prentice Hall), and *Winning Commitment: How to Build and Keep a Competitive Workforce*. His books have been translated into Chinese, Russian, Indonesian, French, Malaysian, Lithuanian, Spanish, and Portuguese, and are being used by students and managers all over the world. He has written numerous articles on employee commitment, organizational behavior, leadership, and quality improvement, has consulted for businesses in the U.S. and abroad, and for ten years wrote the syndicated "Job Talk" column for the *Miami Herald*.

PREFACE

"This book is more than words. It's more than just a way to get new facts and information. It's a window into the world of what managers actually do, and a place to start learning new management practices."

You can't master something just by reading about it, you've got to do it. That's why I emphasize the practical and applied nature of business management in my books. Things today are moving too fast and are too competitive for new managers to spend months on the job figuring out how to transfer what they learned in a book to the real world. As managers, they have to hit the ground running. They have to make decisions, write plans, reorganize employees, lead teams, and keep things under control from day one.

That is why carefully studying this book is so important. This edition cuts through the fads and jargon. That is why this edition takes you back to basics. It provides you with the basic management principles and practices you'll need to succeed as a manager, and to succeed, not just today but tomorrow.

Gary Dessler

■■■ HOW DOES GARY DO THIS?

He accomplishes this in three basic ways. First, this management text is like no other, in that it integrates management principles with management applications and techniques. Every chapter contains practical applications, models, checklists and forms that all managers can use every day.

Second, he's included a *Manager's Portfolio*, a special section containing a wealth of realistic exercises to reinforce concepts learned in the chapters. Once you learn the concepts, it's important to practice applying them in real management situations, so he created a series of video-driven scenarios that allow students to practice their new management skills. Students can view the specially designed video clips on the accompaning CD-ROM and act as a consultant to solve the company's problem.

Third, he's filled every page (and just about every paragraph) with *illustrative, real-life examples* of how managers are actually using the concepts and ideas on that page—how they're putting them into practice. Readers will never have to stop and say, "What does he mean by that?" or "How could I use that in practice?" Instead, he shows you how to apply it, each step of the way.

Management: Principles and Practices for Tomorrow's Leaders provides students in basic Management/ Organization courses with a complete and highly applied review of essential management concepts and techniques in a very readable and understandable form. The book blends traditional management process coverage with a practical and applied management skills emphasis that is totally unique in management textbooks today.

In addition to the new and distinctive applied-skills theme, there are other significant changes in this third edition.

- Unlike most books, *Management, 3e* gets you into the core course material right away. By moving the managment principles chapters forward, students focus on the fundamentals.

- Entreprenuership is a key topic: Every manager is an entreprenuer. Strategically placed to follow the priniciples chapters, this new chapter will teach students how entreprenuers really use managment principles and practices to manage their companies.

- Consolidation of operations management appendices into a new managing World Class Operations chapter.

■■■ KEY PEDAGOGICAL FEATURES OF THE THIRD EDITION

New Management Challenge   Every chapter begins with a description of a management dilemma at a well-known company. Within the chapter, readers learn how the management principles introduced in the chapter were used to resolve this management challenge.

New Checklists Ranging from self-assessments to management guidelines, this new feature provides quick reference to the fundamental principles and practices successful managers possess. These include:

- How to develop a business plan
- How to be a better listener
- How to rate the adequacy of an organization structure
- How to conduct a new business feasibility study
- and much more

CHECKLIST 4.1 ■ How to Develop a Plan

☑ *Set an objective.* "Where do we want to end up at the end of the planning period?" Do we want to own a successful consulting firm by 2005? Cut costs next year by $3 billion? Making this decision—setting these goals—means the manager must address the right problem ("is cutting costs the problem?"). Always ask, "Are we *sure* we've defined the problem correctly?"

☑ *Develop forecasts and planning premises.* This situation analysis provides the information you need to decide how you're going to get from where you are now to where you want to be (and may even help you fine-tune your objectives).

☑ *Determine your options.* Every plan consists of a goal and a course of action for getting there. For any goal, there are usually several options or alternative courses of action for getting there. DaimlerChrysler could save that $3 billion in many ways. It could sell Chrysler, for instance, cut costs across the board, or just cut costs at Chrysler or just at Daimler. Use your creativity and decision-making skills to produce several options.

☑ *Evaluate alternatives.* A plan is a decision you make today for how you're going to do something tomorrow. Therefore, apply all your decision-making skills to evaluating your options. Think through the consequences of each possible course of action.

☑ *Choose your plan, and start to implement it.* Remember, in making this decision: Increase your knowledge, use your intuition, weigh the pros and cons, don't overstress the decision's finality, and make sure the timing is right.

☑ *Go to level 2.* As at Sunbeam, plans tend to be multilayered. For your career plan, setting an overall goal—for instance, start your own consulting firm—is just the beginning. You'll also need supporting plans. These will include your program of studies, your plans for summer internships, your job search plans for that first consulting job, and a budget.

New Management in Action Feature 70+ Management in Action features are included, giving students a birds-eye view into well-known companies and the management challenges key managers have faced.

New Global Manager Feature Similar to Management in Action, the Global Manager focuses on well-known international or multi-national companies.

■ *The Global Manager: Wal-Mart* Deciding how much authority each manager in the chain of command should have is especially tricky when managing a global business. Trying to tell someone 10,000 miles away how to run his or her store can mean ordering that person to do something—like selling the wrong products—that his or her customers don't like. Thus, when Wal-Mart first expanded abroad, it reportedly tried to simply transplant its way of doing business. Some of Wal-Mart's German managers objected to being told how to do things by Wal-Mart "mentors" who couldn't even speak German.[2] Today, Wal-Mart's new head of international operations is working hard to make sure that Wal-Mart's local managers abroad have the authority they need to make decisions that make sense for their stores.

New Managing Without Boundaries This new feature provides vivid examples of how managers use technology to strip away the boundaries between themselves and their customers, vendors, and the company's internal activities.

Webnotes This well-received feature reappears in the new edition. Webnotes provide students with illustrated sources for related information on important topics.

MANAGING WITHOUT BOUNDARIES

Planning and the Boundaryless Supply Chain

Wal-Mart needs to know how many size 30 Levi's jeans it needs to order for each of its stores, Dell needs to know how many laptops to produce next week, and Prentice Hall needs to know whether to reprint this book for the fall. Anticipating and forecasting supply and production requirements is a big part of the manager's job. Traditionally, managers use qualitative and quantitative sales forecasting tools like those above to make these decisions. For example, Prentice Hall might use sales reps' estimates of probable sales to help predict fall semester demand for a book, Coors Beer uses a new Internet-based forecasting tool to estimate future sales. The idea is to ensure that the company

Internet-based Systems Other firms use the Internet to improve their forecasts by expediting the collection of sales estimates. For example, Coors Brewing Company's distributors can use the firm's new **CoorsNet.com** to place orders, and to help analyze the impact of advertising and other promotional activities. Because it takes about four weeks from wholesaler forecast to the shipment of product from the brewery, one supply chain consultant says, "Forecasting demand is a huge problem for these folks. So many times, they are reacting instead of planning ahead. What happens is that they make distributors order too far in advance, and they aren't ready to quantify how much they need to order."[39]

Coors expects its new its new Internet-based system to improve performance. Coors will be able to receive real-time orders. Its distributors should be able to predict more accurately how advertising campaigns and other promotional events will affect sales. Wal-Mart also uses sophisticated technology to forecast sales; the "Managing @ the Speed of Thought" feature provides an example.

exactly the PC you want, and then you click "go." That information then speeds via the Internet to all the participants in Dell's supply chain. Dell's suppliers (including the firm that makes the computer display you ordered) instantaneously know when and to whom to ship their products. Dell production sees instantaneously what PC to assemble for you and when. UPS sees when to pick up your PC and where it goes. And you can actually monitor your PC's progress on Dell's order processing Web site.

With a system like this, Wal-Mart would not need to keep large quantities of Levi's jeans in the store or local warehouse: Levi's would know, on a real-time basis, how many size 30 jeans ... needed in each ... laptops: It would ... orders were com... order. Think of how ... in fact, do) save by ... ostly inventories. ... ted demand means ... ry simply ties up ... ems "just-in-time" ... ished when they're

... chain systems inte... components of the ... manufacturer, and ... l-Mart, and Dell do ... orecasts. They can ... s based on actual

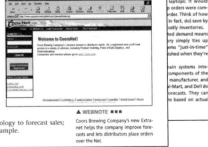

▲ **WEBNOTE** ■ ■ ■
Coors Brewing Company's new Extranet helps the company improve forecasts and lets distributors place orders over the Net.

MANAGING @ THE SPEED OF THOUGHT

Demand Forecasting at Wal-Mart

When it comes to retailing, Wal-Mart is larger than its three closest competitors combined, and that's not just because it buys its merchandise inexpensively. Wal-Mart has what is probably the most sophisticated information technology system in all of retailing, and it uses that system's power to give its customers what they want, while squeezing every bit of extra cost from its operation.

Wal-Mart's data warehouse is a good example of how the company does this. The data warehouse collects information on things like sales, inventory, products in transit, and product returns from Wal-Mart's 3,000 stores. These data are then analyzed to help Wal-Mart's managers analyze trends, understand customers, and more effectively manage inventory. As one example, Wal-Mart is implementing a new demand-forecasting system. Its data warehouse tracks the sale by store of 100,000 products. This powerful system lets Wal-Mart managers examine the sales of individual items for individual stores, and it also creates seasonal profiles for each item. Armed with this information, managers can more accurately plan what items will be needed for each store and when.

Wal-Mart is also teaming with vendors like Warner-Lambert to create an Internet-based collaborative forecasting and replenishment (CFAR) system. Wal-Mart collects data (on things like sales-by-product and by-store) for Warner-Lambert products. Managers at Wal-Mart and Warner-Lambert then collaborate to develop forecasts for sales by store for Warner-Lambert products such as Listerine. Once Warner-Lambert and Wal-Mart planners decide on mutually acceptable forecast figures, a purchase plan is finalized and sent to Warner-Lambert's manufacturing planning system. So far, CFAR has helped cut the supply-cycle time for Listerine from 12 weeks to 6. That means less inventory, lower costs, and better buys for Wal-Mart customers.[40] ■■■

Managing @ the Speed of Thought This feature illustrates how managers are using the Internet to manage organizations today.

Margin Glossary Key terms appear in boldface within the text, and with their definitions in the margin. For added reinforcement, readers will also find the terms at the end of the chapter. In addition, a complete Glossary appears at the end of the book.

■■■ END OF CHAPTER FEATURES

Chapter Summaries   Each chapter contains a concise chapter summary students can use to quickly refresh their memories and get a synopsis of what they've read in that chapter.

Skills and Study Materials

Experiential Exercises   Individual and team exercises provide an opportunity for students to reinforce their understanding of the principles and practices introduced in the chapter. Using exercises (written for this edition by Gary Dessler) students get an opportunity to apply what they learned in the chapter.

Case Studies   These short cases provide students an opportunity to apply the principles learned in the chapter to a common management situation.

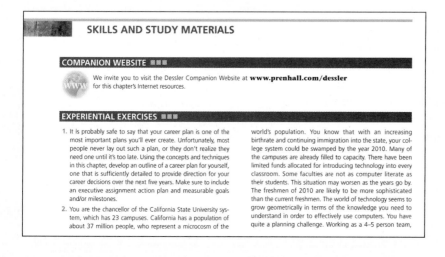

SKILLS AND STUDY MATERIALS

COMPANION WEBSITE ■■■

We invite you to visit the Dessler Companion Website at **www.prenhall.com/dessler** for this chapter's Internet resources.

EXPERIENTIAL EXERCISES ■■■

1. It is probably safe to say that your career plan is one of the most important plans you'll ever create. Unfortunately, most people never lay out such a plan, or they don't realize they need one until it's too late. Using the concepts and techniques in this chapter, develop an outline of a career plan for yourself, one that is sufficiently detailed to provide direction for your career decisions over the next five years. Make sure to include an executive assignment action plan and measurable goals and/or milestones.

2. You are the chancellor of the California State University system, which has 23 campuses. California has a population of about 37 million people, who represent a microcosm of the

world's population. You know that with an increasing birthrate and continuing immigration into the state, your college system could be swamped by the year 2010. Many of the campuses are already filled to capacity. There have been limited funds allocated for introducing technology into every classroom. Some faculties are not as computer literate as their students. This situation may worsen as the years go by. The freshmen of 2010 are likely to be more sophisticated than the current freshmen. The world of technology seems to grow geometrically in terms of the knowledge you need to understand in order to effectively use computers. You have quite a planning challenge. Working as a 4–5 person team,

New "You Be the Consultant" Case Featuring JetBlue   These provide students with actual challenges facing managers at JetBlue Airways. They give students an opportunity to act as a consultant, applying what they learned in the chapters to the problem at hand.

YOU BE THE CONSULTANT ■■■

PLANNING IN THE FACE OF UNCERTAINTY

jetBlue AIRWAYS®   David Neeleman attributes much of JetBlue's initial success to the fact that he and his team stuck closely to his original concept and plan. As Neeleman says, "We're Southwest with seat assignments, leather seats, and television."[60] The foundations of his original plan called for strong financing, fleet homogeneity (so maintenance people and pilots and flight service crews could easily switch from plane to plane), high fleet utilization, attractive pricing, and experienced management.

To a large extent, things are working out according to plan. JetBlue is flying about 80% full, versus an industry average of about 68%. JetBlue is also profitable, an impressive feat given the fact that virtually all of its competitors are racking up losses.[61] While its fleet of brand new Airbus A-320 jets meant higher purchase and/or leas-

ing costs, they are also much less expensive to fly; they burn less fuel and require virtually no expenditures on heavy maintenance (since Airbus warranties them for the first few years). As Mr. Neeleman says, "The way to have low-cost is to buy brand new airplanes."[62]

However, any plan is only as good as the assumptions it's based on, and no manager is ever dealing with an entirely predictable future. On the one hand, some things have worked in JetBlue's favor. For example, right after JetBlue began flying out of JFK, LaGuardia was hit with months of record delays, making JFK a more attractive alternative. Furthermore, Neeleman's most basic assumption—that there was a huge, pent-up demand for flights from places like Fort Lauderdale to JFK on a low-cost airline with new planes and top-quality service—proved very accurate.

On the other hand, many other things were impossible to predict. No one, for instance, expected the 9/11 attacks or the decline

An Integrated Learning Package

In addition to the in-chapter learning features, the third edition includes an exciting new learning tool—the *Manager's Portfolio*—at the end of the book. To enhance your student's understanding of the key principles of management, we provide a three-tiered skills mastery program.

Learn It With these fill-in-the-blank exercises, students can check their knowledge of each chapter's concepts and management principles.

Practice It Let's go to the video! The accompanying customized CD-ROM contains 18 special video clips. These illustrate for each chapter specific management scenarios, and thus give students a chance to apply their new knowledge and skills in solving real-life managerial problems. Gary Dessler wrote special questions and exercises to guide students in addressing the issues in the scenarios. Questions and activities are provided to guide students' understanding of how using management principles would affect this company.

In-chapter self assessments and management checklists are included in the CD-ROM for additional practice.

Apply It The next "layer of learning" challenges students to view the process of management as a whole. Drawing on cases and exercises throughout the book, these special exercises challenge students to apply what they learned in an integrated, cross-functional way. For example: How did the leader's style inadvertently influence the plan his or her team came up with? And, how did JetBlue's plan influence how it decided to organize?

MANAGING GROUPS **AND TEAMS** CHAPTER 13

LEARN IT
Test Your Understanding

1. I was surprised to learn that many managers rate _____ _____ programs as their biggest productivity boosters.

2. A _____ is distinguished by the fact that its members are committed to a common purpose or set of performance goals, while a _____ is two or more persons who are interacting with one another in such a manner that each person influences and is influenced by each other person.

3. Members of our work group always "cover" for each other when someone is having a bad day, but members of Chaz's group tend to stick to more rigidly defined roles. The behavior of either group could be labeled a group _____.

4. _____ competition, such as bowling tournaments between teams, tend to boost cohesiveness, whereas _____ competition among team members tends to undermine it.

5. Our work team has a lot of influence in the activities in our own work area, such as setting our own goals and scheduling our work, but we know that Tom is still the supervisor. We are a _____ team.

6. Five of us have been assigned to the task of identifying workable alternatives for increasing productivity by 15 percent. We could be called a _____ team.

7. I wish that I were a member of Farah's team. They set their own work schedule, establish their own goals, hire and train team members, and deal with vendors on their own. They are obviously a _____ team.

Manager's PORTFOLIO

...d creative ideas and that has its ...s within broad guidelines, is a

...useful to utilize _____ ...d, they rely upon information

...ith a cocktail party at which we ...expectations for the team. I'm ...enthusiastic about our goal. All

...rs of our team are notably less ...port to on a daily basis. Yet our ...ge of team creation."

...of group decision-making by

13. One or two members of Lisa's group will inevitably try to dominate a group. Lisa has decided that in order to avoid this situation, she will appoint one person to defend the proposed group solution, and another person to argue against the proposed solution. Lisa is using the _____.

14. Our organization discovered the hard way that although social support is important, _____ _____ such as timely information, resources, and rewards that encourage group, rather than individual, performance are more important in ensuring cohesiveness.

15. Perhaps the most important determinant in producing cohesive and effective teams isn't demographic similarity, but creating teams whose members share _____ _____.

MP 31

PRACTICE IT
Video for Managing Groups and Teams

CanGo is preparing for an IPO. If the IPO is successful, CanGo will have the funds it needs to expand. Before an IPO can happen, it is important that potential investors have a good understanding of what CanGo does and why it will be successful as a publicly owned company. The video revolves around an early stage in the process of taking CanGo public. It involves developing a presentation which makes the case that CanGo is ready for an IPO. Management needs to provide detailed information about all aspects of the business. This is a huge and immensely important task, because if the presentation fails, so may CanGo's IPO. It is not a project for just one person. The task is too big, the timing is too tight, and it requires integrating different areas of expertise. It calls for the work of a cohesive team. The video is focused on the formation of a work team to develop CanGo's presentation. As you watch, pay close attention to how the team is formed and to the directions and guidance the team gets.

Watch the video, and answer the following questions:

1. Based on what you learned in Chapter 13, analyze this team situation and discuss at least eight reasons why the team does or does not have the necessary building blocks to function effectively.

2. List at least six specific reasons why the team is not performing effectively.

3. List and discuss at least five reasons why you believe Nick (as usual, the funny man at CanGo) is or is not a team player.

4. Use the two checklists in Chapter 13, How To Build a Productive Team and How To Improve a Team's Performance, to suggest how you would improve the CanGo team's performance.

APPLY IT

As is often the case, few decisions that managers have to make involve a single function. The manager's actions in this video, for example, seem to reflect widespread inadequacies in how she plans, organizes, and gives orders. Pinpoint at least 4 non-teamwork-related managerial principles or practices she seems to be failing to apply effectively.

MP 32

◼◼◼ *MANAGEMENT: PRINCIPLES AND PRACTICES FOR TOMORROW'S LEADERS, 3E* SUPPLEMENTS

Instructor's Resource Manual   In the new edition of the Instructor's Resource Manual, instructors will find chapter summaries, learning objectives, lecture outlines with space for instructors' notes, answers and suggestions for all in-chapter elements, answers to all end-of-chapter materials, as well as video guide material for the BusinessNOW segments. Also includes instructor's materials for the *Manager's Portfolio*.

Test Item File   Over 100 questions per chapter including multiple choice, true/false, short answer, and essays. Every question includes a page reference that ties the question to the text and level of difficulty (easy, moderate, or challenging).

PowerPoint Presentation   Included on the Instructor's Resource CD-ROM, and available for faculty download on the Companion Website, this comprehensive set of PowerPoints contains over 500 color slides. The presentation contains lecture content, as well as all of the tables and figures found in the text.

Instructor's Resource CD-ROM   On a single CD, professors can find the Instructor's Manual, PowerPoint presentation, and the Win/PH Test Manager. Containing all of the questions in the printed Test Item File, Test Manager is a comprehensive suite of tools for testing and assessment and allows educators to easily create and distribute tests for their courses.

 **BusinessNOW Video Series**   Brand new to this edition, Prentice Hall is pleased to offer exciting BusinessNOW video cases. BusinessNOW is a fast-paced television news magazine that takes viewers on location and behind closed doors to look at America's most interesting companies and the corporate executives who run them. These videos offer interesting up-to-date content pertaining to the topics raised in *Management: Principles and Practices for Tomorrow's Leaders*, 3e.

Management Skills Video   Video segments offer dramatizations that highlight various management skills. They allow students to see what it's like to conduct an interview, make management decisions, and more. The videos provide excellent starting points for classroom discussion and debate.

MyCW Companion Website   The format of our website has been updated, and includes the same great features in a more user-friendly format. Here you will find password-protected instructor's resources, as well as a student section, which features true/false, multiple-choice, and Internet essay questions. The website for Dessler's *Management: Principles and Practices for Tomorrow's Leaders*, 3e can be found at **www.prenhall.com/dessler**.

WebCT, Blackboard, and Course Compass Online Courses   This edition offers a fully developed online course for management.

ACKNOWLEDGMENTS

This book is, like all others, a team effort, and I especially want to emphasize that fact. I have been very fortunate to have had the benefit of truly insightful reviewer comments and suggestions. I particularly want to thank the 19 reviewers who made suggestions for this third edition, and without whose help the book would not have its theme or current form. They are:

John Bigelow	Boise State University
Richard Chruchman	Belmont University
Dan Cochran	Mississippi State University
Ron England	The Medical College of Ohio
Bernard Erven	Ohio State University
Ernest Friday	Florida International University
David Gerth	Nashville State Tech
David Glew	University of Tulsa
Richard Hodgetts	Florida International University
Jim Hoffman	Texas Tech University
Avis Johnson	University of Akron
Laynie Pizzolatto	Nicholls State
Oswald Richards	Lincoln University
Dan Sherman	University of Alabama
Randi Sims	Nova Southeastern University
Richard M. Steers	University of Oregon
Thomas Tang	Middle Tennessee State University
Les Vermillion	Florida International University
Harry Waters, Jr.	California State University-Hayward
Phyllis Webster	Metropolitan State University

Their suggestions and insights helped me build on those from the reviewers of the first and second editions, including:

Second edition:
Ron Beaulieu,	Central Michigan University
Peggy Brewer	Eastern Kentucky University
Mason Carpenter	University of Wisconsin-Madison
Roger Dunbar	New York University
Earnest Friday	Florida International University
Richard Hodgetts	Florida International University
David J. Lemak	Washington State University at Tri-Cities
Bill Price	Howard Payne University
Annette Ranft	West Virginia University
Jeff Tschetter	University of Sioux Falls

First edition:
Clarence Anderson	Walla Walla College
James Bell	Southwest Texas State University
Aleta Best	Texas A&M University
Barbara Boyington	Brookdale Community College
Monica Briedenbach	DeVry Institute of Technology
James H. Browne	University of Southern Colorado
Dr. John Carmichael	Union County College
Bonnie Chavez	Santa Barbara City College
R. J. Dick	Missouri Western State

Paul Fadil	Valdosta State University
Janice Feldbauer	Austin Community College
Kevin McCarthy	Baker University
Mike Peng	University of Hawaii
Preston Probasco	San Jose State University
Rajib Sanyal	The College of New Jersey
Tim Weaver	SVP Corporate Banking

I am also grateful for the wisdom, efforts, and creativity of the Prentice Hall team for *Management*, 3rd edition. Development Editor Jeannine Ciliotta made hundreds of organizational and content recommendations for the book, and to the extent that this edition improves on the last, she deserves much of the credit. Editor-in-Chief Jeff Shelstad coordinated the team's effort and provided decisive direction, along with Management Editor Jennifer Simon, who joined the team to manage the project's successful completion and introduction to the market. Melisssa Steffens, the second edition's management editor, also helped give this edition its new direction. Managing Editor Jessica Sabloff did a superb job of coordinating the reviews and the supplements package; she also helped in countless ways to keep the project moving.

I'm grateful as always to Managing Editor Judy Leale for working tirelessly to keep this project on track, to Production Editor Cindy Spreder for managing its production, and to Art Director Janet Slowik for creating such a beautiful book. The book's evolution and marketing effort benefited greatly from Marketing Manager Shannon Moore's market knowledge, creativity, and hard work. Media Project Manager Michele Faranda produced the innovative media supplement.

I am again deeply grateful to all the professionals in the Prentice Hall sales force, who have enthusiastically promoted the previous editions of this and my other books. The success of this new edition of *Management: Principles and Practices for Tomorrow's Leaders* now rests in their capable hands, and I thank them for their efforts.

At Florida International University I appreciate the support I received on this book from all of my colleagues, including Earnest Friday, Herman Dorsett, Donald Roomes, Ronnie Silverblatt, Randall Martin, Jack Kleban, Kent Hippolyte, Jim Musarra and of course Ruth Chapman and Sarah Latham.

This edition's all new continuing cases feature JetBlue Airways, which could not have happened without the enthusiastic response and assistance I received from members of the JetBlue management team. I especially want to thank Gareth Edmondson-Jones, Holly Nelson, and Vincent Stabile for taking the time to tell me about JetBlue. After speaking with them and reading dozens of articles and filings about their company, it's easy to see why so many airlines today seem to be trying to imitate JetBlue's way of doing things.

Closer to home, I again want to acknowledge the support of my wife, Claudia, and her willingness to tolerate my disappearance for more evenings and weekends than I should have been gone while working on this book. However, when all the acknowledgments are said and done, if there can be a single inspiration for a book entitled *Management: Principles and Practices for Tomorrow's Leaders* it is again my son Derek, for whom I wrote this book in as practical and useful a way as I could, and whose unswerving support was the only motivation I needed.

Gary Dessler

The Environment and Foundations of Modern Management

THE MANAGEMENT CHALLENGE

Andrea Jung Takes over at Avon

Avon products was in trouble.[1] Fewer people were signing on as Avon sales reps. It was taking the firm's research and development department 3 years to develop new products. The market was changing: People wanted products that not only made them look good, but also resulted in healthier skin. But while firms like L'Oréal and Estée Lauder spent 1.3 to 3% of their sales on research and development (R&D), Avon spent less than 1%. The whole "back end" operation—buying from suppliers, taking orders, and distributing products to local sales reps—lacked automation. Sales reps still took orders by hand. One-third of the orders the firm shipped then went out wrong. Sales rep motivation was down. Few people ordered online. While competitors could sell through department stores and pharmacies, Avon stuck doggedly to its local sales rep network. The stock market was up, but Avon stock had sagged. It seemed apparent that the situation begged for new, decisive management. The company's board of directors knew it had to do something. What it did was appoint Andrea Jung as CEO. The question now was this: What should she do to turn the company around?

CHAPTER OBJECTIVES

After studying this chapter and the case exercises at the end, you should be able to:

1. List the specific management tasks facing the person in charge.

2. Identify the manager, and explain how that person's job differs from that of others.

3. Answer the question, "Do I have what it takes to be a manager?"

4. List and describe five things a manager can learn from the evolution of management thought.

5. Explain what environmental forces are influencing the manager's business.

6. List the reasons why a manager should use a particular management approach.

As we'll see in this chapter, Andrea Jung did a tremendous job of reviving Avon. She succeeded because she was an effective manager. The purpose of this book is to make you a more effective manager. The main purpose of this first chapter is to explain what managers do and to provide you with some of the basic vocabulary of management. The topics we'll address include what managers do, and the environment and foundations of modern management.

■■■ WHAT MANAGERS DO

Managers can have the most remarkable effects on organizations. IBM floundered through much of the 1980s and early 1990s, losing market share, seeing costs rise, and watching its stock price dwindle from almost $180 per share to barely $50. Within three years, new CEO Louis Gerstner had turned the company around. He revamped the company's product line, dramatically lowered costs, changed the company's culture, and oversaw a quadrupling of IBM's stock price.[2] Dell CEO Michael Dell created a $12 billion company in just 13 years. He did it by installing one of the world's most sophisticated direct-sales operations, eliminating resellers' markups and the need for large inventories, and keeping a viselike grip on costs.[3] Within a year of taking over as CEO, Andrea Jung had raised Avon's sales by tens of millions of dollars—and boosted profitability by improving operations and cutting costs.

And "manager" effects like these don't happen at just giant corporations. Right now, as you read these words, managers at thousands of small businesses—diners, dry cleaners, motels—are running their businesses well, with courteous, prompt, first-class service, high-morale employees, and a minimum of problems like "My dinner's cold," or "You didn't press my pants." What do you think would happen if you took the competent managers out of those businesses and dropped in managers without training or skills? You know the answer because you've probably experienced the effects yourself—untrained or unprepared staff, orders not prepared on time, lost reservations, dirty rooms. About 90% of the new businesses started this year will fail within five years, and Dun & Bradstreet says the reason is usually poor management. Management is as—or more—important for the tiny start-up as it is for the giant firm.

The effect of good management is nothing short of amazing. Take an under-performing—even chaotic—organization and install a skilled manager, and he or she can soon get the enterprise humming. Take a successful enterprise that's been managed well for years—say, a neighborhood stationery store—and watch as a new, less-competent manager takes over. Shelves are suddenly in disarray, products out of stock, bills unpaid. One study of 40 manufacturing firms concluded that effective management was more important than factors like market share, firm size, industry average rate of return, or degree of automation.[4] Another study concluded that organizations with better managers had lower turnover rates, and higher profits and sales per employees.[5]

Organization Defined

organization ■ *a group of people with formally assigned roles who work together to achieve the stated goals of the group.*

All these enterprises—IBM, Dell, the diner, the dry cleaner, and the stationery store—are organizations. An organization consists of people with formally assigned roles who work together to achieve stated goals. All organizations have several things in common.

First, organizations are never (or shouldn't be) aimless. Thirty strangers on a bus from New York to Maine are not an organization, since they're not working together to accomplish some singular aim. Second, organizations needn't just be business firms; the definition applies equally well to colleges, local governments, and nonprofits like the American Red Cross. The U.S. government is an organization—certainly a not-for-profit one—and its head manager, or chief executive officer, is the president.

Organizations are also (hopefully) "organized": Even your dry cleaner has an *organizational structure*. People know who does what (pressers press, for instance and cleaners clean) and how the work (in this case, the incoming clothes) will flow through the store and get done.

Whether organizations achieve their goals depends on how they are managed. This is because organizations, by their nature, cannot simply run themselves. Review the definition of an organization again, and you'll see why. Who would ensure that each of the people actually knew what to do? Who would ensure that they work together, more or less harmoniously? Who would decide what the goals should be? The answer is, "the manager."

Management Defined

If you walked into a company, how could you tell who the managers are? Management expert Peter Drucker says that management ". . . is the responsibility for contribution."[6] In other words, it is the manager who is responsible for making sure that the company achieves its goals. A manager is someone who is responsible for accomplishing an organizational unit's goals and who does so by planning, organizing, leading, and controlling the efforts of other people.

That definition highlights three aspects of managerial work. First, a manager is always "responsible for contribution"—on his or her shoulders lies the responsibility for accomplishing the organization's goals. Therefore managers may apply management theories, but management is never just theoretical. That is why former GE vice chairman and Honeywell CEO (and successful manager) Lawrence Bossidy named his recent book *Execution: The Discipline of Getting Things Done*.

Second, managers always get things done through other people. The owner/entrepreneur running a small florist shop without the aid of employees is not managing. She may be an entrepreneur, but she is not (yet) a manager. She is doing all the work herself. She opens the store, places orders, handles customers, and delivers the orders and reconciles the store's books after she goes home at night. It is only when she starts hiring people and trying to get things done through them that she can call herself a manager. She'll have to train her new employees and put controls in place so that the person who closes the store won't borrow any of her day's receipts. She'll have to motivate her workers.

Some entrepreneurs—the people who provide the sparks that get new businesses off the ground—never make it to manager. When it comes to hiring people, putting systems in place, or giving orders, they just can't cut it. The same happens in big companies, too. You will often hear the phrase, "They took a great salesperson (or engineer, mechanic, accountant—or whatever) and turned the person into an awful sales (or some other) manager." Bernard Baker, founder of Fuel Cell Energy Inc. in Danbury, Connecticut, handed over the CEO job several years ago. He said, "My first love was research and development . . . I wasn't a businessman and I knew I wasn't a businessman."[7]

The third aspect of management refers to what managers actually do (and why some people turn out to be better at managing than others). That third aspect is this: Managers must be skilled at planning, organizing, leading, and controlling if they are to accomplish the organization's goals through other people. Management writers traditionally refer to the manager's four basic functions—planning, organizing, leading, and controlling—as the management process.

- *Planning.* Planning is setting goals and deciding on courses of action, developing rules and procedures, developing plans (both for the organization and for those who work in it), and forecasting (predicting or projecting what the future holds for the firm).
- *Organizing.* Organizing is identifying jobs to be done, hiring people to do them, establishing departments, delegating or pushing authority down to subordinates, establishing a chain of command (in other words, channels of authority and communication), and coordinating the work of subordinates.
- *Leading.* Leading means influencing other people to get the job done, maintaining morale, molding company culture, and managing conflicts and communication.
- *Controlling.* Controlling is setting standards (such as sales quotas or quality standards), comparing actual performance with these standards, and then taking corrective action as required.

Some people think that managing is easy and that anyone with half a brain can do it. After all, you will find no exotic mathematical formulas or discussions of nuclear physics in this book. But, if it is so easy, why do 90% of new businesses fail within five years due to poor management? Why did Kmart have to declare bankruptcy after a new

manager ■ *a person who plans, organizes, leads, and controls the work of others so that the organization achieves its goals.*

management process ■ *refers to the manager's four basic functions of planning, organizing, leading, and controlling.*

CEO turned the company in the wrong direction? The words in this book are easy to read. However, don't let that lull you into thinking that anyone can be a manager or that managing is easy.

■ *Application Example: You Too Are a Manager* Managing is something we're often called upon to do every day. In business, for instance, even a nonmanagerial employee may have to do some managing once in a while. The VP of marketing might ask a marketing analyst to head a small team to analyze a new product's potential. Or, the CEO might ask her assistant to manage preparations for an end-of-season company party. Everyone who works should therefore know something about how to manage. You never know when an opportunity might arise.

Furthermore, just as organizations needn't be business firms, you don't have to be in business to need management skills. For example, let's suppose that you and some friends have decided to spend next summer abroad in France. None of you know very much about France or how to get there, so you've been elected "summer tour master" and asked to manage the trip. Where would you start? (Resist the urge to call a travel agent and delegate the whole job to him or her, please.)

You might start with *planning*. Among other things, you'll need to plan the dates your group is leaving and returning, the cities and towns in France you'll visit, the airline you'll take there and back, how the group will get around in France and where you'll stay when you're there. You would not want to arrive at Paris's Charles DeGaulle Airport with a group of friends depending on you—and not know what you're doing next.

Of course, you'll need some help. You'll want to divide up the work and create an *organization*. For example, you might put Rosa in charge of checking airline schedules and prices, Ned in charge of checking hotels, and Ruth in charge of checking the sites to see in various cities as well as the means of transportation between them. However, the job won't get done with Rosa, Ned, and Ruth simply working by themselves. Each requires guidance and coordination from you. Rosa obviously can't make any decisions on airline schedules unless she knows what city you're starting and ending with, and Ned can't schedule hotels unless he knows from Ruth what sites you'll be seeing and when. You'll either have to schedule weekly manager's meetings or coordinate the work of these three people yourself.

Leadership could be a challenge, too. Ned and Ruth don't get along too well, so you'll have to make sure conflicts don't get out of hand. Rosa is a genius with numbers, but tends to get discouraged. You'll have to make sure she stays focused and motivated.

Finally, you'll have to ensure that the whole project stays "in control." If something can go wrong, it often will, and that's certainly the case when a group of people is traveling together. At a minimum, you'll have to make sure that all those airline tickets, hotel reservations, and itineraries are checked and checked again to make sure there are no mistakes.

What Else Do Managers Do?

Most management experts would probably agree that "planning, organizing, leading, and controlling" don't convey the full richness and complexity of what mangers do. For example, Merrill Lynch's former CEO David Komansky recently had to meet with New York's attorney general to negotiate a settlement that ended a suit by the state against his company. The time Komansky spent negotiating that settlement wouldn't easily fit into one of the four management functions, but his efforts helped the company avoid litigation.

Mintzberg's Managerial Roles The point is that other roles and duties fit under the umbrella of what managers do. Some time ago, Henry Mintzberg conducted a study of what managers actually do. Mintzberg found that as they went from task to task, managers didn't just plan, organize, lead, and control. Instead, they filled various roles, including:

- *The figurehead role.* Every manager spends some time performing ceremonial duties.
- *The leader role.* Every manager must function as a leader, motivating and encouraging employees.[8]
- *The liaison role.* Managers spend a lot of time in contact with people outside their own departments, essentially acting as the liaison between their departments and other people within and outside the organization.
- *The spokesperson role.* The manager is often the spokesperson for his or her organization.
- *The negotiator role.* Managers spend a lot of time negotiating; the head of an airline, for instance, might try to negotiate a new contract with the pilots' union.

The Manager as Innovator In today's fast-changing world, managers also have to make sure their companies have what it takes to innovate new products and to react quickly to change. Therefore, say management experts Sumantra Ghoshal and Christopher Bartlett, successful managers can't afford to just focus on designing organization charts or drawing up plans.[9] Instead, successful managers improve their companies' ability to be more innovative. They do this by cultivating three processes in their companies:

- *The entrepreneurial process.*[10] In their study of 20 companies in Japan, the United States, and Europe, Ghoshal and Bartlett found that successful managers focused much of their time and energy on getting employees to think of themselves as entrepreneurs. To do this, managers emphasized giving employees the authority, support, and rewards that self-disciplined and self-directed people need to run their operations as their own.
- *The competence-building process.* Bartlett and Ghoshal also found that "in a world of converging technologies, large companies have to . . . exploit their big-company advantages, which lie not only in scale economies but also in the depth and breadth of employees' talents and knowledge."[11] Successful managers, therefore, work hard to create an environment that lets employees really take charge. This means encouraging them to take on more responsibility, providing the education and training they need to build self-confidence, allowing them to make mistakes without fear of punishment, and coaching them to learn from their mistakes.[12]
- *The renewal process.* Successful managers also foster what Bartlett and Ghoshal call a renewal process.[13] In other words, managers have to make sure that they and all their employees guard against complacency. They encourage employees to question why they do things as they do—and if they might do them differently.

Innovation is not just for scientists and engineers. For example, one South Carolina manufacturer uses a machine that now runs five times faster than anticipated when the firm ordered it. What accounts for the machine's superspeed? The employees made over 200 small improvements to boost its efficiency.[14]

Types of Managers

You already know that there are different types of managers. In your college, for instance, there are presidents, vice presidents, provosts, deans, and department chairs. There are also administrators, such as human resource managers and the head of public safety.

In practice, we can differentiate managers in three ways: Based on their *organization level* (top, middle, first-line), *position* (manager, director, or vice president, for instance), and *functional title* (such as "sales manager" or "vice president for finance"). Figure 1.1 helps to illustrate this. The managers at the top, of course, are the firm's top management. These are the managers we call executives. Typical positions here are president, senior vice president, and executive vice president (in a university, you might also add provost). Functional titles here include "chief executive officer" (CEO), "vice president for sales," "general manager," and "chief financial officer" (CFO). This chapter's Managing @ the Speed of Thought feature provides a snapshot of what it's like to be a CEO. This feature, which focuses on managing in a fast-changing environment, will appear in each chapter.

executives ■ *the managers at the top of an organization.*

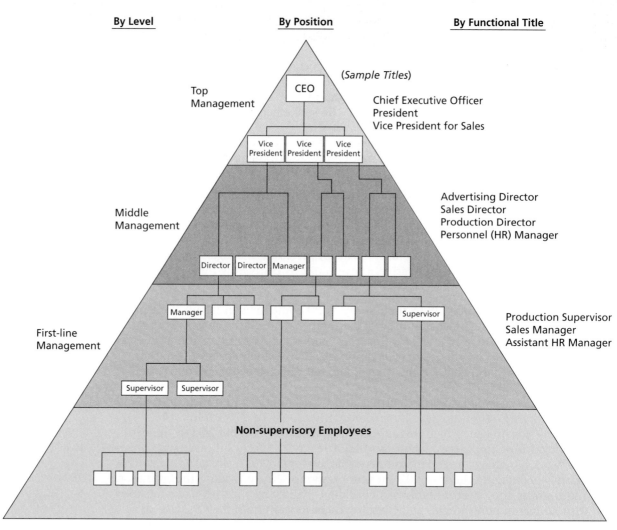

By Level   By Position   By Functional Title

(Sample Titles)

Top
Management

CEO

Chief Executive Officer
President
Vice President for Sales

Vice President | Vice President | Vice President

Middle
Management

Advertising Director
Sales Director
Production Director
Personnel (HR) Manager

Director | Director | Manager

First-line
Management

Manager   Supervisor

Production Supervisor
Sales Manager
Assistant HR Manager

Supervisor | Supervisor

Non-supervisory Employees

▲ **FIGURE 1–1** ■ ■ ■
Types of Managers

first-line manager ■ *managers*
at the lowest rung of the
management ladder.

Beneath the top management level (and reporting to it) may be one or more levels of middle managers. The positions here usually include the terms *manager* or *director* in the titles. (Particularly in larger companies like IBM, managers report to directors, who in turn report to top managers like vice presidents.) Examples of functional titles here include "production manager," "sales director," "HR manager," and "finance manager." First-line managers are at the lowest rung of the management ladder. Positions here might include supervisor or assistant manager. Functional titles might include "production supervisor" and "assistant marketing manager."

All managers have a lot in common. They all plan, organize, lead, and control. All managers at all levels and with every functional title also spend an enormous amount of their time with people—talking, listening, influencing, motivating, and attending meetings.[16] In fact, even chief executives (whom you might expect to be somewhat insulated from other people, up there in their executive suites) reportedly spend about three-fourths of their time dealing directly with other people.[17] However, there are two big differences among the management levels. First, top and middle managers both have managers for subordinates. In other words, they are in charge of other managers. Supervisors have workers—nonmanagers—as subordinates. Managers at different levels also use their time somewhat differently. Top managers tend to spend more time planning and setting goals (like "double sales in the next two years"). Middle managers then translate these goals into specific projects (like "hire two new salespeople and introduce three new products") for their subordinates to execute. First-line supervisors then concentrate on directing and controlling the employees who actually do the work on these projects.

The E-CEO

What is it like being an e-CEO, the chief executive of an e-commerce company? To hear the executives themselves tell it, speed is the word that sums up their experience best. For example, Roger Siboni, CEO of E.piphany, a company that creates the software that helps e-corporations get the most from their customer data, says, "You're driving too fast—you feel the exhilaration—you must turn left and right at death-defying speed without blinking—never blink—if you go up and down with the news, you'll never make it."[15] E-CEOs must also be brutally honest with themselves and others, because if they let a problem fester a day or two, they'll see someone in their rearview mirror coming after them, says Siboni.

With their markets changing so fast, e-CEOs must also constantly focus their companies' and their employees' attention on the company's mission. These companies are deluged with competitive information and new ideas, so it's relatively easy for the employees to become distracted. It's the e-CEO's job to keep everyone focused.

Table 1.1 highlights some differences between traditional and e-CEOs. For example, e-CEOs tend to be more comfortable with ambiguity and speed, and concerned with monitoring market trends and competitors' moves to ensure that their companies aren't blindsided by unanticipated events.

| TABLE 1–1 | E-CEOs Are a Brand-New Breed . . . |

Operating with a great deal of uncertainty, e-CEOs need a new set of qualities to thrive.

Traditional CEO	E-CEO
Encouraging	Evangelizing
Alert	Obsessed
Cordial	Brutally frank
Infotech semiliterate (at best)	Infotech literate (at least)
Clearly focused	Intensely focused
Fast moving	Faster moving
Hates ambiguity	Likes ambiguity
Suffers from technology-confrontation anxiety	Suffers from bandwidth-separation anxiety
A paragon of good judgment	A paragon of good judgment
Age: 57	Age: 38
Rich	Really rich

Source: Fortune, 24 May 1999, p. 107. © 1999 Time Inc. Reprinted by permission.

Do You Have the Traits to Be a Manager?

If you're thinking of becoming a manager, there's a wealth of research to help you to decide whether that's the occupation for you.

Personality and Interests Career counseling expert John Holland says that personality (including values, motives, and needs) is an important determinant of career choice. Specifically, he says that six basic "personal orientations" determine the sorts of careers to which people are drawn. Research with his Vocational Preference Test (VPT) suggests that almost all successful managers fit into at least one of two personality types or orientations:

- *Social orientation.* Social people are attracted to careers that involve working with others in a helpful or facilitative way (managers as well as others, like clinical psychologists and social workers, would exhibit this orientation). Generally speaking, socially oriented people find it easy to talk with all kinds of people; are good at helping people who are upset or troubled; are skilled at explaining things to others; and enjoy doing social things like helping others with their personal problems, teaching, and meeting new people.[18] It's hard to be a manager if you're not comfortable dealing with people.

■ *Enterprising orientation.* Enterprising people tend to like working with people in a supervisory or persuasive way in order to achieve some goal. They especially enjoy verbal activities aimed at influencing others (lawyers and public relations executives would also exhibit this orientation). Enterprising people often characterize themselves as being good public speakers, as having reputations for being able to deal with difficult people, as successfully organizing the work of others, and as being ambitious and assertive. They enjoy influencing others, selling things, serving as officers of groups, and supervising the work of others.

Comptencies Edgar Schein says career planning is a continuing process of discovery. He says each person slowly develops a clearer occupational self-concept, in terms of what his or her talents, abilities, motives, and values are. Based on his study of MIT graduates, Schein concluded that managers have a strong managerial competence career anchor.[19] These people show a strong motivation to become managers, "and their career experience enables them to believe that they have the skills and values necessary to rise to such general management positions." A management position with high responsibility is their ultimate goal.

What have these people learned about themselves that makes them think they can be good managers? They see themselves as competent in three areas. One is *analytical competence.* This is the ability to identify, analyze, and solve problems under conditions of incomplete information and uncertainty. A second is *interpersonal competence* (the ability to influence, supervise, lead, manipulate, and control people at all levels). The third is *emotional competence.* They were stimulated, not exhausted, by emotional and interpersonal crises. They had intestinal fortitude.

Achievements Research also suggests that your achievements provide some insights. Industrial/organizational psychologists at AT&T conducted two long-term studies of managers to determine how their premanagement achievements related to success on the job.[20] Those who went to college rose (on average) much faster and higher in management than did those in the noncollege sample. People with higher college grades showed greater potential for promotion early in their careers, and they rose higher in management than did those with lower grades. The quality of the college attended meant more early in the person's management career than it did later. Those who had attended "better-quality" colleges at first ranked higher as potential managers; however, within several years, college quality had little effect on who got promoted.

College major did seem to have a big effect, however, and here there were some surprises. Managers who had majored in humanities and social sciences scored higher as potential managers, and also moved faster up the corporate ladder.[21] Business administration majors ranked second. Math, science, and engineering majors ranked third. Why? At least in this study, the humanities majors scored the highest in decision-making, intellectual ability, written communication skills, creativity in solving business problems, and motivation for advancement. Both the humanities/social science majors and the business majors ranked higher in leadership ability, oral communication skills, interpersonal skills, and flexibility than did the math, science, and engineering majors.[22]

Findings like these obviously don't suggest that business and science majors are lost; they may just be unique to this specific group of managers—or to AT&T. However, the findings do suggest that, whatever your major, it's important to work on improving things like decision-making, creativity, and written communication skills. Managers also need strong social skills, because managing is a highly people-oriented occupation. The following Management in Action feature illustrates why.

Honeywell Corporation and Allied-Signal merged in 1999, forming a new, much larger Honeywell Corporation. The merger was made possible by the rising fortunes of Allied-Signal, which had vastly improved under its chairman and CEO, Lawrence A. Bossidy.[23]

How did Bossidy turn Allied-Signal around? Bossidy's people skills had a remarkable effect on this huge industrial supplier of aerospace systems, automotive parts, and chemical products.[24] He took over a troubled company that was "hemorrhaging cash."[25] After just three years, Allied-Signal's net income (profits) had doubled to $708 million, profit margins had doubled, and the company's market value (the total value of its shares) had more than doubled as well, to almost $10 billion.

What did Bossidy do to bring about such a dramatic transformation in just three years? A lot of his changes were operational. Under his guidance, the company merged business units, closed factories, reduced suppliers from 9,000 to 3,000, and cut 19,000 salaried jobs from the payroll.[26] Much of what Bossidy focused on, however, was behavioral in nature. In other words, he focused on applying his knowledge of how people, as individuals and groups,

Lawrence Bossidy at a news conference on June 7, 1999, at which he announced the purchase of Honeywell.

act within organizations to help bring about change. For example, in his first two months on the job, he said, "I talked to probably 5,000 employees. I would go to Los Angeles and speak to 500 people, then to Phoenix and talk to another 500. I would stand on a loading dock and speak to people and answer their questions. We talked about what was wrong and what we should do about it."[27]

His job, as he saw it, was not just to cut jobs and merge operations, since actions like these would have only short-term effects on profitability. In the longer run, Bossidy knew, he had to excite his giant firm's many employees by promoting "our employees' ability to win," by uniting the top management team "with vision and values," and in general by convincing all of his employees that there was a tremendous need to change—that their "platform was burning," as Bossidy put it.[28]

That's why Bossidy says that when he looks for managers, he looks for those who have a gift for working with and turning on employees. As he put it:

> Today's corporation is a far cry from the old authoritarian vertical hierarchy I grew up in. The cross-functional ties among individuals and groups are increasingly important. There are channels of activity and communication. The traditional bases of managerial authority are eroding. In the past, we used to reward the lone rangers in the corner offices because their achievements were brilliant even though their behavior was destructive. That day is gone. We need people who are better at persuading than at barking orders, who know how to coach and build consensus. Today, managers add value by brokering with people, not by presiding over empires.[29]

■■■ THE MANAGERIAL SKILLS

Successful managers like Andrea Jung and Lawrence Bossidy don't just have the right traits and competencies; they also have the right skills. In management (as in most other human endeavors), personality gets you only so far. At some point, the person must prove that he or she can actually get the job done. *Skills*—like writing, making forecasts, or communicating effectively, reflect how the person acts and what he or she can actually do. Managers need three sets of skills: technical, interpersonal, and conceptual.[30] *Building management skills* is a basic theme of this book. The book should help to provide you with many of the hands-on skills managers need to succeed, such as how to write business plans, how to discipline subordinates, and how to make better decisions. Let's look at a brief overview of what those skills are. We will then cover them in detail in each of the following chapters.

Technical Skills

Managers have to be technically competent. First, they need to know how to plan, organize, lead, and control. For example, they should know both how to develop a plan and how to write a job description. Chapters 2–17 address these management skills. Managers also should be technically competent in their area of expertise. For example, accounting managers need accounting skills, and sales managers should know what works (and does not work) when it comes to selling.

Interpersonal Skills

Researchers at The Center for Creative Leadership in Greensboro, North Carolina, studied why managers fail, and came to some interesting conclusions. Some managers simply didn't do their jobs, and thought more about being promoted than about the jobs they had.[31] However, the other failures were more interpersonal. Managers failed because they had abusive or insensitive styles, disagreed with upper management about how the business should be run, left a trail of bruised feelings, failed to adapt to the management culture, or didn't resolve conflicts among subordinates.

Managers, therefore, need good interpersonal skills. Interpersonal skills "include knowledge about human behavior and group processes, ability to understand the feelings, attitudes, and motives of others, and ability to communicate clearly and persuasively."[32] They include tact and diplomacy, empathy, persuasiveness, and oral communications ability. Managers with these skills have more cooperative relationships and can better accomplish a wide range of daily managerial chores, such as listening attentively and sympathetically when a subordinate has a problem. Chapters 10–13 will help you learn many of these skills.

Conceptual Skills

Studies also show that effective leaders tend to have more cognitive ability, and that their intelligence (and subordinates' perception of that intelligence) tend to be highly rated.[33] Conceptual (or "cognitive") skills "include analytical ability, logical thinking, concept formation, and inductive reasoning."[34] Conceptual skills manifest themselves in things like good judgment, creativity, and the ability to see the "big picture" when confronted with information.

Of course, intelligence is one thing, good judgment another. As Lawrence Bossidy puts it, "If you have to choose between someone with a staggering IQ and elite education who is gliding along, and someone with a lower IQ but who is absolutely determined to succeed, you'll always do better with the second person."[35] Chapter 3 will help you hone your conceptual skills.

It turned out that Andrea Jung had the skills to be a great manager, as the Management in Action feature shows.

MANAGEMENT IN ACTION   Avon

Within about 20 months, Avon's new CEO had turned her company around. Andrea Jung did it by overhauling "everything about the way Avon does business: how it advertises, manufactures, packages, and even sells its products."[36] She started with a turnaround plan. The plan included launching a new line of businesses, developing new products, building the sales force, and selling Avon products at retail stores.

Next came execution. Several months after taking over as CEO, she boosted Avon's research and development budget by almost 50%. She told R&D, "You've got two years. I need a breakthrough, and that's the goal."[37] By the end of the year, she had her product (Retroactive, an anti-aging cream that soon grossed $100 million). With the sales reps already in their customers' homes, Jung also got Avon to expand the products they could sell. They were soon selling vitamins under Avon's new Wellness line. Several months later, Avon began selling a special new line in JC Penney stores. At the same time, Jung appointed a new chief operating officer, who helped cut $400 million in costs.[38] She also turned her attention to beefing up the sales force and instituted a program called Leadership. Under this program, Avon now pays its sales reps ("Avon ladies") to recruit other reps. As one Avon lady put it, "I spend my Saturdays outside the supermarket trying to talk people into being an Avon lady."[39]

The new CEO's managerial actions are clearly bearing fruit. After growing about 4% per year throughout the 1990s, operating profits recently jumped 7%.

■■■ THE FOUNDATIONS OF MODERN MANAGEMENT

To understand how to manage today, one should understand how management evolved over time. This is because much of what managers do today is surprisingly similar to what managers did, even in ancient times. In terms of managerial planning, for instance, one ancient Egyptian father told his son, "The leader ought to have in mind the days that are yet to come."[40] In terms of control, the Pharaoh's vizier (manager) got this pithy advice: "Furthermore, he shall go in to take counsel on the affairs of the king, and there will be reported to him the affairs of the two lands in his house every day."[41] We can actually learn quite a bit from the managers who came before us.

The Classical and Scientific School

Modern management had its roots in the Industrial Revolution, when machines replaced human labor. Business boomed, but success created a problem—how to manage the new, large enterprises. There were no management principles, no management gurus, and no management textbooks (or business schools). Business people turned for management techniques to the only big organizations they knew—military and religious organizations—for guidance. These organizations had (and still tend to have) centralized decision-making, rigid chains of command, specialized divisions of work, and autocratic leadership.

But being big and centralized only gets the businessperson so far.[42] As their companies grew, and as competition became more intense, managers needed new ways to cut costs and boost efficiency. They needed better management theories. It was out of this environment that the classical school of management emerged.

Frederick Winslow Taylor and Scientific Management Frederick Winslow Taylor was among the first of the classical management writers. Writing mostly in the early 1900s, he developed a set of principles and practices that he called scientific management. Taylor's basic theme was that managers should scientifically study how work was done in order to identify the "one best way" to get a job done. He based his framework for scientific management on four principles:

1. *The "one best way."* Management, through scientific observation, must find the "one best way" to perform each job.
2. *Scientific selection of personnel.* Management must uncover each worker's limitation, find his or her "possibility for development," and give each worker the required training.
3. *Financial incentives.* Taylor knew that putting the right worker on the right job would not ensure high productivity. He proposed a system of financial incentives, in which each worker was paid in direct proportion to how much he or she produced.
4. *Functional foremanship.* Taylor called for a division of work between manager and worker such that managers did all planning, preparing, and inspecting, and the workers did the actual work. Specialized experts, or "functional foremen," would be responsible for specific aspects of a job, such as choosing the best machine speed and inspecting the work.[43]

Frank and Lillian Gilbreth and Motion Study The work of this husband-and-wife team also illustrates the classical/scientific management approach. Born in 1868, Frank Gilbreth began as an apprentice bricklayer, and he became intrigued by the idea of improving efficiency.[44] In 1904, he married Lillian, who had a background in psychology. Together, they developed motion-study principles and practices to scientifically analyze tasks. For example, "The two hands should begin and complete their motions at the same time" and "The two hands should not be idle at the same time except during rest periods."[45]

Henri Fayol and the Principles of Management The work of Henri Fayol also illustrates the classical approach. Fayol had been a manager with a French iron and steel firm for 30 years before writing his book, *General and Industrial Management*. In it, Fayol said that managers performed five basic functions: planning, organizing, commanding, coordinating, and controlling. (Sound familiar?) He also outlined a list of management principles he had found useful. Fayol's 14 principles include his famous *principle of unity of command*: "For any action whatsoever, an employee should receive orders from one superior only."[46]

Max Weber and the Bureaucracy Max Weber's work, first published in Germany in 1921, provides further insight into the contributions of the classical management writers. At the time, managers still had few principles they could apply in managing organizations. Weber, therefore, created the idea of an ideal or "pure form" of organization, which he called bureaucracy. Bureaucracy, for Weber, was the most efficient form of organization. Managers, he said, would do well to organize their companies along these lines:

1. A well-defined hierarchy of authority
2. A clear division of work
3. A system of rules covering the rights and duties of position incumbents
4. A system of procedures for dealing with the work situation
5. Impersonality of interpersonal relationships
6. Selection for employment, and promotion based on technical competence.[47]

The Behavioral School

"Design the most highly specialized and efficient job you can," assumed the classicist, and "plug in the worker, who will then do your bidding if the pay is right." Classicists by and large viewed workers as cogs in the machinery of industrialization. By the 1920s, however, things were changing. People moved from farms to cities and became more dependent on each other for goods and services. Businesses mechanized their factories, and jobs became more specialized and interdependent.[48] Government became more involved in economic matters. Social reformers worked at both establishing a minimum wage and encouraging trade unions. These developments and the great economic depression that began at the end of the decade made people start to question whether hard work, individualism, and maximizing profits—the building blocks of the classical management era—might actually have some drawbacks.

The Hawthorne Studies In 1927, the Hawthorne studies began at the Chicago Hawthorne plant of the Western Electric Company. Researchers from Harvard conducted several studies, one of which is known as the relay assembly test studies. They isolated a group of workers. Then they studied them as the researchers made changes (such as modifying the length of the workday and altering the morning and afternoon rest breaks). The researchers found that these changes did not greatly affect performance. They concluded that performance depended on factors other than physical conditions or rate of pay—a stunning discovery at the time.

They found that it was the social situations of the workers, not just the working conditions, that influenced behavior at work. The researchers discovered that their observations had inadvertently made the workers feel they were special. The "observer" had changed the workers' situation by "his personal interest in the girls and their problems. He had always been sympathetically aware of their hopes and fears."[49] Scientists call this phenomenon the Hawthorne effect. It's what happens when the scientist, in the course of an investigation, inadvertently influences the participants.

The Hawthorne studies were a turning point in the study of management. As the research became more widely known, managers and management experts began to acknowledge that human behavior at work can't be programmed. The *human relations movement*, inspired by this realization, emphasized that workers were not just "givens" in the system. They had needs and desires that the organization had to accommodate.

Changing Environment Hawthorne wasn't the only reason for this new point of view: The environment was changing, too. Having grown large and then made their companies more efficient, many managers were turning to research and development to develop new products. For example, after World War II, companies such as U.S. Rubber and B.F. Goodrich, which had concentrated on tire manufacturing, began developing and marketing new consumer products such as latex, plastics, and flooring.

R&D and diversification affected management theory in several ways. For one thing, efficiency was no longer a manager's main concern. With more diversified product lines, managers had to *decentralize*—that is, set up separate divisions to manage each new product. In addition, with more products, managers had to let lower-level employees make more decisions. That meant managers had to pay more attention to their employees' motivation. Because of the Hawthorne findings and the other social changes taking place after World War II, managers started taking a much more people-oriented approach to managing employees.

Douglas McGregor: Theory X and Theory Y The work of Douglas McGregor is a good example of this new approach. According to McGregor, the classical organization was not just a relic of ancient times. Instead, it reflected certain basic assumptions about human nature.[50] McGregor somewhat arbitrarily classified these assumptions as Theory X. These assumptions held that most people dislike work and responsibility and prefer to be directed; that they are motivated not by the desire to do a good job, but simply by financial incentives; and that, therefore, most people must be closely supervised, controlled, and coerced into achieving organizational objectives.

McGregor questioned this view. He felt that management needed new organizations and practices to deal with diversification, decentralization, and participative decision-making. These new management practices, which he called Theory Y, had to reflect a new set of assumptions about human nature. Theory Y held that people wanted to work hard, could enjoy work, and could exercise substantial self-control. You could trust your employees if you treated them right.

Rensis Likert and the Employee-Centered Organization What new management practices are called for? Researcher Rensis Likert concluded that effective organizations differ from ineffective ones in several ways. Less effective "job-centered" companies focus on specialized jobs, efficiency, and close supervision of workers. Effective "employee-centered" organizations "focus their primary attention on endeavoring to build effective work groups with high performance goals."[51] Therefore, said Likert, "widespread use of participation is one of the more important approaches employed by the high-producing managers."[52]

Chris Argyris and the Mature Individual Chris Argyris reached similar conclusions, but he approached the problem differently.[53] Argyris argued that healthy people go through a maturation process. Gaining employees' compliance by assigning them to highly specialized jobs with no decision-making power and then closely supervising them encourages workers to be dependent, passive, and subordinate. It's better to give workers more responsibility and broader jobs.

Bridging the Eras: The Administrative School

The work of experts like Chester Barnard and Herbert Simon does not fit neatly into any one school of management theory. Their research spanned several schools and contributed to the development of an integrated theory of management.

Chester Barnard was president of New Jersey Bell Telephone Company and, at various times, president of the Rockefeller Foundation and Chair of the National

Science Foundation. As a management theorist, he focused on the "willingness of persons to contribute their individual efforts to the cooperative system."

How do you get the employees to "contribute their individual efforts"?[54] Barnard devised what he called the person's zone of indifference. He said each individual has a range of orders (a "zone of indifference") he or she will willingly accept without consciously questioning their legitimacy.[55] Barnard said the manager had to provide sufficient inducements (and not just financial ones) to make each employee's zone of indifference wider.

Herbert Simon viewed getting employees to do what the organization needed them to do as a major issue facing managers. How can managers influence employee behavior?[56] According to Simon, managers can ensure that employees carry out tasks in one of two ways. They can *impose control* by closely monitoring subordinates and insisting that they do their jobs as ordered (using the classicists' command and control approach). Or, managers can *foster employee self-control* by providing better training, encouraging participative leadership, and developing commitment and loyalty (thus, take a more behavioral approach).

The Quantitative/Management Science School

More recently, management theorists began to apply quantitative techniques to solving management problems. Writers usually refer to this movement as *operations research* or *management science*. It is "the application of scientific methods, techniques, and tools to problems involving the operations of systems so as to provide those in control of the system with optimum solutions to the problems."[57]

The Management Science Approach Historian Daniel Wren points out that operations research/management science has "direct lineal roots in scientific management."[58] Like Taylor and the Gilbreths, today's management scientists try to find optimal solutions to problems through research and analysis. However, modern-day management scientists have much more sophisticated mathematical tools and computers. And, management science's goal is not to try to find a science of management so much as it is to use scientific analysis and tools to solve management problems.

The Systems Approach The management science approach is closely associated with the systems approach to management. A system is an entity—a hospital, city, company, or person, for instance—that has interdependent parts and a purpose. Systems-approach advocates argue that viewing an organization as a system helps managers remember that the firm's different parts, departments, or subsystems are interrelated, and that all must contribute to the organization's purpose. Focusing on the interrelatedness of the subsystems (and between the subsystems and the firm's environment) is an essential feature of systems thinking. For example, a manager can't change one subsystem without affecting the rest. Hiring a new production manager might have repercussions in the sales and accounting departments.

Similarly, according to systems experts, managers can't understand how companies operate without understanding their environments. (For example, product diversification at the tire companies meant they faced an environment with more diverse markets and competitors. That meant companies had to split themselves into separate divisions to address the different markets.) The organization and how you manage are contingent on the environment.

The Situational/Contingency School

In the early 1960s, at about the same time the systems approach was popular, studies in England and the United States began to emphasize the need for a situational or contingency view of management. This approach held that the organization and how its managers should manage it were contingent on the company's environment and on its technology.

Tom Burns and G. M. Stalker analyzed several industrial firms in England. They concluded that whether what they called a "mechanistic" or an "organic" management approach was best depended on the company's environment. For example, they studied a textile mill. Here, it was important to have long, stable production runs, so that management didn't have to shut down huge, specialized machines. Management had to keep sales and demand stable. In a stable environment, Burns and Stalker found that within the company, a mechanistic (or classical) management approach worked best. Management emphasized efficiency, specialized jobs, and making everyone stick to the rules. Burns and Stalker found that high-tech firms faced a lot more innovation and unpredictability. These companies, therefore, used the more flexible, people-oriented, organic approach. Here, the important thing was learning as fast as possible what competitors were doing and being able to respond quickly by letting even lower-level employees make fast decisions. These companies didn't confine employees to specialized jobs.

▪▪▪ TODAY'S MANAGEMENT ENVIRONMENT

Management experts continue to add to what we know about how managers should plan, organize, lead, and control. But (as we've seen from our brief survey of management), the environment of the time helps to explain why firms are organized and managed as they are. Let's therefore consider the environmental forces managers cope with today.

If there are two things that characterize the environment that managers face today, they are "competition and change." For example, after more than 230 years of stability, Encyclopaedia Britannica was almost put out of business in the early 1990s by Microsoft's $50 Encarta CD-ROM. Suddenly, Britannica's environment became much more unpredictable. Today, Britannica has a whole new management structure and system. It had to streamline. It disbanded its door-to-door sales force and is now offering its encyclopedia without charge via the Internet. It hopes that revenue from online ads and sponsorships will be enough to make the company grow again. Web designers, high-tech employees, and advertising sales reps have replaced the company's traditional way of selling door-to-door around the world.

Several basic trends account for the kind of environmental competition, pressure, and change Britannica's managers had to face. Let's start with globalization.

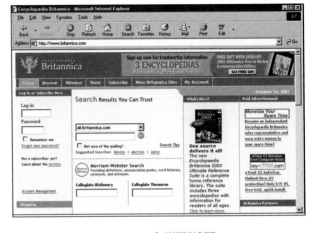

Globalization

Doing business internationally is big business today. For example, U.S. imports and exports jumped from $907 billion in 1991 to $2.5 trillion in 2000, and they now equal about 11% of what America produces.[59]

Globalization refers to the tendency of firms to extend their sales, ownership, and/or manufacturing to new markets abroad. Examples are all around us. Toyota produces the Camry in Kentucky, while Dell produces and sells PCs in China. Firms outside America own four out of five "American" textbook publishers (like Prentice Hall, Harcourt, Houghton-Mifflin, and Southwestern). Free trade areas—agreements that reduce tariffs and barriers among trading partners—further encourage international trade. NAFTA (the North American Free Trade Agreement) and the EU (the European Union) are examples.

More globalization means more competition, and more competition means more pressure to improve—to lower costs, to make employees more productive, and to do things better and less expensively. As one expert put it, "The bottom line is that the growing integration of the world economy into a single, huge marketplace is increasing the intensity of competition in a wide range of manufacturing and service industries."[60]

Managers react in various ways. Some, like Levi Strauss, transfer operations abroad, both to seek cheaper labor and to tap what *Fortune* magazine calls "a vast new supply of skilled labor around the world."[61] Others, as we'll see, apply world-class management practices, such as flexible manufacturing and self-managing teams, to stay competitive.

globalization ▪ *the extension of a firm's sales or manufacturing to new markets abroad.*

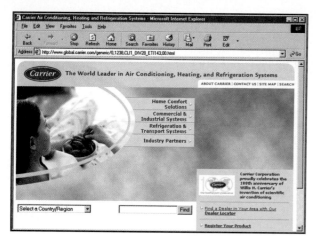

Technological Advances

Many of these world-class improvements involve technology. For example, Carrier Corp.—with $10 billion in sales and 40,000 employees, the world's largest manufacturer of air conditioners—saves an estimated $100 million per year with the Internet. In Brazil, for instance, Carrier handles all its transactions with its channel partners (its 550 dealers, retailers, and installers) over the Web. "The time required to get an order entered and confirmed by our channel partners has gone from six days to six minutes."[62] A vast array of technological advances—from cell phones to the Internet—pressure managers to make sure their firms can compete. Competitors that can't match Carrier's Web technology are lost.

The Nature of Work

Technology is also changing the nature of work. Even factory jobs are becoming more technologically demanding. For one thing, "knowledge-intensive high-tech manufacturing jobs in such industries as aerospace, computers, telecommunications, home electronics, pharmaceuticals, and medical instruments" are replacing factory jobs in steel, auto, rubber, and textiles.[63] Even traditional manufacturing jobs are going high-tech. At Alcoa Aluminum's Davenport, Iowa, plant, a computer stands at each workpost to help each employee control his or her machines. *Fortune* magazine says, "Practically every package delivery, bank teller, retail clerk, telephone operator, and bill collector in America works with a computer [today]."[64] As Microsoft Corporation chairman Bill Gates put it, "In the new organization, the worker is no longer a cog in a machine but is an intelligent part of the overall process. Welders at some steel jobs now have to know algebra and geometry to figure weld angles from computer-generated designs."[65]

Technology is not the only trend driving this change from "brawn to brains." Today, over two-thirds of the U.S. workforce is employed in producing and delivering services, not products. Between 1998 and 2008, the number of jobs in goods-producing industries will stay almost unchanged, at about 25.5 million, while the number in service-producing industries will climb from 99 million to 118.8 million.[66]

For managers, this all means a growing emphasis on "knowledge workers" and human capital.[67] Human capital refers to the knowledge, education, training, skills, and expertise of a firm's workers.[68] Today, "the center of gravity in employment is moving fast from manual and clerical workers to knowledge workers, who resist the command and control model that business took from the military 100 years ago."[69] Managers need new world-class management systems and skills in order to select, train, and motivate these employees and to get them to work more like committed partners.

The Workforce

At the same time, workforce demographics are changing. For one thing, the workforce is becoming more diverse as women, minority-group members, and older workers enter it.[70] Between 1992 and 2005, workers classified as "Asian and other" will jump by just over 81%. Hispanics will represent 11% of the civilian labor force in 2005, up from 8% in 1992.[71] Women represented 46% of the workforce in 1994, and will represent an estimated 47.8% by 2005.[72] About two-thirds of all single women (separated, divorced, widowed, or never married) are in the labor force today, as are almost 45% of mothers with children under three years old.

The labor force is also getting older. The median age in 1995, 37.8 years, will rise to 40.5 years by 2005.[73] Employees will also likely remain in the workforce past the age at which their parents retired, due to Social Security and Medicare changes and the termination of traditional benefit plans by many employers.[74]

Creating unanimity and "human capital" from such a diverse workforce won't be easy. Most managers say they encourage diversity, but most management systems—how companies recruit, screen, and train and promote employees—". . . will not allow diversity, only similarity."[75] Establishing management programs that turn a diverse workforce into highly skilled knowledge workers can thus be a challenge.[76]

■■■ *A knowledge worker: Engineer running a space shuttle heat test simulation.*

Category Killers

Where does an 800-pound gorilla sit? Wherever it wants to, just like category killers such as Office Depot, Wal-Mart, and Lowe's. These mammoth "big box" stores use economies of scale and wide selections to drive down costs and prices. Most small competitors—neighborhood hardware stores, stationery stores, and bookstores, for instance—can't get their costs or prices low enough. This competition squeezes out the weaker firms unless their managers have the skills to compete.

Similarly, many smaller retail chains (like Macy's) have been absorbed into giant chains, like Federated Department Stores, with powerful centralized purchasing departments. When one giant chain accounts for half your company's sales (or more), it's hard to negotiate prices. This squeezes manufacturers to reduce prices. Only the most efficient survive.

Modern Management Thought

To compete in such a fast-changing, globally competitive environment, modern management writers propose new models to describe the ideal approach to managing. Two McKinsey & Co. consultants, Thomas Peters and Robert Waterman Jr., studied eight "excellent" companies. They concluded that these firms were excellent because of how they were managed. Managers here stressed "a bias toward action," "simple form and lean staff," "continued contact with customers," "productivity improvement via people," "operational autonomy to encourage entrepreneurship," "one key business value," "doing what they know best," and "simultaneous loose and tight controls" (in other words, making sure that employees buy into the company's values so that they are able to control themselves).[77]

Rosabeth Moss Kantor studied companies like IBM, AT&T, Ford, and CBS. She concluded that fewer management levels, a greater responsiveness to change, and strategic alliances helped these firms succeed.[78] Several management theorists think that in today's fast-changing environment, the best companies are "intelligent enterprises," or "learning organizations." James Brian Quinn studied what he calls "Intelligent Enterprises." These companies (like IBM) depend on converting their employees' "intellectual resources" (such as engineering knowledge) into services and products. Companies like these, says Quinn, must "leverage"—take maximum advantage of—their intellectual capital by ensuring that ideas can flow quickly among employees. Managers do this in many ways, such as by encouraging informal communications.[79] Similarly, Peter Senge argues for creating "the Learning Organization." These are "organizations where people continually expand their capacity to create the results they truly desire . . . and where people are continually learning how to learn together."[80] Among other things, learning organizations' managers encourage "systems thinking," "personal mastery," "building shared vision," and "team learning."

■■■ MANAGING TODAY

Theories and findings like these characterize managing today. Figure 1.2 presents an overview. A fast-changing, high-pressure environment means more competition, change, and unpredictability. Managers have responded by making their companies more streamlined, efficient, and faster-acting. ABB is an example, as demonstrated in the accompanying Management in Action feature.

Changes	Leads To	So Companies Must Be
• Explosion of technological innovation • Globalization of markets and competition • Deregulation • Changing demographics • New political systems • Category killers • Service and knowledge jobs	• Increased competition • Uncertainty, turbulence, and rapid change • More consumer choices • Mergers and divestitures • Joint ventures • More complexity • Short product life cycles • Market fragmentation • More uncertainty for managers • Record number of business failures	• Fast, responsive, and adaptive • Flat organizations • Downsized • Quality conscious • Empowered • Smaller units • Decentralized • Human capital oriented • Boundaryless • Values and vision oriented • Team based

▲ **FIGURE 1–2** ■ ■ ■

Fundamental Changes Facing Managers

A series of forces—globalized competition, technology revolution, new competitors, and changing tastes—are creating outcomes that include more uncertainty, more choices, and more complexity. The result is that the organizational winners of today and tomorrow will have to be responsive, smaller, flatter, and oriented toward adding value through people.

MANAGEMENT IN ACTION   ABB

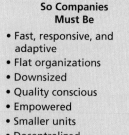

Electrical equipment maker ABB (Asea Brown Boveri) makes huge machines like electric power generators. It competes with giants like GE around the world for customers. Its business requires a unique combination of efficiency (since competitors like GE are highly efficient) and responsiveness (since each local customer's needs are unique and require local technical assistance and attention). When he took over this $30 billion firm, former chairman Percy Barnevik knew he had to take dramatic steps to turn his company into an efficient and responsive competitor. He did four things.[81]

1. First, he split its 215,000 employees into 5,000 *minicompanies*, each averaging only about 50 workers.[82] For example, he made the ABB hydropower unit in Finland a minicompany that serves just Finnish customers. Each of ABB's 50-person units is run by its own manager and three or four lieutenants.

2. Next, to speed decision-making, the 5,000 minicompanies' employees were *empowered*—given the authority—to make most of their own business decisions. Suppose a customer has a complaint about a $50,000 machine. A minicompany employee can approve a replacement on the spot rather than wait for review by several levels of management. This meant faster decision-making.

3. Next, ABB *delayered* its organization. Now its 215,000-employee organization had just three management levels (a comparably sized company might have seven or eight). There was a 13-member top-management executive committee based in Zurich. Below this was a 250-member executive level that includes country managers and executives in charge of groups of businesses. A third level consisted of the 5,000 minicompany managers and their management teams. Barnevik sliced out layers of management and let lower-level employees make more of the decisions. Now ABB employees could respond more quickly to customers' needs and competitors' moves.

4. Letting local employees make more decisions produced another benefit. Barnevik could now *strip away* most headquarters staff. When he became CEO, he found 2,000 people at headquarters basically reviewing and analyzing the decisions of the firm's lower-level employees. He cut the staff to 200.   ■ ■ ■ ■

Basic Management Features Today

ABB's experience helps to illustrate what today's organizations and management systems look like: smaller, more entrepreneurial organizational units; team-based, boundaryless organizations; empowered decision-making; flatter organizational structures; new bases of management power; knowledge-based management; an emphasis on vision; and the realization that leadership is key. Let's take a closer look.

Smaller, More Entrepreneurial Organizational Units First, as at ABB, the operating units in many companies are smaller. Even big firms are encouraging employees to be more like small-business entrepreneurs. For example, T. J. Rogers, president of Cypress Semiconductor, believes that large companies stifle innovation. Thus, when a new product must be developed, he doesn't do it within the existing corporation. Instead, he creates a separate start-up company under the Cypress umbrella. Rogers already has four successful start-ups under development.[83]

Team-Based and Boundaryless Organizations Managers are extending this "small is beautiful" philosophy to how they organize the work itself. Many companies today organize around small, cross-functional teams that manage themselves. GM's Saturn Corporation subsidiary is a famous example. Virtually all shop floor work is organized around work teams of 10 to 12 employees. Each team is responsible for a complete task, such as installing door units, checking electrical systems, or maintaining automated machines. The teams don't have traditional supervisors. Instead, highly trained workers do their own hiring, control their own budgets, monitor the quality of their own work, and generally manage themselves.

Many firms extend this idea to creating interdepartmental teams. Companies like these encourage free-flowing interdepartmental communication unhampered by the usual departmental boundaries. GE's former chairman, Jack Welch, calls this the **boundaryless organization**. To speed decision-making, employees reach across the company to interact with whomever they must to get the job done.[84]

> **boundaryless organization** ■ *an organization in which the widespread use of teams, networks, and similar structural mechanisms means that the boundaries separating organizational functions and hierarchical levels are reduced and more permeable.*

Empowered Decision-Making Self-managing teams can't manage themselves if they haven't the authority and training to do so. Worker empowerment is thus a core idea in modern management thought. Writers like Karl Albrecht say that empowering workers often involves "turning the typical organization upside-down."[85] The company should put the customer—not the CEO—on top, to emphasize that every move the company makes is aimed at satisfying the customer. This philosophy requires empowering front-line employees—the front-desk clerks at the hotel, the cabin attendants on the plane, and the assemblers at the factory. Such employees need the authority to respond quickly to customers. The main purpose of managers in this "upside-down" organization is to support the front-line employees. The manager becomes more of a coach; he or she sees to it that employees have what they need to do their jobs.

Flatter Organizational Structures, Knowledge-Based Management The tall pyramid-shaped organization, with its seven or more layers of management, is disappearing. In its place, relatively flat organizations with just three or four levels prevail. Many companies, like ABB, have already cut the management layers from a dozen to six or fewer—and, therefore, the number of managers.[86] As the remaining managers are left with more people to supervise, they are less able to meddle in the work of their subordinates, who thus have more autonomy.

New Bases of Management Power In today's organizations, says management theorist Rosabeth Moss Kanter, leaders can no longer rely on their formal authority to get employees to follow them.[87] Instead, "success depends increasingly on tapping into sources of good ideas, on figuring out whose collaboration is needed to act on those ideas, and on working with both to produce results. In short, the new managerial work implies very different ways of obtaining and using power."[88] Peter Drucker put it this way: "You have to learn to manage in situations where you don't have command authority, where you are neither controlled nor controlling."[89]

■ ■ ■ *Worker empowerment: Rooms control clerk at the front desk, the New York Marriott, Brooklyn.*

Knowledge-Based Management Management experts say companies today are *knowledge based*. Highly trained and educated employees apply their knowledge in a setting in which they direct and discipline their own activities.[90] This requires a new knowledge-based approach: Managers have to help employees get their jobs done by training and coaching them, by removing roadblocks, and by getting them the resources they need. Yesterday's manager thinks of himself or herself as a "manager" or "boss." The new manager is a "sponsor," a "team leader," or an "internal consultant." The old-style manager hoards information to build his or her personal power; the new manager shares information to help subordinates get their jobs done.[91]

An Emphasis on Vision In companies with fewer bosses, formulating a clear vision of where the firm is heading becomes more important. Peter Drucker says today's companies, which are staffed by professionals and other employees who largely control their own behavior, require "clear, simple, common objectives [a vision] that translate into particular actions."[92] The vision is like a signpost. Even without a lot of supervisors to guide them, employees can steer themselves by the company's vision.

Leadership Is Key Like ABB's Percy Barnevik, today's managers have to be leaders and agents of change. As GE's Jack Welch put it, "You've got to be on the cutting edge of change. You can't simply maintain the status quo, because somebody's always coming from another country with another product, or consumers' tastes change, or the cost structure does, or there's a technology breakthrough. If you are not fast and adaptable, you are vulnerable."[93]

Today's environment puts a premium on effective leadership. In a fast-changing, team-oriented environment, managers need effective leadership skills so they can motivate knowledge workers, build self-managing teams, and lead transformations like the one at ABB.

Using Technology and E-Based Management

Moving fast means getting the information you need now, when you need it. For example, when you sit with Larry Carter, Cisco Systems' CFO, you can see the whole company's activities laid out before you.[94] This is because Cisco, a manufacturer of networking hardware and software, is in the vanguard of firms using sophisticated real-time computerized financial systems to give their top executives access to data almost instantaneously. As a relatively young company (founded in 1984), Cisco "doesn't have a bunch of incompatible, old record-keeping systems gumming things up." It could, therefore, start with a clean slate and computerize the entire financial control system so that top management could detect changes relatively quickly.[95]

As another example, consider the Spanish retailer Zara. Zara doesn't need the long production runs and expensive inventories that burden competitors like The Gap. Zara operates its own Internet-based worldwide distribution network, produces much of its own materials, and does much of its own manufacturing. It also has a sophisticated information technology system that lets it monitor store sales on a daily basis. As soon as it sees that a particular style is in demand at one of its worldwide stores, its "flexible manufacturing system" swings into action. It dyes the required fabric, manufactures the item, and speeds it to that store.[96]

Few things illustrate the changes in management today like managers' use of the Internet to improve their operations. In the chapters that follow, we'll use "Managing Without Boundaries" (as we do on page 21 to show how Dell has turned itself into an Internet-based company). We will also use short illustrated "Webnotes" to show how managers are using the power of the Internet to help them better manage their companies today.

As you can see, the basic theme of managing today (and of theorists like Kantor, Quinn, and Senge) is that managers need to make their companies more flexible, learning-oriented, and entrepreneurial. To paraphrase two management theorists, "a growing band of management thinkers has encouraged companies to transform from a corporate model based on control to one based on entrepreneurialism."[103]

However, flexible may not always be best. First, this management approach is not easy to implement. For example, it requires charismatic leaders, and it is

Virtual Integration at Dell Computer

How do you build a $12 billion company in just 13 years?[97] For Dell Computer, the answer meant using technology and information to "blur the traditional boundaries in the value chain among suppliers, manufacturers, and the end users."[98] What does this mean? As summarized in Figure 1.3, it basically means that there are no intermediaries like wholesalers or retailers to come between Dell and its customers and suppliers; thus, Dell can be a much faster-moving company than it might otherwise be.[99] For most computer companies, the manufacturing process is like a relay race: Components come in from suppliers, these components are assembled into computers, and the computers are then handed off to be distributed through wholesalers and retailers (such as CompUSA) to the ultimate customers. Dell's system changes all that. For example (see Figure 1.3), Dell interacts with and sells to customers directly, so it eliminates the activities of the wholesalers and retailers in the traditional distribution chain.[100]

"Virtual integration"—linking Dell with its suppliers and customers via the Internet—speeds things up even more. Consider one example: Computerized information from Dell continually updates suppliers regarding the number of components to be delivered every morning, so the "outside" supplier actually starts to look and act more like an "inside" part of Dell. Similarly, instead of stocking its own monitors, "We tell Airborne Express or UPS to come to Austin and pick up 10,000 computers a day and go over to the Sony factory in Mexico and pick up the corresponding number of monitors. And while we're all sleeping, they match up the computers and the monitors, and deliver them to the customers . . . [O]f course, this requires sophisticated data exchange."[101]

The result of what Michael Dell calls "this virtual integration" of suppliers, manufacturing, and customers is a lean, efficient, and fast-moving operation that can turn on a dime if the products demanded by customers change. He states,

> There are fewer things to manage, fewer things to go wrong. You don't have the drag effect of taking 50,000 people with you. . . . If we had to build our own factories for every single component of the system, growing at 57% per year just would not be possible. I would spend 500% of my time interviewing prospective vice-presidents because the company would have not 15,000 employees but 80,000. Indirectly, we employ something like that many people today . . . but only a small number of them work for us. Their contract is with other firms. . . . The vast majority [of customers] think [those people] work for us, which is just great. That's part of virtual integration.[102]

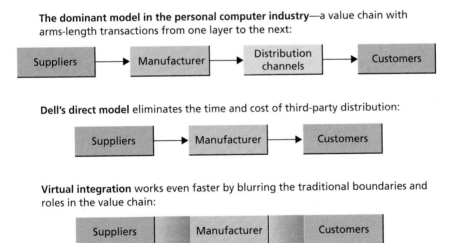

The dominant model in the personal computer industry—a value chain with arms-length transactions from one layer to the next:

Suppliers → Manufacturer → Distribution channels → Customers

Dell's direct model eliminates the time and cost of third-party distribution:

Suppliers → Manufacturer → Customers

Virtual integration works even faster by blurring the traditional boundaries and roles in the value chain:

Suppliers | Manufacturer | Customers

◄ **FIGURE 1–3** ■ ■ ■

The Evolution of a Faster Business Model

Source: Harvard Business Review, March–April 1998, p. 82. Copyright © 1998 by the President and Fellows of Harvard College. All rights reserved.

complicated to manage because the emphasis on informality "can lead to a loss of control."[104] Second, it is not clear from the research that this approach really is always best.[105] Some of the new management research is more anecdotal than scientific, and some of these "excellent companies" have actually performed quite poorly in the past few years. As Chris Argyris, a well-known management expert, says, many businesspeople, therefore, end up accepting advice that is fundamentally flawed.[106]

Third, while many tasks today do favor using the "Organic/Adaptive/ Intelligent/Learning" management approach, this doesn't mean it is always best. Table 1.2 briefly summarizes characteristics of the Classical/Mechanistic and

TABLE 1–2   **Different Management Approaches for Different Situations**

CHARACTERISTIC	TYPE OF MANAGEMENT APPROACH	
	Classical/Mechanistic	**Behavioral/Organic/Adaptive**
Type of environment	Stable	Innovative
Main challenge	Efficiency	Innovation, responsiveness
Similar to	Classical school	Behavior school
Other similarities	Theory X	Theory Y/Intelligent Enterprise/Learning Organization
Theorists	Taylor, Fayol, Gilbreth, Weber	McGregor, Argyris, Peters, Kanter, Quinn, Senge
Adherence to chain of command	Close adherence	Flexible: chain of command often bypassed
How specialized are jobs?	Specialized	Unspecialized: jobs change daily with situation
Emphasis on sticking to the rules	Yes	No
Where are decisions made?	Centralized	Decentralized
Span of control	Narrow	Wide
How are employees motivated?	Incentives and close supervision	Fostering self-control

Behavioral/Organic/Adaptive approaches. We've seen in this chapter that there are times when a more classical, structured approach is best. When he became CEO of a struggling IBM, for instance, Louis Gerstner reportedly said that what the company needed was not a vision but "basic blocking and tackling"—in other words, the application of both traditional and more modern management principles. Similarly, we'll see (in Chapter 17) that managing in a different culture—in, say, China or India—might call for a more classical approach.

The purpose of a management book is not to give you a set of ideas that you can use only until the next management fad comes along. The aim is to give you concepts and skills that will last your management lifetime. Remember that for all the new theories, what managers do today is in many respects similar to what they did even in ancient times. Managers who can't plan, organize, lead, or control would have been kicked off the pyramid job site in ancient Egypt just as quickly as they would be fired by Kmart today. This book aims to provide you with the basic concepts and skills you'll need to manage effectively in any situation. And, it hopefully supplies the wisdom you'll need for knowing when and under what conditions a particular management approach is best.

SUMMARY ■■■

1. An organization consists of people who have formally assigned roles and who must work together to achieve the organization's goals. Organizations needn't be just business firms.

2. Organizations are run by managers. A manager is someone who plans, organizes, leads, and controls the people and the work of the organization in such a way that the organization achieves its goals.

3. Management writers traditionally refer to the manager's four basic functions of planning, organizing, leading, and controlling as the management process.

4. We can classify managers based on organizational level (top, middle, first-line), position (executives, managers or directors, supervisors), and functional title ("vice president of production," "sales manager"). All managers get their work done through people and by planning, organizing, leading, and

controlling. Top managers spend more time planning and setting goals. Lower-level managers concentrate on implementing goals and getting employees to achieve them.

5. Managers play other roles too—for instance, figurehead, leader, liaison, spokesperson, negotiator. They also engage in entrepreneurial, competence-building, and renewal processes.

6. Almost everything a manager does involves interacting with and influencing people. The bottom line is that the leading, or people, side of what managers do is not just another step in the management process; it is an integral part of the manager's job.

7. Managers and their organizations have to confront rapid change and intense competition today. Trends contributing to this change and unpredictability include globalization, technological advances, deregulation, changing political systems, the diverse workforce, category killers, and an emphasis on service and knowledge work.

KEY TERMS ▪▪▪

organization 2
manager 3
management process 3
executives 5

first-line manager 6
managerial competence 8
career anchor 8
bureaucracy 12

globalization 15
boundaryless organization 19

SKILLS AND STUDY MATERIALS

COMPANION WEBSITE ▪▪▪

We invite you to visit the Dessler Companion Website at **www.prenhall.com/dessler** for this chapter's Internet resources.

EXPERIENTIAL EXERCISES ▪▪▪

1. Most people tend to think of organizations as pyramid-shaped hierarchies, with authority and decision-making flowing from the top down. The boss gives the orders, and the employee does the work. As this chapter points out, today's changing environment demands new forms of organization.

   As a team of 4–5 students, graphically depict some of the newer organizational designs mentioned in this chapter. First, draw the shapes you think represent the "organization charts" of the new boundaryless, team-focused organizations. Then write a brief (1–2 page) summary describing what you have drawn and what you think the implications of these designs are for planning, organizing, leading, and controlling organizations today.

2. While most organizations do tend to be hierarchies with bosses telling employees what to do, colleges and universities have long been somewhat different. For example, many universities traditionally have faculty senates that make decisions about what new programs to approve, and on what bases the university will evaluate and appraise professors. Similarly, many universities have students evaluate the faculty—still an unusual arrangement even in progressive companies.

   As a team, answer the following questions: (1) In a university in which students evaluate the faculty and the faculty is "the boss" when it comes to deciding on new programs, how can you determine who the "managers" and "employees" are? (2) What five specific recent environmental trends do you think have had the most pronounced effect on the methods used to manage your college or university today? (3) List several ways in which you believe these trends have influenced the way in which the college or university's managers plan, organize, lead, and control.

3. Write a short essay on this topic: "The tasks I've performed that I most enjoyed, was proudest of, and was most successful at." (Perhaps, if you're lucky, one task fills the bill!) Now do the same for the task or tasks you least enjoyed, were least proud of, and were least successful at. Now answer this question: Based on what you know about what managers do and what it takes to be a manager, do you think you have what it takes to be a manager?

CAN YOU BE DIFFERENT AND STILL WIN?

Chris Sullivan and the founders of Outback Steakhouse, Inc., developed a unique vision for a restaurant concept and the management system that would make it work. Having worked for other chain restaurants in the past, Sullivan and his team wanted to do things very different. They wanted a restaurant that exceeded customer expectations for quality and that was a fun place for employees to work. Could Sullivan's concept of a fun place to work capture the fancy of customers and employees?

Sullivan and his cofounders had originally planned to build just a few restaurants and then play a lot of golf. Life didn't work out that way. The company they created captured the imagination and appetites of the restaurant-going public. Within its first six years, Outback Steakhouse had become the fastest-growing restaurant chain in the casual dining segment of the restaurant industry. Outback's management team took the company public, to the delight of its shareholders. It has won numerous awards for business growth, including Entrepreneur of the Year awards from both *Inc.* magazine and the Kauffman Foundation.

Part of Outback's success has come from its unorthodox management system. First, Sullivan and his colleagues wanted restaurateurs to be able to make a career as store managers. In many restaurant chains, the best-paying positions are in the corporate office, not directly serving customers. Top store managers in those systems leave the restaurant to move to corporate in order to make a good salary.

To attract managers, Outback offered very strong financial packages (in many cases offering the manager equity in the local restaurant), assignment to a location for a minimum of five years, and a work environment serving dinner only. Outback's unique employment offers aren't just for the top employees. Recently, the company rolled out a benefits program for part-time employees. In contrast to many other companies, the less you make at Outback, the less you are required to pay for health insurance.

Sullivan insists that one key for a successful restaurant is for the local team to have fun. Local Outback managers have noted that one of the first questions CEO Sullivan asks them when visiting their location is, "Are you still having fun?" Management's casual style and its fiercely entrepreneurial culture echo the corporate motto: "No rules, just right."

Discussion Questions

1. What management roles does Sullivan fulfill, based on this case?

2. List at least 10 specific management tasks he will have to attend to in a typical week.

3. Is Sullivan using a Classical/Mechanistic or an Organic/Flexible management approach, and why do you think he is doing so, given his environment and situation?

4. What environmental forces that you can think of are acting to influence Outback's business and management style, for good or for ill?

JETBLUE IS AIRBORNE

jetBlue AIRWAYS In the 20 or so years since Congress deregulated the airline industry, dozens of new airlines have launched and then failed. The airline burial grounds are filled with companies like Pan Am, Eastern, Braniff, and National—airlines that had been in business for years but simply couldn't compete in the face of the new efficiencies demanded by deregulation. Airlines that even industry experts had assumed would survive—like United and USAir—were struggling. One major airline that went out of business in 2002, Swissair, was hit by an ill-conceived expansion plan and by fierce, industrywide competition. There continues to be a tough environment for airlines.

David Neeleman stepped into this environment with plans to launch a low-cost airline. Neeleman is no industry novice; he brought to the table a twenty-year record of effective management. Raised in Utah, Neeleman dropped out of college to start a travel agency in 1981. In 1984 he agreed to help another travel agent, Joan Morris, run a charter business that grew into discount airline Morris Air, which they then sold to Southwest Airline in 1993 for $129 million in stock. Prohibited from running a U.S. airline for 5 years by his Southwest buyout, Neeleman headed north to help start the Canadian airline

WestJet, and then headed a company that created electronic reservation systems. Meanwhile, he was making plans for a new airline.[107]

By 1998, Neeleman was speaking to investors about plans for a new airline. This presented investors with a dilemma. On the one hand, Neeleman had a twenty-year record of starting and managing travel and airline businesses. On the other hand, the competition had proved deadly to many other startups. As one article noted, "Low fares and a cute name only kept Kiwi international airlines afloat seven years before it liquidated its assets in August 1999. And despite millions in loans from General Motors Corp., DaimlerChrysler, and the United Auto Workers, ProAir had filed for bankruptcy in September, after the federal aviation administration grounded the airline for safety and maintenance violations.[108]

There were additional aspects of Neeleman's plan that investors might have had doubts about. For example, he planned to initiate service between Fort Lauderdale and JFK. That route certainly needed a low-cost competitor. However, major airlines like American and Delta were already flying the route and could be expected to respond to JetBlue by lowering their own prices. Furthermore, many customers viewed New York's JFK as congested and delay-prone and too far from the city (it takes about a half an hour more to get from JFK to New York than it does from LaGuardia). Neeleman also planned to go "first-class" and to keep costs low. He planned to buy new planes to avoid maintenance costs for the first 5 years or so, install leather seats (which cost more but last twice as long as regular seats), and install a TV at every seat to boost passenger comfort levels.

The question was, could he do all that and offer low-cost pricing? Some of the world's most sophisticated investors, including Chase Capital and George Soros, decided that the answer was "yes." Together, investors put together the $130 million in financing that helped launch JetBlue.

Having a great idea is one thing, implementing it is another. Now that David Neeleman had his $130 million, it was time to get his airline launched. And it turned out that he was going to have to launch JetBlue in an environment that included not just the "usual" threats like cutthroat competition, but also the 9/11 terrorist attacks, which reduced air travel by 30%. It was going to be a challenging few years for David Neeleman.

Assignment

You and your team are consultants to Mr. Neeleman, who is depending on your management expertise to help him navigate the launch and management of JetBlue. Here's what he wants to know from you now:

1. I have the money we need to start the airline but no organization of any kind at this point. What ten specific management tasks am I going to have to attend to during the next 12 months?

2. "He who neglects the past is doomed to repeat it." I'm a bit of a management history buff. List and briefly describe five things I can learn from a study of the evolution of management thought that can help me create JetBlue.

3. List and briefly describe five environmental forces that are influencing my business.

4. List three specific reasons why I should use a classical/mechanistic, or organic/flexible management approach, given JetBlue's situation. (Hint: Fill in a chart similar to Table 1.2).

2 Managing in a Cultural and Ethical Environment

CHAPTER OBJECTIVES

After studying this chapter and the case exercises at the end, you should be able to:

1. Correctly identify both ethical and unethical decisions.

2. Rate your own ethics level.

3. Assess and quantify the ethical culture of an organization.

4. Design a specific plan for improving ethical behavior in a company.

5. Specify the steps a manager should take to change a company's ethical culture.

6. Design a specific diversity management plan.

THE MANAGEMENT CHALLENGE

John Pepper's Dilemma

Several years ago, his managers told Procter & Gamble chairman John Pepper that units in the company were running an extensive intelligence-gathering campaign against one of its competitors, Unilever. Procter & Gamble had reportedly long engaged in what it calls "competitive analysis" to study and predict competitors' moves. However, in this case, it seemed apparent to Pepper that the company's agents had gone too far. P&G managers had hired a general contractor who in turn hired about a dozen subcontractors to spy on Unilever. They ran the operation out of a safe house they called "the Ranch" in Cincinnati, where P&G is headquartered. These subcontractors allegedly trespassed on Unilever property, dug around in its garbage dumpsters, and misrepresented themselves to Unilever employees as market analysts. By doing so, they apparently got plenty of competitive data on Unilever's products. A P&G spokesperson said that P&G had obtained all the Unilever materials legally, but that the methods had "violated our [company's] competitive business information-gathering policy."[1] What would you do if you were John Pepper and just got this news?

Chapter 1 explained the importance of managers' effectiveness in planning, organizing, leading, and controlling skills. However, as is apparent from the rash of Enron/Arthur Andersen/Worldcom management scandals, if you can't exercise good ethical judgment, it does not matter how good you are at planning, organizing, leading, and controlling: Both you and your company are probably doomed to fail. Therefore, before we turn to the management functions (beginning with planning, in Chapter 3), let us look at the ethics of managing. The main purpose of this chapter is to make you both more effective at recognizing an unethical decision when you see it and more effective at making ethical decisions. The main topics covered include the meaning of ethics, factors that influence ethical behavior, and how to foster ethics at work.

■■■ WHAT IS ETHICAL BEHAVIOR?

People face ethical choices every day. Consider this dilemma: Your best friend sits next to you in a large college class and can't afford to miss any more sessions because attendance counts so much in the final grade. She just called to ask that you sign the class roll for her tomorrow. You know that she does have a family emergency. There are 190 students in the hall, so the chance the professor will catch you is virtually zero. Should you help your best friend? How can you decide?

Dilemmas like that represent just the tip of the ethical-dilemma iceberg. For example, is it wrong to use company e-mail for personal reasons? Is a $50 gift to a boss unacceptable?

Compare your answers to those of other Americans surveyed by answering the quiz in Figure 2.1. You'll find the answers to the quiz on page 51. How do you make decisions like these? Let's start by defining ethics.

▼ **FIGURE 2–1** ■■■
The Wall Street Journal Workplace-Ethics Quiz

The spread of technology into the workplace has raised a variety of new ethical questions, and many old ones still linger. Compare your answers with those of other Americans surveyed, on page 51.

Source: Wall Street Journal, 21 October 1999, pp. 81–84. Ethics Officer Association, Belmont, Mass.; Ethics Leadership Group, Wilmette, Ill.; surveys sampled a cross-section of workers at large companies and nationwide.

Office Technology

1. Is it wrong to use company e-mail for personal reasons?
   ☐ Yes   ☐ No

2. Is it wrong to use office equipment to help your children or spouse do schoolwork?
   ☐ Yes   ☐ No

3. Is it wrong to play computer games on office equipment during the workday?
   ☐ Yes   ☐ No

4. Is it wrong to use office equipment to do Internet shopping?
   ☐ Yes   ☐ No

5. Is it unethical to blame an error you made on a technological glitch?
   ☐ Yes   ☐ No

6. Is it unethical to visit pornographic Web sites using office equipment?
   ☐ Yes   ☐ No

Gifts and Entertainment

7. What's the value at which a gift from a supplier or client becomes troubling
   ☐ $25   ☐ $50   ☐ $100

8. Is a $50 gift to a boss unacceptable?
   ☐ Yes   ☐ No

9. Is a $50 gift FROM the boss unacceptable?
   ☐ Yes   ☐ No

10. Of gifts from suppliers: Is it OK to take a $200 pair of football tickets?
    ☐ Yes   ☐ No

11. Is it OK to take a $120 pair of theater tickets?
    ☐ Yes   ☐ No

12. Is it OK to take a $100 holiday food basket?
    ☐ Yes   ☐ No

13. Is it OK to take a $25 gift certificate?
    ☐ Yes   ☐ No

14. Can you accept a $75 prize won at a raffle at a supplier's conference?
    ☐ Yes   ☐ No

Truth and Lies

15. Due to on-the-job pressure, have you ever abused or lied about sick days?
    ☐ Yes   ☐ No

16. Due to on-the-job pressure, have you ever taken credit for someone else's work or idea?
    ☐ Yes   ☐ No

The Meaning of Ethics

Ethics refers to "the principles of conduct governing an individual or a group,"[2] and specifically to the standards you use to decide what your conduct should be. Ethical decisions always involve normative judgments.[3] A normative judgment implies that "something is good or bad, right or wrong, better or worse."[4] "You are wearing a skirt and blouse" is a nonnormative statement. "That's a great outfit!" is a normative one.

Ethical decisions also always involve morality, which is society's accepted standards of behavior. Moral standards differ from other standards in several ways.[5] They address matters of serious consequence to society's well-being, such as murder, lying, and slander. They cannot be established or changed by decisions of authoritative bodies like legislatures,[6] and they should override self-interest. Many people believe that moral judgments are never situational. They argue that something that is morally right (or wrong) in one situation is right (or wrong) in another. Moral judgments tend to trigger strong emotions. Violating moral standards may make you feel ashamed or remorseful.[7]

It would simplify things if it was always clear which decisions were ethical and which were not. Unfortunately, it is not. Ethics—principles of conduct—are rooted in morality, so in many cases it's clear what is ethical. (For example, if the decision makes the person feel ashamed or remorseful or involves a matter of serious consequence such as murder, then chances are it's probably unethical.) On the other hand, perhaps in some places bribery is so widely ingrained that people there don't view it as wrong. In that frame of reference, bribery may simply be how people get things done.

Good and Evil

For many philosophers, the study of ethics is the study of good and evil. Since biblical times people have asked, "What is good and what is evil?"[8] To some of these philosophers, what is good and what is evil does not vary from situation to situation. Religious codes like the Ten Commandments reflect this absolute view. The Ten Commandments lay out what is right and what is wrong irrespective of the situation, "at all times and in all places."[9] The Greek philosopher Socrates believed in such principles. People, he said, should pursue what is good and what is true regardless of the consequences (and he was put to death as a result). At the other extreme, some have long believed (and still do) that "both good and evil are relative to the conditions of the time and place, and that which is good in one place and time will be evil in another."[10] For example, most people would agree that telling the truth is good. But if a person who intends to cause harm asks you where his victim has gone, would telling him the truth be a good thing? Perhaps not.[11] Similarly, is it wrong to lie when doing so helps your employer to survive and you to keep your job? (That is a question managers at Enron and Arthur Andersen perhaps asked themselves.)

Philosophers have names for these two points of view. A *teleologist* evaluates good or evil and right or wrong based on the consequences or results of the proposed actions. A *deontologist* (like Socrates) evaluates whether actions are good or bad, right or wrong, based on "whether or not they conform to certain principles you feel bound to obey or follow regardless of their consequences."[12] Various other positions fall between these two extremes. For example, *utilitarianism* also links right and wrong to consequences. Utilitarians believe that one should make decisions that result in the greatest total utility—that is, achieve the greatest benefit for all those affected by a decision.[13] Table 2.1 summarizes the main moral philosophies.

■ *Application Example* These points of view sometimes lead to different moral decisions. For example, consider this situation:

> You are a railroad switch operator sitting in a watchtower controlling a switch that allows trains to travel over the regular track or switches them to a siding. One morning, you face a terrible dilemma. The New York Zephyr is traveling at high speed on the main track, and a school bus filled with children (at least 50) has stalled on the main track as it crosses Elm Street. The bus driver is trying to restart the engine, but it is clear to you that the bus will not get off the track in time. On the siding track is a homeless man who has fallen down with his foot under a rail. It's clear that he is also stuck.

TABLE 2–1 **A Comparison of Several Moral Philosophies**

Teleology	Stipulates that acts are morally right or acceptable if they produce some desired result, such as the realization of self-interest or utility
Egoism	Defines right or acceptable actions as those that maximize a particular person's self-interest as defined by the individual
Utilitarianism	Defines right or acceptable actions as those that maximize total utility, or the greatest good for the greatest number of people
Deontology	Focuses on the preservation of individual rights and on the intentions associated with a particular behavior rather than on its consequences
Relativist	Evaluates ethicalness subjectively on the basis of individual and group experiences
Virtue ethics	Assumes that what is moral in a given situation is not only what conventional morality requires, but also what the mature person with a "good" moral character would deem appropriate

Source: O. C. Ferrell and John Fraedrich, *Business Ethics*, 3rd ed. (New York: Houghton Mifflin, 1997), p. 54.

In 15 seconds, you must decide whether to use the switch to send the train to the siding—thereby killing the homeless man—or to do nothing and allow the train to take its normal course and thereby hit the bus and probably kill most if not all of the 50 schoolchildren on board."[14] *Here, taking action means knowingly killing the homeless man. But not taking action means the children will proboably die. How would each moral philosophy approach this situation? What would you do?*

Ethics and the Law

The law would probably be of little help to the switch operator, which raises another important point. Something may be legal but not right, and something may be right but not legal. You can make a decision that involves ethics (such as firing an employee) based on what is legal. However, that doesn't mean the decision will be ethical, since a legal decision can be unethical (and an ethical one illegal). Firing a 38-year-old employee just before she has earned the right to her pension may be unethical, but still legal. Charging a naïve customer an exorbitant price may be legal but unethical. Patrick Gnazzo, vice president for business practices at United Technologies Corp. (and a former trial lawyer) put it this way: "Don't lie, don't cheat, don't steal. We were all raised with essentially the same values. Ethics means making decisions that represent what you stand for, not just what the laws are."[15]

One ethicist suggests viewing your ethical options as a continuum, as in Figure 2.2 The "selfish egoist" basically says, "Might makes right." Such people make their decisions based on what they think they can get away with.[16] To stop (or at least slow down) these people, countries and states make laws. In competing with other companies, for instance, some managers voluntarily follow the law, although some powerful selfish egoists may still try to flaunt it.[17] Other managers and professionals voluntarily adhere to the (usually) more exacting professional standards of their professions or professional associations. (For example, the professional association of executive recruiters has rules regarding how long a recruiter should wait before approaching a manager whom he or she placed about a new position.) Finally, there is the person who makes his or her decisions based on the highest standard of all. "The person of integrity stands as the most admired of all who value the standards of the profession. This person accepts the constraints and limitations of the profession—and more."[18]

X	Y	Z	Z+
Selfish egoism standard	Legal standard	Professional practice standard	Integrity standard

◀ **FIGURE 2–2** ■ ■ ■

The Ethical Continuum

Source: Michael Boylan, *Business Ethics* (Upper Saddle River, NJ: Prentice Hall, 2001), p. 119.

There is no one simple answer to the question, "What influences ethical behavior at work?" From the research, it's clear that ethical (or unethical) behavior isn't caused by any one thing.

For example, one review of the research concluded that it's not just the employee's ethics, since even ethical employees can have their decisions influenced by *organizational* factors.[19] The *environment* is important, too. In several laboratory studies, researchers concluded that unethical behavior was more prevalent both in competitive environments and in situations in which the company rewards such behavior.[20] Other research similarly suggests that "ethical decisions are the result of the interaction of the person and the situation."[21] Thus, ethical or unethical decisions seem to be a function of things like the person, the company, and the pressures of the situation.

Individual Factors

Personal predispositions are certainly one important factor behind ethical behavior. People bring to their jobs their own ideas of what is morally right and wrong. The individual must, therefore, shoulder much of the credit (or blame) for the ethical decisions he or she makes. Researchers conducted a survey of CEOs of manufacturing firms to explain the CEOs' intentions to engage (or to not engage) in two questionable business practices: soliciting a competitor's technological secrets and making payments to foreign government officials to secure business. The researchers concluded that a CEO's personal predispositions more strongly affected his or her decisions than environmental pressures or organizational characteristics.[22]

It's hard to generalize about the characteristics of ethical or unethical people, but age is a factor. One study surveyed 421 employees to measure the degree to which age, gender, marital status, education, dependent children, region of the country, and years in business influenced responses to ethical decisions. (Decisions included "doing personal business on company time," "not reporting others' violations of company rules and policies," and "calling in sick to take a day off for personal use.") Older workers in general had stricter interpretations of ethical standards and made more ethical decisions than younger employees. Other characteristics had no effect. Others have also found this ethical generation gap.[23] This age factor is compounded because most people tend to have a distorted view of how ethical they really are.[24] It's therefore easy to be lulled into a false sense of security regarding the ethics of one's actions.

How would you rate your own ethics? Figure 2.3 presents a short self-assessment survey to help you answer that question.

Organizational Factors

If people did unethical things at work because of a desire for personal gain, it might be understandable (though inexcusable). The scary thing about unethical behavior at work is that it's usually not driven by personal interests. Table 2.2 summarizes the results of one survey of the principal causes of ethical compromises, as reported by six levels of employees and managers. It's apparent that characteristics of the organization and how it's managed also influence the level of ethics.

As you can see, dealing with scheduling pressures was the number one factor in ethical lapses. For most of these employees, "meeting overly aggressive financial or business objectives" and "helping the company survive" were the other top two reported causes. "Advancing my own career or financial interests" ranked toward the bottom of the list. Thus, at least in this case, most ethical lapses occurred because employees were under pressure to do what they thought was best to help their companies. Several years ago, for example, three former CUC International executives pleaded guilty to federal charges in what authorities called "the largest and longest" accounting fraud in history; the fraud had gone on for 12 years. The former executives said they had done so to keep the price of the company stock high.[25]

The process is insidious and feeds on itself. As the famous investor Warren Buffett put it, "Once a company moves earnings from one period to another, operating shortfalls that occurred thereafter require it to engage in further accounting maneuvers

INSTRUMENT

Indicate your level of agreement with these 15 statements using the following scale:

1 = Strongly disagree

2 = Disagree

3 = Neither agree or disagree

4 = Agree

5 = Strongly agree

1. The only moral of business is making money.	1	2	3	4	5
2. A person who is doing well in business does not have to worry about moral problems.	1	2	3	4	5
3. Act according to the law, and you can't go wrong morally.	1	2	3	4	5
4. Ethics in business is basically an adjustment between expectations and the ways people behave.	1	2	3	4	5
5. Business decisions involve a realistic economic attitude and not a moral philosophy.	1	2	3	4	5
6. "Business ethics" is a concept for public relations only.	1	2	3	4	5
7. Competitiveness and profitability are important values	1	2	3	4	5
8. Conditions of a free economy will best serve the needs of society. Limiting competition can only hurt society and actually violates basic natural laws.	1	2	3	4	5
9. As a consumer when making an auto insurance claim, I try to get as much as possible regardless of the extent of the damage.	1	2	3	4	5
10. While shopping at the supermarket, it is appropriate to switch price tags on packages.	1	2	3	4	5
11. As an employee, I can take home office supplies; it doesn't hurt anyone.	1	2	3	4	5
12. I view sick days as vacation days that I deserve.	1	2	3	4	5
13. Employees' wages should be determined according to the laws of supply and demand.	1	2	3	4	5
14. The business world has its own rules.	1	2	3	4	5
15. A good businessperson is a successful businessperson.	1	2	3	4	5

ANALYSIS AND INTERPRETATION

Rather than specify "right" answers, this instrument works best when you compare your answer to those of others. With that in mind, here are mean responses from a group of 243 management students. How did your responses compare?

1. 3.09	6. 2.88	11. 1.58
2. 1.88	7. 3.62	12. 2.31
3. 2.54	8. 3.79	13. 3.36
4. 3.41	9. 3.44	14. 3.79
5. 3.88	10. 1.33	15. 3.38

◄ **FIGURE 2–3** ■ ■ ■

How Do My Ethics Rate?

Source: Stephen P. Robbins, *Self-Assessment Library: Insights into your Skills, Abilities and Interests* (Upper Saddle River, NJ: Prentice Hall, 2002), pp. 36–37. Adapted from A. Reichel and Y. Neumann, *Journal of Instructional Psychology*, March 1998, pp. 25–53. With permission of the authors.

TABLE 2–2		Principal Causes of Ethical Compromises					

%	Senior Mgmt.	Middle Mgmt.	Front Line Supv.	Prof. Non-Mgmt.	Admin. Salaried	Hourly
Meeting schedule pressure	1	1	1	1	1	1
Meeting overly aggressive financial or business objectives	3	2	2	2	2	2
Helping the company survive	2	3	4	4	3	4
Advancing the career interests of my boss	5	4	3	3	4	5
Feeling peer pressure	7	7	5	6	5	3
Resisting competitive threats	4	5	6	5	6	7
Saving jobs	9	6	7	7	7	6
Advancing my own career or financial interests	8	9	9	8	9	8
Other	6	8	8	9	8	9

Note: 1 is high, 9 is low

Source: O. C. Ferrell and John Fraedrich, *Business Ethics*, 3rd ed. (New York: Houghton Mifflin, 1997), p. 28. Adapted from Rebecca Goodell, *Ethics in American Business: Policies, Programs, and Perceptions* (1994), p. 54. Permission provided courtesy of the Ethics Resource Center, 1120 6th Street, NW, Washington, DC, 20005.

that must be even more 'heroic.' These can turn fudging into fraud."[26] It's this kind of evolution that may have finally tripped up Enron. As one article said at the time, "To meet the outside world's unrealistic expectations, it began to fudge the figures. To disguise liabilities, it wrapped them up in private partnerships and took them off its balance sheet. And to satisfy the wishful thinkers' insatiable demand, it brought earnings forward by selling shares and other off-balance sheet partnerships, and counting the proceeds as revenues."[27]

In 2001, Enron was one of the largest companies in the world, and Arthur Andersen was one of the world's big five accounting firms. One year later, Enron was in bankruptcy, and Andersen, which was convicted in a case brought by the Justice Department, had ceased to exist by August 2002. Both firms had very good managers, but that didn't do them any good. In violation of its own ethical policies, Enron let some executives set up special "off the books" partnerships. Enron then allegedly used these partnerships to hide costs and puff up revenues. Andersen, its auditor, had controls in place that questioned this dubious accounting. However, Andersen shunted off the partners who did the questioning to other jobs, allegedly to help keep Enron as a client.

Having rules forbidding this sort of thing does not, by itself, seem to work. For example, in 2002, New York's Attorney General filed charges against Merrill Lynch, alleging that several of its analysts had issued optimistic ratings on stocks, while privately expressing concerns about those same stocks. The allegation was that they did so to aid and support Merrill Lynch's investment banking relationships with these companies—in violation of Merrill's own rules.

■ *Application Example: Toxic Toys* You are a regional sales manager of Kaolin Toys. The company has just come out with a line of toys that encourage building skills. There are concerns about safety. Should asthmatic children eat the smallest pieces of the building set and then drink several glasses of milk, they might experience severe digestive problems. The company has put a warning label on all sets. This problem is expected to affect only 75 children (based on the estimated total number of children using the sets).

You realize, however, that claims involving children are always sensitive. A competitor recently was sued on a frivolous claim that cost it millions of dollars. Thousands of people on the net "chatted" about the claim and spread rumor and innuendo about the product. You want to avoid falling into the same situation. What actions would you take to protect yourself and the company?[28] Would that be ethical?

The really worrisome thing about unethical behavior at work, to repeat, is that employees often don't think they're doing anything wrong; they think they're doing right (for their employers). As one writer said (after prosecutors found that Sears service writers were inflating service bills in what was basically an organized scheme), "The people involved were probably ordinary men and women for the most part, not very different from you and me. They found themselves in a dilemma, and they solved it in a way that seemed to be the least troublesome. The consequences . . . probably never occurred to them."[29]

The Influence of Top Management

Top managers (and bosses in general) react to ethical crises in different ways. When he found out about his company's spying operation, P&G Chairman John Pepper was reportedly shocked. He ordered the campaign to stop, and he fired the managers responsible for hiring the spies. Then, he "blew the whistle" on his own company. He had P&G inform Unilever of what his firm had done. Unilever, among other things, demanded that P&G retain a third-party auditor to make sure it does not take advantage of the documents its spies stole from Unilever's trash bins.[30]

On the other hand, even after an Enron vice president warned him that Enron might be an "elaborate accounting hoax," Chairman Kenneth Lay allegedly went online to urge the company's employees to buy Enron shares.[31]

The leader's actions may be "the single most important factor in fostering corporate behavior of a high ethical standard."[32] The boss sets the tone for the company, and by his or her actions sends signals about what is right or wrong. A study by the American Society of Chartered Life Underwriters found that 56% of all workers felt some pressure to act unethically or illegally—and that the problem seems to be getting worse.[33] One writer gives these examples of how supervisors knowingly (or unknowingly) lead subordinates astray ethically:

- Tell staffers to do whatever is necessary to achieve results.
- Overload top performers to ensure that work gets done.
- Look the other way when wrongdoing occurs.
- Take credit for others' work or shift blame.[34]

Ethics Policies and Codes

An ethics policy and code is one way to signal that the firm is serious about ethics.[35] For example, IBM's code of ethics has this to say about tips, gifts, and entertainment:

> No IBM employee, or any member of his or her immediate family, can accept gratuities or gifts of money from a supplier, customer, or anyone in a business relationship. Nor can they accept the gift or consideration that could be perceived as having been offered because of the business relationship. "Perceived" simply means this: If you read about it in the local newspaper, would you wonder whether the gift just might have had something to do with a business relationship? No IBM employee can give money or a gift of significant value to a customer, supplier, or anyone if it could reasonably be viewed as being done to gain a business advantage."[36]

One study found that 56% of large firms (and about 25% of small firms) had corporate codes of conduct. Two things make ethics codes more important today. Diversity is one: It may be more necessary to emphasize explicit rules, expectations, and ethics codes because it's more difficult to infuse common values and beliefs in a diverse workforce.[37] New U.S. federal sentencing guidelines are another. Under the new guidelines, the more effort management can show it made to ensure ethical behavior, the lower the fine the company can expect to pay if it is sued for unethical practices and loses.[38] Similarly, in 2002, President Bush signed into law new legislation requiring CEOs to personally certify their companies' financial reports, and toughening consequences for mangers whose firms break the law.

Sometimes ethics codes work, however, and sometimes they don't. Enron's ethical principles were widely available on the company's Web site. They said, among other things, that "as a partner in the communities in which we operate, Enron believes it has a responsibility to conduct itself according to certain basic principles." Those values include "respect, integrity, communication and excellence."[39] In general, though, an ethics code does send a strong signal to the company's employees. One study consisted of structured interviews with 766 subjects over a two-year period.[40] The researchers drew two main conclusions.

First,

> the existence of a corporate code of ethics affected both employees' ethical behavior and the perception of ethics in several ways. Respondents who worked for companies having a code of ethics judge subordinates, co-workers, themselves and especially supervisors and top managers to be more ethical than respondents employed in organizations not having a formal code of ethics. Employees in companies with an ethics code also gave higher ratings of the company's support for ethical behavior, reported higher levels of satisfaction with outcomes of ethical dilemmas, more frequently reported being encouraged to behave ethically, and felt somewhat less pressure to behave unethically than respondents from companies without an ethics code.[41]

Second, it seemed to be the mere presence of the code (rather than its content) that influenced the employees. "In fact, we found that although most respondents could not recall specific features of their company's ethics code, employees of companies having a code had very different perceptions of ethical climate and behavior than employees of companies lacking a code."[42] Therefore, the important function of the code may be communicating the importance of appropriate behavior, rather than educating employees about what specifically constitutes ethical behavior.

■ *The Global Manager* Around the world, managers face a wide range of ethical standards. Bribes and unethical behavior are the price of doing business in many countries. Some estimate that in Albania, for instance, businesses pay out bribes equal to about 8% of their sales (about one-third of their potential profits) as a cost of doing business.[43] Similarly, some estimate that in one recent year, U.S. businesses lost $15 billion in orders abroad to firms from countries that allow bribes. (Bribes are prohibited in the United States by the Foreign Corrupt Practices Act). In India, where many patients are too poor to see doctors and rely on their pharmacist for medical advice and drugs, a pharmacy owner was proud of the 29-inch color television he received as a gift from the pharmacy company GlaxoSmithKline PLC. This particular pharmacist ordered 600 vials of one antibiotic and 100 boxes of another—many times what he'd normally stock—apparently because he wanted the TV.[44]

Businesspeople hope a number of steps, among them an antibribery treaty signed by 34 trading nations, will reduce the incidence of corruption. Some executives are pushing for a global corporate ethics standard under the auspices of the International Standards Organization (ISO). The ISO now provides quality (ISO 9000) and environmental (ISO 14,000) standards. "We want a simple, effective way to operate internationally—one that meets all the criteria of doing business overseas, whether it's proving assurance of quality or ethical business practices,"[45] says one executive. ISO ethical standards would provide a detailed list of criteria that companies have to meet in order to prove that they do business ethically, including procedures to ensure compliance.

■■■ HOW TO FOSTER ETHICS AT WORK

We've seen that there's no single cause of unethical behavior at work, so it is not surprising that there's no one "silver bullet" to prevent it. Instead, managers must take several steps to ensure ethical behavior by their employees.[46] As two experts say, methods for fostering ethics range from "create[ing] an ethical workforce by recruiting and selecting individuals who have dispositions or work histories that suggest they are less likely to engage in workplace wrongdoing. . . . " to instituting training, ethics codes, and a more ethical culture.[47]

TABLE 2–3	Code of Ethics Implementation

Six Steps to Effective Implementation of a Code of Ethics

1. Distribute the code of ethics comprehensively to employees, subsidiaries, and associated companies.

2. Assist employees in interpreting and understanding the application and intent of the code.

3. Specify management's role in the implementation of the code.

4. Inform employees of their responsibility to understand the code, and provide them with the overall objectives of the code.

5. Establish grievance procedures.

6. Provide a conclusion or closing statement, such as this one from Cadbury Schweppes:

> The character of the company is collectively in our hands. Pride in what we do is important, and let us earn that pride by the way we put the beliefs set out here into action.

Source: O. C. Ferrell and John Fraedrich, *Business Ethics*, 3rd ed. (New York: Houghton Mifflin, 1997), p. 176. Adapted from Walter W. Manley II, *The Handbook of Good Business Practice* (London: Routledge, 1992), p. 16.

Activities That Foster Ethics

These and other researchers conclude that fostering ethics involves the following sets of activities (see Checklist 2.1)

CHECKLIST 2.1 ■ How to Foster Ethics

☑ Emphasize top management's commitment.

☑ Publish an ethics code.

☑ Establish compliance mechanisms.

☑ Involve personnel at all levels.

☑ Train employees.

☑ Measure results.

Emphasize Top Management's Commitment As two researchers put it, "To achieve results, the chief executive officer and those around the CEO need to be openly and strongly committed to ethical conduct, and give constant leadership in tending and renewing the values of the organization."[48]

Publish an Ethics Code Firms with effective ethics programs set forth principles of conduct for the whole organization in the form of written documents.[49] Table 2.3 summarizes six steps for effectively implementing an ethics code. Raytheon has its own method, as the accompanying Management in Action feature demonstrates.

MANAGEMENT IN ACTION   Raytheon

Some firms urge employees to apply a quick "ethics test" to evaluate whether what they're about to do fits the company's code of conduct. For example, the Raytheon Company asks employees who are faced with ethical dilemmas to ask:

■ Is the action legal?

■ Is it right?

■ Who will be affected?

■ Does it fit Raytheon's values?

■ How will it "feel" afterwards?

■ How did it look in the newspaper?

■ Will it reflect poorly on the company?[50]

Establish Compliance Mechanisms Pay attention to candidates' values and ethics in recruiting and hiring; emphasize corporate ethics in training; institute communications programs to inform and motivate employees; and audit to ensure compliance.[51]

Involve Personnel at all Levels Use both roundtable discussions among small groups of employees regarding corporate ethics and surveys of employee attitudes regarding the state of ethics in the firm.[52]

Train Employees Training plays an important role in publicizing a company's ethics values and policies. For example, based on one survey, 89% of surveyed ethics officials said their companies use the new hire orientation to convey ethics codes, and 45% use annual refresher training. Other details of this survey are shown in Figure 2.4.

Measure Results One study of effective ethics programs found that all 11 firms used surveys or audits to monitor compliance with ethical standards.[53] The results of audits should then be discussed among board members and employees.[54] Many firms use technology to keep tabs on ethical results. We'll turn to this next.

Using Technology to Foster Ethics

Technology has been a double-edged sword for employee ethics. On the one hand, the Internet may have caused a rise in the time employees spend on personal pursuits during the day—shopping online, for instance, or sending messages to friends. (UPS caught one employee using the company computer to run a personal business.)

On the other hand, technology also provides the means for monitoring all kinds of potentially unethical actions. For example, Turner Broadcasting System Inc. noticed that

▶ **FIGURE 2–4** ■ ■ ■

The Role of Training in Ethics

Source: Susan Wells, "Turn Employees into Saints," *HRMagazine*, December 1999, p. 52.

Company ethics officials say they convey ethics codes and programs to employees using these training programs:

New hire orientation
89%

Annual refresher training
45%

Annual training
32%

Occasional but not scheduled training
31%

New employee follow-up sessions
20%

No formal training
5%

Company ethics officials use these actual training tools to convey ethics training to employees:

Copies of company policies
78%

Ethics handbooks
76%

Videotaped ethics programs
59%

Online assistance
39%

Ethics newsletters
30%

employees at its CNN London business bureau were piling up overtime claims. CNN installed new software to monitor every Web page every worker used. As the firm's network security specialist put it, "If we see people were surfing the Web all day, then they don't have to be paid for that overtime."[55] One study suggests that about 75% of all U.S. firms now record and review some type of employee communications and/or activity, such as e-mail, phone calls, computer files, and Internet use. That's about double the 1997 figure.[56]

New software can secretly record everything your spouse, children, and employees do on-line on a particular computer. Other software lets the user find out everything your spouse, children, and employees do online via e-mail. "This program works so well it's scary,"[57] says someone who has used it. The accompanying Managing @ the Speed of Thought feature presents some examples.

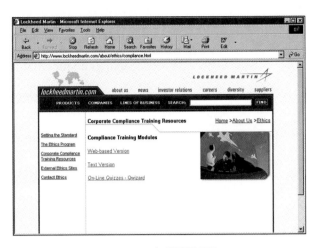

▲ WEBNOTE ■ ■ ■

Lockheed's Intranet allows its employees to take ethics and legal compliance training online; it also allows Lockheed to keep track of who takes the courses and how well employees are maintaining high ethical standards.

www.lockheedmartin.com

Source: © 2002 Lockheed Martin Corporation. Used with permission.

MANAGING @ THE SPEED OF THOUGHT

BellSouth and Lockheed Martin

Internet monitoring is just one example of how managers use technology to keep closer tabs on their employees. When cable repairman Johnny Cupid starts his service truck, his employer, BellSouth, knows exactly where he is. Thanks to BellSouth's new global positioning satellite (GPS) units, BellSouth supervisors know every time Cupid stops at a stoplight, and where he is as he makes his daily rounds. "I feel like they got their eye on me all the time" is what he says. "I can't slow down anywhere anymore." A BellSouth spokeswoman says, "GPS was not installed as an employee monitoring system. It's an efficiency tool, just like the wireless laptops and cellphones our technicians have." However, apparently not all employees feel the same way. Union workers filed about 50 grievances about the system in the last half of one recent year. Cupid says, "They're nitpicking us to death. I love my job (but) I don't need any more stress."[58]

Lockheed Martin is using "rocket science" to make sure it's employees maintain the company's ethical standards. For example, Lockheed uses its intranet to help its 160,000 employees take ethics and legal compliance training on-line. Each short course addresses topics ranging from insider trading to sexual harassment. The system also keeps track of who (and who is not) taking the required courses. Lockheed's electronic ethics software also keeps track of how well the company and its employees are doing in terms of maintaining high ethical standards.[59] For example, the program helped top management see that in one recent year, 4.8% of the company's ethics allegations involved conflicts of interest. It shows that it takes just over 30 days to complete an ethics violation internal investigation.[60] It also shows that several years ago, 302 Lockheed employees were sanctioned for ethical violations. ■ ■ ■

■ ■ CREATING THE RIGHT CULTURE

When it comes to ethical behavior, it's not just what you say that's important; it's what you do. Parents can talk about being ethical, but if their children see them always cutting ethical corners—bringing home "free" office supplies from the office, for instance—the children may assume that "being unethical is really OK."

The same is true at work. The manager—especially the top manager—sets values and creates a culture through what he or she says and does. Employees then take their

■ ■ *Cloudberry employee using global positioning software to track an employee's movements.*

signals from that behavior and from that culture, and act accordingly. Often, for instance, unethical behavior occurs because employees rightly or wrongly believe they are doing what their boss would want them to do. It's therefore important to send clear signals about what is and isn't acceptable behavior in your company.

What Is Organizational Culture?

organizational culture ■ *the characteristic set of values and ways of behaving that employees in an organization share.*

Organizational culture is the characteristic values, traditions, and behaviors a company's employees share. A value is a basic belief about what is right or wrong, or about what you should or shouldn't do. ("Honesty is the best policy" would be a value.) Values are important because they guide and channel behavior. Managing people and shaping their ethical (and other) behavior therefore depends on shaping the values they use as behavioral guides.

To an outside observer, a company's culture reveals itself in several ways. You can sense it from **patterns of behavior**, such as ceremonial events and written and spoken comments. For example, managers and employees may engage in behaviors such as hiding information, politicking, or expressing honest concern when a colleague requires assistance. You can also sense it from *physical manifestations*, such as written rules, office layouts, organizational structure, and dress codes.[61]

patterns of behavior ■ *in organizational behavior, the ceremonial events, written and spoken comments, and actual behaviors of an organization's members that contribute to creating the organizational culture.*

In turn, these cultural symbols and behaviors tend to reflect the firm's shared values, such as "the customer is always right" or "don't be bureaucratic." If management and employees really believe that "honesty is the best policy," the written rules they follow and the things they do will hopefully reflect this value. Of course, these standards—these **values and beliefs**—lay out what ought to be, not what is.[62] Like the parent in the example above, if management's stated values differ from what the managers actually value, it will show up in the managers' behavior. You have to "Walk the Talk" to set the right culture. Culture, then, reflects the firm's values and patterns of behavior, and the values' physical manifestations (such as written rules, rewards systems, and dress codes).

values and beliefs ■ *the guiding standards of an organization, such as "the customer is always right" or "don't be bureaucratic," that affirm what should be practiced, as distinct from what is practiced.*

Ethics and Corporate Culture

Ethical behavior and corporate culture are a little like Siamese twins. One does not "cause" the other. Instead, they feed on each other—it's a two-way street. *The company's culture influences its ethics:* The manager's stated values, rules, and reward systems send signals about what is right or wrong, and influence how employees behave. And, *the manager's ethics influence the culture* that he or she sets: Like the parent saying one thing and doing another, the manager's ethical decisions will tell his or her "employee family" what the real values are. Suppose a university president turns a blind eye to infractions on the part of coaches regarding the regulations governing recruiting and paying athletes. The president's ethics influence the school's culture. And, the school's culture influences how it deals with ethical dilemmas.[63] Table 2.4 provides a brief survey for auditing and assessing how ethically oriented an organization's culture is.

Culture and the Manager

When it comes to creating a corporate culture, the anecdote about the parent is particularly useful. Organizational culture (as noted previously) means the characteristic values, traditions, and behaviors a company's employees share. Things like these don't just reflect what the manager says. They also reflect what he or she actually does. Managers, therefore, have to think through how they're going to send the right signals to their employees. They do so in the following ways (see Checklist 2.2)

CHECKLIST 2.2 ■ How to Create the Corporate Culture

- ☑ Clarify expectations.
- ☑ Use signs and symbols.
- ☑ Provide physical support.
- ☑ Use stories.
- ☑ Organize rites and ceremonies.

TABLE 2–4		**Organizational Culture Ethics Audit**

Answer YES or NO for each of the following questions*

YES	NO	1. Has the founder or top management within the company left an ethical legacy to the organization?
YES	NO	2. Does the company have methods for detecting ethical concerns within the organization and in the external environment?
YES	NO	3. Is there a shared value system and understanding of what constitutes appropriate behavior within the organization?
YES	NO	4. Are there stories and myths embedded in daily conversations with others about appropriate ethical conduct when confronting ethical situations?
YES	NO	5. Are there codes of ethics or ethical policies that are communicated to employees?
YES	NO	6. Are there ethical rules or procedures in training manuals or other company publications?
YES	NO	7. Are there penalties that are publicly discussed for ethical transgressions?
YES	NO	8. Are there rewards for good ethical decisions even if they don't always result in a profit?
YES	NO	9. Does the company recognize the importance of creating a culture concerned about people and their self-development as members of the business?
YES	NO	10. Does the company have a value system of fair play and honesty toward customers?
YES	NO	11. Do employees treat each other with respect, honesty, and fairness?
YES	NO	12. Do people in the organization spend their time on what is valued by the organization in a cohesive manner?
YES	NO	13. Are there ethically based beliefs and values about how to succeed in the company?
YES	NO	14. Are there heroes or stars in the organization that communicate a common understanding about what is important in terms of positive ethical values?
YES	NO	15. Are there day-to-day rituals or behavior patterns that create direction and prevent confusion and mixed signals on ethics matters?
YES	NO	16. Is the firm more focused on the long run than on the short run?
YES	NO	17. Are employees satisfied or happy, with low employee turnover?
YES	NO	18. Do the dress, speech, and physical setting of work prevent an environment of fragmentation, inconsistency, and the lack of a coherent whole about what is right?
YES	NO	19. Are emotional outbursts with role conflict and role ambiguity very rare?
YES	NO	20. Has discrimination and/or sexual harassment been eliminated?
YES	NO	21. Is there an absence of open hostility and severe conflict?
YES	NO	22. Do people act in a way on the job that is consistent with what they say is ethical?
YES	NO	23. Is the firm more externally focused on customers, the environment, and the welfare of society than internally focused in terms of its own profits?
YES	NO	24. Is there open communication between superiors and subordinates that allows them to discuss ethical dilemmas?
YES	NO	25. Have there been instances where employees have received advice on how to improve ethical behavior or were disciplined for committing unethical acts?

*Add the number of yes answers. The greater the number of yes answers, the less ethical conflict will be experienced in the organization.

Source: O. C. Ferrell and John Fraedrich, *Business Ethics*, 3rd ed. (Boston: Houghton Mifflin, 1997), p. 121.

Clarify Expectations First, make it clear what your expectations are with respect to the values you want subordinates to follow. Publishing a corporate ethics code is one way to do this. For example, Johnson & Johnson says, "We believe our first responsibility is to the doctors, nurses and patients, to mothers and fathers and all others who use our products and services."[64]

Use Signs and Symbols "Walk the talk." *Symbolism*—what the manager actually does and thus the signals he or she sends—ultimately does the most to create and sustain the company's culture. For example, Southwest Airlines is known for its fun (some say zany) work attitude.[65] However, the company doesn't talk about fun or

signs and symbols ■ *practices and actions that create and sustain a company's culture.*

JC Penney management employees being inducted into the "Penney Partnership."

humor in its mission statement. Instead, it sets the tone by what it does from the first day a person is hired. For example, new employees "are welcomed with balloons, games, toys, and gifts. New hires, even pilots, learn company songs or cheers during orientation."[66] Greg Moore, vice president of audit for Tricon Global Restaurants Inc. (the parent of KFC, Pizza Hut, and Taco Bell) wants to create a culture that supports the free exchange of information. He therefore schedules "Greg Moore days," so any auditor can come into his office to share ideas or concerns. He also demonstrates the importance of open and honest communication by sharing the results of his own performance evaluations with his staff. These include not just what his superiors say about how he is doing, "but also feedback from his colleagues and employees."[67]

Provide Physical Support The physical manifestations of the manager's values—the firm's incentive plan, appraisal system, and disciplinary procedures, for instance—send strong signals regarding what employees should and should not do.

stories ■ *the repeated tales and anecdotes that contribute to a company's culture by illustrating and reinforcing important company values.*

Use Stories Managers use stories to illustrate important company values. For example, IBM has stories, such as how IBM salespeople took dramatic steps (like driving all night through storms) to get parts to customers.

rites and ceremonies ■ *traditional culture-building events or activities that symbolize the firm's values and help convert employees to these values.*

Organize Rites and Ceremonies For example, at JC Penney, new management employees are inducted at ritualistic conferences into the "Penney Partnership." At these rites and ceremonies, they commit to the firm's ideology as embodied in its statement of core values. Each inductee solemnly swears allegiance to these values and then receives his or her "HCSC. lapel pin." These letters symbolize JC Penney's core values of honor, confidence, service, and cooperation.

The following Management in Action feature provides an example of culture in action.

MANAGEMENT IN ACTION   Corporate Culture at Procter & Gamble

Procter & Gamble's culture reflects what one expert called the firm's legendary emphasis on "thoroughness, market-testing, and ethical behavior," values that are transmitted to new employees through selection, socialization, and training processes.[68]

The culture's basic elements go back to founders William Procter and James Gamble. They started P&G in Cincinnati in 1837 to produce relatively inexpensive household products that were technically superior to those of the competition, quickly consumed, and an integral part of their customers' lifestyles.[69] Their intention was to "foster growth in an orderly manner, and to plan and prepare for the future."[70]

This philosophy translated into the core P&G values. The emphasis on orderly growth manifests itself in "tremendous conformity."[71] A new recruit soon learns to say "we" instead of "I."[72] This conformity bolsters thoroughness and a methodical approach. Its result, according to one past chair, is a "consistency of principles and policy that gives us direction, thoroughness, and self-discipline."[73]

Various management practices help sustain P&G's culture. The firm recruits college graduates and immdiately places them in competitive situations. Those who can't learn the system are quickly weeded out; the remainder enjoy promotion from within. As a result, no one reaches middle management without 5 to 10 years of scrutiny and training. This system in turn creates what one researcher called "a homogeneous leadership group with an enormous amount of common experience and strong set of shared assumptions."[74]

Authority is centralized. New recruits assume major responsibility for projects almost immediately. However, committees of managers far up the chain of command make most big decisions. Nearly everything must be approved through a written memo process. Stories abound that reinforce this process; one describes the decision about the color of the Folger's coffee lid, supposedly made by the CEO after four years of extensive market testing.[75]

Internal competition is fostered by the brand management system. Brands compete for internal resources, have their own advertising and marketing, and act as independent cost centers. The extensive use of memos, the continual rechecking of each other's work, and the rigid timeline for promotions also contribute to (and reflect) P&G's strong culture and emphasis on thoroughness. ■■■

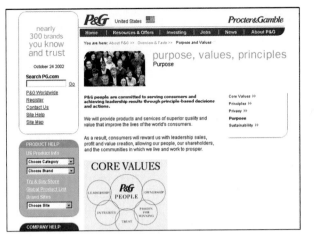

▲ WEBNOTE ■■■

Procter & Gamble's culture is reflected on its Web page, which presents its core values and principles.

www.pandg.com

Source: © 2002 Procter & Gamble.

■■■ MANAGERS AND SOCIAL RESPONSIBILITY

Corporate social responsibility refers to the extent to which companies should and do channel resources toward improving one or more segments of society other than the firm's owners or stockholders. Socially responsible behavior might include creating jobs for minorities, controlling pollution, or supporting educational facilities or cultural events. The socially responsible corporation is the ethical corporation, one which applies high ethical standards to everything it does.

The phrase "social responsibility" tends to trigger images of charitable contributions and helping the homeless, but it actually refers to much more. For example, it refers to the honesty of the company's advertising; to the actual quality of the parts it builds into its products; and to the honesty, ethics, and "rightness" of dealings with customers, suppliers, and employees. So, the socially responsible corporation doesn't just make charitable contributions and avoid selling dangerous products. It is also socially responsible in the sense that it does what's right in everything its managers and employees do.

social responsibility ■ *the extent to which companies should and do channel resources toward improving the quality of life of one or more segments of society other than the firm's own stockholders.*

Ethics and Social Responsibility

In practice, the dividing line between ethics and social responsibility is therefore usually pretty unclear. For example, Eli Lilly Corp. recently faced several lawsuits. Based on usage records, an Eli Lilly salesperson suspected that a pharmacist was diluting an Eli Lilly cancer drug before dispensing it, but said nothing. Only after a physician contacted the FBI about his concerns and implicated the salesperson did the latter admit to his suspicions. For its part, the company points out that its code of conduct emphasizes "proper overall business conduct, possible conflicts of interest, compliance with laws, and confidentiality of proprietary information." For Eli Lilly, is this a matter of ethics or of social responsibility? The answer is, "both." Ethics—what's right or wrong—is the bedrock of socially responsible behavior. Those pressing the lawsuits believe that Eli Lily did not do all it could have done to protect its users and patients.[76]

This raises an interesting question, which has stimulated much heated debate: "To whom should the corporation be responsible?" Most would agree, as two ethicists say, that "the socially responsible corporation is a good corporation."[77] But is a company that tries to do its best only for its owners any less good than one that tries to help customers, vendors, and employees too? The answer depends on what you believe is the purpose of a business. Many perfectly ethical people believe that a company's only social responsibility is to its stockholders. Others disagree.

Managerial Capitalism The classic view is that a corporation's main purpose is to maximize profits for stockholders. Today, this view is most notably associated with economist and Nobel laureate Milton Friedman, who said:

> The view has been gaining widespread acceptance that corporate officials and labor leaders have a "social responsibility" that goes beyond the interest of

their stockholders or their members. This view shows a fundamental misconception of the character and nature of the free economy. In such an economy, there is one and only one social responsibility of business—to use its resources and engage in activities designed to increase its profits so long as it stays within the rules of the game, which is to say, engages in open and free competition, without deception and fraud. . . . Few trends could so thoroughly undermine the very foundation of our free society as the acceptance by corporate officials of a social responsibility other than to make as much money for their stockholders as possible.[78]

Friedman says the stockholders are a company's owners, and so the firm's profits belong to them and to them alone.[79] Furthermore, stockholders deserve their profits, because these profits derive from a voluntary contract among the various corporate stakeholders—the community receives tax money, suppliers are paid, employees earn wages, and so on. Everyone gets his or her due, and additional social responsibility is unnecessary.

Stakeholder Theory An opposing view is that business has a social responsibility to serve *all* the corporate stakeholders affected by its business decisions. A corporate stakeholder is "any group which is vital to the survival and success of the corporation."[80] As in Figure 2.5. six stakeholder groups are traditionally identified: stockholders (owners), employees, customers, suppliers, managers, and the local community (although others could conceivably be identified as well).[81] Stakeholder theory holds that "[t]he rights of these groups must be ensured, and, further, the groups must participate, in some sense, in decisions that substantially affect their welfare."[82] To stakeholder advocates, being socially responsible means more than just maximizing profits; being up-front with employees (unlike the manager in the cartoon) is important too.

The Moral Minimum Between the extremes of Friedman's capitalism and stakeholder theory is an intermediate position. Moral minimum advocates agree that the purpose of the corporation is to maximize profits, but it must do so in conformity with the moral minimum. This means that the firm should be free to strive for profits so long as it commits no harm.[83] A business would certainly have a social responsibility not to produce exploding cigarette lighters or operate chemical plants that poison the environment. However, it's unlikely that the firm's social responsibilities, for instance, would extend to donating to charity or educating the poor.

Don't assume that this brief discussion summarizes the whole complicated field of corporate responsibility. For example, the moral minimum is not the only intermediate position between managerial capitalism and stakeholder theory. Indeed, many find the idea that "maximizing profits is acceptable, as long as the company adheres to the moral minimum of committing no harm"—itself unacceptable. Furthermore, while many view managerial capitalism as a worthy goal, others would say that, in reality, ignoring the interests of nonowner stakeholders—for instance, ignoring the needs of the community in which the corporation has facilities—is bound to undermine profits. The bottom line is that when it comes to being socially responsible, there are many options.

corporate stakeholder ■ *any person or group that is important to the survival and success of the corporation.*

moral minimum ■ *the idea that corporations should be free to strive for profits so long as they commit no harm.*

▶ **FIGURE 2–5** ■ ■ ■

A Corporation's Major Stakeholders

One view of social responsibility is that a firm must consider and serve all the stakeholders that may be affected by its business decisions.

"Some things, Morris, are more easily expressed through puppets."

Why Are Companies Socially Responsible?

Hidden in Hong Kong's Kowloon area is the tiny headquarters of the Asia Monitor Resource Center, which monitors working conditions in China. Its aim is to uncover and publicize unacceptable working conditions in plants producing products for global firms. It hopes to thereby improve working conditions for China's factory workers.

What sorts of unethical practices does the center report? Its Disney report alleged that some mainland Chinese employed by Disney contractors were working up to 16 hours a day, seven days a week, and paid little or no overtime. Another report, on China's toy industry, describes what some have called Mattel's "sweatshop Barbie" assembly lines, because of abuses including long work hours and heavy fines for workers.

Reports like these have an impact.[84] Both Disney and Mattel now have codes of conduct. Disney has done tens of thousands of inspections of its contractors' plants to make sure they comply, and cut off one of its noncomplying factories. Mattel has now received the certificate of workplace standards that Asia Monitor itself calls for.

In practice, the lengths to which the manager goes to be socially responsible depends on several things. It depends on the person's philosophy—whether he or she believes in managerial capitalism, stakeholder theory, or, the moral minimum, for instance. Perhaps the classic example was Ben & Jerry's Ice Cream. Its former owners used to play up the fact that its Rainforest Crunch ice cream contained nuts collected by Amazon "forest peoples" (although it subsequently turned out that "to compensate for quality problems, the nut supplier . . . bought 95% of the nuts from commercial vendors").[85]

Sometimes (as at Disney and Mattel), social responsibility is aided by the watchful eyes of outside monitors and pressure groups. These days, social responsibility advocates have increasingly sophisticated ways to make their positions known. For example, on St. Patrick's Day 2000, shoppers in several Home Depot stores heard a surprising announcement: "Attention shoppers. On aisle 7, you'll find mahogany ripped from the heart of the Amazon."[86] Store managers scampered around looking for pranksters with megaphones, but there were none. It turned out that Rainforest Action Network activists had cracked the security code of Home Depot's intercom systems and were delivering the messages electronically.

All this has led some firms to reduce the decibel level of their claims of social responsiveness.[87] Daniel Grossman, who runs toy maker Wild Planet, says he's very

Top-Rated Companies for Social
Responsibility

Source: Ronald Alsop, "Perils of Corporate
Philanthropy," *Wall Street Journal,* 16
January 2002, pp. B1. 2001 Harris Interactive/
Reputation Institute Survey.

1. Johnson & Johnson
2. Coca-Cola
3. Wal-Mart
4. Anheuser-Busch
5. Hewlett-Packard
6. Walt Disney
7. Microsoft
8. IBM
9. McDonald's
10. 3M
11. UPS
12. FedEx
13. Target
14. Home Depot
15. General Electric

careful not to say his company is socially responsible, just that "we strive to be." For example, while he and his managers screen the factories that manufacture their toys in China, Grossman acknowledges he'd have more control over working conditions if the toys were made in America. Economically, though, he believes doing so wouldn't be practical in the low-cost markets where he's chosen to compete.[88] Figure 2.6 lists the top-rated companies for social responsibility based on a recent Harris poll.

How to Improve the Company's Social Responsiveness

Managers improve their companies' social responsiveness by instituting policies and practices that encourage socially responsible behavior. These include social audits, "whistle blowing," and joining responsibility advocacy groups.

corporate social audit ■ *a rating system used to evaluate a corporation's performance with regard to meeting its social obligations.*

The Social Audit Given a commitment to being socially responsible, how can firms ensure that they are in fact responsive? Some firms monitor how well they measure up to their aims by using a rating system called a corporate social audit.[89]

The Sullivan Principles for Corporate Labor and Community Relations in South Africa is the classic example here.[90] The Reverend Leon Sullivan was an African American minister and General Motors board of directors member. For several years during the 1970s, he had tried to pressure the firm to withdraw from South Africa, whose multiracial population was divided by government-sanctioned racist policies, known as apartheid.

As part of that effort, Sullivan formulated the code, the purpose of which was "to guide U.S. business in its social and moral agenda in South Africa."[91] Like all social audits, it was basically a measurement system. The code provided measurable standards by which U.S. companies operating in South Africa could be audited. For example, there were standards for nonsegregation of the races in all eating, comfort, and work facilities, as well as "equal pay for all employees doing equal or comparable work for the same period of time."[92] In the 1990s, he proposed a new code for companies returning to South Africa after apartheid

■ ■ ■ *Whistleblowing: Enron executives, including VP of Corporate Development Sharon Watkins, who blew the whistle, former CEO Jeffrey Skilling, and President and COO Jeffrey McMahon, being sworn in before the Senate Commerce Committee, February 2002.*

had ended stressing the protection of equal rights and the promotion of education and job training.

Whistle-Blowing Many firms have a reputation for actively discouraging whistle-blowing, the activities of employees who report organizational wrongdoing. Yet many arguments can be made for encouraging whistle-blowers. In a firm that adheres to the moral minimum view, for instance, whistle-blowers can help the company avoid doing harm. As one writer put it, whistle-blowers "represent one of the least expensive and most efficient sources of feedback about mistakes the firm may be making."[93] Other firms find that trying to silence whistle-blowers doesn't pay.[94] Once the damage has been done—whether it is asbestos hurting workers or a chemical plant making hundreds of people in the community ill—the cost of making things right can be enormous.[95] When John Pepper of P&G found out about his company's spying operation, he did a laudable thing: He blew the whistle on his own company and told Unilever about P&G's transgression.

Social Responsibility Networks Other firms, such as Rhino Records, join organizations like the Social Venture Network (**www.svn.org**) and Businesses for Social Responsibility (**www.bsr.org**). These organizations promote socially responsible business practices and help managers to establish socially responsible programs.[96]

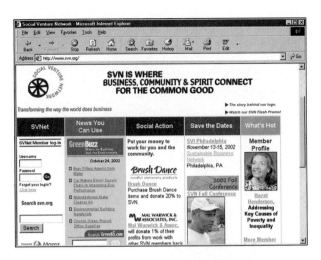

■ ■ ■ MANAGING DIVERSITY

Of all the firm's nonowner stakeholders, perhaps none has so obvious a claim on getting socially responsible treatment as do its employees. To a great extent, the company *is* its people, and their efforts largely determine if the company will succeed or fail. So, a firm that exposes its employees to deadly toxins, for example, is the antithesis of socially responsible. Similarly, the way it manages its employee diversity is a measure of how socially responsible it is.

Managing diversity means "planning and implementing organizational systems and practices to manage people so that the potential advantages of diversity are maximized while its potential disadvantages are minimized."[97] Managing diversity refers to questions like, How much effort should a manager make to employ minorities? How diverse should the company be? How much effort should managers make to manage the resulting diversity?

whistle-blowing ■ *the activities of employees who try to report organizational wrongdoing.*

managing diversity ■ *planning and implementing organizational systems and practices to manage people in a way that maximizes the potential advantages of diversity while minimizing its potential disadvantages.*

Boosting Performance by Managing Diversity

We can certainly argue for equitable and fair treatment of minorities and women just on ethical (and legal) grounds, but these reasons are being overrun today by demographics and globalization. Today, white males no longer dominate the labor force. Women and minorities represent the lion's share of labor force growth over the foreseeable future. Globalization requires that employers hire minority members with the cultural and language skills global companies need.

Managers are therefore striving for racial, ethnic, and sexual workplace balance as a matter of enlightened economic self-interest. Managers today generally understand that they have to recruit and maintain a diverse workforce to compete successfully in a global marketplace. One study found that cultural diversity contributes to improved productivity, return on equity, and market performance.[98] As another writer recently put it:

> *What does it take to win in the global economy? A commitment to mixing people, experiences, and ideas. Companies and countries that embrace diversity to stimulate creativity will be the ones that own the future.[99] The best corporations set the pace in diversity. Their mission is to match people and needs, regardless of nationality, race, or ethnicity. . . . Hybrid teams are the new corporate ideal.[100]*

■ ■ ■ *Winning with diversity: The night crew at Home Depot.*

Bases for Diversity

Diversity means different things to different people. However, there is general agreement regarding its components. In one study, most respondents listed race, gender, culture, national origin, disability, age, and religion as the demographic building blocks that represent diversity. They are what people often think of when they are asked what diversity means.[101]

A workforce is diverse when it is composed of two or more groups, each of whose members are identifiable and distinguishable based on demographic or other characteristics, such as:[102]

diverse ■ *describes a workforce comprised of two or more groups, each of which can be identified by demographic or other characteristics.*

- *Racial and ethnic groups.* African Americans, Pacific Islanders, Asian Americans, Native Americans, and other people of color now comprise about 25% of the U.S. population.
- *Gender.* Women will represent about 48% of the U.S. workforce by 2005.
- *Older workers.* By 2005, the average age of the U.S. worker will be 40, up from an average of 36 in 1990 and reflecting the gradual aging of the workforce and the larger number of older people remaining at work.
- *People with disabilities.* The Americans with Disabilities Act makes it illegal to discriminate against people with disabilities who are otherwise qualified to do a job. This act has highlighted the large number of people with disabilities in the U.S. workforce.
- *Sexual/affectional orientation.* Experts estimate that 5%–10% of the population is gay. This may make gays a larger percentage of the workforce than some racial and ethnic minorities.[103]
- *Religion.* Domestic and world events are underscoring differences, similarities, and tensions relating to the diversity of religions among most employees in a given firm.

Barriers in Dealing with Diversity

Unfortunately, differences like these can produce behavioral barriers that prevent collegiality and cooperation. Managers who want to manage diversity have to address these barriers if they want their employees to work together productively. The barriers include:

stereotyping ■ *attributing specific behavioral traits to individuals on the basis of their apparent membership in a group.*

Stereotyping and Prejudice Stereotyping and prejudice are two sides of the same coin. Stereotyping is a process in which someone ascribes specific behavioral traits to individuals based on their apparent membership in a group.[104] Prejudice is a bias that results from prejudging someone based on some trait.

prejudice ■ *a bias that results from prejudging someone on the basis of the latter's particular trait or traits.*

Most people develop lists of behavioral traits that they associate with certain groups. For example, stereotypical "male" traits might include strong, aggressive, and loud; "female" traits might include cooperative, softhearted, and gentle.[105] When someone allows traits like these to bias them for or against someone, then we say the person is prejudiced.

ethnocentrism ■ *a tendency to view members of one's own group as the center of the universe and to view other social groups less favorably than one's own.*

Ethnocentrism Ethnocentrism is prejudice on a grand scale. It is a tendency to view members of one's own group as the center of the universe and other social groups less favorably. For example, managers have been found to attribute the performance of some minorities less to their abilities and effort and more to help they received from others; conversely, such managers attributed the performance of nonminorities to their own abilities and efforts.[106]

discrimination ■ *a behavioral bias toward or against a person based on the group to which the person belongs.*

Discrimination Discrimination is prejudice in action. Whereas prejudice means a bias toward prejudging someone based on that person's traits, discrimination means taking specific actions toward or against the person based on the person's group.[107]

In many countries, including the United States, it's generally illegal to discriminate at work based on a person' age, race, gender, disability, or country of national origin.

But in practice, discrimination is still a barrier to managing diversity. Discrimination is often subtle. For example, many argue that an invisible "glass ceiling," enforced by an "old boys' network" and friendships built in places like exclusive clubs, effectively prevents women from reaching the top ranks of management.

Tokenism Tokenism occurs when a company appoints a small group of women or minority-group members to high-profile positions, rather than more aggressively seeking full representation for that group. Tokenism is a diversity barrier when it slows the process of hiring or promoting more members of the minority group.

Token employees often fare poorly. Research suggests, for instance, that token employees face obstacles to full participation, success, and acceptance in a company. The extra attention their distinctiveness creates magnifies their good or bad performance.[108]

tokenism ■ appointing a small number of minority-group members to high-profile positions instead of more aggressively achieving full representation for that group.

Gender Roles Discrimination against women goes beyond glass ceilings. Working women also confront gender-role stereotypes, the tendency to associate women with certain (frequently nonmanagerial) jobs. In one study, attractiveness was advantageous for female interviewees when the job was nonmanagerial. When the job was managerial, there was a tendency for a woman's attractiveness to reduce her chances of being hired.[109]

gender-role stereotype ■ usually, the association of women with certain behaviors and possibly (often lower-level) jobs.

How to Manage Diversity Successfully

Diversity can be a blessing or—if mismanaged—a curse. Bringing together people with different values and views can ensure they attack problems in a richer, more multifaceted way. On the other hand, diversity can make it harder to create smoothly functioning teams.[110] *Managing diversity* means taking steps to maximize diversity's potential advantages while minimizing the potential barriers—such as prejudice and bias—that can undermine the functioning of a diverse workforce. See Checklist 2.3 for a summary of steps to take.

CHECKLIST 2.3 ■ How to Manage Diversity

☑ Provide strong leadership.

☑ Assess your situation regularly.

☑ Provide diversity training and education.

☑ Change the culture and management systems.

☑ Evaluate the diversity program.

Managing diversity requires taking both legally mandated and voluntary actions. There are, of course, many legally mandated actions. For example, employers should avoid discriminatory employment advertising (such as "young man wanted for sales position") and prohibit sexual harassment. However, legally required steps are rarely enough to blend diverse employees into a close-knit community. Other, voluntary steps and programs are required. As in Figure 2.7, one diversity expert suggests the following:

Provide Strong Leadership Leaders of firms with exemplary diversity management reputations champion diversity. They take strong personal stands on the need for change, become role models for the behaviors required for the change, write a statement that defines what they mean by diversity and how diversity is important to the business, and provide financial and other support needed to implement the changes.[111]

After settling a class-action suit by black employees in November 2000, Coca-Cola instituted a variety of steps aimed at improving its diversity management record. For example, it established a formal mentoring program. It is also spending $500 million to support minority suppliers.[112]

Assess Your Situation Regularly For example, use surveys to measure current employee attitudes and perceptions toward different cultural groups in the company. Conduct audits of your minority and female hiring and staffing practices. Interview selected people.

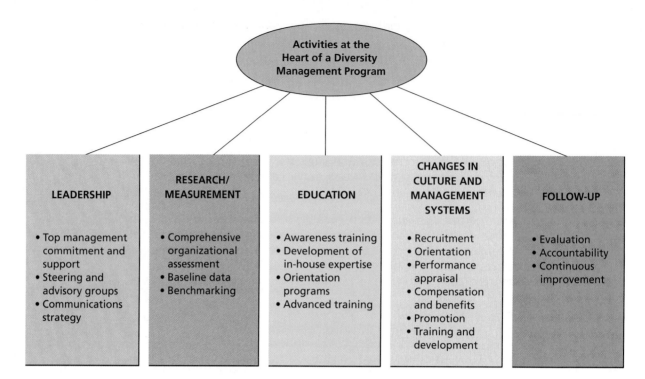

▲ **FIGURE 2–7** ■ ■ ■
Activities Required to Better Manage Diversity

Provide Diversity Training and Education "The most commonly utilized starting point for . . . managing diversity is some type of employee education program."[113] A one-to-two day seminar involving a diverse group of employees is typical. Topics include "What does diversity mean to you?" and "What does it mean to our organization?"[114]

After 9/11, Ford Motor Company sponsored a one-day "Islamic perspective on the events of September 11" event for hundreds of Ford employees of many faiths. Ford also supports an interfaith dialogue group and a support group for employees of Middle Eastern descent. As one Middle Eastern Ford employee said of the one-day event, "I've worked here for 15 years. I like to see my co-workers understand what Islam is about. We need . . . to help people understand all of this."[115]

Change the Culture and Management Systems In diversity management too, "it's not what you say, it's what you do." Managers have to send the right signals. For example, change the performance appraisal procedure to appraise supervisors based partly on their success in minimizing intergroup conflicts. As another example, institute mentoring programs. Mentoring is "a relationship between a younger adult and an older, more experienced adult in which the mentor provides support, guidance, and counseling to enhance the protégé's success at work and in other arenas of life."[116] Mentoring can contribute to the success of diversity management. Why attract a diverse workforce and then leave the new people to sink or swim?[117]

Sending signals can cut both ways. For example, six women recently filed a sexual discrimination class-action suit in federal court against Wal-Mart.[118] Among other things, they asserted that they did not get the raises or promotions their male colleagues received, and that they were exposed to hostile comments and actions by male employees (including, allegedly, offers to "get one of them pregnant"). Wal-Mart denies any systematic discrimination, and points out that it has policies forbidding sexual harassment of any kind. However, some lawyers argue that it's not what Wal-Mart says but what it does. Wal-Mart has long had a policy of vigorously defending itself in such lawsuits and, some allege, of possibly disregarding adverse legal judgments. If true, such actions could send the wrong signals. They could prompt some employees to believe that "we don't take sexual harassment all that seriously here."

mentoring ■ *a relationship between two people in which the more experienced mentor provides support, guidance, and counseling to enhance the protégé's success at work and in other areas of life.*

Evaluate the Diversity Program For example, do your surveys suggest an improvement in employee attitudes toward diversity? How many employees have entered into mentoring relationships? Do these relationships appear to be successful?

SUMMARY ▪▪▪

1. Managers face ethical choices every day. Ethics refers to the principles of conduct governing an individual or a group. Ethical decisions always include both normative and moral judgments.

2. Being legal and being ethical are not necessarily the same thing. A decision can be legal but still unethical, or ethical but still illegal.

3. Several factors influence whether specific people in specific organizations make ethical or unethical decisions. The individual making the decision must ultimately shoulder most of the credit (or blame) for any decision he or she makes. However, the organization itself—including its leadership, culture, and incentive/compensation plan—also shapes an individual employee's behavior.

4. Ethics policies and codes send a strong signal that top management is serious about ethics, and are a sign that the company wants to foster a culture that takes ethics seriously.

5. Managers can take several steps to foster ethics at work: They can emphasize top management's commitment, publish a code, establish compliance mechanisms, involve personnel at all levels, and measure results.

6. Organizational culture may be defined as the characteristic, values, traditions, and behaviors employees share. Values are basic beliefs about what you should or shouldn't do and what is and is not important.

7. Several things contribute to creating and sustaining the corporate culture. One is a formal values statement. Leaders also play a role in creating and sustaining culture. One of a leader's most important functions is to influence the culture and shared values of an organization. Managers also use signs and symbols, stories, and rites and ceremonies to create and sustain their companies' cultures.

8. Social responsibility is largely an ethical issue, since it involves questions of what is morally right or wrong with regard to the firm's responsibilities. People differ in their answer to the question, To whom should the corporation be responsible? Some say solely to stockholders, and some say to all stakeholders. Some take an intermediate position: They agree that the purpose of the corporation is to maximize profits, but subject to the requirement that it must do so in conformity with the moral minimum.

9. As the workforce becomes more diverse, it becomes more important to manage diversity so that the benefits outweigh any potential drawbacks. Potential barriers to managing diversity include stereotyping, prejudice, ethnocentrism, discrimination, and tokenism. Managing diversity involves taking steps such as providing strong leadership, assessing the situation, providing training and education, changing the culture and systems, and evaluating the program.

KEY TERMS ▪▪▪

ethics 28
normative judgment 28
morality 28
organizational culture 38
patterns of behavior 38
values and beliefs 38
signs and symbols 39
stories 40

rites and ceremonies 40
social responsibility 41
corporate stakeholder 42
moral minimum 42
corporate social audit 44
whistle-blowing 45
managing diversity 45
diverse 46

stereotyping 46
prejudice 46
ethnocentrism 46
discrimination 46
tokenism 47
gender-role stereotype 47
mentoring 48

SKILLS AND STUDY MATERIALS

COMPANION WEBSITE ▪▪▪

 We invite you to visit the Dessler Companion Website at **www.prenhall.com/dessler** for this chapter's Internet resources.

1. You work for a medical genetics research firm as a marketing person. You love the job. The location is great, the hours are good, and the work is challenging and flexible. You receive a much higher salary than you ever anticipated. However, you've just heard via the rumor mill that the company's elite medical team has cloned the first human, the firm's CEO. It was such a total success that you have heard that the company may want to clone every employee, so that it can use the clones to harvest body parts as the original people age or become ill. You are not sure you believe in cloning. You joined the firm because of its moral and ethical reputation. You feel that the image presented to you was one of research and development on lifesaving drugs and innovative medical procedures. The thought of cloning was never on your mind, but now it must be.

   In teams of four or five students, answer the following questions: Is there an ethical decision to be made? If so, why, and what is the ethical decision to be made? What would you do? Why? Do you think cloning will become a more controversial ethical and moral issue in the future as cloning becomes increasingly feasible?

2. In teams of four or five class members, research and then write about the ethical philosophies and attitudes toward business in the following nations: Russia, India, Egypt, Israel, the Congo, Norway, Saudi Arabia, and Australia. Compare and contrast their respective approaches to ethics and corporate social responsibility. Explain why there are differences.

3. You were taking a month's holiday in Europe. In your first week there, you became very ill with a recurring ailment for which you have been previously treated with limited success in the United States. It is a chronic condition that is inhibiting your ability to advance your career. The doctors who treated you in Europe have given you some medication that is legal there but has not been approved by the U.S. Food and Drug Administration (FDA). You feel better than you have in years. Because the European drug laws allow this drug to be purchased across the counter without a prescription, you are able to buy a year's supply. However, you know that it is listed as an illegal drug in the United States and that you must pass through customs. What is the ethical decision here? What would you do? What are the ethical and moral dilemmas facing you? Is there any action you can take as an individual to change the situation? If your decision is to smuggle the drug in and you are successful, what will you do in a year?

4. The CEO of Procter & Gamble obviously wants to make sure his company does not have any more problems like the one with the people who spied on Unilever. (Please see the chapter opening vignette). In teams of four or five students, write out, on a single sheet of paper, the outline of an ethics program that will guard against any recurrence of this situation.

ALLSTATE'S DISAPPEARING AGENTS

Like many companies, Allstate faces pressure both to be cost competitive and to provide new services to its customers. It also faces pressure for continuous improvement in its financial performance from its shareholders. Assuming that for Allstate to survive and prosper it needs to respond both to customers and shareholders, what responsibilities does it have toward another important group of stakeholders, its employees?

Here is the situation. Several years ago, the Allstate Corporation announced a series of strategic initiatives to expand its selling and service capabilities, buy back company shares to raise its stock price, and cut expenses by reducing the workforce. As part of its restructuring, Allstate would transfer its existing agents to an exclusive independent contractor program, whereby Allstate agents would become basically self-employed "independent contractors." This would markedly reduce the need for Allstate to provide agency support staff. In its press release on this initiative, Allstate management also announced it would eliminate 4,000 current nonagent positions by the end of 2000, or approximately 10 percent of the company's nonagent workforce.

Said Allstate's CEO,

Now, many of our customers and potential customers are telling us they want our products to be easier to buy, easier to service and more competitively priced. We will combine the power of our agency distribution system with the growth potential of direct selling and electronic commerce. . . . This unique combination is without parallel in the industry and will make Allstate the most customer-focused company in the marketplace.

Proponents of this type of restructuring might argue that Allstate is simply taking the steps needed to be competitive. They might even say that if Allstate did not cut jobs to create the cash flow needed to fund new competitive initiatives, it might ultimately fail as a business, putting all 54,000 of its employees at risk.

Yet Allstate's program raises concerns. One analyst noted that by encouraging customers to purchase insurance products directly via the Internet, Allstate could threaten the commissions of its more than 15,000 agents. The announcement of cost cutting came one day after Allstate announced it would meet its regular quarterly dividend of $0.15 per share. The company has raised its dividend annually since 1993.

Discussion Questions

1. Is reducing the number of employees in a company in and of itself unethical? Why or why not?

2. If you decided it was generally ethical, what would the company have to do to make the employee dismissals unethical?

3. What responsibilities does a company like Allstate have toward its employees?

4. Is there a moral dimension to the question of marketing Allstate insurance via the Internet? If so, what is it?

ETHICS, JETBLUE, AND THE IPO

jetBlue AIRWAYS
Can you trust a security analyst's recommendation, when that analyst owns tens of thousands of shares of the recommended company's stock? For many years, securities firms more or less looked the other way with respect to stocks that the analyst did or did not own. This all changed in early 2002. It was then that New York's attorney general accused Merrill Lynch's analysts of making self-serving recommendations. (One allegation went something like this: Based on e-mail messages, some analysts were bad-mouthing the same stocks that they were recommending to the public, and they were recommending them to the public so the firm could win more investment banking business from these firms, and thereby generate more income for the security analysts). It was not a pretty scene. Merrill Lynch ended up paying a $100 million fine—although the company did not, in so doing, agree that it had done anything wrong.

Morgan Stanley was the investment banking firm that took the lead in preparing JetBlue's $125 million initial public offering of stock. When the public found out that Morgan Stanley employed an airline industry analyst who owned more than 42,000 shares of JetBlue, the discovery raised many questions. For one thing, the analyst was allegedly in violation of Morgan Stanley's new (post-Merrill Lynch) rule forbidding analysts from owning shares in companies they cover.[119] Indeed, Morgan Stanley's new rule also extends to the analyst's associates, assistants and relatives. Analysts had until early 2002 to sell their stocks, but this analyst allegedly did not comply. So, Morgan Stanley was now in the position of being the lead underwriter trying to sell a new issue of stock in an airline in which its chief airline industry analyst held stock. Many of the customers buying the new JetBlue stock would probably turn to the analyst's recommendation in trying to decide whether to buy this new issue. The situation therefore did raise the possibility of a conflict of interest.

Of course, there are arguments pro and con. On the "con" side, would an analyst who owns stock in the company not want to see the stock go up, and therefore give that stock and overly optimistic analysis? On the other hand, would you want to buy a stock from someone who didn't think enough of it to buy it? For example, when a friend recommends a stock to you, isn't one of your first questions, "Do you own the company's shares yourself?" In other words, don't you want to make sure that that person is really committed to the company?

In any event, its analyst's ownership of the shares created complications for Morgan Stanley. It apparently could not insist that the analyst unload the shares, because there were certain contractual agreements requiring that he hold onto the shares for a particular length of time. So, why didn't Morgan Stanley simply say that they would not help JetBlue with its IPO? One outsider had this answer: "It's big money; fees are fees." In its defense, Morgan Stanley said that it was clamping many new restrictions on this analyst's stockholdings. For example, the analyst would have to "lock up" his shares (not sell them) for three years. Furthermore, he couldn't issue analyses of JetBlue stock unless he did so with an independent analyst, one who was not his subordinate. Some people were satisfied with that. Some were not.

Assignment

You and your team are consultants to Mr. Neeleman, who is depending on your management expertise to help him navigate the launch and management of JetBlue. Here's what he wants to know from you now.

1. List both the ethical and unethical decisions that were made by the analyst, and by Morgan Stanley.

2. Provide a brief description of the ethical culture at the investment banker, Morgan Stanley.

3. Provide a one-page outline of plan for improving the ethical behavior of the country's securities firms.

4. Tell us, what we should do now?

ETHICS QUIZ ANSWERS ■■■

Quiz is on page 27

1. 34% said personal e-mail on company computers is wrong
2. 37% said using office equipment for schoolwork is wrong
3. 49% said playing computer games at work is wrong
4. 54% said Internet shipping at work is wrong
5. 61% said it's unethical to blame your error on technology
6. 87% said it's unethical to visit pornographic sites at work
7. 33% said $25 is the amount at which a gift from a supplier or client becomes troubling, while 33% said $50, and 33% said $100
8. 35% said a $50 gift to the boss is unacceptable
9. 12% said a $50 gift *from* the boss is unaceptable
10. 70% it's unacceptable to take the $200 football tickets
11. 70% said it's unacceptable to take the $120 theater tickets
12. 35% said it's unacceptable to take the $100 food basket
13. 45% said it's unacceptable to take the $25 gift certificate
14. 40% said it's unacceptable to take the $75 raffle prize
15. 11% reported they lie about sick days
16. 4% reported they take credit for the work or ideas of others

PART 1

CHAPTER

3   Decision Making

CHAPTER OBJECTIVES

After studying this chapter and the case exercises at the end, you should be able to:

1. Spell out what triggered the problem.

2. List at least four ways to define the problem, and choose the best definition.

3. Propose at least five objectives for the person making the decision.

4. Recommend at least four possible alternative solutions.

5. Develop a Consequences Matrix for the decision.

6. Develop a Decision Matrix for the decision.

THE MANAGEMENT CHALLENGE

Reviving Kmart

Charles Conaway, Kmart's new CEO, decided several years ago to save Kmart by beating Wal-Mart at its own low-cost game. For years, Kmart had attracted customers with circulars in weekly magazines. Conaway's research showed that the circulars accounted for over 10% of Kmart's operating expenses (compared with about 2% at Target, and 1% at Wal-Mart.)[1] He believed Kmart had to reduce that expense. Conaway and his team thus decided to change their marketing approach. They abolished the circulars, slashed prices on about 40,000 products, and started advertising that "Kmart's prices were lower than Wal-Mart's." Given Wal-Mart's size, those were gutsy decisions.

They were also disastrous. Wal-Mart's day-to-day operating costs were way below Kmart's, so Wal-Mart simply dropped its own prices even more. Conaway's decisions left Kmart with higher prices, and no circulars. Customers stopped showing up. "We made a mistake by cutting too much advertising too fast," is how Conaway put it. In December 2001—typically a retailer's busiest month— Kmart's sales fell 1%, while Wal-Mart's rose 8%. One month later, Kmart sought bankruptcy protection. Conaway's last big decision was to close 284 stores and fire 22,000 Kmart employees. In March 2002, Conaway himself left the firm. Now Kmart's board of directors has some decisions to make: Where did we go wrong? What should we do now?

In the previous chapters, we discussed what managers do and the ethical and cultural basis for managers' decisions. In this part we turn to *managerial planning*. The main purpose of this first planning chapter is to improve your effectiveness in making decisions. The topics we'll discuss include basic aspects of decision making, how managers make decisions, and how to make better decisions.

■■■ UNDERSTANDING DECISION MAKING

Everyone continually faces the need to choose—the route to school, the job to accept, or the strategy to pursue. A decision is a choice from among the available alternatives. Decision making is the process of developing and analyzing alternatives and making a choice.

Problems prompt most decisions. A problem is a discrepancy between a desirable and an actual situation. If you need $50 for a show but can afford to spend only $10, you have a problem. However, decisions don't always involve problems. (For example, deciding what to buy your friend for her birthday is not, strictly speaking, a "problem.") On the other hand, the problem-solving *process* is the same as that for making decisions. It is "the process of developing and analyzing alternatives and making a choice." We will, therefore, use the terms *decision making* and *problem solving* interchangeably.

Judgment refers to the cognitive, or "thinking," aspects of the decision-making process.[2] We'll see in this chapter that decision making is often subject to distortions and biases, precisely because it is usually a judgmental, not a mechanical, process.

Decisions are a big part of everything managers do. Planning, organizing, leading, and controlling are the basic management functions. However, as illustrated in Table 3.1, each of these functions calls for decisions—which plan to implement, what goals to choose, which people to hire.

Similarly, every manager, regardless of title or level makes decisions that are germane to that person's specific job. Table 3.2 illustrates this idea. For example, the accounting manager decides what outside auditing firm to use and whether to extend credit to a customer. The sales manager decides which sales representatives to use in

decision ■ *a choice made between available alternatives.*

decision making ■ *the process of developing and analyzing alternatives and choosing from among them.*

problem ■ *a discrepancy between a desirable and an actual situation.*

TABLE 3–1	Everything Managers Do Involves Making Decisions
Management Function	**Representative Decisions**
Planning	What do we want to achieve?
	What are our goals?
	What are the main opportunities and risks we face?
	What competitive strategy should we pursue?
Organizing	What are the main tasks we have to accomplish?
	How should we divide up the work that needs to be done?
	Should I make these decisions or let subordinates make them?
	How should we make sure the work is coordinated?
Leading	What leadership style should I use in this situation?
	Why is this employee doing what he or she is doing?
	How should I motivate this employee?
	How can I get this team to perform better?
Controlling	How am I going to control this activity?
	Are the goals on which these controls are based out of date?
	Does this performance deviation merit corrective action?

TABLE 3–2

Manager	Decisions
Accounting Manager	What accounting firm should we use?
	Who should process our payroll?
	Should we give this customer credit?
Finance Manager	What bank should we use?
	Should we sell bonds or stocks?
	Should we buy back some of our company's stock?
Human Resource Manager	Where should we recruit for employees?
	Should we set up a testing program?
	Should I advise settling the equal employment complaint?
Production Manager	Which supplier should we use?
	Should we build the new plant?
	Should we buy the new machine?
Sales Manager	Which sales rep should we use in this region?
	Should we use this advertising agency?
	Should we lower prices in response to our competitor's doing so?

each region and which advertising agency to use. The production manager decides between alternative suppliers and whether or not to recommend building a new plant.

Types of Decisions

Not all decisions are alike. For example, some decisions are bigger and harder to change (more "strategic") than others. Leasing a car is less strategic than buying a house. Some decisions are also more obvious than others. They are "no-brainers." If your car is out of gas, you have to fill the tank. Decisions also differ in the extent to which you can anticipate and program them—that is, set things up so that the decisions get made more or less automatically.

Programmed and Nonprogrammed Decisions Many (indeed, most of) the decisions businesses make are recurring and routine. At Macy's, for example, clerks need to know what to do when a customer wants to return some shoes. No Macy's manager wants to be drawn into making decisions like these repeatedly. Managers therefore program as many of these decisions as possible. They do this by making them a matter of company policy. **Programmed decisions** can be solved using rules and procedures that can be laid out in advance.[3] Managers create policy, procedure, and rule manuals mostly to facilitate the routinizing and standardizing of decisions in their companies. In contrast, **nonprogrammed decisions** (like those facing Kmart's board) generally can't be laid out in advance. They tend to blindside the manager and to require considerable intuition, creativity, and decision-making prowess. Strategic decisions ("Should we expand overseas?") usually don't lend themselves to programming—managers want to analyze these decisions carefully, and weigh their options and pros and cons.

Some experts estimate that 90% of all management decisions are programmed.[4] In many universities, the decision concerning which students to admit is made by mathematically weighting each candidate's test scores and grades. Most firms try to program inventory decisions, such as "reorder 10 units of item 'A' when the number of item A's in the bin drops to two." When you swipe your credit card at a point of purchase, the computerized card-acceptance decision is a programmed one. The cashier refers the decision to a credit manager only if there's a problem.

Managers distinguish between programmed and nonprogrammed decisions for two main reasons. First, the manager's time is precious. The more decisions he or she can

programmed decision ■ *a decision that is repetitive and routine and can be made by using a definite, systematic procedure.*

nonprogrammed decision ■ *a decision that is unique and novel.*

program or make routine, the less time he or she needs to devote to them. The manager's subordinates or systems can make these decisions more or less automatically. The Principle of Exception says, "Only bring exceptions to the way things should be to the manager's attention. Handle routine matters yourself." The second reason for distinguishing between the two stems from the first: You solve programmed and nonprogrammed decisions using different methods.

Making Programmed and Nonprogrammed Decisions As noted earlier, managers can use standard rules or methods to make programmed decisions more or less automatically. For example, to expedite its refund process, a department store may use this rule: "If the customer returns a jacket, you may give that person a refund if the tag is not removed, if the jacket is not damaged, and if the purchase was made within the past two weeks."

Rules and regulations are among the most familiar programmed decisions. Managers use forms like the one in Figure 3.1 to expedite applying rules. Table 3.3 further illustrates this point. It shows a typical list of programmed decisions—in this case, a master list of the disciplinary rules for Relsedco.

Nonprogrammed decisions generally require a very different decision-making methodology. These decisions, remember, are unexpected and unique. It's difficult or impossible to preplan (program) how you'll respond to a problem that is unexpected and unique. These are the kinds of decisions managers get paid to make.[5] Strategic decisions ("Should we expand abroad?") fall into this category. Kmart's decision to drop its advertising circulars and compete head-to-head with Wal-Mart is another example. What Kmart's board should do now is yet another example. Deciding what career to pursue, which job to take, whether to move across the country, and who to marry are personal nonprogrammed decisions. These decisions all involve a vast array of factors. They rely heavily on judgment. We will spend much of this chapter showing how to do a better job of making these decisions. Table 3.4 compares programmed and nonprogrammed decisions.

◄ **FIGURE 3–1** ■ ■ ■

Procedure and Form to Use for Developing a Workplace Rule

Source: Copyright Gary Dessler, Ph.D.

Any manager or employees wishing to recommend a workplace policy, procedure, or rule for use at Relsedco should complete the following form and submit it to the Human Resources Director

Title of Policy, Procedure, or Rule _____
_____
_____

Purpose and Goal of the Policy, Procedure, or Rule _____
_____
_____

Statement of the Policy, Procedure, or Rule _____
_____
_____

Consequences of violating Policy, Procedure, or Rule _____
_____
_____

Contact person for information, follow-up, or reporting violations _____
_____
_____

Other supporting information(relevant laws, company support programs [if any])
_____
_____
_____

TABLE 3–3   **List of Disciplinary Rules**

RELSEDCO—POLICIES, PROCEDURES, RULES
701—Employee Conduct and Work Rules

Effective Date: 4/18/02

To ensure orderly operations and to provide the best possible work enviromnent, Relsedco expects employees to follow rules of conduct that will protect the interests and safety of all employees and the organization.

It is not possible to list all the forms of behavior that are considered unacceptable in the workplace. The following are examples of infractions of rules of conduct that may result in disciplinary action, up to and including termination of employment:

* Theft or inappropriate removal or possession of property

* Falsification of timekeeping records

* Working under the influence of alcohol or illegal drugs

* Possession, distribution, sale, transfer, or use of alcohol or illegal drugs in the workplace, while on duty, or while operating employer-owned vehicles or equipment

* Fighting or threatening violence in the workplace

* Boisterous or disruptive activity in the workplace

* Negligence or improper conduct leading to damage or employer-owned or customer-owned property

* Insubordination or other disrespectful conduct

* Violation of safety or health rules

* Smoking in prohibited areas

* Sexual or other unlawful or unwelcome harassment

* Possession of dangerous or unauthorized materials, such as explosives or firearms, in the workplace

* Excessive absenteeism or any absence without notice

* Unauthorized absence from workstation during the workday

* Unauthorized use of telephones, mail system, or other employer-owned equipment

* Unauthorized disclosure of business "secrets" or confidential information

* Violation of personnel policies

* Unsatisfactory performance or conduct

Employment with Relsedco is at the mutual consent of Relsedco and the employee, and either party may terminate that relationship at any time, with or without cause, and with or without advance notice.

Source: Policies Now! Knowledgepoint
   1129 Industrial Avenue
   Petaluma, CA 94952

As noted earlier, top-level managers like CEOs tend to face more nonprogrammed decisions, while lower-level managers face more programmed ones. Lower-level managers spend more time addressing recurring, programmable decisions, such as "How many employees should I put on the assembly line today, given our production quota?" The production supervisor has rules and methods he or she can apply to make decisions like these. Top managers face more decisions like "How should we respond to our competitors' moves?" There's usually no simple formula for making nonprogrammed decisions like these. This chapter explains some methods you can use.

Decision-Making Models

You own a retail store and must decide which of several trucks to buy for deliveries. If you are like most people, you probably assume that you would be quite rational in your approach to such a decision. For example, would you not size up all your options

TABLE 3–4

Comparing Programmed and Nonprogrammed Decisions

	Programmed	Nonprogrammed
Type of Decision	Programmable; routine; generic; computational	Nonprogrammable; unique; innovative
Nature of Decision	Procedural; predictable; well-defined information and decision criteria	Novel; unstructured; incomplete channels of information; unknown criteria
Decision-Making Strategy	Reliance on rules and computation	Reliance on principles; judgment; creative problem-solving processes
Decision-Making Technique	Management science; capital budgeting; computerized solutions; rules	Judgment; intuition, creativity

and carefully weigh the pros and cons of each one? Perhaps, and perhaps not. There are two main schools of thought (or "models") regarding how people make decisions.

The Classical Approach The idea that managers are totally rational has a long and honorable tradition in economic and management theory. Early, classical economists needed a simplified way to explain economic phenomena, such as how demand affects prices. Their solution was to accept a number of assumptions about how managers made decisions. Specifically, they assumed that the rational manager:

1. Had complete or "perfect" information about the situation, including the full range of goods and services available on the market and the exact price of each good or service.
2. Could distinguish perfectly between the problem and its symptoms.
3. Could identify all criteria and accurately weigh all the criteria according to his or her preferences.
4. Knew all alternatives and could assess each one against each criterion.
5. Could accurately calculate and choose the alternative with the highest perceived value.[6]
6. Could, therefore, be expected to make an "optimal" choice, without being confused by "irrational" thought processes.

The Administrative Approach You probably sense from your own experiences that these assumptions leave something to be desired. For example, does anyone really (even with the Internet) ever have perfect knowledge of all the options? Do they really, unemotionally, analyze every single option?

Herbert Simon and his associates have proposed a decision-making model they believe better reflects these realities. They agree that decision makers try to be rational, but they point out that such rationality is, in practice, subject to many constraints: "The number of alternatives [the decision-maker] must explore is so great, the information he would need to evaluate them so vast that even an approximation to objective rationality is hard to conceive . . . "[7]

We're all familiar with situations like these. For example, how many people, faced with too many final exams and other pressing problems, have said, "I can't take this any more"? Experiments support this common-sense notion. In one classic series of studies, participants were required to make decisions based on the amount of information transmitted on a screen. Most people quickly reached a point of "information overload" and began adjusting in several ways. Some omitted or ignored some of the information; others began making errors by incorrectly identifying some of the information; others gave only approximate responses (such as "about 25" instead of "24.6"). Based on a review of other evidence, one expert concluded, "Even the simplest decisions, expressed in the conventional form of a decision tree, rapidly overwhelm human cognitive capabilities."[8]

Based on realities like these, Simon argues that "bounded rationality" more accurately represents how managers actually make decisions.[9] **Bounded rationality**,

bounded rationality ■ *the boundaries on rational decision making imposed by one's values, abilities, and limited capacity for processing information.*

"It was precisely this kind of indecisiveness that got us into trouble in the first place!"

means a manager's decision making is only as rational as his or her unique values, abilities, and limited capacity for processing information permit him or her to be.

There are two main implications. One concerns the manager's search for solutions. The classicist's "rational" manager is an optimizer who continues to review potential solutions until he or she finds the optimal one. Simon's "administrative man" (bounded rational) managers satisfice. They look for solutions until they find a satisfactory one. They look for the optimal solution only in exceptional cases.[10] The accompanying Management in Action feature gives an example. A second implication is that many cognitive biases and traps lie in wait for unsuspecting managers. Wise managers thus make it a point to take their own values, biases, abilities, and various other psychological traps into account before blundering into decisions. After the following example of satisficing, we'll look more closely at the decision-making process and at how to improve your decision-making skills.

satisfice ■ *to stop the decision-making process when satisfactory alternatives are found, rather than to review solutions until an optimal alternative is discovered.*

MANAGEMENT IN ACTION So Many Decisions, So Little Time

Management in practice often reflects the emphasis on finding satisfactory (but not necessarily optimal) solutions. Consider Dominic Orr, president and CEO of Alteon WebSystems Inc. Ask him what his main management problem is, and he responds that "like a lot of young companies in new industries, we have to make choices every day about competitive strategy and product development. So how can we make decisions that we trust without wasting valuable time?"[11] As he puts it,

Fast execution and fast delivery—that's easy. Fast decision-making is harder. Young industries and start-ups are constantly changing—which means that even day-to-day decisions take on huge strategic importance . . . [Therefore] making high-stakes decisions as a team is important. But we don't have time for endless debate or for office politics. . . . We focus on collecting as many facts as quickly as we can, and then we decide on the best—but not necessarily the perfect—solution.[12]

The people element is particularly important in Alteon's decision-making process. For example, the firm aims to encourage lively debate while avoiding dysfunctional, personal comments. As Orr says,

There's no silent disagreement, and no getting personal, and definitely no "let's take it off-line" mentality. Our goal is to make each major decision in a single meeting. People arrive with a proposal or a solution—and with the facts to support it. After an idea is presented, we open the floor to objective—and often withering—critiques. And if the idea collapses under scrutiny, we move onto another: no hard feelings. We're judging the idea, not the person. At the same time, we don't really try to regulate emotions. Passionate conflict means that we're getting somewhere, not that the discussion is out of control. But one person does act as referee—by asking basic questions like these: "Is this good for the customer?" or "Does it keep our time to market advantage intact?" By focusing relentlessly on the facts, we're able to see the strains and weaknesses of an idea clearly and quickly."[13]

HOW TO MAKE DECISIONS: THE PROCESS

Some people assume that good judgment is like a good singing voice—either you have it or you don't. However, that's not quite true. As with singing, it certainly helps to have the raw material. But a conscientious effort at improving decision-making skills can turn almost anyone into a much better decision maker. In this section, we'll look at each step in the decision-making process, and at how to improve each decision-making skill. Checklist 3.1 summarizes the five-step decision-making process. The accompanying Management in Action feature describes what Kmart did to solve its problem.

CHECKLIST 3.1 ■ The Decision-Making Process

☑ Define the problem.

☑ Clarify your objectives.

☑ Identify alternatives.

☑ Analyze the consequences.

☑ Make a choice.

MANAGEMENT IN ACTION Kmart's Board Takes Over

With the company in bankruptcy and its decisions closely monitored by the courts, Kmart's board knew it had to make the right decisions if the company was to survive. After dismissing Conaway (and giving him $9.5 million in severance pay), the board appointed turnaround expert James Adamson as the new CEO. Adamson faced an interesting problem. Kmart had gone through 20 years (and five CEOs), trying to find a solution for its inability to compete effectively with Wal-Mart. Solutions had ranged from cutting costs to new advertising campaigns to buying other companies—yet here was Kmart, in bankruptcy.

Adamson said he'd first focus on cutting costs and improving store operations. He started by closing about 15% of Kmart's stores and writing off about $1 billion of the company's assets. However, that approach was similar in many respects to what his predecessor, Conaway, had done. Many people in the industry wondered if Adamson was on the right track and whether Kmart was even addressing the right problem. Perhaps the main problem was not finances, but the fact that people needed a reason to shop at Kmart, with Wal-Mart just down the road.

Step 1. Define the Problem[14]

Problems prompt most decisions, but identifying or "defining" the problem is trickier than it may appear. Common mistakes include emphasizing the obvious and being misled by symptoms.[15] Here is a classic example. Office workers in a large office building were upset because they had to wait so long for an elevator to pick them up, and many tenants were threatening to move out. The owners called in a consulting team and told them the problem was that the elevators were running too slow.

If you agree with defining the problem as "slow-moving elevators," then the potential solutions are all quite expensive. The elevators were running about as fast as they could, so speeding them up was not an option. You could ask the tenants to stagger their work hours, but that could cause more animosity than the slow-moving elevators. Adding more elevators would be too expensive.

The point is that the alternatives you identify and the decisions you make reflect how you define the problem. What the consultants actually did in this case was define the problem as, "The tenants are upset because they have to wait for an elevator." The solution they chose was to have full-length mirrors installed by each bank of elevators so the tenants could admire themselves while waiting! The solution was both inexpensive and satisfactory: The complaints virtually disappeared. The moral of the story? *Never* take the statement of the problem for granted.

How to Define the Problem The consultants' clever solution illustrates the first (and perhaps most important) step in defining problems: Always ask, "What triggered this problem?" Doing so will help guide you to more accurately define it. Luckily for the owners, the consultants did not jump to any conclusions. They asked themselves, "What triggered the problem?" The answer, of course, was the tenant's complaints, complaints triggered by frustration at having to wait. The problem then became: How do we reduce or eliminate frustration with having to wait?

There are some useful hints to keep in mind here.[16] *Start by writing down your initial assessment of the problem.* Then, dissect it. Ask, "What triggered this problem (as I've assessed it)? Why am I even thinking about solving this problem? What is the connection between the trigger and the problem? That's how the consultants approached defining the problem—and how you should, too.

■ *Application Example* Harold has had his job as marketing manager for Universal Widgets, Inc., for about five years, and has been happy with his job and with the company. However, the recent recession wreaked havoc with the company's business, and it had to cut about 10% of the staff. Harold's boss gave him the bad news: "We like the work you've been doing here, but we're closing the New York office. We want you to stay with Universal, though, so we found you a similar position with our plant in Pittsburgh." Harold is thrilled. As he tells his parents, "I have to move to Pittsburgh, but at least I still have a job. The problem is, where should I live?" He immediately starts investigating housing possibilities in Pittsburgh. His father thinks Harold may be jumping the gun. What do you think? What would you do?

Harold's father is right. Harold jumped to the conclusion that his problem now is finding a place to live in Pittsburgh. Is that really the main decision he has to make? Why is Harold even thinking about solving this problem? What triggered this problem? What is the connection between the trigger and the problem? The trigger was his boss's comment that Universal no longer needed his services in New York and that it was, therefore, transferring him to Pittsburgh. What's the real problem Harold must face here? The issue—and the decision Harold really must make—is this: Should I move to Pittsburgh with Universal Widgets? Or should I try to get the best marketing manager job I can, and if so, where?[17]

Step 2. Clarify Your Objectives

Most people want to achieve several aims when making a decision. For example, in choosing a location for a new plant, the manager typically is concerned with several things, including distance from the company's markets; location of raw materials; availability of transportation; quality and availability of the labor supply; and perhaps preference issues, such as where the manager wants to live.

Have More Than One Objective Therefore, few managers would make a decision like this with just a single objective in mind. (There are exceptions. The great football coach Vince Lombardi once reportedly summed this up by saying, "Winning isn't everything. It's the only thing.") However, for most decisions, most people haven't the luxury of focusing like a laser on just a single objective. When deciding on a new laptop computer, you may want to get the most memory, portability, and reliability you can for the price. You'd buy the one that, on balance, best satisfied all these objectives. Hopefully, you'd avoid the trap of making your decision on the assumption that your main aim, such as minimizing price, was your only aim.

How to Clarify Objectives   Your objectives should provide an explicit expression of what you really want. If you don't have clear objectives, you will not be able to evaluate your alternatives. For example, if Harold isn't clear about whether or not he wants to stay close to New York, wants at least a 10% raise, or wants to stay in the widget industry, how could he possibly decide whether to stay with Universal Widgets or leave—or which of several job offers were best? The answer is, he could not.

It's easy to improve your objectives-setting skills. Here is a useful five-step procedure.[18]

1. *Write down all the concerns you hope to address through your decision.* Don't worry about repetition. Looking at the same concern in different ways may help you clarify what your concerns really are. Some people compose a wish list. The idea here is to make a comprehensive list of everything you hope to accomplish with your decision. Harold's concerns include the impact of his decision on his long-term career; enjoying what he's doing; living close to a large urban center; and earning more money than he earns now.

2. *Convert your concerns into specific, concrete objectives.* Your objectives should be measurable. Harold's concerns translate into these objectives: getting a job that puts him in a position to be marketing director within two years; a job with a consumer products company preferably in the widgets industry; being within a one-hour drive of a city with a population of at least one million people; and earning at least $1,200 per week.

3. *Separate ends from means to establish your fundamental objectives.* This step helps you zero in on what you really want. One way to do this is to ask, several times, "Why?" For example, Harold asks himself, "*Why* do I want to live within a one-hour drive of a city with a population of at least one million people?" Because he wants to make sure he can meet many other people who are his own age and because he enjoys what he sees as big city benefits such as museums, theater, and opera. This helps clarify what Harold really wants. For example, a smaller town might do if the town has the right demographics and cultural attractions.

4. *Clarify what you mean by each objective.* You want to banish fuzzy thinking. For example, "getting a raise" would be a fuzzy objective. Harold, to his credit, has already clarified what he means by his financial objective. He wants to "earn at least $1,200 per week."

5. *Test your objectives to see if they capture your interests.* This is your reality check. Harold carefully reviews his full list of final objectives to make sure they completely capture what he wants to accomplish by his decision. Checklist 3.2 summarizes these steps.

CHECKLIST 3.2 ■ How to Clarify Your Objectives

☑ Write down all the concerns you hope to address through your decision.

☑ Convert your concerns into specific, succinct objectives.

☑ Separate ends from means to establish your fundamental objectives.

☑ Clarify what you mean by each objective.

☑ Test your objectives to see if they capture your interests.

Step 3. Identify Alternatives

You must have a choice in order to make an effective decision. When you have no choice, there really isn't any decision to make—except perhaps to "take it or leave it." Wise managers, therefore, usually ask, "What are my options? What are my alternatives?"

Decision-making experts call alternatives "the raw material of decision-making." They say alternatives represent "the range of potential choices you'll have for pursuing your objectives."[19]

How to Identify Alternatives There are several ways to generate good alternatives. Be *creative*; start by trying to generate as many alternatives as you can yourself. (We'll address creativity in more detail below.) Then *expand your search*, by checking with other people, including experts. Another useful technique is to look at each of your objectives and *ask*, "*how*?" For example, Harold might ask, "How could I get a position that would lead to a marketing director's job within two years?" One alternative is certainly to take a senior marketing manager's job. Another might be to go after the senior director's job right away. One caveat here is this: *Know when to stop*. Remember what Simon and his colleagues say about decision-making in practice: Most managers "satisfice." It's rarely practical to spend the time and energy required to find the optimal solution.

■ *Application Example* Through this process, Harold generates several feasible alternatives. He can take the Pittsburgh Universal Widget job, or he can leave. If he leaves, his search for alternatives turns up four other possibilities: a job with a dot-com as senior manager in New York; a marketing director's job with Ford in Detroit; and two other marketing managers jobs, one with a pet food company in Newark, and one with Nokia in Washington, D.C.

Step 4. Analyze the Consequences

There is a danger in making decisions, and it is this: You make them today, but you feel them tomorrow. You buy a computer today, and tomorrow you discover that it doesn't really satisfy your needs because your memory requirements are now higher. Harold decides today to stay with Universal. Then he finds out next year that his prospects of promotion are almost nil because the company already has two Pittsburgh marketing directors, who have no plans to leave. "If only I'd thought of that," you and Harold say.

The next decision-making question to address, therefore, is this: How does each alternative stack up, given your objectives? Should Harold stay with Universal, or leave? Should he seek his fortune with another company? And, if so, which?

One expert says, "This is often the most difficult part of the decision-making process, because this is the stage that typically requires forecasting future events."[20] Classical economists assumed decision makers faced completely rational conditions and could therefore precisely assess the consequences of choosing each alternative. However, such perfect conditions rarely exist. Harold needs a practical way to compare each of his options will fare. To do this, he must understand the consequences of pursuing each option.

How to Analyze the Consequences Your job is to think through, for each alternative, what the consequences of choosing that alternative will be for each of your objectives. Your aim is to make sure you never have to say, "Why didn't I think of that?" Here is a basic process you can use.[21]

First, *mentally put yourself into the future*. For example, imagine that you bought that new computer, and that you're actually using it now, six months later. How do you like it? Has anything changed in your life that should have influenced your decision six months ago? Looking into the future is a crucial analytical skill. One way to improve this skill is through *process analysis*.

Process analysis means solving a problem by thinking through the process involved from beginning to end, imagining, at each step, what actually would happen.[22] Consider this problem. A frugal person named Joe can make one whole cigar from every five cigar butts he finds. How many cigars can he make if he finds 25 cigar butts? Before you answer "five," think through Joe's cigar-making process, step by step. There he sits on his park bench, making (and smoking!) each of his five cigars. As he smokes each cigar, he ends up with one new cigar butt. Putting yourself in Joe's place (figuratively speaking) and actually "experiencing"—thinking through—each step in the process and its outcomes, you can see something you may not have noticed before: In smoking his five handmade cigars, Joe ends up with five new butts, which he in turn

process analysis ■ solving problems by thinking through the process involved from beginning to end, imagining, at each step, what actually would happen.

combines into a sixth whole new cigar.[23] In this case, process analysis meant envisioning Joe sitting on his park bench and then thinking through each of the steps he would take as if you were there.

Second, *eliminate any clearly inferior alternatives*. For example, if Harold does his homework and thinks through the consequences of each of his alternatives, it should be obvious that his prospects for promotion to marketing director are virtually nil if he stays with Universal Widgets. Therefore, why even continue considering this alternative? He crosses it off his list.

Third, *organize your remaining alternatives into a Consequences table*. A consequences matrix (or table) lists your objectives down the left side of the page and your alternatives along the top. In each box of the matrix, put a brief description that shows the consequences of that alternative for that objective. This provides a concise, bird's-eye view of the consequences of pursuing each alternative.

▓ *Application Example* Harold started with five alternatives, and four basic objectives. Here they are in consequences matrix form, along with what he sees as the consequences for each one:

Objective / Alternative	Marketing director in two years	Consumer products company	One-hour drive from major city	Earn at least $1,200 per week
Marketing manager, Universal Widgets, Pittsburgh	Little or no possibility—eliminate this option	NA (Eliminated)	NA (Eliminated)	NA (Eliminated)
Senior manager, dot-com, NY	High probability—if company survives that long	Consumer-oriented, but does not really sell products	Yes, excellent	$1,250 plus stock options
Marketing manager, Ford, Detroit	Moderate possibility—bigger company, longer climb	Yes, but not as interesting as selling widgets. I may get bored	Yes	$1,100 plus great benefits (discount on new T-bird)
Marketing manager, pet foods, Newark	High probability—small, growing company with little marketing expertise now	Yes, but not quite as interesting as selling widgets	Yes	$1,200
Marketing manager, Nokia, Washington DC	Fairly high probability—fast growing company	Yes—exciting industry	Yes—exceptional cultural attractions, and demographics	$1,200

Step 5. Make a Choice

Your analyses are useless unless you make the right choice. Under perfect conditions, doing so should be straightforward. Simply review the consequences of each alternative, and choose the alternative that maximizes your benefits. But in practice, as you know, making a decision—even a relatively simple one like choosing a computer—usually can't be done so accurately or rationally. However, several techniques can help anyone make a better choice.

▬▬ HOW TO MAKE BETTER DECISIONS

Let's look at some techniques to help you improve the quality of your decisions. We begin with an important one: Increase your knowledge.

Increase Your Knowledge

"Knowledge is power," someone once said, and that's particularly true in making decisions. Even the simplest decisions—like mapping your route to work each morning—become difficult without basic information, such as the traffic report. And, complex decisions rely on information even more. To increase your knowledge:

Ask questions Always use the six main question words—Who? What? Where? When? Why? How?—to probe and to boost your knowledge. In buying a used car, for instance ask "*Who* is selling the car, and who previously owned it?" "*What* do similar cars sell for?" "*What* is wrong with this car?" "*Where* did the owner service it?" "*When* did the owner buy it?" "*Why* does the owner want to sell?" "*How* much do you think you could buy it for?" Most people could save themselves a lot of aggravation by arming themselves for their decision with some good pointed questions.

Get experience For many endeavors, there's simply no substitute for experience. That's certainly true on a personal level. Many students find that interning in a job similar to the occupation they plan to pursue can help enormously in clarifying whether that's the right occupation for them. It is also true when managing organizations. For example, some companies expand abroad by opening their own facilities, while others enter into joint ventures. What determines which route a company's managers choose? Experience has a lot to do with it. Multinational corporations that already have a great deal of experience in doing business in a particular country generally opt for full ownership of foreign affiliates. Less experienced companies tend to establish joint ventures in foreign markets, in part so they can develop the required expertise.[24]

Use consultants Managers use the consultants' experience (such as in personnel testing or strategic planning) to supplement their own lack of experience in particular areas. These needn't be management consultants, of course. Sometimes, just talking the problem over with other people can help, particularly if they've had experience solving similar problems.

Do your research Whatever the decision, there's usually a wealth of information you can tap. For example, thinking of moving from New York to D.C.? How do salaries in Washington compare with those in New York? Web sites like **careers.yahoo.com/cities/salaries** easily answer that question.

Force yourself to recognize the facts when you see them It is always easy to overlook or give too much importance to some facts when you really want to do something. For example, it's easy to make the financials of a vacation look better when you want to take that vacation. Therefore, endeavor to maintain your objectivity; base your decision on an objective review of the facts as they really are.

■ *Application Example* Information's value depends on its timeliness. For example, it used to take Cisco Systems 14 days to close its accounting books and to determine its financial performance for the previous period. With modern systems, the company can now aggregate all that information and close its books in just one day. Alcoa is another company that can make faster decisions by getting information earlier. Several years ago, Alcoa's sensitive marketing information systems gave management an early warning that the demand in its aerospace markets was diminishing. Alcoa was able to quickly shift production to other, growing markets—and thereby maintain its profitability.[25]

The following Managing @ The Speed of Thought feature provides another example.

Knowledge Management

In today's highly competitive business environment, it's often the company with the best information that's the most successful. As one expert recently put it, "It is a competitive advantage if your company is learning faster than the competition."[26] As a result, many managers today are emphasizing what they call knowledge management. Knowledge management refers to any efforts aimed at enabling the company's managers and employees to better utilize the information available anywhere in their companies.

Part of the problem in effectively managing knowledge is that, as one expert puts it "only two percent of information gets written down—the rest is in people's heads."[27] For any company—and especially a large one—to capture such information and transform it into knowledge that others can use can be quite a challenge.

Xerox provides a useful example of how one company dealt with this challenge. As an example of the magnitude of the knowledge-management problems Xerox faced, the company has 23,000 repair technicians around the world fixing copiers at clients' sites. In many cases, the repair solutions exist "only in the heads of experienced technicians, who can solve complex problems faster and more efficiently than less experienced ones."[28] The challenge for Xerox was to find a way to access all that brain-based knowledge and translate it into a usable form. What could Xerox do to give the company's entire 23,000-person worldwide repair force access to this knowledge?

Xerox's solution was to create an intranet-based communications system named Eureka, linked to a corporate database. The company encourages repair technicians around the world to share repair tips by inputting them into the database via Eureka. Xerox gave all technicians laptop computers to facilitate this. Soon, more than 5,000 tips were in the database. This experienced-based knowledge is easily accessible by other service reps around the world.

knowledge management ■ *the efforts aimed at enabling a company's managers and employees to better utilize the information available anywhere in the company.*

Use Your Intuition

The psychiatrist Sigmund Freud made this interesting observation on making decisions:

> *When making a decision of minor importance, I have always found it advantageous to consider all the pros and cons. In vital matters, however, such as the choice of a mate or a profession, the decision should come from the unconscious, from somewhere within ourselves. In the important decisions of our personal life, we should be governed, I think, by the deep inner needs of our nature.*[29]

Another expert puts it this way: He says you can usually tell when a decision fits with your inner nature, because it brings an enormous sense of relief. Good decisions, he says, are the best tranquilizers ever invented; bad ones often increase your anxiety. [30]

These experts are talking about intuition. Intuition is a cognitive process whereby a person instinctively makes a decision based on his or her accumulated knowledge and experience.

Psychologist Gary Klein tells this story to illustrate intuitive decision making. A fire commander and his crew encounter a fire at the back of a house. The commander leads his team into the building. Standing in the living room, they blast water onto the smoke and flames, which appear to be consuming the kitchen; yet the fire roars back and continues to burn. The fire's persistence baffles the commander. His men douse the "kitchen fire" again, and the flames subside; but then they flare up with an even greater intensity. The firefighters retreat a few steps to regroup. Suddenly, an uneasy feeling grips the commander. His intuition (which he calls his "sixth sense") tells him to vacate the house. He orders everyone to leave. Just as the crew reaches the street, the living room floor caves in. The fire was in the basement, not the kitchen. Had they still been in the house, the men would have plunged into an inferno.[31]

As this story shows, we reach intuitive decisions by quickly (and, often, unthinkingly) comparing our present situation to situations we've confronted in the past. For example, in his study of firefighters, Klein found they accumulate experiences and "subconsciously categorize fires according to how they should react to them."[32] The fire commander did this: The fire, based on his experience, just didn't make sense. Why? Because it wasn't up ahead in the kitchen, but below, in the basement. The floor muffled the sounds of the fire and retarded the transfer of heat. The commander, standing with his men in the living room, felt that something was wrong: The "kitchen fire" seemed too quiet and too cool. His intuition saved the day.

Yet, in practice, intuition has its limitations. For one thing, "various traits of human nature can easily cloud our decision-making."[33] For example, people tend to take higher than normal risks when they want to recover a loss. They might thus foolishly "bet the ranch" with what (they think) is simply an intuitive counteroffer when a competitor seems to be close to winning a merger race. People also tend to be overconfident—for instance, when sizing up an applicant's honesty.[34] The Management in Action feature gives another example of overconfidence.

MANAGEMENT IN ACTION   Overconfidence Can Be Fatal

A rising executive with a Fortune 100 manufacturing company led his firm into a disastrous expansion in Asia, in the face of negative evidence. He first discussed the opportunity with his executive staff and consultants; this rational analysis indicated it was a very risky venture. The market data looked barely favorable, and the political and cultural factors were huge unknowns; yet the executive blundered ahead. His overconfidence led him to assume that his associates really shared his view but that they were being overcautious. What would you have done if you were in his shoes?[35] He went ahead with his expansion, a decision that proved disastrous.

The bottom line is this: Be sure to challenge your "gut" reactions with some rational analysis.[36] Good managers do this. For example, in the 1990s, the commercial-waste collection division of Browning-Ferris Industries had a problem retaining customers. Its customers defected to competitors at a rate of about 12% per year. Even when the firm's management focused on raising customer satisfaction, the defections continued.[37] A careful analysis helped managers trace customer retention back to customer satisfaction—and then back to specific problems the firm could correct. Defection rates soon dropped below 10%.

Some people seem to be more naturally intuitive than others. Research shows that *systematic decision makers* take a more logical, step-by-step approach to solving a problem.[38] At the other extreme, *intuitive decision makers* use a more trial-and-error approach. They disregard much of the information available and bounce from one alternative to another to get a feel for which seems to work best. One study compared "systematics" with "intuitives." The former systematically searched for information, and thoroughly evaluated all alternatives. The latter sought information nonsystematically, and then quickly evaluated just a few favored alternatives. The intuitive approach was usually best.[39] The lesson seems to be that plodding through all the options may be fine if time permits. However, don't get bogged down in the process. It's often best to follow your instincts and "just do it," as Nike says.[40]

We can measure intuitiveness. The short test in Figure 3.2 provides an approximate reading on whether you are more systematic or intuitive in your decision making.[41]

Weigh the Pros and Cons

Intuition is important, but it's often useful to quantitatively weigh each option's merits as well. Doing so can help you take into consideration the relative importance of each of your objectives. For example, in buying a car, price may be more important than style, and style may be more important than dealer quality (since you can always have it serviced somewhere else). Weighing the pros and cons lets you quantify such realities. The weighting process permits another, more concrete analysis of your options. To accomplish the weighting, it's helpful to use a decision matrix like the one in Figure 3.3. (The appendix explains some other analytical techniques.)

◄ **FIGURE 3–2** ■ ■ ■

Are You More Rational or More Intuitive?

Source: Adapted and reproduced by permission of the Publisher, Psychological Assessment Resources. Inc., Odessa FL 33556, from the Personal Style Inventory by William Taggart, Ph.D., and Barbara Hausladen. Copyright 1991, 1993 by PAR, Inc.

WHAT IS MY ORIENTATION?

You can get a rough idea of your relative preferences for the rational and intuitive ways of dealing with situations by rating yourself on four items. For each statement, rank yourself on a six-point scale—from I (never), 2 (once in a while), 3 (sometimes), 4 (quite often), 5 (frequently but not always), 6 (always)—and place your response in the box to the right of the item:

1. When I have a special job to do, I like to organize it carefully from the start. ☐

2. I feel that a prescribed, step-by-step method is best for solving problems. ☐

3. I prefer people who are imaginative to those who are not. ☐

4. I look at a problem as a whole, approaching it from all sides. ☐

Now add the values for the first two items for one total and for the last two items for another total. Subtract the second total from the first. If your total has a positive value, your preference is *Rational* by that amount, and if your total has a negative value, your preference is *Intuitive* by that amount. Ten represents the maximum possible rational or intuitive score from the equally preferred midpoint (0). Mark your position on the range of possible scores:

Intuitive ◄———————————————► Rational
−10 −9 −8 −7 −6 −5 −4 −3 −2 −1 0 1 2 3 4 5 6 7 8 9 10

These items are taken from a 30-item Personal Style Inventory (PSI) assessment of preferences for Rational and Intuitive behavior created by William Taggert.

Don't Overstress the Finality of Your Decision[42]

In making your choice, remember that few decisions are forever. There is more reversibility in most decisions than we realize. Some strategic decisions are hard to reverse. When Ford decided in 2002 to stop producing the Taurus in one of its plants and to make its new "Cross-Trainer" SUV instead, it was a decision it would have to live with for several years. However, most decisions—even bad ones—won't mean the end of the world. Don't become frozen with an unrealistic fear that a decision can't be changed or modified.

Knowing when to quit is sometimes the smartest thing a manager can do. The London City government lost millions as its efforts to automate the London Stock Exchange collapsed due to technical difficulties. Experts studying the problem subsequently said the venture might have been a victim of what psychologists call escalation. Escalation is the act of making a wrong decision and then losing even more through a continued adherence to that decision.[43] So, once the decision is made, stick with it if you believe you're on the right track. But know "when to fold" if the decision turns out to be a poor one.

▼ **FIGURE 3–3** ■ ■ ■ Decision Matrix

Harold's Objectives	Relative importance of each objective	Marketing manager, Universal Pittsburg*	Senior manager, dotcom, NY*	Marketing manager, Ford Detroit*	Senior Marketing manager pet foods, Newark*	Marketing manager, Nokia, Washington DC*
Marketing director in two years	0.50	1	2	2	5	4
Consumer products company	0.20	5	2	3	3	5
One hour drive from major city	0.15	5	5	5	5	5
Earn at least $1,200 per week	0.15	3	4	3	4	4
	1.00	Sum= 2.70**	2.55	2.80	4.10	4.35

* 1 is low, 5 is high. ** $1 \times 0.50 + 5 \times 0.20 + 5 \times 0.15 + 3 \times 0.15 = 2.20$

Note: Rate each alternative on how well it achieves each of your objectives (such as with a 1-5). Then multiply that rating by the objective's importance score to get a numerical weighted score for each alternative.

Make Sure the Timing Is Right

You've probably noticed that, as with most people, your moods affect your decisions. Deliberately cut off by another driver while speeding down the highway, even a usually placid driver might unwisely decide to retaliate. At work, a small business owner we'll call Tom is famous (or perhaps infamous) among his workers for his passing moods. After a bad night at home or after losing a big sale, Tom is prone to lash out at anyone and anything around. His managers, therefore, learned long ago to avoid asking him for decisions when he's in a dark mood. Researchers know that when people feel "down," their actions tend to be aggressive and destructive. When they feel good, their behavior swings toward balance and tolerance. Similarly, people tend to be lenient when they're in good spirits and tough when they are grouchy.

The lesson is clear. Whether it's appraising an employee, hiring a supervisor, or buying a new machine, do a quick reality check to make sure you're not suffering from an unwelcome mood swing. Good managers tend to have stable, mature personalities. The successful ones avoid sudden decisions when their moods are extreme.

■ ■ *Traders on the floor of the London Exchange on the first day of the euro, January 4, 1999.*

CHECKLIST 3.3 ■ Making a Choice

- ☑ Increase your knowledge.
- ☑ Use your intuition.
- ☑ Weigh the pros and cons.
- ☑ Don't overstress the finality of your decision.
- ☑ Make sure the timing is right.

■ *Application Exercise: Harold's Choice* So, which alternative should Harold choose? He starts by doing some research. He learns that there are two marketing directors at the Pittsburgh plant. Because the prospects of a promotion are virtually nil, he discards that option. That leaves four options—the dot-com in New York, Ford in Detroit, pet food in Newark, and Nokia in D.C. How would you proceed if you were Harold?

He reviews his Consequences Matrix. For three of the jobs—the dot-com, Ford, and pet foods—his research and intuition suggest they probably lack the direct interaction with consumers and consumer products that he prefers. Promotion to senior director would probably take him more than two years at Ford, which in 2002 was suffering some reversals. He asks himself where he'll be six months from now if he takes the dot-com job, and is dissuaded by the high failure rate of dot-coms. Six months from now, he might well be out of a job!

Based on his Decision Matrix (page 67), the pet food and Nokia jobs look like the best bets. The pet food job is a real possibility. In terms of senior director, it's a good career move. However, he's a little less enthusiastic about the pet food business, although it scores a bit higher than the Nokia position. Harold has a good feeling about the Nokia job. It satisfies his objectives, and his research suggests that living costs are comparable to New York. He's excited about the cell phone business. Looking down the road, he sees this industry's fast growth opening many new options for him. He can definitely see himself living in Washington, D.C. He takes the job.

■ *The Global Manager* As companies extend their operations abroad, they need to make sure that all their managers have access to the latest decision-making aids. For example, Honeywell Corporation's Solutions division, based in Phoenix, Arizona, helps Honeywell improve the decisions in each step in its purchasing-manufacturing-distribution supply chain. In one situation, CMAC, a Honeywell supplier in Mexicali, Mexico, had a problem. CMAC was supposed to apply a protective coating to circuit boards, but was coating parts of the boards that were not meant to be coated. How to identify and solve the problem? Honeywell Industry Solutions provided special decision-making training to CMAC employees, so they could analyze the problems themselves. For example, Honeywell showed CMAC how to create special "process maps." These maps laid out each step in the coating process and showed, for each step, what might go wrong. CMAC used this decision aid to identify and solve the problem.[44]

How to Use Creativity to Make Better Decisions

Decision making is not a mechanical process. To make good decisions, the manager needs to be creative—for instance, in how he or she defines the problem. Creativity—the process of developing original, novel responses to a problem—is thus an integral part of making good decisions. Techniques for cultivating creativity include the following.

creativity ■ *the process of developing original, novel responses to a problem.*

Create a Culture of Creativity A major airline reportedly spent hundreds of thousands of dollars training its employees to be creative in their thinking, but the money was largely wasted. After spending several days learning how to be creative, the employees returned to their cubicles, where a bureaucratic environment discouraged them from recommending risky, innovative solutions. "This was an organization dogged by rules and regulations. What the airline had not realized was that while you can increase the level of creativity by training, the more important element is making sure that the corporate environment allows people to exercise what they've learned."[45]

Management therefore has to be proactive about creating an environment in which creativity can flourish. Doing so involves several things. Management should make it clear by word and deed that creativity is not only accepted, but desired. Managers should recognize (and, if appropriate, reward) innovative ideas. Do not cultivate yes men. (If all you do is encourage people to agree with you, it hardly pays to draw on their experience and points of view). Also be willing to tolerate failure. If you punish your employees for mistakes, they'll tend to avoid creative decisions because creativity involves risk.

Encourage Brainstorming Meetings called to discuss problems often turn out to be useless. The participants may come to the meeting willing and even enthusiastic to define a problem and to provide solutions to it. However, if a participant's suggestion is immediately met with comments like "that's ridiculous" or "that's impossible," people are unlikely to make risky, innovative suggestions.

brainstorming ■ *a creativity-stimulating technique in which prior judgments and criticisms are specifically forbidden from being expressed in order to encourage the free flow of ideas*

Brainstorming is a technique aimed at banishing this problem. It involves requiring that all participants withhold any criticism and comment on recommended alternatives, until all suggested alternatives are on the table. One important point here is that people should feel comfortable about making suggestions even if the suggestions seem strange. In an environment where everyone can build on everyone else's suggestions, it's often the most implausible idea that eventually produces the perfect solution.

Suspend Judgment Suspending judgment is the heart of brainstorming, but doing so works equally well when making decisions "solo." One problem to be aware of here is reasoning by analogy. People tend to approach situations by comparing them to similar experiences they've faced in the past. "Unfortunately, . . . [no] two situations are identical. Many decision makers spot the similarities between situations very quickly but . . . ignore critical differences."[46] Your first solution may well be correct, if the new situation really is similar. However, what if it's not? Particularly if time permits, Stanford business professor Michael Ray suggests suspending judgment. Don't automatically go with your first reaction. Suspend your judgment, instead of going back to something that you did previously in a similar situation.

▲ **WEBNOTE** ■ ■ ■

MBA Ware.com sells specialized business software like ThoughtPath, an award-winning program that helps businesses generate ideas and promote creativity.

www.mbaware.com

Source: MBAWare.com.

Get More Points of View When it comes to creativity, more points of view are usually better than fewer, and diverse points of view are better than homogeneous ones. "Creativity works better when you have a group of three or four than it does with one,

■■■ *Boosting creativity: Making sure meeting rooms are well equipped for helping participants exercise creativity.*

because you have the synergistic effect where people are working with each other, building on others' ideas," says one creativity expert. Try to obtain different opinions. For example, rather than just having production people analyze a production problem, get input from other departments as well.

Provide Physical Support for Creativity For example, the America Online facility in Dulles, Virginia has a creativity room with leopard print walls, oversize cartoon murals, and giant paint cans that appear to spill over. "We felt the standard conference rooms weren't casual and comfy enough to allow people to let go" says the room's creator. Similarly, provide plenty of bulletin boards and flat spaces to accommodate the decision-making and creativity process, as well as basics like flip charts, notecards, markers, and Post-it® notes.

Encourage Anonymous Input Even in the most supportive environment, members of your group may be simply too introverted to participate fully. Allowing for anonymous and/or written input can help encourage people like these to participate more.[47]

CHECKLIST 3.4 ■ How to Be More Creative

- ☑ Create a culture of creativity.
- ☑ Encourage brainstorming.
- ☑ Suspend judgment.
- ☑ Get more points of view.
- ☑ Provide physical support for creativity.
- ☑ Encourage anonymous input.

■■■ AVOIDING PSYCHOLOGICAL TRAPS

Don't let the apparent rationality of the decision-making process mislead you. In practice, sprinkled across the decision-making terrain are numerous decision-making traps. The frightening thing is that the manager whose decision the trap undermines probably won't even realize what's happened. Let's look at some of these psychological traps.

Decision-Making Shortcuts

heuristic ■ *a rule of thumb or an approximation applied as a shortcut to decision making.*

People have their own instinctive way of programming many of the decisions they have to make. They do this by using heuristics, decision-making shortcuts, or "rules of thumb." For example, mortgage lenders typically abide by the heuristic that "people shouldn't spend more than 28% of their gross monthly income on mortgage payments and other house-related expenses."[48]

Managers consciously or unconsciously apply heuristics all the time. For example, in the 1990s and early 2000s, former Tyco International CEO Dennis Kozlowski reviewed hundreds of potential acquisitions every year. Carefully analyzing each of them was too time-consuming. He streamlined his decision process by using two decision rules. He only considered deals that (1) were friendly (no hostile takeovers) and (2) would immediately add to Tyco's earnings.[49] (With Tyco's stock price down, some now wonder if he was not too informal in his approach.)

Heuristics manifest themselves in many ways. For example, a manager might (unwisely) predict what a subordinate's performance will be, based on that person's similarity to others with the same ethnic background that the manager has known. Another shortcut involves basing decisions on what happened most recently. Thus, supervisors tend to appraise employees based on the person's past few weeks' performance, since that's what's most readily recalled. Based on 150 interviews with decision makers, one researcher concluded, "Relatively few decisions are made using analytical processes such as generating a variety of options and contrasting their strengths and weaknesses."[50] Instead, most people tend to use cognitive shortcuts, such as rules governing what to do in new situations that are similar to those addressed in the past.

Anchoring

Anchoring means unconsciously giving too much weight to the first information you hear. It can cause you to define the problem incorrectly.

Anchors pop up in the most unexpected ways. Assume you're selling your car, which you know is worth about $10,000. Joe has responded to your classified ad; when he arrives, he offhandedly remarks that the car is only worth about $5,000. What would you do? On the one hand, you know that Joe is probably just positioning himself to get a better deal, and you know that $5,000 is ridiculous. On the other hand, Joe is the only game in town (one other person called, but never showed up). So you start bargaining with Joe. He says $5,000; you say $10,000; and before you know it, you've arrived at a price of $8,000 (for your $10,000 car), which Joe graciously points out is "better than splitting the difference" from your point of view.

What happened? You just got anchored (to put it mildly). Without realizing it, you gave disproportionate weight to his offhand "$5,000" comment, and your decision making (and bargaining) from then on revolved around his price, not yours. What should you have done? One response might have been "$5,000? Are you kidding? That's not even in the ballpark!" At least that might have loosened that subliminal anchor, so the bargaining could take place on your terms, not his.

anchoring ■ unconsciously giving disproportionate weight to the first information you hear.

Psychological Set

Not "thinking out of the box" is another decision-making trap. The technical term for this is psychological set, which means the tendency to focus on a rigid strategy or point of view when solving a problem.[51] Doing so can severely limit a manager's ability to create alternative solutions. Figure 3.4 presents a classic example. Your assignment is to connect all nine dots with no more than four lines running through them, and to do so without lifting your pen from the paper. Hint: Don't take a rigid point of view.

To avoid the trap, always question your assumptions. Look again at the problem of the nine dots in Figure 3.4. Remember that your instructions were to connect all nine dots with no more than four lines running through them and to do so without lifting your pen from the paper. How would you do it? Start by checking your assumptions.

Most people view the nine dots as a square—they're victims of psychological set. Viewing them as a square limits your solutions. There is actually no way to connect all the dots as long as you assume the dots represent a square. Figure 3.5 shows one creative solution. The key was checking your assumptions about how you could solve the problem. Now solve the problem in Figure 3.6.

The psychological-set trap helps explain why many decisions go bad. For example, the owners of the building with the "slow elevators" were victims of psychological set. They could only see the problem in one way, and they did not question their assumptions. Luckily, the consultants didn't fall into the same trap.

psychological set ■ the tendency to rely on a rigid strategy or approach when solving a problem.

Perception

The fact that we don't always see things as they really are is another psychological trap. Perception is the selection and interpretation of information we receive through our senses and the meaning we give to the information. Many things, including our

perception ■ the unique way each person defines stimuli, depending on the influence of past experiences and the person's present needs and personality.

◀ **FIGURE 3–4** ■ ■ ■

Looking at the Problem in Just One Way

Source: Lester A. Lefton and Laura Valvatine, *Mastering Psychology,* 4th ed. Copyright © 1992 by Allyn & Bacon. Reprinted by permission.

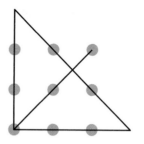

individual needs, influence how we perceive stimuli. For example, a thirsty person in the desert may perceive distant heat waves as an oasis, while his healthy rescuer sees nothing but sand. Things like this happen every day. You might be less happy with a B in a course after finding out that your friend got an A with about the same test grades.[52] Similarly, in organizations, prior experiences and position influence how a person perceives a problem and reacts to it.

A classic study illustrates this point. Researchers asked 23 executives, all employed by a large manufacturing firm, to read a business case.[53] Researchers found that a manager's position influenced how he or she defined the most important problem facing the company. For example, of six sales executives, five thought the most important problem was a sales problem. Four out of five production executives, but only one sales executive and no accounting executives, mentioned organization problems. The managers looked at the same case, but they drew very different conclusions. Each would probably have taken action based on his or her view of the problem. Each would think they'd done a rational analysis. Each would instead have probably fallen into the perception trap.

▶ **FIGURE 3–6** ■ ■ ■

Using Creativity to Find a Solution

How many squares are in the box? Now, count again. Only sixteen? Take away your preconception of how many squares there are. Now, how many do you find? You should find thirty!

Source: Applied Human Relations, 4th ed., by Benton/Halloran cW 1991. Reprinted by permission of Prentice Hall, Upper Saddle River, NJ.

SUMMARY ■ ■ ■

1. A decision is a choice from among available alternatives. Decision making is the process of developing and analyzing alternatives and making a choice.

2. Decisions can be either programmed (repetitive and routine) or nonprogrammed (unique and novel). Nonprogrammed decisions require more intuition and judgment of decision makers.

3. Rational decision making assumes ideal conditions, such as an accurate definition of the problem and complete knowledge about all relevant alternatives and their values.

4. In contrast, decision making in reality is bounded by differences in managers' ability to process information, and by

reliance on heuristics or shortcuts, framing, anchoring, escalation, psychological set, and factors in the organization itself.

5. *Bounded rationality* describes decision making in reality and often implies satisficing, or accepting satisfactory (as opposed to optimal) alternatives.

6. Guidelines for making better decisions include increase your knowledge, use creativity, use intuition, don't overstress finality, and make sure the timing is right.

7. Psychological traps include decision-making shortcuts, anchoring, psychological set, and preception.

SKILLS AND STUDY MATERIALS

COMPANION WEBSITE ▪▪▪

 We invite you to visit the Dessler Companion Website at **www.prenhall.com/dessler** for this chapter's Internet resources.

EXPERIENTIAL EXERCISES ▪▪▪

1. While sitting on the banks of a river, Taoist thinker Chuang-tse was approached by two representatives of the Prince of Ch'u, who offered him a position at court. Chuang-tse watched the water flowing by as if he had not heard. Finally, he remarked, "I am told that the Prince has a sacred tortoise, over 2,000 years old, which is kept in a box, wrapped in silk and brocade." "That is true," the officials replied. "If the tortoise has been given a choice," Chuang-tse continued, "which do you think he would have liked better—to have been alive in the mud or dead within the palace?" "To have been alive in the mud, of course," the men answered. "I too prefer the mud," said Chuang-tse. "Goodbye."[54]

   Working as a team, answer the following questions. Based on his clever answer, how do you think Chuang-tse defined the problem that the two representatives presented?

   What exactly triggered the problem? What did he decide was the solution to the problem? List two other ways Chuang-tse could have defined the problem.

2. Most colleges and universities have grievance procedures in place to address inappropriate behavior by both students and faculty. Working as a team, obtain the student and/or faculty grievance procedures for your college or university, and answer the following questions: What provision (if any) does the procedure make for allowing the parties to define the (student's or faculty member's) problem? Assuming a student has accused a faculty member of "giving me a lower grade then I deserve, based on the grading policies laid out in the course syllabus," propose at least five objectives for the committee which must decide who is right and who is wrong.

CASE STUDY ▪▪▪

BRITISH PETROLEUM

Shareholders of British Petroleum (BP) faced a challenging decision. BP's CEO, Sir John Browne, had recommended that the huge British company purchase long-time American competitor Amoco for $57 billion.

Browne had led BP in the purchase of Atlantic Richfield just six months earlier for $27 billion. If the shareholders approved the new deal, BP-Amoco would become the second largest oil producer in the world—impressive for a company that had been in financial trouble just seven years earlier.

In a presentation to press and industry analysts, Sir John presented his view of the merger. Browne's presentation to shareholders was straightforward. The merger would make BP a "super-major"

oil company, controlling the third largest volume of oil and gas reserves in the world. Browne portrayed the new company as having distinctive assets, global reach, and strongly competitive returns.

Management would partially reorganize/restructure the firm. The resulting efficiencies gained by the new firm would result in a net $2 billion pretax savings. The merger would also geographically diversify BP, improving the balance in its revenues between the United States, Europe, and the rest of the world.

BP's earnings in 1997 were $4.6 billion, and Amoco's totaled $2.7 billion. Combined revenues of the two giants would total $108 billion. The current combined market capitalization (the total value of its shares) of some $110 billion would create Britain's largest company.

Critics of the proposal said it was not so simple. They said that, among other things, Browne had to develop a strategy for BP's natural gas assets. The merger would make BP the world's third largest producer of natural gas (only the Russian giant Gazprom and the U.S. company Exxon were bigger). Analysts had predicted that demand for natural gas would grow twice as fast as that for oil, yet there were questions about BP's knowledge and skills in this area. Former Amoco executives said the company did not understand the global nature of the gas business.

There was also concern that Browne might not be able to expand the new business. Browne had shown great skill in cutting costs and gaining efficiencies, but analysts were still concerned. It takes a different set of skills to cut a company than to grow it. For all his success, Browne had not clearly demonstrated to everyone's satisfaction that he could move a company to sustained growth.

Still, the numbers presented by Browne and his management team were impressive. They carefully documented the sources of their estimated $2 billion in cost savings, and they provided assurances that they'd carefully planned these moves. Furthermore, the management team suggested its numbers were actually conservative. For example, they did not reflect any synergies that might occur in revenue generation—only those that came from cost cut-

ting. In addition, the management team at BP had linked its own management compensation to meeting the strategic cost targets.

In describing the merger to BP shareholders, Browne described the BP-Amoco linkup in glowing terms—as "a superb alliance of equals with complementary strategic and geographical strengths which effectively creates a new super-major that can better serve our millions of customers worldwide."

There was a great deal of information to consider when making the decision. The Securities and Exchange Commission (SEC) filings alone concerning the acquisition were more than 100 pages long. There were strong opinions for and against the acquisition.

Discussion Questions

1. How has BP management defined the problem, and how do you think the problem should be defined?

2. What criteria do you think an investor should use in making his or her decision about the wisdom of the merger?

3. Using your own estimates when necessary, develop both a Consequences Matrix and a Decision Matrix for an investor who has to make this invest/don't invest in BP decision.

4. What decision do you think the shareholders should make, and why?

YOU BE THE CONSULTANT ■■■

WHICH ROUTES TO FLY?

jetBlue AIRWAYS®   As an experienced airline manager, David Neeleman knows there are no more important decisions he has to make than those concerning the routes JetBlue will fly. The right decision will maximize ridership and minimize competitive retaliation, by offering low-cost flights that competitors aren't now providing. The wrong decision will confront Neeleman's fledgling airline with fast and sure competitive retaliation, in which case JetBlue could be out of business before it really takes off.

The first and biggest route decision probably revolved around whether to choose New York's JFK as his first major gateway. [55] There was a time when JFK was actually the headquarters for several U.S. airlines, but most moved on to other cities and airports where costs were lower and spaces were easier to come by. From JetBlue's point of view, JFK has several advantages. It is in the middle of one of the ten busiest air passenger markets in the United States. New York's political leaders badly wanted a low-cost airline for their state that would help reduce the cost of flying from the New York City area to upper New York State. And, while JFK did have heavy delays, it actually was less busy than the New York's other major airport, LaGuardia, for the time slots JetBlue was looking at.

Neeleman and his team have considered other airport alternatives. At Boston's Logan Airport, for instance, Neeleman says, "No one will give us gates." In other words, there's so much competition from American Airlines and US Airways that JetBlue can't get the gates it needs, even though, according to Neeleman, the gates at Logan are now underutilized.

In terms of what he looks for in choosing routes, Neeleman says one thing his company must watch out for is spreading

itself too thin. Spreading his flights among too many destinations runs the risk of lowering the utilization rate of each plane—there'd be too much downtime, without enough passengers on each route. As he says, "I just want passengers on the planes." The basic idea, therefore, is to go into a few major gateways, like JFK, and to use the traffic and population base around these gateways to fly into smaller cities that are not adequately served by low-cost airlines. For example, he wants to fly passengers from JFK to Buffalo, New York, and Fort Lauderdale (instead of Miami). The problem is, "Where should JetBlue fly next?"

Getting the slots (the permissions to fly in and out at specific times) at a busy airport like JFK is not going to be easy. He set up a lobbying operation in Washington, D.C., in order to help convince New York's congressional delegation that New York cities like Buffalo, Syracuse, and Rochester needed JetBlue's low-cost alternative flights from New York City. In turn, New York congressional members will have to work on convincing the Department of Transportation that the needs of New Yorkers (and JetBlue) are important enough to put JetBlue's interest ahead of those of major airlines like American and USAir.

Getting the slots doesn't mean JetBlue is home free. For example, it was able to obtain numerous arrival and departure slots at California's Long Beach airport. However, those slots came with the condition that they must all be utilized within several years. American Airlines is already battling to take over some of those slots, and is lowering prices to Long Beach, and increasing incentives (such as adding more frequent-flier miles for those who fly there from JFK). In the not too distant future, Neeleman also would like to see JetBlue fly abroad—for instance, to Canada and Mexico.

Assignment

You and your team are consultants to Mr. Neeleman, who is depending on your management expertise to navigate the launch and management of JetBlue. He wants you to:

1. Accurately spell out what triggered the route-decision problems stated in the case.

2. List at least four ways that Neeleman can define the "Where should we fly next" problem, and then choose the best alternative.

3. Propose at least five objectives for Neeleman, who must make the decision regarding routes and gateways.

4. Propose at least four alternatives to solve the situation. Develop a Consequences Matrix for the situation.

5. Develop a Decision Matrix for the position.

Chapter Appendix

QUANTITATIVE DECISION-MAKING AIDS

Many decisions (particularly programmed ones) lend themselves to quantitative analysis. Here are several of the more popular quantitative decision-making techniques.

■■■ BREAKEVEN ANALYSIS

breakeven analysis ■ *a financial analysis decision-making aid that enables a manager to determine whether a particular volume of sales will result in losses or profits.*

In financial analysis, the breakeven point is that volume of sales at which revenues just equal expenses, and you have neither a profit nor a loss. Breakeven analysis is a decision-making aid that enables a manager to determine whether a particular volume of sales will result in losses or profits.[1]

Breakeven Charts

Breakeven analysis makes use of four basic concepts: fixed costs, variable costs, revenues, and profits. *Fixed costs* (such as for the plant and machinery) are costs that basically do not change with changes in volume. In other words, you might use the same machine to produce 10 units, 50 units, or 200 units of a product. *Variable costs* (such as for raw material) rise in proportion to volume. *Revenue* is the total income received from sales of the product. For example, if you sell 50 dolls at $8 each, then your revenue is $8 × 50, or $400. *Profit* is the money you have left after subtracting fixed and variable costs from revenues.

A breakeven chart, as in Figure A3.1, is a graph that shows whether a particular volume of sales will result in profits or losses. The fixed costs line is horizontal. Variable costs, however, increase in proportion to output and are shown as an upward sloping line. The total costs line is then equal to variable costs plus fixed costs at each level of output. The breakeven point is the point at which the total revenue line crosses the total costs line. Beyond this point (note the shaded area in Figure A3.1), total revenue exceeds total costs. In this example, an output of about 4,000 units

▶ **FIGURE A3–1** ■■■

A Breakeven Chart

The breakeven point is that number of units sold at which total revenues just equal total costs.

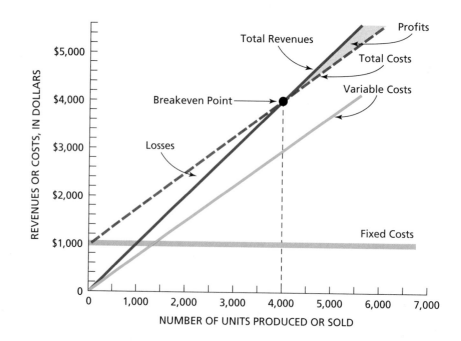

is the breakeven point. Above this, the company can expect to earn a profit. If sales are fewer than 4,000 units, the company can expect a loss.

Breakeven Formula

The breakeven chart provides a picture of the relationship between sales volume and profits. However, a chart is not required for determining breakeven points. Instead, you can use a formula:

$$P(X) = F + V(X)$$

where

$$F = \text{fixed costs}$$

$$V = \text{variable costs per unit}$$

$$X = \text{volume of output (in units)}$$

$$P = \text{price per unit}$$

Rearranging this formula, the breakeven point is $F/(P - V)$. In other words, the breakeven point is the volume of sales where total costs just equal total revenues. If, for example, you have a product in which

$$F = \text{fixed costs} = \$1,000.00$$

$$V = \text{variable costs per unit} = \$.75$$

$$P = \text{price per unit} = \$1.00 \text{ per unit,}$$

then the breakeven point is $\$1,000/(\$1.00 - \$.75) = 4,000$ units.

■■■ LINEAR PROGRAMMING

Breakeven analysis is only one of many quantitative techniques. Decision-science techniques are another category of programmed decision-making aids. These tools all rely on mathematics. For example, linear programming is a mathematical method used to solve resource allocation problems that arise "whenever there are a number of activities to be performed, [with] limitations on either the amount of resources or [on] the way they can be spent."[2]

linear programming ■ *a mathematical method used to solve resource allocation problems.*

You can use linear programming to determine the best way to:

■ Distribute merchandise from a number of warehouses to a number of customers;
■ Assign personnel to various jobs.
■ Design shipping schedules.
■ Select the product mix in a factory to make the best use of machine and labor hours available while maximizing the firm's profit.
■ Route production to optimize the use of machinery.

In order for managers to apply linear programming successfully, the problem must meet certain basic requirements. There must be a stated, quantifiable goal, such as "minimize total shipping costs"; the resources to be utilized must be known (a firm could produce 200 of one item and 300 of another, for instance, or 400 of one or 100 of another); all the necessary relationships must be expressed in the form of mathematical equations or inequalities; and all these relationships must be linear in nature. An example can help illustrate:

Shader Electronics has five manufacturing plants and 12 warehouses scattered across the country. Each plant is manufacturing the same product and operating at full capacity. Since plant capacity and location do not permit the closest plant to fully support each warehouse, Shader would like to identify the factory that should supply each warehouse in order to minimize total shipping costs. Applying linear programming techniques to this problem will provide an optimum shipping schedule.

■■■ WAITING-LINE/QUEUING TECHNIQUES

Waiting-line/queuing techniques are mathematical decision-making techniques for solving waiting-line problems. For example, bank managers need to know how many tellers they should have. If they have too many, they are wasting money on salaries; if they have too few, they may end up with many disgruntled customers. Similar problems arise when selecting the optimal number of airline reservations clerks, warehouse loading docks, highway tollbooths, supermarket checkout counters, and so forth.

waiting-line/queuing techniques ■ *mathematical techniques used to solve waiting-line problems such that the optimal balance of employees available to waiting customers is attained.*

■■ STATISTICAL DECISION THEORY TECHNIQUES

Managers use statistical decision theory techniques to solve problems for which information is incomplete or uncertain. Suppose a shopkeeper can stock either Brand A or Brand B, but not both. She knows how much it will cost to stock her shelves with each brand, and she also knows how much money she would earn (or lose) if each brand turned out to be a success (or failure) with her customers. However, she can only estimate how much of each brand she might sell, so her information is incomplete. Using statistical decision theory, the shopkeeper would assign probabilities (estimates of the likelihood that the brand will sell or not) to each alternative. Then she could determine which alternative—stocking Brand A or Brand B—would most likely result in the greatest profits.

Three Degrees of Uncertainty

Statistical decision theory assumes that a manager may face three degrees of uncertainty in making a decision. Managers make some decisions under conditions of certainty. Here, the manager knows in advance the outcome of the decision. From a practical point of view, for example, you know that if you buy a $50 U.S. savings bond, the interest rate you will earn to maturity on the bond is, say, 6%. Managers rarely make decisions under such conditions.

At the opposite extreme, they make some decisions under conditions of uncertainty. Here, the manager cannot even assign probabilities to the likelihood of the various outcomes. For example, a shopkeeper may have several new products that could be stocked, but no idea of the likelihood that one brand will be successful or that another will fail. Conditions of complete uncertainty are also relatively infrequent. Most management decisions are made under conditions of risk. Under these conditions, the manager can at least assign probabilities to each outcome. In other words, the manager knows (either from past experience or by making an educated guess) the chance that each possible outcome (such as Product A being successful or Product B being successful) will occur.

Decision Tree

A decision tree is one technique for making a decision under conditions of risk. With a decision tree like the one in Figure A3.2, an expected value can be calculated for each alternative. Expected value equals (1) the probability of the outcome multiplied by (2) the benefit or cost of that outcome.

For example, in the figure, it pays our shopkeeper to stock Brand B rather than Brand A. Stocking Brand A allows a 70% chance of success for an $800 profit, so the shopkeeper has to balance this possible expected $560 profit against the possibility of the $90 loss (.30 × possible loss of −$300). The expected value of stocking Brand A is thus $470. By stocking Brand B, though, the expected value is a relatively high $588.

▶ **FIGURE 3–2** ■ ■ ■

Example of a Decision Tree

The expected value of each alternative is equal to (1) the chance of success or failure times (2) the expected profit or loss.

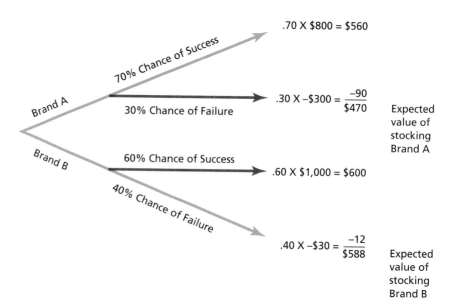

$$.70 \times \$800 = \$560$$

70% Chance of Success

Brand A

$$.30 \times -\$300 = \frac{-90}{\$470}$$

30% Chance of Failure

Expected value of stocking Brand A

Brand B

60% Chance of Success

$$.60 \times \$1,000 = \$600$$

40% Chance of Failure

$$.40 \times -\$30 = \frac{-12}{\$588}$$

Expected value of stocking Brand B

The Basic Planning Process

THE MANAGEMENT CHALLENGE

Dieter Zetsche's Forecasts

German carmaker Daimler's plan to build a stronger global car firm was heading toward disaster. Daimler was known for the incomparable quality of its cars; its huge profits reflected that reputation. Daimler assumed that its new Chrysler division could show it how to cut costs and boost profits. (Chrysler, after all, had fought its way out of bankruptcy in the 1980s by slashing costs and introducing new models all built on a single chassis.) But by the early 2000s, costs of the newly merged Daimler and Chrysler were spiraling out of control, and revenues were plummeting. For 2001, the Chrysler unit's CEO, Dieter Zetsche, had forecast that revenues would grow by $1 billion; instead, they fell by $4.4 billion. DaimlerChrysler's chairman, Juergen Schrempp, was under pressure to show that his decision to buy Chrysler was not a mistake. In a world with new imponderables like the 9/11 terrorist attacks, Zetsche faced a tricky situation. Consumer spending was a question mark in 2001–2002. Zetsche not only had to cut costs by billions of dollars, but had to boost the number of new models Chrysler would introduce, and raise Chrysler's market share (its share was actually slipping). Then he had to lay out specific goals his managers could focus on. He needed a new plan, but how could he make forecasts under such uncertainty? What planning tools should he use?

CHAPTER OBJECTIVES

After studying this chapter and the case exercises at the end, you should be able to:

1. Develop a usable plan for an organization.

2. Write an outline of the required business plan, and provide specific examples of its component functional plans.

3. Express the necessary plan in descriptive, graphic, and financial formats.

4. Explain what the manager did right and did wrong with respect to setting goals for subordinates.

5. Explain the forecasting tools you think the manager should use, and why.

Few of the decisions managers make are more important than those that go into forming their company's plans. The main purpose of this chapter is show you how to develop a plan. The topics we'll focus on include the nature and purpose of planning, the management planning process, how to set objectives, and how to develop planning premises and make forecasts. In Chapter 5, we'll turn to a special type of planning—companywide, long-term strategic planning.

■■■ THE NATURE AND PURPOSE OF PLANNING

plan ■ *a method for doing or making something, consisting of a goal and a course of action.*

goal ■ *a specific result to be achieved; the end result of a plan.*

objectives ■ *specific results toward which effort is directed.*

planning ■ *the process of setting goals and courses of action, developing rules and procedures, and forecasting future outcomes.*

Planning is something we all do, every day. For example, if you are like most readers of this book, you're probably reading it as part of a management course. Chances are the course is part of your program of studies. This program is a plan. It identifies your goal (say, getting a business degree in two years), and it identifies how you will reach that goal by specifying the courses you'll need to graduate and, roughly, the sequence in which you'll take them. Plans are devices that answer the questions: What will we do? When will we do it? Who will do it? How much will it cost?[1] All plans specify or imply *goals* (such as "boost sales by 10%") and *courses of action* (such as "hire a new salesperson and boost advertising by 20%"). Plans are, therefore, methods for achieving a desired result. Goals or objectives are specific results you want to achieve. Planning is thus "the process of establishing objectives and courses of action prior to taking action."[2]

Your own plans may not end with earning the degree. You may also have a broader goal, a vision of where you're headed in life. If you do, then your degree may be just one step in a longer-term plan. For example, suppose you dream of running your own consulting firm by the time you are 35. You, therefore, ask yourself, "What must I do to achieve this goal?" The answer may be to work for a nationally known consulting firm, thus building up your experience and your reputation in the field. So here is your plan: "Take this course to get the degree, get the degree to get the consulting job, and then work as a consultant to achieve my dream." You are well on the way to setting up "Acme Consulting, LLC."

What Planning Entails

Planning really means making tomorrow's decisions today. Planning entails choosing goals and the courses of action to achieve them. Therefore, when you make a plan, you're actually deciding now what you are going to do in the future. In that sense, a plan is simply a set of premade decisions that will allow you to achieve a future goal. As such, planning lets you assess today the consequences tomorrow of your various courses of action.

■ *Application Example: The Trip to Paris* Suppose you're planning a trip to Paris. Your plan might consist of the following decisions (among others): the date you leave, how you get to the airport, your airline and flight, the airport of arrival, how you'll get into Paris, your hotel, and (of course) a fairly detailed itinerary (or plan, or set of decisions) for each day you're in Paris.

Of course, you could just wing it, and many people do. Suppose you *don't* decide ahead of time (plan) how you're getting to or from the airport, or what you'll be doing each day in Paris. What will happen? Maybe nothing. More likely, you'll have to make many last-minute decisions under stressful conditions. Instead of arranging to have a friend take you to the airport, you may be scrambling to find a cab. Instead of researching and pricing your transportation alternatives ahead of time, you may find yourself at Charles de Gaulle Airport, tired and faced with a bewildering variety of buses and cabs. And instead of deciding ahead of time, in the comfort of your home (and with all your guidebooks), what you'll do each day, you may kill several hours each day deciding what to do and what is open—or drifting aimlessly through the Paris streets (which is not necessarily bad, of course).

What Planning Accomplishes

The point of the Paris example is that planning gives you the luxury of deciding ahead of time what you're going to do, and it helps you anticipate the sorts of things that might spoil your plans. As with the Paris trip, planning, first, allows you to *make your decisions ahead of time*, in the comfort of your home (or office), and with the luxury of having the time to research and weigh your options. It also helps you to *anticipate the consequences* of various courses of action, and to think through the practicality and feasibility of each one without actually having to commit the resources to carry out that course of action. Why plan on spending your first five nights in Paris if it turns out that the museums will be closed on the fourth and fifth days?

Planning also provides *direction and a sense of purpose.* "If you don't know where you're going, any path will get you there," the Mad Hatter tells Alice as she stumbles into Wonderland. The same is true for all your endeavors: Knowing ahead of time that your goal is to own a consulting firm provides a sense of direction and purpose for all the career decisions you have to make, such as what to major in and what experience you'll need along the way. Someone once said, "The world parts and makes a path for the person who knows where he or she is going." Planning provides that sense of purpose.

A plan also, therefore, provides a *unifying framework* against which to measure decisions and thus helps you *avoid piecemeal decision making*— making decisions that are not consistent with your goal or with each other. For example, R.R. Donnelley prints documents and other materials for a broad range of clients, including some of the world's largest financial transactions such as initial public offerings and mergers and acquisitions. The company is a leading printer of books, magazines, and catalogs, and is also one of the world's largest managers, storers, and distributors of books in electronic form.[3] R.R. Donnelley's planning led its managers to anticipate a demand for global printing caused by the globalization of its customers. The company therefore invested heavily in advanced technology and a worldwide electronic network. Now, with the help of satellites, R.R. Donnelley can print a securities prospectus simultaneously in many locations around the globe.[4]

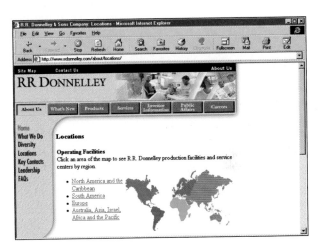

▲ WEBNOTE ■ ■ ■

R.R. Donnelley uses the Web to help customers stay in touch with the company.

www.rrdonnelley.com

Source: Used with permission.

It would have been wasteful for Donnelley to spend its investment dollars building more printing factories in the United States. The globalization of its customers demanded— and technological advances made possible—the capability of transmitting and creating documents via satellite around the globe. Donnelley's plan for doing so helped ensure that the firm channeled its resources toward those desired results, and avoided activities—such as building unneeded domestic printing plants—that were inconsistent with its overall direction. Its plan helped it avoid making piecemeal, internally inconsistant decisions.

Planning's benefits don't stop there. Management theorist Peter Drucker says that planning also helps *identify potential opportunities and threats* and reduce long-term risks.[5] For example, Donnelley's planning process helped identify the opportunity for satellite-based global printing.

Finally, *planning facilitates control.* Control means ensuring that activities conform to plans, and it entails three steps: Set standards, measure performance against these standards, and identify and correct deviations. Planning is the first step in this cycle. Thus, a company's plan may specify that its profits will double within five years. This goal becomes the standard against which to measure, compare, and control a manager's performance. Planning and control are the Siamese twins of the management process. You can't have controls without a plan, and it's useless to have a plan if you don't monitor how you're doing.

■■■ THE MANAGEMENT PLANNING PROCESS

You already know quite a lot about the management planning process. Consider the five steps you might take to plan a career.

1. *Set a career goal,* such as "work as a management consultant."
2. *Analyze the situation* to assess your skills and to determine the prospects.

3. Determine your *alternative courses of action*—the paths you might follow (college major, summer experiences, etc.) to reach your goal.
4. *Evaluate your alternatives.*
5. Finally, *formulate your plan* (including a budget).

It's a logical process and one that parallels how you would make any decision.

That's really all there is to the management planning process. It hardly matters if you're planning your career, or a trip to France, or how you're going to market your firm's new product. The basic process always involves setting objectives, analyzing the situation and making forecasts, determining alternative courses of action, evaluating those options, and then choosing and implementing your plan.

The process is the same when managers plan for their firms, with two small complications. First, there's usually a *hierarchical aspect* to corporate planning: Top management approves a long-term plan; and each department creates its own budgets and other plans to fit and to contribute to the company's long-term plan.

Second—and related to the first complication—the process may involve much interaction and give-and-take among departments and organizational levels. In other words, corporate planning in practice is *iterative* (sort of like a tennis game): Top management formulates its plans at least in part based on upward feedback from the departments, and the departments in turn draft plans that make sense in terms of top management's plan. Let's look more closely at this process.

The Planning Hierarchy

As you can see from this discussion, Step 5 ("formulate your plan") is not the final step. In a sense, it's just the start for round 2, because top management's goals then become the targets for which the departments craft derivative plans. In other words, the planning process produces a hierarchy of plans. This hierarchy includes (1) the companywide plan and goals and (2) various levels of subsidiary units' derivative plans and objectives, each of which contributes to achieving the goals of the next higher unit's plans. A hierarchy of plans thereby evolves; consider Sunbeam.

hierarchy of plans ■ *a set of plans that includes the company-wide plan and the derivative plans of subsidiary units required to help achieve the enterprisewide plan.*

MANAGEMENT IN ACTION   Sunbeam

Several years ago, Sunbeam Corporation, which makes kitchen appliances, decided to reduce costs by at least 20%, by shrinking the firm. Top management's overall plan was to reduce the number of employees by half, roll out 30 new products per year, and shrink the number of factories and warehouses from more than 40 to just 13.

With those goals providing a framework for planning, lower-level managers devised plans for their departments. Managers for each product group had to formulate and receive approval for plans for which products they would add and drop. The production head had to craft plans showing which plants he would close to meet the goal.

Then, third-level managers needed operational plans. For example, once the Human Resources (HR) manager knew which plants were closing, he or she would need operational plans for handling the dismissals. And, each plant manager would need specific monthly production plans, once he or she knew the targets top management had set for the facility. The result was a hierarchy of plans; managers at each level devised plans of increasing specificity (and of shorter time horizon) from the top of the firm to the bottom.

Because of its hierarchical nature, developing a full set of plans typically takes several months. In most companies, top management and the board formulate a few strategic themes (such as "improve productivity") at the start of the year. The divisions then complete reviews of their current businesses in April and forward them to corporate planning. In June, the board adopts a set of planning assumptions (for instance, "The industry will expand by 10%") and guidelines prepared by the corporate planning department. At the same time, the planning group might be preparing financial forecasts, again based in part on projections from the divisions.

President's Strategic Goals
- Have a minimum of 55% of sales revenue from customized products by 2005
- Boost overall corporate profitability by 10%
- Increase sales revenue by 20% in two years

VP of Marketing's Goals
- Complete market study on sales potential for customized products

VP of Sales' Goals
- Increase sales of customized products to 25% in year one

VP of Manufacturing's Goals
- Convert Building C to customized manufacturing

VP of Human Resources' Goals
- Change compensation structure to create incentives for customized sales

Purchasing Director's Goals
- Purchase and install new equipment

Engineering Director's Goals
- Complete feasibility study of conversion requirements

▲ **FIGURE 4–1** ■ ■ ■ Hiearchy of Goals

In, say, July, the board reviews and sets the firm's financial objectives, and in early August these goals are sent to each business unit. The units then use these financial targets (as well as the firm's strategic goals) to prepare their own plans. They submit these plans for approval in January. Once the divisions receive approval for their plans, departments can develop shorter-term tactical and operational plans. Once adopted, top management monitors their progress, perhaps via quarterly reports from the operating units.

The Goals Hierarchy

The planning process obviously produces a hierarchy not just of *plans* but also of *goals*.[6] Figure 4.1 illustrates this. At the top, the president and staff set strategic goals (such as to have a minimum of 55% of sales revenue from customized products by 2005). Lower level managers (in this case, starting with the vice presidents) then set goals to achieve these targets (such as to "convert Building C to customized manufacturing operations") that make sense in terms of the goals at the next higher level. "In this way, the company creates a hierarchy of supporting departmental goals, down to tactical and functional goals and finally short-term day-to-day operational goals."[7]

The hierarchical planning process needn't be complicated. When Gregg Foster purchased the troubled metal-converting Elyria Foundry, he knew the key to long-term prosperity was setting goals and then getting employees—from the shop floor to the top—committed to achieving them. "Goals are specific, but they also create a picture of how we want to be."

Foster used a hierarchical approach. First, he set a few strategic goals to lay out a broad direction for the firm. He next turned to his department managers, who each submitted five to ten supporting goals. Next, input from lower-level employees yielded goals ranging from retirement plan participation to qualifying for ISO 9000 (International Standards Organization quality management) certification.

The goals hierarchy showed how each level's efforts would contribute to attaining the goals at the next higher level and for the foundry as a whole. It also helped identify the things employees and

■ ■ *Gregg Foster of Elyria Foundry: He turned around a sick company by setting goals.*

managers felt the company had to fix if the firm were to achieve Foster's overall goals. The resulting plan was also realistic, since it used input from managers and employees who were actually "at ground level", and doing the job on a day-to-day basis. We'll discuss how to set goals in more detail later in this chapter.

The experience at Sunbeam and at Elyria help to illustrate the steps in the basic planning process, which we summarize in Checklist 4.1.

CHECKLIST 4.1 ■ How to Develop a Plan

☑ **Set an objective.** "Where do we want to end up at the end of the planning period?" Do we want to own a successful consulting firm by 2005? Cut Daimler's costs next year by $3 billion? Making this decision—setting these goals—means the manager must address the right problem ("is cutting costs the problem?"). Always ask, "Are we *sure* we've defined the problem correctly?"

☑ **Develop forecasts and planning premises.** Next, "situation analysis" provides the information about opportunities, threats, and trends you'll need to start formulating intelligent alternatives. This step provides the basic assumptions (premises), such as "the economy will expand by 5% per year for the next 4 years" on which you'll build your plan.

☑ **Determine your options.** Every plan consists of a goal and a course of action for getting there. For any goal, there are usually several options or alternative courses of action for getting there. DaimlerChrysler could save that $3 billion in many ways. It could sell Chrysler, for

instance, cut costs across the board, or just cut costs at Chrysler or just at Daimler. Use your creativity and decision-making skills to produce several options.

☑ **Evaluate alternatives.** A plan is a decision you make today for how you're going to do something tomorrow. Therefore, apply all your decision-making skills to evaluating your options. Think through the consequences of each possible course of action.

☑ **Choose your plan, and start to implement it.** Remember, in making this decision: Increase your knowledge, use your intuition, weigh the pros and cons, don't overstress the decision's finality, and make sure the timing is right.

☑ **Go to level 2.** As at Sunbeam, plans tend to be multilayered. For your career plan, setting an overall goal—for instance, start your own consulting firm—is just the beginning. You'll also need supporting plans. These will include your program of studies, your plans for summer internships, your job search plans for that first consulting job, and a budget.

Who Does the Planning?

Who actually does the planning depends on the size of the firm. The basic process—set goals, develop background information such as forecasts, determine your options, evaluate options, and finalize the plan—is standard. But in a small business, the entrepreneur will do most of the planning himself or herself, perhaps informally bouncing around ideas with several employees or using business planning software.

In large firms, there may be a central corporate planning group whose role it is to work with top management and each division to solicit, challenge, and refine the company's plan. However, over the past few years, most firms have decentralized their planning.[8] Today, the main planners even in big firms are not headquarters specialists. Instead, they are the firms' product and divisional managers, perhaps aided by small headquarters advisory groups. The assumption is that line managers are in the best position to sense changes in customer, competitive, and technological trends and to react to them. Headquarters planning groups mostly compile data, develop standard reports and forms, and do planning-related research and training.[9]

■■■ THE BUSINESS PLAN AND ITS COMPONENTS

You can see that whether it's a tiny firm or GM, it's usually not accurate to refer to the company's "plan." Every firm has not one but a *hierarchy* of plans. There's typically an overall plan guiding the business. Then departmental plans lay out the methods each unit is to follow if top managers are to achieve the firm's overall goals.

We can illustrate this with an example. Assume you are now the owner-president of your own company, Acme Consulting, LLC. Your business is growing, and you see the potential of selling your firm to a major consulting or accounting firm for a great deal of money several years down the road. Accomplishing this goal will take a lot of effort over several years. However, your immediate challenges are these: First, you'll need bank financing to support the expansion of services you anticipate over the next five years. Second, (and related to this) you need a business plan. You need the business plan because no bank will lend you money without seeing such a plan. And, you also need the business plan to provide you and your colleagues with a road map that spells out what they're expected to do, as well as when, how, and at what cost.

That last point bears repeating: In business, you must decide today what you want to be doing tomorrow. If selling Acme means that you must have $2 million is sales at the end of five years, then you must plan today how you expect to achieve that goal, in terms of what kinds of clients to add, how to market your services, what people to hire, and so forth. What you plan to do should generally guide your actions. You can't build a $2 million dollar business without a plan, any more than you would try to get a college degree without thinking through your major, your program of studies, and how you intend to pay for it all. How else would you know what courses to take each semester?

The Components

Let's look at some of the main types of plans you're going to need to build Acme Consulting.

The Business Plan The company's business plan provides a comprehensive overview of the firm's situation today and of its companywide and departmental goals and plans for the next three to five years. Managers most often use the term *business plan* in relation to smaller businesses—and particularly to the sort of plan that investors or lenders want to see before providing money to the firm. However, small businesses don't have monopolies on business plans. Even a GM or a Microsoft will have a version of a comprehensive plan like this (although they may label it their "long-term" or perhaps "strategic" plan).

Figure 4.2 displays the contents of a typical full business plan. There are no rigid rules regarding what such plans must contain. However, they usually include, at a minimum, a (1) *description of the business* (including ownership and products or services), (2) *the marketing plan*, (3) *the financial plan*, and (4) *the management* and/or *personnel plan*. We'll discuss each of these plans in a moment.

You'll see other important business plan elements in Figure 4.2. The *executive summary* provides a brief (usually one to two pages) summary of the plan, including a snapshot of the business that it is in, as well at the company's goals, competitive strengths, financial situation, and a synopsis of its plans. The firm's *mission* is generally a one to two paragraph synopsis that answers the question, "What business are we in?" It " . . . serves to communicate 'who we are, what we do, and where we're headed.'" A *strategic plan* specifies the business or businesses the firm will be in and the major steps it must take to get there. A *strategy* is a course of action. It shows how the enterprise will move from the business it is in now to the business it wants to be in (as stated in its mission as well as in its strategic goals), given its opportunities and threats and its internal strengths and weaknesses. (For example, will Acme continue focusing on the same types of local clients that it has in the past, or will it extend its market base to new types of clients overseas?) *Strategic planning* often provides the foundation on which a business builds other plans. It requires special planning techniques, which we discuss fully in the following chapter.

The Marketing Plan To have a successful business, you must have customers; and to have customers, you must have a plan for marketing your products or services to them. Acme may have the best consultants in the state. However, if the potential clients don't know of its existence, its business prospects are limited, to say the least. The marketing plan specifies the nature of your *product* or service (for instance its variety, quality, design, and features), as well as the approaches you plan to take with respect to *pricing* and *promoting* the product or service, and getting it sold and *delivered* to your target customers. (Marketing managers call these "the four Ps"—product,

► **FIGURE 4–2** ▪ ▪ ▪

Business Plan Table of Contents

Source: Adapted from Business Plan Pro, Palo Alto Software, Palo Alto, CA.

price, promotion, and place, and the marketing plan shows how you plan to address each "P.")

Marketing plans can range from simple to complex. Some marketing plans are quite comprehensive. Figure 4.3 demonstrates the contents of one such plan. It includes a full-blown analysis of the markets as they stand now, as well as detailed product, pricing, promotional, and distribution plans and budgets for realizing those plans.

Your marketing plan for Acme may not be so comprehensive. It might start with a market analysis that projects the potential growth of each segment of your potential market—your segments or target markets are U.S. High Tech, European High Tech, Latin America, and Other. Figure 4.4 shows this part of your plan. Figure 4.5 shows the product, pricing, and sales forecast portions of your marketing plan. You would also want to include summaries of how you plan to promote and distribute your product or service. Like any plan, your marketing plan should show (in this case for each of the four Ps) what will be done, when it will be done, who is to do it, and how much it will cost and/or produce in sales and revenues.

The Personnel/Management Plan To serve its customers, Acme will need consultants, managers, and secretarial staff. Your human resources needs tend to reflect your sales projections. The projected number of clients and amount of planned consulting will help determine how many consultants you'll need in each year of the plan. This will in turn determine your needs for clerical and management staff.

Figure 4.6 summarizes your personnel plan in financial terms. You might also want to accompany this financial summary with a detailed monthly schedule showing specific job titles for which you'll be hiring, and when. You might further supplement this schedule with a breakdown showing the specific duties of each employee, as well as what their skills and experience should be.

Outline of a Marketing Plan

Source: Adapted from Philip Kotler and Gary Armstrong, *Principles of Marketing* (Upper Saddle River, NJ: Prentice Hall, 2001), p. 70.

Section	Purpose
Executive summary	Presents a brief summary of the main goals and recommendations of the plan for management review.
Current marketing situation	Describes the target market and company's position in it, including information about the market, product performance, competition, and distribution. This section includes: • A *market description* that defines the market and major segments, then reviews customer needs and factors in the marketing environment. • A *product review* that shows sales, prices, and gross margins of the major products in the product line. • A review of *competition*, which identifies major competitors and assesses their market positions and strategies. • A review of *distribution*, which evaluates recent sales trends and other developments in major distribution channels.
Threats and opportunity analysis	Assesses major threats and opportunities that the product might face.
Objectives and issues	States the marketing objectives that the company would like to attain during the plan's term and discusses key issues that will affect their attainment.
Marketing strategy	Outlines specific strategies for each marketing mix element and explains how each responds to the threats, opportunities, and critical issues spelled out earlier in the plan.
Action programs	Spells out how marketing strategies will be turned into specific action programs that answer the following questions: *What* will be done? *When* will it be done? *Who* is responsible for doing it? *How* much will it cost?
Budgets	Details a supporting marketing budget that is essentially a projected profit-and-loss statement.
Controls	Outlines the control that will be used to monitor progress.

▶ **FIGURE 4–4** ■ ■ ■

Market Analysis of Acme's
Potential Market Segments

Source: Business Plan Pro, Palo Alto Software, Palo Alto, CA.

The most important market segment for Acme is the large manufacturer of high-technology products, such as Apple, IBM, Microsoft, Siemens, or Olivetti. These companies will be calling on Acme for product development functions that the companies believe are better outsourced.

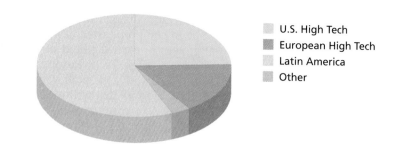

- U.S. High Tech
- European High Tech
- Latin America
- Other

Market Analysis

Potential Customers	Growth	2003	2004	2005	2006	2007
U.S. High Tech	10%	5,000	5,500	6,050	6,655	7,321
European High Tech	15%	1,000	1,150	1,323	1,521	1,749
Latin America	35%	250	338	456	616	832
Other	2%	10,000	10,200	10,404	10,612	10,824
Total	**62%**	**16,250**	**17,188**	**18,233**	**19,404**	**20,726**

The Production/Operations Plan Implementing your marketing plan will undoubtedly require adequate productive assets. This is perhaps most obvious in manufacturing firms. It takes factories and machines to assemble Dell's PCs, and Dell must, therefore, plan well in advance for how it will meet its projected demand. It will have to decide, in writing, well in advance how it plans to satisify its projected manufacturing needs.

▶ **FIGURE 4–5** ■ ■ ■

Product, Pricing, and Sale
Forecasts: Marketing Plan
Components

Source: Business Plan Pro, Palo Alto Software, Palo Alto, CA.

Product

Acme will focus on three geographical markets (the United States, Europe, and Latin America) and in limited product segments (personal computers, software, networks, telecommunications, personal organizers, and technology integration products).

The target customer is usually a manager in a larger corporation, and occasionally an owner or president of a medium-sized corporation in a high-growth period.

Pricing

Acme Consulting will be priced at the upper edge of what the market will bear, competing with the name-brand consultants. The pricing fits with the general positioning of Acme as providing high-level expertise. Consulting should be based on $5,000 per day for project consulting, $2,000 per day for market research, and $10,000 per month and up for retainer consulting.

Sales Forecast

Sales forecasts as follows:

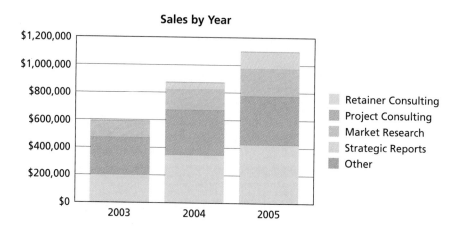

Sales by Year

- Retainer Consulting
- Project Consulting
- Market Research
- Strategic Reports
- Other

◀ **FIGURE 4–6** ■ ■ ■

Personnel Plan

Source: Business Plan Pro, Palo Alto Software, Palo Alto, CA.

Personnel	2003	2004	2005
Partners	$144,000	$175,000	$200,000
Consultants	$0	$50,000	$63,000
Editorial/graphic	$18,000	$22,000	$26,000
VP Marketing	$20,000	$50,000	$55,000
Sales people	$0	$30,000	$33,000
Office Manager	$7,500	$30,000	$33,000
Secretarial	$5,250	$20,000	$22,000
Other	$0	$0	$0
Other	$0	$0	$0
Total Payroll	$194,750	$377,000	$432,000
Total Headcount	7	14	20
Fringe Benefits	$27,265	$52,780	$60,480
Total Payroll Expenditures	$222,015	$429,780	$492,480

Again, the firm's sales projections tend to determine what its production requirements will be. Since Acme is a service business, Figure 4.7 simply shows Acme's projected sales by type of service for January and February 2003. (A manufacturing firm might also create a weekly Master Planning Schedule to lay out its weekly production plans, showing how much it will produce by product.) Acme may also use a Gantt Chart (named after Henry Gantt, who developed this tool) to plan and thus better gauge how many days of consultant time each order will take. (See Figure 4.8.)

Acme Consulting probably won't have to worry about factories. However, it will require productive assets such as office space, computers, and communications systems. For your production plan, you'll have to project these needs on a monthly basis (probably as a function of how many people you'll have working) and then convert these needs to dollars and cents. You may also be able to make use of production planning tools like the Gantt chart to help you visualize how much of your firm's office space and computers each consulting job you have will consume.

The Financial Plan "What's the bottom line?" is the first question many managers and bankers ask. The question underscores a truism about business and management. At the end of the day, most of your plans, goals, and accomplishments will end up being expressed in financial terms, in a *financial plan*. Figure 4.9 shows part of Acme's financial plan. This includes a projected (or pro forma or planned) profit-and-loss (P&L) statement. The P&L shows the revenue, cost, and profit (or loss) implications of Acme's business, marketing, production, and personnel plans. The P&L says this: If your plans work out as you anticipate, these are the revenues, costs, and profits or losses you should produce each month (or quarter, or year). It shows you the bottom line.

Sales by Consulting Service	January	February
Retainer Consulting - Projects	$9,000	$9,000
Project Consulting - Projects	$12,300	$14,200
Market Research - Projects	$6,700	$7,800
Strategic Reports - Projects	$17,000	$22,000
Total Sales	**$45,000**	**$53,000**

◀ **FIGURE 4–7** ■ ■ ■

Sales Forecast by Service: Two-Month Sales Plan for Acme Consulting, 2003

Since Acme is a service business, its "Production Plan" simply shows projected sales by type of service.

Gantt Scheduling Chart for Acme *Strategic Report* Projects, January 1–15, 2003

This Gantt Chart helps Acme's managers to plan their consultants' time and to keep track of each project's progress. Similar Gantt Charts help managers in factories plan machine usage for building different products.

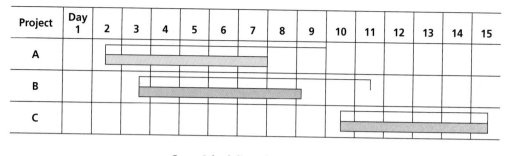

Gantt Scheduling Chart Symbols

	Start of Project		Scheduled Time Allowed
	End of Project		Actual Work Progress

► **FIGURE 4–9** ■ ■ ■

Acme Consulting Profit and Loss

Source: Business Plan Pro, Palo Alto Software, Palo Alto, CA.

Pro Forma Profit and Loss (Income Statement)	2003	2004	2005
Sales	$592,000	$875,000	$1,100,000
Direct Cost of Sales	$159,000	$219,000	$289,000
Other	$0	$0	$0
Total Cost of Sales	$159,000	$219,000	$289,000
Gross Margin	$433,000	$656,000	$811,000
Gross Margin %	73.14%	74.97%	73.73%
Operating expenses:			
Advertising/Promotion	$36,000	$40,000	$44,000
Public Relations	$30,000	$30,000	$33,000
Travel	$90,000	$60,000	$110,000
Miscellaneous	$6,000	$7,000	$8,000
Travel	$0	$0	$0
Miscellaneous	$0	$0	$0
Payroll Expense	$194,750	$377,000	$432,000
Payroll Burden	$27,265	$52,780	$60,480
Depreciation	$3,600	$0	$0
Leased Equipment	$18,000	$7,000	$7,000
Utilities	$0	$12,000	$12,000
Insurance	$0	$2,000	$2,000
Rent	$0	$0	$0
Other	$0	$0	$0
Contract/Consultants	$0	$0	$0
Total Operating Expenses	$423,615	$587,780	$708,480
Profit Before Interest and Taxes	$9,385	$68,220	$102,520
Interest Expense Short-term	$1,800	$6,400	$10,400
Interest Expense Long-term	$5,000	$5,000	$5,000
Taxes Incurred	$646	$14,205	$21,780
Net Profit	$1,939	$42,615	$65,340
Net Profit/Sales	0.33%	4.87%	5.94%

Planning Tools

Managers need a way to convert business, marketing, production, personnel, and financial plans into the concrete goals their subordinates must achieve. Many use the Executive Assignment Action Plan to document the goals and plans emerging from this hierarchical business planning process. Table 4.1 shows an example. Its purpose is to link management's goals at one level to the derivative plans at the next level down.[10]

The Executive Action Assignment Plan Table 4.1 spells out each executive's assignment for carrying out the overall plan. In this case, one long-term top management goal is to "have a minimum of 55% of sales revenue from customized products by 2005." The action plan summarizes the targets each department needs to achieve if that long-term goal is to be met. Thus, the vice president of marketing is to "complete market study on sales potential for customized products" within one year. The vice president of manufacturing is to "convert Building C to customized manufacturing operation by 2005."

TABLE 4–1   Executive Assignment Action Plan for Achieving a Long-Term Objective

LONG-TERM OBJECTIVE: HAVE A MINIMUM OF 55% OF SALES REVENUE FROM CUSTOMIZED PRODUCTS BY 2005

Executive Assignments/ Derivative Objectives	Accountability		Schedule		Resources Required			Feedback Mechanisms
	Primary	Supporting	Start	Complete	Capital	Operating	Human	
1. Complete market study on sales potential for customized products	VP Marketing	VP Sales	Year 1	Year 1		$10,000	500 hrs.	Written progress reports
2. Revise sales forecasts for Years 1, 2, and 3 to reflect changes	VP Sales	VP Marketing		Year 1			50 hrs.	Revised forecasts
3. Convert Building C to customized manufacturing operation by 2003	VP Mfg.	VP Engineering VP Administration	Year 1	Year 2	$500,000	$80,000	1,100 hrs.	Written progress reports
4. Change compensation structure to incentivize customized sales	VP HR	VP Sales	Year 1	Year 1		$50,000	100 hrs.	Revised structure report
5. Train sales staff in new technology	Director of Training	VP Sales	Year 2	Year 2		$50,000	1,000 hrs.	Training plan reports
6. Expand production of customized products —to 25% —to 30% —to40% —to 50% to 55%	VP Mfg.	VP Engineering	Year 1	Year 2 Year 2 Year 3 Year 3		Budgeted	Budgeted	Production reports
7. Increase sales of customized products —to 25% —to 30% —to 40% —to 55%	VP Sales	VP Marketing	Year 1	Year 2 Year 2 Year 3 Year 3				Sales reports
8. Revise sales forecasts	VP Sales	VP Marketing		Year 3				Revised forecasts

Note: This executive assignment action plan shows the specific executive assignments required to achieve top management's long-term objective, "Have a minimum of 55% of sales revenue from customized products by 2005."

Source: Adapted from George Morrisey: *A Guide to Long-Range Planning.* (San Francisco: Jossey-Bass, Inc. 1996), pp. 72–73.

TABLE 4–2   Action Plan for a Specific Executive Assignment

EXECUTIVE ASSIGNMENT: CONVERT BUILDING C TO CUSTOMIZED MANUFACTURING OPERATION BY 2005*

Assignments/ Derivative Objectives	Accountability		Schedule		Resources Required			Feedback Mechanisms
	Primary	Supporting	Start	Complete	Capital	Operating	Human	
1. Complete feasibility study on conversion requirements	Director Engineering	VP Manufacturing	Year 1	Year 1		$10,000	100 hrs.	Written progress reports
2. Complete converted production line design and equipment specifications	Director Engineering	VP Manufacturing		Year 1		$50,000	500 hrs.	Design review meetings
3. Purchase and install new equipment	Purchasing	VP Manufacturing	Year 1	Year 1	$400,000		100 hrs.	Written progress reports
4. Modify existing equipment	VP Mfg.	VP Engineering	Year 1	Year 1	$100,000	$10,000	100 hrs.	Written progress reports
5. Train production staff	Director of Training	VP Manufacturing	Year 1	Year 1		$10,000	300 hrs.	Training plan reports
6. Initiate customized production line	VP Mfg.	VP Engineering				Budgeted	Budgeted	Production reports
7. Increase production of customized products —to 25% —to 30% —to 40% —to 50% to 55%	VP Mfg.	VP Engineering	Year 1	Year 2 Year 2 Year 3 Year 3		Budgeted	Budgeted	Production reports
8. Reassess future production capacity	VP Mfg.	VP Engineering		Year 3				Production forecast

*Note: This action plan shows the subsidiary assignments required to achieve the specific executive assignment, "Convert Building C to customized manufacturing operations by 2005."

Source: Reprinted with permission from George Morrisey: A Guide to Long-Range Planning. Copyright © 1996 Jossey-Bass, Inc. All rights reserved.

Each vice president's assigned goals then become the targets for which they must develop their own plans. Table 4.2 illustrates this. Here, the manufacturing vice president's goal of "converting Building C to customized manufacturing" is the goal for which she'll have to craft a supporting plan. For instance, converting Building C will entail completing a feasibility study and purchasing and installing new equipment. In this way, developing an Executive Assignment Action Plan helps ensure coordinated, purposeful effort by the management team.

The Importance of Teamwork   No single person usually formulates and implements a plan for a complex organization alone.[11] Therefore, creating a cohesive and cooperative top-management team (including the CEO and his or her subordinates) is a precondition if a firm is to execute its plans and achieve its goals. Teamwork is important because:[12]

■ The CEO has a complex coordination task and cannot be effective unless he or she is working closely with the people who are in charge of the company's major activities (such as functions, products, or regions).

- The CEO's subordinate officers usually possess greater expertise about the operating components of the organization and their own fields of expertise than does the CEO.
- The team members can be more understanding of and supportive of the CEO's strategic decisions if they have a voice in shaping those decisions.
- Teamwork among the members of the top-management team enhances communication and coordination among them.
- Innovations will be more likely when team members have more opportunity for cross-functional communication.

Most CEOs, therefore, spend considerable time creating a cohesive team. Former chairman and CEO Stephen Wolf of United Airlines reportedly worked closely on a daily basis with the executives in charge of areas like finance, marketing, and employee relations. His success in turning that company around partly reflects his ability to assemble a talented top-management team that could work together to create an effective plan.[13]

Types of Plans

It should be apparent from all this that plans come in a variety of types and formats. For example, we've seen that plans differ in their *functional orientation*. They range from comprehensive, overall business plans to functionally specialized marketing, production, personnel, and financial plan.

You can express your plans in a variety of *formats*. Descriptive plans, like your program of studies or the marketing plan in Figure 4.3 state in words what is to be achieved, by whom, and when, as well as at what cost. Plans stated in financial terms are budgets. Graphic plans like those in Figures 4.4 and 4.8 show what is to be achieved and how, and when, in the form of charts or in graphical networks.

Plans also differ in the *time span* they cover. Top management usually engages in long-term (three-to-five-year) business or strategic planning. Middle managers focus on developing midterm tactical plans (of up to two to three years' duration). Tactical plans (also sometimes called functional plans) pick up where strategic plans leave off: These are your firm's marketing, production, and personnel plans. They show each department's role in helping carry out the company's overall strategic plan. First-line managers focus on short-term operational plans. This means they focus on detailed, day-to-day planning. The Gantt chart in Figure 4.8 helps show exactly which workers the supervisor plans to assign to which machines or exactly how many units will be produced on a given day.

Finally, some plans are made to be used once, and others over and over. For example, some plans are single-use programs; these present in an orderly fashion all the steps in a major one-time project. Your program of studies is an example.

In contrast, managers design standing plans to be used repeatedly as the need arises.[14] Like all plans, standing plans are methods that are formulated beforehand for doing or making something. They are all decisions you make today to guide decision making tomorrow. They are (to use decision making terminology) programmed decisions. Like all plans, they specify (or imply) *what's* to be accomplished, *when*, by *whom*, and at *what* cost. Policies, procedures, and rules are examples of standing plans. They routinize and standardize decision making for managers. Policies set broad guidelines. For example, it might be the policy at Saks Fifth Avenue that "we sell only high-fashion apparel and top-of-the-line jewelry." How is this a plan? Because it tells all of the firm's apparel and jewelry buyers what general course of action they should follow in choosing merchandise to buy for their stores.

Procedures spell out what to do if a specific situation arises. For example, "before refunding the customer's purchase price, the salesperson should carefully inspect the garment and then obtain approval for the refund from the floor manager." Finally, a rule is a highly specific guide to action. For example, "under no circumstances will the purchase price be refunded after 30 days." Managers

descriptive plan ■ *a plan that state's what is to be achieved and how.*

budget ■ *a financial plan, showing financial expectations for a specific period.*

graphic plan ■ *a plan that shows graphically or in charts what is to be achieved and when.*

tactical plan ■ *a plan that shows how top management's plans are to be carried out at the departmental, short-term level.*

functional plan ■ *a tactical short-term plan showing how each department of a business will contribute to top management's plans.*

operational plan ■ *a short-term plan that shows the detailed daily steps of business operations.*

program ■ *a plan that lays out all the steps in proper sequence to a single-use, often one-time business project.*

standing plan ■ *a plan established to be used repeatedly, as the need arises.*

policy ■ *a standing plan that sets broad guidelines for the enterprise.*

procedure ■ *a plan that specifies how to proceed in specific situations that routinely arise.*

rule ■ *a highly specific guide to action.*

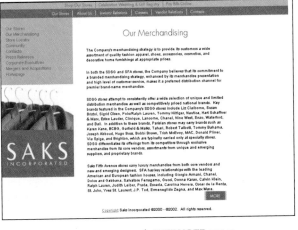

▲ **WEBNOTE** ■ ■ ■

Saks merchandising policy appears on its Web site.

www.saksincorporated.com

Source: Used with permission.

usually write standing plans like procedures or rules so that the plan's goal or purpose is implied, but clear. Figure 4.10 presents one company's policy and procedure regarding reporting improper behavior.

■ *Application Exercise Creating the Acme Plan* So, there you sit, trying to decide how to create the plan you'll need to get Acme Consulting financed and how to provide direction for the firm for the next few years. Where would you start?

The basic thing to remember is this: There is nothing mysterious about what a plan is. Any plan, in essence, simply answers four questions: (1) What are you going to do? (2) When are you going to do it? (3) Who is going to do it? (4) What will implementing the plan cost and what will it produce in dollars and cents? You may lay out your plan in terms of words, graphs, or budgets; it doesn't matter.

The planning process is equally straightforward: Set an objective; develop your forecasts and planning premises; determine what your options are; evaluate your alternatives; choose your plan, and start to implement it; then go to level 2.

You'd probably want to start your Acme plan at the end and work back. What is your objective? To sell Acme in about five to six years. What do you have to do over the next five or so years to accomplish that goal? You have to get Acme up to about $2 million in sales. How do you get from (let's say) $80,000 sales today to $2 million? Here's where your analyses and forecasts come in handy. You've got a great many options. However, you decide to focus on adding four types of clients over the next five years: U.S. High Tech, European High Tech, Latin America, and Other.

That analysis provides a barebones outline for your overall business plan. Now you can go to level 2, and do your functional plans. First draft a marketing plan that lays out your basic product, price, promotion, and place policies and plans for the next few years. Then decide what that plan means in terms of how many and what sorts of personnel you'll have to hire and train. Project what your plans to this point mean operationally in terms of the computers, phones, and office space and supplies you'll

▶ **FIGURE 4–10** ■ ■ ■

Reporting Improper Behavior

Source: James Jenks, *The Hiring, Firing (and everything in between) Personnel Forms Book* (Ridgefield, CT: Round Lake Publishing, 1996), pp. 224–25.

POLICY ON REPORTING IMPROPER BEHAVIOR

PURPOSE

To provide a means through which employees can report incidents of suspected improper activity.

POLICY

It is the policy of this company to comply with all laws, regulations, and principles of ethical conduct which apply to the company and its business. Each employee must observe this policy. Each employee is also responsible for assisting in its application by reporting any instance in which it appears that legal, regulatory, or ethical standards have been violated.

The company is responsible for preventing or, if necessary, correcting any such violation. Not only is this a legal obligation, but failure to do so could seriously affect the company's reputation with the public, its customers, and government authorities.

PROCEDURE

Any employee who has reason to believe this policy has been violated must report this belief. Normally, the violation should be reported to the employee's immediate supervisor. If that is not practical, or if the employee is dissatisfied with the supervisor's response, the employee should file a written report of the complaint with the Director of Personnel.

Any executive, manager, or supervisor who receives a report of possible improper activity shall forward the report immediately to the Director of personnel. The individual who receives the complaint should immediately begin an investigation to determine the facts of the case. The Director of Personnel may designate some other party to conduct the investigation.

All records of the complaint, including the identity of the employee who filed it must be kept confidential and made available only as necessary to conduct a full investigation and to give the accused party a fair opportunity to respond to the complaint. There is to be no retaliation in any form against any employee who in good faith reports a violation even if the investigation determine there has been no violation.

need. Produce a financial plan that lays out in dollars and cents both what each element of your plan (advertising, rent, PCs, personnel, and so on) will cost and what that should mean in terms of profits or losses. Use the Executive Assignment Action Plan to formalize the goals for your managers. Complete your plans with a set of policies and procedures (How do we pay accounts receivables? How do we interview applicants and check references? And so on). You may decide to use an off-the-shelf policies software package like PoliciesNow! (from **www.knowledgepoint.com**) to help you here.

Then perhaps turn to level 3, and to putting together more detailed short-term plans. Each year, put together short-term plans (at least budgets), which show in some detail what you expect each group to be doing each month. For example, they show what (how many clients, and so forth) your U.S. high-tech consultants should be working on in June and when you expect to have to go to the bank to draw down some of your financing. You've thus produced a set of long- and short-term goals for you and your colleagues. Let's now look more closely at how to set objectives or goals.

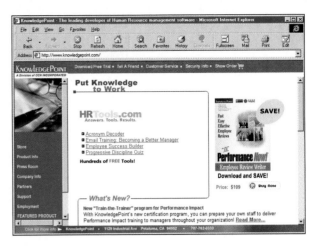

▲ WEBNOTE ■ ■ ■

Knowledgepoint.com's Web site shows some of the products and services it provides.

www.knowledgepoint.com

Source: Used with permission.

■ ■ ■ HOW TO SET OBJECTIVES

As a manager you can always expect to be judged on at least one thing—on the extent to which you achieved your unit's goals. Whether you're in charge of a door-assembly team or all of GM, you are expected to move the unit ahead, and this means visualizing where the unit must go and helping it get there. Organizations exist to achieve some purpose, and if they fail to move forward and achieve their aims, to that extent they have failed. As Peter Drucker put it, "There has to be something to point to and say, [W]e have not worked in vain."[15] DaimlerChrysler's experience is an example.

MANAGEMENT IN ACTION Cost Cutting at DaimlerChrysler

Goals drive the best companies forward. Faced with mounting losses at its Chrysler unit, DaimlerChrysler management set very aggressive cost-cutting goals. The firm lost $4.4 billion in 2001, compared with profits of $450 million in 2000. Its management declared that the firm's units had to slice $3.1 billion in costs to bring the firm to profitability. Managers, including Chrysler CEO Dieter Zetsche, laid out three-year recovery plans to achieve these goals. At Chrysler, the plan included closing six to seven plants and cutting 26,000 jobs. Managers actually cut $3.3 billion, earning themselves large bonuses in the process. At DaimlerChrysler, challenging goals drove an effective management corps to turn around the company.[16] ■ ■ ■ ■

How to Put SMART Goals into Words

DaimlerChrysler's goals had the desired effect in part because they were well-designed. The goals were "SMART." They were *specific* and clearly stated the desired results. They were *measurable* and answered the question, "How much?" They were *attainable*. They were *relevant* and clearly derived from the crucial need to turn Chrysler around. Finally, they were *timely* and reflected deadlines and milestones.[17]

Planning expert George Morrisey presents a four-point model (see Table 4.3 to use in actually expressing what the goal should be. He advises expressing your goal like this:

To (1) (action/verb)
    (2) the (single measurable result)
by (3) (target date/time span)
    (4) at (cost in time and/or energy)

Morrisey's Four-Point Model

To (1) (*action/verb*)	(2) (single measurable *result*)
by (3) (*target* date/time span)	(4) at (*cost* in time and/or energy)

Examples or Objectives That Follow the Model

- To (1, 2) complete the Acme project by (3) December 31 at a (4) cost not to exceed $50,000 and 500 work-hours.

- To (1) decrease the (2) average cost of sales by a minimum of 5%, effective (3) June 1, at an (4) implementation cost not to exceed 40 work-hours.

- To release (1, 2) product A to manufacturing by (3) September 30 at a cost not to (4) exceed $50,000 and 5,000 engineering hours.

- To (1) reduce (2) average turnaround time on service requests from eight to six hours by (3) July 31 at an implementation cost (4) of 40 work-hours.

Source: Reprinted with permission from George Morrisey, *A Guide to Tactical Planning*. Copyright © 1996 Jossey-Bass, Inc. All rights reserved.

For example, to sell $2 million of product X next year at a cost not to exceed $200,000."

The areas (be they sales, costs, or some other category) for which you set goals need to meet some important conditions. They should be *relevant*. At this particular point in time, DaimlerChrysler simply had to focus on cutting costs; it hardly made sense to spend a lot of of time on important but perhaps temporarily secondary issues like developing more fuel-efficient cars. The goals (as we'll see in a moment) also need to be *complete*. People will emphasize those areas they know you're measuring, and this can sometimes trigger bizarre behavior. Chrysler's CEO obviously would not want his managers to focus on cost-cutting to the exclusion of driving up sales. (A bizarre example: Eliminating all advertising would certainly cut costs but might have a disastrous effect on sales.) You can therefore be sure that his managers' goals also touched on areas like "market share" and "units sold."

In practice, the areas for which managers can set goals is practically limitless. A partial list would include:

1. Market standing
2. Innovation
3. Productivity
4. Physical and financial resources
5. Profitability
6. Managerial performance and development
7. Worker performance and attitude
8. Public responsibility[18]

One planning expert listed more than a dozen other areas in which objectives may be set, including the following:

1. Market penetration
2. Future human competencies
3. Revenues/sales
4. New product
5. New/expanded market development
6. Program/project management
7. Technology
8. Research and development
9. Customer relations/satisfaction

10. Cost control/management
11. Quality control/assurance
12. Process improvement
13. Production capability/capacity
14. Cross-functional integration
15. Supplier development/relations
16. Unit structure (reorganization)[19]

One thing that's clear is that setting goals just for profit maximization is not enough. You have heard that in economic theory (and in practice) managers aim to maximize profits (although we saw in Chapter 2 that other goals, including social responsibility, are important too). However, telling a marketing manager or production supervisor or even a CEO that his or her departmental goal is to maximize profits would not provide that manager with much guidance, nor would it make much sense. Remember, managers need goals in areas that are *relevant to their responsibilities*. Setting goals for areas like market penetration and customer service is therefore the only practical way of ensuring that each manager's goals and actions (in this case the sales manager's goals and actions) will in fact contribute to boosting profits.

How To Set Motivational Goals

You know from your own experience that some goals are simply ridiculous. You might be the best marathon runner in the world, but you'd view the goal of "run the Boston marathon in 42 minutes" as so absurdly unrealistic that even a $10 million prize would not motivate you to try it.

The point is that goals are only useful to the extent that employees are motivated to achieve them. Chrysler's managers not only met their cost-cutting goals but also exceeded them. What is it about the goal or how it is set that makes it motivational? Research known as the goal-setting studies provides useful insights into setting motivational goals. The study results suggest four steps to take:

Assign Specific Goals Employees who are given specific goals usually perform better than those who are not. Researchers conducted one study in an Oklahoma logging operation.[20] The subjects were truck drivers whose job was to load logs and drive them to the mill. An analysis of the truckers' performance showed that they often did not fill their trucks to the maximum legal net weight. The researchers believed this happened largely because the workers were simply urged to "do their best" when it came to loading the truck.

The researchers arranged to communicate a specific goal ("94% of a truck's net weight") to each driver. Performance (in terms of weight loaded on each truck) jumped markedly as soon as the truckers got their specific goals, and it generally remained at this much higher level. This and other evidence shows that setting specific goals with subordinates, rather than setting no goals or telling them to "do their best," improves performance in a wide range of settings.[21]

Assign Measurable Goals[22] Express goals in quantitative terms, and include target dates or deadlines. Goals set in absolute terms (such as "an average daily output of 300 units") are often less confusing than goals set in relative terms (such as "improve production by 20%"). If measurable results will not be available, then "satisfactory completion"—such as "satisfactorily attended workshop" or "satisfactorily completed his or her degree"—is the next best thing. In any case, target dates or deadlines should always be set.

Assign Challenging but Doable Goals Goals should be challenging, but not so difficult that they appear impossible or unrealistic (remember that 42-minute marathon).[23] Particularly in areas such as sales management, where immediate and concrete performance is obvious and highly valued, goals consistent with past sales levels—realistic yet high enough to be challenging—are widely used.[24]

When is a goal "too difficult"? One expert says:

> *A goal is probably too easy if it calls for little or no improvement in performance when conditions are becoming more favorable, or if the targeted*

goal-setting studies ■
organizational behavior research that provides useful insights into how to set effective goals.

level of performance is well below that of most other employees in comparable positions. A goal is probably too difficult if it calls for a large improvement in performance when conditions are worsening, or if the targeted level of performance is well above that of people in comparable positions.[25]

Encourage Participation Throughout your management career (and often several times a day), you'll be faced with this decision: Should I just tell my employees what their goals are, or should I let them participate in setting their goals? Sometimes, of course, the situation is out of your hands. You've been given a target to reach (like Chrysler's "cut costs by $3.1 billion"), and your employees will simply need to do it. Most of the time, though, you will have some discretion, and the research suggests that participation can be a good thing. Here is what you need to know:

1. Employees who participate in setting their own goals do perceive themselves as having had more impact on setting those goals than do employees who just get their goals from their managers.[26]
2. Participatively set goals tend to be higher than the goals the supervisor would normally have assigned.[27]
3. Even when participatively set goals are more difficult than those assigned, the employees don't perceive them as such.[28]
4. Participatively set goals do not consistently result in higher performance than assigned goals, nor do assigned goals consistently result in higher performance than participatively set ones. *It is only when the participatively set goals are more difficult than the assigned ones that the participatively set goals produce higher performance.* It's the fact that the goal is more difficult, not that it was participatively set, that explains the higher performance.[29]

However, that last point is usually the key. Participatively set goals do tend to be more challenging. Thus, there's usually a value in discussing goals with your employees before they are set, since the resulting goals will probably be both more difficult and more accepted (assuming you keep the pressure on a bit). And, there is an added benefit. Most people aren't crazy about taking orders ("Clean your room NOW!"). Simply telling an employee what his or her goal is may therefore trigger at least some low-level resistance. Participation creates a sense of ownership in the goals, and can reduce resistance.[30]

■ *The Global Manager* Sometimes, managers don't have the luxury of taking a participative approach. When Ford's European operations posted a big loss, its European head, David Thursfield, had to swing into action. The former rugby player got his managers together in the firm's "war room" and laid out what had to be done: Close the firm's 80-year old plant outside London, slash 600,000 units of capacity, cut 1,400 jobs; and cut costs by at least $850 million. The vice president of manufacturing says that when Thursfield called him recently, the first question was, "How much money have you saved for me today?" Thursfield's plans may not have been popular, but they got the job done. Ford Europe was on track to break even within a year.[31]

Using Management by Objectives

How do you translate the goals of the company and its departments into specific, meaningful goals for each employee? For the company's managers, the Executive Assignment Action Plan is one alternative. Management by objectives (MBO) is another. MBO is a technique in which supervisor and subordinate jointly set goals for the latter and periodically assess progress toward those goals. Managers use MBO to facilitate setting organizationwide goals, and to set goals for subsidiary units and their employees. A manager may engage in a modest MBO program by setting goals with his or her subordinates and periodically providing feedback. However, MBO usually refers to a comprehensive organizationwide program, and is usually reserved for managerial and professional employees.

management by objectives (MBO) ■ *a technique in which supervisor and subordinate jointly set goals for the latter and periodically assess progress toward those goals.*

Peter Drucker, the creator of MBO, emphasizes thinking of it as a philosophy, not as a rigid sequence of steps. The point, he says, is that "the goals of each manager's job must be defined by the contribution he or she has to make to the success of the larger unit of which they are part." In general, the MBO process consists of five steps:

1. *Set organization goals.* Top management sets strategic goals for the company.
2. *Set department goals.* Department heads and their superiors jointly set supporting goals for their departments.
3. *Discuss department goals.* Department heads present department goals and ask all subordinates to develop their own individual goals.
4. *Set individual goals.* Goals are set for each subordinate, and a timetable is assigned for accomplishing those goals.
5. *Give feedback.* Supervisor and subordinate meet periodically to review the subordinate's performance and to monitor and analyze progress toward his or her goals.[32]

MBO has its advantages. Corporate planning tends to be hierarchical anyway, so using MBO provides a process for working through how the goals at each level will relate to those above, and to those below. It also taps the advantages of participation, which we listed earlier. The downside is that MBO is time-consuming. These programs often involve numerous meetings among employees and supervisors, and then extensively documenting each person's goals in various electronic or hard-copy formats. It's useful to remember that MBO's aim is simply to integrate the goals of the individual, of the unit in which the individual works, and of the company as a whole.[33] As in the Gregg Foster/Elyria Foundry example (page 83), doing this doesn't have to be complicated.

Checklist 4.2 summarizes the principles of goal setting.

CHECKLIST 4.2 ■ Principles of Goal-Setting

☑ Set *SMART* goals—make them *specific, measurable, attainable, relevant*, and *timely*.

☑ Choose *areas* (sales revenue, costs, and so forth) that are relevant and complete.

☑ Assign *specific* goals.

☑ Assign *measurable* goals.

☑ Assign doable but *challenging* goals.

☑ Encourage *participation*.

☑ Use executive assignment action plans, or *management by objectives*.

■■■ FORECASTING AND DEVELOPING PLANNING PREMISES

People build plans—whether for careers, trips to Paris, or cutting costs at DaimlerChrysler—on *premises*, assumptions they make about the future. Wal-Mart expands to Europe because it forecasts a burgeoning market for low-cost consumer goods there. People reduce their travel to areas hit by terrorist threats. Chrysler cuts costs because forecasts show it can't survive with the losses it will sustain at its current rate of expenditures. And, students choose careers based in part on the projected future demand for workers in particular occupations.

Managers use several techniques to produce the premises on which they build their plans. These include forecasting, marketing research, and competitive intelligence. Let's look more closely at these, to round out our discussion of the basic planning process.

Sales Forecasting Techniques

Forecast means "to estimate or calculate in advance or to predict."[34] In business, forecasting often starts with predicting the direction and magnitude of the company's sales. Most business activities—production, finance, and hiring employees, for instance—depend on the level of sales.

forecast ■ *to estimate or calculate in advance or to predict.*

■■ Interior of a new Wal-Mart in Bristol, UK, the first 24-hour superstore in Bristol.

quantitative forecasting ■ *a type of forecasting in which statistical methods are used to examine data and find underlying patterns and relationships; includes time-series methods and causal models.*

qualitative forecasting ■ *predictive techniques that emphasize human judgment.*

time series ■ *a set of observations taken at specific times, usually at equal intervals, to identify fundamental patterns.*

causal methods ■ *forecasting techniques that develop projections based on the mathematical relationship between a company factor and the variables believed to influence or explain that factor.*

causal forecasting ■ *estimating a company factor (such as sales) based on other influencing factors (such as advertising expenditures or unemployment levels).*

Managers use either quantitative or qualitative sales forecasting methods (or a combination of the two). Quantitative forecasting uses statistical methods to examine data and find underlying patterns and relationships. Qualitative forecasting emphasizes human judgment.

Quantitative Forecasting Methods Quantitative methods include time-series methods and causal models. They all produce forecasts by assuming that past relationships will continue into the future. A time series is a set of observations taken at specific times, usually at equal intervals. Examples of time series are the yearly or monthly gross domestic product of the United States over several years, a department store's total monthly sales receipts, and the daily closing prices of a share of stock.[35]

If you plot time-series data on a graph for several periods, you may note various patterns. For example, if you were to plot monthly sales of air conditioning units, you would find seasonal increases in late spring and summer, and reduced sales in the winter months. For some time series, you may see an irregular pattern, such as a sudden blip in the graph that reflects unexplained variations in the data: For instance, airline ticket sales plummeted for a time after the World Trade Center tragedy in September 2001. The basic purpose of time-series forecasting methods is to identify irregular and seasonal patterns and to allow managers to identify fundamental trends.

Sometimes, simply tracking activity over time is not enough. Instead, managers may need to understand the causal relationship between two variables. For example, the sales department at General Motors needs to know the causal relationship between car sales and an indicator of economic activity, like disposable income. The basic idea of *causal models* is this: If you can discover a causal relationship between one factor (for example, car sales), and a second, more predictable, factor (for example, disposable income), you can use that relationship to forecast your sales.[36] Causal methods develop a forecast based on the mathematical relationship between a company factor and those variables that management believes influence or explain the company factor.[37] Causal forecasting estimates the company factor (such as sales) based on other factors (such as advertising expenditures or level of unemployment). Managers like Chris Kochan of Rack Room shoes (see the accompanying Management in Action feature) use statistical techniques such as correlation analysis, which shows how closely the variables are related, to identify the necessary relationships.

MANAGEMENT IN ACTION   Rack Room Shoes

Charlotte, North Carolina-based Rack Room Shoes has more than 340 stores and opens 20 to 40 new stores per year. For many years, the firm's real estate committee made site location decisions subjectively. The committee consisted of the firm's president, CFO, and vice presidents for store operations and real estate. When the firm hired Chris Kochan as its new market research manager, his first job was to create a sales forecasting model to improve the accuracy of location decisions. Based on Rack Room's historical sales experience, Kochan was able to correlate sales to demographics (such as the ages and income levels of people in various locales). Today, a number of services make it easy to identify demographics by zip code. Kochan's sales forecasting model therefore enables Rack Room to predict how much sales a new store might generate if placed in a particular zip code. As Kochan says, "Our forecasts now come within 20% of actual sales about 75% of the time. The gut-feel approach was within 20% of actual sales only 34% of the time."[38]

Internet-based Systems Other firms use the Internet to improve their forecasts by expediting the collection of sales estimates. For example, Coors Brewing Company's distributors can use the firm's new **CoorsNet.com** to place orders, and to help analyze the impact of advertising and other promotional activities. Because it takes about four weeks from wholesaler forecast to the shipment of product from the brewery, one supply chain consultant says, "Forecasting demand is a huge problem for these folks. So many times, they are reacting instead of planning ahead. What happens is that they make distributors order too far in advance, and they aren't ready to quantify how much they need to order."[39]

Coors expects its new its new Internet-based system to improve performance. Coors will be able to receive real-time orders. Its distributors should be able to predict more accurately how advertising campaigns and other promotional events will affect sales. Wal-Mart also uses sophisticated technology to forecast sales; the "Managing @ the Speed of Thought" feature provides an example.

▲ WEBNOTE ■ ■ ■

Coors Brewing Company's new Extranet helps the company improve forecasts and lets distributors place orders over the Net.

www.coorsnet.com

MANAGING @ THE SPEED OF THOUGHT

Demand Forecasting at Wal-Mart

When it comes to retailing, Wal-Mart is larger than its three closest competitors combined, and that's not just because it buys its merchandise inexpensively. Wal-Mart has what is probably the most sophisticated information technology system in all of retailing, and it uses that system's power to give its customers what they want, while squeezing every bit of extra cost from its operation.

Wal-Mart's data warehouse is a good example of how the company does this. The data warehouse collects information on things like sales, inventory, products in transit, and product returns from Wal-Mart's 3,000 stores. These data are then analyzed to help Wal-Mart's managers analyze trends, understand customers, and more effectively manage inventory. As one example, Wal-Mart is implementing a new demand-forecasting system. Its data warehouse tracks the sale by store of 100,000 products. This powerful system lets Wal-Mart managers examine the sales of individual items for individual stores, and it also creates seasonal profiles for each item. Armed with this information, managers can more accurately plan what items will be needed for each store and when.

Wal-Mart is also teaming with vendors like Warner-Lambert to create an Internet-based collaborative forecasting and replenishment (CFAR) system. Wal-Mart collects data (on things like sales-by-product and by-store) for Warner-Lambert products. Managers at Wal-Mart and Warner-Lambert then collaborate to develop forecasts for sales by store for Warner-Lambert products such as Listerine. Once Warner-Lambert and Wal-Mart planners decide on mutually acceptable forecast figures, a purchase plan is finalized and sent to Warner-Lambert's manufacturing planning system. So far, CFAR has helped cut the supply-cycle time for Listerine from 12 weeks to 6. That means less inventory, lower costs, and better buys for Wal-Mart customers.[40] ■ ■ ■

Forecasting and Computerized Monitoring Information is the foundation of any forecast, and accuracy depends on how accurate and sensitive a company's information systems are. For example, toward the end of 2000, many analysts expected the sales of software makers like Oracle, SAP, and Siebel systems to rise dramatically. However, as discussed in the Management in Action feature, monitoring a computer screen filled with various types of sales reports, Siebel Systems CEO Thomas Siebel could see that those estimates were wrong.

Among its broad range of software offerings, Siebel Systems sells sales management software that helps managers monitor and control a multitude of performance measures. These range from salesperson hiring costs to how many deals the firm's salespeople have actually closed. As the 2001 sales year opened, Siebel Systems own monitoring systems sent an alarm: Sales were falling off. For example, by February 2001, company executives could see that customers were scaling back orders, and that many contracts that were supposed to close weren't getting signed. The firm's special sales-control software gave them enough time to change their plans and take evasive action. They dramatically reduced expenses, increased pressure on the sales force, and supplemented the sales force with special executive-led teams to focus on big-ticket customers. In an otherwise bleak year for software makers, Siebel Systems' revenues were up 84% in 2001, while profits more than doubled.[41]

Qualitative Forecasting Methods Qualitative forecasting tools emphasize human judgment. They gather, in as logical, unbiased, and systematic a way as possible, all the information and human judgment that can be brought to bear on the factors being forecast.[42]

Don't underestimate the value of qualitative forecasting. It's true that in developing adequate plans, hard data and numbers are usually very important. However, it's also true that if you want realistic plans, there's usually no substitute for a human analysis of the situation and of its possible consequences. Indeed, there are times when quantitative tools are of little use. For example, quantitative tools are virtually useless when data are scarce, such as for a new product with no sales history.[43] These tools also tend to ignore unforeseeable, unexpected occurrences. Yet it is unexpected occurrences that often have the most profound effects.

The banking firm Wells Fargo & Co. provides an example. Wells Fargo's managers typically design yearly budgets that don't vary from the final results by more than about 5%. But after the September 11 terrorist attacks, the firm said it would probably formulate five budgets for the coming year and choose one depending on how events unfurled. Similarly, for years, British Airways built its plans—it's hiring, advertisements, schedules, and aircraft seat configurations—around the basic idea of catering to business travelers. September 11 changed all that. With the falloff in business travel, British Airways (BA) had to quickly revise its plans. By the end of 2001, BA had canceled flights on 10 routes, sold airplanes, and embarked on a new plan to attract budget passengers to its European networks. Sometimes, great uncertainty makes the human, subjective side of planning more important.[44]

On the other hand, basing plans solely on subjective sales forecasts can be perilous. During the summer of 2000, Nortel Networks Corp. planned to meet "explosive customer demand" by spending almost $2 billion to boost production and by adding 9,600 jobs.[45] Throughout 2000, Nortel executives questioned their largest customers to compile sales estimates. Unfortunately, those subjective estimates were way off. Nortel's CEO later found that some of his largest customers were telling him Nortel had to gear up to ship them more equipment, even as diminishing demand was making it harder for them to pay for that equipment.

Nortel did have professional researchers helping it compile forecasts. But, ironically, the researchers relied heavily on feedback from the firm's sales force, and the sales force estimates simply reflected the customers' overly optimistic estimates. By June 2001, Nortel had announced it would lose $19 billion in that quarter alone and would fire 10,000 people, over and above the 20,000 it had already cut.

The same thing happened at Cisco Systems. In early 2001, Cisco Systems customers were saying they needed more of the firm's networking equipment. However, it soon became obvious that the customers—thousands of dot-coms—were either

▲ **WEBNOTE** ■ ■ ■

Nortel Networks is a supplier of information and products through its Web site.

www.nortelnetworks.com

Source: Used with permission.

overoptimistic or just plain wrong. Cisco's inventory ballooned, and the firm had to reduce the value of its inventory by over $2 billion.[46]

Such imperfections notwithstanding, qualitative forecasts are valuable when used correctly. For example, the jury of executive opinion technique involves asking a jury of key executives to forecast sales for, say, the next year. Generally, each executive receives data on forecasted economic levels and anticipated corporate changes. Each jury member then makes an independent forecast. Differences are reconciled by the president or at a meeting of the executives.

The sales force estimation method gathers the opinions of the sales force regarding what they think sales will be in the forthcoming period. Each salesperson estimates his or her next year's sales, usually by product and customer. Sales managers review each estimate, compare it with the previous year's data, and discuss changes with each salesperson. The sales manager then combines the separate estimates into a sales forecast for the firm.

jury of executive opinion ▪ *a qualitative forecasting technique in which a panel of executives are given pertinent data and asked to make independent sales forecasts, which are then reconciled in an executive meeting or by the company president.*

sales force estimation ▪ *a forecasting technique that gathers and combines the opinions of the sales people on what they predict sales will be in the forthcoming period.*

Marketing Research

Sales forecasting tools can help managers explore the future and thereby develop better planning premises. But there are times when, to formulate plans, managers want to know not just what may happen in the future, but also what customers are thinking today. Marketing research refers to the procedures used to develop and analyze customer-related information that helps managers make decisions.[47]

Marketing researchers depend on two main types of information. One source is *secondary data*, or information collected or published already. Good sources of secondary data include the Internet, libraries, trade associations, company files and sales reports, and commercial data (for instance, from companies such as A. C. Nielsen). *Primary data* refer to information specifically collected to solve a current problem. Primary data sources include mail and personal surveys, in-depth and focus-group interviews, and personal observation (watching the reactions of customers who walk into a store).[48]

marketing research ▪ *the procedures used to develop and analyze current customer-related information to help managers make decisions.*

Competitive Intelligence

Developing useful plans requires knowing as much as possible about what competitors are doing or are planning to do. Competitive intelligence (CI) is a systematic way to obtain and analyze public information about competitors. Although this sounds (and is) a lot like legalized spying, it has become much more popular over the past few years. According to one report, the number of large companies with CI groups tripled in one recent 10-year period—to about 1,000.[49]

competitive intelligence ▪ *systematic techniques used to obtain and analyze public information about competitors.*

CI practitioners use various tools to discover what clients' competitors are doing. These tools include keeping track of existing and new competitors by having specialists visit their facilities, hiring their workers, and questioning their suppliers and customers. CI firms also do extensive Internet searches to unearth information about competitors, as well as mundane searches, like reading stock analysts' reports on the competitors' prospects. CI consulting firms use former prosecutors, business analysts, and FBI and Drug Enforcement Agency (DEA) employees to ferret out the sorts of information you might want before entering into an alliance with another company, or before deciding to get into some business.

CI firms can be quite useful. They help client companies (see Table 4.4) learn more about competitors' strengths and vulnerabilities, product strategies, investment strategies, financial capabilities, and current or prior behavior. Other CI services include evaluating the capabilities, weaknesses, and reputation of potential or existing joint-venture partners, identifying the major players in a new market or industry the firm is thinking of

▪ ▪ *Gathering primary data: Videotaping a focus group through a two-way mirror.*

TABLE 4–4	Competitive Intelligence; Kroll's Business Intelligence and Analysis Services and Capabilities

CI Can Address Four Critical Management Concerns	By Providing Intelligence Like This on Companies, Industries, and Countries
COMPETITION: Learning enough about competitors to devise proactive and reactive strategies, including competitors' strengths and vulnerabilities, product strategies, investment strategies, financial capabilities, operational issues, and anticompetitive behavior.	**Operations:** Nature of business, sales, locations, headcount. **Financial:** Ownership, assets, financing, profitability.
BUSINESS RELATIONSHIPS AND TRANSACTIONS: Evaluating the capabilities, weaknesses, and reputation of potential or existing joint venture partners; strategic alliances; acquisitions; distributors; licensees/licensors; critical suppliers/vendors; and project finance participants.	**Management:** Organization structure, decision makers, integrity/reputation, management style, history as partner, political connections. **Marketing/Customers:** Market position, major accounts, pricing, distribution, sales force, advertising.
ENTRY INTO NEW MARKETS: Developing entry strategies into new geographic and/or product markets, including identifying players in an industry, analyzing industry structure and trends, assessing local business practices, and ascertaining entry barriers, government regulation, and political risk.	**Manufacturing:** Plant and equipment, capacity, utilization, sourcing materials/components, shifts, labor costs, unions. **Technology:** New products and processes, research and development practices, technological assessment.
SALES OPPORTUNITIES: Maximizing opportunities to win contracts, develop major new customers, or maintain existing ones, including identifying purchasing decision-makers and critical factors, determining current suppliers, understanding the competition, and assessing the status of bids.	**Strategic Directions:** Business priorities, diversification, geographic strategy, horizontal/vertical integration, strategic relationships. **Legal:** Lawsuits, judgments, potential liabilities environmental exposure.

entering, and helping planners boost sales opportunities (for instance, by identifying the decision makers who actually do the purchasing and the critical factors they look for in vendors).

The Internet and CI The Internet has turned out to be a gold mine for competitive intelligence investigations. For example, Amazon.com recently used this approach to analyze a new business move by a competitor. Barnes & Noble had just listed three new product category tabs on its homepage. Amazon.com hired a competitive intelligence firm to review the site and to analyze Barnes & Noble's Web activity with Internet service providers. Amazon thereby found out that only one of the new **barnesandnoble.com** product tabs was popular with shoppers.

Unearthing competitive intelligence over the Web is easier than you might think. Suggestions for doing so include:[50]

- Use a search engine such as Alta Vista.com to get a list of all the Web pages your competitor has opened on the Internet, by typing in **url://companyname.com**
- Find all the Web sites linked to your competitor's site by typing in **link:// www.companyname.com**
- Comb through your competitor's Web site looking for information on things like the firm's business goals.
- If your competitor is publicly traded, carefully review its investor relations site. This contains public information (like quarterly profits reports and unusual expenses) required by law and convenient to have in one place.
- On the Web site, review your competitor's press releases. They may provide insights into potential problems, like those indicated by restructuring plans.
- Carefully review your competitor's listed job openings. For example, is one of its product lines listing many new job openings? That might point to an expected expansion.
- Check out message boards and chat rooms dedicated to the company. They often contain customer and/or employee complaints that provide insights into the firm's plans and or weaknesses.

Ethics and CI Is using the Internet to unearth competitive intelligence ethical? The answer seems to be "yes." For example, a spokesperson for the society of competitive intelligence professionals says that as long as the firm publicly lists the information on the Web, using it is roughly comparable to walking through a competitor's store to see what he or she is up to. However, you cross the line, says one ethics expert, if you anonymously pry private information from unsuspecting competitors.[51]

[illegible] pped over the line. For example, as discussed in Chapter [illegible] intelligence managers allegedly hired outsiders to gather [illegible] re products. These outsiders (P&G now calls them "rogue [illegible] ctivities like digging through Unilever's dumpsters on [illegible] isrepresenting themselves to Unilever employees. When [illegible] red the operation, he was appalled and reported it to [illegible] nicals firm confronted a similar situation. Here, former [illegible] chemicals company, posing as journalists to unearth [illegible] e firm. Another firm allegedly offered a former reporter [illegible] aper to publish a negative article about the company.[53]

[illegible] Management

[illegible] prove the quality of their forecasts by linking them- [illegible] chain partners. The Wal-Mart example shows how [illegible]

[illegible] UNDARIES

[illegible] Supply Chain

[illegible] y size 30 Levi's jeans it [illegible] es, Dell needs to know [illegible] and Prentice Hall needs [illegible] r the fall. Anticipating [illegible] quirements is a big part [illegible] ers use qualitative and [illegible] those above to make [illegible] l might use sales reps' [illegible] fall semester demand [illegible] based forecasting tool [illegible] ure that the company [illegible] can in turn supply its [illegible] than simply making [illegible]

[illegible] lart, or Coors, every [illegible] sical entities, such as [illegible] conveyances, retail [illegible] are linked together [illegible] om sources through [illegible] *management* is to [illegible] into one boundary- [illegible]

[illegible] ne a customer buys [illegible] oves electronically [illegible] The replenishment [illegible] d just-in-time. The [illegible] ell computer. You [illegible] part of a sophisticated and boundaryless supply chain management system. You use Dell's Web site to design exactly the PC you want, and then you click "go." That information then speeds via the Internet to all the participants in Dell's supply chain. Dell's suppliers (including the firm that makes the computer display you ordered) instantaneously know when and to whom to ship their products. Dell production sees instantaneously what PC to assemble for you and when. UPS sees when to pick up your PC and where it goes. And you can actually monitor your PC's progress on Dell's order processing Web site.

With a system like this, Wal-Mart would not need to keep large quantities of Levi's jeans in the store or local warehouse: Levi's would know, on a real-time basis, how many size 30 jeans were being sold and would, therefore, be needed in each store. Dell would not have to inventory laptops: It would know, on a real-time basis, how many laptop orders were coming in, and it would build each machine to order. Think of how much money Wal-Mart and Dell could (and, in fact, do) save by stripping their supply lines of the need for costly inventories.

Producing items in anticipation of projected demand means those items must be stored, and such inventory simply ties up money, labor, and space. Producing the items "just-in-time" means the items simply appear or get replenished when they're needed.

Boundaryless Internet-based supply chain systems integrate—link together via the Internet—all components of the supply chain, such as the customer, supplier, manufacturer, and shipper. To a large extent, firms like Levis, Wal-Mart, and Dell do not have to depend on short-term sales forecasts. They can make their supply and production decisions based on actual demand.

The Safeway supermarket chain in the United Kingdom also recently put in place a supply-chain management system. Safeway conducted a market research study to find out what customers most disliked about shopping in its stores. "Waiting on line at the checkout counter" topped the list. Safeway responded by installing special scanners; customers can now scan and bag their own items if they choose to do so. Number 2 on the "don't like" list was "not being able to buy out-of-stock items." Safeway's first reaction was to suggest substitute items. Shoppers didn't like that idea, so Safeway switched to a boundaryless supply-chain system. It had been reluctant to do so for fear of divulging competitive information to its suppliers. However, it now saw that it had to take steps to eliminate the out-of-stock problem. With new point-of-sale computerized registers, Safeway started sharing customers' real-time sales with its suppliers.[55] In doing so, Safeway turned suppliers into partners—a hallmark of boundaryless organizations. Suppliers now get real-time information regarding sales of their products. That gives them the information they need to replenish Safeway's shelves just-in-time.

■■■ A FINAL WORD: THERE IS NO ONE BEST PLANNING PROCESS

Planning can sometimes be more trouble than it's worth. Even for something as simple as a trip to Paris, blind devotion to the plan could cause you to miss a great last minute opportunity. In a business, such inflexibility can be deadly. For example, department stores would have been foolish to ignore the possibility of Internet catalog sales just because the word *Internet* didn't appear in their long-term plans in the late 1990s.

Inflexibility isn't the only potential problem. A plan is only as good as its implementation, and it is worthless if top management can't coax divisional managers to actually do things differently. Some top managers go too far in the opposite direction, by naïvely insisting on counterproductive changes to their division managers' proposed plans. As one planning expert says, top managers have only limited time to devote to analyzing the plans of the firm's separate businesses, so "the potential for [giving] misguided advice is high, especially in diversified companies."[56] The more unpredictable things are, the more likely this will happen.

The bottom line is that a planning process that works for one firm won't necessarily work for another. A good planning process:

> . . . is not a generic process but one in which both analytic techniques and organizational processes are carefully tailored to the needs of the businesses as well as to skills, insight, and experiences of senior corporate managers. A mature electrical-products business, for example, has different planning needs than a fast growing entertainment business or a highly cyclical chemicals business.[57]

Each company needs a planning process that's right for it. Perhaps the most important question here is what the manager wants the planning process to achieve. For example, Granada (a British conglomerate with businesses in television broadcasting, hotels, catering, and appliances) prides itself on pushing its managers to find new business opportunities. Therefore, its planning process deliberately discourages managers from comparing or benchmarking their financial results to those of competitors. When you do that, the CEO says, "You lock yourself into low ambitions."[58] Instead, Granada's relatively informed planning process aims to challenge its managers to find ways to achieve huge leaps in their divisions' sales and profitability. "Planning [at Granada] is about raising ambitions and helping businesses get more creative in their search for ways to increase profits."[59]

On the other hand, Dow Chemical Corporation operates in a relatively tranquil and cost-conscious environment. Dow's planning process aims to find small, incremental improvements in processing costs—such as a 2% savings in maintenance costs—since in the slow-growth chemicals industry, costs are crucial. The planning process at Dow is, therefore, relatively formal, analytical, comparative, and numbers-oriented. The point, again, is that managers must decide what they want to achieve with their planning before establishing a planning process.

1. Plans are methods formulated for achieving desired results. Planning is the process of establishing objectives and courses of actions prior to taking action. Plans differ in format, timetable, and frequency (programs versus standing plans).

2. The management-planning process consists of a logical sequence of steps: establish objectives; forecast/conduct situation analysis; determine alternative courses of action; evaluate alternatives; and choose and implement the plan. In practice, this method produces a planning hierarchy because top management's goals become the targets for which subsidiary units must formulate derivative plans.

3. Every manager can expect to be appraised on the extent to which he or she achieves assigned objectives, which makes setting objectives an essential management skill. The areas for which objectives can be set are virtually limitless, ranging from market standing to innovation and profitability.

4. Goal-setting studies suggest these guidelines: Assign specific goals; assign measurable goals; assign challenging but doable goals; and encourage participation where feasible.

5. In setting goals, managers need to emphasize SMART—specific, measurable, attainable, relevant, and timely.

6. Among the techniques for developing planning premises are forecasting, marketing research, and competitive intelligence. Forecasting techniques include quantitative methods such as time-series analysis and causal methods. Qualitative forecasting methods such as sales-force estimation and jury of executive opinion emphasize human judgment.

KEY TERMS ◼◼◼

plan 80	operational plan 93	qualitative forecasting 100
goal 80	program 93	time series 100
objectives 80	standing plan 93	causal methods 100
planning 80	policy 93	causal forecasting 100
hierarchy of plans 82	procedure 93	jury of executive opinion 103
descriptive plan 93	rule 93	sales force estimation 103
budget 93	goal-setting studies 97	marketing research 103
graphic plan 93	management by objectives (MBO) 98	competitive intelligence (CI) 103
tactical plan 93	forecast 99	
functional plan 93	quantitative forecasting 100	

SKILLS AND STUDY MATERIALS

COMPANION WEBSITE ◼◼◼

 We invite you to visit the Dessler Companion Website at **www.prenhall.com/dessler** for this chapter's Internet resources.

EXPERIENTIAL EXERCISES ◼◼◼

1. It is probably safe to say that your career plan is one of the most important plans you'll ever create. Unfortunately, most people never lay out such a plan, or they don't realize they need one until it's too late. Using the concepts and techniques in this chapter, develop an outline of a career plan for yourself, one that is sufficiently detailed to provide direction for your career decisions over the next five years. Make sure to include an executive assignment action plan and measurable goals and/or milestones.

2. You are the chancellor of the California State University system, which has 23 campuses. California has a population of about 37 million people, who represent a microcosm of the world's population. You know that with an increasing birthrate and continuing immigration into the state, your college system could be swamped by the year 2010. Many of the campuses are already filled to capacity. There have been limited funds allocated for introducing technology into every classroom. Some faculties are not as computer literate as their students. This situation may worsen as the years go by. The freshmen of 2010 are likely to be more sophisticated than the current freshmen. The world of technology seems to grow geometrically in terms of the knowledge you need to understand in order to effectively use computers. You have quite a planning challenge. Working as a 4–5 person team,

outline how you would use the information provided in the chapter about planning and setting objectives to formulate a plan for the California State University system. Assume that there is increased funding, along with increased pressures to educate a larger percentage of the population as 2010 approaches.

3. Based on what you know about DaimlerChrysler's plans to date, and on what you learned in this chapter, list at least three things that the company's top managers seem to have done right—and done wrong—with respect to planning.

4. Present your career plan (see exercise 1) in descriptive, graphic, and financial terms.

CASE STUDY ■■■

OPENING THE HOLLYWOOD KNITTING FACTORY

You don't raise $5 million and run a successful, growing business for more than 10 years unless you know where you're going. But when it comes to making detailed business plans, managers at KnitMedia—a company that runs jazz clubs called the Knitting Factory in several cities—still have some doubts. For example, when asked if the company does much planning, Michael Dorf, the firm's CEO, replies,

> Sure, we actually are, you know, starting to use budgets—I can't even say it because it's so hard for me to adhere to them, but, you know, we are using budgets to some extent. [In fact], every so often, I put together the business plan and I talk with every team member and try and consolidate all our ideas and our plans. [However], it's difficult to be very fast-moving, especially at Internet speeds, if everything has to be constricted to a pure schedule and plan.

In fact, Dorf's dilemma is often the dilemma that all start-ups (and especially technology-oriented start-ups) face every day. As he says, KnitMedia's managers have to adapt very quickly to stay ahead of the competition, and it's not easy to do that if every step was decided several months or years ago.

Alan Fried, KnitMedia's chief operating officer, makes much the same point. As he says,

> I mean, we are very much a media company and as some of the clichés around go, Internet years happen much quicker than calendar years. And if you have to move so fast, you have to move fast because if you're thinking of it, some-

body else's thinking of it and first player advantage means a lot. So, sometimes we don't have the good fortune to just sort of sit down and plan everything. [What we do, though], is have an idea, and we have some meetings about it and we just move where I think we have to.

That way, the company is always moving in the new direction even though it doesn't have a rigid, predetermined plan.

The problem is that Dorf and his team are not entirely convinced that this more or less seat-of-the-pants approach to planning is necessarily the best, although it's certainly worked so far. Furthermore, as more people invest money in the business, it's become increasingly important to develop formal plans so others will know where you're planning to go.

The management team has approached you to help it formalize KnitMedia's planning process. Working as a team, use what you learned in this chapter to answer the following questions.

Discussion Questions

1. At a minimum, what sorts of plans do you think management should develop and use at KnitMedia? Why?

2. Their immediate task is to open the new Hollywood, California, club. What forecasting tools do you suggest they use? Provide them with an outline of an Executive Assignment Action Plan that they can use to guide them in opening that location.

3. Is it possible for them to assign specific goals to department managers even though they don't have a formal planning process? If so, how?

YOU BE THE CONSULTANT ■■■

PLANNING IN THE FACE OF UNCERTAINTY

jetBlue AIRWAYS® David Neeleman attributes much of JetBlue's initial success to the fact that he and his team stuck closely to his original concept and plan. As Neeleman says, "We're Southwest with seat assignments, leather seats, and television."[60] The foundations of his original plan called for strong financing, fleet homogeneity (so maintenance people and pilots and flight service crews could easily switch from plane to plane), high fleet utilization, attractive pricing, and experienced management.

To a large extent, things are working out according to plan. JetBlue is flying about 80% full, versus an industry average of about 68%. JetBlue is also profitable, an impressive feat given the fact that virtually all of its competitors are racking up losses.[61] While its fleet of brand new Airbus A-320 jets meant higher purchase and/or leas-

ing costs, they are also much less expensive to fly; they burn less fuel and require virtually no expenditures on heavy maintenance (since Airbus warranties them for the first few years). As Mr. Neeleman says, "The way to have low-cost is to buy brand new airplanes."[62]

However, any plan is only as good as the assumptions it's based on, and no manager is ever dealing with an entirely predictable future. On the one hand, some things have worked in JetBlue's favor. For example, right after JetBlue began flying out of JFK, LaGuardia was hit with months of record delays, making JFK a more attractive alternative. Furthermore, Neeleman's most basic assumption—that there was a huge, pent-up demand for flights from places like Fort Lauderdale to JFK on a low-cost airline with new planes and top-quality service—proved very accurate.

On the other hand, many other things were impossible to predict. No one, for instance, expected the 9/11 attacks or the decline in air travel that followed it. Furthermore, while competition was to be expected, even JetBlue's managers were surprised by the aggressiveness of some of their competitors. For example, in a February 22, 2002, letter to Chris Kunze, the manager of Long Beach Airport, American Airlines pointed out that JetBlue was using few of its slots at the airport and that "it is important that American receive (4) slots so that another air carrier cannot deprive us of the right to operate at Long Beach." Under the terms of its agreement, JetBlue has several years before it must fully utilize its slots. However, American Airlines can file suit to try to win some of those slots and thereby compete head-to-head with JetBlue. Soaring oil prices and a slowing economy didn't help JetBlue in 2001–2002. One problem small airlines can't hedge against is rising fuel costs, because they haven't the financial wherewithal to do so. The big carriers can.[63] As someone who ran a company that developed and marketed airline scheduling and reservation forecasting systems, Neeleman is well-positioned to understand how to develop sophisticated forecasting systems. However, those sophisticated scheduling and reservation systems require several years experience on which to build their forecasts. Neeleman and his team, therefore, have to make decisions (like how many planes to add to particular routes and what fares to charge) more on instinct than on quantitative techniques. As the firm's chief financial officer put it, "The peak last Christmas was far deeper, stronger and longer than expected. This year they'll be fewer discounts. For now, we're heavily biased to working manually."[64] Partly as a result of all this, JetBlue, which is still in strong financial condition, was quickly accumulating debt as late as 2002.

Assignment

You and your team are consultants to Mr. Neeleman, who is depending on your management expertise to help him navigate the launch and management of JetBlue. Here's what he wants to know from you now:

1. From what you know, how well did my team and I do in applying effective planning procedures? Please list what we did right and wrong.

2. Develop an outline of a business plan (just the main headings, please), including the component functional plans we will need for the company as a whole.

3. Give me examples of how JetBlue can use descriptive plans, graphical plans, and financial plans.

4. List four forecasting tools you think we should apply and why.

5 Strategic Management

CHAPTER OBJECTIVES

After studying this chapter and the case exercises at the end, you should be able to:

1. Develop a workable strategic plan for an organization using SWOT analysis.

2. Identify a company's current corporate strategies, and list its strategic options.

3. Develop a vision and mission statement.

4. Accurately identify a company's "core competence."

5. Explain each of the strategic planning tools you think the CEO should use, and why.

THE MANAGEMENT CHALLENGE

Robert Nardelli's New Home Depot Strategy

For 20 years, Home Depot pursued a strategy of rapid growth. Starting with one store, by 2000 the company had nearly 1,300 stores worldwide, revenues of about $46 billion, and status as the third largest retailer in the United States. As one business writer put it, "Over the space of two decades, [founders] Bernie Marcus and Arthur Blank turned a no-frills, hangar-sized, home-improvement store in Atlanta into a phenomenon."[1] The company rode a period of economic prosperity to become the industry leader. However, by 2001, Home Depot's environment was changing—and fast. As consumers tightened their belts, home improvement sales began to lag. More worrisome was the fact that Home Depot was running out of runway. Analysts estimated that there was room for only about 3,500 such home centers in the United States. Home Depot and competitor Lowe's would run out of communities in which to build new U.S. stores within five years.

The founders brought in ex-GE top executive Robert Nardelli as its new CEO, and stepped aside so he could decide what to do. Should Home Depot accelerate its expansion abroad? Diversify into new businesses? Close less profitable stores and boost operating performance? Many strategies were feasible. But Nardelli also knew that choosing the wrong one could spell disaster for his firm.

Chapter 4 discussed the basic planning process and the techniques managers use to set an overall strategy for the firm, and then develop subsidiary plans. We saw in that chapter that all the company's plans stem from that overall strategic plan. The main purpose of this chapter is to provide you with the knowledge and tools you need to develop a strategy for a company. The main topics we'll discuss include the strategic planning process, types of strategies, creating strategic plans, and strategic planning in practice.

■■■ KNOWING YOUR BUSINESS

The plans you designed for Acme Consulting in Chapter 4 assume one thing: They assume you know what business Acme is in—for instance, in terms of your products or services, how you'll compete, and where you will sell. Let's say your business will provide computer-systems consulting services for high-tech firms. That determines what kinds of consultants you hire, the clients you pursue, the way you market your services, and how much money you need to run the business. All your plans (or most of them) would change if you were in a different business, such as providing accounting services to grocery stores (or even to high-tech companies). The bottom line is this: You have to be able to answer the question "what business are we in?" before you can do any business planning. You need a strategy for your company—a basic course of action, and you then build all your plans on that foundation.

It's the same thing on a more personal level. To see why, consider your own career plans. Defining your occupational business as "management consultant" will lead you to make short-term plans—regarding which college to attend and which courses to take, for instance—which are vastly different than if you had decided to be a dentist. Knowing the business you want to be in provides a path and a sense of direction for everything you do. Without it, you may simply drift.

Peter Drucker put it this way: He says top management's primary task is thinking through the mission of the business—that is, asking the question, "What is our business and what should it be?" "This leads to the setting of objectives, the development of strategies and plans, and the making of today's decisions for tomorrow's results."[2] Knowing that they're running the world's low-cost leader retail chain provides Wal-Mart managers with a clear sense of what they must do: expand their satellite-based logistics system, open more stores in relatively low-cost locations, and drive down apparel manufacturing costs. Could they make decisions like these if they did not know the business they were in? The answer is no. *Strategic planning*—the subject of this chapter—involves defining the mission of the business, and laying out the broad strategies or courses of action the firm will use to achieve that mission.

Strategic planning is a type of planning, and thus has a lot in common with the planning process described in Chapter 4. Both involve assessing your situation today and predicting the future; both involve setting objectives; and both involve crafting courses of action to get you from where you are today to where you want to be tomorrow. But strategic planning is also in a class of its own. For one thing, it relies on special tools and techniques. For another, it's often highly subjective. Tom Peters, another management guru, reportedly once offered $1,000 to the first manager who could demonstrate that he or she had created a successful strategy from a planning process.[3] His point was that a careful planning process may actually produce worse—not better—strategic plans.

How could this be? The problem is that strategic planning is a very creative, judgmental process. Unlike shorter-term plans ("What courses should I take this term?"), strategic planning ("What occupation is best for me?") requires looking far ahead, and using insight and creativity to make sense of many imponderables. (For your personal strategic plan, these might include: "Will I be a good consultant?" "Will I enjoy that career?" "Will there be enough jobs in five years to make being a consultant worthwhile?"). Two experts put it this way: "Planning processes are not designed to accommodate the messy process of generating insights and molding them into a winning strategy."[4]

The techniques in this chapter can help make you a better strategic planner. However, don't let them mislead you into believing that strategic planning is mechanical. Insight and creativity always play a big role.

∎∎∎ THE STRATEGIC MANAGEMENT PROCESS

Strategic planning is the process of identifying the business of the firm today and the business of the firm for the future, and then identifying the course of action it should pursue, given its opportunities, threats, strengths, and weaknesses. It specifies with whom the firm will compete, and how it will compete with them.

Strategic planning is part of the firm's strategic management process. As in Figure 5.1, strategic planning includes the first five strategic management tasks. It includes evaluating the firm's internal and external situation, defining the business and developing a mission, translating the mission into strategic goals, and crafting a strategy or course of action. **Strategic management** includes the implementation phase. It is the process of identifying and executing the organization's mission, by matching the organization's capabilities with the demands of its environment.[5] Basic strategic planning, however, is simple: Decide what business you're in now, and which ones you want to be in, then formulate a strategy for getting there, and execute your plan.

The strategic management process consists of several related tasks (see Figure 5.1). Let's look at the main ones (see Checklist 5.1).

CHECKLIST 5.1 ∎ The Strategic Management Process

☑ Define the business and its mission.

☑ Perform external and internal audits.

☑ Translate the mission into strategic goals.

☑ Generate and select strategies to reach strategic goals.

☑ Implement the strategy.

☑ Evaluate performance.

▼ **FIGURE 5–1** ∎ ∎ ∎ A Comprehensive Strategic-Management Model

Source: Adapted from Fred David, *Strategic Management* (Upper Saddle River, NJ: Prentice Hall, 2001), p. 77.

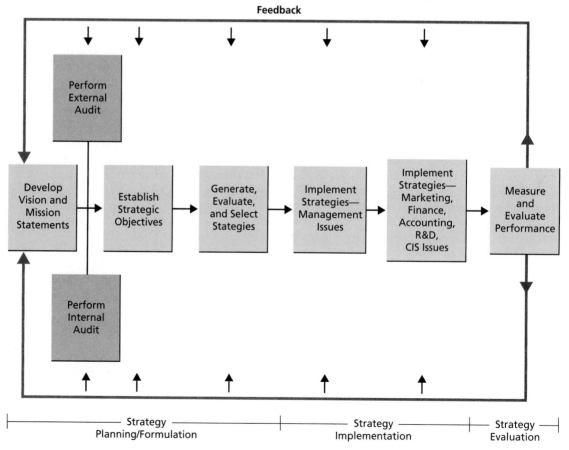

Step 1: Define the Business and Its Mission[6]

The fundamental strategic decisions managers face are these: "Where are we now in terms of the business we're in, and what business do we want to be in, given our company's opportunities and threats, and its strengths and weaknesses?" Managers then choose strategies—courses of action such as buying competitors or expanding overseas—to get the company from where it is today to where it wants to be tomorrow. Making these decisions involves analyzing the company's strategic situation—in terms of competitive trends, for instance.

We'll discuss how to do this later in this chapter. First, however, you should recognize that defining the firm's business is trickier than it might appear. Ferrari and Toyota both make cars. However, Ferrari specializes in high-performance cars, and its competitive advantage depends on high-speed performance. Toyota produces a range of cars, and its competitive advantage depends on cost-efficient production and a strong dealer network. We can't simply say they're all in the car business. How would the CEO know what kinds of engines to build, what people to hire, or how to advertise? Defining one's business thus requires some precision.

Defining a company's business involves identifying several things. Even in the same industry, companies differ in their *product scope*, in the range and diversity of products they sell. They differ in the extent to which they are *vertically integrated*, in the degree to which they produce their own raw materials, or distribute their own products. They differ in *geographic scope*—some firms operate just locally, while others may be statewide, national, or global. They also differ in *how they compete*. Toyota builds cars for reliability, while Ferrari stresses speed. Defining the company's business requires a great deal of thought.

Management experts use the terms *vision* and *mission* to help define a company's current and future business. Some use the terms interchangeably. However, in general usage, vision tends to be the broader and more future-oriented of the two. The company's **vision** is a "general statement of its intended direction that evokes emotional feelings in organization members."[7] As Warren Bennis and Bert Manus say,

> *To choose a direction, a leader must first have developed a mental image of a possible and desirable future state for the organization. This image, which we call a vision, may be as vague as a dream or as precise as a goal or mission statement. The critical point is that a vision articulates a view of a realistic, credible, attractive future for the organization, a condition that is better in some important ways than what now exists.*[8]

vision ■ *a general statement of an organization's intended direction that evokes emotional feelings in its members.*

Rupert Murdoch, chairman of News Corporation (which owns the Fox network and many newspapers and satellite TV operations) has a vision of an integrated global satellite-based news-gathering, entertainment, and multimedia firm. AOL-Time Warner chairman Steve Case has a vision of "AOL Anywhere"—access to the Web from your PC, wireless, or TV. WebMD CEO Jeffrey Arnold launched his business based on a vision of a Web site supplying everything a consumer might want to know about medical-related issues.[9]

MANAGEMENT IN ACTION   Monsanto

Some visions might have been better left unsaid. In the mid-1990s, Monsanto CEO Robert Shapiro envisioned his firm as a sort of life sciences factory, using biochemistry to change the genetic and other characteristics of crops. He saw this as a way to create new food products that could, for instance, lower cholesterol.[10]

Unfortunately, that's not quite how Monsanto's vision worked out. The idea of tampering with the chemistry and genetic structure of crops proved so controversial that Monsanto has now largely abandoned the idea. Monsanto poured lots of dollars into trying to implement the vision. Now, with its strategic vision in tatters, Monsanto may even risk losing its independence. It may have to merge with another firm.

mission statement ■ *a statement that broadly outlines the enterprise's purpose and serves to communicate "who the organization is, what it does, and where it's headed."*

The firm's **mission** is more specific and shorter-term. It "... serves to communicate 'who we are, what we do, and where we're headed.'"[11] Whereas visions usually lay out in

APEX ELEVATOR

To provide a high-reliability, error-free method for moving people and products up, down, and sideways within a building

UNITED TELEPHONE CORPORATION OF DADE

To provide information services in local-exchange and exchange-access markets within its franchised area, as well as cellular phone and paging services.

JOSEPHSON DRUG COMPANY, INC.

To provide people with longer lives and higher-quality lives by applying research efforts to develop new or improved drugs and health-care products.

GRAY COMPUTER, INC.

To transform how educators work by providing innovative and easy-to-use multimedia-based computer systems.

very broad terms what the business should be, the mission lays out what it is supposed to be now. For example, the mission of the California Energy Commission is to "assess, and act through public/private partnerships to improve energy systems that promote a strong economy and a healthy environment." (The Commission's *vision*, by way of comparison, is "for Californians to have energy choices that are affordable, reliable, diverse, safe, and environmentally acceptable"). Figure 5.2 presents some other examples.

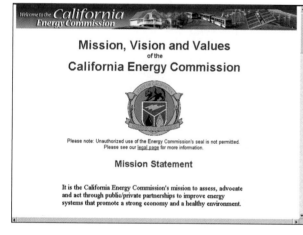

▲ WEBNOTE ■ ■ ■

An accurate, timely analysis of events in the real world might have helped the California Energy Commission avoid—or at least be prepared for—drastic changes in its environment that would seriously affect its mission.

www.energy.ca.gov/commission

Source: California Energy Commission.

Step 2: Perform External and Internal Audits

Events can throw even relatively stable industries into disarray. Electric power sources and needs are supposedly easy to plan for. But, despite its clear mission, the California Energy Commission got a rude surprise a few years ago. Energy deregulation caused power prices to surge, and for months the state faced an energy crisis. To avoid nasty surprises, managers base their strategic plans on methodical analyses of their external and internal situations. The basic point of a plan should be to choose a direction for the firm that makes sense, in terms of the external opportunities and threats it faces, and the internal strengths and weaknesses it possesses. To do this, special tools are required. (We'll learn how to use strategic analysis tools later in this chapter.)

Step 3: Translate the Mission into Strategic Goals

Saying your mission is to "assess and act through public/private partnerships to improve energy systems . . ." is one thing. Operationalizing that mission for your managers is another. You and the firm's other managers need strategic, long-term goals. For example, what exactly does that mission mean, for the next five years, in terms of how many and what specific types of partnerships to form, with whom, and when?

Business managers, of course, need the same specificity. WebMD's sales director needs goals regarding the number of new medical-related content providers—vitamin firms, hospitals, (HMOs)—it must sign up per year, as well as sales revenue targets. The business development manager needs goals regarding the number of new businesses—such as using WebMD to help manage doctors' offices online—he or she is to develop and sign.

Similarly, a global financial powerhouse like Citicorp can't function solely with the broad mission "to provide integrated, comprehensive financial services worldwide." It needs specific goals in areas including building shareholder value through sustained growth in earnings-per-share; continuing its commitment to building customer-oriented business worldwide; maintaining superior rates of return; building a strong balance sheet; and balancing the business by customer, product, and geography.[12]

"Never choose a mission statement on a dark, rainy day."

Step 4: Formulate a Strategy to Achieve the Strategic Goals

The firm's strategy is a bridge connecting where it is today with where it wants to be tomorrow. The question is, "how do we get from here to there?" A strategy is a course of action. It shows how the enterprise will move from the business it is in now to the business it wants to be in (as stated in its vision, mission, and strategic goals), given its opportunities and threats and its internal strengths and weaknesses. For example, Wal-Mart years ago decided to pursue the strategic goal of moving from being a small, southern-based chain of retail discount stores to becoming the national leader (in terms of market share) in low-cost merchandise. To accomplish this, Wal-Mart chose several strategies. One was to pursue a lost-cost leader strategy—and, specifically, to reduce distribution costs and minimize inventory and delivery times through a satellite-based distribution system. A firm can pursue several basic strategies. We'll discuss them later in this chapter.

strategy ■ *a course of action that explains how an enterprise will move from the business it is in now to the business it wants to be in.*

Step 5: Implement the Strategy

Strategy implementation means translating the strategy into actions and results—by actually hiring (or firing) people, building (or closing) plants, and adding (or eliminating) products and product lines. In other words, strategy implementation involves drawing on and applying all the management functions: planning, organizing, leading, and controlling.

Employees can't and won't implement strategies they don't buy into. Top companies therefore craft strategies whose basic principles are easy to communicate. Figure 5.3 illustrates this. For example, the essence of Dell's strategy has always been "be direct." Wal-Mart's strategy boils down to the familiar "low prices, every day."

COMPANY	STRATEGIC PRINCIPLE
America Online	Consumer connectivity first—anytime, anywhere
Dell	Be direct
eBay	Focus on trading communities
General Electric	Be number one or number two in every industry in which we compete, or get out
Southwest Airlines	Meet customers' short-haul travel needs at fares competitive with the cost of automobile travel
Vanguard	Unmatchable value for the investor-owner
Wal-Mart	Low prices, every day

◀ **FIGURE 5–3** ■ ■ ■

Strategies in Brief

Source: Arit Gadiesh and James Gilbert, "Frontline Action," *Harvard Business Review,* May 2001, p. 74.

A knowledge of and commitment to the strategy helps ensure that employees make decisions consistent with the company's needs. For example, the executive team's deep understanding of Nokia's strategy helps explain how the firm can make thousands of decisions each week so coherently.[13]

Step 6: Evaluate Performance

Strategies don't always work out. For example, when General Motors recently sold the last of its Hughes Electronics assets, it was the end of a strategy put in place about 12 years earlier. In the 1980s, GM had bought both Electronic Data Systems and Hughes Electronics, with the idea of using these technology firms to automate and reinvigorate automobile production and sales. GM did make a big profit when it sold those two companies. However, many believe the acquisitions were actually such a distraction that they helped push GM's market share down from about 60% to 28% in the interim.[14] Similarly, Procter & Gamble recently announced it was selling its remaining food businesses—Jif, Crisco, and Folgers coffee—because management wants to concentrate on household and cosmetics products.[15]

Managing strategy is thus an ongoing process. Competitors introduce new products, technological innovations make production processes obsolete, and societal trends reduce demand for some products or services while boosting demand for others. Managers must be alert to opportunities and threats that might require modifying or totally redoing their strategies. And, they must be alert to problems that may be hampering their efforts to implement the current plan.

strategic control ■ *the process of assessing progress toward its strategic objectives and taking corrective action as needed to ensure optimal implementation.*

Strategic control keeps the company's strategy up to date. It is the process of assessing progress toward strategic goals and taking corrective action as needed. Ideally, this is a continuing process. Management monitors the extent to which the firm is meeting its strategic goals, and asks why deviations exist. Management simultaneously scans the firm's strategic situation (competitors, technical advances, customer demographics, and so on) to see if it should make any adjustments. Strategic control addresses several important questions: "Are all the resources of our firm contributing as planned to achieving our strategic goals?" "What is the reason for any discrepancies?" And, "Do changes in our situation suggest that we should revise our strategic plan?" See Checklist 5.2.

CHECKLIST 5.2 ■ How to Test the Quality of Your Strategy

☑ *Does your strategy fit with what's going on in the environment?* Does your strategy provide profit potential?

☑ *Does your strategy exploit your key resources?* Can you pursue this strategy more economically than competitors?

☑ *Will competitors have difficulty keeping up with you?* Does your strategy include a program for continuous innovation?

☑ *Are the elements of your strategy internally consistent?* Do all the elements of your strategy reinforce each other?

☑ *Do you have enough resources to pursue this strategy?* Do you have the money, managerial talent, and other capabilities to do all you envisioned?

☑ *Can your strategy be implemented?* Will your key constituencies allow you to pursue this strategy? Are you and your management team willing and able to lead the required changes?[16]

corporate-level strategy ■ *a plan that identifies the portfolio of businesses that comprise a corporation and how they relate to each other.*

competitive strategy ■ *a strategy that identifies how to build and strengthen the business's long-term competitive position in the marketplace.*

functional strategy ■ *the overall course or courses of action and basic policies that each department is to follow in helping the business accomplish its strategic goals.*

■■■ TYPES OF STRATEGIES

There are three main types of strategies, as summarized in Figure 5.4. Many companies consist of a portfolio of several businesses. For instance, Disney includes movies, theme parks, and the ABC-TV network. These companies need a corporate-level strategy that identifies the portfolio of businesses which make up the corporation and the ways in which these businesses fit together.

The question, then, is "How will each of these portfolio businesses compete?" Each business needs a business-level or competitive strategy. This strategy identifies how to build and strengthen the company's long-term competitive position in the marketplace.[17] It identifies, for instance, how Disney films will compete with Warner films (such as by focusing more on G-rated films).

Each business (such as Disney films) is in turn composed of departments, such as production, marketing, and HR. Functional strategies identify the basic courses of

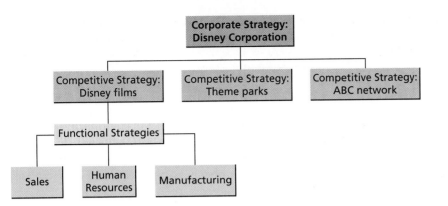

◀ **FIGURE 5–4** ■ ■ ■

Relationships Among Strategies
in Multiple-Business Firms

Companies typically formulate three
types of strategies: Corporate strategies, business-level/competitive strategies, and functional strategies.

action each functional department will pursue to help attain the business's competitive goals. (Thus, Disney film's production strategy might include guidelines regarding the types of stories that are acceptable, and how directors should film them.) We'll look at each type of strategy in turn.

Corporate-Level Strategies

Every company must decide the number of businesses in which it will compete and the relationships that will exist among those businesses. In other words, they must have a corporate-level strategy. Companies can pursue one or more of the following corporate strategies when deciding what businesses to be in and how these businesses should relate to each other.

Concentration With a concentration/single business strategy, the company offers one product or product line, usually in one market. Firms with single-business strategies include McDonald's, KFC, and WD-40 Company. The main advantage here is that the company can concentrate on the business it knows well. It can specialize. This should allow it to do that one thing better than competitors. Gerber, for example, emphasizes the fact that "baby foods are our only business."

The main disadvantage is the risk in putting all one's eggs into one basket. If for some reason hamburgers fall out of favor, McDonald's might find itself with no backup businesses. After years of concentrating in the hamburger franchise business, McDonald's tried unsuccessfully to diversify into franchising children's play areas in covered shopping malls. Harley Davidson, on the other hand, successfully diversified from motorcycles into clothing, restaurants, and finance. Concentration can also leave the firm open to seasonal or cyclical swings in earnings, as demand for the company's product or service ebbs and flows. Adding a line of lawnmowers can help a snowmobile maker even out its yearly production.

Concentrating in a single line of business doesn't mean the firm can't or won't try to grow. Some traditional concentrators, like the Coca-Cola Company, have achieved very high growth rates through concentration. They do this in one of four ways.[18] Some grow through market penetration. This means taking steps to boost sales of present products by more aggressively selling and marketing into the firm's current markets. Geographic expansion is another alternative. The *Wall Street Journal* has achieved above-average growth rates while concentrating on its traditional business by aggressively expanding into new geographic markets, both domestic and overseas. Firms can also achieve growth through product development, which means developing improved products for current markets. Horizontal integration, acquiring ownership or control of competitors in the same or similar markets with the same or similar products, is another option. For example, the Humana Hospitals chain has grown rapidly while remaining a concentrator by acquiring hundreds of hospitals.

■ *The Global Manager* Many companies have little or no choice but to expand geographically, often overseas. For example, restaurant chains like McDonald's and KFC face slow growth in their main U.S. markets. One way for them to grow fast is to expand abroad.

market penetration ■ *a growth strategy to boost sales of present products by more aggressively permeating the organization's current markets.*

geographic expansion ■ *a strategic growth alternative of aggressively expanding into new domestic and/or overseas markets.*

product development ■ *the strategy of improving products for current markets to maintain or boost growth.*

horizontal integration ■ *acquiring ownership or control of competitors who are competing in the same or similar markets with the same or similar products.*

That is what Tricon Global Restaurants is doing. Several years ago, when former owner PepsiCo saw that its drinks-oriented managers could not devote enough attention to the firm's KFC, Pizza Hut, and Taco Bell chains, they spun them off as a separate company, under the Tricon Global name. PepsiCo managers then turned to concentrating on the drinks businesses. The first thing the new Tricon's managers did was to commit to a new, vigorous global expansion strategy. For example, KFC has about 5,000 U.S. stores, and 6,000 abroad. It has restaurants in countries from Saudi Arabia to Australia, Japan, Malaysia, and Swaziland.

Expanding abroad doesn't mean just duplicating "there" what made you famous "here." Tricon's managers found it was important to adjust offerings to fit local tastes. So, it sells tempura strips in Japan, potatoes and gravy in England, and rice with soy in Thailand.

Vertical Integration The firm need not concentrate on one business. One way to expand into other businesses is through a vertical integration strategy (the other is diversification, discussed below). Vertical integration means owning or controlling the inputs to the firm's processes and/or the channels through which it distributes its products or services. (The former is backward integration, and the latter is forward integration.) Polo Ralph Lauren and Levi's have both integrated forward by opening their own retail stores.

Some firms integrate vertically because that's what their customers want. For example, many electronic devices (including cell phones) aren't built by the firms whose names appear on the products. Instead, huge contract manufacturers like Solectron and Flextronics assemble them. In turn, these contract manufacturers are also vertically integrating. They're buying up design and even shipping firms, because "many are trying to provide cradle to grave services from designing to final ship to customers. They are doing it because that's what customers are requiring," says the head of one industry consulting firm.[19]

Diversification Diversification is a strategy of expanding into related or unrelated products or market segments.[20] Diversification helps the firm spread the risk among several products or markets. However, diversification adds a new risk. It forces the company and its managers to split their attention and resources among several products or markets. To that extent, diversification may undermine the firm's ability to compete successfully in its chosen markets.

A firm can diversify in several ways. Related diversification means diversifying into other industries in such a way that a firm's lines of business still possess some kind of fit.[21] When women's-wear maker Donna Karan expanded into men's clothing, that was related diversification. Campbell's Soup purchased Pepperidge Farm Cookies because it felt that Pepperidge Farm's customer base and channels of distribution were a good fit. British Telecom recently took steps aimed at adding television to its telephone and Internet services.[22] Conglomerate diversification, in contrast, means diversifying into products or markets not related to the firm's present businesses or to one another. For example, Getty Oil diversified into pay television.

Amazon.com pursues related and unrelated diversification. It originally specialized in selling books over the Net. It then expanded its offerings to music and electronics. Recently, it formed partnerships with companies like Toys "R" Us to manage these companies' Internet-based sales. Amazon.com has now formed a partnership with Disney to display showtimes, advertisements, and movie reviews on the Amazon Web site.[23] As illustrated in the accompanying Managing Without Boundaries feature, FedEx recently diversified to better serve its customers.

vertical integration ■ a growth strategy in which a company owns or controls the inputs to its processes and/or its distribution channels.

diversification ■ a corporate strategy of expanding into related or unrelated products or market segments.

related diversification ■ a strategy of expanding into other industries or markets related to a company's current business lines, so that the firm's lines of business still have some kind of fit.

conglomerate diversification ■ diversifying into other products or markets that are not related to a firm's present businesses.

MANAGING WITHOUT BOUNDARIES

The Endless Supply Chain and FedEx

By the end of the 1990s, FedEx founder and president Frederick Smith faced some tough strategic choices. E-mail reduced the need for the firm's famous next-day deliveries. Competitors like UPS were expanding their ground delivery services. And, perhaps most troubling, FedEx customers were finding it less and less necessary to send last-minute emergency packages, because their increasingly efficient just-in-time supply chain management systems were making emergency shipments less and less necessary.

To Fred Smith, the problem contained the seeds of the solution. If our customers want boundaryless supply chains, why not build our strategy around supplying what they want? Why should our customers rely on faxes and phone calls to create the necessary supply chain links among their own customers, vendors, factories, and warehouses? As Smith saw it, FedEx would create software programs that enabled its customers to have what amounted to "off-the-shelf" boundaryless supply chains. Its new strategy would not just be to deliver packages; FedEx would provide the information technology foundation for boundaryless supply chains. In this way, FedEx customers might even be able to eliminate all or most of their warehouses. (After all, you don't need a warehouse if you don't have to store and inventory your products, and you don't have to store and inventory them if they're going to be assembled and delivered just in time to your customers.) To round out his new strategy, Smith is also expanding FedEx's traditional services by adding more land-based trucks and delivery systems. That way, whatever a customer's delivery needs, he or she will be able to depend on FedEx.[24]

Status Quo Strategies Sometimes, the manager will assess the situation and decide that no change in strategy is advisable. A stability or status quo strategy is a more conservative approach. It assumes the organization is satisfied with its rate of growth and product lines. Operationally, this means maintaining its present strategy and continuing to concentrate on its present products and markets. Status quo is one corporate strategy pursued by the lubricant company that makes WD-40: It rarely advertises or aggressively pursues increased market share.

Investment Reduction Strategies Sometimes it turns out that the firm's reach exceeds its grasp. Investment reduction and defensive strategies are corrective actions. They are reactions to overexpansion, ill-conceived diversification, or some other financial emergency. For example, Levi Strauss, suffering a dramatic loss of market share, closed many of its U.S. clothing plants. Retrenchment means the reduction of activities or operations. IBM engaged in a massive retrenchment effort, dramatically reducing (downsizing) the number of its employees and closing many facilities. Divestment means selling or liquidating individual businesses. Divestment usually means the sale of a viable business, while liquidation denotes the sale or abandonment of a nonviable one.

retrenchment ■ *the reduction of activities or operations.*

divestment ■ *selling or liquidating the individual businesses of a larger company.*

For some firms, retrenchment, like discretion, is the better part of valor. For example, Toys "R" Us recently announced that it would lay off almost 2,000 people and close 64 stores in an effort to reduce its costs and compete more effectively against Wal-Mart.[25]

Strategic Alliances and Joint Ventures Some firms want to diversify or integrate or expand abroad, but can't (or don't want to) use their own resources to do so. *Strategic alliances* or *joint ventures* are often the strategies of choice here. They are formal agreements between two or more separate companies, the purpose of which is to enable the organizations to benefit from complementary strengths.

Joint ventures involve joint ownership and operation of a business. For example, as the cell phone market became increasingly competitive, some firms began creating joint ventures. Ericsson and Sony now jointly produce and market cell phones, while Japan's NEC Corp. and Matsushita have discussed a similar alliance. Joint ventures are central to textile maker Frisby Technologies' strategy. To help move the firm into Europe, Frisby formed a joint venture there with Schoeller Textiles. It then signed another partnership with Reh Band, a manufacturer of sport braces in Sweden. Information technology is facilitating global partnerships like these. As Duncan Russell, Frisby's president says, "The Internet era has helped usher in global partnerships because of the ease and speed of communication."[26]

Joint ventures are one example of strategic alliances—agreements between actual or potential competitors to achieve some strategic aim. For example, international airlines like Delta want to offer passengers easier access to continuing flights and services as they travel abroad. Thus, a typical Delta passenger to France might want to transfer easily from an overseas Delta flight to Charles de Gaulle in Paris, to a local flight to

Cannes. Delta could expand globally by buying or merging with a French carrier. Instead, like many airlines, it forms strategic alliances. Delta and Air France are part of the Star Alliance. Passengers on either airline can use the other facilities. The airlines derive many of the benefits of a horizontal integration strategy without actually merging.

The Internet is making competitors' alliances much more common. For example, General Motors, Ford, and Chrysler together created an online exchange to help automate their procurement processes.[27] Suppliers—particularly suppliers of commodity products like gaskets and spark plugs—use the exchange to review the buyer's product specifications, and to bid on the various projects. The exchange gives these giant corporate buyers something akin to their own eBay, since suppliers actively bid for their business online. Other competitors creating exchanges include forest products producers Georgia-Pacific and International Paper, and department store chains Sears and Carrefour.

virtual corporation ■ *a temporary network of independent companies linked by information technology.*

The **virtual corporation** is a modern version of the strategic alliance. It is "a temporary network of independent companies—suppliers, customers, even erstwhile rivals—linked by information technology to share skills, costs, and access to one another's markets."[28] Virtual corporations don't have headquarters staffs, organization charts, or the organizational trappings that we associate with traditional corporations. In fact, they generally aren't corporations at all, in the traditional sense of common ownership or a chain of command. Instead, they are networks of companies, each of which lends the virtual corporation/network its special expertise. Information technology (computer information systems, fax machines, electronic mail, and so on) enables the virtual corporation's far-flung company constituents to stay in touch and make their contributions.[29]

Successful virtual corporations rely on trust and on a sense of "co-destiny." This means recognizing that the fate of each partner and of the whole enterprise is dependent on each partner doing its share.[30] For example, when start-up company TelePad came up with an idea for a handheld, pen-based computer, a virtual corporation was how it breathed life into the idea. An industrial design firm in Palo Alto, California, designed the product; Intel engineers helped with engineering details; several firms helped develop software for the product; and a battery maker helped produce the power supply.[31] (Unfortunately, the idea didn't click, and TelePad went out of business.)

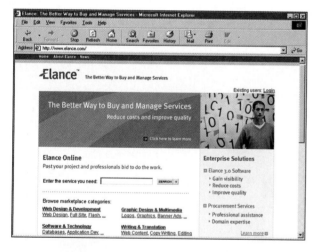

The Internet is also enabling more firms and people to form and to work together through virtual arrangements. The Web site eLance (**www.elance.com**) lets freelance consultants and graphic designers sell their services to businesses; it allows them to post information about their skills and fees.[32] Denver-based graphic designer Serena Rodriguez gets about 10% of her business through that site. She works on projects— virtually and long distance—without seeing or being a formal part of clients like pharmaceuticals manufacturer Merck. Getting a big project often means recruiting other free agents to join your virtual team. For example, says Web designer Andrew Keeler, "I work with lots of people here in San Francisco whom I've never even met. . . . "[33]

Competitive Strategies

Whether a company concentrates on a single business or diversifies into a dozen or more, each business needs a competitive strategy. Michael Porter defines competitive strategy as a plan to establish a profitable and sustainable competitive position against the forces that drive industry competition.[34] The competitive strategy specifies how the company will compete—for instance, based on low cost (Wal-Mart) or high quality (Mercedes Benz). Firms generally pursue one of three competitive strategies: cost leadership, differentiation, or focus.[35] The Marriott experience with Renaissance is an example (see the Management in Action feature).

Without a clear competitive strategy, customers don't know what to make of your product or service. When Marriott International, Inc., bought the Renaissance hotel chain, "nobody knew what to do with [Renaissance]," according to one Marriott senior vice president. The problem was that Renaissance didn't have the clear brand image it needed to differentiate it from other hotel chains. As a result, it really couldn't compete effectively against the Marriott and Starwood chains. After many focus groups and consultations, Marriott decided to turn Renaissance into a chain of chic, up-market hotels. Marriott recently built 15 new Renaissance hotels that fit that image, and it is renovating existing hotels in cities like Miami.[36]   ▪▪▪

Cost Leadership Many well-known firms, such as Southwest Airlines, distinguish themselves by relentlessly minimizing costs. Of course, most firms try to hold down costs. A cost leadership competitive strategy goes beyond this. A business that pursues this strategy aims to be the low-cost leader in an industry. It does this by pursuing absolute cost advantages from all possible sources. Wal-Mart is the classic industry cost leader. It minimizes distribution costs through a satellite-based distribution system linked to suppliers, its stores are plain, and it negotiates the lowest prices from suppliers.

Pursuing a cost leadership strategy requires a tricky balance between low costs and acceptable quality. Southwest Airlines, for instance, keeps its cost per passenger mile below those of most other major airlines while still providing service as good as or better than that of its competitors. Good management—for instance, in terms of maintaining exceptionally high employee morale—help explain such performance.

Differentiation Most firms would love to have a monopoly in order to be able to offer something buyers can get only from them. For many firms, a differentiation strategy is the next best thing. With a differentiation strategy, a firm seeks to be unique in its industry along some dimensions that are valued by buyers.[37] In other words, it picks one or more attributes of the product or service that its buyers perceive as important, and then it positions itself to meet those needs better than its competitors.

As anyone who watches television knows, there's no end to the ways you can try to differentiate your product from those of your competitors. In practice, the dimensions along which you can differentiate range from the product image offered by cosmetics firms to concrete differences such as the product durability emphasized by Caterpillar. Volvo stresses safety, Apple Computer stresses usability, and Mercedes-Benz emphasizes quality.

Focus A business pursuing a focus strategy selects a narrow market segment; it then builds its competitive strategy on serving the customers in that niche better or more cheaply than its generalist competitors. Differentiators (like Volvo) and low-cost leaders (like Wal-Mart) are generalists when it comes to the market. They tend to aim their business at all or most potential buyers.

The basic reason to be a focuser is so you can specialize. Therefore, the manager must ask this: "By focusing on a narrow market, can we provide our target customers with a product or service better or more cheaply than our generalist competitors?" If the answer is "yes" (and if the market is big enough), it may pay to focus. A Pea in the Pod, a chain of maternity stores, focuses on selling stylish clothes to pregnant working women. By specializing in working woman maternity clothes, the company can provide a wider range of such clothes to its target customers than can generalist competitors like Macy's or JCPenney.

The Five Forces Model How a company competes—its competitive strategy—depends on the intensity of the competition in its industry. Years ago, when competition was not so keen in the auto industry, GM was not so concerned with competing on cost and quality. As competition increased, GM (and its competitors) had to seek ways to

cost leadership ▪ *a competitive strategy by which a company aims to be the low-cost leader in its industry.*

differentiation strategy ▪ *a competitive strategy aimed at distinguishing a company from its competitors by focusing on the attributes of its products or services that consumers perceive as important.*

focus strategy ▪ *a strategy in which a business selects a narrow market segment and builds its strategy on serving those in its target market better or more cheaply than its generalist competitors.*

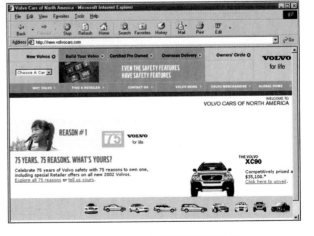

▲ **WEBNOTE** ▪▪▪

Volvo's Web site carries through its product image of safety with a banner that says: "Even the Safety Features Have Safety Features."

www.volvocars.com

Source: ©2002 Volvo Cars of North America, LLC. All rights reserved.

A Pea in the Pod store: Serving a narrow market better.

competitive advantage ■ the basis for superiority over competitors and thus for hoping to claim certain customers.

compete more effectively. They needed to fine-tune their competitive strategies.

To formulate a competitive strategy, the manager should understand the company's competitive situation. For example, how intense are the rivalries among the industry's competitors? What is the nature of that competition—on what basis do the firms compete? Based on that analysis, the manager must find a sustainable competitive advantage, "a basis on which to identify a relative superiority over competitors." Wal-Mart's satellite system is a main source of its competitive advantage. Southwest Airlines has a unique management system that helps it minimize aircraft turnaround time and thus keep its costs lower than its competitors.

All managers strive (or should strive) to find competitive advantages for their firms. Like castle moats, these advantages can help stop or delay new competitors from entering the marketplace. Drug companies like Merck endeavor to invent patentable medicines. Other firms use technology. For example, making it costly for customers to switch to competitors is a potentially powerful entry barrier. Thus, once a travel agent signs up for Sabre, the American Airlines computerized reservation system, it's expensive for that agent to switch to the Delta system. For years, American used its system to maintain an advantage over potential rivals.

Michael Porter's *five forces model* is one tool managers use to analyze their competitive situations and to think through what their competitive advantages should be. Using the model means analyzing what Porter says are the five main forces molding competitive intensity in an industry. Figure 5.5 summarizes these. The model helps managers systematically study each of these five sources of competitive pressure: threat of entry, rivalry among competitors, pressure from substitute products, buyers' bargaining power, and suppliers' bargaining power.[38]

Competition can arise from *new competitors entering* or changing the industry. For example, the competitive landscape for Encyclopaedia Britannica changed dramatically when Microsoft introduced Encarta. Suddenly the market for hard-copy encyclopedias plummeted.

The more easily new competitors can enter the business, the more intense the competition—and, to that extent, the more unattractive the industry. Industries differ in their ease-of-entry. Some industries are so capital-intensive that only the wealthiest companies could even contemplate entering them: The average person couldn't start a car manufacturing business, for instance (although almost anyone could start a lawn service).

Some industries are more warlike than others. *Rivalry among existing competitors* manifests itself in tactics like price competition, advertising battles, and increased

▶ **FIGURE 5–5** ■ ■ ■

Forces Driving Industry Competition

Source: Reprinted with the permission of The Free Press, a division of Simon & Schuster from *Competitive Strategy: Techniques for Analyzing Industries and Competitors* by Michael E. Porter. Copyright © 1980 by The Free Press.

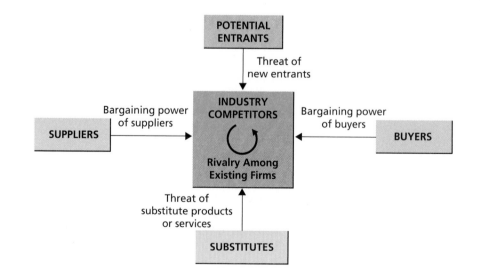

customer service.[39] For many years, for example, the rivalry among law firms and CPA firms was low-key. It is now quite cutthroat. This has prompted most of these firms to cut costs, to offer special pricing plans to clients, and to merge. It has also driven them to find new ways to distinguish themselves from their competitors (in other words, to revamp their competitive strategies). Some differentiate by advertising that they can serve global clients. Others focus (for instance, by specializing entirely in personal accident work). Others went the low-cost route (for instance by advertising "Incorporations—Only $150"). A competitive advantage like American's Sabre reservations system can also help fend off current rivals (not just new ones).

Three other forces shape the nature of an industry's competition. One is *pressure from substitute products*. Substitute products perform the same or similar functions. For example, frozen yogurt is a substitute for ice cream, and synthetics are a substitute for cotton. The more substitute products, then, in effect, the more competitive the industry. The *buyers' bargaining power* is another competitive force. Thus, Toyota has a lot of clout with its suppliers. In general, when the products are standard or undifferentiated (such as apparel elastic), and when buyers face few switching costs, buyers tend to have more power. Sometimes, the *bargaining power of suppliers* molds the competition in an industry. In its lawsuit, for example, the U.S. government claimed that Microsoft exerted tremendous power as the only Windows supplier.

Managers use five forces analysis in two main ways. First, it helps them decide which industries are (or are not) intensely competitive. They use this information to decide which industries they should enter or leave. Figure 5.6 helps illustrate this. For

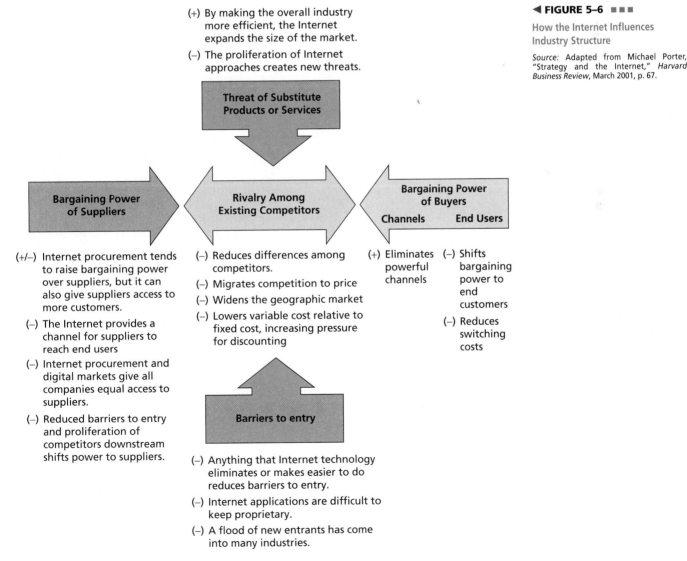

◀ **FIGURE 5–6** ■ ■ ■

How the Internet Influences
Industry Structure

Source: Adapted from Michael Porter, "Strategy and the Internet," *Harvard Business Review*, March 2001, p. 67.

(+) By making the overall industry more efficient, the Internet expands the size of the market.

(−) The proliferation of Internet approaches creates new threats.

Threat of Substitute Products or Services

Bargaining Power of Suppliers

Rivalry Among Existing Competitors

Bargaining Power of Buyers

Channels   End Users

(+/−) Internet procurement tends to raise bargaining power over suppliers, but it can also give suppliers access to more customers.

(−) The Internet provides a channel for suppliers to reach end users

(−) Internet procurement and digital markets give all companies equal access to suppliers.

(−) Reduced barriers to entry and proliferation of competitors downstream shifts power to suppliers.

(−) Reduces differences among competitors.

(−) Migrates competition to price

(−) Widens the geographic market

(−) Lowers variable cost relative to fixed cost, increasing pressure for discounting

(+) Eliminates powerful channels

(−) Shifts bargaining power to end customers

(−) Reduces switching costs

Barriers to entry

(−) Anything that Internet technology eliminates or makes easier to do reduces barriers to entry.

(−) Internet applications are difficult to keep proprietary.

(−) A flood of new entrants has come into many industries.

example, by making it easier for consumers of, say, airline tickets to compare prices, the Internet has made that industry much more competitive. As you can see (and probably know), it shifted the bargaining power for ticket purchases to the end consumer. And since everyone everywhere can now easily compare the prices and pros and cons of a product or service, the Net turned a wide range of products and services into commodities. Similarly, the ability to create a bookstore on the Web inexpensively means the Internet helps create many "new entrant" and "substitution" threats.

Second, the five forces model helps managers think through the competitive landscape and identify potential competitive advantages. The need to keep passengers (who can easily switch to any carrier—remember the buyers' bargaining power) loyal prompted American Airlines to introduce its AAdvantage frequent flyer program, for instance.

Functional Strategies

A functional strategy lays out a department's basic operating policies. Functional strategies flow from and must make sense in terms of the business's overall competitive strategy. Wal-Mart competes as the industry's low-cost leader. To implement this competitive strategy, it formulated departmental functional strategies that made sense for moving Wal-Mart toward its desired competitive position. For example, the distribution department pursued a strategy (satellite-based warehousing) that ultimately drove down distribution costs to a minimum; the company's land development department found locations that fit the firm's customer profile and kept construction costs to a minimum; and the merchandise buyers found sources capable of providing good-quality merchandise at the lowest possible prices. Robert Nardelli's turnaround of retailer Home Depot (see the Management in Action feature) illustrates how a firm's functional strategies flow from its competitive and corporate strategies.

MANAGEMENT IN ACTION   The Home Depot

■■ ■ *A Home Depot megastore in Paramus, New Jersey.*

When Home Depot needed a new strategic plan, CEO Robert Nardelli responded quickly. First, the firm dumped its corporate strategy emphasis on growth and adding new stores, and replaced it with a strategy of improving operating performance throughout its system of stores and warehouses. Today, Nardelli says, "We are generating better operational efficiencies, while rededicating ourselves to customer service as we focus on neighborhood family friendly stores."[40]

Home Depot's new functional strategies mirror the firm's new competitive emphasis on customer service. For example, Nardelli and his team revised store management policies to eliminate customer-unfriendly activities such as stocking the towering shelves during the day. The human resources department got new marching orders to boost customer service training for employees.

Home Depot has not written off the need to grow. It continues to expand abroad. Home Depot is also diversifying—for example, it is expanding its offerings to provide at-home services for consumers who don't want to do the work themselves. (This is potentially a huge opportunity. Home improvement is a $180 billion market, of which Home Depot currently has barely a 1% market share.) Home Depot is also experimenting with new types of stores, including flooring specialty shops, and the Expo Design Center, an upscale home improvement store.

■■ ■ STRATEGIC PLANNING METHODS

Managers don't craft strategic plans in a vacuum. Their plans (hopefully) reflect an intelligent analysis of the strategic situations they face. The aim, you'll recall, is to devise strategies that balance the firm's external opportunities and threats with its internal strengths and weaknesses. The strategy should capitalize on evolving opportunities and address potential threats, so the manager must understand the trends that are driving the industry. At the same time, the strategy must be achievable. It should capitalize on the company's strengths and avoid (or compensate for) the firm's current weaknesses. In this section, we'll discuss the tools managers use for creating their strategies.

However, the availability and popularity of these tools should not lead managers to assume that strategic planning can ever be an entirely mechanical process. The complexity of the factors involved—from global opportunities to competitors' potential moves—is too great for that. Insight and creativity, therefore, always play a vital role. This is especially important at the strategy formulation stage. A *Fortune* article relates how the 17 companies that topped the Fortune 1000 in shareholder return one year did so in large part based on insightful and creative strategies. For example: "While many of its competitors in the biotech industry let the disease lead them to the science, Amgen stays ahead by taking the opposite approach. It develops its drugs by identifying areas of promising research that may lead to breakthrough products."[41]

The creativity-boosting methods discussed in Chapter 2 are useful here. One strategy expert suggests having the top management team spend several hours brainstorming all the possible forces that might influence the firm.[42] Others use the Delphi method and have experts develop alternative future scenarios. The Managing @ the Speed of Thought feature illustrates the Internet's effect on strategizing.

MANAGING @ THE SPEED OF THOUGHT

Strategy for the Internet

Strategies can't be crafted today without considering how information technology (IT) and the Internet could and should affect the company's strategy.

This is nothing new. Wal-Mart has grown quickly thanks to its satellite-based warehouse and distribution system. UPS, the world's largest air and ground package distribution company, has maintained its competitive edge in large part due to the $1 billion annually invested in information technology. UPS drivers use handheld computers to capture customers' signatures, along with pickup, delivery, and time card information, and automatically transmit this information to headquarters via a cellular telephone network. For companies like these and thousands more, IT lies at the heart of their strategies.

But it's likely that the Internet's effect on companies' strategies will be even more profound. Online companies like Amazon.com are perhaps the most obvious examples here. Consider how the strategies of traditional booksellers like Barnes & Noble and countless smaller ones have had to change. Barnes & Noble has had to create its own on-line bookstore. Many smaller booksellers have had to reconsider whether they even want to or can remain in business, given the new competitive landscape. And in 2000, AOL and Time Warner combined. Their new strategy (less than fully successful to date) involved using Time Warner's cable access and content along with AOL's system to reach hundreds of millions of customers.

It's not just information businesses that must adapt to the Internet.[43] Two experts argue that even manufacturing businesses are or will be highly dependent on the Net. For example, GE's divisions used to purchase supplies from firms with which they had long and established relationships. Today, GE has created special online purchasing Web sites, and any supplier can bid on the GE orders. That drives down GE's purchasing costs and gives it a new competitive advantage; meanwhile, its former suppliers must adapt their strategies to make themselves a lot more Web friendly.[44] GE's divisions have also been told to create Internet businesses that could replace their traditional brick-and-mortar businesses.

Choosing the Right Strategic Planning Tools

Strategic planning always involves predicting the future, but some futures are more predictable than others. This means managers must adjust their strategic analysis methods to the needs of the situation. For example, the president of Delta Airlines needs a strategy for dealing with low-cost airlines, such as JetBlue, that are entering Delta's markets. While such planning involves some uncertainty, this situation and the range of Delta's strategic options are fairly predictable. On the other hand, Delta (and the other airlines) were blindsided by the 9/11 terrorist attacks. How do you plan for things you may not even realize may occur? Managers use different tools to cope with planning for predictable and less predictable situations. Let's look at some specifics.

Tools for When the Future Is More Predictable

Imagine you are the president of Delta Airlines. You need a strategy to deal with the possible entrance of a low-cost, no-frills airline into one of your major markets. What strategies might you pursue? Options include introducing a low-cost Delta service, surrendering the low-cost niche to the new entrant, or competing more aggressively on price and service to drive the entrant out of the market.[45]

The question is, What information do you need to make your decision? Generally, the manager needs the sorts of information provided by traditional planning tools like those explained in Chapter 4. For example, you need *market research* on the size of the different markets and on the likely responses of customers in each market segment to different combinations of pricing and service. You need *competitive information* about the new entrant's competitive objectives. In addition, the manager has available a number of traditional strategic planning tools. These include SWOT analysis, environmental scanning, benchmarking, the TOWS matrix, and portfolio analysis (BCG Matrix). Let's look at these.

SWOT Analysis The company's strengths, weaknesses, opportunities, and threats loom large in any strategic analysis. Strategic planning involves identifying the strategic actions that will balance (1) the firm's strengths and weaknesses with (2) its external opportunities and threats. The manager wants to take advantage of opportunities, while capitalizing on company strengths. He or she wants to anticipate and make accommodations for threats, and to reduce (or avoid businesses that might depend on) weaknesses. *Opportunities* might include the possibility of serving additional customers in the face of weakening competition, or the chance to enter foreign markets due to falling trade barriers. *Threats* might include the likely entry of new lower-cost foreign competitors, rising sales of substitute products, and slowing market growth. *Strengths* might include adequate financial resources, economies of scale, and proprietary technology. *Weaknesses* include lack of strategic direction, obsolete facilities, and lack of managerial depth and talent.

SWOT analysis ■ *a strategic planning tool for analyzing a company's strengths, weaknesses, opportunities, and threats.*

Managers use SWOT analysis (see Figure 5.7) to consolidate information regarding the firm's internal strengths and weaknesses and external opportunities and threats. SWOT analysis serves two purposes: (1) It supplies illustrative generic opportunities, threats, strengths, and weaknesses to guide the manager's analysis; and (2) It provides a standardized four-quadrant format for compiling the company's situational information.

▶ **FIGURE 5–7** ■ ■ ■

SWOT Matrix with Examples of a Company's Strengths, Weaknesses, Opportunities, and Threats

POTENTIAL STRENGTHS	POTENTIAL WEAKNESSES
• Market leadership	• Large inventories
• Strong research and development	• Excess capacity for market
• High-quality products	• Management turnover
• Cost advantages	• Weak market image
• Patents	• Lack of management depth
POTENTIAL OPPORTUNITIES	**POTENTIAL THREATS**
• New overseas markets	• Market saturation
• Falling trade barriers	• Threat of takeover
• Competitors failing	• Low-cost foreign competition
• Diversification	• Slower market growth
• Economy rebounding	• Growing government regulation

Economic Trends
(such as recession, inflation, employment, monetary policies)

_____

_____

_____

_____

Competitive Trends
(such as competitors' strategic changes, market/customer trends, entry/exit of competitors, new products from competitors)

_____

_____

_____

_____

Political Trends
(such as national/local election results, special interest groups, legislation, and regulation/deregulation)

_____

_____

_____

_____

Technological Trends
(such as introduction of new production/distribution technologies, rate of product obsolescence, trends in availability of supplies and raw materials)

_____

_____

_____

_____

Social Trends
(such as demographic trends, mobility, education, evolving values)

_____

_____

_____

_____

Geographic Trends
(such as opening/closing of new markets, factors affecting current plant/office facilities location decisions)

_____

_____

_____

_____

Environmental Scanning Managers traditionally scan six key areas (Figure 5.8) to identify opportunities or threats to list in their SWOT analyses. **Environmental scanning** is the process of gathering and compiling information about relevant environmental forces. The six traditional areas to scan include:

environmental scanning ■ *the process of gathering and compiling information about relevant environmental forces.*

1. *Economic trends.* The level of economic activity and the flow of money, goods, and services. For example, the U.S. government now projects that the country's economic growth through 2006 will be below that of 1995–2000. What opportunities and threats would such a trend imply for businesses thinking of expanding in the United States and abroad?
2. *Competitive trends.* Actions taken or to be taken by current and potential competitors. For example, Microsoft's move into Internet browsers helped push Netscape into the waiting arms of AOL, which acquired it.

3. *Political trends*. Factors related to actions of local, national, and foreign governments. For example, R. J. Reynolds must monitor trends in the regulation of cigarette smoking around the globe, and most cigarette firms have diversified into other businesses as regulations have become more widespread.

4. *Technological trends*. The development of new or existing technology, including electronics, machines, tools, and processes. Between 1998 and 2000, many firms invested heavily by expanding into the Internet; others, such as Disney, held back, wisely predicting that the Internet bubble would soon burst.

5. *Social and demographic trends*. The way people live and the nature of the people in a society, including what they value. In the United States for instance, the proportion of Hispanic people is rising quickly. This prompted NBC to purchase the Spanish language network Telemundo.

6. *Geographic trends*. Climate, natural resources, and so forth. In Florida, for instance, a long-term cooling trend has reduced the growing area for oranges. Florida growers have formed alliances with South American firms, which now supply much of the "Florida oranges."

Managers actually "scan" in several ways. Some have employees monitor key areas (economic, social), by scouring publications like the *New York Times* and the *Wall Street Journal* as well as the Internet, consultants' reports, information services, and industry newsletters. Others use consultants called environmental scanners. These experts read a variety of publications to search for environmental changes that could affect the client firm. Some firms set up Internet news services to continuously and automatically screen thousands of news stories and provide precisely the types of stories in which they're interested.

Benchmarking Sometimes, a company must build its strengths or reduce its weaknesses to become a stronger competitor. To do so, the manager first wants to discover how his or her firm compares to other firms. For example, why create a new way to handle customer inquiries, when L.L. Bean already has a world-class system for doing so? Managers often analyze L.L. Bean's order taking and fulfillment system. Most experts view it as a best-practice company for the way it expeditiously handles customers' questions and fulfills orders. **Benchmarking** is the process through which a company learns how to become the best in some area by carefully analyzing the practices of other companies that already excel in that area (best-practices companies). The basic process typically follows several guidelines, as shown in Checklist 5.3.[46]

benchmarking ■ *a process through which a company learns how to become the best in one or more areas by analyzing and comparing the practices of other companies that excel in those areas.*

CHECKLIST 5.3 ■ How to Benchmark

☑ Focus on a specific problem and define it carefully—for example, "What order-fulfillment processes do best-practices companies use in the mail-order business?"

☑ Use the employees who will actually implement those changes to identify the best-practices companies and to conduct on-site studies.

☑ Be willing to share information with others.

☑ Avoid sensitive issues such as pricing, and don't look for new product information.

☑ Keep information you receive confidential.

The TOWS Matrix The TOWS matrix helps managers answer this question: "What are the strategies—the courses of action—we can pursue, given our firm's opportunities, threats, strengths, and weaknesses?

The TOWS matrix picks up where SWOT analysis (and scanning and benchmarking) leaves off. The manager uses the **TOWS matrix** to help visualize what strategies to use to address the firm's strengths, weaknesses, opportunities, and threats. Figure 5.9 shows a TOWS matrix for a large cinema company. You fill in the TOWS by:

TOWS matrix ■ *a strategic planning tool that presents possible strategies for addressing the firm's strengths, weaknesses, opportunities, and threats.*

1. Filling in the opportunities, threats, strengths, and weaknesses from your environmental scan, benchmarking, and SWOT analyses.

2. You develop four possible sets of strategies. SO strategies capitalize on your strengths to take advantage of your opportunities. WO strategies capitalize on

opportunities to overcome your weaknesses. ST strategies use your strengths to address impending threats. WT strategies aim to reduce your weaknesses and address your threats.

Portfolio Analysis: The BCG Matrix Most firms (especially large ones) are in several businesses at once. For example, PepsiCo pursued corporate strategies of diversification and vertical integration, and now it has business divisions for things like PepsiCola and Frito-Lay. How do you decide which businesses to keep in (or drop from) a portfolio? Managers use portfolio analysis tools like the BCG (for Boston Consulting Group) matrix to help them decide. The BCG matrix helps managers identify the relative attractiveness of each of a firm's businesses. Like the TOWS matrix, it helps managers decide the best strategy to pursue for each of their company's businesses.

The BCG matrix assumes that a business's attractiveness depends on two things—on the growth rate of the business, and on the business's market share. As

> **BCG matrix** ■ *a strategic planning tool that helps a manager assess a business unit's attractiveness based on its growth rate and market share.*

▼ **FIGURE 5–9** ■ ■ ■

Cineplex Odeon TOWS Matrix

Source: Fred David, *Strategic Management* (Upper Saddle River, NJ: Prentice Hall, 2001), p. 207.

	STRENGTHS—S	WEAKNESSES—W
	1. Located in large population centers 2. Positive cash flow 3 years running 3. Double the industry concession sales rate 4. Many cost-cutting measures in place 5. Upgraded audio in many places 6. Profitable in Canada	1. Poor labor relations 2. Current ratio of 0.25 3. Flat operating cost through falling revenue 4. Triple the G&A expenses of Carmike 5. Significant losses in the United States 6. Management concentrating on market share 7. Restrictive covenants set by lenders
OPPORTUNITIES—O 1. Approached by most major chains for potential merger 2. Opening economies in Eastern Europe 3. Rebounding attendance (up 6.4%) 4. Videotape industry worth estimated $18 billion vs. $6.4 billion for movie theaters 5. Foreign per capita income growth outpacing the United States	**SO STRATEGIES** 1. Open theaters in Eastern Europe (S1, O2, O5)	**WO STRATEGIES** 1. Pursue merger with American Cinemas (O1, O2, W3, W4, W5, W6)
THREATS—T 1. 80% of all households own VCRs 2. Aging population 3. Dependence on successful movies 4. Switch from bid to allocation for licenses 5. Seasonality for movie releases 6. Increased competition in exhibition	**ST STRATEGIES** 1. Open 50 video rental stores in 10 markets (S1, S6, T1, T3, T5) 2. Construct 20 multidimensional entertainment complexes (S1, T3, T5, T6)	**WT STRATEGIES** 1. Reduce corporate overhead (W3, W4, T3, T5, T6) 2. Divest U.S. operations (W2, W3, W4, W5, W6, T6)

After the position of each of the company's businesses is plotted, a decision can be made regarding which businesses will be cash resources and which will be cash users.

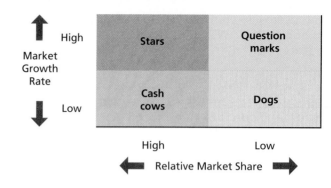

shown in Figure 5.10, you do this by mapping growth rate and relative competitive position (market share) for each of the company's businesses. *Stars* are businesses in high-growth industries in which the company has a high relative market share. For example, Intel's microprocessor business has a high growth rate, and Intel has a relatively high market share. Star businesses usually require large infusions of cash to sustain growth. Their strong market positions help them generate the needed cash.

Question marks are businesses in high-growth industries that have low market shares. These business units face a dilemma: They are in attractive high-growth industries, but they have such low market shares that they can't fend off larger competitors. A company must either divert cash from its other businesses to boost the question mark's market share or get out of the business.

Cash cows are businesses in low-growth industries that enjoy high relative market shares. Being in a low-growth, unattractive industry argues against making large cash infusions into these businesses. However, their high market share generally allows them to generate high sales and profits for years, even without much new investment. Cash cows can help drive a firm's future success. For example, Kodak's consumer film unit is a classic cash cow: The market is shrinking, but Kodak has a commanding market share. In one recent year, Kodak was, therefore, able to generate over $1 billion in free cash flow to help nurture growth businesses like digital photography.[47]

Finally, *dogs* are low market-share businesses in low-growth, unattractive industries. Having a low market share puts the business in jeopardy relative to its larger competitors. As a result, dogs can quickly become "cash traps," absorbing cash to support a hopeless and unattractive situation. Managers usually sell dogs to raise cash for stars and question marks.

■ ■ ■ *Kodak's new digital camera, PalmPix, at its debut in 2000 at the world's largest computer trade fair.*

A Tool for Dealing with Less Predictable Occurrences

It's sometimes not the predictable threats but the unpredictable ones that have the most profound effects on a company's business. Late in 2001, most airlines had elaborate SWOT, TOWS, and BCG-type planning models showing how they would respond if two or more of their competitors decided to merge, or if a new competitor entered one of their markets. What most of them didn't have was a plan to deal with a massive terrorist attack, or with the human and economic consequences of such a disaster. Yet, it was such an attack that molded the future course of many airlines after September 11.

Predicting the unpredictable is, of course, something of a contradiction in terms. In endeavoring to do so, many firms use the scenario planning method. You might think of scenario planning as "imagining alternative futures." Proponents define scenarios as

scenario ■ *a hypothetical sequence of events constructed for the purpose of focusing attention on causal processes and decision points and thereby helping the manager anticipate events and thus create plans for them.*

hypothetical sequences of events constructed for the purpose of focusing attention on causal processes and decision points. They answer two kinds of questions: (1) Precisely how might some hypothetical situation come about, step by step, and (2) What alternatives exist, for each situation at each step, for preventing, diverting, or facilitating the process?[48]

Shell Oil has long used this approach (it's also known as "The Shell Method").[49] As one of its officers said, "The Shell approach to strategic planning is, instead of forecasting, to use scenarios, which are 'stories' about alternative possible futures. These stories promote a discussion of possibilities other than the 'most likely' one, and encourage the consideration of 'what-if' questions."[50]

Management typically asks the planners to produce scenarios that address specific possibilities. For example, in one exercise, Shell's planners were asked to write stories about their "worst possible nightmares, given the forces they deemed most crucial to their company."[51] Shell was thus reportedly the only oil company prepared when, some years ago, a few oil-producing countries took control away from the oil firms and triggered huge price increases. Shell calls its most recent scenarios "The Spirit of the Coming Age" and "Dynamics as Usual." The first foresees a gradual shift from fossil fuels to renewable energy; the second outlines what might happen if a technical breakthrough triggers a more sudden shift.

Companies don't just use scenario planning to produce nightmare scenarios. Some managers just ask planners to develop narratives of a fundamentally different but better world.[52] For example, one Austrian insurance firm used scenarios to anticipate changes in eastern and central Europe and to enter new markets there. Electrolux uses it to spot new consumer markets; and Krone, a wiring and cable supplier in Berlin, uses scenario planning to develop new product ideas.

One obvious reason to do scenario planning is to shake management out of its traditional ways of thinking. The scenario planning process should, therefore, force managers to "think out of the box" by confronting them with new and innovative possibilities, and with their implications. To do this, keep these scenario planning principles in mind (see Checklist 5.4):

CHECKLIST 5.4 ■ Scenario Planning Principles

☑ Scenarios have value only to the extent that they inform decision makers and influence decision making.

☑ Scenarios add value to decision making only when managers and others use them to systematically shape questions about the present and the future, and to guide how to go about answering them.

☑ In each step of developing scenarios, the emphasis must be on identifying, challenging, and refining the substance of managers' mindsets and knowledge.

☑ Alternative projections about a given future must challenge managers' current mental models by creating tension among ideas, hypotheses, perspectives, and assumptions.

☑ The dialogue and discussion spawned by the consideration of alternative futures should directly affect managers' knowledge.

☑ Scenarios should include enough indicators so that managers can track how the future is actually evolving so that the learning and adaptations stimulated by the scenarios are continuous.[53]

■ *Application Example* Your cousin, who owns a small travel agency in Naples, Florida, has just come to you with your first-ever consulting assignment. He needs a strategic plan, and he needs it quickly. This is March 2002, and Delta Airlines has just basically eliminated sales commissions on all or most ticket sales. The airlines want to sell the tickets themselves, preferably over the Internet. He's going to have to start charging his customers to book tickets for them. Many may simply do it for free on the Internet. He may lose (he fears) half his clientele. So, he needs a new strategic plan. Where would you start? Now is your opportunity to apply all you've learned about strategic planning.

What can he tell you about his current situation? He's basically in three businesses now. About a third of his business comes from corporate clients. Another third comes from selling tour packages to places like Disney World and the Caribbean. The final third comes from selling cruises, mostly to the Caribbean. Ten percent of his business comes in over the Internet. The rest is from past clients or from word of mouth, all local. He's not sure he has any huge competitive advantage. However, he does have a fine reputation. And, he has exceptionally good relationships with the firms that package the tours he sells. He has 6 employees and earns about $60,000 for himself each year, after paying all expenses.

You interview him, speak with travel associations, and do some Internet and library research to create a situational analysis for his industry. (Luckily, you find that several stockbroker firms, such as Merrill Lynch, have already published travel industry analyses for their clients.) You use the environmental scan and SWOT to compile what you find. In brief, *opportunities* include a fast-growing cruise market, more retirees looking for tours, and a booming business for selling travel services via the Net. *Threats* include airlines continuing to squeeze agents, growing competition among agents to sell cruises, and more consolidation (with big firms like Liberty Travel gobbling up smaller firms, and some, like Rosenbluth Travel, specializing in servicing corporate clients). *Strengths* include a good "Rolodex" of clients, good relationships with tour packagers, a successful Web site, and five very loyal and competent employees. *Weaknesses* include too small a scale to adequately serve the corporate clients (who require a great deal of time), inadequate funds to advertise, and a diminishing source of revenues, now that airlines are cutting commissions.

You compile all this in a TOWS matrix. Two of the many possible strategies you come up with are:

1. *An "SO" strategy.* Use your strong relationship with tour packagers to take advantage of the opportunity to sell more tours to retirees.
2. *A "WO" strategy.* Form one or more joint ventures with retirees' associations (such as AARP) to split the cost of advertising your tours to their members.

You also do a BCG analysis. For your cousin's firm in the Naples area, the corporate travel business is basically a cash cow. He has a decent market share. However, companies are cutting back—for instance, using more video conferencing—so the market isn't growing. Both the cruise and tour businesses fall in the question-mark quadrant. He has a decent market share, and both markets are growing fast. Perhaps he can reduce his corporate business marketing efforts, and use the revenues that the existing corporate clients generate to expand his cruise and tour efforts.

So, here is your suggestion. In terms of corporate strategy, start to concentrate more on the cruises and tours. Use your strong relationship with tour packagers to take advantage of the opportunity to sell more tours to retirees. (Try to sign exclusive sales agreements with the tour packagers for the Naples area.) Form joint ventures with one or more local and national retirees' associations (such as AARP) to split the cost (and revenues) of advertising cruises and tours to members. Keep your current corporate clients for now, but gradually phase out this part of your business.

Your suggested competitive strategies include differentiation (for now) and focus (probably, in the near future). Differentiate the firm by offering the only tour packages in the Naples area from these particular tour packagers. Consider moving to a focus strategy, in which the travel agency starts to focus on the Naples area retiree market and its needs.

Next, lay out a few specific goals: revenues next year from each business line; how many tour packagers to sign agreements with, and by when; and how many retirees' associations to form joint ventures with, and by when. Your cousin is set to embark on his new strategy.

■■■ STRATEGIC PLANNING IN PRACTICE

Managers in practice invariably come face to face with a dilemma: Given a firm's opportunities and threats, and its strengths and weaknesses, should we simply "fit" our capabilities to the opportunities and threats that we see, or, should we stretch well beyond our capabilities to take advantage of an opportunity? On this issue, there are two points of view.

Achieving Strategic Fit

Strategic planning expert Michael Porter emphasizes the "fit" point of view. He says that all of the firm's activities must be tailored to or fit its strategy, by ensuring that the firm's functional strategies support its corporate and competitive strategies: "It's this 'fit' that breathes life into the firm's strategy."[54]

For example, Southwest Airlines pursues a low-cost leader strategy, and then "tailors all its activities to deliver low-cost convenient service on its particular type of short-haul route."[55,56] It gets fast, 15-minute turnarounds at the gate, so it can keep its planes flying longer hours than rivals, and have more departures with fewer aircraft. It also shuns frills like meals, assigned seats, and premium classes of service on which other full-service airlines build their competitive strategies.

■ ■ *A busy Southwest ticket counter at Albany's International Airport in upstate New York.*

Figure 5.11 illustrates this. The larger circles represent the activities at the heart of Southwest's low-cost activity system: limited passenger services; frequent, reliable departures; lean, highly productive ground and gate crews; high aircraft utilization; very low ticket prices; and short-haul, point-to-point routes. Various subactivities and decisions support each of these activities. For example,

▼ **FIGURE 5–11** ■ ■ ■

The Southwest Airlines' Activity System

Companies like Southwest tailor all their activities so that they fit and contribute to making their strategies a reality.

Source: Reprinted by permission of *Harvard Business Review*. From "What Is Strategy?" by Michael E. Porter, November–December 1996. Copyright © 1996 by the President and Fellows of Harvard College; all rights reserved.

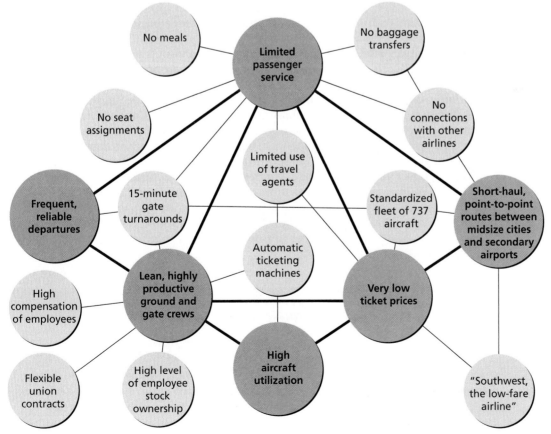

limited passenger service means things like no meals, no seat assignments, no baggage transfers, and limited use of travel agents. Highly productive ground crews mean high compensation, flexible union contracts, and a high level of employee stock ownership. Southwest's success is more than just its low-cost strategy; it's a product of a well-managed system in which each functional component fits each other component and the firm's low-cost strategy and strengths perfectly.

Strategy As Stretch and Leverage

leverage ■ *to gain a competitive edge by concentrating a company's resources on key strategic goals or competencies.*

Strategy experts Gary Hamel and C. K. Prahalad caution against becoming too enamored with the notion of strategic fit.[57] They agree that every company "must ultimately effect a fit between its resources and the opportunities it pursues."[58] However, they argue that being preoccupied with fit can limit growth. They argue for "stretch." They say that leveraging resources—supplementing what you have and doing more with what you have—can be more important than just fitting the strategic plan to current resources. For example, "If modest resources were an insurmountable deterrent to future leadership, GM, Phillips, and IBM would not have found themselves on the defensive with Honda, Sony, and Compaq."[59] Thus, Wal-Mart years ago focused its relatively limited resources on building a satellite-based distribution system, thereby gaining a competitive advantage that helped it overtake Kmart.

The Strategic Role of Core Competencies

core competencies ■ *the collective learning in the organization, especially the knowledge of how to coordinate diverse design and production skills and integrate multiple streams of technologies.*

According to Hamel and Prahalad, it's the firm's "core competencies" that it should leverage. They define core competencies as "the collective learning in the organization, especially [knowing] how to coordinate diverse production skills and integrate multiple streams of technologies."[60]

Canon Corporation provides one example. Over the years it developed three core competencies: precision mechanics, fine optics, and microelectronics. These competencies reflect collective learning and skills that cut across traditional departmental lines; they are dispersed among employees throughout the company, ready to be drawn upon by Canon. They are the end result of how Canon has hired, trained, and nurtured its employees.

Canon builds its new businesses on these core competencies. It starts by drawing on these core competencies to produce core component products like miniature electronic controls and fine lenses. Then, it builds products and businesses—digital cameras, laser printers, and fax machines, for instance—around these core products.

Growing its businesses and products out of a few core competencies makes it easier for Canon to change its product mix quickly. Regardless of how the demand for products shifts—for instance, from one type of fax machine to another—Canon's "assets" are in its core competencies (precision mechanics, fine optics, and microelectronics). If Canon's managers foresee changes in customer demand, they can reach across departmental lines to marshal these competencies. Suppose they sense the need for a new consumer electronic product, like a tiny camera, that takes PC-based pictures. Canon managers can "harmonize know-how in miniaturization, microprocessor design, material science, and ultra thin precision casting—the same skills it applies in its miniature card calculators, pocket TVs, and digital watches—to design and produce the new camera."[61]

Managers must guard against misdefining their core competencies, as the Management in Action feature shows.

MANAGEMENT IN ACTION Circuit City

In the early 1990s, Circuit City managers decided to start the CarMax chain. Between 1993 and 1998, they opened 23 CarMax stores in seven states. With more store openings planned, it suddenly became apparent that their strategy wasn't working. *Barron's* magazine called CarMax "a disaster." Analysts felt that CarMax's losses were driving down Circuit City's results. As new car prices fell or held steady, it became harder for CarMax to sell its top-of-the-line used cars.

What prompted Circuit City to enter the used car business in the first place? Some argue it's because managers misdefined the company's core competency. Management may have felt its core competency was not "selling televisions and other electronics" but "operating superefficient megastores with sophisticated distribution systems." If so, management may have been mistaken.[62]

Starbucks recently ran into a similar situation with its ill-fated foray into serving sandwiches. The idea was to sell prepackaged, high-quality sandwiches made fresh each morning by employees at a central location and then to sell the sandwiches in the stores throughout the day. But customers wanted fresh sandwiches, not prepackaged ones, and the typical Starbucks isn't set up to make sandwiches. Today, Starbucks is back to selling mostly coffee. As founder Howard Schultz put it, "We recognize more than ever our core competency is roasting and selling the best coffee in the world."[63]

SUMMARY ▪▪▪

1. A primary task of top management is to think through the mission of the business and ask, "What is our business, and what should it be?" Strategic management is the process of identifying and pursuing the organization's mission by aligning internal capabilities with the external demands of the environment.

2. There are five steps in the strategy management process: define the business and develop a mission; perform external and internal analyses; translate the mission into strategic objectives; formulate a strategy to achieve the strategic objectives; implement the strategy; and evaluate performance and initiate corrective adjustments as required. Strategic planning includes the first three steps of this process.

3. There are three main types of strategies. Corporate-level strategy identifies the portfolio of businesses that in total will comprise the corporation and the ways in which these businesses will relate; competitive strategy identifies how to build and strengthen the business's long-term competitive position in the marketplace; and functional strategies identify the basic courses of action that each department will pursue to contribute to the attainment of its goals.

4. Each type of strategy includes specific standard or generic strategies. Generic corporate strategies include concentration, market penetration, geographic expansion, product development, horizontal integration, vertical integration, and diversification, as well as status quo and retrenchment.

5. Generic competitive strategies include being a low-cost leader, differentiator, or focuser. Formulating a specific competitive strategy requires understanding the competitive forces that determine how intense the competitive rivalries are and how best to compete. The five forces model helps managers understand the five big forces of competitive pressure in an industry: threat of entry, intensity of rivalry among existing competitors, pressure from substitute products, bargaining power of buyers, and bargaining power of suppliers.

6. Creating strategic plans involves identifying environmental forces, formulating a plan, and creating implementation plans. Useful techniques include SWOT analysis, environmental scanning, benchmarking, the TOWS matrix, portfolio analysis, and scenario planning.

7. Implementing the organization's strategy involves several activities, among them achieving strategic fit, leveraging the company's core competencies, and effectively leading the change process.

KEY TERMS ▪▪▪

strategic planning 112
strategic management 112
vision 113
mission 113
strategy 115
strategic control 116
corporate-level strategy 116
competitive strategy 116
functional strategy 116
market penetration 117
geographic expansion 117

product development 117
horizontal integration 117
vertical integration 118
diversification 118
related diversification 118
conglomerate diversification 118
retrenchment 119
divestment 119
virtual corporation 120
cost leadership 121
differentiation strategy 121

focus strategy 121
competitive advantage 122
SWOT analysis 126
environmental scanning 127
benchmarking 128
TOWS matrix 128
BCG matrix 129
scenario 130
leverage 134
core competencies 134

COMPANION WEBSITE ■■■

 We invite you to visit the Dessler Companion Website at **www.prenhall.com/dessler** for this chapter's Internet resources.

EXPERIENTIAL EXERCISES ■■■

1. With three to four other students in the class, form a strategic management group for your college or university. Your assignment is to develop the outline of a strategic plan for the college or university, including such things as mission and vision statements; strategic goals; corporate, competitive, and functional strategies; and a summary of what "business" your college or university is in. In preparing your plan, make sure to produce a SWOT chart, showing the main strengths, weaknesses, opportunities, and threats the college or university is facing. If possible, prior to meeting, interview some adminis-trators, faculty members, and students about their knowledge of the current strategic plan.

2. You are the newest member of the design team for a major toy manufacturer. You just saw a show on the A&E channel that identified the most popular toys of the last century. The top five were, in ascending order, Playdoh, Lionel trains, Barbie, crayons, and the yo-yo. Your job is to design a new toy that could be the top toy of the twenty-first century. In a team of four to five students, do a strategic analysis for the purpose of developing such a toy, and propose a toy.

CASE STUDY ■■■

STRATEGY TIME AT MARTHA STEWART LIVING

Very few new companies begin the initial public offering (IPO) stage of their history with the brand identity of Martha Stewart Living Omnimedia (stock symbol MSO). On the day of her company's IPO, Martha Stewart came to Wall Street to serve croissants, muffins, and scrambled egg brioches to startled traders on the floor of the stock exchange. By the end of the day, Stewart's small company (only 385 employees) had raised $2.3 billion in capital. The question is, with the recent problems of its founder and CEO, does MSO have the strategy required to gain and sustain competitive success?

Stewart describes her firm as a leading creator of how-to content and related products and services for homemakers and other consumers. The firm's prospectus makes clear that MSO intends to leverage the well-known Martha Stewart brand name to gain access to key promotional and distribution channels.

Stewart's business is built around seven core content areas: home, cooking and entertaining, gardening, crafts, holidays, keeping, and weddings. For each of these areas, the MSO team puts together a library of articles, books, television programs, newspaper columns, radio segments, and products. The firm has two strategic objectives: Provide original how-to content and information to as many consumers as possible, and turn consumers into doers by offering them the information and products they need for do-it-yourself ingenuity the "Martha Stewart way."

MSO distributes its content through a broad media platform that includes two magazines, an Emmy Award–winning television program, a weekly TV segment on *CBS Early Show* (interrupted intermittently when Ms. Stewart refused to answer on-air questions from CBS staff about her financial dealings), a daily cable TV program, a weekly syndicated newspaper column, a radio program, periodic primetime television broadcasts, and 27 how-to books to date. Stewart's two magazines alone, *Martha Stewart Living* and *Martha Stewart Weddings*, have an estimated readership of 9.9 million per month. MSO also has a Web site that now boasts close to one million registered users.

In addition to its impressive communication outlets, the company has created what it calls its "omnimerchandising" platform. The platform consists of products with the Martha Stewart name. At the time of the IPO, the company had more than 2,800 distinct variations of products, including bed and bath products, interior paints, craft kits, outdoor furniture, and garden tools, as well as a line of branded products sold at Kmart. The Kmart partnership recently raised concerns when Kmart filed for bankruptcy protection. Products are also marketed through national department stores, the upscale catalogue *Martha by Mail*, and the online store.

While Stewart's brand name has given her firm a great start, to sustain advantage, MSO plans to position itself as "a leading authority across key categories of domestic arts." To accomplish this goal, the firm plans to capitalize on what it sees as a number of key strengths besides its brand name: a highly experienced team of creative and business personnel; strong relationships with key distribution, fulfillment, and marketing channels; an extensive research and development process; and an extensive library of high-quality products and designs.

The firm has very specific strategies to build revenue over the next few years. These include plans to expand the company's merchandising along its core content lines, amortize (spread) the cost of developing high-quality content by sharing it across media and merchandising platforms, exploit the revenue potential of the Internet, and cross-sell and promote its brands.

One of MSO's strategies is somewhat controversial. The firm has publicly stated that it plans to "evolve our brands through team-based content and reduce dependence on our founder." Some analysts feel it is dangerous to remind the market of Stewart's vulnerability, since so much of the promotional strategy depends on her many media appearances. The company has taken out a $67 million life insurance policy to reduce its exposure to risk in the event that it loses Stewart for any reason. However, even this move has made some investors edgy. At age 59, Stewart is only six years away from the time the average person retires. Recent questions about her possibly trading on inside stock information prompted additional concerns. Currently, Martha Stewart owns 62% of the outstanding shares of MSO.

Consumer companies generally face tremendous pressure. First, consumer preferences can be unpredictable. Fads like Furbys and Pokémon are nearly impossible to predict. There has also been significant consolidation in retail distribution channels. The risk here is that in losing one key distributor, MSO could lose several chains of stores. Furthermore, MSO's competitors will not sit still.

Stewart's new publicly traded firm is off to a great start. She clearly has a well-known brand name, and her slogan, "It's a good thing," is memorable. Now, MSO will have to move past image and slogans to the difficult task of effectively implementing strategy.

Discussion Questions

1. Which of the generic corporate strategies seems best to describe MSO? What competitive strategy does it seem to be pursuing for most of its lines?

2. Based on what you know about MSO or can find out, to what extent do the firm's activities seem to reflect a well-thought-out policy of strategic fit?

3. Perform a SWOT analysis for MSO.

4. Based on your results from question 3, have Stewart and her team positioned MSO so that it can gain and sustain a competitive advantage? If yes, what is the advantage?

5. What are the strategic implications of having a company like MSO so dependent on a single "star," and what strategies would you suggest to deal with those implications?

YOU BE THE CONSULTANT ■■■

JET BLUE: A WINNING STRATEGY

In the hugely competitive airline industry, you'd better have the right strategy, or it doesn't pay to open for business. In the 20 or so years since the U.S. government deregulated the airline industry, dozens of airlines have gone out of business, either because they had the wrong strategy, or a less-than-competent management, or both.

In terms of its corporate-level strategy, JetBlue's plan wasn't that different from the plan followed by other industry start-ups. Its management stuck to the airline business and (in terms of geography) started small, with several flights from JFK to Fort Lauderdale and from JFK to upper New York State. Gradually, it pursued geographic expansion, adding a JFK-to-Long Beach route, and it soon contemplated new routes—to Washington State, and to Canada, for instance. The basic idea is to take care of all of its airplane servicing in-house, but for now contractors at some airports, such as JFK, handle JetBlue's servicing.

It is with respect to its competitive strategy that JetBlue really distinguished itself. Most companies opt to be either differentiator, low-cost leader, or focuser. In the airline industry, for instance, American Airlines tries to be a differentiator by doing things like offering its passengers strong Internet support and a strong frequent-flier program. Southwest Airlines is a low-cost leader. Every decision Southwest makes—from the routes it chooses to the planes it flies—is aimed at minimizing costs so that it can pass the savings onto passengers. Other airlines, (such as the small airlines that specialize in emergency medical evacuations from Europe to the United States) focus on serving very specific niche markets.

In terms of competitive strategy, JetBlue seems to be following a hybrid approach. It seeks to combine the advantages of being a low-cost leader with the kind of high-quality service you'd expect to find only on major differentiator airlines such as American Airlines and Delta. JetBlue keeps costs down by flying new, low-maintenance planes; eliminating meals; training teams of employees to turn aircraft around quickly; and flying only one type of aircraft so that all pilots and crew can easily switch from plane to plane.[64] At the same time, JetBlue aims to provide, not "cut rate," but topnotch service for its passengers. They get leather seats, each with its own TV monitor. JetBlue's Airbus seats are about one inch wider than those on most Boeing economy class seats. Managers carefully select and train employees to provide upbeat, courteous service. As with the majors, passengers flying JetBlue get reserved seats. (You don't get your seat assignment at the airport, as on such low-cost airlines as Southwest). And, while JetBlue eliminated meals, it does provide baskets of unlimited snacks (including blue potato chips, made from "natural blue potatoes").[65]

This competitive strategy has worked until now, but the competition is becoming much more fierce. When JetBlue was "not on the radar screens" of competitors like American Airlines, it had the low-cost flights from some airports, such as Fort Lauderdale, pretty much to itself. However, its own success has increased the attention that it's getting from its competitors. David Neeleman, therefore, knows that he's going to have to monitor events very carefully to make sure, among other things, that his "quality service/low-cost" hybrid competitive strategy doesn't become difficult to maintain.

Assignment

You and your team are consultants to Mr. Neeleman, who is depending on your management expertise to help him navigate the launch and management of JetBlue. Here's what he wants to know from you now:

1. Develop a vision and mission statement for JetBlue.

2. On a single sheet of paper, write the outline of a workable strategic plan for JetBlue.

3. Identify JetBlue's current corporate strategies, and list our strategic options.

4. Accurately identify JetBlue's "core competencies."

5. List the strategic planning tools you think we should use, and why.

6 Fundamentals of Organizing

CHAPTER OBJECTIVES

After studying this chapter and the case exercises at the end, you should be able to:

1. Develop an organization chart for a company.

2. Draw the company's current organization chart, and list its pros and cons.

3. Show how a company could install a network organization.

4. Reorganize a company's tasks around a "horizontal organization."

THE MANAGEMENT CHALLENGE

Howard Schultz Takes Starbucks Abroad

People who think Starbucks is just a local coffee chain don't know much about the company.[1] Howard Schultz, Starbucks' chairman, got the idea for what is now Starbucks while traveling in Italy about 20 years ago. Impressed with the popularity of espresso bars in Milan, he brought the idea back to Seattle, and the rest, as they say, was history. From small beginnings, Schultz methodically opened more stores, first in Oregon, then California, and then across the United States. At the same time, Schultz was branching out, signing partnership deals with Barnes & Noble and United Airlines, opening new roasting plants, and then expanding abroad—to Japan, China, the Philippines, Switzerland, Austria, Israel, and Oman.

Today, with more than 4,700 stores worldwide (including 300 in Japan), organizing the company is no easy task. There must be training departments to turn college students into café managers (who know, for example, that every espresso must be pulled within 23 seconds or be thrown away), departments to sell coffee to United Airlines and supermarkets; and a way to manage stores in places as remote as the Philippines and Beijing. How to organize is, therefore, not an academic issue for Starbucks. What should its organization chart look like?

The plans the manager makes need to be transformed into action, and the first step in doing so usually involves deciding who exactly is responsible for doing what. Part 1, Chapters 3– 5, focused on planning. This chapter starts the "organizing" part of this book. Chapter 6's main purpose is to give you the skills you need to develop organization charts and to understand the basic terminology of managerial organization. The main topics we'll address include authority and the chain of command, departmentalization, network-based organizations, and the span of control. This chapter addresses the fundamentals of organizing—its basic building blocks. In the following chapter, we'll explain how the manager actually chooses and combines these elements into an organization structure.

■■■ WHAT IS ORGANIZING?

In Chapter 1, we saw that an organization consists of people whose specialized tasks are coordinated to contribute to the company's goals. It is the manager's job to create that organization. Specifically, he or she must decide how to divide the work, who does what, who reports to whom, and how to coordinate the organization's various activities. Organizing means arranging activities in such a way that they systematically contribute to the company's goals. Chapters 3–5 discussed how to plan; in this and the next two chapters, we'll discuss how to organize.

> organizing ■ arranging the activities of the enterprise in such a way that they systematically contribute to the enterprise's goals.

From Planning to Organizing

Managers like Howard Schultz know that the organization should grow out of the plan. When Starbuck's was small, its strategy was to offer high-quality coffee drinks through small, specialized local coffee houses. This plan suggested the main jobs for which Schultz had to hire lieutenants—for example, for store management, purchasing, and finance and accounting. Departments then grew up around these tasks.

As Schultz's plan evolved, so did his organization design. As Starbuck's expanded across the United States, and then abroad, he established regional divisions to oversee the stores in each area. Today, with Starbucks coffee also sold to airlines, bookstores, and supermarkets, the company's structure includes new departments that sell to and service the needs of these new markets. Schultz's organization grew out of his plan—that is, structure followed strategy.

■ *Application Example* The manager, in organizing, should always keep this structure-strategy link in mind. Let's return to the management task we first tackled in Chapter 1–your assignment as summer tour master. What's your organization's strategic mission? To plan, organize, and execute a successful trip to France. What division of labor does that imply? One way to organize (and the one we chose in Chapter 1) is to break the job into the main functions you need performed. So we put Rosa in charge of airline scheduling, Ned in charge of hotels, and Ruth in charge of city sites.

Suppose next year your friends promote you (you lucky thing). You are now in charge of simultaneously planning several trips—to England, to Sweden, and to the south of France. Your organization's strategic mission has therefore changed, too. It is now to plan, organize, and execute three successful trips—and to do so more or less simultaneously. How would you organize now? Perhaps you'd put each of last year's trusted lieutenants in charge of a country (say, Rosa—England, Ned—Sweden, and Ruth—south of France). You'd then have a sort of "regional" organization. Each lieutenant might, in turn, hire trusted friends to arrange for airline tickets, hotels, and sites to see. Again, the tasks you need done—and thus how you organize—flow logically from your plan.

Authority and the Chain of Command

The usual way of depicting an organization is with an organization chart. It shows the structure of the organization—specifically, the title of each manager's position and, by means of connecting lines, who is accountable to whom and who has authority for each area. The organization chart also shows the chain of command (sometimes called the scalar chain or the line of authority) between the top of the organization and the

> organization chart ■ a chart that shows the structure of the organization including the title of each manager's position and, by means of connecting lines, who is accountable to whom and who has authority for each area.

chain of command ■ *the path that a directive and/or answer or request should take through each level of an organization; also called a scalar chain or the line of authority.*

authority ■ *the right to take action, to make decisions, and to direct the work of others.*

lowest positions in the chart. The chain of command represents the organization's hierarchy of authority. It shows the path a directive should take in traveling from the president to employees at the bottom of the organization chart or from employees at the bottom to managers at the top.

Authority is a central concept in organizations; it generally refers to a person's legal right or power to take action, to make decisions, and to direct the work of others. In a corporation, authority stems from the owner/stockholders of the company. They elect a board of directors and authorize the board to represent the owners' interests; the owners, through the board, are at the top of the chain of command. The board's main functions are to choose the top executives, to approve strategies and long-term plans, and to monitor performance to make sure management is protecting the owners' interests. The board and its chairperson then delegates (we discuss delegation in more detail in Chapter 7) to the CEO the authority to actually run the company—to develop plans, to hire subordinate managers, and to enter into agreements. This is how an organization chart and chain of command evolve.

■ *The Global Manager: Wal-Mart* Deciding how much authority each manager in the chain of command should have is especially tricky when managing a global business. Trying to tell someone 10,000 miles away how to run his or her store can mean ordering that person to do something—like selling the wrong products—that his or her customers don't like. Thus, when Wal-Mart first expanded abroad, it reportedly tried to simply transplant its way of doing business. Some of Wal-Mart's German managers objected to being told how to do things by Wal-Mart "mentors" who couldn't even speak German.[2] Today, Wal-Mart's new head of international operations is working hard to make sure that Wal-Mart's local managers abroad have the authority they need to make decisions that make sense for their stores.

Line and Staff Authority

line manager ■ *a manager who is (1) in charge of essential activities such as sales and (2) authorized to issue orders to subordinates down the chain of command.*

staff manager ■ *a manager without the authority to give orders down the chain of command (except in his or her own department); generally can only assist and advise line managers in specialized areas such as human resources management.*

functional authority ■ *narrowly limited power to issue orders down the chain of command in a specific functional area such as personnel testing.*

Managers distinguish between line and staff authority. Line managers (like the president, production manager, and sales manager) have *line* authority. This means they (1) are always in charge of essential activities, such as sales and (2) can issue orders down the chain of command. Staff managers have *staff* (or *advisory*) authority. They generally cannot issue orders down the chain of command (except in their own departments). They can only assist and advise line managers. Line managers run line departments (or line organizations); staff managers run staff departments. The HR manager is the classic example of a staff manager. An HR manager—even a vice president—can *advise* a production supervisor regarding the types of selection tests to use. However, it would be unusual for the HR manager to order the supervisor to hire a particular employee. On the other hand, the production supervisor's boss—the production manager—can usually issue such orders.

There is an exception to this rule. A staff manager may also have functional authority. Functional authority means that the manager can issue orders down the chain of command within the very narrow limits of his or her authority. For example, the president might order that no screening tests be administered without first getting the HR manager's approval. That manager then has functional authority over personnel testing.

Some small organizations use only line managers, but most large ones have departments headed by staff managers too—they are, therefore, line and staff organizations. Typical line positions include the CEO, and the managers for sales and production. Typical staff positions include the managers for marketing research, accounting, security, quality control, legal affairs, and, of course, HR.

The Informal Organization

A manager's authority is not always what it seems. An executive, hoping to amuse his audience, opened his speech with the following story.

> *A young and enthusiastic lion, straight out of lion school, was hired by a circus. After his first day on the job, the trainer gave the lion, not a bowl of meat, but a bunch of bananas. The lion stormed over to the ringmaster and*

said, "I'm the lion. What are you doing feeding me bananas?" "Well, the problem is," the ringmaster said, "our senior lion is still around, so you're down on the organization chart as a monkey."

The point is that an organization's chain of command isn't always what it appears to be, based on its formal organization chart. One thing the organization chart does not show is the informal organization. This is the informal, habitual contacts, communications, and ways of doing things employees develop. Thus, a salesperson might call the plant manager directly to check the status of an order. The formal route—asking her sales manager, who in turn asks the plant manager—may simply take too long. Similarly, the chart may show the president's assistant as a secretary, but as the president's gatekeeper, he or she may wield enormous authority. And, young lions occasionally get hired thinking they're going to be the president—only to find that the president lingers as chair of the board, second-guessing almost all the president does. You have to exercise some healthy skepticism when reviewing a company's organization chart.

informal organization ■ *the informal contacts, communications, and habitual ways of doing things that employees develop.*

◼◼◼ DEPARTMENTALIZATION: CREATING DEPARTMENTS

Every enterprise carries out many activities in order to accomplish its goals. In a company, these activities include manufacturing, sales, and accounting. In a town or city, they include fire, police, and health protection. In a hospital, they include nursing, medical services, and radiology. Departmentalization is the process through which the manager groups the enterprise's activities together and assigns them to subordinates; it is the organizationwide division of work. (The logical groupings of activities go by the names department, division, unit, section, or some other similar term.) The manager's central organizational task is thus to decide, "How should I divide up the work that needs to be done?"

departmentalization ■ *the process through which an organization's activities are grouped together and assigned to managers; the organizationwide division of work.*

But of course, it's not so simple. The basic management question is, "Around what activities should I organize the departments?" As editor in chief of the student newspaper, should you organize the main departments around functions like editing, production, and sales? Or should you appoint one lieutenant for each quarterly issue you plan to publish, and let each of these individuals recruit people for their own production, editorial, and advertising units? In managing a summer tour of France, should you organize your people around *functions* such as airline scheduling and hotels, or around *places* such as England and the south of France? In a company, should you organize departments for sales and manufacturing? Or should there be separate departments for industrial and retail customers, each of which then has its own sales and manufacturing units?

Managers traditionally have two basic choices when it comes to organizing departments. They can organize departments around *functions*. Or, they can organize departments around self-contained *divisions* or *purposes*. For example, the editor in chief can appoint functional department heads for editing, production, and ads. Or, he or she can organize departments around some self-contained purpose, such as by appointing editors for each of the paper's four editions—Fall, Winter, Spring, and Summer. The latter would be self-contained divisions; each edition's editor would have within her department her own editorial, production, and advertising editors. There are four types of divisional, self-contained arrangements—by product, customer, marketing channel, or territory.

The decision on which kind of departmentalization to use usually depends more on experience, logic, and common sense than on any formula. We'll look at the traditional options for organizing departments in this section. Then, in Chapter 7, we'll look more closely at the factors that determine why you would choose one option over another. Let's begin with functional organizations.

Organizing Departments by Function

Functional departmentalization is the simplest and most obvious way to organize. It means grouping activities around essential functions, like manufacturing, sales, and finance. These functions are essential because, regardless of how the manager organizes, someone must perform them if the firm is to survive.

functional departmentalization ■ *a form of organization that groups a company's activities around essential functions such as manufacturing, sales, or finance.*

► FIGURE 6–1 ■ ■ ■

Functional Departmentalization

This chart shows *functional* organizations, with departments for basic functions like scheduling, reservations, and sightseeing (STO), and finance, sales, and production (ABC)

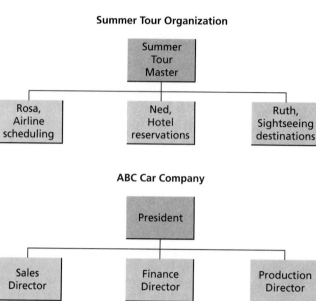

FUNCTIONAL ORGANIZATIONS

Summer Tour Organization

ABC Car Company

Figure 6.1 shows the organizational structures for STO (your summer tour organization) and for the ABC Car Company. At ABC, management organized each department around a different business function—sales, finance, and production. Here, the production director reports to the president and manages ABC's production plants. The directors carry out the sales, finance, and production functions.

The functions that are essential for one type of enterprise may be unnecessary in another. For example, a university's essential functions typically include academic affairs, business affairs, and student affairs. Banks typically have functional departments for operations, control, and loans. Your group tour to France has one person in charge of transportation, one in charge of hotels, and another in charge of sightseeing. Some managers organize by *managerial functions*. This means putting supervisors in charge of departments like planning, control, and administration. Within production, *technological functions* may include plating, welding, or assembling. In any event, the basic idea of functional departmentalization is to group the firm's activities (departmentalize) around the functions that are necessary for the enterprise to survive.

Advantages   Organizing by functions has several advantages.

1. *It is simple, obvious, and logical.* By definition, the enterprise must somehow carry out these functions to survive. Therefore, organizing by putting people in charge of these functions is a simple and obvious way to do things.
2. *It can promote efficiency.* Organizing by function can promote efficiency in three ways. First, functional departments are specialized departments—they focus on doing one thing—and everyone tends to get better with practice. Second, organizing by function means that departments (like sales or production) serve all the firm's products or services. This can mean increased economies of scale (for instance, one large plant and more efficient equipment for manufacturing all the company's products). Third, organizing by function minimizes duplication of effort. For example, there is one production department for all the company's products, rather than separate ones for each product.
3. *It can simplify executive hiring and training.* The duties of the managers running these departments are specialized; the enterprise therefore needs fewer general managers—those with the breadth of experience to administer several functions at once.
4. *It can facilitate the top manager's control.* Functional department managers tend to receive information on and focus on just the activities that concern their own specialized activities. They often have to rely on their boss (the top manager) to coor-

dinate their efforts. A functional organization can therefore make it easier for the top manager to control what's happening in the organization.

Disadvantages Organizing by function also has disadvantages.

1. *It increases the coordination workload for the executive to whom the functional department heads report.* Functional departmentalization can increase the top manager's control, but the other side of the coin is that responsibility for all products and services rests on that person's shoulders. For example, the CEO may be the only one in a position to coordinate the work of the functional departments. This may not be a problem in a small business, or when a firm has just one or two products. But as size and diversity of products increase, the job of coordinating production, sales, and finance for many different products or markets may prove too much for one person.

2. *It may reduce the firm's sensitivity to and service to the customer.* For example, if JC Penney management decided to organize nationally around the functions of merchandising, purchasing, and personnel, all of its U.S. stores might tend to get the same products to sell, even if customers' tastes in Chicago were different from those in El Paso.

3. *It produces fewer general managers.* A functional organization fosters an emphasis on specialized managers (finance experts, production experts, and so forth). This can make it more difficult to cultivate managers with the breadth of experience required for jobs like CEO.

Organizing Departments by Self-Contained Divisions/Purposes: *Products*

Sometimes, the disadvantages of departmentalizing functionally outweigh the advantages. Managers then turn to organizing departments around self-contained "purposes," such as by product, customer, marketing channel, or geographic area.

With *product departmentalization*, the manager organizes his or her departments around the company's products or services, or each family of products or services. Managers often refer to this as a divisional organization. The editor in chief who decides to appoint lieutenants for each of the paper's four editions is organizing around products. Each edition is an identifiable product. With this type of organization, the department heads are generally responsible for both producing and marketing the product or service. As with the Spring Edition editor, they have all or most of the resources in their units (in this case, editorial, production, and advertising editors) to get the entire product or service (the Spring Edition) produced.

The divisional organization in Figure 6.2 illustrates this. Here, the CEO for a pharmaceuticals company organized the firm's top-level departments so that each

divisional ■ *a form of organization in which the firm's major departments are organized so that each one can manage all or most of the activities needed to develop, manufacture, and sell a particular product or product line.*

▼ **FIGURE 6–2** ■ ■ ■ Divisional Organization for Pharmaceuticals Company

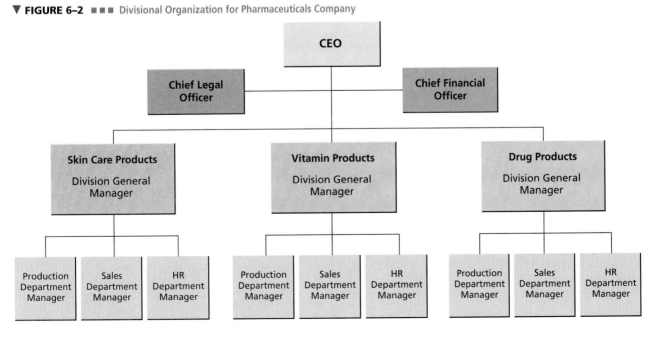

contains all the activities required to develop, manufacture, and sell a particular product (skin care, vitamins, drugs). The general manager of each division has functional departments—for production, sales, and personnel—reporting to him or her. Each of these product divisions is self-contained. Each controls all or most of the resources required to create, produce, and supply its product or products. Kodak recently reorganized for the second time in about two years. The new structure consists of five product-business units, each focused on product lines such as cameras. Divisional organizations help ensure that each product (or customer or geographic area) gets the attention of a dedicated department, but at the cost of having duplicate functional departments for each product.

Organizing Departments by Self-Contained Divisions/Purposes: *Customers*

customer departmentalization ■ *similar to product organization except that generally self-contained departments are organized to serve the needs of specific groups of customers.*

Customer departmentalization is similar to product departmentalization, but the manager organizes departments around the company's customers. Figure 6.3, for instance, shows the organization chart for the Grayson Steel Company. The company's main divisions are organized to serve particular customers, such as metals and chemicals customers, packaging systems customers, aerospace and industrial customers, and the international group. With one management team and unit focused on each customer, customers can expect faster, better service than with functional arrangements, particularly when customers' needs are very different. A main disadvantage is duplication of effort. The company may have several production plants instead of one, and several sales managers, each serving the needs of his or her own customers, instead of one.

Organizing Departments by Self-Contained Divisions/Purposes: *Marketing Channels*

marketing-channel departmentalization ■ *an arrangement in which departments of an organization focus on particular marketing channels, such as drugstores or grocery stores.*

marketing channel ■ *the conduit through which a manufacturer distributes its products to its ultimate customers.*

With marketing-channel departmentalization, management organizes the departments around each of the firm's marketing channels (instead of products or customers). A marketing channel is the conduit (wholesaler, drugstore, grocery, or the like) through which a manufacturer distributes its products to its ultimate customers.

This approach differs from the customer departmentalization approach in two main ways (see Figure 6.4. First, of course, the marketing channels are conduits to the firm's ultimate customers; they're not the ultimate users of the company's products. Second, customer-oriented departments (such as for industrial customers, retail customers, and municipal customers), traditionally market *and manufacture their own products* for their customers. Marketing-channel departments (like those at soaps and cosmetics maker Caswell-Massey) typically market the same product (such as soap) through two or more channels (such as drug stores and grocery stores). Management here typically chooses one department to manufacture the product for all the marketing-channel departments.

Managers use this structure when it's important to cater to each marketing channel's unique needs. For example, Revlon sells through department stores and discount drugstores, and the demands of the two channels are quite different. The department store may want Revlon to supply specially trained salespeople to run concessions in its stores. The discount druggist may just want quick delivery and minimal inventory. Putting a manager and department in charge of each channel helps ensure that Revlon meets these diverse needs quickly and satisfactorily. As in product and customer departmentalization, the resulting duplication—in this case, of sales

▶ **FIGURE 6–3** ■ ■ ■

Customer Departmentalization, Grayson Steel Company

With customer departmentalization, separate departments are organized around customers, such as aerospace as well as metals and chemicals customers.

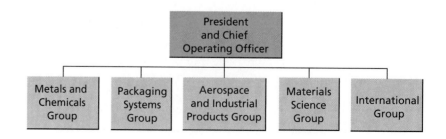

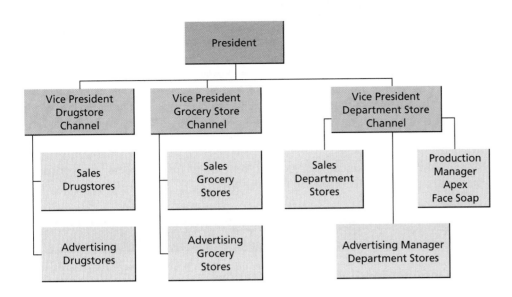

◀ **FIGURE 6–4** ■ ■ ■

Marketing Channel
Departmentalization

With marketing channels, the main
departments are organized to focus
on particular marketing channels,
such as drugstores and grocery stores.
Note: Only the department-store
channel produces the soap, and each
channel may sell to the same ultimate
consumers.

forces—is the main disadvantage. Better serving the marketing channel's needs is the main advantage.

Organizing Departments by Self-Contained Divisions/Purposes: Geographic Area

With geographic, or territorial, departmentalization, the manager establishes separate departments for each of the territories in which the enterprise does business. Each territorial division gets its own management team, and is often self-contained (with its own production, sales, and personnel activities). Like other purpose-oriented structures, territorial departmentalization can help ensure quick, responsive reaction to the needs of the company's clients. Thus, JC Penney might organize territorially to cater to the tastes and needs of customers in each area. On the other hand, territorial departmentalization may also lead to duplicate production and other facilities, and compartmentalization and isolation of one territory from another.

■ *The Global Manager* Organizing geographically grew in popularity as firms expanded across national borders. Years ago, when relatively limited communications made it difficult to take the pulse of consumer needs or to monitor operations abroad, it made sense to let local managers run regional or country businesses as more or less autonomous companies. Two trends are making this structure less popular today. First, *information technology* is reducing the impediments to cross-border communication. The existence of Internet-based video conferencing, e-mail, fax, and computerized monitoring of operations means that an executive in one region—say, the United States—can more easily keep his or her finger on the pulse of operations around the world. Second, *global competition* is so intense that firms can't afford to miss an opportunity to transfer product improvements from one region to another. For example, if H.J. Heinz in Japan discovers a new way to formulate one of its soups, Heinz will want to make sure it quickly applies the improvement elsewhere.

MANAGEMENT IN ACTION   Heinz, P&G, and the INS

Many firms are now switching from geographic to product organizations. Heinz CEO William Johnson said he was ending the company's system of managing by country or region.[3] Instead, Heinz will organize by products or categories. Managers in the United States will then work with those in Europe, Asia, and other regions to apply the best ideas from one region to another. Similarly, Procter & Gamble's new organization eliminates its four regional business units. Seven new executives each manage product groups like baby care, beauty, and fabric and home care for all regions. The company believes the reorganization will speed decision making and send products to market faster.[4]

Other enterprises are moving from geographic back to functional organizations. After September 11, it was apparent that the geographically compartmentalized U.S. Immigration and Naturalization Service (INS) was not focusing enough on functions like country-wide enforcement. Each area INS manager had his or her own applications processing and enforcement units. There was relatively little enforcement at the national level. One of the internal changes under consideration was to reorganize INS from geography to functions. Functions would include immigration services (for processing applications) and immigration enforcement (such as guarding borders).[5]

Advanced telecommunications tools make it easier for managers to organize their ear-flung enterprises as the following feature shows.

MANAGING @ THE SPEED OF THOUGHT

Using the Internet for Global Communications

Companies like Heinz can use the Internet in many ways to improve global communications. Videoconferencing is one of them. For the cost of a local telephone call, companies now have global, face-to-face communications that help eliminate the barriers that distance formerly placed in the way of such face-to-face talk.[6]

CU-SeeMe is one of the systems companies use to hold multiparty videoconference meetings over the Internet. This system uses a reflector program, which sends simultaneous transmissions to every participant. While the system is used primarily for talking head meetings (each participant appears on the screen in a 4-inch box), it provides an inexpensive and effective way to hold long-distance meetings.

The World Bank, with headquarters in Washington, D.C., is an example of how one organization uses CU-SeeMe. With offices or partners in 180 countries, the World Bank has an urgent need to communicate quickly and efficiently across borders. It uses CU-SeeMe to conduct small meetings and virtual seminars. While the images may be small and the video may not always be very smooth, the system's

■ ■ *A participant using the CU-SeeMe videoconferencing system. The camera is on top of the computer monitor.*

low cost and ease of use makes it easy for the World Bank and other organizations and companies to communicate instantly and face to face around the globe. It, therefore, reduces the need to depend so heavily on a global territorial organization structure. ■ ■ ■

Advantages and Disadvantages of the Divisional Approach

Divisionalization (whether by product, customer, territory, or marketing channel) can be advantageous in several ways.

1. *The product or service gets the single-minded attention of its own general manager and unit, and so its customers may get better, more responsive service.* A general manager oversees all the functions required to produce and market each particular product or service. That general manager and division specialize in that product or service. The net effect should be that the product or service (and its customers) get focused,

more responsive attention with this type of organization than they would in a functional organization (in which, for instance, the same sales manager must address the needs of multiple products).

2. *It's easier to judge performance.* If a division is (or is not) doing well, it is clear who is responsible, because one general manager is managing the whole division. This may, in turn, better motivate the general manager.

3. *It develops general managers.* Divisions can be good training grounds for an enterprise's executives, since they are miniature companies that expose managers to a wider range of functional issues.

4. *It reduces the burden for the company's CEO.* In selling, the North American president has to coordinate the tasks of selling, producing, and staffing for each of the company's many products. He or she thus faces an enormous number of problems. This is why virtually all very large companies, as well as many small ones with diverse products and customers, divisionalize.[7] Here is how Bill Harris, then executive vice president of software company Intuit, explained his firm's reorganization:

> . . . it was becoming clear that the bigger we got, the more being organized by functions was a liability. . . . The executive team had become a real bottleneck. We needed a new structure [and decided] to bust the organization apart. [Our new CEO] created eight business units, each with its own general manager and customer mission. The basic goal was to flatten the organization and fragment the decision-making process. Each business unit would be the size that Intuit had been a few years ago, and each would focus on one core product or market.[8]

Intuit's reorganization was effective. Top management previously made or approved most product-related decisions. Now these decisions are left to the business units, and within these units, the managers usually leave these decisions to individual product teams. With smaller, product-oriented divisions that are closer to their customers, Intuit is more responsive and effective at serving its customers, and at responding to and managing change.

The disadvantages of organizing around divisions can include the following:

1. *It involves duplication of effort.* Being self-contained is a two-edged sword. The very fact that each product-oriented unit is self-contained implies that each unit has its own production plants, sales force, and so on.

▼ **FIGURE 6–5** ■ ■ ■ Divisional Organizations Facilitate Coordination

Note: Unless the president, North America, sets up separate divisions for skin care, vitamins, and drugs, he or she will have to personally coordinate sales, production, and personnel for all three sets of products.

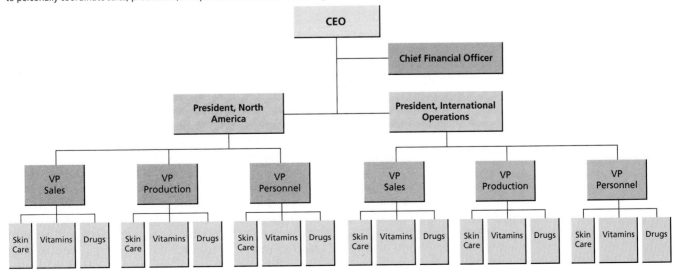

2. *It leads to diminished top management control.* At Intuit, the business units now make decisions that top management used to make. The business units have more autonomy. The net effect is that top management tends to have less control over day-to-day activities. A division might, for instance, run up excessive expenses before top management discovers there's a problem. Striking a balance between providing each division with enough autonomy while maintaining top management control is the central issue in organizing in this way.

3. *It requires more managers with general management abilities.* Each product division is, in a sense, a miniature company, with its own production plant, sales force, personnel department, and so forth. This means these firms must work diligently to identify and develop managers with general management potential.

4. *It can breed compartmentalization.* One problem with any type of divisionalization is that establishing semiautonomous units can inhibit the spread of innovation from one division to another.

■■■ *Anne Robinson, CEO of Caswell-Massey.*

matrix organization ■ *an organization structure in which employees are permanently attached to one department but also simultaneously have ongoing assignments in which they report to project, customer, product, or geographic unit heads.*

■ *Application Example: Caswell-Massey* That is what happened at toiletries marketer Caswell-Massey. For years, managers organized the firm around marketing channels, with catalogue, retail, and wholesale channels run as separate businesses. CEO Ann Robinson says the problem was that each channel was oblivious to what the others were doing: "Retail wasn't listening to catalog and vice versa. The items featured on the catalog's cover were not necessarily in the store window. There was little synergy between brands." Part of her solution was to start marketing Caswell-Massey's products on a more unified basis, by coordinating the marketing effort among the channels.[9]

Creating Matrix Organizations

Sometimes, managers want to leave employees in their specialized functional departments, but also have those employees focus on particular projects, products, or customers. How do they accomplish both? Some opt for a matrix organization. A matrix organization, also known as *matrix management*, is an organization structure in which employees are permanently attached to one department but also simultaneously have ongoing assignments in which they report to project, customer, product, or geographic unit heads.[10]

Figure 6.6 illustrates one example. Management organized the firm's automotive products division functionally, with departments for project management, production, engineering, materials procurement, personnel and accounting. However, in this case, each of Universal's big customers had special new-product development needs that required attention. Universal management therefore established three project groups—for the Ford project, the Chrysler project, and the GM project. Each of these project groups has its own project leader. One or more employees from each functional department (like production and engineering) is temporarily assigned to each project. Employees report to both their functional and customer-product heads.

Matrix structures come in several varieties—they needn't just merge functional and project organizations. For example, some blend customer and geographic organizations.[11] Investment banks tend to be organized geographically, with separate management teams and employees attached to, say, Goldman Sachs France; Goldman Sachs UK; and Goldman Sachs USA. How, though, can a geographically organized bank like this ensure that it adequately serves the global interests of major customers like IBM? The answer is that the bank's employees in each region simultaneously report to their regional heads and also to project heads for major customers like IBM. J.P. Morgan uses a matrix structure. Managers around the world answer to two bosses: their regional head and the head of their product area. A J.P. Morgan investment banking manager in Mexico City would report to both her investment banking head back in New York, and to Eduardo Cepeda, who heads J.P. Morgan's Mexico City office.[12]

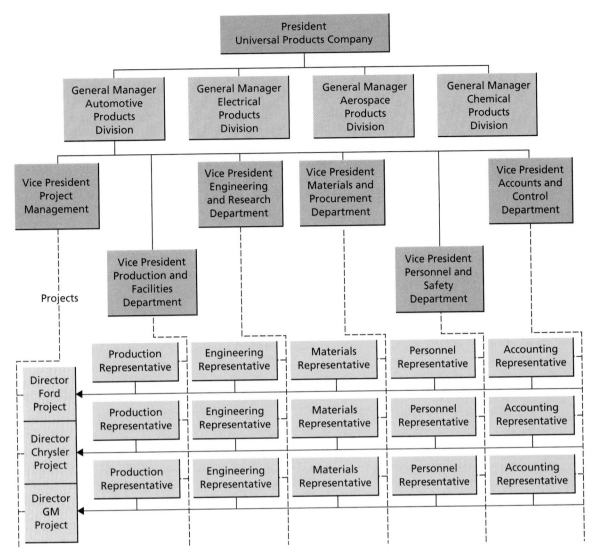

▲ **FIGURE 6–6** ■ ■ ■ Matrix Organization Departmentalization

With a matrix organization, a project structure is often superimposed over a functional organization.

Some matrix organizations are more permanent than others. Sometimes, temporary project managers provide coordination across functional departments for some short-term project. Other firms add a permanent administrative system (including, for instance, project employee appraisal forms) to help emphasize a project's or customer's ongoing importance.[13] Many firms (including Citicorp; TRW Systems; NASA and many of its subcontractors; UNICEF; and various accounting, law, and security firms) have used matrix management successfully.[14] The following Management in Action feature provides an illustration.[15]

MANAGEMENT IN ACTION Implementing Matrix Management at Texas Instruments

Texas Instrument's Sensors and Controls (S&C) division specializes in the design of low-cost, high-quality, customer-specific sensors, controls, and materials. As the industry's product life cycle—the time required to design, introduce, and then redesign or replace a product—became shorter, the company decided it needed to develop new products faster. Called the Materials and Controls division at the time, S&C had a functional organization, with separate departments for design, engineering, manufacturing, purchasing, and quality engineering. After participating in a training course on project management, the division's management and staff became enthusiastic about organizing around projects, but decided that doing so would require a matrix management structure.[16]

In the division's new "balanced matrix" organization, "the project managers and functional managers share roughly equal authority and responsibility for the project."[17] Project managers were appointed and project teams assigned. Team members reported to both a project manager and their existing functional managers. This new structure "required the teams and their managers . . . actively to commit themselves to a project."[18]

Getting that kind of commitment in the face of the ambiguities created by dual reporting turned out to be easier said than done. For example, some of the new project managers reportedly lacked the required skills, time, or commitment; management replaced them. S&C's managers also discovered that having project teams meant they had to cultivate more of a team culture, and better team-building skills. Implementing the matrix structure therefore led management to introduce team-building activities.

Even this wasn't enough. The teams seemed to divide into two factions, one focusing on manufacturing employees, and one on design engineers. Management organized meetings to promote interaction, but, as the researcher notes, promoting interaction is one thing, getting collaboration is another. Ultimately, Texas Instruments' S&C got its matrix structure to work right, but doing so required enormous attention to the people side of managing.

Advantages and Disadvantages To some extent, matrix management provides the best of both worlds. It gives the employees the stability and benefits of belonging to permanent departments. And, it gives the firm most of the advantages of having units and employees focused on specific projects, products, or customers. Thus, the J.P. Morgan investment banker can continuously tap the expertise of her New York-based investment banking colleagues, while also focusing on the needs of her local Mexico City clients.

However, the matrix organization also has some special drawbacks. These include:

- *Confusion.* Having two bosses can cause confusion. Dual reporting lines are appropriate only for complex tasks and uncertain environments in which ambiguity is a reasonable price to pay for dealing more effectively with rapid change.[19]
- *Power struggles and conflicts.* Authority—"Who's in charge of what?"—tends to be more ambiguous and up for grabs in matrix organizations.
- *Lost time.* Matrix organizations tend to result in more inter- and intragroup meetings, which can be time-consuming.
- *Excessive overhead.* Matrix organizations may raise costs, because hiring dual sets of managers and support staff raises overhead.

Checklist 6.1 summarizes the advantages and disadvantages of functional and divisional organizations.

CHECKLIST 6.1 ■ Functional vs. Divisional Organizations

☑ Functional Organization Advantages
1. It is simple, obvious, and logical.
2. It fosters efficiency.
3. It can simplify executive hiring and training.
4. It can facilitate the top manager's control.

☑ Functional Organization Disadvantages
1. It increases the workload on the executive to whom the functional department heads report.
2. It may reduce the firm's sensitivity to and service to the customer.
3. It produces fewer general managers.

☑ Divisional Organization Advantages
1. The product or service gets the single-minded attention of its own general manager and unit, and its customers may get better, more responsive service.
2. It's easier to judge performance.

3. It develops general managers.
4. It reduces the burden for the company's CEO.

☑ Divisional Organization Disadvantages
1. It creates duplication of effort.
2. It may diminish top management's control.
3. It requires more managers with general management abilities.
4. It can breed compartmentalization

Departmentalization in Practice: A Hybrid

All but the smallest firms usually use several types of departments—in other words, they are structural hybrids. Figure 6.7 illustrates this. Within the United States, there are separate product departments for business systems, programming systems, and so forth. Globally, however, this firm uses territorial departmentalization, with separate officers in charge of the United States, the Americas, Asia/Pacific, and the Europe/Middle East/Africa. Management organized the headquarters staff around managerial functions (general counsel, finance and planning, and law).

Managers mix the types of departmentalization for three reasons. One is *hierarchical considerations*: If the top level departments are based on, say, products, then each product department will probably have subsidiary departments for functions like sales and manufacturing. The second is *efficiency*: Product, customer, and territorial departments tend to result in duplicate sales, manufacturing, and other functional departments. One way to minimize this source of inefficiency is to have a single production department serving multiple customer departments. The third is *common sense*: Departmentalizing is still more an art than a science. Managers don't arrive at organization structures through a mathematical formula. A variety of factors—including what management plans to achieve, and the unique needs of the firm's customers, territories, and products—all influence the decision.

MANAGEMENT IN ACTION   Rosenbluth International

Rosenbluth International is a fast-growing 1,000-office global travel agency. However, the way it's organized grew out of what CEO Hal Rosenbluth learned on a cattle farm.

Standing on a field in rural North Dakota several years ago, Rosenbluth made a discovery. "The family farm is the most efficient type of unit I've ever run across, because everybody on the farm has to be fully functional and multifaceted." He decided to look for an organizational design that would get all his employees involved in helping to run the company. He knew that doing so would help his managers succeed.

His company shows how smart managers blend several organizational styles to build successful firms. Rosenbluth broke his company into more than 100 geographic units, each functioning like a farm, serving specific regions and clients. Corporate headquarters became more like what Rosenbluth calls "farm towns," where "stores" like human resources and accounting are centralized so that all the farms can use them. The firm's computerized Global Distribution Network links each of its travel agents to the company's minicomputers in Philadelphia. There, centralized data on clients help ensure that the work of all offices is coordinated to serve the needs of Rosenbluth clients.[20]

Hal Rosenbluth, Chairman and CEO of Rosenbluth International, illustrates quality service by serving tea to new associates attending orientation at the company's world headquarters in Philadelphia. New associates learn how all business units interact with the central service centers at headquarters.

■ *Application Example: The Summer Tour* As your summer-tour organizing fame spreads, more of your friends (and your friends' friends) want to join your summer tours. You're now heading into your third summer tour. What started as a simple mission—

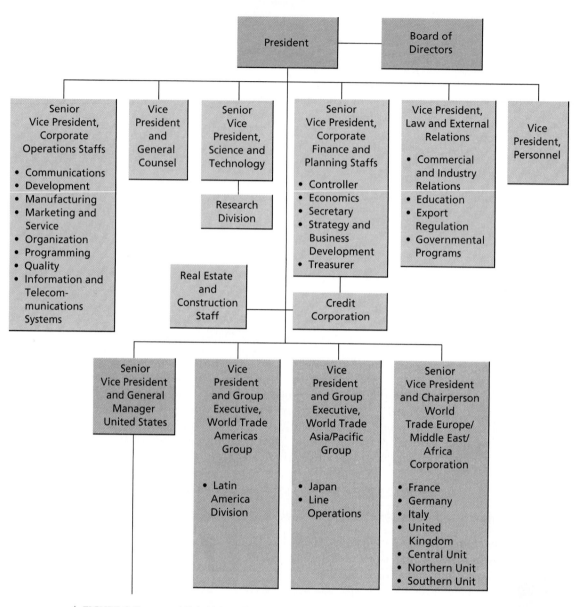

▲ **FIGURE 6–7** ■ ■ ■ A Hybrid Organization

Particularly in large organizations, several types of departmentalization are typically combined, in this case functional, product, and geogrphic.

to plan, organize, and execute a successful trip to France—has now blossomed into much more. You have tour groups going to France, England, Greece, Hong Kong, Nepal, and Japan, and they're all leaving at about the same time. You stand to earn (as a college senior) almost $20,000 if all goes well. However, you have to decide how you should organize, and who should do what.

Organizing your first summer tour was relatively straightforward. Recall that you decided to break the task into the main functions you needed performed. You put Rosa in charge of airline scheduling, Ned in charge of hotels, and Ruth in charge of city sites. The second year's tour got more complicated. You were now in charge of simultaneously planning several trips—to England, to Sweden, and to the south of France. You decided on a divisional/geographic allocation of duties. You put each of last year's trusted lieutenants in charge of a country (Rosa—England, Ned—Sweden, and Ruth—south of France). Each lieutenant in turn hired trusted friends to arrange for airline tickets, hotels, and sites to see.

How did last year's regional organization work out? From your point of view, it was good, but not perfect. Everyone was happy with his or her vacation—certainly your

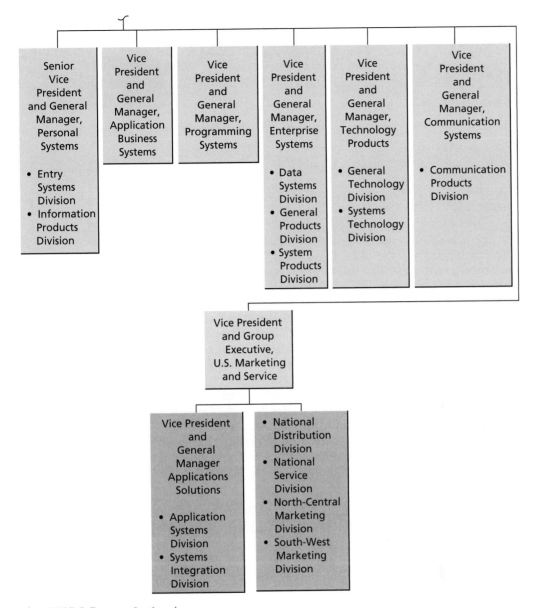

▲ **FIGURE 6–7** ■ ■ ■ Continued

main criterion. Rosa, Ned, and Ruth each did a fine job of seeing to it that everything went smoothly within each of "their" countries. However, there were two problems. First, Rosa, Ned, and Ruth were so on top of the detailed planning for their countries that you often felt out of the loop. The advantage was that they did their own planning without using up much of your time. But that was a disadvantage, too. If they had gotten you more involved, you'd have scheduled more time in London, and less in Oxford, for instance. Second, there was a lot of compartmentalized decision making by country. For example, instead of everyone buying discounted tickets via London from British Air, Rosa, Ned, and Ruth each made their own plane reservations. They therefore spent a lot more than they would have if ticket purchasing had been a separate, specialized function.

What does this tell you about how to organize for the upcoming, worldwide tours? What would you do? Going back to a pure functional structure doesn't seem to make sense. You would like to supply some oversight for each country's plans, and make suggestions when they're relevant. However, getting into the nitty-gritty of coordinating the travel plans to and within six different countries would exceed your knowledge, time,

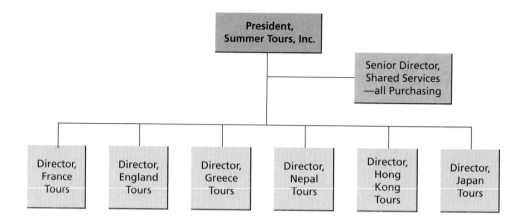

and capabilities. On the other hand, going back to a pure divisional organization by country won't work, either. You want to be able to exercise more oversight regarding the details of each country manager's plans than you did last year. And, someone must ensure that your groups use their total buying power to get the best possible deal on the tickets.

Organizationally, you make three decisions. First, you appoint experienced people from last summer's tour to head the tours to France, England, Greece, Hong Kong, Nepal, and Japan—basically, a regional division structure. Second, you appoint Ruth, who's done a stellar job the past two years, to head a separate Shared Services department. She and her assistant will do all the actual negotiating and purchasing of airline, hotel, and other travel services for all the tours. Figure 6.8 shows your new organization chart. Third, you institute a new formal planning system. Henceforth, the country tour division heads need to work out detailed daily itineraries and submit them to you (and Ruth) for approval by March 1. That gives you an opportunity to suggest fine-tuning for each itinerary. And, once you approve the plans, Ruth can get the best prices on air, hotel, and travel services. Your third-year tours are on their way.

■ ■ ■ TALL AND FLAT ORGANIZATIONS, AND THE SPAN OF CONTROL

Establishing departments is not the only organizational task the manager faces. Whether it's the college's editor-in-chief or the CEO of General Motors, the manager also has to decide what his or her *span of control* is going to be. That will in turn determine if the organizational hierarchy is "flat" or "tall." Let's look at this next.

The Span of Control

span of control ■ *the number of subordinates reporting directly to a supervisor.*

The span of control is the number of subordinates reporting directly to a supervisor. In the country-based geographic organization shown in Figure 6.9, the span of control of the country general manager is 13: There are 6 business managers, 5 directors, 1 innovation manager, and 1 manufacturing manager.

The average number of people reporting to a manager determines the number of management levels in the organization. For example, if an organization with 64 workers to be supervised has an average span of control of 8, there will be 8 supervisors directing the workers and 1 manager directing the 8 supervisors (a *flat* organization). If, on the other hand, the span of control were 4, the same number of workers would require 16 supervisors. The latter would, in turn, be directed by 4 managers. These 4 managers would, in turn, be directed by 1 manager (a *tall* organization).

Tall vs. Flat Organizations

Whether tall or flat is best has long been a matter of debate. Classic management theorists such as Henri Fayol said that tall organizational structures (with narrow spans of control) improved performance by guaranteeing close supervision.[21] The thinking

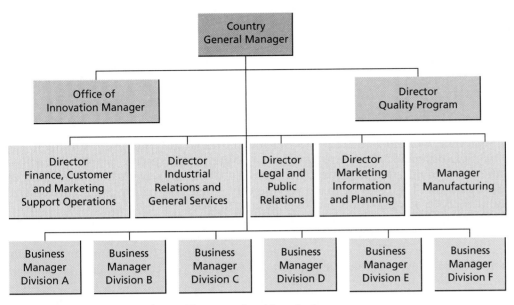

▲ **FIGURE 6–9** ■ ■ ■ Spans of Control in Country-Based Organization

In this chart, the span of control of the general manager is 13—6 business managers, 5 directors, 1 innovation manager, and 1 manufacturing manager.

was that having six to eight subordinates was ideal, since beyond that it became increasingly difficult to monitor and control what your subordinates do. The counterargument is that flat is better: Flat means wide spans, which means less meddling with (and a more motivational experience for) subordinates. The trend today is definitely toward flat.

Some believe that a tall chain of command slows decisions, by forcing each decision to pass through more people at more levels. Several weeks after the United States began bombing Afghanistan in 2001, reporters asked defense secretary Rumsfeld if having several layers of officers making tactical decisions about the ground attacks was slowing the ground forces' responsiveness. (His answer was no.)

The consensus today seems to be that flat is better.[22] For one thing, flattening a firm cuts out levels and managers, and to that extent, it may save the company money. There is also the feeling that eliminating layers does push the point at which decisions are made closer to the customer, and to that extent, flat firms may make faster, more responsive decisions. Having wider spans also implies that the manager monitors his or her subordinates less, and this (not coincidentally) is more practical today, with the trend toward highly trained and empowered employees. The Management in Action feature illustrates this.

MANAGEMENT IN ACTION   The GE Experience

The classic example of flattening occurred in the late 1980s. GE's new CEO at the time, Jack Welch, believed he had to make dramatic organizational changes—and fast. He had climbed the ranks and believed GE's chain of command was draining the firm of creativity and responsiveness. Business heads needed approval from the headquarters staff for almost every big decision they made. In one case, the light bulb business managers spent $30,000 producing a film to demonstrate the need for some production equipment they wanted to buy. The old GE, Welch knew, was wasting hundreds of millions of dollars and missing countless opportunities, because managers at so many levels were busily checking and rechecking each others' work.

The first thing Welch did was to eliminate redundant organizational levels. Before he took over, "GE's business heads reported to a group head, who reported to a sector head, who reported to the CEO. Each level had its own staff in finance, marketing, and planning, checking and double-checking each business."[23] Welch disbanded the group and the sector levels, thus dramatically flattening the organizational chain of command. When he was done, no one stood between the business heads and the CEO's office. The effect was to eliminate both the organizational bottlenecks they caused and the salaries of almost 700 corporate staff. The new GE was much leaner and more responsive. It was probably the first major example of the benefits of organizational streamlining. ■■■

■■■ NETWORK-BASED ORGANIZATIONS

Classical organizations (like the pre-Welch GE) stressed the wisdom of "sticking to the chain of command." Each employee had a position, and specific people with whom he or she could communicate. This arrangement usually worked well, as long as decisions didn't have to be made very quickly. There was plenty of time to analyze (and reanalyze) each problem as it ground its way up and down the chain of command.

Some of today's organizations would probably shock the classicists. Not only is "sticking to the chain of command" not a high priority; these companies actually encourage almost everyone to communicate with almost everyone else. In terms of organization structure, these are *networked* companies. An organizational network is a system of interconnected or cooperating individuals.[24] Through various devices, these firms encourage communications to flow freely without respect to departmental or organizational level. We'll look at seven such arrangements: *informal, formal,* and *electronic organizational networks; team-based* and *horizontal organizations*; and *federal* and *virtual organizations.* They all share the same core idea—to link employees from different functions, departments, levels, and geographic areas so that they can communicate and get their jobs done through relatively free-flowing interactive communications.[25] The aim is to expedite the flow of information and the speed at which employees can respond to customers' needs.

organizational network ■ *a system of interconnected or cooperating individuals.*

Informal Networks

Much of this linking goes on through the firm's informal organizational network. The idea that communications in any organization just follow the formal chain of command was always, of course, slightly ridiculous. As mentioned earlier, a sales manager who wants to know the status of an order may well contact the plant manager directly, rather then funneling the question through the chain of command. Informal networks like this exist in every organization. They consist of cooperating individuals who willingly share information and help solve each other's problems, using the personal knowledge of each other's expertise. Thus, if a Shell Latin America sales manager needs an introduction to a new client, she might call a Shell Zurich manager she knows, who has a contact at the client firm. It's hard to imagine how most firms could function at all, without at least some such informal give-and-take.

Networks like these always arise spontaneously, but firms today, always seeking ways to be more responsive, also nurture them. They do this by helping to develop the personal relationships on which they depend. Some—Phillips and Shell are two examples—build personal relationships through international executive development programs. They bring managers from around the world to work together in training centers in New York and London. "Here, creating confidence in the work of colleagues around the world and building up personal relationships are the key factors."[26] Moving managers from facility to facility around the world is a similar approach. In one case,

> [International mobility] has created what one might call a "nervous system" that facilitates both corporate strategic control and the flow of information throughout the firm. Widespread transfers have created an informal information network, a superior degree of communication, and mutual understanding between headquarters and subsidiaries and between subsidiaries themselves, as well as a stronger identification with the corporate culture, without compromising the local subsidiary cultures.[27]

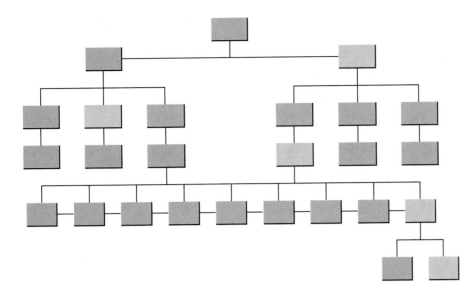

◀ **FIGURE 6–10** ■ ■ ■

How Networks Reshape Organizations

The members of a formal network may be selected from various departments and organizational levels.

Source: Reprinted by permission of *Harvard Business Review*. From "How Networks Reshape Organizations—For Results," by Ram Charan, September–October 1991. Copyright © 1991 by the President and Fellows of Harvard College; all rights reserved.

Formal Networks

Managers also increasingly create formal organizational networks. A formal organizational network is

> *A recognized group of managers [or other employees] assembled by the CEO and the senior executive team. . . . The members are drawn from across the company's functions, business units, and geography, and from different levels of the hierarchy. The number of managers involved almost never exceeds 100 and can be fewer than 25—even in global companies with tens of thousands of employees.[28]*

The blue boxes in Figure 6.10 represent a typical formal network. Note the number of organizational levels and departments represented by the blue boxes. Management decides what tasks it needs a network for, and then assigns employees from various departments, levels, and locations to the formal network. The Management in Action feature gives other examples.

formal organizational network
■ *a recognized group of managers or other employees assembled by the CEO and the other senior executive team, drawn from across the company's functions, business units, geography, and levels.*

MANAGEMENT IN ACTION   Conrail and Electrolux

Many firms use formal networks with great success. At the railroad firm Conrail, 19 middle managers from various departments and levels constitute the firm's Operating Committee, which helps make most of the firm's key operating decisions. The Operating Committee is a formal network. Members meet for several hours on Monday mornings to review and decide on tactical issues (delivery schedules and prices, for instance) and to work on longer-term issues such as five-year business plans.[29] However, as a formal network, they also communicate continuously during the week to monitor operations activities across their departments.

Electrolux provides another example. When Leif Johansson took charge, the firm offered more than 20 products, and had more than 200 plants in many countries. Each country's operation presented unique capabilities, plant capacities, and competitive situations. He wanted to keep these local strengths. But Johansson knew he also had to derive maximum economies of scale from his firm's multiproduct, multiplant, multinational operations. To

■ ■ ■ *Conrail uses a formal network system to run its railroad: An Operating Committee meets weekly and communicates continuously to monitor operations.*

accomplish this goal, he had to find a way to link the various countries' operations. He knew that abandoning the local brands (for instance, by offering similar products across all markets) would jeopardize existing distribution channels and customer loyalty. How could Johansson capitalize on the benefits of Electrolux's multicountry scale while maintaining local brand autonomy?

Johansson created a formal network composed of managers from various countries. He entrusted the network with coordinating cross-border operations. That way, local managers still had wide authority to design and market local brands. But the formal network helped to provide the overall multinational and multiproduct coordination in areas like production and inventory management that helped Electrolux obtain economies of scale.[30]

Electronic Organizational Networks

Information technology has been a boon to organizational electronic networking. This means networking through technology-supported devices such as e-mail, video-conferencing, and collaborative computing software like Lotus Notes.

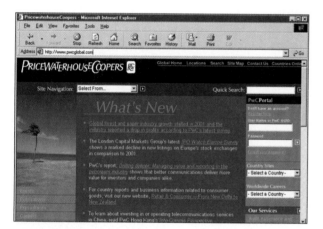

Electronic networking supports the firm's informal and formal networks. For example, PricewaterhouseCoopers' 18,000 accountants stay connected via electronic bulletin boards. A Dublin employee with a question about dairy plant accounting might have her question answered by a networked colleague half a world away.[31] Collaborative group decision support systems packages (like Lotus Notes) provide another example.[32] One, called IP Team 3.0, includes tools that automate and document the making of engineering decisions. One key feature is that it integrates suppliers and contractors into the product development cycle. It lets a geographically dispersed group of employees from the company and its suppliers work together to develop a product.[33] *OneSpace* is another. It allows several design teams "to collaborate over the Internet and across firewalls in real-time by working directly on the 3D solid model. . . .[34]

team ■ *a group of people committed to a common purpose, set of performance goals, and approach for which they hold themselves mutually accountable.*

Team-Based Organizations

You know from your own experience that teams don't typically communicate through a chain of command. The L.A. Lakers, dribbling down the court, are not about to stop, (except for time-outs) for committee meetings. Instead, they continuously interact visually and audibly with each other, as they interactively pursue their single-minded goal of getting a basket. On the court, passing the ball from one to another, the Lakers are, organizationally, a mini-network.

Many firms apply the logic of organizational networking on a micro basis. They do this by organizing individual activities around self-managing work teams. A **team** is a group of people who work together and share a common work objective.[35] In firms like these, teams are often self-managing and responsible for an entire body of work, such a building a jet engine from start to finish. Since they're a team, the individual team members are "networked": They are continually in touch with and interacting with one another. The GE jet engine plant in Durham, North Carolina, illustrates how this works. More than 170 employees work here as members of small, self-managing teams. There's only one manager—the plant manager.[36] The plant doesn't have a conventional organizational hierarchy or chain of command. The well-trained teams manage their own activities.

The GE plant's team organization illustrates the basic characteristics of the team approach.[37] Traditional firms organize with individuals, functions, or departments as the basic work units or elements. This is evident in the typical organization chart, which might show separate boxes for each functional department—and perhaps separate tasks for individual workers at the bottom of the chart.

Team-based organizations are different. Here, the team is the basic work unit. Employees work together in teams, and do much of the planning and decision making you'd often expect a firm's supervisors to do. The teams in a plant like Durham are responsible for things like receiving materials, installing parts, and dealing with vendors who ship defective parts. The teams replace many (or most) of the supervisors in a traditional chain of command. The result is a flat organization in which teams of employees report to a relative handful of traditional managers.

At Johnsonville Foods in Wisconsin, the CEO organized most of the firm's activities around self-managing, 12-person work teams. These teams are responsible for operating and maintaining the firm's packaging equipment. Typical Johnsonville team duties include:

- Recruit, hire, evaluate, and fire (if necessary) team members.
- Conduct quality control inspections, subsequent troubleshooting, and problem solving.
- Establish and monitor quantitative standards for productivity and quality.
- Suggest and develop prototypes of possible new products and packaging.[38]

Consider another example. One Chesebrough Ponds U.S.A. plant replaced it's functional organization with one organized around self-directed teams. Employee teams now run the plant's four production areas. Team members make employee assignments, schedule overtime, establish production times and changeovers, and even handle cost control, requisitions, and work orders. They are also solely responsible for quality control under the plant's Continuous Quality Improvement Challenge. Quality acceptance is now 99.25%. Annual manufacturing costs are down $10.6 million; work-in-process inventory has been reduced 86%; and total inventory is down 65%.[39]

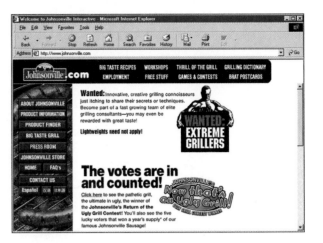

Horizontal Corporations Horizontal corporations are a type of team-based organization. Their uniqueness lies in how management organizes the teams. Here, teams don't just focus on doing things like building an engine. Instead, the team's tasks cut across several business functions. Figure 6.11, illustrates the "horizontal corporation" team organization approach. The organization consists of (1) multidisciplinary teams, (2) each performing *customer-oriented processes* such as new-product development, sales fulfillment, and customer support.

The rationale is as follows. In a traditionally organized firm, management might organize a process like sales fulfillment to look something like a relay race. The order comes into the sales department, which processes it and hands it off to manufacturing, which in turn hands it off to shipping. The horizontal approach is different. Here, one multidisciplinary "sales fulfillment team" is responsible for the entire process. Working together, the team memebers receive the order, and then produce it and make sure it's shipped. This eliminates wasted steps, and the errors that creep into the system when departments pass tasks from one to another. It may also boost morale, by giving each employee and team a more interesting task.

Organizing teams to perform customer-oriented processes that may slice through many steps and functions requires *reengineering* the company's processes. Reengineering means "the fundamental rethinking and radical redesign of businesses processes, to achieve dramatic improvements in . . . cost, quality, service, and speed."[40] In practice, reengineering involves asking, "Why do we perform this activity the way we do?"—and then combining several of the activity's specialized jobs into more enlarged jobs. The employees end up with more authority to perform these newly enlarged jobs. (We'll look at an example on page 161.)

Again, the basic idea for organizing around horizontal teams is to have one tightly integrated multidisciplinary team work in unison on all the formerly discrete steps in the process. Defining the firm's core processes is thus the essence of creating the horizontal organization. Figure 6.12 illustrates this. Managers organize one or more teams around each of these core processes. Once the process teams are in place, the firm can eliminate most functional departments and organizational levels. Checklist 6.2 shows important steps in "going horizontal."

horizontal corporation ■ *a structure that is organized around customer-oriented processes performed by multidisciplinary cross-functional teams rather than by formal functional departments.*

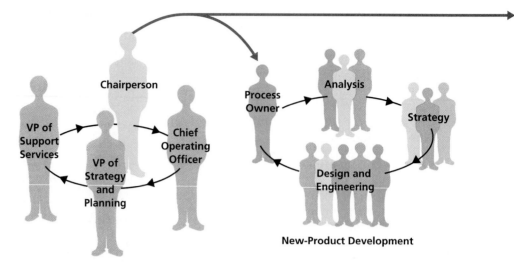

▲ **FIGURE 6–11** ■ ■ ■ The Horizontal Corporation

In the horizontal corporation, the work is organized around cross-functional processes with multifunction teams carrying out the tasks needed to service the customer. Thus the sales fulfillment team carrys out all the tasks required for billing an order.

Source: John A. Byrne, "The Horizontal Corporation," *Business Week*, 20 December 1993, p. 80.

CHECKLIST 6.2 ■ Building Horizontal Organizations

☑ Make responsibilities overlap. Design individual jobs as broadly as possible, and keep the number of job titles to a minimum.[41]

☑ Base rewards on unit performance to emphasize the importance of working together.

☑ Change the physical layout to promote collective responsibility. Let people see each other's work.

☑ Redesign work procedures, provide computer terminals, use the e-mail network, and make sure managers are available.

In practice, these horizontal units don't run themselves. As Michael Hammer (a developer of reengineering and of the horizontal organization) put it, "The most visible difference between a process enterprise and a traditional organization is the existence of process owners. [Usually] senior managers with end-to-end responsibility for individual processes, [these] process owners are the living embodiment of the company's commitment to its processes."[42]

The Management in Action feature provides some illustrative examples.

Identify strategic objectives.

Analyze key competitive advantages to fulfill objectives.

Define core processes, focusing on what's essential to accomplish your goals.

Organize around processes, not functions. Each process should link related tasks to yield a product or service to a customer.

Eliminate all activities that fail to add value or contribute to the key objectives.

▲ **FIGURE 6–12** ■ ■ ■ How to Create a Horizontal Corporation

Creating a horizontal organization involves several steps, starting with determining the firm's strategic objectives and including such steps as flattening the hierarchy and using teams to accomplish the work.

Source: Reprinted from the December 20, 1993, issue of *Business Week* by special permission. Copyright © 1993 by the McGraw-Hill Companies, Inc.

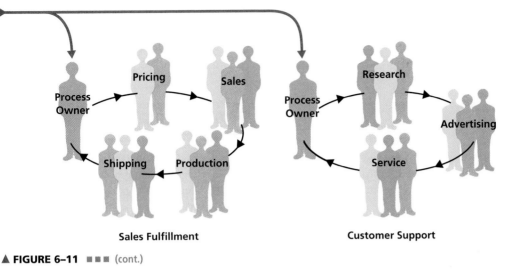

Sales Fulfillment   Customer Support

▲ **FIGURE 6–11** ■ ■ ■ (cont.)

MANAGEMENT IN ACTION   Ryder Systems

At Ryder Systems, purchasing a vehicle for subsequent leasing by Ryder required as many as 17 hand-offs, as the relevant documents made their way from one department to another. Since such hand-offs occurred both horizontally and vertically, the amount of time and energy wasted was enormous.

Ryder corrected the situation by reengineering the vehicle purchase process. Now, a single multispecialist-"horizontal"-vehicle-purchase team handles all the tasks in the vehicle-purchasing process. By organizing these teams, Ryder was able to dramatically streamline each customer's vehicle purchase. Each corporate customer got its order assigned to and quickly processed by a single team. The old procedure would have involved handing the customer's file from the sales department to the credit department, and so on.   ■■■■

As at Ryder, horizontal organizations typically eliminate functional departments and instead sprinkle functional specialists throughout the key process teams.[43] AT&T is another example. AT&T's Network Services division, with 16,000 employees, identified 13 core processes around which to reorganize. GE's lighting business similarly organized around multidisciplinary teams, each carrying out one of more than 100 processes, from new-product design to improving manufacturing machinery efficiency.

Federal-Type Organizations

Some "companies" don't organize as companies in the traditional sense, with a single board of directors and a conventional chain of command. Instead, these companies are actually networks, consisting of several firms and entities all working toward the same aim. In these federal organizations (as in federal governments), power is shared among a central authority and several independent but constituent units, and the central unit's

federal organization ■ *an organization in which power is distributed between a central unit and a number of constituents, but the central unit's authority is intentionally limited.*

▼ **FIGURE 6–12** ■ ■ ■ (cont.)

| **Cut** function and staff departments to a minimum, preserving key expertise. | **Appoint** a manager or team as the "owner" of each core process. | **Create** multidisciplinary teams to run each process. | **Set** specific performance objectives for each process. | **Empower** employees with authority and information to achieve goals. | **Revamp** training, appraisal, pay, and budgetary systems to support the new structure and link it to customer satisfaction. |

authority is intentionally limited.[44] The federal approach lets a company accomplish something it might not be able to accomplish in any other way. Thus, it might enable a tiny firm with a great idea for a new product to quickly marshal the resources it needs, by letting several independent companies each work on a piece of the project.[45]

Consider the organization at TCG.[46]

MANAGEMENT IN ACTION TCG

TCG develops a wide variety of products such as portable and handheld data terminals. It is organized around 13 individual small firms—"Like a cell in a large organism, each firm has its own purpose and ability to function independently, but [it] shares features and purposes with all of its sister firms."[47]

▶ **FIGURE 6–13** ■ ■ ■

TGC's Cellular Organization

Source: Reprinted with permission of the *Academy of Management Executive,* from "Organizing in the Knowledge Age: Anticipating the Cellular Form," Raymond Miles, vol. 11, no. 4, © 1997; permission conveyed through Copyright Clearance Center, Inc.

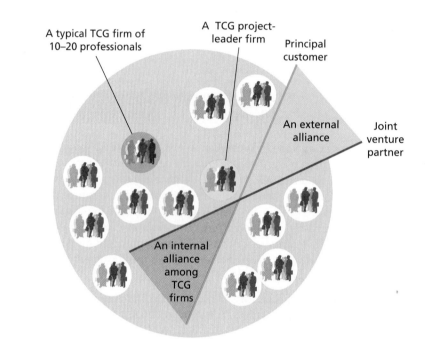

Figure 6.13 shows how TCG's structure works. Each of TCG's individual (but TCG-owned) firms continually searches for new product and service opportunities. When it finds an attractive opportunity, it incubates it. Then, when the new product shows concrete progress, the initiating firm acts as project leader for what TCG calls its "triangulation" process. Triangulation means that the initiating firm creates and leads a three-way partnership (or "cell") consisting of (1) one or more TCG firms, (2) an external joint venture partner, and (3) a principal customer for the product or service.[48] The triangulation process and mutual support among the 13 TCG firms help make TCG more than the sum of its parts. Its firms learn from one another, have access to one another's customers and resources, and help to capitalize and fund one another's projects.

TCG has found that, to be effective, each "cell" must follow three principles.

1. Each firm must accept its entrepreneurial responsibilities, and aggressively identify new project opportunities, and pursue customers.
2. Each must be self-contained, and function with "both the ability and freedom" to respond quickly and creatively to customer and partner needs.
3. Each firm must have the responsibility to be profitable and to have the opportunity to invest in—and even own stock in—the other TCG firms.

Virtual Organizations

Sometimes, a company has to organize substantial resources to accomplish some big project, but can't afford the time or expense of acquiring and owning those resources itself. For many firms, the answer (as we first saw in Chapter 5) is a virtual organization, "a temporary network of independent companies—suppliers, customers, perhaps even rivals—linked by information technology to share skills, costs, and access to one another's markets."[49] Virtual organizations (or "virtual corporations") are networks of companies, each of which brings to the virtual corporation its special expertise and is linked with the rest through information technology.

Virtual organizations have two main features. First, "the central feature of virtual organizations is their dependence on a federation of alliances and partnerships with other organizations."[50] A virtual organization operates as a federated collection of enterprises tied together by partial ownership arrangements such as joint ventures, strategic alliances, minority investments, consortia, coalitions, outsourcing, and franchises.[51]

The second feature stems from the first: Corporate self-interest, not authority, generally keeps everyone in line. In traditional organizations, the employees who actually do the work are supposed to follow orders. In virtual organizations, it's not the company's employees who are doing the work, but the principals and employees of its virtual partners. Giving orders and relying on a chain of command is usually not too constructive here. Instead, the trick is to pick competent and reliable partners, and to provide for equitable incentives.[52] Responsibility and self-interest then hopefully keep all partners in line. The Management in Action feature gives an entrepreneurial example.

MANAGEMENT IN ACTION   Indigo Partners

Virtual organizations enable some small businesses to take on projects they would not have dreamed of years ago. For example, consider Indigo Partners (**www.indigohq.com**). Begun in 1996 by Jennifer Overholt and Michelle Lee as an informal support group for marketing consultants, the company now has dozens of customers. Indigo's projects range from market analyses for Fortune 500 companies to revising business plans for start-ups.[53]

For a consulting company, Indigo Partners is stunning for what it lacks. It has no overhead and no assets to manage. It has no headquarters office and no secretarial pool. The firm's six partners work on projects individually or in small teams. For large projects, they tap into a pool of specialized freelancers. For these entrepreneurs, Indigo provides the best of both worlds. They can tap the sum total of all their knowledge and expertise to bid on projects, and to get each other's advice as they manage their own projects. At the same time, their virtual organization frees them from the hassles of having to manage bricks and mortar assets like an office, furniture, and office staff. ■■■■

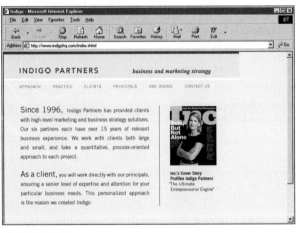

▲ WEBNOTE ■■■

Indigo Partners is a virtual organization: it has a Web site, but no headquarters office, no overhead, and no assets to manage.
www.indigohq.com

Source: Copyright ©1997–2002 Indigo® Instruments. All rights reserved.

SUMMARY ■■■

1. Organizing means arranging an enterprise's activities in such a way that they systematically contribute to the enterprise's goals. An organization consists of people whose specialized tasks are coordinated to contribute to the organization's goals.

2. Authority is the right to take action, to make decisions, and to direct the work of others. Managers usually distinguish between line and staff authority.

3. Departmentalization is the process through which management groups an enterprise's activities together, and assigns them to managers. Managers group activities by functions, products, customer groups, marketing channels, or geographic areas.

4. A matrix organization—sometimes called matrix management—is an organization in which one or more forms of

departmentalization are superimposed on an existing one. In practice, most enterprises are hybrids and use several forms of departmentalization.

5. Many companies are adopting flatter structures in an effort to eliminate duplication of effort, inspire creativity, and increase responsiveness. The span of control in a company is the number of subordinates reporting directly to a supervisor.

6. Many firms superimpose organizational networks over existing structures. A network is a system of interconnected or cooperating individuals. It can be formal or informal, and it can be electronically based. The basic idea is to link managers from various departments, levels, and geographic areas so that they form a multidisciplinary team whose members communicate across normal organizational boundaries. Team-based organi-

zations, federal organizations, virtual organizations, and horizontal organizations are all networked organizations.

7. The horizontal corporation is a structure organized around basic processes such as new-product development, sales fulfillment, and customer support. Everyone works together in multidisciplinary teams, with each team assigned to perform one or more of the processes.

8. Federal organizations are organizations in which power is distributed between a central unit and a number of a constituent units, but the central unit's authority is intentionally limited. A virtual organization is a collection of independent enterprises tied together by contracts and other means, such as partial ownership arrangements.

KEY TERMS ▪▪▪

organizing 139
organization chart 139
chain of command 140
authority 140
line manager 140
staff manager 140
functional authority 140

informal organization 141
departmentalization 141
functional departmentalization 141
divisional 143
customer departmentalization 144
marketing-channel departmentalization 144
marketing channel 144

matrix organization 148
span of control 154
organizational network 156
formal organizational network 157
team 158
horizontal corporation 159
federal organization 161

SKILLS AND STUDY MATERIALS

COMPANION WEBSITE ▪▪▪

WWW We invite you to visit the Dessler Companion Website at **www.prenhall.com/dessler** for this chapter's Internet resources.

EXPERIENTIAL EXERCISES ▪▪▪

1. Colleges are interesting from an organizational viewpoint, because the employees (the faculty) tend to make so many of a college's decisions and run so many of its projects. It's not unusual, for instance, to have the faculty elect a faculty senate, which in turn appoints committees for things like promotions and curricula; the committees then often have a major say in who gets promoted, what programs the college offers, and so on. Similarly, the students often evaluate the faculty, as well as elect their own student governments, which, in turn, decide how the students' fees are spent.

Some critics say that all of this is a little like "letting the inmates run the asylum." And, indeed, the pace of criticism has picked up in the past few years. With more colleges and universities going online, students have more educational choices. As a result, tuition fees are under pressure, and universities are scrambling to cut costs and be more efficient. Since efficiency is not something most people instinctively associate with academia, the pressures to reduce costs have caused a lot of soul-searching. Boards of trustees are reviewing everything about how their colleges do things—from how many courses faculty members teach, to how professors are appraised, and to how to decide which programs to offer or drop.

Form teams of four to five students, and answer the following questions:

1. Draw an organization chart for your college or university. What type(s) of departmentalization does it use? How would you show, on the chart, the authority exercised by the faculty and faculty committees (teams)?

2. The chapter argues that having a network structure tends to speed decisions. However, some people think that even though colleges are networked, they are still the most bureaucratic organizations they've ever dealt with. To what extent and in what way is your college networked? Do you consider it bureaucratic, and, if so, what explains why a networked organization produces such bureaucracy?

3. How would you reorganize the college if streamlining and more efficiency were your goals?

4. How would you reorganize your college as a horizontal organization? (Make sure to indicate what the "customer processes" would be.)

2. As noted in this chapter, experts have made numerous proposals regarding how to reorganize the U.S. government's law enforcement apparatus in order to strengthen its antiterrorism campaign. One recent suggestion is to require the CIA and FBI to share their intelligence information with the new Department of Homeland Security. Others suggest removing the enforcement function from the INS and giving it to the Justice Department. Assume your goals are to minimize the possibility of a new attack, and to maximize the government's ability to stop potential terrorists from entering the country. Prior to coming to class, spend about an hour on the Internet learning about what the United States and its homeland security chief are now doing to achieve those goals. Then, in class, meet in teams of four to five students to devise an organization structure for achieving those two goals.

ORGANIZING GREENLEY COMMUNICATIONS

Louis Greenley has to make a difficult decision. Greenley Communications was a diversified communications company that operated primarily in the western United States. The firm owned and operated newspapers and radio and television stations. For years, there had been an "invisible wall" between the print operations and radio and television.

Greenley's existing structure was organized by industry. There was a newspaper division, a radio division, and a television production division. Each division had its own bookkeeping, sales, marketing, operations, and service divisions. Accounting and financial management were handled at the corporate level.

In the newspaper division, there was a clear distinction between the news and the sales/financial sides of the business. Coming from a family of journalists, Greenley was always concerned that the sale of advertising to local clients would influence the paper's coverage of the news—editors might ignore potential stories that might reflect negatively on an advertiser.

The vice president of broadcast operations in Greenley's television arm proposed a major structural change. The proposal called for organizing Greenley Communications geographically. This would allow regional managers to have a single sales force that could sell advertising in any form: print, radio, or TV. The approach had some appeal. There was significant overlap at Greenley—the company tended to own multiple sales forces in the same region, for instance, often calling on the same customer. Certainly, there would be savings in personnel, since the company would need a far smaller sales staff. However, Greenley is not yet persuaded. He is trying to decide what to do.

Discussion Questions

1. Draw Greenley's current organization chart as best you can.

2. What factors should influence Greenley's decision to restructure?

3. What risks does the proposed restructuring create?

4. What are the pros and cons of the vice president's new proposed structure?

5. If you were Greenley, how exactly would you reorganize (if at all), and why?

JETBLUE'S BASIC ORGANIZATION

jetBlue AIRWAYS' An airline like JetBlue has basic tasks it must attend to, and so it has organized a number of departments. These departments include flight operation (pilots), in-flight (flight attendants), reservations, systems operations (the dispatchers that work with the pilots to determine flights paths), technical operations (mechanics, engineers, quality control), human resources, finance/accounting/treasury, airport (customer service), security, marketing, sales, public relations and communications, information technology, real estate and facilities, legal, and safety. Furthermore, in addition to its CEO and president, JetBlue also has vice presidents for reservations management (in charge of a group determining aircraft load factors and what to charge for each ticket) as well as for planning and scheduling.

While the company obviously has an organization, it has no published organization chart. There are several reasons for this, according to the company's head of HR. For one thing, JetBlue wants to avoid the sense of bureaucracy that often arises when employees start getting preoccupied with organization charts. Furthermore, he points out that "we've been very fluid," and after growing from zero employees to 3,200 in less than three years, the reality is that any published organization chart is quickly out of date. There are also some practical, competitive reasons for not publishing the chart. For example, why spend time and effort recruiting, selecting, and hiring the best employees, and then make it easy for competitors to recruit those employees from you, by showing them who's in charge of what at your company?

Internally, however, employees do have access to the sort of information you'd normally expect on an organization chart. For instance, JetBlue does have, as already noted, departments with specific responsibilities. These departmental assignments and the employees in them are available to JetBlue employees on the company's intranet in the form of a spreadsheet. So if an employee has a question regarding, say, accounts receivables, he or she can check the JetBlue intranet in order to find the right person to talk to. However, while the company currently deemphasizes organization charts, there's no doubt that as JetBlue grows in size, it will need more structure and may well move toward a more conventional organization chart-based structure.

Questions

1. Based on the information in this case and on whatever information you can obtain from the JetBlue Web site, develop a workable organization chart for the company.

2. List the pros and cons of Jet Blue's current approach to organizing—and particularly its emphasis on avoiding formal organization charts.

3. Based on the information in this case and on anything else you know about JetBlue, show specifically, in chart and narrative form, how the company could install a network organization.

4. Given JetBlue's current organization and list of departments, what specifically would you recommend if the company wanted to reorganize its tasks around "horizontal organizations"?

7 Designing Organizational Structures

CHAPTER OBJECTIVES

After studying this chapter and the case exercises at the end, you should be able to:

1. Explain what the situation calls for in terms of organizing the firm's lines of authority, departmentalization, degree of specialization of jobs, delegation and decentralization, and span of control.

2. Design an organization structure for a company.

3. Reorganize a company from its current structure to that of a "learning organization."

4. Explain why a company is not achieving coordination and how you would correct the situation.

5. Explain what the manager is doing wrong about delegating authority and how you would correct the situation.

THE MANAGEMENT CHALLENGE

Rick Wagoner Organizes Saturn

General Motors created the Saturn Car Company in the mid-1980s in part to learn more about Japanese methods (like teamwork). GM made Saturn a separate division, insulating it from GM's usual ways of doing things. GM called it "a new kind of car company," and it was. It had its own president and did its own product design, manufacturing, and marketing. Employee teams ran the Saturn plant. Saturn president Richard Lefauve reported directly to GM's president.

Saturn's autonomy meant some duplication and inefficiencies for General Motors. GM, for example, might have produced the Saturn in one of GM's other plants more efficiently. Similarly, one of GM's other car divisions could have easily handled Saturn's marketing. However, GM believed that the benefits of letting Saturn alone outweighed the disadvantages. By keeping Saturn autonomous, GM could learn more about what was then the famous Japanese team approach to building high-quality cars.

By 2001, GM's goals had changed. Saturn had been losing money for years, small cars were no longer as popular, and GM, like most car manufacturers, had already adopted all the Japanese methods it wanted to adopt. GM's CEO, Rick Wagoner, had some decisions to make. Should he leave Saturn independent, or risk reducing Saturn's uniqueness by absorbing it into another car division?

Chapter 6 covered the basic building blocks of organization, including authority, chain of command, and the various ways managers divide the work or departmentalize. The main purpose of Chapter 7 is to show you how to choose one element over another for the particular situation that you face—in other words, how to organize. The main topics we'll discuss include the factors that determine how managers organize, how to create learning organizations, how to achieve coordination, and how to delegate and decentralize authority.

■■ ■ WHAT DETERMINES HOW A COMPANY ORGANIZES?

Organizing is part art and part science. The managers' plans help determine what tasks they want their organizations to do. Then managers apply experience, knowledge, and common sense to decide what the organization should look like. However, organizing need not (and should not) involve just common sense. There is also considerable scientific knowledge that managers can apply. The research findings and knowledge managers can use to answer the question "How should we organize?" fits under organization theory. It is the body of knowledge used to explain how to organize an enterprise. We'll start with the basics of organization theory.

Management and organization theory got its start about 100 years ago, when industrialization and mass production techniques were spreading. Entrepreneurs focused on making their firms as big as possible because large size meant economies of scale. And, economies of scale meant efficiency and lower costs; lower costs, in turn, meant more sales and more profits. Entrepreneurs needed rational management methods to run these new, large-scale enterprises. As we noted in Chapter 1, they turned to the classical writers, like Frederick Taylor, Max Weber, and Henri Fayol.

Henri Fayol and the Principles of Management

The work of Henri Fayol illustrates the classical approach to organizing. In his book *General and Industrial Management*, this steel company executive outlined a list of management principles he had found useful during his years as a manager. Most of these principles addressed how to organize. He wrote,

1. *Division of work.* The worker, always [working] on the same part, and the manager, concerned always with the same matters, acquired ability, sureness, and accuracy, which increased their output.
2. *Authority and responsibility.* Authority is the right to give orders and the power to exact obedience. Distinction must be made between official authority, deriving from office, and personal authority, compounded of intelligence, experience, moral worth, and ability to lead.
3. *Discipline.* The best means of establishing and maintaining [discipline] are good superiors at all levels; agreements as clear and fair as possible; sanctions [penalties] judiciously applied.
4. *Unity of command.* For any action whatsoever, an employee should receive orders from one superior only.
5. *Unity of direction.* There should be one head and one plan for a group of activities serving the same objective.
6. *Subordination of individual interests.* In a business, the interests of one employee or group of employees should not prevail over those of the concern.
7. *Remuneration of personnel.* Remuneration should be fair and as far as possible afford satisfaction to both personnel and the firm.
8. *Centralization.* The question of centralization or decentralization is a simple question of proportion; it is a matter of finding the optimum degree for the particular concern. What appropriate share of initiative may be left to intermediaries depends on the personal character of the manager, on his moral worth, on the reliability of his subordinates, and also on the conditions of the business.
9. *Scalar chain.* The scalar chain is the chain of superiors ranging from the ultimate authority to the lowest ranks. It is an error to depart needlessly from the line of

authority, but it is an even greater one to keep to it when detriment to the business ensues.

10. *Order.* For social order to prevail in a concern, there must be an appointed place for every employee, and every employee must be in his or her appointed place.

11. *Equity.* For the personnel to be encouraged to carry out its duties with all the devotion and loyalty of which it is capable, it must be treated with kindliness, and equity results from the combination of kindness and justice. Equity excludes neither forcefulness nor sternness.

12. *Stability of tenure of personnel.* Time is required for an employee to get used to new work and succeed in doing it well, always assuming he possesses the requisite abilities.

13. *Initiative.* Thinking out a plan and ensuring its success is one of the keenest satisfactions for an intelligent person to experience. This power of thinking out and executing is what is called initiative. It represents a great source of strength for business.

14. *Esprit de corps.* "Union is strength." Harmony, union among the personnel of a concern, is a great strength in that concern.[1]

These principles were not rigid. Experts like Fayol were practical people; they were savvy enough to know that there are times when sticking to the chain of command results in slow decisions and slow responses. Fayol, for instance, said that orders and inquiries should generally follow the chain of command. But in very special circumstances, a "bridge" communication could occur, say, between a salesperson and a production supervisor. Yet for the most part, the classical emphasis was on a more centralized, functional chain-of-command approach. The resulting organizations were quite militaristic.

A Changing Environment

Prescriptions like these worked well in the environment of Fayol's time. Competition was local, not global. New-product introductions were relatively slow. Consumers were less demanding. Things didn't change too quickly. Organizing by giving employees specialized jobs and making them stick to the chain of command worked well. But as the number of unexpected problems and issues—new competitors, new product and technological innovations, customers suddenly going out of business, and so on—become unmanageable, a classical-type organization gets overloaded and errors start to mount.

■ *Application Example* Consider this example. Your family owns a small chain of supermarkets in the northeastern United States. For many years, your traditional structure (a fairly large central staff of produce and food buyers, a layer of regional managers, a layer below that of store managers, each with two or three layers of department managers) worked well.

It worked well, in part, because things weren't changing very quickly. You've had basically the same competitors for the past 30 years. You all sold more or less the same line of products. And you all used more or less the same technology—telephones and fax machines and an occasional personal computer—to run your operations. No one was much more efficient than anyone else, no one was introducing new technologies, and everyone was selling at about the same prices, since they all had about the same costs. You were kept quite busy, but you didn't have to make a lot of split-second decisions. Nor did you face a lot of unforeseen events. Life was good.

Now things are changing. Two of your competitors just merged and became the new number one chain, and it's building superstores complete with pharmacies. It can also now consolidate backroom operations (functions like accounting and purchasing) and thus drive down costs and prices. As if that weren't enough, you just read that Wal-Mart is building a superstore right outside of town, as is Costco. You know that with their superefficient satellite-based distribution systems, costs and prices are going to fall even more. The decision-making pace is picking up.

Suddenly, managers are coming to you with emergencies, with complaints, and with problems they want you to solve. They can no longer wait weeks for your office to make or approve a decision. You're going to have to make your whole organization structure a lot smarter and faster-moving than it's ever been before. You can't afford to have so many people passing requests for decisions up and down the chain of command like some kind of relay race. You have to make it easier for decisions to get made. The question is, "How?" Should you let your store managers make more decisions themselves? Should you set up regional divisions? Should you give your store managers more support staff? What would you do, and what body of knowledge could you draw on? There is some research evidence you can use. Experts in the United Kingdom conducted some of the earliest and best research in this area.

Organization and Environment: The Burns and Stalker Study

Tom Burns and G. M. Stalker conducted one particularly astute research program.[2] They saw that the world faced by classical management experts like Fayol was much more sedate than that faced by modern managers. The classical environment has several distinguishing characteristics. Demand for the organization's product or service is stable and predictable, there is an unchanging set of competitors, and technological innovation and new product developments are evolutionary rather than revolutionary. Modern firms' environments—with their high-tech product innovations—change more quickly and unexpectedly. Could the type of environment influence how the manager should organize?

Burns and Stalker first studied a textile mill that operated in a more classical, stable environment. To succeed, this firm had to minimize costs and stress efficiency. Its existence depended on keeping unexpected occurrences to a minimum in order to maintain steady, high-volume production runs. This firm had a very militaristic (Burns and Stalker called it "mechanistic") organization structure. Mechanistic organizations, they said, are characterized by close adherence to the chain of command; a functional division of work; highly specialized jobs; use of the formal hierarchy for coordination; and detailed job descriptions that provide a precise definition of rights, obligations, and technical methods for performing each job. This organization fits the needs of the stable environment.

mechanistic organization ■ *an organizational structure characterized by close adherence to the established chain of command, highly specialized jobs, and vertical communications.*

At the other extreme, some companies had to compete in fast-changing innovative environments. Here, (1) demand for the organization's product or service can change drastically, sometimes overnight; (2) sudden, unexpected changes can occur in the nature of the organization's competitors;[3] and (3) an extremely rapid rate of technological innovation and new product development is common.

Several electronics firms were competing in such an environment. Survival depended on being able to introduce innovative products and on being alert for innovations by competitors. Creativity, fast decisions, and entrepreneurial activities are what mattered most. These firms developed new types of responsive, flexible, networked organization structures to fit these new demands. Burns and Stalker called them "organic" organizations.

■■■ *(a) Mechanistic organization: Toyota truck assembly line.*

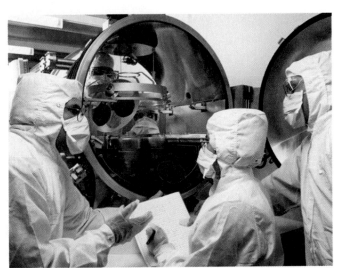

(b) Organic organization: Microelectronic Research Center, making chips.

Organic organizations were the antithesis of mechanistic organizations. Managers organized organic structures for speed, not efficiency. For example, managers don't insist that employees "follow the rules" or stick to the chain of command. Managers also decentralize decision making, by letting more decisions get made farther down the chain of command. Jobs and departments are less functionally specialized.[4] Organic firms tended to have divisional structures. Employees didn't view job responsibility as a limited field of rights and obligations (employees don't respond to requests by saying, "That's not my job"). And there was an emphasis on networked rather than on vertical communication, and on consultation rather than command. Table 7.1 summarizes the features of organic and mechanistic organizations.

In terms of organizational structure, we can summarize the Burns and Stalker findings as follows:

■ *Lines of authority.* In mechanistic organizations, the lines of authority are clear, and everyone adheres to the chain of command. In organic organizations, employees' jobs are always changing, and the lines of authority are not so clear. There is less emphasis on sticking to the chain of command in organic organizations. Employees simply speak directly with the person who can answer the problem.

■ *Departmentalization.* In mechanistic organizations (with their emphasis on efficiency), functional departmentalization prevails. In organic organizations (where flexibility is the rule), product/divisional departmentalization prevails.

■ *Degree of specialization.* In mechanistic organizations, each employee has a highly specialized job at which he or she is expected to become an expert. In organic organizations, job enlargement is the rule.

■ *Degree of Decentralization.* Mechanistic organizations centralize most important decisions. Lower-level employees in organic organizations tend to make more important decisions; these firms are more decentralized.

■ *Span of control.* The span of control is narrow in mechanistic organizations, and there is close supervision. Spans are wider in organic organizations, and supervision is more general.

■ *Type of Coordination.* Managers tend to achieve coordination by "sticking to the chain of command" in mechanistic organizations. In faster-changing organic organizations, there is more emphasis on committees and cross-functional liaisons.

Organization and Technology: The Woodward Studies

British researcher Joan Woodward's contribution is her discovery that a firm's production technology (the processes it uses to produce its products or services) affects how management should organize the firm. Woodward and her associates spent

TABLE 7–1	Burns and Stalker's Approach to Organizing	
	Type of Organization	
Characteristics	Mechanistic	Organic
Type of Environment	Stable	Innovative
Comparable to	Classical organization	Behavioral organization emphasis on self-control
Adherence to Chain of Command	Firm	Flexible—chain of command often bypassed
Type of Departmentalization	Functional	Divisional
How Specialized Are Jobs?	Specialized	Unspecialized—jobs change daily, with situation
Degree of Decentralization	Decision making centralized	Decision making decentralized
Span of Control	Narrow	Wide
Type of Coordination and Communications	Hierarchy and rules, chain of command	Committees, liaisons, and special integrators, networking

months analyzing volumes of data on each company's history and background, size, and policies and procedures. Surprisingly, none of this analysis seemed to explain why some successful firms had classic, mechanistic structures while others were more networked and organic (to use Burns and Stalker's phrases).

In search of an answer, Woodward decided to classify the companies according to their production technologies. *Unit and small-batch production firms* produced one-at-a-time prototypes and specialized custom units (like fine pianos) to customers' requirements. They, therefore, had to be very responsive to customer needs. *Large-batch and mass-production firms* produced large batches of products on assembly lines (like automobiles). They emphasized efficiency. *Process production firms* produced products (such as paper and petroleum products) with continuously running facilities. Highly trained technicians had to be ready to respond at a moment's notice to any production emergency.

Once Woodward's team classified the firms this way, it became obvious that a different type of organizational structure was appropriate for each type of technology. Table 7.2 summarizes Woodward's findings. Note that networked, organic structures were usually best in the unit and process production firms. Mass production firms usually did best with mechanistic structures. The reason (as with Burns and Stalker) may be this: When responding fast is paramount, organic structures work best. For pure efficiency and when demand is more predictable, classical, mechanistic structures seem to work best.

In terms of organizational structure, we can summarize the Woodward findings as follows:

- *Lines of authority.* The lines of authority and adherence to the chain of command are rigid in mass production firms, but more informal and flexible in unit and process production firms.
- *Departmentalization.* There is a functional departmentalization in mass production firms, and a product type of departmentalization in unit and process production firms.
- *Degree of specialization.* Jobs are highly specialized in mass production firms and less so in unit and process production firms.
- *Delegation and decentralization.* Organizations tend to be centralized in mass production firms and decentralized in unit and process production firms.
- *Span of control.* Unit and process production firms have smaller supervisory level spans of control than do mass production firms.

Synthesis: A Contingency Approach to Organizing

Burns and Stalker's findings as well as Woodward's suggest that different organizational structures are appropriate for, and contingent on, different tasks. At one extreme are organizations for dealing with predictable, routine tasks like running a rayon mill. Here, management wants to emphasize efficiency, and successful organizations, therefore, tend to be mechanistic. They stress adherence to rules and to the chain of command, are highly centralized, and have a more specialized, functional departmentalization.

TABLE 7–2	Summary of Woodward's Research Findings		
	Unit and Small-Batch Firms (Example: Custom-Built Cars)	Large-Batch and Mass Production (Example: Mass-Produced Cars)	Process Production (Example: Oil Refinery)
Chain of Command	Not Clear	Clear	Not Clear
Span of Control	Narrow	Wide	Narrow
Departmentalization	Product	Function	Product
Overall Organization	Organic	Mechanistic	Organic
Specialization of Jobs	Low	High	Low

Note: Summary of findings showing how production technology and organization structure are related.

At the other extreme, some organizations have more unpredictable tasks, since they continually face the need to invent new products and respond quickly to emergencies. Here, management must emphasize creativity and entrepreneurial activities, and to encourage these activities, such organizations tend to be organic. They do not urge employees to "play by the rules" or to abide closely to the chain of command. Similarly, decision making is pushed down lower in the chain of command (it is more decentralized), and jobs and departments are less specialized.

Organizing: Always Keep Your Goals in Mind

These findings illustrate an important management principle. The manager's goals should guide how he or she organizes—structure follows strategy. For example, boosting efficiency typically suggests (as Woodward found) one structural approach, while being able to react quickly to customers' concerns suggests another.

There are many contemporary examples of how the manager's goals drive organization. In March 2002, President Bush was appalled when the U.S. Immigration and Naturalization Service—six months after the attack of September 11—mailed pilots' visas for two accused World Trade Center pilots to the school in Florida where they had learned to fly. How could this have happened?

Bush's homeland security team concluded that the problem was partly organizational. INS and Border Patrol were part of the Justice Department, while Customs was in the Treasury Department. Both departments exercised some aspect of enforcement when it came to guarding America's borders. This split arrangement made sense when Customs' main goal was ensuring that tariffs were paid and when the INS goal was screening immigrants. Today, the goals of both Customs and the INS are the same—securing the borders and preventing "illegals" from entering the country. Bush's team, therefore, recommended merging Customs with the INS and the Border Patrol. Merging them would consolidate their enforcement capabilities and thus help achieve today's border-protection goals. The Management in Action feature describes another example of how goals drive organization.

MANAGEMENT IN ACTION   Saturn

▬▬▬ *Annette Clayton, Saturn President, in a new Saturn Vue at the plant in Spring Hill, Tennessee.*

For more than a decade, running Saturn as a separate company made sense for General Motors. GM wanted to learn more about and adopt Japanese production methods (like teamwork). To do that, GM felt it had to insulate Saturn from GM's somewhat bureaucratic, efficiency-oriented way of doing things. Fast forward to 2001. Now Saturn was losing money, and GM had already adopted all the Japanese methods it wanted to adopt. When the plans and goals for Saturn changed, GM changed the Saturn organization (see Figure 7.1).

In January 1991, Saturn was a separate division, and its president, Richard LeFauve, reported directly to GM's president. With the reorganization in August 2001, management absorbed Saturn into the giant GM structure. Saturn's president, Annette Clayton, now reports to one of 28 GM vice presidents and is, essentially, the Saturn factory manager. And now, instead of reporting to the Saturn president, Saturn's chief designer, engineering vice president, and marketing vice president all report to the corresponding GM vice presidents. ▬▬

IBM provides another example. When he arrived at IBM in the 1990s, Louis Gerstner found the firm preoccupied with its organization charts. As one writer described them, "These foldout charts were minor masterpieces of craftsmanship and printing, an intricate latticework of lines, color-coded boxes, and asterisks. Lovely to behold, they recalled the engineering drawings of Leonardo da Vinci, according to one executive.

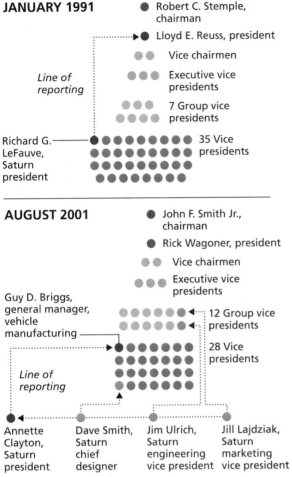

◀ **FIGURE 7–1** ■ ■ ■

Back in the Corporate Fold

Source: Keith Bradsher, "The Reality Behind the Slogan," *New York Times*, 23 August, 2001, p. C1, and General Motors.

JANUARY 1991

● Robert C. Stemple, chairman

▶● Lloyd E. Reuss, president

● ● Vice chairmen

● ● ● Executive vice presidents

● ● ● 7 Group vice
● ● ● ● presidents

Line of reporting

Richard G. LeFauve, Saturn president

35 Vice presidents

AUGUST 2001

● John F. Smith Jr., chairman

● Rick Wagoner, president

● ● Vice chairmen

● ● ● Executive vice presidents

Guy D. Briggs, general manager, vehicle manufacturing

● ● ● ● ● ● ◀ 12 Group vice
● ● ● ● ● ● ◀ presidents

28 Vice presidents

Line of reporting

● ◀ Annette Clayton, Saturn president

Dave Smith, Saturn chief designer

Jim Ulrich, Saturn engineering vice president

Jill Lajdziak, Saturn marketing vice president

Back in the Corporate Fold

Saturn's president once reported to G.M.'s president and oversaw the entire Saturn operation. Now, the Saturn president reports to a G.M. vice president, and runs its factories. Design, engineering and marketing report to other G.M. executives.

Producing them was a cottage industry within IBM, and thousands of them were pinned on the office walls of its workers."[5]

Gerstner wanted more competitiveness and much more focus on the customer. It's, therefore, not surprising that one of his first moves was to eliminate the preoccupation with organization charts. He told his employees that anyone asking for an organization chart was focusing on the wrong thing. In the future, the important thing was building IBM from the customer back, not from the company out.

Organizing: Use Logic and Common Sense

In the final analysis, there is no formula that managers like Gerstner can apply to answer this question: "How should we organize?" Research findings like those of Woodward and Burns and Stalker provide useful input. However, organizing is still an art, and so logic and common sense should prevail.

This helps explain why organizing tends to be a process of continuous fine-tuning. Consider Exide Corporation. In 2000, new CEO Robert Lutz found a company structured geographically around 10 separate country organizations. This facilitated local decision making. However, Lutz felt it was also encouraging the country managers to compete with each other. He therefore reportedly spent $8 million creating a new structure, one based around product lines (such as global divisions for car batteries and industrial batteries). But stripped of their local authority, many European managers soon resigned, causing Lutz to turn to fine-tuning Exide's structure (before leaving for a new post at GM).

Ford is another example. In the late 1990s, management embarked on a reorganization campaign called "Ford 2000." Among other things, this campaign involved reorganizing Ford worldwide around huge global functional departments, such as new car development. This did make it easier to design and introduce new cars. However, Ford soon found its European market share plummeting, probably because it had lost some local spontaneity by moving away from the geographic structure. Ford management was soon back to using logic and common sense in fine-tuning Ford's structure.

Again, this sort of fine-tuning reflects the complexities involved in deciding what structure is best. Organizing is never an exact science. Understanding the firm's environment and technology provides a good start for knowing what the organization structure should look like. However, the manager then has to factor in things like his or her goals and the pros and cons of the various options. This is particularly evident in the persistent issue (as at Exide and Ford) of whether to departmentalize by product, function, or geographic area. The dilemma (as we saw in Chapter 6) is that they all have pros and cons. Thus, product divisions may facilitate introducing product improvements around the world faster, while a geographic approach facilitates attention to local buyers' needs.[6]

In terms of building blocks such as type of departmentalization, adherence to the chain of command, degree of specialization of jobs, degree of decentralization, and width of span of control, important determinants include the factors in Checklist 7.1.

CHECKLIST 7.1 ■ What Determines Organization Structure

☑ *Environment.* Fast-changing environments tend to require more adaptive, organic structures (including product departments, less specialization, and more delegation); placid, slowly changing environments tend to favor classical, mechanistic structures. (See Table 7.1 page 170.)

☑ *Technology.* Unit and continuous production processes tend to favor organic structures. Mass production processes favor mechanistic structures.

☑ *Goals.* Ask, "What are the main goals we want to achieve via this organization?" (Improving attention to local buyers' needs might suggest organizing geographically.)

☑ *Pros and cons.* Each approach to departmentalization has pros and cons. For example, product divisions mean increased duplication, whereas functional departments may mean less attention focused on the customer's needs. (See "Advantages and Disadvantages," Chapter 6, pages 142 and 143).

☑ *Logic and common sense.* For example, why organize around product divisions if the company has no managers to fill the general manager slots? Logic and common sense must prevail, and the structure must be fine-tuned as required.

■ *The Global Manager* Applying such guidelines is especially important when competing in a global arena. Dissatisfied customers are usually easier to notice when you see them every day than when they're 10,000 miles away.

That's one reason Hewlett-Packard-Compaq CEO Carly Fiorina decided to reorganize HP's global organization. The problem was that, with HP's geographic structure, multinational customers found themselves being served by numerous, separate HP sales offices around the world. That meant the multinational customer often couldn't get a unified, companywide sales effort from HP. Fiorina changed that. By establishing special HP customer sales groups, HP can be sure customers will now get the dedicated services of an HP team.

■■■ HOW TO CREATE LEARNING ORGANIZATIONS

A company taps into an online marketplace, thereby linking the firm with its suppliers and customers through the Web. This should mean better prices and faster service, but in this case, it does not. The company just can't seem to take advantage of the Web's real-time pricing. What is going wrong?

The answer is that, it didn't reorganize as a "learning organization." This company joined the online marketplace to get instant, best prices. However, it continued to make its purchasing decisions centrally, once or twice a month. It was the lower-level sales and purchasing people who actually followed and traded on the fast-moving marketplace, and they had to make quick, on-the-spot decisions. The way this firm was organized, these managers had to wait two weeks for a top management decision. Learning in this company proceeded at a snail's pace. The managers didn't learn of the great prices for a week, and the employees doing the buying didn't learn about their managers' decisions for another week. Therefore, the online marketplace did the firm little good. The company couldn't move fast enough to take advantage of the online marketplace's good deals.[7]

Whether launching product innovations, getting the best prices, or figuring out what your customers in London really want, companies must be able to learn faster today than they have in the past. This company wasn't set up to do this. Contrast that with how Brady Corp. did things; see the following Managing Without Boundaries feature.

MANAGING WITHOUT BOUNDARIES

Brady Corps' Boundaryless Supply Chain

Brady Corp., which manufactures identification and safety products, is one company that intends to do things right. Top management has earmarked about $50 million to roll out a new system that will link Brady's suppliers, customers, and distributors over the Internet. However, only about a third of that money is for the technology itself. Top management is spending the rest on restructuring the firm's organization and processes.

For example, Brady customer service employees used to get the orders and pass them on to the firm's production department. Then orders would move on to shipping. The organization structure and processes Brady is putting in place to support its new boundaryless supply chain is very different. Customers with simple orders will send them directly online to manufacturing. In manufacturing, Brady reengineered the operation, creating a horizontal process. One factory floor person will oversee the entire production and shipping process. Management expects the new horizontal organization and processes to cut about five steps out of the current 15 step sale-manufacturing-

shipping process and to cut the processing cost per order by about a third, to $32. Brady is creating an organization structure that learns faster than it did before. ■ ■ ■

▲ WEBNOTE ■ ■ ■

Brady Corp. is committed to the boundaryless supply chain: it is investing not only in the Internet technology, but also in restructuring its own organization and processes

www.whbrady.com

Source: © Brady Corporation. All rights reserved.

What Are Learning Organizations?

Like many other firms today, Brady Corp. knows that to succeed, it must become a learning organization.[8] As the head of planning for Royal Dutch/Shell says, "The ability to learn faster than your competitors may be the only sustainable competitive advantage."[9] *Learning organizations* are generally (1) organic, networked organizations that (2) encourage employees to think outside the boundaries of their own jobs, and which (3) cultivate their employees' personal mastery, so that (4) they have "the capacity to adapt to unforeseen situations, to learn from their own experiences, to shift their shared mindsets, and to change more quickly, broadly, and deeply than ever before."[10] Let's look at each of these characteristics.[11]

What Do Learning Organizations Look Like?

Assume that you want to download the latest Eminem recording (and, since this is just hypothetical, assume you're not concerned, for now, with legality). One option is to methodically check each of your friends, by sending each an e-mail note or making a phone call. Going one by one through your checklist, you hit paydirt (so to speak) after only 17 calls. Your other option is to join a Napster-type network. Here, everyone's record files are shared, so everyone can learn instantaneously who's got the record he or she wants. The genius of Napster (aside from the software) was the idea of networking everyone's files.

Some years ago, psychologists conducted a study of group communications. They arranged groups of five persons in one of the communication networks shown in Figure 7.2. They placed each person in a compartment at a table in such a way that his or her

In the "centralized" wheel networks, each subject could communicate only with the hub subject; in the all-channel "decentralized" network, each subject could communicate with every other subject so that ambiguous problems could be solved more quickly.

Source: Harold Leavitt, "Some Effects of Certain Communication Patterns on Group Performance, " *Journal of Abnormal and Social Psychology* 46, 1972

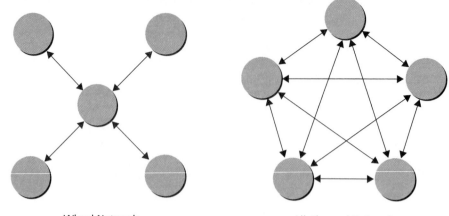

Wheel Network   All-Channel Network

communication was restricted. Each person in the all-channel network could communicate with any other person. People in the wheel network could communicate only with the person in the central position (hub) of the network. This central person could communicate with the four other people in his or her network. (The lines all show two-way linkages.) All each person knew was to whom messages could be sent and from whom messages could be received.

The researchers found that the best communication network depended on the problem they assigned.[12] Where the problem was simple and amenable to a clear-cut yes or no answer (such as, "Is this marble blue?"), the wheel structure was best. But for complex, ambiguous problems that required lots of learning and give-and-take, the all-channel network was best. Here, for instance, two people looking at identical marbles could describe them quite differently; what one might view as "greenish-yellow," another might call "aqua." The person in the center of the wheel network could not himself or herself quickly decide what color was common to all the marbles. Therefore, the all-channel network, where communications could flow freely to and from everyone, arrived at the fastest decision for ambiguous problems. The moral is that, as with Napster, when a lot of learning must take place quickly and you want to process a lot of information, it helps to be networked.

So what do learning organizations look like? Learning organizations don't necessarily have to be structurally networked, but it helps. Learning organizations like Brady Corp. use formal, electronic, or informal networks; team-based organizations; virtual teams; horizontal, process-oriented structures; or federal type structures (as described in Chapter 6) to make sure that the people who need the information can get it—and fast.

Nokia is organized this way. Nokia's network structure helps account for much of the firm's wireless phone success. There is such a deemphasis on organization charts at Nokia that, according to one HR manager, "people who join Nokia spend a few months trying to figure it out . . . You really have to figure out a network of people to get things done."[13]

How To Abolish Organizational Boundaries

Anyone who has tried to register for a closed course or to return an item without a receipt knows that traditional organizations have boundaries. Vertically, the chain of command means there are *authority boundaries*. The president gives orders to the vice president, who gives orders to the managers, and so on down the line. There are also horizontal or *departmental boundaries*. Some call this the "smokestack" approach to organizing. The whole firm consists of departmental smokestacks. The production department has its own responsibilities and point of view, the sales department has its own, and so on. And there's often not much enthusiastic interaction among them.[14]

The point is this: It hardly pays to network an organization or to create horizontal team-based structures (as at Brady Corp.) if boundaries like these stand in the way of information flow. Networking and creating true learning organizations assumes you can abolish some or all of these boundaries. In a **boundaryless organization**, management strips away the "walls" which typically separate organizational functions

boundaryless organization ■ *an organization in which management strips away the "walls" which typically separate organizational functions and hierarchical levels, through the widespread use of teams, networks, and similar structural mechanisms.*

	KEY QUESTIONS	TENSIONS DEVELOPING DUE TO THIS BOUNDARY
Authority Boundary	"Who is in charge of what?" →	How to lead but remain open to criticism. How to follow but still challenge superiors.
Task Boundary	"Who does what?" →	How to depend on others you don't control. How to specialize yet understand other people's jobs.
Political Boundary	"What's in it for us?" →	How to defend one's interests without undermining the organization. How to differentiate between win–win and win–lose situations.
Identity Boundary	"Who is—and isn't—'us'?" →	How to feel pride without devaluing others. How to remain loyal without undermining outsiders.

◄ **FIGURE 7–3** ▪ ▪ ▪

The Four Organizational Boundaries That Matter

In setting up a boundaryless organization, four boundaries must be overcome, but doing so means dealing with the resulting tensions.

Source: Reprinted by permission of *Harvard Business Review.* "The Four Organizational Boundaries that Matter," from "The New Boundaries of the Boundaryless Company," by Larry Hirschorn and Thomas Gilmore, May–June 1992. Copyright © 1992 by the President and Fellows of Harvard College. All rights reserved.

and hierarchical levels.[15] Doing so begins with understanding what the four main boundaries are (see Figure 7.3).

The Authority Boundary Bosses and subordinates deal with an authority boundary, which represents the authority differentials produced by the company's chain of command. The problem is that, to achieve the openness required of a learning-type network structure, just issuing and following orders is no longer good enough.[16] For example, a manager in a formal network who happened to be a vice president would inhibit the network's effectiveness if she demanded the right to give orders based solely on the fact that she was the network's highest-ranking person. A network should rely more on knowledge and expertise.

Piercing an authority boundary requires three things. Bosses must learn how to accept orders from lower-ranking employees who happen to be experts on the problem at hand. And, they must learn how to lead while still welcoming criticism. Subordinates must learn how to follow but still challenge superiors if necessary.

The Task Boundary Managers today also need to pierce the task boundary—in other words, the tendency employees have to focus on just their own individual tasks. Managing this boundary means getting employees to rid themselves of the "It's not my job" attitude. More and more jobs today call for a coordinated, team effort.[17]

The Political Boundary Organizational politics can also present a barrier. Here, individuals or groups scheme for their own interests, often at the expense of the firm's. Two managers, for instance, may be quietly politicking for the same promotion. The result of such opposing agendas can be a conflict at the departments' political boundary.

Realistically, employees are always going to ask, "What's in it for me?" And they will ask this question even in boundaryless organizations. Still, the manager should encourage them to take a more collegial, consensus-oriented approach and to "walk the talk" while doing so. The aim should be to have employees defend their own interests without undermining the best interests of the team, network, or organization.

The Identity Boundary Everyone identifies him- or herself with several groups—for instance, with family, school, profession, department, and company. We tend to identify with groups with which we have shared experiences and with which we share basic values. The identity boundary problem arises because we tend to trust and prefer dealing with those with whom we identify, but we tend to distrust others. This distrust can undermine the free-flowing cooperation that networked or team-based organizations require.

authority boundary ▪ *the boundary created by differences in organizational level or status across which communications may be distorted or constrained due to the status difference.*

task boundary ▪ *the boundary created by the tendency of employees to focus on their own specialized tasks.*

political boundary ▪ *the boundary created special interests or agendas within an organization that may oppose each other.*

identity boundary ▪ *the boundary created by identifying with those groups with which one has shared experiences and with which one believes one shares fundamental values.*

The solution for the manager is to expand the "group" with which his or her employees identify. For example, emphasize that while team spirit is laudable, employees must avoid belittling the contributions of other teams.[18] Similarly, emphasize to new employees that you expect them to identify first with the company and its goals, not just with their own departments or teams. IBM's labs is a good example.

MANAGEMENT IN ACTION   IBM's Labs

Abolishing boundaries isn't just an academic exercise.[19] For example, IBM has eight laboratories worldwide, employing about 3,000 researchers. The labs generated $1.3 billion in licensing revenues in one recent year. Why are they so productive? Many believe it's partly because IBM takes a boundaryless approach to developing and implementing innovations. Abolishing IBM's new-product-development boundaries took a great deal of effort. As the senior vice president for research put it, "The [product] development side is highly disciplined, with a lot of checkpoints, tests, and milestones. . . . The research side is the exact opposite; it's much more freewheeling." Left unattended, such differences could create barriers and impede the development and commercialization of new products.

However, that hasn't happened. By reducing the disruptive barriers created by authority, task, political, and identity boundaries, IBM has been able to blend the work of two very different departments into a collaborative team effort.

How To Streamline Organizational Decision Making

Most firms haven't become learning organizations overnight. For example, GE did not suddenly go from bureaucratic to boundaryless. Like almost all companies making such transitions, it moved gradually, first streamlining its structure in a series of specific organizational moves, including the following.

Downsize As globalization and deregulation (of banks and airlines, for instance) increased the intensity of competition, many firms (including GE) downsized. **Downsizing** means dramatically reducing the size of a company's workforce.[20] For example, faced with dwindling demand several years ago, Ford Motor Company cut well over 10,000 white-collar jobs, as a way to reduce expenses.

downsizing ■ dramatically reducing the size of a company's workforce.

Reduce Management Layers Reducing management layers—first mentioned in Chapter 6—is another popular way to help streamline an organization. Eliminating layers ('flattening' the chain of command) can reduce costs and boost productivity by cutting salaries. It may also speed decision making both by reducing the number of people whose approvals and reviews are required, as well as letting people "on the ground" actually make the decisions. Union Pacific's experience is a good example.

MANAGEMENT IN ACTION   Union Pacific

The experience of former Union Pacific Railroad (UPRR) CEO Mike Walsh provides a classic example. He took over the troubled company and inherited a bureaucratic and slow-moving organization. As Walsh said,

> Suppose a customer was having difficulty [finding] a railroad car—it was either not the right one, or wasn't where the customer needed it for loading or unloading. The customer would go to his UPRR sales representative—who "went up" to the district traffic manager, who in turn "went up" to the regional traffic manager. The regional boss passed the problem from his sales and marketing organization, across a chasm psychologically wider than the Grand Canyon, to the operations department's general manager. The general manager then "went down" to the superintendent, who "went down" to the train master to find out what had gone wrong.[21]

Then the whole process went into reverse. The information went up the operations chain and then down the sales and marketing chain, until the annoyed customer finally got his or her answer—often several days later. Multiplied hundreds or thousands of times a week, that sort of

◀ **FIGURE 7–4** ■ ■ ■

Union Pacific Railroad Hierarchy:
Before and After

Source: From *Liberation Management* by
Tom Peters. Copyright © 1992 by Excel, a
California Limited Partnership. Reprinted by
permission of Alfred A. Knopf, Inc.

Figure A	Figure B
Before	**After**
Reorganization	**Reorganization**
Executive VP Operations	Executive VP Operations
VP Operations	VP Field Operations
General Manager	Superintendent Transportation Services
Assistant General Manager	Manager Train Operations
Regional Transportation Superintendent	Yardmaster
Divisional Superintendent	*Railroaders*
Division Superintendent	
Transportation	
Trainmaster/Terminal Superintendent	
Assistant Trainmaster/ Terminal Trainmaster	
Yardmaster	
Railroaders	

unresponsiveness, Walsh knew, helped explain why UPRR was losing customers, revenues, and profits.

The first thing he did was flatten the firm's 30,000-person operations department, by squeezing out five middle-management layers (see Figure 7.4). When Walsh arrived, there were nine layers of managers between the executive vice president of operations and the railroaders themselves. In about three months, five layers and 800 middle managers were stripped from the chain of command.[22]

Establish Miniunits When it comes to streamlining, many managers conclude that smaller is better. They advocate splitting companies into minicompanies.

Many firms have taken this route. At Intuit, the new CEO broke the company into eight separate businesses, each with its own general manager and mission.[23] Hal Rosenbluth fragmented Rosenbluth International into more than 100 business units, each focused on specific regions or clients.[24] (However, the miniunit approach has its drawbacks. It can mean leaving the firm without the concentrated firepower it needs to compete effectively. That's why Japan Telecom recently said it was merging three of its wireless units into a fourth, which it called J-phone Communications Company. It hopes that by consolidating its wireless resources, it will be better positioned to compete with Japanese leaders like DoCoMo.)

How To Cultivate Personal Mastery

You know from your own experience that you can't create a learning organization just by tinkering with the organization chart. Learning organizations have the capacity "to adapt to unforeseen situations, to learn from their own experiences, to shift their shared mindsets, and to change more quickly, broadly, and deeply than ever before."[25] If employees don't want to learn or are reluctant to express their views, it's not likely that even the most streamlined, boundaryless, networked organization will make them do so. It takes something more. Here are some steps managers need to take.

■ *Provide continuous learning opportunities.* Learning organizations offer extensive opportunities for on-and-off the job training. This increases every employee's personal mastery with respect to what he or she knows and how quickly he or she can learn it.

■ *Foster inquiry and dialogue.* Make people feel safe to share openly and take risks. Set the right tone. Make sure that all of the company's systems and procedures, as well as all the signals that managers send, encourage open inquiry and dialogue.

■ *Establish mechanisms to ensure that the organization is continuously aware of and can inter-act with its environment.* For example, encourage formal and informal environmental scanning activities, and establish more boundaryless supply-chain–type relationships.

■■■ HOW TO ACHIEVE COORDINATION

We saw that departmentalization is the process through which managers divide up work among lieutenants. The editor in chief appoints editors for editorial, production, and ads. In the France tour, you assign jobs to Rosa, Ned, and Ruth. However, *dividing* the work is only part of the organizational job: The manager must ensure that the work is then *coordinated*. What good would it do for your trip to France if Rosa got airline tickets that weren't coordinated with Ned's hotel reservations or with Ruth's sightseeing plans? The only way their efforts (and the trip) will work is if Rosa's, Ned's, and Ruth's activities are all coordinated.

coordination ■ *the process of achieving unity of action among interdependent activities.*

Coordination is the process of achieving unity of action among interdependent activities. Coordination is required whenever two or more interdependent individuals, groups, or departments must work together to achieve a common goal. Departmentalization creates differentiated jobs, such as managers for production and for sales, or for product A and product B. Somewhere along the line, the work of these people must be coordinated so that the company achieves it's goals.

Methods for Achieving Coordination

You know from your own experience that there are many ways to coordinate an activity. For example, you could coordinate the work of Rosa, Ned, and Ruth by appointing a committee and having the three meet twice a week to discuss their progress and to fine-tune their plans. Or you could coordinate their efforts yourself (use 'the chain of command') by speaking with each one several times a day and making sure each person's work fits with that of the others. Let's look at the basic techniques managers use to achieve coordination.[26,27]

mutual adjustment ■ *achieving coordination through face-to-face interpersonal interaction.*

Use Mutual Adjustment Mutual adjustment means achieving coordination by relying on face-to-face interpersonal interaction. This is an obvious and widely used approach. In simple situations (such as two people moving a heavy log), you could achieve coordination by having one person count, "one, two, three, lift," at which time both people lift the log in unison. Mutual adjustment is often the technique of choice in the most complex situations, too. Thus, the members of a special forces squad may carefully follow the chain of command when planning their attack. But when they hit the ground, most coordination will likely take place through a real-time process of mutual adjustment. The soldiers will continually interact with and respond to one another as they confront unanticipated problems. Today's networked organizations facilitate just this type of mutual adjustment, by letting employees throughout the firm freely interact without the usual structural constraints of authority and other organizational boundaries.

Use Rules and Procedures Rules and procedures are useful for coordinating routine, recurring activities. They specify what course of action each employee should take if a particular situation should arise. Thus, a restaurant manager could have a rule that "bussers will clear tables as soon as customers finish eating." This ensures that the work of the waiters and bussers is coordinated.

Standardize In most human endeavors, *standardization* helps ensure that the components fit together properly. Ford builds cars from standardized parts, so that the parts all slide into place as the car moves down the assembly line. Professors give standardized tests, so that the results among students are comparable. Managers also use standardization to achieve coordination. They standardize three things—*goals*, *skills*, and *values*—to help ensure that coordination takes place.

Setting *specific goals* is one option. For example, as long as the sales, finance, and production managers attain their assigned goals, the president can be reasonably sure that there will be enough financing and production capacity to meet the sales target. Managers also standardize *skills*. Imagine the culinary chaos if waiters don't know how to process customers' orders, bussers don't know when to clean, and chefs can't cook. Nothing will go right. Firms like Saturn therefore spend millions each year training workers. Each team member knows how his or her efforts fit with the others and how to proceed. This means less work for the team's immediate supervisor.[28]

Similarly, many companies endeavor to standardize *values* among employees. For example, every year, Unilever gives about 150 of its worldwide managers temporary assignments at corporate headquarters.[29] This helps give the visiting managers a strong sense of Unilever's values. As one of its managers put it; "The experience initiates you into the Unilever club and the clear norms, values, and behaviors that distinguish our people—so much so that we really believe we can spot another Unilever manager anywhere in the world."[30] This helps to ensure that, wherever they are around the world, Unilever managers are consistent with Unilever's values.

▲ WEBNOTE ■ ■ ■

Unilever's Web site features its values, especially its programs for the environment and society.

www.unilever.com

Source: © Unilever 2001.

Exercise Direct Supervision: Use the Chain of Command Direct supervision achieves coordination by having one person coordinate the work of others, issuing instructions and monitoring results[31]—in other words, "Let's ask the boss." When problems arise that the rules or procedures don't cover, subordinates bring the problem to the manager. In addition to using rules and mutual adjustment, all managers use the chain of command in this way to achieve coordination.

Divisionalize Functional departmentalization creates heavy coordination demands on top management. This is because the work of the functional departments (like sales and production) is both specialized and interdependent. Organizing by product, customer, or geographic divisions reduces interdependence and reduces the coordination burden. The president puts each lieutenant in charge of a self-contained operation. The lieutenants coordinate their own operations. The divisions are relatively independent. The president can then coordinate less and plan more. (In the case of the worldwide tours, that's one reason to appoint separate country tour heads for each destination country and also to let them, in turn, coordinate all the tourist activities in their assigned countries.)

Appoint Staff Assistants Coordinating can be demanding from the point of view of the person in charge. He or she must monitor the activities of the subordinate departments as well as analyze and address questions from lieutenants. Some managers hire staff assistants to help with these tasks. When subordinates bring a problem to the manager, the assistant can compile information about the problem, research it, and offer advice. This effectively boosts the manager's ability to handle problems and coordinate the work of subordinates.

Appoint Liaisons When the volume of contacts between two departments grows, some firms use special liaisons to facilitate coordination. For example, the sales department manager might appoint a salesperson to be his or her liaison with the production department. This liaison stays in the sales department but travels frequently to the factory to learn as much as possible about the plant's production schedule and the status of various orders. Then, only deviations come to the manager's attention.

Appoint Committees One way to make sure a project like your France trip is coordinated is to have Rosa, Ned, and Ruth meet with you before making any final decisions. Many firms achieve coordination by appointing interdepartmental committees, task forces, or teams composed of representatives of the interdependent departments. They meet periodically to discuss common problems and ensure interdepartmental coordination.

Organize Independent Integrators An **independent integrator** is a separate individual or group that coordinates the activities of several interdependent

independent integrator ■ *an individual or a group that coordinates the activities of several interdependent departments, but is independent of them.*

departments.[32] Integrators differ from liaisons in that integrators are independent of the departments they coordinate. They report to the manager who oversees those departments. Homeland Security is a good example of an independent integrator.

MANAGEMENT IN ACTION   Homeland Security

Tom Ridge, America's first homeland security chief, led an independent integrator department. In 2001, President George W. Bush charged it with coordinating (integrating) the homeland security-related efforts of dozens of U.S. agencies, including the FBI and CIA. The department had no line authority over these agencies—it couldn't issue orders to the CIA, for instance.

Figure 7.5 summarizes (as an approximation) the task Ridge faced. Hundreds of departments were involved. Ridge had to try to get his job done by working with Congress and all those departments, and tapping into the president's authority. Doing so wasn't easy. Congress was soon working with the president on a plan to give Homeland Security cabinet status—and more clout. Legislation to create the Department of Homeland Security was signed in November 2002, with Tom Ridge named as the first secretary of this new cabinet seat.

▼ FIGURE 7–5 ■ ■ ■

Part of the "Independent Integrator" Challenge Facing Homeland Security Director

Source: Alison Mitchell, "Disputes Erupt over Ridges Needs for His Job," *New York Times*, 9 November 2001, p. B7.

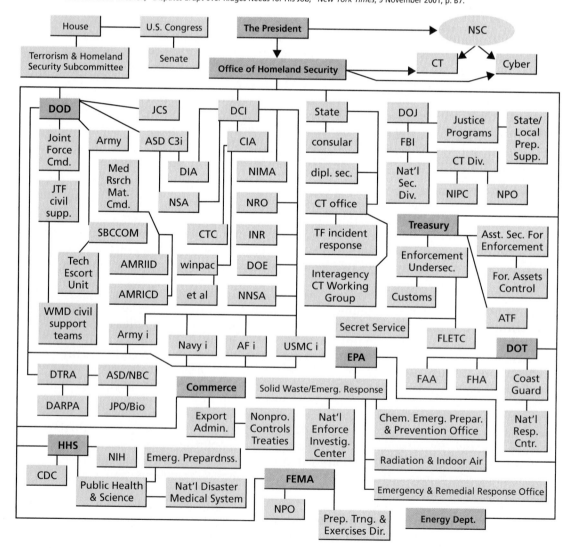

Managers also use technology and the Internet to help coordinate activities. The following feature provides an illustration.

MANAGING @ THE SPEED OF THOUGHT

Construction Central

Coordination is a real and obvious challenge in the construction industry. Particularly when huge projects are involved—Boston's 15-year, $10 billion "big dig," New York City's planned Second Avenue subway, or the San Francisco Giants new stadium, for instance—coordinating the work of hundreds or thousands of suppliers and contractors can be an overwhelming job.

That's why several companies—including Citadon, a San Francisco, California-based company—are providing Web-based software that some refer to as "construction junction." This software helps construction companies that are managing jobs to coordinate all the hundreds or thousands of parties involved. One former Citadon manager said, "We link companies together and streamline information from design to completion. Our application enables the effective flow of information."[33]

By using the Internet and a PC, everyone involved in the project—from owners and architects to contractors and subcontractors—receives instantaneous updates regarding design changes and construction status. That way, instead of having to send time-consuming reports back and forth or to coordinate personally or by phone and fax, any of the parties in the project need only to click on their PC to see the project status and to know when their activity is scheduled to start and end.

Determinants of Coordination

What determines whether the manager uses committees, liaisons, integrators, or some other device to achieve coordination? Much of what we know about how to coordinate stems from a classic study by Harvard professors Paul Lawrence and Jay Lorsch. They addressed the basic question, "What kind of organization does it take to deal with various economic and market conditions?"[34] They focused on companies in the plastics, food, and container industries. These industries displayed differences in the speed with which they were changing and, in particular, in their rates of technological change.

Lawrence and Lorsch focused on what they called *differentiation* and *integration*. Differentiation referred to the degree to which there were differences in the structures, interpersonal orientations, and goals and time orientations of the employees in each of the departments. *Integration* basically meant coordination. They found three things.

> First, the plastics and food firms faced a lot more uncertainty than did the container firms. Container firms had to construct plants years in advance near customers like Pepsi, so they had to be able to predict demand fairly far in advance. There was much more unexpected technical and product change in the plastics and foods industries.
>
> Second, the more rapid technological change and uncertainty facing the plastics and food firms were associated with a greater spread in the differences among departments. For example, the plastics firms' marketing and research and development departments had to be forward-looking, while their manufacturing departments had to concentrate on efficiency. On the other hand, all the departments in the container firms tended to face more similar, predictable tasks.
>
> Third, the degree of differentiation among departments influenced how the companies achieved coordination. Departments in the container firms faced similar tasks, were less differentiated, and therefore used traditional interdepartmental coordination techniques, like having managers stick to the chain of command, and relying on rules and procedures. Departments in the plastics and food firms faced more varied tasks, and therefore differed in how they organized and viewed the world. These differences among departments made it harder to achieve coordination. Plastics firms therefore organized special "independent integrator" units to do the coordinating.[35]

☑ *Consider all available tools:* Mutual adjustment; rules and procedures; standardization; direct supervision; divisionalizing; appointing staff assistants, liaisons, or committees; and organizing independent integrators.

☑ *Ask, "How unpredictable is the task?"* When things are changing quickly, put more emphasis on devices like mutual adjustment, networked organizations, standardizing shared values, and product divisions.

☑ *Ask, "How differentiated are the units we want to coordinate?"* Companies whose departments face differentiated tasks may need special independent integrator departments to achieve coordination.

☑ *Use logic and common sense.* For example, even independent integrator departments will make use of rules and the chain of command to some extent.

How To Organize To Reduce Interunit Conflict

Coordinating the efforts of several departments can be futile when there's conflict among the people in those departments. Opposing parties put their own aims above the company's. Time they could have used productively evaporates, as people hide information and jockey for position. Line-staff conflict is a typical example. Such conflict might result when line managers feel staff managers are encroaching on their prerogatives, or when staff managers feel line managers are resisting good advice. Or it might stem from personality differences. One recent study concluded that "staff personnel were more modest and accurate in their self-assessment, while line managers were more service-oriented but significantly weaker at relationships, openness to new ideas, demonstrating respect, and adaptability to change."[36]

Interdepartmental conflict isn't necessarily counterproductive; sometimes, it's best, to have a healthy airing of an issue's pros and cons, for instance. However, good or bad, you want to keep such conflict under control. Structural ways to do so include the following.

Appeal to Power and the Chain of Command[37] The traditional way to resolve a conflict is to appeal to the boss. One study found that even in decentralized firms, the CEO's power was the most widely used way of solving disagreements. The CEO did this either through decree or by acting as mediator or arbitrator.[38]

Reduce Interdependence Conflicts rarely arise among groups not required to work together. Therefore, one way to reduce conflict is to reduce the required interdepartmental interdependencies. James Thompson distinguished three levels of interdependencies—pooled, sequential, and reciprocal.[39] *Pooled* interdependence (see Figure 7.6) is minimal interdependence. A company with separate product divisions is an example. Here, the divisions are relatively self-contained and independent. *Sequential* interdependence means the output of one unit is the input to a second unit. (For example, the production department depends on and gets its raw materials from the purchasing department.) This makes the task of coordinating the departments more demanding. The most demanding interdependence is *reciprocal*. For example, consider an airline, with both operations and maintenance units. The output of the maintenance unit is an input for operations, in the form of a serviceable aircraft. The product or byproduct of operations is an input for maintenance in the form of an aircraft needing maintenance.[40]

line–staff conflict ■
disagreements between a line manager and the staff manager who is giving him or her advice.

▶ **FIGURE 7–6** ■ ■ ■

Types of Interdependence

Source: Based on James Thompson, *Organizations in Action* (New York: McGraw-Hill, 1967), Chapter 2.

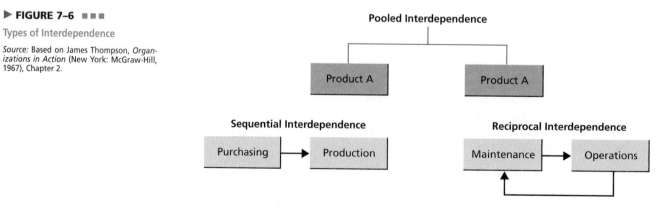

Reducing interdependence reduces the potential for conflict, so this is one obvious structural way to manage conflict. Reduce the degree to which the units need to work together or to depend on each other. For example, if conflict between sales and production in your functionally organized company is out of control, reorganize around divisional departments. Let each product division manager have his or her own smaller, more dedicated sales and production units. You thereby move from reciprocal or sequential to pooled interdependence.

Exchange Personnel Sometimes, it helps to see things from the other side's point of view. Conflict theorists therefore advise having conflicting groups trade personnel for a specific time.[41] In one study, 62 three-person groups composed of students each acted as either a "manufacturer" or a "wholesaler" of medical instruments. Their goal was to get agreement on the selling price and quantity of these instruments.

Thirty minutes into the bargaining session, a random selection of groups got a memo that said the chief executive officers of each firm had decided to undertake a temporary exchange of personnel. The "manufacturer's salesperson" and "wholesaler's purchasing agent" traded positions for 30 minutes. Then, when 20 minutes had elapsed, the "salesperson" and the "purchasing agent" returned to their "home" companies. The bargaining then continued until the trial ended. The researchers concluded that the exchange of personnel helped to reduce conflict and speed agreement.

■■■ HOW TO DELEGATE AUTHORITY

We've seen that authority is an essential part of organizing, because the owners and officers must authorize the firm's managers and employees to carry out the jobs assigned to them. What use would it be to put a sales manager in charge of sales if she has no authority to hire salespeople, visit customers, or close a sale?

Sources of Authority

We've also seen that in corporations, authority stems from the owner-stockholders. They pass down (or delegate) authority first to the board of directors and then to the CEO. This is how the chain of command (or hierarchy of authority) evolves. Authority, therefore, derives in part from a person's rank or position. The president of software manufacturer Intuit has more authority based on rank than does one of his senior vice presidents.

Authority can also stem from other sources. Some people have authority because of *personal traits*, such as intelligence or charisma. People defer to and follow the instructions of such individuals because of the power of their personalities. Others have authority because they are *experts* in an area or have knowledge that requires others to depend on them.

Some astute management writers argue that, regardless of source, authority always depends on subordinates' acceptance of supervisors' orders. Theorist Chester Barnard was an early proponent of this view. Barnard argued that for orders to be carried out, they must lie within a subordinate's "zone of acceptance"—in other words, they must be viewed as acceptable. Experts often argue that getting employees' acceptance is increasingly important today, given the emphasis on empowered workers and team-based organizations.

Principles of Delegation

Organizing would be useless without delegation, which is the pushing down of authority from supervisor to subordinate. The assignment of responsibility for some department or job traditionally goes hand in hand with the delegation of authority to get the job done. It would be inappropriate, for example, to assign a subordinate the responsibility for designing a new product and then deny him or her the authority to hire designers to create the best design.

A well-known management saying is, "You can delegate authority, but you cannot delegate responsibility." The CEO is ultimately responsible for whatever occurs on his or her watch. Similarly, any manager is ultimately responsible for ensuring that the job he or she is in charge of gets done properly. Because the person doing the delegating always retains the ultimate responsibility, delegation of authority always entails the

delegation ■ *the act of passing down authority from supervisor to subordinate.*

creation of accountability. Subordinates become accountable—or answerable—to the supervisor for the performance of the tasks assigned to them, particularly if things go wrong. The boss may fire or discipline the subordinate who fails to do the job; however, the boss is still, strictly speaking, responsible for all that goes wrong (or right) in the department.

Managers are people who get things done through others, and so knowing how to delegate is a crucial management skill. Principles for delegating include:[42]

Clarify the Assignment Make it clear what you want your subordinate to accomplish, the results you expect, and by when you want those results. Frequently, when employees don't perform up to par, it is not because they're not motivated, but because they're not sure what you expect them to do.

Delegate, Don't Abdicate Shortly after assuming the CEO position at Motorola, Chris Galvin sat in on several meetings with the company's mobile phone group. At the time, the group was working on a new phone (code-named Shark) for Europe. Galvin knew that Europeans preferred light, inexpensive phones, so he asked if the market data supported the idea that the relatively heavy Shark would appeal to customers. The manager said, "Yes," and that's reportedly where Galvin left it. He didn't follow up or dig deeper. He let his managers move ahead and launch the product, which subsequently failed.[43] The moral is this: Never delegate without challenging your employees or without thinking through how you're going to monitor their results. Just giving a person a job and not following up is abdication, not delegation.

Know What to Delegate Larry Bossidy, the executive who turned AlliedSignal around and helped it merge with Honeywell, says there is "one job no CEO should delegate—finding and developing great leaders."[44] Bossidy said he spent "between 30% and 40% of [his] day for the first two years hiring and developing leaders. That's a huge amount of time for a CEO to devote to any single task." But for AlliedSignal, it was essential. He knew he had to build a strong management team.

In Bossidy's case, finding and developing great leaders was "the job no CEO should delegate." For a manager in a different company and at a different level, there will be other tasks that he or she cannot (or should not) delegate. These are the tasks—such as actually checking and paying for the tickets for your trip to France—that are too important for the unit's well-being to be assigned to a subordinate.

Specify the Subordinate's Range of Discretion You should give the subordinate enough authority to do the task successfully, but not so much that any actions can have adverse effects outside the areas for which you have made the person responsible. For example, if you want to delegate the task of finding the best airline tickets for France, tell Rosa you are authorizing her to check the Internet and make the calls necessary to accomplish that task. Do not leave her with the impression that she has the authority to actually commit you to buying the tickets. Decide up front how much discretion you want the person to have. There is always a range from low (1) to high (5)—for example, (1) "wait to be told what to do"; (2) "ask what to do"; (3) "recommend, then take action"; (4) "act, then report results immediately"; and (5) "take action, and report only routinely."

Authority Should Equal Responsibility A basic principle of management is that "authority should equal responsibility." The person should have enough authority to accomplish the task.

Make the Person Accountable for Results Make it clear to the subordinate that he or she is accountable to you for results. This means that there must be predictable and acceptable measures of results.

Beware of Backward Delegation A famous *Harvard Business Review* article years ago was titled "Who's got the monkey?" It explains what happens to an unsuspecting manager whose subordinate comes into his office to discuss a problem. The subordinate says, "I have a problem with the job you gave me to do." After a few minutes of discussion, the manager, pressed for time, says, "I'll handle it." Like a monkey, the job has jumped from the subordinate's to the unsuspecting manager's shoulders. The point is this: Beware of backward delegation. When your subordinate says the task isn't working out as planned, you have several good options. You can suggest some solutions or insist that your subordinate take the initiative in solving the problem. Do not carelessly let the task you delegated bounce back to you.

CHECKLIST 7.3 ■ Principles of Delegation

☑ The manager can delegate authority but cannot delegate responsibility.

☑ Clarify the assignment.

☑ Delegate, don't abdicate.

☑ Know what to delegate.

☑ Specify the subordinate's range of discretion.

☑ Authority should equal responsibility.

☑ Make the person accountable for results.

☑ Beware of backward delegation.

■■■ HOW TO DECENTRALIZE

Managers sometimes use the words *delegation* and *decentralization* as if they mean the same thing, but the words, while related, actually have different meanings. When managers say, "Decentralize," they generally mean one of two things.[45] First, they mean where decisions are made in the chain of command. In a *centralized* organization, more decisions are made closer to the top. In a *decentralized* one, more decisions are made lower down. The more areas in which the president delegates authority, the more decentralized the organization.

Second, decentralization means *the extent to which employees must channel all their communications through the head* (CEO).[46] For example, must the finance, production, and sales managers communicate with each other only through the CEO, or can they communicate directly to arrive at a joint decision? The more they are required to channel communications through the CEO, the more centralized the firm. The more managers can communicate directly with one another, the more decentralized the firm.

In practice, a decentralized organization is one in which (1) authority for most departmental decisions is delegated to the department heads, while (2) control for major companywide decisions is maintained at the headquarters office. Managers may departmentalize "decentralized companies" around product, customer, or geographic divisions. However, managers usually use the term *decentralized* in conjunction with product divisions. (Indeed, for this reason, they often use the words *divisionalized* and *decentralized* synonymously.) Managers of product divisions often run what amounts to their own miniature companies. They have the authority to make most decisions that have anything to do with their products, with little or no communication with the firm's CEO. However, the CEO retains authority over major, companywide decisions.

You can't have a decentralized company without effective, centralized controls; consider the problems Arthur Andersen had auditing Enron's books a few years ago.

decentralized organization ■ *an organization in which (1) authority for most departmental decisions is delegated to the department heads, while (2) control for major companywide decisions is maintained at the headquarters office.*

MANAGEMENT IN ACTION   Andersen and Enron

Andersen's Houston office apparently wanted to take a particularly aggressive approach to letting Enron account for some transactions. Andersen Worldwide had a special, centralized Professional Standards Group (PSG) at its Chicago headquarters that apparently told local Houston Andersen managers *not* to use the approach. It appears someone at Andersen Houston may have approved the transaction anyway, with disastrous results for Andersen Worldwide. Managers at Andersen Worldwide had decentralized most decisions to its branches, with the understanding that the branches would abide by the PSGs centralized oversight and control. In this case, those controls may not have been adequate. Local managers overrode the PSG's decision.[47]   ■■■

In practice, decentralization must always represent a shrewd balance between delegated authority and the centralized control of essential functions. On the one hand, division managers get the autonomy and resources they need to service local customers. On the other hand, headquarters maintains the control it needs by centralizing major decisions regarding activities like capital appropriations, incoming cash receipts, and setting profitability goals. The art is in delegating enough to get the job done, while centralizing (or retaining) enough authority and tight enough control over the right activities so that you avoid gross deviations. Here is how two famous management writers put this a number of years ago:

> ... [D]ecentralization cannot mean autonomy, in that it implies establishment of policies to guide decision-making along the desired courses, and in that ... not being an abdication of responsibility, it must be accompanied by controls designed to ensure that delegated authority is used to further goals and plans. Although the art of authority delegation lies at the base of proper decentralization ... it is apparent that the mere act of delegation is not enough to ensure decentralization.[48]

Why Decentralize?

A classic study by economic historian Alfred Chandler helps explain why companies decentralize.[49] Chandler analyzed the histories of about 100 of the largest U.S. industrial enterprises. He got information from annual reports, articles, and government publications, and from interviews with senior executives. Chandler wanted to discover why companies like GE had adopted decentralized, divisionalized, organizational structures, while others, such as steel industry firms, had remained functionally departmentalized. Chandler concluded that "structure follows strategy," or that a company's organizational structure has to fit its strategy. He said,

> The prospect of a new market or the threatened loss of a current one stimulated [strategies of] geographical expansion, vertical integration, and product diversification. ... [In turn] expansion of volume, ... growth through geographical dispersion, ... [and finally] the developing of new lines of products ... brought the formation of the divisional structure.[50]

This was an important insight. A diversification strategy at firms like GE led to multiple product lines for these firms. This meant that GE had to manage an increasingly diverse range of products—and an increasingly diverse range of customers. Having to deal with so many products and customers made the firm's original, functional structures obsolete. The comments of one early Westinghouse executive neatly summarize this:

> All of the activities of the company were [originally] divided into production, engineering, and sales, each of which was the responsibility of a vice president. The domain of each vice president covered the whole diversified and far-flung operations of the corporation. Such an organization of the corporation's management lacks responsiveness. There was too much delay in the recognition of problems and in the solution of problems after they were recognized.[51]

The steel industry was at the other extreme. Here, the strategy was to concentrate on one product, and the main strategic goal was boosting efficiency. These CEOs had little concern about multiple products. In fact, the duplication inherent in setting up separate product divisions would have been inefficient. These companies generally stayed centralized and functionally departmentalized.

What to Decentralize

The trick lies in knowing which decisions to centralize—and which to decentralize. One rule is this: *Decentralize decisions that will affect just that one division or area and that would take a great deal of time for you to make. Centralize decisions that could adversely affect the entire firm and that you can make yourself fairly quickly and easily.* So to use our France trip example, decentralize the ticket research, but centralize the actual purchase. Cirque du Soleil, producer of international traveling circuses, is a good example of decentralization.

Cirque du Soleil's headquarters are in Montreal, with offices in Amsterdam, Las Vegas, and Singapore. Its 2,100 employees worldwide come from 40 different countries and speak more than 15 languages. Two-thirds of the employees work outside Montreal. It has simultaneous, multiple tours. How does Cirque du Soleil manage an operation like that? The answer is decentralization.

Each tour is like a separate, small-town circus. Everyone works for Cirque du Soleil, but most of the employees travel with the local, geographic-division tours. Management delegates decisions for matters like human resources to the separate tour managers, since employment law, for example, can vary drastically from country to country. Management centralizes other decisions—for instance, regarding major investments. The company maintains a sense of unity through its strong culture of shared values and beliefs. It posts jobs on the Internet, and employees write the company newspaper. Members of the Las Vegas finance department videotape themselves on the job and swap tapes with the casting crew in Montreal to keep the community feeling. The result is that, by decentralizing, Cirque du Soleil takes advantage of its size while keeping the separate tours more like small family businesses.

Cirque du Soleil's new creation, Varekai, has a cast of more than 50 artists representing 12 countries.

Sometimes firms go backwards, and recentralize one or more departments. For example, before their merger, most of AOL's and Time Warner's separate units carried out their own marketing efforts. After the merger, AOL Time Warner needed a more centralized approach. It created a new central Global Marketing Solutions Group. This unit now markets and sells ads for all of AOL Time Warner's online, magazine, and television media properties. This helps it accomplish one of the main goals of the merger. Management wanted to enable advertisers to create special types of promotions that they could market simultaneously through multiple AOL Time Warner media properties, including online, magazine, and television. Recentralizing marketing helped them do that.[52]

SUMMARY ■■■

1. Managers use organization theory to help them design organization structures that are right for their situations. Burns and Stalker's findings, as well as Woodward's, suggest that different organizational structures are appropriate for—and contingent on—different tasks. At one extreme are organizations for dealing with predictable, routine tasks like running a rayon mill. Here, the organization tends to be mechanistic. At the other extreme, some organizations have more unpredictable tasks. Here, management must emphasize creativity and entrepreneurial activities, and so it must encourage these activities. Such organizations tend to be organic.

2. Basic factors to consider when deciding on an organization structure include environment, technology, goals, pros and cons, and logic and common sense.

3. Learning organizations are generally (1) organic, networked organizations that (2) encourage employees to think outside the boundaries of their own jobs, and which (3) cultivate their employees' personal mastery, so that (4) they have "the capacity to adapt to unforeseen situations, to learn from their own experiences, to shift their shared mindsets, and to change more quickly, broadly, and deeply than ever before."

4. Managers can make a number of basic structural changes to make their organizations operate more responsively. Simplifying or reducing structure by reducing layers of management, creating miniunits, reassigning support staff, and widening spans of control are examples.

5. Coordination is the process of achieving unity of action among interdependent activities. It is required when two or more interdependent entities must work together to achieve a common goal. Techniques for achieving coordination include mutual adjustment; the use of rules or procedures; the standardization of targets, skills, or shared values, direct supervision; divisionalizing; the use of a staff assistant, a liaison, a committee; and/or, independent integrators.

6. Principles of delegation include delegating authority, not responsibility; clarifying the assignment; delegating, not abdicating; knowing what to delegate; specifying the range of discretion; having authority equal responsibility; making the person accountable for results; and avoiding backward delegation.

7. In practice, a decentralized organization is one in which (1) authority for most departmental decisions is delegated to the department heads, while (2) control for major companywide decisions is maintained at the headquarters office. Managers usually use the term *decentralized* in conjunction with product divisions.

mechanistic organizations 169
organic organizations 170
boundaryless organization 176
authority boundary 177
task boundary 177

political boundary 177
identity boundary 177
downsizing 178
coordination 180
mutual adjustment 180

independent integrator 181
line–staff conflict 184
delegation 185
decentralized organization 187

SKILLS AND STUDY MATERIALS

COMPANION WEBSITE ■■■

We invite you to visit the Dessler Companion Website at **www.prenhall.com/dessler** for this chapter's Internet resources.

EXPERIENTIAL EXERCISES ■■■

1. Management experts consider the German sociologist Max Weber to be the intellectual father of the mechanistic or bureaucratic organization. Writing in the late 1800s and the early 1900s, Weber was analyzing the ushering in of what management expert Charles Handy has called "The Century of Organizations." Weber emphasized the need for having a well-defined chain of command, a clear division of work, and an emphasis on following rules and procedures. For Weber, the new large-scale organizations would emphasize authority: "In the past the man has been first, in the future the system must be first."

Questions

1. What do you think he meant by that statement? How would Weber react to and explain today's team-based, learning, boundaryless organizations? List five specific things you would do to turn Weber's bureaucratic type of organization into a learning organization.

2. In *The Horizontal Organization* (Oxford: Oxford University Press, 1999), Frank Ostroff argues that the vertical organization design, with its chain of command, is of the past and that the flat, horizontal organization design is for now and the future. The vertical organization, he says, has inherent shortcomings in our competitive, technological, and workforce-focused environment. Among the shortcomings are its internal focus on functional goals rather than an outward-looking concentration on delivering value and winning customers, the loss of information as knowledge travels up and down multiple levels and across the functional departments, the added expense involved in coordinating overly fragmented work and departments, and the stifling of creativity and initiative of the workers at lower levels.

Among the reasons Ostroff gives for saying the horizontal corporation is the structure of today and the future are that horizontal organizations organize around core processes, not tasks or functions. In other words, they install process owners or managers who will take responsibility for the core process in its entirety. Furthermore, teams, not individuals, are the cornerstone of this organizational design and performance. And, these organizations empower people by giving them the tools, skills, motivation, and authority to make decisions essential to the team's performance.

Working in teams of four to five students, list the organizations (including student groups) in which you've worked that you would consider (1) vertical or (2) horizontal organizations. What makes you say they were vertical or horizontal? What were your experiences in terms of getting things done, and what problems arose? List five specific ways vertical and horizontal organizations differ in how they achieve coordination.

3. Since you are in college to learn, it is reasonable to assume that your college (in general) and this management class (in particular) are learning organizations. (After all, your class does have an organization structure in terms of who does what, whether authority is centralized or dispersed, and so on.) In teams of four to five students, answer these questions: If you were the "manager" taking over this class, what would you say are the main goals you want this class to achieve? Based on that, what are the main tasks the class's organization must perform? Draw the organization chart of this class as it is now. Then list five specific things you would do to reorganize this class as a learning organization. To what extent is the class subject to the various boundaries discussed in this chapter?

W. L. GORE & ASSOCIATES: STRUCTURING FOR CONTINUOUS CHANGE

Would you offer someone a high-salary position without knowing what job they would have? W. L. Gore & Associates does. It is one of the many unusual practices that have helped Gore, makers of the waterproof fabric GORE-TEX^W, to be repeatedly named to the Fortune list of 100 Best Companies to Work for in America, recently ranking as the 11th best firm. Gore has revenues in excess of $1 billion, and it operates in 45 countries while employing only 6,100 people.

Gore operates a high-tech company in a market (textiles) that is traditionally low-tech. As a high-tech company, Gore must be prepared to change rapidly when the market changes. To do this, Gore's structure and processes are distinguished by three unique characteristics: sponsors rather than bosses, a "lattice" organization, and the "waterline principle."

Gore believes that these three characteristics are what set it apart from its competitors. Gore shuns bureaucracy and sees hierarchies as the enemies of innovation. Gore hires "associates" (not employees) into general work areas. When hired, these employees don't have specific job titles or positions. With the help of their Gore sponsors (bosses), associates select and commit to projects that seem to match their skills and interests. One of each sponsor's jobs is to help associates find a place in Gore that will offer personal fulfillment and maximize their contribution to the enterprise. Gore does not assign managers. In the company's view, leaders are people who have followers. If the organization is left on its own, leaders will emerge naturally by demonstrating the character, knowledge, and skills that attract followers. To become a leader at Gore, you need to perform in a way that attracts followers.

This self-selecting process leads to what Gore calls the lattice organization. In the lattice, there are no chains of command; instead, decision making is delegated to the point where the decision must be made. Gore assumes that employees are sufficiently concerned about the good of the organization to make sound decisions on behalf of the organization. Gore's lattice has no preestablished channels of communication. Sponsors coach new associates to communicate directly with each other. Associates work in multidisciplinary teams and are accountable to each other. The goal of this innovative structure is to unleash the creative potential of all of the associates, thus allowing Gore to become a truly innovative company.

Many cite Gore's last commitment—to the waterline principle—as a key to its successful ability to adapt. The company is viewed as a ship. Holes above the waterline are unattractive and even uncomfortable, but they are not deadly. Holes below the waterline would sink the ship. If you are a Gore associate and you see an action or event that could hit Gore below the waterline, then it is your individual responsibility to do something, even if the event or action happens outside your department or area. Failing to act on a waterline issue would earn you a severe reprimand from your peers, the other associates. After all, it is the role of every employee to protect the ship. With these principles firmly in place, Gore has been able to be remarkably flexible and to change constantly to meet the needs of current and future clients.

The results of Gore's structure and processes have been impressive. Its world-renowned fluoropolymer technology has allowed it to extend the product line far beyond the well-known GORE-TEX^W brand. The same technology has allowed the company to produce Glide^W, a nonstick dental floss, and Elixir^W, a corrosion-resistant guitar string. Lesser-known but equally impressive products—including next-generation materials for printed circuit boards and fiber optics and new methods to detect and control environmental pollution—are marketed in the industrial sector. Experts have also recognized Gore for its work in advancing the science of regenerating tissue destroyed by injuries.

The company's founder, Bill Gore, originally articulated the company's unique structure and culture. To Gore, the company would be successful only if it could create an environment that was naturally conducive to the highest levels of innovation and productivity. Gore said associates should be committed to four basic principles: (1) fairness to each other and everyone you came in contact with; (2) freedom to encourage and help other associates to grow in knowledge, skill, and scope of responsibility; (3) the ability to make one's own commitments and keep them; and (4) consultation with other associates before undertaking actions that could affect the reputation of the company by hitting it "below the waterline."

While all this has worked in the past, many of these organizational techniques are no longer unique. Just as Saturn, in the past 20 years, has lost its position as the only "Japanese-method" American car company, so Gore has seen many competitors adopt its once-unique organizational ways. Gore, therefore, now has to decide if a new approach would be worthwhile.

Discussion Questions

1. Review Gore's Web site at **www.gore.com**. Note Gore's various divisions and its many geographical locations. Based on what you find there and in the case, draw an organization chart for the company.

2. List the ways Gore's lattice structure is similar to the structures discussed in this chapter.

3. In what ways does Gore's lattice structure make it well suited to respond to change?

4. Gore asserts that its structure makes it more innovative. Could a traditionally structured company be as innovative as W. L. Gore & Associates? How?

5. What difficulties might you encounter if you tried to apply Gore's structural principles to an existing company?

6. What modern organizational techniques, described in this and the previous chapter, could Gore apply to improve its competitive situation?

COORDINATING JETBLUE

jetBlue AIRWAYS® JetBlue does not publish a formal organization chart, and, indeed, it currently endeavors to minimize employees' preoccupation with organization charts in order to maintain its "think small," start-up, entrepreneurial culture. However, in an industry in which safety is always the main concern, the company has obviously had to take steps to ensure that the work of all of its departments is coordinated and that, in a manner of speaking, "the left hand knows what the right hand is doing."

JetBlue accomplishes this coordination in a variety of ways. It holds monthly meetings within each department at which employees are kept apprised of what their colleagues are doing. Within departments, such as human resources, there are also weekly meetings (such as between the recruiting and training groups). HR's meetings address questions such as what open jobs the company is trying to fill (typically more than 100 jobs open at any time) and training schedules. There is a daily conference call every morning, in which all general managers and corporate managers participate, and in which any other JetBlue employee can also listen in, insofar as it is an open phone call. This daily phone conference addresses problems and issues that may have arisen during the previous 24 hours, such as weather problems, unusual events (such as the president visiting New York), and the status of the company's aircraft. The company also holds monthly officer meetings. One of Jetblue's underlying themes is that if it treats its people right, they will perform in a way that creates prosperity for them and the company. The company, therefore, organizes the agenda for these monthly officer meetings around what it calls the "3-Ps"—people, performance, and prosperity. JetBlue is also considering formalizing these sorts of monthly meetings at the next organizational level down and having its directors meet at monthly meetings.

Given the company's rapid growth and successful financial performance, it's organizational arrangements seem to be working well. However, management is still considering the need to reorganize—and, in particular, to institute a more structured approach than it now uses. The company's growth seems to demand doing so. For example, not too long ago there was a three-person benefits group within the HR department, and each employee tackled any benefits issues that came his or her way. The department is now up to five employees with a manager, and it has become necessary to divide the benefits work in a more formal manner, and to assign specific tasks to each benefits employee. It is also important to institute a more structured approach, because the amount of work that managers need to do is now considerably more than it was just six months or a year ago, given the company's rapid growth. Management knows that much of its success is a direct result of the fact that senior managers—including the CEO, president, and head of HR—spend a great deal of their time out in the field, speaking with customers and employees. Even working 80-hour weeks, that doesn't leave much time for them to tackle the day-to-day technical aspects of their jobs. One way to deal with that problem is to add more subordinates and to delegate specific tasks to them.

The bottom line is that it seems obvious that JetBlue is going to have to take the sorts of steps that leave it open to possibly adding some bureaucracy in the organization (such as putting more emphasis on organization charts, delegating specific duties, and a chain of command), while trying hard to maintain its small, company, entrepreneurial culture.

Questions

1. Based on what you know about the airline industry and JetBlue's environment, where, on a continuum, would you say it should be (in terms of Burns and Stalker's mechanistic and organic types of organizations) with respect to lines of authority, departmentalization, degree of specialization of jobs, delegation and decentralization, coordination, and span of control?

2. Explain what the company is now doing right and now doing wrong with respect to achieving coordination, and explain how you would improve the situation in light of findings like those of Lawrence and Lorsch.

3. Based on what you know about JetBlue, list the specific things you would do to reorganize the company from its current structure to that of a 'learning organization'.

4. Design an organization structure for JetBlue as you think it should be.

Managing Organizational Change

THE MANAGEMENT CHALLENGE

Ghosn Arrives to Save Nissan

At the time, Renault's 1999 decision to plow $5.5 billion into buying part of Nissan motors seemed a ridiculously risky bet. In 1999 alone, Nissan had lost $5.7 billion, had debts of about $11 billion, and had watched its share of the Japanese car market fall for 25 years. In 2000, Nissan sold 80% of its cars at a loss. The situation wasn't helped by the nature of the task facing Carlos Ghosn, the person Renault sent to Japan to turn Nissan around.

He knew the only way to save Nissan was to take some decidedly un-Japanese steps: Close 5 domestic plants, cut 21,000 jobs, sell assets, and impose merit-based pay. As he said, "There were no sacred cows, no constraints, no taboos . . . "[1] Yet, as a French citizen flying in to save a Japanese company, Ghosn faced a particularly tricky dilemma. How could he implement the widespread cuts and changes he knew were required, when doing so might trigger resentment and resistance on the part of the firm's Japanese workers and customers? Ghosn could only succeed by applying everything he knew about how to change an organization. The question was, how should he do that and what should he do first?

CHAPTER OBJECTIVES

After studying this chapter and the case exercises at the end, you should be able to:

1. Decide if the company should reorganize, and, if so, what the new structure should look like.

2. "Read" the company's organization culture and make specific recommendations to improve it.

3. Tell the manager what he or she did wrong in implementing the change.

4. Decide what conflict-resolution style is right for the situation.

Chapters 6 and 7 explained the basics of organizing, and the factors that influence whether managers organize one way or another. However, as Carlos Ghosn knew, managers usually don't have the luxury of just dictating the changes that must be made. They have to size up what needs to be changed, and then implement those changes in a way that minimizes employee resistance. The purpose of this chapter is to show you how to successfully implement an organizational change. The main topics we'll focus on include how to decide what to change and how to change it, a nine-step process for implementing organizational change and managing interpersonal conflict.

■■■ AN OVERVIEW OF THE ORGANIZATIONAL CHANGE PROCESS

Leading an organizational change can be treacherous, even for CEOs with lots of clout. The change may require the cooperation of dozens or even hundreds of managers and supervisors, resistance may be considerable, and the manager will probably have to complete the change while the firm continues to serve its customer base. In 2000–2001, Ford CEO Jacques Nasser tried to press through changes aimed at making Ford "one of the world's best-run companies." He tried to change how the firm produced and marketed its cars, and how it evaluated, trained, and rewarded its employees. As CEO, Nasser had enormous clout. However, it wasn't enough to overcome the resistance of the firm's managers, employees, and dealers. His board forced him out in less than a year.

Not all organizational changes are as broad or complex as those facing Carlos Ghosn or Jacques Nasser. For example, you may just want to stop two departments from bickering, install a new computer, or get your employees to be less risk-averse.

However, whether the required change is simple or complex, the basic organizational change process remains basically the same. Figure 8.1 presents an overview of this process. As illustrated, the "change agent" (usually the manager leading the change) needs to ask him- or herself three basic questions.

▼ **FIGURE 8–1** ■■■

Model for Planned Organizational Change

Source: Adapted from Larry Short, "Planned Organizational Change," *MSU Business Topics*, Autumn 1973, pp. 53–61; ed. Theodore Herbert, *Organizational Behavior: Readings and Cases* (New York: McMillan, 1976), p. 351.

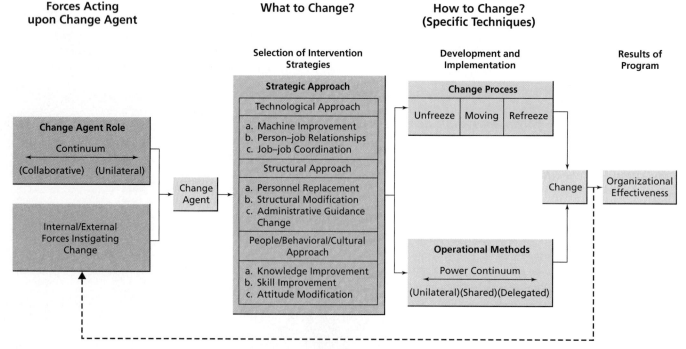

1. *What are the forces acting upon me?* In other words, what are the pressures I should take into consideration as I decide what to change and how I should change it? For example, what are the external pressures prompting the change—such as lackluster financial performance, inadequate new product development, or new competitors gaining market share—and how quickly must we respond to them? In terms of internal pressures, how am I usually inclined to lead a change? For example, am I normally more collaborative/people-oriented or more unilateral/task-oriented in my approach to doing things? Will my usual approach work in this case?

2. *What should we change?* Should the changes be strategic and companywide or relatively limited? Sometimes, the firm needs a strategic, organizationwide change. As at Nissan, this meant reformulating the firm's strategy (what business are we in, and how should we compete?) as well as changing Nissan's organization structure, production technologies, and the "people side" of the company—it's employees' knowledge, skills, and attitudes. But, often, the required change can be more limited in scope. Perhaps one department needs reorganizing, or the firm just needs to install a new technology. We'll discuss *how to decide what to change* in the following section.

3. *How should we change it?* The next question is, "How should we actually implement the change?" The manager's basic concern here is making sure that the change is both successful and timely. No manager wants the nightmare Nasser ran into at Ford. Overcoming employee resistance will, therefore, loom large in the implementation decision. "Should I force through the change or get the employees involved, and (if the latter) how involved should they be?" We'll see later in the chapter that the basic approach generally involves a process psychologist Kurt Lewin called "unfreeze, moving, refreeze." It underscores the importance of provoking the employees out of their traditional ways of doing things. However, before turning to deciding how to implement the change, let us look at how managers decide what to change.

■■■ DECIDING WHAT TO CHANGE

The manager's change program can aim to alter one of four basic things: The firm's strategy, technology, structure, and people/behavior/culture. We'll look at each in this section. However, remember that in practice, such changes are rarely compartmentalized. Instead, the manager needs to take a coordinated view of the change and its implications. Thus, a recent decision by Aetna Insurance to change its strategy and downsize also prompted changes in the firm's structure and in how it trains the sales force.

Strategic Change

Changing the firm's strategy is one option. For example, faced with declining profits, Aetna Insurance recently pulled back from its high-growth strategy. The firm had emphasized adding more policyholders. Its new strategy is to emphasize fewer but more profitable ones. Management reduced policyholders from 22 million to 14.4 million. By focusing on more profitable policyholders, Aetna was able to boost profits by 10 times—to $108 million in one recent quarter. Similarly, faced with surprising competition from digital cameras, Kodak's former CEO refocused the company, redeploying assets to build the firm's competencies in digital photography.

While often unavoidable and required for survival, strategic changes like these are risky. This is especially true when the firm faces what researchers call discontinuous change. This is an unexpected change that triggers a crisis, as when digital photography suddenly started crowding conventional film off the shelves. Changes like these have companywide impact, frequently (as at Aetna) prompting changes in the firm's structure, technology, and people. They're often made under short time constraints. They are usually reactions to uncontrollable outside events like deregulation, intensified global competition, and dramatic technological innovations such as the Internet.[2] Managers faced with the need to make such a change would do well to keep the research evidence in mind:

strategic change ■ *a change in a firm's strategy.*

1. *Strategic changes are usually triggered by factors outside the company.* External threats or challenges, such as deregulation, intensified global competition, and dramatic

technological innovations like the Internet usually prompt organizations to embark on companywide, strategic changes.[3]

2. *Strategic changes are often required for survival.* Researchers found that making a strategic change did not guarantee success, but that firms which didn't change failed to survive. This was especially true when discontinuous environmental change—change of an unexpected nature—required quick and effective strategic change, such as when the Internet suddenly made bookselling more competitive.

3. *Strategic changes implemented under crisis conditions are highly risky.* Strategic changes made under crisis conditions and with short time constraints were the riskiest and most prone to fail. Changes like these eventually trigger changes companywide—for instance, to the firm's structure, technologies, people, and culture and core values. Core values (such as "don't make any risky moves") are especially hard to change, so trying to change them tends to trigger the most employee resistance—as Ford's Jacques Nasser discovered.

Technological Change

technological change ■ *changing the way the company creates and markets its products or services.*

Technological change is a second basic approach. Technological change means changing the way the company creates and markets its products or services. Here, for example, the manager might want to improve operations by (1) installing or modifying the firm's computer systems or machinery, (2) modifying the relationship between the employees and their physical environment, or (3) modifying the interface of the employees with the technology itself—for instance, improving the workflow or reducing the discomfort caused by bending over a machine. The following Management in Action feature illustrates technological change.

MANAGEMENT IN ACTION   Bill Zollars at Yellow Freightways

When Bill Zollars became CEO at Yellow Freightways, the firm was just coming off an appalling year. It had just lost about $30 million, laid off workers, and had a Teamsters union strike. Previously a senior vice president at Ryder Corp., Zollars had built its high-tech integrated logistics unit into a $1.5 billion business. He believed that saving Yellow Freightways would require extensive technological change.

One of Zollars' biggest changes, therefore, involved upgrading the firm's technology. Yellow has now spent over $80 million per year in the past few years on new integrated information systems. Now, for instance, when customers call 1–800-go-yellow, the service representative automatically sees the profile corresponding to that caller's phone number.[4] That automatically tells the sales representative where the customer's company is located, what kind of shipments it typically makes, what sort of loading dock it has, and the firm's previous shipping destinations. This dramatically reduced the time it took to process an order—to as little as 15 seconds in most cases.

Zollars and his team also equipped each dockworker with a wireless "mobile data terminal." Now, even before the truck arrives, the worker can see what's on board and when it's pulling into the dock. And, if the worker takes longer to unload the pallets than the system estimates it should take given the amount of freight, an alert is sent to the mobile data terminal.[5] Managers back at headquarters can monitor progress, and send in additional employees if help is required.

As is usually the case with changes like these, changing the technology needs to go hand in glove with changing the people. It's futile to install a new system that employees cannot or will not use properly. Before making his changes, Zollars, therefore, carefully explained his plan to all the employees. With 25,000 people in hundreds of locations around the country, Zollars spent over a year going from terminal to terminal, standing on loading docks and explaining the changes. The new technology gives the employees the information they need to solve problems quickly. But this meant Zollars had to make sure that the employees got the additional decision-making authority they required, as well as training on the new equipment. Another effect of all these changes has been to change Yellow's culture. Linking employees with the new technology and giving them the authority to make fast, on-the-spot decisions (empowering them) helped to win their commitment and dedication to getting the job done fast.

Structural Change: How to Reorganize

Structural change means changing one or more aspects of the company's organization structures. Structural changes may involve several things. Managers may *reorganize*—change the firm's organization chart and structural elements. (Thus, GE's new CEO, Jeffrey Immelt, recently reorganized his firm's huge GE Capital division. He broke it into four divisions, with their four managers reporting directly to him rather than to the former GE Capital head.) Managers may also change the structure by simply replacing, dismissing, or adding personnel. Or they may change the firm's infrastructure by changing its policies, procedures, and rules (such as the firm's performance appraisal system).

structural change ▪ *changing one or more aspects of the company's organization structures.*

In any case, structural changes tend to trigger resistance. New structures mean new reporting relationships, so some may view the change as a demotion. New structures may also mean new tasks and job descriptions ("task redesign") for employees. For example, Kodak assigned new tasks to its new Digital Photo division employees. People often have an affinity for predictability and the status quo. Not everyone welcomes new tasks.

Reorganizing is a familiar organizational change technique in today's fast-changing times. For example, after dismissing thousands of employees, Lucent needed a new organization design. Former CEO Richard McGinn had organized the company around 11 different businesses.[6] When the board of directors dismissed McGinn, his successor, Harry Schacht, argued that the 11-division structure was too unwieldy; he chopped the design down to five units. More recently (as Lucent continues to downsize), it announced it was reorganizing from five units down to two main units (and laying off 80 executives in the process). One unit, Integrated Network Solutions, will handle landline-based businesses, such as optical networks and phone-call switching. Mobility Solutions will focus on Lucent's wireless products.

Reorganizations confront the manager with two basic questions: (1) Do we really need a new structure? (2) How exactly should the new structure look?

Is a New Structure Really Required? An organizational problem doesn't necessarily mean that a dramatic structural overhaul is required. The current structure may simply need some fine-tuning. Figure 8.2 helps the manager make this determination. Start by determining if just fine-tuning is in order. For example, ask if it might be sufficient to just clarify employees' responsibilities or reporting relationships.

How Exactly Should the New Structure Look? Fine tuning is not always sufficient. As at GE or Lucent, an entirely new organization structure and chart—a major organizational redesign—may be required. How does the manager decide what the structural problem is, and what the new structure should look like? In general, of course, the guidelines in Chapters 6 and 7 apply. For example, fast-changing *environments* tend to require more adaptive, organic, networked "learning organization"-type structures. Mass production technologies favor mechanistic structures. Also consider the firm's *strategy and goals*. When INS and Customs goals evolved after 9/11 from taxes to security, that goal virtually mandated reorganizing those two department's enforcement units into a single, more powerful unit. We also saw that managers have to use *logic and common sense* when organizing.

▲ WEBNOTE ■ ■ ■

Lucent Technologies now has a new organizational design that focuses on two main units: landline-based businesses and wireless products.

www.lucent.com

Source: Lucent Technologies

To help managers enhance their use of logic and common sense, two researchers developed several tests the manager can apply to better gauge (1) the problem with the current structure, and (2) what the new organization structure should look like. These nine tests are as follows.[7]

► FIGURE 8–2 ■ ■ ■

Is a New Structure Really
Required?

Source: Adapted from Michael Goold and
Andrew Campbell, "Do You Have a Well-
Designed Organization?" *Harvard Business
Review*, March 2002, p. 124.

When you identify a problem with your design, first look for ways to fix it without substantially altering it. If that doesn't work, you'll have to make fundamental changes. Here's a step-by-step process for resolving problems:

STEPS NOT INVOLVING MAJOR DESIGN CHANGE

Modify without changing the units.

- Refine the allocation of responsibilities (for example, clarify powers and responsibilities).
- Refine reporting relationships and processes.
- Refine lateral relationships and processes (for example, define coordination mechanisms).
- Refine accountabilities (for example, define more appropriate performance measures).

Redefine Skill Requirements and Incentives.

- Modify criteria for selecting people.
- Redefine skill development needs.
- Develop incentives.

Shape Informal Context.

- Clarify the leadership style needed.
- Define norms of behavior, values, or social context.

STEPS INVOLVING MAJOR DESIGN CHANGE

Make Substantial Changes in the Units.

- Make major adjustments to unit boundaries.
- Change unit roles (for example, turn functional units into business units or shared services).
- Introduce new units or merge units.

Change the Structure.

- Change reporting lines.
- Create new divisions.

1. *The market advantage test.* Does your design direct sufficient management attention to your sources of competitive advantage in each market? "The first and most fundamental test of a design . . . is whether it fits your company's market strategy."[8] The firm's strategy must identify both the markets in which the company will compete, and what the firm's competitive advantages will be. The organization structure must then support that strategy. For example, if the strategy involves expanding overseas, an organization structure that had no provision for addressing the markets abroad should raise a red flag. The two experts say that the rule of thumb here is this: "If a single unit is dedicated to a single segment, the segment is receiving sufficient attention. If no unit has responsibility for the segment, the design is fatally flawed and needs to be revamped." Smaller firms or those facing other strategic concerns may not be able to afford the duplication inherent in creating a structure that addresses multiple markets. However, the basic test remains: "Does your design direct sufficient management attention to your sources of competitive advantage in each market?"

   For example, Volkswagen recently considered reorganizing its nine brands into three operational divisions—one for premium cars, one for mass-market cars, and one for commercial vehicles.[9] One intent of this reorganization is to enable the firm to better focus on what it increasingly sees as VW's three separate market segments. These are premium brands (Audi, Bugatti, Bentley, and Lamborghini), mass brands (Volkswagen), and commercial vehicles.

2. *The parenting advantage test.* Does your design help the corporate parent add value to the organization? For example, GE is a highly diverse conglomerate. So some might ask, "Would it not be more efficient for each of GE's separate divisions to spin off and run themselves rather than to remain part of GE's overall structure?" GE says, "No." It argues that the GE corporate parent brings enormous additional value to each subsidiary. For example, the current structure helps ensure that modern management techniques (such as using the Internet to build a boundaryless supply chain) devised in one unit quickly spread to the others. Suppose ensuring that such sharing of man-

agement know-how is an advantage the parent firm expects to provide. Then, to pass the *parenting advantage test*, the firm's structure should facilitate such sharing.

3. *The people test.* Does your design reflect the strengths, weaknesses, and motivations of your people? The point is that "if an organization is not suited to the skills and attitudes of its members, the problem lies with the design, not the people."[10] The basic question here is whether the organization structure provides the appropriate responsibilities and relationships and wins employee commitment. For example, after PepsiCo purchased Quaker Oats Co., PepsiCo reorganized some business units partly because of the strengths of some executives it inherited with the Quaker purchase. For example, Robert Morrison, Quaker's CEO, quickly assumed responsibility for PepsiCo's Tropicana juice unit, while continuing to oversee the original Quaker business.

■ ■ *Hundreds of new VW Beetles delivered to the Boston Auto Port at Charlestown.*

4. *The feasibility test.* Have you taken into account all the obstacles that may impede the implementation of your design? The basic question here is, "What could stand in the way of successfully implementing my new organization design?" Constraints may include government regulations, the interests of the company stakeholders (including its employees and unions), the firm's information systems, and its corporate culture. For example, in terms of culture, "[3M] is a homegrown place with a collegial atmosphere where the emphasis on being nice to each other means issues haven't always surfaced in an honest way" says one 3M senior vice president.[11] That could have meant resistance on the part of employees to making the hard-nosed structural decisions its new CEO had to make, including consolidating purchasing units and moving some manufacturing abroad. However, he anticipated the potential constraints and dealt with them successfully.

5. *The specialist culture test.* Does your design protect units that need distinct cultures? For example, 3M is known for the number of new products its engineers produce (including Scotch tape, and Post-it notes). Reorganizing R&D, therefore, required addressing its special cultural needs. As its new CEO says, "3M people wake up every morning thinking about what new product they can bring to market. Innovation is in their DNA—and if I kill that entrepreneurial spirit, I will have failed. My job is to build on that strength, corral it, and focus it."[12]

6. *The difficult-links test.* Does your design provide coordination solutions for the unit-to-unit links that are likely to be a problem? In other words, have you addressed the hard-to-coordinate relationships? For example, recall (from our discussion in Chapter 7) that Lawrence and Lorsch found that the product development process in plastics firms required a special coordinated effort. Here, managers installed special "independent integrator" departments. These ensured ongoing coordination among the development, sales, and manufacturing departments under rapidly changing conditions.

7. *The redundant-hierarchy test.* Does your design have too many levels and units? For example, when he became CEO of GE, Jack Welch (now former CEO) found that GE had a hierarchy of what he believed were redundant "parent units." There was a corporate headquarters staff; and then below that, there were various group-level executive vice president staffs; and below that, there were business-level groups. One of the first steps Welch took was to pare the corporate staff, eliminate division groupings, and let most of the heads of the largest independent business units report directly to him and his team.

8. *The accountability test.* Does your design support effective controls? For example, is the company organized in such a way that if a problem arose (such as a dramatic sales decline) for a particular product line, you could quickly identify the manager responsible?

9. *The flexibility test.* Does your design facilitate the development of new strategies and provide the flexibility required to adapt to change? The question here is

whether your organization structure "provides ways for a company to pursue innovation and allows for adaptability to changing circumstances."[13] The aim is to make sure the organization structure doesn't become an impediment to identifying opportunities and pursuing them. For example, several years ago, the magazine publisher Emap saw that new media and Internet-based publishing could be a significant new publishing opportunity. Management knew the firm's current magazine-focused business units might not want to risk diluting their own efforts by pursuing new digital opportunities. Emap management, therefore, created a new digital business function to deal with these opportunities

People/Behavioral/Cultural Change

Strategic, technical, and structural changes invariably trigger various changes in the behavioral side of the firm, including the employees' attitudes, values, and skills. Sometimes, employees simply don't have the *knowledge* or *skills* to do the job. Here, managers such as Yellow Freightways' Bill Zollars call on training and development techniques to improve employees' skills. (We address training and development in Chapter 9). At other times, the "people" problems stem from *misunderstanding* or *conflict*. Here, organizational development interventions or conflict-resolution efforts (like those discussed shortly) may be in order.

Finally, the manager may want to change the firm's organizational or corporate culture—the *basic values* its employees share and the ways in which these values manifest themselves in behavior. For example, some attribute Motorola's recent lackluster performance to the company's culture, which one writer describes as "stifling bureaucracy, snail-paced decision making, . . . engineering bigotry that subordinates customer focus, and internal competition so fierce that [CEO] Galvin himself has referred to it as a 'culture of warring tribes.'[14]

The first step in changing the culture is to understand what it is now. Checklist 8.1 can be of use here.

CHECKLIST 8.1 ■ How to Read an Organization's Culture[15]

☑ **Observe the physical surroundings.** Look at how the employees are dressed, the degree of openness among offices, the pictures and photographs on the walls, the type of furniture and its placement, and any signs (such as a long list of activities that are "prohibited here"!)

☑ **Sit in on a team meeting.** How do the employees treat each other? Are there obvious differences in how each rank of employee is treated? Are the communications open or decidedly one-sided?

☑ **Listen to the language.** Is there a lot of talk about "quality," "perfection," and "going the extra mile?" Or is there more emphasis on "don't rock the boat," "don't tell those people what we're doing," or "be nice."

☑ **Note to whom you are introduced and how they act.** Is the person casual or formal, laid-back or serious? Does it seem that you're only being introduced to a limited number of people—or to everyone in the unit?

☑ **Get the views of outsiders, including vendors, customers, and former employees.** What do they think of the firm? Do you get responses like "they're so bureaucratic that it takes a year to get an answer"? Or do they say things like "they're open and flexible and always willing to accommodate?"

The Basics of Changing Culture You know from your own experience that changing someone's values entails more than just talk. Parents might tell their children to eat only healthy foods. But suppose the children see their parents saying one thing and doing another? Chances are that the parents' actions will mold their children's values about what's right or wrong when it comes to food.

The same is true of cultural change at work: You have to send the right signals. When he decided to transform Kodak, for instance, the former CEO knew he had to do more than talk. Top executives who weren't performing were replaced, and new incentive plans and more results-oriented appraisal systems were instituted. The net effect was to send a strong signal to employees throughout the firm. It said, "The values of being efficient, effective, and responsive are a lot more important today than they were the week before."

Creating and Sustaining the Right Corporate Culture

The board makes you CEO of a struggling company. The firm is known for its culture of backbiting, bureaucratic behavior, and disdain for clients. What steps would you take to change the company's culture? Experts suggest the following broad tactics:[16]

■ ■ *Ben (Cohen) and Jerry (Greenfield) at the October 2000 grand opening of the Ben & Jerry's Scoop Shop in Minneapolis. Proceeds from the shop will fund programs to provide educational and employment opportunities for low-income people in the community.*

1. *Make it clear to your employees what you pay attention to, measure, and control.* For example, direct your employees' attention toward controlling costs or serving customers if those are the values you want to emphasize. Use management policies and practices to send strong signals about what is or is not acceptable. At Toyota, for example, "quality and teamwork" are desirable values. It therefore makes sense that Toyota's employee selection and training process emphasizes the candidate's quality and teamwork orientation.

2. *React appropriately* to critical incidents and organizational crises. For example, if you want to emphasize the value that "we're all in this together," don't react to declining profits by laying off operating employees and middle managers while giving top managers a raise.

3. *Use "signs, symbols, stories, rites, and ceremonies"* to signal your values. At Ben & Jerry's, signs and symbols help sustain the company's culture. The "joy gang" team distributes awards to worthy B&J teams. The team's existence is a concrete symbol of the firm's values, which emphasize charity, fun, and goodwill. At JC Penney, loyalty and tradition are values. To support this, the firm inducts new management employees into the "Penney Partnership" at formal conferences, where they commit to the firm's core values of "honor, confidence, service, and cooperation."

4. *Deliberately role model, teach, and coach the values you want to emphasize.* For example, Wal-Mart founder Sam Walton lived the values "hard work, honesty, neighborliness, and thrift" that he wanted Wal-Mart employees to follow. He was one of the richest men in the world, but he drove a pickup truck. He explained this by saying, "If I drove a Rolls Royce, what would I do with my dog?"

5. *Communicate your priorities by how you allocate rewards.* Leaders communicate their priorities by how they link raises and promotions to particular behaviors. For example, General Foods decided several years ago to reorient its strategy from cost control to diversification and sales growth. It therefore revised the firm's pay plan. Management linked bonuses to sales volume and to new-product development rather than just to increased earnings.

6. *Make your HR procedures and criteria consistent* with the values you espouse. When he became chairman and CEO of IBM, Louis Gerstner instituted new appraisal systems and pay plans to reinforce his focus on performance.

Lawrence Weinbach's efforts to change the culture at Unisys are a good example of how to create the right corporate culture.

MANAGEMENT IN ACTION   Weinbach at Unisys

Lawrence Weinbach, chairman and CEO of Unisys, took many steps to change the culture of that firm—and particularly to focus employees on performance and execution. For example, "... We've moved to a pay-for-performance approach, to make sure that we're properly recognizing the people who are doing things right. ... in some cases, we've needed to tell people to seek opportunities elsewhere where they will be happier. ... we've invested in training and education and created Unisys University, where employees can find courses and programs on a range of ... business related topics. We've also spent a lot of time communicating and educating people about the importance of execution. I think we've done pretty well at getting everyone here to understand what we're good at, what our core competencies are, and then driving home the fact that you have to deliver every single day."[17]

DECIDING HOW TO IMPLEMENT THE CHANGE

After deciding what to change, the manager must decide, "How should we actually implement the change?" As noted earlier, the manager's basic concern is to ensure that the change is both successful and timely. The basic issue here is how to deal with and minimize employee resistance. Functionally, the manager's options range from unilaterally ramming through the change to having the employees themselves decide what to change and how to change it.

Why Do People Resist Change?

Overcoming resistance is often the hardest part of leading a change. Niccolò Machiavelli, a shrewd observer of 16th-century Italian politics, put it this way: "There is nothing so difficult to implement as change, since those in favor of the change will often be small in number while those opposing the change will be numerous and enthusiastic in their resistance to change."[18]

The fact that a change is advisable or even mandatory doesn't mean employees will accept it. In fact, even the company's key people—perhaps including some top and middle managers—may (perhaps slyly) resist it. They may just prefer the status quo.

Application Example It's easy to see how such resistance might arise. Take a personal example. Suppose you've been attending a management class with the college's best professor. Several weeks into the semester, the dean comes in and announces that some students will have to move. They must move to another professor and class because the fire marshal says the lecture hall is overcrowded.

The dean asks you to move. What would go through your mind? Probably several things: that moving might adversely affect your grade; that you don't want to leave the friends you've made here and start all over again; that it might be just a tad embarrassing to have to get up and leave (although obviously it's not your fault); and that it's not fair you should be one of those singled out. The change makes sense—and indeed is quite benign. But in spite of that, you don't want to go!

Years ago, Professor Paul Lawrence said it's usually not the technical aspects of a change employees resist, but its social consequences—"the changes in their human relationships that generally accompany the technical change."[19] Thus, they may see in the change diminished responsibilities for themselves and, therefore, lower status in the organization and less job security. Sometimes, it's not fear of the obvious consequences, but rather apprehension about the unknown consequences that produces resistance. For example, how much do you know about the professor who'll be teaching that new class you're being moved to—and about the new classmates? Not much, unfortunately.

Sources of Resistance

Resistance has many sources. For example, in his book *Beyond the Wall of Resistance*, consultant Rick Maurer says resistance like this can stem from two main sources. What he calls *Level 1* resistance stems from lack of information or honest disagreement over the facts. *Level 2* resistance is more personal and emotional. Here, people are afraid—that the change may cost them their jobs, or to lose face, for instance. Maurer says that treating all resistance as if it were Level 1 can undermine the manager's change efforts. For example, using "slick visual presentations to explain change with nice neat facts, charts, and time lines, when what people really want to hear is: 'What does this mean to them?'" can be a recipe for disaster.[20]

Furthermore, some people are more resistant to change than others—they always seem to be fighting the system. As you might imagine, they are usually not the sorts of employees who contribute in a positive way to organizational change. One study focused on six organizations—two European companies, two Australian banks, a U.S. university, and a Korean manufacturing firm. Its aim was to determine how managers' personality traits influenced their reactions to change. Three personality traits—

tolerance for ambiguity, having a positive self-concept, and being more tolerant of risk—significantly predicted effectiveness in coping with change.[21] Managers with the lowest self-image, least tolerance for ambiguity, and least tolerance for risk appeared, as expected, to be the most resistant.

Sometimes, employees say they want to change (and may actually mean it), and yet they resist the program. What accounts for this? Two organizational psychologists recently suggested that this resistance may be the result of "competing commitments." In other words, the employees say they want to change (and may even think they do), but in fact, a competing commitment makes them resist it.

Figure 8.3 provides a few examples. For example, "Helen" says and may believe that she is committed to the new initiative. However, she has an unstated competing commitment: "Do not upset my relationship with my boss by leaving the [mentored] role." She's therefore actually not pushing her team to implement the new initiative.

Uncovering competing commitments like these requires a diagnostic process. First, notice and record the person's actual, current behavior (since it's not what they say they *want* to do but what they're *actually* doing that is important to you as a manager). Second, speak with the person and lead him or her to understand what the competing commitments really are.

Overcoming Resistance to Change

Psychologist Kurt Lewin proposed a famous model to summarize the basic process for implementing a change with minimal resistance. To Lewin, all behavior in organizations was a product of two kinds of forces: those striving to maintain the status quo, and those pushing for change. Implementing change thus meant either reducing the forces for the status quo or building up the forces for change. Lewin's process consists of three steps: unfreezing, moving, and refreezing.

Unfreezing means reducing the forces pressing for the status quo. The usual way to accomplish this is by presenting a provocative problem or event. The goal is to get employees to recognize the need for change and to search for new solutions. Attitude surveys, interview results, or participatory informational meetings often provide such provocative events. As we'll see in a moment, some managers accomplish this by creating a crisis—such as by suggesting that bankruptcy might be imminent if things don't change fast.

unfreezing ■ *a step in psychologist Kurt Lewin's model of change that involves reducing the forces for the status quo, usually by presenting a provocative problem or event to get people to recognize the need for change and to search for new solutions.*

▼ **FIGURE 8–3** ■ ■ ■

How Immune Is the Person to Change?

Source: Robert Kegan and Lisa Lahey, "The Real Reason People Won't Change," *Harvard Business Review,* November 2001, p. 89.

Stated commitment *I am committed to . . .*	What am I doing, or not doing, that is keeping my stated commitment from being fully realized?	Competing commitments	Big assumptions
Helen . . . *the new initiative.*	I don't push for top performance from my team members or myself; I accept mediocre products and thinking too often; I don't prioritize.	I am committed to not upsetting my relationship with my boss by leaving the [mentored] role.	I assume my boss will stop supporting me if I move toward becoming his peer; I assume that I don't have what it takes to successfully carry out a cutting-edge project.
Bill . . . *being a team player.*	I don't collaborate enough; I make unilateral decisions too often; I don't really take people's input into account.	I am committed to being the one who gets the credit and to avoiding the frustration or conflict that comes with collaboration.	I assume that on one will appreciate me if I am not seen as the source of success; I assume nothing good will come of my being frustrated in conflict.
Jane . . . *turning around my department.*	Too often, I let things slide; I'm not proactive enough in getting people to follow through with their tasks.	I am committed to not setting full sail until I have a clear map of how we get our department from here to there.	I assume that if I take my group out into deep waters and discover I am unable to get us to the other side, I will be seen as an incompetent leader who is underservingof trust or responsibility.

Once you have employees' attention, you must move them in the desired direction. Lewin's second step, *moving*, aims to shift or alter the behavior of the employees. Moving means developing new behaviors, values, and attitudes by applying one or more organizational change techniques. We discuss organizational change technique options later in this chapter.

Lewin was shrewd enough to know that just making a change is not enough. People and organizations tend to revert to their old ways of doing things unless management reinforces the new ways. Whether it's a new diet, a new saving plan, or a new organizational procedure, Lewin knew you had to reinforce the change. If you did not, you run the risk that the change won't be permanent. That's what Lewin meant by refreezing. He said you had to institute new systems and procedures that would support and maintain the changes that you made.

Choosing the Right Tool for Overcoming Resistance

Table 8.1 summarizes some tools that managers use to overcome resistance—and when to use them. For example, "education and communication" are appropriate where inaccurate or missing information is contributing to employee resistance. "Coercion"—forcing through the change—can be a fast way of pushing through a change, particularly when speed is essential. This can work when the manager has the power to force the change, but can be risky if it leaves influential employees with the will and ability to undermine the change. The Managing @ the Speed of Thought feature illustrates one application of the change process.

TABLE 8–1	Six Methods for Dealing with Resistance to Change		
Method	**Commonly Used in Situations**	**Advantages**	**Drawbacks**
Education + communication	Where there is a lack of information or inaccurate information and analysis.	Once persuaded, people will often help with the implementation of the change.	Can be very time-consuming if lots of people are involved.
Participation + involvement	Where the initiators do not have all the information they need to design the change, and where others have considerable power to resist.	People who participate will be committed to implementing change, and any relevant information they have will be integrated into the change plan.	Can be very time-consuming if participators design an inappropriate change.
Facilitation + support	Where people are resisting because of fear and anxiety.	No other approach works as well with employee adjustment problems.	Can be time-consuming and expensive, yet still fail.
Negotiation + agreement	Where someone or some group will clearly lose out in a change, and where that group has considerable power to resist.	Sometimes, it is a relatively easy way to avoid major resistance.	Can be too expensive in many cases if it prompts others to negotiate.
Manipulation + co-optation	Where other tactics will not work or are too expensive.	It can be relatively quick and inexpensive solution to resistance problems.	Can lead to future problems if people feel manipulated.
Coercion	Where speed is essential, and the change initiators possess considerable power.	It is speedy and can overcome any kind of resistance.	Can be risky if it leaves people angry at the initiators.

Source: Adapted and reprinted by permission of *Harvard Business Review.* "Six Methods for Dealing with Change," from "Choosing Strategies for Change," by John P. Kotter and Leonard A. Schlesinger, March–April 1979. Copyright © 1979 by the President and Fellows of Harvard College; all rights reserved.

Business Process Reengineering

One firm's experience reengineering its processes illustrates some of the issues involved in implementing a successful change. Business reengineering is "the radical redesign of business processes, combining steps to cut waste and eliminate repetitive, paper-intensive tasks in order to improve cost, quality, and service, and to maximize the benefits of information technology."[22] The basic approach is to (1) identify a business process to be redesigned (such as approving a mortgage application); (2) measure the performance of the existing processes; (3) identify opportunities to improve these processes; and (4) redesign and implement a new way of doing the work, usually by (5) assigning ownership of formerly separate tasks to an individual or team that use new computerized systems to support the new arrangement.

A system installed at Bank One Mortgage provides an example. As illustrated in Figure 8.4, Bank One redesigned its mortgage application process so that it required fewer steps and reduced processing time from 17 days to 2. In the past, a mortgage applicant completed a paper loan application that the bank then entered in its computer system. A series of specialists such as

business reengineering ▪ the radical redesign of business processes to cut waste; to improve cost, quality, and service; and to maximize the benefits of information technology, generally by questioning how and why things are being done as they are.

▼ **FIGURE 8–4** ■■■

Redesigning Mortgage Processing at Bank One

By redesigning its mortgage processing system and the mortgage application process, Bank One will be able to handle the increased paperwork as it moves from processing 33,000 loans per year to processing 300,000 loans per year.

Shifting from a traditional approach helped Bank One Mortgage slash processing time from 17 days to 2

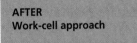

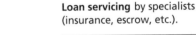

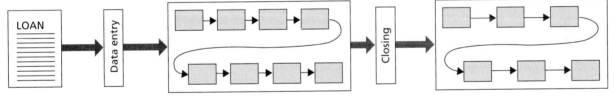

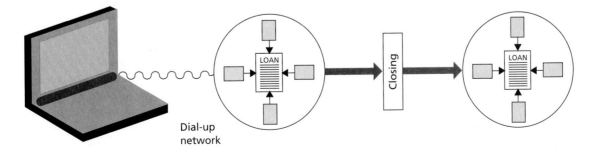

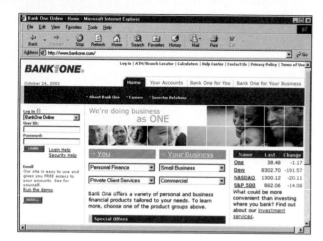

credit analysts and underwriters evaluated the application individually as it moved through eight different departments.

Bank One replaced the sequential operation with a work-cell, or team, approach. Loan originators in the field now entered the mortgage application directly into laptop computers, where software checked it for completeness. The information then went electronically to regional production centers. Here, specialists (like credit analysts and loan underwriters) convened electronically, working as a team to review the mortgage together—at once. After they formally closed the loan, another team of specialists took on the task of servicing the loan. ■■■

Companies' experiences with reengineering help illustrate the importance of applying an effective organizational change process. Many such programs have been successful, but failure rates run as high as 70%.[23] When reengineering does fail, it is often due to behavioral factors. Sometimes, employees resist and undermine the new procedures. Reengineering without considering the new skill requirements, training, and reporting relationships can aggravate the situation. As John Champy, a long-time reengineering proponent, has said, "In short, reducing hierarchy, bureaucracy, and the rest of it is not just a matter of rearranging the furniture to face our customers and markets. It is [also] a matter of rearranging the quality of people's attachments—to their work and to each other. These are *cultural* matters."[24] The basic need is to prepare employees for the change, both to reduce resistance and to provide them with the knowledge, skills, and attitudes they need to do their new jobs.

■■■ A NINE-STEP PROCESS FOR LEADING ORGANIZATIONAL CHANGE

Lewin's unfreeze–moving–refreeze model provides a powerful framework for making a change, but the devil, of course, is in the details. In particular, what specific steps should a manager use to carry out the change? Experts have proposed many multistep models. Change experts Wendel French and Cecil Bell Jr. describe six such multistep models, for instance.[25] The following nine-step list provides a useful change process for managers.

Create a Sense of Urgency[26]

You know something's wrong. What do you do now? Do you just paper over the problems (see the cartoon)? Or do you take remedial action? Most experienced leaders instinctively know that before taking action, they have to unfreeze the old habits. They have to create a sense of urgency.

Creating a sense of urgency has a double-barreled benefit. For those who might want to resist the change, it can convince them of the need for the change. And it may jar those who might simply be neutral (or who simply don't care) out of their complacency. Techniques managers use to create a sense of urgency include:[27]

- *Create a crisis* by allowing a financial loss or exposing managers to major weaknesses relative to competitors.
- *Eliminate examples of excess* such as company-owned country club facilities, numerous aircraft, or gourmet executive dining rooms.
- *Set targets* for revenue, income, productivity, customer satisfaction, and product development cycle time so high that they can't be reached by those conducting business as usual.
- *Send more data* about customer satisfaction and financial performance to more employees, especially information that demonstrates weaknesses relative to competitors.

© 1997 Randy Glasbergen.

GLASBERGEN

**"Your job will be to walk funny and look really cute,
so nobody notices how horrible it is to work here."**

Decide What to Change

You've just taken over as CEO of a troubled company. You know you have to make changes. What are your options—what is it about the company that you can change? In practice, as explained earlier, you can change the firm's strategy, technologies, and structure, as well as the culture, attitudes, and skills of its people.

Create a Guiding Coalition and Mobilize Commitment

Leading a change is one thing. Trying to do it all by yourself is another. Major transformations—such as the one CEO McNerney achieved by transforming 3M—are often associated with one highly visible leader. But no leader can accomplish a major change alone. That's why most leaders create a *guiding coalition* of influential people. Such individuals become the vanguard—the missionaries and implementers of change. The coalition should work as a team and should include people with enough power to lead the change effort.

You must choose the right lieutenants. One reason is to gather political support. The leader therefore has to ensure that there are enough key players "on board," so that those left out can't easily block progress.[28] The coalition should also have the expertise, credibility, and leadership skills required to explain and implement the change. One option is to create one or more broad, employee-based task forces to diagnose the company's problems. Doing so can produce a shared understanding of and commitment to what the company can and must improve. Leaders can also be trained to lead change, as the following Management in Action feature shows.

MANAGEMENT IN ACTION Training Leaders to Lead Change

Power, respect, and influence drive coalition-member choice, but some otherwise logical candidates may lack the leadership skills to play a forceful role. Can you train these employees to be better leaders of change? The answer, based on one recent study, is yes.

This study focused specifically on training the employees to be transformational leaders. Such leaders tend to act charismatic, stimulating, and inspirational.[29] The study took place at a large bank in Canada.[30] The trainers randomly assigned managers of the 20 branches in one region to receive transformational leadership training—or not to receive it.

The first part of the two-part training program consisted of a one-day training session that familiarized participants with the meaning of transformational leadership. The trainers explained and illustrated how to implement transformational leadership in the managers' branches. The second part consisted of several one-on-one booster sessions. Here a trainer met individually with each of the managers to go over the latter's leadership style. The two developed personal action plans

■■ ■ *Barry Gibbons, who supplied the vision that gave Spec's Music and its stakeholders a direction to follow.*

for the manager, to enable him or her to become more of a goal-oriented, transformational leader.

The results were quite positive. For example, the subordinates of the transformation-trained managers subsequently perceived their managers as higher on intellectual stimulation and charisma than did subordinates of managers in the no-training group. Supporting otherwise qualified change-coalition members to be more effective at taking leadership roles in the change thus seems quite feasible. ■■■■

Develop and Communicate a Shared Vision

Beyond the guiding coalition, the firm's other employees also need a vision they can rally around, a signpost on which to focus. As we saw in Chapter 5, a vision is "a general statement of the organization's intended direction that evokes emotional feelings in organization members." When Barry Gibbons became CEO of a struggling Spec's Music retail chain, its employees, owners, and bankers—all of its stakeholders—required a vision around which to rally. Gibbons's vision of a leaner Spec's offering both concerts and retail music helped to provide the needed sense of direction.

Having a vision is useless unless the employees share that vision. Change expert John Kotter says, "The real power of a vision is unleashed only when most of those involved in an enterprise or activity have a common understanding of its goals and direction."[31] Key steps in communicating a vision include:

- *Keep it simple.* Here is an example of a good statement of vision: "We are going to become faster than anyone else in our industry at satisfying customer needs."
- *Use multiple forums.* Try to use every channel possible—big meetings and small, memos and newspapers, formal and informal interaction—to spread the word.
- *Use repetition.* Ideas sink in deeply only after people have heard them many times.
- *Lead by example.* "Walk the talk" so that your behaviors and decisions are consistent with the vision you advocate.

Empower Employees To Make the Change

Some leaders then confront a dilemma. They need the active assistance of their employees to implement the change. But the employees haven't the tools, skills, authority or freedom to do what's needed to help. For example, in a study of change in major companies like Sears Roebuck & Co., Royal Dutch Shell, and the U.S. Army, the researchers found that employees were rarely able or willing to do what it took to carry out the change if they thought they lacked the power to do so. Therefore, ask "Do employees believe they can affect organizational performance? Do they believe they have the power to make things happen?"[32]

There are many potential barriers to empowerment—and, therefore, many ways to remove them (see Figure 8.5). At Allied Signal (now Honeywell), CEO Lawrence Bossidy put all of his 80,000 people through quality training. He also created area "councils" (for instance, for Asia). These councils allowed employees who were undertaking initiatives in those areas to get together, share market intelligence, and compare notes.[33]

Generate Short-Term Wins

Most people can't wait years before deciding if they're going in the right direction. They need periodic feedback: what some call "short-term wins."[34] The guiding coalition in one company set its sights on producing one highly visible and successful new product about 20 months after the start of its organizational renewal effort.[35] It selected the new product in part because the coalition knew that the introduction was doable. Accomplishing it sent a strong signal that the broader, longer-term change was also doable.

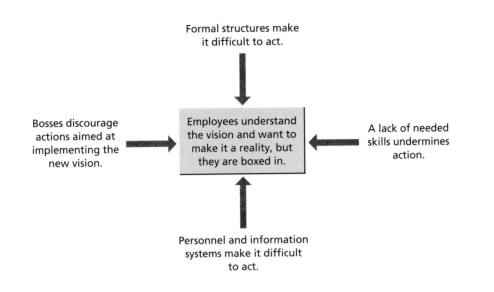

Formal structures make it difficult to act.

Bosses discourage actions aimed at implementing the new vision.

Employees understand the vision and want to make it a reality, but they are boxed in.

A lack of needed skills undermines action.

Personnel and information systems make it difficult to act.

◀ **FIGURE 8–5** ■ ■ ■

Barriers to Empowerment

Source: Reprinted by permission of Harvard Business School Press. From *Leading Change* by John P. Kotter. Boston,. MA. 1996, p. 102. Copyright © 1996 by the President and Fellows of Harvard College, all rights reserved.

Consolidate Gains and Produce More Change

The challenge, now, is to capitalize on the short-term wins. This is the time to press ahead and extend your gains. You have increased credibility from the short-term wins. Use it to change all of the systems, structures, and policies that don't fit well with the company's new vision.

Anchor the New Ways of Doing Things in the Company Culture

As you consolidate and extend the gains, remember that you will need a parallel change in the company's values and culture. Perhaps you want a "team-based, quality-oriented, adaptable organization." However, that is not going to happen if the firm's shared values still emphasize "selfishness, mediocrity, and bureaucratic behavior." Changing the culture is, therefore, crucial. It is one of the manager's most challenging jobs. We discussed cultural change earlier in the chapter.

Monitor Progress and Adjust the Vision as Required

Finally, monitor the effectiveness of the change. Continually compare results to goals. One firm appointed an oversight team composed of managers, a union representative, an engineer, and several others. They monitored the functioning of the firm's new self-managing teams. Another firm used morale surveys to monitor employees' reactions to the changes. The Management in Action feature that follows describes what Carlos Ghosn did at Nissan.

MANAGEMENT IN ACTION   Ghosn and Nissan

The approach used by Carlos Ghosn in his dramatic turnaround of Nissan Motors illustrates how a manager can use his firm's employees to devise and implement the change. When the Renault executive agreed to head up the turnaround at Renault's new strategic partner, Nissan had lost billions of dollars, and it had billions more in debts. It was utilizing only about 53% of its auto producing capacity, and it was losing $1,000 on every car it sold in the United States. Purchasing costs were 15–25% higher than at Renault.[36]

Ghosn knew he had to make big changes—and fast. Another CEO (especially one with such extensive experience in the auto business) might have assumed that the way to go was to formulate and force through the changes. However, as Ghosn puts it, "I knew that if I had tried simply to impose the changes from the top, I would have failed. Instead, I decided to use as the centerpiece of the turnaround effort a set of cross-functional teams."[37]

Team	Purchasing	Manufacturing & Logistics	Sales & Marketing	Phaseout of Products & Parts Complexity Management	Organization
CFT Leaders	• executive VP of purchasing • executive VP of engineering	• executive VP of manufacturing • executive VP of product planning	• executive VP of overseas sales & marketing • executive VP of domestic sales & marketing	• executive VP of domestic sales & marketing • executive VP of product planning	• executive VP of finance (CFO) • executive VP of manufacturing
CFT Pilot	• general manager of purchasing	• deputy general manager of manufacturing	• manager of overseas sales & marketing	• manager of product planning	• manager of human resources
Functions Represented	• purchasing • engineering • manufacturing • finance	• manufacturing • logistics • product planning • human resources	• sales & marketing • purchasing	• product planning • sales & marketing • manufacturing • engineering • finance • purchasing	• product planning • sales & marketing • manufacturing • engineering • finance • purchasing
Team Review Focus	• supplier relationships • product specifications and standards	• manufacturing effieicney and cost effectiveness	• advertising structure • distribution structure • dealer organization • incentives	• manufacturing efficiency and cost effectiveness	• organizational structure • employee incentive and pay packages
Objectives Based on Review	• cut number of suppliers in half • reduce costs by 20% over three years	• close three assembly plants in Japan • close two power-train plants in Japan • improve capacity utilization in Japan from 53% in 1999 to 82% in 2002	• move to a single global advertising agency • reduce SG&A costs by 20% • reduce distribution subsidiaries by 20% in Japan • close 10% of retail outlets in Japan	• reduce number of plants in Japan from seven to four by 2002 • reduce number of platforms in Japan from 24 to 15 by 2002 • reduce by 50% the variation in parts (due to differences in engines or cars).	• create a worldwide corporate headquarters • create regional management committees • empower program directors • implement performance-oriented compensation.

▲ **FIGURE 8–6** ■ ■ ■

Some of Nissan's Cross-Functional Teams (CFTs)

Source: Adapted from Carlos Ghosn, "Saving the Business Without Losing the Company," *Harvard Business Review*, January 2002, pp. 40–41.

Figure 8.6 summarizes Ghosn's approach. As you can see, he organized cross-functional teams, each with responsibilities for the main tasks required for Nissan to have a successful turnaround. He appointed teams for business development, purchasing, manufacturing and logistics, research and development, sales and marketing, general and administrative, financing costs, phaseout of products, and organization. (The figure shows 5 of the teams). Each team had a set of executive 'leaders', a day-to-day operational 'pilot,' and specific assignments. Each consisted of about 10 members, all middle managers with line responsibilities (except for the "executive leaders").

Based on recent results, the changes designed and pushed through by Nissan's teams were quite successful. For example, net profit rose from a loss of $5.7 billion in fiscal year 1999 to a profit of about $2.8 billion in fiscal year 2001. Automotive debt dropped from $11.2 billion in 1999 to $5.8 billion in 2002. ■■■■

A Special Kind of Change: Becoming an E-Business

Every business is becoming an e-business today. For example, Bank One sponsored an Immersion Day in New York City to introduce its new Internet bank, **wingspanbank.com**.[38] As *Fortune* recently put it, "e or be eaten": Either link your business to the Web, or say goodbye to your business.

The problem is that "blending old business and e-business—'clicks and mortar'—is for the most part a

■■■ *In November 1999, Arthur C. Martinez, then Sears chairman and CEO, introduced an expanded Sears Web site that includes a new feature called Tool Territory, the only place online shoppers can find top brands in every major tool category.*

difficult, awkward process."[39] The merger of AOL and Time Warner is one striking example. Here Time-Warner's more buttoned-down, conservative culture sometimes clashed with AOL's entrepreneurial values. And consider Sears's Internet operation. Most Sears headquarters employees are housed in comfortable offices in the firm's Chicago tower. Over at their Internet division in Hoffman Estates, Illinois, Sears's e-employees, including its former treasurer, have small cubicles. "Boxes lie everywhere."[40]

What changes can you expect when moving from a conventional to an Internet-based business? "Entering the e-commerce realm is like managing at 90 mph. E-business affects finance, human resources, training, supply-chain management, customer-resource management, and just about every other corporate function. This puts the managers of these departments in a new light," says the chief strategist for one e-business.[41]

As at AOL/Time Warner, how to structure the new enterprise is a big issue. For one thing, you'll have to decide whether to blend the new e-business into the company's current structure or organize it as a separate entity. If you blend the two entities, what role should the e-business play? Some argue for assigning one manager responsibility for the e-business initiative. Others say that "it's far better to develop an organizational structure that puts the Web and e-business at the central focus of a cross-departmental business group, rather than merely adding Web responsibilities to a preexisting task list."[42] Greg Rogers heads up Whirlpool Corporation's e-commerce operation. He says that the company's strategy will have to change too: "Internet strategy is really business strategy."[43] The company's new business strategy will have to reflect the fact that the company now embraces e-commerce as part of its competitive advantage.

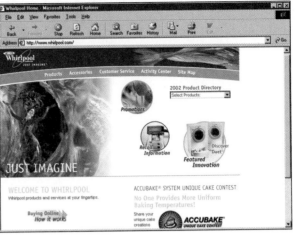

■■■ USING ORGANIZATIONAL DEVELOPMENT TO CHANGE ORGANIZATIONS

Organizational development (OD) is a special approach to organizational and cultural change, in which the employees formulate and implement the change, usually with the aid of a trained facilitator. OD has three distinguishing characteristics:

1. It is based on action research, which means collecting data about a group, department, or organization, and then feeding that data back to the employees. Then the group members themselves analyze the data and develop hypotheses about what the problems in the unit might be.
2. It applies behavioral science knowledge in order to improve the organization's effectiveness.
3. It changes the organization in a particular direction—toward improved problem solving, responsiveness, quality of work, and effectiveness.[44]

The range of OD applications (also called OD interventions or techniques) has increased over the years. OD got its start with human process interventions. These aimed to help employees better understand and modify their own and others' attitudes, values, and beliefs—and thereby improve the company.

Today (see Table 8.2), OD practitioners aren't just involved in changing participants' attitudes, values, and beliefs. Now, they also directly alter the firm's structure, practices, strategy, and culture. However, OD's distinguishing characteristic has stayed the same: to have the employees themselves analyze the situation and develop the solutions. Let's look at the four main types of OD interventions: human process, technostructural, HR management, and strategic.

Human Process Applications

Human process applications aim at improving employees' human relations skills. The goal is to provide employees with the insight and skills they need to analyze their own and others' behavior more effectively. With this new insight, they should be able to

organizational development (OD) ■ *an approach to organizational change in which the employees themselves formulate the change that's required and implement it, usually with the aid of a trained consultant.*

action research ■ *the process of collecting data from employees about a system in need of change, and then feeding that data back to the employees so that they can analyze it, identify problems, develop solutions, and take action themselves.*

human process interventions ■ *organizational change techniques aimed at enabling employees to develop a better understanding of their own and others' behaviors for the purpose of improving that behavior such that the organization benefits.*

TABLE 8–2	Examples of OD Interventions and the Organizational Levels They Affect		

| Interventions | Primary Organizational Level Affected | | |
	Individual	Group	Organization
HUMAN PROCESS			
T-groups	x	x	
Process consultation		x	
Third-party intervention	x	x	
Team building		x	
Organizational confrontation meeting		x	x
Intergroup relations		x	x
TECHNOSTRUCTURAL			
Formal structural change			x
Differentiation and integration			x
Cooperative union-management projects	x	x	x
Quality circles	x	x	
Total quality management		x	x
Work design	x	x	
HUMAN RESOURCE MANAGEMENT			
Goal setting	x	x	
Performance appraisal	x	x	
Reward systems	x	x	x
Career planning and development	x		
Managing workforce diversity	x		
Employee wellness	x		
STRATEGIC			
Integrated strategic management			x
Culture change			x
Strategic change			x
Self-designing organizations		x	x

solve interpersonal and intergroup problems more intelligently. *Sensitivity training, team building,* and *survey research* are three classic techniques here.

Sensitivity training (aka laboratory or t-group training) was one of the earliest OD techniques. It aims to increase the participant's insight into his or her own behavior and the behavior of others by encouraging an open expression of feelings in the training group. Typically, 10 to 15 people meet, usually away from the job. The focus is on the feelings and interactions of group members. Participants are encouraged to portray themselves as they are now, in the group, rather than in terms of past experiences.[45] T-group training is obviously very personal in nature, so it's not surprising that it is controversial and that its use has diminished markedly.[46]

OD's action research emphasis is perhaps most evident in team building. This is a special process for improving the effectiveness of a team. The facilitator collects data concerning the team's performance and then feeds it back to the members of the team.

sensitivity training ■ *also called laboratory or t-group training, the basic aim of this organizational development technique is to increase participants' insight into their own behavior and that of others by encouraging an open expression of feelings in a trainer-guided group.*

team building ■ *the process of improving the effectiveness of a team through action research or other techniques.*

The participants examine, explain, and analyze the data. They then develop specific action plans or solutions for solving the team's problems.

Before the meeting, the consultant interviews each group member.[47] He or she asks what their problems are, how the group functions, and what obstacles are preventing the group from performing better. The consultant might then categorize the interview data into themes and present the themes to the group at the beginning of the meeting. (Themes like lack of cohesion might be culled from statements such as, "I can't get any cooperation around here.") The group then explores and discusses the themes, examines the underlying causes of the problems, and works on solutions.

Some firms use survey research to create a sense of urgency. Here, the facilitator/consultant has employees throughout the company fill out attitude surveys. He or she then feeds back the data to top management and to the appropriate group or groups. The survey data provide a convenient method for unfreezing an organization's management and employees. It provides a lucid, comparative, graphic illustration of the fact that the organization has problems.

survey research ■ the process of collecting data from attitude surveys filled out by employees of an organization, then feeding the data back to workgroups to provide a basis for problem analysis and action planning.

Technostructural Applications

As noted above, OD practitioners no longer limit themselves to human process applications (such as team-building). Instead, they are increasingly involved in efforts to change the structures, methods, and job designs of firms. Compared with human process interventions, technostructural interventions (as well as HR management interventions and strategic interventions) focus directly on productivity improvement and efficiency. For example, in a formal structure change program, employees collect data on existing structures and analyze them. The purpose is to jointly redesign and implement new organizational structures. OD practitioners also assist in implementing employee-involvement programs, including quality circles and job redesign.

formal structure change program ■ an intervention technique in which employees collect information on existing formal organizational structures and analyze it for the purpose of redesigning and implementing new organizational structures.

HR Management Applications

OD practitioners use action research to help employees analyze and change personnel practices. Targets of change include the performance appraisal system and reward system. Another typical effort involves using action research to institute workforce diversity programs. These aim to boost cooperation among a firm's diverse employees.

Strategic Applications

Strategic interventions are companywide OD programs aimed at achieving a better fit among a firm's strategy, structure, culture, and external environments. Integrated strategic management is one example. It involves four steps:

1. *Analyze current strategy and organizational design.* Senior managers and other employees utilize models such as the SWOT matrix (explained in Chapter 5) to analyze the firm's current strategy and organizational design.
2. *Choose a desired strategy* and organizational design. Based on the analysis, senior management formulates a strategic vision, objectives, and plan, and an organizational structure for implementing them.
3. *Design a strategic change plan.* The group designs a strategic change plan. This "is an action plan for moving the organization from its current strategy and organizational design to the desired future strategy and design."[48] The plan explains how management will implement the strategic change. It includes specific activities as well as the costs and budgets associated with them.
4. *Implement the strategic change plan.* The final step is to implement the strategic change plan and then measure and review the results.[49]

strategic intervention ■ an organization development application aimed at effecting a suitable fit among a firm's strategy, structure, culture, and external environments.

integrated strategic management ■ an organizational development program to create or change a company's strategy by analyzing the current strategy, choosing a desired strategy, designing a strategic change plan, and implementing the new plan.

■ *The Global Manager* OD practices such as sensitivity training that may be acceptable in one context may be frowned upon in another. Managers thinking of using OD interventions abroad, therefore, need to consider the cultural context.

A recent study of OD usage by U.S., Japanese, and European Multinational Corporations and local Chinese firms in Hong Kong illustrates this. Although the firms were all operating in the same Hong Kong environment, the results suggest that OD usage was largely a function of the firms' countries of origin. In particular, there were distinct differences in OD usage between Western and Asian firms. For example, Chinese and Japanese firms generally practiced all types of OD interventions less frequently than did Western firms. In this study, the researchers also found that the individual development types of intervention (like sensitivity training) were least used, even for the American firms, and that the Chinese firms were even less open to individual and personal level interventions like these than were European and U.S. firms.

The researchers concluded that the Chinese tended to be more skeptical of personal and confrontation-type interventions then were the European and U.S. firms. On the other hand, local Chinese firms used HR-type, system-level OD interventions, for instance to strengthen their reward systems and personnel and succession planning. These HR activities "have a long-term orientation, [and] are [therefore] more often practiced in local Chinese firms. This phenomenon is consistent with the cultural perspective that Chinese have long-term and collective values."[50]

■ ■ ■ MANAGING INTERPERSONAL CONFLICT

Few things are potentially as deadly for a company's performance as uncontrolled conflict among employees or departments. Opposing parties put their own aims above those of the organization, and the organization's effectiveness suffers. Time that they could have used productively evaporates, as people hide information and jockey for position. Opponents may become so angry that their health suffers. Managing conflicts like these is a major part of all managers' organizational change responsibilities.

Sometimes these conflicts are structural in nature, sometimes not. Where conflicts stem from structural sources like interdepartmental differences and points of view, structural solutions (as per Chapter 7) include exchanging personnel and minimizing interdependencies. However, many (or most) conflicts require the manager's personal intervention. It is at this point that the manager must become something of a diplomat. He or she must size up the situation and decide what conflict-resolution style to use.

Every diplomat knows that there are different ways ("conflict-resolution styles") to settle an argument—and that some are better than others, depending on the situation. For example, having both parties meet to confront the facts and hammer out a solution is usually better than simply smoothing over the conflict by pushing problems under a rug. Yet there are undoubtedly times when letting things just cool down is advisable. Knowing which approach to use—and when—is an art.

Interpersonal Conflict-Resolution Styles

Different conflict experts have slightly different ways of describing the conflict resolution styles a person can use. One popular approach involves thinking of conflict resolution styles in terms of a *dual concern model*.[51] This approach views conflict resolution styles as based on two things—the individual's concern for his or her *own* outcomes and for the outcomes of *others*. This produces a matrix, as in Figure 8.7, and four (or five) styles (depending on the expert).

Accommodators are high in concern for others and low in concern for self. They tend to sacrifice their own goals and to satisfy the needs of others. *Avoiders* are low in concern for both self and others. They "allow conflicts to go unresolved or permit others to take responsibility for solving the problem."[52] *Competitors* maximize their own outcomes while disregarding the effects on others. For them, conflict is always a win–lose situation. *Collaborators* pursue a win–win style. They are high in their concern for self and for others. They "... try to integrate the needs of both parties into a solution that will maximize the interests of both."[53] *Compromisers* fall in the middle of both sides.

Figure 8.8 provides a self-assessment exercise for sizing up your own conflict-resolution style, using a similar list of styles. One thing to remember is that people seem to be capable of adapting their style to the situation and of using several styles at once.

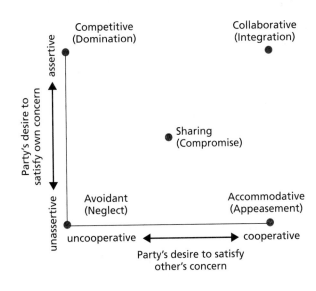

◄ **FIGURE 8–7** ■ ■ ■

Conflict Handling Styles

Source: Kenneth W. Thomas, "Organiza-
tional Conflict," ed., Steven Kerr, *Organiza-
tional Behavior* (Columbus, OH: Grid
Publishing, 1979), in Andrew DuBrin,
Applying Psychology (Upper Saddle River,
NJ: Prentice Hall, 2000), p. 223.

A Study of Interpersonal Conflict Styles

In practice, people usually don't rely on a single conflict-resolution mode; they use several simultaneously.[54] A study of supervisors and subordinates illustrates this.

The researchers studied how supervisors used several possible conflict-resolution styles. Table 8.3 presents all of them (along with definitions). The researchers' basic question was this: Is some combination of these styles more effective at resolving conflicts than others? They analyzed videotapes of 116 male police sergeants handling a standardized, scripted conflict with either a subordinate or a superior. The possible styles in this study (with examples) included:

■ *Confrontation.* "In recent meetings we have had a thrashing around about our needs. At first, we did not have much agreement. However, we kept thrashing the issues around, and we finally agreed on the best solution." Confronting the issue head-on is often the best approach. This is especially so when the parties are willing to confront and air their differences in a civil, problem-solving manner.

■ *Forcing.* "If I want something very badly and I am confronted by a roadblock, I go to top management for the backing I need to get the decision made. If there is a conflict, then I take the decision to somebody higher up."[55] Forcing can be effective as a brute show of power. However, remember the old saying: "The person convinced against his will is of the same opinion still." Forcing compliance can backfire if the person you're forcing can wiggle out of the deal later.

■ *Avoidance.* "I'm not going to discuss that with you." Avoidance or smoothing over usually won't resolve a conflict. In fact, doing so may actually make it worse if bad feelings fester. However, some problems—especially small ones—sometimes do go away by themselves. And avoidance may be your only option if one or both parties are highly emotional.

avoidance ■ *moving away from or refusing to discuss a conflict issue.*

smoothing over ■ *in conflict management, diminishing or avoiding a conflict issue.*

■ *Process controlling.* "We're going to follow my agenda for this meeting, and solve this problem my way." Process controlling means dominating the conflict resolution process to one's own advantage.

process controlling ■ *dominating the conflict resolution process to one's own advantage.*

■ *Compromise and collaboration.* "I'm sure we can figure out a way to solve this together." "We're all in the same boat." Compromise means each person gives up something in return for reaching agreement. This approach can work well. However, it assumes a high level of maturity and willingness on both parties' parts. And it can leave one or both parties feeling that they could have done better if they'd bargained harder. Collaboration meant both rider work together to achieve agreement.

compromise ■ *settling a conflict through mutual concessions.*

collaboration ■ *a conflict-management style in which both sides work together to achieve agreement.*

■ *Accommodating.* "Calm down so we can work this out."[56] Accommodation can help calm an opponent who is not uncontrollably irate. However, this is a stop-gap measure. You'll have to take up the issue again later, since the matter remains unresolved.

accommodation ■ *giving in to the opponent in an attempt to end a conflict.*

Your Conflict Resolution Style

Source: Thomas J. Von de Embse, *Supervision: Managerial Skills for a New Era* (New York: Macmillian Publishing Company, 1987), in Stephen Robbins and Philip Hunsaker, *Training in Interpersonal Skills* (Upper Saddle River, NJ: Prentice Hall, 1996), pp. 217–19.

Indicate how often you do the following when you differ with someone.

WHEN I DIFFER WITH SOMEONE:

	Usually	Sometimes	Seldom
1. I explore our differences, not backing down, but not imposing my view either.	☐	☐	☐
2. I disagree openly, then invite more discussion about our differences.	☐	☐	☐
3. I look for a mutually satisfactory solution.	☐	☐	☐
4. Rather than let the other person make a decision without my input, I make sure I am heard and also that I hear the other out.	☐	☐	☐
5. I agree to a middle ground rather than look for a completely satisfying solution.	☐	☐	☐
6. I admit I am half wrong rather than explore our differences	☐	☐	☐
7. I have a reputation for meeting a person halfway.	☐	☐	☐
8. I expect to get out about half of what I really want to say.	☐	☐	☐
9. I give in totally rather than try to change another's opinion.	☐	☐	☐
10. I put aside any controversial aspects of an issue.	☐	☐	☐
11. I agree early on rather than argue about a point.	☐	☐	☐
12. I give in as soon as the other party gets emotional about an issue.	☐	☐	☐
13. I try to win the other person over.	☐	☐	☐
14. I work to come out victorious, no matter what.	☐	☐	☐
15. I never back away from a good argument.	☐	☐	☐
16. I would rather win than end up compromising.	☐	☐	☐

Scoring Key and Interpretation

Total your choices as follows: Give yourself 5 points for "Usually"; 3 points for "Sometimes"; and 1 point for "Seldom." Then total them for each set of statements, grouped as follows:

Set A: items 13–16   Set C: items 5–8

Set B: items 9–12   Set D: items 1–4

Treat each set separately.

A score of 17 or above on any set is considered high;

Scores of 8 to 16 are moderate;

Scores of 7 or less are considered low.

Sets A, B, C, and D represent conflict-resolution strategies:

A = Forcing/domination. I win, you lose.

B = Accommodation. I lose, you win.

C = Compromise. Both win some, lose some.

D = Collaboration. I win, you win.

Everyone has a basic or underlying conflict-handling style. Your scores on this exercise indicate the strategies you rely upon most.

TABLE 8–3	Conflict-Resolution Modes
Component	**Definition**
Forcing	Contending the adversary do what you say in a direct way
Confronting	Demanding attention to the conflict issue
Process controlling	Dominating the conflict-resolution process to one's own advantage
Problem solving	Reconciling the parties' basic interests
Compromising	Settling through mutual concessions
Accommodating	Giving in to the opponent
Avoiding	Moving away from the conflict issue

Source: Evert Van De Vliert, Martin C. Euwema, and Sipke E. Huismans, "Managing Conflict with a Subordinate or a Superior: Effectiveness of Conglomerated Behavior," *Journal of Applied Psychology*, April 1995, pp. 271–81. Copyright © 1995 by the American Psychological Association. Reprinted by permission.

It was obvious that to resolve the conflict, the sergeant had to use several styles simultaneously. For example, problem solving tended to enhance the sergeant's effectiveness, especially if he or she combined it with some forcing. However, process controlling—dominating the conflict-resolution process to one's own advantage, for instance, by not letting the conversation stray off track—was even more effective. It was better than trying to force the issue by insisting that the adversary follow orders. Some sergeants also boosted their conflict-management effectiveness by being somewhat accommodating.

The bottom line seems to be this: At least for these police sergeants, using three styles together—*problem solving* while being moderately *accommodating* and still maintaining a strong hand in controlling the conflict-resolution process—was an especially effective combination. Multiple styles seems to be the way to go.

SUMMARY ▪▪▪

1. Whatever the change, the basic organizational change process remains basically the same. The change agent (usually the manager leading the change) needs to ask him- or herself three basic questions: What are the forces acting upon me? What should we change? How should we change it?

2. The manager's change program can aim to alter one of four basic things: The firm's strategy, technology, structure, and people/behavior/culture. In practice, such changes are rarely compartmentalized. Instead, the manager needs to take a systems view of the change and it's implications.

3. The hardest part of leading a change is overcoming resistance. Resistance stems from several sources: habit, resource limitations, threats to power and influence, fear of the unknown, and altering employees' personal compacts.

4. Methods of dealing with resistance include education and communication, facilitation and support, participation and involvement, negotiation and agreement, manipulation and co-optation, and coercion. Lewin suggests unfreezing the situation, perhaps by using a dramatic event to get people to recognize the need for change.

5. A nine-step process for actually leading organizational change includes creating a sense of urgency; deciding what to change; creating a guiding coalition and mobilizing commit-

ment to change through a joint diagnosis of business problems; developing and then communicating a shared vision; removing barriers to the change and empowering employees; generating short-term wins; consolidating gains and producing more change; anchoring the new ways of doing things in the company's culture; and monitoring progress and adjusting the vision as required.

6. Organizational development (OD) is a special approach to organizational change that basically involves letting the employees themselves formulate and implement the change that's required, often with the assistance of a trained consultant. Types of OD applications include human process applications, technostructural interventions, HR management applications, and strategic applications.

7. Different conflict experts have slightly different ways of describing the conflict resolution styles a person can use. One popular approach involves thinking of conflict resolution styles in terms of a "dual concern model." This approach views conflict resolution styles as based on two things—the individual's concern for his or her *own* outcomes and for the outcomes of *others*. This produces a matrix and four (or five) styles (depending on the expert): *accommodators*, *avoiders*, *competitors*, and *collaborators*.

strategic change 195
technological change 196
structural change 197
unfreezing 203
moving 204
refreezing 204
business reengineering 205
organizational development (OD) 211

action research 211
human process interventions 211
sensitivity training 212
team building 212
survey research 213
formal structure change program 213
strategic intervention 213
integrated strategic management 213

avoidance 215
smoothing over 215
process controlling 215
compromise 215
collaboration 215
accommodation 215

SKILLS AND STUDY MATERIALS

COMPANION WEBSITE ■■■

We invite you to visit the Dessler Companion Website at **www.prenhall.com/dessler** for this chapter's Internet resources.

EXPERIENTIAL EXERCISES ■■■

1. In teams of 4–5 students, use what you learned about organizational culture in this chapter to describe the organizational culture in this class. List the specific things that you believe contributed to creating that culture and what specifically you would do to fine-tune the culture.

2. You are the professor in a management class, and you have a problem. Classes started last week, and the class did not get off to a good start. You arrived late, were snappy with the students, and gave them the impression that you'd be running a tough, dictatorial classroom. Several students dropped the course, and most of the others probably stayed only because the other sections are full. You don't want to spend a miserable semester. Form teams of 4–5 students, and write out an outline, using the nine-step change process from this chapter that shows what exactly you would change in your class (if you were the professor) and how you would change it, to have a more pleasant and productive class.

3. Working in teams of 4–5 students, explain specifically how you would apply each of the three steps in Lewin's change process to overcome resistance to change in the following situations: (1) Your brother is 200 pounds overweight. How would you get him to go on a diet? (2) Your professor gave you an A-minus instead of an A, because you compiled a 91.9 average instead of the required 92, and you want the grade changed to A. (3) You want to go to France on vacation this year, but your significant other is concerned with the risks of flying and of being out of the United States. How can you get that person to change his or her mind? (4) You just applied for a job as marketing manager for a local department store. The head of HR says that you seem like a very good candidate but that you don't have quite enough experience. How would you overcome his or her resistance?

CASE STUDY ■■■

IMMELT SPLITS GE CAPITAL

In his first major reorganization since taking over as CEO of General Electric, Jeffrey Immelt said he was splitting GE's huge GE capital finance division into four major parts. GE Capital produces about 40% of all of GE's earnings, and the heads of its individual insurance, consumer finance, commercial finance, and equipment units formally reported to GE capital chief executive Denis Nayden. He, in turn, reported to Jeffrey Immelt, along with the heads of GE's various other businesses, including NBC, appliances, and medical equipment. Under the new organization, Immelt eliminated the position of GE Capital chief executive, and the heads of GE Capital's four main insurance, consumer finance, commercial finance, and equipment units will now report directly to Immelt.

In making the change, Immelt basically said he wanted more direct day-to-day control over GE Capital's huge financial services businesses. He said, "This will create a clearer line of sight on how our financial services businesses operate and enhance growth." The reorganization will, therefore, give him the same direct control over each of the GE capital divisions that he now has with respect to GE's other businesses, such as appliances and jet engines. Another benefit of the change, according to GE, is that "our external reporting will mirror this organizational structure, providing greater clarity for investors." In other words, investors will now receive financial reports on each of the four GE Capital businesses rather than on just GE Capital as a whole.

While the reorganization seems to make sense, several observers have criticized it. The range of businesses and the number of people reporting to Immelt is already quite large, and the new organization means he'll have three additional people reporting directly to him. Furthermore, there are some obvious synergies among the four separate GE Capital divisions; therefore, it's now going to be up to Immelt to ensure that he provides the required coordination so that those synergies take place. Others point out that the sorts of improvements that Immelt says he wants—such as giving him a clearer idea of what each of the four divisions is doing—could have been accomplished without a major reorganization. In the past, for instance, GE's former CEO, Jack Welch, rou-tinely personally reviewed major GE Capital transactions. Another analyst pointed out that "... Whenever a high-level executive [such as Nayden] departs, you have to be a little bit skeptical, and it raises a red flag that perhaps there may be another shoe."[57]

Questions.

1. Use Figure 8.2 to answer this question: Was this reorganization really necessary? What other knowledge that you have about how to reorganize would you apply to answering that question, and what conclusions would you arrive at?

2. Use the nine "test" questions (such as the market advantage test) in this chapter both to analyze the organization that Immelt decided upon and to answer this question: How would you have reorganized GE Capital?

YOU BE THE CONSULTANT ■■■

FINE-TUNING AN EFFECTIVE ORGANIZATIONAL CULTURE AT JETBLUE

jetBlue AIRWAYS® Anyone who's flown in the past few years (including the industry's most experienced, "elite-status" flyers) knows how frustrating flying can be, because of the long security lines, testy employees, and (when you finally get on the plane) lack of food. It hasn't been pleasant, and David Neeleman knew that building JetBlue meant putting "pleasant" back into flying. He also knows there's more to building a great airline than buying brand-new planes and offering low fares and seatback TVs (although that certainly helps). Great companies have great cultures, values, and expected behaviors that guide everything employees do. As he says in his "Welcome from our CEO" memo to passengers on JetBlue's Web site, "... We set out to bring humanity back to air travel and to make traveling more enjoyable." That's why Neeleman and his team have worked so hard to create the right culture at JetBlue.

In building the right culture, he and his team have taken several tangible steps. The Culture page on its Web site lays out the company's five values: safety, caring, integrity, fun, and passion. The Diversity page follows up with management's commitment to "encourage a diverse environment where teamwork prevails over cultural or ethnic differences." Creating the right culture means hiring people who have the sorts of values and behavior patterns JetBlue is looking for. If you browse through JetBlue's online job listings, you will, therefore, find numerous references to values and behavior. For example, the customer service crew needs to be "[a]ble to demonstrate a Passion for taking Care of customers with Integrity while having Fun and doing it all Safely." Its people should "find a way to say 'YES' to the cus-tomer." Other job listings—such as that for the manager of operations—similarly stress the need to exhibit a passion for the work of that position. JetBlue's online employment application form requires applicants to "[t]ell us your 'shining moment' story ... ," when you've "gone out of your way to meet the needs of a customer or fellow employees." It also asks the applicant to describe an instance when he or she had "FUN on the job."

Neeleman and his team also take other culture-building steps. For example, you will often find him or members of his top-management team on the planes, speaking with passengers and crew to judge the level of service. They also pitch in with the ground crews, helping them load and unload planes and sort baggage.

Assignment

You and your team are consultants to Mr. Neeleman, who is depending on your management expertise to help him navigate the launching and management of JetBlue. Here's what he wants to know from you now:

1. Develop a form we can use to "read" how employees see our culture now. Could we use the same form to measure our passengers' perceptions of our culture? Tell us how we should go about doing the latter.

2. Write a brief (one-paragraph) summary of the sort of culture we are shooting for now. Then tell us what you would do to fine-tune that target culture, to delete aspects you think are unwise, or to add aspects you believe are necessary. Explain your changes, please.

3. Based on anything you know about JetBlue, list at least five other tangible things the company does (other than those in the case above) to create JetBlue's culture.

Staffing and Human Resource Management

THE MANAGEMENT CHALLENGE

Terry Lutz Needs a "New Kind of Employee"

Wisconsin-based Signicast Corp.'s president, Terry Lutz, knew his company had to build a new, high-tech plant if it was going to grow. Signicast produces metal parts from a casting process. Workers use wax molds to create ceramic molds, which they then use to cast metal parts. The basic process is actually ancient, although Signicast has improved it dramatically. To compete, the firm knew it had to reinvent itself by building a new, highly automated plant. But it discovered that "in the real world, new automation technology requires a new kind of employee"—one capable of working in teams, managing his or her own work, and utilizing the new computerized equipment at the firm's new plant. Lutz and his management team, therefore, faced many questions. Should they just design the new plant themselves, or should they get employees (only some of whom would end up working at the new plant) involved in the planning? And, how should Signicast select, train, and organize the employees so the new plant would have the sorts of new tech-friendly people it needed to be a success?[1] Lutz knew his plans for the company hinged on human resource management.

Chapters 6–8 focused on designing the company's organization structure. However, organization charts don't show what employees actually do, or what kinds of skills they need to do their jobs. After designing the organizational superstructure of the company, managers, therefore, turn to staffing their organizations—in other words, to actually filling their firms' positions. Staffing, personnel, or (as it is usually called today) **Human Resource (HR) Management** is the management function devoted to acquiring and training the organization's employees—and then appraising and paying them. The purpose of this chapter is to give you the basic skills you need to staff your organization. The main topics we cover include writing job descriptions, interviewing and selecting employees, and training and appraising the firm's new workers.

human resources (HR) management ■ *the management function devoted to acquiring, training, appraising, and compensating employees.*

■■■ THE STRATEGIC ROLE OF HUMAN RESOURCE MANAGEMENT

Most large firms have Human Resource (HR) departments with their own HR managers. However, all managers are, in a sense, personnel managers: They all get involved in recruiting, interviewing, selecting, and training employees. All managers therefore need basic staffing skills, such as writing job descriptions, recruiting and interviewing employees, training new employees, appraising them, and managing their compensation. Figure 9.1 shows this basic step-by-step HR process. We'll focus on each set of skills in this chapter.

Terry Lutz's experience at Signicast says much about how human resource management has changed in the past few years. Managers used to view HR (or, as it was known, "personnel management") as strictly operational: as "putting out small fires—ensuring that people are paid on the right basis; the job advertisement meets the newspaper deadline; and a suitable supervisor is recruited for the night shift by the time it goes ahead . . ."[2] Today, managers such as Lutz know that in flattened, downsized, and high-performing organizations, trained and committed employees—not machines—are the firm's competitive advantage. As at Signicast, automated machines are useless without highly trained and capable workers to run them. All firms have access to the same high-tech machines and devices. It's the employees who set their firms apart. That is why human resource management—the function responsible for acquiring, training, appraising, and compensating employees—plays a bigger role in companies' strategic success.

Managers call this **strategic human resource management**. It means aligning the firm's human resource management goals and policies with the strategic goals of the enterprise in order to improve business performance. Ideally, HR and top management work together to craft the company's business strategy. That strategy then shapes specific HR policies such as where to recruit, who to hire, and how to pay employees. That's basically what Signicast's managers did in designing and opening the new plant.

strategic human resource management ■ *the linking of the human resource function with the company's strategies to accomplish that strategy.*

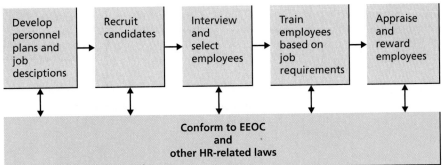

◀ **FIGURE 9–1** ■■■

The Basic HR Process

HR's involvement at Signicast began at the plant design stage. HR people invited employees from the existing facility to participate in planning and design meetings. They solicited suggestions on matters ranging from how to design a new piece of equipment to the workflow in the new plant: "Employees would come up with suggestions; we'd implement them, and bring them back to [employees] for confirmation."

HR's role in the building of this new plant was apparent in other ways. HR had to select and train the new workforce. The new automated plant would produce parts almost five times faster than the old plant. This would leave no time for rework or errors. The employees would therefore have to have more responsibility. In many ways, they would have to be more highly trained and carefully selected than their counterparts at the old facility.

Selection standards were thus tighter. At the old plant, for example, the only hiring requirements were a high school diploma and a good work ethic. The 135 employees at the new plant would require the same high school degree and work ethic plus team orientation, good trainability, good communication skills, and a willingness to do varied jobs over a 12 hour-shift. HR also had to create a cross-training program, so that employees could do each other's jobs to avoid getting bored or tired during 12-hour shifts.[3] A new compensation plan paid workers not just for performance, but also for knowledge and for the number of jobs at which they became competent. HR, therefore, played a crucial role in implementing Signicast's expansion strategy.

■■■ WRITING JOB DESCRIPTIONS AND RECRUITING EMPLOYEES

Human resource management starts with staffing, which means actually filling a firm's open positions. As in Figure 9.2, this encompasses job analysis, recruiting, selecting, and training employees.

Job Analysis and Personnel Planning

Developing an organization chart (Chapters 6–8) creates jobs the firm must fill. Job analysis is the procedure through which you determine the duties of the jobs, and the kinds of people (in terms of skills and experience) to hire for them.[4] You then use this information to develop job descriptions (a list of duties showing what the job entails), and job specifications (a list of the skills and aptitudes sought in people hired for the job). It is impossible to know what kinds of people to recruit or select—or how to train them—if you don't understand the jobs they have to do.

The job description, as in Figure 9.3, identifies the job, provides a brief job summary, and then lists specific responsibilities and duties. There is no standard format for writing a job description. However, most descriptions contain sections covering job

staffing ■ actually filling a firm's open positions; also, the personnel process that includes six steps: job analysis, personnel planning; recruiting, interviewing, testing and selection, and training and development.

job analysis ■ the procedure used to determine the duties of particular jobs and the kinds of people (in terms of skills and experience) who should be hired for them.

job description ■ a document that identifies a particular job, provides a brief job summary, and lists specific responsibilities and duties of the job.

job specification ■ the human qualifications in terms of traits, skills, and experiences required to accomplish a job.

▼ **FIGURE 9–2** ■ ■ ■

Steps in the Recruitment and Selection (staffing) Process

The recruitment and selection process is a series of hurdles aimed at selecting the best candidate for the job.

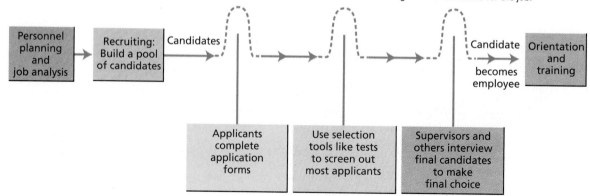

OLEC CORP.
Job Description

Job Title: Marketing Manager
Department: Marketing
Reports To: President
FLSA Status: Non Exempt
Prepared By: Michael George
Prepared Date: April 1, 2002
Approved By: Ian Alexander
Approved Date: April 15, 2002

SUMMARY

Plans, directs, and coordinates the marketing of the organization's products and/or services by performing the following duties personally or through subordinate supervisors.

ESSENTIAL DUTIES AND RESPONSIBILITIES include the following. Other duties may be assigned.

Establishes marketing goals to ensure share of market and profitability of products and/or services.

Develops and executes marketing plans and programs, both short and long range, to ensure the profit growth and expansion of company products and/or services.

Researches, analyzes, and monitors financial, technological, and demographic factors so that market opportunities may be capitalized on and the effects of competitive activity may be minimized.

Plans and oversees the organization's advertising and promotion activities including print, electronic, and direct mail outlets.

Communicates with outside advertising agencies on ongoing campaigns.

Works with writers and artists and oversees copywriting, design, layout, pasteup, and production of promotional materials.

Develops and recommends pricing strategy for the organization, which will result in the greatest share of the market over the long run.

Achieves satisfactory profit/loss ratio and share of market performance in relation to preset standards and to general and specific trends within the industry and the economy.

Ensures effective control of marketing results and that corrective action takes place to be certain that the achievement of marketing objectives are within designated budgets.

Evaluates market reactions to advertising programs, merchandising policy, and product packaging and formulation to ensure the timely adjustment of marketing strategy and plans to meet changing market and competitive conditions.

Recommends changes in basic structure and organization of marketing group to ensure the effective fulfillment of objectives assigned to it and to provide the flexibility to move swiftly in relation to marketing problems and opportunities.

Conducts marketing surveys on current and new product concepts.

Prepares marketing activity reports.

SUPERVISORY RESPONSIBILITIES

Manages three subordinate supervisors who supervise a total of five employees in the Marketing Department. Is responsible for the overall direction, coordination, and evaluation of this unit. Also directly supervises two non-supervisory employees. Carries out supervisory responsibilities in accordance with the organization's policies and applicable laws. Responsibilities include interviewing, hiring, and training employees; planning, assigning, and directing work; appraising performance; rewarding and disciplining employees; addressing complaints and resolving problems.

QUALIFICATIONS

To perform this job successfully, an individual must be able to perform each essential duty satisfactorily. The requirements listed below are representative of the knowledge, skill, and/or ability required. Reasonable accommodations may be made to enable individuals with disabilities to perform the essential functions.

EDUCATION and/or EXPERIENCE

Master's degree (M.A.) or equivalent; or four to ten years related experience and/or training; or equivalent combination of education and experience.

LANGUAGE SKILLS

Ability to read, analyze, and interpret common scientific and technical journals, financial reports, and legal documents. Ability to respond to common inquiries or complaints from customers, regulatory agencies, or members of the business community. Ability to write speeches and articles for publication that conform to prescribed style and format. Ability to effectively present information to top management, public groups, and/or boards of directors.

MATHEMATICAL SKILLS

Ability to apply advanced mathematical concepts such as exponents, logarithms, quadratic equations, and permutations. Ability to apply mathematical operations to such tasks as frequency distribution, determination of test reliability and validity, analysis of variance, correlation techniques, sampling theory, and factor analysis.

REASONING ABILITY

Ability to define problems, collect data, establish facts, and draw valid conclusions. Ability to interpret an extensive variety of technical instructions in mathematical or diagram form.

identification, job summary, responsibilities and duties, authority of incumbent, standards or performance, working conditions, and job specifications (the human requirements of the job).

job analysis questionnaire ■ *a form used by managers to determine the duties and functions of a job through a series of questions that employees answer.*

Managers can use a **job analysis questionnaire** Figure 9.4 to ascertain a job's duties and responsibilities. It requires employees to provide detailed information on what they do. Employees do this by briefly stating their main duties in their own words,

▶ FIGURE 9–4 ■■■

Job Analysis Questionnaire for Developing Job Descriptions

Use a questionnaire like this to interview job incumbents, or have them fill it out.

Source: **www.hrnext.com** (accessed July 28, 2001).

Job Analysis Information Sheet

Job Title____________________ **Date** __________

Job Code__________________ **Dept.** __________

Superior's Title ____________________

Hours worked ______ **AM to** _______ **PM**

Job Analyst's Name ____________________

1. **What is the job's overall purpose?**

2. **If the incumbent supervises others,** list them by job title; if there is more than one employee with the same title, put the number in parentheses following.

3. **Check those activities** that are part of the incumbent's supervisory duties.
   - ❐ Training
   - ❐ Performance Appraisal
   - ❐ Inspecting work
   - ❐ Budgeting
   - ❐ Coaching and/or counseling
   - ❐ Others (please specify) ____________________

4. **Describe the type and extent of supervision** received by the incumbent.

5. **JOB DUTIES:** Describe briefly WHAT the incumbent does and, if possible, HOW he/she does it. Include duties in the following categories:
   a. daily duties (those performed on a regular basis every day or almost every day)

   b. periodic duties (those performed weekly, monthly, quarterly, or at other regular intervals)

   c. duties performed at irregular intervals

6. Is the incumbent performing duties he/she considers unnecessary? If so, describe.

7. Is the incumbent performing duties not presently included in the job description? If so, describe.

8. **EDUCATION:** Check the box that indicates the educational requirements for the job (not the educational background of the incumbent).
   - ❐ No formal education required
   - ❐ Eighth grade education
   - ❐ High school diploma (or equivalent)
   - ❐ 2-year college degree (or equivalent)
   - ❐ 4-year college degree (or equivalent) (specify:)
   - ❐ Graduate work or advanced degree
   - ❐ Professional license (specify:)

describing the conditions under which they work, and listing any permits or licenses required to perform duties assigned to their positions. Supervisors and/or specialists from the company's HR department then review this information. They question the employees and decide exactly what each job does—or should—entail. Checklist 9.1 provides typical questions. The Managing @ the Speed of Thought feature shows how firms use the Internet to create their job descriptions.

◀ FIGURE 9–4 ■ ■ ■

(continued)

9. **EXPERIENCE:** Check the amount of experience needed to perform the job.

- ❑ None
- ❑ Less than one month
- ❑ One to six months
- ❑ Six months to one year
- ❑ One to three years
- ❑ Three to five years
- ❑ Five to ten years
- ❑ More than ten years

10. **LOCATION:** Check location of job and, if necessary or appropriate, describe briefly.

- ❑ Outdoor
- ❑ Indoor
- ❑ Underground
- ❑ Pit
- ❑ Scaffold
- ❑ Other (specify)

11. **ENVIRONMENTAL CONDITIONS:** Check any objectionable conditions found on the job and note afterward how frequently each is encountered (rarely, occasionally, constantly, etc.)

- ❑ Dirt
- ❑ Dust
- ❑ Heat
- ❑ Cold
- ❑ Noise
- ❑ Fumes
- ❑ Odors
- ❑ Wetness/humidity
- ❑ Vibration
- ❑ Sudden temperature changes
- ❑ Darkness or poor lighting
- ❑ Other (specify)

12. **HEALTH AND SAFETY:** Check any undesirable health and safety conditions under which the incumbent must perform, and note how often they are encountered.

- ❑ Elevated workplace
- ❑ Mechanical hazards
- ❑ Explosives
- ❑ Electrical hazards
- ❑ Fire hazards
- ❑ Radiation
- ❑ Other (specify)

13. **MACHINES, TOOLS, EQUIPMENT, AND WORK AIDS:** Describe briefly what machines, tools, equipment, or work aids the incumbent works with on a regular basis:

_____

14. Have concrete work standards been established (errors allowed, time taken for a particular task, etc.)? If so, what are they?

_____

15. Are there any personal attributes (special aptitudes, physical characteristics, personality traits, etc.) required by the job?

_____

16. Are there any exceptional problems the incumbent might be expected to encounter in performing the job under normal conditions? If so, describe.

_____

17. Describe the successful completion and/or end results of the job.

_____

18. What is the seriousness of error on this job? Who or what is affected by errors the incumbent makes?

_____

19. To what job would a successful incumbent expect to be promoted?

[**Note:** This form is obviously slanted toward a manufacturing environment. but it can be adapted quite easily to fit a number of different types of jobs.]

CHECKLIST 9.1 ■ Job Analysis Questions

- ☑ What is the job being performed?
- ☑ What are the major duties of your position? What exactly do you do?
- ☑ What are the education, experience, skill, and [where applicable] certification and licensing requirements?
- ☑ In what activities do you participate now?
- ☑ What are the job's responsibilities and duties?
- ☑ What are the basic accountabilities or performance standards that typify your work?

- ☑ What are your responsibilities?
- ☑ What are the environmental and working conditions involved?
- ☑ What are the job's physical demands? Its emotional and mental demands?
- ☑ What are the health and safety conditions?
- ☑ Does the job expose you to any hazards or unusual working conditions?

MANAGING @ THE SPEED OF THOUGHT

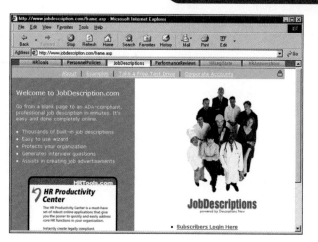

▲ WEBNOTE ■■■

The whole process of creating a job description online is quick and easy using Jobdescription.com.

www.jobdescription.com

personnel planning ■ *the process of determining the organization's future personnel needs, as well as the methods to be used to fill those needs.*

personnel replacement chart ■ *company records showing present performance and promotability of inside candidates for the most important positions.*

position replacement card ■ *a card prepared for each position in a company to show possible replacement candidates and their qualifications.*

recruiting ■ *attracting a pool of viable job applicants.*

www.jobdescription.com

Most employers still write their own job descriptions, but more are turning to the Internet. One site, **www.jobdescription.com**, illustrates why. The process is simple. Search by alphabetical title, keyword, category, or industry to find the desired job title. This leads you to a generic job description for that title—say, "computers & EDP systems sales representative." You can then use the wizard to customize the generic description for this position. For example, you can add specific information about your organization, such as job title, job codes, department, and preparation date. And you can indicate whether the job has supervisory responsibilities and choose from a number of possible desirable competencies and experience levels.[5]

Job analysis is part of personnel planning. **Personnel planning** is the process of determining the organization's future personnel needs, as well as the methods to be used to fill those needs. It includes developing job descriptions and specifications to determine what sorts of people the company will need to staff, say, a new department. It also involves deciding ahead of time (planning) where those new employees will come from (within or outside the company's employee pool) and how to train them.

Many employers use **personnel replacement charts** (see Figure 9.5) to keep track of inside candidates for their most important positions. These show the present performance and promotability for each potential replacement for important positions. An alternative is a **position replacement card**. You make up a card for each position, showing possible replacements as well as present performance, promotion potential, and training required by each candidate. Thanks to computers, personnel planning is increasingly sophisticated. Many firms maintain databanks containing information on hundreds of traits (like special skills, product knowledge, work experience, training courses, relocation limitations, and career interests) for each employee.

Employee Recruiting

Once you know the jobs to fill, **recruiting**—attracting a pool of viable job applicants—becomes very important. If you have only two candidates for two openings, you may have little choice but to hire them. But if many applicants appear, you can use techniques like interviews and tests to hire the best. Managers recruit candidates in various ways.

Current Employees Promotion from within is one option. On the plus side, employees see that the firm rewards competence, which may, in turn, enhance morale and performance. Inside candidates are also known quantities in terms of performance

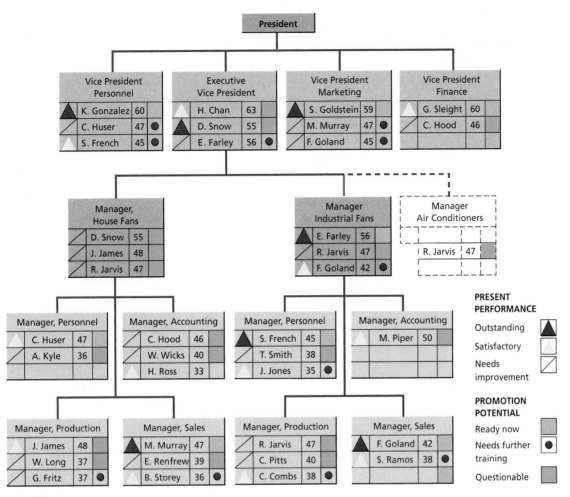

▲ FIGURE 9–5 ■ ■ ■

Management Personnel Replacement Chart

and skills, and they are more likely to be committed to the company and its goals. However, employees who unsuccessfully apply for jobs may become demoralized. And when an entire management team has come up through the ranks, there may be a tendency to maintain the status quo. Many long-term promotion-from-within firms like Delta Airlines have thus gone outside to hire their CEOs.

Promotion from within generally requires job postings.[6] Job posting means publicizing the open job to employees (often by literally posting it on bulletin boards and intranets) and listing the job's attributes, like qualifications, supervisor, working schedule, and pay rate (see Figure A9.1). Some union contracts require job postings to ensure that union members get first choice of new and better positions. Job posting can be a good practice, even in nonunion firms, if it facilitates the transfer and promotion of qualified inside candidates.[7]

job posting ■ *publicizing an open job to employees (often by literally posting it on bulletin boards and intranets) and listing its attributes, like qualifications, supervisor, working schedule, and pay rate.*

Advertising As you know from the many help-wanted ads that appear online and in your local newspaper, advertising is a major way to attract applicants. The main issue here is selecting the best advertising medium, be it the local paper, the *Wall Street Journal*, a technical journal, or the Net.

The Internet A large and fast-growing proportion of employers use the Internet as a recruiting tool. The percentage of Fortune 500 companies recruiting via the Internet jumped from 10% in 1997 to virtually 100% today.

Managers use Internet recruiting in numerous ways. A Boston-based recruiting firm posts job descriptions on its Web page. NEC Electronics, Unisys Corp., and LSI Logicorp have all posted Internet based "cyber fairs" to recruit for applicants.[8] Cisco

TABLE 9–1 Sample List of Recruiting Web Sites

America's Job Bank www.ajb.dni.us

On this site, candidates can search for jobs by occupation, location, education and experience levels, and salary. Those with a military background can search for civilian jobs that match their areas of expertise. Employers can cull a pool of nearly 2 million job seekers.

CareerBuilder www.careerbuilder.com

CareerBuilder offers information about career advancement and workplace trends, including tips and news for students and recent grads. Users can search more than 50 leading job sites that are part of the CareerBuilder network, with access to more than 3 million job postings.

CareerMosaic www.careermosaic.com

CreerMosaic offers insider profiles on such companies as Microsoft and Canon. Job seekers can search for openings by geographic area, job description, or company name. CareerMosaic has links to more than a dozen countries in North America, Europe, and the Pacific Rim.

CareerShop.com www.careershop.com

In addition to providing easy searches for job seekers and a pool of nearly 300,000 résumés for employers, CareerShop offers a marketplace for freelancers and employers, guidance for employers on human resource issues, and a variety of counseling services.

ComputerJobs.com www.computerjobs.com

ComputerJobs.com is the leading information technology employment site, with job opportunities organized by specific skills and regional markets. As part of its virtual recruiting service for employers, ComputerJobs.com will do online behavioral testing and credit checks of candidates.

Dice.com www.dice.com

This is the first place to look for many IT professionals. This site lists over 150,000 job openings, both permanent and contractual.

Employment911.com www.employment911.com

This metasite can speed your search by quickly scanning it own listings and those of 35 other sites.

JobOptions www.joboptions.com

Contemplating a move? On the JobOptions site, users can compute comparable salaries for different cities based on housing and other factors, and they can search by job classification, location, and qualifications. Employers can search more than 250,000 résumés.

Jobs.com www.jobs.com

Get the inside scoop on working for major companies with jobs.com's Testify section. Jobs.com offers free software that simplifies the process of writing and delivering a résumé via the Internet. The site features interactive career fairs (with chat and video Web casts) with employers.

JobTrak.com www.jobtrak.com

JobTrak.com is the largest site for college students and alumni. It has partnerships with more than 1,000 university career centers, MBA programs, and alumni associations. Students can receive advice from college counselors, they can contact alumni, and they can learn to negotiate a salary package.

Monster.com www.monster.com

The big daddy of job boards with 3 million résumés, Monster.com has "communities" for students, techies, and the self-employed. Users can create a career management account where they can store up to five résumés, track applications, and receive news tailored to their interests.

Systems, Inc. has a Web site with a "Careers at Cisco" page. This page links to such things as hot jobs (job descriptions for hard-to-fill positions), Cisco culture (a look at Cisco worklife), Cisco College (internships and mentoring program information), and Cisco jobs (jobs and job listings). Table 9.1 lists some popular recruiting Web sites.

Employment Agencies An employment agency is an intermediary whose business is to match applicants with positions. There are three basic types.

Public employment agencies, often called job service or unemployment service agencies, exist in every state. They are good sources of blue-collar and clerical workers, but firms use them for professional and managerial-level applicants as well. Other employment agencies are associated with *not-for-profit organizations*. For example, most professional and technical societies have units to help members find jobs.

Private agencies charge a fee for each applicant they place. Market conditions determine whether the employer or the candidate pays the fee, but the trend is toward "fee paid" jobs, in which the employer pays. These agencies are important sources of clerical, white-collar, and managerial personnel. Checklist 9.2 shows the points to keep in mind when dealing directly with employment agencies.

CHECKLIST 9.2 ■ How to Use an Employment Agency[9]

☑ Give the agency an accurate and complete job description.

☑ Tests, application blanks, and interviews should be a part of the agency's selection process.

☑ Periodically review data on candidates accepted or rejected by your firm and by the agency.

☑ Develop a long-term relationship with one or two agencies.

☑ Screen the agency. Check with other managers. What is its reputation in the community and with the Better Business Bureau?

Contingent Workers and Temporary Help Agencies Employers often supplement their permanent workforce by hiring contingent or temporary workers, often through temporary help employment agencies. Also known as part-time or just in time workers, the contingent workforce is big and growing. It recently accounted for about 20% of all new jobs created in the United States. Such workers are broadly defined as workers who don't have permanent jobs.[10]

Today's contingent workforce isn't limited to clerical or maintenance staff. In one year, almost 100,000 people found temporary work in engineering, science, or management support occupations, for instance. And growing numbers of firms use temporary workers as short-term chief financial officers—or even chief executive officers. It's estimated that 60% of the total U.S. temporary payroll is not clerical and includes "CEOs, human resource directors, computer systems analysts, accountants, doctors, and nurses." Over 84% of employers now reportedly use temp agencies, and their use is on the rise.[11]

> **contingent (or temporary) worker** ■ a temporary worker hired by an employer to fill short-term needs; not a permanent full-time or part-time employee.

Executive Recruiters Executive recruiters (also ominously called headhunters) are agencies retained by employers to look for top management talent, usually in the $70,000 and up category. They have extensive contacts and a file of potential recruits, and are adept at contacting qualified employed candidates who aren't looking to change jobs. They can also keep the client firm's name confidential until late in the search process. The recruiter saves management time by advertising the position and screening what could turn out to be hundreds of applicants.

> **executive recruiter** ■ an agency retained by employers to seek out top management talent.

Digging up the initial long list of candidates used to take months, but that's not practical anymore. Most search firms are therefore creating Internet-linked computerized databases, the aim of which, according to one recruiter, is "to create a long list [of candidates] by pushing a button."[12] Recruiter Korn/Ferry International launched an Internet service called Futurestep to draw more managerial applicants into its files; in turn, it teamed up with the *Wall Street Journal*, which runs its own career Web site.[13]

Referrals and Walk-ins Particularly for hourly workers, walk-ins—people who apply directly at the office—are a major source of applicants. Encouraging walk-ins may be as simple as posting help-wanted signs on the door.

Some firms use employee referral campaigns to encourage applicants. They print announcements of openings and requests for referrals in the company's newsletter, on the intranet, or on bulletin boards. Of the firms responding to one survey, 40% said they use employee referral systems and hire about 15% of their employees through referrals. A cash award for referring hired candidates is the most common incentive. Some experts contend that the most effective recruiting method is to encourage existing employees to refer qualified friends and colleagues.[14] Recruiting high-tech employees is especially amenable to such programs.

▲ WEBNOTE ■ ■ ■

Korn/Ferry International's Web site shows the range of its services.

www.kornferry.com

Source: Copyright © 2002 Korn/Ferry International. All rights reserved.

College Recruiting College recruiting—sending employers' representatives to college campuses to prescreen applicants and create an applicant pool from the graduating class—is an important source of management, professional and technical employees. One study of 251 staffing professionals concluded that firms filled about 38% of all externally filled jobs requiring a college degree with new college grads.[15]

What do recruiters look for in new college grads? The report presented in Figure 9.6 is typical. Traits assessed include motivation, communication skills, education, appearance, and attitude.[16]

Almost three-quarters of all college students take part in an internship before they graduate, and many students get their jobs through these internships.[17] Internships can be win–win situations for both students and employers. For students, it may mean being able to hone business skills, check out potential employers, and learn more about their occupational likes (and dislikes). Employers can use interns to make useful

▼ **FIGURE 9–6** ■ ■ ■

Campus Applicant Interview Report

Source: Adapted from Joseph J. Famularo, *Handbook of Personnel Forms, Records, and Reports* (New York: McGraw-Hill, 1982), p. 70.

CAMPUS INTERVIEW REPORT

Name_____ Anticipated Graduation Date _____

Current Address _____
    If different than on placement form

Position Applied For_____
_____

If Applicable (Use Comment Section if necessary)

    Driver's License   Yes _____   No _____

    Any special considerations affecting your availability for relocation?
    _____
    _____

    Are you willing to travel? _____   If so, what % of time? _____
_____

EVALUATION	Outstanding	Above Average	Average	Below Average
Education: Courses relevant to job? Does performance in class indicate good potential for work?	_____	_____	_____	_____
Appearance: Was applicant neat and dressed appropriately?	_____	_____	_____	_____
Communication Skills: Was applicant mentally alert? Did he or she express ideas clearly?	_____	_____	_____	_____
Motivation: Does applicant have high energy level? Are his or her interests compatible with job?	_____	_____	_____	_____
Attitude: Did applicant appear to be pleasant, people-oriented?	_____	_____	_____	_____

COMMENTS: (Use back of sheet if necessary)
_____
_____
_____
_____

Given Application   Yes _____   No _____   Received Transcript Release Authorization _____

Recommendations Invite _____   Reject _____

Interviewed by:_____ Date:_____

Campus _____

contributions, while evaluating them as possible full-time employees.

Recruiting a More Diverse Workforce Recruiting a diverse workforce isn't just socially responsible; it's a necessity. Minorities will represent over 20% of the workforce in 2005. It's therefore unrealistic to think that any firm can do much hiring today without tapping minority sources.

Tools here include diversity databanks, word-of-mouth, and minority-oriented applicant sources. Hispan-Data is one example. Recruiters from firms like McDonald's get access to its computerized databank; it costs a candidate $5 to register.[18] Firms increasingly make use of specialized minority-oriented Internet Web sites.

As another option, Marriott International hired 600 welfare recipients under its Pathways to Independence program. The heart of the program is a six-week preemployment training program that teaches work and life skills "designed to rebuild workers' self-esteem and instill positive attitudes about work."[19]

Recruiting a diverse workforce: Many companies are actively recruiting older workers, minorities, and women.

▪▫▫ INTERVIEWING AND SELECTING EMPLOYEES

With a pool of applicants, managers turn to selecting the best, using one or more screening techniques. These include application blanks, interviews, tests, and reference checks to assess and investigate an applicant's aptitudes, interests, and background. The manager then chooses the best candidate, given the job's requirements.

Employee selection is important for several specific reasons. Your own performance as a manager always hinges on your subordinate's performance. A poor performer drags a manager down, and a good one enhances the manager's and the firms' performance. Hiring employees is also expensive, so it is best to do it right. Hiring a manager who earns $60,000 a year may cost as much as $40,000 or $50,000, including search fees, interviewing time, and travel and moving expenses. The cost of hiring even nonexecutive employees can be $3,000 to $5,000 or more. Establishing the right screening process can have a decisive effect on a firm's success, as the following Management in Action feature shows.

MANAGEMENT IN ACTION   City Garage

Consider the experience of City Garage, a 200-employee chain of 25 auto service and repair shops in Dallas-Fort Worth. The company had expanded rapidly since its founding in 1993. However, its growth was hampered by the problems it was having hiring and keeping good managers and employees.[20] One thing it discovered was that not all its managers had the same level of interviewing and hiring skills. The result was excessive turnover and too few managers to staff new stores. For a firm planning to expand to 50 or 60 shops throughout Texas in the next few years, City Garage knew that poor screening would prevent growth.

City's original hiring process consisted of a paper and pencil application and one interview, immediately followed by a hire/don't hire decision. This was particularly unsatisfactory for a fast-growing operation. For one thing, local shop managers didn't have the time to evaluate every applicant. "If they had been shorthanded too long, we would hire pretty much anybody who had experience," said training director Rusty Reinhold. City's solution was to purchase the Personality Profile Analysis (PPA) online test from Dallas-based Thomas International USA. Now, after a quick application and background check, likely candidates take the 10-minute, 24-question PPA. City Garage staff then enter the answers into the PPA software system; test results are available in less than two minutes, and show whether the applicant is high or low on four personality characteristics. The PPA also produces follow-up questions about areas that might cause problems. As Reinhold says, "At a minimum, we feel like we'll be able to put $500,000 on the bottom line each year, if [the PPA] does what we expect it to [do] in terms of retention and right hiring." ▪▪▫

Application Forms

For most employers, the application form is the first step in the selection process. (Some firms first require a brief prescreening interview.) The application is a good way to quickly collect verifiable historical data from the candidate. It usually includes information about such areas as education, prior work history, and hobbies. Figure 9.7 is an example.

In practice, most organizations need several application forms. For technical and managerial personnel, the form may require detailed answers to questions concerning

▼ **FIGURE 9–7** ■ ■ ■

Employment Application

FEDERAL BUREAU OF INVESTIGATION

FIELD OFFICE USE ONLY
Right Thumb Print

Preliminary Application for
Special Agent Position
(Please Type or Print in Black Ink)

Div: _____ Program: _____

Date: _____

I. PERSONAL HISTORY

Name in Full   (Last, First, Middle)

List College Degree(s) Already Received or Pursuing, Major, School, and Month/Year:

Marital Status: ☐ Single ☐ Engaged ☐ Married ☐ Separated ☐ Legally Separated ☐ Widowed ☐ Divorced

Birth Date (Month, Day, Year)
Birth Place:

Social Security Number: (Optional)

Do you understand FBI employment requires availability for assignment anywhere in the U.S.?

Current Address

Street   Apt. No.

Home Phone

Area Code   Number

City   State   Zip Code

Work Phone

Area Code   Number

Are you: CPA ☐ Yes ☐ No   Licensed Driver ☐ Yes ☐ No   U. S. Citizen ☐ Yes ☐ No

Have you served on active duty in the U. S. Military? ☐ Yes ☐ No If yes, indicate branch of service and dates (month/year) of active duty. Include military school attendance (month/year):

How did you learn or become interested in FBI employment as a Special Agent?

Have you previously applied for FBI employment? ☐ Yes ☐ No If yes, location and date:

Do you have a foreign language background? ☐ Yes ☐ No List proficiency for each language on reverse side.

Have you ever been arrested for any crime (include major traffic violations such as Driving Under the Influence or While Intoxicated, etc.)? ☐ Yes ☐ No If so, list all such matters on a continuation sheet, even if not formally charged, or no court appearance or found not guilty, or matter settled by payment of fine or forfeiture of collateral. Include date, place, charge, disposition, details, and police agency on reverse side.

II. EMPLOYMENT HISTORY

Identify your most recent three years FULL-TIME work experience, after high school (excluding summer, part-time and temporary employment).

From Month/Year	To Month/Year	Title of Position and Description of Work	# of hrs. Per week	Name/Location of Employer

III. PERSONAL DECLARATIONS

Persons with a disability who require an accommodation to complete the application process are required to notify the FBI of their need for the accommodation.

Have you used marijuana during the last three years or more than 15 times? ☐ Yes ☐ No

Have you used any illegal drug(s) or combination of illegal drugs, other than marijuana, more than 5 times or during the last 10 years? ☐ Yes ☐ No

All information provided by applicants concerning their drug history will be subject to verification by a preemployment polygraph examination.

Do you understand all prospective FBI employees will be required to submit to an urinalysis for drug abuse prior to employment? ☐ Yes ☐ No

Please do not write below this line.

I am aware that willfully withholding information or making false statements on this application constitutes a violation of Section 1001, Title 18, U.S. Code and if appointed, will be the basis for dismissal from the Federal Bureau of Investigation. I agree to these conditions and I hereby certify that all statements made by me on this application are true and complete, to the best of my knowledge.

Signature of applicant as usually written (**Do Not Use Nickname**)

education and experience. The form for hourly factory workers might focus on the tools and equipment the applicant used.

Testing for Employee Selection

A test is a sample of a person's behavior. Employers use tests to predict success on the job. About 45% of 1,085 companies surveyed by the American Management Association tested applicants for basic skills (defined as the ability to read instructions, write reports, and do arithmetic at a level adequate to perform common workplace tasks).[21] Another survey concluded that 38.6% of companies said they performed psychological testing on job applicants, ranging from tests of the applicants' cognitive abilities to "honesty testing."[22] Try the short test in Figure 9.8 to see how prone you might be to on-the-job accidents.

Uses of Tests Tests are not just for low-level workers. For example, consultants McKinsey & Co. flew 54 MIT M.B.A. students to Miami for two days of multiple-choice business knowledge tests, case-oriented case studies, and interviews. Barclays Capital gives graduate and undergraduate job candidates aptitude tests instead of first-round interviews.

While popular, there are many legal and ethical constraints on the use of tests. It is useless (and often illegal) to use a test that lacks validity or reliability. *Test validity* answers the question, "Does this test measure what it supposed to measure?" (In practical terms, does performance on the test predict subsequent performance on the job?) A test that does not meet that standard and which unfairly screens out minority or female candidates might well run afoul of various equal employment laws. *Reliability* is a test's consistency. For example, if a person scores 90 on an intelligence test on Monday and 130 on Tuesday, you probably wouldn't have much faith in the test's reliability.

Types of Tests Many types of tests are available. Employers use intelligence (IQ) tests like the Stanford-Binet, the Wechsler, or Wonderlic to measure general intellectual abilities. For some jobs, managers are also interested in testing other abilities. The Bennett Test of Mechanical Comprehension (see Figure 9.9) helps assess an applicant's understanding of basic mechanical principles; it would be useful for predicting success on a job such as machinist or engineer. Other tests measure personality and interests. For example, you probably wouldn't hire someone for an entry-level job as an accounting clerk if he or she had no measurable interest in working with numbers![23] Most of us have had some experience dealing with service people who are obviously not psychologically suited for such jobs. A personality test might have screened them out.

◀ **FIGURE 9–8** ■ ■ ■

Sample Test

Source: Courtesy of NYT Permissions.

CHECK YES OR NO	YES	NO
1. You like a lot of excitement in your life.		
2. An employee who takes it easy at work is cheating on the employer.		
3. You are a cautious person.		
4. In the past three years, you have found yourself in a shouting match at school or work.		
5. You like to drive fast just for fun.		

Analysis: According to John Kamp, an industrial psychologist, applicants who answered no, yes, yes, no, no to questions 1, 2, 3, 4, and 5 are statistically likely to be absent less often, to have fewer on-the-job injuries, and, if the job involves driving, to have fewer on-the-job driving accidents. Actual scores on the test are based on answers to 130 questions.

► **FIGURE 9–9** ◼◼◼

Bennett Test of Mechanical Comprehension, Example

Human resource managers often use personnel tests, like this one, to measure a candidate's skills and aptitudes.

Source: Bennett Mechanical Comprehension Test. Copyright 1942, 1967–1970, 1980 by The Psychological Corporation, a Harcourt Assessment Company. Reproduced by permission. All rights reserved. "Bennett Mechanical Comprehension Test" and "BMCT" are registered trademarks of The Psychological Corporation.

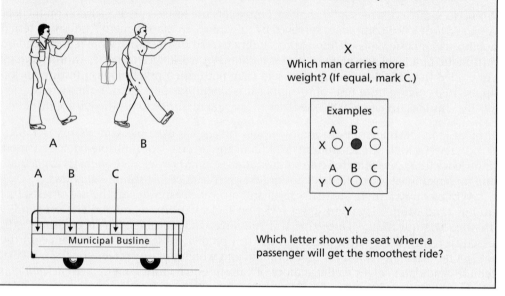

Look at Sample X on this page. It shows two men carrying a weighted object on a plank, and it asks, Which man carries more weight? Because the object is closer to man B than to man A, man B is shouldering more weight; so blacken the circle under B on your answer sheet. Now look at Sample Y and answer it yourself. Fill in the circle under the correct answer on your answer sheet.

X
Which man carries more weight? (If equal, mark C.)

Examples

A B C
X ○ ● ○

A B C
Y ○ ○ ○

Y

Which letter shows the seat where a passenger will get the smoothest ride?

---

management assessment center ◼ *a development and/or selection device wherein management candidates spend two or three days performing realistic management tasks under the observation of appraisers.*

A **management assessment center** is another testing technique. In such centers, about a dozen candidates spend two or three days performing realistic management tasks, while expert appraisers observe them. They assess each candidate's potential.[24] The center's activities might include individual presentations, objective tests, interviews, and participation in management games. Participants engage in realistic problem solving, usually as members of two or three simulated companies that are competing in a mock marketplace.

Computerized Testing These tests are increasingly replacing conventional paper and pencil and manual testing. In one large manufacturing company, experts developed a computerized testing procedure for selecting clerical personnel.[25] They developed eight test components to represent actual work performed by secretarial personnel, such as maintaining and developing databases and spreadsheets, and handling travel arrangements. For the word processing test, applicants had three minutes (monitored by the computer) to type as much of a letter as possible. The computer recorded and corrected the manuscript. For the "travel expense form completion" test, applicants had to access the database file, use some of the information there to compute quarterly expenses, and transfer this information to the travel expense form. The Webnote illustrates a site that offers computerized testing.

With all the aptitudes, skills, and traits for which managers can test applicants, there is still one thing that's usually not tested for but that perhaps should be—at least if some recent research findings are valid. Particularly in companies facing downsizings and competitive pressures, there's much to be said about hiring people who are inclined to remain happy even in

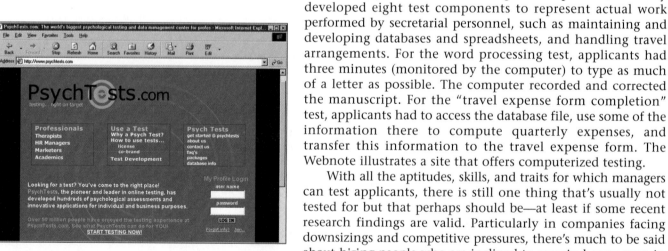

▲ **WEBNOTE** ◼◼◼

PsychTests.com illustrates some of the many employment tests available, and lets you take a sample test and scores it for you while you wait.

www.psychtest.com

Source: Copyright © 1996–2002 PsychTests.com

the face of unhappy events. As illustrated in the following feature, a recent line of research suggests that it might be possible to do so.

◼ *Application Exercise* Basically, this research suggests that happiness is largely determined by the person's genetic makeup. In other words, some people are simply born to be somewhat happier than others.[26] The theory, in a nutshell, says that people have a "set point" for happiness, a genetically determined happiness level to which the person quickly tends to gravitate, no matter what failures or successes he or she experiences. So confront a high-happiness-set-point person with the prospect of a demotion or an unattractive lateral transfer, and he or she will soon return to being relatively happy once the short blip of disappointment has dissipated. On the other hand, send an inherently low-set-point, unhappy person off on a two-week vacation or give him or her a sizable raise or a new computer, and chances are he or she will soon be as unhappy as before the reward.

Several lines of research lend support to this theory. A study of lottery winners found that they were on the whole no happier a year after their good fortune than they were before. Several studies show that even people with spinal-cord injuries tend to rebound in spirits.[27] Studies of identical twins led one psychologist to conclude that life circumstances like salary, education, or marital status predicted only 2% of the happiness variation within each pair of twins, and that much of the rest was simply determined by the person's genes. In fact, the results of several long-term studies that followed people over many years suggest that the people who are happiest today will also be the happiest 10 years from now.

Like testing employees for any traits, coming up with a set of tests or interview questions to identify happier, high-set-point people requires careful consideration and probably the help of a licensed psychologist. However, the following might provide some insight into the tendency to be relatively happy:

Indicate how strongly (high, medium, low) you agree with the following statements:

- "When good things happen to me, it strongly affects me."
- "I will often do things for no other reason than they might be fun."
- "When I get something I want, I feel excited and energized."
- "When I'm doing well at something, I love to keep at it."

Agreeing with more statements and agreeing with them more strongly may correlate with a higher happiness set point.[28]

Interviews

The interview is the most widely used selection device, and it would be very unusual for a manager to hire a subordinate without at least a brief personal interview. The problem is that while almost everyone gets a job interview, most interviews don't produce very reliable information. However, a manager can boost the usefulness of selection interviews by following sound procedures like these:[29]

Plan the Interview Begin by reviewing the candidate's application and résumé, and note any areas that are vague or may indicate strengths or weaknesses. Review the job specification. Start the interview with a clear picture of the traits of an ideal candidate.

Structure the Interview The main problem with most interviews is that they are much too informal. The interviewer gives little thought to the sorts of questions that might actually set a top applicant apart. And the whole process is one in which subjectivity rules, with hard-to-measure or easy-to-fake questions like "What are your main strengths?" playing too big a role.

Therefore, rather than the usual subjective questions, ask questions that are clearly relevant to success on the job. Emphasize *situational* questions. Such questions make the person explain how he or she would handle a hypothetical situation, such as "If you were a supervisor here, what would you do if one of your subordinates came in consistently late?" and "What program would you use to design this Web site?" Also ask job-relevant questions about the applicant's *past behavior*. For example (if the job calls for making cold calls) ask, "Tell me about a time when you had to make an unsolicited sales call. How did you do it? What happened? What was the result?" Ask relevant *background* questions like "what work experiences, training, or other qualifications do you have for working in a team work-environment?" *Job-knowledge* questions are important too—for instance, "What factors should you consider when developing a TV advertising campaign?"

Interviews based on a structured guide, as in Figure 9.10, usually give the best results.[30] At a minimum, write out your questions prior to the interview.

► **FIGURE 9–10** ■■■

Structured Interview Form
for College Applicants

CANDIDATE RECORD NAP 100 (10/77)

CANDIDATE NUMBER U 921 NAME (LAST NAME FIRST) COLLEGE NAME COLLEGE CODE
(1–7) (8–27) (28–30)

INTERVIEWER NUMBER 0
(33–40)

INTERVIEWER NAME

SOURCE (41)	RACE (42)	SEX (43)	DEGREE (53)	AVERAGE (A = 4.0)	CLASS STANDING (59–59)
Campus ☐ C	White ☐ W	Male ☐ M	Bachelors ☐ B	Overall ☐☐ (54-55)	Top 10% ☐ 10
Walk-in ☐ W	Black ☐ B	Female ☐ F	Masters ☐ M	Acctg. ☐☐ (56-57)	Top 25% ☐ 25
Intern ☐ I	Asian ☐ A	Init.	Law ☐ L		Top Half ☐ 50
Agency ☐ A	Hispanic ☐ H	Cont.	Majors		Bottom Half ☐ 75
	Native Am. ☐ NA	Date			

CAMPUS INTERVIEW EVALUATIONS

ATTITUDE – MOTIVATION – GOALS

POOR ☐   AVERAGE ☐   GOOD ☐   OUTSTANDING ☐
(POSITIVE, COOPERATIVE, ENERGETIC, MOTIVATED, SUCCESSFUL, GOAL-ORIENTED)
COMMENTS:

COMMUNICATIONS SKILLS – PERSONALITY – SALES ABILITY

POOR ☐   AVERAGE ☐   GOOD ☐   OUTSTANDING ☐
(ARTICULATE, LISTENS, ENTHUSIASTIC, LIKEABLE, POISED, TACTFUL, ACCEPTING, CONVINCING)
COMMENTS:

EXECUTIVE PRESENCE – DEAL WITH TOP PEOPLE

POOR ☐   AVERAGE ☐   GOOD ☐   OUTSTANDING ☐
(IMPRESSIVE, STANDS OUT, A WINNER, REMEMBERED, LEVELHEADED, AT EASE, AWARE)
COMMENTS:

INTELLECTUAL ABILITIES

POOR ☐   AVERAGE ☐   GOOD ☐   OUTSTANDING ☐
(INSIGHTFUL, CREATIVE, CURIOUS, IMAGINATIVE, UNDERSTANDS, REASONS, INTELLIGENT, SCHOLARLY)
COMMENTS:

JUDGMENT – DECISION MAKING ABILITY

POOR ☐   AVERAGE ☐   GOOD ☐   OUTSTANDING ☐
(MATURE, SEASONED, INDEPENDENT, COMMON SENSE, CERTAIN, DETERMINED, LOGICAL)
COMMENTS:

LEADERSHIP

POOR ☐   AVERAGE ☐   GOOD ☐   OUTSTANDING ☐
(SELF-CONFIDENT, TAKES CHARGE, EFFECTIVE, RESPECTED, MANAGEMENT MINDED, GRASPS AUTHORITY)
COMMENTS:

CAMPUS INTERVIEW SUMMARY

INVITE (Circle) Yes No	AREA OF INTEREST (Circle)	SEMESTER HRS.	OFFICES PREFERRED:	SUMMARY COMMENTS:
DATE AVAILABLE	AUDIT TAX	Acct'g. _____	No. 1 _____	
	MCS ABC	Audit _____	No. 2 _____	
	OTHER	Tax _____	No. 3 _____	

Establish Rapport The main purpose of the interview is to find out about the applicant, and it's thus helpful to put the person at ease. Greet the candidate and start by asking a noncontroversial question—perhaps about the weather or the traffic conditions that day. As a rule, all applicants—even unsolicited drop-ins—should receive friendly, courteous treatment, not only on humanitarian grounds, but also because your reputation is on the line.

Ask Questions Try to follow your structured interview guide or the questions you wrote out ahead of time (see the earlier section entitled "Structure the Interview"). Some suggestions for asking questions include these:

- Avoid questions the candidate can answer with a simple yes or no.
- Don't put words in the applicant's mouth or telegraph the desired answer (for instance, by nodding or smiling when the right answer is given).
- Don't interrogate the applicant as if the person were a criminal, and don't be patronizing, sarcastic, or inattentive.
- Don't monopolize the interview by rambling, and don't let the applicant dominate the interview.
- Listen to the candidate and encourage him or her to express thoughts fully.

- Don't just ask for general statements about accomplishments, also ask for specific examples.[31]
- If the candidate lists specific strengths or weaknesses, follow up with, "What are specific examples that demonstrate each of your strengths? Give an example of an incident that shows a weakness."

Delay Your Decision Interviewers often make snap judgments even before they see the candidate, perhaps based on the application or résumé. Keep a record of the interview, and review it afterward. Make your decision then.[32]

Close the Interview Toward the end of the interview, leave time to answer any questions the candidate may have and, if appropriate, to promote your firm to the candidate. Tell the applicant whether there is an interest in him or her and, if so, what the next step will be. Make rejections diplomatically with a statement like, "Although your background is impressive, there are other candidates whose experience is closer to our requirements."

Guidelines for Interviewees Before interviewing applicants, you will have to navigate some job interviews yourself. Guidelines here include:

1. *Prepare.* Before the interview, learn all you can about the employer, the job, and the people doing the recruiting. Look through business periodicals and Web sites to find out what is happening in the company and industry.
2. *Make a good first impression.* Most interviewers make up their minds about the applicant during the early minutes of the interview. Bad first impressions are almost impossible to overcome.
3. *Uncover the interviewer's real needs.* Determine what the person is looking for and what problems he or she needs solved. Sample questions include "Would you mind describing the job for me?" "What's the first problem you'd want me to address?" and "Could you tell me about the people who would be reporting to me?"
4. *Relate your answers to the interviewer's needs.* Start by saying something like, "One of the problem areas you've said is important to you is similar to a problem I once faced." Then state the problem, describe your solution, and reveal the results.
5. *Think before answering.* Answering a question should be a three-step process: pause, think, speak. Pause to make sure you understand what the interviewer is driving at, think about how to structure your answer, and then speak.
6. *Watch your nonverbal behavior.* In most interviews, the interviewee's nonverbal behavior broadcasts more about the person than what the person says. Maintain eye contact. Speak with enthusiasm, nod agreement, and remember to take a moment to frame your answer (pause, think, speak) so that you sound articulate and fluent.[33]

Other Selection Techniques

Managers use several other selection techniques to screen applicants.

Background Investigations and Reference Checks Employers should verify the applicant's background information and references.[34]This is necessary to verify the information the candidate provides and to uncover other, potentially damaging information (about an unrevealed conviction, for instance). Don't underestimate the importance of checking the applicant's background. For example, BellSouth's security director estimates that between 15% and 20% of applicants conceal a fabrication: "It's not uncommon to find someone who applies and looks good, and then you do a little digging and you start to see all sorts of criminal history."[35]

The most commonly verified background areas are legal eligibility for employment (to comply with immigration laws), dates of prior employment, military service (including discharge status), education, and identification (including date of birth and address).[36] Figure 9.11 shows a form you can use.

EMPLOYMENT REFERENCE CHECK FORM

Applicant: 1. Please print out this Reference Check Form.
2. Fill out the top section of the form.
3. Send it to a former employer to complete and return to:

Human Resources Department
Winter Sports, Inc./Big Mountain Ski & Summer Resort
PO Box 1400, Whitefish, MT 59937\or Fax to: 406-862-2955

REFERENCE CHECK FORM   Please Type or Print Legibly
To Be Completed by Applicant _____
Applicant's Name _____
Name of Reference _____
Business Name _____
I have applied for a position with Winter Sports, Inc. at Big Mountain Ski and Summer
Resort. In order to be considered for employment, they have requested information from my
previous employers. I would appreciate your cooperation in providing the answers to the
following questions. I have been advised this information will be held in confidence by
the Winter Sports, Inc. Human Resource Department.

_____   _____
                    Applicant's Signature   Date

To be Completed by Employer:

Employed From_____ To_____
Position(s) Held
Reason for Separation: ____ Quit ____ Laid-off ____ Discharged
                    Other _____
Comments: _____
_____
_____

As an employee, was this person:
Responsible? ____YES ____ NO
Able to work well with others? ____YES ____ NO
Trustworthy? ____YES ____ NO
Dependable (Attendance)? ____YES ____ NO
Eligible for rehire? ____YES ____ NO
A positive customer service representative? (if applies) ____YES ____ NO
Please comment briefly on "NO" responses: _____
_____
_____
_____

Additional comments from supervisor, if possible _____
_____
_____

Signature of person filling out form: _____
Title: _____ Date: _____

Most companies try to verify an applicant's current or previous position and salary with the current employer by telephone. Others call current and previous supervisors to discover more about the person's motivation, technical competence, and ability to work with others. Some employers also get background reports from commercial credit-rating companies; this can provide information about an applicant's credit standing, indebtedness, reputation, character, and lifestyle. Others use special *preemployment information services*. These firms use Internet and computerized databases to access and accumulate stacks of information about matters such as applicants' compensation histories, credit histories, driving records, and conviction records. Today, you can place a call and obtain data on a person's credit, driving, workers' compensation, and criminal records for as little as a few dollars.

Honesty Testing Many employees work in jobs for which honesty is crucial—as bank tellers or cashiers, for instance—and so paper-and-pencil "honesty testing" is a miniindustry.[37] These tests ask questions (such as "Have you ever made a personal phone call on company time?") aimed at assessing a person's tendency to be honest.

Experts initially questioned the validity of tests like these, but the consensus today is that they can predict which applicants may be dishonest. However, in practice, detecting dishonest candidates involves not just tests, but also comprehensive antitheft screening procedures. Checklist 9.3 summarizes what the manager can do here.

CHECKLIST 9.3 ■ How to Screen Potentially Dishonest Candidates

☑ **Ask blunt questions.**[38] "Have you recently held jobs other than those listed on your application?" "Have you ever been fired or asked to leave the job?" "What reasons would past supervisors give if they were asked why they let you go?"

☑ **Do a credit check.** Include a clause in your application form giving you the right to conduct background checks, including credit checks and motor vehicle reports.

☑ **Carefully check all employment and personal references.**

☑ **Use paper and pencil honesty tests and psychological tests.**

☑ **Tests for drugs.** Devise a drug-testing program, and give each applicant a copy of the policy.

☑ **Establish a search and seizure policy.** The policy should state that all lockers, desks, and similar property remain the property of the company and may be inspected routinely.[39] Give each applicant a copy of the policy, and require each to return a signed copy.

Health Exams The selection process often ends with sending the candidate for a physical examination and drug screening test. Employers use the medical exam to confirm that the applicant qualifies for the physical requirements of the position, and to discover any medical limitations they should take into account. By identifying health problems, a physical exam can also reduce absenteeism and accidents and detect communicable diseases that may be unknown to the applicant.

With respect to drug screenings, the most common practice is to test candidates just before they're formally hired. Many also test current employees when there is reason to believe the person has been using drugs—after a work accident or in the presence of obvious behavioral symptoms, chronic lateness, or high absenteeism. Some firms routinely administer drug tests on a random or periodic basis, while others require a drug test when they transfer or promote employees to new positions.[40]

■ *The Global Manager* The processes firms use to select managers for their domestic and foreign operations obviously have many similarities. For either assignment, the candidate should have the technical knowledge and skills to do the job and the intelligence and people skills to be a successful manager.

However, foreign assignments are somewhat different. There is the need to cope with colleagues whose cultural inclinations may be very different from one's own, and with the stress that being alone in a foreign land can put on the single manager. And if spouse and children share the assignment, there are the complexities and pressures that the family will have to confront—from learning a new language to finding new friends and attending new schools.

Selecting managers for these assignments therefore sometimes means testing them for traits that predict success in adapting to new environments. Important traits here tend to include job knowledge and motivation, relational skills, flexibility/adaptability, extracultural openness, and family situation (spouse's positive opinion, willingness of spouse to live abroad, and so on).

With flexibility and adaptability important, *adaptability screening* is sometimes part of the expatriate screening process. Often conducted by a psychologist or psychiatrist, adaptability screening aims to assess the assignee's and spouse's probable success in handling the foreign transfer, and to alert them to issues (such as the impact on children) the move may involve.

Here, experience is often the best predictor of future success. Companies like Colgate-Palmolive therefore look for overseas candidates whose work and nonwork experience, education, and language skills already demonstrate a commitment to and facility in living and working with different cultures. Even several successful summers spent traveling overseas or participating in foreign student programs would seem to provide some concrete basis for believing that the potential transferee can accomplish the required adaptation when he or she arrives overseas.

▪▪▪ ORIENTING AND TRAINING EMPLOYEES

Once employees are hired, they must be prepared to do their jobs; this is the purpose of *orientation and training*. Most people have had experience with inadequately trained personnel—the waiter who doesn't say "hello" or the dry cleaner who does not properly press your jacket. Designing and implementing training programs are essential managerial activities. Do not underestimate their importance. It is, basically, futile to carefully select new employees and then to put them on the job with little or no training.

Orienting Employees

orientation ▪ *the process of providing new employees with basic information about the employer, such as company policies, working hours, or parking arrangements.*

Employee **orientation** means providing new employees with basic information on things like work rules and vacation policies. In many companies, employees receive a hard copy or Internet-based handbook containing this information. Orientation aims to familiarize the new employee with the company and his or her coworkers; provide information about working conditions (coffee breaks, overtime policy, and so on); explain how to get on the payroll, how to obtain identification cards, and what the working hours are; and generally reduce the jitters often associated with starting a new job. Figure 9.12 outlines a typical orientation program.

Training Employees

Orientation usually precedes training, which is a set of activities aimed at giving the employee the knowledge and skills needed to perform the job.[41]

Training is one of the things that distinguish superior firms and managers. Superior firms invest time and money training employees.[42] For example, why do you think the coffee always tastes good at Starbucks? It's not just the beans; it's the training. "Brewing the perfect cup" is one of five classes that all Starbucks employees take during their first six weeks on the job.[43] They learn that they must steam milk at temperatures of at least 150°F, that orders are called out (such as "triple-tall nonfat mocha"), and that coffee should never sit on the hot plate for more than 20 minutes.

training program ▪ *the process of providing new employees with information they need to do their jobs satisfactorily.*

Training programs consist of five steps. The first, or *needs analysis* step, identifies the specific job performance skills needed; analyzes the skills and needs of the prospective trainees; and develops specific, measurable knowledge and performance objectives. In the second step, *instructional design*, you decide on, compile, and produce the training program content, including workbooks, exercises, and activities. There may be a third, *validation* step, in which the firm works the bugs out of the training program by presenting it to a small representative audience. The fourth step is to *implement* the program by actually training the targeted employee group. Fifth is an *evaluation and follow-up step*, in which management assesses the program's successes or failures.

Most managers do not (and need not) create their own training materials, since many materials are available on- and off-line. For example, the professional development site Click2learn.com offers a wide range of Web-based courses that employees can take online. And many firms, including American Media Inc. of West Des Moines, Iowa, provide turnkey training programs on various topics. The programs include a training leaders guide, self-study book, and a video for improving skills in areas such as customer service, documenting discipline, and appraising performance.

▪▪▪ *Lexus, the luxury car division of Toyota, uses a computerized simulation called Fact Lab for sales training. A simulation test shows four digital images of sales scenarios.*

NEW EMPLOYEE DEPARTMENTAL ORIENTATION CHECKLIST
(Return to Human Resources within 10 days of Hire)

NAME:	HIRE DATE:	SSN:	JOB TITLE:
DEPARTMENT:	NEO DATE:	DEPARTMENTAL ORIENTATION COMPLETED BY:	

TOPIC	DATE REVIEWED	N/A
1. HUMAN RESOURCES INFORMATION		
a. Departmental Attendance Procedures and UCSD Healthcare Work Time & Attendance Policy	a. _____	☐
b. Job Description Review	b. _____	☐
c. Annual Performance Evaluation and Peer Feedback Process	c. _____	☐
d. Probationary Period Information	d. _____	☐
e. Appearance/Dress Code Requirements	e. _____	☐
f. Annual TB Screening	f. _____	☐
g. License and/or certification Renewals	g. _____	☐
2. DEPARTMENT INFORMATION		
a. Organizational Structure-Department Core Values Orientation	a. _____	☐
b. Department/Unit Area Specific Policies & Procedures	b. _____	☐
c. Customer Service Practices	c. _____	☐
d. CQI Effort and Projects	d. _____	☐
e. Tour and Floor Plan	e. _____	☐
f. Equipment/Supplies	f. _____	☐
• Keys issued	_____	☐
• Radio Pager issued	_____	☐
• Other _____	_____	☐
g. Mail and Recharge Codes	g. _____	☐
3. SAFETY INFORMATION		
a. Departmental Safety Plan	a. _____	☐
b. Employee Safety/Injury Reporting Procedures	b. _____	☐
c. Hazard Communication	c. _____	☐
d. Infection Control/Sharps Disposal	d. _____	☐
e. Attendance at annual Safety Fair (mandatory)	e. _____	☐
4. FACILITES INFORMATION		
a. Emergency Power	a. _____	☐
b. Mechanical Systems	b. _____	☐
c. Water	c. _____	☐
d. Medical Gases	d. _____	☐
e. Patient Room	e. _____	☐
• Bed	_____	☐
• Headwall	_____	☐
• Bathroom	_____	☐
• Nurse Call System	_____	☐
5. SECURITY INFORMATION		
a. Code Triage Assignment	a. _____	☐
b. Code Blue Assignment	b. _____	☐
c. Code Red – Evacuation Procedure	c. _____	☐
d. Code 10 – Bomb Threat Procedure	d. _____	☐
e. Departmental Security Measures	e. _____	☐
f. UCSD Emergency Number 6111 or 911	f. _____	☐

This generic checklist may not constitute a complete departmental orientation or assessment. Please attach any additional unit specific orientation material for placement in the employee's HR file

I have been oriented on the items listed above_____

Training Techniques

Training techniques range from simple to complex. On-the-job training (OJT) means having a person learn a job by actually performing it. Just about every employee gets some OJT. In many firms, OJT is the only training available. It usually involves assigning new employees to experienced workers or supervisors, who then do the actual training.[44] It's important not to take on-the-job training for granted. Employees should get job descriptions and training manuals that explain their jobs. Checklist 9.4 shows how to use OJT techniques.

CHECKLIST 9.4 ■ How to Conduct an On-the-Job Training Program

☑ Step 1. Prepare the learner.

1. Put the learner at ease—relieve tension.
2. Explain why he or she is being taught.
3. Create interest, encourage questions, find out what the learner already knows.
4. Explain the whole job, and relate it to some job the worker already knows.
5. Place the learner as close to the normal working position as possible.
6. Familiarize the worker with equipment, materials, tools, and trade terms.

☑ Step 2. Present the operations.

1. Explain quantity and quality requirements.
2. Go through the job at the normal workplace.
3. Go through the job at a slow pace several times, explaining each step.
4. Go through the job again at a slow pace several times; explain the key points.
5. Have the learner explain the steps as you go through the job at a slow pace.

☑ Step 3. Do a tryout.

1. Have the learner go through the job several times, slowly, explaining each step to you.
2. Run the job at the normal pace.
3. Have the learner do the job, gradually building up skill and speed.
4. As soon as the learner demonstrates ability to do the job, let the worker begin, but don't abandon him or her.

☑ Step 4. Follow-up

1. Designate to whom the learner should go for help.
2. Gradually decrease supervision, checking work from time to time.
3. Correct faulty work patterns before they become a habit.
4. Compliment good work; encourage the worker until he or she is able to meet the quality and quantity standards.[45]

Much training today is technologically advanced. For example, instead of sending new rental agents to weeklong classroom-based training courses, Value Rent-a-Car now provides them with interactive, multimedia-based training programs that utilize CD-ROMs. These programs help agents learn the car rental process by walking them through various procedures, such as how to operate the rental computer system.[46]

Many firms are creating their own Internet-based learning portals for their employees. These portals let the company contract with training content-providers, which offer their training content to the firms' employees via the portal. ADC Telecommunications is an example.

MANAGEMENT IN ACTION ADC Telecommunications

ADC supplies equipment and services for broadband communications, and it has 16,000 employees worldwide. The firm's training department concluded that its existing instructor-led training was not meeting its needs. The company decided that the solution was to deliver training programs online. To accomplish this, ADC turned to Click2learn.com, which installed a version of its standard portal for ADC. As one ADC manager put it, "Our Click2learn learning site gives ADC personnel access to the wide variety of online courses available on the learning network . . . and, all displayed in a way that makes it easy for users to find what they're looking for. And with a pay-as-you-go model, we're only paying to train those who need it."[47]

■■■ APPRAISING AND MAINTAINING EMPLOYEES

Once employees are recruited, hired, oriented and trained, the manager turns to appraising their performance and to providing for their compensation and working conditions.

Employee Appraisal

Once employees have been at work for some time, you should appraise (evaluate) their performance. Performance appraisal means evaluating an employee's current or past performance relative to his or her performance standards. Probably the most familiar performance appraisal method involves using a *graphic rating scale*. This lists several job characteristics (like quality of work) and provides a rating scale (from outstanding to unsatisfactory), along with short definitions of each rating.

The form in Figure 9.13 is relatively objective, because it calls for numerical ratings. However, it also provides space in the comments column for more subjective examples of particularly good or particularly bad performance. Some firms use the critical incidents method instead. Here the manager compiles brief examples of the

performance appraisal ■ *a manager's evaluation of and feedback on an employee's work performance.*

critical incidents method ■ *compiling brief examples of good/bad performance, and using them to support appraisal and development needs.*

◀ **FIGURE 9–13** ■■■

Performance Appraisal Form

Source: Gary Dessler, *Human Resource Management*, 9th ed. (Upper Saddle River, NJ: Prentice Hall, 2000).

Performance Appraisal for:

Employee Name _____ Title _____

Department _____ Employee Payroll Number _____

Reason for Review:
☐ Annual   ☐ Promotion   ☐ Unsatisfactory Performance
☐ Merit   ☐ End Probation Period ☐ Other _____

Date employee began present position _____ / _____ / _____

Date of last appraisal _____ / _____ / _____   Scheduled appraisal date _____ / _____ / _____

Instructions: Carefully evaluate employee's work performance in relation to current job requirements. Check rating box to indicate the employee's performance. Indicate N/A if not applicable. Assign points for each rating within the scale in the corresponding points box. Points will be totaled and averaged for an overall performance score.

RATING IDENTIFICATION

O – **Outstanding**—Performance is exceptional in all areas.
V – **Very Good**—Results clearly exceed most position requirements.
G – **Good**—Competent and dependable level of performance. Meets performance standards.
I – **Improvement Needed**—Performance is deficient in certain areas.
U – **Unsatisfactory**—Results are generally unacceptable and require immediate improvement.
N – **Not Rated**—Not applicable or too soon to rate.

GENERAL FACTORS	RATING	SCALE	COMMENTS
1. **Quality**—The accuracy, thoroughness, and acceptability of work performed.	O ☐ V ☐ G ☐ I ☐ U ☐	100–90 90–80 80–70 70–60 below 60	Points
2. **Productivity**—The quantity and efficiency of work produced in a specified period of time.	O ☐ V ☐ G ☐ I ☐ U ☐	100–90 90–80 80–70 70–60 below 60	Points
3. **Job Knowledge**—The practical/technical skills and information used on the job.	O ☐ V ☐ G ☐ I ☐ U ☐	100–90 90–80 80–70 70–60 below 60	Points
4. **Reliability**—The extent to which an employee can be relied upon regarding task completion and follow up.	O ☐ V ☐ G ☐ I ☐ U ☐	100–90 90–80 80–70 70–60 below 60	Points
5. **Availability**—The extent to which an employee is punctual, observes prescribed work break/meal periods, and the overall attendance record.	O ☐ V ☐ G ☐ I ☐ U ☐	100–90 90–80 80–70 70–60 below 60	Points

employee's good or bad performance and then uses them to support both the person's appraisal and development needs. Some combine rating scales with critical incidents.

forced distribution method ▪ *placing predetermined percentages of ratees into performance categories*

The forced distribution method is similar to grading on a curve. With this method, you place predetermined percentages of ratees into performance categories. For example, you may decide to distribute employees as follows:

- 15% high performers
- 20% high average performance
- 30% average performers
- 20% low average performers
- 15% low performers

More firms are adopting this practice. Sun Microsystems recently began forced ranking of all its 43,000 employees. Managers appraise individual employees in groups of about 30, and 10% of each group gets 90 days to improve. If they're still at the bottom 10% in 90 days, they get a chance to resign and take severance pay. Some decide to stay, but "if it doesn't work out," the firm fires them without severance.[48]

Many experts and managers dislike what they see as the potential ruthlessness of this approach. For example, the newly hired HR vice president at Electronic Data Systems left abruptly when the CEO instituted a plan like this despite employee resistance. Instituting such a system played a role in the quick demise of Jacques Nasser as Ford CEO. Experts like W. E. Deming argue that forced ranking systems foster fear and are unfair. His basic argument is that performance is more often a product of the person's training and of the company's support, so employees shouldn't be summarily dismissed for poor performance. Deming recommends, among other things, using "360 degree feedback," and having employees sign performance contracts laying out the steps they and the company will take to get each person's performance back up to par. Based on one study, 29% of the responding employers use 360-degree feedback, and another 11% had plans to implement it.[49]

360-degree feedback ▪ *a performance evaluation method that involves collecting performance information on an employee all around that person— for instance, from subordinates, supervisors, peers, and internal and external customers.*

With 360-degree feedback, performance information is collected "all around" an employee—from supervisors, subordinates, peers, and internal or external customers.[50] The employee's peers, supervisors, subordinates, and customers complete appraisal surveys. These surveys take many forms, but (for managers) they often include supervisory skill items such as "returns phone calls promptly," "listens well," and "my manager keeps me informed."[51] Computerized systems compile the feedback into individualized reports for the ratee.[52] The feedback is generally used for training and development rather than for deciding pay raises.[53]

The Appraisal Interview An appraisal typically culminates in an appraisal interview. It is safe to say that most people look forward to these interviews with some trepidation. Few people like to receive—or give—negative feedback. Checklist 9.5 summarizes the suggested approach.

CHECKLIST 9.5 ▪ How to Conduct the Appraisal Interview

☑ **Prepare for the interview.** Assemble the data, study the person's job description and performance, and give the person at least a week's notice to review his or her work.

☑ **Be direct and specific.** Talk in terms of objective work data. Use examples such as absences, tardiness, quality records, and inspection reports.

☑ **Don't get personal.** Try to compare the person's performance to a standard ("These reports should normally be done within ten days.").

☑ **Encourage the person to talk.** Ask open-ended questions. Use a command such as "Go on" or "Tell me more."

☑ **Don't tiptoe around.** Make sure the person leaves knowing specifically what he or she is doing right and doing wrong.

☑ **Create a plan.** The employee should leave the meeting with a plan to correct any deficiencies.

Compensation

After being appraised, employees expect to be paid. **Employee compensation** refers to all work-related pay or rewards that go to employees.[54] It includes direct financial payments in the form of wages, salaries, incentives, commissions, and bonuses, as well as indirect payments in the form of financial fringe benefits like employer-paid insurance and vacations.

A **fixed salary** or **an hourly wage** is the centerpiece of most employees' pay. For example, clerical workers usually receive hourly or daily wages. Some employees—managerial, professional, and often secretarial—are salaried. They are paid by the week, month, or year.

A **financial incentive** is any financial reward that is contingent on performance (some call this "pay for performance"). Salespeople get financial incentives called *commissions*, generally in proportion to the items or services they actually sell. Production workers may receive a financial incentive called *piecework*, which is a standard sum for each item the worker produces. Many employees periodically receive *merit pay* or a merit raise, which is a salary increase awarded to an employee based on individual performance. Merit pay differs from a *bonus*, which is a one-time financial payment. (We discuss incentives further in Chapter 11, Motivation.)

Employee benefits are supplements to pay based on working for the organization. They typically include health and life insurance, vacation, pension, and education plans. Many of these benefits are legally mandated. For example, under federal and state law, **unemployment insurance** is available to most employees, and is paid by state agencies to workers who lose their jobs through no fault of their own. The funds come from a tax on the employer's payroll. **Workers' compensation**, another legally mandated benefit, is a payment aimed at providing sure, prompt income and medical benefits to victims of work-related accidents or their dependents, regardless of fault. Social Security is another federally mandated benefit, paid for by a tax on an employee's salary or wages.

Discipline and Grievances

Supervisors sometimes discipline subordinates, usually when the latter violate a rule. A company should have clear rules (such as "No smoking allowed when dealing with customers"), as well as a series of progressive penalties that all employees know the firm will enforce if the rule is broken. In assessing the need for discipline, some supervisors follow the so-called **FRACT model**: Get the **F**acts, obtain the **r**eason for the infraction, **a**udit the records, pinpoint the **c**onsequences, and identify the **t**ype of infraction before taking remedial steps. Some use the **discipline without punishment** approach. Here, an employee first gets an oral reminder if he or she breaks a rule—and then a written reminder if it occurs again. The person gets a paid one-day "decision-making leave" if another incident occurs in the next few weeks. If the rule is broken again, a dismissal may be in order. Discipline guidelines include those in Checklist 9.6.

employee compensation ■ *all forms of pay or rewards that go to employees and arise from their employment.*

fixed salary ■ *compensation based on an agreed rate for a set period of time.*

hourly wage ■ *compensation based on a set hourly pay rate for work performed.*

financial incentive ■ *any financial reward that is contingent on a worker's performance, such as commissions or piecework.*

employee benefits ■ *supplements to wages or pay that employees get as a result of their working for an organization.*

unemployment insurance ■ *legally mandated insurance that is paid by state agencies to workers who are terminated through no fault of their own; the funds come from a tax on the employer's payroll.*

workers' compensation ■ *a legally mandated benefit that pays income and medical benefits to work-related accident victims or their dependents, regardless of fault.*

FRACT model ■ *A procedure for assessing the need for discipline, consisting of the steps get the facts, find the reason, audit the records, pinpoint consequences, and identify the type of infraction.*

discipline without punishment ■ *a multistage disciplinary technique that uses oral reminders of the violated rule; then written reminders; followed by a paid one-day leave; and finally, if the behavior is not corrected, dismissal.*

CHECKLIST 9.6 ■ Guidelines for Disciplining an Employee

- ☑ Make sure the evidence supports the charge.
- ☑ Protect the employee's due process rights.
- ☑ Warn the employee of the disciplinary consequences.
- ☑ The rule allegedly violated should be "reasonably related" to the efficient and safe operation of the work environment.
- ☑ Fairly and adequately investigate the matter.
- ☑ Be sure there is substantial evidence of misconduct.
- ☑ Apply rules, orders, or penalties even-handedly.

- ☑ Make sure the penalty is reasonably related to the misconduct and to the employee's past work history.
- ☑ Maintain the employee's right to counsel.
- ☑ Don't rob your subordinate of his or her dignity.
- ☑ Remember that the burden of proof is on you.
- ☑ Get the facts. Don't base your decision on hearsay or "general impression."
- ☑ Don't act while angry.

grievance ■ *a complaint that an employee lodges against an employer, usually one regarding wages, hours, or some condition of employment, such as unfair supervisory behavior.*

A grievance is a complaint an employee lodges against an employer, usually regarding wages, hours, or some condition of employment like supervisory behavior. Most union contracts contain a grievance procedure whereby the employer and the union determine whether there's been a violation of some clause of the contract. For example, a terminated employee might file a grievance stating that the supervisor had issued no warnings as called for in the union agreement and that the firing was unwarranted. Grievance steps typically include discussing the problem with a supervisor, and then referring the matter to the department head, the personnel department, and finally the head of the facility. Many nonunion companies voluntarily offer grievance procedures. One way to avoid grievances is to adhere to disciplinary guidelines.

■■■ UNDERSTANDING HR'S LEGAL FRAMEWORK

When it comes to personnel practices, managers can't just do whatever they please. Thousands of federal, state, and local laws prescribe what companies can and can't do when it comes to employee recruitment and selection, compensation and benefits, and safety-related working conditions. Most federal laws cover larger employers. However, that certainly doesn't mean the small local café or dry cleaner isn't covered. State and local laws cover these employers.

Equal Employment Laws and Affirmative Action

Equal employment opportunity laws aim to ensure that supervisors conduct the full range of the firm's personnel activities in a nondiscriminatory way. For example, employers should verify that the selection tests they use do not unfairly screen out minorities, and interviews should avoid delving into an applicant's ethnic, racial, or marital status. Employers today generally cannot advertise for "help wanted—male" or "help wanted—female," generally cannot institute height or weight requirements for jobs (such as "minimum weight of 150 pounds"), generally cannot use arrest records, and generally can't pay a man more than a woman for doing exactly the same job under exactly the same working conditions. The basic idea is this: with respect to employment, all employees should be on a level playing field. The manager should not discriminate against an applicant or employee based on that person's age, race, sex, religion, national origin, color, or disability.

For example, Title VII of the 1964 Civil Rights Act bars discrimination because of race, color, religion, sex, or national origin (see Table 9.2). (The Equal Employment Opportunity Commission [EEOC]), a five-member commission appointed by the president with the advice and consent of the Senate, enforces these laws. It receives, investigates, and may file charges regarding job discrimination complaints on behalf of aggrieved individuals.) Other important antidiscrimination laws include the Equal Pay Act of 1963, which requires equal pay for men and women performing similar work; and the Pregnancy Discrimination Act of 1978, which prohibits discrimination in employment against pregnant women.

The Americans with Disabilities Act (ADA) of 1990 prohibits employment discrimination against qualified disabled individuals. Employers with 15 or more workers are prohibited from discriminating against qualified individuals with disabilities with regard to applications, hiring, discharge, compensation, advancement, training, or other terms, conditions, or privileges of employment. Employers must also make "reasonable accommodations" for physical or mental limitations unless doing so imposes an "undue hardship" on the business. The EEOC's guidelines say that an individual is disabled when he or she has a physical or mental impairment that substantially limits one or more major life activities.

Sexual Harassment Sexual harassment is a special type of discriminatory behavior. It is

unwelcome sexual advances, requests for sexual favors, and other verbal or physical conduct of a sexual nature that occurs under conditions including the following: when such conduct is made, either explicitly or implicitly, a term or condition of an individual's employment; when submission to or rejection of such conduct by an individual is used as the basis for employ-

Action	What It Does
Title VII of 1964 Civil Rights Act, as amended	Bars discrimination because of race, color, religion, sex, or national origin; instituted EEOC
Executive orders	Prohibit employment discrimination by employers with federal contracts of more than $10,000 (and their subcontractors); establish office of federal compliance; require affirmative action programs
Federal agency guidelines	Used by federal agencies for enforcement of laws barring discrimination based on sex, national origin, and religion, as well as employee selection procedures; for example, they require validation of tests
Supreme court decisions: *Griggs* v. *Duke Power Co.*, *Albemarie* v. *Moody*	Ruled that job requirements must be related to job success; that discrimination need not be overt to be proved; that the burden of proof is on the employer to prove that the qualification is valid
Equal Pay Act of 1967	Requires equal pay for men and women for performing similar work
Age Discrimination in employment Act of 1967	Prohibits discriminating against a person 40 years or over in any area of employment because of age
State and local laws	Often cover organizations too small to be covered by federal laws
Vocational Rehabilitation Act of 1973	Requires affirmative action to employ and promote qualified disabled persons and prohibits discrimination against disabled persons
Pregnancy Discrimination Act of 1978	Prohibits discrimination in employment against pregnant women or workers with related conditions.
Vietnam Era Veteran's Readjustment Assistance Act of 1974	Requires affirmative action in employment for veterans of the Vietnam War era
Wards Cove v. *Atonio*; *Patterson* v. *McLean Credit Union*	These Supreme Court decisions made it more difficult to prove a case of unlawful discrimination against an employer
Morton v. *Wilks*	This case allowed consent decrees to be attacked and could have had a chilling effect on certain affirmative action programs
Americans with Disabilities Act of 1990	Strengthens the need for most employers to make reasonable accommodations for disabled employees at work; prohibits discrimination
Civil Rights Act of 1991	Reverses *Wards Cove*, *Patterson*, and *Morton* decisions; places burden of proof back on employer and permits compensatory and punitive money damages for discrimination

Source: Gary Dessler, *Human Resource Management*, 7th ed. (Upper Saddle River, NJ: Prentice Hall, 2000), 52.

> *ment decisions affecting the individual; or when such conduct has the purpose or effect of unreasonably interfering with an individual's performance or creating an intimidating, hostile, or offensive work environment.*

In addition to being unfair and detestable, sexual harassment is also illegal. In one famous case, *Meritor Savings Bank, FSB* v. *Vinson*, the U.S. Supreme Court indicated that employers should establish meaningful complaint procedures and head off charges of sexual harassment before they occur. They should:

1. Take all complaints seriously. As one manual for managers and supervisors advises, "When confronted with sexual harassment complaints or when sexual conduct is observed in the workplace, the best reaction is to address the complaint or stop the conduct."[55]
2. Issue a strong policy statement condemning such behavior.
3. Inform all employees about the policy prohibiting sexual harassment and of their rights under the policy.
4. Establish a complaint procedure so that employees understand the chain of command in filing and appealing sexual harassment complaints.
5. Establish a management response system that includes an immediate reaction and investigation by senior management when charges of sexual harassment are made.
6. Hold training sessions with supervisors and increase their own awareness of the issues.
7. Discipline managers and employees involved in sexual harassment.

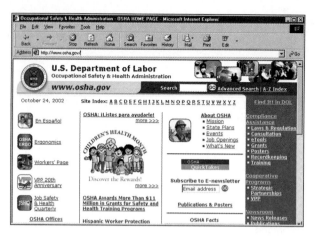

affirmative action ■ *a legislated requirement that employers make an extra effort to hire and promote those in a protected (women or minority) group.*

Affirmative Action Whereas equal employment opportunity aims to ensure equal treatment at work, affirmative action requires employers to make an extra effort to hire and promote those in a protected group (such as women or minorities). Affirmative action thus includes taking specific actions (in recruitment, hiring, promotions, and compensation) designed to eliminate the present effects of past discrimination. An example would be setting a goal of promoting more minorities to middle management jobs.

Occupational Safety and Health

The Occupational Safety and Health Act was passed by Congress "to assure so far as possible every working man and woman in the nation safe and healthful working conditions and to preserve our human resources." It sets safety and health standards that apply to almost all workers in the United States. The standards themselves cover just about any hazard one could think of, including, for instance, what sorts of ladders to use, appropriate fire protection, and ways to guard against accidents when using machines and portable power tools. The Occupational Safety and Health Administration (OSHA), a U.S. government agency, administers these laws.

Companies can take a variety of steps to improve the safety and health of their workforces. One is to reduce unsafe *conditions* that can lead to accidents. This is an employer's first line of defense. The occupational safety laws specify the sorts of unsafe conditions firms should attend to. A brief checklist like that in Figure A9.2 can be useful. Reducing unsafe *acts* is another matter, since careless employees may have accidents even where unsafe conditions are minimal. Screening out potentially careless employees, training employees to work carefully, and rewarding those who act properly are some methods employers use to reduce unsafe acts.

Labor–Management Relations

Under the laws of the United States and many other countries, employees may organize into unions. In the United States, the Norris–LaGuardia Act guarantees each employee the right to bargain with employers for union benefits. The Wagner Act outlaws unfair labor practices such as employers interfering with, restraining, or coercing employees who are exercising their legally sanctioned rights of organizing themselves into a union. The Taft–Hartley Act prohibits unfair labor practices by unions against employers (like refusing to bargain with the employer). The Landrum-Griffin Act protects union members from unfair practices perpetrated against them by their unions.

Other Employment Law Issues

Other employment-related laws affect virtually every HR-related decision that managers make. For example, the Fair Labor Standards Act specifies a minimum wage ($5.15 per hour as of 2002), as well as child-labor and overtime pay rules. The Employee Polygraph Protection Act of 1988 outlaws almost all uses of the polygraph, or lie-detector machine, for employment purposes.

SUMMARY ■ ■ ■

1. Human resource management is the management function devoted to acquiring, training, appraising, and compensating employees. As workers become more fully empowered, the HR function has grown in importance.

2. Staffing—filling a firm's open positions—starts with job analysis and personnel planning. Recruiting—including the use of internal sources, advertising, the Internet, employment agencies, recruiters, referrals, college recruiting, and recruiting a more diverse workforce—is then used to create a pool of applicants.

3. With a pool of applicants, the employer can turn to screening and selecting, using one or more techniques—including application blanks, interviews, tests, and reference checks—to assess and investigate an applicant's aptitudes, interests, and background.

4. Once employees have been recruited, screened, and selected, they must be prepared to do their jobs; this is the role of employee orientation and training. Orientation means providing new employees with basic information about the employer; training ensures that the new employee has the basic knowledge required to perform the job satisfactorily.

5. Once they've been on the job for some time, employees are appraised.

6. Employee compensation refers to all work-related pay or rewards that go to employees. It includes direct financial payments in the form of wages, salaries, incentives, commissions, and bonuses, as well as indirect payments in the form of financial fringe benefits like employer-paid insurance and vacations.

7. In disciplining employees, managers should be sure they have all the facts, and that the discipline is defensible and fair.

8. The HR function is subject to the constraints of numerous federal, state, and local laws. The equal employment laws prohibiting employment discrimination are among the most important of these personnel laws and include Title VII of the Civil Rights Act, various executive orders, the Equal Pay Act of 1963, and the Americans with Disabilities Act of 1990. The Occupational Safety and Health Act sets safety and health standards that apply to most U.S. workers. Other laws govern union–management relations and include the Wagner Act.

KEY TERMS ■■■

human resources (HR) management 221
strategic human resources
    management 221
staffing 222
job analysis 222
job description 222
job specification 222
job analysis questionnaire 224
personnel planning 226
personnel replacement chart 226
position replacement card 226
recruiting 226

job posting 227
contingent (or temporary) workers 229
executive recruiter 229
application form 232
management assessment center 234
orientation 240
training program 240
on-the-job training (OJT) 242
performance appraisal 243
critical incidents method 243
forced distribution method 244
360-degree feedback 244

employee compensation 245
fixed salary 245
hourly wage 245
financial incentive 245
employee benefits 245
unemployment insurance 245
workers' compensation 245
FRACT model 245
discipline without punishment 245
grievance 246
affirmative action 248

SKILLS AND STUDY MATERIALS

COMPANION WEBSITE ■■■

We invite you to visit the Dessler Companion Website at **www.prenhall.com/dessler** for this chapter's Internet resources.

EXPERIENTIAL EXERCISES ■■■

1. Working in teams of 4–5 students, conduct a job analysis and develop a job description for the instructor of this course. Make sure to include a job summary, as well as a list of job duties and a job specification listing the human requirements of the job. If time permits, compare your job description with one from a Web site such as **www.jobdescriptions.com**.

2. Using that job description as a guide, develop a recruiting plan for the job of teaching this course, as well as list of interview questions your team would use to screen instructor applicants.

3. Working in teams of 4–5 students, spend 30 minutes using Figure A9–2 to assess the safety of the college building you are in. Then develop a performance appraisal procedure and form for the instructor in this course.

CASE STUDY ■■■

THE OUT-OF-CONTROL INTERVIEW

Maria Fernandez is a bright, popular, and well-informed mechanical engineer who graduated with an engineering degree from State University in June 2001. During the spring preceding her graduation, she went out on many job interviews, most of which she thought were courteous and reasonably useful in giving both her and the prospective employer a good impression of where each of them stood on matters of importance to both of them. It was, therefore, with great anticipation that she looked forward to an interview with the one firm in which she most wanted to work, Apex Environmental. She had always had a strong interest in cleaning up the environment and firmly believed that the best use of her training and skills lay in working for a firm like Apex, where she thought she could have a successful career while making the world a better place.

The interview, however, was a disaster. When Maria walked into the room, five men, including the president of the company, two vice presidents, the marketing director, and another engineer, began throwing questions at her that she felt were aimed primarily at tripping her up rather than finding out what she could offer through her engineering skills. The questions ranged from unnecessarily discourteous ("Why would you take a job as a waitress in college if you're such an intelligent person?") to irrelevant and sexist ("Are you planning on settling down and starting a family anytime soon?"). Then after the interview, she met with two of the gentlemen individually (including the president), and the discussions focused almost exclusively on her technical expertise. She thought that these later discussions went fairly well. However, given the apparent aimlessness and even mean-spiritedness of the panel interview, she was astonished when several days later she got a job offer from the firm.

The offer forced her to consider several matters. From her point of view, the job itself was perfect—she liked what she would be doing, the industry, and the firm's location. And, in fact, the president had been quite courteous in subsequent discussions, as had the other members of the management team. She was left wondering whether the panel interview had been intentionally tense to see how she'd stand up under pressure, and, if so, why the panel members would do such a thing.

Discussion Questions

1. How would you explain the nature of the interview Maria had to endure? Specifically, do you think it reflected a well-thought-out interviewing strategy on the part of the firm or carelessness on the part of the firm's management? If it was carelessness, what would you do to improve the interview process at Apex Environmental?

2. Would you take the job if you were Maria? If you're not sure, is there any additional information that would help you make your decision, and if so, what is it?

3. The job of applications engineer for which Maria was applying requires (1) excellent technical skills with respect to mechanical engineering; (2) a commitment to working in the area of pollution control; (3) the ability to deal well and confidently with customers who have engineering problems; (4) a willingness to travel worldwide; and (5) a very intelligent and well-balanced personality. What questions would you ask when interviewing applicants for the job?

JETBLUE: STAFFING THE BLUE SKIES

jetBlue
AIRWAYS
When airline passenger traffic declined after September 11, most airlines responded predictably, by dramatically downsizing their staffs. Throughout the industry, company after company laid off employees as passenger traffic declined and the airlines cut flights.

David Neeleman and his management team bucked the industry trend.[56] Neeleman's first reaction was to not lay off any of JetBlue's 2,000 employees. It wasn't easy. "We are probably carrying half as many (passengers)," as one JetBlue spokesperson said.[57] Neeleman's decision reflects his approach to human resource management. JetBlue's management team works hard to make sure that it has highly qualified, people-oriented employees and that those employees like what they do and how they're treated. JetBlue's managers believe that one of the best ways to keep service standards up is to make sure the employees who are providing that service enjoy what they're doing and love dealing with people.

JetBlue's HR process starts by hiring the right people in the first place. As David Neeleman says, "It's really focused on whether or not you like people."[58] How does JetBlue make sure it hires people who like people? One way is by asking applicants the right questions. For example the company will ask prospective employees to tell it about a specific time in their past work experience when they did something out of the ordinary for their job description and helped someone. One of JetBlue's best flight attendants is a 60-year-old retired fireman. His answer to the interview question was, "I was in a burning building, and some of my guys were inside, and the building was coming down, and I had to go in to get them out of there." The man was hired on the spot.

At an airline like JetBlue, keeping costs down means having highly committed employees, ones who are willing to pitch in when the plane comes in—to make sure bags are loaded, passengers embark, and that the airplane gets turned around as quickly as possible. JetBlue's employment interviewers therefore look for employees who are used to pitching in; they want employees "who aren't regimented to the point where they say, 'That's not my job; that's your job.'"[59] At JetBlue, when the plane comes in, every employee—from the CEO, to marketing executives, to the pilots—are expected to help get the plane turned around and out as fast as possible. Therefore, anyone who's not willing to pitch in and get his or her hands dirty need not apply.

JetBlue also takes a nontraditional approach to the way it hires and manages its telephone reservations agents. Here, flexibility is the rule. For example, instead of being crammed into office cubicles answering phones all day, JetBlues's 350 reservationists work out of their homes.[60] That approach has a double-barreled benefit. "It's efficient for us," says JetBlue's manager for corporate communications, since JetBlue saves on office space. "But it also allows people to have a job and be able to pick their kids up from school." Partly because of that flexibility, JetBlue's reservationist turnover rate is less than 1%.

JetBlue extends its flexible staffing approach to its flight attendants. For example, it has the JetBlue Friend's Crew program. In this program, JetBlue hires two people to share a schedule. The two friends interview together. If JetBlue hires them, it gives them a flight schedule and leaves it to them to decide who works when. JetBlue doesn't care who shows up for the flight, as long as one of them does. For example, one JetBlue Friend's Crew is a mother-daughter duo. They share a flight schedule and the daughter's child-care responsibilities.

Assignment

You and your team are consultants to Mr. Neeleman, who is depending on your management expertise to help navigate the launching and management of JetBlue. Here's what he wants to know from you now:

1. Write a job description for the positions of reservations agents and JetBlue Friend's Crew member.

2. Provide me with a recruiting plan for the jobs of reservations agents and JetBlue Friend's Crew Member. Please make sure to tell me specifically how you would recruit for these employees.

3. Explain what we are doing right and wrong with respect to interviewing for our positions now, and what, if anything you think we should do to improve our process. Please be sure to provide me with at least five specific questions we should be asking prospective flight attendants, and also five questions for reservation clerks.

Chapter Appendix

Source: Bureau of National Affairs, Inc., *Recruiting and Selection Procedures* (Washington, DC, 1988), p.35.

NO. ____

POSTED: _____
CLOSING: _____

_____

There is a full-time position available for a _____ in the _____ Department.   This position is/is not open to outside candidates.

PAY SCALE

Minimum	Midpoint	Maximum
$ _____	$ _____	$ _____

or
SALARIED

DUTIES
See attached job description.

REQUIRED SKILLS AND ABILITIES
(Must possess all the following skills and abilities to be considered for this position.)
1. Demonstrated successful performance at past/present positions including:
   – ability to perform tasks in a complete and accurate manner
   – demonstrated timeliness and follow-through on duties and assignments
   – ability to work well with other people
   – ability to communicate effectively
   – reliability and good attendance
   – good organizational skills
   – problem solving attitude and approach
   – positive work attitude: enthusiastic, confident, outgoing, helpful, committed

DESIRED SKILLS AND ABILITIES
(These skills and abilities will make a candidate more competitive.)

Application procedure FOR   EMPLOYEES is as follows:

1. Apply by phoning _____ , on ext. _____ , by 3:00 p.m.
_____

2. Ensure that a completed Internal Job Application and up-to-date résumé/application is delivered to _____ by the same date.
Applicants will be pre-screened according to the above qualifications.
Selection will be made by the _____ .
   is an equal opportunity employer.
0255M/1

◄ **FIGURE A9–2** ■ ■ ■

Checklist of Mechanical or Physical
Accident-Causing Conditions

Source: Courtesy of the American Insurance
Association. From "A Safety Committee
Man's Guide," pp. 1–64.

I. GENERAL HOUSEKEEPING

Adequate and wide aisles—no materials protruding into aisles

Parts and tools stored safely after use—not left in hazardous positions that could cause them to fall

Even and solid flooring—no defective floors or ramps that could cause falling or tripping accidents

Waste and trash cans—safely located and not overfilled

Material piled in safe manner—not too high or too close to sprinkler heads

All work areas clean and dry

All exit doors and aisles clean of obstructions

Aisles kept clear and properly marked; no air lines or electric cords across aisles

II. MATERIAL HANDLING EQUIPMENT AND CONVEYANCES

On all conveyances, electric or hand, check to see that the following items are all in sound working conditions:

Brakes—properly adjusted

Not too much play in steering wheel

Warning device—in place and working

Wheels—securely in place; properly inflated

Fuel and oil—enough and right kind

No loose parts

Cables, hooks or chains—not worn or otherwise defective

Suspended chains or hooks conspicuous

Safely loaded

Properly stored

III. LADDERS, SCAFFOLD, BENCHES, STAIRWAYS, ETC.

The following items of major interest to be checked:

Safety feet on straight ladders

Guardrails or handrails

Treads, not slippery

No splintered, cracked, or rickety

Properly stored

Extension ladder ropes in good condition

Toeboards

IV. POWER TOOLS (STATIONARY)

Point of operation guarded

Guards in proper adjustment

Gears, belts, shafting, counterweights guarded

Foot pedals guarded

Brushes provided for cleaning machines

Adequate lighting

Properly grounded

Tool or material rests properly adjusted

Adequate work space around machines

Control switch easily accessible

Safety glasses worn

Gloves worn by persons handling rough or sharp materials

No gloves or loose clothing worn by persons operating machines

V. HAND TOOLS AND MISCELLANEOUS

In good condition—not cracked, worn, or otherwise defective

Properly stored

Correct for job

Goggles, respirators, and other personal protective equipment worn where necessary

VI. ELECTRICITY

No frayed, cracked, or deteriorated cords

All portable, as well as fixed machinery grounded by three-wire connectors

No dangling wires

Ground-fault circuit interrupters used in humid conditions

VII. SPRAY PAINTING

Explosion-proof electrical equipment

Proper storage of paints and thinners in approved metal cabinets

Fire extinguishers adequate and suitable; readily accessible

Minimum storage in work area

VIII. FIRE EXTINGUISHERS

Properly serviced and tagged

Readily accessible

Adequate and suitable for operations involved

CHAPTER

10   Being a Leader

CHAPTER OBJECTIVES

After studying this chapter and the case exercises at the end, you should be able to:

1. Decide whether the person has the traits and skills to be a leader.

2. Identify the leadership style the leader is now using.

3. Recommend, specifically, the extent to which the leader should let his or her employees participate in a decision, and why.

4. Size up the leadership situation and recommend the leadership style to use, and why.

5. Explain how a leader can strengthen his or her power base.

THE MANAGEMENT CHALLENGE

Jacques Nasser's Reign at Ford

By the time he became CEO of Ford Motor Company, Jacques Nasser had spent 30 years at the carmaker, going from success to success. Now, as Ford's CEO, Nasser's plan was to lead a vast transformation of Ford and to turn it into the world's premier consumer-products company. He wanted Ford and all its employees to be the best. He said, "Five years from now, we will be a different company, and five years from then, we'll be another different company."[1]

Nasser set about leading that transformation by instituting numerous changes. In a move that upset Ford's dealer network, Ford bought several of its dealers with an eye toward possibly expanding its ownership of dealers and of selling cars directly over the Web. To boost employee performance, he installed a new performance appraisal system. Henceforth, those rated C for two years running would be out. He forced out many long-serving middle and senior managers. Nasser decided that this was no time for participative leadership. He wanted the new appraisal system, and he drove it through. But as Ford's sales and quality fell, many inside and outside Ford began questioning his leadership ability. Nasser—and Ford's board—had to decide what to do.

Managers like Jacques Nasser know that after plans are set and the organization and employees are in place, nothing will happen without *leadership*. Leadership breathes life into the manager's plans by translating the company's plans and organization into action. In any company, conflicts must be resolved, employees motivated, and organizational values set if plans are to become results. *Leading* is thus the third main function in the management process. The first two, planning and organizing, are useless without it. The main purpose of this chapter is make you a more effective leader. The main topics we'll cover include what leaders do, the traits and skills of leadership, leader behaviors, situational theories of leadership, and how to improve your leadership skills.

■■■ WHAT DO LEADERS DO?

Leadership means influencing others to work willingly toward achieving the firm's objectives. It is the distinctly behavioral and interpersonal facet of what managers do. In the previous parts of this book, we've covered the management functions of planning and organizing. Now, we turn to the concepts and skills involved in actually influencing the organization's employees to implement the company's plans. We turn to being a leader—and to leadership.

leadership ■ *one person influencing another to willingly work toward a predetermined objective.*

The Leadership Function in the Management Process

Leadership has two meanings for managers. First, as noted above, it means "influencing others to work willingly toward achieving the firm's objectives." Second, leadership also refers to the third basic function of the management process (the others are planning, organizing, and controlling). In this sense, managers use *leadership* as an umbrella term to cover all or most of the behavioral (or people-oriented) things managers do, like motivation, communication, groups, conflict, and change.[2] The knowledge contained in this chapter—"Being a Leader"—is therefore only part of what managers/leaders must know about leading. This chapter will get you started. To be a more effective leader, you'll need the following three chapters, too. Here's what they cover:

■ *Chapter 11: Influencing Individual Behavior and Motivation.* Individual differences (for example, in aptitudes and skills) that help to account for why people do what they do, and several theories that help to explain how leaders motivate employees
■ *Chapter 12: Improving Communication Skills.* The barriers that can undermine effective communications, and what a manager has to know about communicating to be an effective leader
■ *Chapter 13: Managing Groups and Teams.* What leaders can do to create cohesive teams, and the group dynamics leaders should take into consideration when supervising their own teams.

Together, these chapters provide a wealth of information about leadership and behavioral science concepts and skills. After studying them, you should be able to apply the right leadership skill in the right situation. Don't be overwhelmed by the number of leadership concepts and skills in this and the next three chapters. Instead, think of each as a tool in your leadership toolbox, each useful in its way and under the right conditions.

Studying Leadership

The question of what makes some leaders more effective than others has long perplexed and fascinated organizational observers and experts. Machiavelli, a shrewd advisor to kings and princes, addressed the question 400 years ago, and the Bible has many references to the actions leaders should take to be more effective. Certainly, medieval kings, pharaohs, and even the earliest "team leaders" who led bands of cave dwellers across the plains must have asked themselves, "What makes some people more effective as leaders than others?"[3]

Yet it has only been in the past 60 or so years that experts have made a concerted effort to investigate this question. The current thinking, in brief, is this: Effective leadership reflects a balance of (1) traits and skills, and (2) leadership styles or behaviors, all (3) combined in a way that's right for the situation. Leadership, in other words, reflects who we "are" (in terms of traits and skills) and how we behave (our leadership style) in particular situations.

The three main scientific approaches to studying leadership have been to focus on the leader's *traits and skills*, on his or her *behavior*, or on how the *situation* influences what type of leader is best. We'll look at these three main approaches in this chapter, and then we'll translate them into practice in the final section. Let's start with leadership traits and skills.

■ ■ THE TRAITS AND SKILLS OF LEADERSHIP

Most people readily recognize the names of great American Civil War leaders, such as Abraham Lincoln, Ulysses S. Grant, and Robert E. Lee. But, have you ever heard of Major General Gustave Smith? Probably not. In the midst of a battle in May 1862, command of the South's largest army was thrust on Smith when his commander was wounded. So why did Smith not earn his place alongside the war's great leaders? Because faced with the enormity of his new responsibilities, Smith simply froze. He was incapable of even deciding what to do. The next day, Confederate President Jefferson Davis replaced Smith with Robert E. Lee.[4] In terms of leadership, Smith didn't have "the right stuff." He didn't have the traits and skills required to be a great leader.

The idea that leaders have certain traits or skills that distinguish them from nonleaders is not new. In fact, it is an idea that probably resonates with most people, since it's something we've all had some experience with. Who hasn't had a classmate whose charisma and decisiveness made him or her stand out as the most likely to succeed? Who hasn't had a boss whose intelligence and authority and empathy haven't made us want to follow her? On the other hand, who hasn't worked for someone whose traits or skills—perhaps indecisiveness, lack of confidence, or dishonesty—would characterize the person as "the worst leader I've ever met"? It is, therefore, not surprising that early researchers believed that if they studied the personality and intelligence of great leaders, they would stumble on the combination of traits and skills that made these people great.

In thinking about what it is about the leader that determines his or her effectiveness, experts usually don't focus just on leadership traits; they talk of both traits and skills. Traits (such as self-confidence) are more or less unchanging characteristics of the person that predispose someone to act in a particular way. Skill "refers to the ability to do something in an effective manner."[5] Intelligence and self-confidence might be examples of traits. Skills include technical skills (such as knowing how to program a computer), interpersonal skills (such as being able to empathize with other people), and conceptual skills (such as creativity and being able to solve complex problems).

What Are the Leadership Traits and Skills?

Most of the early leadership trait research was inconclusive. Most researchers administered personality inventories to assess the traits leaders had. Some merely asked leaders to describe their leadership traits. In any case, researchers found that specific traits corresponded to effectiveness in some situations but not in others. There seemed to be no single set of "great leader" traits. Interest in this approach began to fade.

Gradually, however, the trait approach has come back into vogue. For example, after reviewing 163 studies of leadership traits some years ago, Ralph Stogdill put it this way:

> *The leader is characterized by a strong drive for responsibility and task completion, vigor and persistence in pursuit of goals, venturesomeness and originality in problem solving, drive to exercise initiative in social situations, self-confidence and sense of personal identity, willingness to accept consequences of decision and action, readiness to absorb interpersonal stress, willingness to tolerate frustration and delay, ability to influence other person's behavior, and capacity to structure social interaction systems to the purpose at hand.[6]*

Table 10.1 summarizes the leadership traits and skills that Stogdill concluded were important.

More recent research has made it clear that successful leaders are not like other people. "The evidence indicates that there are certain core traits which significantly

traits ■ *the unchanging characteristics of a person that predisposes someone to act in a particular way.*

skills ■ *the ability to do something in an effective manner.*

TABLE 10–1	Traits and Skills Differentiating Leaders from Nonleaders

Traits	Skills
Adaptable to situations	Clever (intelligent)
Alert to social environment	Conceptually skilled
Ambitious, achievement oriented	Creative
Assertive	Diplomatic and tactful
Cooperative	Fluent in speaking
Decisive	Knowledgeable about the work
Dependable	Organized (administrative ability)
Dominant (power motivation)	Persuasive
Energetic (high activity level)	Socially skilled
Persistent	
Self-confident	
Tolerate of stress	
Willing to assume responsibility	

Source: Based on Ralph Stogdill *Handbook of Leadership: A Survey of the Literature* (New York: Free Press, 1974), p. 237.

contribute to business leaders' success."[7] Six traits or skills on which leaders differ from nonleaders include drive, the desire to lead, honesty and integrity, self-confidence, cognitive ability, and knowledge of the business:

Leaders Have Drive They are action-oriented people with a high desire to achieve. They get satisfaction from successfully completing challenging tasks. Leaders are more ambitious than nonleaders. They have high energy because "working long, intense work weeks (and many weekends for many years) requires an individual to have physical, mental, and emotional vitality."[8] Leaders are also tenacious and better at overcoming obstacles than are nonleaders.[9]

Leaders Are Motivated to Lead Leaders are motivated to influence others. They prefer to be in leadership rather than subordinate roles, and they willingly shoulder the mantle of authority. Other traits seem to underlie the motivation to lead. For example, there is evidence that whether a person is motivated to lead depends on his or her extraversion, agreeableness, conscientiousness, openness to experience, and emotional stability. (Some psychologists call these "The Big 5" traits, because they are a foundation of personality.)[10]

Leaders Have Honesty and Integrity If your followers can't trust you, why should they follow you? Studies have found that people tend to rate leaders as more trustworthy and reliable in carrying out responsibilities than they rate followers.[11] Some believe that Secretary of Health and Human Services Tommy Thompson crippled his leadership potential after September 11, 2001, by speculating that the first anthrax victim got the disease by drinking from a North Carolina stream.[12]

Leaders Have Self-Confidence As two experts summarize, "Self-confidence plays an important role in decision-making and in gaining others' trust. Obviously, if the leader is not sure of what decision to make, or expresses a high degree of doubt, then the followers are less likely to trust the leader and be committed to the vision."[13] After General Smith asked President Jefferson Davis what *he* thought of how to fight the battle, Davis wisely replaced him the next day with Robert E. Lee.

Leaders Have Cognitive Ability No one will keep following someone who always makes the wrong decisions. By definition, the leader is the one who must pick the right direction and then put the mechanisms in place to get there. The leader's intelligence and decision-making ability—and the subordinates' perceptions of those abilities—are, therefore, important leadership traits.[14]

The Leader Knows the Business Effective leaders are exceptionally knowledgeable about the company and the industry; their information helps them make informed decisions and anticipate the implications of those decisions.[15] Sometimes, there seem to be exceptions. With no computer experience, former IBM CEO Louis Gerstner Jr. became CEO after years with R.J. Reynolds, and he excelled at the job. However, such exceptions make the rule. Gerstner has high cognitive ability, he quickly immersed himself in the details of IBM, and he happens to have an engineering degree!

■ *The Global Manager* With most companies doing business globally today, it's reasonable to ask, "Do managers from different countries share the same leadership traits?" For example, do traits like cognitive ability distinguish managers in all cultures, or only in some, such as in the United States?

There is evidence pro and con on this issue. Some researchers found that as much as 52% of the variance in managers' behavior could be attributed to nationality—even within a single multinational firm. Others similarly conclude that the strongest predictors of leadership behaviors are "consistently due to national differences."[16] This would seem to suggest that leadership traits and skills vary from country to country. On the other hand, some researchers contend that leadership behaviors "are largely free from the influence of national culture."[17]

■ ■ *Louis Gerstner, former chairman of IBM, in his office. Gerstner's leadership skills turned IBM around.*

A recent study sheds some light on this matter. The researcher collected data on the leaders' traits and values from 79 American and 87 Taiwanese CEOs from small and medium-sized firms in the United States and Taiwan. To assess personality, the researchers used a personality instrument known as the Myers-Briggs Type Indicator (MBTI). They assessed values using an instrument known as Rokeach's Value Survey (RVS).

The researchers found significant differences between the American and Taiwanese managers. For example, in terms of the MBTI measures, 51% of the American managers were Intuitive Thinkers (who like solving new problems and tend to jump to conclusions), while 74% of the Taiwanese managers were Sensing Thinkers (who dislike new problems and prefer to apply methodical, routine ways to solve them). Cultural background thus did seem to influence how these CEOs went about making decisions.

The CEOs' values also varied by nationality. For example, the American CEOs placed a higher emphasis on self-respect, an exciting life, a sense of accomplishment, and happiness/contentedness than did the Taiwanese CEOs. In contrast, the Taiwanese CEOs placed a higher emphasis on equality, wisdom, pleasure, inner harmony, a comfortable life, and social recognition. The two groups of CEOs essentially rated several values—including family security, freedom, and true friendship—the same.

These findings underscore a truism about doing business abroad: What makes a great leader in one culture may not be the same as in another. All the people in this study were CEOs—and, thus, were probably fairly accomplished leaders. Yet the American and Taiwanese CEOs differed, often dramatically, in terms of personality traits and values.

Power and Leadership

Perhaps you've had the unfortunate experience of being in charge of something—only to find that your subordinates ignore your instructions. This underscores a fact of leadership: *A leader without power is really not a leader at all, since he or she has zero chance of influencing anyone to do anything.* Skillful leaders, therefore, know how to build their power bases.

Sources of Power A leader's power can derive from several sources. It most commonly stems, first, from the *position* he or she holds. Positions like sales manager or president have formal authority attached to them, and some positions in the chain of command (like CEO) have more position power than do others (like plant manager). As a leader, you also have power based on your authority to *reward* employees who do well, or to *coerce* or *punish* those who don't. You may have *expert* power and be such an authority in your area that people do what you ask because they respect your expertise. And perhaps you possess *referent* power based on your personal magnetism, so people follow you because of your charisma.

Control over *information* is another important and familiar source of power. Some people in a gatekeeper position (like the president's executive assistant) control access to information—and thereby exercise control and exert power over others. *Experts* (like the computer expert to whom the president turns for advice about logging on for investment advice in a recent TV commercial) are another example. John Kotter points out, however, that power based on information is easily lost, and so those depending on this kind of power must continually cultivate information sources.

gatekeeper ■ *someone who controls access to information or other resources.*

Whatever your source of power, it must be *legitimate* if you want to call yourself a leader. A mugger may have a gun and thus power to threaten your life. However, he or she wouldn't qualify as a leader. Remember, *leading* means influencing people to work willingly toward achieving your or your organization's goals. That is not to say that fear can't be a good thing for leaders—at least occasionally. Here's how Machiavelli summed this up in his book *The Prince*:

> One ought to be both feared and loved, but as it is difficult for the two to go together, it is much safer to be feared than loved, for love is held by a chain of obligation which, men being selfish, is broken whenever it serves their purpose; but fear is maintained by a dread of punishment which never fails.[18]

Command and Control? Power is not an absolute; it's partly in the eye of the beholder. Chester Barnard wrote that managers are essentially powerless unless their followers grant them the authority to lead.[19] It usually doesn't matter how much authority you have (or think you have). What matters is how much authority your followers are willing to accept that you have. You may be charisma-less to most people, but if your subordinates think you're great, that may be all that matters. Similarly, your father, who owns the business, may make you CEO; but if your subordinates don't respect you, your orders may go unfulfilled. You always have to think through how you're going to convince your followers that you have the right to lead them.

The issue of power is especially tricky in today's empowered organizations. Managers increasingly organize around self-managing teams in which the employees control their own activities. Influencing people to get their jobs done by relying too heavily on your own formal authority is thus a dubious tactic. The command and control approach to leadership is increasingly giving way to a more collegial system.

This is even true in situations in which you'd least expect it. For example, General Peter Schoomaker is former commander in chief of the U.S. Special Operations Command (which includes the U.S. Army's Delta Force, the Green Berets, the Rangers, and the Navy Seals). He argues that the traditional military way of issuing orders that soldiers obey unquestioningly is often an outmoded, inaccurate, and dangerous model for leadership today.[20] That's because the armies (and companies) that win today will be those that marshal "creative solutions in ambiguous circumstances"—diffusing ethnic tensions, delivering humanitarian aid, and rescuing U.S. civilians trapped in overseas uprisings. In situations like these, "everybody's got to know how to be a leader."[21]

Beyond the Leadership Foundations Having power and the right skills and traits won't guarantee you'll be a successful leader—they are only a foundation, a precondition. Having them gives you leadership potential.[22] As Kirkpatrick and Locke put it, "Traits only endow people with the potential for leadership. To actualize this potential, additional factors are necessary."[23] The leader must engage in the *behaviors* required to get his or her people to move in the desired direction. Let's turn to leadership style and how leaders behave.

■■■ LEADER BEHAVIORS

"I wouldn't work for him again if he were the last person left on earth" sums up how some people feel about a particularly disagreeable former boss. At the other extreme are those gifted leaders whose employees say, "I'd follow her through a burning building if she asked." What is it about how a leader behaves that triggers such emotions?

Researchers have spent years trying to explain how a leader's style or behavior relates to effectiveness. The assumption underlying most of these studies is that leaders perform two main functions—accomplishing the task and satisfying followers' needs. This assumption makes a good deal of sense. The leader's task-oriented functions include making it clear to subordinates what they must do and then making sure they focus on doing it. The leader's social or people-oriented role is to reduce tension, make the job more pleasant, boost morale, and crystallize and defend the values, attitudes, and beliefs of the group. A number of specific leadership styles and schools of thought are associated with these task and people dimensions.[24] We'll look at them next.

The Ohio State Studies

Research aimed at studying leader behavior began years ago at the Bureau of Business Research at Ohio State University. Ralph Stogdill led this effort for many years. He and his team developed a survey called the Leader Behavior Description Questionnaire (LBDQ), which was then further refined by subsequent researchers.[25] The two leadership styles it measures—consideration and initiating structure—have become synonymous with what experts call The Ohio State Dimensions of Leadership:[26]

- *Consideration.* Leader behavior indicative of mutual trust, friendship, support, respect, and warmth. (Example: "The leader is friendly and approachable.")
- *Initiating structure.* Leader behavior by which the person organizes the work to be done and defines relationships or roles, the channels of communication, and ways of getting jobs done. (Example: "The leader lets group members know what is expected of them.")

The researchers' basic question was, "Which of these styles makes a leader more effective?" The studies here were voluminous, but the results are somewhat inconclusive. That people are more satisfied when they have considerate leaders is not in doubt. The findings led researcher Gary Yukl to conclude, "[I]n most situations, considerate leaders will have more satisfied subordinates."[27] However, while morale is important, it's essential to get high performance, too. Here, considerate leadership is not always the solution. Many considerate leaders had low performing groups. Leaders high in initiating structure often don't fare much better. They often have high-performing groups. However, in one representative study, structuring activities by the leader seemed to trigger employee grievances. Thus, being task-oriented seems to produce low morale.

What explains such inconclusive findings? First—as we'll see in the next section—the style that's right for one situation might be wrong for another; leadership is situational. For example, you might need one style for leading a research team and another for leading a platoon under enemy fire. Second, it's usually not one style or the other but a balance that works best. Even the Ohio State researchers found that leader structure did not trigger grievances (reduce morale) for those leaders who were also very considerate.[28]

In practice, balance is quite important. Leaders particularly have to avoid what some experts call the "country club" leader style: all consideration and no focus on the work.[29]

MANAGEMENT IN ACTION   Herb Kelleher of Southwest

Showing respect for employees, keeping them happy, providing support, and generally being considerate of their material and psychological needs are certainly important. But setting goals and getting things done is what the leader is usually there to do. Leaders such as Herb Kelleher of Southwest Airlines balance supportiveness with a clear expectation that employees are there to get their jobs done. As he says, "I've tried to create a culture of caring for people in the totality of their lives, not just at work. You have to recognize that people are still most important. How you treat them determines how they treat people on the outside."[30] However, he also keeps all of his employees relentlessly focused on the company's cost-cutting goals, and Southwest thus remains a leader in airline efficiency

The University of Michigan Studies

While the Ohio State researchers were working with their LBDQ, Rensis Likert and his team at the University of Michigan were conducting a parallel series of leadership style studies. They identified two leadership styles. Employee-oriented leaders focus on the individuality and personality needs of their employees and emphasize building good interpersonal relationships. Job-centered leaders focus on production and the job's technical aspects. Based on his review of the research results, Likert recommended a balanced approach. He said that supervisors with the best record of performance focus on the human aspects of their subordinates' problems and on endeavoring to build effective work groups with high performance goals.[31]

Other University of Michigan researchers studied what they termed close and general leadership styles. Close supervision is at "one end of a continuum that describes the degree to which a supervisor specifies the roles of subordinates and checks up to see that they comply with these specifications."[32] The laissez-faire leader who follows a completely hands-off policy with subordinates is at the other extreme, while a general leader is toward the middle of the continuum.

It's clear that most people don't like being closely supervised, since close supervision was usually associated with lower employee morale.[33] Yet, in practice, knowing when to put your foot down and when to back off is a continuing leadership dilemma, as the following Management in Action demonstrates.

employee-oriented leader ■ *a leader who focuses on the needs of employees and emphasizes building good interpersonal relationships.*

job-centered leader ■ *a leader who focuses on production and on a job's technical aspects.*

close supervision ■ *a leadership style involving close, hands-on monitoring of subordinates and their work.*

laissez-faire leader ■ *a leader who takes a hands-off approach toward supervising subordinates.*

general leader ■ *a leader who takes a middle-ground approach between close supervision and laissez-faire leadership.*

MANAGEMENT IN ACTION   Close Leadership Style

After the 9/11 attacks, Greg Malever, CEO of Lante Technology Group, tried to be sensitive to his employees' new anxieties.[34] But when an employee brought in a TV so he could watch the news all day, the CEO felt he'd gone too far. "He just plugged into the wall and pulled up the rabbit ears . . . I marched over to his office and told him to turn it off. Enough is enough." And then there is Mr. Bertelli, who runs the Italian luxury goods company Prada. Some Italians call him Toscanaccio, or "rough Tuscan."[35] Angered that some employees were not parking in their assigned factory parking spots, he walked through the lot smashing headlights. Bertelli says he paid to repair the lights—but from that point on, the employees parked in their assigned spots. ■■■

While the Michigan researchers found that close supervision seemed to undermine morale, they found no consistent relationship between closeness of supervision and employee performance. Some "close" leaders had high performing groups, some did not. It was apparent that in some situations, employees did need to have a supervisor specify their roles and carefully check up on them if the work was to get done right. Findings like these further underscored the notion that leaders had to adjust their styles to fit the task.

Participative and Autocratic Styles

Participative and autocratic styles also roughly parallel the basic people and task dimensions; however, they focus on the extent to which the leader lets the followers make decisions themselves rather then unilaterally making the decisions for them. Faced with the need to make a decision, autocratic leaders solve the problem and make the decision alone, using the information available at the time.[36] Participative leaders share the problem with subordinates as a group. Then, together they and their groups generate and evaluate alternatives and try to reach consensus on a solution.[37] Some experts view participation as a continuum, for instance:

- *Autocratic.* . . . The leader makes the decision alone.
- *Consultation.* . . . The leader asks the followers for their opinions and then makes the decision him- or herself.
- *Joint decision.* . . . The leader and followers discuss the problem and make the decision together.

autocratic leader ■ *leader who solves problems and makes the decisions alone, using the information available at the time.*

participative leader ■ *leader who shares the problem with subordinates as a group so that together, they can generate and evaluate alternatives in order to reach consensus on a solution.*

"When the boss isn't around to watch us,
he loads up this screen saver."

- *Delegation. . . .* The leader gives the individual or group the authority and responsibility to make the decision themselves.[38]

Encouraging employees to make and implement decisions affecting their jobs has advantages, and much research supports the wisdom of doing so. For example (as explained in Chapter 4) employees who participate in setting goals tend to set higher goals than the supervisor would normally have assigned.[39] Participation also brings more points of view to bear and can improve the chances that participants will buy into the final decision. Consider the following example of what happened when former Ford CEO Jacques Nasser tried to force through his numerous changes.

MANAGEMENT IN ACTION   Nasser at Ford

With his new performance appraisal system, Nasser wanted about 5% of all managers to get C performance grades each year; two consecutive Cs would mean dismissal. He instituted his new system unilaterally without checking with the managers. Unfortunately, some participatory decision making would have revealed how deeply his employees (and their union) resented the new system. The board soon forced Nasser out as CEO—in part due to the antagonism (and litigation) he triggered with the new system.

In some respects, it's easy to appreciate what Nasser was trying to do. He wanted to propel Ford to a higher level of excellence, and he believed that the new appraisal system would help him to do that. He set a direction and tried to get his employees to follow. Isn't that what leaders are supposed to do? It is. But as one historian put it, "Leadership is always about advancing an agenda, and you aren't likely to achieve that without empathy for other viewpoints."[40] Yet in practice, there are obviously situations (like a sinking ship) where autocrats are exactly what's called for. Here too (as with knowing when to use close supervision or some other leadership style), it seems that great leaders know how to adjust their styles to the needs of the situation.

Are There Gender Differences in Leadership Styles?

Although the number of women in management jobs has risen to almost 40%, barely 2% of top management jobs are held by women.[41] Women like HP's Carly Fiorina are the exception. Most women managers are having trouble breaking into the top ranks. The question is, "Why?"

The evidence suggests that it's not due to some inherent inability of women to lead—hardly a surprising conclusion given leaders such as Elizabeth I, Joan of Arc, Margaret Thatcher, and many successful business leaders. Instead, there are other barriers. Glass ceiling *institutional biases* explain part of the problem: Women often simply don't get access to the same old boy network their male colleagues so easily draw on.

Persistent, *inaccurate stereotypes* are another problem. Managers tend to identify masculine (competitive) characteristics as managerial and feminine (cooperative and communicative) characteristics as nonmanagerial.[42] Women tend to be seen as less capable of being effective managers; men are viewed as better leaders. Another stereotype is that women managers fall apart under pressure, respond impulsively, and have difficulty managing their emotions.[43]

Such stereotypes don't hold up under scrutiny. Studies suggest few measurable differences in the leader behaviors women and men use on the job. Women managers were somewhat more achievement-oriented, and men more candid with coworkers.[44] In another study, the only gender differences found were that women were more understanding than men.[45] Women and men who score high on the need for power (the need to influence other people) tend to behave more like each other than like people with lower power needs.[46]

■ ■ *Carly Fiorina of Hewlett-Packard: one of the very few women in top management jobs.*

How do women managers rate when compared with men? On the job and in joblike work simulations, women managers perform much like men. In actual organizational settings, "Women and men in similar positions receive similar ratings."[47] In an assessment center, in which managers had to perform realistic leadership tasks (such as leading problem-solving groups and making decisions), men and women managers performed similarly. Only in several off-the-job laboratory studies did men score higher in performance.[48]

There was one interesting difference, though. Women often score higher on measures of patience, relationship development, social sensitivity, and communication. And these may be precisely the skills managers will need to manage diversity and the empowered members of self-managing teams.[49]

Transformational Leadership Behavior

Creating a new company from an old one can require a major transformation. As we saw in Chapter 8, doing so often involves massive organizational change. Boundaries must be stripped from between the organization's departments and levels; new, formal, informal, and electronic network-based structures must be installed; and the culture and systems must be changed so that employees are open and willing to learn. Nasser's experience at Ford illustrates what happens when the leader is unable to exercise the leadership needed to transform an organization.

James McGregor Burns wrote a book called *Leadership*, in which he addressed this issue. In it, he argued for a new type of leadership style.[50] Burns argued that all leadership behavior is either *transactional* or *transformational*.[51] Transactional behaviors are "largely oriented toward accomplishing the tasks at hand and at maintaining good relations with those working with the leader [exchanging promises of rewards for performance]."[52] Leader behaviors like initiating structure and consideration, he suggests, are based on quid pro quo transactions: "You do something for me, and I'll do something for you." ("You do this, and you'll get a raise," for instance.) Burns says that this style doesn't work when the task requires inspiring people to want to make a big change.

transactional behaviors ■
leadership actions that focus on accomplishing the tasks at hand and on maintaining good working relationships by exchanging promises of rewards for performance.

Today, leaders of even giant companies like Merrill Lynch must transform their companies, seemingly overnight. In the days following the September 11 attacks, Merrill's new president, E. Stanley O'Neal, swept into action. As Merrill executives streamed from their offices, he ordered them to go to different locations: "We shouldn't be in one place."[53] He organized the effort to find new offices and then pressed on with the launch of the new streamlining and restructuring he'd been working on. He demoted some executives and promoted others. He instituted a review that aimed to cut

$2 billion (10%) of Merrill's expenses. And he put in place a new strategy calling for brokers to focus more on wealthy clients—those worth at least $1 million. Result: He transformed the company.

What Transformational Leaders Do Burns says changes like these require the guidance of transformational leaders. Transformational leadership refers to the process of influencing major changes in the attitudes and assumptions of organization members and building commitment for the organization's mission, objectives and strategies.[54] Transformational leaders are those who bring about "change, innovation, and entrepreneurship."[55] They are responsible for leading a corporate transformation that "recognizes the need for revitalization, creates a new vision, and institutionalizes change."[56]

Transformational leaders have the knack for inspiring their followers to want to make the change and to throw themselves into doing so. Such leaders encourage—and obtain—performance beyond expectations by formulating visions and then inspiring subordinates to pursue them. Transformational leaders cultivate employee acceptance and commitment to those visions.[57] They "attempt to raise the needs of followers and promote dramatic changes in individuals, groups, and organizations."[58]

Perhaps you've worked with such a person. From the vantage point of their followers, transformational leaders come across as charismatic, inspirational, considerate, and stimulating.[59] Specifically, they are:

- *Charismatic.* Employees often idolize and develop strong emotional attachments to them. A typical questionnaire answer is, "I am ready to trust him or her to overcome any obstacle." Charisma isn't an either-or thing; it depends on both the leader and the followers. Just as "beauty is in the eye of the beholder," so too is charisma. "Most [charismatic leadership] theorists now view charisma as the result of follower perceptions and attributions influenced by actual leader traits and behavior, by the context of the leadership situation, and by the individual and collective need of the followers."[60]
- *Inspirational.* "The [transformational] leader passionately communicates a future idealistic organization that can be shared. The leader uses visionary explanations to depict what the employee work group can accomplish."[61] Employees are then motivated to achieve these organizational aims. The transformational leader "provides [a] vision of what lies ahead."[62]
- *Considerate.* The transformational leader treats employees as individuals and stresses developing them in a way that encourages the employees to become all they can be: He or she "treats me as an individual rather than as just a member of the group."
- *Stimulating.* They use *intellectual stimulation.* The transformational leader encourages "employees to approach old and familiar problems in new ways."[63] This enables employees to question their own beliefs and use creative ways to solve problems by themselves: He or she "shows me how to think about problems in new ways."

Using Transformational Leadership The evidence suggests that a transformational leadership style is not just for leaders who want to build learning organizations or to implement major organizational changes. In other words, transformational leadership can also help produce routine change. One study found that successful champions of relatively small-scale technological change (leading the introduction of a new product, for instance) used more transformational leader behaviors than did less successful champions.[64] Another study[65] found that high-performing managers in an express delivery firm used significantly more transformational leader behaviors than did less successful managers.[66] Other findings suggest that transformational leadership was more closely associated with leader effectiveness and employee satisfaction than were transactional styles such as general or laissez-faire leadership.[67] All leaders are responsible for moving their followers forward. To that extent, it appears that most can benefit from transformational-type leadership behaviors. Checklist 10.1 presents these behaviors.

CHECKLIST 10.1 ■ How to Be a Transformational Leader[68]

☑ Articulate a clear and appealing vision.

☑ Explain how the vision can be attained.

☑ Act confident and optimistic.

☑ Express confidence in followers.

☑ Provide opportunities for early successes.

☑ Celebrate successes.

☑ Use dramatic, symbolic actions to emphasize key values.

☑ Lead by example.

☑ Empower people to achieve the vision.

The Level 5 Leadership Style

Is there one style of leadership that can make a good company great? That is one of the questions researchers Jim Collins and Jerry Porras pursue in their book *Built to Last: Successful Habits of Visionary Companies*.[69] Collins and Porras focused on 11 companies that had started out years earlier as "good" (competent, but nothing spectacular) and then ended up in the mid-1990s as "great." The market values of these "good-to-great" companies grew eight to nine times faster than did the stock market as a whole.

What sort of leaders led these good-to-great companies? Collins and Porras found that most good-to-great companies were led by CEOs who exhibited what Collins calls the Level 5 Leadership Style. Figure 10.1 summarizes the main behaviors associated with this style. As you can see, Level 5 leadership is a unique blend of personal humility and professional will. On the one hand, Level 5 leaders are modest, calm, and willing to take the blame when things go wrong. At the same time, they demonstrate an unwavering resolve to do whatever must be done to produce the best long-term results; they not only set high standards, but they also settle for nothing less.

That seems to be the style that epitomizes Dieter Zetsche, the executive DaimlerChrysler sent from Germany to turn around its Chrysler unit. A recent article about him notes that he is tactful ("I would rather talk about what I like than criticize

Personal Humility	Professional Will
Demonstrates a compelling modesty, shunning public adulation, never boastful.	Creates superb results, a clear catalyst in the transition from good to great.
Acts with quiet, calm determination; relies principally on inspired standards, not inspiring charisma, to motivate.	Demonstrates an unwavering resolve to do whatever must be done to produce the best long-term results, no matter how difficult.
Channels ambition into the company not the self; sets up successors for even more greatness in the next generation.	Sets the standard of building an enduring great company; will settle for nothing less.
Looks in the mirror, not out the window, to apportion responsibility for poor results, never blaming other people, external factors, or bad luck.	Looks out the window, not in the mirror, to apportion credit for the success of the company—to other people, external factors, and good luck.

◄ **FIGURE 10–1** ■ ■ ■

The Main Behaviors of Level 5

Source: Jim Collins, "Level 5 Leadership," *Harvard Business Review*, January 2001, p. 73.

► **FIGURE 10–2** ■■■

Six Leadership Styles at a Glance

Source: Daniel Goleman, "Leadership That Gets Results," *Harvard Business Review*, March–April 2000, pp. 82–83.

	Coercive	Authoritative
The leader's distinctive behavior	Demands immediate compliance	Mobilizes people toward a vision
The style in a phrase	"Do what I tell you."	"Come with me."
Underlying emotional intelligence traits	Drive to achieve, initiative, self-control	Self-confidence, empathy, change catalyst
When the style works best	In a crisis, kick-start a turnaround, or with problem employees	When changes require a new vision, or when a clear direction is needed
Overall impact on climate	Negative	Most strongly positive

something"); avoids executive airs ("eat in the employee cafeteria"); is responsive, not aloof ("my style is talking to people and listening . . . "); and likes "schmoozing" (he joked with a small group of reporters for hours).[70] At the same time, Zetsche is certainly no pushover. He has driven Chrysler to slash costs and introduce new, more competitive models.

Leadership Styles and Emotional Intelligence

Some experts argue that a manager's leadership style always reflects, to some extent, his or her level of emotional intelligence. People who score high on emotional intelligence tests usually act self-confidently, are trustworthy, strive to achieve, are culturally sensitive, and are very persuasive. Those scoring low act quite the opposite. A person's emotional intelligence reflects his or her unique mix of the underlying emotional intelligence traits—namely self-confidence, trustworthiness, the need to achieve, cross-cultural sensitivity, and persuasiveness.

A person's emotional intelligence reveals itself in his or her leadership styles. Researchers from the consulting firm Hay/McBer studied a sample of 3,810 executives. They concluded that these executives typically used one or more of six leadership styles in trying to influence their followers (see Figure 10.2): coercive, authoritative, affiliative, democratic, pacesetting, and coaching. Each style emphasizes (for better or worse) different aspects, traits, or facets of the leader's emotional intelligence. For example, the coercive leader is a do-what-I-tell-you leader. This style tends to reflect facets of emotional intelligence such as the drive to achieve and self-control. Democratic leadership taps emotional intelligence facets such as collaboration and communication.

The researchers came to two conclusions. First, "[l]eaders with the best results do not rely on only one leadership style; they use most of them in any given week—seamlessly and in different measure—depending on the business situation." In other words, they use several styles.[71] To the Hay/McBer researchers, the six leader styles are akin to the clubs in a golf pro's bag. "Over the course of a game, the pro picks and chooses clubs based on the demands of the shot."[72] The second conclusion stems from the first: The best style for one situation might not work for another. A golfer wouldn't use a driver to make a putt; nor would he or she use a putter to tee off. You need to fit the style to the situation.

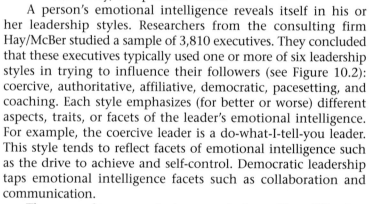

■■■ SITUATIONAL THEORIES OF LEADERSHIP

Two things are clear from the research on leadership traits and styles. First, skills or styles that might be right in one situation may backfire in another. Thus, Jacques Nasser's results with an autocratic style were less than optimal, although the approach

Affiliative	Democratic	Pacesetting	Coaching
Creates harmony and builds emotional bonds	Forges consensus through participation	Sets high standards for performance	Develops people for the future
"People come first."	"What do you think?"	"Do as I do, now."	"Try this."
Empathy, building relationships, communication	Collaboration, team leadership, communication	Conscientiousness, drive to achieve, initiative	Developing others, empathy, self-awareness
To heal rifts in a team or to motivate people during stressful circumstances	To build buy-in or consensus, or to get input from valuable employees	To get quick results from a highly motivated and competent team	To help an employee improve performance or develop long-term strengths
Positive	Positive	Negative	Positive

probably worked for him the past. Second, leaders can use several styles simultaneously: Most managers are (or can be) "multistyled." Andy Pearson illustrates the flexible nature of leadership styles in the following example.

MANAGEMENT IN ACTION Pearson's Management Styles

When he ran PepsiCo, Andy Pearson increased revenues from $1 billion to over $8 billion. He did this through what one writer describes as "fear, surprise, and a fanatical devotion to the numbers."[73] In fact, *Fortune* magazine named him one of the "ten toughest bosses in the United States."

Today, Pearson is running a different kind of company, and he has adapted his leadership style as a result. He runs Yum! Brands, which owns K. F. C., Pizza Hut, and Taco Bell. Yum! Brands' situation calls for a more participative approach. At one recent meeting, "someone suggested opening an all-night restaurant. Pearson doesn't think it would work, but he doesn't say so, at least [not] directly. He finds some nugget of intelligence in the idea, and offers what he sees as 'the challenge.' He says, 'For Kinko's, being open all-night is a big thing.'[74] He goes on to let the person who suggested the idea research the matter more fully." What Pearson is doing now is sharing the decision-making. Same person. Different style.

Of course, the $64 question is this: When and under what conditions do I use one style or another? When should I be people-oriented, and when should I clamp down? When should I let my subordinates participate, and when should I make the decisions myself? Managers obviously must have answers to questions like these. Researchers have studied and put forth several models to help managers decide how to fit their leadership style to the situation. We turn to these models next.

Fiedler's Contingency Theory of Leadership

Working at the University of Illinois, Fred E. Fiedler and his team originally sought to determine whether a leader who was lenient in evaluating associates was more likely or less likely to have a high-producing group than a leader who was demanding and discriminating.[75] He measured leadership style with his Least Preferred Co-worker (LPC) scale. Leaders who describe their least preferred coworker favorably (pleasant, smart, and so on) are "high LPC" and are considered more people-oriented. "Low LPCs" describe least preferred coworkers unfavorably; they're less people-oriented and more task-oriented. Figure 10.3 presents the Fiedler LPC scale. Those scoring high (4.9 or above) on it are high LPCs, whereas those scoring low (1.8 or below) are low LPCs.

According to Fiedler's theory, three situational factors combine to determine whether the high-LPC or the low-LPC style is appropriate:

1. *Leader position power.* The degree to which the position itself enables the leader to get group members to comply with and accept his or her decisions and leadership
2. *Task structure.* How routine and predictable the work group's task is
3. *Leader-member relations.* The extent to which the leader gets along with workers and the extent to which they have confidence in and are loyal to him or her

▶ **FIGURE 10–3** ■ ■ ■

Fiedler's LPC Leadership Scale

Source: Fred E. Fiedler, *A Theory of Leadership Effectiveness* (New York: McGraw-Hill, 1967), p. 41.

Look at the words at both ends of the line before you put in your "X". Please remember that there are *no right or wrong answers*. Work rapidly; your first answer is likely to be the best. Please do not omit any items, and mark each item only once.

LPC

Think of the person *with whom you can work least well.* He or she may be someone you work with now, or he may be someone you knew in the past.

He or she does not have to be the person you like least well, but he or she should be the person with whom you had the most difficulty in getting a job done. Describe this person as he or she appears to you.

Pleasant	8 7 6 5	4 3 2 1	Unpleasant
Friendly	8 7 6 5	4 3 2 1	Unfriendly
Rejecting	1 2 3 4	5 6 7 8	Accepting
Helpful	8 7 6 5	4 3 2 1	Frustrating
Unenthusiastic	1 2 3 4	5 6 7 8	Enthusiastic
Tense	1 2 3 4	5 6 7 8	Relaxed
Distant	1 2 3 4	5 6 7 8	Close
Cold	1 2 3 4	5 6 7 8	Warm
Cooperative	8 7 6 5	4 3 2 1	Uncooperative
Supportive	8 7 6 5	4 3 2 1	Hostile
Boring	1 2 3 4	5 6 7 8	Interesting
Quarrelsome	1 2 3 4	5 6 7 8	Harmonious
Self-assured	8 7 6 5	4 3 2 1	Hesitant
Efficient	8 7 6 5	4 3 2 1	Inefficient
Gloomy	1 2 3 4	5 6 7 8	Cheerful
Open	8 7 6 5	4 3 2 1	Guarded

Fiedler concluded that the appropriateness of the leadership style "is contingent upon the favorableness of the group-task situation."[76] Basically, he argued that where the situation is either favorable or unfavorable for the leader (where leader–member relationships, task structure, and leader position power all are either very high or very low), a more task-oriented, low-LPC leader is appropriate. In favorable situations, the leader could get away with just focusing on the task. In unfavorable situations, the leader basically had no choice but to focus on the task. In the middle range, where these factors are more mixed and the task is not as clear-cut, a more people-oriented, high-LPC leader is appropriate. Of the three situational factors, Fiedler wrote that leader–member relations seem to be the key: "A leader who is liked, accepted, and trusted by his members will find it easy to make his [or her] influence felt."[77] Figure 10.4 summarizes both the relationships involved and how to apply Fiedler's model. Many subsequent research findings produced mixed results, and the usefulness of Fiedler's theory, including its more recent variants, remains in dispute.[78]

Path–Goal Leadership Theory

Path–goal leadership theory assumes that the leader's job is to ensure that followers are motivated to do their jobs, and is based on the *expectancy theory of motivation.* Expectancy theory says that whether a person will be motivated depends on two things: whether the person believes he or she has the *ability* to accomplish a task, and on his or her *desire* to do so.

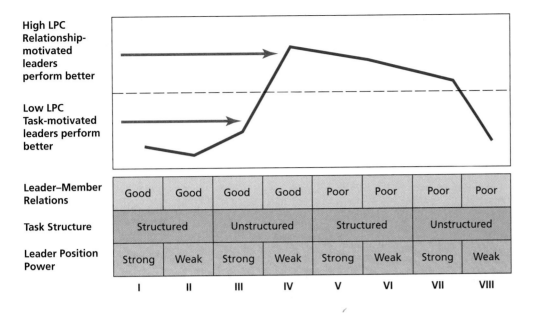

◄ **FIGURE 10–4** ■ ■ ■

How Style of Effective Leadership
Varies with Situation

Source: Adapted and reprinted by permission of the *Harvard Business Review.* "How the Style of Effective Leadership Varies with the Situation" from "Engineer the Job to Fit the Manager" by Fred E. Fiedler, September–October 1965. Copyright © 1965 by the President and Fellows of Harvard College; all rights reserved.

High LPC Relationship-motivated leaders perform better							

Leader–Member Relations

Good	Good	Good	Good	Poor	Poor	Poor	Poor

Task Structure

Structured		Unstructured		Structured		Unstructured	

Leader Position Power

Strong	Weak	Strong	Weak	Strong	Weak	Strong	Weak
I	II	III	IV	V	VI	VII	VIII

Path–goal leadership theory says the leader's job is to increase the personal rewards subordinates receive for attaining goals and to make the path to these goals easier to follow by reducing roadblocks—setting goals, explaining what needs to be done, and organizing the work, for instance. Stripped to its essentials, path–goal theory says this: If the job is ambiguous, structure it. If it is demoralizing or the employees lack confidence, be supportive and considerate. And always make it clear how an effort on the job will lead to rewards.

Leadership expert Robert J. House developed path–goal leadership theory, which originally focused on two leadership styles: the Ohio State LBDQ leader dimensions of consideration and initiating structure.[79] Today, path–goal theory has expanded to focus on four leadership styles: directive leadership, supportive leadership, participative leadership, and achievement-oriented leadership. *Directive leaders* "let subordinates know what is expected of them, give specific guidance as to what should be done and how it should be done," and schedule the work to be done. *Supportive leaders* are "friendly and approachable" and show concern for their followers' status and well-being. *Participative leaders* consult with subordinates and solicit their suggestions. *Achievement-oriented leaders* "set challenging goals, expect subordinates to perform at their highest level . . . [and] continuously seek improvement in performance, and show a high degree of confidence that the subordinates will assume responsibility."[80]

Path–goal theory says that the "right" style of leadership depends on the nature of the task and on the capabilities of the followers. Under this theory, the preferred leadership style, therefore, depends on three things: on the (1) structure of the task, and on the (2) self-confidence and (3) morale of the employees. For example, if subordinates lack confidence in their ability to do the jobs, they may need more consideration and support. Or if subordinates aren't clear about what to do or how to do it, the leader should provide structure (in terms of instructions, for instance), as required.[81] Again, the idea is that if people don't know what to do, or think they can't do it, or don't see how effort leads to rewards, they won't do the job. The theory thus makes a good deal of intuitive sense.

Table 10.2 shows how to apply the theory. In ambiguous, unstructured situations, *directive* leaders have a motivational effect on their followers by reducing ambiguity and by showing followers how their effort will lead to performance and to rewards. For subordinates dealing with frustrating or demoralizing tasks, *supportive* leaders increase self-confidence and make the task more bearable. For challenging but ambiguous tasks, *participative* leaders can help clarify expectations and reduce ambiguity (at least for employees who are not overly frightened by unstructured tasks). Finally, *achievement-oriented* leaders boost employee confidence by clarifying goals when the task is ambiguous and challenging.

TABLE 10–2

Fitting the Style to the Situation with Path–Goal Theory

Leader Behavior	Situational Factors	Motivational Effects
Directive	Ambiguous, unstructured	Reduces role ambiguity; increases follower beliefs that effort will result in good performance and that performance will be rewarded.
Supportive	Frustrating, routine, stressful, or dissatisfying tasks. Employees may lack self-confidence.	Increases self-confidence; increases the personal value of job related effort.
Participative	Ambiguous, nonrepetitive, challenging	Reduces ambiguity, clarifies expectations, increases consistency of subordinate and organizational goals, increases involvement with and commitment to organizational goals.
Achievement-oriented	Ambiguous, nonrepetitive, challenging	Increases subordinate confidence and the personal value of goal-directed effort.

Source: Adapted from Jon Howell and Dan Costley, *Understanding Behavior for Effective Leadership* (Upper Saddle River, New Jersey: Prentice Hall, 2001), p. 43.

Research on path–goal theory has yielded mixed results.[82] As one expert recently noted, "[D]espite the large number of studies that have tested the theory, the results were inconclusive."[83] Most of the evidence regarding fitting directive leadership behavior to the task was not supported, while supportive leadership tends to have a positive relationship with morale regardless of the task. And "not enough studies were available to provide an adequate test of hypotheses about situational moderators of participative and achievement-oriented leadership."[84]

Substitutes for Leadership Theory

Path–goal theory basically suggests that the leader's role is to in some way substitute for the nature of the situation. For example, Robert House (in explaining this theory) essentially says this: If the task is already so routine and structured that it's clear how to do it, then leaders who use a high-initiating structure style will trigger worker resentment. Similarly, the more satisfying the task already is, the less important it is for the leader to be highly considerate and supportive.[85] In other words, leadership (and, in particular, the specific leadership style) is, to some extent, a necessary substitute for the inherent structure and satisfaction of the task.

Steve Kerr and J.M. Jermier propose a "Substitutes for Leadership" theory that expands on this idea.[86] Their theory focuses on the need for two basic leadership styles—supportive/considerate leadership and instrumental/initiating structure leadership. They suggest that various characteristics of the subordinates, the task, and the organization may either *substitute for* (render unnecessary) direct intervention by the leader or *neutralize* (prevent) the leader's best efforts.

Table 10.3 lists these substitutes and neutralizers as well as their likely interplay with each leadership style. For example, if your subordinates are highly professional (you're leading a dedicated team of engineers, for instance), their professional orientation should substitute for (reduce the need for) either supportive or instrumental leadership. The existence of adequate organizational rules and procedures should make structuring that much less necessary.

TABLE 10–3	Specific Substitutes and Neutralizers for Supportive and Instrumental Leadership	

Characteristics that may be Substitute or Neutralizer	Effect on Supportive Leadership	Effect on Instrumental Leadership
A. SUBORDINATE CHARACTERISTICS		
1. Experience, ability, training		Substitute
2. Professional orientation	Substitute	Substitute
3. Indifference toward rewards	Neutralizer	Neutralizer
B. TASK CHARACTERISTICS		
1. Structured, routine task		Substitute
2. Feedback provided by task		Substitute
3. Intrinsically satisfying task	Substitute	
C. ORGANIZATION CHARACTERISTICS		
1. Cohesive work group	Substitute	Substitute
2. Low position power	Neutralizer	Neutralizer
3. Formalization (roles, procedures)		Substitute
4. Inflexibility (rules, policies)		Neutralizer
5. Dispersed subordinate work sites	Neutralizer	Neutralizer

Source: Based on Steve Kerr and J. M. Jermier "Substitutes for Leadership: Their Meaning and Measurement," *Organizational Behavior and Human Performance* 22 (1978); as printed in Gary Yukl, *Leadership in Organizations,* (Upper Saddle River, NJ: Prentice Hall, 1998), p. 274.

This theory has some practical implications. It suggests that as a leader, you can "set the stage" to make your job easier.[87] Here are two examples.

- *Choose the Right Followers.* If you select and train your followers well, there may be less need to exercise leadership on a daily basis. The greater your subordinates' ability, the more their experience, the better their training, and the more professional their behavior, the less direct supervision they will need. Some followers are inherently more effective than others. Choose followers who are cooperative, flexible, and trustworthy and who have initiative and are good at solving problems.[88]
- *Organize the Task Properly.* You may also be able to adjust organizational factors to reduce the need for day-to-day leadership. For example, jobs for which the performance standards are clear or for which there is plenty of built-in feedback may require less leadership.[89] Similarly, employees engaged in work that is intrinsically satisfying (work they love to do) require less leadership.[90] Cohesive work groups with positive norms also require less leadership (as do, by definition, self-managing teams).

Leader–Member Exchange Theory

Although a leader may have one prevailing style, most leaders don't treat all subordinates the same. The leader-member exchange (LMX) theory says that leaders may use different styles with different members of the same work group.[91] In this theory, leaders also adapt their styles to the situation, but it is *the quality of the relationship between the leader and the subordinate* that determines what the situation is.

LMX theory says leaders tend to divide their subordinates into an in group and an out group (and you can guess who gets the better treatment!). What determines whether you're part of a leader's in or out group? The leader usually decides based on very little real information, although perceived leader–member similarities—gender, age, or attitudes, for instance—are usually important.[92]

leader–member exchange (LMX) theory ■ *the theory that leaders may use different leadership styles with different members of the same workgroup, based in part on perceived similarities and differences with the leader.*

One study is illustrative. Researchers received completed attitude surveys from 84 full-time registered nurses and 12 supervisors in 12 work groups at a large hospital in the southern United States.[93] Of the supervisors (leaders), 83% were women, with an average age of 39 years; the nurses (followers) were mostly women (88.1%), with an average age of 36 years. Researchers measured various things, including the strength and quality of leader–member relationships or exchanges (friendliness between leader and member, rewards given to members, and so on).

The leader's perceptions of two things—similarity of leader–follower attitudes and follower extroversion—seemed to determine the quality of leader–member relations. Leaders assessed the similarity between themselves and their followers in terms of attitudes toward six items: family, money, career strategies, goals in life, education, and overall perspective. Leaders were more favorably inclined toward followers with whom they shared similar attitudes. Followers also completed questionnaires that enabled the researchers to label them as introverted or extroverted. The extroverted nurses were more likely to have high-quality leader–member exchanges than were the introverts, presumably because they were more outgoing and sociable in general.

This suggests two practical implications. First, members of the in-group tend to perform better than do those in the out-group, so leaders should strive to make the in-group more inclusive. For followers, the findings underscore the attraction of being in your leader's in-group—and thus the need for emphasizing similarities rather than differences in politics, for instance, and of endeavoring to be sociable.

The Vroom–Jago–Yetton Model

Leadership experts Victor Vroom, Arthur Jago, and Philip Yetton focus on participative leadership styles. They argue that being participative is not an either/or decision, since there are different degrees of participation. They developed a model that enables leaders to analyze a situation and decide how much participation is called for. Their technique consists of three components: (1) A set of management decision styles; (2) a set of diagnostic questions; and (3) a decision tree for identifying how much participation the situation calls for.

The Management Decision Styles We've seen in this chapter that there are degrees of participation. As in Figure 10.5, Vroom and his associates propose a situational model based on a continuum of five decision styles. At one extreme is style AI—no participation. Here, the leader solves the problem and makes the decision alone. GII,

▶ **FIGURE 10–5** ■ ■ ■

Types of Management Decision Styles

AI. You solve the problem or make the decision yourself, using information available to you at that time.

AII. You obtain the necessary information from your subordinates, then decide on the solution to the problem yourself. You may or may not tell your subordinates what the problem is when getting the information from them. The role played by your subordinates in making the decision is clearly one of providing the necessary information to you, rather than generating or evaluating alternative solutions.

CI. You share the problem with relevant subordinates individually, getting their ideas and suggestions without bringing them together as a group. Then you make the decision, which may or may not reflect your subordinates' influence.

CII. You share the problem with your subordinates as a group, collectively obtaining their ideas and suggestions. Then you make the decision, which may or may not reflect your subordinates' influence.

GII. You share a problem with your subordinates as a group. Together, you generate and evaluate alternatives and attempt to reach agreement (consensus) on a solution. Your role is much like that of a chairperson. You do not try to influence the group to adopt "your" solution, and you are willing to accept and implement any solution that has the support of the entire group.

total participation, is at the other extreme. Here, the leader shares the problem with subordinates, and they reach an agreement together. You can see in Figure 10.5 that between these two extremes are style AII, CI, and CII, each with more participation.

The Diagnostic Questions In this leadership model, the appropriate degree of participation depends on several attributes of the situation. The situational attributes include both the importance of the quality of the decision and the extent to which the leader has enough information to make a high-quality decision alone. The manager can assess the presence or absence of these attributes by asking the following sequence of diagnostic questions:

- A. Is there a quality requirement such that one solution is likely to be more rational than another?
- B. Do I have sufficient information to make a high-quality decision?
- C. Is the problem structured?
- D. Is acceptance of the decision by subordinates critical to effective implementation?
- E. If you were to make the decision by yourself, is it reasonably certain that it would be accepted by your subordinates?
- F. Do subordinates share the organizational goals to be obtained in solving this problem?
- G. Is conflict among subordinates likely over preferred solutions?

The Decision Tree The decision tree in Figure 10.6 puts this all together. This chart enables the leader to quickly choose the appropriate degree of participation. By starting on the left of a chart and answering each sequential diagnostic question with a yes or no, you can work your way across the decision tree and determine which leadership style is best. For example, when the problem (A) does not possess a quality requirement (in other words, when the decision is not exceptionally important) and (D) when acceptance of the decision by subordinates is not important for effective implementation, then any of the styles (including the most directive style) would be appropriate. On the other hand, even if there is no particular quality requirement (Question A) but if acceptance of the decision by subordinates is important for implementation (Question D) and it's likely your decision won't be accepted if you make it yourself (Question E), then style GII—sharing the problem with your subordinates as a group—is the way to go.

Studies generally support this model or variations of the model. In one study, Vroom and Jago found an average success rate of about 62% for decisions made in accordance with the model, versus 37% for those that were not.[94] However, remember that this model focuses only on participative leadership; in practice, as we've seen, leaders may have to tap other types of leadership styles, too. For that, other models, like the following one, are available.

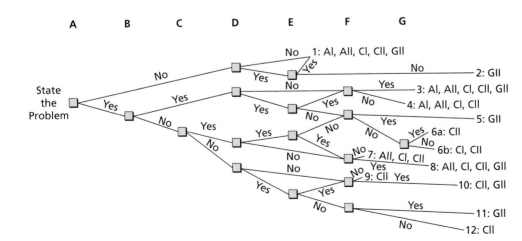

◄ FIGURE 10–6 ■■■

Vroom and Yetton Decision Process Flow Chart

Source: Adapted from *Leadership and Decisionmaking* by Victor H. Vroom and Philip W. Yetton, by permission of the University of Pittsburgh Press. Copyright © 1973 by University of Pittsburgh Press.

The Hersey–Blanchard Situational Leadership Model

The *Situational Leadership model* aims to provide a practical way for a leader to decide how to adapt his or her style to the task.[95] This model focuses on four leadership styles, and was developed by management development experts Paul Hersey and Kenneth Blanchard:

- The *delegating style* lets the members of the group decide what to do.
- The *participating style* asks the members of the group what to do, but makes the final decisions.
- The *selling style* makes the decision but explains the reasons.
- The *telling style* makes the decision and tells the group what to do.

As summarized in Figure 10.7, each style is appropriate in a specific situation:

- Delegating works best when followers are willing to do the job and know how to go about doing it.
- Participating works best when followers are able to do the job but are unwilling and so require emotional support.
- Selling works best when followers are neither willing nor able to do the job.
- Telling works best when followers are willing to do the job but don't know how to do it.

Figure 10.8 provides detailed guidance on what to look for when deciding which style to use. For example:

- **S4:** When followers are "able and willing or confident," a *delegating* leader who turns over responsibility for decisions and implementation is the style of choice. Delegating leaders encourage autonomy, provide support and resources, and delegate activities.
- **S3:** When followers are somewhat less ready to be led—when they are "able but unwilling or insecure"—a *participating style* is best. Participating leaders "share ideas and facilitate the decision making." They share responsibility for decision making with their followers, focus on results, and (where necessary) discuss their followers' apprehensions.
- **S2:** When followers are even less ready to be led—where they are "unable but willing or confident," the *selling style* is best. The selling leader "explains decisions and provides opportunity for clarification." He or she is somewhat less participatory than the previous two leaders. The selling leader seeks to get his or her followers to buy into the decision by persuading them, checks their understanding of the task, encourages questions, explains why, and emphasizes "how-to."
- **S1:** Finally, followers may be relatively unprepared for the task: They are "unable and unwilling, or insecure." This calls for a *telling style*. Here the leader "provides specific instructions and closely supervises performance." The leader's main job here is structuring what employees need to do. The leader provides specific instructions, closely supervises what followers are doing, positively reinforces small improvements, and considers the possibility of instituting some negative consequences for nonperformance.

▶ **FIGURE 10–7** ■■■

Summary of Situational Leadership Model

Source: Jerald Greenberg, *Managing Behaviour in Organizations: Science in Service* (Upper Saddle River, NJ: Prentice Hall, 1996). Reprinted by permission.

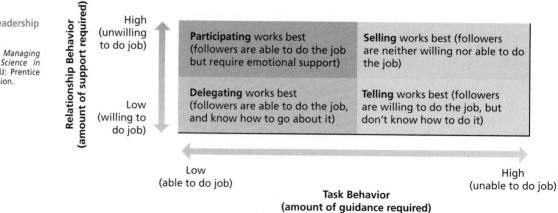

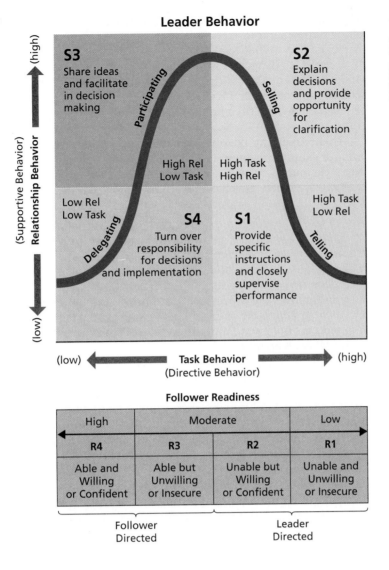

Leader Behavior

S3
Share ideas and facilitate in decision making

Participating

High Rel
Low Task

S2
Explain decisions and provide opportunity for clarification

Selling

High Task
High Rel

Low Rel
Low Task

Delegating

S4
Turn over responsibility for decisions and implementation

S1
Provide specific instructions and closely supervise performance

High Task
Low Rel

Telling

(high) / (low) — (Supportive Behavior) Relationship Behavior

(low) ◄───── **Task Behavior** ─────► (high)
(Directive Behavior)

◄ **FIGURE 10–8** ■ ■ ■

Applying the Situational Leadership Model

Source: Adapted from Paul Hersey, *Situational Selling* (Escondido, CA: Center for Leadership Studies, 1985), p. 19. Reprinted with permission.

Follower Readiness

High	Moderate		Low
R4	R3	R2	R1
Able and Willing or Confident	Able but Unwilling or Insecure	Unable but Willing or Confident	Unable and Unwilling or Insecure

Follower Directed   Leader Directed

■■■ HOW TO IMPROVE YOUR LEADERSHIP SKILLS

Being a leader means taking the steps required to boost your effectiveness at filling the leader's role. No formula can guarantee that you can be a leader. However, based on the research in this chapter, you certainly can improve the chances that in a leadership situation, you will be effective. Doing so requires strengthening your leadership skills, as follows.

Skill 1: How to Think Like a Leader

We've seen in this chapter that there are many tools and models in the leadership tool chest, and many situations in which to apply them. The prudent leader therefore resists acting impulsively. He or she sizes up the situation, and thinks through the options like a leader. Knowing how to think like a leader is thus the first leadership skill.

■ *Application Example* Consider this example. Gus owns an engineering company in New York. He's a genius at what he does, and his company now employs about 200 people, including 80 engineers. Though successful, the firm has a persistent problem. An engineering team will work on a project and send off the proposal, but if the client doesn't like the design, the project team members will just give up and shelve the project. They don't say a word to Gus. Gus, therefore, is often seen storming around the office, yelling, "Why didn't you tell me we didn't get that deal?!"

Unfortunately, all this yelling is getting Gus nowhere. His engineers still avoid telling him when they lose a job, and morale is starting to slip as well. Gus has turned to you for advice. "What can I do to make those irresponsible engineers let me know before these projects fall apart?" is how he puts it. You know Gus faces a leadership dilemma. The question is, What is the problem, and how should he solve it? Are his employees actually "irresponsible"? Is Gus lacking in the traits that effective leaders should have? Is he less participative then he should be? Is the pay scale so low that the engineers simply don't care?

There are many possible explanations, and you don't want to choose the wrong one. For example, being more participative won't help Gus if the problem is not leadership style, but the pay. Nor will it help him if the situation calls for a more "telling" or "selling" approach. Gus has to learn to "think like a leader."

The Process Leadership experts at the U.S. Military Academy (West Point) say that "thinking like a leader" isn't a mysterious talent. In training cadets to be leaders, they suggest a logical and scientific three-step approach. They say the leader should step back and look at the situation he or she is facing, and then (1) *identify what is happening*, (2) *explain why it is happening*, and (3) decide *what you are going to do about it*.[96] Figure 10.9 summarizes the process. Let's see how Gus might apply this three-step process.

What is happening here? In Gus's case, two facts seem clear: For some reason, his engineers are not giving him the bad news. And when he does discover that they've lost a job, he reacts angrily.

Why is it happening? The *what* was simple; the hard part now is *explaining what is happening*. For years, Gus assumed his engineers were irresponsible. However, he's been reading up on leadership, and now he's not so sure. He sees that thinking like a leader involves understanding why something is happening. And he knows that answering that question involves applying leadership, motivation, communications, and teamwork behavioral science theories and concepts. Gus needs to formulate a cause–effect relationship (or hypothesis) between *what* has occurred and *why*. For example, "The engineers here refuse to divulge bad news (the effect) *because* they are punished when they do so by having Gus yell at them (the cause)." The key to solving the leadership problem lies in formulating that cause–effect link.

In figuring out "why is it happening," don't miss the forest for the trees. View the situation as a coherent whole, but at the same time look for logical cause–effect connections. Be logical. Do the engineers know they're doing something wrong? Are they irresponsible? What typically happens when they tell Gus they may have lost the job? How does he react? Are they just reacting to Gus's habit of responding quickly and harshly to any negative news? How does Gus's apparent leadership style enter into the equation?

You may discover that more than one of the leadership or behavioral science concepts covered in this and the next three chapters (Motivation, Communications, and Teams) applies. (For example, perhaps the engineers *are* a bit irresponsible, *and* dissatisfied with their pay, *and* hesitant to expose themselves to Gus's tirades.) Don't be

► **FIGURE 10–9** ■ ■ ■

How to Think Like a Leader

Source: Adapted from Jeffrey A. McNally, Stephen J. Gerra, and R. Craig Bollis, "Teaching Leadership at the U.S. Military Academy at West Point." *Journal of Applied Behavioral Science*, 32:2, p. 178, copyright © 1996 by Sage Publications. Reprinted by permission of Sage Publications.

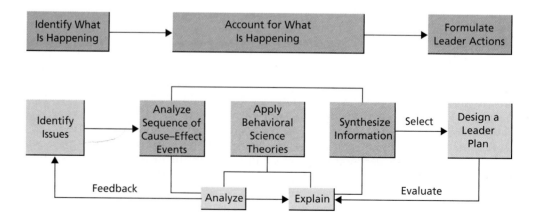

put off if more than one theory or concept helps explain the problem. That is really quite normal. You may combine several possible explanations for what has gone wrong, or choose the one you'll take action on first.

What should I do about it? Once you've answered the questions *What is happening?* and *Why is it happening?*, you can address the question *What should I do about it?* Doing so means applying your knowledge of behavioral science from this and the next three chapters—such as choosing the right leadership style for the situation, or deciding how to motivate your employees, or how to boost their teamwork.

What actions would you take to help resolve Gus's problem? After discussing the situation with you, Gus comes to several conclusions. No doubt, he's been too quick-tempered when people bring him bad news. The engineers know he'll yell at them. So at a minimum, his own temper is something he will have to address. Good possibilities for leadership actions for Gus include:

- *Get some counseling to deal with "emotional intelligence" needs.* In this chapter, we saw that a leader's emotional intelligence—ability to interact in a healthy manner—with subordinates manifests itself in one or more of these leadership styles: *coercive, authoritative, affiliative, democratic, pacesetting,* and *coaching.* Gus's overuse of the coercive, punitive style does not seem to be working. He must recognize why he's behaving that way—and change his behavior.
- *Decide what leadership style is best for this situation.* What do the situational leadership theories tell us about the style Gus should use? The Path–Goal and Substitutes for Leadership theories tell us that Gus's employees are professionals and should be able to manage themselves. Hersey-Blanchard's Situational Leadership Theory suggests that Gus and his engineers are in an "S3"-type situation. The engineers seem "able but unwilling or insecure" about doing their jobs. This model suggests using a "participating" leader style: Gus should "share ideas and facilitate decision making" (for instance, by giving the engineers an opportunity to tap his considerable expertise when they're doing or reworking their proposals).
- *Meet with the engineers* to explain that things are going to be different—and then behave consistently like a high-emotional intelligence manager.
- *Set up a new profit-sharing plan* that rewards engineers partly based on the number of new projects the company sells.

Remember not to limit the behavioral science knowledge you apply to just the material in this chapter. You'll need to apply what you learn in subsequent chapters on motivation, communications, and teams. Fit that knowledge into your assessment of the situation as you account for what is happening and formulate a response. Do not be overwhelmed by the number of theories and concepts that might apply. Instead, think of them as tools in your leadership toolbox. There may well be more than one way to solve the problem.

Skill 2: How to Know What Leadership Style to Use

Most people (like Gus) may well have one prevailing leadership style, but great leaders usually fit their style to the situation. A skillful football coach won't treat a mistake by a new player fresh out of college the way he'd treat the same blunder by a 10-year veteran (at least, not the first time). Leader styles (as noted earlier) are like the clubs in the golf-pro's bag, each appropriate to the situation.

In picking the right style, there are several situational leadership theories to choose from and apply (as you did for Gus). Review Tables 10.2 (page 270) and 10.3 (page 271) to get a sense (from the Path–Goal and Substitutes theories) of whether the situation is already sufficiently structured and/or satisfying that it doesn't warrant additional structure and/or support. Decide if (in line with LMX) you are treating one or two favored employees different from the rest. If the leadership question you face seems to be "to what extent should I let my subordinates participate in making the decision?" apply the Vroom-Jago-Yetton model presented above (Figure 10.6, page 273). If the situation seems to call for a more varied range of leader styles, apply the Hersey-Blanchard model (Figure 10.8, page 275).

Skill 3: How to Pick the Right Leadership Situation

What do you do if you know from experience that (while most people seem to be somewhat flexible) your style is your style and can't be easily changed? (Let us hope the autocratic Gus does not fit in that category.)

One solution is to gravitate toward leadership situations that do fit your favored leadership style. To do this, use the situational leadership models to choose the right situations for your style (rather than to choose a style). For example, suppose you're a more authoritarian, "telling"-type leader. A tough turnaround situation in which your employees can't or won't do their jobs may be right for you, Hersey-Blanchard would say. If you tend to be participatory and to prefer delegating most decisions, then unstructured situations with employees who tend to have the right answers may be best for you, say Vroom, Jago, and Yetton. Similarly, Fiedler suggests recruiting and hiring managers based on the types of situations in which they're expected to lead. He says, "The organization must . . . be aware of the type of leadership situations into which the individual should be successively guided. . . ."[97]

Skill 4: How to Build Your Power Base

Remember that a powerless leader is not a leader at all, because employees must need to or want to follow you. Therefore, bolster your leadership potential by enhancing your authority. How much power do you have, and how can you accumulate more? Managers with more power generally have:

Reward power if they can:

1. Increase pay levels and specific benefits.
2. Control or influence getting a raise or a promotion.

Coercive power if they can:

3. Give undesirable work assignments and make the job difficult or unpleasant.
4. Discipline and/or dismiss employees.

Legitimate position power if they have:

5. A clear position in the chain of command, with unambiguous line authority
6. Clear and visible support of their superiors.
7. Clear and visible support from their peers.

Expert power if they can:

8. Provide needed technical knowledge.
9. Share considerable experience and/or training.
10. Provide sound job-related advice.

Information power if they can:

11. Control access to important information, people, or schedules.

Referent power if they can:

12. Exercise emotional intelligence.
13. Use the right leadership style for the situation.
14. Be transformational and charismatic by articulating a clear and appealing vision; by explaining how the vision can be attained; by acting confident and optimistic; by expressing confidence in followers; by providing opportunities for early successes; by celebrating successes; by using dramatic, symbolic actions to emphasize key values; and by leading by example.
15. Exercise good judgment.

Skill 5: How to Exercise Better Judgment

No one wants to be led by someone who keeps making bad decisions. Decisiveness and good judgment ("cognitive ability") are thus important leadership traits. In Chapter 3, we saw that the following steps can improve your judgment:

1. *Correctly define the problem.* Don't install new elevators when mirrors will do!
2. *Clarify your objectives.* To do this, write down all the concerns you hope to address through your decision; convert your concerns into succinct objectives; separate ends from means to establish your fundamental objectives; clarify what you mean by each objective; and test your objectives to see if they capture your interests.
3. *Identify the alternatives.*
4. *Analyze the alternatives;* use a consequences matrix.
5. *Make a choice,* weighing the pros and cons with a decision matrix.
6. *And, remember these hints:*

   - *Increase your knowledge.* The more you know about the problem and the more facts you can marshal, the better the decision.
   - *Free your judgment of bias.* Cognitive or decision-making biases can distort a manager's judgment. Reducing or eliminating biases like stereotyping is therefore a crucial step toward making better decisions.
   - *Be creative.* The ability to develop novel responses—creativity—is essential for decision-making activities like developing new alternatives and correctly defining the problem.
   - *Use your intuition.* A preoccupation with analyzing problems rationally and logically can sometimes backfire by blocking someone from using his or her intuition.
   - *Don't overstress the finality of your decision.* Remember that very few decisions are forever; there is more give in more decisions than we realize.
   - *Make sure the timing is right.* Passing moods affect decisions. Decision makers should therefore, consider their emotions before making important decisions. Don't do anything impulsively.

Skill 6: How to Improve Your Other Leadership Traits and Skills

We saw that leaders have traits that distinguish them from nonleaders and that these traits are not set in stone. Just as you can improve your cognitive ability, leaders can develop and cultivate these leadership traits.

For example, leaders exhibit *self-confidence.* Although developing self-confidence is a lifelong process, you can enhance yours in several ways. Gravitate toward situations in which you're already more self-confident, such as those in which you are an expert. (As someone once said, "Knowledge is power." A stamp collector might exhibit more self-confidence as president of his or her stamp club than in coaching a baseball team, for instance.) Act like a leader: Make decisions and stick with them—and act somewhat reserved. Display *honesty and integrity;* apply high ethical standards to everything you do.

Your *knowledge of the business* is among the easiest traits to modify. Immerse yourself in the details of your new job. Learn as much about the business as you can and as fast as you can.

SUMMARY ■■■

1. Leadership means influencing others to work willingly toward achieving objectives. Being a leader requires more than having a command of leadership theories. It also means motivating employees; managing groups, teams, and conflict; and facilitating communications.

2. To be a leader, one must also have the potential to be a leader. Some traits on which leaders differ from nonleaders include drive, the desire to lead, honesty and integrity, self-confidence, cognitive ability, and knowledge of the business.

3. Legitimate power and authority are elements in the foundation of leadership, because a leader without power is not a leader at all. Sources of leader power include position, rewards, coercion, expertise, and referent power or personal magnetism.

4. Leadership style or behaviors include structuring and considerate styles, participative and autocratic styles, employee-centered and production-centered styles, close and general styles, and transformational behavior.

5. Although there are some differences in the way men and women lead, they do not account for the slower career progress of most women managers. Institutional biases such as the glass ceiling and persistent, inaccurate stereotypes are contributing factors.

6. Situational leadership theories like those of Fiedler, Vroom, House, and Hersey–Blanchard underscore the importance of fitting the style to the situation.

7. Thinking like a leader means reviewing a situation and *identifying* what is happening, *explaining* what is happening (in terms of leadership and other behavioral science theories and concepts), and *formulating* leader actions.

SKILLS AND STUDY MATERIALS

COMPANION WEBSITE ■■■

 We invite you to visit the Dessler Companion Website at **www.prenhall.com/dessler** for this chapter's Internet resources.

EXPERIENTIAL EXERCISES ■■■

1. Several years ago, *Fortune* magazine traced the concept of leadership over the twentieth century by decade. The point was that each era gives rise to its own popular vision of what leadership means. In the early 1900s, industrialists and bankers like J. P. Morgan epitomized leadership. In the 1910s, it was "the government as regulator," such as the government's leadership role in breaking up the Standard Oil Company. By the 1920s, leadership meant celebrities such as Charles Lindbergh, with their media-driven prominence. The union worker led the Depression-era 1930s. In the 1940s, the United States led the rebuilding of Europe. In the 1950s, it was the Organization Man or the "man in the gray flannel suit" who represented the cadres of managers working diligently to build the era's great companies. By the 1960s, the conglomerators who led the building of huge companies of the era like Gulf & Western symbolized the times. Women emerged as leaders in the 1970s. In the 1980s the MBA consultant was the leader. In the decade of the 1990s, the e-leaders such as Jeff Bezos of Amazon.com reinvented old business models for a wired world.

   In teams of 4–5 students, think about what will epitomize leadership in the 2000s, 2010s, 2020s, and 2030s. Base your thinking on what the book discussed to this point and on your knowledge of current events. What implications do your conclusions have for the career you choose?

2. Leaders come in all backgrounds, genders, and races. Your task is to meet in teams of 4–5 students, to discuss the following people, and then to write a brief, one-page analysis of what has made them effective (or less than effective) as leaders. The people are President George W. Bush; former Vice President Al Gore; Reverend Jesse Jackson; Senator Hillary Clinton; and Microsoft Chairman Bill Gates.

3. Some people say that being a great professor requires having great leadership skills, insofar as teaching a class and dealing effectively with students is a challenging leadership situation. In teams of 4–5 students, answer these questions: Do you agree that being a great professor requires leadership? Why or why not? If the answer is yes, list the leadership traits and skills you believe a professor should have. Finally, use one or more of the situational leadership theories from this chapter to describe the leadership style that is right for the professor in this class.

CASE STUDY ■■■

TURNING AROUND THE U.S.S. *BENFOLD*

While "leadership" may seem a little theoretical in some situations, that's certainly not the case when it comes to the U.S. Navy. When you're the captain of the ship, the lives of all the people on that ship are in your hands. Leadership style can have a corrosive effect on sailors' morale and on their—and the ship's—performance.

For several years, in fact, the U.S. military was in what one officer calls "deep trouble." Commander Mike Abrashoff says, "People aren't joining. More people are leaving. The attrition rates are going through the roof. In the navy, 33% of those who join never complete their first tour of duty. Combat readiness is declining."[98] Given those trends, Commander Abrashoff's experience in instituting a new leadership initiative when he took over as captain of the U.S.S. *Benfold* is all the more remarkable. In the two years he was leading the ship, the *Benfold* retention rate went from about 25% to 100% in most of the ship's top job categories. Attrition went from more than 18% to less than 1%, and mission-degrading casualties dropped from 75 to 24. During his final 12 months in command, the ship even ran on 75% of its operating budget, and returned millions of dollars to the navy. How did he do it?

To a large extent, this turnaround in attitudes was a consequence of a remarkably simple initiative on Abrashoff's part: He brought a new leadership style to the U.S.S. *Benfold* when he took command. Abrashoff says that when he took over, he decided right away that before he could fix the problems on the ship, he had to find out what those problems were. He started his command by interviewing every crew member individually. He'd start each interview with several questions, such as "Where are you from?" "Why did you join the navy?" "What are your goals in the navy?" "What are your goals in life?" Then he asked three more questions: "What do you like most about the *Benfold*?" "What do you like least?" "What things would you change if you could?"

As Abrashoff puts it, "The minute I started these interviews, our performance took off like a rocket. Whenever I got an outstanding idea from a sailor—and about 70% of the ideas that I got were, in fact, outstanding—I would implement that idea right on the spot."[99] He used the public address system to tell the rest of the crew what the new idea was, which sailor the idea came from, and that he was implementing it immediately and needed their support in doing so.

Mike Abrashoff says that whenever he needed a reminder about what leadership was all about, he took out an index card he kept in his wallet. On the card were the eight leadership traits he always used as personal guidelines: A leader is trusted. A leader takes the initiative. A leader uses good judgment. A leader speaks with authority. A leader strengthens others. A leader is optimistic and enthusiastic. A leader never compromises his absolutes. A leader leads by example.[100]

Questions

1. How would you describe Commander Abrashoff's leadership style in comparison with the leadership styles described in this chapter?

2. Abrashoff's index card contains eight leadership traits. How do these eight traits compare with the foundation traits of leadership covered in this chapter? In what ways are they similar? Different?

3. Which situational leadership theories would you have applied in Abrashoff's situation? Apply one of those theories, and explain why you believe his leadership style is (or is not) right for the situation.

4. In addressing the problems on the U.S.S. *Benfold*, did Abrashoff think like a leader? Explain your answer.

5. As ship's captain, Abrashoff has about as much authority as any leader anywhere. With all that power, why (if at all) does he even have to be concerned with his leadership style? Can't he just count on giving orders and having them obeyed? Why?

JETBLUE LEADERSHIP

jetBlue AIRWAYS® To ask whether David Neeleman is an effective leader is probably unnecessary. You don't start and manage three very successful airline businesses before you're 40 if you don't have what it takes to be a leader. Particularly during the start-up period, it's the leader, by force of his or her personality and vision, who keeps the firm's employees focused. There is no doubt that Neeleman has done this not once but three times. As one person who knows him says, "He's low-key, and he's totally directed." One business writer, watching him make a presentation, said, "The man can be completely, utterly riveting."[101]

However, he does not just have a "just decide and give orders" directive style. For example, at an employee orientation for new baggage handlers, he carefully explained JetBlue's philosophy, including how JetBlue can make money when the big airlines don't. He shared details about the company's plans, and he answered personal questions. He spends most of his time when he flies JetBlue talking to customers and crew.[102] He talks to flight attendants and passengers to find out their concerns and solicits their comments, and he spends time walking through the cabin helping to serve snacks. He spends time in the cabin with the pilots, and back at the airport, he works with the baggage handlers "throwing bags."

An incident after 9/11 helps provide some more insight into Neeleman's leadership approach. The decision to make was, "What should our first response be with respect to communicating with the flying public?" Neeleman's first reaction was to draft a personal letter from him and run it as a full-page ad. However, his team thought the message was a bit too personal. Other airlines were placing ads that basically tried to convince the flying public that it was patriotic to fly and important to show that "we're not afraid to fly." Neeleman's feeling was that his personal letter was the way to go—and that this was the perfect time to publicize JetBlue's low price fares. But as driven as he is as an entrepreneur, Neeleman went with his team's advice. As he says, "I'm being patient because I think the situation demands it. I have to trust the instincts of the people around me."[103]

Assignment

You and your team are consultants to Mr. Neeleman, who is depending on your management expertise to help in navigating the launch and management of JetBlue. Here's what he wants to know from you now:

1. Do you think I have the traits and skills to be a leader? Specifically, why or why not in terms of leadership models and theory?

2. What leadership style did I use with respect to the decision to make our first response after 9/11? Do you think I used the right style? Use one or more of the leadership theories in this chapter to explain why you think I did or did not use the right style.

3. What do some of the other incidents in the case tell you about the other leadership styles I typically use? What do you think my prevailing style is? Why?

11 Influencing Individual Behavior and Motivation

CHAPTER OBJECTIVES

After studying this chapter and the case exercises at the end, you should be able to:

1. Explain to the manager why the pay-for-performance incentive plan is not working.

2. Explain to the manager why his or her attempts to empower the employees have been ineffective.

3. Determine if the job is amenable to job enrichment and explain in detail how to enrich it.

4. Develop a behavior management program for the job in question.

5. Analyze the performance problem and recommend how to solve it.

THE MANAGEMENT CHALLENGE

Gordon Bethune Turns Continental Around

When he became CEO of Continental Airlines in the mid-1990s, Gordon Bethune faced a daunting task. Continental was close to bankruptcy, with annual losses of over $600 million. In terms of industry standards like "on-time departures," his firm was a perpetual also-ran. Continental had reached this state of affairs in part by following a cost-cutting strategy. In the 1980s, for instance, former CEO Frank Lorenzo had broken union agreements, slashed costs, and emerged from bankruptcy with the lowest labor costs in the airline industry.[1] Unfortunately, a deeply demoralized workforce was the downside of this strategy.

Bethune knew he had to jump-start Continental's performance. But what could he do—quickly—to get the firm's now-35,000-plus employees to buy into the need to improve? Another CEO might have said, "Let's just cut costs further." Bethune's solution was to build his strategy around his employees—and to begin by instituting new motivation plans. The question was, "Which plans, and how to institute them?"

Planning and organizing are useless if your employees won't do their jobs—or won't do them well. Managers thus need motivational skills. Psychologists define motivation as the intensity of a person's desire to engage in some activity. Motivating employees is part of a manager's leadership activities. We focused on leadership traits and skills in the previous chapter. The purpose of this chapter is to show you how to motivate employees. The main topics we'll cover include what managers should know about individual behavior; need-based, process, and learning/reinforcement approaches to motivation; and how to apply motivation theories in practice.

motivation ■ the intensity of a person's desire to engage in some activity.

■■■ YOU ARE A MOTIVATION EXPERT

The question "How should I motivate people?" underlies almost everything managers do. Every time you set a goal, delegate a task, or set out to lead a new department, you will have to draw on your knowledge of how to motivate employees. Luckily, like most people, you are already something of a motivation expert. Let's see what you already know.

■ Application Exercise

1. *You know what sorts of activities motivate you.* Ask yourself, "What are the things I am driven to do, just because I *want* to do them?" From the time he was four, Charles (not his real name, but a true story nevertheless) watched the street-cleaning machines with their rotating brushes move through his neighborhood, sweeping the gutters clean. When he turned 18, Charles knew what job he wanted. He was soon driving one of those cleaners. Things like hobbies and the job you love are things you'd gladly do for hours each day, even if you were not paid to do them or were paid less than on a different job. You are *motivated* to do them—and doing them motivates you.

2. *You know why they motivate you.* Most people (thank goodness) don't sit around asking themselves *why* they're doing the things they love; they just do them. But if you did ask why you do the things you love, you'd probably have a good answer. Chances are, when you ask yourself, "Why do I love to do the things I love to do?" the answer has a lot to do with the feedback you get from doing them. It may be the built-in satisfaction you get from doing the task or the feedback you get from your peers (or both). In any case, these activities motivate you because the feedback you get from doing them makes you feel good.

3. *You know that different things motivate different people.* George is a well-known lawyer who is respected in his field. He is ordinary—except for about a week before the NFL draft. During that week, George goes incommunicado. He buys and downloads all of the rosters, lists, and scouting reports he can find, and he lays them all out on his living room floor. Then he spends days assessing all the collegiate prospects and each NFL team's needs. His aim is to predict the actual draft choices the teams will make on draft day. The point of this (true) story is this: You know that the things that will motivate one person might not motivate another. Different people have different needs, and so it takes different things to satisfy different people. John might happily work nights for an extra $2,000. George thinks nothing of foregoing twice that amount to put together his roster.

4. *You know how to motivate people.* Most people become motivation experts when they are about two minutes old. Infants instinctively "know" exactly how to motivate their parents. The sequence goes something like this: I'm hungry; I cry; they feed me. As an adult, you naturally know even more about how to motivate people. Here are some things you already know: that people don't like to be punished; that people do like to get rewards; that people are motivated by the feedback they get by doing jobs they love to do; that people like doing what they like to do; that people probably won't even bother trying to do things that they know (or believe) they can't do; that (as noted in 3) you have to appeal to the person's needs if you want to motivate him or her; and that some needs are more important to some people than they are to others.

WHAT MANAGERS SHOULD KNOW ABOUT INDIVIDUAL BEHAVIOR

law of individual differences ■ *a psychological term representing the fact that people differ in their personalities, abilities, self-concept, values, and needs.*

In terms of motivation, you know that any stimulus—an order from the boss, an offer of a raise, or the threat of being fired—has different effects on different people. John might jump whenever the boss gives orders, while Jane might laugh them off.

These behavioral differences reflect what psychologists call the law of individual differences—in other words, the fact that people differ in personalities, abilities, self-concept, values, and needs. As illustrated in Figure 11.1, these factors act much like filters, adding to, detracting from, and often distorting the effect of any stimulus. Psychologists have taken three main approaches to studying what motivates people: These are the need-based, process-based, and learning/reinforcement-based approaches. However, so we can understand these theories better, let's first review the factors that influence individual behavior.

Personality and Behavior

Personality is probably the first thing that comes to mind when you think about what determines behavior. We tend to classify people as introverted, dominant, mature, or paranoid, for instance, and these labels invoke images of particular kinds of behavior.

personality ■ *the characteristic and distinctive traits of an individual, and the way these traits interact to help or hinder the adjustment of the person to other people and situations.*

Personality Defined Many psychologists would define personality as "the characteristic and distinctive traits of an individual, and the way the traits interact to help or hinder the adjustment of the person to other people and situations." They assume that everyone possesses traits like friendliness or aggressiveness to some degree, and that these traits are the basis for who the person "is" and how he or she behaves.

What the basic traits are (and even how many there are) is a matter of some dispute. Psychologist Raymond Cattell used observations and questionnaires to identify 16 primary personality traits, which he then expressed in pairs of words, such as submissive/dominant, and trusting/suspicious.[2] Based on this work, Cattell and his colleagues developed a questionnaire that produced a personality profile for individuals. Figure 11.2 presents a classic example. It shows the average personality profiles for people in two sample occupational groups: airline pilots and business executives.

On the other hand, psychologists today often emphasize the "big five" personality dimensions as they apply to behavior at work: extraversion, emotional stability, agreeableness, conscientiousness, and openness to experience. Many studies lead psychologists to conclude that these five traits represent the fundamental structure of personality—and thus influence how the person behaves.[3] For example, in one study of police officers, professionals, managers, sales workers, and unskilled and semiskilled workers, *conscientiousness* showed a consistent relationship with all job performance criteria for all occupations. *Extraversion* was tied to performance for managers and sales employees, two occupations which involve much social interaction.[4]

authoritarian personality ■ *a personality type characterized by rigidity, intolerance of ambiguity, the tendency to stereotype others as being good or bad, and conformity to the requirements of authority.*

As noted, personality traits are important in part because they mold how people behave—the person is "extraverted," or "conscientious," for instance. At work, you will encounter many unique personalities (each supposedly growing out of a unique mix of traits). For example, the authoritarian personality is rigid, intolerant of ambiguity, tends to stereotype people as good or bad, and conforms to the requirements of

▶ **FIGURE 11–1** ■ ■ ■

Some Individual Determinants of Behavior

A particular stimulus may evoke different behaviors among individuals, because each person's values, personality, self-concept, abilities, and needs influence how he or she reacts.

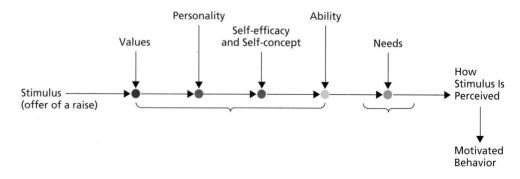

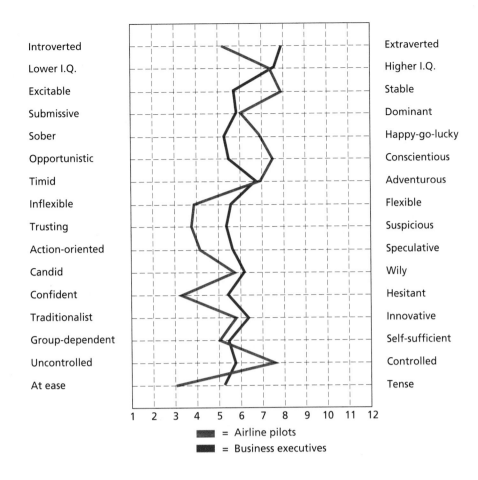

Introverted														Extraverted
Lower I.Q.														Higher I.Q.
Excitable														Stable
Submissive														Dominant
Sober														Happy-go-lucky
Opportunistic														Conscientious
Timid														Adventurous
Inflexible														Flexible
Trusting														Suspicious
Action-oriented														Speculative
Candid														Wily
Confident														Hesitant
Traditionalist														Innovative
Group-dependent														Self-sufficient
Uncontrolled														Controlled
At ease														Tense

1 2 3 4 5 6 7 8 9 10 11 12

= Airline pilots
= Business executives

◀ FIGURE 11–2 ■ ■ ■

Cattell's 16 Personality Factors

The personalities of various people and even various groups of people are characterized by particular packages of traits, such as introverted, dominant, excitable, and innovative.

Source: Adapted from Gregory Northcraft and Margaret Neale, *Organizational Behavior* (Fort Worth, TX: Dryden Press, 1994), p. 87.

authority, perhaps while being dictatorial to subordinates. The **Machiavellian personality** (the name refers to the writings of the sixteenth-century Italian political advisor Niccolò Machiavelli) tends to be oriented toward manipulation and control, with a low sensitivity to the needs of others.[5]

Machiavellian personality ■ *a personality type oriented toward manipulation and control, with a low sensitivity to the needs of others, the name of which refers to the sixteenth-century political advisor Niccolò Machiavelli.*

Measuring Personality The Myers-Briggs Type Indicator (MBTI) is one popular tool for measuring personality, particularly in the work setting. The MBTI classifies people as extraverted or introverted (E or I), sensing or intuitive (S or N), thinking or feeling (T or F), and perceiving or judging (P or J). The MBTI questionnaire classifies people into 16 different personality types (a 4 × 4 matrix); these 16 types are, in turn, classified into one of four cognitive (thinking or problem-solving) styles:

- ■ Sensation–thinking (ST)
- ■ Intuition–thinking (NT)
- ■ Sensation–feeling (SF)
- ■ Intuition–feeling (NF)

Classifying personality types and cognitive styles in this way has several applications. Some employers match the MBTI styles to particular occupations. Figure 11.3 illustrates this. People with the ST approach to problem solving are often well suited to occupations like auditor and safety engineer, for instance.

Abilities and Behavior

Of course, personality traits don't by themselves determine how a person will behave; for instance, a conscientious but unskilled individual may not be a high performer. Therefore, individual differences in abilities also influence how we behave and perform.[6] Even the most highly motivated person will not perform well unless he or she also has the ability to do the job. Conversely, the most able employee will not perform satisfactorily if not motivated. In other words, Performance = Ability × Motivation.

	Thinking Style	Feeling Style
Sensation Style	People with this combined thinking/sensation style tend to be *thorough*, *logical*, and *practical* and to make good *CPAs* or *safety engineers*.	People with this combined sensation/feeling style tend to be *conscientious* and *responsible* and to make *good social workers* and *drug supervisors*.
Intuitive Style	People with this combined intuitive/thinking style tend to be *creative*, *independent*, and *critical* and to make good *systems analysts*, *professors*, and *lawyers*.	People with this combined intuitive/feeling style tend to be *people-oriented*, sociable, and often *charismatic* and to make good *human resource managers*, *public relations directors*, and *politicians*.

There are several types of abilities. Mental, cognitive, or thinking abilities include intelligence and its building blocks, such as memory, inductive reasoning, and verbal comprehension. Mechanical ability would be important for mechanical engineers or machinists. Psychomotor abilities include dexterity, manipulative ability, eye–hand coordination, and motor ability. Such abilities might be important for employees who put together delicate computer components or who work as dealers in Las Vegas. People also differ in visual skills—for example, in their ability to discriminate between colors and between black and white detail.

In addition to these general abilities, people also have specific abilities learned through training, experience, or education. Companies test for these abilities when they are interested in assessing proficiency for jobs such as computer programmer or chemical engineer.

Self-Concept and Behavior

self-concept ■ *the perceptions people have of themselves and their relationships to people and other aspects of life.*

Humanist psychologists like Carl Rogers emphasize the role of self-concept in personality and behavior. They argue that who we are and how we behave is largely driven by our perceptions of who we are and how we relate to other people. For example, psychologist Saul Gellerman says we are all driven to become and to be treated as the kinds of people we think we should be.[7] Self-concept, therefore, looms large as a determinant of motivation and behavior for humanist psychologists.

Some people have rigid self-concepts and can't modify how they view themselves, even in the face of contrary evidence.[8] Turn the person down for a raise, and he'll write it off as office politics or as your incompetence (not his). To some degree, everyone tries to protect his or her self-concept. However, most psychologists would probably agree that "people with healthy self-concepts can allow new experiences into their lives and can accept or reject them."[9]

self-efficacy ■ *being able to influence important aspects of one's world; the belief that one can accomplish what one sets out to do.*

Self-efficacy—a person's belief about his or her capacity to perform a task—is part of self-concept.[10] Self-efficacy affects how people perform and even whether they try to accomplish a task. Research shows that self-efficacy is associated with work performance in a wide range of settings: life insurance sales, faculty research productivity, career choice, learning and achievement, and adaptability to new technology, to name a few.[11]

Perception and Behavior

perceptions ■ *how our personalities and experiences cause us to interpret stimuli.*

We all react to stimuli that reach us via our sense organs. However, how we define or perceive these stimuli reflects our experiences and our needs and personalities.[12] In other words, our behavior is motivated by our perceptions of those stimuli, by the way our personalities and experiences cause us to interpret them.

Perception obviously affects how we see inanimate objects. When we look down a row of arches, as in Figure 11.4, the farthest one looks smaller than the closest one, and its perspective size is, in fact, smaller (because it is farthest away). Based on experience,

◀ FIGURE 11–4 ■ ■ ■

Perception affects how we "see" the arches' sizes.

The farthest arch looks to be about one-third the size of the closest, but we know they're actually the same size.

however, we know that the arches are actually equal in size. Therefore, what we perceive is a compromise between the perspective size of the arch and its actual size. *Our desire to see objects as we expect them to be causes us to perceive things as we expect them to be.*

The same phenomenon applies to work relationships. For example, some people associate characteristics like industriousness and honesty with certain socioeconomic classes, but not with others, a process called stereotyping. We tend to stereotype people according to age, gender, race, or national origin. We then attribute the characteristics of this stereotype to everyone we meet who is of that age, gender, race, or national origin.[13]

Perceptions depend on many things, including *personality and needs*. For example, an insecure employee might think an upcoming meeting is about his being fired, although it actually involves vacation schedules. *Self-efficacy*, *values* (such as a strong personal code of ethics), *stress*, and one's *position* in the company are some other things that influence perception.

stereotyping ■ *associating certain characteristics with certain socioeconomic classes but not with others.*

Attitudes and Behavior

When people say things like "I like my job" or "I don't care about my job," they are expressing attitudes. An attitude is a tendency to respond to objects, people, or events in either a positive or negative way.[14] Attitudes are important because they can influence how people behave on the job.

Job satisfaction is probably the most familiar example of attitudes at work. It is "an evaluative judgment about one's job . . ."[15] One popular job satisfaction survey, the Job Descriptive Index, measures the following five aspects of job satisfaction:

attitude ■ *a predisposition to respond to objects, people, or events in either a positive or negative way.*

job satisfaction ■ *the measure of an employee's attitude about his or her job.*

1. *Pay.* How much pay is received, and is it perceived as equitable?
2. *Job.* Are tasks interesting? Are opportunities provided for learning and for accepting responsibility?
3. *Promotional opportunities.* Are promotions and opportunities to advance available and fair?
4. *Supervisor.* Does the supervisor demonstrate interest in and concern about employees?
5. *Coworkers.* Are coworkers friendly, competent, and supportive?[16]

Good (or bad) attitudes can but do not necessarily translate into good (or bad) performance.[17] For example, dissatisfied engineers may continue to do their best because their performance may be governed by their professional standards.

In summary, a person's behavior depends on many things, including his or her personality, abilities, self-concept, values, and attitudes; motivation explains only part of why people behave as they do. However, motivating employees is always a key to a manager's success. Let's, therefore, now turn to the three main approaches to studying motivation, and how to apply them.

■■■ NEED-BASED APPROACHES TO MOTIVATION

The defense attorney paced back and forth in front of the jury and asked, "Ladies and gentlemen, what possible motive would my client have for committing this crime?" That question is crucial: After all, if there's no motive, then why do it?

A **motive** is something that incites the person to action or that sustains and gives direction to action.[18] When we ask why a defendant might have done what he did, or why a football player works to stay in shape all year, or why a sales manager flies all night to meet with a client, we are asking about motives.

Motives play a central role at work. Gordon Bethune knew he couldn't turn Continental around unless he gave his employees a reason (a motive) to work harder. When professional baseball players threatened to go on strike, the owners scramble to understand their motives and to give them a reason not to leave the game.

A motive can be aroused or unaroused. Everyone carries within him or her **motivational dispositions** or **needs**—motives that, like seeds in winter, go unaroused until the proper conditions bring them forth. You may have a motivational disposition to enjoy yourself at the movies, but that motive is dormant until Saturday night, when you can put your studies aside. **Aroused motives** are motives that express themselves in behavior.[19] When the conditions are right—when the studies are over, the quiz is done, and the weekend arrives—the movie-attendance motive is aroused, and you may be off to see your favorite film.

Need-based approaches to motivation focus on how needs (or motivational dispositions) drive people to do what they do. Which needs or motivational dispositions are most important? How and under what conditions do they become aroused and transformed into behavior? These are the sorts of questions studied by psychologists like Abraham Maslow, David McClelland, and Frederick Herzberg.

Maslow's Needs-Hierarchy Theory

Maslow's needs hierarchy is typical of need-based approaches, and is also the basis for the other approaches discussed in this section. Abraham Maslow argued that people have a hierarchy of five increasingly higher-level needs: physiological, security, social, self-esteem, and self-actualization. According to his *prepotency process principle*, people are motivated first to satisfy the lower-order needs and then, in sequence, each of the higher-order needs.[20]

We usually envision Maslow's hierarchy as a stepladder or pyramid, as in Figure 11.5. The satisfaction of lower-level needs triggers the potency of the higher-order needs.[21] The higher-level needs aren't too important in motivating behavior unless the lower-level needs are pretty well satisfied.

That's how the theory is usually presented, but there's actually not much research supporting the idea that needs form a hierarchy. One expert says that illustrating Maslow's theory in the form of a pyramid (with the physiological needs on bottom and

motive ■ *something that incites a person to action or that sustains and gives direction to action.*

motivational dispositions or needs ■ *motives that lie dormant until the proper conditions arise to bring them forth or make them active.*

aroused motive ■ *a motive that expresses itself in behavior.*

▶ **FIGURE 11–5** ■ ■ ■

Maslow's Hierarchy of Needs

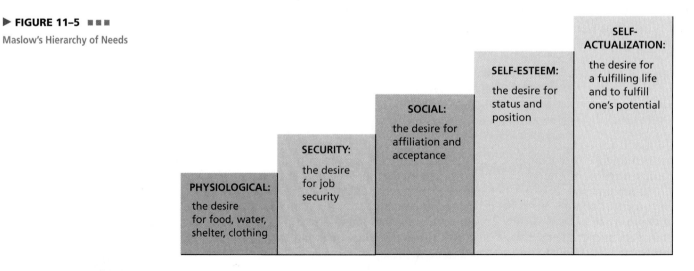

SELF-ACTUALIZATION: the desire for a fulfilling life and to fulfill one's potential

SELF-ESTEEM: the desire for status and position

SOCIAL: the desire for affiliation and acceptance

SECURITY: the desire for job security

PHYSIOLOGICAL: the desire for food, water, shelter, clothing

the self-actualization needs on top) "is one of the worst things that has happened to the theory."[22] What Maslow wanted to do was emphasize that people have different needs and that, quite possibly, as they grow older, "higher level" needs become more important.[23] The pyramid or ladder idea makes the whole process seem more inflexible than Maslow meant it to be. (Later in his career, Maslow actually suggested it might be useful to think of needs as a two-step, not a five-step, hierarchy.[24]) In any event, the five Maslow needs are as follows.

Physiological Needs People are born with physiological needs. These are the basic survival needs, including the needs for food, water, clothing, and shelter.

Security Needs When physiological needs are reasonably satisfied—when a person is no longer thirsty and has enough to eat, for instance—then security, or safety, needs become aroused. Thus, if you are in the middle of a desert with nothing to drink, the lower-level need for water will drive your behavior. You might risk your safety to satisfy that need. But once you have enough to drink, personal safety and security start to motivate your behavior. When American Airlines announced in 2002 that it would lay off 7,000 employees, the airline activated its employees' safety needs; the announcement surely prompted many to think less about promotions and colleagues, and more about keeping their jobs.

Social Needs Once you have had enough to eat and drink and feel reasonably secure, social needs start to drive your behavior. These are the needs to give and receive affection and to have friends. At work, social needs manifest themselves in the work groups and alliances employees form—and with whom they choose to spend their time.

Self-Esteem Needs In Maslow's theory, *self-esteem needs* include needs for things like independence, achievement, competence, status, recognition, position, and the respect of others.[25] Like the social, security, and physiological needs, self-esteem needs supposedly don't motivate behavior until the person has pretty much satisfied the lower-level needs.

However, they differ from social, security, and physiological needs in two ways. First, self-esteem (and the next higher-level need for self-actualization) are relatively *insatiable*—we never get enough of them. Thus, people are endlessly motivated by the need to achieve, to be competent, and to gain the respect of others, both on and off the job. In contrast, lower-level needs (like physiological, security, and, to some extent, social needs) are quickly satiated. People only need so much food and security. Second, it usually requires factors *intrinsic to the task* (like a job's challenge and sense of responsibility) to satisfy self-esteem needs (although a windowed office may provide sufficient recognition for some people). It's generally extrinsic factors like pay and supervision that satisfy the lower-level needs.

Self-Actualization Needs Finally, Maslow says there's an ultimate need that only begins to dominate behavior once all lower-level needs have been quite satisfied. This is the need for self-actualization or fulfillment, the need we all have to become the person we feel we have the potential to become. Employees seeking to better themselves by taking evening classes toward a degree are motivated in part by the need to self-actualize.

Existence Relatedness Growth (ERG) Theory

Clay Alderfer's theory of human needs expands on Maslow's. Alderfer focuses on three needs: existence, relatedness, and growth. His *existence* needs are similar to Maslow's physiological needs, and to the physical components of Maslow's security needs (such as concern for losing your job and salary). *Relatedness* needs are those that require interpersonal interaction to satisfy the needs for things like prestige and esteem from others. *Growth* needs are similar to Maslow's needs for self-esteem and self-actualization.

Maslow's and Alderfer's models differ in two main ways. Maslow emphasized (at least originally) five sets of needs; Alderfer focuses on three. Maslow suggests that each need must be nearly satisfied before the next level of needs become active. Alderfer contends that existence, relatedness, and growth needs are all active simultaneously.[26]

Herzberg's Hygiene-Motivator (Two-Factor) Approach

Frederick Herzberg's famous Hygiene–Motivator motivation theory divides Maslow's hierarchy into lower-level (physiological, safety, social) and higher-level (ego, self-actualization) needs. He says that the best way to motivate someone is to arrange the job so that it helps satisfy the person's higher-level needs, since these needs are relatively insatiable. Herzberg called the two factors at the heart of the theory *hygienes* and *motivators*.

Hygienes and Motivators Herzberg says the factors (hygienes) that satisfy lower-level needs are different from those (motivators) that satisfy, or partially satisfy, higher-level needs. If hygiene factors (factors outside the job itself, such as working conditions, salary, and supervision) are not adequate, employees become dissatisfied. But—and this is very important—adding more of these hygiene factors (like salary) to the job (providing what Herzberg calls *extrinsic motivation*) is a poor way to try to motivate someone, because lower-level needs are quickly satisfied. Soon, the person says, in effect, "What have you done for me lately? I want another raise."

Job content, or *motivator factors*, are different. First, motivator factors (like opportunities for achievement, recognition, responsibility, and challenge on the job) are intrinsic to the work itself. It's the sense of enjoyment and accomplishment that provides the motivation, not some external factor like more pay. Second, motivator factors aim to appeal to the employee's self-esteem and self-actualization needs, needs that are rarely satiated. According to Herzberg, the best way to motivate employees is to build challenges and opportunities for achievement into jobs—to make sure the job provides *intrinsic motivation*, in other words. That way the job itself turns the employee on, much as the thought of working on a favorite hobby may motivate you.

Distilled to its essentials, Herzberg's theory accomplished two main things. It popularized the important role of intrinsic motivation—motivation that comes from within the person—in motivating employees. And it popularized the idea that the nature of the job therefore plays a central role in employee motivation. Today's emphasis on enriching jobs (discussed later in this chapter) and on organizing work around empowered, self-managing teams largely derives from this thinking.

Research Studies Herzberg's theory didn't stem from an experiment, but from a literature review he and his colleagues made of employee satisfaction studies. They concluded that there was a relationship between job satisfaction and certain types of work behaviors (such as challenging work and more responsibility), and also between job dissatisfaction and different work behaviors (like inadequate pay). Figure 11.6 summarizes Herzberg's findings.

Herzberg's motivator factors (those that seemed to cause satisfaction) ranged in importance from getting a sense of achievement (from doing the job) down to recognition, the work itself, responsibility, advancement, and, finally, growth. The hygiene factors that (when poorly designed or administered) caused dissatisfaction ranged from company policy and administration, to supervision and relationship with supervisor, salary, and relationship with peers. Herzberg's conclusion was, that "if you want to motivate someone, make sure [the] pay is adequate (to prevent dissatisfaction); then build challenge and opportunities for achievement into the job to ensure intrinsic motivation."[27]

Most independent studies failed to find such a consistent relationship.[28] A more recent study concluded that sustained job performance was directly related to intrinsic feelings that produce positive attitudes, a finding consistent with Herzberg's theory.[29] The findings notwithstanding, Herzberg's ideas have had a powerful effect on job design and employee empowerment and motivation.

Needs for Achievement, Power, and Affiliation

David McClelland and John Atkinson agree with Herzberg that managers should appeal to employees' higher-level needs. They focused on three needs they believe are especially important—the needs for *achievement, power,* and *affiliation*. To understand the nature of these needs, try the following exercise.

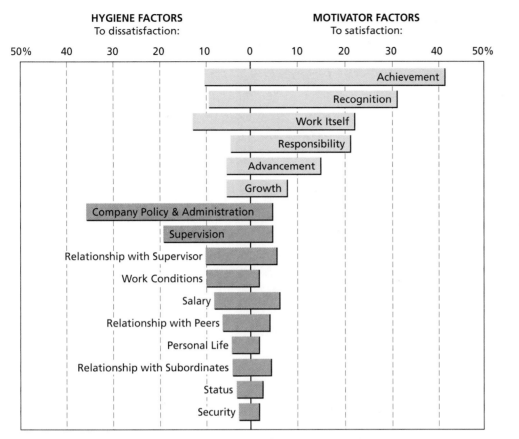

◀ **FIGURE 11–6** ■ ■ ■

Summary of Herzberg's
Motivator–Hygiene Findings

Source: Adapted from Frederick Herzberg,
"One More Time: How Do You Motivate
Employees," *Harvard Business Review*,
January–February 1968.

Take a quick look (just 10 to 15 seconds) at Figure 11.7. Now allow yourself up to five minutes to write a short essay about the picture, touching on the following questions:

1. What is happening? Who are the people?
2. What has led up to this situation? That is, what happened in the past?
3. What is being thought? What is wanted? By whom?
4. What will happen? What will be done?

The questions are only guides, so don't just answer each one. Instead, make your story continuous and let your imagination roam. Once you have finished writing, resume reading the text.

The picture is one from the Thematic Apperception Test (TAT). McClelland and his associates use the TAT, which is made up of a number of pictures, to identify a person's needs. The pictures are intentionally ambiguous, so when you wrote your essay, you were probably reading into the picture ideas that reflected your own needs and drives. McClelland says the test is useful for identifying the level of a person's achievement, power, and affiliation needs.[30]

The Need for Achievement Achievement motivation is present in your essay when any one of the following three things occurs:

1. Someone in your story is concerned about a standard of excellence—for example, he wants to win or do well in a competition, or has self-imposed standards for a good performance. You can infer standards of excellence from the use of words such as *good* or *better* to evaluate performance.
2. Someone in the story is involved in a unique accomplishment, such as an invention or an artistic creation.
3. Someone in the story is involved in a long-term goal, such as having a specific career or being a success in life.

People high in the need to achieve have a predisposition to strive for success. They are highly motivated to obtain the satisfaction that comes from accomplishing a

► **FIGURE 11–7** ■ ■ ■

What's Happening Here?

Source: David A. Kolb, Irwin M. Rubin, and James M. McIntyre, *Organizational Psychology: An Experiential Approach* (Upper Saddle River, NJ: Prentice Hall, 1971), p. 55.

challenging task or goal. They prefer tasks for which there is a reasonable chance for success, and they avoid those that are too easy or too difficult. They prefer specific, timely feedback about their performance.

The Need for Power Power motivation is present in your essay when any of the following three things occurs:

1. Someone in the story is emotionally concerned about getting or maintaining control of the means of influencing a person. Wanting to win a point, to show dominance, to convince someone, or to gain a position of control—as well as wanting to avoid weakness or humiliation—are examples.[31]
2. Someone is actually doing something to get or keep control of the means of influence, such as arguing, demanding or forcing, giving a command, trying to convince, or punishing.
3. Your story involves an interpersonal relationship that is culturally defined as one in which a superior has control of the means of influencing a subordinate. For example, a boss is giving orders to a subordinate, or a parent is ordering a child to shape up.

People with a strong need for power want to influence others directly by making suggestions, giving their opinions and evaluations, and trying to talk others into things. They enjoy roles requiring persuasion, such as teaching and public speaking, as well as positions as leaders and members of the clergy.

How the need for power manifests itself depends on the person's other needs. A person with a high need for power but a low need for warm, supportive relationships might become dictatorial, while one with high needs for comradeship might become a member of the clergy or a social worker. McClelland believed that "a good manager is motivated by a regimented and regulated concern for influencing others"—in other words, good managers do have a need for power, but one that is under control.[32]

The Need for Affiliation Affiliation motivation is present in your essay when one of the following three things occurs:

1. Someone in the story is concerned about establishing, maintaining, or restoring a positive emotional relationship with another person. Friendship is the basic example. Other relationships, such as father–son, reflect affiliation motivation only if they have the warm, compassionate quality implied by the need for affiliation.
2. One person likes or wants to be liked by someone else. Affiliation motivation is also present if someone is expressing sorrow or grief about a broken relationship.

3. Affiliative activities are taking place, such as parties, reunions, visits, or relaxed small talk. Friendly actions, such as consoling or being concerned about the well-being or happiness of another person, usually reflect a need for affiliation.

People with a strong need for affiliation are highly motivated to maintain strong, warm relationships with friends and relatives. In group meetings, they try to establish friendly relationships, often by being agreeable or giving emotional support.[33]

Employee Needs in Practice

You know from your own experience that what appeals to one person may mean nothing to another. One driver, on the way to work, may find the risk of cutting from lane to lane exciting. Another prefers the security of a more temperate pace. One manager may push herself to obtain a promotion, whereas another, while equally secure, is happier on a slower track if that means spending more time with the spouse.

As another example, needs drive career choices, often in ways we don't notice. Psychologist Edgar Schein found that peoples' needs (what he called "career anchors") guided their occupational choices. Some people had a strong *technical/functional career anchor*. They made decisions that enabled them to remain in their chosen technical or functional fields. Some had *managerial competence* as a career anchor. They showed a strong motivation to become managers (as first mentioned in Chapter 1). Some needed to express their *creativity*. Many of these people went on to be successful entrepreneurs.

For some, *autonomy and independence* drove their career decisions. These people seemed driven by the need to be on their own, free of the dependence that can arise when a person elects to work in a large organization. Finally, some were mostly concerned with long-run career stability and *job security*; they did what was required to maintain job security, a decent income, and a stable future, including a good retirement program and benefits.[34] In summary, needs theories tend to explain motivation and what people do based on their needs.[35]

■■ ■ PROCESS APPROACHES TO MOTIVATION

Process approaches explain motivation not in terms of specific needs, but in terms of the decision-making process through which motivation takes place. We'll focus on the work of psychologists J. S. Adams, Edwin Locke, and Victor Vroom.

Adams's Equity Theory

Adams's equity theory assumes that people have a need for—and, therefore, value and seek—fairness at work. Equity theory states that if a person perceives an inequity, a tension or drive will develop in the person's mind, and the person will be motivated to

equity theory ■ *J. S. Adams's theory that people have a need for, and therefore value and seek, fairness in employer–employee relationships.*

© 1996 Randy Glasbergen

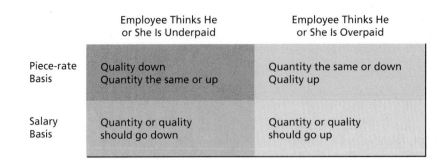

► **FIGURE 11–8** ■ ■ ■

How a Perceived Inequity Can
Affect Performance

According to equity theory, how a person
reacts to under- or overpayment depends
on whether he or she is paid on a piece-rate
or salary basis.

reduce or eliminate the tension and the perceived inequity. Employees can do this by reducing what they put into the job, or by boosting the magnitude of the rewards they take out (or both).

Equity theory takes reality into account. Thus, a person might not envy a colleague's higher salary if it's obvious that the colleague actually does work harder or longer. Rewards, in equity theory, are also somewhat substitutable. Thus, a person might accept a lower salary in return for either a more prestigious title or the satisfaction that comes from doing charitable work. However, individual differences, of course, play a central role. It matters less what the reality is than how the person perceives his or her inputs and outputs as compared with the other person's.[36]

Equity theory's predictions depend on how the person is paid. Figure 11.8 summarizes this. For example, someone paid on a piece-rate plan who thinks he or she is underpaid should react by lowering quality or (perhaps) by boosting output (since the latter should increase pay). The same person, paid a salary, would have little choice but to reduce the quality and/or quantity of what he or she produces. Similarly, paying somewhat more than the going rate should lead to higher quality (if the person is on incentive pay) or to a rise in quality and quantity (for those paid a salary).

In reality, things don't always work out that way. The findings, at least regarding underpayment, are consistent with Adams's theory. People paid on a piece-rate basis, per item produced, typically boost quantity and reduce quality when they believe they are not earning enough. Those paid a straight hourly rate tend to reduce both quantity and quality when they think they're underpaid. However, overpayment inequity does not always have the positive effects on either quantity or quality that Adams's theory would predict for it.[37]

Locke's Goal Theory of Motivation

Locke's **goal theory** assumes that people regulate their behavior in such a way as to achieve their goals.[38] Psychologist Edwin Locke and his colleagues contend that goals provide the mechanism through which unsatisfied needs are translated into action.[39] In other words, unsatisfied needs prompt the person to seek ways to satisfy those needs; the person then formulates goals that prompt action.[40] For example, a person wants to be an artist. To become one, she must go to college for a fine arts degree, so she sets the goal of graduating from Columbia University's fine arts program. That goal (which is prompted by her need) then motivates her behavior—she signs up and goes to college.

The research here is strikingly more extensive and scientific than that on most other motivation theories (in part because goal-setting lends itself more easily to analysis).[41] The findings suggest that setting goals is a simple, effective way to motivate employees. Specifically, they show that

> "... specific, challenging goals lead to higher task performance than specific, unchallenging goals, or vague goals or no goals, providing that: (1) there is feedback showing progress in relation to the goals; (2) appropriate task strategies are used [to show how to do the task] when the task is complex; (3) individuals have adequate ability ... and (4) there is a commitment to the goals ... "[42]

It therefore seems apparent that the most straightforward way to motivate an employee may simply be to make sure that he or she has (and understands) an acceptable, challenging goal, and has the ability to achieve it.

Vroom's Expectancy Theory

Most people won't pursue rewards they find unattractive; nor will they take on tasks where the odds of success are very low. Psychologist Victor Vroom's motivation theory echoes these common-sense observations. He says that a person's motivation to exert some level of effort is a function of three things: the person's expectancy (in terms of probability) that his or her effort will lead to performance;[43] instrumentality, or the perceived relationship between successful performance and obtaining the reward; and valence, which represents the perceived value the person attaches to the reward.[44] In Vroom's theory, motivation is thus a product of these three things: Motivation = $(E \times I \times V)$, where, of course, E represents expectancy, I instrumentality, and V valence. Like equity theory and goal-setting theory, expectancy theory views people as conscious agents; it assumes people are continually sizing up situations in terms of their perceived needs and then acting in accordance with these perceptions.

expectancy ■ *in motivation, the probability that a person's efforts will lead to performance.*

instrumentality ■ *the perceived correlation between successful performance and obtaining the reward.*

valence ■ *in motivation, the perceived value a person ascribes to the reward for certain efforts.*

Research Findings Vroom actually developed expectancy theory to try to better understand and explain why people choose the jobs that they do.[45] Here, results do suggest that expectancy, instrumentality, and valence combine to influence motivation to choose specific jobs.[46] However, studies of the expectancy approach also provide moderate-to-strong support for its usefulness in explaining and predicting other types of work motivation.[47] One expert used Vroom's theory to explain why and how fast employees who were injured on the job and then rehabilitated would return. He conducted a study of 32 public sector employees who were off work and receiving compensation for a work-related condition. He concluded that expectancy and valence were both related to the speed with which the employees intended to return to work. Those who saw a clear link between returning to work (and being able to do the job successfully and earn the reward) were more likely to return to work more quickly.[48] Not all findings are supportive. One study reviewed 77 prior studies of expectancy theory and concluded the results are at best mixed.[49]

Practical Implications Vroom's theory has some obvious implications for how managers motivate employees. First, without an *expectancy* that effort will lead to performance, no motivation will take place. Managers therefore must ensure that their employees have the skills to do the job and know they *can* do the job. In other words, not all motivation problems are "won't do" problems. Instead, some are "can't do" problems: Employees don't know what to do or how to do it—or think they can't do it. That's one reason training, job descriptions, and confidence building and support are important for improving performance.

Second, employees must see the *instrumentality* of their efforts—that successful performance will, in fact, lead to getting the reward. Managers ensure this in many ways—for instance, by creating easy-to-understand incentive plans and by communicating success stories. Finally, managers should think through how to boost the *valence* or perceived value their subordinates attach to the rewards. Two extra days off may be more important to one person, whereas another prefers two days' extra pay.

■■ ■ LEARNING/REINFORCEMENT APPROACHES TO MOTIVATION

Learning can be defined as a relatively permanent change in a person that occurs as a result of experience.[50] For example, we learn as children that being courteous is rewarded by our parents—through their smiles, or some material reward—and we thus may be motivated to be courteous throughout our lives. Motivation like this (such as being courteous) tends to be instinctive rather than a product of a deliberate thought process (as is process-based motivation like Vroom's). Few people consciously think about the pros and cons of being courteous when they behave in a courteous way.

learning ■ *a relatively permanent change in a person that occurs as a result of experience.*

There are several theories about how people learn. In this section, we'll focus on what may be called learning/reinforcement approaches to motivating employees. These deal with how consequences mold behavior.

B. F. Skinner and Operant Behavior

Psychologist B. F. Skinner's findings provide the foundation for much of what we know about learning. Consider an example. Suppose you wanted to train your dog to roll over. How would you do it? You'd probably encourage the dog to roll over (perhaps by gently nudging it down and around), and then you'd reward it with some treat. Your dog would soon come to associate rolling over with the treat. It would *learn* that if it wanted a treat, it would have to roll over. Fido would soon be rolling through your house.

In Skinner's theory, the dog's rolling over is operant behavior, because the act of rolling over operates on the dog's environment, specifically by causing its owner to give it a treat. (So who's training whom, you might ask!) The process (training the dog to roll over in return for a treat) is *operant conditioning*, and the main question is how to strengthen the association between the contingent reward (in this case the treat) and the operant behavior.[51] (For instance, what can you do to make it really clear to Fido that rolling over leads to a treat?).

operant behavior ■ *behavior that appears to operate on or have an influence on the subject's environment.*

contingent reward ■ *a reward that is contingent or dependent on performance of a particular behavior.*

Behavior Modification

behavior modification ■ *the technique of changing or modifying behavior through the use of contingent rewards or punishments.*

Managers and psychologists apply the principles of operant conditioning at work through behavior modification. Behavior modification means changing or modifying behavior through rewards or punishment that are contingent on performance. Behavior modification has two basic principles: (1) Behavior that appears to lead to a positive consequence (reward) tends to be repeated, whereas behavior that appears to lead to a negative consequence (punishment) tends not to be repeated. (2) Therefore, it is possible to get a person to learn to change his or her behavior by providing the properly scheduled rewards.[52] We'll see how to apply this (and the other) motivation theories in the following section.

■ ■ ■ MOTIVATION IN ACTION: TEN METHODS FOR MOTIVATING EMPLOYEES

Managers apply the motivation theories through various methods. As Table 11.1 shows, each of these methods is based on one or more motivation theories. For example, *job redesign* reflects experts' (including Herzberg's) attempts to find a practical way to apply

| TABLE 11–1 | The Motivational Underpinnings of 10 Motivation Methods |

Foundations of Behavior and Motivation	Goal Setting	Pay for Performance
Self-Concept: People seek to fulfill their potential.		
Self-Efficacy: People differ in their estimates of how they'll perform on a task: self-efficacy influences effort.		
Maslow's Needs Hierarchy: High-level needs are never totally satisfied and aren't aroused until lower-level needs are satisfied.		
Alderfer: All needs may be active, to some degree, at the same time.		
McClelland's (Achievement, Power, Affiliation): Needs for achievement, power, and affiliation are especially important in the work setting.		
Herzberg's Dual Factor: Extrinsic factors prevent dissatisfaction; intrinsic factors motivate workers.		
Vroom's Expectancy Approach: Motivation is a function of expectancy that effort leads to performance, performance leads to reward, and reward is valued.		x
Locke's Goal Setting: People are motivated to achieve goals they consciously set.	x	
Adams's Equity Theory: People are motivated to maintain balance between their perceived inputs and outputs.	x	
Reinforcement: People will continue behavior that is rewarded and cease behavior that is punished.		x

Source: Copyright © 1997 by Gary Dessler, Ph.D.

his ideas about how to build intrinsic motivation into employees' jobs. *Positive reinforcement* programs reflect experts' attempts to operationalize learning theories of motivation in industrial settings. We'll focus on ten widely used motivation methods in this section.

Set Goals

The manager's first option for motivating employees is usually simply to ensure that the employee has a doable goal and that he or she agrees with it. It makes little sense to try to motivate employees in other ways (such as with financial incentives) if they don't know their goals or don't agree with them. As noted above, the research evidence on this point is quite clear. Checklist 11.1 contains the goal-setting steps first presented in Chapter 5, for your review.

CHECKLIST 11.1 ■ Setting Effective Goals

- ☑ Set *SMART* goals—make them *specific, measurable, attainable, relevant,* and *timely.*
- ☑ Choose *areas* (sales revenue, costs, and so forth) that are *relevant* and *complete.*
- ☑ Assign *specific* goals.
- ☑ Assign *measurable* goals.
- ☑ Assign doable but *challenging* goals.
- ☑ Encourage *participation.*
- ☑ Use *management by objectives.*

Use Pay for Performance

Pay for performance refers to any compensation method that ties pay to the quantity or quality of work the person produces. In terms of motivation theory, pay for performance plans should motivate employees by reinforcing desirable behaviors and (per expectancy theory) by making it clear that performance is instrumental in producing a coveted reward. Several such plans are popular today.

Variable pay plans are pay-for-performance plans that put a portion of the employee's pay at risk, in return for the opportunity to earn additional pay. In one plan at DuPont, employees voluntarily put up to 6% of their base pay at risk.[53] If their

pay for performance ■ *any compensation method based on merit or performance rather than across-the-board nonoutput-based pay.*

variable pay plan ■ *a compensation plan that may reduce or increase some portion of the individual employee's pay, depending on whether the company meets its financial goals.*

Merit Raises	Spot Rewards	Skill-Based Pay	Recognition Awards	Job Redesign	Empower Employees	Positive Reinforcement	Lifelong Learning
		x	x	x	x		x
		x			x		x
x	x		x	x	x		x
x	x		x	x	x		x
		x	x	x	x		x
			x	x	x		x
x	x		x				
					x		
x	x		x				
x	x		x			x	

■■ ■ *Starbucks' first retail coffee store in Beijing. The company offers its employees a number of opportunities to participate in its success.*

gainsharing plan ■ *an incentive plan that engages many or all employees in a common effort to achieve a company's productivity objectives and in which they share in the gains.*

departments met their earnings projections, the employees got that 6% back, plus additional percentages, depending on how much the department exceeded its goals.

Gainsharing plans are group incentive plans that engage many or all employees in a common effort to achieve productivity goals.[54] The basic idea is this: If the employees' efforts succeed, they share in the financial gains. Typically, managers choose specific performance measures (such as "cost per unit produced") and a funding formula (such as "47% of savings go to employees"). Then, if employees achieve cost savings in line with their performance goals, they share in the resulting gains.[55]

Sometimes, the pay for performance comes in the form of stock options. *Stock options* are rights to purchase company stock at a discount some time in the future. People associate stock options with high-priced executives, but many firms actually offer stock options to all or most employees.[56] As Bradley Honeycutt, a former Starbucks HR executive put it, "We established Bean Stock [the firm's employee stock option plan] in 1991 as a way of investing in our partners and creating ownership across the company; it's been a key to retaining good people and building loyalty."[57]

MANAGEMENT IN ACTION   Continental's Pay-for-Performance Plans

Pay for Performance plans can have impressive results. In the mid-1990s, Continental Airlines was close to bankruptcy. When Gordon Bethune, the firm's new CEO took over, one of his first steps was to install a new incentive plan for Continental's 35,000 nonmanagerial employees.[58]

The plan was simple: Any month Continental ranked among the top five airlines in terms of on-time departures, every employee would get a $65 cash bonus. Some experts might have predicted such a plan would never work. For example, everyone got the $65, so wouldn't "free rider" employees just slack off, and let their harder working colleagues carry the brunt of the increased load? It turned out that everyone pitched in. By 1997, the firm's profits were up to almost $400 million. The plan was successful because it had:

■ *The right performance measure.* Continental could easily measure "On-time departures" and compare it to the competition's performance. It was a measure that crew members and airport staff could definitely affect.

■ *Mutual monitoring.* Although the firm had over 35,000 employees, most of them worked locally in very small teams, so the team members themselves helped to keep each other's performance in line.

■ *Visible rewards.* Management was careful not to hide the monthly $65 bonus in each employee's paycheck. Each worker got a separate monthly check for the full $65.

■ *Program kick-start.* Bethune "kick-started" the program by immediately modifying the firm's flight schedules to make on-time performance easier to achieve. This virtually ensured that employees would get their bonuses in the first month, which they did. It provided immediate reinforcement for the employees' renewed efforts. ■■■■

As with Bethune's incentive plan, managers build successful incentive plans on a firm foundation of motivation theory. For example, Vroom's expectancy approach says that motivation depends on employees' seeing the link between performance and rewards—and on the value of the reward to the recipient. Therefore, make sure of the following: that the employee knows he or she can do the job, sees the link between performance and reward, and values the reward. Checklist 11.2 shows the motivation-based steps for implementing an effective incentive plan.

☑ **Make sure effort and rewards are directly related.** The incentive plan should reward employees in direct proportion to increased productivity or quality.

☑ **Make the plan easy to understand.** Employees should be able to calculate their rewards for various levels of effort.

☑ **Set effective standards.** Make standards high but reasonable—there should be about a 60 percent to 70 percent chance of success. The goal should also be specific.

☑ **View the standard as a contract with your employees.** Once the plan is working, use caution before decreasing the size of the incentive.

☑ **Get employee support for the plan.** Restrictions by peers can undermine the plan.

☑

Use good measurement systems. As at Continental Airlines, make sure the standard and the employees' performance are both easy to measure.

☑ **Emphasize long-term as well as short-term success.** For example, just paying plant managers based on yearly productivity may be shortsighted if one or two of them decide to get around the requirement by skimping on machine maintenance.

☑ **Take the system into account.** From the employees' point of view, incentive plans don't exist in isolation. For example, trying to motivate employees with a new incentive plan when they either don't have the skills to do the job or are demoralized by unfair supervisors might well fail.[59]

Improve Merit Pay

A merit raise is a salary increase—usually permanent—based on individual performance. The motivational basis for such raises is sound. The prospect of the raise should focus the employee on the link between effort, performance, and rewards, consistent with Vroom's expectancy model. Getting it should provide reinforcement, consistent with learning theory. The merit raise should also reflect the fact that rewards are distributed equitably, consistent with equity theory.

merit raise ■ a salary increase—usually permanent—based on individual performance.

Unfortunately, merit raises often fail on all three counts. Many supervisors try to avoid bad feelings by awarding raises across the board—regardless of merit—thus severing the performance-reward link and crippling the merit pay's incentive value. Merit plans depend on annual appraisals, and some firms' appraisal procedures don't effectively distinguish between those who do well or poorly. (One study focused on the relationship between performance ratings and merit pay raises for 218 workers in a nuclear waste facility. The researchers found a "very modest relationship between merit pay increase and performance rating."[60]) Furthermore, a year is a long time to wait for a reward, so the reinforcement benefits of merit pay are somewhat suspect.[61]

The solution is to apply merit raises more intelligently. First, clarify performance standards before the measurement period begins. Second, institute a performance appraisal system that you can use to systematically and accurately evaluate performance. Third, train all supervisors to award merit pay based on merit rather then across the board. Fourth, conduct the award allocations biannually, and/or combine the merit plan with other, more timely financial (and other) rewards—such as recognition.

Use Recognition

Recognizing an employee's contribution is a simple and effective motivational tool. It provides an inexpensive and timely form of feedback, and it contributes to a person's sense of self-esteem. Herzberg found recognition to be an important motivator.

Studies show that recognition has a positive impact on performance, either alone or in combination with financial rewards. For example, in one study, combining financial rewards with nonfinancial ones (like recognition) produced a 30% performance improvement in service firms—almost twice the effect of using each reward alone.[62] When the Minnesota Department of Natural Resources conducted a study of recognition, respondents said they highly valued day-to-day recognition from supervisors, peers, and team members. More than two-thirds said it was important to believe that others appreciated their work.[63]

■ ■ *Ed Matsumoto, an employee of Scitor, a Sunnyvale, California, systems engineering consulting firm, bought himself a refrigerator by saving up his "Be Our Guest" bonuses.*

Many companies therefore formalize the employee recognition process. According to one survey, 78% of CEOs and 58% of HR vice presidents said their firms were using performance recognition programs.[64]

Dallas-based Texas Instruments offers bonuses as well as nonfinancial recognition, including personalized plaques, parties, movie tickets, golf lessons, and team shirts and jackets. The number of individual Texas Instruments employees recognized in this way jumped by 400% in one recent year—from 21,970 to 84,260.[65] At Metro Motors in Montclair, California, the name of the employee of the month appears on the electronic billboard over the dealership.[66] Managers at American Skandia (which provides insurance and financial planning products and services) regularly evaluate their customer service reps. Those who exceed their standards receive a plaque, a $500 check, their photo and story on the firm's internal Web site, and a dinner for them and their teams.[67]

■ *The Global Manager* When Shred-it, a Toronto-based mobile document shredding service, decided to expand its employee recognition program abroad, it discovered that incentives that work in one country don't necessarily work in others. "The key is to see how people are motivated differently around the world," says the consultant who helped Shred-it develop its new plan. For example, a cash award is highly taxed in Scandinavia, and Asians tend to prefer team awards. Therefore, installing an incentive plan to be used around the world means ". . . you have to do your homework and find out what motivates the most people, regardless of culture."[68]

Use Positive Reinforcement

"Positive reinforcement" is one of the most loosely used terms in management. Every time a manager thanks or recognizes an employee, awards a raise, or gives someone a promotion, the manager probably thinks, "I'm using positive reinforcement." Indeed, as you can see from the illustrative list in Figure 11.9 the variety of potential positive reinforcements—rewards—you can use is quite large. Just a short list would include salary increases, bonuses, discount airline tickets, promotions, job rotation, department parties, compliments, encouragement, and (of course) a bigger desk. (We'll address *behavior management*, a more complex form of positive reinforcement, in the following section).

Positive reinforcement's popularity stems from its solid basis in motivation theory. Numerous studies of learning and reinforcement confirm the motivational benefits of providing employees with positive rewards. But implementing programs like these can create administrative headaches for employers. For example, many programs let employees choose from a long list of gifts and other rewards. This may entail considerable paperwork in maintaining brochures and administrating the logistics of the program. The Managing @ the Speed of Thought feature describes how companies use the Web to facilitate such programs.

Going Online with Incentives

Companies use technology to improve their positive reinforcement programs.[69] For example, the ASPIRE 1.5 (Automated System Promoting Incentives that Reward Excellence) software package takes incentive planners through the steps required to design a corporate incentive program. HR can use the program both to indicate how the winners will be judged (such as percentage of sales growth over past performance), and to choose rewards from a menu of incentives options (such as travel, gifts, checks, or paid time off from the office). Another program, Bob Nelson's Reward Wizard, "keeps performance records for all employees in a department or organization, along with their career objectives, personal preferences, hobbies and family circumstances. Space is also provided to enter their accomplishments, award criteria, time allotted to win an award and individual award preferences."[70] Once running, Reward Wizard can generate prize suggestions adapted to each employee's needs, such as extra Mondays off for Gary and a bigger computer screen for Jeannine.

Many firms—including Nortel Networks, Nextel Communications, Levi Strauss & Co., Barnes & Noble, Citibank, and Wal-Mart—also partner with online incentive firms to improve and expedite the whole positive reinforcement process. Management consultant Hewitt Associates uses **www.bravanta.com** to help its managers more easily recognize exceptional employee service with special awards. Internet incentive sites include **bravanta.com, premier choiceaward.com, givenanything.com, incentivecity.com, netcentives.com, salesdriver.com,** and **kudoz.com.**

In learning theory, the best reinforcement usually comes at once. A **spot award** is one you give "on the spot," as soon as you observe the praiseworthy performance.[71] For example, Scitor, a systems engineering consulting firm based in Sunnyvale, California, has a program called Be Our Guest.[72] Be Our Guest bonuses (which usually range from $100 to $300) are given by employees to their coworkers for doing something beyond the call of duty. If (in the giver's eyes) the recipient does something exceptional—stays late on a project, for instance—the giver fills out a card indicating the amount of the bonus—and then it's the recipient's to spend as he or she likes.

spot award ■ *a financial reward given to an employee as soon as laudable performance is observed.*

MONETARY

Salary increases or bonuses

Company-paid vacation trip

Discount coupons

Company stock

Extra paid vacation days

Profit sharing

Paid personal holiday (such as birthday)

Movie or athletic event passes

Free or discount airline tickets

Discounts on company products or services

Gift selection from catalog

JOB AND CAREER RELATED

Empowerment of employee

Challenging work assignments

Job security (relatively permanent job)

Favorable performance appraisal

Freedom to choose own work activity

Promotion

Having fun built into work

More of preferred task

Role as boss's stand-in when he or she is away

Role in presentations to top management

Job rotation

Encouragement of learning and continuous improvement

Being provided with ample encouragement

Being allowed to set own goals

FOOD AND DINING

Business luncheon paid by company

Company picnics

Department parties

Holiday turkeys and fruit baskets

SOCIAL AND PRIDE RELATED

Compliments

Encouragement

Comradeship with boss

Access to confidential information

Pat on back

Expression of appreciation in front of others

Note of thanks

Employee-of-the-month award

Wall plaque indicating accomplishment

Special commendation

Company recognition plan

STATUS SYMBOLS

Bigger desk

Bigger office or cubicle

Exclusive use of fax machine

Freedom to personalize work area

Private office

Cellular phone privileges

On-line service privileges

◀ **FIGURE 11–9** ■ ■ ■

Positive Reinforcement Rewards

Source: Several items under the job- and career-related category are from Dean R. Spitzer, "Power Rewards: Rewards That Really Motivate," *Management Review,* May 1996, p. 48.

TABLE 11–2   Order of Importance of Various Job Factors

Job Factors	Survey of Employees	Survey of Bosses
Full appreciation of work done	1	8
Feeling of being in on things	2	10
Sympathetic help on personal problems	3	9
Job security	4	2
Good wages	5	1
Interesting work	6	5
Promotional growth in organization	7	3
Personal loyalty to employees	8	6
Good working conditions	9	4
Tactful disciplining	10	7

Source: LeDue, A. I., Jr. (1980). *Motivation of Programmers.*

Whether it's recognition, a spot award, or some other positive reinforcement, managers have to make sure their perceptions of what's important to employees is consistent with their employees' perceptions. Table 11.2 illustrates why. In this survey of employees, "full appreciation of work done" was ranked No. 1 by employees, but only No. 8 by their bosses. Bosses assumed "good wages" were most important, whereas the employees themselves ranked wages as No. 5.[73]

Use Behavior Management

Some experts would challenge using the label *positive reinforcement* to cover such a wide array of reward programs. Some prefer to limit the term to formal *behavior management* programs. These apply the concepts and principles of learning/reinforcement (discussed earlier) to motivating employees at work. Managers applying behavior modification at work must address two basic issues: the *type of reinforcement* (reward or punishment) and the *schedule of reinforcement*.

positive reinforcement ■ *the act of rewarding desired behavior; or the actual rewards, such as praise or bonuses, given each time the desired behavior occurs.*

extinction ■ *the behavioral modification technique of withholding positive reinforcement so that the undesired behavior disappears over time.*

negative reinforcement ■ *reinforcing the desirable behavior by removing something undesirable from the situation.*

punishment ■ *a behavioral modification option that applies penalties for the undesired behavior to reduce the possibility that it will recur.*

Types of Reinforcement There are four types of reinforcement. **Positive reinforcement** is a positive consequence, or reward, such as praise or a bonus, that results when the desired behavior occurs. In **extinction**, managers withhold reinforcement so that the undesired behavior disappears over time. Managers use extinction when they discover they've been inadvertently rewarding someone for doing the wrong thing. For example, suppose your subordinate learns that arriving late invariably leads to a scolding by you, which, in turn, leads to laughter and congratulations from the worker's peers. Here, use extinction: Start disciplining that person in the privacy of your office, thereby removing the attention and the laughter—the reward—that the worker gets from his or her friends. **Negative reinforcement** means reinforcing the desirable behavior by removing something undesirable that results from performing the behavior. Making safety helmets more comfortable is an example.

Punishment, as you know, is in a class by itself. It means adding something undesirable to change a person's behavior. Reprimands and discipline are familiar examples. Punishment is the most controversial method of modifying behavior. Skinner recommends extinction rather than punishment for decreasing the frequency of the undesired behavior.

As in Figure 11.10, modifying behavior is like balancing a scale. Suppose wearing a safety helmet is the desired behavior and not wearing it is the undesired behavior. One way to increase the desired behavior is to add a positive consequence—for instance, by praising the worker each time he or she wears the helmet. Another option is to remove

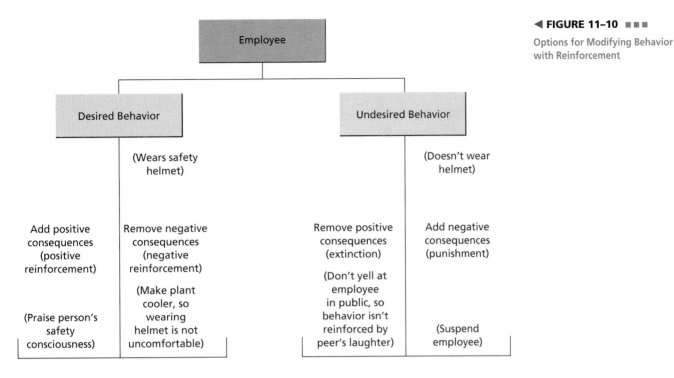

the negative consequences of wearing the helmet, by lowering the temperature to cool the plant or by making the helmet less cumbersome. Most psychologists say it's best to focus on improving desirable behaviors rather than on decreasing undesirable ones. If the employee fails to wear a safety helmet, emphasize improving the desired behavior (wearing the helmet) rather than reducing the undesirable behavior (not wearing the helmet).

The Schedule of Reinforcement In behavior modification, it's not just the type of reinforcement, but the *schedule* you use to apply it that's important. Here, the research findings suggest the following:

1. The fastest way to get someone to learn is not to put him or her on a schedule at all. Instead, reinforce the desired behavior every time it occurs. This is *continuous reinforcement*. The drawback is that the desired behavior also diminishes very quickly once you stop reinforcing it.
2. *Variable* (also called partial) *reinforcement* is the one that is the most powerful at sustaining behavior. Here, you don't reinforce the desired behavior each time it occurs, but every few times, around some average number of times. This is very powerful. As with Las Vegas-type slot machines, people are always expecting to "hit the jackpot" on the next try, so they continue producing the desired behavior for a long time even without reinforcement.

The Basic Procedure To a behaviorist (a behavior management expert), any behavior is, to put it simply, a product of its consequences. If the person comes to work late all the time, you are not providing the right consequences for coming to work on time, or you are inadvertently reinforcing coming in late. The way to motivate the right behavior, a behaviorist would say, is to identify the desired behaviors and then carefully reinforce them. The process involves four steps.[74]

1. *Pinpoint behavior:* Identify and define the specific behavior(s) you wish to change.
2. *Record:* Count the occurrence of the pinpoint behavior.
3. *Change Consequences:* Analyze the consequences of the behavior as they are now, and arrange for new or improved consequences to follow the behavior.
4. *Evaluate:* Ask, "Did the behavior improve, and if so, how much?"

Figure 11.11 illustrates an application of this approach. Here, the *general problem* was that the accounting department was making too many payroll errors. The consultants *pinpointed the behaviors* (the number of errors reported back to them by department managers) and *counted and recorded* the reported errors. They then *formulated consequences* for the behavioral change. In this case, the consequences included both the feedback the bookkeepers got from keeping their errors-graphs and the feedback from the managers.

■ *Application Example Emery Air Freight* The Emery Air Freight Company program grew out of management's discovery that the containers used to consolidate air freight shipments were not being fully utilized.[75] In this case, the workers used containers only about 45% of the time, while they reportedly thought they were using them about 90% of the time. Management wanted them to boost the actual usage rate to 90% to 95%.

Consultants installed a behavior management program. It included an instruction book for managers that detailed how to use recognition, rewards, feedback, and various other types of social, intrinsic, and tangible consequences. Each dockworker also received a checklist to mark each time he or she used a container (so the worker, in effect, gave him- or herself positive feedback). In 80% of the offices where Emery installed it, container usage rose from 45% to 95% in a single day.

Criticisms Many people disapprove of this approach to motivating behavior. As one psychologist said, "If human behavior were regulated solely by external outcomes, people would behave like weathervanes, constantly shifting direction to conform to

► **FIGURE 11–11** ■ ■ ■

Performance Improvement Project Worksheet

Source: Lawrence Miller, *Behavior Management: The New Science of Managing People at Work* (New York: John Wiley, 1978), p. 18.

1. General Statement of Problem

The accounting department was making too many payroll errors. This increased cost by taking up managers' time and accounting time. It also caused a lot of frustration on the part of employees.

2. Pinpointed Behaviors

The accounting department was instructed to count the number of errors reported back to it by department managers.

3. Count and Record

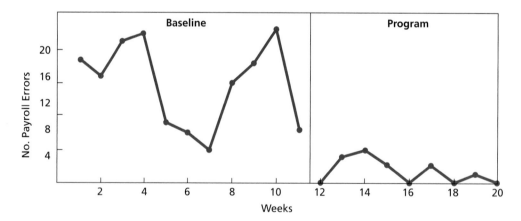

4. Consequences for Behavior Changes

Each bookkeeper in the accounting department started keeping a graph of the number of errors for which he or she was responsible. The accounting manager discussed each error with the bookkeepers and assigned responsibility. The manager verbally reinforced those bookkeepers who showed improvement on their graphs or who displayed low rates of error to begin with.

5. What Changes Occurred.

The number of errors dropped from an average 11.6 errors per week to 1.17 errors per week.

whatever momentary social influence happens to impinge upon them. In actuality, people possess self-reflective and self-reactive capabilities that enable them to exercise some control over their thoughts, feelings, motivations, and actions."[76] However, as a manager you may well face situations in which this approach does apply and in which you can apply it in a civilized way.

Empower Employees

Empowerment means giving employees some degree of control over their jobs and enabling them to employ suitable power to make their work lives more effective.[77] Empowerment, in motivation theory, helps to satisfy employees' higher-level needs. Psychologists such as Maslow and Herzberg would argue that the satisfaction one gets from doing a job and doing it well is highly motivating, and that empowering employees is one way to provide that satisfaction. Empowerment should boost feelings of self-efficacy, and also enable employees to use their potential. In so doing, it appeals to employees' higher-level needs for achievement, recognition, and self-actualization.

Empowering employees, therefore, is not just theoretical. Doing so requires taking specific steps, such as providing employees with a clear vision and goals, fostering their personal mastery, and providing them with needed support. Table 11.3 suggests actions managers can take to empower employees.[78]

empowerment ■ *the act of giving employees the authority, tools, and information they need to do their jobs with greater autonomy and confidence.*

TABLE 11–3   Practical Suggestions for Empowering Others

ARTICULATE A CLEAR VISION AND GOALS
- ☐ Create a picture of a desired future.
- ☐ Use word pictures and emotional language to describe the vision.
- ☐ Identify specific actions and strategies that will lead to the vision.
- ☐ Establish SMART goals.
- ☐ Associate the vision and goals with personal values.

FOSTER PERSONAL MASTERY EXPERIENCES
- ☐ Break apart large tasks and assign one part at a time.
- ☐ Assign simple tasks before difficult tasks.
- ☐ Highlight and celebrate small winds.
- ☐ Incrementally expand job responsibilities.
- ☐ Give increasingly more responsibility to solve problems.

MODEL SUCCESSFUL BEHAVIORS
- ☐ Demonstrate successful task accomplishment.
- ☐ Point out other people who have succeeded.
- ☐ Facilitate interaction with other role models.
- ☐ Find a coach.
- ☐ Establish a mentor relationship.

PROVIDE SUPPORT
- ☐ Praise, encourage, express approval for, and reassure.
- ☐ Send letters or notes of praise to family members of coworkers.
- ☐ Regularly provide feedback.
- ☐ Foster informal social activities to build cohesion.
- ☐ Supervise less closely and provide time slack.
- ☐ Hold recognition ceremonies.

(continued)

TABLE 11–3 **Practical Suggestions for Empowering Others** (*continued*)

AROUSE POSITIVE EMOTIONS

☐ Foster activities to encourage friendship formation.

☐ Periodically send lighthearted messages.

☐ Use superlatives in giving feedback.

☐ Highlight compatibility between important personal values and organizational goals.

☐ Clarify impact on the ultimate customer.

☐ Foster attributes of recreation in work: clear goals, effective scorekeeping and feedback systems, and out-of-bounds behavior.

PROVIDE INFORMATION

☐ Provide all task-relevant information.

☐ Continuously provide technical information and objective data.

☐ Pass along relevant cross-unit and cross-functional information.

☐ Provide access to information or people with senior responsibility.

☐ Provide access to information from its source.

☐ Clarify effects of actions on customers.

PROVIDE RESOURCES

☐ Provide training and development experiences.

☐ Provide technical and administrative support.

☐ Provide needed time, space, or equipment.

☐ Ensure access to relevant information networks.

☐ Provide more discretion to commit resources.

CONNECT TO OUTCOMES

☐ Provide a chance to interact directly with those receiving the service or output.

☐ Provide authority to resolve problems on the spot.

☐ Provide immediate, unfiltered, direct feedback on results.

☐ Create task identity or the opportunity to accomplish a complete task.

☐ Clarify and measure effects as well as direct outcomes.

CREATE CONFIDENCE

☐ Exhibit reliability and consistency.

☐ Exhibit fairness and equity.

☐ Exhibit caring and personal concern.

☐ Exhibit openness and honesty.

☐ Exhibit competence and expertise.

Source: David A. Whetton and Kim S. Cameron, *Developing Management Skills* (Upper Saddle River, NJ: Prentice Hall, 2002), pp. 426–27.

Enrich the Jobs

job enrichment ■ *the inclusion of opportunities for achievement and other motivators in a job by making the job itself more challenging.*

One way to empower employees is to enrich their jobs. Job enrichment means building motivators into the job by making it more interesting and challenging. Managers often do this by *vertically loading* the job. This means giving the worker more autonomy and allowing the person to do much of the planning and inspection normally done by the person's supervisor. Job enrichment has its roots in the work of Frederick Herzberg. It is the method he recommends for applying his motivator–hygiene approach.

Using Job Enrichment Successfully applying this approach requires understanding several things. The first question is, "How does one know if a job (or set of jobs) is ripe for this approach?" There is no one sure-fire way.[79] However, managers need to start somewhere, and Figure 11.12 provides a guide. It is a form for evaluating the appropriateness of job enrichment. According to the form's creators, "a lower rating (1.0–1.9) indicates that a job is a prime candidate for enrichment; and if properly implemented, it has a high expected return on investment. A job enrichment rating of 2.0–3.9 identifies jobs that can be enriched that may have a marginal return on investment in terms of productivity measures. A high rating (4.0–5.0) identifies jobs that for all practical purposes cannot be enriched at the present time."[80]

▼ **FIGURE 11–12** ■ ■ ■

A Job Enrichment Evaluation Form

Source: Theodore T. Herbert, *Organizational Behavior: Readings and Cases* (New York: Macmillan Publishing Co., Inc., 1976), pp. 344–45.

The Job Itself

1. Quality is important and attributable to the worker | /1/2/3/4/5/ | Quality is not too important and/or is not controllable by the worker..

2. Flexibility is a major contributor to job efficiency. | /1/2/3/4/5/ | Flexibility is not a major consideration.

3. The job requires the coordination of tasks or activities among several workers. | /1/2/3/4/5/ | The job is performed by one worker acting independently of others.

4. The benefits of job enrichment will compensate for the efficiencies of task specialization. | /1/2/3/4/5/ | Job enrichment will eliminate substantial efficiencies realized from specialization.

5. The conversion and one-time set-up costs involved in job enrichment can be recovered in a reasonable period of time. | /1/2/3/4/5/ | Training and other costs associated with job enrichment are estimated to be much greater than expected results.

6. The wage payment plan is not based solely on output. | /1/2/3/4/5/ | Workers are under a straight piece-work wage plan.

7. Due to the worker's ability to affect output, an increase in job satisfaction can be expected to increase productivity. | /1/2/3/4/5/ | Due to the dominance of technology, an increase in job satisfaction is unlikely to significantly affect productivity.

Technology

8. Changes in job content would not necessitate a large investment in equipment and technology | /1/2/3/4/5/ | The huge investment in equipment and technology overrides all other considerations.

9. Employees are accustomed to change and respond favorably to it. | /1/2/3/4/5/ | Employees are set in their ways and prefer the status quo.

10. Employees feel secure in their jobs; employment has been stable. | /1/2/3/4/5/ | Layoffs are frequent, many employees are concerned about the permanency of employment.

11. Employees are dissatisfied with their jobs and would welcome changes in job content and work relationships. | /1/2/3/4/5/ | Employees are satisfied with their present jobs and general work situation.

12. Employees are highly skilled blue- and white-collar workers, professionals, and supervisors. | /1/2/3/4/5/ | Employees are semi- and unskilled blue- and white-collar workers.

13. Employees are well educated, with most having college degrees. | /1/2/3/4/5/ | The average employee has less than a high school education.

14. Employees are from a small town and rural environment. | /1/2/3/4/5/ | The company is located in a large, highly industrialized metropolitan area.

15. The history of union-management (if no union, worker–management) relations has been one of cooperation and mutual support. | /1/2/3/4/5/ | Union-management (worker-management) relations are strained, and the two parties are antagonistic to one another.

Management

16. Managers are committed to job enrichment and are anxious to participate in its implementation. | /1/2/3/4/5/ | Managers show little interest in job enrichment and even less interest in having it implemented in their departments.

17. Managers have attended seminars, workshops, and so forth; are quite knowledgeable of the concept; and have had experience in implementing it. | /1/2/3/4/5/ | Managers lack the training and experience necessary to develop and implement job enrichment projects.

18. Management realizes that substantial payoffs from job enrichment usually take one to three years to materialize. | /1/2/3/4/5/ | Management expects immediate results (within six months) from job enrichment projects

Total Score _____ ÷ 18 = _____

Job Enrichment Rating

The second question is, "What specific actions can I take that will 'enrich' an employee's job?" Managers enrich jobs in several ways:[81]

1. *Form natural work groups.* For example, put a team in charge of an identifiable body of work, such as building the entire engine.
2. *Combine tasks.* Let one person assemble a product from start to finish instead of having it go through separate operations performed by different people.
3. *Establish client relationships.* Let the worker have contact as often as possible with the client of that person's work.
4. *Vertically load the job.* Have the worker, rather the supervisor, plan, schedule, troubleshoot, and control his or her job.
5. *Open feedback channels.* Find more and better ways for the worker to get quick feedback on performance.

■ *Application Example* Numerous firms have applied this approach. At Saturn Corporation, for instance, the plant's self-managing work teams all have enriched jobs. Figure 11.13 lists specific things that make their jobs enriched.

Job design Job enrichment is one example of a management method called job design (or job redesign). Job design refers to manipulating the number and nature of activities in a job. The basic issue in job design is whether jobs should be more specialized or, at the other extreme, more enriched and nonroutine. Job enlargement assigns workers

---

job design ■ *the number and nature of specific tasks or activities in a job.*

job enlargement ■ *an increase in the number of similar tasks assigned to a job.*

▶ **FIGURE 11–13** ■ ■ ■

Sample of Saturn Work Team's Functions

Source: Reprinted with permission from *Saturn Work Team Functions*, a training document.

EACH SATURN TEAM WILL:

1. *Use consensus decision making:* No formal leader [will be] apparent in the process. . . . All members of the work unit that reaches consensus must be at least 70% comfortable with the decision and 100% committed to its implementation.

3. *Make their own job assignments:* A work unit . . . ensures safe, effective, efficient, and equal distribution of the work unit tasks to all its members.

5. *Plan their own work:* The work unit assigns timely resources for the accomplishment of its purpose to its customers while meeting the needs of the people within the work unit.

6. *Design their own jobs:* This should provide the optimum balance between people and technology and include the effective use of manpower, ergonomics, machine utilization, quality, cost, job-task analysis, and continuous improvement.

8. *Control their own material and inventory:* Work directly in a coordinated manner with suppliers, partners, customers, and indirect/product material resource team members to develop and maintain necessary work unit inventory.

9. *Perform their own equipment maintenance:* Perform those tasks that can be defined as safe and those they have the expertise, ability, and knowledge to perform effectively.

13. *Make selection decisions of new members into the work unit:* A work unit operating in a steady state has responsibility for determining total manpower requirements, and selection and movement of qualified new members from a candidate pool will be in accordance with the established Saturn selection process.

14. *Constantly seek improvement in quality, cost, and the work environment:* The work unit is responsible for involving all work unit members in improving quality, cost, and the work environment in concert with Saturn's quality system.

18. *Determine their own methods:* The work unit is responsible for designing the jobs of its team members consistent with the requirements of the Saturn production system and comprehending the necessary resources and work breakdown required.

21. *Provide their own absentee replacements:* the work unit is responsible for the attendance of its members. . . . The work unit will be required to plan for and provide its own absentee coverage.

22. *Perform their own repairs:* The work unit will have the ultimate responsibility for producing a world-class product that meets the needs and requirements of the customer. In the event a job leaves the work unit with a known or unknown nonconformance to specification, the originating work unit will be accountable for corrective action and repair.

additional similar tasks. For example, the worker who previously only bolted the seat to the chair legs might also attach the back. Job rotation systematically moves workers from job to job. Job enrichment is more extensive (and assumedly motivational) than both. It also vertically loads the job, establishes client relationships, forms natural work groups, and opens feedback channels.

Use Skill-Based Pay

Having employees work on self-managing, enriched-work teams presents a dilemma as far as pay is concerned. Most firms pay employees based on specific jobs. Presidents make more than vice presidents, and sales managers make more than assistant sales managers. How do you pay workers when you want to encourage them to move from one team job to another, when the jobs may entail considerably different skill levels?

Skill-based pay is one solution. Here, employers pay employees for the range and depth of their skills and knowledge, rather than for the jobs they currently hold.[82] As an example, a General Mills plant boosted the flexibility and skill level of its workforce by implementing a pay plan that encouraged employees to develop greater skills.[83] The plan paid workers based on attained skill levels. For each of the several types of jobs in the plant, workers could attain three levels of skill: *limited ability* (ability to perform simple tasks without direction); *partial proficiency* (ability to apply more advanced principles on the job); and *full competence* (ability to analyze and solve problems associated with that job).

After starting a job, workers got tests periodically to see if they had earned certification at the next higher skill level. If they had, they received higher pay even though they kept the same job. The plant's overall skill level increased, as did its ability to switch employees from job to job.

Provide Lifelong Learning

Programs like job enrichment and skill-based pay obviously demand a higher level of knowledge and skills from employees. Lifelong learning is a formal, companywide effort aimed at making sure employees have the skills they need—from remedial skills to decision-making techniques to college degrees—to work effectively throughout their careers. It usually includes programs that range from in-house training, to making community-college courses available at the plant's facility, to providing tuition reimbursement for relevant college coursework.

Lifelong learning is inherently motivational. It boosts employees' sense of self-efficacy; and it provides an enhanced opportunity for the employee to self-actualize, fulfill his or her potential, and gain the sense of achievement that psychologists argue is important in motivation.

Lifelong learning is not the sort of tool (like incentives or merit pay) that springs to mind when you think about motivating employees. However, the motivational effect of giving employees an opportunity to develop their skills and to self-actualize appears to be considerable. One study concluded that "productivity improvements, greater workforce flexibility, reduced material and capital costs, a better motivated workforce, and improved quality of the final product or service are all identified as advantages [of lifelong learning] for commercial enterprises."[84]

An Integrating Model: How to Analyze Performance-Motivation Problems

Your employee is not performing up to par. You want to understand what is happening—and why—and correct the problem.

To help you reduce the vast number of potential causes and to simplify your analysis, you may find Figure 11.14 useful. The model, based on what we discussed in this chapter, assumes that inadequate performance may have three main sources: Either the person (1) does not know what to do in terms of his or her goals; or (2) could not do the job if he or she wanted to; or (3), is not motivated to do the job. Use the model to analyze and solve the performance-motivation problem.

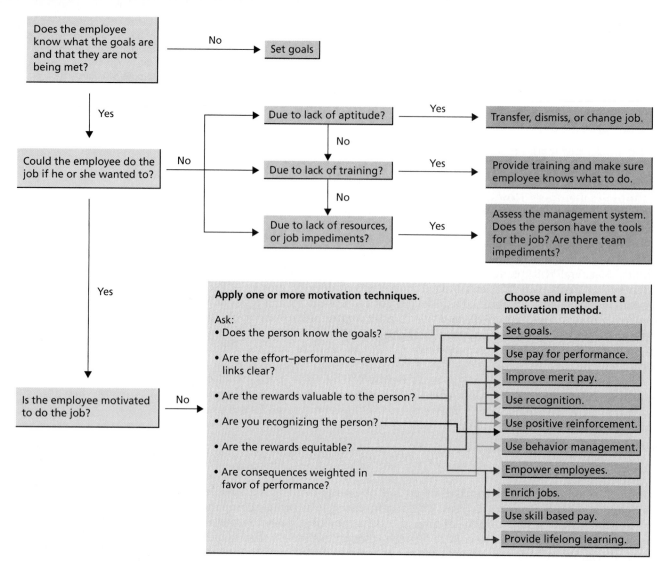

▲ **FIGURE 11–14** ■■■

How to Analyze Performance-Motivation Problems

Source: Copyright Gary Dessler, Ph.D. Suggested in part by "Performance Diagnosis Model," David Whetton and Kim Cameron, *Developing Management Skills* (Upper Saddle River, NJ: Prentice Hall, 2001), p. 339.

SUMMARY ■■■

1. Motivation is the intensity of the person's desire to engage in some activity. Need-based approaches to motivating employees—such as those of Maslow and Herzberg—emphasize the role played by motivational dispositions or needs, such as the need for achievement and for self-actualization.

2. An employee's thought process also influences motivation. Thus, people seek equity in their inputs and rewards. Having decided to pursue a goal, they regulate their behavior to try to ensure that they reach that goal. Their expectations—that effort will lead to performance, that performance will lead to reward, and that the reward is valuable enough to pursue in the first place—also influence motivation.

3. Behavior modification means changing or modifying behavior through the use of contingent rewards or punishment. It assumes, for instance, that behavior that appears to lead to a positive consequence or reward tends to be repeated, whereas behavior that leads to a negative consequence or punishment tends not to be repeated.

4. Methods based on motivational approaches like Maslow's theory and behavior modification include pay for performance, spot awards, merit raises, empowerment, goal setting, positive reinforcement, and lifelong learning.

SKILLS AND STUDY MATERIALS

COMPANION WEBSITE ■■■

 We invite you to visit the Dessler Companion Website at **www.prenhall.com/dessler** for this chapter's Internet resources.

EXPERIENTIAL EXERCISES ■■■

1. In teams of 4–5 students, use Figure 11.12 to analyze your professor's job for its enrichment potential. To what extent would you say it is enriched now? Why? What specifically would you do to enrich it more?

2. You like everything your professor does, with one glaring exception: He insists on spending much of each lecture with his back toward the class. His excuse is that he's busy writing on the board. However, in an average 80-minute class, he probably turns his back to the class and talks 30 to 35 times, and it is driving everyone to distraction. One student said, half in jest, that it would be less distracting if he'd at least give his lectures with a baseball cap on backwards. In teams of 4–5 students, develop a behavior management program to cure your professor of his annoying behavior.

3. The business school dean decided to put her professors on an incentive plan and did the following. She said that henceforth, faculty members would get a 1% raise each year for every 0.10 points that their average student evaluations are above 4.00 (out of 5.00). (Thus, someone with a 4.2 average would get a 2% raise.) Professors with average evaluations equal to or under 4.00 get no raise. Students now use a simple form that asks them to rate professors from 1 to 5 on several traits, including preparation, accessibility, and fairness. The Dean's professors are now upset. They say the plan is ambiguous, unfair, and unscientific. In teams of 4–5 students, evaluate the dean's incentive plan, and make specific suggestions for improving it.

CASE STUDY ■■■

DAYTON-HUDSON CORPORATION: LEARNING TO MOTIVATE EMPLOYEES

Dayton-Hudson Corporation (DHC) wants to run "the best stores in town." The owner of Dayton's, Hudson's, Mervyn's, Marshall Fields, and Target, DHC understands that to have the best stores, it needs to attract, retain, and motivate the best employees. Since women consumers account for most of the retail-shopping dollars spent, DHC also wants to attract and motivate women managers; it has therefore developed various policies to make the company attractive to prospective women employees.

DHC has been successful in its efforts to promote women managers. The company's most recent Equal Employment Opportunity (EEO) report noted that in senior management, 26% of DHC managers at the level of vice president or higher are women. Of middle management at the company, 37% are women. Women recently comprised more than 66% of DHC's employee population.

Each of DHC's major divisions has its own program of compensation-related HR policies and benefits, but they all have several common features:

■ Pretax salary set-asides to help pay for dependent care

■ Child-care resource and referral information

- Employee participation in alternative work arrangements, such as telecommuting, job-sharing, working at home, flex-time, and part-time employment
- Time off to care for a sick child or seriously ill family member
- Generous leaves for pregnancy
- 401(k) plan and employee stock option/stock ownership plan that includes a dollar-for-dollar match for the first 5% of salary
- Additional programs in individual divisions, such as expense reimbursement for adoption and prenatal and well-baby care programs

Working Mother magazine has six times named DHC one of the top workplaces for women with children. It has noted a number of key features in the DHC programs, including the publication of its overall benefits program.

The stakes are very high in the retail industry. Consider the Target division of DHC. Since opening the first Target store in May 1962 in suburban St. Paul, Minnesota, the company has grown to nearly 900 stores in 44 states. Target provides employment for approximately 189,000 people. The parent company, DHC, is America's fourth largest general merchandise retailer, with more than a quarter of a million team members. However, profit margins have been eroding for years as customers seek ever-better sales, and it's obvious that only the most efficient retailers are going to survive.

Discussion Questions

1. DHC has hired you as a consultant to evaluate the motivational potential of its various compensation programs. Write a brief report titled "The Motivational Potential of DHC's Family-Friendly Compensation Program." Please make sure to explain (in terms of the motivation theories in this chapter) the extent to which each program (such as preset salary set-asides) is or is not motivational.

2. Why (if at all) do you think DHC's compensation programs would help to motivate women in particular to work in its stores and /or offices?

3. In your opinion, does DHC have all the programs it needs to motivate managers? Why or why not? Based on what you know about the retail store business, propose three specific motivational programs you would recommend that Target use for the salespeople in its stores.

YOU BE THE CONSULTANT ■■■

JETBLUE: KEEPING THE TROOPS HAPPY

jetBlue AIRWAYS® One reason JetBlue's costs are low is that it doesn't have labor unions. It can, therefore, "require higher productivity from its 2,100 employees while paying them lower wages than unionized airlines."[85]

However, employees are not foolish; they know when they're working harder than their colleagues at other airlines for about the same pay. Yet without that higher productivity, JetBlue would not be as competitive. The question is, "How does JetBlue keep morale and motivation up so that its workers are willing to work harder for the same or less pay?"

JetBlue accomplishes this in several ways. One is by providing very flexible working conditions. For example, its staff of 350 or so reservation agents work from special minicall centers in their homes, and so they needn't travel to work.[86] JetBlue also lets its flight attendants decide how many hours they want to work. For example, they have some flight attendants on traditional schedules and some on a more flexible college student flight attendant program. The JetBlue Friend's Crew Program is another example. In this program, JetBlue hires people to share a schedule.[87] Thus, two friends might share one flight attendant's schedule, and decide between themselves who flies when.

JetBlue also has several pay and benefits programs aimed at keeping morale and motivation high. Its new, high-tech planes and new systems mean JetBlue can fly with fewer employees per plane. That means pay at JetBlue is quite competitive. Furthermore, JetBlue employees like the company's profit-sharing plan. Asked how the company's profit-sharing plan increases employees productivity, CEO David Neeleman gave the following answer: "One day in December, there were a lot of cancellations in the New York City area, and we operated our flights deep into the night, but we got them all done. I got e-mail from employees who picked up passengers off canceled flights from all these other carriers from LaGuardia, and they wrote 'profit sharing' in big bold letters."[88]

JetBlue also keeps some employee benefits higher than those at other airlines. For example, rather than wait until a new employee has completed his or her 90-day probationary period, he or she starts getting benefits almost at once. Similarly, whereas most airlines don't pay for new employees benefits (such as hotel expenses) while they're being trained, JetBlue pays them during training.

For much of this, JetBlue can probably thank Ann Rhoades. They hired her as the HR chief from Southwest Airlines, which has a reputation for high morale. However, in that regard, a recent news item might raise some concern for JetBlue's management. Recently, Southwest Airlines has been running into some unexpected turbulence with regard to its employee relations. Its mechanics want a federal mediator to help settle a two-year contract battle. Its flight attendants and reservations agents are demanding new contracts. Ground workers sued the airline because of how Southwest is disciplining its employees. And its pilots were reluctantly voting on a Southwest contract offer that their own pilot union leaders said was insufficient.[89] Since Southwest is in many respects, the model that David Neeleman used in creating JetBlue, Southwest's recent employee turbulence may be a warning sign. As one writer noted, "Neeleman obsesses over keeping employees happy, and with good reason. Airline watchers say JetBlue's ability to stay union free is critical to its survival as a low-cost carrier."[90] Analysts seem to agree that JetBlue's managers know what it takes to keep employees happy. the question is "Can they do what's necessary to avoid the sorts of problems that Southwest seems to be running into?"

You and your team are consultants to Mr. Neeleman, who is depending on your management expertise to help in navigating the launch and management of JetBlue. Here's what he wants to know from you now.

Assignment

1. What are the pros and cons of the JetBlue profit-sharing incentive plan? Are there any changes you would recommend?

2. Assume that a consultant has recommended to JetBlue that, if it wants to keep its labor costs down, it should use job enrichment, either for its pilots, mechanics, or flight attendants. Do you agree that JetBlue can substitute "job enrichment" for "pay"—in other words, make the job itself so motivating that people will willingly work hard even if the pay is not as good as it might be at another airline? Next, choose the pilots', mechanics', or flight attendants' jobs. Ascertain (from what you know about such jobs) if the job is amenable to job enrichment, and explain in detail how you would enrich it.

3. David Neeleman and his managerial colleagues work very hard to make sure they hire sociable, friendly people to be JetBlue employees, because they want to make sure JetBlue's customer service remains among the best in the industry. Assume that you want to develop a behavior management program for flight attendants. You want to focus on improving "customer service." Define the specific activity you will use to measure customer service, and then develop a behavior management program for this activity for the flight attendants.

12 Improving Communication Skills

CHAPTER OBJECTIVES

After studying this chapter and the case exercises at the end, you should be able to:

1. Identify the communications barriers the managers seem to be ignoring.

2. List and explain what the manager can do to improve interpersonal communications.

3. Conduct an effective appraisal interview using the facts and roles in a scenario.

4. Persuade a colleague to carry out a task.

5. Explain why a manager is not getting good results in tryng to encourage upward feedback.

THE MANAGEMENT CHALLENGE

Emily Liu Gets Zapped

Asia-based customer service representative Emily Liu had spent several years building a good working relationship with her U.S. colleague. She knew that when a customer service problem arose, she could e-mail or phone the colleague and quickly solve the problem. She had met with and spoken often with this person, and they'd become a team. Liu was, therefore, disturbed to receive an e-mail from managers in the United States. It said that management had just eliminated the firm's customer service operation from U.S. headquarters. Her e-mailed instructions were brusque and businesslike.[1] In the future, if she had a customer service problem that required U.S.-based help, she should contact the appropriate marketing representative for each product. The e-mail didn't specify who Liu should contact for each product.

Liu's former customer service colleague sent her a short note of regret, and said the firm had transferred him to another department. Emily Liu was upset. She found it insulting to learn so impersonally about something she considered so important. "At least they could have done it by videoconference—not by e-mail," she said.[2] Other customer service reps, also notified by e-mail, were even more upset. Several soon left the company. Management had to decide what (if anything) to do to rectify the blunder—and to make sure it didn't happen again.

Just about everything managers do requires communicating. One study found supervisors spent 53% of their time in meetings, plus 15% writing and reading, plus 9% on the phone.[3] Another found that, including meetings and interacting with customers and colleagues, managers spent 60% to 80% of their time communicating.[4] As Emily Liu well knows, communication is also important for employees' peace of mind. One study concluded, "Communication with one's superior was a significant predictor of job satisfaction, irrespective of job level."[5]

The purpose of this chapter is to make you a better communicator. The main topics we'll address include barriers to effective communication; how to improve interpersonal, organizational, and informal communications; and how to use technology to improve communications.

The word *communication* derives from the Latin verb *communicare*, "to make common."[6] How you communicate—whether by talking, writing letters, sending e-mails, or giving lectures—is beside the point. Those are just means to an end. Communication means exchanging information in such a way that you create a common basis of understanding and feeling. This chapter will show you how to do this easily and effectively.

communication ■ *the exchange of information and the transmission of meaning.*

■■■ WHAT EVERY MANAGER SHOULD KNOW ABOUT COMMUNICATING

A man drove up to a gasoline pump to fill his tank. The gas station attendant noticed three penguins in the back seat of the car and, curious, asked about them.

"I don't know how they got there," the driver said. "The penguins were there when I took the car out of the garage this morning."

The attendant thought for a moment. "Why don't you take them to the zoo?"

"Good idea," the driver said, and drove away.

The next day, the same man returned to the station. In the back seat were the same three penguins, but now they wore sunglasses.

The attendant looked at them in surprise. "I thought you took them to the zoo!" said the attendant. "I did," the driver said, "and they had such a good time that now I'm taking them to the beach."

The Communication Process

The problem, of course, is that, like our friend with the penguins, what one person says is not always what the other person hears. As you already know from your own experiences, many things—misunderstandings, semantics, or even fear—can distort the meaning of what people think you're trying to say.[7] Barriers like these can ruin your management career. They can cripple even the simplest supervisory tasks, such as giving instructions, setting goals, and motivating and coaching your employees.

To better understand how such problems arise, it helps to walk through the communication process. Figure 12.1 depicts that process. As you can see, the process includes five main components, and problems can arise in any one.[8] Assume you're about to give your subordinate a semiannual appraisal interview. Where might communication problems arise?

- *The information source.* The information source is the message, idea, thought, or fact that you want to communicate. In this case, your subordinate (let's call him Joe) has not performed well. The basic thought you want to get across to him is this: "Your performance this past six months has been below par, and if it doesn't improve by the end of the year, we're going to have to let you go."
- *The signal.* The signal is the stream of words, images, or gestures you use to actually express the message. The signal is what you actually say to Joe when you meet with him, as well as the gestures you use to help communicate your point.
- *The transmission,* and *the channel or medium.* The day of the appraisal interview arrives, and you sit down with Joe. The *transmission* is the act of actually sending, delivering, or transferring the message to Joe, which you do using a *medium* or *channel,* such as a report, image, speech, or (in this case) a one-on-one interview.

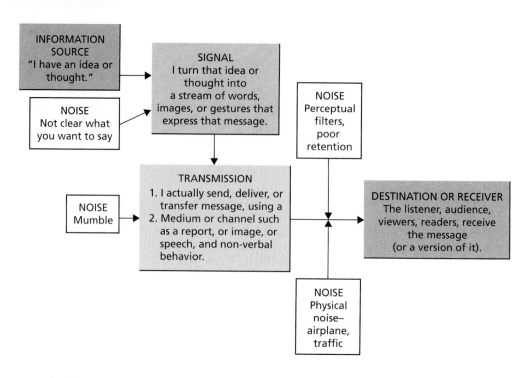

- *The destination or receiver.* The destination or receiver is the listener, audience, viewer, or reader that you're actually aiming your message at—in this case, Joe.
- *The noise.* Noise is any barrier that blocks, distorts, or in any way changes the *information source* (the idea, thought, or fact that you originally started out to communicate) as it makes its way to the destination/receiver. Noise can arise at each step in the communication process.

■ *Application Example* The appraisal interview does not go well. The *signal*—the stream of words, images, or gestures—that you actually used to express your message was muddled. Hoping to set the stage for a positive outcome, you made the mistake of opening the meeting by talking about the local football team's recruiting problems. You sent a mixed signal. Joe, having worried about this meeting for two weeks, starts getting agitated and drumming his fingers on the table. The more agitated he gets, the more uptight you get. You're soon mumbling and looking down at your feet. Annoyed with yourself, you finally make your point (while still looking down): "Your performance this past six months has been well below par, and if you don't improve by the end of the year, we're going to have to let you go." At this point, Joe is only hearing about 10% of what you say. He hears "have to let you go," and he starts arguing that you can't fire him without warning, especially since he's had such good performance—"considering my family situation" (his mother has been ill). You have not delivered your message, he's missed your point, and you're both agitated. This is hardly an example of creating a "common basis of understanding and feeling." There is little likelihood of using this meeting to improve Joe's performance. You ignored the potential noise/problems/barriers at each step of the communication process. Let's look more closely at each of these barriers.

Noise: Barriers to Effective Communication

The situation with Joe did not have to occur. You could have had a productive meeting by (1) keeping the goal of "creating a common basis for understanding and feeling" in mind and (2) by anticipating the communication problems that could arise.[9] These potential barriers include the following.[10]

Ambiguous, Muddled Messages "Say what you mean, and mean what you say," one expert advises, and that is good advice indeed. Few things cause communication breakdowns more often than ambiguous, muddled messages. *Ambiguity of meaning* means the person receiving the message isn't sure what the person who sent it meant. (Does "We're going to have to let you go" mean immediately or next year?) *Ambiguity* *of intent* means the words may be clear, but the sender's intentions aren't. ("This is an appraisal interview. Why is he talking to me about the football team?") *Ambiguity of effect* means the receiver is uncertain about what the message's consequences might be. ("Is he actually going to fire me?") In any case, the solution is to formulate and send a clear, unambiguous message.

Semantics Words mean different things to different people. The attendant said, "Take the penguins to the zoo," but he didn't mean as tourists. Luckily for the penguins, the driver misinterpreted his meaning. Telling a hospital administrator that she has "scabs" in her hospital may mean a sign of recuperation to her, but something different to the head of the local union.

Physical Barriers Physical barriers range from obvious to subtle. Street noise, frequent interruptions, and the clattering of machines are obvious distractions. Indecipherable writing and tiny font are less obvious sources of noise. Even discomfort is a source of noise. A recent ad for a desk chair says, "Think of what your brain could be accomplishing now, if it didn't have to worry about your back."

Loss of Transmission Everyone with cable TV is familiar with this problem, but loss of transmission along the line is not limited to cables and wires. People rarely relay messages without snipping from (or adding to) them in some way. You, therefore, cannot assume that the message you send will be exactly the one that reaches the destination.

Failing to Communicate Problems like those cited previously assume that you've taken the time to send a message, but failing to communicate at all is a problem in itself. For example, the manager may just assume that "everyone knows" and not follow up by sending a message.

Competition Barriers As every professor knows, the person you're speaking to is not "yours" alone. The students in the lecture hall may have matters they want to discuss with each other; the employee you're appraising may have his mind on his sick mother;

TABLE 12–1	**Some Differences Between Japanese and American Communication Styles**
Japanese *Ningensei* Style of Communication	**U.S. Adversarial Style of Communication**
Indirect verbal and nonverbal communication	More direct verbal and nonverbal communication
Strategically ambiguous communication	Prefers more to-the-point communication
Delayed feedback	More immediate feedback
Patient, longer-term negotiators	Shorter-term negotiators
Uses fewer words	Favors verbosity
Cautious, tentative	More assertive, self-assured
Softer, heartlike logic	Harder, analytic logic preferred
Makes decisions in private venues, away from public eye	Frequent decisions in public at negotiating tables
Decisions via *ringi* and *nemawashi* (complete consensus process)	Decisions by majority rule and public compromise are more commonplace
Uses go-betweens for decision making	More extensive use of direct person-to-person, player-to-player interaction for decisions
Understatement and hesitation in verbal and nonverbal communication	May publicly speak in superlatives, exaggerations, nonverbal projection
Uses qualifiers; tentative; humility as communicator	Favors fewer qualifiers; more ego-centered
Shy, reserved communicators	More publicly self-assertive
Distaste for purely business transactions	Prefers to "get down to business" or the "nitty gritty"
Utilizes *matomari*, or "hints," for achieving group adjustment and saving face in negotiating	More directly verbalizes management's preference at negotiating tables

Source: Adapted from *International Journal of Intercultural Relations* 18, no. 1, A. Goldman, "The Centrality of 'Ningensei' to Japanese Negotiating and Interpersonal Relationships: Implications for U.S.-Japanese Communications," copyright 1994.

and that e-mail you send may simply get lost among two dozen messages your manager has to deal with that day. Many other things are competing for your audience's time and attention. It's usually a mistake to assume that you've got the person's full attention.

Cultural, Linguistic, and Diversity Barriers There is always the potential for a Tower of Babel effect in today's diverse and globalized organizations. Words and gestures often mean different things in different ethnic and cultural groups. Table 12.1 illustrates this fact. For example, the Japanese tend to be indirect and relationship-oriented, while U.S. managers are more direct and "get to the point"-oriented.

An informal survey of managers from 15 countries helps highlight this point. The managers mentioned lack of cultural understanding as the biggest challenge in communicating with people around the world. Other challenges (in order) were "being thorough and very careful with interpretations," "careful audience research," "keeping communication simple," "respecting everyone," "using technology as an asset," "knowing similarities as well as differences," and "teaching the value of a globally accepted language."[11]

Not Listening Many communication efforts fail because one of the parties simply does not or will not listen. We'll see that "active listening" skills are crucial for managers.

Nonverbal Communication

The people who said "It's not what you say, but how you say it" were wiser than they realized. This is because "[i]t has been estimated that in a conversation involving two people, verbal aspects of a message account for less than 5% of the meaning, whereas nonverbal aspects of a message account for 95% of the meaning."[12] In other words (to use our terms), the *channel or medium* you use to make your point is not always just the one you consciously choose. People also draw conclusions about who you are and what you mean from your manner of speaking, facial expressions, bodily posture, and so on—from your nonverbal communication. And this can present a problem.

Here's how one expert interprets some common nonverbal behaviors:

1. Scratching your head indicates confusion or disbelief.
2. Biting your lips signals anxiety.
3. Rubbing the back of your head or neck suggests frustration or impatience.
4. A lowered chin conveys defensiveness or insecurity.
5. Avoiding eye contact conveys insincerity, fear, evasiveness, or (at the very least) lack of interest in what's being discussed.
6. A steady stare suggests a need to control, intimidate, and dominate.
7. Crossing your arms in front of your chest communicates defiance, defensiveness, resistance, aggressiveness, or a closed mind.
8. Handwringing is a strong sign of anxiety verging on terror.
9. In North America, getting a limp, dead-fish handshake is almost always a disappointment.[13]

> **nonverbal communication** ■ *the nonspoken aspects of communication, such as a person's manner of speaking, facial expressions, or body posture, that express meaning to others.*

The nonverbal aspects of communication can especially complicate the task of communicating internationally. For one thing, gestures have different meanings in different cultures. The A-OK sign means "everything's fine" in New York, but it may be a crude insult in South America.

The nonverbal part of communicating is more important in some societies than in others.[14] For example, a sales manager in Michigan might e-mail an unsolicited sales pitch to a potential customer in Taiwan, and be surprised when the person ignores the message. Yet, to the Taiwanese, ignoring such a message is quite understandable. In the United States, Canada, and northern Europe, the verbal content of a message tends to be more important than the setting in which the message is delivered. In such "low-context" cultures, an e-mail is often accepted as an efficient substitute for an in-person meeting.[15] But in many "high-context" countries, including many in Asia and the Middle East, context (or setting), with its nonverbal cues, can convey far more meaning than the words of a given message. Here business transactions tend to be ritualized, and the ritual is all-important. There's more emphasis both on face-to-face interaction and on after-hours socializing. You can see why the Michigan sales manager's efforts failed: Her e-mail lacked the nonverbal content and nuances so important to doing business in Asia.

■ **The Global Manager** Cultural differences like these help explain where Emily Liu's managers went wrong. Liu's low-context U.S. managers made the mistake of sending an important message to high-context Asia, as if the context didn't matter. In this case (as Liu said), a videoconference (with its opportunity for face-to-face interaction) might have helped avoid the ill will. Ironically, technology can thus actually hinder rather than aid global communication. It can make it too easy to lob an impersonal message from culture to culture and to forget that the people there may have different cultural needs.

Psychological Barriers

In addition to these barriers, psychology also plays a role in whether what one person says is the same as what another hears. Psychological barriers include perception, experience, emotions, and defenses.

Perception Misperceptions can wreck communications. This is because people's needs and situations shape how they see things. If you're concerned about losing your job, you may be jumpy if your boss schedules a meeting with you.

Perception problems manifest themselves in several ways. There is the selectivity/exposure filter: Here, you block out unpleasant things that you don't want to hear, or you "hear" things that may not be there. Thus, after buying a new car, people tend to screen out negative data about the car, and to be more aware of good news about it. There's the retention filter: You remember things that feel good, and tend to forget those that are painful.

Experiential Barriers Peoples' experiences also affect what they hear. For example, most people find it more difficult to understand things they haven't experienced themselves. So convincing employees who've never been injured at work that it's important to work safely may fall on deaf ears. The converse is that people find it easier to understand things they can identify with personally. The director of one large research lab wanted to make the point to his firm's board of directors that managing research scientists was no easy matter. He made it by saying that managing the lab "is like trying to herd a pack of alley cats." Most of the board members had never experienced managing research scientists (or cats). However, they could identify with the difficulty of getting two dozen screaming and independent-minded alley cats all going in the same direction. He made his point by linking it to something his audience could personally identify with.

Emotions You know from your own experience that your emotions influence what you say and how you hear things. An angry or frustrated person (like your appraisee, Joe) may ignore even the most persuasive argument. Someone in a good mood may be much more agreeable.

Defensiveness Defenses are adjustments people make, often without thinking, to avoid acknowledging personal inadequacies that might reduce their self-esteem. Accuse someone of poor performance and his or her first reaction may well be *denial*. Denial, here, is a defense mechanism. By denying fault, the person avoids having to question or analyze his or her own competence. People who react this way aren't ignoring what you said. They're simply "hearing" and reacting to it in a way that protects their self-esteem. What they are hearing is as real to them as what you're saying is to you.[16]

■■■ HOW TO IMPROVE INTERPERSONAL COMMUNICATION

Tasks that require interpersonal communication—communication between two people—fill the manager's day. The supervisor disciplines an employee for breaking the rules, shows a new employee how to improve her performance, and tries to convince production to get an order out early. Barriers like ambiguity and defensiveness can cripple any manager's efforts to make him- or herself understood—and thus his or her ability to lead.

interpersonal communication ■
*communication that occurs
between two individuals.*

Methods for Improving Interpersonal Communications

Managers who want to improve their interpersonal communications can use several methods.

TABLE 12–2   Guidelines for Written and Oral Work

Written Work	Oral Presentations
1. *Make sense.* Express your ideas in a coherent, orderly way.	1. *Speak up.*
2. *Back up your assertions.* Consider the use of examples, anecdotes, citation of authorities, statistics, and other forms of support.	2. *Achieve rapport quickly.* Use the first few moments to orient audience members and show them that you feel comfortable with them.
3. *Write for your audience.* Select language, length, arguments, and evidence that suit your audience.	3. *Look at your listeners.*
4. *Edit and revise.* Eliminate deadwood, provide transitions between ideas, and repair every error in grammar and spelling.	4. *Use gestures to express your ideas.*
5. *Format for readability.* Use word-processing to create easy-to-read, attractive documents.	5. *Move freely, without pacing.* Use the available space to move naturally.
6. *Write to express, not to impress.* Get to the point.	6. *Use notes (if necessary) as unobtrusively as possible.* Notes function best as "thought triggers."
7. *Prefer common language to difficult verbiage.* Mark Twain vowed "never to write 'metropolis' when I get paid the same for writing 'city'."	7. *Highlight key ideas.* Use voice volume, pauses, graphic aids, and "headlining" (telling listeners that a point is particularly important) to emphasize key points.
8. *Give credit to your sources.* Ideas, sentences, phrases, and terms that aren't your own must be footnoted.	8. *Channel nervous energy into an enthusiastic delivery.*
9. *Use graphic aids where necessary to capture and highlight ideas.*	9. *Watch your audience for signs of comprehension or misunderstanding.*
10. *Write with energy and conviction.*	10. *End with a bang, not a whimper.* Your concluding words should be memorable.

Source: Adapted from Arthur H. Bell and Dayle M. Smith, *Management Communication* (New York: Wiley, 1999), p. 14.

Pay Attention *Communication* means "exchanging information in such a way that you create a common basis of understanding and feeling." You are unlikely to create such a common understanding if you don't listen attentively and make it clear that the person has your full and undivided attention.

Make Yourself Clear "Say what you mean and mean what you say." If you mean immediately, say "immediately," not "as soon as you can." If you are there to discuss the employee's appraisal, don't muddy the waters by prefacing your remarks with something irrelevant. Also, make sure your tone, expression, and words convey a consistent meaning. Table 12.2 provides guidelines for clear written and oral work.

Be an Active Listener Communications pioneer Carl Rogers says that "active listeners" don't just listen to what the speaker says; they also try to understand and respond to the feelings behind the words.[17] They try to understand the person from his or her point of view and to convey the message that they do understand. Checklist 12.1 presents a guideline for honing your active listening skills.

CHECKLIST 12.1 ■ Active Listening

☑ **Listen for total meaning.** For example, if the sales manager says, "We can't sell that much this year," the typical knee-jerk response might be "Sure you can." An active listener would strive to understand the underlying feelings (such as the pressure the sales manager is under): "I know how you feel, so let's see what we can work out."

☑ **Reflect feelings.** Show the person that his or her message is getting through. For example, say something like, "They're pushing you pretty hard, aren't they?"

☑ **Note all cues.** Remember that not all communication is verbal. Facial expressions and gestures reveal feelings, too.

☑ **Give the person your full attention.** Turn off the phone, ignore the computer screen, don't look at your watch. Don't listen only for what you want to hear; don't think ahead to what you plan to say next; don't interrupt or finish people's sentences.

☑ **Show that you are listening with an open mind.** Avoid killer phrases ("You've got to be kidding.") and "Yes, but . . ."; avoid judgmental body language (rolling one's eyes).

☑ **Encourage the speaker to give complete information.** Ask open-ended questions; confirm your understanding by paraphrasing, summarizing, and asking if your paraphrase or summary was the message the speaker intended.

Source: Adapted from Paula J. Caprioni, *The Practical Coach: Management Skills for Everyday Life* (Upper Saddle River, NJ: Prentice Hall, 2001), p. 86.

Don't Attack the Person's Defenses Criticizing, arguing, even giving advice can trigger defensiveness, as the other person tries to protect his or her self-image. For example, don't try to explain a person to him- or herself by saying things like, "You know the reason you're using that excuse is that you can't bear to be blamed for anything." Instead, focus your comments on the act itself ("Production levels are too low"). Sometimes, it's best to do nothing—postpone action until you both cool down.

Get Feedback It's no coincidence that where life hangs in the balance, feedback (confirming that the message was received and understood) is mandatory. In situations like these, communication failures are simply unacceptable. Thus, the operating room nurse repeats, "scalpel," when the surgeon says, "scalpel." When the pilot orders, "Wheels down," the co-pilot says, "wheels down." However, getting feedback is obviously not limited to life-and-death situations. Asking the person to repeat his or her understanding of your point is always a straightforward way to confirm understanding.

How to Be More Persuasive

Many management tasks require persuading others. The coach who wants to motivate her team, the director who wants to sell his plan to the board, the supervisor who wants a new computer, and the manager who wants to get an employee to do better all need to be persuasive. This is especially true today, when leaders must often persuade, rather than order, their teams to go in a particular direction.

One person who has studied senior business leaders says many managers underestimate the power of and need for persuasive skills. As he says, "Persuasion is widely perceived as a skill reserved for selling products and closing deals."[18] In fact, he says that persuasiveness is a skill managers need in a variety of situations.

Studies suggest that people tend to make several mistakes when trying to persuade others.[19] They assume that the way to persuade is by *overwhelming the other party* with a barrage of ideas, facts, and figures. In actuality, this sales pitch is more often a turnoff,

HERMAN®   by Jim Unger

9-17   © Jim Unger/dist. by United Media, 1999

"Is that your final answer?"

and it gives the other party specific targets to attack. *They resist compromise.* By failing to compromise, the manager sends the signal that he or she is not interested in reaching a common basis of understanding—and, is thus not communicating. *They assume the secret of persuasion lies in presenting great arguments.* In fact, the person's credibility—and making the proposal in a way that makes sense to recipients—is as or more important. Finally, *they assume persuasion is a one-shot effort.* More often, persuasion is a process, one in which ideas are floated, positions are tested, and new, more "salable" positions arrived at incrementally.

Research also suggests that "persuasion works by appealing to a limited set of deeply rooted human drives and needs, and it does so in predictable ways. Persuasion, in other words, is governed by basic principles that can be taught, learned, and applied."[20] Checklist 12.2 includes suggestions for being more persuasive.

CHECKLIST 12.2 ■ How to Be More Persuasive

☑ **1. Establish your credibility.** It is difficult to persuade anyone to do anything if they think you don't know what you're talking about or if they don't trust you. To establish your creditability marshall *the facts* underlying your position, underscore your *expertise* (perhaps by listing what you've accomplished), and cultivate and mention *relationships* that help prove your credibility.

☑ **Frame for common ground.** Present your argument in terms that appeal to the person you're trying to persuade.

☑ **Connect emotionally.** Facts and figures only get you so far. A recent ad for a Mitsubishi automobile shows four 20-something people gliding in their new Mitsubishi, miming rock lyrics with the music in the background. Like most ads, this one aims to persuade by connecting emotionally with its audience.

☑ **Provide evidence.** Once you've established your credibility, framed for common ground, and connected emotionally, persuasion becomes a matter of presenting supporting evidence. "The most effective persuaders . . . supplement numerical data with examples, stories, metaphors, and analogies to make their positions come alive."[21]

☑ **Use peer power whenever it's available.** It's easier to persuade someone to do something once you've made the point that others they identify with have already done something similar.[22]

☑ **Have the person make the commitment active, public, and voluntary.** Remember that people tend to align their actions with the commitments they've made.

How to Improve Your Negotiating Skills

"Everything," someone once said, "is a negotiation." Whether you're buying a car, requesting a raise, getting a better seat on a plane, or trying to get an employee to improve, negotiations are involved.

One expert says that negotiators typically make several big mistakes and suggests these ways to prevent them:[23]

- *Neglecting the other side's problems.* Like other forms of communication, negotiations usually go best when they aim to achieve a common basis of understanding. Good negotiating therefore involves striving to understand the other person's problems and point of view.
- *Letting price overwhelm other interests.* Some negotiators let the negotiations fall apart over price, when discussing the deal's other terms might have saved the day. For example, a higher price for the new computer system may look less foreboding if the store will finance the purchase.
- *Searching too hard for common ground.* Sometimes, the best way to proceed is to accept that the parties have different agendas. For example, the potential buyer for a small company wants to do the deal but is much less optimistic about the firm's future prospects than the firm's current owner. Here, structure a deal that takes into account these differences. For example, negotiate a deal whereby an initial payment is followed by a series of payments contingent on the performance of the business.
- *Neglecting BANTRAs.* In their book *Getting To Yes*, Robert Fisher, Bill Ury, and Bruce Patton stress the importance of knowing your "best alternative to a negotiated agreement" (BANTRA). For example, the best alternative may not be "doing" the deal, but walking away, approaching another buyer, or making the product in-house. Don't become so swept up in the negotiations that you forget other alternatives.

Experienced negotiators also use several tactics to improve their bargaining positions. *Leverage* refers to the factors that help or hinder a party in a bargaining situation. You want all the leverage you can muster, of course.[24] Necessity, desire, competition, and time are leveraging factors. The seller who must sell (of *necessity*) is at a disadvantage: It's being able to walk away from a deal (or to look like you can) that wins a negotiator the best terms. That is one reason why having an offer of another job is so persuasive when you're negotiating for a raise. Similarly, the new car may not be a necessity, but if your *desire* is too obvious, it will undercut your bargaining power. *Competition* is important, too. There is no more convincing ploy then telling the other party that someone else wants to make the deal. *Time* (and particularly deadlines) can also tilt the tables—for or against you.

Furthermore, in negotiations, "knowledge is power." Going into the negotiation armed with *information* about the other side and about the situation puts you at a relative advantage (of course, the opposite is also true). *Credibility* is important: The people on the other side will be trying to decide if you're bluffing, so convincing them otherwise is an important negotiating skill. Good negotiators also use good *judgment*: They have the ability to "strike the right balance between gaining advantages and reaching compromises, in the substance as well as in the style of [their] negotiating technique."[25]

▪▪▪ IMPROVING ORGANIZATIONAL COMMUNICATION

Organizational communication means exchanging information in such a way that you create a common basis of understanding and feeling among two or more individuals or groups throughout the organization. *Downward communications* go from superior to subordinate, and they consist of communiqués regarding things like what a job entails, where the firm is heading, and what the firm's required procedures and practices are. *Lateral* (horizontal) *communications* move between departments or between people in the same department. *Upward communication* (from subordinates to superiors) provides management with insights into the company and its employees and competitors.

organizational communication
▪ *communication that occurs among several individuals or groups.*

Special Barriers to Organizational Communication

Since people are usually involved, *interpersonal barriers* (such as ambiguities, semantics, and perception) also affect organizational communication. In addition, however, the nature of organizations (the fact that they're hierarchical and comprised of various departments, for instance) means that communications in them also suffer from some special barriers. For example, managers need to contend with the *authority, task, political,* and *identity boundaries* discussed in Chapter 8. For example, subordinates may act deferential toward their bosses and withhold unwelcome information. Politicking can prompt departments to withhold information from each other, although the company might suffer as a result.

Who says what to whom also tends to reflect the *organizational culture* of the firm. Some cultures encourage communication better than others do. Even in college, for example, some professors set a tone that encourages students to participate, while others prefer a more formal, teacher-oriented arrangement. We've also seen that some *organization structures* are more organic and open to free-flowing communications than are others. Thus, we saw in Chapters 6–9 that learning organizations emphasize networked flows of communications and eliminating organizational boundaries, and that employees in such organizations communicate easily with colleagues vertically and laterally throughout the chain of command.

The presence of barriers like these means that managers need to take some special steps to improve organizational communications. This means improving upward, downward, lateral, and organizationwide communications flows.

Improving Upward Communication

Encouraging upward communication can be quite advantageous. Doing so helps management know whether subordinates understand orders and instructions. It encourages subordinates to volunteer ideas. It provides management with valuable input on which to base decisions,[26] encourages gripes and grievances to surface,[27] and

► **FIGURE 12–2** ■ ■ ■

Getting Upward Feedback

Source: Adapted from Paula J. Caproni, *The Practical Coach* (Upper Saddle River, NJ: Prentice Hall, 2001), p. 21.

- Request feedback from people whom you trust and who will be honest with you.
- If the feedback is too general ("You're doing a fine job" or "There's room for improvement"), ask for examples of specific, recent behavior.
- Don't be defensive, make excuses, or blame others when you hear criticism.
- Do not overreact or underreact to feedback.
- Once the feedback is complete, summarize what the speaker said to make sure that you understand.
- Explain what you are going to do in response to the feedback, do it, evaluate the consequences on performance, and then let the feedback-giver know of the outcome.
- Thank the person for his or her concern and advice.

cultivates acceptance and commitment by giving employees an opportunity to express ideas and suggestions.[28] It helps employees "cope with their work problems and strengthen their involvement in their jobs and with the organization."[29] And it enables managers to see how subordinates feel about their jobs, superiors, and the organization.

On the other hand, getting upward feedback is more difficult than you might imagine. A major challenge is that some subordinates aren't eager to share bad news with their supervisors; there's thus a tendency for bad news to stay submerged. The commonsense solution here is to make sure that bringing you bad news does not produce a negative experience for your employee. Other suggestions include, don't be defensive, blame others, make excuses, or overreact. Don't "shoot the messenger." Be discreet about sources. Be accessible and approachable. Figure 12.2 summarizes these and other commonsense prescriptions. One expert says, "By far the most effective way of tapping the ideas of subordinates is sympathetic listening in the many day-to-day, informal contacts within the department and outside the workplace."[30] The Management in Action feature shows how one new president learned this simple lesson.

MANAGEMENT IN ACTION   Feedback at Harvard

■ ■ ■ *Lawrence Summers, inaugurated in October 2001 as Harvard's president.*

Lawrence Summers, Harvard University's new president, has an interesting way of eliciting upward communication: He starts debates (and some say arguments) with the people with whom he is talking.[31] For example, shortly after arriving at Harvard, Summers reportedly astonished law school professors who had invited him to meet Harvard's legal scholars. Says one professor, "He seemed to regard that the way to get to know the faculty was to have abstract debate, as opposed to just asking questions about the law school or politely inquiring about our research." (In this case, he triggered a heated debate by arguing that it was fair to use age as a factor in awarding tenure to professors.) At about the same time, members of the university's governing board had to get him to tone down his approach after he angered senior black professors by getting into a public feud with one of their colleagues, Cornell West, about the latter's performance. (West subsequently accepted a professorship at Princeton.)

To some on the Harvard campus, the contrast between Summers and his predecessor, Neil Rudenstine, is particularly stark. As one former Harvard officer said, "Neil had a soft approach. He spent his entire life in the academy. He believed in academic collegiality and exercising leadership through quiet persuasion." Whereas Rudenstine would say that something is "complicated" when he thought it was a bad idea, Summers would say it is "outrageous and stupid" even if what he really meant was that he was willing to listen to a good argument. Rudenstine would get information by gentle probing. Summers asks questions, restates the person's position, and then "smiles and refutes it." The effect on his professors can apparently be more than a little disconcerting.

On the other hand, there are some who believe that Summers' more direct style is exactly what Harvard needs now. The university is driving to revamp undergraduate education, hire hundreds of new professors, and take a number of other bold steps—and some believe this effort requires a more forceful, less collegial communication style.   ■ ■ ■

◀ FIGURE 12–3 ■ ■ ■

Sample Suggestion Program
Procedures LearnInMotion.com

Source: Business Plan Pro, Palo Alto
Software, Palo Alto, CA.

806 Suggestion Program

Effective Date: 4/23/02

As employees of LIM, you have the opportunity to contribute to our future success and growth by submitting suggestions for practical work-improvement or cost-savings ideas.

All regular employees are eligible to participate in the suggestion program.

A suggestion is an idea that will benefit LIM by solving a problem, reducing costs, improving operations or procedures, enhancing customer service, eliminating waste or spoilage, or making LIM a better or safer place to work. Statements of problems without accompanying solutions, or recommendations concerning coworkers and management are not appropriate suggestions.

All suggestions must be submitted on a suggestion form and should contain a description of the problem or condition to be improved, a detailed explanation of the solution or improvement, and the reasons why it should be implemented. If you have questions or need advice about your idea, contact your supervisor for help.

Submit suggestions to the Human Resources Director and, after review, they will be forwarded to the Suggestion Committee. As soon as possible, you will be notified of the adoption or rejection of your suggestion.

Special recognition will be given to employees who submit a suggestion that is implemented.

Familiar Techniques Other simple, effective methods for fostering upward organizational communication include:

1. *Social gatherings* (including departmental parties, picnics, and recreational events) provide opportunities for informal, casual communication.
2. *Union publications* provide useful insights into employee attitudes.
3. *Regular meetings* with subordinates, in addition to the informal contacts that take place every day, can be a good source of information.
4. *Performance appraisal meetings* are good opportunities to seek employees' opinions about their jobs and job attitudes.
5. *Grievances* provide top management with insights into operational problems.
6. *Attitude surveys* provide answers to (and help management address) questions like, "Are working hours and shift rotations perceived as reasonable?" "Do employees feel the boss has favorites?" and "Do employees consider cafeteria prices fair and the quality of the food good?"
7. *A suggestion system,* even a suggestion box, can encourage upward communication. Figure 12.3 shows one firm's suggestion program policy and procedure.
8. *An open door* policy lets employees express concerns through a channel outside the normal chain of command—and can thus act as a safety valve. (It can also be abused and undercut a supervisor's authority.)
9. *Indirect measures,* including absences, turnover rates, and safety records, are useful indicators of festering problems at the operational level.
10. *E-Mail:* Many firms, including Microsoft, encourage all employees to e-mail concerns and questions directly to top management.

Managers should not underestimate the usefulness of simple devices like these. Consider the results presented in the following Management in Action feature.

MANAGEMENT IN ACTION   Saved by Sheep

Techniques such as suggestion plans can sometimes lead to surprising solutions. For example, the Northern Ireland Electric Company has about 15 acres of grassy area under the overhead lines that it uses for training its employees. This land has to be mowed and maintained on a regular basis, no easy chore given the metal and bolts and nuts that get sprinkled around it.[32] How do you keep those acres mowed? The solution was so simple and so obvious that it took top management by surprise. As part of an employee suggestion plan, one employee suggested using sheep to graze the land and to keep it neat. The idea at first seemed unusual (to say the least). However, it has so far saved the company about £64,000 (about $100,000) over five years. ■■■

Comprehensive Programs Many firms install formal, comprehensive programs to encourage upward communication. For example, at its Lexington, Kentucky, plant, Toyota tells its employees, "Don't spend time worrying about something . . . Speak up!" The firm has what it refers to as "The Hotline." Employees can use any plant phone to dial the Hotline extension (the number is posted on the plant bulletin board) and deliver their messages to a recorder, 24 hours a day. Toyota guarantees that an HR manager will review and investigate all inquiries—and that the process is anonymous. If it's decided that a question would be of interest to other Toyota team members, then the question, with the firm's response, is posted on plant bulletin boards. If the employee wants a personal response, he or she can leave a name.[33]

Upward Appraisals Some firms now have provision for letting employees formally appraise their bosses. Studies suggest that this approach can have merit. In one study, researchers collected subordinates' ratings for 238 managers in a large firm at two points in time, six months apart.[34] Subordinates were asked to rate a variety of supervisory behaviors, such as "Regularly challenged me to continuously improve my effectiveness," "Took steps to resolve conflict and disagreement within the team," and "Treated me fairly and with respect."[35]

The prospect of upward appraisals didn't seem to affect the performance of managers whose original appraisals were high; their ratings were about the same six months later. It was a different story with the managers whose initial appraisals were moderate or low. Six months later, their ratings had jumped up. The researchers say, "This is encouraging, because these are the managers [who] most need to improve from the organization's (as well as the subordinates') perspective."[36] Interestingly, it didn't seem to matter whether the managers actually got feedback in six months regarding how they were doing. They improved with no feedback. It seemed that just knowing they'd be appraised was enough to get the bosses to improve their behavior at work.

Communicating with Your Supervisor The last thing a manager needs is a misunderstanding with his or her boss. Your boss wants results, expects you to contribute, and may not be an active listener. Therefore, avoid phrases that may inadvertently signal a lack of responsibility on your part. These include "I'm only human," "I'm overworked," "It slipped past me," "It's not my fault," "It's not my problem," and "You don't appreciate me."[37] Similarly, avoid counterproductive body language. Nonverbal mannerisms to avoid include cringing; looking down; rushing to be seated; slouching in your chair; bringing your hands to your face, mouth, or neck (this suggests anxiety and evasion); and crossing your arms in front of your chest.

Improving Downward Communication

Downward communication includes a variety of essential types of information regarding, for instance, job instructions, rationales for jobs (including how jobs are related to other jobs and positions in the organization), organizational policies and practices, employee appraisal results, and the organization's mission.[38] Much of what happens in companies requires downward communication. Indeed, the whole mechanism of making companies work, including giving orders, training employees, and informing employees about policies and practices and the company's mission, fits under the heading of "downward communication."[39]

Today's team-based, empowered companies are especially dependent on this type of information. Facilities like Toyota's Camry and GM's Saturn plants are largely run by knowledgeable and empowered employees, who are aware of and committed to the company's vision and strategy. The employees are more like partners, and as such, they require more company information than they might in more conventional situations.

Firms like these, therefore, make heroic efforts to keep their employees informed. At Saturn, assemblers "get information continuously via the internal television network and from financial documents."[40] The firm also has monthly town-hall meetings, usually with 500 to 700 attendees. The result is that all employees are familiar with Saturn's activities and performance. At Toyota, a closed-circuit TV at each worksite runs continuously, presenting plantwide information from the in-house

Toyota Broadcasting Center. The company sponsors quarterly roundtable discussions between top management and selected nonsupervisory staff, as well as an in-house newsletter. The plant's top managers are often on the shop floor, fielding questions, providing plant performance information, and ensuring that all team members are "aware of Toyota's goals and where we are heading."[41]

◼◼◼ *Toyota employees watch in-house programming during a break on the assembly line.*

Open-Book Management Other firms install open-book management programs. Open-book management "is a way of managing a company demonstrably, without concealment, that motivates all employees to focus on helping the business grow profitably and increasing the return on its human capital."[42] It means literally opening the company's books to its employees. The firm shares its financial data, explains its numbers, and rewards workers for improvements in performance.[43]

The basic idea behind open-book management is to foster trust and commitment among employees by treating them more like partners than employees. Manco, a Cleveland-based manufacturer of industrial products,[44] distributes its financial information to employees in three ways. Every month, each department gets four books, designated by color, with financial information broken down by company, department, product line, and customer. Monthly meetings are held so that employees can see whether they're on track to earn their bonuses and what, if anything, can be and is being done to see that they stay on track. Between meetings, management posts daily companywide sales totals. Employees can take accounting classes to help them understand the numbers.

open-book management ◼ *a management style in which a company opens its books to the employees, sharing financial data, explaining numbers, and rewarding workers for improvement.*

Communicating with Subordinates On a more micro basis, there are several things to keep in mind when communicating directly with one or more of your subordinates. Fairness and the appearance of fairness are key. You don't want to undermine your authority by behaving unprofessionally. In any case, going into attack mode will likely just trigger defensiveness on the person's part—and bring a halt to constructive discussion. Words to avoid with subordinates thus include *blame, catastrophe, demand, destroyed, idiotic,* and *misguided.* Phrases include *better shape up, don't come to me about it, don't want to hear it, figure it out for yourself, you don't understand,* and *you'd better.*

In terms of body language, "come across as open and receptive."[45] Maintain eye contact, smile, keep hands away from your face and mouth, use open-handed gestures, and (if you must achieve some subtle domination) direct your glance at the subordinate's forehead rather than meet his or her eyes directly.[46]

Improving Horizontal Communication

One sure route to managerial oblivion is to fail to get along with one's colleagues. You depend on them for help to get your job done, and your career progress and day-to-day peace of mind usually depend, to some extent, on how you get along with your peers. Therefore, belligerent-sounding words and phrases like *absurd, bad, can't, crazy, doomed, unworkable,* and *are you out of your mind?* are best left unsaid. Mannerisms to avoid include shaking your head no, avoiding eye contact, frowning, and pushing gestures (that is, using the hands as if to push people or things away).[47]

In terms of organizational design issues, we saw in Chapter 7 that managers can improve horizontal (interdepartmental) communication in several ways. These include:

- *Appoint liaison personnel.* For example, house a sales employee in the factory to help coordinate order processing.
- *Organize committees and task forces.* These meet periodically to discuss and solve common problems and to ensure interdepartmental communication and coordination.
- *Use independent integrators* to improve communication among departments.

Improving Organizationwide Communication

Communication flows more freely in some firms than in others. Getting your special order approved in one firm might take two minutes, while another keeps you waiting two years.

We saw in Chapters 6–9 that managers use various structural methods to improve organization-wide communication. For example, many superimpose formal, informal, or electronic *networks* over their existing organizational structures. These make it easier for managers from various departments, levels, and geographic areas to communicate directly, unencumbered by normal organizational boundaries. Stripping away the authority, task, identity, and political *boundaries* that can inhibit communication is another method.

However, structure alone rarely explains why one firm has free-flowing communication while another does not. In addition, the *organizational cultures* of some firms encourage communication, while discouraging it in others. If the firm's values say, "Don't rock the boat by letting your boss know something is wrong," bad news is unlikely to travel fast. Furthermore, it's often not the formal organization but the *informal organization* that determines how freely communication actually flows. We'll look at how to foster informal communications next.

■■■ IMPROVING INFORMAL COMMUNICATIONS

A number of years ago, two consultants, Tom Peters and Robert Waterman, conducted a study of what they called excellent, highly innovative companies. Their aim was to discover what those firms were doing that caused them to be excellent. One of their more notable findings was that these firms put enormous effort into fostering *informal communication*—communication that flows outside the firm's formal chain of command. In turn, this wealth of informal communication seemed to enable these firms to be quicker on thier feet, and also more innovative.[48] Some firms subsequently fell off most experts' lists of excellent companies. However, Peters and Waterman's findings regarding the techniques such companies used to encourage informal communication are worth noting.

How Excellent Companies Foster Informal Communications

Peters' and Waterman's main conclusion here was that "The excellent companies are vast networks of informal, open communications. The patterns and intensity cultivate the right people getting into contact with each other, regularly, and the chaotic/anarchic properties of a system are kept well under control simply because of the regularity of contact and its nature."[49] In these firms, "[t]he intensity and sheer volume of communications are unmistakable and usually start with a stress on informality."[50] Furthermore, "[t]he astonishing byproduct is the ability to have your cake and eat it too; that is, rich informal communication leads to more action, more experiments, more learning, and simultaneously to the ability to stay in touch and on top of things."[51] Here is what these companies do to accomplish this:

1. *They emphasize informality.* At Walt Disney productions, for instance, everyone from the president down wears a name tag with just his or her first name on it. (Employees wear these in the theme parks on a regular basis.) At 3M there are numerous meetings; most are characterized by the casual getting together of people from different disciplines who talk about problems in a campuslike, shirtsleeves atmosphere.
2. *They maintain communication intensity at an extraordinary level.* These excellent companies encourage an open confrontation of ideas, in which people are blunt and straightforward in going after the issues. For example, they hold meetings at which "the questions are unabashed; the flow is free; everyone is involved. Nobody hesitates to cut off the chairman, the president, or board members."[52]
3. *They provide physical support for informal communication.* In one high-tech firm, for instance, all employees from the president down work not in offices but in six-foot high doorless cubicles that encourage openness and interaction among employees. Corning Glass installed escalators rather than elevators in its new engineering building to increase the chance of face-to-face contact.[53] Another firm eliminated its four-person dining room tables; they replaced them with long rectangular ones

that encourage strangers to come into contact, often across departmental lines. Blackboards and open offices facilitate and encourage frequent informal interaction. The firm encourages managers to get out of their offices, walk around, and strike up conversations with employees in and outside their own departments.

Management by Wandering Around

Some dub that last technique "management by wandering (or walking) around." As one executive put it, "Go visit the department heads—chat with them, ask questions, learn what they do for a living. Ask them what is frustrating for them in their business process, and they will talk all day if you let them. You'll learn a great deal about how the cogs mesh . . ."[54]

For example, J. W. Marriott Jr. logs over 160,000 miles per year in plane travel, visiting his company's hotels, walking through their lobbies, guest rooms, and kitchens, and speaking with the employees. This not only helps him notice things that may need improvement. It also gives him direct access to what his firm's first-line employees are thinking and doing in all his hotels.

It's useful to keep in mind that wandering around doesn't automatically produce useful information. The communications skill here is not in the wandering but in the interpersonal communications skills you can bring to bear when you're speaking with the employees. These skills include paying attention, making yourself clear, listening actively, and listening sympathetically.

Dealing with Rumors and the Grapevine

When it comes to informal organizational communications, rumors and the grapevine are probably king-of-the-hill. Rumors are spread by the grapevine (the original organizational "network"), often at great speed.[55] In one classic study of 100 employees, the researcher found that when management made an important change in the organization, most employees heard the news first through the grapevine. Hearing news from a supervisor and official memorandums ran a poor second and third, respectively.[56] The Web site **www.greedyassociates.com** (a big hit with associates at major law firms) announced recently that "I heard Shearman [& Sterling, a Wall Street law firm] partners are sacrificing, in a bloody, gruesome manner, 1 of each 10 associates at midnight during the next full moon." The firm did indeed soon lay off about that many.[57]

Some rumors are accurate and some are not. Researcher Keith Davis said that there are three main reasons rumors get started: Lack of information, insecurity, and conflicts.[58] When employees don't know what's happening, they are likely to speculate about a situation—and a rumor is born. (Thus, employees who observe an unscheduled disassembly of a machine may erroneously assume that the firm will soon lay off the machine's operators.) Insecure employees are especially prone to react that way. Conflicts—such as those between union and management—may trigger rumors as each side uses propaganda to interpret the situation in a way most favorable to itself. Davis advises releasing the truth as quickly as possible, since the more the rumor spreads, the more people will believe it.

■■■ COMMUNICATING AT THE SPEED OF THOUGHT

Most people today understandably can't imagine communicating without thinking of technology-based devices like e-mail and the Internet. Let's, therefore, consider how managers use technology to improve communications.

Telecommunications

It looks like the control room of the USS *Enterprise*, but it's actually the Littleton, Colorado, network-reliability operations center of phone company USWest.[59] As at USWest, telecommunications—the electronic transmission of information—plays a big role in managing organizations today. The center's blinking screens let the 700 USWest employees there instantly see how the firm is performing in terms of phone problems

telecommunications ■ *the electronic transmission of data, text, graphics, voice (audio), or image (video) over any distance.*

in 14 western states. USWest once had 100 minicenters. These didn't provide the comprehensive, 14-state real-time information the company needed to react quickly if, for instance, a problem (like a massive storm sweeping across the area) was about to tie up more phones.

The Littleton center's high-tech communications capabilities mean its staff can provide fast, coordinated responses when emergencies arise. One or more employees from every major technical group (including engineering and repair) are in the room. Eight large screens alert workers to outages throughout the firm's 14-state region.[60] When a team monitoring the screens noted a mysterious gridlock in one area, the problem turned out to be the result of "thousands of people trying to call one merchant that had just received a shipment of beanie babies."[61] The solution was to put controls on the number of calls into that store's region so that the store's neighbors could start making calls again.

Telecommunications is also crucial for technology-based management systems. Levi Strauss uses such a system to link its inventory and manufacturing facilities with point-of-sale processing devices at retail stores. Computers analyze sales information instantaneously. Management can then make more accurate inventory and production plan decisions. JC Penney uses telecommunications to manage in-store inventories. Its buyers get instant access to sales information from the stores and can modify their purchasing decisions accordingly. Ford designers at the company's Dearborn, Michigan, headquarters use computers to design new cars like the Lincoln Continental. Digitized designs then go electronically to Ford's Turin, Italy, design facility. There, the system automatically reproduces the designs and creates styrofoam mockups of them.

Videoconferencing

Videoconferencing is a telecommunications-based method that lets group members interact directly with other team members via televised links.[62] The links may be by phone or satellite-based; or they may use one of the popular PC-based video technologies. Most let users send live video and audio messages with no more then a few seconds delay.[63] For example, the team developing the Boeing 777 made extensive use of videoconferencing for meetings with engine suppliers and airlines to discuss the new aircraft's design.[64] After 9/11, more U.S. firms began substituting videoconferences for on-site meetings.

Electronic Mail

As everyone knows, electronic mail (e-mail) is a computerized information system that lets people electronically create, edit, and communicate messages to one another, using electronic mailboxes. An *electronic bulletin board* lets one or more group members file messages on various topics that are to be picked up later by other group members.

More firms today configure their e-mail systems to automate communication tasks. For example, the e-mail software Eudora Pro helps one company manage its sales operation. The owner set up a computer to check all customers' accounts every 10 minutes, so he never misses a rush order. It also lets him sort messages based on key words like *brochure* (so requests for his brochures are automatically routed to the person in charge of mailing them).[65]

As e-mail use has proliferated, communications experts have suggested rules governing its use. For example:[66]

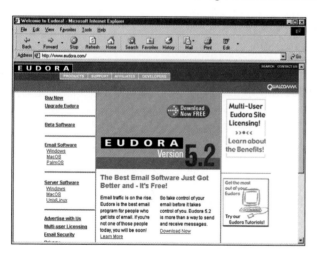

▲ WEBNOTE ■ ■ ■

Eudora's specialty is software to help companies manage e-mail efficiently.

www.eudora.com

1. *Use the right medium for the message.* Dealing with sensitive topics or trying to be persuasive is probably best left to more personal, rich media. E-mail is particularly useful for sending simple factual messages, for tasks such as setting up meetings, and for matters that you can cover in a paragraph or so. For more complex matters, consider snail mail, a phone call or meeting, or (at least) attaching your note as a document.

2. *Think before you hit the "send" key.* Don't send anything that you wouldn't want posted in a public place—or that you think you may be sorry about tomorrow.[67] While just about everyone who uses e-mail knows this is the case, it's something

that even CEOs still disregard at their peril. For example, the following e-mail from one corporate CEO quickly ended up on several Internet bulletin boards:

> *Hell will freeze over before this CEO implements any other employee benefit in this culture. We are getting less than 40 hours of work from a large number of our KC-based employees. The parking lot is scarcely used at 8 AM; likewise at 5 PM. As managers—you either do not know what your employees are doing; or you do not care . . . You have a problem and you will fix it or I will replace you . . . What you're doing, as managers, with this company makes me sick.[68]*

3. *Be professional.* Among other things, this means be concise, clear, respectful, and also sensible about who you add to your distribution list.

Work Group Support Systems

Telecommunications also powers "work group support systems." These are technology-based systems that make it easier for work-group members to work together. Team members might all be at a single site, or they may be dispersed around the city or the world. In any case, firms increasingly rely on all or most of the following work group support systems to help their employees get their jobs done. Table 12.3 summarizes the more popular digital-based work group collaboration systems, which include:

TABLE 12–3	Digital Work Group Support and Collaboration Systems	
Tool	**Description**	**Issues**
Electronic messaging systems	Messaging infrastructures such as e-mail or instant messenger systems	☐ rules governing use ☐ integration of multiple systems ☐ security
Electronic meeting systems	Real-time conferencing systems that may be managed by either local or remote sources	☐ scheduling ☐ postmeeting follow-up ☐ cost ☐ facilitation ☐ standard systems ☐ number of people who can work on system simultaneously and efficiently
Asynchronous conferencing systems	Content exchange that can occur instantly or over time using such tools as bulletin board systems	☐ facilitation ☐ follow-up on action items ☐ maximizing discussion
Document handling systems	Group document management, storage, and editing tools	☐ security ☐ work flow ☐ data integrity ☐ page mark-up standards ☐ standard systems ☐ ensuring user compatibility
Online communities	Web sites organized by subject matter where members access interactive discussion areas and share content, reference tools, and Web links	☐ facilitation ☐ value of shared content ☐ updating of content and resources
Workflow management systems	Project management, process diagramming, and routing tools	☐ establishing workflow standards ☐ making decisions ☐ establishing processes and systems
Group decision-support systems	Tools used to integrate collaboration and team management systems across computer platforms, operating systems, and network architectures	☐ security ☐ updating of systems ☐ customization

Source: Adapted from Jennifer Salopek, "Digital Collaboration" *Training and Development*, June 2000, v. 54, 6, 38.

The Ventana Corporation demonstrates the features of its GroupSystems for Windows electronic meeting software, which helps people create, share, record, organize, and evaluate ideas in meetings, between offices, or around the world.

decision support systems (DSS) ■ *an interactive computer-based communications system that facilitates the solution of unstructured problems by a team of decision makers.*

Group Decision-Support Systems A decision support system (DSS) is an interactive computer-based communications system that facilitates the solution of unstructured problems by a decision-making team.[69] It lets a team get together (often in the same room) and make better and faster decisions and complete their task more quickly. The DSS (as pictured in Figure 12.4) lets team members interact via their PCs and use several software tools to assist in decision making and project completion. These software tools include electronic questionnaires, electronic brainstorming tools, idea organizers (to help team members synthesize ideas generated during brainstorming), and tools for voting or setting priorities (so that recommended solutions can be weighted and prioritized).

A DSS can help a group avoid many of the decision-making barriers that often plague traditional face-to-face groups. For example, there's less likelihood that one assertive person will monopolize the meeting, since all the brainstorming and listing of ideas—and the voting—is governed by the computerized programs.

collaborative writing systems ■ *a computerized support system that lets group members work simultaneously on a single document from a number of interconnected or network computers.*

Other Work Group Support Systems Managers use other systems to facilitate group work. Collaborative writing systems let group members create long written documents (such as proposals) while working simultaneously at a network of interconnected computers. As team members work on different sections of the proposal, each member has automatic access to the rest of the sections and can modify his or her section to be compatible with the rest.

Instant messaging can support conference-call operations. For example, instant messaging (real-time, interactive e-mail) allows two managers to confer quietly, on the side, as a conference call among several people takes place.[70]

group scheduling system ■ *a computerized support system that allows each group member to put his or her daily schedule into a shared database so that each can identify the most suitable times to schedule meetings or to attend currently scheduled meetings.*

A group scheduling system provides a shared scheduling database. Each group member put his or her daily schedule into the shared database. This facilitates identifying the most suitable times for meetings. A workflow automation system uses an e-mail type of system to automate the flow of paperwork.[71] For example, if a proposal requires four signatures, the workflow automation system can send it electronically from mailbox to mailbox for the required signatures.

workflow automation system ■ *an e-mail type of system that automates the flow of paperwork from person to person.*

Telecommuting

Today, millions of people do most of their work at home and commute to their employers electronically. Telecommuting is the substitution of telecommunications and computers for the commute to a central office.[72]

telecommuting ■ *the substitution of telecommunications and computers for the commute to a central office.*

There are three types of telecommuters. Some are not employees at all, but are independent entrepreneurs who work out of their homes—perhaps developing new computer applications for consulting clients. The second (and largest) group of telecommuters includes professionals and highly skilled people who work at jobs that involve a great deal of independent thought and action. These employees—computer programmers, regional salespersons, textbook editors, and research specialists, for instance—typically work at home most of the time, and come to the office only occasionally, perhaps for monthly meetings.[73] The third telecommuter category includes those who carry out relatively routine and easily monitored jobs like data entry or making reservations.[74]

Internet-Based Communications

Firms today increasingly rely on Internet-based networks to link employees electronically—and to, therefore, provide instantaneous communication organizationwide. For example, when the PriceWaterhouseCoopers accounting manager Rick Richardson arrives at his office each morning, he checks his computer to review the average 20-to-25 e-mail messages he gets in a typical day. PriceWaterhouseCoopers also maintains electronic bulletin boards on more than 1,000 different jobs. About 18,000 of its employees in 22 countries use these electronic bulletin boards to get updates on matters such as how to handle specialized projects on which they are working.[75] Real estate firm Cushman & Wakefield's Internet-based communication system (see the following Managing @ the Speed of Thought feature) provides another example.

MANAGING @ THE SPEED OF THOUGHT

Communicating via the Internet

In addition to being a commercial real estate broker, Cushman & Wakefield manages office buildings, factories, and other commercial properties around the world. With about 2,000 employees, keeping the firm's personnel files up-to-date was an expensive logistical nightmare. For example, each time an employee was out sick, took a vacation, completed a college course, got a raise, or changed his or her job, the person's personnel files had to be changed. Keeping track of all this manually and through traditional telecommunications systems was very expensive.

Since almost all employees already had Internet access, Cushman & Wakefield decided to use the Internet's low-cost and interactive features to create an Internet-based employee communication network.[76] It then turned out that the firm's policies, procedures, and forms were already being stored electronically as Microsoft Word documents; as a result; converting existing documents so they could be displayed on the Web was fairly inexpensive. The new system cost the company less than $10,000 to develop. Then, with all the policies and forms online, it was relatively easy for every office to update its files. Managers (or, more often, the employees themselves) just typed the changes into the Web-based documents using Microsoft Word. The company's new software converted these documents and transferred them through the company's new Internet-based Employee Resource System.[77]

Cushman & Wakefield soon added other communication applications to its Internet system. One uses an internal, intranet-based system to calculate employee commissions, so agents and brokers can get the commission data they want. Another, Site Solutions, is a property tracking system that maintains detailed information on thousands of commercial properties worldwide, including available office space. Today, in other words, more and more of the company's communications, computations, and record-keeping are handled by the Net.

Building Internet-Based Virtual Communities

Many firms are blurring the boundaries between themselves and their customers and suppliers by building "virtual communities." For example, as prime contractor in an effort to win a $300 million navy ship deal, Lockheed-Martin "established a virtual design environment with two major shipbuilders, via a private internet existing entirely outside the firewalls of the three individual companies."[78] Eventually, about 200 suppliers would also be connected to the network via special, secure Internet links. This Internet-based network "allows secure transfer of design, project management, and even financial data back and forth among the extended design team via simple browser access, with one homepage as its focal point."[79] Lockheed-Martin got the contract and built the ship in one-third the time and at one-half the cost of previous contracts. Home Depot (see the accompanying Managing Without Boundaries feature) provides another, more familiar example.

Home Depot

Home Depot is using new communications technology to blur the boundaries between itself and its suppliers and customers, with the aim of improving performance. For example, imagine an employee pulling up to a local Home Depot store. The employee then uses a keypad to log on to a high-tech mobile cart that will transmit his or her progress and sales as he or she helps shoppers in the store's lumberyard. What is unusual here is that this employee doesn't work for Home Depot, but for one of its large suppliers, Georgia-Pacific Corp.

It's all part of a trial program. Home Depot and Georgia-Pacific want to see whether working together without boundaries can improve their sales and profit performance. This particular program will let Home Depot and Georgia-Pacific compare sales and inventory information. The firms hope this will provide insights about what they can do to reduce inventories and boost sales in Home Depot's lumber departments.

That's just one example of how Home Depot managers are using advanced communications, including the Internet, to manage without boundaries. For example, they installed their first electronic data interchange network in 1992. Today, "85 percent of all the Company's dealings with suppliers—from ordering to invoicing—are conducted electronically."[80] Home Depot is also sharing real-time information from its point-of-sale cash registers; this helps its suppliers lower their inventory costs (and, therefore, the prices Home Depot has to pay).

With successes like these, more vendors are introducing Internet-based "virtual community construction kits." Tribal Voice is one example. Its features include instant messaging (sending a message that will pop up on the receivers' screens), text to speech (hearing text as it appears in a window), file transfer (exchanging files), a buddy list (keeping track of regular online contacts), a whiteboard (exchanging drawings), and cruising (starting a meeting or conversation with a few people and then directing their Web browsers to the pages of your choosing).[81]

Tribal Voice lets a group of employees who share a common interest get together via the Internet. For example, says the vice president of marketing for the company that created Tribal Voice, "the sales department could hold forums and share information in an interactive community. A salesperson in a remote location could join this online department and ask for advice on a particular company he wants to call on."[82]

Tools like Tribal Voice can be useful in the right situations. The following Management in Action feature describes some research that helps managers decide what those situations are.

MANAGEMENT IN ACTION   The Media Richness Model

If you are an emergency room doctor and have to diagnose a patient who is obviously turning green, would you do it face-to-face, use e-mail, or send personal notes back and forth?

The question highlights what communications researchers call the Media Richness Model. This line of research says that the communication media or channels used—which may include face-to-face contact, telephone, personally addressed documents, or unaddressed documents, for instance—differ in their media richness. Figure 12.5 summarizes this idea. Media richness means

▶ **FIGURE 12–5** ■ ■ ■

Hierarchy of Media Richness and Application for Managerial Applications

Source: Adapted from Richard L. Daft and Robert H. Lengel, "Information Richness: A New Approach to Managerial Information Processing and Organization Design," in Barry Staw and Larry L. Cummings, eds., *Research in Organizational Behavior*, vol. 6 (Greenwich, CT: JAI Press, 1984), pp. 191–233. Reprinted from R. Daft and R. Steers, *Organizations: A Micro/Macro Approach* (Glenview, IL: Scott, Foresman, 1986) p. 532.

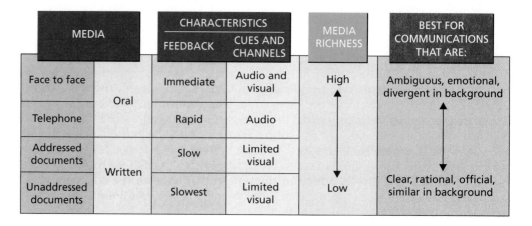

MEDIA		CHARACTERISTICS		MEDIA RICHNESS	BEST FOR COMMUNICATIONS THAT ARE:
		FEEDBACK	CUES AND CHANNELS		
Face to face	Oral	Immediate	Audio and visual	High	Ambiguous, emotional, divergent in background
Telephone		Rapid	Audio		
Addressed documents	Written	Slow	Limited visual		
Unaddressed documents		Slowest	Limited visual	Low	Clear, rational, official, similar in background

the capacity of the media to resolve ambiguity. Four aspects of the media—speed of feedback, number of cues and channels employed, personalness of the source, and richness of the language used—determine its richness.

Face-to-face oral communication is the richest medium. As you know from your own experience, it provides instantaneous audio and visual feedback, not just through the person's words, but through his or her body language and tone as well. At the other extreme, unaddressed documents (like companywide memos impersonally distributed to all employees) are low in media richness.

Research like this has some practical implications. Organizations and people often wisely rely more on rich media for addressing ambiguous, fast-changing situations. Face-to-face meetings, videoconferencing, and phone calls often make more sense than memos (especially impersonal memos) in these situations. Employers such as Emily Liu's (from the chapter opener) would do well to keep the richness of the media in mind when deciding how to communicate their point.

Is There a Company Portal in Your Future?

While most people today are using portals like Yahoo! to surf the Net, many are also using their employers' company-based business portals.

A business portal is, like other Yahoo!-type portals, a window to the Internet.[83] But unlike general-purpose portals, business portals are special company and/or function-oriented gateways to Internet-based information. Through their business portals, categories of employees—secretaries, engineers, salespeople, and so on—can access all the corporate applications they need to use as well as "get the tools you need to analyze data inside and outside your company, and see the customized content you need, like industry news and competitive data."[84] Thus, a sales manager could use the portal to access all the information her company has on sales trends, market analyses, and competitors' sales.

Many companies are in the business of designing business portals for corporate customers. Netscape (now a division of AOL Time Warner) has created business portals for FedEx and Lucent. Another firm, Concur Technologies, installed business portals for Hearst Corporation's 15,000 employees. Thousands of specialized business portals—ranging from benefits portals for letting employees update their benefits to training portals for letting employees take courses online—are also in use. If communication is indeed "exchanging information in such a way that you create a common basis of understanding and feeling," it looks like a company portal will soon be in most employees' futures. It will help employees zero in on just the information they need to do their jobs, and it will help them to organize and make sense of all the information that's out there. The Management in Action feature describes what GM has done.

MANAGEMENT IN ACTION   GM's mySocrates

General Motors calls its employee portal mySocrates, and it's not hard to see why it picked that name. Like other firms' Internet portals, mySocrates lets GM's 200,000 North American employees handle many routine HR tasks, such as making online 401(k) allocation changes, changing their personal data, and registering for benefits online.

But mySocrates goes well beyond this. If GM gets its way, mySocrates will become the main work *and nonwork* portal for all of its employees. At work, mySocrates not only facilitates the sorts of HR activities noted above, but it lets GM employees easily link with hundreds of thousands of other GM Web sites and information sources to help them do their jobs better. (Assembly workers can get updates on new decision-making methods, for instance). When the employee is back home, GM hopes mySocrates will turn out to be a sort of "myYahoo" for all of its employees. The aim is to make mySocrates the portal of choice for all of its employees—the first thing that opens when they log onto the Net. GM thereby hopes to use it as way to market new products and services (such as financial services from GM's financial services arm) to all its employees. Now, that is communications![85]

Personal Digital Assistants

Firms are also increasingly using personal digital assistants (PDAs) like PalmPilots to improve their communications. For example, the consumer markets division of Countrywide Home Loans gave personal digital assistants that can quickly supply mortgage information to all sales representatives. Now, "I can't go into a restaurant or a grocery store without running into someone who's talking about buying a home," says one manager. And "now, wherever I am, I pull out my Palm VII, say 'how can I help you?', and demonstrate exactly what Countrywide can do for them."

■■■ *Using a Palm Pilot to stay in touch while out of the office.*

SUMMARY ■■■

1. Communication means exchanging information *in such a way that you create a common basis of understanding and feeling.* Always remember that your aim is to create a common basis of understanding and feeling.

2. There are five elements in the communication process, and errors can occur at any one: source, signal, transmission and channel, destination/receiver, and noise.

3. Several interpersonal communication barriers can distort messages and inhibit communication. These barriers include ambiguity, errors in perception, semantics, and nonverbal communication.

4. You can improve interpersonal communication by being an active listener, avoiding triggering defensiveness, providing feedback, and clarifying your ideas before communicating.

5. Because organizational communication involves people, it is susceptible to all of the problems of interpersonal communication and some special problems, including organizational culture, structural restrictions, and boundary differences.

6. Upward communication can be encouraged through techniques like upward appraisals, sympathetic listening, social gatherings, internal (or union) publications, scheduled meetings, and formal suggestion systems. Toyota's Hotline is another example. Downward communication is encouraged through the usual channels (like face-to-face and written messages), as well as through techniques like open book management and closed-circuit televisions.

7. Horizontal organizational communication can often be improved through liaison personnel, committees and task forces, and independent integrators.

8. To influence and improve organizationwide communication, a leader can foster informal communication, use networks, reduce boundaries, and use electronic networking.

9. Telecommunications and the Internet play an important role in managing communications. Companies use sophisticated telecommunications systems to link their inventory and manufacturing facilities with point-of-sale processing devices at retail stores. Work group support systems allow geographically dispersed employees to interact in real-time as teams. Internet-based communications systems let companies use the relatively inexpensive Internet to substantially reduce their communications costs. More companies are establishing Internet-based virtual communities.

KEY TERMS ■■■

communication 315
nonverbal communication 318
interpersonal communication 319
organizational communication 323

open-book management 237
telecommunications 329
decision support system 332
collaborative writing system 332

group scheduling system 332
workflow automation system 332
telecommuting 332

SKILLS AND STUDY MATERIALS

COMPANION WEBSITE ■■■

We invite you to visit the Dessler Companion Website at **www.prenhall.com/dessler** for this chapter's Internet resources.

EXPERIENTIAL EXERCISES ■■■

1. As the Management in Action feature about Larry Summers at Harvard shows, different university presidents have different ways of communicating with their university communities. As a student, you've undoubtedly had some experience with this yourself (although you may not have thought much about it at the time). Form teams of 4–5 students, and answer the following questions: What methods has the president of your college or university used to elicit upward communication from members of the college or university community? What methods does he or she use to foster downward communication from the president to the students? What do the president's communication methods tell you about the organizational culture that person is trying to create (or is inadvertently creating) at your university or college?

2. Like most students, you have probably faced a situation in which you had to speak with a professor about a problem— you thought your grade should be higher, or you had to miss a test, or you wanted an override into the person's class, for instance. In teams of 4–5 students, discuss the experiences you've had with various professors along these lines. Then choose a professor, and make a list of what that person did right and wrong with respect to the interpersonal communication skills (how to be an active listener, and so on) in this chapter. What communication barriers did this person seem to be ignoring?

3. You desperately need to take a class from Professor Smith to graduate on time, but it's not offered next semester. She has made you this proposition: If you can persuade 15 other students to sign up for the course, she will offer it. In teams of 4–5 students, use what you learned in this chapter to write out a script you will use to persuade other students to join you in this course.

CASE STUDY ■■■

APPROACHING DIVERSITY: BARRIERS OR BREAKTHROUGHS?

You have just been hired by a traditional, paternalistic restaurant chain that has been successfully sued by former employees five times in the last five years for racial and gender discrimination. The company is starting to lose business because of its poor image in the community. Employees are also leaving, and others are threatening to sue if conditions do not improve. The workforce is 65% women, of which 55% are women of color. Twenty-one percent of the male workforce consists of men of color. Middle management and above are all white males.

The board of directors has fired the CEO and replaced her with a young Latina to try to change the company. You are the new COO. The new CEO has asked you to help her implement a diversity program to reach all aspects of operations. She needs your report by the end of the week.

Discussion Questions

1. What communications barriers and problems might you expect to unearth in this situation?

2. What means of communication might you use to help the new CEO reach the employees? What exactly would you suggest?

3. Given that you are new on the job, how would you collect information to do your analysis in less than a week?

Source: Gillian Flynn, "Do You Have the Right Approach to Diversity?" *Personnel Journal*, October 1995, 68–76.

YOU BE THE CONSULTANT ■■■

KEEPING COMMUNICATION OPEN AT JETBLUE

jetBlue AIRWAYS® Management has built JetBlue based on five values—safety, caring, integrity, fun, and passion—and keeping communications open and transparent is vital for adhering to all of them. Indeed, the company feels so strongly about these values that they appear on all employees' identification cards.

Most employees' first exposure to JetBlue's brand of open communication comes during their initial, one-hour orientation, when the company's president and CEO explain how JetBlue makes money. The officers go so far as to do the math with the new employees, and then show how each of the employees' jobs affects every aspect of the company's expenses and revenues. The basic idea is to get the new employee to think, "If I do this—that's what happens." The basic theme is that JetBlue can succeed as a low-cost, high-quality airline only if every employee gives his or her best, and so employees have to think of themselves more as partners than employees. Indeed, there are no employees at JetBlue—just "crewmembers."

JetBlue's monthly pocket sessions provide another example of open communications. The pocket sessions meetings include the company CEO, president, and head of HR with about 200 JetBlue employees, at the company's main crew lounge at JFK airport. These meetings usually involve short presentations by each officer and then a period of frank and open questions and answers between officers and employees. Again, given JetBlue's emphasis on open, transparent communication, the officers work hard to answer even the thorniest questions forthrightly. For example, at one recent meeting, a flight attendant asked why the officers get stock options, while the flight attendants do not. (The answer was that they play different roles and that early on management and the board of directors made the decision that only managers, pilots, and others in the company requiring professional licensing and degrees would be eligible for stock options. However, other employees are eligible for profit sharing and other benefits.)

Another employee pointed out that because of bad weather, many employees had to work mandatory overtime for three days. This particular employee "didn't like the fact that it was mandatory" and complained that the supervisor shouldn't have put the order in "mandatory" terms. Management responded that if the order was less than courteous, they would look into it, but the bottom line was that everyone joining JetBlue had to understand that it is everyone's responsibility to pitch in and help during periods like these and that those who could not do so might not be happy at JetBlue. Finally, the company also issues periodic "Blue notes"—companywide e-mails covering important news and press releases—as another communication aid.

However, JetBlue does not have some of the trappings of formal communication you might expect from a company this size. For example, there is no employee manual. (The company is con-

sidering publishing one, tentatively titled "the JetBlue route map," sometime in the future.) New employees do get a "Blue book"— a 13-page pamphlet summarizing major policy issues, for instance, concerning equal employment opportunity and sexual harassment. There are also several benefits documents describing matters such as sick leave and vacation pay. The company has disciplinary procedures but does not publicize them or distribute them to employees. JetBlue simply emphasizes that it will treat employees with respect. Then, if there is a problem, employees receive a warning and a description of the progressive disciplinary policy.

Employee appraisal at JetBlue similarly tends to be an open, give-and-take discussion, one in which the employee's commitment to JetBlue looms large. JetBlue managers call the annual appraisal the "Flight plan." JetBlue also has a yearly crew member experience survey. This is an attitude survey that monitors employee impressions of various matters, ranging from supervision to pay. Generally, according to the company's head of HR, this survey contains few surprises, but rather tends to validate things that management already knows. This is because managers, and particularly top managers, spend so much time out in the field—in the terminal, in the aircraft, and so on—talking to and interacting with employees and passengers.

Discussion Questions.

1. Are there any interpersonal or organizational communication barriers that JetBlue seems to be ignoring, and if so, how would you suggest the company remedy the situation?

2. List and explain the things you would do to improve organizational communication at JetBlue.

3. Make a list of the specific vehicles JetBlue is currently using to encourage upward communication, downward communication, and interdepartmental communication. Do you think these are adequate for a company in JetBlue's situation? What would you suggest Jetblue do to improve organizational communication?

Managing Groups and Teams

THE MANAGEMENT CHALLENGE

Big Apple Circus

Paul Binder, Big Apple Circus's founder and head, faces an interesting question when he staffs and organizes his shows. He wants great entertainers, ones who'll bring a unique experience to the circus. That means he typically ends up with "virtuosos"—potential prima donnas who are not just good but great at what they do. He also invariably finds himself with a highly diverse crew—the acts in one recent year came from China, Poland, Denmark, France, England, and the United States. The combination of star power and diversity could mean that each person will insist on doing things his or her own way. Binder's question therefore is, "How can I put together a crew made up of individual stars who will also work together as a close-knit team?"

CHAPTER OBJECTIVES

After studying this chapter and the case exercises at the end, you should be able to:

1. Specify the level of employee involvement in a team situation.

2. Analyze a team situation and list at least six specific reasons why the team is not performing effectively, and what you would suggest doing about it.

3. Analyze a team situation and discuss at least seven reasons why you believe the team does or does not have the necessary characteristics to perform productively.

4. Explain specifically why you believe a person is or is not a potential "team player."

5. Conduct a productive group decision-making meeting.

Anyone who's watched a baseball or football game knows there's a reason why some teams do better than others. Some have better, more committed players. Some have better coaches. Some have better training. And some have higher morale. The main purpose of this chapter is to improve your ability to create and manage high-performing teams. The main topics we cover include how companies use teams at work, the building blocks of productive teams, and how to lead productive teams and use groups to make better decisions.

■■■ TEAMS: EMPLOYEE INVOLVEMENT IN ACTION

Teams, not departments or individuals, do much of America's work today.[1] The Center for the Study of Work Teams at the University of North Texas suggests that about 80% of Fortune 500 companies have half their employees on teams. Another study concluded that 82% of all U.S. firms organized at least some of their employees into work groups identified as teams. Thirty-five percent of all U.S. organizations also have at least one team classified as self-directed or semiautonomous (which generally means that the team supervises itself).[2] Yet another study, by the Hay Group, a Philadelphia-based consulting firm, found that 66% of the employers surveyed planned to increase the level of employee participation in teams.

Based on one brief survey of executives, cross-functional project groups were by far the most common types of teams, followed by service, marketing, and operations teams. Team size ranged from 3 to 25 members. The average size was about 8.4 members per team; most had 5 members. The most frustrating aspect of managing teamwork programs (from most to least) was developing/sustaining high motivation, minimizing confusion/coordination problems, managing conflict productively, and managing people problems.[3]

In general, the popularity of teams has paralleled the need to improve the performance and responsiveness of companies in the face of rising global competition. Reasons given for organizing more work around teams included improving product quality (chosen by 69% of these respondents), improving productivity (64%), improving employee morale (17%), and improving staffing flexibility (13%).[4] The basic idea is to use the team approach to encourage employees to become more involved in their work.

Work teams are examples of *employee involvement programs*. An **employee involvement program** is any formal program that lets employees participate in formulating important work-related decisions or in supervising all or part of their own jobs.[5] The assumption—often correct—is that employees involved in this way will be more committed and perform better than those who are not.

Employee involvement is not an either-or situation; there are degrees. Consider an example (see Figure 13.1). Involvement might range from *information sharing* (managers make all important operational decisions, inform employees, and then respond to employee questions), to *intergroup problem solving* (experienced, trained, cross-functional teams meet regularly with managers to solve problems across several organizational units),[6] to *total self-direction* (every employee belongs to a self-directed team, starting with a high-level executive team).[7] Here[8] (as we saw in Chapter 8), management arranges the organizational structure and systems around team-based work assignments.[9]

Managers rate involvement programs as their biggest productivity boosters. For example, several years ago, the editors of *National Productivity Review* found that "increased employee involvement in the generation and implementation of ideas was ranked the highest priority productivity improvement action by the [survey's] respondents." Employee involvement "was similarly ranked number one as the top cause of improvement over the past two years at these firms." (The other eight sources of improvement, in *descending* order, were quality programs, improved process methods, top management, equipment, technology, training, computers, and automation.) We'll focus, in this chapter, on how to create team-based involvement programs.[10]

employee involvement program ■ *any formal program that lets employees participate in formulating important work decisions or in supervising all or part of their own work activities.*

1. *Information sharing:* Managers make decisions on their own, announce them, and then respond to any questions employees may have.

2. Managers usually make the decisions, but only after seeking the views of employees.

3. Managers often form temporary employee groups to recommend solutions for specified problems.

4. Managers meet with employee groups regularly—once per week or so—to help them identify problems and recommend solutions.

5. *Intergroup problem solving:* Managers establish and participate in cross-functional employee problem-solving teams.

6. Ongoing work groups assume expanded responsibility for a particular issue, like cost reduction.

7. Employees within an area function full time, with minimal direct supervision.

8. *Total self-direction:* Traditional supervisory roles do not exist; almost all employees participate in self-managing teams.

◀ **FIGURE 13–1** ■ ■ ■

Employee Involvement in Your Company: An Informal Checklist

Source: Adapted from Jack Osborn et al., *Self-Directed Work Teams* (Homewood, IL: Business One Irwin, 1990), p. 30.

■ *The Global Manager* Yet, it is dangerous to use involvement programs indiscriminately, particularly when other cultures are involved. In one recent study, researchers investigated how worker involvement affected employee satisfaction in four countries—the United States, Mexico, Poland, and India. Of these four cultures, India is reportedly the most "vertical," in that "those who are at the top are expected to take charge, to be in control, to give orders, and to know what is right."[11] Worker involvement programs were not only less successful in India, but "[t]he negative paths [relationships] from involvement to satisfaction in the Indian sample, arguably the most vertical sample, were in stark contrast to the positive paths in the other three samples."[12]

■ ■ GROUP DYNAMICS

All teams are *groups*. A group is defined as two or more persons who are interacting in such a way that each person influences and is influenced by each other person.[13] Five people traveling by bus from Miami to New York may comprise a group, insofar as they interact and talk and have meals together. However, groups like these don't necessarily exhibit a team's unity of purpose. Whether it's a football team, a commando team, or a self-managing work team, a team is always "committed to a common purpose, set of performance goals, and approach for which [the team members] hold themselves mutually accountable."[14] Team members also usually hold one another accountable for achieving team goals.[15] Yet while a group isn't necessarily a team, all teams are groups. Therefore, much of what we know about building effective teams comes from small-group research. We'll look at this next.

Group Norms

Peer pressure—wanting to look "right" from the point of view of our peers—drives much of what we do, including what we wear and how we behave. It takes a strong-willed person to deliberately defy one's reference group—the people we'd like to emulate. The same is true at work. For example, the study "Monkey See, Monkey Do: The Influence of Workgroups on the Antisocial Behavior of Employees" looked at how the antisocial behavior of coworkers influenced individual team members' antisocial behavior. The researchers found that ". . . a work group was a significant predictor of an individual's antisocial behavior at work."[16] In fact, the more antisocial the group became, the more it was able to pressure its individual members into taking antisocial actions.[17] Experts on gangs might not be surprised by such findings, but it was something of a surprise to find they applied to people in a work setting. The point is that ignoring the group's potential influence can be calamitous to the manager.

Groups exert their influence largely through group norms. Group norms are "the informal rules that groups adopt to regulate and regularize group members' behavior."[18] They are "rules of behavior, proper ways of acting, which have been accepted as legitimate by members of a group [and which] specify the kind of behaviors that are expected of group members."[19]

group ■ *two or more persons who are interacting in such a way that each person influences and is influenced by each other person.*

team ■ *a group of people committed to a common purpose, set of performance goals, and approach for which the team members hold themselves mutually accountable.*

group norms ■ *the informal rules that groups adopt to regulate and regularize group members' behavior.*

Group norms may have a positive or negative (or neutral) effect from the company's point of view. At the Toyota plant in Kentucky, positive group norms include "always do your best" and "build these cars like you own the company." Creating an environment that leads to norms like these can obviously be beneficial to an employer. On the other hand, negative group norms like "don't exceed 10 units per hour no matter what the manager says" can hinder management by causing workers to limit their efforts.

It's hard to overestimate the power of group norms. Studies show that "group norms may have a greater influence on the individual's performance than the knowledge, skills and abilities the individual brings to the work setting."[20] Researchers first stumbled across that fact during a project known as the Hawthorne Studies. The Hawthorne researchers described, for instance, how production levels that exceeded the group's norms triggered what the workers called "binging." Here, the worker's teammates slapped her hand for exceeding group production norms.[21]

Group Cohesiveness

group cohesiveness ■ the degree of interpersonal attractiveness within a group, dependent on factors like proximity, similarities, attraction among the individual group members, group size, intergroup competition, and agreement about goals.

In turn, the extent to which a group can enforce its norms and influence its members' behavior depends to some extent on the group's attraction for its members—on its group cohesiveness.[22] Members of cohesive teams "sit closer together, focus more attention on one another, shows signs of mutual affection, and display coordinated patterns of behavior"[23]—and, of course, they are more likely to enforce the group's rules or norms.

In turn, group cohesiveness depends on several things. One is *proximity*, since geographically dispersed people are less likely to form friendships. *Similarities* then seem to become important. Individuals tend to be attracted to a group because they find its activities or goals attractive, rewarding, or valuable, or because they believe they can accomplish something through the group that they can't accomplish individually. *Agreement regarding goals*, therefore, boosts cohesiveness, while differences reduce it.[24]

While the old saying "opposites attract" is occasionally true, people usually choose friends based on similarities. For example, in early studies, students tended to choose friends based on similarities such as age, gender, and (to some extent) academic achievement and intelligence.[25]

People also tend to choose their friends based on similarities of interest or values. In one early study of high school students, 49-to-70% of all the friendships were with social class equals.[26] When given a chance to form friendships with any other student, a large percentage of the students tended to choose friendships based on religious similarities. Personality is another factor. In one study, for instance, "subjects chose others whom they described as being similar to their own positive traits and rejected those whom they described as being similar to their own negative traits."[27]

Intergroup competition can boost cohesiveness (particularly for the winning group), whereas intragroup competition (among the group's members) tends to undermine it.[28] Similarly, abrasive, antagonistic, or inflexible team members can undermine group cohesiveness. Group cohesiveness also tends to decline as group size increases beyond five to six members.[29]

Group size affects cohesiveness for several reasons. "Members are generally less satisfied with the group if the size is increased" [beyond five to seven members].[30] Larger groups tend to split into two or more, often opposing, subgroups. And the group's leader in large groups has less time to spend communicating with each of the members. Based on much small-group research (at least for small discussion groups), the optimum size seems to be five or six members.[31]

■■■ HOW COMPANIES USE TEAMS AT WORK

Employers use teams in numerous ways.[32] We'll look next at the more popular choices.

Suggestion/Problem-Solving Teams and Quality Circles

Firms use teams to involve employees in solving problems and making improvements at work. Usually, no one knows the job as well as the employees themselves. Employers, therefore, often wisely ask the employees to analyze work-related problems and to suggest improvements.

There are several levels of such involvement. Suggestion teams are temporary teams whose members work on specific analytical assignments, such as how to cut costs or raise productivity. Problem-solving teams are more formal and semipermanent. They "are involved in identifying and researching activities and in developing effective solutions to work-related problems."[33] They usually consist of the supervisor and five to eight employees from a common work area; quality circles are an example.[34] A quality circle is a team of 6 to 12 specially trained employees who meet once a week to solve problems affecting their work area.[35] The team first gets training in problem-analysis techniques (including basic statistics). Then it applies the problem-analysis process (problem identification, problem selection, problem analysis, solution recommendations, and solution review by top management) to solve problems in its work area.[36]

The quality circle process today is generally more structured and directed than it was some years ago. Many of the original quality circle programs failed to produce measurable cost savings. Some circles' bottom-line goals were too vague. In other firms, having the employees choose and analyze their own problems proved ineffective.[37] In a typical reaction, one corporation replaced about 700 of its original quality circles with 1,000 new work teams. These teams are not voluntary. They include most shop floor employees. And, in contrast to the early circles that chose their own problems, they work on problems assigned by management.[38]

Suggestion team ■ *a team formed to work in the short term on a given issue such as increasing productivity.*

problem-solving team ■ *a team formed to identify and solve work-related problems.*

quality circle ■ *a team of 6 to 12 employees who meet about once per week on company time to solve problems affecting their work area.*

Project, Development, or Venture Teams

Project, development, or venture teams are small groups that operate as semiautonomous units to create and develop new ideas.[39] They often consist of professionals like marketing experts or engineers. They work on specific projects like designing new processes (process-design teams), new products (product-development teams), or new businesses (venture teams). The classic example is the IBM team organized in Boca Raton, Florida, to develop and introduce IBM's first personal computer. As is usually the case with venture teams, the IBM unit was fairly autonomous: It had its own budget and leader as well as the freedom to make decisions within broad guidelines.

IBM's experience illustrates the pros and cons of the venture-team approach. Working more or less autonomously outside IBM's usual network of rules and policies, the team created the new PC computer and brought it to market in less than two years. This project might have taken IBM years to accomplish under its usual hierarchical, "check with me first," product-development approach. However, many believe the venture team's autonomy eventually backfired. Not bound by IBM's traditional policy of using only IBM parts, the team went outside to Microsoft (for its DOS, or disk operating system) and to Intel (for the computer processor). Unfortunately for IBM, this allowed Intel and Microsoft to sell the same PC parts to any manufacturer, and it led to the proliferation of IBM clones.[40] The bottom line is that team autonomy can be good, but it should be tempered by the required controls.

venture team ■ *a small team of people who operate as semiautonomous units to create and develop a new idea.*

Transnational Teams

How do you carry out a project involving activities in several countries at once? Increasingly, managers are solving that problem by creating transnational teams composed of multinational members whose activities span many countries.[41]

Firms use transnational teams in many ways. Fuji-Xerox sent 15 experienced Tokyo engineers to a Xerox Corporation facility in Webster, New York. They worked there for five years with a group of U.S. engineers to develop a "world copier," a product that was a huge success in the global marketplace.[42] Managers and technical specialists from IBM-Latin America formed a transnational team to market, sell, and distribute personal computers in Latin American countries. A European beverage manufacturer, Heineken, formed a 13-member transnational team called the European Production Task Force, with members from five countries. Its task was to analyze how many factories the firm should operate in Europe, what size they should be, and where they should be placed.[43]

Transnational teams face special challenges.[44] They tend to work on complex, important projects. They must operate over vast distances. And they are composed of

transnational team ■ *a work team composed of multinational members whose activities span many countries.*

people with different languages, interpersonal styles, and cultures. What can you do to make these teams more effective?

- *Clarify the team's goal.* With big distances between team members, it's especially important for each member to be able to focus his or her efforts on accomplishing the team's common goal.[45]
- *Facilitate communications.* The preferred information technology includes videoconferencing as well as telephone, voice mail, e-mail, and fax. Decision-support systems—PC-based groupware that permits, for instance, simultaneous computerized discussions of issues—are important, too.
- *Build trust and teamwork.* Fostering group cohesiveness is especially important, given the diverse and multicultural makeup of these groups. "Successful [transnational] teams are characterized by leaders and members who trust each other, are committed to the team's mission, can be counted on to perform their respective tasks, and enjoy working with each other."[46] We'll explain how to accomplish this shortly.
- *Demonstrate mutual respect.* For example, rotate conference times so that the same members in remote time zones don't always have to do business in the wee hours of the morning. Hold staff meetings at various geographic locations. Learn words expressing respect and gratitude in the languages of other team members.[47]

Virtual Teams

Transnational team members (or members of other widely-dispersed teams) sometimes don't meet face to face at all, but they work instead in a virtual environment. Their meetings take place mostly via telecommunications. Virtual teams are groups of geographically and/or organizationally dispersed coworkers who are assembled and who interact using a combination of telecommunications and information technologies to accomplish an organizational task.

Virtual teams are increasingly popular. Globalization is one reason. Global operations require that teams communicate at great distances, but rarely face to face. Strategic partnerships and joint ventures are another reason. Employees of partner companies frequently act together as a team, although they work for different companies and may be in different locales. Virtual teams may be temporary, existing only to accomplish a specific task. Or they may be permanent and address ongoing matters, such as strategic planning. In either case, membership is often fluid, evolving according to changing task requirements.[48]

Technology and Virtual Teams Virtual teams depend on information technology for communications. Desktop videoconferencing systems are often the heart around which firms build the teams' technologies. Systems like these re-create the face-to-face interactions of conventional groups. Communication among team members can thus include the rich body language and nuances of face-to-face communications.[49] (However, some experts contend that the technology most often used by virtual groups is still the jet plane.)

Collaborative software systems (specifically, the work-group support systems/decision support systems discussed in Chapter 12) further facilitate virtual decision making. For example, one consulting team used a collaborative software system to research and write a proposal for a major project. This enabled each member to access in real-time the contribution of each other member while inputting his or her own contribution. Microsoft offers a NetMeeting conference system. When this system is combined with new products like Framework Technologies Corp.'s ActiveProject 5.0, virtual team members can hold live project reviews and discussions and then store the sessions on the project's Web site.[50] Figure 13.2 shows Websites that help virtual teams work better.

Other firms use their intranets. With all the team's required forms and documents available on a firm's internal Web site, these intranets "allow virtual teams to archive

Site	What it does	Strength	Weakness	Cost
GroupVine www.groupvine.com	Lets you create members-only discussion boards so that a team can post audio files, comments, documents, or pictures concerning a project.	Perfect for groups on the go. GroupVine allows users to view and respond to discussions on the board via Web-enabled mobile phones or PalmPilots.	Although you can post documents for team members to review, there are currently no other collaboration tools.	Free
Intranets.com www.intranets.com	An instant intranet. In less than 3 minutes, a company or a department can have a central place to keep everyone in a group up-to-date on work, reports, and so on.	From group contacts and a calendar to group e-mail and discussion boards, this site has the word *group* written all over it.	Don't want everyone in the group to know about something? With a few exceptions, anything added to this site is for group consumption.	Free, but tech-support calls are $29.95 each.
ScheduleOnline www.scheduleonline.com	A group calendar that lets users schedule events, invite people to meetings, and reserve physical resources, such as conference rooms or equipment.	If a meeting is already scheduled or if a resource is already booked, the system automatically alerts you and shows you alternate times.	Although the site offers other group-oriented functions, like helping people keep track of action items and to-do lists, its strong suit is scheduling.	Free
TeamWave www.teamwave.com	Technically, a shared whiteboard that allows users to draw, add text, and capture what gets created.	What makes this service special is TeamWave's ability to add shared tools to the whiteboard, including address books, calendars, message boards, and to-do lists.	The user interface is neither the most elegant to look at nor the most intuitive to navigate.	A free version is available at TeamWave's StuffinCommon.com, a companion site. Client/server software starts at $1,499 for 50 users.

▲ **FIGURE 13–2** ■ ■ ■

Web-Based Tools for Virtual Teams

Source: Adapted from Gina Imperato, "Read Tools for Virtual Teams," *Fast Company* July 2000, p. 382.

text, visual, audio, and numerical data in a user-friendly format, [and] allow virtual teams to keep other organizational members and outside constituents such as suppliers and customers up-to-date on the team's progress."[51] The I-Many and Accenture experiences described in the Management in Action feature are good examples.

MANAGEMENT IN ACTION   Working with Virtual Teams

At I-Many, a Maine-based software company, having an employee meeting is no easy task. Leigh Powell, the firm's chief executive, lives in New Jersey. His COO lives in St. Louis. The customer service vice president lives in Denver. And that vice president's customer service staff is in Portland, Maine. To keep this geographically dispersed team operating, the firm relies on computers, cellphones, and instant messaging. As Powell says, "We're constantly bouncing ideas off each other. . . . We talk about everything. Ultimately, the people in this company have a lot of authority to make decisions. But very often, we're making decisions in a highly collaborative way."[52]

As a marketing manager in consulting firm Accenture's human performance group, Joanne McMorrow has had a similar experience. When she was a consultant, her usual schedule involved flying off Sunday night to be with clients on Monday. Now as a marketing manager, she has had to readjust her activities to work harmoniously with her virtual team. Accenture's technology support helps her do this. She uses its Knowledge eXchange to share documents and check project progress.[53] She uses NetMeeting and her phone to participate in team meetings. And she uses www.mylearning.com to take courses. She's careful to tell team members when she's stepping away for a brief break during a long virtual meeting. And once a quarter, she and her team meet in person to renew acquaintances.

Building Trust in Virtual Teams Given the lack of in-person interaction in geographically dispersed virtual teams, building trust is especially important. One study found that virtual teams with the highest levels of trust had several characteristics. First, team members began their projects by *introducing themselves* and providing some personal background rather than by immediately focusing on the team's task.[54] Second, each member had a *specific task and role*. Third, high-trust virtual teams had the *right attitude*. Team members "consistently displayed eagerness, enthusiasm, and an intense action orientation in all their messages." Fourth, effective teams also respect *cultural differences*. One expert suggests removing cultural idioms (like "apples to oranges") from communications and using multiple channels (such as videoconferencing and e-mail) to build in redundancy to ensure that the message—both verbal and nonverbal—is understood.[55]

Rotating Leadership in Virtual Teams Finally, many firms rotate virtual team leadership across countries and divisions. As one person who has studied transnational teams said, "By rotating and diffusing team leadership across countries, managers in several subsidiaries gain an appreciation for cross-border coordination and learn to iron out conflicts and to use teams to achieve their objectives."[56] Procter & Gamble uses this approach. As John Pepper, chairman, put it, "We set up a brand team on Lenor, another on Pampers, another on Pantene, and so on. We assign different country managers to lead these; really wanting to get everybody into the fire, so to speak, experiencing it. What made the teams work was the mutual interdependency that grew."[57]

Self-Directed Work Teams

self-managing/self-directed work team ■ *a highly trained team of employees, including 6 to 18 people on average, who are fully responsible for turning out a well-defined segment of finished work.*

Self-managing work teams are the 1000-pound gorillas of employee involvement today. A **self-managing/self-directed work team** is "a highly trained group of around eight employees, fully responsible for turning out a well-defined segment of finished work."[58] The well-defined segment might be an entire jet engine or a fully processed insurance claim. In any case, the distinguishing features of self-directed teams are (1) they are empowered to direct and do virtually all of their own work, and (2) their work results in a singular, well-defined item or service. They represent the highest level of employee involvement.

Firms often organize the work of an entire facility around self-managing teams. The GE aircraft engine plant in Durham, North Carolina, is a self-managing team-based facility. The plant's 170 workers work in teams, all of which report to one boss, the factory manager.[59] Johnsonville Foods is another example. Here, self-managing teams recruit, hire, evaluate, and (if necessary) fire on their own. Many of the workers have little or no college background. However, they also "train one another, formulate and track their own budgets, make capital investment proposals as needed, handle quality control and inspection, develop their own quantitative standards, improve every process and product, and create prototypes of possible new products."[60]

Such empowerment can be very motivational, and it can trigger vast improvements in productivity. As the vice president of one midwestern U.S. consumer goods company said about organizing his firm around teams, "People on the floor were talking about world markets, customer needs, competitors' products, making process improvements—all the things managers are supposed to think about."[61]

■■■ THE BUILDING BLOCKS OF PRODUCTIVE TEAMS

Requiring several people to work together doesn't make them a team—and certainly not a productive one. Let's look at what managers can do to build effective teams.

Does Teamwork Work?

The evidence regarding work-team productivity is quite mixed. Some programs have been quite successful. After Kodak's consumer film finishing division instituted a team-based structure, its division manager reported that unit costs declined by 6% per year over six years. Productivity increased by over 200% in six years, from 383 units per employee to 836.[62] Another study analyzed the impact of work teams on manufacturing performance in a unionized plant operated by a Fortune 500 firm.[63] During a 21-month period, the plant was converted to a team structure. The researchers found that "quality and labor productivity improved over time after the introduction of work teams."[64] Yet other programs failed, as the Management in Action feature shows.[65]

MANAGEMENT IN ACTION   The Levi Strauss Experiment

One highly publicized failure occurred in the mid-1990s, in the U.S. factories of Levi Strauss. The firm prided itself on its "made in USA" philosophy. However, as competitors with cheaper sources overseas cut into Levi's sales, the firm sought a way to keep its U.S. factories open but with higher productivity. The idea it hit on was the Work Team Program. The results are informative.

At the time, most of the firm's U.S. plants operated on the piece-work system. The firm paid each worker a sum for each specialized task (like attaching belt loops) that he or she finished.[66] The Work Team Program changed that. Now a pair of pants would be constructed entirely by a group of 10 to 35 workers, who would share all the tasks and be paid according to the total number of pants the group finished each day. The idea was to boost productivity by, among other things, enabling employees to do several jobs instead of one on the assumption that this would reduce boredom.

Unfortunately, it didn't work out that way. High-performing, faster workers in a group found their wages pulled down by slower-working colleagues (who, conversely, saw their hourly wages rise).

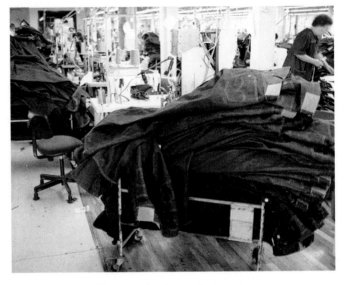

Inside a Levi Strauss jeans factory in San Francisco.

Morale fell, arguments ensued, and at some plants, like the Morrilton, Arkansas, factory, a pair of Dockers that previously cost $5 to stitch together now cost $7.50. The results weren't entirely grim. Teams that were more homogeneous (in terms of work skills) did see productivity rise. Average turnaround—the time from when an order is received to when the products are shipped to retail stores-improved from 9 weeks to 7. Levi Strauss decided to continue the Work Team Program at its remaining U.S. plants, but for 6,000 of its U.S. employees, that is now irrelevant. Levi's soon announced it was closing 11 U.S. plants and dismissing one-third of its U.S. employees.

The mixed results at Levi's highlight a fact of life with regard to implementing programs like these: You should view them as just part of a more comprehensive organizational change effort. When managers introduce teams, they also flatten the management hierarchy, cut personnel, restructure tasks, change incentive plans, and take other steps. All these steps need to be consistent with and make sense in light of the new team-based organization. At Levi Strauss, for instance, it wasn't necessarily the effort to organize around teams that created the problem, but the team-based incentive plan implemented with it. Failing to understand the systemic nature of a program like this is enough to doom it. However, it is only one of several potential problems.

What Causes Unproductive Teams?

The list of other things that can undermine a team-based program is, unfortunately, quite long. Teams should harness divergent skills to achieve their aims. However, divergent points of view may instead trigger tension and conflict.[67] A team member may simply be ignored, thus eliminating a potentially valuable resource.[68] Power struggles may cripple the team, as when individual members undermine potentially productive ideas with the goal of winning their point. An intentionally confusing or provocative team member may spread turmoil: "One bad apple can spoil the bunch," as the saying goes.[69] An unequal distribution of workload among team members, and a lack of management support can further undermine the team.[70]

Power struggles, provocation, and divergent points of view often stem, in turn, from larger problems, in particular inadequate leadership, focus, and/or capability (a

► **FIGURE 13–3** ■ ■ ■

Why Teams Fail: The Leadership, Focus, and Capability Pyramid

Each of three factors—leadership, focus, and capability—requires a different improvement strategy to overcome traps that lead to declines in team effectiveness.

Source: Adapted from Steven Rayner, "Team Traps: What They Are, How to Avoid Them." *National Productivity Review.* Summer 1996, p. 107. Reprinted by permission of John Wiley & Sons, Inc.

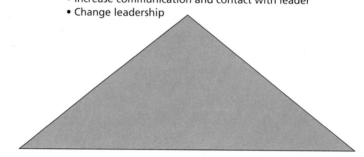

Leadership

Lack of support, consistency of direction, vision, budget, and resources.
  Improvement strategy:
  • Plan events to demonstrate the firm's support of the leader
  • Increase budget and resources
  • Increase communication and contact with leader
  • Change leadership

Focus

Lack of clarity about team purpose, roles, strategy, and goals.
  Improvement strategy:
  • Establish and clarify team mission
  • Ensure open channels for communications and information transfer
  • Clarify team member roles
  • Establish regular team meetings

Capability

Lack of critical skill sets, knowledge, ongoing learning, and development.
  Improvement strategy:
  • Staff the team with the right employees
  • Provide appropriate education and training
  • Establish individual development plans
  • Regularly assess team effectiveness

point summarized in Figure 13.3. For example, in some team situations, the *leadership* is absent or ineffective. Where there is (or should be) an elected or appointed team leader, this person is not providing the direction or vision, or he or she isn't fighting hard enough for the team's resources. Improving the situation here may mean changing the leader—or at least getting him or her to provide the necessary direction.

"No decision. They're still sleeping on it."

Sometimes, it's a lack of *focus*. Here, if you spoke with the team members, you'd find a lack of clarity about the team's purpose, roles, strategy, and goals. Comments here might include, "Why are we organized this way, and what are we supposed to be doing?" The solution here is to clarify the team's mission, and the team members' roles. Some teams lack the *motivation or capability*. Employees may lack critical skills, or they may not have the knowledge they need to do their jobs. Eliminating this problem requires staffing the teams with the right employees, providing appropriate education and training, and launching the right incentive plan for the team and its members. The Management in Action feature illustrates how things may go wrong.

■ ■ *Team members at Rodel, Inc., a Delaware manufacturing firm, after completing a rigorous leadership-training program aimed at building trust, teamwork, and leadership.*

MANAGEMENT IN ACTION   Nut Island

For many years, the Nut Island sewage treatment plant in Quincy, Massachusetts, and its team of dedicated workers did an exemplary job of keeping pollution from flowing into Boston Harbor. Then, in one six-month period a number of years ago, they released 3.7 billion gallons of raw sewage into the harbor. In hindsight, one expert who studied Nut Island thinks several things contributed to this team's failure.[71] First, management assigned "vital, behind-the-scenes tasks" to the team and gave it considerable autonomy. Second, management took the team's self-sufficiency for granted and ignored requests for help and signs of trouble. Third, as problems mounted, the team developed an "us against the world mentality." Soon, both the team and management were operating with a false sense of reality—the team thought it was doing a good job, and management blinded itself to bad news. In this case, too much authority, too little oversight, and ignoring danger signs meant 3.7 billion gallons of raw sewage in Boston Harbor. ■ ■ ■ ■

Characteristics of Productive Teams

Of course, you don't want unproductive teams; you want productive ones. Experienced managers who have worked successfully with teams have clear notions about what makes teams successful. For example, H. David Aycock, the former chairman, CEO, and president of steel maker Nucor Corp., says successful teams have seven key ingredients:

1. The company must clearly define and articulate the mission, and everybody has to understand it. That includes an understanding of the project's purpose.
2. All team members have to be positive thinkers.
3. Selfish people spell doom for a team effort.
4. Each team member must have enough self-confidence and self-respect to respect other team members.
5. The team leader must always be on the lookout for distractions, tensions, and unproductive or ancillary issues. If the leader spots the project going astray, it is our responsibility to get it back on track—fast.
6. Each member must trust the motives of the other members.
7. The team has to be as small as possible. If you have more people than are absolutely necessary on a team, members will start functioning like a committee.[72]

Or, consider the experience of Big Apple Circus.

MANAGEMENT IN ACTION   Big Apple Circus

This traveling circus is famous for the skills of its artists as well as for their ability to work together as a team in the show. Working together collegially to present a seamless show is no easy matter when you consider how diverse the team is. In a typical year, "the Circus is made up of 25 performers, including Chinese acrobats, Russian and Polish aerialists, elephant trainers from the United States, a French clown, the Danish equestrian, and a bird trainer from England."[73] How does Big Apple's founder and director Paul Binder put together a troop that is both diverse and collaborative? As he says, "...The most important part of putting together and managing a great diverse team is picking the right people at the start... They're people with talent, of course. But they're also people who get along—who can engage with others. After all, we don't just work together, we travel together, we see one another every day."[74]

How does he select his performers?

> *When I find out about potential acts for the Circus, I visit with them and I watch them. I'm looking for skill. They have to be a great act; they have to bring something dazzling to the audience. But along with that, I try to spend quite a bit of time talking with them. What I'm listening for is a certain kind of flexibility—a willingness to work outside their own conceptions of what "has to be." For instance, I might say to them, "You know, I think we might want to change your costumes or music. How do you feel about that?" I want to hear openness. I want to get a sense right off that they're willing to create something bigger than their individual act.[75]*

Team Member Traits Coworker diversity can be a tricky issue when it comes to team performance.[76] On the one hand, "a team with a variety of members whose skills and experiences differ and complement each other can take on a wide range of tasks."[77] On the other hand, "be on the alert... for teams whose membership is excessively varied, because conflict and communications breakdown can result."[78] What is the ideal mix of traits?

One study examined the impact of various types of traits (demographic, value, and behavioral style preference) on coworkers' attitudes and behaviors.[79] Demographic traits included age, level of education, country of citizenship, and gender. Information about values included the relative importance that individuals placed, for example, on a world at peace, happiness, freedom, and self-determination. Team members also rated such things as how much they liked each team member and their willingness to work with each of them in the future

The basic research question was, "How did coworkers' similarities influence how much they liked each other and how they felt about working with other team members in the future?" Demographic similarity (age, education, citizenship, and gender) was the strongest predictor of social liking and coworker preference,—but only at the start of the training. Three weeks after the teams had begun work, demographic similarity ceased to be significant in social liking and coworker preference. Working together successfully apparently overcame any such differences.

After three weeks of working together, however, similarity of personal values still predicted both liking and preference. Therefore, creating teams with members who share personal values—beliefs about what is good or bad and what one should or should not do—is quite important for building long-term team cohesiveness. Differences in things like age, education, country of citizenship, and gender seem to fade in significance as the team members work together successfully.

In summary, the building blocks of effective teams include those in Checklist 13.1.[80]

CHECKLIST 13.1 ■ How to Build a Productive Team

☑ **A clear mission/purpose.** Effective teams have a clear purpose, such as "Build a world-class quality car."

☑ **Commitment to a mission.** "The essence of a team is a common commitment. Without it, groups perform as individuals; with it, they become a powerful unit of collective performance."[81] Members believe, "We are all in this together."[82] "The best teams invest a tremendous amount of time and effort exploring, shaping, and agreeing on a purpose that belongs to them both collectively and individually."[83]

☑ **Specific performance goals.** Productive teams translate their common purpose (such as "build world-class qual-

ity cars") into specific team goals (such as "reduce new-car defects to no more than four per vehicle"). In fact, "transforming broad directives into specific and measurable performance goals is the surest first step for a team trying to shape a purpose meaningful to its members."[84]

☑ **Right size, right mix.** High-performing teams generally (but not always) have fewer than 25 people—usually 7 to 14. Team members' skills should be complementary, and members should share basic values. Teams composed of agreeable and conscientious employees receive higher supervisory ratings and better objective measures of team accuracy and completion.[85]

☑ **An agreed-upon structure appropriate to the task.** Team members agree about who does particular jobs, how schedules are set and followed, what skills need to be developed, what members have to do to earn continuing membership in the team, and how to make decisions.

☑ **The authority to make the decisions needed, given their mission.**

☑ **Access to or control of the resources needed to complete their mission.**

☑ **A mix of group and individual rewards.**

☑ **Longevity and the stability of team membership.**

Symptoms of Unproductive Teams Managers don't have to wait for team-based programs to fail before knowing something is wrong. Various early-warning signs signal that there's an unproductive team. Checklist 13.2 shows what to look for.[86]

CHECKLIST 13.2 ■ Symptoms of Unproductive Teams

☑ **Nonaccomplishment of goals.** The team should have specific goals and milestones. If these aren't met, the program is not working.

☑ **Cautious, guarded communication.** When team members fear ridicule or a negative reaction, they may say nothing or be cautious in what they say.

☑ **Lack of disagreement.** Lack of disagreement among team members may reflect an unwillingness to share true feelings and ideas.

☑ **Malfunctioning meetings.** As in the cartoon on page 348, unproductive teams often have meetings characterized by boredom, lack of enthusiastic participation, failure to reach decisions, or dominance by one or two people.

☑ **Conflict within the team.** A suspicious, combative environment and personal conflict among team members may signal problems in the team.

What It Takes to Be a Team Player

Whether at work, school, or sports, we've all served on teams with people who did more harm than good. These people weren't team players: They would not put the team's needs above their own, they would not do their share of the work, and their continual argumentativeness often caused turmoil and grief. As one writer put it, "Some people . . . find it difficult to subordinate their inner drive to that of their team members. Like it or not, they end up being labeled as 'not team players' and may have hurt their career potential because of their behavior."[87] Managers and prospective managers should, therefore, ask themselves if they have what it takes to be team players.

Personality Experienced managers know what they're looking for when it comes to hiring team players. As noted earlier, Nucor's H. David Aycock wants "positive thinkers." He says, "Selfish people spell doom for a team effort," each team member must have enough "self-confidence and self-respect to respect other team members," and "each member must trust the motives of the other members." Big Apple Circus's Paul Binder looks for "a certain kind of flexibility—a willingness to work outside one's own conceptions of what 'has to be'."

To some extent, the likelihood of your being a team player reflects your tendency to be "individualistic" or "collectivist" in how you approach tasks and people. Individualists tend to prefer to work alone, while collectivists prefer working with others. Figure 13.4 provides a rough measure of the extent to which these labels fit you. Add your answers to arrive at your score. In one study of 492 undergraduate students, the average score was about 89. Scores below 65 to 70 may suggest a strong preference for working alone. Scores above 110 or so may indicate a "preference for collaborating with others."[88]

Skills Personality is important, but studies show that people also need various interpersonal skills to work effectively in teams.[89] In terms of *conflict resolution skills*, for instance, team members need the ability (1) to recognize and encourage desirable (but discourage undesirable) conflict; (2) to recognize the type and source of conflict and be able to implement appropriate conflict resolution strategies; and (3) to use

► FIGURE 13–4 ■ ■ ■

Do You Have a Team Mentality?

Source: Adapted from J. A. Wagner III, "Studies of Individualism–Collectivism: Effects on Cooperation in Groups." *Academy of Management Journal*, February 1995, p. 162.

Circle the answer that most closely resembles your attitude.

	Strongly Disagree						Strongly Agree
1. Only those who depend on themselves get ahead in life.	7	6	5	4	3	2	1
2. To be superior, a person must stand alone.	7	6	5	4	3	2	1
3. If you want something done right, you must do it yourself.	7	6	5	4	3	2	1
4. What happens to me is my own doing.	7	6	5	4	3	2	1
5. In the long run, the only person you can count on is yourself.	7	6	5	4	3	2	1
6. Winning is everything.	7	6	5	4	3	2	1
7. I feel that winning is important in both work and games.	7	6	5	4	3	2	1
8. Success is the most important thing in life.	7	6	5	4	3	2	1
9. It annoys me when other people perform better than I do.	7	6	5	4	3	2	1
10. Doing your best is not enough; it is important to win.	7	6	5	4	3	2	1
11. I prefer to work with others in a group rather than work alone.	7	6	5	4	3	2	1
12. Given a choice, I would rather do a job where I can work alone rather than doing a job where I have to work with others in a group.	7	6	5	4	3	2	1
13. Working with a group is better than working alone.	7	6	5	4	3	2	1
14. People should be made aware that if they are going to be part of a group, then they are somethimes going to have to do things they do not want to do.	7	6	5	4	3	2	1
15. People who belong to a group should realize that they are not always going to get what they personally want.	7	6	5	4	3	2	1
16. People in a group should realize that they sometimes are going to have to make sacrifices for the sake of the group as a whole.	7	6	5	4	3	2	1
17. People in a group should be willing to make sacrifices for the sake of the group's well-being.	7	6	5	4	3	2	1
18. A group is most productive when its members do what *they* want to do rather than what the group wants to do.	7	6	5	4	3	2	1
19. A group is most efficient when its members do what *they* think is best rather than do what the group wants them to do.	7	6	5	4	3	2	1
20. A group is most productive when its members follow their own interests and concerns.	7	6	5	4	3	2	1

Add your answers to calculate your score. The higher your score, the higher your collectivist orientation, so high scores are more compatible with being a team player.

integrative, rather than disruptive, approaches to negotiation. In terms of *collaborative problem solving skills*, team members need the ability to (1) choose the proper degree of participation for the task and to (2) recognize obstacles to collaborative problem solving and then implement corrective actions. In terms of *communication skills*, they need the ability to (1) let everyone contribute, (2) communicate openly and in a supportive way, (3) listen nonevaluatively and use active listening, and (4) engage in small talk and ritual greetings. Not everyone is suited to exercise such skills.

Given that many teams manage their own activities, their members also need to develop various managerial skills. These include the ability (1) to help establish specific, challenging, and accepted team goals, and (2) to monitor, evaluate, and provide feedback on performance. Team players also need the ability to (1) coordinate and synchronize activities, information, and tasks among team members, and (2) to help establish task and role assignments for individual team members and ensure proper balancing of workloads. Again, not all team candidates will have the potential or inclination to exercise such skills.

Top Management Teams Some consultants who have worked with top management teams say top managers sometimes make the worst team players. Says one, "CEOs often have team-averse personality types. In a way, the problem is too much talent at the table . . . you get a CEO running a team composed essentially of five other CEOs—the heads of divisions of businesses—and there is a natural tendency to wonder, who is really the boss here? These are super accelerators, ambitious people, and there is only one step higher than the one they're now occupying: the top job. . . . You would be amazed at the level of threat some executives perceive from one another."[90]

■■ ■ LEADING PRODUCTIVE TEAMS

In many respects, *team leadership* is what springs to mind when most of us think of leading. We think of the captain leading her team, the soldier leading his squad, or the scientist leading the team that makes some brilliant discovery. Since *team leadership* is so representative of leading, the leadership techniques from Chapter 10 are fully applicable to team leader situations. For example, you can use the Situational Leadership Model to help decide the style (telling, selling. participating, or delegating) that's best for your team's situation.

However, leading productive teams often does present special challenges. For example, it often requires a lot more emphasis on coaching and much less emphasis on being the boss. It also, therefore, often requires being able to surrender some of the trappings of supervisory authority. This is particularly the case when the team is supposed to manage itself.

What Are Team Leader Skills?

The collegial nature of team leadership suggests that team leaders need three special skills. First, they *coach, they don't boss*. In this context, the leader-coach's main role is to help people develop their skills. It is not your job to tell people what to do or to sell your own ideas, but to help others define, analyze, and solve problems.[91] Here, the leader stimulates employee initiative and autonomy by raising questions, by helping team members identify alternatives, by providing general direction, by encouraging employees to contribute their own ideas, and by supplying feedback.[92] Second, they *encourage participation*. They solicit input into decisions, share decision-making responsibility, and delegate specifically identified decisions to the team. Third, they are *facilitators*.[93] They give the other team members the self-confidence, authority, information, and tools they need to get their jobs done.

What Are Team Leader Values?

Skills and behaviors like these don't come easily to some people. For instance, not everyone is philosophically prepared to surrender the trappings of being the boss. Such situations are not at all like running a traditional assembly line. Leaders like these, therefore, need to be able to internalize the following values.

People Deserve Respect Effective team leaders respect each individual. At Saturn, for instance, team members carry a card that lists Saturn's values, one of which says, "We have nothing of greater value than our people. We believe that demonstrating respect for the uniqueness of every individual builds a team of confident, creative members possessing a high degree of initiative, self-respect, and self-discipline.[94]

Toyota, long known for it's exemplary team approach, also reflects this "people first" philosophy. Here's how one manager puts it:

> In all our meetings and in every way, all Toyota top managers continually express their trust in human nature. Mr. Cho [the chief executive of the company] continually reminds us that the team members must come first and that every other action we take and decision we make must be adapted to that basic idea; I must manage around that core idea.[95]

Team Members Can Be Trusted Effective team leaders have what Douglas McGregor called Theory Y assumptions: They trust team members to do their best. They assume team members can and want to do a good job, and they focus their attention on ensuring that team members have what they need to do their jobs.

Teamwork Comes First Team leaders believe in the wisdom of stripping away the barriers that can undermine teamwork. For example, they have to be willing to minimize status differences, since such differences build barriers to team member relations. At Toyota's manufacturing facility in Lexington, Kentucky, none of the managers—not even the president—have private offices or executive parking spaces. Team leaders say, "We are here to support our teams and to eliminate barriers." They believe their main responsibility is to help their teams get their jobs done.

Typical Leader Transition Problems

Moving from traditional in-charge supervisor to facilitator-coach isn't easy. As one former executive put it:

> *Working . . . under the autocratic system was a lot easier, particularly when you want something done quickly and you are convinced you know the right way to do it. It is a lot easier to say, "OK, we're going to Chicago tomorrow," rather than sit down and say, "All right, first of all, do we want to go out of town? And where do we want to go—east or west?"*[96]

You can expect four things to make it hard to transition from boss to coach. Knowing them may make the transition easier.

Perceived Loss of Power or Status Moving from supervisor to team leader often involves a loss of power and/or status.[97] One day you're the boss, with the authority to give orders and have others obey. The next day, the pyramid is upside-down. Now you're a facilitator/coach, focused on making sure that your team has what it needs to do its job—to a large extent, without you.

Unclear Team Leader Roles Team leadership—particularly when the team is a self-managing one—leaves the leader in a somewhat ambiguous situation. The very loss of power that often typifies this type of leadership can leave the leader unsure of what he or she is there to do. Some companies aggravate the situation by overemphasizing what the former supervisor (now team leader) is not: You're not the boss; you are not to control or direct any more, and you are not to make all the hiring decisions any more. This can leave the leader with the question, "What exactly am I supposed to be doing?"

In fact, team leaders do have important duties—for instance, as coaches, facilitators, and boundary managers (representing his or her team's interests to top management, for instance). Management's job is to ensure that the team leaders understand what their new duties are—and how they can do their new jobs effectively.

Job Security Concerns Telling former supervisors/new team leaders that they're not in charge anymore understandably undermines their sense of security. After all, it's not unreasonable for someone to ask, "Just how secure is the job of managing a self-managing team?" For example, General Mills claims much of the productivity improvement from its self-directed work teams came from eliminating middle managers.

Companies handle this problem in several ways. Many of the new teams still need a facilitator/coach, so some supervisors will find new jobs as team leaders. As another example, when chemical firm Rohm and Haas's Louisville, Kentucky, plant changed over to self-directing work teams, it turned the redundant supervisors into training coordinators. The firm made them responsible for managing the continuing educational requirements of the plant's new teams.[98]

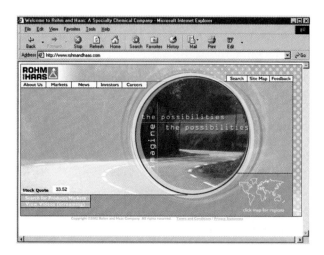

The Double Standard Problem Some supervisors will feel that the company is treating them like second-class citizens compared with the employees who are being trained to be team members. The solution here is to create and implement a development and transition plan for the supervisors too—one that clarifies their new duties and identifies the training they'll receive as they make the transition from supervisor to team leader.

The Leader's Role in Creating a Self-Managing Team

Working in self-managing teams can be unsettling to employees who haven't done so before, since people who are used to having bosses may feel adrift. It is therefore useful for team leaders to understand how such teams evolve. That way, they can anticipate the problems that may arise at each stage of the process. Most experts describe the five main team creation stages as *forming, storming, norming, performing,* and *adjourning.* We'll look at them.

In practice, the process usually begins before the team itself is formed. It starts with an executive steering committee. Often working with employee input, this committee analyzes the feasibility of a team-based arrangement, and takes steps to implement the program. It also identifies measurable goals for the program, chooses the initial sites for the program, and makes an initial division of work among teams.

Forming Once the committee announces plans for the team program's nature and structure, the teams themselves begin *forming.* The teams and their leaders begin working out their specific responsibilities. They also start building friendships and working through any issues they may have with the team's purpose, structure, and leadership.[99]

Training is usually one of the leader's main tasks here. For example, the employees have to learn how to communicate and how to listen, how to use administrative procedures and budgets, and how to work together as a team. All this effort requires team-building exercises as well as considerable support from the team's leader. During this stage, the leaders themselves have to learn how to become facilitators and coaches rather than bosses.[100]

Some team-building exercises have been known to cause more problems than they solve. For example, many companies try to make their corporate team-building exercises entertaining (such as by sending six vice presidents to a cooking class together). Not everyone will be pleased (nor should they be) to have to abandon busy schedules for what they see as a dubious exercise. As one participant said, "We had deadlines to meet [back on our jobs], and people's minds were on that."[101]

Storming In the *storming* stage, questions typically arise regarding who is leading the team and what its structure and purpose should be. In other words, it is a period of some confusion. Now the initial enthusiasm has worn off. Team members may become concerned about whether their new higher work standards may backfire at compensation time, and whether they'll be able to manage themselves. Supervisors may become increasingly concerned about their shrinking role in day-to-day operations.

The chief danger now is that rather than remaining self-directed, the team lets a team member become its de facto boss. Rather than making decisions by consensus and letting all members contribute to the team's direction, they allow someone—perhaps one of their own—to supervise them. One way to avoid this is to make sure everyone "continues to learn and eventually exercise leadership skills . . . [and] allow anyone to exercise leadership functions as needed."[102] Ideally, the team's confidence grows as members master their new skills and find better ways to accomplish their work.

Norming At this point, team members agree on matters like purpose, structure, and leadership and are prepared to start performing. Cooperation, mutual support, and agreement regarding team norms, therefore, characterize this third, *norming* stage. Misplaced loyalty is a potential danger at this stage. The team's newfound cohesiveness, loyalty, and norms can prompt it to cover for poorly performing members. The leader's job is to emphasize the need for the team to temper cooperation with the responsibility to supervise its own members. The organization can then move to what one researcher calls "the period of true [team] self-direction."[103]

Performing The *performing* stage is hopefully a period of productivity, achievement, and pride as the team members work together to get the job done.

Adjourning Finally, with some teams (such as temporary project teams), there may be an *adjourning* stage as the team splits up. Here, the team members face the mixed emotions of both separation and satisfaction over a job well done.

How to Improve Team Performance

Earlier in this chapter, we saw that productive teams require certain building blocks, such as a clear purpose and "right size, right mix." Actions that team leaders can take to put these building blocks in place include:

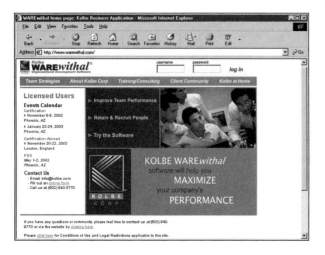

- *Select members for skill and teamwork.* Teams need people who are able to work together collegially and learn new skills. Choose team members both for their existing skills and for their potential to learn new ones. Create teams with the smallest number of employees required to do the work.[104] Do what companies like Toyota do: Recruit and select employees who have a history of preferring to work in teams and of being good team members. Internet-based applications are available to help managers match employees to team needs. For example, Kolbe WAREwithal® online (**www.warewithal.com**) lets potential team members take an online test. This identifies and classifies employees based on four basic team behaviors—fact finder, follow-thru, quick start, and implementer.[105]

- *Establish challenging performance standards.* Teams need challenging goals, clear performance standards, and intermediate milestones.

- *Emphasize the task's importance.* Team members need to know that what they're doing is important for the company. Emphasize the task's importance in terms of customers, other employees, the organization's mission, and the company's overall results.

- *Assign whole tasks.* Strive to make the team responsible for a complete item, such as an entire product, project, or segment of the business. This can boost each team member's sense of responsibility and ownership.

- *Send the right signals.* Demonstrate that you're committed to the team approach. Particularly during the early team formation stage, employees will monitor management's actions to assess its commitment to the process. For example, if a senior executive leaves the kickoff meeting "to take a phone call" and then never returns, the message is that he or she doesn't care about the team.

- *Encourage social support.* Teams are more effective when members support each other. A manager should take concrete steps to encourage and reinforce positive interactions and cohesiveness within the team.

- *Make sure there are unambiguous team rules.* To ensure cooperative behavior, teams need rules governing what members can and cannot do. The critical rules pertain to attendance (for example, "no interruptions to take phone calls"), discussion ("no sacred cows"), confidentiality ("the only things to leave this room are what we agree on"), the analytic approach ("facts are friendly"), end-product orientation ("everyone gets assignments and does them"), constructive confrontation ("no finger pointing"), and perhaps the most important, contributions ("everyone does real work").

- *Challenge the group regularly with fresh facts and information.* New information—about performance or new competitors—helps a team redefine and enrich its understanding of the challenges it faces. It also helps the team reshape its common purpose and refine its goals.

- *Train and cross-train.* Training should be broad and ongoing. Consider the team training program for BMW's new Spartansburg, South Carolina, auto plant. It includes sessions on problem solving, communication, and how to deal with conflict within and between teams. During the teams' first 18 months, workers received more than 80 more hours of team-skills training,—for instance, in problem analysis. As the HR director for BMW Manufacturing put it, training employees about technical matters is straightforward; teaching them how to work well with others is much harder.[106]

- *Provide the necessary tools and material support.* Training and support are useless if the teams don't have the tools and infrastructure they need to do their jobs. One study found these to "be more important than [just] ensuring group members are cohesive."[107] The researchers found that support should include timely information, resources, and rewards that encourage group, rather than individual, performance. The findings also suggest that ". . . organizations should determine if the necessary support resources are available before creating teams."[108]

■ *Encourage "emotionally intelligent" team behavior.* For example, acknowledge and discuss group moods, communicate your sense of what is happening in the team, tell your teammates what you're thinking and how you are feeling, ask whether everyone agrees with the decision, ask quiet members what they think, "call" members on errant behavior, support members and volunteer to help them if need be; protect members from attack, and never be derogatory or demeaning.[109]

Provide an Organizational Context That Supports Teams[110]

The manager heading up the overall organizational team effort needs to keep in mind that the organizational context of the program is important. On a micro level, setting clear missions, providing support, and encouraging emotionally intelligent behavior won't work if the context of the company, including its policies and systems, is inconsistent with the team approach. Experience suggests that the firm must have the right philosophy, structure, systems, policies, and employee skills (see Figure 13.5).

Organizational Philosophy For example, organizing self-managing teams and then showing employees you don't trust them is self-defeating. The team approach, therefore, calls for a new managerial mindset. The people in top management have to make it clear by word and deed that they're sincere about involving and trusting employees.

Organizational Structure In team-based companies, teams are the basic work units. The teams carry out supervisory tasks ranging from scheduling overtime to actually doing the work. These firms have flat hierarchies with relatively few supervisors, and they delegate much decision-making authority to the work teams.

Organizational Systems Every company depends on standard operating systems to ensure that everything goes smoothly. These range from performance appraisal and incentive systems to the systems used to gather marketing data and to monitor sales and production levels.

Organizing around teams means thinking through how to make the firm's systems compatible with the team approach. For example, managers will want to pay financial incentives to the team as a whole rather than to individual employees. Similarly, they may institute a 360-degree appraisal system to capture feedback from all the worker's teammates, not just the facility's managers.

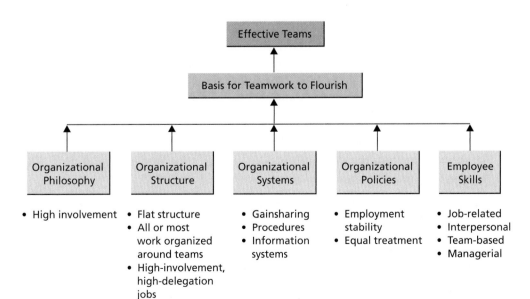

◀ **FIGURE 13–5** ■ ■ ■

Designing Organizations to Manage Teams

Source: Adapted from James H. Shonk, *Team-Based Organizations* (Homewood, IL: Irwin, 1997), p. 36.

Organizational Policies Every company uses organizational policies (such as "we only use fresh ingredients") to guide employee decisions. Team-based firms need team-friendly policies. For example, organizing around self-managing teams requires some employment stability. It hardly pays to spend years building self-managing teams if the firm fires employees at the first signs of a slowdown. *Employment stability* is thus one policy firms like these try to adhere to. At Toyota's Camry facility in Lexington, Kentucky, for instance, slack demand might mean that more employees spend time training to develop new skills rather than being laid off. Consider another example: Rigid policies such as "any employee coming to work more than 12 minutes late will not be allowed on the premises" would be counterproductive. The teams, after all, are supposed to be responsible for supervising themselves.

Figure 13.6 provides diagnostic questions team leaders can use to see if they're doing what's necessary to address critical factors for team success (such as setting a clear direction and formulating an effective team rewards program).

▶ **FIGURE 13–6** ■ ■ ■

Critical Success Factors: Diagnostic Questions for Team Leaders

Source: Ruth Wageman, *Organizational Dynamics*, Summer 1997, pp. 49–61.

1. CLEAR DIRECTION

   Can team members articulate a clear direction, shared by all members, of the basic purpose that the team exists to achieve?

2. A REAL TEAM TASK

   Is the team assigned collective responsibility for all of the team's customers and major outputs?

   Is the team required to make collective decisions about work strategies (rather than leaving it to individuals)?

   Are members cross-trained, able to help each other?

   Does the team get team-level data and feedback about its performance?

   Is the team required to meet frequently, and does it do so?

3. TEAM REWARDS

   Counting all reward dollars available, are more than 80 percent available to teams only, and not to individuals?

4. BASIC MATERIAL RESOURCES

   Does the team have its own meeting space?

   Can the team easily get basic materials needed for the work?

5. AUTHORITY TO MANAGE THE WORK

   Do the team members have the authority to decide the following (without first receiving special authorization)?

   • How to meet client demands.

   • Which actions to take, and when.

   • Whether to change their work strategies when they deem necessary.

6. TEAM GOALS

   Can the team members articulate specific goals?

   Do these goals stretch their performance?

   Have they specified a time by which they intend to accomplish these goals?

7. STRATEGY NORMS

   Do team members encourage each other to detect problems without the leader's intervention?

   Do members openly discuss differences in what members have to contribute to the team?

   Do members encourage experimentation with new ways of operating?

   Does the team actively seek to learn from other teams?

■■■ USING GROUPS TO MAKE BETTER DECISIONS

Anyone who has been on a committee can attest to the fact that when it comes to making decisions, groups can be a force for good or ill. Being able to lead a group discussion is, therefore, an important team-leadership skill.

Pros and Cons of Group Decision Making

The old saying that "two heads are better than one" can be true when you bring people together to discuss a problem. Pooling the experiences and points of view of several people obviously means you may bring more points of view to bear. This may lead to more ways to define the problem, more possible solutions, and more creative decisions in general. Groups that come up with their own decisions also tend to "buy into" those decisions; this acceptance boosts the likelihood that the group will work harder to implement the decision once it's put into effect.[111]

However, while advocates say "two heads are better than one," detractors say "a camel is a horse put together by a committee." This is because several things can go wrong when groups make decisions. The desire to be accepted tends to silence disagreement and to favor consensus, a fact that can actually reduce creative decisions instead of enhancing them.[112] In many groups, a dominant individual emerges who effectively cuts off debate and channels the rest of the group to his or her point of view. When groups are confronted by a problem, there is also a tendency for individual members to become committed to their own solutions; the goal then becomes winning the argument rather than solving the problem. Groups also take longer to make decisions.

Other strange things happen when groups make decisions. In one study, researchers had group members read an example of poor performance, and then they asked the group how it would discipline the poor-performing employee. Individually, each group member's decision was rather lenient. But when the group got together to discuss the punishment, its consensus decision was more severe than the average of the individual decisions.[113]

Groupthink is a special problem. It is "a mode of thinking that people engage in when they are deeply involved in a cohesive group, when the members' desire for unanimity overrides their personal motivation to realistically appraise alternative courses of action."[114] The classic example involved the Kennedy administration's disastrous decision to invade Cuba at the Bay of Pigs in 1961. Midway through the National Security Council's discussions of the pros and cons of the invasion, then-Attorney General Robert Kennedy reportedly told one detractor, "You may be right and you may be wrong, but President Kennedy has made his decision, so keep your opinions to yourself." The desire for unanimity overrode the potential advantage of including more varying points of view and contributed to what turned out to be a bad decision. Figure 13.7 presents groupthink's warning signs. However, groupthink may not be without benefits. In one study, groupthink was associated with "feelings of

groupthink ■ the mode of thinking in a cohesive group in which the desire to achieve group consensus overrides the potentially valuable individual points of view of its members.

"Don't ask, don't question."	Group members censor themselves, refuse to ask probing questions, and withhold disagreement.
"You must conform."	Someone, probably a group member, pressures others to withhold dissent and to go along with the group decisions.
"We all agree."	Group members press on with making their decisions under the erroneous impression that all group members agree—possibly due to dissenters' silence.
"We're on a mission."	Group members frame their arguments in terms of what's right for the group's mission—electing the U.S. president, attacking a country, or beating a competitor, for instance—and assume, therefore, that what they're doing is right and ethical.
"Masters of the world."	Group members come to believe that the group is totally in command of the mission and can, therefore, do anything, regardless of the risks—they come to feel invulnerable.

◀ **FIGURE 13–7** ■■■

Signs That Groupthink May Be a Problem

Source: Adapted from information provided in Irving James, *Group Think: Psychological Studies of Policy Decisions and Fiascos*, 2nd ed. (Boston: Houghton Mifflin, 1982).

invulnerability, immortality, and unanimity." This, in turn, boosted the team's morale, confidence, motivation, and feelings of group identity.[115] The downside is that this can blind team members to fallacies in their thinking.

Improving Group Decision Making

The manager's job is to use his or her team in such a way that the advantages of group decision making outweigh its disadvantages. For this task, managers use several group decision-making techniques.[116]

Devil's-Advocate Approach One way to avoid groupthink is to formalize the criticism process. The devil's-advocate approach does this. An advocate defends the proposed solution, and the group appoints a second person to be the devil's advocate, to prepare a detailed counterargument. That person lists what is wrong with the solution and why the group should not adopt it. The aim is to ensure a full and objective airing of the proposal's pros and cons.

Brainstorming Brainstorming is a group problem-solving technique whereby group members introduce all possible solutions before evaluating any of them.[117] The technique is aimed at fostering creative solutions by encouraging everyone to make suggestions without fear of criticism. Brainstorming has four main rules:

1. Avoid criticizing others' ideas until all suggestions are out on the table.
2. Share even wild suggestions.
3. Offer as many suggestions and supportive comments as possible.[118]
4. Build on others' suggestions to create your own.[119]

Electronic brainstorming is a recent innovation. Here, group members interact via PCs instead of face-to-face. This actually results in a relatively large increase in the number of high-quality ideas generated by the group, compared with face-to-face groups, perhaps because it reduces inhibitions.[120]

PC-Based Decision Support Systems Computerized group decision support systems can improve a group's decision-making effectiveness. In one study, researchers split 216 midlevel managers who were participating in a five-day training session into three-person decision-making groups. Researchers asked participants to help the fictitious Consolidated Commodities Inc. select a product manager for a new division. All participants read descriptions of three hypothetical candidates. Then they met in three-person groups to decide on whom to recommend.[121]

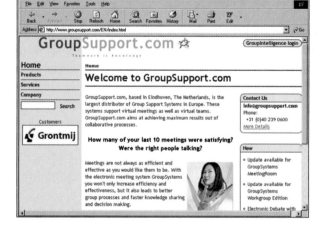

There were two types of groups. Some worked in a conventional setting, with verbal interaction among team members. Others worked in a computer-assisted decision room. Here, group members could communicate only through the computerized group decision support system. They could not communicate verbally. In this study, the computer-assisted groups significantly outperformed the traditional groups in agreeing on the superior candidate. Eliminating the verbal interactions apparently reduced potential group decision-making problems like groupthink.

The Delphi Technique This is a multistage group decision-making process aimed at eliminating the problems (like inhibitions or groupthink) that arise when group members must meet face to face. It involves obtaining the opinions of experts (the Delphi of ancient Greece) who work independently; these experts' written opinions from one stage provide the basis for other experts' analyses of each succeeding stage. The steps are as follows:

1. Identify a problem.
2. Solicit experts' opinions anonymously and individually through questionnaires (for example, on a problem such as "What do you think are the five biggest breakthrough products our computer company will have to confront in the next five years?").

3. Analyze, distill, and then resubmit these opinions to other experts, for a second round of opinions.
4. Continue this process for several more rounds until the experts reach a consensus.

The Nominal Group Technique   The nominal group decision-making technique is hardly a group decision-making process at all. Participants do not attempt to arrive at a solution as a group. Instead, they meet and vote secretly on all the solutions proposed after privately ranking the proposals in order of preference.[122] It is called the nominal group technique because the "group" is a group in name only: Members vote on solutions not as a group, but individually.

The process is this:

1. Each group member writes down his or her ideas for solving the problem at hand.
2. Each member then presents his or her ideas orally, and the person writes the ideas on a board for other participants to see.
3. After all ideas are presented, the entire group discusses all ideas simultaneously.
4. Group members individually and secretly vote on each proposed solution.
5. The solution with the most individual votes wins.

The Stepladder Technique   This is another way to reduce the potentially inhibiting effects of face-to-face meetings. It's the "stepladder" technique because you add group members one-by-one at each stage of the process so that their input is untainted by the previous discussants' points of view. The process involves these steps:

1. Individuals A and B are given a problem to solve, and each produces an independent solution.
2. A and B then meet, develop a joint decision, and meet with C, who had independently analyzed the problem and arrived at a decision.
3. A, B, and C jointly discuss the problem and arrive at a consensus decision, and they are joined by person D, who has individually analyzed the problem and arrived at his or her own decision.
4. A, B, C, and D meet and arrive at a final group decision.[123]

How to Lead a Group Decision-Making Discussion

The discussion leader has an enormous effect on whether the group's decision is useful. The chairperson who monopolizes the discussion and constantly shoots down others' ideas while pushing his or her own is unlikely to influence others to express their points of view. One who encourages input, delays criticism, and creates a supportive environment in which people want to express their opinions will more likely have a productive meeting.

According to one series of group decision-making studies, an effective discussion leader, therefore, has a responsibility to do the following:

1. See that all group members participate and contribute. As discussion leader, this is your responsibility. Doing so can help ensure that different points of view emerge and that everyone takes ownership of the final decision.
2. Distinguish between idea getting and idea evaluation. These studies conclude that evaluating and criticizing proposed solutions and ideas actually inhibit the process of getting or generating new ideas. Yet in most group discussions, one person presents an alternative, and others begin immediately discussing its pros and cons. Discussion leaders should distinguish between the idea-getting and idea-evaluation stages—forbid criticism until all ideas are on the table.
3. Do not respond to each participant or dominate the discussion. Remember that the discussion leader's main responsibility is to elicit ideas from the group, not to supply them.
4. Direct the group's effort toward overcoming surmountable obstacles. Focus on solving the problem rather than on discussing historical events that you cannot change. You cannot change the past. As discussion leader, your job is to focus the group on obstacles that the organization can overcome and on solutions it can implement.[124]

5. Don't sit down. In one study, researchers compared 56 five-member groups that conducted meetings while standing with 55 groups that conducted meetings while sitting. Sit-down meetings were 34 percent longer than standup meetings. However, the sit-down meetings produced decisions that were no better than those arrived at in standup meetings.[125]

SUMMARY ■■■

1. Work teams are examples of employee involvement programs, which let employees participate in formulating important work decisions or in supervising all or most of their work activities. Managers rank such programs as their biggest productivity boosters.

2. Several aspects of group dynamics are especially important for team leaders. Group norms are important because they're the rules groups use to control their members. Group cohesiveness determines the attraction of the group for its members, and it reflects things like proximity, interpersonal attractiveness, homogeneity of interests or goals, and intergroup competition.

3. Leaders can use several types of teams in organizations, including suggestion teams, problem-solving teams, transnational teams, virtual teams, and self-managing teams.

4. Symptoms of unproductive teams include cautious or guarded communication, lack of disagreement, malfunctioning meetings, failure to accomplish goals, and conflict within the team. Characteristics of productive teams include commitment to a mission, specific performance goals, and the right size and mix of people.

5. How can a leader go about building a high-performing team? Guidelines include establish demanding performance standards; select members for skill and skill potential; set clear rules of behavior; move from boss to coach; choose people who like teamwork; train team members, assign whole tasks; and encourage social support. When teams do not succeed, the problem often lies in one of three contextual factors: leadership, focus, or capability.

6. Team leaders have special skills. They coach, encourage participation, are boundary managers, and are facilitators. Moving from boss to team leader can cause transition problems stemming from the perceived loss of power or status, unclear team leader roles, job security concerns, and problems with double standards.

7. Not everyone has the values to be an effective leader of self-managing teams. A successful team leader must adhere to the right values, including respecting people, putting team members first, and trusting team members to do their best.

8. Group discussion leader skills include seeing that all group members participate, distinguishing between idea getting and idea evaluation, not responding to each participant or dominating the discussion, and directing the group's effort toward overcoming surmountable obstacles.

KEY TERMS ■■■

employee involvement program 340
group 341
team 341
group norms 341
group cohesiveness 342

suggestion team 343
problem-solving team 343
quality circle 343
venture team 343
transnational team 343

virtual team 344
self-managing/self-directed work team 346
groupthink 359
brainstorming 360

SKILLS AND STUDY MATERIALS

COMPANION WEBSITE ■■■

 We invite you to visit the Dessler Companion Website at **www.prenhall.com/dessler** for this chapter's Internet resources.

EXPERIENTIAL EXERCISES ■■■

1. In many of the exercises throughout this book, you have been working in teams. Now, in teams of 4 or 5 students, compare team cohesiveness as the semester or quarter has progressed. Has it increased or decreased? What accounts for this? What group norms have evolved? How have these influenced group functioning? List the ways your team does or does not have the necessary building blocks to be a highly effective team.

2. Lecturing to a class is similar in many respects to leading a discussion group. The discussion leader's role is to get everyone involved in contributing. In teams of 4 or 5 students, discuss your professor's use of the discussion leader skills as explained in this chapter, and list what skills he or she seems to consistently apply or to not apply.

3. You have undoubtedly worked on teams at school, at work, or socially with someone who obviously did not have what it takes to be a team player. In teams of 4 or 5 students, discuss your nominees for "the worst team player I ever worked with" (no names, please), including what he or she did to win your nomination. List five reasons why you believe the person is not suited to be a team player.

STUDY CASE ■■■

TEAM BUILDING AT THE COLORADO SYMPHONY ORCHESTRA

Anyone checking the Web site of the Colorado Symphony Orchestra (CSO) in 2000 would have found a friendly message that the weekend concert series was sold out. A first-time visitor to the site would not realize that this orchestra, both artistically and financially successful, was largely the same group of musicians who watched the Denver Symphony Orchestra (DSO) declare bankruptcy a few years earlier. The musicians then decided to create a new team approach to orchestra management, and a new orchestra, the CSO, was born.

The DSO had served the community in one form or another for over 55 years before its board dissolved it for failing to meet its debts. The board had told orchestra members they could accept a 20 percent cut in pay or the organization would file for bankruptcy. With some reluctance, the musicians accepted the cut and agreed to a three-year contract. While the orchestra's future seemed more promising, further difficulties lay ahead. Soon, the board announced yet another $700,000 shortfall. It asked the musicians to reopen their contract, but they refused.

By the early 1990s, the situation was bleak. The board announced a "comeback season," with a new barebones budget that included a 50 percent pay cut for the musicians. The board offered musicians a salary of $11,000 for the 21-week season. The musicians unanimously rejected the proposed salary package. Thirty days later, 50 musicians gathered at the Boettcher Hall concert site and voted the CSO into existence.

DSO's traditional orchestra management model was complicated. Ticket sales were never enough to fund the full cost of production, so orchestras relied heavily on contributions from patrons to cover costs. These patrons often had advisory roles, and they could exert financial pressure by withholding gifts. An executive director usually manages the business side of an orchestra, while a music director manages the artistic side. Musicians were usually unionized. At DSO, there was a long history of labor–management problems. There were four work stoppages, the longest of which lasted more than 11 weeks.

The newly organized CSO musicians opted for a different model—a partnership, or cooperative team. The basic concept was that all the stakeholders—musicians, staff members, and board—were to share in making decisions that affected the outcomes for the CSO. They planned to share the risks and potential rewards of running the orchestra as a team. According to Erin Lehman, program director of The Arts & Culture Initiative at Harvard University's Kennedy School of Government, no other orchestra in the country was managed like the CSO.[126]

One of the key elements that made the agreement unique was the high level of musician involvement in managing the business. The musicians made a substantial financial commitment to the orchestra. They agreed to accept a low salary for the potential to share in surpluses generated at year-end. The goal was to keep musicians' salaries at no more than 50% of the operating budget. Since the musicians were making such a strong financial commitment, they also got a stronger voice in the operation of the orchestra. They held one-third of the seats on all governing committees and the majority of seats on the artistic committee (an area usually under the sole control of the artistic director).

The results were extraordinary. Ticket sales, a direct measure of customer satisfaction, increased more than 2.5 times in the 1990s. There were also substantial increases in contributions. The organization operated in the black for the entire decade. There was also a big increase in other types of volunteer support. However, the CSO isn't standing still. It has hired an experienced professional named Tom Bacchetti, former director of the Atlanta Symphony for over a decade, as executive director. Under Bacchetti's leadership, the Atlanta Symphony performance revenues grew from $1.9 million to $9.4 million. The organization has also invested in developing future audiences with an aggressive youth education program, including two series of free concerts for school groups.

Recently, although the orchestra has still not achieved the level of contributions it had hoped for, it is financially stable. The team-based structure at the CSO, which is such a radical departure from its DSO past, has proved to be a solid base from which to lead the orchestra.

Discussion Questions

1. Based on what you read in this chapter, what team-building values, concepts, and techniques did the CSO musicians (perhaps inadvertently) apply to build their new team approach to managing the orchestra? List at least eight reasons why you believe the CSO team does or does not have the necessary building blocks to function effectively as a team.

2. Specifically, what managerial role do you see Tom Bacchetti playing in CSO's team-based organization? What skills do you think he'll need? Why? How do you believe the addition of a new strong executive director will change the dynamics of the CSO's team-based structure?

3. To what extent could CSO's team-based structure work in other orchestras? Why?

4. Is giving a concert similar to managing the CSO's day-to-day operations? Do you think the orchestra could apply the same team approach to conducting its presentations without a conductor? Why or why not?

BUILDING TEAMWORK AT JETBLUE

jetBlue AIRWAYS® Although JetBlue is organized departmentally rather than around teams, teamwork plays a central role in the company's success. For one thing, at any point in time, JetBlue does have 30 or 40 "Tiger teams" working on specific, short-term projects. Furthermore, JetBlue knows that maintaining its lead as a low-cost–high-quality airline means making sure that in everything it does, JetBlue emphasizes teamwork—and it does this in a variety of ways.

First, it makes sure that the employees it hires are team players. The company uses a screening device known as "Targeted selection." Targeted selection is a structured interview aimed at uncovering the extent to which the candidate follows (and has followed in the past) the company's five basic values of safety, caring, integrity, fun, and passion. The targeted-selection interview questions go far beyond the usual "tell me your strengths and weaknesses" types of questions that other companies tend to emphasize during interviews. For example, the JetBlue interviewer might ask a pilot candidate, "Describe a situation that challenged your skills as a pilot, and how you dealt with it." Similarly, JetBlue does extensive background screening to screen out those who might not fit well into the JetBlue team. For example, rather than just check with the 6–7 personal references the candidate provides, JetBlue interviewers ask these references, "Who do you know who might be able to give me some insights into this candidate?"—and then the interviewers check with those people.

JetBlue takes other steps to foster a sense of teamwork. For example, everyone makes a conscious effort to avoid unproductive meetings and in general to be very respectful of one another's time. In fact, every meeting the company holds typically has one or two self-appointed "time cops," who make sure the meeting doesn't last any longer than is necessary.

In general, therefore, there is a pervasive effort, both formally and informally, to hire team players, as well as to encourage a sense that "we're all in this together" and that teamwork is crucial for JetBlue's success. However, from a practical point of view, it seems likely that as JetBlue grows, it will become harder to maintain this team atmosphere (particularly as more employees get more specialized assignments.). JetBlue is working hard to maintain its start-up, entrepreneurial atmosphere, and it knows that doing so was always going to be easier when the company was small than when it's much larger.

Assignment

You and your team are consultants to Mr. Neeleman, who is depending on your management expertise to help him navigate the launch and management of JetBlue. Here's what he wants to know from you now:

1. What do you think of the steps JetBlue is now taking to ensure that it hires only team players? Create and list five specific structured interview questions you would use to help screen out nonteam players in order to supplement the current targeted selection interview.

2. Many of JetBlue's meetings now have "time cops" to make sure that everyone's time is respected and that the meetings last no longer than necessary. Based on the information in this chapter, list five other specific steps you would suggest JetBlue take in order to ensure that meetings are as short and productive as possible.

3. Show, in organization-chart form, what JetBlue's organization might look like if it made the decision to organize the company around teams.

Controlling and Building Commitment

THE MANAGEMENT CHALLENGE

Michael Buckley Institutes New Controls

*A*llfirst, the U.S. division of Ireland's Allied International Bank (AIB), recently revised its financial statements because $691 million was missing from the company's treasury. The money was supposedly profits earned by an Allfirst currency trader for the company. However, it turned out that the trader never actually made many of the trades and that the profits he reported were just an illusion. The loss wipes out Allfirst's profits for the previous four years.[1] It was clear to AIB CEO Michael Buckley that Allfirst's trading had been out of control.

It didn't have to be that way. In 1998, AIB had begun installing software to ensure that it could control its trading operations. Among other things, the software was supposed to track the company's foreign currency transactions and report any discrepancies (such as trades in which buyers don't match sellers or in which the size of the trades exceeds the company's limits) to the company's management. But in this case, the managers apparently didn't notice or simply ignored the problems because of their misplaced trust in the trader's judgment. As CEO Michael Buckley put it, "It's very clear now that this [trader] targeted every control point of the system and systematically found ways around them, and built a web of concealment that was very sophisticated." Now, Buckley had to figure out where the system went wrong, and what AIB could do to improve the company's controls.

CHAPTER OBJECTIVES

After studying this chapter and the case exercises at the end, you should be able to:

1. Rate the adequacy of the manager's control system.

2. Recommend specific feedforward, concurrent, and feedback controls that the manager can use to control the activity.

3. Write a simple budget for the manager.

4. Specify a specific strategic ratio the manager should have employees focus on.

5. List five measures the manager can use to build a balanced scorecard.

6. Make five specific suggestions for improving a company's employee commitment.

Chapter 4   The Basic Planning Process ▪▪▪   **365**

Michael Buckley is just one of thousands of managers trying to keep their businesses under control. Sometimes, being out of control isn't catastrophic, as when your cleaner is an hour late delivering your blouse. Often, though, as at Allfirst, the consequences are severe. Once plans are set and the manager has organized and motivated the employees, he or she has to ensure that all is going as planned—that things are under control. The main purpose of this chapter is to give you the tools you need to create and manage a company's basic control systems. The main topics we'll cover include the fundamentals of controls, traditional control systems, how people react to controls, and how to use employee commitment-based control systems.

■■■ THE FUNDAMENTALS OF AN EFFECTIVE CONTROL SYSTEM

control ■ *task of ensuring that activities are getting the desired results.*

Control is the task of ensuring that activities are providing the desired results. All control systems collect, store, and transmit information on profits, sales, or some other measure. And all control systems try to influence behavior. (This is one reason why "controlling someone" often has negative overtones.) Control also requires that targets, standards, or goals be set. This is why managers often use the word *planning* along with the word *control*. Controlling involves setting a target, measuring performance, and taking corrective action. Allfirst is one example of what happens when things swing out of control. As one expert says, "The goal [of the control system] is to have no unpleasant surprises in the future."[2]

If you could be sure that every plan you made and every task you assigned would be perfectly executed, you really wouldn't need control. There would be no surprises. Unfortunately, things rarely go this smoothly. People vary widely in abilities, motivation, and ethics. Furthermore, why assume that the plans might not suddenly become outdated? (Imagine the scrambling that the big accounting firms had to do when Arthur Andersen began to fall apart.) Managers aren't paid just to introduce a plan and then to leave its execution to chance. They earn their pay for getting results. But there's no way to be sure you're progressing toward those results unless you are in control.

Many people associate control with large, companywide accounting systems, but those systems are just part of what control is all about. Control actually applies to monitoring every task—large and small—that you delegate. Some tasks may be so unimportant (or your subordinates so able) that you don't need to bother with controls. However, most managers know that abdication like this is a risky way to manage. As someone once said; "A poor manager delegates nothing, and a mediocre manager delegates everything. An effective manager delegates all that he or she can to subordinates. At the same time, the manager establishes sufficient checkpoints so that he or she knows the work has been performed." For every task you delegate, you'll need to establish some formal or informal control mechanism. Well see how to do that in this chapter.

The Role of Control in the Management Process

The apparent logic of the management process can be misleading. Strictly speaking, managers decide "where we're going" ("Planning," Chapters 3–5), who will do what ("Organizing," 6–9), and how to motivate their troops ("Leading," 10–13). Then (Chapters 14–15), they ensure that things are happening as they should—that things are under control.

However, as you might imagine, *controlling* isn't something managers can just think about once they're finished planning, organizing, and leading. For one thing, in practice, managing isn't so sequential. Imagine, for instance, that you've just become editor in chief of your college paper. Might you not want to find out fast what funds are in your account and what debts you have to suppliers? Would you really want to start planning your next edition before making sure you wouldn't run out of funds by the end of the month? Probably not. So you'd actually start with control in this case.

Furthermore, it's not so easy to separate control from the other three management functions. Indeed there's a control side to everything managers do. Control always requires that some desirable outcomes (like targets, standards, or goals) be set. That is why managers often use the word *planning* along with the word *control*.

Control is also always an issue in how managers organize. For example, we saw that self-contained, autonomous divisions can, due to their relative freedom, easily overspend and spin out of control. Decentralizing, therefore, always requires thinking through how top management will control the division's results. As another example, consider what happened at Enron. When reports began surfacing about misleading financial reports at an Enron subsidiary, Arthur Andersen, its auditors, issued a report. That report criticized Enron's ability to keep track of the financial commitments its managers were making. It said that Enron's financial controls didn't let its officers spot problems early enough.[3] However, an Enron spokesperson quickly pointed out that (in addition to being its auditor), Arthur Andersen was also in charge of Enron's internal financial controls: "As part of that job, [it] would offer suggestions on how to fix any problems that they found."[4] So who was to blame for Enron's inadequate financial controls, Andersen or Enron? It's not clear, because the controls did not reflect and conform to Enron's supposed organizational division of labor.

Leadership similarly relates to control. Leading effectively can dramatically reduce the amount of control the manager must exercise. This is because motivated and committed employees are more likely to exercise self-control. The other side of the coin (as AIB's management found out to their chagrin) is that there's often no practical way to exercise control when an employee is absolutely intent on bending the rules.

Figure 14.1 summarizes what control is and its role in the management process.

The Importance of a Timely Response

It would surely do Michael Buckley little good to discover in June that in March a trader had risked $10 million too much of his company's money. By June, the money might well be lost. Buckley needs a control system that he can monitor continuously. The control system must allow for a timely response.

Managers therefore use three types of control systems: *steering control, concurrent control,* and *feedback control.* **Steering control** (also called *feedforward* or *precontrol*) is any system that lets the manager take corrective action before the activity or project is finished.[5] Steering control is preventive in nature. For example, on a flight to Mars, you would not want to find out after the fact that you missed your mark. Engineers therefore track the flight continuously so they can adjust the trajectory in time to reach the target.

Managers use such steering/feedforward controls all the time. For example, they set intermediate milestones and thus check progress long before the project is complete.

steering control ■ *control that predicts results and takes corrective action before the operation or project is completed.*

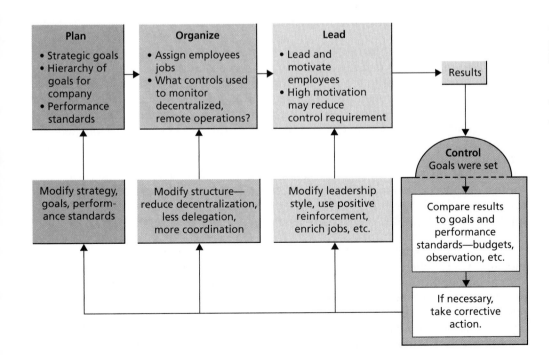

◀ **FIGURE 14–1** ■ ■ ■

Management and the Control Process

Note the control aspects (last bulleted item in first row of chart) of each of the management functions.

Source: © Gary Dessler, PH.D

They put in place procedures to reject defective raw materials, for example, and to test and screen out candidates who may cause problems. Similarly, managers review budgets on a comparative basis so as to better identify trends. Thus, in fiscal year 2000–2001, analysts noted that Gap Inc.'s sales at stores open at least one year had fallen every month. This trend led one legal expert to say, "If you ask anybody who follows retail to name five companies that could have serious problems in the next six months, I'd be shocked the Gap wasn't on the list."[6]

What steering/feedforward control would you suggest for AIB? Perhaps a system that tracks the trend of the total financial risks a trader has made, so that management can take action before the total risks become excessive. The "Managing @ the Speed of Thought" feature that follows illustrates how Boeing uses technology for controlling.

MANAGING @ THE SPEED OF THOUGHT

Controlling on Internet Time

The Internet has vastly improved managers' abilities to make timely midcourse corrections if they see activities trending out of control. Boeing's use of the Web is a good example. Boeing has an Internet-based network used by 1,000 other companies, including aluminum supplier Alcoa, Inc.[7] To gain access to this network, external users (including most of Boeing's suppliers and customers) receive digital certificates from Boeing, with passwords authorizing them to access the network.

The network allows both Boeing and its suppliers to maintain better, more timely control, "by reducing the number of misunderstandings with business partners and customers," according to Boeing's Web program manager. Access to the e-network means suppliers can continually get real-time updates regarding required delivery dates and schedule changes, and they can make course corrections if required. And, since Boeing linked its e-commerce system to tracking tools supplied by delivery services such as FedEx, customers can view the status of their orders at any time over the Web. That minimizes delivery surprises.

Boeing's Internet-based system has improved the timeliness of the company's control system in other ways. For example, employees use the system to monitor production lines: "We use the Web to keep track of shortages on airplane production lines so that everyone in the whole organization can know where the hot spots are, not just management."[8] The system even made it easier to control activities in more specific areas, such as training. For example, as soon as each instructor was required to publish his or her course lists on the Internet-based system, the training department realized different instructors were sometimes teaching the same thing. This allowed the training department to eliminate redundant courses and better control the costs of the courses the company makes available to its employees.

With concurrent (or "yes/no") control, the manager exercises control as the activity takes place (concurrent), *and* the work may not proceed until or unless it is acceptable ("yes/no"). These controls often take the form of policies and rules. For example, most companies have rules forbidding employees from entering into contracts unless the firm's legal staff approves the agreements. Direct supervision—having the supervisor at Cheesecake Factory walk the aisles to make sure all the customers are content—is concurrent control. A quality control chart that lets you plot rejects per minute and repair the machine when the trend is ominous is another example. New computerized controls (like the balanced scorecard discussed later) let managers exercise concurrent control of their operations. What steering/feedforward control would you suggest for AIB? Perhaps a policy that states, "No trader may put more than $1 million of the firm's capital at risk at one time," and a daily reporting system that shows managers the daily totals for each trader.

With feedback (or "post-action") controls, you compare results to the standard after the project is complete. The final inspection on a car assembly line is an example. Semi-annual budgets are also examples, as are the end-of-term grades students receive. The problem with postaction controls, as with grades, is that you usually can't do much to remedy the situation once the results are in. That's why professors (and managers) try to inject an element of timeliness into their controls. Instead of just a final exam, they give a midterm too. Instead of just an end-of-year budget, the manager gets monthly budgets, too. As an example, customer satisfaction is a strategic issue for Siebel Systems, which produces computer systems for businesses.[9] Twice a year, Siebel therefore has a consultant collect data from about 20% of its customers to see how satisfied the customers are with specific Siebel departments and individuals.[10]

As you probably realize, increasing the frequency of such a postaction control makes it function more like a steering/feedforward control. The main difference lies in how often you check the intermediate results. How might AIB apply this technique? Perhaps by having a special accountant do an audit every six months to verify the accuracy of the traders' reported figures.

Sometimes, the control is less responsive than you realize. For example, Cisco Systems has long trumpeted the way it has integrated its manufacturing, marketing, financial, and other accounting systems to produce controls so responsive that Cisco could "close its books" (produce complete financial statements) in one day on any day of the year.[11] Unfortunately, it recently had to lower the value of inventory by over $2 billion. It turned

■ ■ Concurrent control: A manager talks to customers at a Cheesecake Factory in California.

out that management had ordered too much inventory. The control system was "not responsive enough to stop building billions of dollars worth of stuff nobody wanted."[12] It assumed that the customers' estimates for what they'd be ordering were more accurate than they actually were. The Management in Action feature shows how another firm uses its technology for control.

MANAGEMENT IN ACTION   Using Technology to Stay in Control at UPS

UPS is the world's largest air and ground package distribution company, delivering close to three billion parcels and documents each year in the United States and more than 185 other countries. Critical to its success has been the $1.8 billion UPS invested in information technology. Each UPS driver uses a hand-held computer called a Delivery Information Acquisition Device (see photo). It captures customers' signatures, along with pickup, delivery, and time-card information, and lets the driver automatically transmit this information to headquarters via a cellular telephone network.

Through TotalTrack, its automated package-tracking system, UPS can control packages throughout the delivery process. And with its own global communication network called UPSnet, UPS not only tracks its packages, it also electronically transmits documentation on each shipment directly to customs officials prior to arrival. Shipments are therefore either cleared for shipment or flagged for inspection when they arrive.

Today, UPS uses the Internet to help it and its customers monitor and control the progress of all those millions and millions of packages. For example, the UPS Internet-based tracking system lets a customer store up to 25 tracking numbers and then monitor the progress of each package. That not only lets the customer (and UPS) keep on top of each package's progress. It is also a value-added feature for the customer, which can easily keep customers informed about the progress of the ultimate customer's package. ■■■

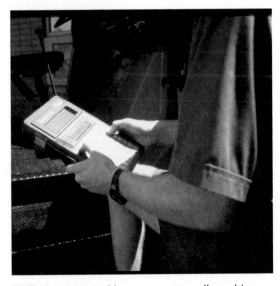

■ ■ The UPS portable scanner system allows drivers to relay information from each delivery to headquarters so the firm can monitor the whereabouts of every package it ships.

The Effective Control System

Timeliness is certainly crucial, but it's not the only basis on which to judge a control system's usefulness. Checklist 14.1 summarizes 10 important requirements. Figure 14.2 presents a chart you can use to rate the adequacy of your control system based on these 10 requirements.

	Yes	No
1. Do the controls reflect the nature and needs of the activity (i.e., budgets for financial goals, sales targets for the sales force)?	—	—
2. Do the *controls report deviations promptly*?	—	—
3. Are the *controls forward-looking*?	—	—
4. Do the *controls point up exceptions at strategic points*?	—	—
5. Are the *controls (standards, corrective actions, etc.) objective*?	—	—
6. Are the *controls flexible (adaptable to each situation)*?	—	—
7. Do the *controls reflect the organizations structure and make it clear who is responsible for what*?	—	—
8. Are *the controls economical*?	—	—
9. Are the *controls understandable*?	—	—
10. Do the *controls indicate the appropriate corrective action*?	—	—
Totals	—	—

CHECKLIST 14.1 ■ Requirements for Adequate Controls[13]

☑ **Controls should reflect the nature and needs of the activity.** In other words, controls must make sense in terms of what you're trying to control. For example, you might use a budget to control expenses and a daily log to control whether your salespeople are using their time effectively.

☑ **Controls should report deviations promptly.** Whether it's feedforward, concurrent, or feedback control, the control is useless if it can't report deviations quickly enough for you to do something about them. That is why most managers get monthly and even weekly and daily reports.

☑ **Controls should be forward-looking.** The information provided by the controls should signal the manager that a trend is taking place. For example, by plotting defects per hour, a quality-control chart lets the manager visualize a trend and take corrective action before quality reaches unacceptable limits.

☑ **Controls should point up exceptions at strategic points.** The *principle of exception* as applied to controls is that the control system should not flood the manager with data that may simply be distracting. A sales manager would be more concerned about being 30% over budget for her department's $1 million travel expenses than she would be about being 60% over in the $500 budgeted for pencils.

☑ **Controls should be objective.** To the greatest extent possible, the manager should endeavor to use objective, measurable standards rather than subjective ones.

☑ **Controls should be flexible.** For example, it might be counterproductive to have a salesperson compile the usual time-consuming weekly report during the week she's working round-the-clock to win a big account.

☑ **Controls should reflect the organization structure.** As at Enron, lack of clarity about who (Enron or Arthur Andersen) is responsible for what can lead to ambiguity about who is at fault.

☑ **Controls should be economical.** The amount of time and resources the manager puts into controlling activities needs to make sense in terms of the magnitude of those activities—and the benefits derived from those controls.

☑ **Controls should be understandable.** Some standards are too complex or hard to compute. Some control forms are too complex. Controls like these breed errors and employee resistance. Ideally, the control should be simple and understandable.

☑ **Controls should indicate corrective action.** Identifying deviations is a useful function of any control system. In addition, however, "an adequate system should disclose where failures are occurring, who is responsible for them, and what should be done about them."[14]

■ ■ ■ TWO APPROACHES TO MAINTAINING CONTROL

You just took over as editor in chief of your college's student paper. What are some of the things you'd want to control? A (very) short list would include advertising revenues, expenses, deadlines for articles, article length and quality, and the format for each issue. How will you make sure things stay under control? You have two basic options: You can use the *traditional control process*, or you can use the *commitment-based process*. Let's compare the two.

The Traditional Control Process

Traditional control methods monitor results via some type of external process. This is what usually springs to mind when most people think of control. Thus, the supervisor controls a team by watching what its members do, or Carly Fiorina controls HP/Compaq through a system of financial controls and budgets. We'll see later in this chapter that there are many types of traditional controls in use. However, the traditional control process always involves three basic steps, as follows.

Step 1: Set a Standard, Target, or Goal This shows what the results *ought* to be. Managers express standards in terms of money, time, quantity, or quality (or a combination of these). Thus, a salesperson might have a (money) quota of $8,000 worth of products per month. You may give your editor until June 1 (time) to submit her column. Production supervisors are usually responsible for producing a specified number of units (quantity) of product per week. Lexus speaks glowingly of its few defects per car (quality).

As in Figure 14.3 the usual procedure is to choose a *yardstick*, and then set a *standard*. For example, "units produced per shift" is a quantity yardstick.[15] "Fourteen units produced per shift" is then one possible standard.

Some things are easier to find yardsticks for than others. At first glance, judging your subordinates' morale or motivation is not as easy as counting defects. However, managers can and do translate subjective measures like these into concrete ones. For example, Fedex conducts annual attitude/morale surveys, the results of which it quantifies and tracks from year to year (by department) for comparison purposes.

Step 2: Measure Actual Performance Against Standards The next step involves comparing actual performance with the standard. There are two basic issues here. First, will you use personal or impersonal tracking techniques? *Personally observing* subordinates is the most common technique. Simply check how they are doing periodically to ensure that things are being done right. Personal observation works as long as the number of subordinates is limited. It becomes increasingly impractical as you add subordinates. One way to handle this is to add supervisors. For example, a hospital director might hire two assistant directors to observe employees on different floors. But in practice, you must at some point supplement personal control with formal, more *impersonal* control techniques. Examples include budgetary and financial reports, quality control reports, and inventory control reports.

The second issue is *timing*. As explained earlier, you need to decide if the situation warrants steering/feedforward, concurrent, or feedback/postaction control. For example, do you just want to check your editor's new article after it's finished (feedback)? Or do you want to see a first draft too (steering)? Do you want the person to check with you before choosing a topic (concurrent)?

Step 3: Take Corrective Action You've now compared actual with planned performance: Are there any significant deviations? If so, you'll have to take corrective action.

This isn't as simple as it may appear. First, defining the problem is essentially a problem-solving process. Perhaps the reason for the deviation is obvious. But (recall Chapter 3, "Decision Making") things are often not what they seem. Perhaps you set the sales target too high. Perhaps the salesperson isn't right for the job. Or perhaps your firm could not supply the products on time because production didn't know what sales was doing. Correcting the deviation then involves more complications. It may involve harnessing any or all of the other management functions. For example, do you need to revise your plans? Are your employee screening or training procedures inadequate?

Area to Control	Possible Yardstick	Standard/Goal to Achieve
Quantity	Number of units produced per shift	Produce 14 units per shift
Quality	Number of rejects	No more than 10 rejects per day
Timeliness	Percentage of sales reports in on time	Return 90% of sales reports on time
Dollars	Percentage of deviation from budget	Do not exceed budgeted expenses by more than 5% during year

◀ **FIGURE 14–3** ■ ■ ■

Examples of Control Standards

Does the deviation stem from low morale? Taking corrective action invariably requires a knowledgeable application of all you know about managing organizations.

The Commitment-Based Control Process

As companies expand worldwide, the problems of relying on traditional controls (like budgets and inspection reports) have become increasingly apparent. Arthur Andersen found that due to lax ethical standards on some employees' parts, financial statements that it should not have approved were approved. The controls, policies, and procedures were in place. It appears that some employees just decided to circumvent or ignore them.

The fact is that (even in accounting firms) traditional controls like budgets and reports only get you so far. There are several reasons for this. No traditional control system can anticipate every possible crisis. Employees (as we'll explain shortly) have many ingenious ways of getting around the system. And in many situations (such as building high-quality cars), you want the employees to *want* to build in quality; you don't want to have to force them to do so, or to have to stand at the end of the line catching every error. Today, markets and situations change quickly. Managers need a way to ensure that the employees themselves watch that activities don't slip out of control. You don't want, as a manager, to have to deal with an Enron or AIB-type situation. There's therefore more emphasis on commitment-based control today. Harvard professor and control expert Robert Simons puts it this way:

> A fundamental problem facing managers [today] is how to exercise adequate control in organizations that demand flexibility, innovation, and creativity. In most organizations operating in dynamic and highly competitive markets, managers cannot spend all their time and effort making sure that everyone is doing what is expected. Nor is it realistic to think that managers can achieve control by simply hiring good people, aligning incentives, and hoping for the best. Instead, today's managers must encourage employees to initiate process improvements and new ways of responding to customers' needs—but in a controlled way.[16]

Two Basic Control Approaches: A Synopsis

This leaves us with the two basic ways to maintain control (see Figure 14.4): *traditional control systems* and *commitment-based control systems*. We can summarize them as follows:

Traditional control systems involve setting standards and then monitoring performance, usually through an external monitoring process. In this chapter we'll discuss three types of traditional controls: diagnostic controls, boundary systems, and interactive controls.[17] Diagnostic controls (such as budgets) allow managers to determine whether the manager's standards have been met and, if necessary, to figure out why they haven't been. Boundary controls are policies such as codes of conduct, that identify the boundaries within which employees are to stay. Ethical rules against accepting gifts from suppliers are an example. Interactive controls involve controlling employees interactively by questioning them personally. We'll discuss each of these in the following section.

diagnostic controls ■ *a control method, such as a budget, that ensures that standards are being met and that variances are diagnosed and explained.*

boundary controls ■ *policies, such as codes of conduct, that establish rules and identify the actions and pitfalls that employees must avoid.*

personal/interactive controls ■ *control methods that involve direct, face-to-face interaction with employees so as to monitor rapidly changing information and respond proactively to changing conditions.*

▶ **FIGURE 14–4** ■ ■ ■
Two Basic Categories of Control Systems

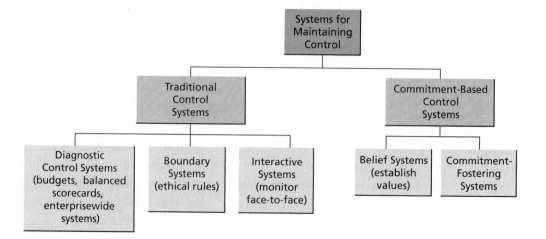

Commitment-based control systems rely on getting the employees themselves to want to do things right—they emphasize self-control. Fostering such self-control isn't easy. Companies like Saturn work hard to create an environment in which employees do a great job because they want to. Doing so means socializing the employees in the company's belief systems and values (such as the importance of quality and respect for people). And it means earning the employees' commitment by allowing them to use all of their potential. The results here can be powerful: Employees do their jobs as if they own the company. We'll spend the rest of this chapter looking at the nuts and bolts of the traditional and commitment-based systems.

■■■ TRADITIONAL CONTROL SYSTEMS

We start by exploring the three main types of traditional control systems: *diagnostic control systems*, *boundary control systems*, and *personal/interactive control systems*.

Diagnostic Controls and Budgetary Systems

Diagnostic controls are formal, preplanned, methodical systems that help managers zero in on discrepancies. When most people think of controls, they think of diagnostic control systems. Budgets and production reports are two examples. Semiannual performance reviews are another.

Diagnostic controls reduce the need for managers to continuously and personally monitor everything for which they are responsible.[18] Once targets are set, managers can (at least in theory) leave the employees to pursue the goals. Supposedly, management can be secure in the knowledge that if the goals aren't met, the deviations will show up as red flags in performance reports. This idea is at the heart of what managers call the principle of exception. The principle of exception (or "management by exception") holds that to conserve managers' time, only significant deviations or exceptions from the standard, "both the especially good and bad exceptions," should be brought to the manager's attention.[19]

The Basic Management Control System Managers—including a student paper's editor in chief—have many things to control. For our editor, these include advertising revenues, expenses, deadlines for articles, article length and quality, and the format for each issue. Yet from a practical point of view, there's no doubt that it's usually the financial aspects—the bottom line—that's first among equals when it comes to control. Financial or *budgetary* controls thus form the heart of a company's basic management control system.

Financial controls start with the firm's planning process. Management formulates an overall strategy and mission for the firm. This provides a framework within which the rest of the planning process can take place. Next, management formulates subsidiary, lower-level plans and a hierarchy of goals. At the top, the president sets strategic goals (such as "have 50% of sales revenue from customized products by 2005"). As we discussed in Chapter 5, each functional vice president—and, in turn, each of his or her subordinates—then receives goals to achieve.

The result is a chain or hierarchy of departmental goals and short-term operational goals. At each step in this hierarchical process, management invariably translates the goals and plans into financial targets—and embodies them in budgets. The president's goal might translate as "$2 million in revenues from the Custom Products Division in 2005." Let's look more closely at these basic budgetary controls.

Budgets are formal financial expressions of a manager's plans. They show targets for things such as sales, cost of materials, production levels, and profit, expressed in dollars. These planned targets are the standards against which the manager compares and controls the unit's actual financial performance. The first step in budgeting is generally to develop a sales forecast and sales budget. The sales budget shows the planned sales activity for each period (usually in units per month) and the revenue expected from the sales.

The manager can then produce various operating budgets. Operating budgets show the expected sales and/or expenses for each of the company's departments for the planning period in question. For example, the production and materials budget (or plan) shows what the company plans to spend for materials, labor, administration, and so forth in order to fulfill the requirements of the sales budget (see Figure 14–5).

principle of exception ■ *sometimes called management by exception, this rule holds that employees should be left to pursue the standards set by management, and only significant deviations from the standard should be brought to a manager's attention.*

budget ■ *formal financial expression of a manager's plans.*

sales budget ■ *shows the number of units to be sold in each period (usually per month) or in general the sales activity to be achieved and the sales revenue expected from the sales.*

operating budget ■ *shows the expected sales and/or expenses for each of the company's departments for the planning period in question.*

► **FIGURE 14–5** ■■■

Example of a Budget

Operating Budget for Machinery Department, June 2000

Budgeted Expenses	Budget
Direct Labor	$2,107
Supplies	$3,826
Repairs	$ 402
Overhead (electricity, etc.)	$ 500
TOTAL EXPENSES	$6,835

The next step is to combine all of these departmental budgets into a profit plan for the coming year. This profit plan is the budgeted income statement or pro forma income statement. It shows expected sales, expected expenses, and expected income or profit for the year. In practice, cash from sales usually doesn't flow into the firm in such a way as to coincide precisely with cash disbursements. (Some customers may take 35 days to pay their bills, for instance, but employees expect paychecks every week.) The cash budget or plan shows, for each month, the amount of cash the company can expect to receive and the amount it can expect to disperse. The manager can use it to anticipate his or her cash needs and to arrange for short-term loans, if need be.

The company will also have a budgeted balance sheet. The budgeted balance sheet shows managers, owners, and creditors what the company's projected financial picture should be at the end of the year. It shows *assets* (such as cash and equipment), *liabilities* (such as long-term debt), and *net worth* (the excess of assets over other liabilities).

Budgets are the most widely used control device. Each manager, from first-line supervisor to company president, usually has an operating budget to use as a standard of comparison. Remember, however, that creating the budget (as in Figure 14.5) is just the standard-setting step in the three-step control process. You must still compare the actual and the budgeted figures. And, if necessary, you'll need to diagnose any problems and take corrective action.

The firm's accountants compile the financial information and feed it back to the appropriate managers. As in Figure 14.6, the performance report shows budgeted or planned targets. Next to these numbers, it shows the department's actual performance numbers. Variances show the differences between budgeted and actual amounts. The report may provide a space for the manager to explain any variances. After reviewing the performance report, management can take corrective action.

The firm's accountants also periodically audit the firm's financial statements. An audit is a systematic process that involves three steps. These are: (1) objectively obtain and evaluate evidence regarding important aspects of the firm's performance; (2) judge the accuracy and validity of the data; and (3) communicate the results to interested users, such as the board of directors and the company's banks.[20] The purpose of the audit is to certify that the firm's financial statements accurately reflect its performance.

Ratio Analysis and Return on Investment Managers also use financial ratio analysis to monitor performance and maintain control. Financial ratios compare one financial measure on a financial statement to another. The rate of return on investment (ROI) is one such ratio. ROI equals net profit divided by total investment; it is a gauge of overall company performance. Rather than measuring net profit as an absolute figure, it shows profit in relation to the total investment in the business. This is often a more informative figure. For example, a $1 million profit is more impressive with a $10 million investment than with a $100 million investment. Figure 14.7 lists some commonly used financial ratios.

income statement ■ *shows expected sales, expected expenses, and expected income or profit for the year.*

cash budget ■ *shows, for each month, the amount of cash the company can expect to receive and the amount it can expect to disperse.*

balance sheet ■ *is a projected statement of the financial position of the firm.*

variance ■ *the difference between budgeted and actual amounts.*

audit ■ *a systematic process of objectively obtaining and evaluating evidence regarding important aspects of the firm's performance, judging the accuracy and validity of the data, and communicating the results to interested users.*

financial ratio ■ *an arithmetic comparison of one financial measure to another, generally used to monitor and control financial performance.*

► **FIGURE 14–6** ■■■

Example of a Performance Report

Performance Report for Machinery Department, June 2000

	Budget	Actual	Variance	Explanation
Direct Labor	$2,107	$2,480	$373 over	Had to put workers on overtime.
Supplies	$3,826	$4,200	$374 over	Wasted two crates of material.
Repairs	$ 402	$ 150	$252 under	
Overhead (electricity, etc.)	$ 500	$ 500	0	
TOTAL	$6,835	$7,330	$495 over	

Name of Ratio	Formula	Industry Norm (As Illustration)
1. Liquidity Ratios (measuring the ability of the firm to meet its short-term obligations)		
Current ratio	$\dfrac{\text{Current assets}}{\text{Current liabilities}}$	2.6
Acid-test ratio	$\dfrac{\text{Cash and equivalent}}{\text{Current liability}}$	1.0
Cash velocity	$\dfrac{\text{Sales}}{\text{Cash and equivalent}}$	12 times
Inventory to net working capital	$\dfrac{\text{Inventory}}{\text{Current assets} - \text{Current liabilities}}$	85%
2. Leverage Ratios (measures the contributions of financing by owners compared with financing provide by creditors)		
Debt to equity	$\dfrac{\text{Total debt}}{\text{Net worth}}$	56%
Coverage of fixed charges	$\dfrac{\text{Net profit before fixed charges}}{\text{Fixed charges}}$	6 times
Current liability to net worth	$\dfrac{\text{Current liability}}{\text{Net worth}}$	32%
Fixed assets to net worth	$\dfrac{\text{Fixed assets}}{\text{Net worth}}$	60%
3. Activities Ratios (measures the effectiveness of the employment of resources)		
Inventory turnover	$\dfrac{\text{Sales}}{\text{Inventory}}$	7 times
Net working capital turnover	$\dfrac{\text{Sales}}{\text{Net working capital}}$	5 times
Fixed-assets turnover	$\dfrac{\text{Sales}}{\text{Fixed assets}}$	6 times
Average collection period	$\dfrac{\text{Receivables}}{\text{Average sales per day}}$	20 days
Equity capital turnover	$\dfrac{\text{Sales}}{\text{Net worth}}$	3 times
Total capital turnover	$\dfrac{\text{Sales}}{\text{Total assets}}$	2 times
4. Profitability Ratios (indicates degree of success in achieving desired profit levels)		
Gross operating margin	$\dfrac{\text{Gross operating profit}}{\text{Sales}}$	30%
Net operating margin	$\dfrac{\text{Net operating profit}}{\text{Sales}}$	6.5%
Sales (profit) margin	$\dfrac{\text{Net profit after taxes}}{\text{Sales}}$	3.2%
Productivity of assets	$\dfrac{\text{Gross income} - \text{taxes}}{\text{Total assets}}$	10%
Return on investment	$\dfrac{\text{Net profit after taxes}}{\text{Total investment}}$	7.5%
Net profit on working capital	$\dfrac{\text{Net operating profit}}{\text{Net working capital}}$	14.5%

Analyzing financial ratios helps managers understand their firm's performance. Figure 14.8 illustrates this. For example, suppose the firm didn't meet its net income target. Ratio analysis shows that low sales or high sales costs may account for this. Similarly, earnings divided by sales (the profit margin) reflects management's success or failure in maintaining satisfactory cost controls. As another example, too much investment may help account for a low ROI. In turn, too much investment might reflect inadequate inventory control, too many accounts receivable, or too much cash.[21]

Ratio Analysis: Factors Affecting
Return on Investment

The firm's overall profitability—its
return on total investments—can be
better understood by analyzing its
components, including earnings as a
percentage of sales and turnover.

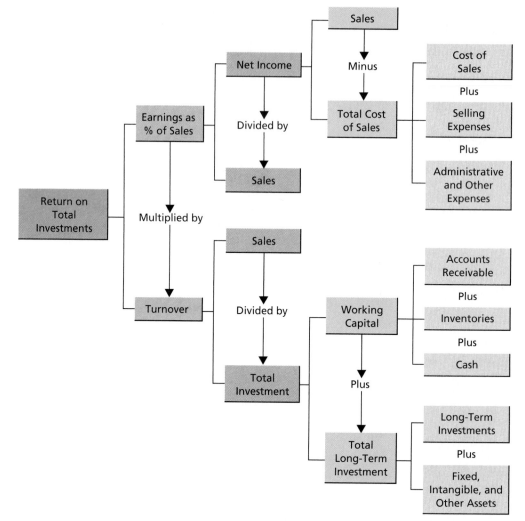

Strategic Ratios In his book *Good to Great*, Jim Collins studied companies that went from good but average to great. He says that one distinguishing characteristic of companies that went from good to great was that they were able to sum up in one simple ratio what their strategy was all about.[22] For example, Gillette bases its strategy in part on selling multiple products repeatedly to customers. It therefore focuses on profit per customer rather than on profit per division as other consumer companies do. Walgreen's wants to be "the place to shop," and it sells a variety of items. It therefore focuses on profit per customer visit rather than on profit per store. The grocery firm Kroger wants to dominate in each local market. It therefore focuses on profit per local population instead of profit per store.

Financial Responsibility Centers In most firms, some or most managers are responsible for specific sets of financial targets. This makes it easier for top management to evaluate each manager's performance. It also makes it easier for the manager to see how the firm will evaluate his or her performance. When the manager has an operating budget tied to specific financial performance targets, we say the manager is in charge of a financial responsibility center. **Financial responsibility centers** are units that are responsible for and measured by a specific set of financial activities.

There are several types. **Profit centers** are responsibility centers whose managers the company holds accountable for profit. (Profit is a measure of the difference between the revenues generated and the cost of generating those revenues).[23] The Allfirst unit of AIB is a profit center. AIB holds the division's head responsible for the profitability of that division. AIB controls that manager's performance partly by monitoring whether the division makes its numbers—in other words, meets its profit goals. **Revenue centers** are responsibility centers whose managers are accountable for generating revenues. Thus, firms generally measure sales managers in terms of the sales produced by their revenue centers/departments.

financial responsibility centers ■ *individuals or groups who are assigned the responsibility for a particular set of financial outputs and/or inputs.*

profit centers ■ *responsibility centers whose managers are held accountable for profit.*

revenue centers ■ *responsibility centers whose managers are held accountable for generating revenues, which is a financial measure of output.*

Activity Based Costing (ABC) Traditional accounting systems can produce misleading results. Most accounting today reflects what accountants call "absorption costing." Basically, this means that as a product moves through the production process, it absorbs costs at each step of the process—for instance, for raw materials or the amount of labor required to produce it.[24]

The problem with this approach is that it can distort what managers think each product really costs. For example, it may not accurately account for factory overhead—the costs of heating and lighting the factory, running its cafeteria, and paying its managers and supervisors. The budget may just list these as plantwide monthly expenses. Similarly, if there's one sales and distribution department for all of the firm's products, the budget may also show them as an overall monthly expense. *All the actual costs of selling a particular product, or distributing it does not get absorbed into the product's calculated cost.* So when a manager asks, "What's the cost of this product?" he or she may well get a misleading answer. The calculated costs usually only include the actual, absorbed, direct production costs.

Activity-based costing (or **ABC**) is a method for allocating costs to products and services that takes all the product's cost drivers (including production, marketing, distribution, and sales activities) into account when calculating the actual cost of each product or service. Doing this isn't easy, as the Management in Action feature shows.

activity-based costing (ABC) ■ *a method for allocating costs to products and services that takes all the product's cost drivers into account when calculating the actual cost of each product or service.*

MANAGEMENT IN ACTION   Reichhold Inc. Installs ABC

When Reichhold Inc., which makes plastics and resins, decided to switch to an ABC system, it established an ABC steering committee. The committee included someone from senior management as well as operational managers from the divisional, manufacturing, and financial units.[25]

Having people who are fully familiar with the production process is especially important in creating ABC. At Reichhold, for instance, the traditional accounting system absorbed raw materials and labor costs into each product based on each product's processing time. It turned out that doing so produced misleading results. The switch to ABC made it apparent that processing time was only one of the activities that drive product costs. The operating managers on the committee knew that product cost also depended on both filtration time and waste disposal.[26] Allocating production and raw materials costs to each product based solely on the time required for processing was, therefore, misleading. Its new ABC costing system helped Reichhold identify the activities that were actually driving costs and enabled it to get a better grip on what its products' costs really were. ■■■

The Balanced Scorecard The basic idea behind the **balanced scorecard** is to give the firm's managers an integrated and instantaneous way to determine the extent to which the firm is addressing its strategic responsibilities. The balanced scorecard itself is typically 15 to 25 interrelated measures, all chosen because they provide insight into the question, "Is this company doing what it needs to do to achieve its strategic objectives?"[27] The scorecard itself is usually a computerized picture of how the firm is doing on those 15 to 25 measures—and what it all means for the firm's strategic success.

The important thing is to choose scorecard measures that make sense in terms of the firm's strategic objectives. For example, consider how Dell Computer could use a balanced scorecard.

balanced scorecard ■ *a management tool, usually a computerized model, that traces a multitude of performance measures simultaneously and shows their interactions.*

MANAGEMENT IN ACTION   Dell

Dell's mission statement (see its Web site) is "to be the most successful computer company in the world at delivering the best customer experience in markets we serve." Given this mission, Chairman Michael Dell has been quoted as saying that looking for value shifts in his company's customer base is his most important leadership responsibility. In other words, Dell needs to constantly monitor what its customers want in terms of value. Given this goal, where does Michael Dell want to focus his employees' attention? He wants to stay in close contact with customers, and he wants to make sure that in everything it does, Dell is addressing its customers' needs.

Therefore, Dell's balanced scorecard should use measures that reflect this need to stay customer-focused. These balanced scorecard measures might include:

- *Training dollars spent per full-time employee, by customer segment.* This would help ensure that well-educated business segment managers provide state-of-the-art advice to customers.
- *Percentage of total hours spent in contact with the customer.*
- *Number of customer-initiated product innovations.*[28]

For Dell, 15 to 25 measures like these would provide the main components of an effective balanced scorecard. The manager chooses measures he or she believes reflect (hypothetical) cause-and-effect relationships. These relationships should link results from specific activities (such as hours spent by Dell employees in contact with customers) with the firm's strategic objectives (like discovering what Dell's customers want).

enterprise resource planning system ■ a companywide integrated computer system that gives managers real-time, instantaneous information regarding the costs and status of every activity and project in the business.

Enterprise Resource Planning (ERP) Systems Balanced scorecards are often components of more comprehensive systems known as enterprise resource planning systems. These are companywide integrated computer control systems. They integrate a firm's individual control systems (such as order processing, production control, and accounting). The aim is to give managers real-time, instantaneous information regarding the costs and status of every activity and project in the business.[29] Some call these systems "the stuff that puts the information age to work for corporations."[30] By linking all of the company's control systems, "managers will now be able to receive daily online reports about the costs of specific business processes, for example, and on the real-time profitability of individual products and customers."[31]

The check-printing company Deluxe Paper Payment Systems used its ERP system to "get a clearer picture of which of its customers were profitable and which were not."[32] For example, its enterprise resource planning system helped it discover that orders for checks from banks were much more profitable when they arrived via electronic ordering. Deluxe then launched a campaign to increase electronic ordering—particularly by its 18,000 bank and small-business customers. The number of checks ordered electronically jumped from 48% to 62% in just a few months. This dramatically improved profits. The Management in Action feature shows how one company installed its ERP system.

MANAGEMENT IN ACTION   Using ERP to Get in Control

While enterprise software systems can be very expensive—one Fortune 500 company reportedly spent $30 million in license fees and $200 million in consulting fees to install one—smaller firms are increasingly using smaller ERPs too.[33] For example, thanks to its new enterprise software system, "three people at Harman Music Group [who] once worked nearly full-time planning what products to make at its factory [have been replaced by] two people who do that work part time each week."[34]

According to Harman's director of operations, Matthew Bush, the stacks of reports (including production schedules, orders, and inventory reports) that he used to analyze each day to begin developing his production plans now come right off his personal computer. "I just call it up and, in a matter of seconds, there it is." Harman hired Hewlett-Packard to install its new software, and Hewlett-Packard assigned a five-person full-time team to the project. The team began by developing a blueprint of how Harman music operates by interviewing employees, mapping out exactly how information (such as a new order) went from one activity to another, and analyzing which managers needed what kind of information.

The team made some interesting discoveries along the way. For example, they discovered that three people at Harman spent part of their workdays literally "taking out the trash," getting rid of scrap and obsolete inventory. When it became obvious how expensive that activity was, the team streamlined the process. There were other discoveries—and many other benefits. For example, while the company reportedly always knew how many units of a model it planned to build in any given week, how many were in stock, and how many were ordered, there was a lot of guesswork in matching all that information. The new system updates the forecast whenever the company gets an order. It also automatically updates production plans, while providing Harman's managers with a real-time estimate of the profitability of each of its products. Now that's control!

As another example, Kohler Co. uses its ERP "to analyze outbound shipments, on-time deliveries, first-time sales, monthly sales trends, and backlog data."[35] "You can drill down and see where in the process things are going wrong," says one Kohler manager.[36]

Boundary Control Systems

Diagnostic controls (like budgets, financial ratios, and ERP) are one traditional way that companies exercise control; boundary control systems are another. Boundary control systems "establish the rules of the game and identify actions and pitfalls that employees must avoid."[37] Boundary controls include ethics standards, codes of conduct, and strategic policies.

It's hard to overestimate the importance of boundary controls in keeping things on track. Asked recently if there's anything he loses sleep over, Jeff Immelt, GE's new CEO, said that he worries about an ethical lapse on the part of some employee: "Some employees just don't get it" as he said. Johnson & Johnson's Credo (see Figure 14.9) is a classic example of a boundary control.

▲ **WEBNOTE** ■ ■ ■

NeuStar's code of conduct. NeuStar is a provider of clearinghouse services that allow communications networks to connect to one another.

www.neustar.com

Source: Copyright 1999–2002 NeuStar, Inc.

MANAGEMENT IN ACTION   J&J's Credo

The Credo contains J&J's conduct guidelines (such as, "We believe our first responsibility is to the doctors, nurses and patients . . . who use our products . . . "). These guidelines provide the boundaries within which Johnson & Johnson employees are to remain. Selling a potentially harmful product would obviously be out of bounds. When several bottles of poisoned Tylenol were found some years back, Johnson & Johnson quickly recalled the entire stock of the product.

Johnson & Johnson was therefore shocked recently when armed federal agents came in and briefly closed down its LifeScan unit's headquarters. Among other things, LifeScan makes a diabetes diagnostic device. Some J&J employees had failed to report that a software glitch made some units show the wrong diagnosis. How could that happen in a company in which all 100,000 employees are supposed to be committed to a strong code of ethics? "Mistakes were made in the LifeScan situation. . . . They were errors in judgment. We did too little, too late." That is how the firm's CEO put it.[38] ■ ■ ■ ■

Codes of conduct are useless unless they trigger action when the boundaries are breached. Employees therefore must understand that the firm takes the boundaries seriously and will monitor results. There's therefore more to establishing boundary controls than just drawing up guidelines. Steps include:

1. Emphasize top management's commitment.
2. Publish a code.
3. Establish compliance mechanisms.
4. Measure results.

Boundary controls aren't limited to ethics or codes of conduct. The company's policies—and particularly its strategic policies—also establish boundaries. Such policies ". . . focus on ensuring that people steer clear of opportunities that could diminish the business's competitive position."[39] As someone once said, "Presidents need strategies so they know what mail to throw out in the morning." Managers at Automatic Data Processing (ADP) use a strategic boundary list. This lays out the types of business opportunities ADP managers should avoid. One large Netherlands-based multinational has a strategic policy of discouraging its executives from forming joint ventures with firms in the United States because of the greater possibility of litigation in U.S. courts.

Our Credo

We believe our first responsibility is to the doctors, nurses and patients,
to mothers and fathers and all others who use our products and services.
In meeting their needs, everything we do must be of high quality.
We must constantly strive to reduce our costs
in order to maintain reasonable prices.
Customers' orders must be serviced promptly and accurately.
Our suppliers and distributors must have an opportunity
to make a fair profit.

We are responsible to our employees,
the men and women who work with us throughout the world.
Everyone must be considered as an individual.
We must respect their dignity and recognize their merit.
They must have a sense of security in their jobs.
Compensation must be fair and adequate
and working conditions clean, orderly and safe.
We must be mindful of ways to help our employees fulfill
their family responsibilities.
Employees must feel free to make suggestions and complaints.
There must be equal opportunity for employment, development
and advancement for those qualified.
We must provide competent management,
and their actions must be just and ethical.

We are responsible to the communities in which we live and work
and to the world community as well.
We must be good citizens—support good works and charities
and bear our fair share of taxes.
We must encourage civic improvements and better health and education.
We must maintain in good order
the property we are privileged to use,
protecting the environment and natural resources.

Our final responsibility is to our stockholders.
Business must make a sound profit.
We must experiment with new ideas.
Research must be carried on, innovative programs developed
and mistakes paid for.
New equipment must be purchased, new facilities provided
and new products launched.
Reserves must be created to provide for adverse times.
When we operate according to these principles,
the stockholders should realize a fair return.

Johnson & Johnson

Personal/Interactive Control Systems

The typical small, entrepreneurial company has one big control advantage over its huge multinational competitors: "Mom and Pop" can talk face to face with almost everyone in the firm. They can thus monitor in real time how everything is going.

Interactive Control Maintaining control by personally monitoring how everyone is doing is interactive control. It is the most basic traditional way to stay in control. Even large firms are turning to this approach.[40] For example, Intuit divided its business into smaller units. In this way, interactions and control in each unit remain more instantaneous and personal.

Even in large firms, interactive control can be very effective. Senior managers at *USA Today* use interactive control.[41] The process starts each Friday morning when they get three weekly reports. These reports provide an overview of how they have done in the previous week and what they may expect in the next few weeks. This Friday packet includes information ranging from advertising sales figures to information about particular advertisers.

Weekly face-to-face meetings among senior managers and key subordinates help apply this information. Regular topics include advertising volume compared to plan and new business by type of client. Senior managers don't just look for unexpected shortfalls. They also look for unexpected successes. These might suggest putting more emphasis on particular areas, such as trying to get more software suppliers to advertise, or instituting a new market-survey service for automotive clients.

Electronic Performance Monitoring and Control When it comes to monitoring employees, the use of electronic methods is on the rise. As two researchers recently put it, "As many as 26 million workers in the United States are subject to electronic performance monitoring (EPM)—such as having supervisors monitor through electronic means the amount of computerized data an employee is processing per day—on the job."[42] The supervisors can then take immediate action by speaking with or contacting the errant employee.

■ ■ The USA Today *newsroom, where managers can meet and monitor both the news and the newspaper's activities, minute by minute.*

Jeffrey Stanton and Janet Barnes-Farrell studied the effects of such monitoring on individuals working on computers in an officelike environment.[43] The 108 participants were recruited from introductory psychology classes. The researchers wanted to study several things: One was whether a worker's feelings of personal control were affected by having the ability to lock out the performance monitoring; another was whether informing the person he or she was being monitored affected performance. The results show why it's important for employees to believe they have some personal control over their environments. "Participants with the ability to delay or prevent electronic performance monitoring indicated higher feelings of personal control and demonstrated superior task performance."[44]

The findings also suggest that if you are going to monitor employees' performance electronically, it's probably best not to let them know when they're actually being monitored. Participants who knew exactly when they were being monitored expressed lower feelings of personal control than did those who were not told when they were being monitored.

Do not assume that electronic performance monitoring applies only to subordinates and not to bosses. For example, the Japanese company that controls 7-Eleven is gradually imposing an EPM system on its store managers in Japan and in the United States. Like all 7-Eleven stores, the ones belonging to Michiharu Endo use a point-of-sale computer to let headquarters know each time he makes a sale. In the case of 7-Eleven's new system, headquarters monitors both how much time Endo spends using the analytical tools built into the computerized cash register to track product sales and how effective he is at weeding out poor sellers. Headquarters then ranks stores by how often their operators use the computer as a measure of how efficient they are.

The system has run into particular resistance in the United States. Many 7-Eleven managers thought they had escaped the bureaucratic rat race by taking over their own stores, and were surprised at the degree of control this new EPM system exposed them to.[45]

■ ■ ■ HOW DO PEOPLE REACT TO CONTROL?

Every manager needs a way to ensure that his or her employees are performing as planned. It may be CEO Jeffrey Immelt trying to control GE's Asian operations. Or it may just be a GE sales manager in Miami asking, "How can I make sure Marie files her sales reports on time?" Both managers would use traditional controls—diagnostic, boundary, or interactive—to accomplish what they want. In other words, they both would depend to some extent on some external, imposed system—like budgets, policies, or close supervision—to keep performance in line. Unfortunately, there is a downside to these traditional control approaches. As at Arthur Andersen and AIB, employees may try to evade them.

The Negative Side of Control

If controlling employees' behavior were the only (or the best) way to ensure effective performance, we could disregard much of this book. For example, we wouldn't need to know much about what motivates people. Nor would managers have to care so much about what leadership style is best or how to foster employee commitment. Managers could just set goals—and then control employees' work.

But the fact is that managers can't rely just on traditional controls for keeping employees in line. For one thing, it's impossible to have a system of rules and controls so complete that you can track everything employees say or do (even with enterprise software). There's no practical way, for instance, to control how the front-desk clerk is greeting guests every minute of the day—and doing so is even more impractical with today's team-based, empowered employees. For another, employees often short-circuit the controls, sometimes with ingenious tactics. Let's look more closely at this second problem.

Some Unintended Behavioral Consequences of Controls

Employees may use several familiar tactics to evade controls. One expert classifies these tactics as behavioral displacement, gamesmanship, operating delays, and negative attitudes.[46]

behavioral displacement ■ *a reaction to being controlled in which the controls encourage behaviors that are inconsistent with what the company actually wants to accomplish.*

Behavioral Displacement Behavioral displacement occurs when the controls encourage behaviors that are inconsistent with what the company actually wants to accomplish. A famous management truism is, "You get what you measure." This is a two-edged sword. Setting performance targets does tend to focus employees' efforts on those targets. The problem arises when the employees focus just on what you're measuring and disregard the company's more important goals.

The problem stems mostly from limiting what you measure to just one or two control standards. For example, Nordstrom set up a policy of measuring employees in terms of sales per hour of performance.[47] Unfortunately simply monitoring "sales per hour" backfired. Without other performance measures, the system didn't work. Some employees claimed their supervisors were pressuring them to underreport hours on the job to boost reported sales per hour. (Nordstrom settled an employee suit for $15 million.)

gamesmanship ■ *management actions that try to improve the manager's apparent performance in terms of the control system without producing any economic benefits for the company.*

Gamesmanship Gamesmanship is another ploy. It refers to management actions that improve the manager's performance in terms of the control system without producing any economic benefits for the firm. For example, one manager depleted his stocks of spare parts and heating oil at year's end. He knew these stocks would have to be replenished shortly thereafter at higher prices. But by reducing his stocks, the manager reduced his expenses for the year and made his end-of-year results look better. In the longer run, the company spent more than it had to.[48] Another manager overshipped products to distributors at year-end. The aim was to ensure that management would meet its budgeted sales targets. It did, but then it had to deal with excess returns the following year.[49]

Operating Delays Managers also must be vigilant for control systems that trigger operating delays—and thus unnecessarily slow things down. For example, a "yes–no" control policy that prohibits signing agreements without your lawyer's approval can help keep the firm out of trouble. However, it may also mean losing a good project if a competitor can move faster to make agreements. GE's former CEO Jack Welch found that it sometimes took a year or more for division managers to get approval to introduce new products. The problem was the long list of approvals required by GE's control system. Streamlining the approval process solved this problem.

Negative Attitudes Most people are programmed from childhood to react skeptically, at best, to efforts to control them. It's therefore not surprising that traditional control systems often trigger negative employee attitudes. One study focused on first-line supervisors' reactions to budgets. It found that the supervisors saw the budgets as pressure devices. In reaction to this perceived pressure, they formed anti-management groups. Their own supervisors then reacted by increasing their compliance efforts.[50]

■ *The Global Manager* Controlling facilities abroad can trigger problems of its own. Two researchers studied management control in China. They say, "Control systems used in firms in market economies [such as the United States] are, in many cases, new to China; may not be acceptable to the host country employees; may require extensive training of host country employees before they can be effectively used; may be expensive to implement; and may not function efficiently without the existence of elaborate supporting services and infrastructure."[51] They analyzed the extent to which nine control techniques (including cost accounting, inventory control systems, individual budgets for each department, and management information systems) were successfully implemented when companies established subsidiaries in China. Larger subsidiaries were more likely to institute control systems. And the use of such systems did influence the subsidiary's performance. Allied International Bank's problems are another illustration of how control systems can backfire.

MANAGEMENT IN ACTION Correcting Flaws in the AIB System

A review of Allied International Bank's (AIB's) control systems after management discovered its currency trading losses made it clear that there were several flaws in the system. AIB had already installed its control software at its headquarters, but only part of the office software was running at its Allfirst facility. As a result, Allfirst still accomplished many of its trading procedures (such as matching trades to confirm that there were real buyers that matched real sellers) manually, which made them subject to human manipulation. The oversight would have allowed the Allfirst trader to enter bogus trades and show fictitious profits.

Buckley and his management team took steps at once to eliminate the weaknesses in Allfirst's control systems. They installed the new software and linked it to Allfirst's existing software. The system now could analyze trades electronically, in real time and flag exceptions at once. The company also installed new risk analysis software. This would immediately report any currency positions that exceeded the trader's trading limitations. However, AIB's management also knows that (as a report on the problem indicated) the new software won't solve the problem if employees are motivated to take advantage of the system's weaknesses. Management knows it is impossible to create a system that an employee can't circumvent if he or she wants to.

■■■ USING COMMITMENT-BASED CONTROL SYSTEMS

Traditional control systems (whether diagnostic, boundary, or interactive) have numerous weaknesses. Employees have many clever ways to evade them. It's not practical to have so many rules and controls that you can track everything employees say or do. And for some activities—such as building high quality cars—you need the employees to want to do a great job, because you can't force them to do it. At some point, therefore, the manager at a company like AIB (or any other) must rely on employees' self-control rather than just on traditional, imposed controls.

Today's emphasis on building global learning organizations makes this fact especially important. Globalized, empowered, team-based organizations complicate the task of keeping everything under control. Distance makes monitoring what your employees are doing day-to-day more difficult. And imposing too much control on self-managing teams is obviously counterproductive. How can you feel empowered if someone else is controlling everything you do? There is therefore a growing need to supplement traditional control efforts with efforts aimed at getting employees to want to control themselves. Management guru Tom Peters explains this well:

> *You are out of control when you are "in control." You are in control when you are "out of control." [The executive] who knows everything and who is surrounded by layers of staffers and inundated with thousands of pages of analyses from below may be "in control" in the classic sense but in fact really only has the illusion of control. The manager has tons of after-the-fact reports on everything, but (almost) invariably a control system and organization that's so ponderous that it's virtually impossible to respond*

fast enough even if a deviation is finally detected. . . . In fact, you really are in control when thousands upon thousands of people, unbeknownst to you, are taking initiatives, going beyond job descriptions and the constraints of their box on the organization chart, to serve the customer better, improve the process, [or] work quickly with a supplier to nullify a defect.[52]

Managers use three basic techniques to accomplish this goal: *motivation techniques, belief systems,* and *commitment-building systems.* Obviously, motivated employees are more likely to exercise self-control and to do their jobs right. We discussed motivation at length in Chapter 11. In the remainder of this chapter, we'll look at how managers use belief systems and commitment-building systems to encourage and foster employee self-control.[53]

Using Belief Systems, Culture, and Values to Foster Self-Control

People's actions tend to reflect what they value and believe. People who value hard work tend to work harder then those who do not. Those who value consensus and teamwork tend to be more team-oriented than those who do not. Managers recognize this, and try to instill the right values in their employees. They assume, usually correctly, that employees with the right values will exercise the sort of self-control the firm requires to compete effectively.

Research tends to support this commonsense conclusion. For example, James Collins and Jerry Porras studied firms that had been successful over many years. The researchers reported their findings in their book, *Built to Last.* In it, they describe how firms like Boeing, Disney, GE, Merck, and Motorola put enormous effort into creating the right shared values. These values answer questions such as "What are we trying to achieve together?" and "What does this organization stand for?"[54] Values include things like "The customer is always right" and "Don't hide information from your colleagues." Collins and Porras concluded that

> *More than at any time in the past companies will not be able to hold themselves together with the traditional methods of control: hierarchy, systems, budgets, and the like. Even "going into the office" will become less relevant as technology enables people to work from remote sites. The bonding glue will increasingly become ideological.*[55]

This is a powerful concept. Collins and Porras emphasize that a strong set of shared values "allows for coordination without control, adaptation without chaos."[56] In other words, employees who buy into the company's values don't need to be coaxed, prodded, or forced into doing the right thing. Management can be reasonably sure that these employees will do the right thing because they believe it's the right thing to do. The employees will control themselves.

This helps to explain why companies work hard (as we explained in Chapter 2) to create a culture that is consistent with what they want to achieve. At the Toyota plant in Lexington, Kentucky, for instance, quality and teamwork are crucial. Its managers therefore steep employees in the culture and values of quality and teamwork. They do this by selecting new employees based on the extent to which they evidence such traits. Then they emphasize quality and teamwork in all their orientation, training, and appraisal and incentive systems. This is important. Camry's superior quality is not just a consequence of technology (since all auto plants have similar machines). Nor is it just a consequence of traditional controls like final inspection. It is largely a product of employee self-control. It reflects the fact that from the moment it starts screening and training employees, Toyota invests heavily in gaining its employees' dedication to the handful of core values that drive their behavior.

Using Commitment-Building Systems to Foster Self-Control

Several years ago, Viacom agreed to sell its Prentice Hall publishing operations to Pearson PLC for $4.6 billion. In announcing the sale, Prentice Hall's president thanked its employees for their "past hard work and dedication." And he reminded them that during the transition, "It's more important than ever to focus on our individual responsibilities to ensure that our company performs at the highest levels."[57]

His message highlights a management dilemma. All companies want and need employee commitment—an employee's identification with and agreement to pursue the company's mission. But, how does a manager obtain employee commitment in the face of downsizing, mergers, and change?[58] How, in other words, do you get employees to exercise self-control and do their jobs as if they own the company when loyalty often seems out of style?

commitment ■ the relative strength of an individual's identification with and involvement in an organization.

Many firms do have high-commitment employees, and research helps explain how these firms accomplish this feat. In brief, the evidence suggests that earning employees' commitment requires an integrated package of concrete managerial actions, one that draws on all of the managers' planning, organizing, leading, and controlling skills. These actions include the following: foster people-first values, guarantee organizational justice, build a sense of shared fate and community, use value-based hiring plus financial rewards, communicate your vision, and encourage personal development and self-actualization. We'll look at each.

Foster People-First Values High-commitment companies are usually managed by people who emphasize their "People-first values." These managers trust their employees, believe in respecting their employees as individuals and in treating them fairly, and are committed to each employee's welfare. Furthermore, values like these tend to pervade the whole chain of command. Here's how one United Auto Workers officer at Saturn's Spring Hill, Tennessee, plant put it

> Our philosophy is, we care about people—and it shows. We involve people in decisions that affect them. . . . Saturn's commitment really comes down to how you feel about people—your attitudes—more than anything, because all the other Saturn programs—the work teams, the extensive training, the way people are paid—all stem from these people attitudes.[59]

Saturn works hard to foster such people-first values. For example, all Saturn employees carry a card that lists the firm's values, one of which is "Trust and respect for the individual: We have nothing of greater value than our people. We believe that demonstrating respect for the uniqueness of every individual builds a team of confident, creative members possessing a high degree of initiative, self-respect, and self-discipline."[60] The idea is to apply values like these to every decision. As one JC Penney officer said,

> Our people's high commitment stems from our commitment to them, and that commitment boils down to the fundamental respect for the individual that we all share. That respect goes back to the Penney idea—"To test every act in this wise: Does it square with what is right and just?" As a result, the value of respect for the individual is brought into our management process on a regular basis and is a standard against which we measure each and every decision that we make.[61]

Guarantee Organizational Justice Commitment assumes that there's a climate of trust, and that, in turn, assumes that employees are treated fairly. Managers in firms like Saturn and FedEx don't just talk about being fair. They institute programs that guarantee the firm will treat employees fairly. Communications programs (as described earlier, in Chapter 12) are crucial here. Specific programs include guaranteed fair treatment programs for filing grievances, "speak up" programs for voicing concerns, periodic surveys for expressing opinions, and top-down programs for keeping employees informed.

Build a Sense of Shared Fate and Community Part of fostering commitment involves making employees feel that "we're all in this together." Rosabeth Moss Kanter found that leaders do this in several ways.[62] They *minimize status differences*. At Hewlett-Packard, managers and employees shared one large space, with movable cubicles, and managers shun status symbols such as executive washrooms. Others foster a sense of community by encouraging *joint effort and communal work*. At Saturn, all employees are on teams, and all teams work on projects together. Others bring individual employees into *regular contact with the group* as a whole.[63] Ben & Jerry's has monthly staff meetings in the receiving bay of its Waterbury, Vermont, plant.

Thanks to the Internet, employees don't have to be at the same location to feel that they're part of a close-knit community. Internet-based group communication systems such as Tribal Voice allow companies to build virtual communities by letting employees communicate easily and in real time, even if they are dispersed around the globe.[64] As one expert puts it, "The sales department could hold forums and share information in an interactive community." Said another, "When people interact in a virtual community, there is an exchange of ideas and information, [an exchange] which becomes powerful and generates excitement."[65]

Use Value-Based Hiring Similarly, Kanter found that commitment to a cause is higher among employees who share the same basic values. High-commitment firms therefore practice value-based hiring. They don't just look for job-related skills in the people they hire. Instead, they look for common experiences and values that may signal the applicant's fit with the firm. Thus, Delta Airlines wants employees who fit in. Even college grads may thus start out by cleaning planes. The idea is that if you don't fit in, you probably won't become committed to the company.

Communicate Your Vision Committed employees need a vision to which to be committed, preferably one that they feel "is bigger than we are." Employees at organizations like the Salvation Army, Saturn, and Ben & Jerry's become, to a certain extent, soldiers in a crusade. Through their employment, they redefine themselves and their goals in terms of the company's mission. The employee, says Kanter, "finds himself anew in something larger and greater [than himself]."[66] The level of employee commitment thus derives in part from the willingness of the employees to submit, if need be, to the needs of the firm for the good of achieving its mission.

Use Financial Rewards and Profit Sharing There's obviously more to building commitment than financial rewards. However, it's also usually futile to try to build commitment when pay is substandard. High-commitment firms generally provide above-average pay and incentives. FedEx, for instance, provides a half-dozen types of incentive awards, including Bravo-Zulu awards that managers can give on the spot.

Encourage Employee Development and Self-Actualization Employees are not foolish. Most understand that becoming committed to an employer is risky in a time of continuing mergers and mass layoffs. They want—and need—a sign that their employers are committed to them. One strong signal is to show employees that the company is committed to their personal development. Being the best at what one can be provides the best job security, whether or not the person stays with the firm. Psychologist Abraham Maslow emphasized that people need to self-actualize, "to become . . . everything that one is capable of becoming." As he said, "What man can be, he must be . . . "[67]

Firms can do this in many ways. Train employees to expand their skills and to solve problems. Enrich their jobs. Empower them. Provide career-oriented interviews. Help them to continue their education and to grow. The results can be dramatic. Here's how one Saturn assembler put it: "I'm committed to Saturn in part for what [it] did for me; for the 300 hours of training in problem solving and leadership that help me expand my personal horizons; for the firm's Excel program that helps me push myself to the limit; and because I know that at Saturn I can go as far as I can go—this company wants its people to be all that they can be."[68]

At FedEx, one manager similarly described his experience as follows: "At Federal Express, the best I can be is what I can be here. I have been allowed to grow with Federal Express. For the people at Federal Express, it's not the money that draws us to the firm. The biggest benefit is that Federal Express made me a man. It gave me the confidence and self-esteem to become the person I had the potential to become."[69]

Summary: How Do You Foster Employees' Self-Control?

Managers can't rely on traditional controls to ensure that results are up to par. Financial statements, policies, budgets, close supervision—all those elements of traditional control systems—only go so far. They cannot fully monitor what an Allfirst trader is buying and selling 8,000 miles away. Nor can traditional controls ensure the kind of continuous attention to detail and initiative that producing high-quality Camrys or Windows XP requires of those working on these projects. Managers have to make the workers want to do their jobs as if they own the company.

There are several ways to do this. *Motivation techniques* can certainly help, since motivated employees should perform better. *Fostering the right values and culture* is another approach. What people do reflects what they believe. If employees believe, for instance, in doing high-quality work, then their performance will more likely reflect such values. Finally, we've seen on the last few pages that *fostering commitment* is another powerful method. Committed employees identify with and agree to pursue the company's mission. They exercise self-control because their companies' missions and goals really are their own and because they, therefore, do their jobs as if they own the company. Getting employees to actually think of the company's goals as their own isn't easy. It requires most of the management skills you learned in this book. It requires an integrated, commitment-oriented management system that

- Fosters people-first values.
- Guarantees organizational justice.
- Builds a sense of shared fate and community.
- Uses value-based hiring.
- Provides a vision.
- Uses financial rewards and profit sharing.
- Encourages self-actualization.

SUMMARY ■■■

1. Control is the task of ensuring that activities are providing the desired results. In its most general sense, controlling therefore means setting a target, measuring performance, and taking corrective action when things go wrong. Experts distinguish between steering controls, yes/no controls, and postaction controls.

2. As companies expand worldwide and compete in fast-changing markets, the problems of relying on a traditional control system (set standards, compare actual to standard, and take corrective action) have become increasingly apparent. Employees have had to become more empowered to be more responsive, and controlling can detract from that.

3. While the classification is somewhat arbitrary, there are three types of traditional control methods. Diagnostic control systems like budgets, performance reports, and balanced scorecards are intended to ensure that goals are being achieved and that variances, if any, are explained. Boundary control systems establish the rules of the game and identify actions and

pitfalls employees must avoid. Personal/interactive control systems are real-time, usually face-to-face methods of monitoring both a plan's effectiveness and the underlying assumptions on which the plan was built.

4. Budgets and ratio analysis are among the most widely used diagnostic control tools. Budgets are formal financial expressions of a manager's plan and show targets for yardsticks such as revenues, cost of materials, production levels, and profits, usually expressed in dollars. Most managers also achieve control by monitoring various financial ratios.

5. Traditional controls can lead to unintended, undesirable, and often harmful employee reactions, such as behavioral displacement, gamesmanship, operating delays, and negative attitudes.

6. Achieving control today also relies on employees' self-control. Motivation techniques and building value systems are two important ways to tap such self-control. Another powerful way is to get employees to think of the company's goals as their own—to earn their commitment.

KEY TERMS ■■■

SKILLS AND STUDY MATERIALS

EXPERIENTIAL EXERCISES ■■■

1. You are one of the founding engineers in your six-month-old firm, and you brought to the firm values of environmental awareness, quality, and excellence. These values have united the original members, but you are concerned that they might change with the addition of 50 new people needed by your fast-growing company to meet demand. In teams of 4 or 5 students, answer the question, "What type of control system would I develop to ensure my values are adhered to, based on the concepts in this chapter?"

2. College students deal with professors all the time, but may not realize how difficult it is for the college's administrators to control what their faculties are doing. The typical professor has a number of responsibilities, including teaching classes, writing research articles, and attending curriculum-development committee meetings. Furthermore, the dean also wants to make sure faculty members are conducting themselves professionally—for instance, in terms of how they interact with their students. Knowing that you are a management student, the dean has asked you to develop a control package for a college of business professors. The package is to include, at a minimum, a list of the things that you want to control and a corresponding list showing how you plan to control them. In teams of 4 or 5 students, develop a package for the dean.

3. Based on what you learned in this chapter, meet with a team of 4 or 5 of your fellow students; then write a one-page document listing what AIB did wrong in controlling its traders and how you would remedy the situation.

4. There is nothing quite like eating in a restaurant where things—from customer service to hygiene—are out of control. Before coming to class, visit 1 or 2 local restaurants, and make a list of the things you see that might suggest that (at least in those areas) things are a bit out of control. Then meet in teams of 4–5 students, compare notes, and create a checklist for assessing the adequacy of a restaurant's control mechanisms. If time permits and if there is an on-campus cafeteria, use your checklist to evaluate the school eating place's controls.

CASE STUDY ■■■

CONTROLLING A RITZ-CARLTON

Many consider business hotels as offering a generic service—a safe, clean, comfortable room in a city away from home. Ritz-Carlton Hotel Company views its business differently. Targeting industry executives, conference and corporate travel planners, and affluent travelers, the Atlanta-based company manages 25 luxury hotels that pursue the goal of being the very best in each market. Ritz-Carlton succeeded with more than just its guests. For example, it received the U.S. government's Malcom Baldridge National Quality Award. Given its mission of true excellence in service, what types of control systems did Ritz-Carlton need to achieve its goals?

In the presentation of the Baldridge award, the committee commended Ritz-Carlton for a management program that included participatory leadership, thorough information gathering, coordinated planning and execution, and a trained workforce empowered "to move heaven and earth" to satisfy customers. Of all the elements in the system, Ritz-Carlton felt the most important control mechanism was committed employees.

The firm trains all employees in the company's "Gold Standards." These set out Ritz-Carlton's service credo and the basics of premium service. The company has translated key product and service requirements into a credo and 20 "Ritz-Carlton Basics." Each employee is to understand and adhere to these standards, which describe processes for solving any problem guests may have.

The corporate motto is "ladies and gentlemen serving ladies and gentlemen." Like many companies, Ritz-Carlton gives new employees an orientation followed by on-the-job training. Unlike other hotel firms, Ritz-Carlton then certifies employees. It reinforces its corporate values continuously by daily lineups, frequent recognition for extraordinary achievement, and a performance appraisal based on expectations explained during the orientation, training, and certification processes.

All workers are required to act at the first sign of a problem, regardless of the type of problem or customer complaint. Employees are empowered to do whatever it takes to provide "instant pacification." Other employees must assist if a coworker requests aid in responding to a guest's complaint or wish. There is never an excuse for not solving a customer problem.

Responsibility for ensuring high-quality guest services and accommodations rests largely with employees. All employees are surveyed annually to determine their understanding of quality standards and their personal satisfaction as a Ritz-Carlton employee. In one case, 96% of all employees surveyed singled out excellence in guest services as the key priority.

Discussion Questions

1. What steps does Ritz-Carlton take to control the quality of its service?

2. What does Ritz-Carlton do to foster its employees' high level of commitment?

3. How does the company's value system foster employee self-control?

YOU BE THE CONSULTANT ■■■

JETBLUE STAYS IN CONTROL

jetBlue AIRWAYS

A recent *Wall Street Journal* article helps illustrate why maintaining control is important for airlines like JetBlue.[70] It compares the efficiency of JetBlue's Flight 112 with United Airlines Flight 235, both of which fly from Dulles International Airport to Oakland California, nonstop. Both fly the same number of miles (2,415), both have six crew members (two pilots and four flight attendants), and both use the same aircraft, the Airbus A320. However, United spends about $23,690 to fly its flight one-way, whereas JetBlue spends $14,546 to fly Flight 112. How is it that with the same aircraft and number of crew members, United spends more than 50% more to operate its flight? By controlling costs in dozens of ways—from lower salaries to not offering meals to quicker turnarounds at the gate—JetBlue maintains its strategy to be the country's premier low-cost airline.

As an airline competing in an environment filled with numerous safety and customer service regulations, controlling its costs is only one of the many areas in which JetBlue has to maintain control. Because the airline industry is governed by various U.S. Department of Transportation (DOT) regulations, JetBlue and other airlines must address at least four main operational metrics: completion factors (did you fly the flight?); on-time performance within 14 minutes; consumer complaints; and baggage delayed, misplaced, or lost. Airlines monitor completion factors and on-time performance on a daily basis, and they monitor consumer complaints and baggage delays monthly.

Airlines also have numerous internal operating measures that they follow closely. For example, all airlines carefully monitor their load factors—in other words, the percentage of filled seats on their aircraft. JetBlue monitors what it calls its "blue turn"—in other words, its target of turning around an aircraft within 35 minutes from the time it first reaches the gate and then takes off again. All airlines also have full budgeting processes in order to plan for and control their expenses. Many of the expense factors are uncontrollable. For example, airlines like JetBlue don't have a great deal of flexibility with regard to what they have to pay for fuel. For JetBlue, the biggest controllable expenses are personnel related, including salaries, bonuses, and benefits.

The DOT and/or the FAA mandate many of the systems to actually control activities like these. For example, the DOT has its own rules for how airlines are to measure and report activities like on-time performance. At JetBlue, cost center managers are usually individually responsible for monitoring many of these activities within their own areas. There is a general manager or director for each city; if a flight doesn't leave on time or arrive on time, he or she has to fill out a clarification report and file it via e-mail with his or her superiors at JetBlue. Similarly, the Federal Aviation Administration (FAA) has issued numerous security directives that airlines are to follow—for instance, with respect to processing passengers and with regard to aircraft parts inspections and acceptability of vendors. JetBlue must also have systems in place to comply with these rules.

For example, when cabin attendants explain the use of safety equipment before the plane takes off and then check to see that everyone's seatback is up, they are enforcing FAA safety regulations. How does the FAA know that the airlines are complying with its regulations? Airlines have their own internal auditors checking selected flights, staffed by people from (in JetBlue's case) their own quality department and safety department. The FAA also has its own inspectors anonymously flying selected flights to ensure that its rules are obeyed.

Although controlling activities with inspectors is certainly essential, there is often no substitute for employee motivation and commitment in ensuring that things are going as planned. JetBlue therefore puts an enormous amount of effort into winning its employees' commitment, starting with a comprehensive orientation with presentations by JetBlue's top management and extending to flexible work rules and profit-sharing plans.

Assignment

You and your team are consultants to Mr. Neeleman, who is depending on your management expertise to help him navigate the launch and management of JetBlue. Here's what he wants to know from you now:

1. Recommend specific feedforward, concurrent, and feedback controls that JetBlue could use to control any five of the activities mentioned in the case.

2. Specify a specific strategic ratio that JetBlue's CEO David Neeleman should have his employees focus on.

3. List 10 measures David Neeleman could use to build a balanced scorecard for JetBlue.

CHAPTER OBJECTIVES

After studying this chapter and the case exercises at the end, you should be able to:

1. Create a Gantt chart for a project.

2. Compute the Economic Order Quantity (EOQ) for an item.

3. Explain what the manager has to do to win a Baldridge quality award.

4. Use a "fishbone"/cause-and-effect diagram to analyze the problem.

5. Quantitatively rate or "read" the effectiveness of the company's production facility.

6. List the reasons why a company is (and is not) "World-Class."

7. List a company's "Moments of Truth" and write a detailed service plan, including a "service audit."

THE MANAGEMENT CHALLENGE

Diane Kokkinos Streamlines Her Factory

If you drive a Dodge Intrepid, Dodge Dakota, Chrysler Concorde, or Chrysler minivan, chances are the interior trim came from Collins & Aikman's automotive trim division plant in Port Huron, Michigan. The 140,000 square foot facility employs 400 workers and makes inside trim products such as armrests. While only 10 years old, the plant has earned many quality and safety awards. However, as Diane Kokkinos, the plant's vice president of operations, says, "We don't want to get carried away. You can't assume that because you're good today, you're going to be good tomorrow. You have to be constantly looking at the next challenge, and what process will take you to a different level than where you are today."[1]

Kokkinos began streamlining her plant's operations several years ago, but as she puts it, "[while] we were already fairly good . . . we wanted to get better." Kokkinos knew that while her manufacturing facility was quite advanced, it had an inventory problem. There was so much finished goods inventory waiting for shipment that it clogged floor space, created production bottlenecks, and forced the plant to lease space to conduct operations it normally would have carried out in the main plant. As Debbie Skinner, the plant's materials manager put it, "Now what were our obstacles? Inventory. We used every bit of floor space. We would have 6 to 10 hours of finished goods inventory easily, which really made it difficult to operate and function." Kokkinos and her team knew they had to do something to streamline their operations and remove the finished goods inventory bottleneck. The question was, "what exactly should we do?"

Kokkinos specializes in operations management, but you don't have to manage a factory to need operations management skills. The HR manager needs to know how to manage the quality of her department's services, the sales manager needs to know how to schedule sales calls, and the office manager needs to lay out the department's workflow as efficiently as possible. Chapter 14 discussed the basic control process. The main purpose of this chapter is to familiarize you with the techniques managers use to control and improve the quality, scheduling, and functioning of their operations. The main topics we'll cover include production systems, operations planning and control techniques, inventory and quality control techniques, world-class operations methods, and techniques for managing services.

■■■ THE BASICS OF OPERATIONS MANAGEMENT

Operations management is the process of managing the resources required to produce the organization's goods and services.[2] Operations managers focus on managing the "five Ps" of the firm's operations: people, plants, parts, processes, and planning and control systems. The *people* include the direct and indirect workforce, such as assembly workers, inventory clerks, and clerical staff. *Plants* are the factories or service branches (like banks) where the firm creates its product or service. *Parts* include the raw materials and other inputs that the firm's operations will transform into finished products or services. *Processes* represent the technology, the equipment, and the steps required to accomplish production. The *planning and control systems* are the procedures management uses to operate the system (such as the methods used to schedule the work) and to control quality.[3] Operations managers include, for instance, plant managers, manufacturing managers, purchasing managers, and logistics (or transportation) managers.

Operations management is not just important for manufacturing firms. All firms— from GE and GM to service firms like KFC and 7-Eleven—have to manage their productive operations. For example, in the new McDonald's kitchen, computers control production and sandwiches come off the line in 45 seconds. Merrill Lynch needs to manage its inventory of securities. American Airlines uses sophisticated operations management planning and scheduling tools to schedule ticket-counter personnel "just in time" and to adjust flight schedules in the face of rough weather. La Quinta Motor Inns uses operations management tools to analyze variables (such as traffic counts and local purchasing power) to identify preferred locations. Mrs. Fields Cookies store managers use special work scheduling software. This predicts hourly demand based on historical trends, and projects the amount and type of cookies to bake. It also charts hourly and daily sales, and tells the manager how many employees he or she will need to staff the store during the day.[4] Even service firms are heavy users of operations management techniques.

In this chapter we'll look at the basic aspects of managing operations, the first of which is managing the production system itself.

■■■ MANAGING THE PRODUCTION SYSTEM

The *production system* is the heart of operations management, and it has three main components—inputs, a conversion system, and outputs (see Figure 15.1). Inputs are all the resources required to create the product or service. These include raw materials and purchased parts, personnel, and capital. Other inputs include data on the competition, the product, and the customer.

Any production system takes inputs and converts them into products or services (outputs). The conversion system (also called the production process or technology) has several components. These include the production machinery and its physical layout, the transport services that bring in the inputs and deliver the final products to customers, and warehousing services for goods awaiting shipment. The production system's outputs may be divided into direct outputs (the actual products or services) and indirect outputs (such as wages and salaries).

The same sequence applies to a service business like a university (see Table 15.1).[5] Here inputs include students, books, supplies, personnel (professors), and buildings. The conversion system consists of the technology used to transmit information to the

operations management ■ *the process of managing the resources that are needed to produce an organization's goods and services.*

input ■ *a resource required for the manufacture of a product or service.*

conversion system ■ *any production system that converts inputs (material and human resources) into outputs (products or services); sometimes called the production process or technology.*

output ■ *a direct outcome (actual product or service) or indirect outcome (taxes, wages, salaries) of a production system.*

► FIGURE 15–1 ■ ■ ■

The Basic Production System

Every production system is built around a conversion process or system that takes various inputs and converts these into outputs such as products or services.

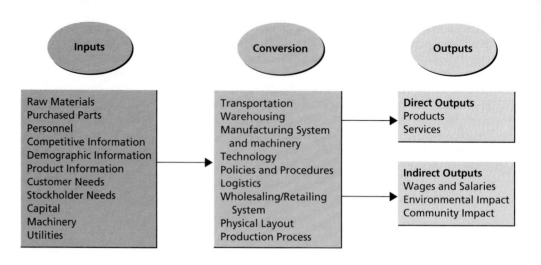

students (lectures, exams, computerized instruction, and so forth). The output is educated persons.

Whether you're producing goods or services, designing a production system requires four basic decisions: Where will the facility be located? What type of production process will be used? What will be the layout of the overall plant or facility? And what will be the layout of the production system itself?

The Facility Location Decision

Deciding where to locate the facility is always crucial. For a service firm like a retail store or fast-food restaurant, even placing the facility on the wrong side of the road can spell disaster. Thus dry cleaners try to place their stores near large supermarkets to make it more convenient for customers to drop off and pick up clothes on the way to do their shopping. The British retailer Marks & Spencer had to close more than 30 of its European stores because it had chosen poor locations. For a manufacturer, plant location influences crucial factors like transportation costs and labor availability.

Locating a facility requires managers to apply both subjective and objective criteria. On the subjective side are things like the owner's personal preferences. If Mr. Suarez loves to sail and his whole family lives in Miami, then the plant may be located in nearby Hialeah, even if transportation costs are somewhat higher than they might be elsewhere.

As production becomes global, selecting a site tends to rest on a variety of country-, region-, and site-specific objective criteria. Typical country-related considerations include, for instance, government rules and attitudes, cultural and economic issues, location of markets, availability of labor and supplies, and exchange rates. Region/com-

TABLE 15–1	Components of Some Typical Production Systems		
Production System	**Primary Inputs**	**Purpose of Conversion System**	**Outputs**
1. Pet food factory	Grain, water, fish meal, personnel, tools, machines, paper bags, cans, buildings, utilities	Converts raw materials into finished goods	Pet food products
2. Public accounting firm	Supplies, personnel, information, computers, buildings, office furniture, machines, utilities	Attracts customers, compiles data, supplies management, information, computes taxes	Management information, tax services, and audited financial statements
3. College or university	Students, books, supplies, personnel, buildings, utilities	Transmits information and develops skills and knowledge via lectures, exams, computerized instruction	Educated persons

Source: Adapted from Norman Gaither, *Production and Operations Management*, 5th ed. (Fort Worth, TX: The Dryden Press, 1992), pp. 22–23.

munity considerations include corporate management's desires as well as the region's attractiveness in terms of things like taxes, labor availability, utilities, environmental regulations, government incentives, and proximity to supplies and customers.

Once management makes these decisions, it turns to finding a specific site. Considerations here include the cost of the site, transportation availability, zoning restrictions, and environmental impact issues.

Managers ignore country, region, and site-specific considerations at their peril, especially if they're looking to expand abroad. For example, the $64 million Hilton Hanoi Opera Hotel stands nearly empty, as do most of the city's eight other new luxury hotels. What went wrong? In the first half of the 1990s, many believed Vietnam was the next great "Asian tiger" in terms of projected economic growth.[6] Now reality has set in. Vietnam is still communist, and it is reportedly "closer to Cuba than to today's market-oriented China."[7] It's also still one of the poorest countries in Asia, with many antibusiness government policies and tariffs. Corruption is reportedly rampant. So it looks like the Hanoi Hilton may be empty for awhile.

■■ ■ Location, location, location: A dry cleaner in a shopping mall allows customers to drop off and pick up clothes on their way to shop for food or other items.

Basic Types of Production Processes

Deciding on a production process is a second crucial decision. We can distinguish between two broad types of systems: *intermittent production systems* and *continuous production systems*.

In intermittent production systems, employees work on the product on a start-and-stop basis.[8] Automobile repair shops, custom-cabinet shops, and construction contractors are examples. Firms like these usually offer made-to-order products. They face relatively low product volumes as well as frequent schedule changes, and tend to use general-purpose equipment that can make a variety of models or products.

Mass production is a special type of intermittent production process. Here, standardized methods and single-use machines produce long runs of standardized items. Most mass production processes use assembly lines. An assembly line is a fixed sequence of specialized (single-use) machines. In a typical assembly line, the product moves from station to station, where one or more employees and/or specialized machines perform tasks such as inserting bumpers or screwing on doors. Mass production systems may, in fact, run more or less continuously and may stop and start very few times over the course of a year.

Mass customization is an increasingly popular hybrid production process, and it falls between intermittent and continuous production (discussed below). Mass customization means designing, producing, and delivering products in such a way that customers get customized products for at or near the cost and convenience of mass-produced items.[9] Dell production process exemplifies this approach. Thanks to mass customization, a customer can call or link with Dell and have a customized PC at a price at or below that of a mass-produced standardized machine. Mass customization consists of three elements:[10]

intermittent production system
■ *a system in which production is performed on a start-and-stop basis, such as for the manufacture of made-to-order products.*

mass customization ■ *designing, producing, and delivering products in such a way that customers get customized products for at or near the cost and convenience of mass-produced items.*

▲ WEBNOTE ■ ■ ■

Dell exemplifies the mass customization approach: Customers can go on Dell's Web site, choose the components they need, and Dell will build a computer to their specifications.

www.dell.com

Source: Copyright 1999–2002 Dell Computer Corporation.

1. *Modular product design.* Design the product to consist of separate modules. Employees can then easily assemble them into different forms of the product. For example, instead of designing its printers with standard power supplies, HP-Compaq designs its printers to have a separate power supply inserted later. Customers around the globe can, therefore, get the power supply they need.
2. *Modular process design.* Similarly, the firm designs the production process so that workers can perform different steps in different places. For example, consider Levi's mass customization jeans production program. The aim is to get a customer a cus-

tomized pair of jeans within a few days. Modular process design is the heart of the Levi's personal pairs program. The jeans get designed at the store (based on the customer's fittings), sewn at the factory, and delivered back to the store. Similarly, the HP-Compaq machine is designed so that it is built in one place, and its power supply is then installed at the distributor's facility.

3. *Agile supply networks.* Mass customization firms design the whole supply chain from vendors to production to distribution to be adept at providing a variety of services. For example, IBM designs some products around modules. Vendors supply components and may do some preliminary assembly, IBM assembles them into modules, and IBM distributors assemble the modules into complete products based on what their customers want.

Mass customization is unique among production processes. In typical intermittent firms, managers must choose between high volume or product variety. Mass customization weds high production volume with high product variety.

continuous production processes ■ *a production process, such as those used by chemical plants or refineries, that runs for very long periods without the start-and-stop behavior associated with intermittent production.*

Continuous production processes run uninterrupted for very long periods. Chemical plants, paper plants, and petroleum refineries are examples. Enormous capital investments are involved in building these highly automated facilities that use special-purpose equipment. Their owners, therefore, usually design them for high volume and little or no variation.

As we will see, the traditional dividing line between intermittent and continuous processes is beginning to blur. For example, computer-assisted manufacturing processes at Mead Corporation, which produces and sells paper, merge the flexibility of intermittent production with the efficiency of continuous production. Similarly, mass-customization processes help firms wed advantages of intermittent and continuous production processes.

Facility and Production Layout

Once the manager decides on a production process, he or she can decide how to lay out the plant or facility.

facility layout ■ *the configuration of all the machines, employee workstations, storage areas, internal walls, and so forth that constitute the facility used to create a firm's product or service.*

Facility Layout Facility layout refers to the configuration of the total facility—not just the machines, but also the employee workstations, storage areas, internal walls, and so forth. Important objectives here usually include reducing materials-handling costs, providing sufficient capacity, and allowing for safe equipment operation and ease of maintenance.

Facility layout is also important for service firms. Retailers lay out their stores to improve sales, raise customer satisfaction, and increase convenience. Thus, food stores typically put products like meats toward the back; to get to them, customers must pass the other aisles. Office managers may use movable partitions to promote communication between departments (while still providing adequate privacy).

product layout ■ *a production system design in which every item to be produced follows the same sequence of operations from beginning to end, such as an assembly line.*

Production System Layout Whether in a factory or a service business like a car wash, there are basically four ways to lay out the production (conversion) system itself. In a **product layout**, every item produced follows the same sequence from beginning to end, moving from one specialized tool and operation to another. An assembly, or production, line is one example. Product layouts are not restricted to manufacturing. For example, automatic car washes use product layouts, as Figure 15.2 illustrates.[11]

▼ **FIGURE 15–2** ■ ■ ■

Product Layout

A car wash is an example of an assembly-line–type product layout, where each special-purpose machine performs its function as the product moves from station to station.

Source: Everett Adam Jr. and Ronald Ebert, *Production and Operations Management* (Upper Saddle River, NJ: Prentice Hall, 1992), p. 254.

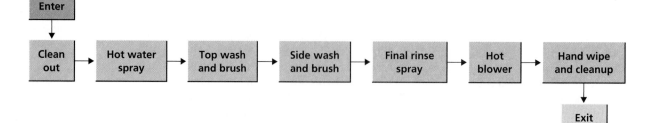

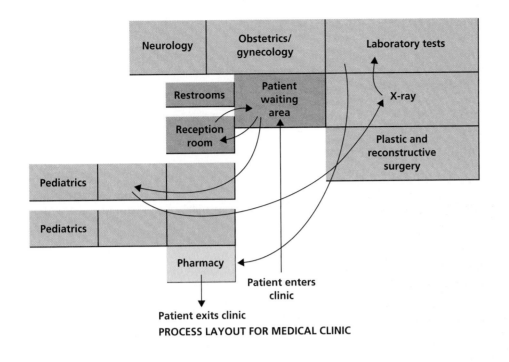

Process Layout

In a process layout like this, each process has its own area, and the "product" (in this case, the patient) is directed to the processes (such as X-ray and pediatrics) that are appropriate.

Source: Everett Adam Jr. and Ronald Ebert, *Production and Operations Management* (Upper Saddle River, NJ: Prentice Hall, 1992), p. 254.

PROCESS LAYOUT FOR MEDICAL CLINIC

process layout ■ *a production system design in which similar machines or functions are grouped together.*

fixed-position layout ■ *a production system arrangement in which the product being built or produced stays at one location and the machines, workers, and tools required to build the product are brought to that location as needed, as for the building of ships or other bulky products.*

cellular manufacturing layout ■ *usually a combination of process and product layouts, in which machines and personnel are grouped into cells containing all the tools and operations required to produce a particular product or family of products.*

In a process layout, the designers group similar machines or functions together. For example, the designers may place all drill presses in one area and all lathes in another. As Figure 15.3 illustrates,[12] service businesses like hospitals are usually organized around process layouts. Separate locations exist for departments like Pediatrics and Neurology, and for testing and X-ray. In a fixed-position layout, the product stays at one location. The manufacturing machines and workers (or machines) bring the tools required to build the product to that location, as needed. Heavy, bulky products like ships and planes are built this way.

In a cellular manufacturing layout, the firm groups machines into cells, each of which contains all the tools and operations required to help produce a particular product or family of products. This is shown in Figure 15.4.[13] Thus, a cell may be dedicated to all the grinding and buffing needed to produce the valves that go into the company's car engines.

Improving Layouts by Moving to the Cellular Manufacturing Concept

Note in both (a) and (b) that U-shaped work cells can reduce material and employee movement. The U shape may also reduce space requirements.

Source: Barry Render and Jay Heizer, *Principles of Operations Management*, 2nd ed., © 1997. Reprinted by permission of Prentice Hall, Inc., Upper Saddle River, NJ.

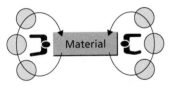

(a) Current layout—workers in small closed areas. Cannot increase output without a third worker.

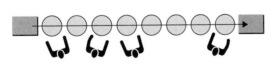

(b) Current layout—straight lines are hard to balance.

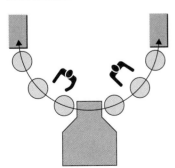

Improved layout—workers can assist each other. May be able to add a third worker.

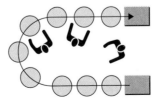

Improved layout—in U shape, workers have better access. Four workers were reduced to three.

■■■ OPERATIONS PLANNING AND CONTROL TECHNIQUES

Whether you're producing cars or Broadway shows, a system for planning and controlling production is required. Operations or production planning is the process of deciding what products to produce and where, when, and how to produce them. Operations or production control is the process of ensuring that the operation is fulfilling its production plans and schedules. We'll look at some important techniques used in these processes.

Scheduling and Gantt Charts

Managers present production schedules on charts that show what operations are to be carried out and when. The Gantt chart shown in Figure 15.5 is one example. It shows the activities required to complete a product or project, and the period in which the manager anticipates performing each activity.

Henry Gantt, a management pioneer, devised several versions of his chart. The example in Figure 15.5 shows time on the horizontal scale. For each order, it shows the start and stop times sequentially. Another type of Gantt chart lists each operation separately in the left column, one under the other, and time along the top or bottom. That way, the start and stop times for all operations in a complex project can be scheduled and tracked.

In practice, production schedulers work from the required delivery date backward. They determine how long each assembly will take, how long it will take to obtain raw materials, and so forth. Based on the results, schedulers can determine whether the firm can meet its required delivery date, and what bottlenecks they must prepare to unclog.

Network Planning and Control Methods

The Gantt chart is adequate for managing simpler projects (with not too many subassemblies or activities). Complex projects usually require computerized network charting tools to show how one activity affects the others.

Network planning and control methods graphically represent the project's steps and the timing and linkages among those steps. A project is a series of interrelated activities aimed at producing a major, coordinated product or service. Examples include introducing a new Ford Taurus or planning a wedding reception.

PERT and CPM are the two most popular network planning and control methods. PERT (program evaluation review technique) and CPM (critical path method) were invented at about the same time and are similar, although several details (for instance, CPM shows the cost of each step) set PERT apart from CPM.

▶ **FIGURE 15–5** ■■■

A Gantt Chart

This Gantt chart shows the steps and timing of each step for each order.

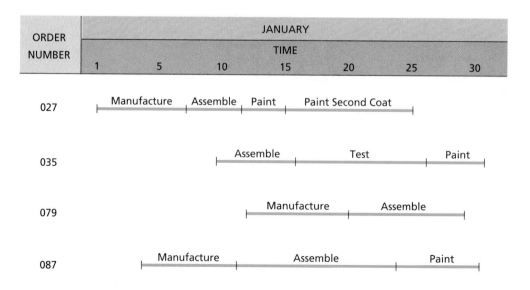

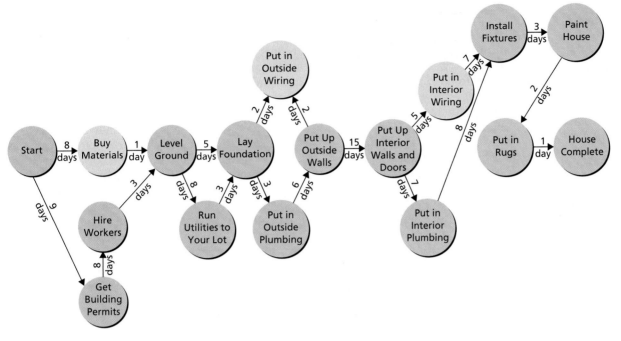

▲ FIGURE 15–6 ■■■

PERT Chart for Building a House

In a PERT chart like this one, each event is shown in its proper relationship to the other events. The blue circles show the critical—or most time-consuming—path.

Events and activities are the two major components of PERT networks. As Figure 15.6 shows, events, depicted by circles, represent specific accomplishments, such as "lay foundation." Arrows represent activities, which are the time-consuming aspects of the project (like laying the foundation). By studying the PERT chart, the scheduler can determine the critical path, the sequence of critical events that, in total, requires the most time to complete. Schedulers use computerized programs (see Figure 15.7 to create PERT networks for complex projects.

events ■ *the specific accomplishments in a project, represented by circles in a PERT chart.*

activities ■ *the time-consuming aspects of a project, represented by arrows in a PERT chart.*

critical path ■ *the sequence of events in a project that, in total, requires the most time to complete.*

◀ FIGURE 15–7 ■■■

Example of a Computerized Network Planning Report

Purchasing

Purchasing departments buy all the materials and parts the firm needs to conduct its business. This includes the raw materials that go into the firm's products as well as machinery, tools, purchased components, and even paper clips and computer paper.

Purchasing is a more important function than many managers realize. Some experts estimate that 60% of a manufacturer's sales dollars are paid to suppliers for purchased materials.[14] Furthermore, manufacturers striving to maintain quality levels know that the quality of the finished products can't be any better than the quality of the components. Purchasing departments can thus affect a firm's cost-effectiveness as well as its reputation. Today, in fact, many firms work closely with suppliers to create better-quality parts. Many firms, such as Ford, send engineers to help suppliers boost their quality-management systems.

Purchasing managers engage in several activities.[15] They maintain a database of available suppliers. They are also responsible for selecting suppliers and negotiating supply contracts. Purchasing managers try to minimize the costs of materials and supplies, but it would be an oversimplification to say that this is their only (or even their main) concern. For many firms, high-quality, reliable, on-time deliveries outweigh costs. And, increasingly, firms are automating their purchase decisions by having suppliers bid for their business via the Internet.

■ *The Global Manager* Multinational production operations often prompt managers to find ways to consolidate regional purchasing as a way to reduce costs. For example, Sony recently grouped various plants in each of four global regions into a new Sony EMCS (engineering, manufacturing, and customer service) operation.[16] One of the first things Sony did was to centralize purchasing for certain plants in each regional EMCS into the EMCS regional headquarters. Sony reportedly hopes to save up to 14% on parts costs with the move. However, some purchasing experts worry that by focusing on minimizing purchasing costs, Sony may drop some local suppliers that have higher costs but can also deliver parts quicker, just-in-time, if need be. If that happened, then the money Sony is saving by paying less for parts could be surpassed by its additional inventory costs, since the Sony plants would have to keep more parts in stock for emergencies.

■■■ INVENTORY MANAGEMENT TECHNIQUES

Firms keep inventories of five types of items.[17] Firms obtain *raw materials and purchased parts* from outside suppliers, and hold them for the production of finished products. *Components* are subassemblies that are awaiting final assembly. *Work in process* refers to all materials or components on the production floor in various stages of production. *Finished goods* are final products waiting for purchase or to be sent to customers. Finally, *supplies* are all items the firm needs that are not part of the finished product, such as paper clips, duplicating machine toner, and tools.

The Role of Inventory Management

inventory management ■ the process of ensuring that the firm has adequate inventories of all parts and supplies needed, within the constraint of minimizing total inventory costs.

Inventory management is the process of ensuring that the firm has enough inventories of all required parts and supplies within the constraint of minimizing total inventory costs.

In practice, inventory managers must address four specific costs. Ordering, or setup, costs are the costs of placing the order or setting up machines for the production run. For purchased items, ordering costs might include order-processing costs (such as clerical time for filling out the order) and the cost of inspecting goods when they arrive. For items made in-house, setup costs include the labor involved with setting up the machine and the cost of preparing the paperwork for scheduling the production run.

ordering, or setup, costs ■ the costs, usually fixed, of placing an order or setting up machines for a production run.

Ordering, or setup, costs are usually fixed, meaning that they are independent of the size of the order. Acquisition costs, the total cost of all the units themselves bought to fill an order, vary with the size of the order. For example, ordering required parts in larger quantities may reduce each unit's cost thanks to quantity discounts. This, in turn, will lower the total acquisition costs of the order, whereas ordering smaller quantities may raise the unit cost.

acquisition costs ■ the total costs of all units bought to fill an order, usually varying with the size of the order.

Inventory managers focus on two other inventory costs. Inventory-holding (or carrying) costs are all the costs associated with carrying parts or materials in inventory. The biggest specific cost here is usually the firm's cost of capital, which in this case is the value of a unit of the inventory times the length of time it is held times the interest rate at which the firm borrows money.[18] Suppose an item costs $10 and stays in inventory for a year, and the firm must pay its bank 5% interest to borrow money. Then it costs the firm 50 cents in finance charges just to hold the item in inventory for a year. Stockout costs are the costs associated with running out of raw materials or finished-goods inventory. For example, if a company cannot fill a customer's order, it might lose both the current order and any profits on future sales to this customer.

inventory-holding (carrying) costs ▪ all the costs associated with carrying parts or materials in inventory.

stockout costs ▪ the costs associated with running out of raw materials, parts, or finished-goods inventory.

Inventory managers want to avoid three basic problems. The first is overinvestment in inventories, which ties up money, crowds available space, and increases losses when stored products deteriorate or become obsolete. At the other extreme, inventory managers want to avoid underinvestment, which leaves the firm unable to fill production orders and discourages customers. The third problem is unbalanced inventory, which means there are some understocked items and some overstocked ones.

Basic Inventory Management Systems

Many quantitative and nonquantitative systems are available for managing inventory. The ABC and EOQ systems are two of the most popular.

ABC Inventory Management Most firms find that a small proportion (25% to 30%) of the parts in their inventory accounts for a large proportion (70% or 80%) of their annual dollar volume of inventory usage. (A part's annual dollar volume is computed by multiplying its cost per part by the number of parts used in a year.)

When using the ABC system, the manager divides the inventory into three dollar-volume categories—A, B, and C—with the A parts being the most active. The manager then concentrates most of his or her checking and surveillance on the A parts. For example, the A parts are ordered most often so that their total in inventory is minimized and so that they are not in the inventory bins too long.

At the other extreme, the inventory manager might find that perhaps 50% of the parts in inventory account for, say, 15% of annual dollar volume. Why spend as much time closely monitoring all those parts when, in total, they account for only 15% of the firm's annual dollar volume of inventory usage? The idea is to focus most on the high-annual-dollar-volume A inventory items, to a lesser extent on the B items, and even less on the C items.

The Economic Order Quantity Inventory Management System The idea behind the economic order quantity (EOQ) system or model is to determine the most economical quantity to order—in other words, the quantity that will minimize total inventory and setup costs. EOQ is the best-known and probably the oldest inventory system.

economic order quantity (EOQ) ▪ an inventory management system based on a simple formula that is used to determine the most economical quantity to order so that the total of inventory and setup costs is minimized.

Figure 15.8 illustrates the relationships involved in EOQ. As shown, the two major costs, inventory carrying costs and ordering/setup costs, vary inversely with each other. For example, ordering in large quantities usually allows the firm to reduce ordering or setup costs, but it means higher storage costs (because the firm would have, on average, more inventory in stock).

In its simplest form the economic order quantity is $Q = \sqrt{\dfrac{2US}{H}}$ where Q is the economic order quantity (the most economical quantity to order), U is the annual usage of the item, S is the restocking or ordering costs, and H is the annual holding cost per unit per year. If a car factory uses 10,000 door handles per year to build its cars, U for the handles is 10,000. S may refer to either restocking or ordering costs. If the car factory orders the handles from a supplier and it costs the factory $200 per order (for forms, clerical support, and so forth) to place the order, then S is $200. If the factory manufactures the door handles in house and must spend $500 (labor to put the new tools in place, and so forth) to set up its machine to produce the order, then S would be $500. Holding (or carrying) costs (H) include such things as pilferage, borrowing costs associated with holding the items in stock, and the costs of the space in which you hold the inventory. H is generally presented on a per-unit basis.

This EOQ equation is widely used, but it is based on some simplifications. For example, it assumes that the same number of units is taken from inventory periodi-

► **FIGURE 15–8** ■ ■ ■

The Economic Order Quantity Model

When order size goes up, ordering costs per order go down, but carrying costs go up because more items are left longer in inventory.

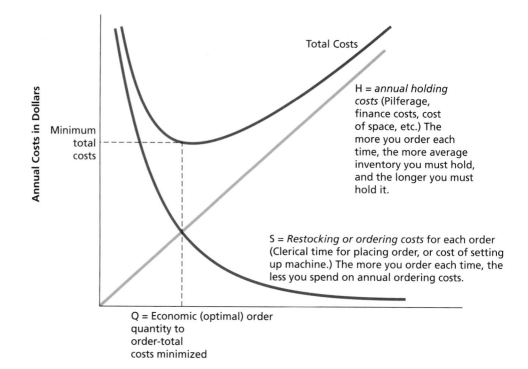

Annual Costs in Dollars

Total Costs

Minimum total costs

H = *annual holding costs* (Pilferage, finance costs, cost of space, etc.) The more you order each time, the more average inventory you must hold, and the longer you must hold it.

S = *Restocking or ordering costs* for each order (Clerical time for placing order, or cost of setting up machine.) The more you order each time, the less you spend on annual ordering costs.

Q = Economic (optimal) order quantity to order-total costs minimized

quality ■ *the extent to which a product or service is able to meet customer needs and expectations.*

ISO 9000 ■ *the quality standards of the International Standards Organization.*

total quality management (TQM) ■ *a specific organizationwide program that integrates all the functions and related processes of a business such that they are all aimed at maximizing customer satisfaction through ongoing improvements.*

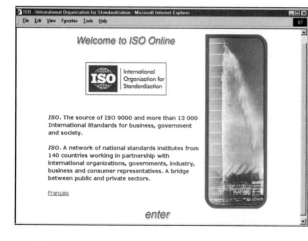

cally, such as 10 units per day. It also assumes that the supplier does not offer quantity discounts for ordering in large batches. More sophisticated EOQ versions are available for handling these and other complications.[19]

■ ■ ■ CONTROLLING FOR QUALITY AND PRODUCTIVITY

Quality refers to the totality of features and characteristics of a product or service that bears on its ability to satisfy given needs. To put this another way, "Quality measures how well a product or service meets customer needs."[20]

This definition highlights several important things about quality. First, the customer's needs are the basic standard for measuring quality. An airplane seat in coach can be as high quality as one in first class in terms of the coach passenger's expectations and the competitor's services. Thus, many coach flyers understandably consider traveling on JetBlue's wider leather coach seats as high quality compared with the typical coach experience. Second, high quality does not have to mean high price. Again, the basic consideration should be the extent to which the product or service meets the customer's expectations.

Quality standards today are international. Doing business often means the firm must show it complies with ISO 9000, the quality standards of the International Standards Organization, to which the U.S. is a signatory.

Total Quality Management Programs

Total quality management (TQM) programs are organizationwide quality-oriented initiatives. They are "programs that aim to integrate all functions of the business such that all aspects of the business, including design, planning, production, distribution, and field service, are aimed at maximizing customer satisfaction through continuous improvements."[21] TQM also goes by the names *continuous improvement, zero defects, Six-Sigma* (which refers to the statistical likelihood of reducing defects to 3.5 per million) or (in Japan) *Kaizen*.[22]

Most regard W. Edwards Deming as the intellectual father of TQM. He based his concept of total quality on the following 14-point system, which he says must be implemented at all organizational levels:

1. Create consistency of purpose toward the improvement of product and service, and translate that goal into a plan.
2. Adopt the new philosophy of quality.
3. Cease dependence on inspection to achieve quality by building quality into the product from the beginning.
4. End the practice of choosing suppliers based solely on price. Move toward a single supplier for any one item and toward a long-term relationship of loyalty and trust.
5. Improve constantly and forever the production and service system in order to improve quality and productivity and thus constantly decrease cost. In other words, aim for continuous improvement.
6. Institute extensive training on the job.
7. Shift your focus from production numbers to quality.
8. Drive out fear so that everyone may work effectively for the company.
9. Break down barriers between departments. People in research, design, sales, and production must work as a team to foresee problems of production as well as problems that may occur after sale, when the product or service is actually used.
10. Eliminate slogans and targets for the workforce that push for zero defects and new levels of productivity, particularly where new methods for achieving these targets are not put into place.
11. Eliminate work standards (quotas) on the factory floor.
12. Remove barriers that rob employees of their right to pride of workmanship. Among other things, this means abolishing the annual merit rating and all forms of management by objectives or management by numbers.
13. Institute a vigorous program of education and self-improvement.
14. Create a structure within top management that will push every day for each of the preceding 13 points. Make sure to put everybody in the company to work to accomplish the transformation.[23]

■ ■ *Clarke American Checks, Inc. employees who received the Malcolm Baldridge award.*

The U.S. Department of Commerce created the Malcolm Baldridge Award to recognize firms that adhere to Deming-type quality principles. (Mr. Baldridge was Secretary of Commerce in the Reagan administration.) Most U.S. manufacturing firms, service firms, and small businesses can apply for the award. In choosing Baldridge winners, the judges (from several agencies, including the U.S. Department of Commerce) focus on seven basic categories, as summarized in Checklist 15.1.

Malcolm Baldrige Award ■ *a prize created in 1987 by the U.S. Department of Commerce to recognize outstanding achievement in quality control management.*

CHECKLIST 15.1 ■ How to Win a Baldridge Award

☑ *Is the company exhibiting senior executive leadership?* Judges look for top management commitment to quality and try to assess the day-to-day quality leadership of the firm's senior staff. Symbolic leadership gestures might include taking the same quality courses as lower-level employees, talking to customers about quality, and meeting with employees regarding quality.

☑ *Is the company obtaining quality information and analysis?* The company must show that it is gathering and using data that demonstrate both quality performance and continuous improvement. *Benchmarking* refers to the process of comparing the manager's own firm's statistical results in key areas with those of other firms. The firm should be

able to show which companies it benchmarked, what it learned, and how it used the information.[24]

☑ *Is the company engaging in strategic quality planning?* Examiners typically review two or three quality-related goals to determine the extent to which the firm is meeting those goals. Goals might include answering all telephone calls from customers by the second ring or increasing on-time customer deliveries by 80%.

☑ *Is the company developing its human resources?* Judges look at the extent to which the firm is using human resource management and organizational behavior techniques (such as worker empowerment, training, and team building) to take advantage of each employee's potential.

☑ **Is the company managing the entire quality process?** Is the firm taking an integrated approach to the quality process? For example, representatives from design, production, and sales might work together to produce a product design that both facilitates production and maximizes customer satisfaction.

☑ **How does the company measure operational results?** Companies have to provide statistical data on quality levels, quality improvement trends, operational performance, and supplier quality. One aim here is to show that the firm is achieving continuous quality improvement.

☑ **Does the company exhibit a customer focus?** Can the company prove with hard data that it has a "focus on the customer" and pursues "customer satisfaction"? The judges will expect the company to track data on things like sales calls, customer surveys, and telephone hot lines.

Quality Control Methods

acceptance sampling ■ *a method of monitoring product quality that requires the inspection of only a small portion of the produced items.*

Managers use various methods to monitor product or service quality. Measurement is usually key. Most firms have formal inspection procedures. Sometimes (such as when producing heart pacemakers), a 100% inspection is typical. More common is acceptance sampling. Here the firm inspects only a portion of the items, perhaps 2% or 5%. Have you ever called an airline and been told, "The conversation may be recorded for quality or training purposes"? That airline is using acceptance sampling to check on the service quality of its reservations clerks.

Firms also use quality control charts like the one in Figure 15.9. There are many charts, but the basic idea is always the same. The manager draws upper and lower control limits to show the range within which some measurable characteristic is to fall. Then employees (or machines) measure the chosen characteristic (such as length or weight). (Thus, Kellogg's foods might want to make sure each box of corn flakes contains no more than 20 ounces and no fewer than 19.5 ounces.)

If the measures begin to move toward the upper or lower control limits, it's time to see what's causing the variation. Some managers use special software to track quality automatically and to report it in various graphic formats.

Employee quality-assurance teams typically use several tools to monitor and analyze quality problems. Figure 15.10 summarizes some of them.[25] For example, a scatter diagram shows the magnitude of one trait (such as the number of defects) versus a second trait (such as time). A cause-and-effect (or fishbone) diagram outlines the four main categories of problems—machine, manpower/people, method, and material—and helps employees analyze the problem and devise solutions.

▶ **FIGURE 15–9** ■ ■ ■

Example of a Quality Control Chart

The idea behind any control chart is to track quality trends to ensure that they don't go out of control.

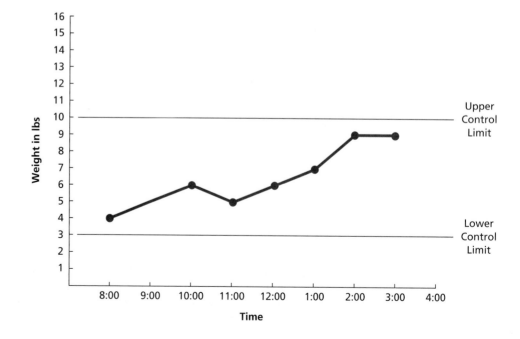

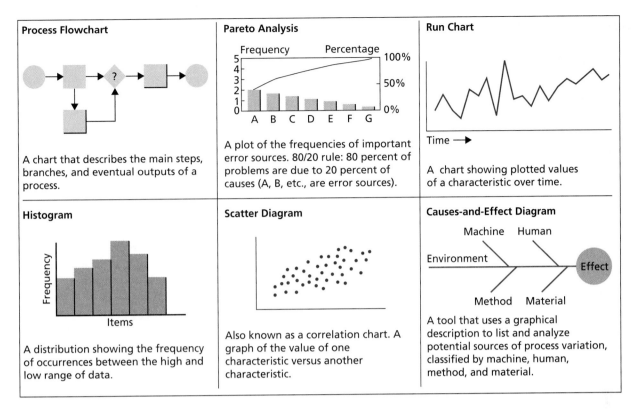

Process Flowchart	Pareto Analysis	Run Chart
A chart that describes the main steps, branches, and eventual outputs of a process.	A plot of the frequencies of important error sources. 80/20 rule: 80 percent of problems are due to 20 percent of causes (A, B, etc., are error sources).	A chart showing plotted values of a characteristic over time.
Histogram	Scatter Diagram	Causes-and-Effect Diagram
A distribution showing the frequency of occurrences between the high and low range of data.	Also known as a correlation chart. A graph of the value of one characteristic versus another characteristic.	A tool that uses a graphical description to list and analyze potential sources of process variation, classified by machine, human, method, and material.

▲ **FIGURE 15–10** ■ ■ ■

Commonly Used Tools for Problem Solving and Continuous Improvement

Source: Adapted from Richard Chase and Nicholas Aquilero, *Production and Operations Management,* 6th ed. (Homewood, IL: Irwin, 1992), p. 197.

Consider two specific examples. In the *fishbone* diagram in Figure 15.11 the problem being addressed is, "What accounts for so many dissatisfied airline customers?" The diagram helps to organize the analysis. Four main categories of problems may be contributing to the situation, namely material, machinery, methods, and manpower/people. The analyst (or employee quality team) uses the diagram to think through specific possible causes. For example, under "material," possible causes include "inadequate special meals on board." The team could then drop down to a second level of analysis—for example, "what is causing the fact that we have inadequate special meals on board?"

Pareto analysis is also widely used. Figure 15.12 presents an example. Pareto analysis (named after Vilfredo Pareto, a nineteenth-century economist) assumes that a small portion of the defects accounts for a large portion of the problems. In Figure 15.12 there are 75 defects, on average, including scratches, porosity, nicks, contamination, and miscellaneous. However, scratches cause 54 defects (or 72%). So eliminating scratches should eliminate most defects.

Design for Manufacturability

Designing for manufacturability means designing products with ease of high-quality manufacturing in mind. Its aims are to develop a product that can

- Exhibit the desired level of quality and reliability.
- Be designed in the least time with the least development cost.
- Make the quickest and smoothest transition into production.
- Be produced and tested with the minimum cost in the minimum amount of time.
- Satisfy customers' needs and compete in the marketplace.[26]

designing for manufacturability
■ *designing products with ease of manufacturing and quality in mind.*

Designing for manufacturability is increasingly important. As one expert points out, "By the time a product has been designed, only about 8 percent of the total product budget has been spent. But by that point, the design has determined 80 percent of the cost of the product!"[27] For example, Hewlett-Packard's original LaserJet III printer

► **FIGURE 15–11** ■■■

Fishbone Chart (or Cause-and-
Effect Diagram) for Problems with
Airline Customer Service

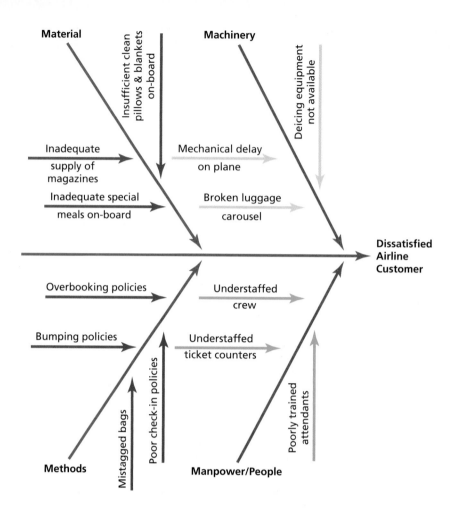

► **FIGURE 15–12** ■■■

Pareto Analysis Chart

The Pareto chart shown indicates that
72%(54 ÷ 75) of the defects were the
result of one cause: scratches. The
majority of defects will be eliminated
when this one cause is corrected.

Source: Jay Heizer and Barry Render,
Operations Management, 6th ed. (Upper
Saddle River, NJ: Prentice Hall, NJ 2001),
p. 182, Example 1.

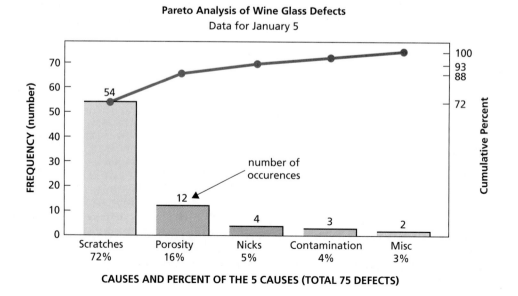

had dozens more parts than the IBM laser printer. Because IBM's printers had fewer points where assembly errors could occur, IBM could manufacture it more quickly, less expensively, and with fewer initial defects. As one expert said, "The design determines the manufacturability."[28]

Designing for manufacturability often means designing products using multidisciplinary teams. Operations managers call this *simultaneous design* or concurrent engineering. It ensures that all departments involved in the product's success contribute to its design.[29]

concurrent engineering ▪ *designing products in multidisciplinary teams so that all departments involved in the product's success contribute to its design.*

How to "Read" a Plant

In the final analysis, all these operations management tools—from plant layout to production scheduling to inventory and quality management—should combine to create a well-run facility. Being able to walk into a production facility and quickly size up its effectiveness is an important management skill. The Rapid Plant Assessment (RPA) provides a tool for doing this. Figure 15.13 presents the RPA rating sheet and its accompanying questionnaire. After inspecting the plant, the manager (or rating team) answers the yes/no questions on the RPA Questionnaire. Note that specific items provide input into the manager's assessments of each of the 11 categories on the Rapid Assessment Rating Sheet (in this case, items 1, 2, and 20 apply to category 1, cutomer satisfaction). The manager can then give his or her ratings (from "poor" to "best in class") for each of the 11 Rating Sheet categories, using the following explanatory category illustrations:[30]

1. *Customer satisfaction.* "Workers in the best plants clearly know who their customers are—both internal and external—and make customer satisfaction their primary goal."[31]
2. *Safety, environment, cleanliness, and order.* "In a clean and orderly plant, parts are easy to find, inventory is easy to count or estimate, and product moves safely and efficiently."
3. *Visual management system.* Tools such as signs that guide employees to their locations and tasks "provide visual cues and directions [and] are readily apparent in well-functioning plants."
4. *Scheduling system.* In the best plants, "demand for products at each work center is triggered by demand at the next." In contrast, notes the RPA's creator, "I visited a tractor factory in the [former] Soviet Union. The plant was diligently producing according to its centralized schedule, but the engine plant wasn't shipping enough engines, so each incomplete tractor was towed out to the yard. I counted a full six months supply of lifeless tractors, each waiting for its final, all-important part."[32] In the best plants, there is a single "pacing process" for each product line. The customer demand at the end of the product line "pulls" demand for the remaining upstream activities.
5. *Use of space, movement of materials, and product line flow.* "The best plants use space efficiently. Ideally, materials are moved only once, over as short [a] distance [as] possible, in efficient containers."
6. *Levels of inventory and work in process.* ". . . the observable number of any component part is a good measure of a plant's leanness."[33]
7. *Teamwork and motivation.* "In the best plants, people consistently focus on the plant's goals for productivity and quality, know their jobs well, and are eager to share their knowledge with customers and visitors."
8. *Condition and maintenance of equipment and tools.* "In the best plants, equipment is clean and well maintained. . . . Maintenance records are posted."
9. *Management of complexity and variability.* For instance, ". . . If you observe many people manually recording data and a large number of keyboards for data entry, the company may be doing a poor job of handling complexity, especially if the data collection is done by hand." Consider another example: Some companies, like Dell, provide training aids, which help workers minimize complexity. For example, they color-code items to make it easier for assemblers to see which parts go together.
10. *Supply chain integration.* "The best operations keep costs low and quality high by working closely with a relatively small number of dedicated and supportive suppliers."
11. *Commitment to quality.* "The best plants are always striving to improve quality and productivity, and it shows."

Rapid Plant Assessment Rating Sheet

Source: R. Eugene Goodson, "Reading A Plant—Fast," *Harvard Business Review*, May 2002, pp. 108–9.

RPA Rating Sheet

Plant _____

Tour date _____

Rated by _____

Team members use the RPA rating sheet to assess a plant in η categories on a scale from "poor" (1) to "excellent" (9) to "best in class" (η). The total score for all categories will fall between η (poor in all categories) and 121 (the best in the world in all categories), with an average score of 55. Factors to consider to rate a plant in each category are described in this article; a more detailed list of evaluative factors appears on the Web at www.bus.umich.edu/rpa. The rating sheet also guides team members to questions in the RPA questionnaire (opposite) that relate specifically to each category.

When plants are rated every year, the ratings for most tend to improve. Ratings are usually shared with plants, and motivated managers first improve their plants in the categories that receive the lowest ratings.

Ratings

Categories	Related questions in RPA questionnaire	poor (1)	below average (3)	average (5)	above average (7)	excellent (9)	best in class (11)	category score
1 Customer satisfaction	1, 2, 20							
2 Safety, environment, cleanliness, and order	3–5, 20							
3 Visual management system	12, 4, 6–10, 20							
4 Scheduling system	11, 20							
5 Use of space, movement of materials, and product line flow	7, 12, 13,20							
6 Levels of inventory and work in progress	7, 11, 20							
7 Teamwork and motivation	6, 9, 14, 15, 20							
8 Condition and maintenance of equipment and tools	16, 20							
9 Management of complexity and variability	8, 17, 20							
10 Supply chain integration	18, 20							
11 Commitment to quality	15, 17, 19, 20							

Total score for 11 categories _____
(*max = 121*)

RPA Questionnaire

The total number of yeses on this questionnaire is an indicator of a plant's leanness: the more yeses, the leaner the plant. Each question should be answered *yes* only if the plant obviously adheres to the principle implied by the question. In case of doubt, answer *no.*

	yes	no
1 Are visitors welcomed and given information about plant layout, workforce, customers, and products?	○	○
2 Are ratings for customer satisfaction and product quality displayed?	○	○
3 Is the facility safe, clean, orderly, and well lit? Is the air quality good, and are noise levels low?	○	○
4 Does a visual labeling system identity and locate inventory, tools, processes, and flow?	○	○
5 Does everything have its own place, and is everything stored in its place?	○	○
6 Are up-to-date operational goals and performance measures for those goals prominently posted?	○	○
7 Are production materials brought to and stored at side of the production line rather than in separate inventory storage areas?	○	○
8 Are work instructions and product quality specifications visible at all work areas?	○	○
9 Are updated charts on productivity, quality, safety, and problem solving visible for all teams?	○	○
10 Can the current state of the operation be viewed from a central control room, on a status board, or on a computer display?	○	○
11 Are production lines scheduled off a single pacing process, with appropriate inventory levels at each stage?	○	○
12 Is material moved only once and as short a distance as possible? Is material moved efficiently in appropriate containers?	○	○
13 Is the plant laid out in continuous product line flows rather than in "shops"?	○	○
14 Are work teams trained, empowered, and involved in problem solving and ongoing improvements?	○	○
15 Do employees appear committed to continuous improvement?	○	○
16 Is a timetable posted for equipment preventive maintenance and ongoing improvement of tools and processes?	○	○
17 Is there an effective project-management process, with cost and timing goals, for new product start-ups?	○	○
18 Is a supplier certification process–with measures for quality, delivery, and cost performance–displayed?	○	○
19 Have key product characteristics been identified, and are fail-safe methods used to forestall propagation of defects?	○	○
20 Would you buy the products this operation produces?	○	○

Total number of yeses _____

Today, no firm—not even one apparently hidden away in small-town USA—can assume that it is immune from global competition.[34] Virtually every industry is globalized. This means that firms face not just local competitors, but foreign ones too. When competition is global, even local competition is more intense. Firms everywhere are striving to improve quality, lead-time, customer service, and costs in the hope of gaining a stronger hold on their markets. It's not easy to do this.

World-class companies are those that can compete based on quality and productivity in an intensely competitive global environment. Firms such as UPS, Sony, and Dell set the performance standards for their industries and are able to respond swiftly and effectively to changing conditions.

World-class manufacturers are world class in part because they use modern production techniques and management systems to boost productivity, quality, and flexibility. These techniques and systems include TQM (already described), just-in-time manufacturing, computer-aided design and manufacturing, flexible manufacturing systems, computer-integrated manufacturing, supply-chain management, and enterprise resource planning. We'll look at each one in turn.

The Basic Components of Just-in-Time Systems (JIT)

just-in-time (JIT) ■ *a production control method used to attain minimum inventory levels by ensuring delivery of materials and assemblies just when they are to be used; also refers to a philosophy of manufacturing that aims to optimize production processes by continuously reducing waste.*

The concept called just-in-time (JIT) has two related definitions. In the narrowest sense, JIT refers to production control methods used to attain minimum inventory levels by arranging delivery of materials and assemblies "just in time"—in other words, just when they are to be used. More broadly, JIT refers to a philosophy of manufacturing that aims to optimize production process efficiency by continuously reducing waste.

Reducing seven main wastes is at the heart of the JIT philosophy.[35] The seven wastes (and examples of how to reduce them) are *overproduction* (reduce by producing only what is needed as it is needed), *waiting* (synchronize the workflow), *transportation* (minimize transport with better layouts), *processing* (ask, "Why do we need this process at all?"), *stock* (reduce inventories), *motion* (reduce wasted employee motions), and *defective products* (improve quality to reduce rework).

lean or value-added manufacturing ■ *a management philosophy that assumes that any manufacturing process that does not add value to the product for the customer is wasteful; also called value-added manufacturing.*

As an example, most firms waste enormous resources "waiting"—to inspect incoming items, for storing raw materials or work in process, or for moving work in process from one step of the process to another. JIT is aimed at reducing or eliminating wastes like these. Why can you often buy a custom-built Dell computer for less than its competitors? Dell uses JIT to strip wastes like these from its processes. JIT is also sometimes called lean or value-added manufacturing (reflecting the fact that any manufacturing process that does not add value to the product for the customer is wasteful).[36]

In practice, JIT-based facilities tend to have several characteristics. They tend to be small, specialized plants rather than large ones. It is easier to manage small plants, and it is easier to design the workflow and to staff specialized, single function plants. Few of these plants have as many as 1,000 employees; most have fewer than 30.[37] And inside their plants, the Japanese (where JIT was invented) tend to lay out facilities around the cell technology we discussed earlier. Typically, all the processes required to complete a major part of the product are together in one place. One employee can then perform all the processes. The worker will have to be more highly trained and flexible, of course. However, the arrangement reduces the moving and waiting time between steps in the process. Each worker tends to be personally responsible for the quality of the item he or she produces. Thus, quality goes in "at the source," when the product is actually made, thus eliminating another potential waste.

■▬■ *JIT-based facilities: Toyota inspectors examine a finished car coming off the assembly line in the company's Miyazaki, Japan, factory.*

Producing 134 door panels, 37 interior car components, and 12 different fabric materials, Diane Kokkinos and her team at the Textron Port Huron plant knew they needed a better way to reduce finished goods inventory.[38] Then a consultant introduced them to the Japanese *Heijunka* system. *Heijunka* is a system for scheduling what is produced based on the specific orders that come into the plant every day.

As the plant receives orders electronically from DaimlerChrysler plants in Michigan, Missouri, and Austria, plant employees fill out *heijunka* cards. Each card contains a specification such as the number of parts (for example, door panels) ordered, and their models, colors, and fabrics. Employees then prioritize the cards by shipping times and place them in a special box. Employees schedule production one card at a time, based on the cards' priorities. In addition to signaling employees what their production line is to produce, the *heijunka* cards show employees which of the plant's production processes they're going to have to use for that order. Based on that information, the employees can complete *kanban* cards. The *kanban* cards signal each production area to order the appropriate supplies, such as paint or materials. Of course, the *heijunka* system, while important, is only part of an integrated, lean manufacturing system that makes the Port Huron plant a consistent award winner. For example, the *heijunka* system itself would be useless without the plant's other lean manufacturing processes, such as quick machine changeover times. ■■■■

Computer-Aided Design and Manufacturing

Computer-aided design (CAD) is a computerized process for designing new products or modifying existing ones. Designers sketch and modify designs on a computer screen, usually with an electronic pencil. CAD facilitates the actual design of the item, makes it easier to modify existing products, and lets designers expose their designs to simulated stresses such as wind resistance.

Computer-aided manufacturing (CAM) uses computers to plan and program the production process or equipment. For example, CAM allows for computerized control of tool movement and cutting speed so that a machine can carry out several sequential operations on a part, all under the guidance of the computer-assisted system.

Operations managers often use CAD and CAM together. For example, with the design already in place within the CAD system, the computer "knows" a component's specifications and can thereby "tell" the production equipment how to cut and machine it. Companies are using the Internet today to expand the potential of such computer-based systems. For example, consider Motorola's plant in Mansfield, Massachusetts.

> **computer-aided design (CAD)** ■ *a computerized process for designing new products, modifying existing ones, or simulating conditions that may affect the designs.*

> **computer-aided manufacturing (CAM)** ■ *a computerized process for planning and programming production processes and equipment.*

When Motorola's Mansfield, Massachusetts, plant got the green light to produce new cable modems, the plant manager knew he needed a faster and cheaper way to get the engineering documents to the assemblers on the plant floor.[39] The manager and his staff created an internal plant intranet. Now with a $500 digital camera to take pictures of each component, digitized images of the parts to be built are simply placed online, along with step-by-step instructions for assembly and testing. This not only eliminates having to produce all those expensive paper engineering drawings; it also helps Motorola update its drawings instantaneously. ■■■■

Flexible Manufacturing Systems

In many firms today, flexible manufacturing systems are at the heart of being world-class. A flexible manufacturing system (FMS) is "a system in which groups of production machines are connected by automated materials-handling and transfer machines, and integrated into a computer system."[40] Computers route parts and components to the appropriate machines, select and load the proper machine tools, and then direct the machines to perform the required operations. Computerized automated guided vehicles (AGV) then move the items from machine to machine. Often, there is a com-

> **flexible manufacturing system (FMS)** ■ *the organization of groups of production machines that are connected by automated materials-handling and transfer machines, and integrated into a computer system for the purpose of combining the benefits of made-to-order flexibility and mass-production efficiency.*

puter-guided cart system. It picks up and delivers tools and parts from multiple workstations. Systems like these depend on automation and robots. Automation is the automatic operation of a system, process, or machine. A robot is a programmable machine capable of manipulating items and designed to move materials, parts, or specialized devices through programmed motions.

Several things contribute to the manufacturing system's flexibility. Computerized instructions reduce machine setup times. Operators can quickly retool each machine to produce a variety of parts. Reduced setup times cut required manufacturing lead times. Automated guided vehicles move parts with relative speed and efficiency. And the firm can respond more quickly to new competing products or changing consumer tastes by using CAD to redesign products and CAM to reprogram its machines. Toshiba's president, Funio Sato, said the aim of flexible manufacturing "is to push Toshiba's two dozen factories to adapt faster to markets . . . customers wanted choices. They wanted a washing machine or TV set that was precisely right for their needs. We needed variety, not mass production."[41]

Flexible manufacturing helps Toshiba combine the advantages of customized, one-at-a-time production with mass production's efficiency. At the Toshiba plant in Ome, Japan, for instance, workers efficiently assemble nine word processor models on one line and 20 laptop computer models on another.[42] Such flexibility helps Toshiba be responsive to customer requirements. The National Bicycle Industrial Company, a subsidiary of electronics giant Matsushita, is another example.[43] With only 20 employees, National Bicycle's factory can produce more than a million variations of 18 bicycle models, each custom-made to a customer's unique requirements.

Computer-Integrated Manufacturing

Many firms integrate automation, JIT, flexible manufacturing, and CAD/CAM into one self-regulating production system. Computer-integrated manufacturing (CIM), is defined as the total integration of all production-related business activities through the use of computer systems.[44] It gives the firm a competitive advantage based on speed, flexibility, quality, and low cost. Figure 15.14 summarizes this integrative process.

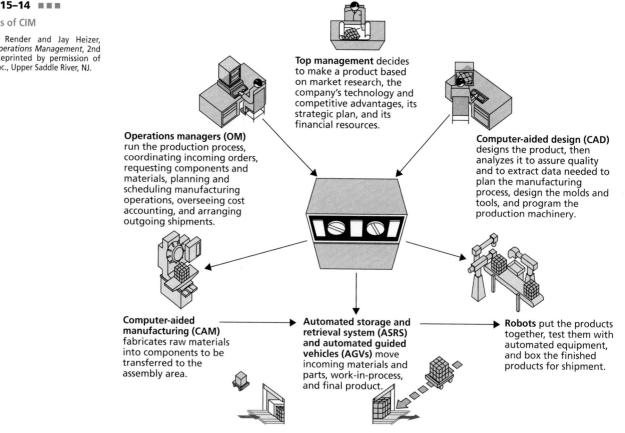

Top management decides to make a product based on market research, the company's technology and competitive advantages, its strategic plan, and its financial resources.

Operations managers (OM) run the production process, coordinating incoming orders, requesting components and materials, planning and scheduling manufacturing operations, overseeing cost accounting, and arranging outgoing shipments.

Computer-aided design (CAD) designs the product, then analyzes it to assure quality and to extract data needed to plan the manufacturing process, design the molds and tools, and program the production machinery.

Computer-aided manufacturing (CAM) fabricates raw materials into components to be transferred to the assembly area.

Automated storage and retrieval system (ASRS) and automated guided vehicles (AGVs) move incoming materials and parts, work-in-process, and final product.

Robots put the products together, test them with automated equipment, and box the finished products for shipment.

approximation, a firm might have to boost sales by $3 to $4 to produce the same bounce in profits that cutting purchasing costs by $1 would produce. Furthermore, the quality of the finished product is usually no better than the quality of its components. You would be very disappointed with your new Dell Computer if the disk drive kept breaking down. Supply chain management helps ensure that the parts you buy are of acceptable quality.

There are other advantages. For example, at GE's power systems division, the firm's Web-based supply chain management system lets its customers monitor the assembly of the huge turbines they ordered as the turbines move through the production process. These power-generating turbines cost $35 million each and contain thousands of parts. Catching errors early and being able to make changes more expeditiously mean big cost savings for the customer and for GE.[55]

Supplier Partnering Two main trends characterize supply chain management. *Supplier partnering* is one. Supplier partnering means choosing to do business with a limited number of suppliers, with the aim of building relationships that improve quality and reliability rather than just improve costs. Supplier partnering often means eliminating the usual competitive bidding process. Rather than getting competitive bids, the customer-company decides to work with a few supplier-partners.

Supplier partnering produces several advantages. The customer company may work with the partner-suppliers to help insure a cost-effective design. At firms like Wal-Mart, supplier partnering means letting the suppliers literally link into the company's point of purchase and inventory systems. This reduces inventory costs, improves just-in-time performance, and reduces administrative costs. Supplier partnering can reduce the customer-company's administration costs (for instance, fewer purchasing agents are required). It can also improve product quality (for instance by enabling the customer-company to insist that the supplier be ISO 9000 certified), squeeze waste out of the supply chain, and still let the firm push for cost reductions (although, perhaps, not quite so hard).

Some companies extend this partnering concept to their distributors. The process utilizes *channel assembly*. With channel assembly, a company such as IBM doesn't send finished products to its distributors, but instead it sends them components and modules. The distributors thus become an extension of IBM's production process. When a retail store calls the distributor for a particular IBM product, the distributor simply plugs together the required components and ships it off.

Internet Purchasing Internet-based purchasing is a second characteristic of supply chain management today. Internet purchasing (also called e-procurement) may simply mean letting vendors interact with the company via the Net (for instance, letting the firms place the order and acknowledge it via the Web). Let's see what GE has done.

> **supplier partnering** ■ *choosing to do business with a limited number of suppliers, with the aim of building relationships that improve quality and reliability rather than just improve costs.*

> **channel assembly** ■ *channel assembly means organizing the product assembly process so that the company doesn't send finished products to its distribution channel partners (such as warehouses, distributors, and retailers), but instead sends the partners components and modules. The partners thus become an extension of the firm's product assembly process.*

MANAGEMENT IN ACTION

GE Streamlines Its Supply Chain

Streamlining its supply chain is one reason why GE is putting most of its administrative operations on the Internet. "We'll have the capability to deal with virtually all of our suppliers electronically," says David Hay, global product manager of GE global exchange.[56] For example, like most large buyers, GE now takes about 60 days to pay a vendor. During that time, the vendor (needing the cash) usually sells its debt to a factoring company. The factor lends the vendor the money and then collects it from GE. The factor, of course, receives a handsome fee for its trouble. With its new Internet-based purchasing system, GE plans to reduce the amount of time it takes to pay the vendor to about 15 days, thus eliminating the need for the factor. By splitting the previously required factoring fee with the vendor, GE estimates it can cut 12% per year from its accounts payable costs.

Increasingly, companies are creating what amounts to their own eBay-type purchasing Web sites or bazaars. They use these sites to allow potential vendors to bid for their business. The thousand-pound gorilla here is the new Web-based purchasing exchange created by America's big three automakers—GM, Ford, and DaimlerChrysler. Every year, these firms will be making about $250 billion worth of purchases via this exchange. As one Ford vice president puts it, "This will be the world's largest Internet company and trade exchange."[57]

Enterprise Resource Planning

Enterprise resource planning (ERP) helps firms capitalize on world-class applications like supply chain management, computer-integrated manufacturing, CAD-CAM, and flexible manufacturing. As we saw in Chapter 14, ERP is a package of business software systems that allow companies to integrate the majority of their business processes and produce and access information on a real-time basis.[58] The accompanying Managing Without Boundaries feature shows how Dell computer uses ERP.

MANAGING WITHOUT BOUNDARIES

Using ERP

ERP software integrates and automates the organizational decision-making and control process. The ERP software and its associated databases link together and integrate all or most of the business's functions, including production and material management, shipping, finance/accounting, HR, and supply chain elements such as distributors and suppliers. Placing an order with a firm using ERP triggers a sequence of automated, interrelated activities. For example, when you order a Dell Computer, Dell's ERP software posts the order and signals manufacturing to plan to produce your PC.

The ERP also signals suppliers (such as the one producing the monitor you want) to prepare to have one picked up. The ERP notifies UPS to pick up your PC from Dell (and the monitor from the supplier) on a particular day and to deliver it all to you, as ordered. At the same time, the ERP notifies the accounting department to send you a bill, and it lists your PC's specifications on the Dell customer service system in case you call or link in with a question. For many firms, it is ERP that makes managing without boundaries possible.

■■■ MANAGING SERVICES

Currently, about 75% of people work in service-producing industries. These industries include transportation; communications; wholesale or retail trade; finance or insurance; government; and the legal, educational, and health sectors. Managing services is, therefore, a growth industry itself.

Managing services is especially challenging because it's different from creating tangible products.[59] First, a service (such as legal advice) is generally created the instant it's used; it can't be produced and held in stock awaiting demand. Second, workers provide most services with little or no supervision: There's usually no supervisor hovering around when the arrogant waiter ruins a customer's meal, for example. The techniques we discussed earlier (such as facilities layout) are equally applicable to most service firms. However, the special nature of services means that some special management skills are also required. We'll discuss these in this final section.

service management ■ *a total organizationwide approach that makes quality of service the business's number one driving force.*

Karl Albrecht, a famous service management expert, defines service management as "a total organizational approach that makes quality of service, as perceived by the customer, the number one driving force for the operation of the business."[60]

Service management thus means more than just managing a service firm. Certainly, Donald Carty is a service manager insofar as he is CEO of American Airlines, a service firm. But service management also means managing an enterprise in such a way that quality of service becomes the basic standard for evaluating everything the company does or should do.

Why Service Management Is Important

Everyone today has to fight harder for customers. Service management is important for at least three specific reasons.

Service Is a Competitive Advantage In Chapter 5 ("Strategic Management"), we saw that one way for a company to compete is to differentiate its product or service by creating something that is perceived as unique.[61] Many firms today differentiate themselves, at least in part, on customer service. For example, Crown Cork and Seal custom-builds a manufacturing plant near each of its major customers, thereby providing customized services for each one of them.

Bad Service Leads to Lost Customers Good service is also important because companies never hear from most of their dissatisfied customers; they just lose them.

This point is illustrated by a classic series of studies undertaken by the Technical Assistance Research Program, Inc. (TARP), in Washington, D.C.[62] It found that the average business never even hears from 96% of its unhappy customers. In other words, if four people complain to a company, there are probably another 96 or so unhappy customers who don't. However, TARP also found that although the company may not hear from these unhappy customers directly, they are out there spreading the word. Each of them will tell an average of 9 or 10 people about the problems they had with the firm. So in addition to reducing its competitive edge, bad service will siphon off many current and potential customers.

Customer Defections Drain Profits Effective service management is also crucial because in most industries, the longer a firm keeps a customer, the more profit it stands to make from that customer.[63]

There are three reasons for this. First, long-term customers tend to spend more than new customers. Second, they tend to generate profits in other ways, such as referrals. Third, customers generally become more profitable over time. For example, it usually costs a credit card company about $51 to recruit a new customer. If that customer then stays only about a year and uses the card once or twice before leaving in disgust over an error on a bill, the credit card company might not even earn back the $51 acquisition cost. On the other hand, if the company can keep that customer for several years, his or her value to the company rises because the customer generates a profit in each of those years through credit card fees. Even world-class service companies aren't immune from occasional service problems as McDonald's experience demonstrates.

MANAGEMENT IN ACTION   McDonald's Service Problems

McDonald's recently reportedly found that "on any given day, 11% of McDonald's customers are dissatisfied with their visit and take the time to share their complaint with the restaurant."[64] Furthermore, "more than half of these dissatisfied customers reduce their visits to McDonald's as a result of how their complaint was mishandled." The dissatisfied customers also tell "as many as 10 other people about their unsatisfactory experience."[65]

The Wall Street Journal, which reviewed the McDonald's documents, reported that the top five McDonald's customer complaints in the U.S. were "rude employees; being out of happy meal toys; slow service; missing product/wrong order; and unclean restaurants."[66] McDonald's reacted quickly with an initiative that included establishing customer recovery teams to improve service at local stores. ■■■

■ ■ *McDonald's prides itself on the kind of first-class service evident here in the Johannesburg store, South Africa's first McDonald's.*

Karl Albrecht's Service Triangle

Most firms, like McDonalds, work hard to avoid and/or rectify service problems. The actual techniques of service management focus on three core concepts: the *moment of truth*, *service cycles*, and the *service triangle*.[67]

moment of truth ■ *the instant when the customer comes into contact with any aspect of a business and, based on that contact, forms an opinion about the quality of your service or product.*

The Moment of Truth The core concept in service management is the **moment of truth**, which service management expert Karl Albrecht defines as "that precise instant when the customer comes into contact with any aspect of your business and, on the basis of that contact, forms an opinion about the quality of your service and, potentially, the quality of your product."[68] It is "the basic atom of service, the smallest indivisible unit of value delivered to the customer."[69] When you as a customer call FedEx, you experience moments of truth, precise instants when you come into contact with any aspect of the business—as when you first reach the Fedex call system, speak to a rep, have the package picked up, and call to track its whereabouts.

On the basis of those accumulated moments of truth, you then form an opinion about the quality of the service you have received and, potentially, about the quality of the product as well.

Here are some typical moments of truth in a supermarket shopping experience:

1. You look for a place to park in the supermarket's lot.
2. You walk to the supermarket from your car.
3. You look for a shopping cart.
4. You get your check approved.
5. You ask a clerk how to find a product.
6. You pick up your item.
7. You wait in the checkout line.
8. Your order is added up.
9. Your items are put in the bag.
10. You take your purchases back to your car.

Even in this simplified example, consider how many opportunities the supermarket's management has to create a good (or bad) impression. If the supermarket was interested in improving service quality, it would have to manage the service experience in such a way that *each of those moments of truth* proved to be as positive an experience as possible. How might management do this? By taking actions like reducing waiting time at the checkout lines, expediting the check approval process, and ensuring that stock clerks are ready and eager to answer your questions.

Indeed, when the moments of truth go unmanaged, the quality of service quickly declines. In other words, if the supermarket manager doesn't actually stop and consider what his or her customer's typical moments of truth are and then make sure that they are positive, they will likely be unhappy experiences. In today's highly competitive world, that could be deadly. Management may stock the shelves with the finest products and even offer competitive prices. But if the customer's experience is bad, the business will lose out to its competitors down the road.

cycle of service ■ *includes all the moments of truth experienced by a typical customer, from first to last.*

The Cycle of Service Albrecht, therefore, suggests thinking of the customer's moments of truth in terms of a **cycle of service**. It begins with the first moment in which a customer comes in contact with any aspect of the firm. It then includes, in sequence, every other moment of truth.

The manager and his or her team should map out a cycle of service for three reasons. First, by carefully thinking through all contacts from beginning to end, they can compile a complete list of all the moments of truth. Second, once identified, the manager can focus on improving each moment. Third, doing so enables management to develop a comprehensive plan for managing the entire service experience. This means creating a service strategy and attending to the service people and the service system.

The Service Triangle Albrecht says it's therefore useful to think of a successful service management effort in terms of a service triangle. The triangle highlights the idea that the firm's service *strategy*, *people*, and *systems* must work together to achieve service quality. Here's how Albrecht describes each of the three elements:

■ *A well-conceived service strategy.* Outstanding organizations have a unifying idea about what they do. This service concept, or service strategy . . . directs the attention of the people in the organization toward the real priorities of the customer. It becomes . . . the nucleus of the message to be transmitted to the customer. For example, McDonald's service strategy focuses on "quality, service, cleanliness, and price."

- *Customer-oriented front-line people.* [T]he managers of such organizations have [also] encouraged and helped the people who deliver the service to keep their attention fastened on the needs of the customer. . . . This leads to a level of responsiveness, attentiveness, and willingness to help that marks the service as superior in the customer's mind. . . .
- *Customer-friendly systems.* The delivery system that backs up the service people is truly designed for the convenience of the customer rather than the convenience of the organization. The physical facilities, policies, procedures, methods, and communication processes all say to the customer, "This apparatus is here to meet your needs."[70]

Jan Carlson's efforts at SAS Airlines a number of years ago provide an example. On becoming CEO, Carlson decided to base SAS's competitive advantage on customer service. His new strategy was to give business travelers top-notch service for which they were willing to pay top-notch prices—special business-class seats and service, for instance.

Carlson knew that to implement his strategy, he had to modify both the people and the systems at SAS. For example, the SAS people had to be specially trained, and they had to be empowered to cut through red tape to help customers. In terms of the systems, Carlson had to eliminate first-class service, expand business-class service, institute new check-in systems for business customers, and install special business equipment that his customers could use.

How to Implement a Service Management Program

According to service management experts Karl Albrecht and Ron Zemke, creating a service-oriented, customer-driven organization involves a five-step process.[71]

Step I: The Service Audit First, conduct a service audit, preferably using a customer report card. The customer report card lists the service attributes for which your customers are looking, as well as the relative weights or priorities of each attribute and how the customers score your company on each of them. If possible, include your competitors' scores on each attribute for comparison purposes. One way to obtain the information is to conduct in-depth interviews with a sample of your (and your competitor's) customers.[72]

Table 15.2 shows an example of a report card for the Ten-Plex Movie Theater. As you can see, the movie theater's customer research found eight service attributes typical theatergoers look for in the Ten-Plex Theater. These attributes include convenient parking, first-run movies, and a clean theater. In the next column, each of these attributes gets a priority ranking. For example, convenient parking, safe parking, and first-run movies are all high-priority services, whereas "courteous clerks" is a lower priority. Finally, the customer report card includes a column called "Our Score." Management can use this space to record how customers rated the Downtown Ten-Plex Movie Theater on each of these service attributes.

customer report card ■ *lists the service attributes for which customers are looking as well as the relative weights or priorities of each attribute and how the customers score your company on each of them.*

TABLE 15–2	Report Card for Downtown Ten-Plex Movie Theater	
Desirable Service Attributes	**Customer Priority**	**Our Score (Based on Audit)**
Convenient parking	High	Medium
Safe parking	High	Low
First-run movies	High	High
Clean theater	High	Medium
Unobstructed view	High	High
Comfortable seats	Medium	Medium
Courteous clerks	Low	Low
Short waits for tickets	Medium	Low

Step 2: Strategy Development Next, formulate a service strategy, which has been defined as "a distinctive formula for delivering service; such a strategy is keyed to a well-chosen benefit premise that's valuable to the customer and that establishes an effective competitive position."[73]

In simplest terms, the service strategy should answer the question, "Why should the customer choose us?" It should be clear and brief enough for management to easily communicate it to the firm's employees. McDonald's strategic emphasis on "quality, service, cleanliness, and price" and Carlson's SAS strategy emphasis on "high-quality service for business travelers" are examples.

Step 3: Education The next step in implementing a service program is to spread the "gospel" of service throughout the company. At companies like SAS, wall-to-wall training is often the method of choice. This means doing short bursts of 100% participation training. The firm trains everyone at about the same time during a one- or two-day period.

Step 4: Implementation The next phase is the "implementation of grassroots improvements in the way the organization produces and delivers its service products."[74]

Several techniques are useful here. *Service quality teams* serve as a source of specific recommendations on how to improve service and the moments of truth. The teams also function as conduits to get information back to their departments. The *application lab* is another implementation technique. Here, a trainer (often a member of the firm's human resources department) meets with a department to discuss the group's service mission, and to identify operational aspects the department would like to improve.

The heart of the implementation is to *redesign the firm's service systems* using what you know about the moments of truth. For example, in one bank, the check-cashing process required that you stand in one line to get a check approved and then that you stand in another, longer line to pick up your money. A process like this would upset customers even with the best, most customer-oriented employees. The bank streamlined the process.

Redesigning service systems can involve making many changes. Grassroots improvements might include modifying the firm's organization—for instance, so a customer doesn't get sales calls from four different divisions. You might change the phone systems (to avoid having to deal with too many voice commands). Implementation may also mean changing customer rules and processes, including serial procedures (the actual sequence of steps used to handle the customer's problem).

Step 5: Maintenance—Making the Change Permanent Making the change permanent requires all of a manager's planning, organizing, leading, and controlling skills. For example, making high-quality service the norm requires leadership—setting the right tone and instituting the right incentives. And it requires control—perhaps polling customers to ensure that the service attributes (such as speed of delivery) have changed.

SUMMARY ■■■

1. Operations management is the process of managing the resources required to produce an organization's goods and services. The direct production resources of a firm are often called the five Ps of operations and production management: people, plants, parts, processes, and planning and control systems.

2. Any production system consists of inputs, a conversion system, and outputs. Inputs are the primary resources used in the direct manufacture of the product or service. The conversion system converts those inputs into useful products or services called outputs.

3. The production system is the heart of the operation. Four production design system decisions include the facility or plant location, the type of production processes that will be used, the layout of the plant or facility, and the layout of the production system itself.

4. Production planning is the process of deciding what products to produce, and where, when, and how to produce them. Production control is the process of ensuring that the specified production plans or schedules are being met.

5. The production schedule is often presented on a chart that shows what operations are to be carried out and when. Network planning and control methods are used to plan and control complex projects. Purchasing departments buy the materials and parts the firm needs to conduct its business.

6. Inventory management ensures that the firm has adequate inventories of all needed parts and supplies within the constraint of minimizing total inventory costs. Many quantitative and nonquantitative systems are available for managing inventory; ABC and EOQ systems are two of the most popular.

7. Quality reflects how well a product or service meets customer needs. Many firms use a process called designing for manu-

facturability to improve quality. Quality control involves a total, companywide effort. A number of quality-control techniques are used to monitor and control product quality, including inspection procedures and acceptance sampling.

8. World-class companies compete based on quality, productivity, and responsiveness in an intensely competitive global environment. World-class manufacturers use modern production techniques and progressive management systems to boost manufacturing productivity, quality, and flexibility. These production techniques and management systems include TQM, JIT manufacturing, CAD and CAM, FMS, CIM, and mass customization.

9. Supply chain management helps the firm achieve more efficient, integrated operations. Supplies partnering involves choosing to deal with a limited number of partners with whom the firm develops closer relationships. Channel assembly means having partners in the supply chain assemble modules to suit their customers' needs.

10. Service management is "a total organizational approach that makes quality of service, as perceived by the customer, the number one driving force for the operation of the business." The actual techniques of service management focus on three core concepts: the *moment of truth, service cycles*, and the *service triangle*. Creating a service-oriented, customer-driven organization involves a five-step process: service audit, strategy development, education, implementation, and maintenance.

KEY TERMS ■■■

operations management 391
input 391
conversion system 391
output 391
intermittent production system 393
mass customization 393
continuous production processes 394
facility layout 394
product layout 394
process layout 395
fixed-position layout 395
cellular manufacturing layout 395
operations or production planning 396
operations or production control 396
Gantt chart 396
network planning and control methods 396

events 397
activities 397
critical path 397
inventory management 398
ordering, or setup, costs 398
acquisition costs 398
inventory-holding (carrying) costs 399
stockout costs 399
economic order quantity (EOQ) 399
quality 400
ISO 9000 400
total quality management (TQM) 400
Malcolm Baldrige Award 401
acceptance sampling 402
designing for manufacturability 403
concurrent engineering 405

just-in-time (JIT) 408
lean or value-added manufacturing 408
computer-aided design (CAD) 409
computer-aided manufacturing (CAM) 409
flexible manufacturing system (FMS) 409
automation 410
computer-integrated manufacturing (CIM) 410
supply chain management 412
supplier partnering 413
channel assembly 413
service management 414
moment of truth 416
cycle of service 416
customer report card 417
service strategy 418

SKILLS AND STUDY MATERIALS

COMPANION WEBSITE ■■■

We invite you to visit the Dessler Companion Website at **www.prenhall.com/dessler** for this chapter's Internet resources.

EXPERIENTIAL EXERCISES ■■■

1. The people managing your school cafeteria (or other restaurant) have discovered that you know all about rating a production facility's effectiveness, and they want to make use of your services. In teams of four or five students, visit your school cafeteria or other restaurant. Use the RPA rating sheet and what you learned in this chapter to assess the cafeteria's effectiveness. Then briefly present your findings in class.

2. You probably will not want to attempt exercise 1 (evaluating your school cafeteria) until you've laid out the schedule for your project. In teams of four or five students, create a Gantt chart for the cafeteria evaluation project.

3. After you have evaluated the school cafeteria, you'll probably identify problems that you want management to address. Use a fishbone/cause-and-effect diagram to analyze the problem.

4. List the school cafeteria's moments of truth, and write a detailed service plan, including a service audit.

5. Your college's cafeteria wants to reduce what it spends on its inventory of paper goods by determining the optimal number of paper plates to obtain per order. Its annual demand for paper plates is 50,000. The ordering cost is $10 per order. The holding cost per plate per year is $0.05. Using the EOQ model, how many plates should the cafeteria manager order each time?

CASE STUDY ■■■

THE PROCESS STRATEGY AT WHEELED COACH

Wheeled Coach, based in Winter Park, Florida, is the world's largest manufacturer of ambulances.[75] Working four 10-hour days, 350 employees make only custom-made ambulances: Virtually every vehicle is different. Wheeled Coach accommodates the marketplace by providing a wide variety of options and an engineering staff accustomed to innovation and custom design. Continuing growth, which now requires that more than 20 ambulances roll off the assembly line each week, makes designing the production process a challenge. Wheeled Coach's response has been to build a focused factory. In other words, it builds nothing but ambulances. Within a focused factory, Wheeled Coach established work cells for every major module feeding an assembly line, including aluminum bodies, electrical wiring harnesses, interior cabinets, windows, painting, and upholstery.

Every work cell feeds the assembly line on schedule, just in time for installation. The chassis, usually that of a Ford truck, moves to a station at which the aluminum body is mounted. Then the vehicle is moved to painting. Following a custom paint job, it moves to the assembly line, where it will spend seven days. During each of the seven workdays, each work cell delivers its respective module to the appropriate position on the assembly line. During the first day, electrical wiring is installed; on the second day, the unit moves forward to the station at which cabinetry is delivered and installed, then to a window and lighting station, on to upholstery, to fit and finish, to further customizing, and finally to inspection and rote testing.

Discussion Questions

1. Why do you think major auto manufacturers do not build ambulances?

2. What is a possible alternative production process to the seven-day assembly line that Wheeled Coach currently uses?

3. Why is it more efficient for the work cells to prepare modules and deliver them to the assembly line than it would be to produce the component (such as the dashboard) as part of the line?

4. List the reasons why you believe Wheeled Coach is (and is not) a world-class manufacturer.

YOU BE THE CONSULTANT ■■■

JETBLUE'S TALKATIVE FLIGHT CREW

jetBlue **AIRWAYS** Superior customer service is one of the foundations on which JetBlue's managers built their business plan. JetBlue's basic strategy is to keep cost down while providing superior service. To that end, it buys only brand-new planes, gives all passengers leather seats, and equips each seat with a monitor that provides dozens of satellite TV programs. To reduce some of the discomfort of waiting on long lines, JetBlue also introduced a hand-held wireless check-in service at its main JFK airport terminal. Specially trained staff are able to check in passengers, print boarding passes, and check luggage virtually anywhere inside or outside the terminal without the passengers having to wait on long lines.

That is why the following story (repeated verbatim from an article in the magazine *Advertising Age*) raised some eyebrows at JetBlue.[76] A reporter for *Advertising Age* and his sister had to fly back to New York from Fort Lauderdale, and they decided to use JetBlue, in part to check out its stellar reputation for high-quality customer service. (JetBlue was listed as the number 2 airline for customer service by both Zagat's and Condé Nast Traveler.) Here's what he says happened:

Beginning with our arrival at JFK, the airline lived up to its advance billing. The woman who checked us in was infec-

tiously friendly. The plane was clean and modern. We took off on time. I tracked the market on my live TV. Then came the flight attendants.

My sister is a nervous flyer who pops a sleeping pill before boarding a plane to sleep through the flight. She had warned me not to talk to her but didn't warn the off-duty flight attendants directly in front of us. After takeoff, members of the on-duty crew joined them. Their discussion was boisterous, but what bothered us was the content. They were complaining about their customers. They complained about our eating habits, our hygiene, our lack of appreciation. One wished for an eject button to rid the plane of its more obnoxious fliers. By the time we got off the flight, [my sister] was steamed. When an employee standing outside the door said, "I hope you enjoyed your flight," she replied, curtly, "actually, we didn't." "You should tell us about it," he said. "I will," she answered, "I plan to send a letter to the president."

"I'm the president," he said. "Tell me about it now." The man was JetBlue president and chief operating officer Dave Barger, recruited by founder CEO David Neeleman from Continental Airlines. He apologized and promised to follow up. They exchanged business cards. Within days, his office called to say the airline would refund the full cost of her ticket.

True story. And it drives home the lessons that front-line employees and the customer experience are far more crucial to a brand's reputation than paid advertising.

The reporter continues: When I called Barger, he remembered his encounter with my sister, and [he] said he talked to her because it was clear she had not had a good experience. "We have orientation sessions with our crew members every five weeks in Fort Lauderdale and we spend a lot of time talking about the brand," Barger said. "We try to provide tools to the front-line staff to take the sting out of a [a bad] situation. It's amazing how much the customer is just looking for someone who cares."

Discussion Questions

1. Do you think Barger handled this situation correctly? Why or why not?

2. Based on your experience as an airline passenger with any airline, list JetBlue's moment of truth. Then create a form for a service audit, and provide an outline of a detailed service plan for the company.

3. Exactly what would you do to make sure a problem like this did not happen again? If you had been Barger, what would you have done to the crew members involved?

16 Managing Entrepreneurial Organizations

CHAPTER OBJECTIVES

After studying this chapter and the case exercises at the end, you should be able to:

1. Explain why you do (or do not) have the traits to be an entrepreneur.

2. List what the entrepreneur is doing right and doing wrong with respect to starting the business.

3. List what the person did right and did wrong with respect to buying a franchise.

4. Conduct an informal business feasibility study.

5. Recommend a start-up structure for the new business.

6. List the activity areas for which the new business owner should establish controls.

THE MANAGEMENT CHALLENGE

Can Shoshana Berger Get ReadyMade *Magazine Funded?*

As 33-year-old entrepreneur Shoshana Berger knowingly put it, making her new magazine succeed will "take a whole lot of luck and a whole lot of pluck."[1] Her magazine, ReadyMade (**www.readymademag.com**) *is a sort of* Martha Stewart Living *for a younger, hipper audience. The first year's editions contained advice for projects such as beds made out of meat carts, fruit bowls made out of melted LPs, and a lamp made from an old hard drive.*

She and co-founder Grace Hawthorne started ReadyMade *with about $150,000 borrowed from friends and relatives. Within a year, the magazine had a total circulation of about 50,000, with 10,000 paid subscribers, healthy newsstand sales, and $385,000 in net profits. ACE hardware, Levi's, and JVC were some of the big name advertisers in early issues. Contributors suggest do-it-yourself projects on ReadyMade's Web site, and local (San Francisco-based) interns provide marketing and design. Shoshana is enormously optimistic about ReadyMade's prospects. She and Grace are working on brand extensions such as a book based on the same offbeat do-it-yourself theme. One of their first challenges is developing a business plan and getting it funded. The question is, how should they do that and where should they turn for funding?*

As we'll see in this chapter, starting and managing a new business is not quite the same as managing a big, going concern. Many new skills are required. Chapters 1–15 focused on providing you with the basic skills all managers need to manage organizations. Now, in this and the following chapter, we turn to managing small entrepreneurial businesses and global businesses. This chapter will provide you with the basic skills managers need to start and manage smaller businesses. The main topics we will discuss include entrepreneurship today, what it takes to be an entrepreneur, getting started in business, and how entrepreneurs plan, organize, lead, and control.

▪▪▪ ENTREPRENEURSHIP TODAY

Shoshana Berger is a classic entrepreneur. Entrepreneurship is the creation of a business for the purpose of gain or growth under conditions of risk and uncertainty.[2] An entrepreneur is thus someone who creates new businesses under risky conditions.[3] Entrepreneurship "requires a vision and the passion and commitment to lead others in the pursuit of that vision [and] a willingness to take calculated risks."[4] Figure 16.1 neatly sums up what entrepreneurship is all about. In the pantheon of management, entrepreneurs are unique. Entrepreneurs "build something of value from practically nothing."[5] Innovation, value-creation, growth, and uniqueness characterize the entrepreneur's efforts.

entrepreneurship ▪ *the creation of a business for the purpose of gain or growth under conditions of risk and uncertainty.*

entrepreneur ▪ *someone who creates new businesses for the purpose of gain or growth under conditions of risk and uncertainty.*

Entrepreneurs and Small Business Management

Since entrepreneurs create something out of nothing, it stands to reason that the firms they create usually start small. Most people therefore tend to associate entrepreneurs with small businesses managers, although that link is, in reality, a bit tenuous. David Neeleman, JetBlue's founder and CEO, is certainly an entrepreneur, although the business he's running is not (and never really was) very small. On the other hand, someone who buys a successful dry cleaner and runs it competently but not innovatively probably is not an entrepreneur in the strictest sense. That person is a small-business owner/manager. Small business management refers to planning, organizing, leading, and controlling a small business. The U.S. Small Business Administration (SBA) sets size limits by industry when it defines which businesses are small enough to be eligible for SBA guaranteed loans. Generally, manufacturing or wholesaling firms with fewer than 100 employees are "small businesses." Retailing or service firms with annual sales under $5 million are small businesses.

small business management ▪ *planning, organizing, leading, and controlling a small business.*

Successful entrepreneurs like Neeleman tend to be good small business managers, since the firms they start either grow successfully or die. However, successful small business managers needn't necessarily exhibit the flair for creating new businesses under risky conditions that is the entrepreneur's forte. We'll focus first on entrepreneurship in this chapter, and then on the techniques small business owners use to successfully manage and grow small businesses.

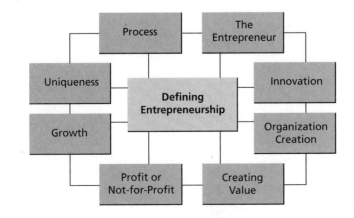

◀ **FIGURE 16–1** ▪▪▪

Common Themes in Definitions of Entrepreneurship

Sources: From Mary Coulter, *Entrepreneurship in Action* (Upper Saddle River, NJ: Prentice Hall, 2001), p. 4; based on W. B. Gartner, "What Are We Talking About When We Talk About Entrepreneurship?" *Journal of Business Venturing* 5, 1990, pp. 15–28.

The Environment of Entrepreneurship

Entrepreneurs like taking risks, but that doesn't mean they are foolish. The good ones continuously size up their opportunities and constraints—their environments.

Some environments are more conducive to entrepreneurship than others. The level of *economic freedom* is one consideration.[6] Some countries (and locales) make it easier to be entrepreneurial than do others. Table 16.1 shows a portion of the Heritage Foundation's index of economic freedom. For instance, in Hong Kong, Singapore, Ireland, and the United States, entrepreneurs encounter relatively few barriers in starting, financing, and growing their businesses. At the other extreme, pity the entrepreneur who wants to start a business in Cuba, Iraq, or North Korea. Here, the combination of governmental and bureaucratic impediments and high taxes are enough to stifle almost any new business idea.

Economic freedom means that companies in some countries also find it easier to *streamline*, *downsize*, and *fire employees at will*, and this affects new business creation, too. For example, when DuPont cut 47,000 employees, 30% returned in some temporary capacity, or as vendors or contractors.[7] In the United States, downsizing triggered the outsourcing of various activities, and entrepreneurial former employees created businesses to fulfill these needs.

Periods of increased economic activity also tend to be associated with increased business creation. As the U.S. economy boomed in the late 1990s, the number of businesses created jumped in 2000 (see Figure 16.2). Business creation also outpaced the number of firms that closed down. However, the latter rose, too, perhaps because boom times also mean that struggling entrepreneurs have other employment opportunities to pursue.

Technological advances (whether steam engine, railroad, telephone, computer, or the Web) also trigger bursts of business creation. Technological advances tend to reflect the level of innovation at any point in time. For example, the rate of patents

	TABLE 16–1	The Index of Economic Freedom: Selected Locales

Overall Rank	Country	Overall Score*
1	Hong Kong	1.35
2	Singapore	1.55
4	Ireland	1.80
4	United States	1.80
9	United Kingdom	1.85
45	France	2.70
60	Mexico	2.90
72	Saudi Arabia	3.00
121	People's Republic of China	3.55
131	Russia	3.70
153	Cuba	4.75
155	Iraq	5.00
155	North Korea	5.00

*Low overall score means higher economic freedom.

Source: © 2001 The Heritage Foundation, 214 Massachusetts Ave NE, Washington, DC 20002-4999, at **www.heritage.org**.

Business Turnover, 1990–2000

THOUSANDS

650

500

350

1990 1992 1994 1996 1998 2000 est.

● Employer firm births ■ Employer firm terminations

◀ **FIGURE 16–2** ■ ■ ■

Business Turnover, 1990–2000

Sources: U.S. Small Business Administration, Office of Advocacy from data provided by the U.S. Bureau of the Census and U.S. Department of Labor, ETA (1999 and 2000 were estimated by Advocacy).

issued by the U.S. patent office rose from single digits in the early 1990s to over 32% in 1998.[8] Many of these patents translated into new business ideas.

In practice, dozens of other environmental opportunities and constraints influence the budding entrepreneur's willingness and ability to create a new business. *Globalization* is one, since the opportunity to sell goods from one country to buyers in another triggers new-business creation. A short list of other environmental factors would include venture capital availability, a technically skilled labor force, accessibility of suppliers, accessibility of customers, the availability of lenders, accessibility of transportation, the attitude of the area's population, and the availability of supporting services (such as roads, electric power, and accounting firms).[9]

Why Entrepreneurship Is Important

When it comes to its impact on the U.S. economy, the phrase *small business* is something of a misnomer. These businesses may be small in terms of individual size, but their aggregate effect on the economy is huge.[10] For example, small businesses as a group account for most of the 600,000 or so new businesses created every year as well as for most of the growth of companies (small firms grow much faster than big ones). Small firms also account for about three-quarters of the employment growth in the U.S. economy—in other words, small businesses create most of the new jobs in the United States.

More than half—68 million out of 118 million—people working in the United States work for small firms. That's why one recent U.S. president's report noted that "a great strength of small businesses is [their] role in renewing the American economy."[11] Small businesses are "an integral part of the renewal process" through which businesses arise to replace those that fail and in doing so provide employment opportunities for tens of millions of people.

Small businesses also account for much of the product and technological innovation in America today. For example, "new small organizations generate 24 times more innovations per research and development dollar spent then do Fortune 500 organizations, and they account for over 95 percent of new and 'radical' product development."[12] The bottom line is that the entrepreneurs who create new businesses have an enormous influence on building our economy, and those who manage small businesses manage over half the people working today.

Corporate Intrapreneurship

Entrepreneurship is not just for entrepreneurs. In this chapter, we'll focus mostly on the activities and management methods of traditional small-business entrepreneurs. However, large companies also work hard at being entrepreneurial. Managers of giant companies understand that entrepreneurial activities drive innovation and that big-company bureaucracy can stifle such activities. They therefore work hard to institute policies and practices that encourage entrepreneurship within big firms.

For example, entrepreneurial activities within Cisco Systems led to the creation of several spin-off companies (including Cordis Corp. and Equinox) that together produced almost $700 million for Cisco.[13] Similarly, QUALCOMM Corporation's entrepreneurial activities led to the wireless Web company Handspring. Sun Microsystems' entrepreneurial activities helped it create and spin off several successful companies, including Caldera Systems.

When large corporations create radically new products or services like this, the process they use to do so is intrapreneurship. Intrapreneurship "is the development, within a large corporation, of internal markets and relatively small autonomous or [semiautonomous] business units, producing products, services, or technologies that employ the firm's resources in a unique way."[14] Intrapreneurship usually does not just mean creating products that are similar to what the company already sells. Instead, it leads to "something new for the corporation and represents, in its fullest manifestations, a complete break with the past."[15] Intel provides an example of what is involved.

intrapreneurship ■ the development, within a large corporation, of internal markets and relatively small autonomous or semiautonomous business units that produce products, services, or technologies that employ the firm's resources in a unique way.

MANAGEMENT IN ACTION Intel's New Business Initiatives

Several years ago, Intel created an in-house new business initiative.[16] "The idea for the whole thing came from our employees, who kept telling us they wanted to do entrepreneurial things . . . " said Intel's CEO. Although Intel is in the microprocessor business, its new business initiative is earmarked specifically for nonmicroprocessor businesses. For example, Intel engineer Paul Scagnetti came up with the idea for a hand-held computer that helps people record and plan their fitness regimens. Intel gave him the funding to launch his product, the Vivonic fitness planner.

■■■ WHAT IT TAKES TO BE AN ENTREPRENEUR

A number of years ago, H. Ross Perot appeared on television to receive an award for his entrepreneurial activities. Someone asked Perot, who had made hundreds of millions of dollars building Electronic Data Systems Inc. and then Perot Systems Inc., what his advice would be for people who hoped to be entrepreneurs. Perot said, "Never give up, never give up, never give up." His advice highlights an interesting entrepreneurial dilemma. On the one hand, there's no doubt that tenacity is a crucial trait for entrepreneurs, since "creating something out of nothing" is inherently so difficult. On the other hand, at what point does one give up? Tenacity, after all, only gets the entrepreneur so far—it is only one entrepreneurial trait among many.

Research Findings What does it take to be a successful entrepreneur? Psychologists have studied this question with mixed results. Based on some studies, researchers say that the entrepreneur's personality characteristics include self-confidence, a high level of motivation, a high energy level, persistence, initiative, resourcefulness, the desire and ability to be self-directed, and a relatively high need for autonomy.[17] Others argue that people high in the need to achieve are more prone to be entrepreneurs, since they like to set goals and achieve them. Yet high-need-for-achievement people seem to be no more likely to start businesses than those with a lower need.[18] One expert concludes that the trait approach to identifying entrepreneurs is "inadequate to explain the phenomenon of entrepreneurship."[19]

Recent studies focus on the proactive personality and on its relationship to entrepreneurship. Proactive behavior reflects the extent to which people ". . . take action to influence their environments."[20] One study of 107 small-business owners found some support for the notion that proactive personality contributes to innovation in some circumstances.[21] Still others study what they call the "dark side" of the entrepreneur. They say entrepreneurs are driven by less positive traits, such as the need for control, a sense of distrust, the need for applause, and a tendency to defend one's operations.[22] This approach doesn't paint too pretty a picture of how some entrepreneurs behave. With respect to the need for control, for instance, "a major theme in the life and personality of many entrepreneurs is the need for control. Their preoccupation with control inevitably affects the way entrepreneurs deal with power relationships and the consequences for interpersonal action. . . . An entrepreneur has a great inner struggle with issues of authority and control."[23]

Anecdotal Evidence A few behaviors do seem to arise consistently in anecdotal/case descriptions of successful entrepreneurs. *Tenacity* is one. Entrepreneurs face so many headwinds when creating a business that if they're not tenacious, they're bound to fail.

For example, consider the challenges facing Asil Hero as he tries to build Broadway Digital Entertainment. Over the past few years, Hero bought the digital rights to over 300 classic Broadway shows, including *The Glass Menagerie* with Katherine Hepburn. For now, Hero sells tapes of the shows to theater buffs through his Internet site. But he hopes to create a TV channel dedicated to Broadway.[24] Doing so will take tenacity. Cable TV already has over 600 channels. He's an outsider facing giants like AOL Time Warner. And selling old Broadway shows is not exactly mainstream entertainment.[25]

Intensity—the drive to pursue a goal with passion and focus—is another trait that often pops up. For example, Sky Dayton started EarthLink in the mid-1990s, and the firm is now one of the largest Internet service providers.[26] Software from his new company, Boingo, will enable people with notebook computers to link to the Web via special Wi-Fi hubs. What kind of person is Dayton? One friend, who watched him surfing, says Dayton "took the sport up with a vengeance. He's as intense and fearless in surfing as he is in business."

▲ **WEBNOTE** ■ ■ ■

Broadway Digital Entertainment's Web site presents the two aspects of this entrepreneurial idea: The Broadway Theater Archive (tapes of classic shows) and Broadway Tonight (broadcasts of shows to global pay TV audiences).

www.broadwaydigitalentertainment. com

Source: © 2001 Broadway Digital Entertainment

Should You Be an Entrepreneur?

Is entrepreneurship for you? As one gauge, take the short survey in Figure 16.3. Then, answer the following questions, compliments of the U.S. Small Business Administration:

- *Are you a self-starter?* No one will be there prompting you to develop projects and to follow through on details.
- *How well do you get along with different personalities?* Business owners need to develop working relationships with a variety of people, including customers, vendors, staff, bankers, and professionals such as lawyers, accountants and consultants. Will you be able to deal with a demanding client, an unreliable vendor, or a cranky employee in ways that advance the best interests of your business?
- *How good are you at making decisions?* Small-business owners make decisions constantly, often quickly, under pressure, and independently.
- *Do you have the physical and emotional stamina to run a business?* Can you handle 12-hour workdays, six or seven days a week?
- *How well do you plan and organize?* Research indicates that good plans could have prevented many business failures. Furthermore, good organization (not just of employees, but also of financials, inventory, schedules, production and all the other details of running a business) can help prevent problems.
- *Is your drive strong enough to maintain your motivation?* Running a business can wear you down. You'll need strong motivation to make the business succeed and to help you survive slowdowns, reversals, and burnout.
- *How will the business affect your family?* The first few years of a business start-up can be hard on family life. The strain of an unsupportive spouse may be hard to balance against the demands of starting a business. There also may be financial difficulties until the business becomes profitable, which could take months or years.[27]

▶ FIGURE 16–3 ▪▪▪

Is Entrepreneurship for Me?

Sources: Based on T. S. Bateman and J. M. Crant, "The Proactive Component of Organizational Behavior: A Measure and Correlates," *Journal of Organizational Behavior*, March 1993, pp. 103–18; and J. M. Crant, "The Proactive Personality Scale as a Predictor of Entrepreneurial Intentions," *Journal of Small Business Management*, July 1996, pp. 42–49.

INSTRUMENT

Respond to each of the 17 statements using the following rating scale:

     1 = Strongly disagree

     2 = Moderately disagree

     3 = Slightly disagree

     4 = Neither agree or disagree

     5 = Slightly agree

     6 = Moderately agree

     7 = Strongly agree

1. I am constantly on the lookout for new ways to improve my life.   1 2 3 4 5 6 7

2. I feel driven to make a difference in my community— and maybe the world.   1 2 3 4 5 6 7

3. I tend to let others take the initiative to start new projects.   1 2 3 4 5 6 7

4. Wherever I have been, I have been a powerful force for constructive change.   1 2 3 4 5 6 7

5. I enjoy facing and overcoming obstacles to my ideas.   1 2 3 4 5 6 7

6. Nothing is more exciting than seeing my ideas turn into reality.   1 2 3 4 5 6 7

7. If I see something I don't like, I fix it.   1 2 3 4 5 6 7

8. No matter what the odds, if I believe in something, I will make it happen.   1 2 3 4 5 6 7

9. I love being a champion for my ideas, even against others' opposition.   1 2 3 4 5 6 7

10. I excel at identifying opportunities.   1 2 3 4 5 6 7

11. I am always looking for better ways to do things.   1 2 3 4 5 6 7

12. If I believe in an idea, no obstacle will prevent me from making it happen   1 2 3 4 5 6 7

13. I love to challenge the status quo.   1 2 3 4 5 6 7

14. When I have a problem, I tackle it head-on.   1 2 3 4 5 6 7

15. I am great at turning problems into opportunities.   1 2 3 4 5 6 7

16. I can spot a good opportunity long before others can.   1 2 3 4 5 6 7

17. If I see someone in trouble, I help out in any way I can.   1 2 3 4 5 6 7

SCORING KEY

To calculate your proactive personality score, add up your responses to all statements, except item 3. For item 3, reverse your score.

ANALYSIS AND INTERPRETATION

This instrument assesses proactive personality. That is, it identifies differences among people in the extent to which they take action to influence their environments. Proactive personalities identify opportunities and act on them; they show initiative, take action, and persevere until they bring about change. Research finds that the proactive personality is positively associated with entrepreneurial intentions. Your total score will range between 17 and 119. The higher your score, the stronger your proactive personality. For instance, scores above 85 indicated fairly high proactivity.

▪▪▪ GETTING STARTED IN BUSINESS

Overcoming all the challenges that stand in the way of going from nothing to something requires tackling at least four main tasks along the way: (1) coming up with the idea for the business, (2) deciding how to get into that business, (3) deciding on a form of business ownership, and (4) getting funded.

The Idea: What Business Should I Be in?

Most entrepreneurs don't come up with the ideas for their businesses by doing an elaborate analysis of what customers want. They seem to stumble upon their ideas.[28] By far, the largest proportion (between 43% and 71%) of those responding to one survey said they got their ideas for their businesses through their *previous employment*. (Ralph

Lauren supposedly got his idea for the Polo line of clothes while working at Brooks Brothers.) Furthermore, "in addition to providing the means to discover opportunities to start a business, this approach has the advantage of being much more forgiving of mistakes arising from inexperience."[29] In other words, it's smart to learn the business at someone else's expense.

After work experience, *serendipity* was the source that most respondents (15% to 20%) mentioned. They just stumbled across them. A relative handful of respondents got their ideas from *hobbies* or from a "systematic search for business opportunities."[30]

Some business ideas do arise quite unexpectedly.[31] Consider Triumph Motorcycle Company. The original Triumph Company had been in business for years before closing down in the 1960s. Then about 20 years ago, housing developer John Bloor was looking for building sites in Coventry, England. He stumbled across the shuttered Triumph factory while looking for potential building sites. He decided not to buy the factory site, but seeing the factory gave him an idea. For about $200,000, he bought the rights to the Triumph motorcycle brand name and to the company's designs and tooling. Today, a former housing developer who just happened to stumble upon the company's factory still manages Triumph.

Methods for Getting into Business

Entrepreneurs actually get into business in several ways: through a family-owned business; by starting a business from scratch; by buying a business; or by buying a franchise.

The Family-Owned Business Perhaps the easiest way to become an entrepreneur (or, more accurately, a small-business manager) is to be the child of one and to take over the family business. A family-owned business "is one that includes two or more members of a family with financial control of the company."[32] Family business is big business. It is estimated that about 90% of all businesses in the United States are family-owned and managed, and that they employ more than 50 million people and account for over half of the country's economic output.[33]

Balancing family and business pressures is not easy. As someone once said, "You can't run a family with your head, and you can't run a business with your heart." Or as Dan Bishop, president of the National Family Business Association has said, "A family is based on emotion, nurturing, and security, but a business revolves around productivity, accomplishment, and profit."[34] These issues manifest themselves in the family business in many ways. Children may fight for the right to gain control of the business. The owner may be torn between doing what's best for the business and a desire to help a child (who may not actually have what it takes) to succeed. Poor planning may exacerbate these problems.

Many owners do little planning to help ease the burden for heirs. One survey showed that only 45 percent of the owners of family firms had selected successors. One expert suggests that the owner should prepare a kit containing items like a list of helpful advisers, the location of key documents, and advice on business strategies and on whether the survivor should sell the firm or continue to run it.[35] At minimum, the owner of the family business should make his or her succession plans clear. "The children should know if they will take over management or if the business will be sold to an outsider. If they spend years working in the business only to find it sold to an outsider, they may have trouble finding positions in other companies."[36]

Starting A New Business When most people think of entrepreneurship, it's "starting a new business" that comes to mind. It is in starting a new business that the entrepreneur supplies the spark that makes something out of nothing—and that brings a new business to life, complete with customers, suppliers, permits, accountants, lawyers, and all the paraphernalia you think of when you think about a business. The overall process of business creation consists of these steps:

- Conduct a feasibility analysis.
- Develop a business plan.
- Project financing needs.
- Secure the needed resources and permits.
- Establish internal control procedures and organization.
- Start serving customers.

Starting a small business isn't something to be taken lightly. To prepare, the entrepreneur should:

1. *List the reasons for wanting to go into business.* Some of the most common reasons for starting a business are that you want to be in your own business, you want financial independence, you want creative freedom, and you want to use your skills and knowledge more fully.
2. Next, *determine what business is right for you.* Ask yourself, "What do I like to do with my time? What technical skills have I learned or developed? What do others say I am good at? Will I make enough to support my family? How much time do I have to run a successful business? Do I have any marketable hobbies or interests?"
3. *Identify the niche your business will fill.* Conduct the necessary research to answer these questions: "What business am I interested in starting? What services or products will I sell? Is my idea practical, and will it really work? What is my competition? What is my business's advantage over existing firms? Can I deliver better quality service than my competitors? Can I create a demand for my business?"
4. *Conduct a prebusiness review.* Now answer these questions: "What skills and experience do I bring to the business? How will I maintain my company's business records? What insurance coverage will I need? What equipment or supplies will I need? What are my resources? What financing will I need? Where will my business be located? What will I name my business?"

Answers to these questions will help you create a business plan. That plan should serve as a blueprint for the business. According to the Small Business Administration, "[The plan] should detail how the business will be operated, managed and capitalized."[37] We'll return to business planning in a moment.

Buying an Existing Business When it comes to being an entrepreneur, buying an existing business is a double-edged sword. On the one hand, it reduces the risks. At least in theory, buying an existing business means the entrepreneur will know what the existing market is, as well as what the company's revenues, expenses, and profits (or losses) are. Buying a business can also mean getting into business faster and with less effort than starting a business from scratch.

On the other hand, as one cynical management consultant once put it, "There's always a reason why the business owner wants to sell, and the reason is never good." One risk is that there is sometimes puffery in the figures the owner reports. Another is that the owner may know that things are about to go wrong. Furthermore, the entrepreneur is buying not just the business's assets but also its liabilities, such as problem employees.

Buying a Franchise To some extent, buying a franchise gives the entrepreneur the best of both worlds. A franchiser is a firm that licenses other firms to use its business idea and procedures and to sell its goods or services in return for royalty and other types of payments. A franchisee is a firm that obtains a license to use a franchiser's business ideas and procedures, and which may get an exclusive right to sell the franchiser's goods or services in a specific territory. Each franchisee owns his or her franchise unit. The franchising agreement is a document that lays out the relationship between the franchiser and franchisee. The agreement creates a franchise, a franchising system, a franchiser, and a franchisee.[38]

This can be a good way to get into business. The franchisee usually gets the right to start his or her business from scratch without the excess baggage of the problems associated with buying an existing business. Yet the franchisee gets much of the start-up, preparatory work done by the franchiser—and also (it is hoped) gets a business that is based on a proven business model. Other benefits include name recognition, management training and assistance, economies in buying, financial assistance, and promotional assistance. One expert suggests looking for the following things when evaluating a franchise:

1. Select a franchising company that is primarily interested in distributing products and services to ultimate customers. Franchisers like Dunkin' Donuts and McDonald's are famous for their emphasis on providing high-quality products and services—they're not just there to sell franchises.
2. Pick a franchiser that is dedicated to franchising as its primary mechanism of product and service distribution. Avoid franchisers with large numbers of company-

---

franchise ■ *a license to use a company's business ideas and procedures and to sell its goods or services.*

franchiser ■ *a firm that licenses other firms to use its business idea and procedures and to sell its goods or services in return for royalty and other types of payments.*

franchisee ■ *a firm that obtains a license to use a franchiser's business ideas and procedures, and which may get an exclusive right to sell the franchiser's goods or services in a specific territory.*

franchising agreement ■ *document that lays out the relationship between the franchiser and franchisee.*

owned stores—or that distribute the product or services through other channels, such as supermarkets.

3. Pick a franchiser that provides products or services for which there is an established market demand.
4. Pick a franchiser that has a well-accepted trademark.
5. Evaluate your franchiser's business plan and marketing system.
6. Make sure your franchiser has good relationships with its franchisees.
7. Deal with franchising companies that provide sales and earnings projections that demonstrate an attractive return on your investment.
8. Meet with your accountant and lawyer, and carefully review the franchiser's Uniform Franchise Offering Circular, a document required by the U.S. Federal Trade Commission (FTC). The FTC oversees the interstate activities of the franchise industry. The uniform franchise offering circular rules require franchisers to disclose all essential information about the business.[39]

The checklist in Figure 16.4 provides additional guidance for evaluating the franchise and the franchiser.

Forms of Business Ownership

In creating the business entity, the entrepreneur needs to decide what the entity's ownership structure will be. The four main forms of business ownership are the sole proprietorship, the partnership, the corporation, and the limited liability company. As we will see, taxation and limiting the owner's liability are always big considerations in choosing an ownership form.

The Sole Proprietorship The sole proprietorship is a business owned by one person. About 70 percent of businesses in the United States are sole proprietorships.

The sole proprietorship is simple to start. There are no laws on setting up the sole proprietorship (although local and state laws require licenses and permits). The sole proprietor usually has to register the firm's name at the county courthouse (to make sure no one else is using the name).[40] As sole owner, the proprietor owns the firm and its profits (or losses) outright; there are no other owners with whom to share the rewards or setbacks. Sole proprietors are their own bosses: they can decide for themselves what hours to work and whether to expand their firms. Because the sole proprietor *is* the firm, he or she pays only personal income taxes on its profits. There is no income tax on the firm as a separate entity. A sole proprietorship is also easy to dissolve. The owner needs no permission to dissolve the business.

They may be simple to start, but the sole proprietorship does have drawbacks. Perhaps most important, the sole proprietor has unlimited financial liability. *Unlimited liability* means that the business owner is responsible for any claims against the firm that go beyond what the owner has invested in the business. If the firm can't pay its debts, liability could extend to the owner's personal property (furniture, car, and personal savings) and, in some states, to the owner's real property (homes and other real estate). Sole proprietors, therefore, risk losing everything they own if their businesses go bust. Furthermore, since there are no other owners, the sole proprietorship form can limit the owner's ability to raise funds for expansion. And, similarly, there is no other owner with whom to share the management burden.

The Partnership Some entrepreneurs therefore opt to form a partnership. Under the Uniform Partnership Act, a partnership is "an association of two or more persons to carry on as co-owners of a business for profit." People form a partnership by entering into a partnership agreement. A partnership agreement is an oral or written contract between the owners of a partnership. It identifies the business, and it lays out the partners' respective rights and duties. The agreement states the name, location, and business of the firm. It also specifies the mutual understanding of each owner's duties and rights in running the business, the method for sharing the profits or losses, and the policies for withdrawing from the business and dissolving the partnership.

There are two basic forms of partnerships. In a *general partnership*, all partners share in the ownership, management, and liabilities of the firm. A *limited partnership* is a business in which one or more, but not all, partners (the limited partners) are liable for the

sole proprietorship ■ *a business owned by one person.*

partnership ■ *an association of two or more persons to carry on as co-owners of a business for profit.*

partnership agreement ■ *an oral or written contract between the owners of a partnership. It identifies the business, and it lays out the partners' respective rights and duties.*

▼ **FIGURE 16–4** ■ ■ ■

Checklist for Evaluating a Franchise

Source: Franchise Opportunities Hanbook (Washington, D.C.: U.S. Government Printing Office, 1988).

THE FRANCHISE

☐ 1. Did your lawyer approve the franchise contract you are considering after he studied it paragraph by paragraph?

☐ 2. Does the franchise call on you to take any steps that are, according to your lawyer, unwise or illegal in your state, county, or city?

☐ 3. Does the franchise give you an exclusive territory for the length of the franchise agreement or can the franchisor sell a second or third franchise in your terriroty?

☐ 4. Is the franchisor connected in any way with any other franchise company handling similar merchandise or service?

☐ 5. If the answer to the last question is yes, what is your protection against this second franchisor organization?

☐ 6. Under what circumstances can you terminate the franchise contract and at what cost to you, if you decide for any reason at all that you wish to cancel it?

☐ 7. If you sell your franchise, will you be compensated for your goodwill, or will the goodwill you have built into the business be lost by you?

THE FRANCHISOR

☐ 8. How many years has the firm offering you a franchise been in operation?

☐ 9. Has it a reputation for honesty and fair dealing among the local firms holding its franchise?

☐ 10. Has the franchisor shown you any certified figures indicating exact net profits of one or more going firms that you personally checked yourself with the franchisee?

☐ 11. Will the firm assist you with

a. A management training program?

b. An employee training program?

c. A public relations program?

d. Capital?

e. Credit?

f. Merchandising ideas?

☐ 12. Will the firm help you find a good location for your new business?

☐ 13. Is the franchising firm adequately financed so that it can carry out its stated plan of financial assistance and expansion?

☐ 14. Is the franchisor a one-person company or a corporation with an experienced management trained in depth (so that there would always be an experienced person at its head)?

☐ 15. Exactly what can the franchisor do for you that you cannot do for yourself?

☐ 16. Has the franchisor investigated you carefully enough to assure itself that you can successfully operate one of its franchises at a profit both to it and to you?

☐ 17. Does your state have a law regulating the sale of franchises, and has the franchisor complied with that law?

YOU—THE FRANCHISEE

☐ 18. How much equity capital will you have to have to purchase the franchise and operate it until your income equals your expenses? Where are you going to get it?

☐ 19. Are you prepared to give up some independence of action to secure the advantages offered by the franchise?

☐ 20. Do you really believe you have the innate ability, training, and experience to work smoothly and profitably with the franchisor, your employees, and your customers?

☐ 21. Are you ready to spend much or all of the remainder of your business life with this franchisor, offering its product or service to your public?

YOUR MARKET

☐ 22. Have you made any study to determine whether the product or service that you propose to sell under the franchise has a market in your territory at the prices you will have to charge?

☐ 23. Will the population in the territory given to you increase, remain static, or decrease over the next five years?

☐ 24. Will the product or service you are considering be in greater demand, about the same, or less demand five years from now than today?

☐ 25. What competition exists in your territory already for the product or service you contemplate selling?

a. Nonfranchise firms?

b. Franchise firms?

firm's debts *only to the extent of their financial investment in the firm*. This helps general partners attract investment dollars from people who do not want unlimited liability—or who do not want to get involved in managing the firm. Under the law, partners are assumed to be general partners unless it is made known that they are limited partners.

The partnership has four main advantages. There are few restrictions on starting one. There are several partners, so a partnership permits the pooling of funds, talents, and borrowing power. The partnership also provides more chance to specialize. (For example, the outside person can specialize in sales, while the inside person specializes in running the business day to day.) Finally, like a sole proprietorship, there's no tax on the business as distinct from the owners. The owners individually, not the firm, are taxed.

Unlimited liability is one disadvantage. In general partnerships, all partners have unlimited liability for the partnership's debts. In a partnership, this means joint liability. Each partner is responsible for business debts incurred by the other. The partners' combined personal property and (in most states) real property are available to business creditors. (In a limited liability partnership, the limited partners are only personally liable up to the amount they invest in the business.) The potential for personal disagreements is another disadvantage. As in most relationships, one must choose one's partners with great care. A partnership agreement can reduce many of the ambiguities. However, disagreements can still arise over questions like how much money each partner is to invest, what the salary of each partner will be, and the duties of each.

The Corporation A corporation is a legally chartered organization that is a separate legal entity, apart from its owners. A corporation comes into being when the incorporators (founders) apply for and receive a charter from the state in which the firm is to reside.

The corporate form has several advantages. It is a *separate legal entity* and can issue stock certificates to shareholders as evidence of ownership. Shareholders (or stockholders) own the corporation. Each owns a part interest in the entire corporation. However, the corporation is a separate legal entity: GM's shareholders are not GM, and GM is not its shareholders. GM is, legally, like a separate "person." Banks lend money to GM, people sue GM, and GM (not the individual shareholders) hires GM's employees.

The corporation's owners also have *limited financial liability*. This is the corporation's main advantage over sole proprietorships and partnerships. The most a shareholder can lose is what he or she paid for the shares. This makes it much easier for the company to raise money. Furthermore, because the corporation is a separate legal entity, it has *permanence*. The death, insanity, or imprisonment of a shareholder does not mean the end of the corporation. This also facilitates transfer of ownership. In a corporation, shareholders just sell their shares of stock.

Corporations also have disadvantages. In sole proprietorships and partnerships, the owners pay the income taxes individually—the government does not separately tax the companies themselves. Corporations are different. Remember that they are entities separate from their owners. The corporation thus pays federal and state taxes on its profits. If the corporation then pays cash dividends to shareholders from its after-tax profits, the shareholders pay personal income taxes on the dividends. So the company's profits are subject to *double taxation*. (Corporations can avoid double taxation by forming an *S corporation*. An S corporation has the option of being taxed like a partnership. It pays no income taxes as a firm.) Each state has its own corporation laws, and some of them are complex. Furthermore, corporations are subject to both state and federal laws and public disclosure requirements.

The Limited Liability Company The limited liability company (LLC) is a cross between a partnership and a corporation. Like a corporation, the LLC limits the liability on its owners (called "members") from personal liability for the company's debts and liabilities. At the same time, the limited liability company's earnings are not subject to separate corporate taxes.[41]

Getting Funded

Generating ideas for the business, developing business plans, creating or buying the business, and deciding on a legal organization are all theoretical exercises if the entrepreneur can't find the money to actually start and run the business. "How will I fund

corporation ■ *a legally chartered organization that is a separate legal entity apart from its owners. A corporation comes into being when the incorporators (founders) apply for and receive a charter from the state in which the firm is to reside.*

limited liability company (LLC) ■ *a cross between a partnership and a corporation.*

■ ■ *One of the swimming pools at the new Royal Palm Crowne Plaza Resort in Miami Beach.*

my business?" is, therefore, a question the entrepreneur should be thinking about from the moment he or she starts thinking about creating a business.

How much money does the entrepreneur need? The actual amount needed will vary with the business and the situation, but the logical way to answer this question is to produce a business plan. Develop a projection of expected first and second year sales. This should produce (with some research) a list of the expenses needed to support these sales—and, thus, an estimate of how much cash the business will need for the first few years.

Overoptimism is a problem. Even experienced businesspeople can make mistakes. The developers of the Royal Palm Crowne Plaza Hotel in South Florida recently completed their new hotel—but two years late and with cost overruns of $16 million above the original $80 million estimate. To pay down some of that debt, they had to sell about 150 of the 422 rooms as condominiums.[42]

The two basic sources of business finance are debt and equity. Equity finance represents an ownership in the venture, whereas debt, of course, is borrowed capital.

Equity For the typical new small business, much of the initial capital traditionally comes from the founder of the business. Family and friends are usually the second-biggest source. No one knows the entrepreneur like his or her family and friends, and it is hoped that this familiarity translates into the faith required to help that person start a business.

Outside equity—either from wealthy private investors ("angels") or from venture capital firms—are two other possibilities. **Angels** are wealthy individuals interested in the high-risk/high-reward potentials of new venture creation. **Venture capitalists** are professionally managed pools of investor money. They specialize in evaluating new venture opportunities and taking equity stakes in worthy businesses. A *Public offering*—selling stock to the public—is usually an option open to relatively few new ventures. When the company first sells stock to outside owners, the firm has "gone public." The process is the **initial public offering (IPO)**. Investment bankers are professionals that walk the entrepreneur through the various registration requirements, thus enabling the company to publicly offer stock.[43]

angels ■ *wealthy individuals interested in the high-risk/high-reward potentials of new venture creation.*

venture capitalists ■ *professionally managed pools of investor money. They specialize in evaluating new venture opportunities and taking equity stakes in worthy businesses.*

initial public offering (IPO) ■ *when a company first sells stock to outside owners.*

Debt Debt, or borrowed capital, is the second main source of business finance. An entrepreneur with good personal credit and a sound business plan may be able to obtain a business loan from a commercial bank. However, banks are not in the venture capital business. The entrepreneur usually guarantees loans like these with his or her personal assets and promise to repay.

Studies suggest that many entrepreneurs dip deeply into their personal debt-paying capacity in order to support the business. By one estimate, the debts of smaller businesses are divided roughly equally among (1) credit lines and loans, (2) business credit card debt, and (3) personal credit card debt.[44] *Asset-based debt* is a popular source of small-business funds. It is debt collateralized (guaranteed) by one or more specific assets of the business. If the business doesn't pay, the lender takes the asset.

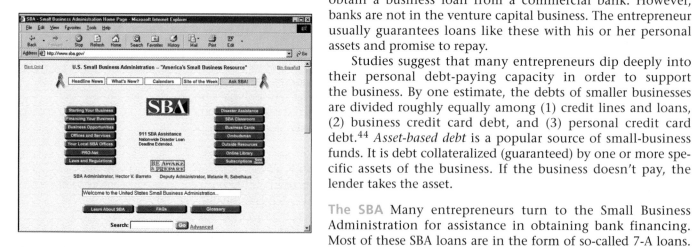

▲ **WEBNOTE** ■ ■ ■

The U.S. Small Business Administration provides a number of tools and services for small business startups.

www.sba.gov

The SBA Many entrepreneurs turn to the Small Business Administration for assistance in obtaining bank financing. Most of these SBA loans are in the form of so-called 7-A loans. The SBA basically guarantees up to 90% of the outstanding loan; the loan itself comes from a commercial bank. Loans generally cannot exceed $750,000. Both the SBA and the bank typically require over 100% collateral for financing things like equipment purchases, real estate purchases, or expanding the company's working capital (the amount of cash it needs to run its business on a day-to-day basis).

Whether raising capital from friends or the SBA, the entrepreneur will have to provide a business plan and evidence that he or she can actually manage the firm. Let's, therefore, turn to the important topic of how entrepreneurs plan. We will then address how entrepreneurs organize, lead, and control their companies.

◼◼◼ HOW ENTREPRENEURS PLAN

To some people, the phrase *entrepreneurial planning* sounds inconsistent. After all (they might argue), entrepreneurs get things done by being fast and innovative and by not playing by the usual rules. Therefore, doesn't the idea of thinking through the next moves run counter to the nature of entrepreneurship?

Yes and no. *Yes*, it turns out that entrepreneurs do cut some corners and streamline the planning process. However, *no*, since successful entrepreneurs don't jump into business without thinking through their moves with some precision. Let's look first at strategic planning by entrepreneurs.

How Entrepreneurs Craft Strategies

Interviews with the founders of 100 of the fastest-growing private companies in the United States (and research on 100 other thriving ventures) showed that entrepreneurs use three general guidelines in formulating strategies:[45]

1. *Screen out losers quickly.* Successful entrepreneurs know how to quickly discard ideas for new products and services that have a low potential. Their decision making tends to emphasize judgment and intuition rather than piles of data.
2. *Minimize the resources devoted to researching ideas.* With limited resources, entrepreneurs can do only as much planning and analysis as necessary. They then make judgment calls, sometimes based on very limited data. Many got the ideas for their businesses by simply replicating or modifying an idea encountered in their previous employment. (Recall Ralph Lauren.) As noted earlier, 15% to 20% got their ideas serendipitously—building a temporary job into a business, developing a family member's idea, or "thinking it up during a honeymoon in Italy," for instance.
3. *Don't wait for all the answers, and be ready to change course.* Entrepreneurs rarely have the time or resources for the "GE approach" to strategic planning: SWOT analyses, scenario planning, and environmental scanning are usually informal, at best. The researchers found that entrepreneurs often "don't know all the answers before they act." They introduce a product or service based on very preliminary market data. Then they quickly drop or modify the product if it doesn't click with customers.

Create Competitive Barriers However, looking at entrepreneurial success stories makes it clear that entrepreneurs can and do make good use of the strategic planning tools covered in Chapter 5. For example, they benefit from being able to formulate a mission and vision for the firm, by being able to formulate both corporate and competitive-level strategies, and by using strategic planning tools (such as SWOT and TOWS). The success of Russ Leatherman and his colleagues at MovieFone illustrates how a smart entrepreneurial company puts competitive strategy tools into practice.

MANAGEMENT IN ACTION   Building Entry Barriers

In 1989, Russ Leatherman dreamed up the idea for an interactive telephone movie guide he called MovieFone. His competitive strategy is a shrewd mix of focus and differentiation. Callers get listings of theater offerings in their area, and they can buy tickets over the phone. The Porter Five-Forces model (discussed in Chapter 5) prompts managers to build competitive barriers that hamper competitors' moves. Leatherman knew that, once his firm was running, he had to build barriers to keep potential competitors like Ticketmaster at bay. He, therefore, established the following competitive barriers:

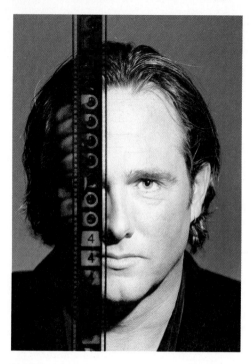

1. *Exclusivity.* MovieFone acquired highly desirable phone numbers in each of its area codes, such as 777-FILM, and registered them as trademarks. The numbers are easy for callers to remember, differentiating MovieFone and keeping competitors out.
2. *Focus.* MovieFone focused on movie listings instead of branching out into other markets such as theaters or sporting events. MovieFone thus became the industry expert when it comes to supplying listings and tickets. It has mastered the hardware, software, and logistics required to obtain, compile, and deliver listings and tickets better than anyone else.
3. *Expert systems.* MovieFone has developed what it calls expert systems, comprising special hardware, software, and electronic "will-call windows," in which customers can automatically pick up tickets. These systems further differentiate MovieFone from its competitors. They also create substantial barriers to any new competitors that might be considering entering the market.
4. *Strategic alliances.* Many of the electronic will-call windows are in movie theaters, with which MovieFone has formed strategic alliances for that purpose.[46] Today, MovieFone is growing fast. Moviegoers can reach it on the Internet, too.

■■ ■ *Russ Leatherman, co-founder of AOL MovieFone.*

Ask, "What Business Are We In?" Chapter 5 explains that the heart of strategic planning is setting a mission and vision—in other words, answering the question, "What business are we in?" Defining the business helps the manager make all other business decisions. Managers can't intelligently choose suppliers, employees, advertising campaigns, or business partners if they don't know what business they are in. That is why it was so important for Shoshana Berger and her team to formulate how they defined *ReadyMade* magazine's business. Entrepreneurs may not always do elaborate strategic analyses. However, the best still define their basic business with great care. Compass Records is another case in point.

MANAGEMENT IN ACTION

Compass Records

Alison Brown and Garry West, both musicians, got their idea for starting Compass Records while talking before a show they were at in Stockholm.[47] Today, Compass Records is booming. Over the last seven or so years, the company has released more than 100 albums, ranging from "collections of centuries old ballads by the British folksinger Kate Rusby to an album of soukous by the Congolese singer guitarist Samba Ngo."[48]

What business is Compass Records in? Compass has built up an audience of discerning listeners by focusing like a laser on roots music-folk music—from whatever country. As Alison Brown says, "Whether we're doing Celtic or Bluegrass or singer-songwriter, it all has that common thread running through it."[49]

Sticking to that vision has taken Compass Records into some interesting musical nooks and crannies. Its first release was an album of music played on a didgeridoo, a wood instrument indigenous to Australia. Other titles "have included sets by the progressive jazz bassist Victor Wooten, the Czech Bluegrass band Druha Trava and the neopop duo Swan Dive."[50] The partners may not have done a lot of strategic analysis. However, they do know exactly what business they are in.

Use the Internet Not surprisingly, the Internet has been a strategic boon to entrepreneurs. The Internet lowers the barriers to entry. For example, an entrepreneur can create a virtual bookstore or other business for a fraction of the time and cost that it would take to create a bricks-and-mortar version. Today, most small businesses have their own Web sites. For example, a survey by National Small Business United shows that about 53% of the small businesses surveyed had a Web page. (See the Managing @ the Speed of Thought feature.)[51]

Choosing a Competitive Strategy

In terms of strategy, the secret of small-business Web success seems to be choosing a niche competitive strategy. Web analyst Carrie Johnson calls this "the fragmentation of the Web."[52] For example, Harris Cyclery is a successful New England business. Sheldon Brown, the veteran mechanic who runs Harris Cyclery, avoids head-on competition with bigger online bicycle retailers by focusing on hard-to-find replacement parts. He also cultivates a competitive advantage by offering free advice over the Web.[53] Ron Davis, who owns and manages a chain of apparel stores called The Shoe Horn, also created a Web site, but he kept it highly focused. He sells dyed wedding shoes online.[54]

Highly focused online entrepreneurs can use giant Web sites to help them promote their wares. Thanks to sites like eBay and Yahoo!'s "Yahoo! small-business" services, even tiny businesses can auction their products to huge audiences online.

▲ **WEBNOTE** ■ ■ ■

The Shoe Horn Web site, which sells only dyed wedding and evening shoes, is part of the company's competitive strategy.

www.theshoehorn.com

Source: Copyright © 2002 Dyeable Shoe Store

The Feasibility Study: Is This Business for Me?

A giant corporation can start a new business and survive even if that new business fails. For example, some years ago, FedEx began a new service called ZapMail. In the days before fax machines became widely available, FedEx's idea was for customers to bring their documents to local FedEx stores. FedEx would then fax them via a proprietary satellite system to other FedEx locations, which then delivered the hard copies to the intended recipient. Unfortunately, the rapid deployment of fax machines into every office and almost every home rendered ZapMail irrelevant. FedEx lost about $350 million on the project.

Most entrepreneurs lack such staying power. When a person quits a job, sinks his or her (and, possibly his or her family's) life savings into a business, and runs up debts to boot, that entrepreneur had better be sure that the business makes sense. Almost as many businesses go out of business every year as start up. Being entrepreneurial is one thing. Not doing a feasibility study is another.

At a minimum, the entrepreneur should study the market, customers, industry, and competitors. One entrepreneurship expert suggests asking the questions listed in Checklist 16.1 when sizing up the market, customers, and industry.[55]

CHECKLIST 16.1 ■ Is the Business Idea Feasible?

☑ **The Market**

1. Can I clearly identify my market (my target customers)?
2. Who are my competitors, how many are there, and will the market sustain another player?
3. How big is the market? How fast is it growing? Does the market consist of segments that I could exploit?
4. What are the keys to succeeding in this market?

☑ **The Customers**

1. What factors are most important to buyers when selecting a product/service? Is it price? Quality? Delivery time? Reliability? What prices are buyers currently paying for comparable products or services?
2. What do I know about the types of people currently buying this product or service in terms of income level, demographics, and so on?

3. What do potential or existing customers like and not like about my competitors' products or services?
4. What makes my product or service unique compared to others in the marketplace? Do any of my competitors seem to be preparing to make any changes in the way they do business?

☑ **The Industry**

1. Is the industry growing? What are the current trends in the industry? Why are the industry leaders so successful?
2. In terms of marketing strategies (advertising, promotion, and direct sales, for instance) what techniques are competitors using successfully?
3. What are the legal and governmental regulations affecting this industry? Are any changes on the horizon?

4. Is the industry sensitive to economic fluctuations?
5. Is there customer loyalty within the industry? If so, what is it based on?
6. What sorts of competitive barriers will we have to overcome?

7. Are there technological changes happening or about to happen? How will they affect the industry?
8. What are the financial characteristics of the industry—for instance, in terms of profit margins, cost structure, and return on investment?

■ *The Global Manager* For many entrepreneurs, expanding sales abroad to foreign markets makes a good deal of sense. It helps firms with seasonal products (like snowmobiles) even out seasonal demand, compensates for declining domestic markets, and enables the manager to take advantage of what may be fast-growing developing markets abroad. Yet attractive as expanding abroad may be, this is not a decision small business owners can make lightly. Dealing with people from different cultures requires a keen awareness of cultural differences: "Getting right down to business" may be a discourteous thing to do when dealing with a businessperson in Japan, for instance. Large distances and inadequate face-to-face communications can prompt misunderstandings. And careful thought must be given to how to get paid.

Small business managers have several government sources they can draw on. Trade Information Center specialists at the U.S. Department of Commerce can advise on things like how to use government programs and can help guide managers through the process. The U.S. Commerce department's Foreign Commercial Service has offices in cities around the United States to assist small business owners. Commerce also set up U.S. export centers as one-stop shops in major cities to help businesses with marketing abroad. The SBA's Export Legal Assistance Network provides export-related legal assistance to small businesses.

The Competition

"Know your enemy" is a well-known bit of military advice, but it is equally applicable to entrepreneurship. With relatively few resources, entrepreneurs often blunder into situations without fully understanding the competition. Marc Andreesen, who helped found Netscape Communications, gave considerable thought to what new business to start after Netscape became part of AOL Time Warner, and he struck out on his own. One criterion was that he did not want to compete in any business in which Microsoft already had a dominant position. He founded Loudcloud. The company provides Internet hosting services for large companies.

Entrepreneurs can use the Competitive Profile Matrix shown in Table 16.2 to assess their potential competitors' strengths and weaknesses. To do so, first identify the fac-

TABLE 16–2	Illustrative Competitive Profile Matrix

Critical Success Factors	Weight	Avon Rating	Avon Score	L'Oreal Rating	L'Oreal Score	Procter & Gamble Rating	Procter & Gamble Score
Advertising	0.20	1	0.20	4	0.80	3	0.60
Product Quality	0.10	4	0.40	4	0.40	3	0.30
Price Competitiveness	0.10	3	0.30	3	0.30	4	0.40
Management	0.10	4	0.40	3	0.30	3	0.30
Financial Position	0.15	4	0.60	3	0.45	3	0.45
Customer Loyalty	0.10	4	0.40	4	0.40	2	0.20
Global Expansion	0.20	4	0.80	2	0.40	2	0.40
Market Share	0.05	1	0.05	4	0.20	3	0.15
TOTAL	1.00		3.15		3.25		2.80

Note: (1) The ratings values are as follows: 1 = major weakness, 2 = minor weakness, 3 = minor strength, 4 = major strength. (2) As indicated by the total weighted score of 2.8, P&G is weakest. (3) Only eight critical success factors are included for simplicity; this is too few in actuality.

Source: Fred R. David, *Strategic Management* (Upper Saddle River, NJ: Prentice Hall, 2001), p. 115.

tors that are critical to success in the proposed business (for instance, price, advertising, or management). Next, weigh their importance (weights should add up to 1.00). Then rate each competitor to identify its strengths and weaknesses—and to help answer the question, "Can we compete successfully in this industry?"

The Business Plan

The business plan is the distinguishing characteristic of entrepreneurial planning. The business plan lays out what the business is, where it is heading, and how it plans to get there. Figure 16.5 summarizes the contents of a typical business plan.

business plan ■ *a plan that lays out what the business is, where it is heading, and how it plans to get there.*

Creating a Business Plan Creating a business plan is an important entrepreneurial skill. As with any managerial planning (as covered in Chapters 4–5), developing the business plan helps the entrepreneur understand his or her options, anticipate problems, and make tomorrow's decisions today. The entrepreneur does not want to find out six months after opening the store that labor costs are twice as high as anticipated and that the store's economics, therefore, make it unlikely that the business can survive. Furthermore, the chances of getting financing without a business plan are virtually nil. No banker, angel, or financier is about to make a cash infusion without a business plan.

Experts in writing business plans underscore the importance of doing this job right. You need to pay particular attention to four things: (1) clearly defining the business, (2) providing evidence of management capabilities, (3) providing evidence of marketing capabilities, and (4) offering an attractive financial arrangement.[56] As one expert says, "Most entrepreneurs and small-business owners can prepare a B or B+ business plan without too much trouble. That would be fine if investors would fund B or B+ plans. Investors, however, fund only A or A+ plans. . . . "[57] *ReadyMade*'s experience is illustrative.

◄ **FIGURE 16–5** ■ ■ ■

Contents of a Good Business Plan

Source: William F. Schoell, Gary Dessler, and John A. Reinecke, *Introduction to Business* (Boston: Allyn & Bacon, 1993), p. 176.

INTRODUCTION
A basic description of the firm—name, address, business activity, current stage of development of the firm, and plans for the future.

EXECUTIVE SUMMARY
An overview of the entire business plan, summarizing the content of each section and inviting the reader to continue.

INDUSTRY ANALYSIS
A description of the industry the firm is competing in, focusing on industry trends and profit potential.

MANAGEMENT SECTION
A description of the management team and whether it is complete—and, if not, when and how it will be completed.

MANUFACTURING SECTION
A description of the complexity and logistics of the manufacturing process and of the firm's production capacity and current percentage of capacity use.

PRODUCT SECTION
A description of the good or service, including where it is in its life cycle (for example, a new product or a mature product); of future product research and development efforts; and of the status of patent or copyright applications.

MARKETING SECTION
A marketing plan, including a customer profile, an analysis of market needs, and a geographic analysis of markets; a description of pricing, distribution, and promotion; and an analysis of how the firm's marketing efforts are different from competitors' efforts.

FINANCIAL SECTION
Financial statements for the current year and the three previous years, if applicable; financial projections for the next three to five years; and assumptions for sales, cost of sales, cash flow, pro forma balance sheets, and key statistics, such as the current ratio, the debt/equity ratio, and inventory turnovers.

LEGAL SECTION
Form of ownership (proprietorship, partnership, or corporation) and a listing of any pending lawsuits filed by or against the firm.

The October 2002 issue of *Inc.* magazine showcased Shoshana Berger, Grace Hawthorne, and *ReadyMade* magazine. *ReadyMade*'s co-founders were seeking $500,000 in initial financing. After $635 in revenues and $385,000 in net profits in year 1 (2002), they estimated they would have $1 million in revenues in 2003 and $4 million in 2004, with substantial losses in both 2003 and 2004. *Inc.*'s reviewers were generally lukewarm about *ReadyMade*'s future. Said one expert, "The major problem is that the founders plan to start working on brand extensions before they've gotten the magazine right." An investment banker who specializes in global publishing said that *ReadyMade*'s founders had identified an unserved niche in a dynamic market, "but their business plan is short on detail—it contains fewer numbers than any business plan I've every analyzed. . . . " However, another evaluator said, ". . . Take heart. A good idea, backed by proper resources, can work." Time will tell if Shoshana and Grace can make a success of *ReadyMade* in a tough environment. ■■■■

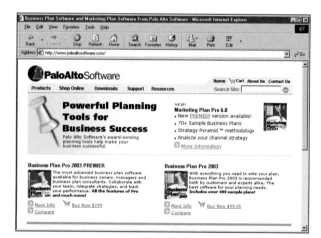

▲ **WEBNOTE** ■ ■ ■

Palo Alto Software's Business Plan Pro includes over 400 sample plans.

www.paloaltosoftware.com

Source: Copyright 2002 Palo Alto Software, Inc.

Using Computerized Business Planning Software There are several business planning software packages available to assist you in writing A+ plans. For example, Business Plan Pro from Palo Alto Software contains all the information and planning aids you need to create a business plan. It contains, for example, 30 sample plans, step-by-step instructions (with examples) for creating each part of a plan (executive summary, market analysis, and so on), financial planning spreadsheets, easy-to-use tables (for instance, for making sales forecasts), and automatic programs for creating color 3D charts for showing things like monthly sales and yearly profits.

Business Plan Pro's Planning Wizard takes the entrepreneur "by the hand" and helps the person develop a business plan step by step. The result is an integrated plan, complete with charts, tables, and professional formatting. For example, click "start a plan," and the Planning Wizard presents a series of questions, including "Does your company sell products, services or both? Would you like a detailed or basic business plan? Does your company sell on credit?" Then as you go to each succeeding part of the plan—such as the Executive Summary—the Planning Wizard shows you instructions with examples, making it easy to create your own executive summary (or other plan section). As you move into the quantitative part of your plan, such as making sales and financial forecasts, the Planning Wizard translates your numbers into tables and charts.

The Planning Process in Practice

In practice, entrepreneurs tend to take an abbreviated approach to ongoing business planning. They compress the forecasting/goal-setting/course-of-action-setting process. Take Gary Steele. When he joined Internet start-up Netiva, the company looked like a sure bet. It had big-name venture-capital backers, and it had a product, the Netiva Internet application system, which let large companies build databases using the Java programming language. However, Steele soon discovered that management had based most of the company's plans on flawed assumptions. For example, the original business plan assumed customers would develop multiple applications based on Netiva's software and would therefore have to pay multiple license fees. But that wasn't happening. Netiva was doing a lot of work for just the one-time license fee of $25,000.

Steele saw that the company was doomed without drastic action. He laid off 40% of the employees at once. Working mostly on his own, he produced a brief, undetailed eight-point plan of action, laying out what the company had to do in the following six weeks. Several weeks later, he and four members of his team held 75 fact-finding meetings with executives at medium- and large-sized firms. This "full court press" approach helped them quickly compile information about what customers wanted—and, thus, what Netiva's basic plan should be.

ServicePort was one new product to come out of these meetings. It is a Web portal for consulting firms. It enables the consultant's employees (who are often out of town) to plug in to their companies' databases and share things like client reports. Now called

Portera (see **www.portera.com/about**), the company has 70 employees. Steele has raised more money, thanks to his ability to quickly create an abbreviated business planning process and plan.[58]

■■■ HOW ENTREPRENEURS ORGANIZE

At first glance, it might seem that organizing is not a topic the entrepreneur needs to address in much detail. After all, what kind of organization chart do you need for managing a three-person store? However, any such conclusion would be misleading. First, many small businesses have dozens or hundreds of employees—and, therefore, do require the sorts of organizational design techniques covered in Chapters 6–9. Furthermore, even the owner of a three-person business has to ensure that each person knows what to do and how his or her efforts mesh with those of the other employees.

Organizing the Small Business

In practice, new small businesses don't start off with conventional organizational structures. Studies (including one by historian Alfred Chandler) suggest they begin life with a simple structure.[59] The entrepreneur typically works interactively with a handful of associates, making all or most of the decisions him- or herself. It would be unusual to have an organization chart.

This informality becomes counterproductive when the company grows to several dozen people. Few entrepreneurs can effectively supervise so many people directly. At this point, an organization structure is born. The entrepreneur institutes a departmentalization—in other words, a formal division of work among employees, including managers and a chain of command. Then, as the company grows, it may evolve into a divisional and then into a multidivisional structure. Figure 16.6 summarizes the typical structural evolution. Netscape Communication provides an example.

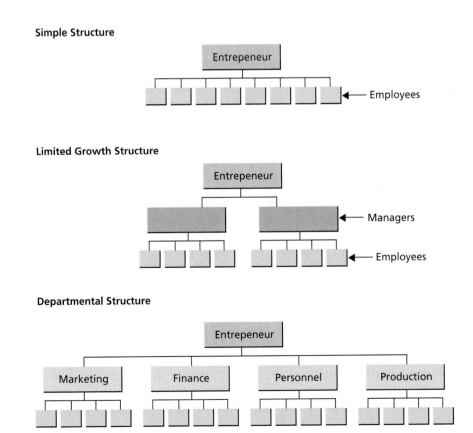

Simple Structure

Limited Growth Structure

Departmental Structure

◀ **FIGURE 16–6** ■ ■ ■

Illustrative Organizational Charts as a Company Grows

Source: Peggy Lambing and Charles R. Kuehl, *Entrepreneurship* (Upper Saddle River, NJ: 2000), p. 44.

etween May 5, 1994 (when it started corporate life as Mosaic Communications) and March 1999 (when AOL bought it), Netscape went from nothing to a company valued at over $10 billion. How it built its organization in such a short time provides some interesting insights into how start-up companies organize under rapidly changing conditions.[60]

Netscape began with a simple functional organization, one with separate departments for activities like marketing, development, legal, and finance. However, it also provided the sort of networked communications that would help it avoid becoming bureaucratic. For example, management divided the technology-development group into small teams of around six engineers each, and it gave each team a lot of autonomy. Netscape also used the Internet to create a virtual development organization. In 1994, Netscape had only 115 employees and so lacked the resources to test and debug its new browser. It therefore posted a beta version of Navigator on the Internet, thus allowing users to serve as a sort of virtual quality assurance team.

As Netscape grew, management replaced its functional organization with one built around product divisions. Netscape executives did this in part because "they believed that combining the functional groups needed to build a product under a single general manager will enable the product groups to be closer to customers, to focus more effectively on specific markets and competitors, and to act more autonomously."[61]

As the size of the product divisions grew, Netscape's top managers needed a more formal way to coordinate their activities. Management made various organizational changes to add more formality, such as creating a new position for quality and customer satisfaction. The company also instituted a more systematic way of doing things by building activities around 36-month plans.

Staffing the Small Business

In advising entrepreneurs, the SBA emphasizes the importance of effective human resource management. It notes, for instance, that "the small business owner should base the firm's personnel policies on explicit, well-proven principles . . . "[62] Therefore, the management skills covered in Chapter 9 ("Staffing and Human Resource Management") certainly apply to starting and managing a small business. Specifically, the entrepreneur needs to write job descriptions for the jobs in question and have a recruiting plan showing the jobs to recruit for and how to recruit for them. The entrepreneur must also effectively interview and screen candidates; train, appraise, and discipline the new employees; and know federal and local equal employment laws. The Duncan Group, Inc. helps illustrate how one entrepreneur went about this.

ne day," as Melba J. Duncan recalls, "I woke up and I knew: This is a business!"[63] After years as administrative assistant to CEOs, Duncan decided to strike out on her own. She correctly believed that top administrative/executive assistants represented an overlooked niche in the employee-search industry. Today, her company successfully places administrative assistants who command salaries ranging from $55,000 to $130,000 per year, not counting bonuses and benefits. Clients include IBM, Home Depot, and the Boston Consulting Group.

With years as a top assistant herself, Duncan combines an understanding of what the job calls for with a comprehensive system for selecting great candidates. To send three great finalists to a client, Duncan knows she must start with a pool of 100. Her recruiters, therefore, work the phones "like air-traffic controllers." They also review their files and their network of contacts. An initial screening cuts the original candidate pool to about 50, who complete a 15-page questionnaire, after which the pool is cut to about 15.[64] Those 15 go through a four-hour testing and profiling process. This helps highlight their written and oral communication and clerical skills as well as their management aptitude and personality. A clinical psychologist spends two days per week in Duncan's office, interviewing candidates and compiling profiles. Duncan's favorite questions for applicants appear in Figure 16.7.[65]

■■ ■ *Melba Duncan of Duncan Group, Inc.: Duncan's screening techniques enable her to successfully place top-ranked executive/administrative assistants.*

HR Start-Up Policies and Procedures

Organizing the paperwork involved in the small business's human resource management activities is essential. Doing so is a crucial aspect of having an organized company.

The paperwork required for even a small business is enormous. For example, just recruiting and hiring an employee might require a notice of available position, a help wanted advertising listing, an employment application, an interviewing checklist, and a telephone reference checklist. The entrepreneur then needs an employment agreement, a confidentiality and noncompete agreement, a hiring-authorization form, and an employee background verification. To keep track of the employee once he or she is on board, the entrepreneur will need—just to start—an employee change form, personnel data sheet, and daily or weekly time records. Then there are the performance appraisal forms; notice of probation; and dozens of other, similar forms. The new business owner without these documents cannot consider his or her business to be organized.

Where does the entrepreneur go to obtain the necessary HR forms and systems? For a start-up business, office supply stores such as Office Depot and OfficeMax sell paper and pencil forms. For example, Office Depot sells packages of individual personnel forms, including an employment application, performance evaluation, and weekly expense reports. However, as your company grows, it becomes increasingly unwieldy and inefficient to rely on manual HR systems. Conducting performance appraisals for a few employees and tracking the results may not be much of a problem for a small store, but for a company with 40 or 50 employees, the management time devoted to conducting appraisals can multiply.

It is at about this stage that most small- to medium-sized firms begin computerizing individual HR tasks. For example, HR supply firms such as G. Neil Companies and

At the Duncan Group, candidates are asked to complete a 15-page questionnaire. It's jammed with mind-benders such as "What does service mean to you?" and "What places, people, ideas, or things arouse your curiosity?" The questionnaire doesn't change, but the questions Duncan is inspired to ask during face-to-face interviews always do. Here are her current favorites, culled from the questionnaire and the interviews:

1. Describe your worst boss and best boss.
("I'm partly thinking about discretion," says Duncan. "How much are you telling me that I shouldn't know?")

2. What would a previous employer have to say about you? ("For perspective on flexibility, judgment, and maturity.")

3. What are some of the qualities that enable you to perform successfully in a support role? ("People are more important than technology in this job; of course you need both, but does the answer reveal a technician?")

4. Given the opportunity, what new activities would you try? ("Are you curious, outgoing, strong, confident? Whiners aren't good.")

5. Please write a brief paragraph on the subject of your own choosing. You may want to focus on your life, your family, your aspirations, your goals, or your achievements.
("There's nothing as important as having people's best interests at heart; I want to guide them into the right position and this answer will help me do that. I want to know they have a sense of direction. I want to know what they care about. Also, attention to detail: please, no typos!")

◄ **FIGURE 16–7** ■ ■ ■

Duncan's Five Fave Questions for Applicants

Source: Reprinted with permission of *Inc. Magazine* from "First Aide," by Nancy Austin, September 1999, copyright © 1999; permission conveyed through Copyright Clearance Center, Inc.

HR-Direct sell off-the-shelf software packages that enable firms to control attendance, keep employee records, write job descriptions, and conduct computerized employee appraisals.

■ ■ HOW ENTREPRENEURS LEAD

Small-business owners face some special challenges when it comes to leading and motivating employees. Many—like Steve Lauer, who runs eight Subway sandwich shops in northern Colorado—have the type of operation that depends heavily on minimum-wage, entry-level workers, many of whom have never worked before.[66] Keeping their workers motivated while trying to manage all the other functions of a small business can be a challenge. That makes the leadership skills covered in Chapters 10–13 especially important. Knowing the right leadership style for the situation, applying a range of motivation tools (from praise to higher pay), knowing how to communicate, and being able to get the most out of the company's work teams can spell the difference between success and failure for the entrepreneur.

Motivation in Small Businesses

Consider some examples. Steve Lauer found that half his stores' turnover occurred in the first 30 days of employment. Remembering his own stress level during his first days on the job, his first step was to get his new hires' stress levels down. He now has someone spend 20 hours periodically coaching new workers.

Leona Ackerly has a slightly different motivation problem. She runs a residential maid service in Georgia called Mini Maid, Inc. Most of her employees are women in their twenties, who have little education and few skills. Many have grown up on welfare. Some were abused. Part of Ackerly's motivation approach is to get her employees to "look at us as their partners in a team effort. We tell them, 'this is what we give you; this is what you give us.'" She makes her new employees feel they are an important part of the company. She builds their self-esteem and sense of self-worth.[67]

Not that Ackerly can't be tough when she needs to be. She hires no one with a police record or history of drug use, and if she catches anyone stealing, she presses charges. She insists that employees be punctual, clean, and neat. They also earn attendance bonuses each day they come to work on time and in uniform.

Richard Kerley, president and CEO of Fine Host Corporation, provides another example. He runs a food service in Greenwich, Connecticut. At any time, he has employees working in convention centers and corporate and college dining facilities, busing tables, cooking, and serving food. In this highly competitive business, wages are necessarily low, but as Kerley says, "Though there may be economic restraints on what we pay them, there are no restraints on the recognition we give them." For example, the company posts workers' names in the company building to acknowledge good work, it gives individual workers quality awards, and it makes sure each employee gets a framed certificate for completing training courses.

The bottom line is that while running a smaller business may have some special challenges, the intelligent use of Chapter 11's motivation tools, such as respect and recognition, can go a long way toward motivating workers who are also entry level and low paid.

Teamwork in Entrepreneurial Organizations

Entrepreneurs can make good use of the teamwork skills covered in Chapter 13. Published Image, Inc. is an example. Almost from the day he founded Published Image, Inc. and organized the company into self-managed teams, Eric Gershman had in mind the day his own position would become unnecessary. He believed that employees capable of preparing their own work schedules, budgets, and bonuses shouldn't have much use for a boss.

With the growth of mutual funds, Gershman had correctly predicted the need for shareholder newsletters. He spent his entire savings getting Published Image off the ground. Eleven clients later, things looked bleak. Turnover was high, morale was low, factual errors were common, and a third of the clients left annually. Gershman came

Dimension	Traditional Organization	Entrepreneurial Organization
Strategy	Status quo, conservative	Evolving, futuristic
Productivity	Short-term focus, profitability	Short and long term, multiple criteria
Risk	Averse, punished	Emphasized and rewarded
Opportunity	Absent	Integral
Leadership	Top-down, autocratic	Culture of empowerment
Power	Hoarded	Given away
Failure	Costly	OK; teaches a lesson
Decision making	Centralized	Decentralized
Communication	By the book, chain of command	Flexible, facilitates innovation
Structure	Hierarchical	Organic
Creativity	Tolerated	Prized and worshiped
Efficiency	Valued, accountants are heroes	Valued if it helps realize overall goals

◀ **FIGURE 16–8** ■ ■ ■

Organizational Culture: A Comparison

Source: Adapted from J. Cornwall and B. Perlman, *Organizational Entrepreneurship* (Homewood, IL: Irwin, 1990).

up with a plan of action. "We blew up the whole company and totally changed people's thinking about what their [jobs are]," Gershman says. He divided Published Image into four independent teams, responsible for client relations, sales, editorial content, and production. Everyone performed a specialty, but everyone shared responsibility for daily deadlines as well. "We work like a unit and pitch in to get out on time whatever has to get done," says account rep Shelley Danse.

Published Image's team approach fostered a sense of ownership of the collective output. It also helped employees appreciate the work of other employees. Planning was easier, and efficiency improved. Clients were impressed. "We have one group of people who know all facets of our job, and we can contact any of them during the process," says Peter Herlihy, vice president of mutual funds marketing at Fleet Financial Group.

Gershman soon got his wish of working himself out of a job. After revenues doubled to more than $4 million, Standard & Poors bought his business.[68]

The Entrepreneurial Culture

While many entrepreneurs (such as Eric Gershman) have no trouble creating just the right culture, for others doing so can be a chore. As noted earlier, one dark side of entrepreneurs is that some have high needs to control. This can translate into a culture of hiding and blame—hardly an entrepreneurial culture.

This darker culture has potential pros and cons. It may help the entrepreneur to keep things under control. On the other hand, it is also the opposite of what a small, innovative company's culture should be. Figure 16.8 sums up what most would view as the preferred entrepreneurial culture. It reflects the fact that entrepreneurial activities need a risk-loving, failure-forgiving, creative and decentralized culture to take root.

■ ■ ■ HOW ENTREPRENEURS CONTROL

The concepts and methods of managerial control are applicable to smaller organizations. For example, entrepreneurs should be able to use budgets, choose strategic ratios, and create a balanced scorecard (see Chapter 14).

What to Control?

The problem is that the entrepreneur who is first opening his or her doors has no control infrastructure to rely on. To that person, the idea that control means "setting standards, measuring performance, and taking corrective action" (Chapter 14) may seem a bit theoretical. The question the entrepreneur has to answer is, "What exactly do I have to 'control'?"[69] The following list provides a starting point. To start with, the entrepreneur should control:

- All approvals for disbursements of cash and regular accounting.
- The review of cash receipts, including reconciliation with the work that the firm actually did for the customer.
- The reconciliation of bank statements.
- The periodic review and reconciliation of inventory records.
- The approval of pricing policies and exceptions.
- The approval of credit policies and exceptions.
- The review of all expenses and commissions.
- The approval of purchasing and receiving policies.
- The review of payments to vendors and employees.
- The approval of signature authorities for payments (in other words, who can sign checks?).
- The review and changes to policies.

To monitor and control these and other activities, entrepreneurs need several operating reports. Control means setting targets, measuring performance, and taking corrective actions. These reports provide the tools for comparing what happened to what the entrepreneur planned. Operating reports provide insights into various facets of the company's operations. Managers typically need operating reports for activities, including:

- New orders and backlog (weekly, monthly).
- Shipments/sales (weekly, monthly).
- Employment (monthly).
- Inventory that is out of stock (weekly, monthly).
- Product quality (weekly, monthly).
- Accounts receivable aging (who owes what, and for how long?).
- Weekly overdue accounts.
- Returns and allowances (monthly).
- Production (weekly, monthly).

Computerized Operations Management and Enterprise Resource Planning

Even small businesses can automate their reporting process.[70] For example, thanks to its new enterprise resource planning system, "three people at Harman Music Group that once worked nearly full time planning what products to make at its factory [have been replaced by] two people who do that work part time each week."[71]

SUMMARY ■■■

1. Entrepreneurship is the creation of a business for the purpose of gain or growth under conditions of risk and uncertainty, and an entrepreneur is, thus, someone who creates new businesses under risky conditions.

2. Some environments are more conducive to entrepreneurship than others. The level of *economic freedom* is one consideration. Others include the ability to *streamline, downsize,* and *fire employees at will; technological advances,* and the level of *economic activity; globalization,* and other environmental factors, such as venture-capital availability; a technically skilled labor force; the accessibility of suppliers; the accessibility of customers; the availability of lenders; the accessibility of transportation; the attitude of the area's population; and the availability of supporting services (such as roads, electric power, and accounting firms).

3. Small businesses as a group account for most of the 600,000 or so new businesses created every year as well as for most of the growth of companies (small firms grow much faster than big ones). Small firms also account for about three-quarters of the employment growth in the U.S. economy—in other words, small businesses create most of the new jobs in the United States.

4. A few behaviors seem to arise consistently in anecdotal/case descriptions of successful entrepreneurs, including *tenacity* and *intensity*—the drive to pursue a goal with passion and focus.

5. Most entrepreneurs seem to stumble upon their ideas for a business. Most of those responding to one survey said they got their ideas for their businesses through their *previous employment. Serendipity* was the next source that most respondents mentioned. A relative handful got their ideas from *hobbies* or from a *systematic search* for business opportunities.

6. In creating the business entity, the entrepreneur needs to decide what the ownership structure will be. The four main forms of business ownership are the *sole proprietorship,* the *partnership,* the

corporation, and the *LLC.* Taxation and limiting the owner's liability are always big considerations in choosing an ownership form.

7. The two basic sources of business finance are debt and equity. Equity financing represents an ownership in the venture, while debt is borrowed capital.

8. While entrepreneurs often do develop detailed business plans to get their financing, in general they tend to abbreviate most steps of the planning process. In formulating strategies, for instance, they screen out losers quickly, minimize the resources devoted to researching ideas, don't wait for all the answers, and stand ready to change course.

9. In practice, new small businesses don't start off with conventional organization structures. The entrepreneur typically works interactively with a handful of associates, making all or most decisions him- or herself. As the firm grows, the manager institutes an organizational structure and chart.

10. Small business owners face some special challenges when it comes to leading and motivating employees. Keeping their workers motivated while trying to manage all the other functions of a small business can be a challenge. Knowing the right leadership style for the situation, applying a range of motivation tools (from praise to higher pay), knowing how to communicate, and being able to get the most out of the company's work teams can spell the difference between success and failure for the entrepreneur.

11. The small business manager needs to be sure he or she is controlling activities crucial to the firm's viability. These include cash disbursements and regular accounting, cash receipts, reconciliation of bank statements, review and reconciliation of inventory records, pricing policies, credit policies, all expenses and commissions, purchasing and receiving policies, payments to vendors and employees, signature authorities for payments, and changes to policies.

KEY TERMS ■■■

entrepreneurship 423
entrepreneur 423
small business management 423
intrapreneurship 426
franchise 430
franchiser 430

franchisee 430
franchising agreement 430
sole proprietorship 431
partnership 431
partnership agreement 431
corporation 433

limited liability company (LLC) 433
angels 434
venture capitalists 434
initial public offering (IPO) 434
business plan 439

SKILLS AND STUDY MATERIALS

COMPANION WEBSITE ■■■

 We invite you to visit the Dessler Companion Website at **www.prenhall.com/dessler** for this chapter's Internet resources.

EXPERIENTIAL EXERCISES ■■■

1. Using the materials in this chapter, write a one page paper on the topic, "Why I would (or would not) make a good entrepreneur."

2. At the library or on the Internet, review sales information on two popular franchises of your choice. Then, in teams of four or five students, evaluate the pros and cons of these franchise businesses, and answer the question, "Should I invest in this franchise?"

3. The dean of your business school is eager to expand her college's programs to new markets. She has decided to try to establish a new online M.B.A. program—the university's first. She has asked you to conduct an informal, quick feasibility study. In teams of four or five students, outline what you would cover in such a study, and then explain why you believe her new program is or is not a good idea.

CASE STUDY ■■■

GETTING BY WITH A LITTLE HELP FROM HIS MOTHER'S FRIENDS

Andrew Morris had almost everything he needed to start his Caribbean-flavored grocery store in a New York City suburb.[72] He had an M.B.A. from Columbia University, a business plan, and a $50,000 loan from the European American bank.

However, after he negotiated the rent on a 1,600 square foot retail space in Hempstead, New York, he found he did not have enough cash left for inventory, payroll, marketing, and licenses. Thanks to his mother—and her friends—he was able to secure an additional $15,000 in resources, which enabled him to stock the shelves with dozens of kinds of hot sauce, curry brands, and reggae music that the growing Caribbean community craves.

Morris got the money from his mother's *susu*, a kind of club or fund developed by West Indian housewives to provide rotating credit for big-ticket household purchases. A *susu*, which means "partner," typically has about 20 members, most of them either relatives or close friends. Each week, every member contributes a fixed sum, or *hand*, into the fund for a 20-week period. Any time during those 20 weeks, each member is entitled to borrow an amount, or *draw*, to use interest-free during that time. For example, if a 20-member *susu* has a set weekly contribution of $100, each member pays $100 into the fund every week—or pays a total of $2,000 over 20 weeks. Each member is then also able to draw $2,000 at any point during that period. Essentially, the *susu* is a kind of planned savings program that pools money to help members of the group who need help with cash flow. The Caribbean *susu* is not really a unique concept in the United States. Asian Americans and other ethnic groups have also developed informal lending networks for their members.

Andrew Morris has dipped into his mother's *susu* a number of times to help his business grow. He used the money to pay a sales tax obligation, to purchase a commercial oven to cook Jamaican meat patties, to produce a special Easter promotion with tradi-tional cheese and sweet bread sandwiches, and to expand his inventory to include unusual but popular items, such as Jamaican Chinese soy sauce. "It's a cash-flow boon," Morris says. After seven years of ongoing *susu* support, Morris's store now has annual revenues of over $1 million. Morris is now counting on *susu* support to help it expand into distributing coffee and developing a Web site. "[The *susu* is] no longer just a Christmas club," he says. "It's a way of life."

Discussion Questions

1. Andrew Morris has approached you for help. List what you believe he is doing right and doing wrong with respect to starting his business. What do you think accounts for the fact that he ran out of money before he opened, even though he had a business plan? What remedy or remedies would you suggest at this point?

2. Develop a one-page outline showing Morris how you would suggest he conduct an informal business feasibility study.

3. List the activity areas for which Morris should establish controls.

4. What other alternative means for obtaining financing would you recommend for Morris, and what are their pros and cons when compared to continuing to use his mothers *susu*?

YOU BE THE CONSULTANT ■■■

JETBLUE THE ENTREPRENEUR

jetBlue AIRWAYS Just about any way you look at it, David Neeleman is your classic entrepreneur. As one friend and airline analyst put it, "He's a genius entrepreneur." Says Neeleman's second in command, "He has an uncanny knack for knowing when an opportunity is right."[73] Neeleman's record speaks for itself. He was one of two people who started Morris Air, and then he sold it for a huge profit to Southwest Airlines. Southwest bought Morris Air on the condition that Neeleman sign a five-year noncompete clause. Neeleman spent the next five years helping to start a (noncompeting) new airline (WestJet) in Canada and a company that created an electronic reservation system. He also spent some time researching what a new, low-cost airline in the United States might look like. Thus, by the time his five-year noncompete agreement had run out, Neeleman had already started three very successful companies over the course of his career, and he had developed the plan for his fourth, which would turn out to be JetBlue.

You could trace Neeleman's strategy for JetBlue back to his experiences at Morris Air and Southwest Airlines. As he tells it, he spent part of his five-year noncompete period thinking through how to build a top-notch, low-fare passenger airline: "We asked, ['How] could we create a preferred product—rather than a secondary or tertiary choice—and do that at the lowest [cost?']"[74]

Several of JetBlue's basic operating policies stem from Neeleman's earlier experiences. For example, at Morris Air, he was one of the airline industry's first executives to implement paperless electronic tickets. He was also one of the first to encourage telecommuting, with many of Morris's reservation agents working from their homes. From the outset, he knew he wanted his new airline to "offer a superior product with everyday low fares." His original plan, therefore, called for new planes, strong financing, high utilization, fleet homogeneity, great pricing, and experienced management. As he put it, "We're Southwest with seat assignments, leather seats and television."[75]

With a strong plan and years of success in creating value for his investors, it's probably not surprising that Neeleman was able to raise about $160 million, making his new airline the best financed new airline in history. His investors included J.P. Morgan Partners, Soros Private Equity Partners LLC, and Weston Presidio Capital, all among the top financiers in America. He soon followed that up with an IPO that raised over $100 million more—and helped pay back several of his initial investors.

Neeleman seems to exhibit some of the traits most people would associate with successful entrepreneurs—as well as some you might not. He is a college dropout as well as "a Mormon with nine kids who won't sip coffee, much less chain-smoke cigarettes and toss back . . . Wild Turkey."[76] He doesn't spend much time partying, and he says his only hobby (other than spending time with his family) is reading history books. Neeleman self-mockingly told one reporter that he sometimes thinks he has attention deficit disorder, apparently because he is so quick to move from one idea to another. On the other hand, friends and associates describe him as highly focused. "He's low-key, and he's totally directed . . .," says one associate. One reporter, after watching him lead an orientation session for new employees, described him as "completely, utterly riveting."[77]

So far, according to virtually all reports, JetBlue has avoided the sorts of poor service and/or spotty performance problems that have tripped up some other start-up airlines.[78] However, some airline industry analysts have expressed some concerns. At the moment, for instance, JetBlue's profitability is high in part because, with brand-new airplanes, it has no maintenance costs—the maintenance is provided as part of the original purchase price of the aircraft. Furthermore, now that JetBlue is more firmly in the radar screen of major airlines like American and United, they are more aggressively resisting JetBlue's incursions onto their turf. Employees at Southwest Airlines (which, remember, served as part of the model for JetBlue) have recently been much more vocal about getting a bigger share of the pie from Southwest management. Furthermore, Neeleman has said that staying small (in terms of maintaining JetBlue's enthusiastic entrepreneurial culture) is "our greatest challenge as we move forward."[79] That will mean maintaining good compensation (including the company's profit-sharing and stock purchase plans), as well as doing whatever else is necessary to keep employees happy and focused on customer service and high productivity.

Discussion Questions

1. In what ways does Neeleman fit the stereotype of the typical entrepreneur? In what ways does he differ? Would you say that he has the traits to be entrepreneur? Why or why not?

2. List in outline form the things you think Neeleman did right and wrong with respect to starting JetBlue.

3. Based on what you know, what are Neeleman and his team doing to maintain an entrepreneurial culture at JetBlue? What else would you suggest that they do?

17 Managing in a Global Environment

CHAPTER OBJECTIVES

After studying this chapter and the case exercises at the end, you should be able to

1. List the socio cultural and legal/political errors managers make when expanding abroad.

2. Tell a manager why a company is (or is not) a suitable candidate for expanding into a specific country, based on the *cultural*, and *geographic* distance between that country and the company's home country.

3. List the reasons why you would (or would not) be a good global manager.

4. Specify the basic global strategy a manager should pursue, and why.

5. Specify the type of basic global organization structure a manager should use, and why.

6. Tell a manager what he or she did wrong in leading and motivating employees abroad.

450

THE MANAGEMENT CHALLENGE

Lincoln Electric's Global Expansion

When it comes to motivating workers, the Lincoln Electric Company of Cleveland, Ohio, is one of the most famous companies in the world. In 1934, it established its Lincoln incentive system, where Lincoln distributes much of the cash it produces each year to its employees as a bonus. Management bases the bonus on the employees' factorywide and individual performances. The plan has made Lincoln's factory workers among the highest paid in the world—many earn $80,000 or more per year.

When Lincoln decided to expand abroad in the late 1980s, its financial performance began to unravel.[1] Lincoln's management made four basic assumptions: the incentive plan would work as well with employees abroad as it did in the United States; that with the highly motivated workforce its incentive plan produced, management would be able to control all foreign operations from the Cleveland headquarters; the company could expand abroad without a core of experienced global managers and corporate directors; and Lincoln's management systems were so good that the company's managers didn't have to study the cultures into which Lincoln was expanding.

By the early 1990s, for the first time in Lincoln's 97-year history, management had to report a multimillion dollar quarterly loss. The problem was foreign operations. Upon taking the reins as CEO, Donald Hastings needed to know the answers to these questions: Where do you think management went wrong? What would you suggest we do about it?

Globalization is a major force in business today, with exports accounting for over 11% of America's total economic activity.[2] Some business leaders say that globalization really means "Americanization." Martin Sorrell, chairman and CEO of UK-based advertising giant WPP Group, says, "You see this in every industry: The strongest global franchises belong to companies that have strong franchises in the United States. If you're not strong in the United States, it's hard to be strong elsewhere. To dominate an industry—whatever the scale, wherever the business—you simply have to have strong representation in United States."[3] Yet as Lincoln's experience shows, being tops in America doesn't necessarily mean you'll succeed overseas. Managing abroad brings its own special challenges. The main purpose of this chapter is to enable you to better size up the pros and cons of expanding abroad, and to better manage your global operations once you do expand. The main topics we'll cover include methods of doing business abroad; the international environment; the management team in a global business; and global management planning, organizing, leading, and controlling techniques.

■■■ DOING BUSINESS ABROAD

Globalization (as noted in Chapter 1) is the tendency of firms to extend their sales, ownership, and/or manufacturing to new markets abroad. Globalization of *markets* is perhaps most obvious. Sony, Calvin Klein, The Gap, Nike, and Mercedes Benz are some firms that market all over the world. *Production* is global too. Toyota produces its Camry in Georgetown, Kentucky. Dell produces computers in China. In turn, the existence of globalized markets and production means that globalized *ownership* makes more sense. For example, firms outside America own four out of five American textbook publishers—Prentice Hall, Harcourt, Houghton Mifflin, and Southwestern (Britain's Pearson owns Prentice Hall). Why do managers take their firms abroad?

Companies expand abroad for several reasons. *Sales expansion* is often the goal. Thus, Lincoln Electric went abroad to open new markets in Europe and elsewhere. Wal-Mart is opening stores in South America. Dell Computer, knowing that China will soon be the world's second biggest market for PCs, is aggressively building plants and selling there.[4]

Firms also go abroad for other reasons. Some manufacturers go seeking *new foreign products* and services to sell, and to *cut labor costs*. Thus, Florida apparel manufacturers have products assembled in Central America, where labor costs are relatively low. Sometimes, high-quality or specialized skills drive firms overseas. For example, Apple Computer enlisted Sony's aid in producing parts for a notebook computer.

The question for the manager is, "*How* should we expand abroad?" Options include exporting, licensing, franchising, foreign direct investment, joint ventures/strategic alliances, and wholly owned subsidiaries. Many things—including the company's goals and resources—determine which option is best.

Exporting

Exporting is often a manager's first choice when expanding abroad. Exporting is a relatively simple and easy approach. It means selling abroad, either directly to customers, or indirectly through sales agents and distributors.[5] Agents, distributors or other intermediaries handle more than half of all exports. They are generally local people familiar with the market's customs and customers.

Carefully selecting intermediaries is important. For example, you can check business reputations via local agencies of the U.S. State Department. Then carefully draft agency and distribution agreements to ensure you have the right representatives.[6] Bird Corporation President Fred Schweser sought out the U.S. Commerce department's trade specialist Harvey Roffman for help in generating overseas business. Roffman recommended advertising in *Commercial News USA*, a government publication designed to inform around 100,000 foreign agents, distributors, buyers, and government officials about U.S. products. The advice worked. Schweser's Elkhorn, Nebraska, Go-Cart company now boasts customers from Japan to the United Kingdom.[7]

Exporting has pros and cons. It avoids the need to build factories in the host country, and it is a relatively quick and inexpensive way of "going international."[8] It's also a good way to test the waters in the host country, and to learn more about its customers' needs. However, transportation, tariff, or manufacturing costs can put the exporter at a disadvantage, as can poorly selected intermediaries. Some avoid this problem by selling

exporting ■ *selling abroad, either directly to target customers or indirectly by retaining foreign sales agents and distributors.*

direct. L.L. Bean, Lands' End, and Sharper Image all export globally via their catalogues and the Internet.[9] Since the Internet is basically borderless, almost any company can market its products or services directly to potential customers anywhere in the world.

Licensing

Licensing is an arrangement whereby the licensor grants a foreign firm the right to exploit intangible ("intellectual") property, such as patents, copyrights, manufacturing processes, or trade names for a specific period. The licensor usually gets royalties—a percentage of the earnings—in return.[10] Licensing enables a firm to generate income abroad from its intellectual property without actually producing or marketing the product or service there.

For example, consider a small U.S. inventor of antipollution materials. Licensing Shell Oil to produce and sell the material in Europe lets the U.S. firm enter that market with little or no investment. However, it might not be able to control the design, manufacture, or sales of its products as well as it could if it built its own facilities there.

Franchising

If you've eaten in McDonald's by Rome's Spanish Steps, you know that franchising is another way to do business abroad. Franchising is the granting of a right by a parent company to another firm to do business in a prescribed manner.[11]

Franchising is similar to licensing. Both involve granting rights to intellectual property. Both are quick and relatively low-cost ways to expand into other countries. However, franchising usually requires both parties to make greater commitments in time and money. A franchisee must generally follow strict guidelines in running the business. It must also make substantial investments in a physical plant (such as a fast-food restaurant). Licensing tends to be limited to manufacturers. Franchising is more common among service firms such as restaurants, hotels, and rental services. Maintaining the franchisee's quality can be a particular problem. For example, an early McDonald's franchisee in France had to close its restaurants when it failed to maintain McDonald's quality standards.

Foreign Direct Investment and the Multinational Enterprise

At some point, managers find that capitalizing on international opportunities requires direct investment. Foreign direct investment refers to operations in one country controlled by entities in a foreign country. A foreign firm might build facilities in another country, as Toyota did when it built its Camry plant in Georgetown, Kentucky. Or a firm might acquire property or operations, as when Wal-Mart bought control of the Wertkauf stores in Germany. A foreign direct investment turns the firm into a multinational enterprise. Strictly speaking, foreign direct investment means owning more than 50% of the operation. But in practice, a firm can gain effective control by owning less than half.

Purchases like these trigger large and small changes. For example, the Italian bank UniCredito Italiano Group purchased Boston's Pioneer Group several years ago. One of its first changes was installing an Italian espresso machine in Pioneer's offices. The Milan bank also installed video cameras and screens. Now investment managers on both sides of the Atlantic can hold videoconferences. Pioneer group managers have begun learning Italian. And the companies integrated their Italian and U.S. investment teams, which then went on to launch several global funds.[12]

Joint Ventures and Strategic Alliances

Foreign direct investments are often strategic alliances. Strictly speaking, strategic alliances are "cooperative agreements between potential or actual competitors."[13] For example, Boeing partnered with several Japanese companies to produce a new commercial jet. Airline alliances, such as American Airlines' One World alliance, are also examples. The airlines don't share investments, but they do share seating on some flights, and they let passengers use alliance members' airport lounges.[14] In practice, most managers define strategic alliances more broadly, as any agreements between firms that are of strategic importance to one or both firms.[15] In that sense, even licensing or franchising agreements might come under the strategic alliance umbrella.

The point of the alliance is usually to quickly gain strengths that would otherwise take time to acquire. General Motors is using alliances to build its Asian presence. It has minority stakes in several Asian auto manufacturers, including Daewoo Motor Company, Suzuki Motor Ltd., Isuzu Motor Ltd., and Fuji Heavy Industries.[16]

A joint venture is "the participation of two or more companies jointly in an enterprise in which each party contributes assets, owns the entity to some degree, and shares risk."[17] A joint venture is a special strategic alliance.[18] Companies execute joint ventures every day. For example, the big Indian media company, Zee Telefilms, recently formed several partnerships with AOL Time Warner. The firms call their new joint venture Zee Turner. It will distribute both partners' television programs in India and neighboring countries.[19]

A joint venture lets a firm gain useful experience in a foreign country by using the expertise and resources of a locally knowledgeable firm. Joint ventures also help both companies share the cost of starting a new operation. But as in licensing, the joint venture partners risk giving away proprietary secrets. And joint ventures usually require the partners to share control.

Joint ventures can be a necessity. In China, foreign companies that want to enter regulated industries (like telecommunications) must use joint ventures with well-connected Chinese partners. The partnership of Britain's Alcatel and Shanghai Bell to make telephone-switching equipment is an example.[20]

joint venture ■ *the participation of two or more companies in an enterprise such that each party contributes assets, owns the entity to some degree, and shares risk.*

Wholly Owned Subsidiaries

Some companies have the knowledge and resources to go it alone. A wholly owned subsidiary is one owned 100 percent by the foreign firm. In the United States, Toyota Motor Manufacturing, Inc., and its Georgetown, Kentucky, Camry facility is a wholly owned subsidiary of Japan's Toyota Motor Corporation. Toys "R" Us, Inc., was the first large U.S.-owned discount store in Japan, and it is now expanding its wholly owned subsidiary there.[21] Wholly owned subsidiaries let the company do things exactly as it wants (subject to local laws and regulations, of course).

wholly owned subsidiary ■ *a firm that is owned 100% by a foreign firm.*

The Language of International Business

To do business abroad, the manager should know the vocabulary of international business. An international business is any firm that engages in international trade or investment.[22] International business also refers to those activities, such as exporting goods or transferring employees, that require the movement of resources, goods, services, and skills across national boundaries.[23] International trade is the export or import of goods or services to consumers in another country. International management is the performance of the management functions of planning, organizing, leading, and controlling across national borders. As Wal-Mart managers expand abroad, for instance, they necessarily engage in international management.

A multinational corporation (MNC) operates manufacturing and marketing facilities in two or more countries; managers of the parent firm, whose owners are mostly in the firm's home country, coordinate the MNC's operations. Firms like GE and GM have long been multinational corporations. However, thousands of small firms are MNCs, too.

The MNC operates in multiple countries and adapts its products and practices to each one. Sometimes, however, the MNC's behavior may still reflect its national roots. Thus, Germany's DeutscheBank recently bought a British bank, and the British managers' high incentive pay created tension between them and their new German bosses.[24]

international business ■ *any firm that engages in international trade or investment; also refers to business activities that involve the movement of resources, goods, services, and skills across national boundaries.*

international management ■ *the performance of the management process across national boundaries.*

international trade ■ *the export or import of goods or services to consumers in another country.*

multinational corporation (MNC) ■ *a company that operates manufacturing and marketing facilities in two or more countries: managers of the parent firm, whose owners are mostly in the firm's home country, coordinate the MNC's operation.*

■ ■ ■ THE MANAGER'S INTERNATIONAL ENVIRONMENT

Tensions like these illustrate a fact of life of doing business abroad: Countries differ in terms of economic, legal, and political systems—and also in their cultures. Managers ignore such differences at their peril, since they'll shape the manager's plans, organization, leadership style, and controls.

The Economic Environment

First, managers should understand the economic environments of the countries they are thinking of entering. This includes each country's *economic system, economic development, exchange rates, trade barriers, economic integration* and *free trade.*

The Economic System Countries differ in the extent to which they adhere to capitalistic economic ideals and policies like America's. For example, like America, Hong Kong is a *market economy*. In a pure market economy, supply and demand determine what is produced, in what quantities, and at what prices. Managers here tend to have much flexibility to compete and set prices without government intervention.

At the other extreme, the People's Republic of China until recently was a pure *command economy* (North Korea still is). Countries like these base their yearly targets on five-year plans set by the government. Then the government establishes specific production goals and prices for each sector of the economy (for each product or group of products), as well as for each manufacturing plant. Managers from abroad usually need government approval before entering these markets and forming partnerships with local firms.

After taking over Hong Kong from Britain several years ago, China agreed to let Hong Kong keep its capitalist system for 50 years. However, Beijing now governs Hong Kong's political administration, and Hong Kong's legislature imposed limits on opposition activities. Developing long-run management plans under such circumstances can be challenging.

In a **mixed economy**, some sectors have private ownership and free market mechanisms, while others are owned and managed by the government.[25] *Mixed* is, of course, a matter of degree. For example, France is a capitalist country. However, it has a mixed economy. The government owns shares of industries like telecommunications (France Telecom) and air travel (Air France).

Economic systems in transition can trigger social instability. This occurred several years ago in the newly capitalized Russia. Free-market economies require commercial laws, banking regulations, and an effective independent judiciary and law enforcement. Without such a political and legal infrastructure in Russia, early business owners had to cope not just with competitors but also with criminals, lax law enforcement, and the control of several industries by friends of powerful politicians. Managers taking their firms into such areas obviously can't just be concerned with running their businesses. There's the added challenge of the turbulence.

mixed economy ■ *an economy in which some sectors are left to private ownership and free market mechanisms, while others are largely owned and managed by the government.*

Economic Development Countries also differ in degree of *economic development*. For example, some countries, such as the United States, Japan, Germany, France, Italy, and Canada, have large, mature economies. They also have extensive *industrial infrastructures*. This includes telecommunications, transportation, and regulatory and judicial systems. These countries' gross domestic products range from about $700 billion for Canada to $8.5 trillion for the United States.[26] Other countries, such as Mexico, are less developed. **Gross domestic product (GDP)** is the market value of all goods and services bought for final domestic use during a period. It is a basic measure of a nation's economic activity.

Some countries are growing much faster than others. The growth rate of mature economies averages around 4% per year. On the other hand, China, India, and Taiwan are growing at about 7.5%, 5.0%, and 5.2%, respectively. Many managers at firms like Wal-Mart are therefore boosting their investments in these high-growth, high-potential countries.[27] A country's economic development level can thus be both a blessing and a curse to the manager thinking of entering it. Low economic development may suggest the potential for rapid development and growth, but it can also mean an absence of adequate roadways, communications, and regulatory and judicial infrastructure.

gross domestic product (GDP) ■ *the market value of all goods and services that have been bought for final use during a period of time, and, therefore, the basic measure of a nation's economic activity.*

Exchange Rates Managers engaged in international business must also juggle exchange rates. The **exchange rate** for one country's currency is the rate at which someone can exchange it for another country's currency. A dramatic drop in the value of the dollar relative to the pound could have a devastating effect on a small U.S. company that suddenly found it needed 30% more dollars than planned to build a factory in Scotland.

exchange rate ■ *the rate at which one country's currency can be exchanged for another country's currency.*

Trade Barriers The Gap store in Paris's Passy area sells jeans that you could buy for two-thirds the price in midtown Manhattan. How can this be? The answer is that trade barriers distort the prices companies must charge for their products. **Trade barriers** are governmental influences aimed at reducing the competitiveness of imported products or services. **Tariffs**, the most common trade barrier, are governmental taxes levied on

trade barrier ■ *a governmental influence that is usually aimed at reducing the competitiveness of imported products or services.*

tariff ■ *government tax on imports.*

goods shipped internationally.[28] The exporting country collects export tariffs. Importing countries collect import tariffs. Countries through which the goods pass collect transit tariffs. Other countries impose quotas—legal restrictions on the import of specific goods.[29] Managers thinking of doing business abroad ignore taxes like these at their peril.

Nontariff trade barriers exist too. For example, cars imported to Japan must meet a complex set of regulations and equipment modifications. Side mirrors must snap off easily if they contact a pedestrian, for example. Some countries make payments called subsidies to domestic producers. These are government payments that can make inefficient domestic producers more competitive.

Economic Integration and Free Trade Free trade agreements among countries are a big part of the economic situation international managers face. Free trade means all trade barriers among participating countries are removed.[30] Free trade occurs when two or more countries agree to allow the free flow of goods and services. This means trade is unimpeded by trade barriers such as tariffs. Economic integration occurs when two or more nations obtain the advantages of free trade by minimizing trade restrictions.

Economic integration occurs on several levels. In a free trade area, member countries remove all barriers to trade among them so that they can freely trade goods and services among member countries. A customs union is the next higher level of economic integration. Here, members dismantle trade barriers among themselves while establishing a common trade policy with respect to nonmembers. In a common market, no barriers to trade exist among members, and a common external trade policy is in force. In addition, factors of production, such as labor, capital, and technology, move freely between member countries, as shown in Figure 17.1.

Economic integration is happening around the world. Back in 1957, founding members France, West Germany, Italy, Belgium, the Netherlands, and Luxembourg established the European Economic Community (now called the European Union, or EU). They signed the Treaty of Rome. It called for the formation of a free trade area, the gradual elimination of tariffs and other barriers to trade, and the formation of a customs union and (eventually) a common market. By 1987, the renamed European Community had added six other countries (Great Britain, Ireland, Denmark, Greece, Spain, and Portugal) and signed the Single Europe Act. This act "envisages a true common market where goods, people, and money move among the twelve EC countries with the same ease that they move between Wisconsin and Illinois."[31] In 1995, Austria, Finland, and Sweden became the 13th, 14th, and 15th members of the EU. Figure 17.2 outlines the organizational structure of the EU. The EU admitted 10 more countries in 2002.

On January 1, 1999, 11 EU countries formed a European Economic and Monetary Union (EMU). On January 1, 2002, the Union's new currency, the Euro, went into circulation. Within two to three months, it entirely replaced these 11 countries' local currencies. Now companies in these countries deal with just one currency within the EU;

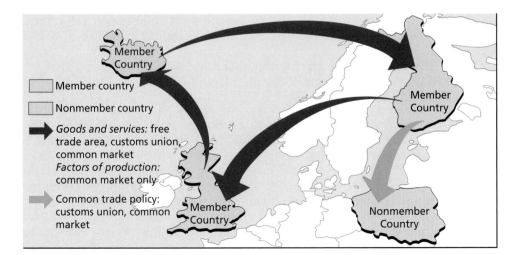

◀ **FIGURE 17–1** ■ ■ ■

Levels of Economic Integration

▶ FIGURE 17–2 ■ ■ ■

EU Organizational Structure

Source: From "Survey of Europe," *The Economist*, October 23, 1999. The Economist Newspaper Group, Inc. **www.economist. com**. Reprinted with permission. Further reproduction prohibited.

How the EU (more or less) works

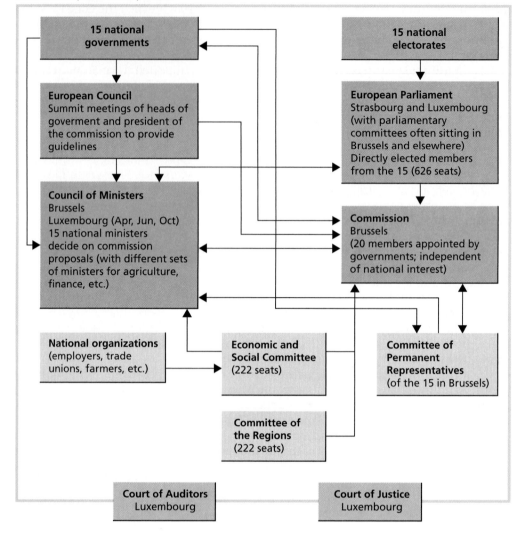

and companies from other countries, like the United States, deal with just two currencies (theirs and the Euro) and with one exchange rate rather than several.

In 1967, Brunei, Indonesia, Malaysia, the Philippines, Singapore, Thailand, and Vietnam organized the Association of Southeast Asian Nations (ASEAN).[32] There is also the Asia Pacific Economic Cooperation (APEC) forum. This is a loose association of 18 Pacific Rim states. Members include Australia, Chile, China, Japan, Malaysia, Mexico, Singapore, and the United States.[33] Africa similarly has several regional trading groups, including the southern African development community, the common market for Eastern and southern Africa, and the economic community of West African states.

Canada, the United States, and Mexico established a North American Free Trade Agreement (NAFTA). NAFTA creates the world's largest free trade market, with a total output of about $6 trillion.

The WTO Governments work together to encourage free trade in other ways.[34] GATT—the General Agreement on Tariffs and Trade—was one example. Formed in 1947 by 23 countries, by the mid-1990s 117 countries were participating. Among other things, GATT sponsored "rounds" or sessions at which members discussed multilateral reductions in trade barriers. The World Trade Organization (WTO) replaced GATT in 1995, and it now has over 130 members. One of the WTO's important functions is granting "most favored nation" (or "normal trade relations") status for countries. This means that the WTO countries' "most favorable trade concessions must apply to all trading partners."[35]

China recently received most favored nation status and joined the WTO. Joining means getting the benefits of normal trade relations with WTO partners, but it also means the new member must reduce its own trade barriers. Several U.S. companies, including New York Life Insurance Company and Metropolitan Life Insurance Co., quickly got the green light to set up 50-50 joint ventures with Chinese partners once China joined the WTO.[36] Even for WTO members, some trade barriers fall faster than others. With WTO membership, China will see its import duties on cars fall drastically (to about 25%).[37] However, within China, Shanghai still has big license fees on cars from neighboring provinces so that Shanghai can protect its locally built Volkswagen.

Economic integration has a big effect on managers. By removing trade barriers (such as tariffs), it promotes regional trade and thus boosts competition.[38] Thus, in Europe, airlines (like British Airways) and telecommunications firms (like France Telecom) had relatively little competition 10 years ago. Now they face new competition from firms like Air France and DeutscheTelecom within their EU trading bloc. Establishing free trade zones also put firms from nonmember countries at a disadvantage. Many U.S. managers are forming joint ventures with European partners to make it easier for them to sell in the EU.

Legal and Political Environment

Global political and legal differences can blindside even the most sophisticated companies. After spending billions of dollars expanding into Germany, for instance, Wal-Mart managers were surprised to learn that Germany's commercial laws discourage advertising or promotions that involve competitive price comparisons.

Legal considerations influence how managers expand abroad.[39] In India, for instance, a foreign investor may own only up to 40% of an Indian industrial company, whereas in Japan, up to 100% of foreign ownership is allowed.[40] Some managers go global by appointing sales agents or representatives in other countries. But in Algeria, for instance, agents can't represent foreign sellers. Other countries view agents as employees subject to those countries' employment laws.[41]

Legal Systems Countries also differ fundamentally in their approaches to the law. England and the United States use *common law* legal systems. Here, tradition and precedent—not written statutes—govern legal decisions. Other countries, like France, follow a *code law system*, or a comprehensive set of written statutes. A businessperson accused of a crime there might also be surprised to find he or she is "guilty till proven innocent," while the U.S. system assumes the accused is innocent. Some countries use a combination of common law and code law. The United States adheres to a system of common law in criminal proceedings but to a written Uniform Commercial Code for governing business activities.

International law is another consideration when expanding abroad. *International law* is less an enforceable body of law than it is agreements embodied in treaties and other types of agreements. International law governs things like intellectual property rights, such as whether someone in Japan can reproduce Motown's music without its permission. Intellectual property piracy (fake brands) can be a big problem where the legal system is inadequate or inadequately enforced. For example, P&G reportedly estimates that about 20 percent of all its products sold in China are fake.[42]

Political Systems Going abroad also means sizing up the political systems and risks with which you'll have to cope. Thus, democratic countries will usually provide a more open environment in which to establish and manage businesses than will dictatorships. Sometimes, the company's fate can change unexpectedly as the political winds shift. For example, in the mid-1990s, the Coca-Cola Company was very successful with its bottling plant in Uzbekistan. One reason, apparently, was that it opened the plant in partnership with the

■ ■ *Global management can have special problems: Lab technician at a Coca-Cola plant near Verona in northern Italy tests samples after several European countries banned Coke drinks because youngsters who drank Coke produced at plants that serve Belgium became ill.*

■ ■ *Store manager Ryota Tsunoda, far right, and other employees serve customers at the opening of Starbucks' first overseas store, in Tokyo's Ginza. The Starbucks style redefined how Japanese drink coffee.*

Uzbekistan president's son-in-law. Recently, when the president's daughter separated from her husband, the bottling company's Uzbek fortunes abruptly took a turn for the worse.[43]

The Sociocultural Environment

People around the world react to events in characteristic ways. For example, a researcher at Georgetown University found that Japanese, German, and U.S. managers tended to take different approaches when resolving workplace conflict.[44] The Japanese prefer the power approach, tending to defer to the party with the most power. Germans tend to emphasize a more legalistic, sticking-to-the-rules approach. U.S. managers tend to try to take into account all parties' interests and to work out a solution that maximizes the benefits for everyone.

Cultural differences like these should influence how managers conduct business abroad. When it opened its new production plant in Valenciennes, France, Toyota had to explain to the French Labor Ministry why management banned the traditional red wine at lunchtime in the company cafeteria. (The reasons given were health and working conditions.)[45]

On the other hand, Starbucks broke some traditions when it opened its first Tokyo store, and it now has over 300 stores in Japan. Starbucks (pronounced "STAH-buks-zu" in Japanese) accomplished this by redefining (not adapting to) the way the Japanese drink coffee. Its nonsmoking, bright, sofa-filled stores are in marked contrast to the dimly lit, smoke-filled stores where many Japanese traditionally drink their coffee from tiny cups. It turned out that Japanese girls preferred Starbucks' nonsmoking stores, and the boys were soon following them there to socialize.[46] We'll look more closely at multicultural issues in management later in this chapter.

The Technological Environment

technology transfer ■ *the transfer, often to another country, of systematic knowledge for the manufacturing of a product, for the application of a process, or for the rendering of a service; it does not extend to the mere sales or lease of goods.*

Doing business abroad often requires technology transfer, which is the "transfer of systematic knowledge for the manufacture of a product, for the application of a process, or for the rendering of a service, and [it] does not extend to the mere sale or lease of goods."[47] When Dell builds a computer factory in China, the plant's success depends on Dell's ability to successfully transfer to local managers knowledge of its sophisticated manufacturing processes.

Successful technology transfer depends on several things. It depends on having a needed and suitable technology. Social and economic conditions must favor the transfer. (Pollution-reducing technology might be economically useless in a country where pollution reduction is not a priority.) Finally, technology transfer depends on the willingness and ability of the receiving party to use and adapt the technology.[48] Opening a new plant or franchising a process require an acceptable level of technical expertise in the receiving country. Without it, the expansion may well fail.

Distance and Global Management

As you can see, geographic distance was just one of the barriers managers like Lincoln Electric's new CEO Donald Hastings faced when Lincoln expanded abroad. They also faced economic, legal/political, sociocultural, and technological barriers.

Studies of international trade show that factors like these are actually more important than geographic distance in explaining a foreign venture's success. For example, studies show that international trade is much more likely among countries that share a common language and that belong to a common regional trading bloc. International trade is greater among countries that formerly shared a colony-colonizer relationship (as between England and Australia). Similarly, common political systems and a common currency translate into less troublesome—and thus greater—trade.

ATTRIBUTES CREATING DISTANCE			
Cultural Distance	**Administrative Distance**	**Geographic Distance**	**Economic Distance**
Different languages	Absence of colonial ties	Physical remoteness	Differences in consumer incomes
Different ethnicities; lack of connective ethnic or social networks	Absence of shared monetary or political association	Lack of a common border	
		Lack of sea or river access	Differences in costs and quality of:
Different religions	Political hostility	Size of country	• natural resources
Different social norms	Government policies	Weak transportation or communication links	• financial resources
	Institutional weakness		• human resources
		Differences in climates	• infrastructure
			• intermediate inputs
			• information or knowledge

◀ **FIGURE 17–3** ■■■

Determinants of Global Distance

Source: Adapted from Pankaj Ghemawat, "Distance Still Matters," *Harvard Business Review*, September, 2001, p. 140.

One researcher says (see Figure 17.3) that managers like Donald Hastings should consider at least four factors before expanding abroad: (1) *cultural distance* (such as languages and religions), (2) *administrative distance* (such as absence of shared monetary or political associations), (3) *geographic distance* (such as physical remoteness), and (4) *economic distance* (such as differences in consumer incomes).

His point is that some cross-border business initiatives are more likely to succeed than are others. Figure 17.4 summarizes this. For example, in the textile industry, geographic distance isn't nearly as important as administrative distance. That's because preferential trading agreements and tariffs determine whether textiles from one country are salable in another. If you're a manager in a textile firm, you'd best take preferential trading agreements into account. Similarly, managers at Campbell Soup should consider cultural distance when launching products abroad (for instance, the Japanese tend to have soup for breakfast).

▼ **FIGURE 17–4** ■■■

Industry Sensitivity to Distance

The various types of distance affect different industries in different ways.

Source: Pankaj Ghemawat, "Distance Still Matters," *Harvard Business Review*, September 2001, pp. 142–43.

Cultural Distance	Administrative Distance	Geographic Distance	Economic Distance
Linguistic Ties	Preferential Trading Agreement	Physical Remoteness	Wealth Differences
		MORE SENSITIVE	
Meat and meat preparations	Gold, nonmonetary	Electricity current	(*economic distance decreases trade*)
Cereals and cereal preparations	Electricity current	Gas, natural and manufactured	Nonferrous metals
Miscellaneous edible products and preparations	Coffee, tea, cocoa, spices	Paper, paperboard	Manufactured fertilizers
Tobacco and tobacco products	Textile fibers	Live animals	Meat and meat preparations
Office machines and automatic data-processing equipment	Sugar, sugar preparations, and honey	Sugar, sugar preparations, and honey	Iron and steel
			Pulp and waste paper
		LESS SENSITIVE	
Photographic apparatuses, optical goods, watches	Gas, natural and manufactured	Pulp and waste paper	(*economic distance increases trade*)
Road vehicles	Travel goods, handbags	Photographic apparatuses, optical goods, watches	Coffee, tea, cocoa, spices
Cork and wood	Footwear	Telecommunications and sound-recording apparatuses	Animal oils and fats
Metalworking machinery	Sanitary, plumbing, heating, and lighting fixtures	Coffee, tea, cocoa, spices	Office machines and automatic data-processing equipment
Electricity current	Furniture and furniture parts	Gold, nonmonetary	Power-generating machinery and equipment
			Photographic apparatuses, optical goods, watches

more sensitive ◀───▶ *less sensitive*

■■■ THE MANAGEMENT TEAM IN A GLOBAL BUSINESS

Globalizing is a two-edged sword from the point of view of the manager. On the one hand, it opens up new markets and productive capabilities. On the other hand, the distances involved as well as factors like legal and cultural differences complicate marketing, producing, and staffing decisions abroad. Let's look at some examples.

▲ WEBNOTE ■■■

Wal*Mart® is expanding all over the world, bringing its merchandising expertise to high-growth, high-potential countries in the hope of making profits as these economies grow and prosper.

www.walmart.com

Global Marketing

Expanding into markets abroad is often a matter of survival. As one expert says, "Even the biggest companies in the biggest countries cannot survive on their domestic markets if they are in global industries."[49] In the late 1990s, Wal-Mart's total company sales rose by 16 percent, but its international sales jumped by 26 percent.[50] About 10 percent—or 135,000—of Wal-Mart's employees are outside the United States. Its Web site (**www.walmart.com**) shows how giants like Wal-Mart (or tiny firms), can market globally, sometimes without even leaving their home countries.

Yet we've seen that expanding abroad confronts marketing managers with many challenges. For some products, like Benetton clothes, consumer preferences in different countries are similar. However, even global firms that emphasize standardized products, like McDonald's, must still fine-tune their products when they go abroad.[51] You won't find beef in McDonald's India restaurants, and you'll find sparkling water on sale on the Champs Elysees. Marketing managers expanding abroad, therefore, can't simply use their domestic marketing and advertising plans. They'll need local market research and analysis before creating new marketing plans.

Globalization of Production

Globalizing production means dispersing components of a firm's production process to locations around the globe. One aim may be to support local markets abroad. Another may be to capitalize on national differences in the cost and quality of production—it might be cheaper to produce in Peru, for instance.

Sometimes, the best strategy is to integrate global production operations into a unified and efficient system of manufacturing facilities around the world.[52] For example, why ship supplies from the United States to Spain, when it's possible to support the Spanish factory with supplies from the south of France? Thus, as mentioned in Chapter 15, Toyota recently reorganized its global production facilities into several regional centers. Xerox is another example.

MANAGEMENT IN ACTION   Xerox

In the 1980s, each Xerox subsidiary in each country had its own suppliers, assembly plants, and distribution channels. Each country's plant managers gave little thought to how their plans fit with Xerox's global needs. This approach became untenable as Canon, Minolta, and Ricoh penetrated Xerox's U.S. and European markets with low-cost copiers.[53]

The competitive threat prompted Xerox's senior managers to coordinate their global production processes. They organized a new central purchasing group to consolidate raw materials purchases, and they, thereby, cut worldwide manufacturing costs. They instituted a "leadership through quality" program to improve product quality, streamline and standardize manufacturing processes, and cut costs. Xerox managers also eliminated over $1 billion of inventory costs with a computer system that linked customer orders from one region more closely with production capabilities in other regions.

Schlumberger integrated its global production facilities using the Internet, as the Managing @ the Speed of Thought feature illustrates.

MANAGING @ THE SPEED OF THOUGHT

Using the Internet as a Global Production Management Tool

Managing a global production operation is always a challenge. The distances involved are usually enormous, and it's easy for home-office managers to lose track of what's going on in the field, especially when the field is 8,000 miles away. If that happens, the benefits of efficiency sought by firms like Xerox in the earlier example will not materialize.

Production managers today are therefore using the Internet to monitor their global operations. Schlumberger Ltd. is a good example. Schlumberger, which manufactures oil-drilling equipment and electronics, has headquarters in New York and Paris. The company operates in 85 countries, and in most of them, employees are in remote locations.[54] How do the company's managers maintain control over so many far-flung locations? Here's how experts describe the company's system:

> To install their own network for so few people at each remote location would have been prohibitively expensive. Using the Internet, Schlumberger engineers in Dubai (on the Persian Gulf) can check e-mail and effectively stay in close contact with management at a very low cost. In addition, the field staff is able to follow research projects as easily as can personnel within the United States. Schlumberger has found that since it converted to the Internet from its own network, its overall communications costs are down 2% despite a major increase in network and information technology infrastructure spending. The main reason for the savings is the dramatic drop in voice traffic and in overnight delivery service charges ([since employees] attach complete documents to their e-mail messages).[55]
>
> At Schlumberger, the Internet plays a central role in creating an efficient world-wide production system.

Global Staffing

Doing business abroad also triggers global staffing concerns. At a minimum, setting up factories abroad requires studying employment laws in the host country, establishing a recruiting office, and ensuring that the firm complies with local staffing regulations.

Global staffing is very important today.[56] 3M produces tapes, chemicals, and electrical parts in Bangalore, India, and HP-Compaq assembles computers and designs memory boards in Guadalajara, Mexico. In Jamaica, 3,500 office workers make airline reservations, process tickets, and handle calls to toll-free numbers via satellite dishes for U.S. companies. Back in Bangalore, a skilled workforce attracted firms like Texas Instruments, Motorola, and IBM, to establish programming centers.[57]

Even apparently minor growth abroad requires a global staffing outlook. For example, sending the company's sales manager abroad for several months to close a deal means deciding how to compensate her for her expenses abroad, what to do with her house here, and how to make sure she knows how to handle the cultural demands of her foreign assignment. And finding globally qualified managers is not easy. Companies like Motorola Inc. therefore use special programs to identify and evaluate potential global managers.[58]

One program involves putting management candidates through two-to-three days of realistic role-playing exercises under the watchful eyes of trained psychologists. As one participant writes, ". . . the telephone calls, unexpected visitors and urgent tasks come so fast and furious that I quickly forget it is only a game."[59] Motorola has used its new program to screen hundreds of local Chinese management candidates so far. One company, French food firm Danone reportedly reduced its expatriate failure rate from 35 percent to 3 percent in three years using similar programs.[60] As other examples, consider the following issues managers ran into when setting up a factory in Mexico.

Managers at one U.S.-owned Mexican factory discovered that they had to carefully consider the people side of managing when staffing their facility.[61]

Workplace Harmony   The Mexican workplace has a low tolerance for adversarial relations. While getting along with others is important in U.S. factories too, Mexican employers put much more emphasis on hiring employees who have a record of working cooperatively with authority. Mexican employers, according to one expert, "tend to seek workers who are agreeable, respectful, and obedient rather than innovative and independent."[62] This can lead to counterproductive behavior—even on the part of supervisors. For example, in attempting to preserve the appearance of harmony, supervisors may hide defective work rather than confront the problem or report it to a manager.

Role and Status   Mexican employees often put a relatively high emphasis on social order and on respecting one's status. In one factory in Chihuahua, Mexico, for instance, a U.S. manager wore jeans and insisted that everyone call him Jim. He assumed those around him would prefer that he reduce the visible status gap between himself and the workers. He was then amazed to learn that the local employees considered him "uncultured and boorish."[63]

Exercising Authority   Mexican employees tend to have a more rigid view of authority than do their U.S. counterparts. Therefore, attempts by U.S. managers to encourage input and feedback from employees may cause confusion.[64]

■ *The Global Manager*   Not everyone is competent to manage in a global arena. Saying you appreciate cultural differences is one thing; being able to act on it is another. Global managers therefore tend to be, first, cosmopolitan in how they view people and the world. Some define *cosmopolitan* as "belonging to the world; not limited to just one part of the political, social, commercial or intellectual spheres; free from local, provincial, or national ideas, prejudices or attachments."[65] Global managers must be comfortable living and working anywhere in the world, and being cosmopolitan helps them to be so.

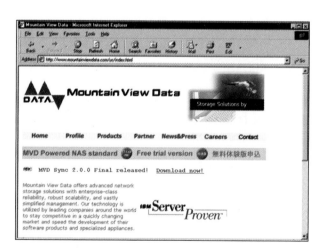

Cliff Miller is an example of how global managers operate. With his wife, he runs Mountain View Data, Inc., which produces powerful software that automatically backs up files in real time.[66] With facilities in San Francisco and Northeast Asia, Miller likes to say that he lives in four places: "San Francisco, Beijing, Tokyo, and United Airlines."[67] He and his wife Iris are continually on the move as they operate branches of their high-tech company in each city.

How can you tell if you're cosmopolitan? Cosmopolitan people are sensitive to what is expected of them in any context, and they have the flexibility to deal intelligently and in an unbiased way with people and situations from other cultures. You needn't have traveled extensively abroad or be multilingual to be cosmopolitan, although such experiences help. The important thing is that you are open to learning about other people's perspectives and to considering them in your own decisions.[68]

In addition to being cosmopolitan, global managers also have what some experts call a *global brain*. They are flexible enough to accept that, at times, their own ways of doing business are not the best. For example, Volkswagen formed a partnership with Skoda, a Czech carmaker. VW trained Skoda's managers in Western management techniques. However, it followed Skoda's suggestions about how to conduct business in the Czech Republic.[69] Being willing to apply the best solutions from different systems is what experts mean by having a global brain.

TABLE 17–1	Characteristics of More Successful International Managers	

Scale	Score	Sample Item
Sensitive to cultural differences		When working with people from other cultures, works hard to understand their perspectives.
Business knowledge		Has a solid understanding of our products and services.
Courage to take a stand		Is willing to take a stand on issues.
Brings out the best in people		Has a special talent for dealing with people.
Acts with integrity		Can be depended on to tell the truth, regardless of circumstances.
Is insightful		Is good at identifying the most important part of a complex problem or issue.
Is committed to success		Clearly demonstrates commitment to seeing the organization succeed.
Takes risks		Takes personal as well as business risks.
Uses feedback		Has changed as a result of feedback.
Is culturally adventurous		Enjoys the challenge of working in countries other than his or her own.
Seeks opportunities to learn		Takes advantage of opportunities to do new things.
Is open to criticism		Appears brittle—as if criticism might cause him or her to break.*
Seeks feedback		Pursues feedback even when others are reluctant to give it.
Is flexible		Doesn't get so invested in things that he or she cannot change when something doesn't work.

*Reverse scored, so 1 is "strongly agree" for this item.

This global point of view (or its absence) tends to reflect itself in a manager's global philosophy. For example, an ethnocentric (home-base-oriented) management philosophy may manifest itself in an ethnocentric or home-market-oriented firm. A polycentric philosophy may translate into a company that is limited to several individual foreign markets. A regiocentric (or geocentric) philosophy may lead managers to create more of an integrated global production and marketing presence.

Would Your Company Choose You as an International Executive? What do companies look for in their international executives? One study focused on 838 lower-, middle-, and senior-level managers from six international firms in 21 countries. The researchers studied the extent to which employers could use personal characteristics such as sensitivity to cultural differences to distinguish between managers who had high potential as international executives and those whose potential was not so high. Fourteen personal characteristics successfully distinguished those identified by their companies as having high potential from those identified as lower performing.

To get an initial impression of how you would rate, look at Table 17.1. It lists the 14 characteristics with sample items. For each, indicate (by placing a number in the space provided) whether you strongly agree (number 7), strongly disagree (number 1), or fall somewhere in between. The higher you score, the more likely you would have scored high as a potential global executive in this study.[70]

ethnocentric ■ *a management philosophy that leads to the creation of home-market-oriented firms.*

polycentric ■ *a management philosophy oriented toward pursuing a limited number of individual foreign markets.*

regiocentric ■ *a management philosophy oriented toward larger areas, including the global marketplace; also called geocentric.*

■■■ PLANNING, ORGANIZING, AND CONTROLLING IN A GLOBAL ENVIRONMENT

Managing globally also complicates the management process. *International management* means carrying out the four management functions we discuss in this book—planning, organizing, leading, and controlling—on an international scale.

Planning in a Global Environment

Planning means setting goals and identifying the courses of action for achieving those goals. Since much of what the manager does—the firm's structure, and its marketing, staffing, and production policies, for instance—will stem from his or her basic global strategy, choosing that strategy is usually of paramount concern.

With respect to global strategy, one thorny question is whether to emphasize standardized versus customized products worldwide. Specifically, managers like Donald Hastings must decide, "How should we balance (1) the need to provide customized products to each country in which we do business with (2) the need to maintain standardized products worldwide so as to exploit economies of scale? Answering that question requires choosing a global strategy. As in any strategic planning (as covered in Chapter 5), this involves defining the mission of the business and laying out the broad strategies or courses of action the firm will use to achieve that mission. Central to this agenda is deciding what products to sell.

Global Strategic Planning With respect to the products it sells, the company can pursue one of three basic global strategies. One is the *global integration strategy*. "To capitalize on the economies of scale and to take advantage of the diverse opportunities for cost reduction that the global market provides, the [best] choice of strategy is global integration."[71] This strategy means taking a centralized, integrated view of where to design and produce the company's product or service. The emphasis here is on producing, say, a standardized "world car" as efficiently as possible. The company then just fine-tunes this standard car for slight differences in national tastes. Managers make production decisions in a globally integrated manner. (For instance, Xerox centralized its global purchasing decisions to minimize costs). The organization structure delegates less decision-making authority to local managers.

Global integration assumes that market similarities and the need to be efficient trump the differences among the markets. U.S. automakers generally take this approach. They build "globalizable" cars and components in different countries (an integrated production strategy). Then they sell more or less the same cars in different countries, with different nameplates.

At the other extreme, the manager may decide that the differences among markets are too numerous to allow them to take this standardized approach. If so, they may choose to pursue a *host country focus strategy*. Each market needs its own autonomous subsidiary. The managers in each country are relatively free to adapt their products or services to local tastes as they see fit. The multinational company's headquarters provides overall coordination, and perhaps tries to minimize unnecessary product duplication among country subsidiaries. Some food companies, like Kellogg's, take this approach.

Many global managers try to get the best of both global strategy worlds. They pursue a *hybrid international strategy*. Here, the manager tries to blend (1) the efficiencies that come from integrating global production with (2) the ability to provide each country with specialized products or services (the host country focus strategy). The trick here is to minimize excessive duplication among country units and to maximize the firm's ability to quickly transfer product innovations from one locale to another. ABB Group Ltd. takes this hybrid approach.

MANAGEMENT IN ACTION   ABB Group

Local ABB units have great autonomy. However, ABB also uses the Internet and information technology to make sure good ideas get fast approval and distribution. For example, if several engineers in France develop a good idea for a new process, they post their idea, with appropriate keywords, on ABB's Internet using a special template. The ABB system amounts to a private bulletin board. ABB managers and engineers worldwide use it to instantaneously broadcast new ideas throughout ABB. That way, they minimize the amount of time they waste "reinventing the wheel."[72] ■■■

Figure 17.5 can help managers decide if global integration, host country focus, or hybrid is best. For example, where the forces for local responsiveness are weak and the forces for global integration strong, global integration is best. All countries here get more-or-less undifferentiated products. Industries fitting here include construction and

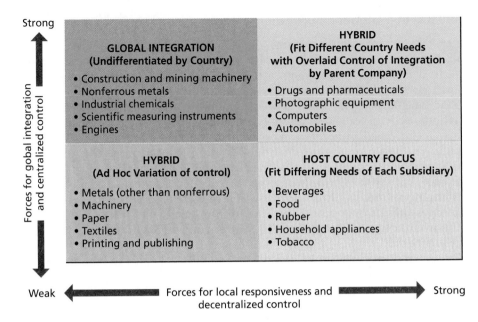

◀ **FIGURE 17–5** ■ ■ ■

Environmental Influences and Global Strategy

Source: Adapted from Figures 2 and 5 and discussion in Sumantra Ghoshal and Nitin Nohria, Reprinted from John Daniels and Lee Radebaugh, *International Business* (Upper Saddle River, NJ: Prentice Hall, 2001), p. 529. "Horses for Courses: Organizational Forms for Multinational Corporations," *Sloan Management Review*, Winter 1993, pp. 23–36.

mining machinery, and industrial chemicals. At the other extreme, where the forces for integration are weak and the forces for local responsiveness strong, host-country focus is best. The beverages, food, and household appliances industries are examples here.

Global Feasibility Planning In general, "domestic and international strategic planning processes are very similar, differing only in the specifics."[73] The planning tools covered in Chapters 3–5 are thus applicable for global planning. The main difference is that companies (like Lincoln Electric) going abroad must conduct particularly thorough feasibility studies.

The reason stems from the national differences discussed earlier. International planners must contend with a multitude of economic, political/legal, socio-cultural, and technological issues. It's easy but risky to assume that things "there" are the same as "here." Furthermore, gathering information abroad—about demographics, production levels, and so on—can be difficult, and the data are often questionable.[74] The Carrefour and Wal-Mart experiences illustrate the problem.

MANAGEMENT IN ACTION Carrefour and Wal-Mart

French retailer Carrefour (Wal-Mart's chief worldwide rival) conducts careful feasibility studies before entering new markets. For example, it avoids entering developing markets—such as Russia—that don't have reliable legal systems.[75] Even in more traditional markets, Carrefour won't proceed without at least a year's worth of on-site research. Carrefour doesn't make many mistakes when it enters a new market. In China, for instance, "Carrefour takes care to chop vegetables vertically—not laterally—so as not to bring bad luck to superstitious shoppers."[76]

With less experience in the international arena, Wal-Mart's first expansions abroad did not go so smoothly. For example, when it opened stores in Argentina, its hardware departments offered tools and appliances wired for 110 volts, although Argentina uses 220. Similarly, "only by trial and error did Wal-Mart learn that far more Argentine customers than Americans were in the habit of shopping at a store each day. The greater traffic meant that aisles always seemed overcrowded and floors always seemed dirty."[77] Wal-Mart adapted by making the aisles wider and installing scuff-proof floors. Wal-Mart is huge. It could, therefore, use trial and error instead of detailed feasibility planning—and not get ruined in the process. A smaller firm (like Lincoln Electric) runs the risk of depleting its cash and having to quickly close down.[78] ■ ■■■

■ ■ ■ *Vincent Rochefort, head of Carrefour Poland, checks the vegetable display in a Carrefour store in Lodz, Poland. Carrefour is careful to carry the products its customers want, arranged as they want to see them.*

Organizing in a Global Environment

In general, the company's international organization reflects the firm's degree of globalization. Figure 17.6 presents the typical options for organizing an international business.[79] In a *domestic organization*, each division handles its own foreign sales. In response to increasing orders from abroad, the firm may move to an *export-oriented structure*. Here, one department (often called an import-export department) coordinates all international activities such as licensing, contracting, and managing foreign sales.

In an *international organization*, management splits the company into domestic and international divisions. The international division focuses on production and sales overseas, whereas the domestic division focuses on domestic markets. Reynolds Metals, for instance, has six worldwide businesses, each with a U.S.-focused group and a separate international group.[80] In a *multinational organization*, each country where the firm does business has its own subsidiary. The oil firm Royal Dutch Shell is organized this way. It has separate subsidiaries for Shell Switzerland and Shell U.S.A. (as well as many other countries).[81]

The organizational principles covered in Chapters 7–8 apply to organizing internationally. This includes the principle that structure follows strategy.[82] For example, a host country focus strategy suggests having separate subsidiaries for each locale. A global integration strategy suggests more emphasis on centralizing functions (such as product design and manufacturing) under a single manager.[83]

As noted earlier, the firm's history and its stage of internationalization will also influence how it organizes its international efforts. Thus, a company at the earliest stages of internationalization (or with few globally qualified managers) will more likely opt for managing its international operations out of a headquarters import-export or international department. It's unlikely to begin its first, tentative forays into exporting abroad by reorganizing as a full-blown multinational organization. Similarly, as noted, the stage of internationalization is important. As the firm adds more foreign subsidiaries, it is more likely to move toward the multinational structure.

Top management philosophy is another consideration. For example (as noted earlier), some managers are more globally oriented, while some are more local (ethnocentric) in their philosophical outlooks. The manager who believes "my country's ways are best" is less likely to delegate much authority to remote local managers. Geographic distance is also important. Managing activities thousands of miles away is no easy matter. The manager will have to pay special attention to making sure his or her remote operations don't slip out of control.

▼ **FIGURE 17–6** ■ ■ ■

International Organizations

As firms evolve from domestic to multinational enterprises, their increasing international operations necessitate a more globally oriented organization.

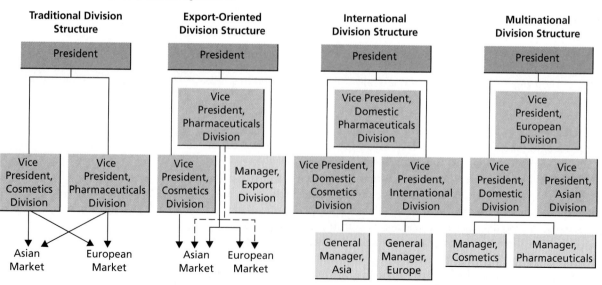

Controlling in a Global Environment

Several years ago, Coca-Cola had a rude surprise when several European countries made it take its beverages off store shelves. Coke has high standards for product quality and integrity, but controlling what's happening at every plant worldwide is a challenge. Chemicals had seeped into the beverages at one of Coke's European plants.

As explained in Chapters 14–15, *control* means monitoring actual performance to ensure it is consistent with the standards that were set. This is hard enough when the people you're controlling are next door; geographic distance complicates the problem. And the other distances (socio-cultural and legal, for instance) complicate it even more. The global manager has to carefully address two things: *what to control*, and *how to control it.*

Deciding What to Control Particularly given the geographic distances involved, the global manager has to choose the activities he or she will control with great care. The manager could, of course, try to micromanage everything—from hiring and firing to product design, sales campaigns, and cash management. However, micromanaging at long distances is less than practical. And in any case, too much control can smother the subsidiary and reduce its ability to respond quickly to customer needs.

In practice, the local manager's autonomy is *least* for financial and capital decisions, and *most* for personnel decisions.[84] Production and marketing decisions tend to fall in the middle. In one study of 109 U.S., Canadian, and European multinational corporations, "these firms exercised stricter financial control, and allowed greater local freedom for labor, political, and business decisions. Also, the home office of these multinational corporations made the decisions to introduce new products and to establish R&D facilities."[85]

Deciding How to Maintain Control Two things characterize the methods global managers use to maintain control. One is the use of computerized information systems. For many years, Kelly Services, Inc., let its offices in each country operate with their own individual billing and accounts receivable systems. However, according to Kelly's chief technology officer, "we are consolidating our operations in all countries and subsidiaries under a standard [information system]. . . . All our customers expect us to deliver consistent practices, metrics, and measurement. Establishing global standards is an important part of meeting and exceeding that expectation."[86]

The second characteristic of how global managers maintain control is the emphasis on self-control and employee commitment. Global managers do use financial and operating reports, visits to subsidiaries, and management performance evaluations to help control their international operations.[87] However, supervision is limited when thousands of miles separate boss and subordinate. Furthermore, as explained in Chapter 15, formal reports, rules, and regulations are not hard to evade. Particularly in global companies, there's wisdom in making sure employees want to do what is right—and that they know what's expected of them in terms of the company's values and goals.

In other words, global companies have to make sure their managers buy into "the way we do things around here."[88] Companies do this in many ways: job rotation from country to country; multicountry management development programs; informal company sponsored events; and using teams from different countries to work on cross-border projects. Motivating managers and employees to do things right is especially important. We'll therefore turn to this next.

■■■ LEADING AND MOTIVATING IN A MULTICULTURAL ENVIRONMENT

Many managers are probably less adept at appreciating cultural differences than they think they are. Most would eagerly take the position that "of course, there are cultural differences among people from different cultures." Yet many, transferred abroad, would blunder into simply treating the people "there" the same as the people "here."[89] The problem stems from what international management writers call the *universality assumption* of motivation: "These theories erroneously assume that human needs are universal."[90] Such assumptions are certainly not uniquely American. There's often a tendency to assume that everyone everywhere thinks and feels more or less like we do. Ironically, the universality assumption seems to be universal.

Yet, for U.S. managers, the problem may be more severe. First, they don't have the same multicultural experience as people living in, say, Europe, where travel between countries is a way of life. Furthermore, U.S. researchers did much of the research on human needs and motivation using U.S. employees. The problem is that those theories and findings don't always apply to people everywhere. (You can't always generalize them to different cultures.) A Chinese believing in Confucianism's emphasis on respect and obedience may react differently to autocratic leadership than would the typical American. One of the biggest mistakes the international manager can make is to fail to see that "to understand why people do what they do, we have to understand the cultural constructs by which they interpret the world."[91]

Values

values ■ *basic beliefs about what is important and unimportant, and what one should and should not do.*

One way people around the world differ is in terms of their values. Values are basic beliefs we hold about what is good or bad, important or unimportant. Values (such as West Point's famous "duty, honor, country") are important because our values shape the way we behave. When Geert Hofstede studied managers around the world, he found that societies' values differ in several ways:

- *Power distance.*[92] Power distance is the extent to which the less powerful members of institutions accept and expect that power will be distributed unequally.[93] Hofstede concluded that acceptance of such inequality was higher in some countries (such as Mexico) than it was in others (such as Sweden).
- *Individualism versus collectivism.* In individualistic countries like Australia and the United States, "all members are expected to look after themselves and their immediate families."[94] In collectivist countries like Indonesia and Pakistan, society expects people to care for each other more.
- *Masculinity versus femininity.* According to Hofstede, societies differ also in the extent to which they value assertiveness (which he called *masculinity*) or caring (*femininity*). Japan and Austria ranked high in masculinity; Denmark and Chile ranked lower.
- *Uncertainty avoidance.* Uncertainty avoidance refers to whether people in the society are uncomfortable with unstructured situations in which unknown, surprising, novel incidents occur. People in some countries (such as Sweden, Israel, and Great Britain) are relatively comfortable dealing with uncertainty and surprises. People living in other countries (including Greece and Portugal) tend to be uncertainty avoiders.[95]

Leadership in a Multicultural Environment

Cultural realities like these can dramatically alter the efficacy of theories like those covered in Chapter 10 ("Leading"). For example, consider the large differences Hofstede found in the "power distance" (inequality) people in different cultures will tolerate.[96] Figure 17.7 lists countries with large and small power distance rankings.

Cultural differences have important implications for how managers apply leadership theories abroad. For example, one might assume that in societies in which large power distances (inequalities) are an accepted way of life, participative leadership may backfire. Says one expert, "For example, if a superior, in a 'large power distance society,' attempts to reduce the distance by acting more accessible and friendly, his or her subordinates may not willingly accept such openness."[97] Indeed, studies suggest that managers in some countries (including Indonesia, Malaysia, Thailand, Turkey, and the Philippines) do prefer to use autocratic leadership; those in others such as Hong Kong prefer less autocratic styles.[98] Table 17.2 helps to illustrate. It shows that leaders in some countries (Spain, Portugal, and Greece) tend to delegate less authority than do leaders in others (Sweden, Japan, Norway, and the United States). The point is that the indiscriminate application of leadership theories abroad can be counterproductive.

◀ FIGURE 17–7 ■ ■ ■

Country Clusters Based on Power Distance

Source: Adapted from G. Hofstede, *Culture's Consequences* (Beverly Hills, CA: Sage Publications, 1984).

Large	Argentina
	Brazil
	Belgium
	Chile
	Colombia
	France
	Greece
	Hong Kong
	India
	Iran
	Italy
	Japan
	Mexico
	Pakistan
	Peru
	Philippines
	Portugal
	Singapore
	Spain
	Taiwan
	Thailand
	Turkey
	Venezuela
	Yugoslavia
Power distance	
	Australia
	Austria
	Canada
	Denmark
	Finland
	Germany
	Great Britain
	Ireland
	Israel
	Netherlands
	New Zealand
	Norway
	Sweden
	Switzerland
Small	U.S.A.

TABLE 17–2	Comparative Leadership Dimensions: Participation

Extent to Which Leaders Delegate Authority

0 = low; 100 = high

Country	Value	Country	Value
Sweden	75.51	Germany	60.85
Japan	69.27	New Zealand	60.54
Norway	68.50	Ireland	59.53
United States	66.23	UK	58.95
Singapore	65.37	Belgium/Lux	54.55
Denmark	64.65	Austria	54.29
Canada	64.38	France	53.62
Finland	62.92	Italy	46.80
Switzerland	62.20	Spain	44.31
Netherlands	61.33	Portugal	42.56
Australia	61.22	Greece	37.95

Source: C. Hampden-Turner and A. Trompenaars, *The Seven Cultures of Capitalism* (New York: Doubleday, 1993). Adapted from Helen Deresky, *International Management*, 2nd ed., NY Addison Wesley Longman, 1997, Exh 11-5, p. 402.

Motivation in a Multicultural Environment

Many of the motivation theories discussed in Chapter 11 ("Influencing Individual Behavior and Motivation") make assumptions about peoples' needs. For example, the Maslow needs hierarchy assumes that peoples' needs form a five-step hierarchy (from basic physiological needs, up to security, social, self-esteem, and self-actualization needs). But can the global manager act as if this assumption applies to his or her local employees?

Not always. Maslow's theory emphasizes the supremacy of self—of satisfying one's own needs and of being all you can be (self-actualization). In other societies, peoples' needs don't revolve around self as much as around social relationships. For example, one researcher concluded that we would have to rearrange the Maslow needs hierarchy to use it in China. Social needs would come first, then physiological, then security, and then, finally self-actualization—but, not to be "all you can be," but "to serve society."[99]

Another popular motivation theory emphasizes the importance of the need to achieve in motivating behavior. Yet an attempt by the originator of this theory to extend it to workers in India failed.[100] Similarly, "money is not an incentive everywhere—it may be accepted gladly, but [it] will not automatically improve performance. Honor, dignity and family may be much more important. Imposing the American style of merit system may be an outrageous blow to a respected and established seniority system."[101] Again, the indiscriminate use of familiar motivation theories abroad can backfire. The manager needs to start by understanding his or her employees and what their needs and values are.

Communications in a Multicultural Environment

Cultural differences also influence communication in obvious and subtle ways. Language barriers are one obvious problem. An American manager negotiating a deal in England can generally make him- or herself fairly well understood using English, but he or she

TABLE 17–3	Implications of Various Nonverbal Behaviors in Different Cultures	

Nonverbal Behavior	Country	Meaning
Thumbs up	United States	An Approval gesture/OK/good job!
	Middle East	A gesture of insult
	Japan	A sign indicating "male"
	Germany	A sign for count of "one"
A finger circulating next to the ear	Argentina	A telephone
	United States	That is crazy!
A raised arm and waggling hand	United States	Goodbye
	India, South America	Beckoning
	Much of Europe	A signal for "no"
Showing the back of the hand in a V-sign	England	A rude sign
	Greece, Middle East	A sign for count of "two"
Showing a circle formed with index finger and thumb	United States	Very good!
	Turkey	Insult gesture/accusation of homosexuality
Eye contact, gazing	United States	A sign of attentiveness
	Japan	A rude behavior/invasion of privacy
	Most Asian countries	Sign of disrespect to senior people
Widening eye	United States	An indication of surprise
	Chinese	An indication of anger
	Hispanic	Request for help
	French	Issuance of challenge
Nodding the head up and down	Western countries	A sign for agreement/yes
	Greece, Bulgaria	A sign for disagreement/no

Source: Adapted from Kamal Fatehi, International Management (Upper Saddle River, NJ: Prentice Hall 1996), Table 6.1, p. 194.

might need an interpreter in France. Even where the other party speaks some English, problems can arise. For example, using a colloquialism (such as "you bet it is") may be incomprehensible to the person with whom you're speaking. Furthermore, as General Motors discovered to its chagrin, words that sound or look the same (such as *Nova* which means "won't go" in Spanish) may have different meanings in different countries.

The problem is not just the words. As we explained in Chapter 12 ("Improving Communication Skills"), as much as 90% of what people hear isn't verbal. It is nonverbal, and it is conveyed via facial expressions and signs and motions of one sort or another. Here is where the novice international manager can really get into trouble. Table 17.3 shows what some typical nonverbal behaviors mean in various countries. It's subtle differences like these that can make international management an adventure!

MANAGEMENT IN ACTION   Lincoln Electric

This chapter should help put the problems Lincoln Electric faced into perspective—and help us to understand what the company needs to do now. Donald Hastings took over as Lincoln Electric Company's CEO just after the failure of its international expansion became evident. As he says, in retrospect, it was apparent that Lincoln Electric made several bad assumptions. "For example, without truly exploring the idea, we assumed that the incentive system would be accepted abroad. We found, however, that the European culture of labor was hostile to the piecework and bonus system."[102]

Another questionable assumption was appointing a vice president for managing the European factories who had no global management experience. In hindsight, says Hastings,

I realize that [this vice president's] appointment reflected a broader problem: our corporate management lacked sufficient international expertise and had little experience running a complex, dispersed organization. Our managers didn't know how to run foreign operations; nor did they understand foreign cultures. Consequently, we had to rely on people in our foreign companies—people we did not know and who didn't know us.[103]

It was soon obvious to Hastings that the whole process of control was breaking down:

I witnessed a troubling pattern. The individual European businesses would submit extremely optimistic sales and profits estimates in their budgets. But they invariably missed the targets—often by quite a bit—and the gaps were getting bigger and bigger. Even more worrisome, nobody seemed to have a handle on why the targets were being missed or what to do about the gaps. When asked, the businesses' managers would say, "We were too optimistic. The recession is worse than we thought. We'll downsize the budget."[104]

Lincoln Electric's debt was soon soaring, and its losses were mounting. In the spring of 1993, Hastings stumbled across the reason why his European managers always missed their sales and profit targets. "The operating budget of the [headquarters] management company in Norway was funded by the individual businesses in each country, and the size of its budget was based on the forecasted, rather than the actual, sales and profits of those businesses. To inflate the management company's own operating budget, its leaders had encouraged the businesses to submit optimistic—rather than realistic—forecasts."[105] Hastings knew he had to do something—and fast. What would you have done?

In June, he handed over responsibility for North American operations to his president and moved to England to take charge of European operations himself. In Europe, some of his discoveries were even more shocking. Every factory was operating at 50% or less of capacity. As he says, "people were not working! On one visit . . . three workers were found sleeping on the job."[106] In Germany, Hastings discovered, the average factory worker worked only about 35 hours per week, in contrast to the average Lincoln worker's 43 to 58 hours. He pushed his local managers to develop plans for boosting market share, but they said, "The only way you increase market share is to buy another company. You never take an account from a competitor, because [it] will retaliate and take one from you."[107]

At a trade show in Germany, exhibitors traditionally spent their time entertaining customers rather than making sales, as they more often do in the United States. Hastings decided to break with tradition. He and his team did some aggressive selling. The sales gave the company a well-needed financial shot in the arm. It also proved that well-made American products would sell in Germany even if they weren't produced there.[108]

Hastings put a turnaround plan in place. The company downsized its operations in Europe. It closed the German factory (as well as manufacturing operations in Brazil, Venezuela, and Japan). Within a year, "our new export strategy—which included selling American-made machines worldwide and rethinking which of our plants around the world could best serve a given market—was a smashing success. Moreover, in countries where we had closed operations, market share actually increased."[109]

The only place where Lincoln was able to successfully implement its incentive system was Mexico City. There, it started small. It asked two employees to try working on the incentive system. Other workers soon asked to join the plan. In about two years; Lincoln's whole Mexico City workforce had adopted its incentive plan.

Today, with its new global integration strategy, Lincoln is thriving. Its balance sheet is strong, and revenues and profits are up. It has also added several new, internationally experienced executives to its board of directors, and it has built its international management team. In retrospect, Hastings says, "competing globally requires a lot more time, money, and management resources than we realized. At least five years before we launched our expansion program in 1987, we should have started building a management team and [board of directors] from whom we could have learned how to proceed."[110]

SUMMARY ▪▪▪

1. Companies can pursue several strategies when it comes to extending operations to foreign markets. Exporting is the route often chosen by manufacturers, and licensing and franchising are two popular alternatives. At some point, a firm may decide to invest funds in another country. Joint ventures and wholly owned subsidiaries are two examples of foreign direct investment.

2. An international business is any firm that engages in international trade or investment. Firms are globalizing for many reasons, the three most common being to expand sales, to acquire resources, and to diversify sources of sales and supplies. Other reasons for pursuing international business include reducing costs or improving quality by seeking products and services produced in foreign countries and smoothing out sales and profit swings.

3. Free trade means removing all barriers to trade among countries participating in the trade agreement. Its potential benefits have prompted many nations to enter into various levels of economic integration, ranging from a free trade area to a common market.

4. Globalizing production means placing parts of a firm's production process in various locations around the globe. The aim is to take advantage of national differences in the cost and quality of production and then integrate these operations in a unified system of manufacturing facilities around the world. Companies are also tapping new supplies of skilled labor in various countries. The globalization of markets, production, and labor coincides with the rise of a new type of global manager, someone who can function effectively anywhere in the world.

5. International managers must be skilled at weighing an array of environmental factors. Before doing business abroad, managers should be familiar with the economic systems, exchange rates, and level of economic development of the countries in which they plan to do business. They must be aware of import restrictions, political risks, and legal differences and restraints. Important socio-cultural differences also affect the way people in various countries act and expect to be treated. Values, languages, and customs are examples of elements that distinguish people of one culture from those of another. Finally, the relative ease with which the manager can transfer technology from one country to another is an important consideration in conducting international business.

6. With respect to the products it sells, the company can pursue one of three basic global strategies. One is the *global integration strategy*. At the other extreme, the manager may choose to pursue a *host country focus strategy*. Many global managers try to get the best of both global strategy worlds and pursue a *hybrid international strategy*.

7. The company's international organization reflects the firm's degree of globalization. In a *domestic organization*, each division handles its own foreign sales. In response to increasing orders from abroad, the firm may move to an *export-oriented structure*. In an *international organization*, management splits the company into domestic and international divisions. In a *multinational organization*, each country where the firm does business has its own subsidiary.

8. Leading, motivating, and communicating abroad is susceptible to what international management writers call the "universality assumption"—the tendency to assume that everyone everywhere thinks and feels more or less like "we" do. In fact, they do not. For one thing, people around the world hold to different values, such as power distance, individualism versus collectivism, masculinity versus femininity, and uncertainty avoidance.

exporting 451
licensing 452
franchising 452
foreign direct investment 452
strategic alliance 452
joint venture 453
wholly owned subsidiary 453
international business 453
international trade 453
international management 453

multinational corporation (MNC) 453
mixed economy 454
gross domestic product (GDP) 454
exchange rate 454
trade barrier 454
tariff 454
quota 455
subsidy 455
free trade 455
economic integration 455

free trade area 455
customs union 455
common market 455
technology transfer 458
ethnocentric 463
polycentric 463
regiocentric 463
planning 464
values 468

SKILLS AND STUDY MATERIALS

COMPANION WEBSITE ■■■

We invite you to visit the Dessler Companion Website at **www.prenhall.com/dessler** for this chapter's Internet resources.

EXPERIENTIAL EXERCISES ■■■

1. You have just taken an assignment to assess the feasibility of opening a branch of your company's business in Russia. Your company manufactures and sells farming equipment. Your company is located in David, California, a community known for a heavy sense of social responsibility, progressive agricultural techniques, and a liberal political atmosphere. You have a month to prepare your report. Working in teams of four or five students, prepare a detailed outline showing the main topic headings you will have in your report, including a note on the management tools you will use to get the information you need for each topic.

2. While Lincoln Electric's new strategy of exporting its welding equipment from the United States to various countries seems to be working well, management is now concerned that local competitors may start eating into its business. Furthermore, some developing countries object to having products enter that may compete with their own. Working in teams of four or five students, use the tools in this chapter, and specify the global strategy you believe Lincoln should pursue now. What global organization structure would that imply?

3. Spend several minutes using the tools and what you learned in this chapter and book to list 10 reasons "Why I would (or would not) be a good global manager."

4. Many rightfully believe that it is the business school's responsibility to familiarize business students with what it takes to be an effective global manager. In teams of four or five students, compile a list, based on this course and any others you've taken here, of what your business school is doing to cultivate a better appreciation of the challenges of doing business internationally.

CASE STUDY ■■■

U.S. BOOKSELLER FINDS A STRONG PARTNER IN GERMAN MEDIA GIANT

When Barnes & Noble was exploring ways to become more competitive in its battle with Amazon.com, there were hundreds of U.S. companies to which it could turn. Research clearly demonstrated that the cultural differences that characterize cross-border ventures made them far more complicated than domestic ones. Yet Barnes & Noble surprised competitors when it chose to form its Internet joint venture with the German media giant Bertelsmann. Was Barnes & Noble mistaken to look abroad for a partner?

Bertelsmann is best known among college students for its record label and music club, BMG (now both owned by Universal). At the time, BMG entertainment was second in the market with $1.9 billion in sales. The BMG music club is well known to U.S. college students with its buy-one, get-10 free CD offers posted on campus bulletin boards nationwide. With $3.9 billion in sales and nearly 65,000 employees, Bertelsmann is much more than a CD club. Its holdings include Random House, the world's largest English-language book publisher, and Offset Paperback, a firm that manufactures nearly 40% of all the paperback books sold in the United States. Bertelsmann had also actively pursued e-commerce on its own. By the end of the twentieth century, Bertelsmann had quietly staked out a position as the world's third largest Internet business.

To fund **barnesandnoble.com**, the two created a separate company and conducted an initial public offering (IPO) to raise capital. The offering raised $421 million for the new venture after commissions and expenses, making it the largest e-commerce offering in history. Since launching its online business in May 1997, **barnesandnoble.com** has quickly become one of the world's largest e-commerce retailers. The company has successfully capitalized on the recognized brand value of the Barnes & Noble name to become the second largest on-line retailer of books. Yet it doesn't seem to have made as much headway as it would have liked in capturing market share from Amazon.

Discussion Questions

1. What may have motivated Barnes & Noble to partner with the German firm Bertelsmann? In general terms, what advantages would Barnes & Noble gain by having an international partner in such an endeavor? Explain the pros and cons of this partnership.

2. Specify the basic global strategy you believe **barnesand noble.com** should pursue, and why? How, in general terms, would you organize this venture?

3. With all its experience in e-commerce, why wouldn't BMG just set up its own competitor to Amazon.com?

4. List three specific planning, organizing, leading, and controlling issues Barnes & Noble's managers probably faced in establishing this new joint venture.

5. Write a one page essay on the topic "Cultural Factors our Barnes & Noble managers should keep in mind when dealing with our colleagues at Bertelsmann."

YOU BE THE CONSULTANT ■■■

MANAGING JETBLUE IN A GLOBAL ENVIRONMENT

jetBlue AIRWAYS® JetBlue's route structure is basically domestic, but that doesn't mean it can ignore its global environment. For one thing, its heavy flight schedule from New York already means that it is also advantageous to fly out of the continental United States—to Puerto Rico. On May 30, 2002, JetBlue, therefore, added three daily JFK-San Juan nonstop flights. Neeleman says that he has no plans to expand to Europe but that Canada, the Caribbean, and Mexico are possibilities sometime in the future.[111]

Furthermore, JetBlue President Barger says he would sign international code-share arrangements (which would make it easier for JetBlue's domestic passengers to switch seamlessly to flights abroad on another airline), if doing so didn't interfere with JetBlue's need for quick turnarounds. (For example, having to change JetBlue's flight schedules in such a way that they had to spend more time on the ground waiting for incoming passengers from abroad might mean longer turnaround time—and, therefore, higher costs for Jetblue.)[112]

It's not just the global aspects of its route structure that are important to JetBlue's management, but the global nature of aircraft purchases and leasing as well. Neeleman's original plan (given the $130 million or more in start-up capital) was to go directly to Airbus or Boeing to buy his firm's first aircraft. However, it turned out that neither Airbus nor Boeing could deliver all the planes the new start-up needed in the years 2000 and 2001. JetBlue therefore had to lease six Airbus A320s from a company called International Lease Finance Corp. and two more from Singapore Aircraft Leasing Enterprise. Then as JetBlue expanded (and in keeping with its desire to maintain a homogeneous fleet so that all mechanics and flight crews could more easily switch from aircraft to aircraft), JetBlue placed an order with the European aircraft manufacturer Airbus for an additional 10 A320s (the planes list for about $54 million each, but they typically sell for less). Based on its expected needs through 2005, JetBlue will therefore end up ordering about 74 of the A320s from Europe's Airbus rather than aircraft from America's Boeing. Neeleman and his team felt that the Airbus 320 best fit their needs, given JetBlue's route structure and the Airbus's economies of operation and emphasis on technology.

Assignment

1. Other start-up airlines (not JetBlue) have made the mistake of expanding abroad too soon. Make a list of five erroneous assumptions you believe these airlines' managers made in expanding abroad.

2. Neeleman says he is only interested in expanding into Mexico, Canada, or the Caribbean in the foreseeable future. Tell him why JetBlue is (or is not) a suitable candidate for expanding into each of these three areas, based on the cultural, administrative, geographic, and economic distance between that country and his.

3. List the reasons why you think Neeleman might (or might not) be a good global manager.

4. Assuming JetBlue decides to expand outside the United States, briefly specify the basic global strategy the company should pursue, and why.

5. Draw an organization chart showing the basic global organization structure JetBlue should use if it begins flying to Canada, Mexico, and the Caribbean in addition to its current domestic U.S.A. flights.

6. What are the *noneconomic* pros and cons to a company like JetBlue in placing such a large order with a foreign rather than with a domestic, supplier?

ENDNOTES

CHAPTER 1

1 Katrina Brooker, "It Took a Lady to Save Avon," *Fortune*, 15 October 2001, pp. 203–8; Emily Nelson, "Avon Calls On Good-Looking Research," *Wall Street Journal*, 23 May 2002, p. B6.

2 David Kirkpatrick, "IBM: From Blue Dinosaur to E-Business Animal," *Fortune*, 26 April 1999, pp. 119–25.

3 Joan Magretta, "The Power of Virtual Integration: An Interview with Dell Computer's Michael Dell," *Harvard Business Review*, March–April 1998, pp. 73–84.

4 In G. Hanson, "Determinants of Firm Performance: An Integration of Economic and Organizational Factors," unpublished doctoral dissertation, University of Michigan Business School, 1986.

5 M. A. Huselid, "The Impact of Human Resource Management Practices on Turnover, Productivity, and Corporate Financial Performance," *Academy of Management Journal*, 1995, p. 647; J. Pfeffer and J. Vega, "Putting People First for Organizational Success," *Academy of Management Executive*" 13, 1999, pp. 37–48

6 Peter Drucker, *An Introductory View of Management* (New York: Harper's College Press, 1977), p. 15.

7 Christina Cheddar, "Boardroom Vets Move to Power Technology—Sector Has Shed Founders Who Thrived in Labs as Skill Needs Change," *Wall Street Journal*, 11 September 2001, p. B8.

8 These are based on Henry Mintzberg, "The Manager's Job: Folklore and Fact," *Harvard Business Review*, July–August 1975, pp. 489–561.

9 Sumantra Ghoshal and Christopher Bartlett, "Changing the Role of Top Management: Beyond Structure to Processes," *Harvard Business Review*, January–February 1995, pp. 86–96

10 Ibid., p. 89.

11 Ibid., p. 91.

12 Ibid., p. 96.

13 Ibid., p. 94.

14 Liz Simpson, "Fostering Creativity," *Training* 38, no. 12, December 2001, pp. 54–57

15 Geoffrey Colvin, "How to be a Great ECEO," *Fortune*, 24 May 1999, pp. 104–10.

16 Mintzberg, op cit., pp. 489–561.

17 See, for example, ibid.; and George Copeman, *The Chief Executive* (London: Leviathan House, 1971), p. 271. See also George Weathersby, "Facing Today's Sea Changes," *Management Review*, June 1999, p. 5; David Kirkpatrick, "The Second Coming of Apple," *Fortune*, 9 November 1998, pp. 86–104; and Jenny McCune, "The Changemakers," *Management Review*, May 1999, pp. 16–22.

18 John Holland, *Making Vocational Choices: A Theory of Careers* (Upper Saddle River, NJ: Prentice Hall, 1973). See also John Holland, *Assessment Booklet: A Guide to Educational and Career Planning* (Odessa, FL: Psychological Assessment Resources, Inc., 1990).

19 Edgar Schein, *Career Dynamics: Matching Individual and Organizational Needs* (Reading, MA: Addison-Wesley, 1978), pp. 128–29.

20 A. Howard and D. W. Bray, *Managerial Lives in Transition: Advancing Age and Changing Times* (New York: Guilford, 1988); discussed in Dwayne Schultz and Sydney Ellen Schultz, *Psychology and Work Today* (New York: Macmillan Publishing Co., 1994), pp. 103–4.

21 Ibid., Schultz and Schultz, p. 104.

22 Ibid.

23 Claudia H. Deutsch, "A Hands-on-the-Helm Leader," *New York Times*, 13 June 1999, Money and Business Section, p. 2.

24 Noel Tichy and Ram Charan, "The CEO as Coach: An Interview with Allied-Signal's Lawrence A. Bossidy," *Harvard Business Review*, March–April 1995, pp. 69–78.

25 Ibid., p. 70.

26 Ibid., p. 73.

27 Ibid., p. 70.

28 Ibid.

29 Ibid., p. 76.

30 Unless otherwise noted, the following discussion is based on Gary Yukl, *Leadership in Organizations* (Upper Saddle River, NJ: Prentice Hall, 1998); pp. 251–55.

31 Joan Lloyd, "Derailing Your Career," *Baltimore Business Journal* 19, 19 October 2000, pp. 21 and 33.

32 Yukl, op cit., p. 252.

33 Shelley Kirkpatrick and Edwin Locke, "Leadership: Do Traits Matter?" *Academy of Management Executive*, May 1991, p. 49.

34 Yukl, op cit., p. 253.

35 Quoted in William Holstein, "Why Big Ideas Often Fall Flat," *New York Times*, 26 May 2002, p. B5. See also Judith Chapman, "The Work of Managers in New Organizational Context," *Journal of Management Development* 20, no. 1, January 2001, p. 55.

36 Brooker, op cit., p. 203.

37 Ibid., p. 204.

38 Ibid., p. 208

39 Ibid.

40 Claude George, *The History of Management Thought* (Upper Saddle River, NJ: Prentice Hall, 1968), p. 6.

41 Ibid., p. 7.

42 Alfred Chandler, *Strategy and Structure* (Cambridge, MA: MIT Press, 1962). See also Daniel Wren, *The Evolution of Management Thought* (New York: John Wiley, 1979).

43 D. S. Pugh, *Organization Theory* (Baltimore: Penguin, 1971), pp. 126–27.

44 Claude George Jr., *The History of Management Thought* (Upper Saddle River, NJ: Prentice Hall, 1972), pp. 99–101.

45 Richard Hopeman, *Production* (Columbus, OH: Charles Merrill, 1965), pp. 478–85.

46 Henri Fayol, *General and Industrial Management*, transl. Constance Storrs (London: Sir Isaac Pitman, 1949), pp. 42–43.

47 Based on Richard Hall, "Intra-Organizational Structural Variation: Application of the Bureaucratic Model," *Administrative Science Quarterly*, December 1962, pp. 295–308.

48 William Scott, *Organization Theory* (Homewood, IL: Richard D. Irwin, 1967).

49 F. L. Roethlisberger and William Dickson, *Management and The Worker* (Boston: Harvard University Graduate School of Business, 1947), p. 21.

50 Douglas McGregor, "The Human Side of Enterprise," ed. Edward Deci, B. Von Haller Gilmer, and Harry Kairn, *Readings in Industrial and Organizational Psychology* (New York: McGraw-Hill, 1972), p. 123.

51 R. Likert, *New Patterns of Management* (New York: McGraw-Hill, 1961), p. 6.

52 Ibid., p. 100.

53 Chris Argyris, *Integrating the Individual and the Organization* (New York: John Wiley, 1964).

54 Chester Barnard, *The Functions of the Executive* (Cambridge, MA: Harvard University Press, 1968), p. 84.

55 Ibid., p. 167.

56 Herbert A. Simon, *Administrative Behavior* (New York: Free Press, 1976), p. 11.

57 C. West Churchman, Russell Ackoff, and E. Leonard Arnoff, *Introduction to Operations Research* (New York: John Wiley, 1957), p. 18.

58 Daniel Wren, *The Evolution of Management Thought* (New York: John Wiley, 1979), p. 512.

59 *The World Almanac and Book of Facts, 1998* (Mahwah, NJ: K-III Reference Corporation, 1998), p. 207.

60 Ibid., p. 9. See also "The Impact of Globalization on HR," *Workplace Visions*, Society for Human Resource Management, no. 5, 2000, pp. 1–8.

61 Bryan O'Reilly, "Your New Global Workforce," *Fortune*, 14 December 1992, pp. 52–66.

62 Paul Judge, "How I Saved $100 Million on the Web," *Fast Company*, February 2001, pp. 174–81.

63 Richard Crawford, *In the Era of Human Capital* (New York: Harper Business, 1991), p. 10.

64 O'Reilly, op cit., p. 63.

65 This discussion is based on Gary Dessler, *Management Fundamentals* (Reston, VA: Reston, 1977), p. 2. See also William Berliner and William McClarney, *Management Practice and Training* (Burr Ridge, IL: McGraw-Hill, 1974), p. 11.

66 Rachel Moskowitz and Drew Warwick, "The 1994–2005 Job Outlook in Brief," *Occupational Outlook Quarterly* 40, no. 1 (Spring 1996), pp. 2–41. See also Mahlon Apgar IV, "The Alternative Workplace: Changing Where and How People Work," *Harvard Business Review* (May–June 1998), pp. 121–36.

67 Ibid.

68 Crawford, op cit., p. 26.

69 Peter Drucker, "The Coming of the New Organization," *Harvard Business Review*, January–February 1988, p. 45. See also Richard Cappelli, "Rethinking the Nature of Work: A Look at the Research Evidence," *Compensation & Benefits Review*, July/August 1997, pp. 50–59.

70 Gerald Ferris, Dwight Frank, and M. Carmen Galang, "Diversity in the Workplace: The Human Resources Management Challenge," *Human Resource Planning* 16, no. 1, 1993 pp. 41–51. See also "Charting the Projections: 2000–10," *Occupational Outlook Quarterly*, Winter 2001–02, pp. 36–41.

71 "Immigrants in the Workforce," *BNA Bulletin to Management Datagraph*, 15 August 1996, pp. 260–61.

72 Howard Fullerton Jr., "Another Look at the Labor Force," *Monthly Labor Review* (November 1993), pp. 31–40; "The American Workforce, 1994–2005," *BNA Bulletin to Management*, 4 January 1996, pp. 4–5.

73 "Workforce Becoming Older, Better Educated," *BNA Bulletin to Management*, 17 October 1996, pp. 332–33.

74 Ibid.

75 Ferris, et al., op cit.

76 For related discussions, see, for example, Felice Schwartz, "Women in American Business: The Demographic Imperative," *Business and the Contemporary World*, Summer 1993, pp. 10–19; and also Karen Stephenson and Valdis Krebs, "A More Accurate Way to Measure Diversity," *Personnel Journal*, October 1993, pp. 66–74.

77 Thomas Peters and Robert Waterman Jr., "In Search of Excellence," ed. Jon Pierce and John Nestrom, *The Manger's Bookshelf* (Upper Saddle River, NJ: Prentice Hall, 2000), p. 45.

78 Rosabeth Moss Kanter, *When Giants Learn to Dance* (New York: Touchstone, 1989).

79 James Brian Quinn, *Intelligent Enterprises* (New York: The Free Press, 1992).

80 Peter Senge, *The Fifth Discipline* (New York: Currency Doubleday, 1994), p. 3.

81 Tom Peters, *Liberation Management* (New York: Alfred Knopf, 1992), p. 9.

82 Ibid., and www.abb.com, 31 December 1999.

83 Bryan Dumaine, "What the Leaders of Tomorrow See," *Fortune*, 3 July 1989, p. 58. See also Weathersby, op cit., p. 5; and Gary Hamel and Jeff Sampler, "The eCorp.: Building a New Industrial," *Fortune*, 7 December 1998, pp. 80–112.

84 These are based on Walter Kiechel III, "How We Will Work in the Year 2000," *Fortune*, 17 May 1993, p. 79.

85 Karl Albrecht, *At America's Service: How Corporations Can Revolutionize the Way They Treat Their Customers* (Homewood, IL: Dow-Jones Irwin, 1998).

86 Bryan Dumaine, "What the Leaders of Tomorrow See," *Fortune*, 3 July 1989, p. 51.

87 Rosabeth Moss Kanter, "The New Managerial Work," *Harvard Business Review*, November–December 1989, p. 88.

88 Ibid.

89 Drucker, "The Coming of the New Organization," p. 45.

90 Peters, op cit.

91 Bryan Dumaine, "The New Non-Managers," *Fortune*, 22 February 1993, p. 81. See also David Kirkpatrick, "IBM: from Big Blue Dinosaur to e-Business Animal," *Fortune*, 26 April 1999, pp. 116–27. See also McCune, pp. 16–22; and Brent Schlender, "Larry Ellison: Oracle at Web Speed," *Fortune*, 24 May 1999, pp. 128–37.

92 Peter Drucker, "The Coming of the New Organization," p. 43.

93 Stratford Sherman, "A Master Class in Radical Change," *Fortune*, 13 December 1993, p. 82. See also McCune, pp. 16–22.

94 Eryn Brown, "Nine Ways to Win on the Web," *Fortune*, 24 May 1999, p. 125.

95 Ibid., p. 125.

96 Carlta Vitzthum, "Just in Time Fashion," *Wall Street Journal*, 18 May 2001, p. B1.

97 Joan Magretta, "The Power of a Virtual Integration: An Interview with Dell Computer's Michael Dell," *Harvard Business Review*, March–April 1998, pp. 73–84.

98 Ibid., p. 74.

99 Ibid., p. 82.

100 Ibid.

101 Ibid., p. 76.

102 Ibid., p. 75.

103 John Micklethwait and Adrian Wooldridge, "The Witch Doctors: What the Management Gurus Are Saying, Why It Matters, and How to Make Sense of It," summarized by Brad Jackson, in Jon Pierce and John Newstrom, op cit., p. 13.

104 Ibid.

105 Ibid.

106 Chris Argyris, "Flawed Advice and the Management Trap," prepared by Kelly Nelson, in Jon Pierce and John Newstrom, op cit., p. 20.

107 "JetBlue," *Fortune Small Business*, 1 March 2001, p. 92; "Fort Lauderdale, Florida-Based Discount Airlines Survives Turbulence," *Knight Ridder/Tribune*, 11 March 2001, item 01070000; Harvey Mackay, "Customer Service from the Ground up Really Flies," *Tampa Bay Business Journal*, 23 November 2001, pp. 36; "JetBlue Scores Top Awards for Onboard Service," JetBlue press release, 23 January 2002; Bill Saporito, "Lessons Learned: Air Travel," *Time*, 31 December 2001, pp. 128–129; Catherine Yung, "Collapse of Two Start of Carriers Puts Focus on Frontier, JetBlue Airlines," *Knight Ridder/Tribune News*, 24 December 2000, item 003 6 000 a.

108 Yung, op cit.

CHAPTER 2

1 This account is based on Andy Serwer, "P&G's Covert Operation," *Fortune*, 17 September 2001, pp. 42–47.

2 Manuel Velasquez, *Business Ethics: Concepts and Cases* (Upper Saddle River, NJ: Prentice Hall, 1992), p. 9. (See also Kate Walter, "Ethics Hot Lines Tap into More Than Wrongdoing," *HRMagazine*, September 1995, pp. 79–85; and Skip Kaltenheuser, "Bribery Is Being Outlawed Virtually Worldwide," *Business Ethics*, May 1998, p. 11.

3 The following discussion, except as noted, is based on Manuel Velasquez, op cit., pp. 9–12.

4 Ibid., p. 9.

5 This discussion is based on ibid., pp. 12–14.

6 Ibid., p. 12. For further discussion, see Kurt Baier, *Moral Points of View*, abbr. ed. (New York: Random House, 1965), p. 88. See also Milton Bordwin, "The 3 R's of Ethics," *Management Review*, June 1998, pp. 59–61.

7 For further discussion of ethics and morality, see Tom Beauchamp and Norman Bowie, *Ethical Theory and Business* (Upper Saddle River, NJ: Prentice Hall, 2001), pp. 1–19.

8 See, for example, S. E. Frost Jr., *Basic Teachings of the Great Philosophers* (New York: Doubleday, 1962), pp. 80–99.

9 Ibid., p. 81.

10 Ibid.

11 Based on ibid., p. 81.

12 S. Morris Engel, *The Study of Philosophy* (San Diego, CA: Collegiate Press, 1987), p. 52.

13 O. C. Ferrell and John Fraedrich, *Business Ethics*, 3rd Ed. (Boston: Houghton Mifflin, 1997), p. 55.

14 Example quoted from Michael Boylan, *Business Ethics* (Upper Saddle River, NJ: Prentice Hall, 2001), pp. 37–38.

15 Richard Osborne, "A Matter of Ethics," *Industry Week* 49, no. 14, 4 September 2000, pp. 41–42.

16 Boylan, op cit., p. 118.

17 Ibid.

18 Ibid., p. 119.

19 J. Fraedrich et al., "Assessing the Application of Cognitive Moral Development Theory to Business Ethics," *Journal of Business Ethics* 13, 1994, pp. 829–38.

20 M. T. Hegarty and H. P. Sims Jr., "Organizational Philosophy, Policies, and Objectives Related to Unethical Decision Behavior:

A Laboratory Experiment," *Journal of Applied Psychology* 64, 1979, pp. 331–38.

21 Janet Adams et al., "Code of Ethics as Signals for Ethical Behavior," *Journal of Business Ethics* 29, no. 3, February 2001, pp. 199–211.

22 Sara Morris et al., "A Test of Environmental, Situational, and Personal Influences on the Ethical Intentions of CEOs," *Business and Society*, August 1995, pp. 119–47.

23 Justin Longnecker, Joseph McKinney, and Carlos Moore, "The Generation Gap in Business Ethics," *Business Horizons*, September–October 1989, pp. 9–14.

24 Thomas Tyson, "Does Believing That Everyone Else Is Less Ethical Have an Impact on Work Behavior?" *Journal of Business Ethics* 11, 1992, pp. 707–17. See also Basil Orsini and Diane McDougall, "Fraud Busting Ethics," *CMA 1973*, June 1999, pp. 18–21.

25 Floyd Norris and Diana Henriques, "Three Admit Guilt in Falsifying CUC's Books," *New York Times*, 15 June 2000, p. C1.

26 "Back to Basics," A Survey of Management, *The Economist*, 9 March 2002, p. 9.

27 Ibid.

28 Quoted from Boylan, op cit., p. 213.

29 Saul Gellerman, "Why Good Managers Make Bad Ethical Choices," *Harvard Business Review*, July–August 1986, p. 86.

30 Julian Barnes, "Unilever wants P&G Placed Under Monitor," *New York Times*, 1 September 2001, p. B1.

31 "Enron Chief Went Online to Urge Stock Purchases," *New York Times*, 19 January 2002, p. B1.

32 For a discussion, see Steen Brenner and Earl Molander, "Is the Ethics of Business Changing?" *Harvard Business Review*, January–February 1977, pp. 57–71. See also Robert Jackyll, "Moral Mazes: Bureaucracy and Managerial Work," *Harvard Business Review*, September–October 1983, pp. 118–30; and Ishmael P. Akaah, "The Influence of Organizational Rank and Role of Marketing Professionals' Ethical Judgments," *Journal of Business Ethics*, June 1996, pp. 605–14.

33 Discussed in Samuel Greengard, "Cheating and Stealing," *Workforce*, October 1997, pp. 45–53.

34 From Guy Brumback, "Managing Above the Bottom Line of Ethics," *Supervisory Management*, December 1993, p. 12.

35 Deon Nel, Leyland Pitt, and Richard Watson, "Business Ethics: Defining the Twilight Zone," *Journal of Business Ethics* 8, 1989, p. 781. See also Brenner and Molander, op cit.; and Daniel Glasner, "Past Mistakes Present Future Challenges," *Workforce*, May 1998, p. 117.

36 Quoted in Beauchamp and Bowie, p. 109.

37 Rochelle Kelin, "Ethnic versus Organizational Cultures: The Bureaucratic Alternatives," *International Journal of Public Administration*, March 1996, pp. 323–44.

38 Lynn Sharpe Paine, "Managing for Organizational Integrity," *Harvard Business Review*, March–April 1994, p. 110.

39 James Kunen, "Enron's Vision (and Values) Thing," *New York Times*, 19 January 2002, p. A19.

40 Adams, et al., op cit.

41 Ibid.

42 Ibid.

43 "A Global War Against Bribery," *The Economist*, 16 January 1999, pp. 22–24.

44 Daniel Pearl and Steve Stecklow, "Pushing Pills," *Wall Street Journal*, 16 August 2001, p. A1.

45 Amy Zuckerman, "Managing Business Ethics in a World of Payola," *World Trade* 14, no. 12, December 2001, pp. 38–39.

46 Marcia Miceli and Janet Near, "Ethical Issues in the Management of Human Resources," *Human Resource Management Review* 11, no. 1, 2001, pp. 1–10.

47 Ibid., p. 6.

48 For a discussion see, for example, Alan Rowe et al., *Strategic Management: A Methodological Approach* (Reading, MA: Addison-Wesley Publishing Co., 1994), p. 101.

49 Ibid., p. 6.

50 Dayton Fandray, "The Ethical Company," *Workforce* 79, no. 12, December 2000, pp. 74–77.

51 Kate Walter, "Ethics Hot Lines Tap into More Than Wrongdoing," *HRMagazine*, September 1995, pp. 79–85.

52 Rowe et al., op cit., p. 7. See also John J. Quinn, "The Role of 'Good Conversation' in Strategic Control," *Journal of Management Studies*, May 1996, pp. 381–95.

53 Ibid., p. 9.

54 Sandra Gray, "Audit Your Ethics," *Association Management*, September 1996, p. 188.

55 Michael McCarthy, "Now the Boss Knows Where You're Clicking," *Wall Street Journal*, 21 October 1999, p. B1.

56 "Study Says Employers Monitor One-Third of Employee e-mail, Internet Use," Knight/Tribune Business News, 01191038.

57 Cynthia Kemper, "Big Brother," *Communication World*, 18, no. 1, December 2000/January 2001, pp. 8–12.

58 Tammy Joyner, "Big Boss Is Watching," *Atlanta Constitution*, 25 July 2001, p. D1.

59 Michael J. McCarthy, "How One Firm Tracks Ethics Electronically," *Wall Street Journal*, 21 October 1999, pp. B1(W) and B1(E).

60 Ibid.

61 James G. Hunt, *Leadership* (Newbury Park, CA: Sage Publications, 1991), pp. 220–24. One writer describes culture as a sort of "organizational DNA," since "it's the stuff, mostly intangible, that determines the basic character of a business." See James Moore, "How Companies Have Sex," *Fast Company*, October–November 1997, pp. 66–68.

62 Hunt, op cit., p. 221. For a recent discussion of types of cultures see, for example, "A Quadrant of Corporate Cultures," *Management Decision*, September 1996, pp. 37–40.

63 For example, see Ferrell and Fraedrich, op cit., p. 117.

64 Richard Osborne, "Core Value Statements: The Corporate Compass," *Business Horizons*, September–October 1991, p. 29.

65 "Promoting Workplace Fun Draws Serious Attention," *BNA Bulletin to Management*, 8 August 1999, p. 215.

66 Ibid.

67 Max Messmer, "Capitalizing on Corporate Culture," *The Internal Auditor* 58, no. 5, October 2001, pp. 38–45.

68 This example is based on Daniel Denison, *Corporate Culture and Organizational Effectiveness* (New York: Wiley, 1990), pp. 147–74.

69 Ibid., p. 148.

70 Ibid.

71 Ibid., p. 151.

72 Ibid.

73 Ibid.

74 Ibid., p. 154.

75 Ibid., p. 155.

76 Curtis Verschoor, "Why Do Unfortunate Things Happen to Good Corporate Citizens?" *Strategic Finance* 83, no. 5, November 2001, pp. 20, 22.

77 Beauchamp and Bowie, op cit., p. 45.

78 Milton Friedman, *Capitalism and Freedom* (Chicago: University of Chicago Press, 1962), p. 133. See also Charles Handy, "A Better Capitalism," *Across the Board*, April 1998, pp. 16–22; and Robert Reich, "The New Meaning of Corporate Social Responsibility," *California Management Review*, Winter 1998, pp. 8–17. Reich also believes both that because of pressure from investors, nonowner stakeholders are being neglected and that the government should step in to protect them.

79 Beauchamp and Bowie, op cit., pp. 49–52. See also Marjorie Kelly, "Do Stockholders 'Own' Corporations?" *Business Ethics*, June 1999, pp. 4–5.

80 Ibid., p. 79.

81 Ibid., p. 60.

82 Ibid., p. 54.

83 John Simon, Charles Powers, and John Gunnermann, "The Responsibilities of Corporations and Their Owners," *The Ethical Investor: Universities and Corporate Responsibility* (New Haven, CT: Yale University Press, 1972); reprinted in Beauchamp and Bowie, op cit., pp. 60–65. See also Roger Kaufman et al., "The Changing Corporate Mind: Organizations, Vision, Missions, Purposes, and Indicators on the Move Toward Societal Payoffs," *Performance Improvement Quarterly* 11, no. 3, 1998, pp. 32–44.

84 "Sweatshop Wars," *The Economist*, 27 February 1999, pp. 62–63.

85 Thea Singer, "Can Business Still Save the World?" *Inc.* 23, no. 5, 30 April 2001, pp. 58–71.

86 Charles Hess and Kenneth Hey, "Good Doesn't Always Mean Right," *Across the Board*, 38, no. 4, July/August 2001, pp. 61–64.

87 Matthew Arnold, "Walking the Ethical Tightrope," *Marketing* 12, July 2001, p. 17.

88 Singer, op ct.

89 Jo-Ann Johnston, "Social Auditors: The New Breed of Expert," *Business Ethics*, March 1996, p. 27.

90 Karen Paul and Steven Ludenberg, "Applications of Corporate Social Monitoring Systems: Types, Dimensions and Goals," *Journal of Business Ethics* 11, 1992, pp. 1–10.

91 Karen Paul, "Corporate Social Monitoring in South Africa: A Decade of Achievement, An Uncertain Future," *Journal of Business Ethics* 8, 1989, p. 464. See also Bernadette Ruf et al., "The Development of a Systematic, Aggregate Measure of Corporate Social Performance," *Journal of Management* 24, no. 1, 1998, pp. 119–33.

92 Paul, op cit., p. 464. See also John S. North, "Living Under a Social Code of Ethics: Eli Lilly in South Africa Operating Under the Sullivan Principles," *Business and the Contemporary World* 8, no. 1, 1996, pp. 168–80; and S. Prakash Sethi, "Working With International Codes of Conduct: Experience of U.S. Companies Operating in South Africa Under the Sullivan Principles," *Business and the Contemporary World* 8, no. 1, 1996, pp. 129–50. Standards similar to the international quality standards that have been used for some time have been put in place for social accountability areas such as child labor and health and safety. See Ruth Thaler-Carter, "Social Accountability 8000: A Social Guide for Companies or Another Layer of Bureaucracy?" *HRMagazine*, June 1999, pp. 106–8.

93 Janet Near, "Whistle-Blowing: Encourage It!" *Business Horizons*, January–February, 1989, p. 5. See also Robert J. Paul and James B. Townsend, "Don't Kill the Messenger! Whistle-Blowing in America: A Review with Recommendations," *Employee Responsibilities and Rights*, June 1996, pp. 149–61; and Nick Perry, "Indecent Exposures: Theorizing Whistle Blowing," *Organization Studies* 19, no. 2, 1998, pp. 235–57.

94 Near, op cit., p. 5. See also Fraser Younson, "Spilling the Beans," *People Management* 11 June 1998, pp. 25–26.

95 Ibid., p. 6. See also David Lewis, "Whistle blowing at Work: Ingredients for an Effective Procedure," *Human Resource Management Journal* 7, no. 4, 1997, pp. 5–11.

96 "The Importance of Business Ethics," *HR Focus* 78, no. 7, July 2001, pp. 1, 13.

97 Taylor Cox, Jr., *Cultural Diversity in Organizations* (San Francisco, CA: Berrett Kohler Publishers, Inc., 1993), p. 11.

98 Richard Orlando, "Racial Diversity, Business Strategy, and Firm Performance: A Resource Based View," *Academy of Management Journal* 43, no. 2, 2000, pp. 164–77.

99 G. Pascal Zachary, "Mighty Is the Mongrel," *Fast Company*, July 2000, pp. 271.

100 Ibid., p. 278.

101 Patricia Digh, "Creating a New Balance Sheet: The Need for Better Diversity Metrics," *Mosaics*, September–October 1999, p. 1.

102 Michael Carrell, Daniel Jennings, and Christina Heavrin, *Fundamentals of Organizational Behavior* (Upper Saddle River, NJ: Prentice Hall, 1997), pp. 282–83.

103 George Kronenberger, "Out of the Closet," *Personnel Journal*, June 1991, pp. 40–44.

104 Cox, op cit., p. 88.

105 Ibid., p. 89.

106 J. H. Greenhaus and S. Parasuraman, "Job Performance Attributions and Career Advancement Prospects: An Examination of Gender and Race Affects," *Organizational Behavior and Human Decision Processes* 55, July 1993, pp. 273–98.

107 Adapted from Cox, op cit., p. 64.

108 Ibid., pp. 179–80.

109 Madeleine Heilmann and Lewis Saruwatari, "When Beauty Is Beastly: The Effects of Appearance and Sex on Evaluation of Job Applicants for Managerial and Nonmanagerial Jobs," *Organizational Behavior and Human Performance*, June 1979, pp. 360–72. See also Tracy McDonald and Milton Hakel, "Effects of Applicant Race, Sex, Suitability, and Answers on Interviewer's Questioning Strategy and Ratings," *Personnel Psychology*, Summer 1985, pp. 321–34.

110 Francis Milliken and Luis Martins, "Searching for Common Threads: Understanding the Multiple Effects of Diversity in Organizational Groups," *Academy of Management Review* 21, no. 2, 1996, p. 415. See also Patricia Nemetz and Sandra Christensen, "The Challenge of Cultural Diversity: Harnessing a Diversity of Views to Understand Multiculturalism," *Academy of Management Review* July 21, 1996, pp. 434–62.

111 Patricia Digh, "Coming to Terms with Diversity," *HRMagazine*, November 1998, p. 119.

112 Jeremy Kahn, "Diversity Trumps the Downturn," *Fortune* 144, no. 1, 9 July 2001, pp. 114–16.

113 Cox, op cit., p. 236.

114 Digh, op cit., p. 119.

115 Danny Hakim, "Ford Motor Workers Get On the Job Training in Religious Tolerance," *New York Times*, 19 November 2001, p. B6.

116 K. Kram, *Mentoring at Work* (Glenview, IL: Scott Foresman, 1985). See also Cox, op cit., p. 198; and Ian Cunningham and Linda Honold, "Everyone Can Be a Coach," *HRMagazine*, June 1998, pp. 63–66.

117 See, for example, G. F. Dreher and R. A. Ash, "A Comparative Study of Mentoring Among Men and Women in Managerial, Professional, and Technical Positions," *Journal of Applied Psychology* 75, no. 5, 1990, pp. 1–8.

118 Michelle Conlon and Wendy Zellner, "Is Wal-Mart Hostile to Women?" *Business Week*, 16 July 2001, Issue 3741, pp. 58–59.

119 "Morgan Stanley Bans the Rules," *Investment Dealers Digest*, 4 March 2002, item 02063001.

CHAPTER 3

1 Amy Merrick, "Expensive Circulars Help Precipitate Kmart President's Departure," *Wall Street Journal*, 18 January, 2002, p. B1.

2 Max Bazerman, *Judgment in Managerial Decision Making* (New York: John Wiley, 1994), p. 3.

3 See, for example, Herbert Simon, *The New Science of Management Decision* (Upper Saddle River, NJ: PrenticeHall, 1971), pp. 45–47.

4 Larry Long and Nancy Long, *Computers*, (Upper Saddle River, NJ: PrenticeHall, 1996), p. M7.

5 Mairead Browne, *Organizational Decision Making and Information* (Norwood, NJ: Ablex Publishing Corporation, 1993), p. 6.

6 Bazerman, op cit., p. 5.

7 Herbert Simon, *Administrative Behavior* (New York: The Free Press, 1977).

8 George Lowenstein, "The Creative Destruction of Decision Research," *Journal of Consumer Research* 38, no. 4, December 2001, pp. 499–505.

9 See, for example, Bazerman, p. 5.

10 James March and Herbert Simon, *Organizations* (New York: Wiley, 1958), pp. 140–41.

11 Cathy Olofson "So Many Decisions, So Little Time," *Fast Company*, October 1999, p. 62.

12 Ibid., p. 62.

13 Ibid.

14 For a discussion see, for example, Bazerman, pp. 4–5.

15 Ibid., p. 4.

16 John Hammond, Ralph Keeney, and Howard Raiffa, *Smart Choices* (Boston: Harvard Business School Press, 1999), pp. 19–30.

17 Of course, this also assumes that Harold wants to stay in marketing.

18 Except as noted, the titles of the steps and the ideas for this section are based on Hammond et al., op cit., pp. 35–41.

19 Ibid., p. 47.

20 Bazerman, op cit., p. 4.

21 Based on Hammond et al., op cit, pp. 67–72.

22 See Bazerman, p. 108.

23 Quoted from ibid., pp. 105–106.

24 Prased Padmanabhan, "Decision Specific Experience in Foreign Ownership and Establishment Strategies: Evidence from Japanese Firms," *Journal of International Studies*, Spring 1999, pp. 25–27.

25 Thomas Stewart, "Making Decisions in Real-Time," *Fortune*, 26 June, 2000, p. 332.

26 Michael Hickins, "Xerox Shares Its Knowledge," *Management Review*, September 1999, p. 42.

27 Ibid., p. 42.

28 Ibid.

29 Quoted in Robert L. Heilbroner, "How to Make an Intelligent Decision," *Think*, December 1990, pp. 2–4.

30 Ibid. See also Theodore Rubin, *Overcoming Indecisiveness: The Eight Stages of Effective Decision Making* (New York: Avon Books, 1985). See also John Hammond et al., op cit.

31 This anecdote is quoted and paraphrased from Bill Breen, "What's Your Intuition?" *Fast Company*, September 2000, pp. 294–95.

32 Ibid., p. 296.

33 Alden Hayashi, "When to Trust Your Gut," *Harvard Business Review*, February 2001, p. 64.

34 J. Wesley Hutchinson and Joseph Alba, "When Business Is a Confidence Game," *Harvard Business Review*, June 2001, pp. 20–21. For an additional perspective see, for example, John Middlebrook and Peter Tobia, "Decision-Making in the Digital Age," *USA Today*, 130, no. 2676, September 2001, p. 50; and Linda Freeman, "Disney Exec Suggests Matrix for Decision-Making," *Credit Union Journal* 5, no. 35, 3 September 2001, p. 7.

35 Robert Cross and Susan Brodt, "How Assumptions of Consensus Undermined Decision-Making," *MIT Sloan Management Review* 42, no. 2, Winter 2001, p. 86.

36 See, for example, Lisa Burke and Monica Miller, "Taking the Mystery Out of Intuitive Decision-Making," *Academy of Management Executive* 13, no. 4, 1999.

37 Mark Epstein and Robert Westbrook, "Linking Actions to Profits in Strategic Decision-Making," *MIT Sloan Management Review* 42, no. 3, Spring 2001, pp. 39–49.

38 Kenneth Laudon and Jane Price Laudon, *Management Information Systems* (Upper Saddle River, NJ: Prentice Hall, 1996), p. 125. See also Bob F. Holder, "Intuitive Decision Making," *CMA*, October 1995, p. 6.

39 Joan Johnson et al, "Vigilant and Hypervigilant Decision Making," *Journal of Applied Psychology* 82, no. 4, pp. 614–622.

40 Studies indicate that you can adjust your style and that decision styles are more preferences than set in stone. See Dorothy Leonard and Susan Straus, "Putting Your Company's Whole Brain to Work," *Harvard Business Review*, July–August 1997, pp. 111–21.

41 See, for example, William Taggart and Enzo Valenzi, "Assessing Rational and Intuitive Styles: A Human Information Processing Metaphor," *Journal of Management Studies*, March 1990, pp. 150–71; and Christopher W. Allinson and John Hayes, "The Cognitive Style Index: A Measure of Intuition—Anaylsis for Organizational Research," *Journal of Management Studies*, January 1996, pp. 119–35.

42 This and the following guideline are from Heilbroner, op cit.

43 Helga Drummond, "Analysis and Intuition in Technological Choice: Lessons of Taurus," *International Journal of Technology Management*, April 1999, pp. 459–67.

44 This discussion is based on Anne Porter, "Just the Facts," *Purchasing* 131, no. 7, 18 April 2002, pp. 25–32.

45 These techniques are based on Monica Elliott, "Breakthrough Thinking," *IIE Solutions* 33, no. 10, October 2001, p. 22; Curtis Sittenfeld, "The Most Creative Man in Silicon Valley," *Fast Company*, June 2000, pp. 275–90; Joy Caldwell, "Beyond Brainstorming: How Managers Can Cultivate Creativity and Creative Problem Solving Skills in Employees," *Supervision*, August 2001, pp. 6–9; "Creativity Rooms Help Brainstormers Become Rainmakers at America Online," *BNA Bulletin to Management*, 24 June, 1999, p. 193; Max Messner, "Encouraging Employee Creativity," *Strategic Finance* 83, no. 6, December 2001, pp. 16–18.

46 As discussed in Michael Roberto, "Making Difficult Decisions in Turbulent Times," *Ivey Business Journal* 66, no. 3, January/February 2002, pp. 14–20.

47 For an additional perspective, see, for example; Ruth Weiss, "How to Foster Creativity at Work," *Training & Development*, February 2001, pp. 61–67; A. Muoio, "Where Do Great Ideas Come From?" *Fast Company*, January–February 2000, pp. 149–64; Charles Fishman, "Creative Tension," *Fast Company*, November 2000, pp. 359–68; Andrew Hargadon and Robert Sutton, "Building an Innovation Factory," *Harvard Business Review*, May–June 2000, pp. 157–166; Michael Michalko, "Jumpstart your Company's Creativity," *Supervision*, 62, no. 1, January 2001, p. 14; and Liz Sampson, "Fostering Creativity: Companies Enhance the Bottom Line by Building Corporate Cultures That Encourage Employee Innovation," *Training* 38, no. 12, December 2001, pp. 54–58.

48 Bazerman, op cit., pp. 6–8; Roberto, op. cit., pp. 14–20.

49 Roberto, pp. 14–20.

50 Lowenstein, op cit., pp. 499–505.

51 Lester Lefton and Laura Valvatne, *Mastering Psychology* (Boston: Allyn and Bacon, 1992), pp. 248–49. See also Daphne Main and Joyce Lambert, "Improving Your Decision Making," *Business and Economic Review*, April 1998, pp. 9–12.

52 See, for example, Janice Beyer et al., "The Selective Perception of Managers Revisited," *Academy of Management Journal*, June 1997, pp. 716–37.

53 Dewitt Dearborn and Herbert A. Simon, "Selective Perception: A Note on the Departmental Identification of Executives," *Sociometry* 21, 1958, pp. 140–44. For a recent study of this phenomenon, see Mary Waller, George Huber, and William Glick, "Functional

Background as a Determinant of Executives' Selective Perception," *Academy of Management Journal*, August 1995, pp. 943–94. While not completely supporting the Dearborn findings, these researchers did also conclude that managers' functional backgrounds affected how they perceived organizational changes. See also Paul Gamble and Duncan Gibson, "Executive Values and Decision Making: The Relationship of Culture and Information Flows," *Journal of Management Studies*, March 1999, pp. 217–40.

54 From Benjamin Hoff, *The Tao of P'u* (London: Methuen, 1982), p. 42.

55 This discussion is based on Joan Feldman, "JetBlue Loves New York," *Air Transport World* 38, no. 6, June 2001, p. 78.

CHAPTER 3 APPENDIX

1 The breakeven point is also sometimes defined more technically as the quantity of output or sales that will result in a zero level of earnings before interest or taxes. See, for example, J. William Petty et al., *Basic Financial Management* (Upper Saddle River, NJ: PrenticeHall, 1993), p. 932.

2 Jay Heizer and Barry Render, *Production and Operations Management* (Upper Saddle River, NJ: PrenticeHall, 1996), pp. 240–50.

CHAPTER 4

1 George L. Morrisey, *A Guide to Tactical Planning* (San Francisco: Jossey-Bass, 1996), p. 61.

2 Leonard Goodstein, Timothy Nolan, and Jay William Pfeiffer, *Applied Strategic Planning* (New York: McGraw-Hill, 1993), p. 3.

3 R.R. Donnelley and Sons Company Web site, 10 November 1999. www.rrdonnelley.com

4 Ronald Henkoff, "How to Plan for 1995," *Fortune*, 31 December 1990, p. 74.

5 Peter Drucker, "Long Range Planning," *Management Science* 5, 1959, pp. 238–49. See also Bristol Voss, "Cover to Cover Drucker," *Journal of Business Strategy*, May–June 1999, Fall 1991, pp. 1–9.

6 Goodstein, Nolan, and Pfeiffer, op cit., p. 170.

7 Leslie Brokow, "One-Page Company Game Plan," *Inc.*, June 1993, 111–13.

8 Arthur Little, *Global Strategic Planning* (New York: Business International Corporation, 1991), p. 3.

9 Melanie Warner, "Nightmare on Net Street," *Fortune*, 6 September 1999, pp. 285–86.

10 This is from George Morrisey, *A Guide to Long-Range Planning* (San Francisco: Jossey-Bass, 1996), pp. 72–73.

11 For a discussion, see Peter Wright, Mark Kroll, and John Parnell, *Strategic Management Concepts* (Upper Saddle River, NJ: Prentice Hall, 1996), pp. 224–25.

12 Ibid.

13 Ibid., p. 225.

14 Harvey Kahalas, "A Look at Planning and Its Components," *Managerial Planning*, January–February 1982, pp. 13–16; reprinted in Phillip DuBose, *Readings in Management* (Englewood Cliffs, NJ: Prentice Hall, Inc., 1988), pp. 49–50. See also Mary M. Crossan, Henry W. Lane, Roderick E. White, and Leo Klus, "The Improvising Organization: Where Planning Meets Opportunity," *Organization Dynamics*, Spring 1996, pp. 20–35.

15 Peter F. Drucker, *The Effective Executive* (New York: Harper & Row, 1966); quoted in Keith Curtis, *From Management Goal Setting to Organizational Results* (Westport, CT: Quorum Books, 1994), p. 101.

16 Jamie Butters, "Chrysler Exceeds Its Cost-Cutting Goals for 2001," *Knight-Ridder/Tribune Business News*, 21 February 2002, Item 02052032.

17 "Setting Departmental Goals You Can Actually Achieve," *InfoTech Advisor Newsletter*, 22 January 2002.

18 Peter F. Drucker, *The Practice of Management* (New York: Harper & Row, 1954), pp. 65–83, 100.

19 Morrisey, *A Guide to Tactical Planning* p. 25.

20 Gary Latham and J. James Baldes, "The Practical Significance of Locke's Theory of Goal Setting," *Journal of Applied Psychology*, February 1975. See also Gary Latham, "The Effects of Proximal and Distal Goals on Performance on a Moderately Complex Task," *Journal of Organizational Behavior*, July 1999, pp. 421–30.

21 See, for example, Gary Latham and Gary Yukl, "A Review of Research on the Application of Goal Setting in Organizations," *Academy of Management Journal* 18, no. 4, 1964, p. 824. See also

Gary Latham and Terrance A. Mitchell, "Importance of Participative Goal Setting and Anticipated Rewards on Goal Difficulty and Job Performance," *Journal of Applied Psychology* 63, 1978, pp. 163–71; and Sondra Hart, William Moncrief, and A. Parasuraman, "An Empirical Investigation of Sales People's Performance, Effort, and Selling Method During a Sales Contest," *Journal of the Academy of Marketing Science*, Winter 1989, pp. 29–39. See also Theresa Libby, "The Influence of Voice and Explanation on Performance in a Participative Budget Setting," *Accounting, Organizations, and Society*, February 1999, p. 125.

22 The rest of this section, except as noted, is based on Gary Yukl, *Skills for Managers and Leaders* (Englewood Cliffs, NJ: Prentice Hall, 1991), pp. 132–33. See also Gary Latham, "Cognitive and Motivational Effects of Participation: A Mediator Study," *Journal of Organizational Behavior*, January 1994, pp. 49–64.

23 Yukl, op cit., p. 133. See also Miriam Erez, Daniel Gopher, and Nira Arzi, "Effects of Goal Difficulty, Self-Set Goals, and Monetary Rewards on Dual Task Performance," *Organizational Behavior & Human Decision Processes*, December 1990, pp. 247–69; and Thomas Lee, "Explaining the Assigned Goal—Incentive Interaction: The Role of Self-Efficacy and Personal Goals," *Journal of Management*, July–August 1997, pp. 541–50.

24 See, for example, Stephan Schiffman and Michele Reisner, "New Sales Resolutions," *Sales & Marketing*, January 1992, pp. 15–16. See also Steve Rosenstock, "Your Agent's Success," *Manager's Magazine*, September 1991, pp. 21–23.

25 Yukl, op cit., p. 133.

26 Gary Latham and Lise Saari, "The Effects of Holding Goal Difficulty Constant on Assigned and Participatively Set Goals," *Academy of Management Journal* 22, 1979, pp. 163–68. See also Mark Tubbs and Steven Ekeberg, "The Role of Intentions in Work Motivation: Implications for Goal Setting Theory and Research," *Academy of Management Review*, January 1991, pp. 180–99; and Cathy Durham, "Effects of Leader Role, Team Set Goal Difficulty, Efficacy, and Tactics on Keying Effectiveness," *Organizational Behavior & Human Decision Processes*, November 1997, pp. 203–32.

27 See Latham and Saari, op cit., pp. 163–68.

28 Gary Latham, Terence Mitchell, and Denise Dorsett, "Importance of Participative Goal Setting and Anticipated Rewards on Goal Difficulty and Job Performance," *Journal of Applied Psychology* 63, 1978, p. 170. See also John Wagner III, "Cognitive and Motivational Frameworks in U.S. Research on Participation: A Meta-analysis of Primary Effects," *Journal of Organizational Behavior*, January 1997, pp. 49–66.

29 See, for example, Anthony Mento, Norman Cartledge, and Edwin Locke, "Maryland Versus Michigan Versus Minnesota: Another Look at the Relationship of Expectancy and Goal Difficulty to Task Performance," *Organizational Behavior and Human Performance*, June 1980, pp. 419–40. See also Robert Renn, "Further Examination of the Measurement Properties of Leifer & McGannons 1986 Goal Acceptance and Goal Commitment Scales," *Journal of Occupational and Organizational Psychology*, March 1999, pp. 107–14.

30 William Werther, "Workshops Aid in Goal Setting," *Personnel Journal*, November 1989, pp. 32–38. See also Kenneth Thompson et al., "Stretch Targets: What Makes Them Effective?" *Academy of Management Review* 11, no. 3, 1997, pp. 48–60; and Theresa Libby, "The Influence of Voice and Explanation on Performance in a Participative Budget Setting," *Accounting, Organizations, and Society*, February 1999, p. 125.

31 Scott Miller, "Tough Tactics Spark Turnaround at Ford Europe," *Wall Street Journal*, 30 November 2001, p. A12.

32 Steven Carroll and Henry Tosi, *Management by Objectives* (New York: Macmillan, 1973).

33 Mark McConkie, "A Clarification of the Goal Setting and Appraisal Processes in MBO," *Academy of Management Review*, December 1991, pp. 29–40. See also Dawn Winters, "The Effects of Learning vs. Outcome Goals on a Simple vs. a Complex Task," *Group and Organization Management*, June 1996, pp. 236–51.

34 *Webster's Collegiate Dictionary of American English* (New York: Simon & Schuster, Inc., 1988).

35 Murray R. Spiegel, *Statistics* (New York: Schaum Publishing, 1961), p. 283.

36 George Kress, *Practical Techniques of Business Forecasting* (Westport, CT: Quorum Books, 1985), p. 13. See also Diane painter, "The Business Economist at Work: Mobil Corp.," *Business Economics*, April 1999, pp. 52–55.

37 See, for example, Moore, p. 5.

38 Connie Robbins Gentry, "Smart Moves," *Chain Store Age*, January 2002, 78, no. 1, pp. 127–30.

39 Chuck Moozakis, "Silver Bullet—Brewer Turns to Web System to Track Orders and Forecast," *Internet Weeks*, 23 July 2001, pp. 14, 46.

40 Kenneth Laudon and Jane Laudon, *Management Information Systems* (Upper Saddle River, NJ: Prentice Hall, 2001), p. 598. See also "Wal-Mart to Triple Size of a Warehouse," *TechWeb*, 10 February 1999. http://192.215.17.45/newsflash/ nf617/ 0210—st6.htm.

41 Jim Chris Better, "Execs at Siebel Systems Knew Trouble Was Brewing So They Put a Cost-Cutting Plan into Action—Fast," *Business Week*, 27 August 2001, p. 112.

42 John Chambers, Santinder Mullick, and Donald Smith, "How to Choose the Right Forecasting Technique," *Harvard Business Review*, July–August 1971, pp. 45–74. See also Moore, *Handbook of Business Forecasting* (New York: Harper Information, 1990), pp. 265–90; and John Mentzer et al., "Benchmarking Sales Forecasting Management," *Business Horizons*, May–June 1999, pp. 48–57. This study of 20 leading U.S. firms found widespread dissatisfaction regarding their current sales forecasting techniques.

43 A. Chairncross, quoted in Thomas Milne, *Business Forecasting*, p. 42.

44 Alan Cowell, "In Shift, British Airways Looks to Coach," *New York Times*, 14 February 2002, p. W1.

45 Dennis Berman, "Lousy Sales Forecasts Helped Fuel the Telecom Mess," *Wall Street Journal*, 9 July 2001, p. B1.

46 Bolaji Ojo, "Cisco—Getting Its House in Order After Gross Miscalculation," *EBN*, 1 October 2001, p. 38.

47 Philip Kotler, *Marketing Management* (Upper Saddle River, NJ: Prentice Hall, 1997), p. 113.

48 E. Jerome McCarthy and William Perreault Jr., *Basic Marketing* (Homewood, IL: Irwin, 1990), pp. 131–32.

49 Stan Crock et al., "They Snoop to Conquer," *Business Week*, 28 October 1996, p. 172.

50 Susan Warren, "I-Spy: Getting the Lowdown on Your Competition Is Just a Few Clicks Away," *Wall Street Journal*, 14 January 2002, p. 14.

51 Ibid.

52 Andy Serwer, "P&G's Covert Operation," *Fortune*, 17 September 2001, pp. 42–44.

53 Douglas Frantz, "Journalists, or Detectives? Depends on Who Is Asking," *New York Times*, 28 July 1999, p. A1.

54 Kenneth Laudon and Jane Laudon, *Management Information Systems* (Upper Saddle River, NJ: Prentice Hall, 1998), p. 57.

55 Janet Perna, "Reinventing How We Do Business," *Vital Speeches of the Day*, 67, no. 19, 15 July 2001, pp. 587–91.

56 Andrew Campbell, "Tailored, Not Benchmarked: A Fresh Look at Corporate Planning," *Harvard Business Review*, March–April 1999, pp. 41–50.

57 Ibid., p. 42.

58 Ibid.

59 Ibid., p. 43.

60 "Case Study JetBlue," *Flight International*, 9 April 2002, p. 39.

61 See Sally Donnelly, "Blue Skies," *Time* 158, no. 4, 30 July 2001, pp. 24–27.

62 Katherine Yung, "Collapse of Two Startup Carriers Puts Focus on Frontier, JetBlue Airlines," *Knight-Ridder/Tribune Business News*, 24 December 2000, item 0036000a.

63 Jeremy Kahn, "Air Startups Hit Unexpected Turbulence," *Fortune* 143, no 2, 22 January 2001, p. 42.

64 Joan Feldman, "JetBlue Loves New York, *Air Transport World*, June 2001, p. 78.

CHAPTER 5

1 Patricia Sellers, "Exit the Builder, Enter the Repairman," *Fortune*, 19 March 2001, pp. 86–88.

2 Peter Drucker, *Management: Tasks, Responsibilities, Practices* (New York: Harper & Row, 1974), p. 611. For an interesting point of view on strategic management, see Daniel W. Greening and Richard A. Johnson, "Do Managers and Strategies Matter? A Study in Crisis," *Journal of Management Studies*, January 1996, pp. 25–52.

3 Andrew Campbell and Marchus Alexander, "What's Wrong with Strategy?" *Harvard Business Review*, November–December 1977, p. 42.

4 Ibid., p. 48.

5 See, for example, Allan J. Rowe et al., *Strategic Management* (Reading, MA: Addison-Wesley Publishing Co., 1989), p. 2; James Higgins and Julian Vincze, *Strategic Management* (Fort Worth, TX: The Dryden Press, 1993), p. 5; Peter Wright, Mark Kroll, and John Parnell, *Strategic Management Concepts* (Upper Saddle River, NJ: Prentice Hall, 1996), pp. 1–15.

6 Arthur Thompson and A. J. Strickland, *Strategic Management* (Homewood, IL: Irwin, 1992), p. 4. See also Fred R. David, *Concepts of Strategic Management* (Upper Saddle River, NJ: Prentice-Hall, 1997), pp. 1–27; and Bob Dust, "Making Mission Statements Meaningful," *Training & Development Journal*, June 1996, p. 53.

7 Higgins and Vincze, op cit., p. 5.

8 Warren Bennis and Bert Manus, *Leaders: The Strategies for Taking Charge* (New York: Harper & Row, 1985); quoted in Andrew Campbell and Sally Yeung, "Mission, Vision and Strategic Intent," *Long-Range Planning* 24, no. 4, p. 145. See also James M. Lucas, "Anatomy of a Vision Statement," *Management Review*, February 1998, pp. 22–26.

9 Melanie Warner, "The Young and the Loaded," *Fortune*, 27 September 1999, pp. 78–118.

10 Scott Kilman and Thomas Burton, "Monsanto Boss's Vision of Life Sciences Firm Now Confronts Reality," *Wall Street Journal*, 21 December 1999, p. A1.

11 Thompson and Strickland, op cit., p. 4. See also George Morrisey, *A Guide to Strategic Planning* (San Francisco: Jossey-Bass, 1996), p. 7.

12 Ibid., p. 8.

13 David Pringle, "CEO, Marking a Decade, Faces Struggling, Quickly Changing Industry," *Wall Street Journal*, 23 January 2002, p. B70.

14 Danny Hakim, "With Hughes Sale, GM Buries a Discarded Strategy," *New York Times*, 30 October 2001, p. C8.

15 Julian Barnes, "Proctor Plans to Jettison Jif and Crisco," *New York Times*, 26 April 2001, p. C1.

16 Adapted from Donald Hambrick and James Frederickson, "Are You Sure You Have a Strategy?" *Academy of Management Executive* 15, no. 4, 2001, p. 59.

17 Allan J. Rowe, et al., op cit., pp. 114–116; and Stephen George and Arnold Weimerskirch, *Total Quality Management* (New York: John Wiley, 1994), pp. 207–21. See also Jeffrey Sampler and James Short, "Strategy in Dynamic Information–Intensive Environments," *Journal of Management Studies*, July 1998, pp. 429–36.

18 This discussion is based on Higgins and Vincze, op cit.. pp. 200–204.

19 Jim Carbone, "Contract Manufacturer Is Moved to Vertical Integration," *Purchasing* 130, no. 20, 18 October 2001, pp. 33–35.

20 Rowe et al., op cit., pp. 246–47.

21 Thompson and Strickland, op cit., p. 169. See also Michael Lubatkin and Sayan Chatterjee, "Extending Portfolio Theory into the Domain of Corporate Diversification: Does It Apply?" *Academy of Management Journal*, February 1994, pp. 109–36.

22 Suzanne Kapner, "Strategy Shift Puts Pictures with Words," *New York Times*, 2, November 2001, p. W1.

23 Amazon.com in Movie Service Deal with Disney," *New York Times*, 19 May 2001, p. B3.

24 Douglas Blackmon, "Overnight, Everything Changes for FedEx: Can It Reinvent Itself?" *Wall Street Journal*, 4 November 2000, p. A1.

25 Constance Hays, "Toys "R" Us Plans to Lay Off 1,900 and Close 64 Stores," *New York Times*, 29 January 2002, p. C1.

26 Emily Waizer, "Remodeling the Middle," *Sporting Goods Business* 35, no. 1, January 2002, pp. 44–45.

27 Peter Henig, "Revenge of the Bricks," *Red Herring*, August 2000, pp. 121–33.

28 John Byrne, Richard Brandt, and Otis Port, "The Virtual Corporation," *Business Week*, 8 February 1993, p. 99. See also Keith Hammonds, "This Virtual Agency Has Big Ideas," *Fast Company*, November 1999, pp. 70–74.

29 See also J. Carlos Jarillo, "On Strategic Networks," *Strategic Management Journal* 9, 1988, pp. 31–41; and William Davidow and Michael Malone, "The Virtual Corporation," *California Business Review*, 12 November 1992, pp. 34–42. See also Hammonds, op cit.

30 Byrne et al., op cit., p. 99.

31 Virtual corporations should not be confused with the Japanese Keiretsus strategy. Keiretsus are tightly knit groups of firms governed by a supraboard of directors concerned with establishing the long-term survivability of the Keiretsus organization. Interlocking boards of directors and shared ownership help distinguish Keiretsus from other forms of strategic alliances, including virtual corporations. See, for example, Byrne et al., op cit., p. 101; Thompson and Strickland, op cit., p. 216; and Kenichi Ohmae, "The Global Logic of Strategic Alliances," *Harvard Business Review*, March–April 1989, pp. 143–54. See also Richard Oliver, "Killer Keiretsu," *Management Review*, September 1999, pp. 10–11.

32 Katherine Mieszkowski, "The E-Lance Economy," *Fast Company*, November 1999, pp. 66–68.

33 Ibid., p. 68.

34 Unless otherwise noted, the following is based on Michael E. Porter, *Competitive Strategy: Techniques for Analyzing Industries and Competitions* (New York: The Free Press, 1980); and Michael E. Porter, *Competitive Advantage* (New York: The Free Press, 1985).

35 Not everyone agrees that the only ways to compete are differentiation, low cost, and focus. For example, one recent *Harvard Business Review* article argues that "managers competing in a business can choose among three distinct ways to fight. They can build a fortress and defend it; they can nurture and leverage unique resources; or they can flexibly pursue fleeting opportunities within simple rules." See Kathleen Eisenhardt and Donald Sull, "Strategy as Simple Rules," *Harvard Business Review*, January 2001, p. 109.

36 In Christina Binkley, "Marriott to Turn Renaissance Units into Eclectic, Surprising Hotels," *Wall Street Journal*, 27 August 2001, p. B2.

37 Porter, *Competitive Advantage*, p. 14.

38 Ibid.

39 Porter, *Competitive Strategy*, p. 17.

40 Debbie Howell, "The Super Growth Leaders—The Home Depot: Diversification Builds Bridge to the Future," *DSN Retailing Today* 40, no. 23, 10 December 2001, pp. 17–18.

41 Gary Hamel, "Killer Strategies That Make Shareholders Rich," *Fortune*, 23 June 1997, p. 83.

42 Clayton Christensen, "Making Strategy: Learning by Doing," *Harvard Business Review*, November–December 1997, pp. 141–56.

43 Philip Evans and Thomas Wurster, "Strategy and the New Economics of Information," *Harvard Business Review*, September–October 1997, p. 72.

44 Ibid., p. 31.

45 Ibid., p. 69.

46 This discussion is based on ibid, p. 116; and George and Weimerskirch, op cit., pp. 207–21.

47 Adrienne Carter, "Kodak's Promising Development," *Money*, 31, no. 2, February 2002, p. 39.

48 Herman Kahn and Anthony Weiner, *The Year 2000: A Framework for Speculation on the Next Thirty-Three Years* (New York: Macmillan, 1967), p. 6; quoted in George A. Steiner, *Strategic Planning: What Every Manager Must Know* (New York: The Free Press, 1979), p. 237. See also Nicholas Georgantzas and William Acar, *Scenario-Driven Planning* (Westport, CT: Quorum Books, 1995); Diann Painter, "The Business Economist at Work: Mobil Corporation," *Business Economics*, April 1999, pp. 52–55; and Peter Bartram, "Prophet Making," *Director* 54, no. 12, July 2001, pp. 76–79.

49 "The Next Big Surprise," *The Economist*, 13 October 2001, p. 60.

50 Adam Kahane, "Scenarios for Energy: Sustainable World vs. Global Mercantilism," *Long-Range Planning* 25, no. 4, 1992, pp. 38–46.

51 Kerry Tucker, "Scenario Planning: Visualizing a Broader World of Possibilities Can Help Associations Anticipate and Prepare for Change," *Association Management*, April 1999, pp. 70–77.

52 Gil Ringland, *Scenario Planning: Managing the Future* (New York: John Wiley, 1998).

53 Liam Fahey, "Scenario Learning," *Management Review*, March 2000, p. 30.

54 Michael E. Porter, "What Is Strategy?" *Harvard Business Review*, November–December 1996, pp. 61–80.

55 This example is based on ibid., pp. 70–75.

56 Ibid., p. 64.

57 Gary Hamel and C. K. Prahalad, "Strategy as Stretch and Leverage," *Harvard Business Review*, March–April 1993, pp. 75–84.

58 Ibid., p. 77.

59 Ibid, p. 78.

60 C. K. Prahalad and Gary Hamel, "The Core Competence of a Corporation," *Harvard Business Review*, May–June 1990, p. 82.

61 Ibid., p. 82.

62 Marlene Piturro, "CarMax: A Cautionary Tale," *Management Review*, September 1999, p. 30.

63 Shirley Leung, "Upper Crust: Fast Food Chains Fight to Carve Out Empire in Pricey Sandwiches," *Wall Street Journal*, 5 February 2002, p. A1.

64 "Strategy Helps New York-Based Airline JetBlue Score," *Knight-Ridder/Tribute Business News*, 19 May 2001, item 01139020.

65 Paul Judge, "How Will Your Company Adapt?" *Fast Company*, no. 53, December 2001, pp. 128–39. See also Elena Harris, "Undercutting the Competition," *Sales and Marketing Management*152, no. 11, November 2000, p. 14.

CHAPTER 6

1 www.starbucks.com/company/timeline.asp211hqv-1a.

2 Wendy Zellner et al., "How Well Does Wal-Mart Travel?" *Business Week*, 3 September 2001, pp. 82–84.

3 Rekha Bach, "Heinz's Johnson to Divest Operations, Scrap Management of Firm by Region," *Wall Street Journal*, 8 December 1997, pp. B10, B12.

4 Jana Parker-Pope and Joann Lublin, "P&G Will Make Jager CEO Ahead of Schedule," *Wall Street Journal*, 10 September 1998, pp. B1, B8.

5 Chris Adams, "INS Is Retooling to Cast Agency as two Bureaus," *Wall Street Journal*, 15 November 2001, p. A18.

6 Kenneth Laudon and Jane Laudon, *Management Information Systems*, 5th edition (Upper Saddle River, NJ: PrenticeHall, 1998), p. 323.

7 "How Can Big Companies Keep the Entrepreneurial Spirit Alive?" *Harvard Business Review*, November–December 1995, pp. 188–89. See also Mary Jo Hatch, "Exploring the Empty Spaces of Organizing: How Improvisational Jazz Helps Redescribe Organizational Structure," *Organization Studies* 20, no. 1, 1999, pp. 75–100.

8 Ernest Dale, *Organization* (New York: AMA, 1967), p. 109. See also Ed Clark, "The Adoption of the Multidivisional Form in Large Czech Enterprises: The Role of Economics, Institutional and Strategic Choice Factors," *Journal of Management Studies*, July 1999, pp. 535–37. Quote from Tom Peters, "Destruction Is Cool . . . ," *Forbes*, 23 February 1998, p. 128.

9 Mark Dale Franco, "Synergies 250 Years in the Making," *Catalog Age*, 18, no. 4, 15 March 2001, pp. 47–48.

10 See, for example, Lawton Burns and Douglas Wholey, "Adoption and Abandonment of Matrix Management Programs: Effects of Organizational Characteristics and Interorganizational Networks," *Academy of Management Journal*, February 1993, pp. 106–38.

11 *Organizing for International Competitiveness* (New York: Business International Corp., 1985), p. 117.

12 John Barham, "The Morgan Matrix," *Latin Finance*, issue 126, April 2001, p. 18.

13 Burns and Wholey, op. cit., p. 106.

14 For a discussion of this type of organization and its problems, see Stanley Davis and Paul Lawrence, *Matrix* (Reading, MA: Addison-Wesley, 1967); and Stanley Davis and Paul Lawrence, "Problems of Matrix Organizations," *Harvard Business Review*, May–June 1978, pp. 131–42. See also Wilma Bernasco, "Balanced Matrix Structure and New Product Development Process at Texas Instruments Materials and Controls Division," *R&D Management*, April 1999, p. 121.

15 Wilma Bernasco, "Balanced Matrix Structure and New Product Development Process at Texas Instruments Materials and Controls Division," *R&D Management*, April 1999, p. 121.

16 Ibid.

17 Ibid.

18 Ibid.

19 John Hunt, "Is Matrix Management a Recipe for Chaos?" *Financial Times*, January 1998, p. 14.

20 Rob Walker, "Down on the Farm," *Fast Company*, February–March 1997, pp. 112–22.

21 See, for example, Henri Fayol, *General and Industrial Management*, trans. Constance Storrs (London: Sir Isaac Putnam, 1949).

22 For a discussion of the contingencies affecting span of control (task uncertainty, professionalism, and interdependence), see, for example, Daniel Robey, *Designing Organizations*, 3rd edition (Homewood, IL: Irwin, 1991), pp. 258–59.

23 Judith H. Dobrzynski, "Jack Welch: How Good a Manager?" *Business Week*, 14 December 1987, p. 94. See also Thomas Stewart, "Brain Power," *Fortune*, 17 March 1997, pp. 105–10.

24 *Webster's New World Dictionary*, 3rd College Ed. (New York: Simon & Schuster, Inc., 1988), p. 911. For a discussion of networked organizations, see James Brian Quinn, *Intelligent Enterprise* (New York: The Free Press, 1992), pp. 213–40.

25 See, for example, John Child and Rita Gunther McGrath, "Organizations Unfettered: Organizational Form in an Information-Intensive Economy," *Academy of Management Journal*, 44, no. 6, 2001, pp. 1135–48.

26 Tom Lester, "The Rise of the Network," *International Management*, June 1992, p. 72.

27 Paul Evans, Yves Doz, and Andre Laurent, *Human Resource Management in International Firms* (London: Macmillan, 1989), p. 123.

28 Ram Charan, "How Networks Reshape Organizations—For Results," *Harvard Business Review*, September–October 1991, pp. 104–15.

29 Ibid., p.108.

30 Christopher Bartlett and Sumantra Ghoshal, "What Is a Global Manager?" *Harvard Business Review*, September–October 1992, pp. 62–74.

31 David Kilpatrick, "Groupware Goes Boom," *Fortune*, 27 December 1993, pp. 99–101.

32 Kenneth Laudon and Jane Laudon, *Essentials of Management Information Systems* (Upper Saddle River, NJ: PrenticeHall, 1997), pp. 413–16. See also Bob Underwood, "Transforming with Collaborative Computing," *AS/400 Systems Management*, March 1999, p. 59.

33 "Product Development Tool Gets Revamped with Java; Ip Team Integrates Suppliers and Contractors," *Computer World*, 24 May 1999, p. 16.

34 Douglas Johnson, "Discuss Changing Models in Real Time," *Design News*, 3 May 1999, p. 96.

35 Tom Peters, *Thriving on Chaos*, (New York: Harper & Row, 1987), p. 256.

36 Charles Fishman, "Engines of Democracy," *Fast Company*, October 1999, pp. 174–202.

37 Except as noted, the remainder of this section is based on James Shonk, *Team-Based Organizations* (Chicago: Irwin, 1997).

38 Tom Peters, *Liberation Management*, (New York: Knopf, 1992), p. 238.

39 William H. Miller, "Chesebrough-Ponds at a Glance," *Industry Week*, 19 October 1992, pp. 14–15.

40 Michael Hammer and John Champy, *Reengineering the Corporation*, (New York: HarperBusiness, 1992), p. 32.

41 Ann Majchrzak and Quinwei Wang, "Breaking the Functional Mind-Set of Process Organizations," *Harvard Business Review*, September–October 1996, pp.93–99.

42 Michael Hammer and Steven Stanton, "How Process Enterprises Is Really Working," *Harvard Business Review*, November–December 1999, pp. 108–18.

43 Except as noted, this section is based on John A. Byrne, "The Horizontal Corporation," *Business Week*, 20 December 1993, pp. 76–81.

44 See, for example, *Webster's New Collegiate Dictionary* (Springfield, MA: G&C Miriam Company), 1973, p. 420.

45 For a discussion of how modularity contributes to flexibility, see, for example, Melissa Schilling and H. Kevin Steensma, "The Use of Modular Organizational Forms: An Industry Level Analysis," *Academy of Management Journal* 44, no. 6, 2001 pp. 1149–168.

46 Raymond Miles et al., "Organizing in the Knowledge Age: Anticipating the Cellular Form," *Academy of Management Executive*, 1997, pp. 7–24.

47 Ibid., p. 13.

48 Ibid., p. 13.

49 John Byrne, Richard Brandt, and Otis Port, "The Virtual Corporation," *Business Week*, 8 February 1993, p. 99.

50 Marie-Claude Boudreau et al., "Going Global: Using Information Technology to Advance the Competitiveness of the Virtual Transnational Organization," *Academy of Management Executive*, 1998, pp. 121–22.

51 Ibid., p. 122.

52 See, for example, Gail Dutton, "The New Consortiums," *Management Review*, January 1999, pp. 46–50.

53 Julie Bick, "The New Fact of Self-Employment," *Inc. Magazine*, 23, no. 5, November 2001, pp. 87–89.

CHAPTER 7

1 Henry Fayol, *General and Industrial Management,* translated by Constance Storrs (London: Sir Issac Pitman, 1949), pp. 42–43.

2 Tom Burns and G. M. Stalker, *The Management of Innovation* (London: Tavistock, 1961), p. 1.

3 Emery and Trist, two other British researchers, referred to this innovative environment as a "turbulent field" environment because changes often come not from a firm's traditional competitors, but from out of the blue. Often, in fact, the changes seem to "arise from the field itself," in so far as they result from interaction between parts of the environment. The very texture of a firm's environment changes because previously unrelated or (from the point of view of the firm) irrelevant elements in its environment become interconnected. See F. E. Emery and E. C. Trist, "The Causal Texture of Organizational Environments," *Human Relations,* August 1965, pp. 20–26. As another example, after 1970 (when digital watches were introduced), calculator firms like Texas Instruments suddenly and unexpectedly became competitors in the watch industry.

4 How can we explain the fact that an organization's environment and technology influence its structure? One plausible explanation is that some environments and technologies require managers to handle more unforeseen problems and decisions than do others. And since each person's capacity for juggling problems and making decisions is limited, an overabundance of problems forces managers to respond—often by reorganizing. Thus, when a manager finds himself or herself becoming overloaded with problems, one reasonable response is to give subordinates more autonomy, to decentralize (thus letting employees handle more problems among themselves), and to reorganize around self-contained divisions. By reorganizing in these ways, the manager may surrender some direct control, but at least the organization avoids becoming unresponsive, as might otherwise have been the case.

5 Steve Lohr, "He Loves to Win. At IBM, He Did," *New York Times,* 10 March 2002, p. C11.

6 Joann Lublin, "Price vs. Product: It's Tough to Choose a Management Model," *Wall Street Journal,* 27 June 2001, p. A1.

7 Karyn Chan, "Overview—From Top to Bottom: Taking Advantage of Online Marketplaces Isn't Just About Changing Technology; It's About Changing an Entire Company," *Wall Street Journal,* 21 May 2001, p. R12.

8 Peter Senge, *The Fifth Discipline: The Art and Practice of the Learning Organizations* (New York: Currency Doubleday, 1994), p. 3.

9 Ibid., p. 4.

10 Robert Rowden, "The Learning Organization and Strategic Change," *SAM Advanced Management Journal* 66, no. 3, Summer 2001, p. 11.

11 Senge, op cit., pp. 8–10 and 139–301.

12 Harold Leavitt, "Some Effects of Certain Communication Patterns on Group Performance," *Journal of Abnormal and Social Psychology* 46, 1972, pp. 38–50.

13 Justin Fox, "Nokia's Secret Code," *Fortune,* 1 May 2000, p. 170.

14 Mary Anne Devanna and Noel Tichy, "Creating the Competitive Organization of the 21st Century: The Boundaryless Corporation," *Human Resource Management,* Winter 1990, pp. 455–71.

15 This is based on Larry Hirschhorn and Thomas Gilmore, "The New Boundaries of the 'Boundaryless' Company," *Harvard Business Review,* May–June 1992, pp. 104–108.

16 Ibid., p. 107.

17 Ibid., p. 108.

18 Ibid., p. 109.

19 Luc Hatlestad, "New Shades of Blue," *Red Herring,* November 1999, p. 126.

20 Except as noted, this section is based on Tom Peters, *Thriving on Chaos* (New York: Harper & Row, 1987), pp. 425–38; and Peters, *Liberation Management,* (New York: Knopf, 1992), pp. 90–95.

21 Peters, *Liberation Management,* p. 88.

22 Ibid., p. 90. Union Pacific also shows the potential downside of eliminating layers. Annual losses after Walsh left were soon approaching $1.3 billion due to severe traffic delays, a lack of rail cars, congestion problems, and accidents. UPRR's merger with another railroad explains part of the problem. However, the elimination of all those experienced midlevel managers probably contributed to it, too. See "Union Pacific's Rail Trouble's Take Toll on Texas Business," *New York Times,* 28 November, 1997, p. A12.

23 "How Can Big Companies Keep the Entrepreneurial Spirit Alive?" *Harvard Business Review,* November–December 1995, pp. 188–89.

24 Rob Walker, "Down on the Farm," *Fast Company,* February–March 1997 pp. 112–22.

25 This quote and the following points are based on Robert Rowden, "The Learning Organization and Strategic Change," *SAM Advanced Management Journal* 66, no. 3, Summer 2001, p. 11.

26 Jay Galbraith, "Organizational Design: An Information Processing View," *Interfaces* 4, no. 3, 1974, pp. 28–36; and Jay Galbraith, *Organizational Design* (Reading, MA: Addison-Wesley, 1977). See also Ranjay Gulati, "The architecture of Cooperation: Managing Coordination Costs and Appropriation Concerns in Strategic Alliances," *Administrative Science Quarterly,* December 1998, pp. 781–84.

27 Henry Mintzberg, *Structure in Fives: Designing Effective Organizations* (Upper Saddle River, NJ: Prentice Hall, 1983), pp. 4–9. See also Cliff McGoon, "Cutting-Edge Companies Use Integrated Marketing Communication," *Communication World,* December 1998, pp. 15–20.

28 Ibid., p. 6.

29 Christopher A. Bartlett and Sumantra Ghoshal, "Matrix Management: Not a Structure, a Frame of Mind," *Harvard Business Review,* July–August 1990, pp. 138–45. See also K. Simon-Elorz, "Information Technology for Organizational Systems: Some Evidence with Case Studies," *International Journal of Information Management,* February 1999, p. 75; and Alexander Gerybadz, "Globalization of R&D: Recent Changes in the Management of Innovation in Transnational Corporations," *Research Policy,* March 1999, pp. 251–53.

30 Ibid., pp. 143–44.

31 Mintzberg, op cit., p. 4.

32 Paul Lawrence and Jay Lorsch, *Organization and Environment* (Cambridge, MA: Harvard University Press, 1967). See also Frank Mueller and Romano Dyerson, "Expert Humans or Expert Organizations?" *Organization Studies* 20, no. 2, 1999, pp. 225–56. Some companies today practice concurrent engineering to improve production coordination, which basically means having all the departments—design, production, and marketing, for instance—work together to develop the product so that its production and marketing is more easily coordinated once the item goes into production. See Hassan Abdalla, "Concurrent Engineering for Global Manufacturing," *International Journal of Production Economics,* 20 April 1999, p. 251.

33 Delia Craven, "Click and Mortar," *Red Herring,* November 1999, p. 208.

34 Paul Lawrence and Jay Lorsch, *Organization and Environment* (Boston: Division of Research, Graduate School of Business Administration, Harvard University, 1967), p. 1.

35 Ibid.

36 Alan Church and Janine Waclawski, "Hold the Line: An Examination of Line vs. Staff Differences," *Human Resource Management* 40, no. 1, Spring 2001, pp. 21–34.

37 Gary Dessler, *Organization Theory* (Englewood Cliffs, NJ: Prentice Hall, 1980), pp. 333–36.

38 Ross Stagner, "Conflict in the Executive Suite," ed. Warren Ennis, *American Bureaucracy,* (Chicago: Aldine, 1970), pp. 85–95.

39 James Thompson, *Organizations in Action* (New York: McGraw-Hill, 1967).

40 Ibid., p. 55.

41 Louis Stern, Brian Sternthal, and C. Samuel Craig, "Strategies for Managing Interorganizational Conflict: A Laboratory Paradigm," *Journal of Applied Psychology* 60, no. 4, August 1975, pp. 472–82.

42 These principles are based on Stephen Robbins and Philip Hunsaker, *Training in Interpersonal Skills* (Upper Saddle River, NJ: Prentice Hall, 1996), pp. 91–95; and David Whetter and Kim Cameron, *Developing Management Skills* (Upper Saddle River, NJ: Prentice Hall, 2002), p. 435.

43 Roger Crockett, "Can Chris Galvin Save His Family's Legacy?" *Business Week,* July 16, 2001, pp. 72–78.

44 Larry Bossidy, "The Job No CEO Should Delegate," *Harvard Business Review* March 2001, pp. 47–49.

45 Kenneth MacKenzie, *Organizational Structure* (Arlington Heights, OH: AHM, 1978), pp. 198–230.

46 Ibid., p. 201.

47 Tom Hamburger et al., "Auditor Who Questioned Accounting for Enron Speaks to Investigators," *Wall Street Journal,* 1 April 2001, p. C1.

48 Harold Koontz and Cyril O'Donnell, *The Principles of Management* (New York: McGraw-Hill, 1964), p. 335.

49 The foundation study for this conclusion is Alfred Chandler, *Strategy and Structure* (Cambridge: MIT Press, 1962). For a recent literature review and test of the strategy-structure link, see Terry Amburgey and Tina Dacin, "As the Left Foot Follows the Right? The Dynamics of Strategic and Structural Change," *Academy of Management Journal* 37, no. 6, 1994, pp. 1427–52.

50 Chandler, op cit., p. 14.

51 Ibid., p. 366.

52 Jared Sandberg, "New AOL Unit Will Promote Marketing Across Multiple Media," *Wall Street Journal*, 20 August 2002, p. B7.

CHAPTER 8

1 Roger Schreffler, "Revivalist Art," *Ward's Auto World* 37, no. 11, November 2001, pp. 38–39.

2 Based on David Nadler and Michael Tushman, "Beyond the Charismatic Leader: Leadership and Organizational Change," *California Management Review*, Winter 1990, p. 80; and Alfred Marcus, "Responses to Externally Induced Innovation: To Their Effects on Organizational Performance," *Strategic Management Journal* 9, (1988), pp. 194–202. See also Steve Crom, "Change Leadership: the Virtues of Obedience," *Leadership & Organization Development Journal*, March–June 1999, pp. 162–68.

3 Nadler and Tushman, p. 80.

4 Chuck Salter, "On the Road Again," *Fast Company*, January 2002, pp. 51–58.

5 Ibid., p. 56.

6 Dennis Berman, "Lucent's Latest Revamp to Split Five Businesses into Two Units," *Wall Street Journal*, 11 July 2001, p. B7.

7 Michael Goold and Andrew Campbell, "Do You Have a Well-Designed Organization?" *Harvard Business Review*, March 2002, pp. 117–24.

8 Ibid., p. 118.

9 Scott Miller, "Volkswagen is Considering a Reorganization into Three Divisions," *Wall Street Journal*, 26 June, 2001, p. 18.

10 Goold and Campbell, op cit., p. 120.

11 Carol Hymowitz, "How a Leader at 3M Got His Employees to Back Big Changes," *Wall Street Journal*, 23 April 2002, p. B1.

12 Ibid., p. B1.

13 Goold and Campbell, op cit., p. 123.

14 John Kador, "Shall We Dance?" *Electronic Business* 28, no. 2, February 2002, p. 56.

15 This checklist is based on Philip Hunsaker, "Training in Management Skills, (Upper Saddle River, NJ: Prentice Hall, 2001), p. 323.

16 Edgar Schein, *Organizational Culture and Leadership* (San Francisco: Jossey-Bass, 1985), pp. 224–37. Peter Wright, Mark Kroll, and John Parnell, *Strategic Management Concepts* (Upper Saddle River, NJ: Prentice Hall, 1996), pp. 233–36; and Benjamin Schneider et al., "Creating a Climate and Culture for Sustainable Organizational Change," *Organizational Dynamics* 24, no. 4, 1996, pp. 7–19.

17 Peter N. Haapaniemi, "How Companies Transformed Themselves," *Chief Executive*, November 2001, pp. 2–5.

18 Niccolò Machiavelli, *The Prince*, trans. W. K. Marriott (London: J. M. Dent & Sons, Ltd., 1958).

19 Paul Lawrence, "How to Deal with Resistance to Change," *Harvard Business Review*, May–June, 1954. See also Andrew W. Schwartz, "Eight Guidelines for Managing Change," *Supervisory Management*, July 1994, pp. 3–5; Thomas J. Werner and Robert F. Lynch, "Challenges of a Change Agent," *Journal for Quality and Participation*, June 1994, pp. 50–54; Larry Reynolds, "Understand Employees' Resistance to Change," *HR Focus*, June 1994, pp. 17–18; Kenneth E. Hultman, "Scaling the Wall of Resistance," *Training & Development Journal*, October 1995, pp. 15–18; and Eric Dent, "Challenging Resistance to Change," *Journal of Applied Behavioral Science*, March 1999, p. 25.

20 John Mariotti, "The Challenge of Change," *Industry Week*, 6 April 1998, p. 140.

21 Timothy Judge et al., "Managerial Coping with Organizational Change: A Dispositional Perspective," *Journal of Applied Psychology* 84, no. 1, 1999, pp. 107–22.

22 Gary Dessler, *Winning Commitment: How to Build and Keep a Competitive Work Force* (New York: McGraw-Hill, 1993), p. 85.

23 Ibid., p. 85. See also Varun Grover, "From Business Reengineering to Business Process Change Management: A Longitudinal Study of Trends and Practices," *IEEE Transactions on Engineering Management*, February 1999, p. 36.

24 Daniel Denison, *Corporate Culture and Organizational Effectiveness* (Hoboken, NJ: John Wiley & Sons, 1990), p. 12. For a recent discussion, see also Daniel Denison, "What Is the Difference between Organizational Culture and Organizational Climate? A Native's Point of View on a Decade of Paradigm Wars," *Academy of Management Review*, July 1996, pp. 619–54.

25 Wendell French and Cecil Bell Jr., *Organization Development*, 6th ed. (Upper Saddle River, NJ: Prentice Hall, 1999), pp. 74–82.

26 John P. Kotter, *Leading Change* (Boston: Harvard Business School Press, 1996), pp. 40–41. See also Gary Hamel, "Waking up IBM," *Harvard Business Review*, July–August 2000, pp. 137–46.

27 Kotter, op cit., p. 44.

28 Ibid., p. 57.

29 For a discussion, see Julian Barling, Tom Weber, and E. Kevin Kelloway, "Effects of Transformational Leadership Training on Attitudinal and Financial Outcomes: A Field Experiment," *Journal of Applied Psychology*, December 1996, pp. 827–32.

30 Ibid.

31 Kotter, op cit., pp. 90–91.

32 Richard Pascale et al., "Changing the Way We Change," *Harvard Business Review*, November–December 1997, p. 129.

33 Noel Tichy and Ram Charan, "The CEO as Coach: An Interview with Allied Signal's Lawrence A. Bossidy," *Harvard Business Review*, March–April 1995, p. 77.

34 This is based on Kotter, op cit.," pp. 61–66.

35 Ibid., p. 65.

36 This is based on Carlos Ghosn, "Saving the Business Without Losing the Company," *Harvard Business Review*, January 2002, pp. 37–45.

37 Ibid., p. 41.

38 Erin Brown, "Big Business Meets the E World," *Fortune*, 8 November 1999, p. 88.

39 Ibid., p. 91.

40 Ibid.

41 David Baum, "Running the Rapids," *Profit Magazine*, November 1999, p. 54.

42 Ibid.

43 Stewart Alsop, "E or Be Eaten," *Fortune*, 8 November 1999, pp. 94–95.

44 Thomas Cummings and Christopher Worley, *Organization Development and Change* (Minneapolis: West Publishing Company, 1993), p. 3.

45 Based on J. T. Campbell and M. D. Dunnette, "Effectiveness of T-Group Experiences in Managerial Training and Development" *Psychological Bulletin* 7, 1968, pp. 73–104, reprinted in W. E. Scott and L. L. Cummings, *Readings in Organizational Behavior and Human Performance* (Homewood, IL: Irwin, 1973), p. 571.

46 Robert J. House, *Management Development* (Ann Arbor, MI: Bureau of Industrial Relations, University of Michigan, 1967), p. 71; Louis White and Kevin Wooten, "Ethical Dilemmas in Various Stages of Organizational Development," *Academy of Management Review* 8, no. 4 (1983) pp. 690–97.

47 Wendell French and Cecil Bell Jr., *Organization Development* (Upper Saddle River, NJ: Prentice Hall, 1995), pp. 171–93.

48 Cummings and Worley, op cit., p. 501.

49 For a description of how to make OD a part of organizational strategy, see Aubrey Mendelow and S. Jay Liebowitz, "Difficulties in Making OD a Part of Organizational Strategy," *Human Resource Planning* 12, no. 4 (1995), pp. 317–29.

50 Chung-Ming Lau and Hang-Yue Ngo, "Organizational Development and Firm Performance: A Comparison of Multinational and Local Firms," *Journal of International Business Studies* 32, no. 1, Spring 2001, p. 95.

51 Christina Gabrielidis et al., "Preferred Styles of Conflict Resolution: Mexico and United States," *Journal of Cross-Cultural Psychology* 28, no. 6, November 1997, pp. 667–78.

52 Ibid.

53 Ibid.

54 This section is based on Evert Van De Vliert, Martin C. Euwema, and Sipke E. Huismans, "Managing Conflict with a Subordinate or a Superior: Effectiveness of Conglomerated Behavior," *Journal of Applied Psychology*, April 1995, pp. 271–81.

55. Paul Lawrence and Jay Lorsch, *Organization and Environment*, (Boston: Harvard University, Graduate School of Business Administration, Division of Research, 1967), pp. 74–75.

56. Kenneth Thomas, "Conflict and Conflict Management," in Marvin Dunnette, *Handbook of Industrial and Organizational Psychology* (Chicago: Rand McNally, 1976), pp. 900–2; and Michael Carrell, Daniel Jennings, and Christina Heavrin, Fundamentals of Organizational Behavior (Upper Saddle River, NJ: Prentice Hall, 1997), pp. 505–9.

57. "One into Four," *The Economist*, 1 August 2002, www.economist.com; see also Philip Klein, "GE Capital to Split into Four," 26 July 2002, biz.yahoo.com.

CHAPTER 9

1. Ben Nagler, "Recasting Employees into Teams," *Workforce*, January 1998, 101–106.

2. Peter Boxall, "Placing HR Strategy at the Heart of Business Success," *Personnel Management* 26, no. 7, July 1994, pp. 32–34.

3. Nagler, op cit., p. 103.

4. See also James Clifford, "Manage Work Better to Better Manage Human Resources: A Comparative Study of Two Approaches to Job Analysis," *Public Personnel Management*, Spring 1996, pp. 89–103.

5. Gary Dessler, *Human Resource Management*, 9th Edition (Upper Saddle River, NJ: Prentice Hall, 2002), pp. 64–76.

6. Arthur R. Pell, *Recruiting and Selecting Personnel* (New York: Regents, 1969), pp. 10–12. See also Katherine Tyler, "Employees Can Help Recruiting New Talent," *HRMagazine*, September 1996, pp. 57–61.

7. Ibid., p. 11.

8. Dessler, op cit., p. 112.

9. Dessler, op cit., p. 104.

10. Allison Thompson, "The Contingent Workforce," *Occupational Outlook Quarterly*, Spring 1995, p. 45.

11. Brenda Palk Sunoo, "From Santas to CEO—Temps Play All Roles," *Personnel Journal*, April 1996, pp. 34–44.

12. "Search and Destroy," *The Economist*, 27 June 1998, p. 63.

13. Ibid.

14. Survey published by Bernard Hodes Advertising, Dept 106, 555 Madison Avenue, New York, NY 10022.

15. Sara Rynes, Marc Orlitzky, and Robert Bretz Jr., "Experienced Hiring versus College Recruiting: Practices and Emerging Trends," *Peronnel Psychology* 50, 1997, pp. 309–39.

16. See, for example, Richard Becker, "Ten Common Mistakes in College Recruiting—or How to Try Without Really Succeeding," *Personnel*, March–April 1975, pp. 19–28. See also Sara Rynes and John Boudreau, "College Recruiting in Large Organizations: Practice, Evaluation, and Research Implications," *Personnel Psychology*, Winter 1986, pp. 729–57.

17. "Internships Provide Workplace Snapshot," *BNA Bulletin to Management*, 22 May 1997, p. 168.

18. Jennifer Koch, "Finding Qualified Hispanic Candidates," *Recruitment Today*, Spring 1990, p. 35. See also Shelley Coolidge, "Minority Grads Sought for Jobs," *Christian Science Monitor*, 5 December 1997, p. 8.

19. "Welfare to Work: No Easy Chore," *BNA Bulletin to Management*, February 13, 1997, p. 56.

20. Gilbert Nicholson, "Automated Assessments for Better Hires," *Workforce* 20, no. 12, December 2000, pp. 102–4.

21. "Workplace Testing and Monitoring," *Management Review*, October 1998, pp. 31–42.

22. Ibid.

23. Mel Kleiman, "Employee Testing Essential to Hiring Effectively in the '90s," *Houston Business Journal*, 8 February 1993, p. 31; and Gerald L. Borofsky, "Pre-Employment Psychological Screening," *Risk Management*, January 1993, p. 47. See also Christina Ron Quist, "Pre-Employment Testing: Making It Work for You," *Occupational Hazards*, December 1997, pp. 38–40.

24. Louis Olivas, "Using Assessment Centers for Individual and Organizational Development," *Personnel*, May–June 1980, pp. 63–67; Tim Payne, Neil Anderson, and Tom Smith, "Assessment Centers, Selection Systems and Cost-Effectiveness: An Evaluative Case Study," *Personnel Review*, Fall 1992, p. 48; Roger Mottram, "Assessment Centers Are Not Only for Selection: The Assessment Center as a Development Workshop," *Journal of Managerial Psychology*,

January 1992, p. A1; and Charles Woodruffe, "Going Back a Generation," *People Management*, 20 February 1997, pp. 32–35.

25. Neal Schmitt et al., "Computer-Based Testing Applied to Selection of Secretarial Candidates," *Personnel Psychology* 46, no. 19, pp. 149–65.

26. This is based on Daniel Goleman, "Forget Money; Nothing Can Buy Happiness, Some Researchers Say," *Wall Street Journal*, 16 August 1996, pp. B5, B9. See also Shari Caudron, "Hire for Attitude," *Staffing: A Workforce Supplement*, August 1997, pp. 20–26.

27. Goleman, op cit., p. B9.

28. Source for questions: Goleman, ibid.; and Dr. Richard Davidson, University of Wisconsin.

29. For a full discussion of this, see Gary Dessler, *Human Resource Management*, 8th ed. (Upper Saddle River, NJ: Prentice Hall, 2000), Chapter 6.

30. R. E. Carlson, "Selection Interview Decisions: The Effects of Interviewer Experience, Relative Quota Situation, and Applicant Sample on Interview Decisions," *Personnel Psychology* 20, 1967, pp. 259–80. See also Linda Thornburgh, "Computer-Assisted Interviewing Shortens Hiring Cycle," *HRMagazine*, February 1998, pp. 73–76.

31. Pamela Paul, "Interviewing Is Your Business," *Association Management*, November 1992, p. 29.

32. William Tullar, Terry Mullins, and Sharon Caldwell, "Effects of Interview Length and Applicant Quality on Interview Decision Time," *Journal of Applied Psychology*, December 1979, pp. 669–74. See also Jennifer Burnett, et. al. "Interview Notes and Validity," *Personnel Psychology*, Summer 1998, pp. 375–96.

33. Gary Dessler, *Human Resource Management*, 7th ed. (Upper Saddle River, NJ: Prentice Hall, 1997), pp. 242–43.

34. See, for example, George Burgnoli, James Campion, and Jeffrey Bisen, "Racial Bias in the Use of Work Samples for Personnel Selection," *Journal of Applied Psychology*, April 1979, pp. 119–23.

35. Edward Robinson, "Beware—Job Seekers Have No Secrets," *Fortune*, December 29, 1997, p. 285.

36. Seymour Adler, "Verifying a Job Candidate's Background: The State of Practice in a Vital Human Resources Activity,"*Review of Business*, 15, no. 2 (Winter 1993) p. 6.

37. John Jones and William Terris, "Post-Polygraph Selection Techniques," *Recruitment Today*, May–June 1989, pp. 25–31.

38. These are based on Commerce Clearing House, *Ideas and Trends*, 29 December 1998, pp. 222–23. See also "Divining Integrity Through Interviews," *BNA Bulletin to Management*, 4 June 1987, p. 184.

39. Dessler, *Human Resource Management*, 9e, op cit., pp. 150–51.

40. Scott MacDonald et al., "The Limitations of Drug Screening in the Workplace," *International Labor Review* 132, no. 1, 1993, p. 98.

41. See, for example, Ann Fields, "Class Act," *Inc. Technology*, 1997, pp. 55–57.

42. "Industry Report 1999," *Training*, October 1999, pp. 37–60.

43. Jennifer Reese, "Starbuck," *Fortune*, 9 December 1996, 190–200.

44. Kenneth Wexley and Gary Latham, *Developing and Training Human Resources in Organizations* (Glenview, IL: Scott, Foresman, 1981), p. 107.

45. William Berliner and William McLarney, *Management Practice and Training* (Burr Ridge, IL: McGraw-Hill, 1974), pp. 442–43. See also Stephen Wehrenberg, "Supervisors as Trainees: The Long-Term Gains of OJT," *Personnel Journal* 66, no. 4, April 1987, pp. 48–51.

46. Shari Caudron, "Your Learning Technology Primer," *Personnel Journal*, June 1996, pp. 120–36.

47. "Creating Portals to Effective Learning," *Training* 538, no. 1, January 2001, pp. 41–42.

48. Del Jones, "More Firms Cut Workers Ranked at Bottom to Make Way for Talent," *USA Today*, 30 May 2001, p. BU01.

49. "360-Degree Feedback on the Rise, Survey Finds," *BNA Bulletin to Management*, 23 January 1997, p. 31. See also Kenneth Nowack et al., "How to Evaluate Your 360-Degree Feedback Efforts," *Training and Development Journal*, April 1999, pp. 48–53.

50. Kenneth Nowack, "360-Degree Feedback: The Whole Story," *Training and Development*, January 1993, p. 69. For a description of some of the problems involved in implementing 360-degree feedback, see Matthew Budman, "The Rating Game," *Across the Board*, February 1994, pp. 35–38.

51. Katherine Romano, "Fear of Feedback," *Management Review*, December 1993, p. 39.

52. See, for instance, Gerry Rich, "Group Reviews—Are You Up to It?" *CMA Magazine*, March 1993, p. 5.

53 Romano, op cit.

54 This is based on Dessler, *Human Resource Management*, 8th ed., op cit., pp. 321–23.

55 This section is based on Gary Dessler, *Human Resource Management*, 8th ed., op cit., pp. 43–44. See also Commerce Clearing House, *Sexual Harassment Manual*, p. 8.

56 See Paul Judge, "How Might your Company Adapt?" *Fast Company*, no. 53, December 2001, pp. 128–39.

57 Deze Khasru, "JetBlue Hopes to Fly Through Tough Times," *Fairfield County Business Journal* 40, no. 41, 8 October 2001, p. 7.

58 "JetBlue," *Fortune Small Business* 11, no. 2, 1 March 2001, p. 92.

59 Ibid.

60 Amy Rottier, "The Skies Are JetBlue," *Workforce* 80, no. 9, September 2001, p. 22.

CHAPTER 10

1 Joseph White and Norihiko Shirouzu, "Backfire: A Stalled Revolution by Nasser, *Wall Street Journal*, 31 October, 2001, p. A1.

2 Jeffrey McNally, Stephen Gerras, and R. Craig Bullis, "Teaching Leadership at the U.S. Military Academy at West Point," *Journal of Applied Behavioral Science*, June 1996, p. 181.

3 See David Waldman, Gabriel Ramirez, Robert J. House, and Phanish Puranam, "Does Leadership Matter? CEO Leadership Attributes and Profitability Under Conditions of Perceived Incremental Uncertainty," *Academy of Management Journal*, 44, no. 1, 2001, pp. 134–43.

4 In Jerry Useem, "What It Takes," *Fortune*, 12 November, 2001, p. 126.

5 Gary Yukl, *Leadership in Organizations*, 3rd ed. (Upper Saddle River, NJ: Prentice Hall, 1998), p. 235.

6 Ralph Stogdill, *Handbook of Leadership: A Survey of the Literature* (New York: Free Press, 1974), p. 81, quoted in Gary Yukl, *Leadership in Organizations*, p. 236.

7 Shelley Kirkpatrick and Edwin A. Locke, "Leadership: Do Traits Matter?" *Academy of Management Executive*, May 1991, p. 49.

8 Ibid., p. 50.

9 Except as noted, this section is based on ibid., pp. 48–60. See also Ross Laver, "Building a Better Boss: Studies Show That the Personality of a Chief Executive Can Have a Major Impact on Profits and Productivity," *Maclean's*, 30 September 1996, p. 41.

10 Kim-Yin Chan and Fritz Dragsow, "Toward a Theory of Individual Differences and Leadership: Understanding the Motivation to Lead," *Journal of Applied Psychology*, 86, no. 3, 2001, pp. 481–98.

11 Kirkpatrick and Locke, op cit., p. 53.

12 Useem, op cit., p. 130.

13 Ibid., p. 54.

14 Ibid., p. 55.

15 Ibid., pp. 5–6.

16 Discussed in William Q. Judge, "Is a Leader's Character Culture-Bound or Culture-Free? An Empirical Comparison of the Character Traits of American and Taiwanese CEOs," *Journal of Leadership Studies* 8, no. 2, Fall 2001, 63.

17 Ibid.

18 Niccoló Machiavelli, *The Prince*, trans. W. K. Marriott (London: J. M. Dent & Sons, Ltd., 1958).

19 Chester Barnard, *The Functions of the Executive* (Cambridge, MA: Harvard University Press, 1938). See also Roger Dawson, *Secrets of Power Persuasion* (Upper Saddle River, NJ: Prentice Hall, 1992); Sydney Finkelstein, "Power in Top Management Teams: Dimensions, Measurement, and Validation," *Academy of Management Journal*, August 1992; and Jeffrey Pfeffer, *Managing with Power: Politics and Influence in Organizations* (Boston: Harvard Business School Press, 1992).

20 Eli Cohen and Noel Tichy, "Operation: Leadership," *Fast Company*, September 1999, p. 280.

21 Ibid., p. 280.

22 See, for example, Kirkpatrick and Locke, op. cit., p. 49.

23 Ibid., p. 56.

24 See John Kotter, "What Leaders Really Do," *Harvard Business Review*, December 2001, pp. 86–95.

25 Ralph Stogdill, *Managers, Employees, Organizations* (Columbus: Bureau of Business Research, Ohio State University, 1965).

26 Ralph Stogdill and A. E. Koonz, "Leader Behavior: Its Description and Measurement" (Columbus: Bureau of Business Research, Ohio State University, 1957). See also Bernard M. Bass, *Bass &

Stogdill's Handbook of Leadership: Theory, Research, & Managerial Applications*, 3rd ed. (New York: The Free Press, 1990).

27 Gary Yukl, "Towards a Behavioral Theory of Leadership," *Organizational Behavior and Human Performance*, July 1971, pp. 414–40. See also Yukl, *Leadership in Organizations*, op cit.

28 Chester Schriesheim, Robert J. House, and Steven Kerr, "Leader Initiating Structure: A Reconciliation of Discrepant Research Results and Some Empirical Tests," *Organizational Behavior and Human Performance*, April 1976. See also Bass, op cit.

29 Robert Blake and Jane Mouton, *The Managerial Grid* (Houston: Gulf Publishing, 1964).

30 Hal Lancaster, "Herb Kelleher Has One Main Strategy: Treat Employees Well," *Wall Street Journal*, 31 August 1999, p. B1.

31 Rensis Likert, *New Patterns of Management* (New York: McGraw-Hill, 1961), pp. 102–6.

32 Robert Day and Robert Hamblin, "Some Effects of Close and Punitive Styles of Leadership," *American Journal of Psychology* 69, 1964, pp. 499–510.

33 See, for example, Nancy Morse, *Satisfaction in the White Collar Job* (Ann Arbor: Survey Research Center, University of Michigan, 1953).

34 Rachel Silverman and Chris Maher, "Bosses' Challenge: So the Workers Get the Job Done," *Wall Street Journal*, 23 October, 2001, B1.

35 "Prada Faces Shaky Future with Slowing Economy," *Wall Street Journal*, 8 November, 2001, p. B12.

36 Victor Vroom and Arthur Jago, "On the Validity of the Vroom-Yetton Model," *Journal of Applied Psychology* 63, no. 2, 1978, pp. 151–62; Madeleine Heilman et al., "Reactions to Prescribed Leader Behavior as a Function of Role Perspective: The Case of the Vroom-Yetton Model," *Journal of Applied Psychology*, February 1984, pp. 50–60. See also Donna Brown, "Why Participative Management Won't Work Here" *Management Review*, June 1992.

37 Vroom and Jago, op cit., pp. 151–62.

38 Based on Yukl, *Leadership in Organizations*, p. 123.

39 See, for example, Mark Tubbs and Steven Akeberg, "The Role of Intentions in Work Motivation: Implications for Goal Setting Theory and Research," *Academy of Management Review*, January 1991, pp. 180–99.

40 Carol Hymowitz, "In Times of Trouble, the Best of Leaders Listen to Dissenters," *Wall Street Journal*, 13 November, 2001, p. B1.

41 C. M. Solomon, "Careers Under Glass," *Personnel Journal* 69, no. 4, 1990, pp. 96–105.

42 See, for example, James Bowditch and Anthony Buono, *A Primer on Organizational Behavior* (New York: John Wiley, 1994), p. 238.

43 Russell Kent and Sherry Moss, "Effects of Sex and Gender Role on Leader Emergence," *Academy of Management Journal* 37, no. 5, 1994, pp. 1335–46; Jane Baack, Norma Carr-Ruffino, and Monica Pelletier, "Making It to the Top: Specific Leadership Skills," *Women in Management Review* 8, no. 2, 1993, pp. 17–23.

44 S. M. Donnel and J. Hall, "Men and Women as Managers: A Significant Case of No Significant Difference," *Organizational Dynamics* 8, 1980, pp. 60–77. See also Jennifer L. Berdahl, "Gender and Leadership in Work Groups: Six Alternative Models," *Leadership Quarterly*, Spring 1996, pp. 21–40.

45 M. A. Hatcher, "The Corporate Woman of the 1990s: Maverick or Innovator?" *Psychology of Women Quarterly* 5, 1991, pp. 251–59.

46 D. G. Winter, *The Power Motive* (New York: The Free Press, 1975).

47 L. McFarland Shore and G. C. Thornton, "Effects of Gender on Self and Supervisory Ratings," *Academy of Management Journal* 29, no. 1, 1986, pp. 115–129; quoted in Bowditch and Buono, op cit., p. 238.

48 G. H. Dobbins and S. J. Paltz, "Sex Differences in Leadership: How Real Are They?" *Academy of Management Review* 11, 1986, pp. 118–27; R. Drazin and E. R. Auster, "Wage Differences Between Men and Women: Performance Appraisal Ratings versus Salary Allocation as the Locus of Bias," *Human Resource Management* 26, 1987, pp. 157–68. See also Nancy DiTomaso and Robert Hooijberg, "Diversity and the Demands of Leadership," *Leadership Quarterly*, Summer 1996, pp. 163–87; and Chao C. Chen and Ellen Van Velsor, "New Directions for Research and Practice in Diversity Leadership," *Leadership Quarterly*, Summer 1996, pp. 285–302.

49 M. Jelinek and N. J. Alder, "Women: World-Class Managers for Global Competition," *Academy of Management Executive* 2, no. 1, 1988, pp. 11–19; J. Grant, "Women as Managers: What Can They

Offer to Organizations?" *Organizational Dynamics*, 16, no. 3, 1988, pp. 56–63. On the other hand, one author suggests that women should be more Machiavellian: "War favors the dangerous woman. Women may love peace and seek stability, but these conditions seldom serve them." [From Harriet Rubin, The Princessa: Machiavelli for Women (New York: Doubleday/Currenly, 1997), quoted in Anne Fisher, "What Women Can Learn from Machiavelli," *Fortune*, April 1997, p. 162.]

50 J. M. Burns, *Leadership* (New York: Harper, 1978).

51 For a discussion, see Ronald Deluga, "Relationship of Transformational and Transactional Leadership with Employee Influencing Strategies," *Group and Organizational Studies*, December 1988, pp. 457–58. See also Philip M. Podsakoff, Scott B. MacKenzie, and William H. Bommer, "Transformational Leader Behaviors as Determinants of Employee Satisfaction, Commitment, Trust, and Organizational Citizenship Behaviors," *Journal of Management* 22, no. 2, 1996, pp. 259–98.

52 Joseph Seltzer and Bernard Bass, "Transformational Leadership: Beyond Initiation and Consideration," *Journal of Management* 4, 1990, p. 694. See also Bernard M. Bass, "Theory of Transformational Leadership Redux," *Leadership Quarterly*, Winter 1995, pp. 463–78.

53 Charles Gasparino, "Bull by the Horns," *Wall Street Journal*, 2 November, 2001.

54 Gary Yukl, "Leadership in Organizations," p. 324.

55 N. M. Tichy and M. A. Devanna, *The Transformational Leader* (New York: Wiley 1986).

56 Seltzer and Bass, op cit., p. 694.

57 Deluga, op cit., p. 457.

58 Frances Yamarino and Bernard Bass, "Transformational Leadership and Multiple Levels of Analysis," *Human Relations* 43, no. 10, 1990, p. 976. See also David Walman, "CEO Charismatic Leadership: Levels of Management and Levels of Analysis Effects," *Academy of Management Review*, April 1999, pp. 266–68.

59 Bernard Bass, *Leadership and Performance Beyond Expectations* (New York: The Free Press, 1985); and Deluga, op cit., pp. 457–58. See also Boas Shamir, "Correlates of Charismatic Leader Behavior in Military Units: Subordinates Attitudes, Unit Characteristics, and Superiors' Appraisals of Leader Performance," *Academy of Management Journal*, August 1998, pp. 387–410.

60 Gary Yukl, *Leadership in Organizations*, pp. 298–99.

61 Deluga, op cit., p. 457.

62 Yamarino and Bass, op cit., p. 981.

63 Ibid.

64 J. M. Howell and C. A. Higgins, "Champions of Technological Innovation," *Administrative Science Quarterly* 35, 1990, pp. 317–41.

65 For a review, see Robert Keller, "Transformational Leadership and the Performance of Research and Development Project Groups," *Journal of Management* 18, no. 3, 1992, pp. 489–501.

66 J. J. Hater and Bernard Bass, "Superiors' Evaluations and Subordinates' Perceptions of Transformational and Transactional Leadership," *Journal of Applied Psychology* 73, 1988, pp. 695–702.

67 Yamarino and Bass, op cit., p. 981.

68 From Yukl, *Leadership in Organizations*, op cit., p. 342.

69 Jim Collins, "Level 5 Leadership," *Harvard Business Review*, January 2001, pp. 67–76.

70 James Healey and David Kiley, "Surprise: Chrysler Loves Its German Boss: 'Car Guy' Eats in the Cafeteria, Hangs Out with Union Members," *USA Today*, 3 May, 2001, p. B01.

71 Daniel Goleman, "Leadership That Gets Results," *Harvard Business Review*, March –April 2000, 78; and Daniel Goleman, "What Makes a Leader?" *Harvard Business Review*, November–December 1998, p. 90.

72 Goleman, "Leadership," p. 80.

73 David Dorsey, "Andy Pearson Finds Love," *Fast Company*, no. 49, August 2001, pp. 78–86.

74 Ibid.

75 Frederick E. Fiedler, *A Theory of Leadership Effectiveness* (New York: McGraw-Hill, 1967), p. 147. See also David Stauffer, "Once a Leader, Always a Leader?" *Across the Board*, April 1999, pp. 14–19.

76 Fiedler, p. 147.

77 Ibid, p. 143.

78 See, for example, Robert J. House and J. V. Singh, "Organizational Behavior: Some New Directions for I/O Psychology," *Annual Review of Psychology* 38, 1987, pp. 669–718; L. H. Peters, D. D. Hartke, and J. T. Pohlmann, "Fiedler's Contingency Theory of Leadership: An Application of the Meta-Analytic Procedures of Schmidt and Hunter," *Psychological Bulletin* 97, 1985, pp. 274–85. See also Fred Fiedler and J. E. Garcia, *New Approaches to Effective Leadership: Cognitive Resources and Organizational Performance* (New York: John Wiley and Sons, 1987); Robert T. Vecchio, "Theoretical and Empirical Examination of Cognitive Resource Theory," *Journal of Applied Psychology*, April 1990, pp. 141–47; and Robert Vecchio, "Cognitive Resource Theory: Issues for Specifying a Test of the Theory," *Journal of Applied Psychology*, June 1992.

79 Gary Dessler, *An Investigation of a Path–Goal Theory of Leadership*, Ph.D. Dissertation, City University of New York, 1972.

80 Robert J. House and Terence Mitchell, "Path–Goal Theory of Leadership," *Journal of Contemporary Business* 3, Autumn 1974, pp. 81–97; reprinted in Donald White, *Contemporary Perspectives in Organizational Behavior* (Boston: Allyn and Bacon, 1982), pp. 228–35.

81 Robert J. House and Terrence Mitchell, "Path–Goal Theory of Leadership," *Contemporary Business* 3, 1974, pp. 81–98; and Abraham Sagie and Meni Koslowsky, "Organizational Attitudes and Behaviors as a Function of Participation in Strategic and Tactical Change Decisions: An Application of Path–Goal Theory," *Journal of Organizational Behavior*, January 1994, pp. 37–48.

82 Yukl, *Leadership in Organizations*, op cit., pp. 268–270.

83 Ibid., p. 269.

84 Ibid.

85 Robert J. House, "A Path–Goal Theory of Leader Effectiveness," *Administrative Science Quarterly* 16, no. 3, September 1971; reprinted in Henry Tosi and W. Clay Hammer, *Organizational Behavior and Management* (Chicago: St. Clair Press, 1974), pp. 459–68.

86 Steve Kerr and J. M. Jermier, "Substitutes for Leadership: Their Meaning and Measurement," *Organizational Behavior and Human Performance* 22, 1978, pp. 374–403.

87 Ibid. See also Philip M. Podsakoff and Scott B. MacKenzie, "An Examination of Substitutes for Leadership Within a Levels-of-Analysis Framework," *Leadership Quarterly*, Fall 1995, pp. 289–328.

88 David Alcorn, "Dynamic Followership: Empowerment at Work," *Management Quarterly*, Spring 1992, pp. 11–13.

89 Jon Howell, David Bowen, Peter Dorfman, Steven Kerr, and Philip Podsakoff, "Substitutes for Leadership: Effective Alternatives to Ineffective Leadership," *Organizational Dynamics*, Summer 1990, p. 23.

90 Ibid.

91 G. B. Graen and T. A. Scandura, "Toward a Psychology of Daidic Organizing," eds. L. L. Cummings and B. M. Staw, *Research in Organizational Behavior*, Vol. 9 (Greenwich, CT: J.A.I. Press, 1987), p. 208. See also David Schneider and Charles Goldwasser, "Be a Model Leader of Change," *Management Review*, March 1998, pp. 41–48; Antoinette Phillips and Arthur Bedeian, "Leader–Follower Exchange Quality: The Role of Personal and Interpersonal Attributes," *Academy of Management Journal* 37, no. 4, 1994, pp. 990–1001; Nancy Boyd and Robert Taylor, "A Developmental Approach to the Examination of Friendship in Leader and Follower Relationships," *Leadership Quarterly* 9, no. 1, 1998, pp. 1–25; Jaesub Lee, "Leader Member Exchange: The 'Pelz Effect' and Cooperative Communication Between Group Members," *Management Communications Quarterly*, November 1997, pp. 266–87; and Christopher Avery, "All Power to You: Collaborative Leadership Works," *Journal for Quality and Participation*, March–April 1999, pp. 36–41.

92 Jerald Greenberg, *Managing Behavior in Organizations* (Upper Saddle River, NJ: Prentice Hall, 1996), p. 215.

93 Phillips and Bedeian, op cit.

94 Yukl, *Leadership in Organizations*, op cit., p. 132.

95 See Robert P. Vecchio, "Situational Leadership Theory: An Examination of a Prescriptive Theory," *Journal of Applied Psychology*, August 1987, pp. 444–51; and Jerald Greenberg, *Managing Behavior in Organizations* (Upper Saddle River, NJ: Prentice Hall, 1996), p. 226.

96 McNally et al., op cit., p. 178.

97 Fiedler, *A Theory of Leadership Effectiveness*, p. 250.

98 Adrian Tomine, "Fast Track 2000," *Fast Company*, March 2000, pp. 246–247.

99 Ibid, p. 268.

100 Ibid.

101 Eryn Brown, "A Smokeless Herb," *Fortune*, 28 May, 2001, pp. 78–79.

102 Paul Judge, "JetBlue," *Fortune Small Business*, 1 March 2001, p. 92.

103 Paul Judge, op cit.

CHAPTER 11

1 Matthew Brelis, "I've Got Trust for Bethune," *Boston Globe*, 3 June 2001.

2 R. Cattel, *The Scientific Analysis of Personality* (Baltimore: Penguin Books, 1965). See also G. Northcraft and M. Neale, *Organizational Behavior* (Hinsdale, IL: Dryden Press, 1994), pp. 64–240.

3 See, for example, Jesus Delgado, "The Five Factor Model of Personality and Job Performance in the European Community," *Journal of Applied Psychology* 82, no. 1, 1997, pp. 30–43; and Robert Beck, *Motivation* (Upper Saddle River, NJ: Prentice Hall, 2000), pp. 323–25.

4 Murray Barrick and Michael Mount, "The Big Five Personality Dimension and Job Performance: A Meta-Analysis," *Personal Psychology*, Spring 1991, pp. 1–26.

5 James Bowditch and Anthony Buono, *A Primer on Organizational Behavior* (New York: John Wiley, 1994), p. 115.

6 Based on Ernest J. McCormick and Joseph Tiffin, *Industrial Psychology* (Upper Saddle River, NJ: Prentice Hall, 1974), pp. 136–74. See also Marilyn Gist and Terence Mitchell, "Self-Efficacy: A Theoretical Analysis of Its Determinants and Malleability," *Academy of Management Review*, April 1992, pp. 183–202.

7 Saul Gellerman, *Motivation and Productivity* (New York: AMACOM, 1963), p. 290.

8 Lester Lefton and Laura Valvatne, *Mastering Psychology* (Boston: Allyn & Bacon, 1992), p. 412.

9 Ibid.

10 Gist and Mitchell, op cit., p. 183.

11 For a review and listing of these studies, see Gist and Mitchell, op cit., pp. 183–202.

12 Ernest R. Hilgard, *Introduction to Psychology* (New York: Harcourt Brace and World, 1962), p. 86.

13 Benson Rosen and Thomas Jerdee, "The Influence of Age Stereotypes on Managerial Decisions," *Journal of Applied Psychology*, August 1976, pp. 428–32.

14 Martin Fishbein and Icek Ajzen, *Attitude, Intention and Behavior: An Introduction to Theory and Research* (Reading, MA: Addison-Wesley, 1975).

15 Craig Pinder, *Work Motivation in Organizational Behavior* (Upper Saddle River, NJ: Prentice Hall, 1998), p. 245.

16 The Job Descriptive Index is copyrighted by Bowling Green State University, and it can be obtained from Dr. Patricia C. Smith, Department of Psychology, Bowling Green State University, Bowling Green, Ohio, 43403.

17 See, for example, M. T. Iaffaldano and M. P. Muchinsky, "Job Satisfaction and Job Performance: A Meta-Analysis," *Psychological Bulletin*, March 1985, pp. 251–73.

18 Ernest R. Hilgard, *Introduction to Psychology* (New York: Harcourt Brace and World, 1962), pp. 124–25.

19 Ibid., p. 124.

20 See, for instance, R. Kanfer, "Motivation Theory," in M. D. Dunnette and L. M. Hough (eds.), *Handbook of Industrial and Organizational Psychology*, (Palo Alto, CA: Consulting Psychologists Press, 1990). See also Robert Hersey, "A Practitioner's View of Motivation," *Journal of Managerial Psychology*, May 1993, pp. 110–15; and Kenneth Kovatch, "Employee Motivation: Addressing a Crucial Factor in Your Organization's Performance," *Employment Relations Today*, Summer 1995, pp. 93–107.

21 See Douglas M. McGregor, "The Human Side of Enterprise," ed. Michael Matteson and John M. Ivancevich, *Management Classics* (Santa Monica, CA: Goodyear, 1977), pp. 43–49. See also Ewart Woolridge, "Time to Stand Maslow's Hierarchy on Its Head?" *People Management*, 21 December 1995, p. 17.

22 John Rowan, "Maslow Amended," *Journal of Humanistic Psychology*, Winter 1998, pp. 81–83. See also Clay Alderfer, "Theories Reflecting My Personal Experience and Life Development," *Journal of Applied Behavioral Science*, November 1989, pp. 351–66.

23 See, for example, Alderfer, op cit., pp. 351–66.

24 Abraham Maslow, *Toward a Psychology of Being*, 2nd ed. (New York: Van Nostrand Reinhold, 1968).

25 McGregor, op cit., p. 45.

26 For a discussion, see, for example, Pinder, op cit., pp. 64–66.

27 Frederick Herzberg et al., *Job Attitudes: Review of Research and Opinion* (Pittsburgh, PA: Pittsburgh Psychological Services, 1957).

28 R. B. Ewen, "Some Determinants of Job Satisfaction: A Study of the Generality of Herzberg's Theory," *Journal of Applied Psychology*, 48, 1964, pp. 161–63.

29 Mark Tietjen and Robert Myers, "Motivation and Job Satisfaction," *Management Decision*, May–June 1998, pp. 226–32.

30 This is based on David Kolb, Irwin Rubin, and James McIntyre, *Organizational Psychology: An Experiential Approach* (Upper Saddle River, NJ: Prentice Hall, 1971), pp. 65–69.

31 These are all from ibid.

32 David McClelland and David Burnham, "Power Is the Great Motivator," *Harvard Business Review*, January–February 1995, pp. 126–36.

33 George Litwin and Robert Stringer Jr., *Motivation and Organizational Climate* (Boston: Harvard University Press, 1968), pp. 20–24.

34 Edgar Schein, *Career Dynamics: Matching Individual and Organizational Needs* (Reading, MA: Addison-Wesley, 1978); and Thomas Barth, "Career Anchor Theory," *Review of Public Personnel Administration* 13, no. 4, 1993, pp. 27–42. See also Jeffrey Colvin, "Looking to Hire the Very Best? Ask the Right Questions, Lots of Them," *Fortune*, 21 June 1999, pp. 19–21.

35 Bob Nelson et al, "Motivate Employees According to Temperament," *HRMagazine*, March 1997, pp. 51–56. See also Donna Mc-Neese-Smith, "The Relationship Between Managerial Motivation, Leadership, Nurse Outcomes and Patient Satisfaction," *Journal of Organizational Behavior*, March 1999, p. 243.

36 Craig Pinder, *Work Motivation in Organizational Behavior* (Upper Saddle River, NJ: Prentice Hall, 1998), pp. 288–99.

37 See, for example, J. Greenberg, "A Taxonomy of Organizational Justice Theories," *Academy of Management Review* 12, 1987, pp. 9–22. See also Armin Falk, "Intrinsic Motivation and Extrinsic Incentives in a Repeated Game with Incomplete Contracts," *Journal of Economic Psychology*, June 1999, pp. 251–54.

38 For a discussion, see Kanfer, op cit., 124.

39 Edwin A. Locke and D. Henne, "Work Motivation Theories," eds. C. L. Cooper and I. Robertson, *International Review of Industrial and Organizational Psychology* (Chichester, England: Wiley, 1986), pp. 1–35. See also Maureen Ambrose, "Old Friends, New Faces: Motivation Research in the 1990s," *Journal of Management*, May–June 1999, pp. 231–37.

40 Kanfer, op cit., p. 125.

41 Craig Pinder, op cit., p. 377.

42 Edwin Locke et al., "The Effects of Intra-Individual Goal Conflict on Performance," *Journal of Management* 20, 1994, pp. 67–91. See also the discussion in Pinder, op cit., p. 383.

43 Kanfer, p. 113.

44 For a discussion, see John P. Campbell and Robert Pritchard, "Motivation Theory in Industrial and Organizational Psychology," ed. Marvin Dunnette, *Industrial and Organizational Psychology* (Chicago: Rand McNally, 1976), pp. 74–75; and Kanfer, op cit., pp. 115–16.

45 Peter Foreman, "Work Values and Expectancies in Occupational Rehabilitation: The Role of Cognitive Values in the Return to Work Process," *Journal of Rehabilitation*, July–September 1996, pp. 44–49.

46 See, for example, Terrence Mitchell, "Expectancy-Value Models in Organizational Psychology," ed. N. P. Feather, *Expectations and Actions: Expectancy-Value Models in Psychology* (Hillsdale, NJ: Erlbaum, 1982), pp. 293–312. See also Mark Tubbs et al., "Expectancy, Valence, and Motivational Force Functions in Goal Setting Research: An Empirical Test," *Journal of Applied Psychology*, June 1993, pp. 36–49; and Peter Foreman, "Work Values and Expectancies in Occupational Rehabilitation: the Role of Cognitive Values in the Return to Work Process," *Journal of Rehabilitation*, July–September 1996, pp. 44–49.

47 Mark Tubbs, Donna Boehne, and James Dahl, "Expectancy, Valence, and Motivational Force Functions in Goal Setting Research: An Empirical Test," *Journal of Applied Psychology*, June 1993, pp. 361–73; and Wendelien Van Eerde and Hank Thierry, "Vroom's Expectancy Model and Work-Related Criteria: A Meta-Analysis," *Journal of Applied Psychology*, October 1996, pp. 575–86. See also Robert Fudge and John Schlacter, "Motivating Employees to Act Ethically: An Expectancies Theory Approach," *Journal of Business Ethics*, February 1999, p. 295; and Barbara Caska, "The Search for

48 Foreman, op cit., pp. 44–49.

49 Van Eerde and Thierry, op cit., pp. 575–86. See also Jason Colquitt, "Conscientiousness, Goal Orientation, and Motivation to Learn During the Learning Process: A Longitudinal Study," *Journal of Applied Psychology*, August 1998, pp. 654–66.

50 For a definition of learning, see Lefton and Valvatne, op cit., p. 161.

51 For a review of operant conditioning, see Fred Luthans and R. Kreitner, *Organizational Behavior Modification and Beyond: An Operant and Social Learning Approach* (Glenview, IL: Scott, Foresman, 1985). See also Nancy Chase, "You Get What You Reward," *Quality*, June 1999, p. 104.

52 W. Clay Hamner, "Reinforcement Theory in Management and Organizational Settings," eds. Henry Tosi and W. Clay Hamner, *Organizational Behavior and Management: A Contingency Approach* (Chicago: Saint Claire, 1974), pp. 86–112. See also Donald J. Campbell, "The Effects of Goal-Contingent Payment on the Performance of a Complex Task," *Personnel Psychology*, Spring 1984, pp. 23–40; and Robert Taylor, "Preventing Employee Theft: A Behavioral Approach," *Business Perspectives*, June 1998, pp. 9–14.

53 Robert McNutt "Sharing Across the Board: DuPont's Achievement Sharing Program," *Compensation & Benefits Review*, July–August 1990, pp. 17–24.

54 Barry Thomas and Madeline Hess Olson, "Gainsharing: The Design Guarantees Success," *Personnel Journal*, May 1988, pp. 73–79. One of the most well-known and well-established plans of this type is in place at the Lincoln Electric Company. See, for example, Kenneth Chilton, "Lincoln Electric's Incentive System: A Reservoir of Trust," *Compensation and Benefits Review*, November 1994, pp. 29–34.

55 See, for example, William Atkinson, "Incentive Pay Programs That Work in Textiles," *Textile World*, February 2001 151, no. 2, pp. 55–57.

56 James Lardner, "Okay Here Are Your Options," *U.S. News and World Report*, 1 March 1999, p. 44.

57 Naomi Weiss, "How Starbucks Impassions Workers to Drive Growth," *Workforce*, August 1998, pp. 61–63.

58 Marc Knez and Duncan Simester, "Making Across-the-Board Incentives Work," *Harvard Business Review*, February 2002, pp. 16–17.

59 Adapted from Gary Dessler, *Human Resource Management* (Upper Saddle River, NJ: Prentice Hall, 2002), p. 356.

60 Michael Harris et al., "A Longitudinal Examination of a Merit Pay System," *Journal of Applied Psychology*, 83, 1998, pp. 825–31.

61 James Brinks, "Is There Merit in Merit Increases?" *Personnel Administrator*, May 1980, p. 60. See also Atul Migra et al., "The Case of the Invisible Merit Raise: How People See Their Pay Raises," *Compensation & Benefits Review*, May 1995, pp. 71–76.

62 Cheryl Comeau-Kirschner, "Improving Productivity Doesn't Cost a Dime," *Management Review*, January 1999, p. 7.

63 Bob Nelson, *1001 Ways to Reward Employees* (New York: Workmen Publishing, 1994), p. 19.

64 Scot Hays, "Pros and Cons of Pay for Performance," *Workforce*, February 1999, pp. 69–74.

65 Ibid., p. 70.

66 Nelson, op cit., p. 5.

67 Leslie Yerkes, "Motivating Workers in Tough Times," *Incentive* 75, no. 10, October 2001, p. 120.

68 Libby Estell, "I See London, I See France . . . ," *Incentive*, August 2001, pp. 58–62.

69 Sarah Braley, "Getting Technical: The Incentive Business Gets Wired Slowly," *Meetings and Conventions*, October 1997, p. 13.

70 Ibid.

71 Nelson, op cit., p. 47.

72 Cora Daniels, "Thank You Is Nice, But This Is Better," *Fortune*, 22 November 1999, p. 370.

73 In David A. Whetten and Kim S. Cameron, *Developing Management Skills* (Upper Saddle River, NJ: Prentice Hall, 2002), p. 324.

74 The following is based on Thomas Connellan, *How to Improve Human Performance: Behaviorism in Business* (New York: Harper & Row, 1978); and Lawrence Miller, *Behavior Management: The New Science of Managing People at Work* (New York: Wiley, 1978), p. 253.

75 This is based on W. Clay Hamner and Ellen Hamner, "Behavior Modification on the Bottom Line," *Organizational Dynamics*, Spring 1976. For recent applications, see Greg LaBar, "Safety Incentives: Q & A Reveals Best Practices," *Occupational Hazards*, November 1996, pp. 51–56.

76 Albert Bandura, "Social Cognitive Theory of Self-Regulation," *Organizational Behavior and Human Decision Processes* 50, 1991, p. 249; quoted in Pinder, op cit., pp. 442–43.

77 Adapted from Pinder, op cit., p. 203.

78 Whetten and Cameron, op cit., pp. 420–21.

79 Sharon Parker, Toby Wall, and John Cordery, "Future Work Design Research and Practice: Towards an Elaborated Model of Work Design," *Journal of Occupational and Organizational Psychology* 74, no. 4, November 2001, pp. 413–40.

80 Quoted in Theodore T. Herbert, *Organizational Behavior: Readings and Cases* (New York: Macmillan, 1976), pp. 344–45.

81 See, for example, J. Richard Hackman et al., "A New Strategy for Job Enrichment," *California Management Review*, 17, no. 4, pp. 57–71.

82 Gerald Ledford, Jr., "Three Case Studies on Skill-Based Pay: An Overview," *Compensation & Benefits Review*, March–April 1991, pp. 11–23.

83 Gerald Ledford Jr. and Gary Bergel, "Skill-Based Pay Case No. 1: General Mills," *Compensation & Benefits Review*, March–April 1991, pp. 24–38.

84 "The Benefits of Lifelong Learning," *Journal of European Industrial Training*, February–March 1997, p. 3.

85 Lawrence Zuckerman, "JetBlue, Exception Among Airlines, Is Likely to Post a Profit," *New York Times*, 7 November 2001, p C3.

86 Amy Rottier, "The Skies Are JetBlue," *Workforce* 80, no. 9, September 2001, p. 22.

87 Ibid.

88 "JetBlue: Odds Are You Won't Start Two Airlines, Revolutionize Your Industry, or Talk George Soros into Investing in Your Company Anytime Soon," *Fortune Small Business* 11, no. 2, p. 92.

89 Michelle Maynard, "Southwest, Without the Stunts," *New York Times*, 7 July 2002, p. BU2.

90 Sally Donnelly, "Blue Skies," *Time* 158, July 2001, pp. 24–27.

CHAPTER 12

1 Ernest Grundling, "How to Communicate Globally", *Training and Development* 53, no. 6, June 1999, pp. 28–32.

2 Ibid.

3 George Miller, *Language and Communication* (New York: McGraw-Hill, 1951), p. 10, discussed in Gary Hunt, *Communication Skills in the Organization*, 2nd ed. (Upper Saddle River, NJ: Prentice Hall, 1989), p. 29.

4 This is discussed in and based on Fred Luthans and Janet Larsen, "How Managers Really Communicate," *Human Relations*, 1986, p. 162.

5 Edward Miles et al., "Job Level as a Variable in Predicting the Relationship Between Supervisory Communication and Job Satisfaction," *Journal of Occupational and Organizational Psychology*, 69, no. 3, September 1996, pp. 277–93.

6 Arthur Bell and Dayle Smith, *Management Communication* (New York: John Wiley, 1999), p. 19.

7 Daniel Katz and Robert Kahn, *The Social Psychology of Organizations* (New York: John Wiley, 1966).

8 This is based on Bell and Smith, op cit., pp. 22–24.

9 This section on dealing with communication barriers is based on R. Wayne Pace and Don Faules, *Organizational Communication*, (Upper Saddle River, NJ: Prentice Hall, 1989), pp. 150–62, unless otherwise noted. See also Tom Geddie, "Leap Over Communications Barriers," *Communication World*, April 1994, pp. 12–17.

10 See, for example, Bell and Smith, op cit., pp. 36–39.

11 Tom Geddie, "Moving Communication Across Cultures," *Communication World*, 16, no. 5, April–May 1998, pp. 37–41.

12 Pace and Faules, op cit., p. 153.

13 Jack Griffin, *How to Say It at Work* (Paramus, NJ: Prentice Hall Press, 1998), pp. 26–28.

14 Ernest Gundling, "How to Communicate Globally," *Training and Development*, June 1999, pp. 28–32.

15 Ibid., p. 29.

16 See Holly Weeks, "Taking the Stress Out of Stressful Conversations," *Harvard Business Review*, July–August 2001, pp. 112–19.

17 Joyce Osland, David Kolb, and Irwin Rubin, eds., *The Organizational Behavior Reader* (Upper Saddle River, NJ: Prentice Hall, 2001), pp. 185–95.

18 Jay Conger, "The Necessary Art of Persuasion," *Harvard Business Review*, May–June 1998, pp. 85–95, reprinted in Osland, Kolb, and Rubin, op cit., pp. 468–78.

19 Conger, op cit.

20 Robert Cialdini, "Harnessing the Science of Persuasion," *Harvard Business Review*, October 2001, pp. 72–81.

21 Conger, op cit., p. 458.

22 Cialdini, op cit., p. 75.

23 James Sebenius, "Six Habits of Merely Effective Negotiators," *Harvard Business Review*, April 2001, pp. 87–95.

24 James C. Freund, *Smart Negotiating* (New York: Simon & Schuster, 1992), pp. 42–46.

25 Ibid., p. 33.

26 Jitendra Sharma, "Organizational Communications: A Linking Process," *The Personnel Administrator*, July 1979, pp. 35–43. See also Victor Callan, "Subordinate–Manager Communication in Different Sex Dyads: Consequences for Job Satisfaction," *Journal of Occupational and Organizational Psychology*, March 1993, pp. 13–28.

27 William Convoy, *Working Together . . . Communication in a Healthy Organization* (Columbus, OH: Charles Merrill, 1976). See also David Johnson et al. "Differences Between Formal and Informal Communication Channels," *Journal of Business Communication*, April 1994, pp. 111–24.

28 Gary Dessler, *Winning Commitment: How to Build and Keep a Competitive Workforce* (New York: McGraw-Hill, 1993).

29 Pace and Faules, op cit., pp. 105–6. See also Joanne Yates and Wanda Orlinkowski, "Genres of Organizational Communication: A Structurational Approach to Studying Communication and Media," *Academy of Management Review*, April 1992, pp. 299–327.

30 Earl Plenty and William Machaner, "Stimulating Upward Communication," ed. Jerry Gray and Frederick Starke, *Readings in Organizational Behavior* (Columbus, OH: Charles Merrill, 1977), pp. 229–40. See also Pace and Faules, op cit., pp. 153–60.

31 This is based on David Abel, "New Leader's Style Shakes up Harvard: Blunt Talk Contrasts With Predecessor's," *Boston Globe*, 12 January 2002, p. B1.

32 Alison Coleman, "Open to Suggestions," *Director* 54, no. 12, July 2001, pp. 27–28.

33 Toyota Motor Manufacturing, USA, *Team-Member Handbook*, February 1988, pp. 52–53.

34 For a recent review and a discussion, see James Smither et al., "An Examination of the Effects of an Upward Feedback Program Over Time," *Personnel Psychology* 48, 1995, pp. 1–34.

35 Ibid., pp. 10–11.

36 Ibid., p. 27.

37 Griffin, op cit., pp. 86–220.

38 See, for example, Pace and Faules, op cit., pp. 99–100.

39 Ibid., pp. 99–100.

40 Personal interview, March 1992.

41 Personal interview, March 1992.

42 Rai Aggarwal and Betty Simkins, "Open Book Management—Optimizing Human Capital," *Business Horizons* 44, no. 5, pp. 5–13.

43 "Employers Profit from Opening the Books," *Bureau of National Affairs Bulletin to Management*, 5 September 1999, p. 288.

44 Ibid.

45 Griffin, op cit., p. 178.

46 Ibid.

47 Griffin, op cit.

48 This is based on Tom Peters and Robert Waterman, *In Search of Excellence* (New York: Harper & Row, 1982), pp. 119–218.

49 Ibid., p. 122.

50 Ibid., pp. 122–23.

51 Ibid., p. 124.

52 Ibid., p. 219.

53 Ibid., p. 22.

54 Greg Saltzman, "Managing By Walking Around," *PC Week* 15, no. 20, 18 May 1998, p. 94.

55 Bob Smith, "Care and Feeding of the Office Grapevine," *Management Review*, February 1996, p. 6.

56 Eugene Walton, "How Efficient Is the Grapevine?" *Personnel*, March/April 1961, pp. 45–49; reprinted in Davis, Organizational Behavior, A Book of Readings (New York: McGraw-Hill, 1977).

57 Laura Mansnerus, "Wall Street Lawyers Being Laid Off as Deals Drop," *New York Times*, 9 November 2001, p. D1.

58 Keith Davis, "Cut Those Rumors Down to Size," *Supervisory Management*, June 1975, p. 206.

59 Ron Lieber, "Information Is Everything," *Fast Company*, November 1999, pp. 246–54.

60 Ibid., p. 253.

61 Ibid.

62 See, for example, Cathleen Moore, "Videoconferencing Takes Control," *InfoWorld* 23, no. 37, 10 September 2001, pp. 40–41.

63 Stephen Loudermilk, "Desktop Video Conferencing Getting Prime Time," *PC Week*, 19 October 1992, p. 81.

64 Paul Saffo, "The Future of Travel," *Fortune*, Autumn 1993, p. 119.

65 Sarah Schafer, "E-mail Grows Up," Inc. Technology 1, 1997, pp. 87–88.

66 Paula Caproni, *The Practical Coach* (Upper Saddle River, NJ: Prentice Hall, 2001), pp. 106–8.

67 For instance, see Andrea Poe, "Don't Touch That Send Button," *HR Magazine* 46, no. 7, July 2001, pp. 74–80.

68 Thomas Burton and Rachel Silverman, "Lots of Empty Spaces in Corner Parking Lot Gets CEO Riled Up," *Wall Street Journal*, 30 March 2001, p. B3.

69 Kenneth Laudon and Jane Laudon, *Essentials of Management Information Systems* (Upper Saddle River, NJ: Prentice Hall, 1997), p. 413.

70 Amy Joyce, "And Maybe IM or Maybe IM Not," *Washington Post*, 3 March 2002, p. 6.

71 David Kroenke and Richard Hatch, *Management Information Systems* (New York: McGraw-Hill, 1994), p. 359.

72 Robert Ford and Michael Butts, "Is Your Organization Ready for Telecommuting?" *SAM Advanced Management Journal*, Autumn 1991, p. 19; and Laudon and Laudon, op cit., pp. 413–16.

73 Ford and Butts, op cit.

74 See Sandra Atchison, "The Care and Feeding of Loan Eagles," *Business Week*, 15 November 1993, p. 58.

75 David Kirkpatrick, "Groupware Goes Boom," *Fortune*, 27 December 1993, pp. 99–100.

76 Kenneth Laudon and Jane Laudon, *Management Information Systems* (Upper Saddle River, NJ: Prentice Hall, 1998), p. 128.

77 Ibid., 128.

78 Tim Stevens, "Internet-Aided Design," *Industry Week*, 23 June 1997, pp. 50–55.

79 Ibid.

80 Paul McDougall, "Collaborative Business," *Information Week*, 7 May 2001, no. 36, pp. 42–86.

81 Joann Davy, "Online at the Office: Virtual Communities Go to Work," *Managing Office Technology*, July–August 1998, pp. 9–11.

82 Ibid.

83 David Kirkpatrick, "The Portal of the Future? Your Boss Will Run It," *Fortune*, 2 August 1999, pp. 222–27.

84 Ibid.

85 Martin Piszczalski, "GM's Smart New Portal," *Automotive Design & Production* 114, no. 2, February 2002, pp. 14–15.

CHAPTER 13

1 Carla Johnson, "Teams at Work," *HRMagazine*, May 1999, p. 30.

2 Jack Gordon, "Work Teams: How Far Have They Come?" *Training*, October 1992, pp. 60–65. See also Cheryl Dahle, "Extreme Teams," *Fast Company*, November 1999, pp. 311–26.

3 Leigh Thompson, *Making the Team: A Guide for Managers* (Upper Saddle River, NJ: Prentice Hall, 2000), pp. 11–14.

4 "Outlook on Teams,"*BNA Bulletin to Management*, 20 March 1997, pp. 92–93.

5 For employee involvement survey data, see Lee Towe, "Survey Finds Employee Involvement a Priority for Necessary Innovation, "*National Productivity Review*, Winter 1989–90, pp. 3–15. See also Bradley Kirkman and Benson Rosen, "Beyond Self-Management: Antecedents and Consequences of Team Empowerment," *Academy of Management Journal*, February 1999, pp. 58–74.

6 Jack Osburn et al., *Self-Directed Work Teams: The New American Challenge* (Homewood, IL: Business One Irwin, 1990), p. 33. See also Kirkman and Rosen, op cit., pp. 58–74.

7 Ibid.

8 See, for example, John Katzenbach and Douglas Smith, "The Discipline of Teams," *Harvard Business Review*, March–April 1993,

pp. 112–13. Note that many researchers do not, however, distinguish between groups and teams. See, for example, Gary Coleman and Eileen M. VanAken, "Applying Small-Group Behavior Dynamics to Improve Action-Team Performance," *Employment Relations Today*, Autumn 1991, pp. 343–53.

9 Osburn et al., op cit., p. 34. See also Charles Manz, "Self-Leading Work Teams: Moving Beyond Self-Management Myths," *Human Relations* 45, no. 11, 1992, pp. 1119–41.

10 Lee Towe, "Survey Finds Employee Involvement a Priority for Necessary Innovation," *National Productivity Review*, Winter 1989–90, pp. 3–15.

11 Christopher Robert et al., "Empowerment and Continuous Improvement in the United States, Mexico, Poland, and India: Predicting Fit on the Basis of the Dimensions of Power Distance and Individuals," *Journal of Applied Psychology* 85, no. 5, 2000, pp. 643–58.

12 Ibid., p. 655.

13 These definitions are from Marvin E. Shaw, *Group Dynamics: The Psychology of Small Group Behavior* (New York: McGraw-Hill, 1976), p. 11.

14 Osburn et al., op cit., p. 34. See also Manz, op cit.

15 Jon Katzenbach and Jason Santamaria, "Firing Up the Front-Line," *Harvard Business Review*, May–June 1999, p. 114.

16 Sandra Robinson and Ann O'Leary-Kelly, "Monkey See, Monkey Do: The Influence of Workgroups on the Antisocial Behavior of Employees," *Academy of Management Journal* 41, no. 6, 1988, 658–72.

17 Ibid., 667.

18 Daniel Feldman, "The Development and Enforcement of Group Norms," *Academy of Management Review* 9, no. 1, 1984, 47–53.

19 A. P. Hare, *Handbook of Small Group Research* (New York: The Free Press, 1962), 24. See also S. Barr and E. Conlon, "Effects of Distribution of Feedback in Work Groups," *Academy of Management Journal*, June 1994, pp. 641–56.

20 See Stephen Worchel, Wendy Wood, and Jeffrey Simpson, *Group Process and Productivity* (Newbury Park, CA: Sage Publications, 1992), pp. 45–50.

21 F. J. Roethlisberger and William J. Dickson, *Management and the Worker* (New York: John Wiley, 1964).

22 For a discussion of the difficulty of measuring and defining cohesiveness, see Peter Mudrack, "Group Cohesiveness and Productivity: A Closer Look," *Human Relations* 42, no. 9, 1989, pp. 771–85. See also R. Saavedra et al., "Complex Interdependence in Task-Performing Groups," *Journal of Applied Psychology*, February 1993, pp. 61–73.

23 Thompson, op cit., p. 79.

24 John R. P. French Jr., "The Disruption and Cohesion of Groups," *Journal of Abnormal and Social Psychology* 36, 1941, pp. 361–77.

25 A. Paul Hare, *Small Group Research*, (New York: The Free Press, 1962), p. 244.

26 Ibid., pp. 157–58.

27 Ibid., p. 161.

28 Robert Blake and Jane Mouton, "Reactions to Inter-Group Competition under Win–Lose Conditions," *Management Science* 7, 1961, p. 432.

29 Stanley C. Seashore, *Group Cohesiveness in the Industry Work Group* (Ann Arbor, MI: Survey Research Center, University of Michigan, 1954), pp. 90–95; See also Joseph Litterer, *The Analysis of Organizations* (New York: John Wiley, 1965), pp. 91–101; and J. Haleblian and S. Finkelstein, "Top Management Team Size, CEO Dominance, and Firm Performance: The Moderating Roles of Environmental Turbulence and Discretion," *Academy of Management Journal*, August 1993, pp. 844–64.

30 Hare, op cit., p. 244.

31 Ibid., p. 245.

32 This material is based on James H. Shonk, *Team-Based Organizations* (Chicago: Irwin, 1997), pp. 27–33.

33 Ibid., p. 28.

34 Katzenbach and Smith, op cit., pp. 116–18.

35 Everett Adams Jr., "Quality Circle Performance," *Journal of Management* 17, no. 1, 1991, pp. 25–39.

36 Ibid.

37 See, for example, Adams, op cit.; and Gilbert Fuchsberg, "Quality Programs Show Shoddy Results," *Wall Street Journal*, 14 May 1992, pp. B1, B4.

38 Gopal Pati, Robert Salitore, and Saundra Brady, "What Went Wrong with Quality Circles?" *Personnel Journal*, December 1987, pp. 83–89.

39 Philip Olson, "Choices for Innovation Minded Corporations," *Journal of Business Strategy*, January–February 1990, pp. 86–90.

40 In many firms, the concept of a venture team is taken to what may be its natural conclusion in that new-venture units and new-venture divisions are established. These are separate divisions devoted to new-product development. See, for example, Christopher Bart, "New Venture Units: Use Them Wisely to Manage Innovation," *Sloan Management Review*, Summer 1988, pp. 35–43; and Robert Burgelman, "Managing the New Venture Division: Research Findings and Implications for Strategic Management," *Strategic Management Journal* 6, 1985, pp. 39–54.

41 Charles Snow, Scott Snell, Sue Canney Davison, and Donald Hambrick, "Use Transnational Teams to Globalize Your Company," *Organizational Dynamics*, Spring 1996, pp. 50–67.

42 Ibid., p. 50.

43 Ibid.

44 Ibid., pp. 53–57.

45 Lynda McDermott, Bill Waite, and Nolan Brawley, "Putting Together a World-Class Team," *Training and Development*, January 1999, p. 48.

46 Snow et al., p. 61.

47 Based on suggestions by David Armstrong, "Making Dispersed Teams Work," *Bureau of National Affairs Bulletin to Management*, 23 May 1996, p. 168.

48 Anthony Townsend, Samuel DiMarie, and Anthony Hendrickson, "Virtual Teams: Technology and the Workplace of the Future," *Academy of Management Executive* 12, no. 3, 1998, pp. 17–29.

49 Ibid., p. 20.

50 Christa Degnan, "ActiveProject Aids Teamwork," *PC Week*, 31 May 1999, p. 35.

51 Ibid., pp. 21–22.

52 Michael Rosenwald, "Long Distance Team Worked as Virtual Offices Spread, Managers and Their Staffs Are Learning to Adapt to New Cultures," *Boston Globe*, 29 April 2001, p. J1.

53 Allison Overhault, "Virtually There," *Fast Company*, no. 56, pp. 108–14.

54 Diane Coutu, "Trust in Virtual Teams," *Harvard Business Review*, May–June 1998, pp. 20–22.

55 Rochelle Garner, "Round-the-World Teamwork," *Computerworld*, 24 May 1999, p. 46.

56 Vijay Govindarajan and Anil Gupta, "Building an Effective Global Business Team," *MIT Sloan Management Review* 42, no. 4, Summer 2001, pp. 63–71.

57 Ibid.

58 Osburn et al., op cit., p. 8.

59 Charles Fishman, "Engines of Democracy," *Fast Company*, October 1999, pp. 173–202.

60 Tom Peters, *Liberation Management* (New York: Alfred Knopf, 1992), pp. 238–39.

61 Osburn et al., op cit., pp. 22–23.

62 "Kodak's Team Structure Is Picture Perfect," *Bureau of National Affairs Bulletin to Management*, 15 August 1996, p. 264.

63 Rojiv Banker, Roger Schroeder, and Kingshuk Sinha, "Impact of Work Teams on Manufacturing Performance: A Longitudinal Field Study," *Academy of Management Journal* 39, no. 4, 1996, pp. 867–88.

64 Ibid., p. 887–88.

65 Ibid., p. 870. After reviewing the evidence, one writer suggested that self-managing teams may turn out to have been a management fad and that proponents overstated the benefits firms derived from them. See Jane Gibson and Dana Testone, "Management Fads: Emergence, Evolution, and Implications for Managers," *The Academy of Management Executive* 15, no. 4, pp. 122–33.

66 Ralph King Jr., "Levi's Factory Workers Are Assigned to Teams, and Morale has Taken a Hit," *Wall Street Journal*, 20 May 1998, pp. A1, A6.

67 Based on Erin Neurick, "Facilitating Effective Work Teams," *SAM Advanced Management Journal*, Winter 1993, pp. 22–26. See also Margarita Alegria, "Building Effective Research Teams When Conducting Drug Prevention Research with Minority Populations," *Drugs & Society*, 1999 14, no. 1–2, pp. 227–45; and George Neuman and Julie Wright, "Team Effectiveness: Beyond Skills and Cognitive Ability," *Journal of Applied Psychology*, June 1999, pp. 376–89.

68 Neurick, p. 23.

69 Joann Keyton, "Analyzing Interaction Patterns in Dysfunctional teams," *Small Group Research*, August 1999, pp. 491–518.

70 Suchitra Mouly and Jayaram Sankaran, "Barriers to the Cohesiveness and Effectiveness of Indian R&D Project Groups: Insights from Four Federal R&D Organizations," ed. John Wagner et al., *Advances in Qualitative Organization Research*, vol. 2 (Stamford, CT: JAI Press, 1999), pp. 221–43.

71 Paul Levy, "When Good Teams Go Wrong," *Harvard Business Review*, March 2001, p. 54.

72 Quoted or paraphrased from Regina Maruca, "What Makes Teams Work?" *Fast Company*, November 2000, p. 128.

73 "Under the Big Top," *Harvard Business Review*, September–October 1999, p. 17.

74 Ibid.

75 Ibid.

76 Michael Campion and A. Catherine Higgs, "Design Work Teams to Increase Productivity and Satisfaction," *HR Magazine*, October 1995, pp. 101–07. See also Michael Campion, Ellen Papper, and Gina Medsker, "Relations Between Work Team Characteristics and Effectiveness: A Replication and Extension," *Personnel Psychology*, Summer 1996, pp. 429–52.

77 Campion and Higgs, p. 102.

78 Ibid., p. 103–4.

79 Joan Glaman, Allan Jones, and Richard Rozelle, "The Effects of Co-Worker Similarity on the Emergence of Effective Work Teams," *Group & Organization Management*, June 1996, pp. 192–215.

80 See, for example, Drew Harris, "Seven Principles for Sustainable Social System: Lessons from Teams, Organizations and Communities," *Competitiveness Review* 10 no. 2, Summer–Fall 2000, pp. 169–73.

81 Katzenbach and Smith, op cit., p. 112. See also C. Meyer, "How the Right Measures Help Teams Excel," *Harvard Business Review*, May–June 1994, p. 112.

82 Neurick, op cit., p. 23.

83 Katzenbach and Smith, op cit., p. 113.

84 Ibid. The evaluation process is important as well. See R. Saavedra and S. Kwun, "Peer Evaluation in Self-Managing Work Groups," *Journal of Applied Psychology*, June 1993, pp. 450–63.

85 Neuman and Wright, op cit., pp. 376–89.

86 The following, except as noted, is based on Glenn H. Varney, *Building Productive Teams: An Action Guide and Resource Book* (San Francisco: Jossey-Bass Publishers, 1989), pp. 11–18. See also P. Bernthal and C. Insko, "Cohesiveness Without Group Think: The Interactive Effects of Social and Task Cohesion," *Group and Organization Management*, March 1993, pp. 66–88; and Vanessa Druskat, "The Antecedents of Team Competence: Toward a Fine-Grained Model of Self-Managing Team Effectiveness," in Margaret Neale and E. Mannix, eds., *Research on Managing Groups and Teams: Groups in Context*, vol. 2, (Stamford, CT: Jai Press, 1999), pp. 201–31.

87 Sal Divita, "Being a Team Player Is Essential to Your Career," *Marketing News* 30, no. 19, 9 September 1996, p. 8.

88 Philip Hunsaker, *Training in Management Skills*, (Upper Saddle River, NJ: Prentice Hall, 2001), p. 286.

89 Michael Stevens and Michael Campion, "Staffing Work Teams: Development and Validation of a Selection Test for Teamwork Settings," *Journal of Management* 25, no. 2, March–April 1999, pp. 207–25.

90 Michael Finley, "All for One, But None for All?" *Across the Board* 39, no. 1, January/February 2002, pp. 45–48.

91 See Shonk, op cit., pp. 133–38; and Andrew DuBrin, *Leadership: Research Findings, Practice and Skills* (Boston: Houghton-Mifflin, 1995), pp. 224–27.

92 Shonk, op cit., p. 133.

93 Kimball Fisher, pp. 151–53.

94 Gary Dessler, *Winning Commitment* (New York: McGraw-Hill, 1992), p. 28.

95 Ibid., p. 30.

96 Ibid., p. 44.

97 These are based on Fisher, op cit., pp. 48–56.

98 Ibid., p. 53.

99 This is based on Hunsaker, op cit., pp. 293–96.

100 Osburn et al., op cit., pp. 20–27.

101 Mark McMaster, "Roping in the Followers," *Sales and Marketing Management* 154, no. 1, January 2002, pp. 36–41.

102 Ibid., p. 21.

103 Ibid., p. 22.

104 The remaining items in this section, except as noted, are quoted from or based on Campion and Higgs, op cit., pp. 101–7. See also Steven G. Rogelberg and Steven M. Rumery, "Gender Diversity, Team Decision Quality, Time on Task, and Interpersonal Cohesion," *Small Group Research*, February 1996, pp. 79–90; Steven E. Gross and Jeffrey Blair, "Reinforcing Team Effectiveness Through Pay," *Compensation & Benefits Review*, September 1995, pp. 34–38; and Joan M. Glaman, Allan P. Jones, and Richard M. Rozelle, "The Effects of Co-Worker Similarity on the Emergence of Affect in Work Teams," *Group and Organization Management*, June 1996, pp. 192–215.

105 John Day, "Warewithal Online: Assemble Teams Based on Employee Instincts," *HRMagazine*, August 1999, pp. 124–30. See also Michael Stevens and Michael Campion, "Staffing Work Teams: Development and Validation of a Selection Test for Teamwork Settings," *Journal of Management* 25, no.2, 1999, pp. 207–28.

106 "Getting the Most from Employee Teams," *Bureau of National Affairs Bulletin to Management*, 20 March 1997, p. 96.

107 David Hyatt and Thomas Ruddy, "An Examination of the Relationship Between Workgroup Characteristics and Performance: Once More into the Breach," *Personnel Psychology*, 1997, p. 577.

108 Ibid., p. 578.

109 Vanessa Druskat and Steven Wolff, "Building the Emotional Intelligence of Groups," *Harvard Business Review*, March 2001, p. 87.

110 This section is based on Shonk, op cit.

111 Michael Carrell, Daniel Jennings, and Christine Heavrin, *Fundamentals of Organizational Behavior* (Upper Saddle River, NJ: Prentice Hall, 1997), p. 346.

112 For a discussion of these and the following points see, for example, ibid.

113 Robert Liden et al., "Management of Poor Performance: A Comparison of Manager, Group Member, and Group Disciplinary Decisions," *Journal of Applied Psychology* 84, no. 6, 1999, pp. 835–50.

114 Irving Janis, *Groupthink: Psychological Studies of Policy Decisions and Fiascos*, 2d edition (Boston: Houghton Mifflin, 1982); See also James Esser, "Alive and Well After 25 Years: A Review of Group Think Research," *Organizational Behavior & Human Decision Processes*, February–March 1998, pp. 116–42; and also Jin Nam Choi and Myung Un Kim, "The Organizational Application of Groupthink and Its Limitations in Organizations," *Journal of Applied Psychology* 84, no. 2, 1999 pp. 297–306.

115 Choi and Kim, ibid.

116 For an additional perspective on many of these issues, see Randy Hirokawa and Marshall Scott Poole, *Communication and Group Decision Making* (Thousand Oaks, CA: Sage Publications, Inc., 1996), pp. 354–64. See also John O. Whitney and E. Kirby Warren, "Action Forums: How General Electric and Other Firms Have Learned to Make Better Decisions," *Columbia Journal of World Business*, Winter 1995, pp. 18–27; Steven G. Rogelberg and Steven M. Rumery, "Gender Diversity, Team Decision Quality, Time on Task, and Interpersonal Cohesion," *Small Group Research*, February 1996, pp. 79–90; Beatrice Shultz, Sandra M. Ketrow, and Daphne M. Urban, "Improving Decision Quality in the Small Group: The Role of the Reminder," *Small Group Research*, November 1995, pp. 521–41.

117 See, for example, Lester Lefton and Laura Valvatne, *Mastering Psychology* (Boston: Allyn and Bacon, 1992), p. 249.

118 Greenberg and Baron, p. 393.

119 See Ron Zemke, "In Search of Good Ideas," *Training*, January 1993, pp. 46–52; R. Brent Gallupe, Lana Bastianutti, and William Cooper, "Unblocking Brainstorms," *Journal of Applied Psychology*, January 1991, pp. 137–42; and Vincent Brown et al., "Modeling Cognitive Interactions During Group Brainstorming," *Small Group Research*, August 1998, pp. 495–526.

120 R. B. Gallupe et al., "Electronic Brainstorming and Group Size," *Academy of Management Journal* 35, 1992, pp. 350–69.

121 Simon Lam and John Schaubroeck, "Improving Group Decisions by Better Pooling Information: A Comparative Advantage of Group Decision Support Sysems," *Journal of Applied Psychology* 85 no. 4, 2000, pp. 565–73.

122 See, for example, Greenberg and Baron, pp. 399–400.

123 See S. G. Rogelberg, J. L. Barnes-Farrell, and C. A. Lowe, "The Stepladder Technique: An Alternative Group Structure Facilitating Effective Group Decision Making," *Journal of Applied Psychology* 57, 1992, pp. 730–37.

124 Norman R. F. Maier and E. P. McRay, "Increasing Innovation in Change Situations Through Leadership Skills," *Psychological Reports* 31, 1972, pp. 30–43. See also Jean Phillips, "Antecedents of Leader Utilization of Staff Input in Decision-Making Teams," *Organizational Behavior & Human Decision Processes*, March 1999, pp. 215–17.

125 Alan Bluedorn, Daniel Turban, and Mary Love, "The Effects of Standup and Sit-Down Meetings Formats and Meeting Outcomes," *Journal of Applied Psychology*, 84 no. 2, 1999, pp. 277–85.

126 Erin Lehman, "Is the Glass Half Empty or Half Full? Organizational Change at the Colorado Symphony Orchestra, 1990–1991 to 1998–1999," in *Lessons Learned, Case Studies* (Washington, DC: National Endowment for the Arts).

CHAPTER 14

1 Sean Gallagher, "Allfirst Financial: Out of Control," *Baseline*, 12 March 2002.

2 Kenneth Merchant, "The Control Function of Management," *Sloan Management Review*, Summer 1982, p. 44.

3 "Enron Ex-Official Says Company Shredded Papers," *New York Times*, 22 January 2002, p. C6.

4 Ibid.

5 This section is based on William Newman, *Constructive Control* (Upper Saddle River, NJ: Prentice Hall, 1995), pp. 6–9.

6 Louise Lee and Nanette Byrnes, "More Than Just a Bad Patch at Gap," *Business Week*, New York, 11 February 2002, p. 36.

7 Kristina Sullivan, "Boeing Achieves Internet Liftoff," *PC Week*, 10 May 1999, p. 67.

8 Ibid.

9 Melanie Warner, "Confessions of a Control Freak," *Fortune*, 4 September 2000, pp. 130–40.

10 Ibid., p. 136.

11 Paula Kaihla, "Inside Cisco's $2 Billion Blunder," *Business 2.0* 3, no. 3, March 2002, pp. 88–90.

12 Ibid.

13 The ten specific italicized requirements are quoted from Harold Koontz and Cyril O'Donnell, *Principles of Management* (New York: McGraw-Hill, 1964), pp. 541–44.

14 Koontz and O'Donnell, op cit., p. 544.

15 Thomas Connellan, *How to Improve Human Performance: Behaviorism in Business and Industry* (New York: Harper & Row, 1978), pp. 68–73.

16 Robert Simons, *Levers of Control: How Managers Use Innovative Control Systems to Drive Strategic Renewal* (Boston: Harvard Business School Press, 1995), p. 80.

17 This classification is based on Simons, op cit., p. 81.

18 For example, see Ibid., p. 82.

19 Daniel Wren, *The Evolution of Management Thought* (John Wiley & Sons, 1994), p. 115.

20 Based on Kenneth Merchant, *Modern Management Control Systems* (Upper Saddle River, NJ: Prentice Hall, 1998), p. 642.

21 For a discussion, see ibid., pp. 542–45.

22 Biff Motley, "Picking the Right Ratio to Measure Performance," *Bank Marketing* 34, no. 1, January/February 2002, p. 44.

23 Merchant, op cit., p. 304.

24 Sydney Baxendale, "Activity Based Costing for the Small Business: A Primer," *Business Horizons* 44, no. 1, January 2001, p. 61.

25 Edward Blocher et al., "Making Bottom-Up ABC Work at Reichhold Inc." *Strategic Finance* 83, no. 10, April 2002, pp. 51–56.

26 See John Lere, "Selling Activity Based Costing," *The CPA Journal* 72 no. 3, March 2002, pp. 54–56.

27 Peter Brewer, "Putting Strategy into the Balanced Scorecard," *Strategic Finance* 83, no. 7, January 2002, pp. 44–52.

28 Examples from ibid.

29 See for example Matt Hicks, "Tuning in to the Big Picture for a Better Business," *PC Week*, 15 July 1999, p. 69.

30 "The Software War," *Fortune*, 7 December 1998, p. 102.

31 Robin Cooper and Tobert Kaplan, "The Promise and Peril of Integrated Costs Systems," *Harvard Business Review*, July–August 1998, p. 109.

32 Hicks, op cit., p. 69.

33 "The Software War," *Fortune*, 7 December 1998, p. 102.

34 Guy Bolton, "Enterprise Resource Planning Software Creates Supply Business Revolution," *Knight Ridder/Tribune Business News*, 9 November 1998.

35 Doug Bartholomew, "Maximizing ERP," *Industry Week* 251, no. 3, March 2002, p. 58.

36 Mark Cross, "Decision Support Systems: Using Technology for Successful Management," *CMA Management*, 75, no. 8, December 2001, pp. 48–50.

37 Simons, op cit., p. 81.

38 Jeffrey L. Seglin, "A Company Credo, as Applied or Not," *New York Times*, 15 July 2001, pp. BU 3–4.

39 Simons, op cit., p. 86.

40 These characteristics are based on ibid., p. 87.

41 This discussion is based on ibid., pp. 87–88.

42 Jeffrey Stanton and Janet Barnes-Farrell, "Effects of Electronic Performance Monitoring on Personal Control, Task Satisfaction, and Task Performance," *Journal of Applied Psychology*, December 1996, p. 738. See also Paul Greenlaw, "The Impact of Federal Legislation to Limit Electronic Monitoring," *Public Personnel Management*, Summer 1997, pp. 227–45.

43 Stanton and Barnes-Farrell, op cit., pp. 738–45.

44 Ibid., p. 738.

45 Norihiko Shirouzu and Jon Bigness, "'7-Eleven' Operators Resist System to Monitor Managers," *Wall Street Journal*, 16 June 1997, pp. B1–B6.

46 The following, except as noted, is based on Kenneth Merchant, *Control in Business Organizations* (Boston: Pitman, 1985), pp. 71–120. See also Robert Kaplan, "New Systems for Measurement and Control," *The Engineering Economist*, Spring 1991, pp. 201–18.

47 This is based on Simons, op cit., pp. 81–82.

48 Merchant, *Control in Business Organizations*, p. 98.

49 "Did Warner-Lambert Make a $468 Million Mistake?" *Business Week*, 21 November 1983, p. 123; quoted in Merchant, *Control in Business Organizations*, pp. 98–99.

50 Chris Argyris, "Human Problems with Budgets," *Harvard Business Review*, January–February 1953, pp. 97–110.

51 Rajiv Sanyal and Turgut Guvenli, "Introducing Modern Management Control Techniques in an Economy in Transition: The Experience of American Firms in China," *Mid-Atlantic Journal of Business* 36, no. 4, December 2000, p. 217.

52 Tom Peters, *Liberation Management* (New York: Knopf, 1992), pp. 465–66.

53 See Eric Krell, "Greener Pastures," *Training* 38, no. 11, pp. 54–59.

54 James Collins and Jerry Porras, *Built to Last: Successful Habits of Visionary Companies* (New York: Harper & Row, 1994).

55 This quote is based on William Taylor, "Control in an Age of Chaos," *Harvard Business Review*, November–December 1994, pp. 70–71.

56 Ibid., p. 71.

57 J. Newcomb, 1998 letter to employees, 17 May 1999.

58 Gary Dessler, "How to Earn Your Employees Commitment," *Academy of Management Executive* 13, no. 2, 1999, pp. 58–67.

59 Personal interview. See Gary Dessler, *Winning Commitment: How to Build and Keep a Competitive Work Force* (New York: McGraw-Hill, 1993), pp. 27–28.

60 Ibid., p. 28.

61 Ibid., p. 30.

62 Rosabeth Moss Kanter, *Commitment and Community* (Cambridge, MA: Harvard University Press, 1972), pp. 24–25.

63 See Dessler, "How to Earn Your Employees Commitment," p. 64.

64 JoAnn Davy, "Online at the Office: Virtual Communities Go to Work," *Managing Office Technology*, July–August 1998, pp. 9–11.

65 Ibid.

66 Dessler, "How to Earn Your Employees Commitment," p. 69.

67 Abraham Maslow, *Motivation and Personality* (New York: Harper & Row, 1954), p. 336.

68 Interview with assembler Dan Dise, March 1992.

69 Personal interview, March 1992.

70 Susan Carey, "Costly Race in the Sky," *Wall Street Journal*, 9 September 2002, p. B1.

CHAPTER 15

1 Peter Strozniak, "Inventory Busters," *Industry Week* 250, no. 13, October 2001, pp. 57–58.

2 Richard Chase and Nicholas Aquilero, *Production and Operations Management*, 6th ed. (Homewood, IL: Irwin, 1992), p. 5.

3 Ibid., p. 5.

4   Based on Jay Heizer and Barry Render, *Operations Management* (Upper Saddle River, NJ: Prentice Hall, 2001), p. 181.

5   Norman Gaither, *Production and Operations Management*, 5E (Fort Worth, TX: The Dryden Press, 1992), p. 22.

6   "Goodnight, Vietnam," *Economist*, 8 January 2000, p. 65.

7   Ibid., p. 65.

8   Gaither, pp. 132–33.

9   See, for example, James Gilmore and Joseph Pine II, "The Four Faces of Mass Customization," *Harvard Business Review*, January–February 1997, pp. 91–101.

10 For a discussion of how another company applies these concepts, see, for example, Edward Feitzinger and Jan Lee, "Mass Customization and Hewlett-Packard: The Power of Postponement" *Harvard Business Review*, January–February 1997, pp. 116–21.

11 Everett Adam Jr. and Ronald Ebert, *Production and Operations Management* (Upper Saddle River, NJ: Prentice Hall, 1992), p. 254.

12 Ibid., p. 254.

13 Gaither, op cit., p. 135. See also Nancy Hyer, "The Discipline of Real Cells," *Journal of Operations Management*, August 1999, pp. 557–59.

14 Barry Render and Jay Heizer, *Principles of Operations Management* (Upper Saddle River, NJ: Prentice Hall, 1997), p. 551.

15 Ibid., pp. 551–53.

16 Jack Robertson, "Sony Centralizes Procurement," *EBN*, 28 January 2002, p. 1.

17 James Evans et al., *Applied Production and Operations Management* (St. Paul, MN: West Publishing Co., 1984), pp. 500–1.

18 Ibid., p. 511.

19 See, for example, Steven Replogle, "The Strategic Use of Smaller Lot Sizes Through a New EOQ Model," *Production and Inventory Management Journal*, Third Quarter 1988, pp. 41–44; and T. C. E. Cheng, "An EOQ Model with Learning Effect on Set-Ups," *Production and Inventory Management Journal*, First Quarter 1991, pp. 83–84.

20 Evans et al., op cit., p. 39.

21 Joel E. Ross, *Total Quality Management: Text, Cases and Readings* (Delray Beach, FL: St. Lucie Press, 1993), p. 1. See also James Gaskin, "Bonner Bets on Total Quality Management," *Internet Week*, 6 September 1999, p. 43.

22 Render and Heizer, op cit., p. 96.

23 Discussed in Ross, op cit., pp. 2–3, 35–36.

24 In Richard Hodgetts, *Blueprints for Continuous Improvement: Lessons from the Baldridge Winners* (New York: American Management Association, 1993), p. 19.

25 Chase and Aquilero, op cit., p. 197.

26 These traits are quoted from David Anderson, *Design for Manufacturability* (Lafayette, CA: CI Press, 1990), p. 9.

27 Ibid., p. 16.

28 Ibid., p. 15. See also F. Robert Jacobs and Vincent Mabert, *Production Planning, Scheduling, and Inventory Control* (Norcross, GA: Industrial Engineering and Management Press, 1986), pp. 96–100; and Otis Port, Zachary Shiller, Gregory Miles, and Amy Schulman, "Smart Factories, America's Turn," *Business Week*, 8 May 1989, pp. 142–48.

29 See, for example, Joseph Martinich, *Production and Operations Management* (New York: Wiley, 1997), pp. 215–16.

30 R. Eugene Goodson, "Reading a Plant—Fast," *Harvard Business Review*, May 2002, pp. 108–9.

31 These are based on R. Eugene Goodson, "Reading a Plant—Fast," *Harvard Business Review*, May 2002, pp. 108–9.

32 Ibid., p. 107.

33 Ibid., p. 110.

34 Valerie Reitman, "Global Money Trends Rattle Shop Windows in Heartland America," *Wall Street Journal*, 26 November 1993, p. A1.

35 Adam and Ebert, op cit., p. 568.

36 These elements are based on Kenneth Wantuck, *The Japanese Approach to Productivity* (Southfield, MI: Bendix Corporation, 1983); and Chase and Aquilero, op cit., pp. 261–72. See also Mike Kaye, "Continuous Improvement: Ten Essential Criteria," *International Journal of Quality & Reliability Management*, April–May 1999, pp. 485–87.

37 Chase and Aquilero, op cit., p. 261.

38 Strozniak, op cit., pp. 57–58.

39 Mary Cronin, "Intranets Reach the Factory Floor," *Fortune*, 18 August 1997, p. 208.

40 Adapted from Gaither, op cit., pp. 6–8. See also David Woodruff, "A Dozen Motor Factories—Under One Roof," *Business Week*, 20 November 1989, pp. 93–94; and Mike Brezonick, "New Vickers Plant Focuses on Flexibility," *Diesel Progress*, North American Edition, January 1999, pp. 32–35.

41 Thomas Stewart, "Brace for Japan's Hot New Strategy," *Fortune*, 21 September 1992, p. 64. See also Bobby Ray Inman, "Are You Implementing a Pull System by Putting the Cart before the Horse?" *Production & Inventory Management Journal*, Spring 1999, pp. 67–72.

42 Ibid., p. 64.

43 Susan Moffat, "Japan's New Personalized Production," *Fortune*, 22 October 1990, pp. 132–35.

44 Mark Vonderem and Gregory White, *Operations Management* (St. Paul, MN: West Publishing, 1988), pp. 44–45. For more information on computer-integrated manufacturing, see Michael Baudin, *Manufacturing Systems Analysis* (Upper Saddle River, NJ: Prentice Hall, 1990), pp. 2–5. See also Patricia Smith, "CAD/CAM for the Cutting Edge," *Machine Design*, 8 July 1999, pp. 25–29.

45 For additional information, see, for example, Alan Luber, "Living in the Real World of Computer Interfaced Manufacturing," *Production & Inventory Management*, September 1991, pp. 10–11; and Jeremy Main, "Computers of the World, Unite!" *Fortune*, 24 September 1990, pp. 115–22. See also John Teresko, "Japan's New Idea," *Industry Week*, 3 September 1990, pp. 62–66; and David Bak, "Shared Intelligence Guides Control System," *Design News*, 18 October 1999, p. 97.

46 Kristina Sullivan, "Boeing Achieves Liftoff," *PC Week*, 10 May 1999, p. 67.

47 John Teresko, "Manufacturing in Japan," *Industry Week*, 4 September 1989, pp. 35 (13). See also Richard Jensen, "How to Be Nimble, How to Be Quick," *CMA Management*, October 1999, pp. 34–38.

48 Brian McWilliams, "Re-Engineering of the Small Factory," *Inc. Technology*, 19 March 1996, pp. 44–47, reprinted in Roberta Russell and Bernard Taylor, *Operations Management* (Upper Saddle River, NJ: Prentice Hall), p. 260.

49 David Upton, "What Really Makes Factories Flexible?" *Harvard Business Review* July–August 1995, p. 75.

50 Ibid., pp. 80–81.

51 Ibid., p. 80.

52 Jay Heizer and Barry Render, *Operations Management*, 6th ed. (Upper Saddle River, NJ: Prentice Hall, 2001), p. 434.

53 Ibid.

54 Ibid.

55 "In the Boom," *Business Week*, 14 February 2000, p. 116.

56 Matt Murray and Jathon Sapsford, "GE Reshuffles its Dotcom Strategy to Focus on Internal 'Digitizing,'" *Wall Street Journal*, 4 May 2001, pp. B1 and B4.

57 Robert Simison et al., "Big Three Carmakers Plan Net Exchange," *Wall Street Journal*, 28 February 2000, p. A3.

58 W. G. Jordan and K. R. Krumweide, "ERP Implementers, Beware," *Cost Management Update*, March 1999, p. 1, quoted in Heizer and Render, op cit., p. 292.

59 Karl Albrecht, *At America's Service: How Corporations Can Revolutionize the Way They Treat Their Customers* (Homewood, IL: Dow Jones-Irwin, 1988), p. 20. For an analysis of how to organize and manage service businesses, see also James Brian Quinn, *Intelligent Enterprise* (New York: The Free Press, 1992).

60 Michael E. Porter, *Competitive Strategy: Techniques for Analyzing Industries and Competitors* (New York: The Free Press, 1980), p. 37.

61 Based on a discussion in Karl Albrecht and Ron Zemke, *Service America!: Doing Business in the New Economy* (Homewood, IL: Dow Jones-Irwin, 1985), p. 6.

62 Based on Frederick F. Reichheld and W. Earl Sasser Jr., "Zero Defections: Quality Comes to Service," *Harvard Business Review*, September–October 1990, pp. 105–11.

63 Based on Philip Sadler, *Managerial Leadership in the Post-Industrial Society* (Aldershot, Hampshire: Ashgate Publishing, Ltd, 1988), as summarized in "When the Product is Service," *Economist*, 7 January 1989, p. 60.

64 Richard Gibson, "McDonald's Finds Angry Customers on Its Menu," *Wall Street Journal*, 16 July 2001, p. A14.

65 Ibid.

66 Ibid.

67 Based on Albrecht and Zemke, op cit., pp. 31–47. Albrecht, op cit., pp. 20–42; and Karl Albrecht and Lawrence J. Bradford, *The Service Advantage: How to Identify and Fulfill Customer Needs* (Homewood, IL: Dow Jones-Irwin, 1990), pp. 24–49.

68 Albrecht and Bradford, op cit., p. 30.

69 Albrecht, op cit., p. 26.

70 Ibid., p. 32.

71 Based on Albrecht and Zemke, op cit., pp. 69–79; and Albrecht, op cit., pp. 157–223.

72 Albrecht, op cit., pp. 162–63; Albrecht and Bradford, op cit., pp. 88–91.

73 Albrecht and Zemke, op cit., p. 174.

74 Albrecht, op cit., p. 198.

75 This case is quoted in Heizer and Render, op cit., p. 277.

76 Scott Donaton, "Flying Lessons: JetBlue Soars When the Front Lines Value Brand," *Advertising Age* 73, no. 6, 11 February 2002, p. 16.

CHAPTER 16

1 Tahl Raz, "This hip house," *Inc.*, Oct. 2002, page 36; see also Sandy Olkowski, "Martha Stewart goes street: an interview with indie Mag dynamo, Shoshana Berger," www.withitgirl.com/life/profile1.htm.

2 Adapted from ibid., p. 5.

3 Ibid.

4 Jeffrey Timmons, "The Entrepreneurial Mind," *Success*, April 1994, p. 48.

5 Ibid.

6 This is based on Marc Dollinger, *Entrepreneurship: Strategies and Resources* (Upper Saddle River, NJ: Prentice Hall, 2003), pp. 7–8.

7 Amy Kover, "Manufacturing's Hidden Assets: Workers," *Fortune*, 10 November 1997, pp. 28–29.

8 U.S. Patent and Trademark Office "Issues and Patent Numbers," April 1999, (www.uspto.gov).

9 W. Gartner, "The Conceptual Framework for Describing the Phenomenon of New Venture Creation," *Academy of Management Review* 10, 1985, pp. 696–706, as cited in Dollinger, op cit., p. 19.

10 "Small Business Economic Indicators 2000," Office of Advocacy, U.S. Small Business Administration, Washington, D.C., 2001, p. 5.

11 This data comes from *Small Business: A Report of the President*, 1998, www.sba.gov/advo/stats.

12 R. J. Arend, "The Emergence of Entrepreneurs Following Exogenous Technological Change," *Strategic Management Journal* 20, no. 1, 1999, pp. 31–47; discussed in Mary Coulter, *Entrepreneurship in Action* (Upper Saddle River, NJ: Prentice Hall, 2001), p. 4.

13 Dollinger, op cit., p. 335.

14 Adapted from R. Nielsen, M. Peters, and R. Hisrich, "Intrapreneurship Strategy for Internal Markets: Corporate, Nonprofit Anti-Government Institution Cases," *Strategic Management Journal* no. 6, April–June 1985, pp. 181–89, quoted in Dollinger, op cit., p. 333.

15 Dollinger, ibid.

16 This is based on Dean Takahashi, "Reinventing the Intrapreneur," *Red Herring*, September 2000, pp. 189–96.

17 Coulter, op cit., p. 18.

18 C. R. Brockhaus, "The Psychology of the Entrepreneur," ed. C. Kent, D. Sexton, and K. Verspers, *Encyclopedia of Entrepreneurship* (Upper Saddle River, NJ: Prentice Hall, 1982), pp. 39–71; discussed in Dollinger, op cit., p. 38.

19 Richard Becherer and John Maurer, "The Proactive Personality Disposition and Entrepreneurial Behavior Among Small Company Presidents," *Journal of Small Business Management* 37, no. 1, January 1999, pp. 28–37.

20 Ibid.

21 Jill Kickul and Lisa Gundry, "Prospective for Strategic Advantage: The Proactive Entrepreneurial Personality and Small Firm Innovation," *Journal of Small-Business Management* 40, no. 2, April 2002, pp. 85–98.

22 S. D. McKenna, "The Darker Side of the Entrepreneur," *Leadership and Organization Development Journal* 17, no. 6, November 1996, pp. 41–46.

23 Ibid.

24 Julie Rose, "The New Risk Takers," *Fortune Small Business* 12, no. 2, March 2002, pp. 28–34.

25 Ibid.

26 Arlene Weintraub, "Can Boingo Wireless, From the Founder of EarthLink, Turn Hot Spots into Money?" *Business Week*, no. 3780, 29 April 2002, p. 106.

27 From "The U.S. Small Business Administration's Small Business Start-Up Kit," downloaded 12 May 2002, www.sba.gov/starting/ask.html.

28 A. Bhide, "How Entrepreneurs Craft Strategies That Work," *Harvard Business Review*, March–April 1994, pp. 150–61, and John Case, "The Origins of Entrepreneurship," *Inc.*, June 1989, pp. 51–62.

29 Peggy Lambing and Charles Kuehl, *Entrepreneurship* (Upper Saddle River, NJ: Prentice Hall, 2000), p. 90.

30 Ibid., p. 91.

31 Stewart Brown, "A Sweet Triumph," *Fortune Small Business* 12, April 2002, pp. 45–54.

32 Norman Scarborough and Thomas Zimmerer, *Effective Small Business Management* (Upper Saddle River, NJ: Prentice Hall, 2002), p. 21.

33 Lambing and Kuehl, op cit., p. 35.

34 Quoted in ibid.

35 Barbara Marsh, "When Owners of Family Businesses Die, Survivors Often Feel Unsuited to Fill the Void," *Wall Street Journal*, 7 May 1990, pp. B1–B2; discussed in William Schoell, Gary Dessler, and John Reinecke, *Introduction to Business* (Boston: Allyn and Bacon, 1993), p. 173.

36 Lambing and Kuehl, op cit., p. 38.

37 Steps 1 to 4 from Small Business Administration, "First Steps: How to Start a Business," downloaded 12 May 2002, www.sba.gov/starting/indexsteps.html.

38 Schoell, Dessler, and Reinecke, op cit., pp. 178–79.

39 Laverne Urlacher, *Small Business Entrepreneurship: An Ethics and Human Relations Perspective* (Upper Saddle River, NJ: Prentice Hall, 1999), pp. 114–19.

40 This section is based on Schoell, Dessler, and Reinecke, op cit., pp. 132–42.

41 John Vinturella, *The Entrepreneur's Field Book* (Upper Saddle River, NJ: Prentice Hall, 1999), pp. 109–10.

42 Cara Buckley, "A Long-Awaited Debut," *Miami Herald*, 15 May 2002, p. C1.

43 Dollinger, op cit., pp. 314–33.

44 U.S. Small Business Administration, "Small Business Frequently Asked Questions," downloaded 12 May 2002, www.sba.gov/addl/stats/spfaq.txt.

45 Michael E. Porter, "What Is Strategy?" *Harvard Business Review*, November–December 1996, pp. 61–80.

46 This example is based on ibid., pp. 70–75.

47 Bill Friskics-Warren, "Tapping an Audience With an Ear to the Ground," *New York Times*, 17 March 2002, pp. 2, 33.

48 Ibid.

49 Ibid.

50 Ibid.

51 Ross Kerber, "dotcoms May be Dead, But Small Businesses Are Still Using the Internet," *Boston Globe*, 15 April 2002, p. C1.

52 Ibid.

53 Ibid.

54 Ibid.

55 This is adapted from John Vinturella, *The Entrepreneur's Field Book* (Upper Saddle River, NJ: Prentice Hall, 1999), pp. 64–65.

56 W. Keith Schilit, *The Entrepreneurs' Guide to Preparing a Winning Business Plan and Raising Venture Capital* (Upper Saddle River, NJ: Prentice Hall, 1990), pp. 4–6.

57 Ibid., p. 5.

58 For a discussion, see Peter Wright, Mark Kroll, and John Parnell, *Strategic Management Concepts* (Upper Saddle River, NJ: Prentice Hall, 1996), pp. 224–25.

59 This is based on Dollinger, op cit., pp. 313–16.

60 David Yoffie, "Building a Company on Internet Time: Lessons from Netscape," *California Management Review*, Spring 1999, p. 8.

61 Ibid.

62 www.sba.gov/sbainfo/manageabusiness/human.txt.

63 Nancy Austin, "First Aide," *Inc.*, September 1999, p. 78.

64 Ibid., p. 72.

65 "Internships Provide Workplace Snapshot," *BNA Bulletin to Management*, 22 May 1997, p. 168.

66 Gary Dessler, "How to Earn Your Employees' Commitment," *Academy of Management Executive* 13, no. 2, 1999, pp. 58–67.

67 Ibid.

68 Michael Selz, "Testing Self-Managing Teams, Entrepreneur Hopes to Lose Job," *Wall Street Journal*, 11 January 1994, p. B1; and Sally Goll Beatty, "Standard & Poors Acquires Published Image, Inc.," *Wall Street Journal*, 2 July 1997, p. B7.

69 The following section is based on "Management Issues for the Growing Business," www.sba.gov/sbainfo/manage-8-business/man.txt.

70 Kenneth Merchant, *Control in Business Organizations* (Boston: Pitman, 1985), p. 98.

71 Guy Bolton, "Enterprise Resource Planning Software Creates Supply Business Revolution," Knight Ridder/Tribune Business News, 9 November 1998.

72 This case is quoted from Dollinger, op cit., p. 37, and it is adapted from Meera Louis, "Pooled Savings Help Jamaicans Build Business," *Wall Street Journal*, 17 October 2000, pp. B1–B2.

73 Eryn Brown, "A Smokeless Herb," *Fortune*, 28 May 2001 143, no. 11, pp. 78–79.

74 Frances Fiorino, "JetBlue Pursues Growth While Staying Small," *Aviation Week & Space Technology* 156, no. 23, 10 June 2002, p. 41.

75 "Case Study JetBlue," *Flight International*, 9 April 2002, p. 39.

76 Brown, op cit.

77 Ibid.

78 "JetBlue Airways," *Air Transport World* 39, no. 2, February 2002, pp. 28–29.

79 Fiorino, op cit.

CHAPTER 17

1 Donald Hastings, "Lincoln Electric's Harsh Lessons from International Expansion," *Harvard Business Review*, May–June 1999, pp. 163–78.

2 Louis Uchitelle, "Trade, Already Off, Faces New Hurdle," *New York Times*, 9 October 2001, p. C1.

3 William Taylor, "The Gurus of Globalization," *Fast Company*, September 1999, p. 231.

4 Neel Chowdhury, "Dell Cracks China," *Fortune*, 21 June 1999, pp. 120–24.

5 Ted Rakstis, "Going Global," *Kiwanis Magazine*, October 1981, pp. 39–43.

6 Thomas Clasen, "An Exporter's Guide to Selecting Foreign Sales Agents and Distributors," *The Journal of European Business*, November–December 1991, pp. 28–32.

7 Albert G. Holzinger, "Paving the Way for Small Exporters," *Nation's Business*, June 1992, pp. 42–43.

8 Charles Hill, *International Business* (Bun Ridge, IL: Irwin, 1994), p. 402.

9 Art Garcia, "It's in the Mail," *World Trade*, April 1992, pp. 56–62.

10 See, for example, John Daniels and Lee Radebaugh, *International Business* (Reading, MA: Addison-Wesley, 1994), p. 544.

11 Michael Czinkota, Pietra Rivoli, and Ilka Ronkinen, *International Business* (Fort Worth: The Dryden Press, 1992), p. 278.

12 Aaron Lucchetti, "Pioneer Group Blazes Trail After Purchase by Milan Bank," *Wall Street Journal*, 9 July 2001, p. R1.

13 Hill, op cit., p. 411.

14 Barry James, "Air France and Delta Pave the Way for the Third Alliance," *International Herald Tribune*, 23 June 1999, p. 1.

15 John Daniels and Lee Radebaugh, *Internaitonal Business* (Upper Saddle River, NJ: Prentice Hall, 2001) p. 12.

16 Gregory White, "In Asia, GM Pins Hope on a Delicate Web of Alliances," *Wall Street Journal*, 23 October 2001, p. A23.

17 Czinkota et al., op cit. p. 320.

18 Kenichi Ohmae, "The Global Logic of Strategic Alliances," *Harvard Business Review*, March–April 1989, pp. 143–54.

19 Saritha Rai, "India Company Reaches Deal with AOL for Programming," *New York Times*, 14 December 2001, p. W1.

20 Wilfred Vanhonacker, "Entering China: An Unconventional Approach," *Harvard Business Review*, March–April 1997, pp. 130–40.

21 Robert Neff, "Guess Who's Selling Barbies in Japan Now?" *Business Week*, December 9, 1991, pp. 72, 74, 76. See also Jeffrey Garten, "Troubles Ahead in Emerging Markets," *Harvard Business Review*, May–June 1997, pp. 38–50 and Yagang Pan and Peter Chi, "Financial Performance and Survival of Multinational Corporations in China," *Strategic Management Journal*, April 1999, p. 359.

22 Hill, op cit., p. 4: See also Dawn Anfuso, "Colgate's Global HR United Under One Strategy," *Personnel Journal*, October 1995,

p. 44ff; Marlene Piturro, "What Are You Doing About the New Global Realities?" *Management Review*, March 1999, pp. 16–22; and Maureen Minehan, "Changing Conditions in Emerging Markets," *HR Magazine*, January 1998, p. 160.

23 For a discussion see, for example, Arvind Phatak, *International Dimensions of Management* (Boston: PWS-Kent, 1989), p. 2.

24 Theodore Levitt, "The Globalization of Markets," *Harvard Business Review*, May–June 1983, pp. 92–102, For an example, see Thomas Stewart, "See Jack. See Jack Run Europe," *Fortune*, 27 September 1999, pp. 124–27.

25 Note that there are few, if any, "pure" market economies or command economies anymore. For example, some of the French banking system is still under government control. And it was only several years ago that the government of England privatized (sold to private investors) British Airways.

26 "Countries with Highest Gross Domestic Product and Per-Capita GDP," *The World Almanac and Book of Facts, 1998* (Mahwah, NJ: K-III Reference Corporation, 1997), p. 112.

27 David Kemme, "The World Economic Outlook for 1999," *Business Perspectives*, January 1999, pp. 6–9.

28 Daniels and Radebaugh, op cit., p. 138.

29 Czinkota et al., op cit., p. 640.

30 For a discussion see, for example, ibid., Chapter 2; and James Flanigan, "Asian Crisis Could Bring New Threat: Protectionism," *Los Angeles Times*, 3 February 1999, p. N1.

31 Czinkota et al., p. 116.

32 Daniels and Radebaugh, op cit. 1994, p. 409.

33 Molly O'Meara, "Riding the Dragon," *World Watch*, March/April 1997, pp. 8–18.

34 This is based on John Daniels and Lee Radebaugh, *International Business* (Upper Saddle River, NJ: Prentice Hall, 2001), pp. 217–19.

35 Ibid., p. 218.

36 Karby Leggett, "Beijing Allows New York Life, Met Life, Nippon to sell in China," *Wall Street Journal*, 12 December 2001, p. A8.

37 Andrew Tanzer, "Chinese Walls," *Forbes*, 168, 12 November 2001, pp. 74–75.

38 See, for example, Susan Lee, "Are We Building New Berlin Walls?" *Forbes*, January 1991, pp. 86–89; Tom Reilly, "The Harmonization of Standards in the European Union and the Impact on U.S. Business," *Business Horizons*, March–April 1995.

39 Laura Pincus and James Belohlav, "Legal Issues in Multinational Business Strategy: To Play the Game, You Have to Know the Rules," *Academy of Management Executive*, November 1996, pp. 52–61.

40 Ibid., pp. 53–54.

41 Ibid., p. 53.

42 Richard Behar, "China's Phony War on Fakes," *Fortune*, 30 October 2000, p. 206. See also Derek Dessler, "China's Intellectual Property Protection: Prospects for Achieving International Standards," *Fordham International Law Journal*, 181 (1995).

43 Steve Levine and Betsy McKay, "Coke Finds Mixing Marriage and Businesses Tricky in Tashkent," *Wall Street Journal*, 21 August 2001, p. A1.

44 Catherine Tinsley, "Models of Conflict Resolution in Japanese, German, and American Cultures," *Journal of Applied Psychology*, April 1998, pp. 316–22.

45 In John Tagliabue, "In the French Factory, Culture Is a Two-Way Street," *New York Times*, 25 February 2001, p. BU4.

46 Ken Belson, "As Starbucks Grows, Japan, Too, Is Awash," *New York Times*, 21 October 2001, p. BU5.

47 United Nations, *Draft International Code of Conduct on the Transfer of Technology* (New York: United Nations, 1981), p. 3; quoted in Michael Czinkota et al., op cit., p. 313.

48 Ibid., p. 314.

49 Jeremy Main, "How to Go Global—and Why," *Fortune*, 28 August 1989, p. 70. See also Kasra Ferdows, "Making the Most of Foreign Markets," *Harvard Business Review*, March–April 1997, pp. 73–88.

50 www.walmart.com/newsroom/firstquarter99.html.

51 Hill, op cit., pp. 5–6.

52 Kenneth Laudon and Jane Laudon, *Management Information Systems* (Upper Saddle River, NJ: Prentice Hall 1998), p. 6. See also Michael McGrath and Richard Hoole, "Manufacturing's New Economies of Scale," *Harvard Business Review*, May–June 1992, p. 94. Thomas Kochan and Russell Lansbury, "Lean Production and Changing Employment Relations in the International Auto Industry," *Economic and Industrial Democracy*, November 1997, pp. 597–620 and John Sheridan, "Bridging the Enterprise," *Industry Week*, 5 April 1999, p. 17.

53 Based on McGrath and Hoole, op cit., pp. 94–102.

54 Laudon and Laudon, op cit., p. 348.

55 Ibid., p. 384.

56 Based on Brian O'Reilly, "Your New Global Workforce," *Fortune*, December 1992, pp. 52–66, See also Charlene Solomon, "Don't Get Burned by Hot New Markets," *Global Workforce*, a supplement to *Workforce*, January 1998, p. 12.

57 O'Reilly, op cit., p. 64. See also Shirley R. Fishman, "Developing a Global Workforce," Canadian Business Review, Spring 1996, pp. 18–21.

58 David Woodruff, "Distractions Make Global Manager a Difficult Role," *Wall Street Journal*, 21 November 2000, p. B1.

59 Ibid., p. B18.

60 Ibid.

61 See Mariah E. DeForest, "Thinking of a Plant in Mexico?" *Academy of Management Executive*, February 1994, pp. 33–40.

62 Ibid., p. 34.

63 Ibid., p. 37.

64 Ibid., p. 38. See also Randall S. Schuler, Susan E. Jackson, Ellen Jackofsky, and John W. Slocum, "Managing Human Resources in Mexico: A Cultural Understanding," *Business Horizons*, May 1996, pp. 55–61.

65 Philip Harris and Robert Moran, *Managing Cultural Differences* (Houston, TX: Gulf Publishing Company, 1979), p. 1.

66 David Armstrong, "Overseas Acumen," *San Francisco Chronicle*, 15 April 15 2001, p. B3.

67 Kamal Fatehi, *International Management* (Upper Saddle River, NJ: Prentice Hall, 1996), p. 41.

68 Gail Dutton, "Building a Global Brain," *Management Review*, May 1999, pp. 34–38.

69 Ibid., p. 35.

70 Gretchen Spreitzer, Morgan McCall Jr., and Joan Mahoney, "Early Identification of International Executive Potential," *Journal of Applied Psychology*, February 1997, pp. 6–29.

71 Fatehi, op cit., p. 59.

72 Gary Anthes, "Think Globally, Act Locally," *ComputerWorld* 35 no. 22, 28 May 2001, pp. 36–37.

73 Fatehi, op cit., p. 41.

74 Anant Negandhi, *International Management* (Newton, MA: Allyn & Bacon, Inc., 1987), p. 61. See also Keith W. Glaister and Peter J. Buckley, "Strategic Motives for International Alliance Formation," *Journal of Management Studies*, May 1996, pp. 301–22.

75 Richard Tomlinson, "Who's Afraid of Wal-Mart?" *Fortune*, 26 June 2000, p. 196.

76 Ibid.

77 Clifford Krause, "Selling to Argentina—as Translated by the French," *New York Times*, 5 December 1999, p. BU7.

78 See, for example, Wendy Zellner et al., "How Well Does Wal-Mart Travel?" *Business Week*, 3 September 2001, pp. 82–84.

79 Richard D. Robinson, *Internationalization of Business: An Introduction* (Hillsdale, IL: The Dryden Press, 1984), pp. 227–28; See also "Organizing for Europe," *International Journal of Retail and Distribution Management*, Winter 1993, pp. 15–16.

80 PR Newswire, 27 March 1997, "Reynolds Metal Announces Organizational and Management Changes."

81 See, for example, S. M. Davis, "Managing and Organizing Multinational Corporations," ed. C. A. Bartlett and S. Ghoshal, *Transnational Management* (Homewood, IL: Irwin, 1992).

82 This is based on Fatehi, op cit., pp. 89–91.

83 See also Thomas Malnight, "Emerging Structural Patterns Within Multinational Corporations: Toward Processed Database Structures," *Academy of Management Journal*, 44, no. 6, 2001, pp. 1187–216.

84 Discussed in Fatehi, op cit., p. 123.

85 Ibid.

86 Ken Siegmann, "Workforce," *Profit*, November 1999, p. 47.

87 Daniels and Radebaugh, op cit., p. 529.

88 Fatehi, op cit., p. 129.

89 See, for example, ibid., p. 230.

90 Ibid.

91 R. G. D'Andrade and C. Strauss, *Human Motives and Cultural Models* (Cambridge: Cambridge University Press, 1992), p. 4.

92 Geert Hofstede, "Cultural Dimensions in People Management," ed. Vladimir Pucik, Noel Tichy, and Carole Barnett, *Globalizing Management*, (New York: John Wiley & Sons, Inc., 1992), pp. 139–58.

93 Ibid., p. 143.

94 Ibid.

95 Ibid., p. 147.

96 Geert Hofstede, "Cultural Constraints and Management Theories," *Academy of Management Review* 7, no. 1, 1993, pp. 81–93; reprinted in Joyce Osland, David Kolb, and Irwin Rubin, *The Organizational Behavior Reader* (Upper Saddle River, NJ: Prentice Hall, 2001), pp. 345–56.

97 Fatehi, op cit., p. 279.

98 Discussed in Helen Deresky, *International Management* (Reading, MA: Addison-Wesley, 1997), pp. 401–2.

99 E. C. Nevis, "Using an American Perspective in Understanding Another Culture: Toward a Hierarchy of Needs for the People's Republic of China," *The Journal of Applied Behavioral Science* 19, no. 3, 1983, pp. 249–64; discussed in Fatehi, op cit., p. 240.

100 D. C. McClelland and D. G. Winter, *Motivating Economic Achievement* (New York: Free Press, 1969).

101 L. Copland and L. Griggs, *Going International: How to Make Friends and Deal Effectively in the Global Marketplace* (New York: Random House, 1985), p. 14; discussed in Fatehi, op cit., p. 251.

102 Hastings, op cit., p. 166.

103 Ibid.

104 Ibid.

105 Ibid., p. 171.

106 Ibid., p. 174.

107 Ibid.

108 Ibid., p. 177.

109 Ibid., p. 178.

110 Ibid.

111 Frances Fiorino, "JetBlue Pursues Growth While Staying Small," *Aviation Week & Space Technology* 156, no. 23, 10 June 2002, p. 41.

112 Joan Feldman, "JetBlue Loves New York," *Air Transport World* 38, no. 6, June 2001, p. 78.

PHOTO CREDITS

CHAPTER 1 Page 1: Mario Tama/Getty Images, Inc—Liaison. Page 9: Marty Lederhandler/AP/Wide World Photos. Page 17: Michael Newman/PhotoEdit. Page 19: AP/Wide World Photos.

CHAPTER 2 Page 26: AP/Wide World Photos. Page 37: Cloudberry. Page 40: AOL Moviefone RLM. Page 44: AP/Wide World Photos. Page 46: Alan Levenson.

CHAPTER 3 Page 52: Donna Terek Photography. Page 68: AP/Wide World Photos. Page 70: Masterfile Corporation.

CHAPTER 4 Page 79: John C. Hillery/Reuters/Getty Images, Inc—Liaison. Page 83: Roger Mastroianni. Page 100: SMAILES ALEX/Corbis/Sygma. Page 103: Spencer Grant/PhotoEdit.

CHAPTER 5 Page 110: AP/Wide World Photos. Page 122: Jim Whitmer/Jim Whitmer Photography. Page 124: Jeff Greenberg/Photo Researchers, Inc. Page 130: AFP PHOTO EPA/DPA/Rainer Jensen/CORBIS. Page 133:© Frank Ordoñez/Syracuse Newspapers/The Image Works.

CHAPTER 6 Page 138: Koji Sasahara/AP/Wide World Photos. Page 146: CuseeMe Networks. Page 148: Caswell-Massey, Co. Ltd. Page 151: Leif Skoogfors/Rosenbluth International. Page 157: Howard Dratch/The Image Works.

CHAPTER 7 Page 166: AFP PHOTO/Yoshikazu Tsuno. Page 169: Mark Richards. Page 169: John Abbott Photography. Page 172: Dayton Daily News. Page 189: AP/Wide World Photos.

CHAPTER 8 Page 193: Koichi Kamoshida/Getty Images, Inc—Liaison. Page 199: AP/Wide World Photos. Page 201: AP/Wide World Photos. Page 208: Brian Smith/The Ward Group Miami. Page 210: AP/Wide World Photos.

CHAPTER 9 Page 220: Signicast Corporation. Page 231: Michael Newman/PhotoEdit.

CHAPTER 10 Page 254: James Schnepf/Getty Images, Inc—Liaison. Page 258: Porter Gifford/Getty Images, Inc—Liaison. Page 263: AFP PHOTO/Doug Kanter/CORBIS.

CHAPTER 11 Page 282: AP/Wide World Photos. Page 287: David Norton /ImageState/International Stock Photography Ltd. Page 298: AP/Wide World Photos. Page 299: Jay Blakesberg

CHAPTER 12 Page 314: Alan Jakubek/CORBIS. Page 324: REUTERS/Jim Bourg/Getty Images, Inc—Liaison. Page 327: Toyota Motor Manufacturing, Kentucky, Inc. Page 332: Ventana Corporation Group Systems. Page 336: Rommel/Masterfile Corporation.

CHAPTER 13 Page 339: Big Apple Circus. Page 347: AP/Wide World Photos. Page 349: James Wasserman/James Wasserman Photography.

CHAPTER 14 Page 365: AIB Group. Page 369: Spencer Grant/PhotoEdit. Page 369: Tony Freeman/PhotoEdit. Page 381: John Neubauer/PhotoEdit.

CHAPTER 15 Page 390: Collins & Aikman, Inc. Page 393: Jim Whitmer/Jim Whitmer Photography. Page 401: Seale Studios. Page 408: Michael S. Yamashita/CORBIS. Page 415: AP/Wide World Photos.

CHAPTER 16 Page 422: Peter DaSilva. Page 434: AP/Wide World Photos. Page 436: AOL Moviefone RLM. Page 443: Erica Freudstein.

CHAPTER 17 Page 450: Spencer Grant /PhotoEdit. Page 457: AP/Wide World Photos. Page 458: AP/Wide World Photos. Page 465: Witold Krassowski/Network/Corbis/SABA Press Photos, Inc.

A

acceptance sampling a method of monitoring product quality that requires the inspection of only a small portion of the produced items.

accommodation giving in to the opponent in an attempt to end a conflict.

acquisition costs the total costs of all units bought to fill an order, usually varying with the size of the order.

action research the process of collecting data from employees about a system in need of change, and then feeding that data back to the employees so that they can analyze it, identify problems, develop solutions, and take action themselves.

activities the time-consuming aspects of a project, represented by arrows in a PERT chart.

activity-based costing (ABC) a method for allocating costs to products and services that takes all the product's cost drivers into account when calculating the actual cost of each product or service.

affirmative action a legislated requirement that employers make an extra effort to hire and promote those in a protected (women or minority) group.

anchoring unconsciously giving disproportionate weight to the first information you hear.

angels wealthy individuals interested in the high-risk/high-reward potentials of new venture creation.

application form a form that requests information such as education, work history, and hobbies from a job candidate as a means of quickly collecting verifiable historical data.

aroused motive a motive that expresses itself in behavior.

attitude a predisposition to respond to objects, people, or events in either a positive or negative way.

audit a systematic process of objectively obtaining and evaluating evidence regarding important aspects of the firm's performance, judging the accuracy and validity of the data, and communicating the results to interested users.

authoritarian personality a personality type characterized by rigidity, intolerance of ambiguity, the tendency to stereotype others as being good or bad, and conformity to the requirements of authority.

authority the right to take action, to make decisions, and to direct the work of others.

authority boundary the boundary created by differences in organizational level or status across which communications may be distorted or constrained due to the status difference.

autocratic leader leader who solves problems and makes the decisions alone, using the information available at the time.

automation the automatic operation of a system, process, or machine.

avoidance moving away from or refusing to discuss a conflict issue.

B

balance sheet is a projected statement of the financial position of the firm.

balanced scorecard a management tool, usually a computerized model, that traces a multitude of performance measures simultaneously and shows their interactions.

BCG matrix a strategic planning tool that helps a manager assess a business units attractiveness based on its growth rate and market share.

behavior modification the technique of changing or modifying behavior through the use of contingent rewards or punishments.

behavioral displacement a reaction to being controlled in which the controls encourage behaviors that are inconsistent with what the company actually wants to accomplish.

benchmarking a process through which a company learns how to become the best in one or more areas by analyzing and comparing the practices of other companies that excel in those areas.

boundary controls policies, such as codes of conduct, that establish rules and identify the actions and pitfalls that employees must avoid.

boundaryless organization an organization in which the widespread use of teams, networks, and similar structural mechanisms means that the boundaries separating organizational functions and hierarchical levels are reduced and more permeable.

boundaryless organization an organization in which management strips away the "walls" which typically separate organizational functions and hierarchical levels, through the widespread use of teams, networks, and similar structural mechanisms.

bounded rationality the boundaries on rational decision making imposed by one's values, abilities, and limited capacity for processing information.

brainstorming a creativity-stimulating technique in which prior judgments and criticisms are specifically forbidden from being expressed and thus inhibiting the free flow of ideas, which are encouraged.

breakeven analysis a financial analysis decision-making aid that enables a manager to determine whether a particular volume of sales will result in losses or profits.

budget a financial plan, showing financial expectations for a specific period.

budget formal financial expression of a manager's plans.

bureaucracy to Max Weber, the ideal way to organize and manage an organization; generally viewed today as a term reflecting an unnecessarily rigid and mechanical way of getting things done.

business plan a plan that lays out what the business is, where it is heading, and how it plans to get there.

business reengineering the radical redesign of business processes to cut waste; to improve cost, quality, and service; and to maximize the benefits of information technology, generally by questioning how and why things are being done as they are.

C

career anchor a dominant concern or value that directs an individual's career choices and that the person will not give up if a choice must be made.

cash budget shows, for each month, the amount of cash the company can expect to receive and the amount it can expect to disperse.

causal forecasting estimating a company factor (such as sales) based on other influencing factors (such as advertising expenditures or unemployment levels).

causal methods forecasting techniques that develop projections based on the mathematical relationship between a company factor and the variables believed to influence or explain that factor.

cellular manufacturing layout usually a combination of process and product layouts, in which machines and personnel are grouped into cells containing all the tools and operations required to produce a particular product or family of products.

certainty the condition of knowing in advance the outcome of a decision.

chain of command the path that a directive and/or answer or request should take through each level of an organization; also called a scalar chain or the line of authority.

channel assembly channel assembly means organizing the product assembly process so that the company doesn't send finished products to its distribution channel partners (such as warehouses, distributors, and retailers), but instead sends the partners components and modules. The partners thus become an extension of the firm's product assembly process.

close supervision a leadership style involving close, hands-on monitoring of subordinates and their work.

collaboration a conflict-management style in which both sides work together to achieve agreement.

collaborative writing systems a computerized support system that lets group members work simultaneously on a single document from a number of interconnected or network computers.

commitment the relative strength of an individual's identification with and involvement in an organization.

common market a system in which no barriers to trade exist among member countries, and a common external trade policy is in force that governs trade with nonmembers; factors of production, such as labor, capital, and technology, more freely among members.

communication the exchange of information and the transmission of meaning.

competition an approach to conflict management and negotiating that presumes a win-lose situation.

competitive advantage the basis for superiority over competitors and thus for hoping to claim certain customers.

competitive intelligence systematic techniques used to obtain and analyze public information about competitors.

competitive strategy a strategy that identifies how to build and strengthen the business's long-term competitive position in the marketplace.

compromise settling a conflict through mutual concessions.

computer-aided design (CAD) a computerized process for designing new products, modifying existing ones, or simulating conditions that may affect the designs.

computer-aided manufacturing (CAM) a computerized process for planning and programming production processes and equipment.

computer-integrated manufacturing (CIM) the total integration of all production-related business activities through the use of computer systems.

concurrent engineering designing products in multidisciplinary teams so that all departments involved in the product's success contribute to its design.

concurrent or yes/no control a control system in which the manager exercises control as the activity takes place, and the work may not proceed until or unless it is acceptable.

conglomerate diversification diversifying into other products or markets that are not related to a firm's present businesses.

contingent (or temporary) worker a temporary worker hired by an employer to fill short-term needs; not a permanent full-time or part-time employee.

contingent reward a reward that is contingent or dependent on performance of a particular behavior.

continuous production processes a production process, such as those used by chemical plants or refineries, that runs for very long periods without the start-and-stop behavior associated with intermittent production.

control task of ensuring that activities are getting the desired results.

conversion system any production system that converts inputs (material and human resources) into outputs (products or services); sometimes called the production process or technology.

coordination the process of achieving unity of action among interdependent activities.

core competencies the collective learning in the organization, especially the knowledge of how to coordinate diverse design and production skills and integrate multiple streams of technologies.

corporate social audit a rating system used to evaluate a corporation's performance with regard to meeting its social obligations.

corporate stakeholder any person or group that is important to the survival and success of the corporation.

corporate-level strategy a plan that identifies the portfolio of businesses that comprise a corporation and how they relate to each other.

corporation a legally chartered organization that is a separate legal entity apart from its owners. A corporation comes into being when the incorporators (founders) apply for and receive a charter from the state in which the firm is to reside.

cost leadership a competitive strategy by which a company aims to be the low-cost leader in its industry.

creativity the process of developing original, novel responses to a problem.

critical incidents method compiling brief examples of good/bad performance, and using them to support appraisal and development needs.

critical path the sequence of events in a project that, in total, requires the most time to complete.

customer departmentalization similar to product organization except that generally self-contained departments are organized to serve the needs of specific groups of customers.

customer report card lists the service attributes for which customers are looking as well as the relative weights or priorities of each attribute and how the customers score your company on each of them.

customs union a situation in which trade barriers among members are removed and a common trade policy exists with respect to nonmembers.

cycle of service includes all the moments of truth experienced by a typical customer, from first to last.

D

decentralized organization an organization in which (1) authority for most departmental decisions is delegated to the department heads, while (2) control for major companywide decisions is maintained at the headquarters office.

decision a choice made between available alternatives.

decision making the process of developing and analyzing alternatives and choosing from among them.

decision support systems (DSS) an interactive computer-based communications system that facilitates the solution of unstructured problems by a team of decision makers.

decision tree a technique for facilitating how decisions under conditions of risk are made, whereby an expected value and gain or loss can be applied to each alternative.

delegation the act of passing down authority from supervisor to subordinate.

departmentalization the process through which an organization's activities are grouped together and assigned to managers; the organizationwide division of work.

descriptive plan a plan that state's what is to be achieved and how.

designing for manufacturability designing products with ease of manufacturing and quality in mind.

diagnostic controls a control method, such as a budget, that ensures that standards are being met and that variances are diagnosed and explained.

differentiation strategy a competitive strategy aimed at distinguishing a company from its competitors by focusing on the attributes of its products or services that consumers perceive as important.

discipline without punishment a multistage disciplinary technique that uses oral reminders of the violated rule; then written reminders; followed by a paid one-day leave; and finally, if the behavior is not corrected, dismissal.

discrimination a behavioral bias toward or against a person based on the group to which the person belongs.

diverse describes a workforce comprised of two or more groups, each of which can be identified by demographic or other characteristics.

diversification a corporate strategy of expanding into related or unrelated products or market segments.

divestment selling or liquidating the individual businesses of a larger company.

divisionalization a form of organization in which the firm's major departments are organized so that each one can manage all or most of the activities needed to develop, manufacture, and sell a particular product or product line.

downsizing dramatically reducing the size of a company's workforce.

E

economic integration the result of two or more nations minimizing trade restrictions to obtain the advantages of free trade.

economic order quantity (EOQ) an inventory management system based on a simple formula that is used to determine the most economical quantity to order so that the total of inventory and setup costs is minimized.

employee benefits supplements to wages or pay that employees get as a result of their working for an organization.

employee compensation all forms of pay or rewards that go to employees and arise from their employment.

employee involvement program any formal program that lets employees participate in formulating important work decisions or in supervising all or part of their own work activities.

employee-oriented leader a leader who focuses on the needs of employees and emphasizes building good interpersonal relationships.

empowerment the act of giving employees the authority, tools, and information they need to do their jobs with greater autonomy and confidence.

enterprise resource planning system a companywide integrated computer system that gives managers real-time, instantaneous information regarding the costs and status of every activity and project in the business.

entrepreneur someone who creates new businesses for the purpose of gain or growth under conditions of risk and uncertainty.

entrepreneurship the creation of a business for the purpose of gain or growth under conditions of risk and uncertainty.

environmental scanning the process of gathering and compiling information about relevant environmental forces.

equity theory J. S. Adams's theory that people have a need for, and therefore value and seek, fairness in employer-employee relationships.

ethics the study of standards of conduct and moral judgment; also, the standards of right conduct.

ethnocentric a management philosophy that leads to the creation of home-market-oriented firms.

ethnocentrism a tendency to view members of one's own group as the center of the universe and to view other social groups less favorably than one's own.

events the specific accomplishments in a project, represented by circles in a PERT chart.

exchange rate the rate at which one country's currency can be exchanged for another country's currency.

executive recruiter an agency retained by employers to seek out top management talent.

executives the managers at the top of an organization.

expectancy in motivation, the probability that a person's efforts will lead to performance.

expected value a calculated value that equals the probability of the outcome multiplied by the benefit or cost of that outcome.

exporting selling abroad, either directly to target customers or indirectly by retaining foreign sales agents and distributors.

extinction the behavioral modification technique of withholding positive reinforcement so that the undesired behavior disappears over time.

F

facility layout the configuration of all the machines, employee workstations, storage areas, internal walls, and so forth that constitute the facility used to create a firm's product or service.

federal organization an organization in which power is distributed between a central unit and a number of constituents, but the central unit's authority is intentionally limited.

feedback or post-action control any control tool in which the project or operation being controlled is completed first, and then results are measured and compared to the standard.

financial incentive any financial reward that is contingent on a worker's performance, such as commissions or piecework.

financial ratio an arithmetic comparison of one financial measure to another, generally used to monitor and control financial performance.

financial responsibility centers individuals or groups who are assigned the responsibility for a particular set of financial outputs and/or inputs.

first-line manager managers at the lowest rung of the management ladder.

fixed salary compensation based on an agreed rate for a set period of time.

fixed-position layout a production system arrangement in which the product being built or produced stays at one location and the machines, workers, and tools required to build the product are brought to that location as needed, as for the building of ships or other bulky products.

flexible manufacturing system (FMS) the organization of groups of production machines that are connected by automated materials-handling and transfer machines, and integrated into a computer system for the purpose of combining the benefits of made-to-order flexibility and mass-production efficiency.

focus strategy a strategy in which a business selects a narrow market segment and builds its strategy on serving those in its target market better or more cheaply than its generalist competitors.

forced distribution method placing predetermined percentages of ratees into performance

forecast to estimate or calculate in advance or to predict.

foreign direct investment operations in one country controlled by entities in a foreign country.

formal organizational network a recognized group of managers or other employees assembled by the CEO and the other senior executive team, drawn from across the company's functions, business units, geography, and levels.

formal structure change program an intervention technique in which employees collect information on existing formal organizational structures and analyze it for the purpose of redesigning and implementing new organizational structures.

FRACT model A procedure for assessing the need for discipline, consisting of the steps get the facts, find the reason, audit the records, pinpoint consequences, and identify the type of infraction.

franchise a license to use a company's business ideas and procedures and to sell its goods or services.

franchisee a firm that obtains a license to use a franchiser's business ideas and procedures, and which may get an exclusive right to sell the franchiser's goods or services in a specific territory.

franchiser a firm that licenses other firms to use its business idea and procedures and to sell its goods or services in return for royalty and other types of payments.

franchising the granting of a right by a parent company to another firm to do business in a prescribed manner.

franchising agreement document that lays out the relationship between the franchiser and franchisee.

free trade all trade barriers among participating countries are removed, so there is an unrestricted exchange of goods among these countries.

free trade area a type of economic integration in which all barriers to trade among members are removed.

functional authority narrowly limited power to issue orders down the chain of command in a specific functional area such as personnel testing.

functional departmentalization a form of organization that groups a company's activities around essential functions such as manufacturing, sales, or finance.

functional plan a tactical short-term plan showing how each department of a business will contribute to top management's plans.

functional strategy the overall course or courses of action and basic policies that each department is to follow in helping the business accomplish its strategic goals.

G

gainsharing plan an incentive plan that engages many or all employees in a common effort to achieve a company's productivity objectives and in which they share in the gains.

gamemanship management actions that try to improve the manager's apparent performance in terms of the control system without producing any economic benefits for the company.

Gantt chart a production scheduling chart (named after management pioneer Henry Gantt) that plots time on a horizontal scale and generally shows, for each product or project, the start-and-stop times of each operation.

gatekeeper someone who controls access to information or other resources.

gender-role stereotype usually, the association of women with certain behaviors and possibly (often lower-level) jobs.

general leader a leader who takes a middle-ground approach between close supervision and laissez-faire leadership.

geographic expansion a strategic growth alternative of aggressively expanding into new domestic and/or overseas markets.

globalization the tendency of firms to extend their sales, ownership, and/or manufacturing to new markets abroad.

goal a specific result to be achieved; the end result of a plan.

goal theory theory that a person's goals provide the mechanism through which unsatisfied needs are translated into actions.

goal-setting studies organizational behavior research that provides useful insights into how to set effective goals.

graphic plan a plan that shows graphically or in charts what is to be achieved and when.

grievance a complaint that an employee lodges against an employer, usually one regarding wages, hours, or some condition of employment, such as unfair supervisory behavior.

gross domestic product (GDP) the market value of all goods and services that have been bought for final use during a period of time, and, therefore, the basic measure of a nation's economic activity.

group two or more persons who are interacting in such a way that each person influences and is influenced by each other person.

group cohesiveness the degree of interpersonal attractiveness within a group, dependent on factors like proximity, similarities, attraction among the individual group members, group size, intergroup competition, and agreement about goals.

group norms the informal rules that groups adopt to regulate and regularize group members' behavior.

group scheduling system a computerized support system that allows each group member to put his or her daily schedule into a shared database so that each can identify the most suitable times to schedule meetings or to attend currently scheduled meetings.

groupthink the mode of thinking in a cohesive group in which the desire to achieve group consensus overrides the potentially valuable individual points of view of its members.

H

heuristics a rule of thumb or an approximation applied as a shortcut to decision making.

hierarchy of plans a set of plans that includes the companywide plan and the derivative plans of subsidiary units required to help achieve the enterprisewide plan.

horizontal corporation a structure that is organized around customer-oriented processes performed by multidisciplinary cross-functional teams rather than by formal functional departments.

horizontal integration acquiring ownership or control of competitors who are competing in the same or similar markets with the same or similar products.

hourly wage compensation based on a set hourly pay rate for work performed.

human process interventions organizational change techniques aimed at enabling employees to develop a better understanding of their own and others' behaviors for the purpose of improving that behavior such that the organization benefits.

human resources (HR) management the management function devoted to acquiring, training, appraising, and compensating employees.

I

identity boundary the boundary created by identifying with those groups with which one has shared experiences and with which one believes one shares fundamental values.

income statement shows expected sales, expected expenses, and expected income or profit for the year.

independent integrator an individual or a group that coordinates the activities of several interdependent departments, but is independent of them.

informal organization the informal contacts, communications, and habitual ways of doing things that employees develop.

initial public offering (IPO) when a company first sells stock to outside owners.

input a resource required for the manufacture of a product or service.

instrumentality the perceived correlation between successful performance and obtaining the reward.

integrated strategic management an organizational development program to create or change a company's strategy by analyzing the current strategy, choosing a desired strategy, designing a strategic change plan, and implementing the new plan.

intermittent production system a system in which production is performed on a start-and-stop basis, such as for the manufacture of made-to-order products.

international business any firm that engages in international trade or investment; also refers to business activities that involve the movement of resources, goods, services, and skills across national boundaries.

international management the performance of the management process across national boundaries.

international trade the export or import of goods or services to consumers in another country.

interpersonal communication communication that occurs between two individuals.

intrapreneurship the development, within a large corporation, of internal markets and relatively small autonomous or semiautonomous business units that produce products, services, or technologies that employ the firm's resources in a unique way.

inventory management the process of ensuring that the firm has adequate inventories of all parts and supplies needed, within the constraint of minimizing total inventory costs.

inventory-holding (carrying) costs all the costs associated with carrying parts or materials in inventory.

ISO 9000 the quality standards of the International Standards Organization.

J

job analysis the procedure used to determine the duties of particular jobs and the kinds of people (in terms of skills and experience) who should be hired for them.

job analysis questionnaire a form used by managers to determine the duties and functions of a job through a series of questions that employees answer.

job description a document that identifies a particular job, provides a brief job summary, and lists specific responsibilities and duties of the job.

job design the number and nature of specific tasks or activities in a job.

job enlargement an increase in the number of similar tasks assigned to a job.

job enrichment the inclusion of opportunities for achievement and other motivators in a job by making the job itself more challenging.

job posting publicizing an open job to employees (often by literally posting it on bulletin boards and intranets) and listing its attributes, like qualifications, supervisor, working schedule, and pay rate.

job rotation the systematic movement of a worker from job to job to improve job satisfaction and reduce boredom.

job satisfaction the measure of an employee's attitude about his or her job.

job specification the human qualifications in terms of traits, skills, and experiences required to accomplish a job.

job-centered leader a leader who focuses on production and on a job's technical aspects.

joint venture the participation of two or more companies in an enterprise such that each party contributes assets, owns the entity to some degree, and shares risk.

jury of executive opinion a qualitative forecasting technique in which a panel of executives are given pertinent data and asked to make independent sales forecasts, which are then reconciled in an executive meeting or by the company president.

just-in-time (JIT) a production control method used to attain minimum inventory levels by ensuring delivery of materials and assemblies just when they are to be used; also refers to a philosophy of manufacturing that aims to optimize production processes by continuously reducing waste.

L

laissez-faire leader a leader who takes a hands-off approach toward supervising subordinates.

law of individual differences a psychological term representing the fact that people differ in their personalities, abilities, self-concept, values, and needs.

leader-member exchange (LMX) theory the theory that leaders may use different leadership styles with different members of the same workgroup, based in part on perceived similarities and differences with the leader.

leadership one person influencing another to willingly work toward a predetermined objective.

lean or value-added manufacturing a management philosophy that assumes that any manufacturing process that does not add value to the product for the customer is wasteful; also called value-added manufacturing.

learning a relatively permanent change in a person that occurs as a result of experience.

leverage to gain a competitive edge by concentrating a company's resources on key strategic goals or competencies.

licensing an arrangement whereby a firm (the licensor) grants a foreign firm the right to use intangible property.

lifelong learning the organizational program of providing continuing education and training to employees throughout their careers.

limited liability company (LLC) a cross between a partnership and a corporation.

line manager a manager who is (1) in charge of essential activities such as sales and (2) authorized to issue orders to subordinates down the chain of command.

linear programming a mathematical method used to solve resource allocation problems.

line-staff conflict disagreements between a line manager and the staff manager who is giving him or her advice.

M

Machiavellian personality a personality type oriented toward manipulation and control, with a low sensitivity to the needs of others, the name of which refers to the sixteenth-century political advisor Niccolò Machiavelli.

Malcolm Baldrige Award a prize created in 1987 by the U.S. Department of Commerce to recognize outstanding achievement in quality control management.

management assessment center a development and/or selection device wherein management candidates spend two or three days performing realistic management tasks under the observation of appraisers.

management by objectives (MBO) a technique in which supervisor and subordinate jointly set goals for the latter and periodically assess progress toward those goals.

management process refers to the manager's four basic functions of planning, organizing, leading, and controlling.

manager a person who plans, organizes, leads, and controls the work of others so that the organization achieves its goals.

managerial competence the motivation and skills required to gain a management position, including intellectual, emotional, and interpersonal skills.

managing diversity planning and implementing organizational systems and practices to manage people in a way that maximizes the potential advantages of diversity while minimizing its potential disadvantages.

market penetration a growth strategy to boost sales of present products by more aggressively permeating the organization's current markets.

marketing channel the conduit through which a manufacturer distributes its products to its ultimate customers.

marketing research the procedures used to develop and analyze current customer-related information to help managers make decisions.

marketing-channel departmentalization an arrangement in which departments of an organization focus on particular marketing channels, such as drugstores or grocery stores.

mass customization designing, producing, and delivering products in such a way that customers get customized products for at or near the cost and convenience of mass-produced items.

matrix organization an organization structure in which employees are permanently attached to one department but also simultaneously have ongoing assignments in which they report to project, customer, product, or geographic unit heads.

mechanistic organization an organizational structure characterized by close adherence to the established chain of command, highly specialized jobs, and vertical communications.

mentoring a relationship between two people in which the more experienced mentor provides support, guidance, and counseling to enhance the protégé's success at work and in other areas of life.

merit raise a salary increase—usually permanent—based on individual performance.

mission statement a statement that broadly outlines the enterprise's purpose and serves to communicate "who the organization is, what it does, and where it's headed."

mixed economy an economy in which some sectors are left to private ownership and free market mechanisms, while others are largely owned and managed by the government.

moment of truth the instant when the customer comes into contact with any aspect of a business and, based on that contact, forms an opinion about the quality of your service or product.

moral minimum the idea that corporations should be free to strive for profits so long as they commit no harm.

morality a society's accepted norms of behavior.

motivation the intensity of a person's desire to engage in some activity.

motivational dispositions or needs motives that lie dormant until the proper conditions arise to bring them forth or make them active.

motive something that incites a person to action or that sustains and gives direction to action.

moving a step in psychologist Kurt Lewin's model of change aimed at using techniques and actually altering the behaviors, values, and attitudes of the individuals in an organization.

multinational corporation (MNC) a company that operates manufacturing and marketing facilities in two or more countries: managers of the parent firm, whose owners are mostly in the firm's home country, coordinate the MNC's operation.

mutual adjustment achieving coordination through face-to-face interpersonal interaction.

N

negative reinforcement reinforcing the desirable behavior by removing something undesirable from the situation.

network planning and control methods ways of planning and controlling projects by graphically representing the projects' steps and the timing and links between these steps.

nonprogrammed decision a decision that is unique and novel.

nonverbal communication the nonspoken aspects of communication, such as a person's manner of speaking, facial expressions, or body posture, that express meaning to others.

normative judgment a comparative evaluation stating or implying that something is good or bad, right or wrong, or better or worse.

O

objectives specific results toward which effort is directed.

on-the-job training (OJT) training in which a person learns a job while he or she is working at it.

open-book management a management style in which a company opens its books to the employees, sharing financial data, explaining numbers, and rewarding workers for improvement.

operant behavior behavior that appears to operate on or have an influence on the subject's environment.

operating budget shows the expected sales and/or expenses for each of the company's departments for the planning period in question.

operational plan a short-term plan that shows the detailed daily steps of business operations.

operations management the process of managing the resources that are needed to produce an organization's goods and services.

operations or production control the process of ensuring that the specified production plans and schedules are being adhered to.

operations or production planning the process of deciding what products to produce and where, when, and how to produce them.

ordering, or setup, costs the costs, usually fixed, of placing an order or setting up machines for a production run.

organic organization an organizational structure characterized by flexible lines of authority, less specialized jobs, and decentralized decisions.

organization a group of people with formally assigned roles who work together to achieve the stated goals of the group.

organization chart a chart that shows the structure of the organization including the title of each manager's position and, by means of connecting lines, who is accountable to whom and who has authority for each area.

organizational communication communication that occurs among several individuals or groups.

organizational culture the characteristic set of values and ways of behaving that employees in an organization share.

organizational development (OD) an approach to organizational change in which the employees themselves formulate the change that's required and implement it, usually with the aid of a trained consultant.

organizational network a system of interconnected or cooperating individuals.

organizing arranging the activities of the enterprise in such a way that they systematically contribute to the enterprise's goals.

orientation the process of providing new employees with basic information about the employer, such as company policies, working hours, or parking arrangements.

output a direct outcome (actual product or service) or indirect outcome (taxes, wages, salaries) of a production system.

P

participative leader leader who shares the problem with subordinates as a group so that together, they can generate and evaluate alternatives in order to reach consensus on a solution.

partnership an association of two or more persons to carry on as co-owners of a business for profit.

partnership agreement an oral or written contract between the owners of a partnership. It identifies the business, and it lays out the partners' respective rights and duties.

patterns of behavior in organizational behavior, the ceremonial events, written and spoken comments, and actual behaviors of an organization's members that contribute to creating the organizational culture.

pay for performance any compensation method based on merit or performance rather than across-the-board nonoutput-based pay.

perception the unique way each person defines stimuli, depending on the influence of past experiences and the person's present needs and personality.

perceptions how our personalities and experiences cause us to interpret stimuli.

performance appraisal a manager's evaluation of and feedback on an employee's work performance.

personal/interactive controls control methods that involve direct, face-to-face interaction with employees so as to monitor rapidly changing information and respond proactively to changing conditions.

personality the characteristic and distinctive traits of an individual, and the way these traits interact to help or hinder the adjustment of the person to other people and situations.

personnel planning the process of determining the organization's future personnel needs, as well as the methods to be used to fill those needs.

personnel replacement chart company records showing present performance and promotability of inside candidates for the most important positions.

plan a method for doing or making something, consisting of a goal and a course of action.

planning the process of setting goals and courses of action, developing rules and procedures, and forecasting future outcomes.

policy a standing plan that sets broad guidelines for the enterprise.

political boundary the boundary created special interests or agendas within an organization that may oppose each other.

polycentric a management philosophy oriented toward pursuing a limited number of individual foreign markets.

position replacement card a card prepared for each position in a company to show possible replacement candidates and their qualifications.

positive reinforcement the act of rewarding desired behavior; or the actual rewards, such as praise or bonuses, given each time the desired behavior occurs.

prejudice a bias that results from prejudging someone on the basis of the latter's particular trait or traits.

principle of exception sometimes called management by exception, this rule holds that employees should be left to pursue the standards set by management, and only significant deviations from the standard should be brought to a manager's attention.

problem a discrepancy between a desirable and an actual situation.

problem-solving team a team formed to identify and solve work-related problems.

procedure a plan that specifies how to proceed in specific situations that routinely arise.

process analysis solving problems by thinking through the process involved from beginning to end, imagining, at each step, what actually would happen.

process layout a production system design in which similar machines or functions are grouped together.

product development the strategy of improving products for current markets to maintain or boost growth.

product layout a production system design in which every item to be produced follows the same sequence of operations from beginning to end, such as an assembly line.

profit centers responsibility centers whose managers are held accountable for profit.

program a plan that lays out all the steps in proper sequence to a single-use, often one-time business project.

programmed decision a decision that is repetitive and routine and can be made by using a definite, systematic procedure.

psychological set the tendency to rely on a rigid strategy or approach when solving a problem.

punishment a behavioral modification option that applies penalties for the unde-sired behavior to reduce the possibility that it will recur.

Q

qualitative forecasting predictive techniques that emphasize human judgment.

quality the extent to which a product or service is able to meet customer needs and expectations.

quality circle a team of 6 to 12 employees who meet about once per week on company time to solve problems affecting their work area.

quantitative forecasting a type of forecasting in which statistical methods are used to examine data and find underlying patterns and relationships; includes time-series methods and causal models.

quota a legal restriction on the import of particular goods.

R

recruiting attracting a pool of viable job applicants.

refreezing a step in psychologist Kurt Lewin's model of change aimed at preventing a return to old ways of doing things by instituting new systems and procedures that reinforce the new organizational changes.

regiocentric a management philosophy oriented toward larger areas, including the global marketplace; also called geocentric.

related diversification a strategy of expanding into other industries or markets related to a company's current business lines, so that the firm's lines of business still have some kind of fit.

retrenchment the reduction of activities or operations.

revenue centers responsibility centers whose managers are held accountable for generating revenues, which is a financial measure of output.

risk the chance that a particular outcome will or will not occur.

rites and ceremonies traditional culture-building events or activities that symbolize the firm's values and help convert employees to these values.

rule a highly specific guide to action.

S

sales budget shows the number of units to be sold in each period (usually per month) or in general the sales activity to be achieved and the sales revenue expected from the sales.

sales force estimation a forecasting technique that gathers and combines the opinions of the sales people on what they predict sales will be in the forthcoming period.

satisfice to stop the decision-making process when satisfactory alternatives are found, rather than to review solutions until an optimal alternative is discovered.

scenario a hypothetical sequence of events constructed for the purpose of focusing attention on causal processes and decision points and thereby helping the manager anticipate events and thus create plans for them.

self-concept the perceptions people have of themselves and their relationships to people and other aspects of life.

self-efficacy being able to influence important aspects of one's world; the belief that one can accomplish what one sets out to do.

self-managing/self-directed work team a highly trained team of employees, including 6 to 18 people on average, who are fully responsible for turning out a well-defined segment of finished work.

sensitivity training also called laboratory or t-group training, the basic aim of this organizational development technique is to increase participants' insight into their own behavior and that of others by encouraging an open expression of feelings in a trainer-guided group.

service management a total organizationwide approach that makes quality of service the business's number one driving force.

service strategy the company's plan for achieving superior service.

signs and symbols practices and actions that create and sustain a company's culture.

skills the ability to do something in an effective manner.

small business management planning, organizing, leading, and controlling a small business.

smoothing over in conflict management, diminishing or avoiding a conflict issue.

social responsibility the extent to which companies should and do channel resources toward improving the quality of life of one or more segments of society other than the firm's own stockholders.

sole proprietorship a business owned by one person.

span of control the number of subordinates reporting directly to a supervisor.

spot award a financial reward given to an employee as soon as laudable performance is observed.

staff manager a manager without the authority to give orders down the chain of command (except in his or her own department); generally can only assist and advise line managers in specialized areas such as human resources management.

staffing actually filling a firm's open positions; also, the personnel process that includes six steps: job analysis, personnel planning; recruiting, interviewing, testing and selection, and training and development.

standing plan a plan established to be used repeatedly, as the need arises.

statistical decision theory techniques techniques used to solve problems for which information is incomplete or uncertain.

steering control control that predicts results and takes corrective action before the operation or project is completed.

stereotyping associating certain characteristics with certain socioeconomic classes but not with others.

stereotyping attributing specific behavioral traits to individuals on the basis of their apparent membership in a group.

stockout costs the costs associated with running out of raw materials, parts, or finished-goods inventory.

stories the repeated tales and anecdotes that contribute to a company's culture by illustrating and reinforcing important company values.

strategic alliance an agreement between potential or actual competitors to achieve common objectives.

strategic change a change in a firm's strategy.

strategic control the process of assessing progress toward its strategic objectives and taking corrective action as needed to ensure optimal implementation.

strategic human resource management the linking of the human resource function with the company's strategies to accomplish that strategy.

strategic intervention an organization development application aimed at effecting a suitable fit among a firm's strategy, structure, culture, and external environments.

strategic management the process of identifying and executing the organization's mission by matching the organizations capabilities with the demands of its environment.

strategic planning identifying the current business of a firm and the business it wants for the future, and the course of action or strategy it will pursue.

strategy a course of action that explains how an enterprise will move from the business it is in now to the business it wants to be in.

structural change changing one or more aspects of the company's organization structures.

subsidy a direct payment a country makes to support a domestic producer.

suggestion team a team formed to work in the short term on a given issue such as increasing productivity.

supplier partnering choosing to do business with a limited number of suppliers, with the aim of building relationships that improve quality and reliability rather than just improve costs.

supply chain management the integration of the activities that procure materials, transform them into intermediate goods and final product, and deliver them to customers.

survey research the process of collecting data from attitude surveys filled out by employees of an organization, then feeding the data back to workgroups to provide a basis for problem analysis and action planning.

SWOT analysis a strategic planning tool for analyzing a company's strengths, weaknesses, opportunities, and threats.

T

tactical plan a plan that shows how top management's plans are to be carried out at the departmental, short-term level.

tariff government tax on imports.

task boundary the boundary created by the tendency of employees to focus on their own specialized tasks.

team a group of people committed to a common purpose, set of performance goals, and approach for which the team members hold themselves mutually accountable.

team building the process of improving the effectiveness of a team through action research or other techniques.

technological change changing the way the company creates and markets its products or services.

technology transfer the transfer, often to another country, of systematic knowledge for the manufacturing of a product, for the application of a process, or for the rendering of a service; it does not extend to the mere sales or lease of goods.

telecommunications the electronic transmission of data, text, graphics, voice (audio), or image (video) over any distance.

telecommuting the substitution of telecommunications and computers for the commute to a central office.

360-degree feedback a performance evaluation method that involves collecting performance information on an employee all around that person-for instance, from subordinates, supervisors, peers, and internal and external customers.

time series a set of observations taken at specific times, usually at equal intervals, to identify fundamental patterns.

tokenism appointing a small number of minority-group members to high-profile positions instead of more aggressively achieving full representation for that group.

total quality management (TQM) a specific organizationwide program that integrates all the functions and related processes of a business such that they are all aimed at maximizing customer satisfaction through ongoing improvements.

TOWS matrix a strategic planning tool that presents possible strategies for addressing the firm's strengths, weaknesses, opportunities, and threats.

trade barrier a governmental influence that is usually aimed at reducing the competitiveness of imported products or services.

training program the process of providing new employees with information they need to do their jobs satisfactorily.

traits the unchanging characteristics of a person that predisposes someone to act in a particular way.

transactional behaviors leadership actions that focus on accomplishing the tasks at hand and on maintaining good working relationships by exchanging promises of rewards for performance.

transformational leadership the leadership process that involves influencing major changes in the attitudes and assumptions of organization members and building commitment for the organization's mission, objectives, and strategies.

transnational team a work team composed of multinational members whose activities span many countries.

U

uncertainty the absence of information about a particular area of concern.

unemployment insurance legally mandated insurance that is paid by state agencies to workers who are terminated through no fault of their own; the funds come from a tax on the employer's payroll.

unfreezing a step in psychologist Kurt Lewin's model of change that involves reducing the forces for the status quo, usually by presenting a provocative problem or event to get people to recognize the need for change and to search for new solutions.

V

valence in motivation, the perceived value a person ascribes to the reward for certain efforts.

value-based hiring the practice of screening and hiring people whose values are consistent with those of the company rather than looking just at an applicant's job-related skills.

values basic beliefs about what is important and unimportant, and what one should and should not do.

values and beliefs the guiding standards of an organization, such as "the customer is always right" or "don't be bureaucratic," that

affirm what should be practiced, as distinct from what is practiced.

variable pay plan a compensation plan that may reduce or increase some portion of the individual employee's pay, depending on whether the company meets its financial goals.

variance the difference between budgeted and actual amounts.

venture capitalists professionally managed pools of investor money. They specialize in evaluating new venture opportunities and taking equity stakes in worthy businesses.

venture team a small team of people who operate as semiautonomous units to create and develop a new idea.

vertical integration a growth strategy in which a company owns or controls the inputs to its processes and/or its distribution channels.

virtual corporation a temporary network of independent companies linked by information technology.

virtual team groups of geographically and/or organizationally dispersed coworkers

who are assembled and who interact using a combination of telecommunications and information technologies to accomplish an organizational task.

vision a general statement of an organization's intended direction that evokes emotional feelings in its members.

W

waiting-line/queuing techniques mathematical techniques used to solve waiting-line problems such that the optimal balance of employees available to waiting customers is attained.

whistle-blowing the activities of employees who try to report organizational wrongdoing.

wholly owned subsidiary a firm that is owned 100% by a foreign firm.

workers' compensation a legally mandated benefit that pays income and medical benefits to work-related accident victims or their dependents, regardless of fault.

workflow automation system an e-mail type of system that automates the flow of paperwork from person to person.

Career anchor, defined, 8
Careers at Cisco, 228
Cash budget, defined, 374
Cash cows, in strategic planning, defined, 130, 130f
Causal forecasting, defined, 100
Causal methods, defined, 100
Cellular manufacturing layout, 395, 395f
  defined, 395
Ceremony(ies), rites and, defined, 40
Certainty, defined, 78
Chain of command
  appeal to power and, in coordination, 184
  in coordination, 181
  defined, 140
  in organizations, 139–140
Channel assembly, 413
  defined, 413
CIA, 182
CIM. See Computer-integrated manufacturing (CIM)
Classical school, of modern management, 11–12
Classical/mechanistic management approach, 21–22, 22t
Close supervision, defined, 261
Coalition, guiding, in organizational change, 207
Code law system, 457
Cognitive ability, of leaders, 257
Collaboration, defined, 215
Collaborative writing system, defined, 332
Collaborator(s), described, 214, 215f
College recruiting, 229–230, 230f
Columbia University fine arts program, 294
Command and control, 259
Commercial News USA, 451
Commission(s), defined, 245
Commitment
  controlling and building, 365–389
  defined, 385
  in organizational change, mobilizing of, 207
Commitment-based control process, 372
Commitment-based control systems, uses of, 383–387, 386f
Committee(s), in coordination, 181
Common law, 457
Common market, defined, 455
Common sense, in organization, 173–174
Communicating, with subordinates, 327
Communication
  active listening in, 320–321
  barriers to, 316–319, 317t, 318t
  defined, 315, 320
  downward, 323
  guidelines for, 320, 320t
  horizontal, improvements in, 327
  informal, improvements in, 328–329
  Internet-based, 333
  interpersonal. See Interpersonal communication
  Japanese *vs.* American styles of, 317t, 317–318,
  lateral, 323
  in multicultural environment, 470–472, 470t
  nonverbal, 318–319
  organizational. See Organizational communication
  organizationwide, improvements in, 328
  process of, 315–316, 316f
  at speed of thought, 329–336, 330t, 331t, 332f, 334f, 336f
  upward, 323–325, 324t
  of vision, 386

what managers should know about, 315–319, 316f, 317t
Communication skills, improvements in, 314–338
Community(ies)
  sense of, 385–386
  virtual, Internet-based, building of, 333–335, 334f
Compensation, 245
  defined, 245
  types of, 245
Competence
  analytical, 7–8
  managerial, defined, 8
Competence-building process, 5
Competency(ies), of managers, 8
Competition
  business, 438–439, 438t
  defined, 215, 323
Competitive advantage, defined, 122
Competitive intelligence (CI), 103–105, 103f, 104t
  defined, 103
  ethics and, 105
  Internet and, 104
Competitive Profile Matrix, 438, 438t
Competitive strategies, 120–124, 121f-124f
  cost leadership, 121
  defined, 116, 120
  differentiation strategy, 121
  five forces model, 121–124, 122f-124f
  focus strategy, 121
Competitor(s), described, 214, 215f
Compromise, defined, 215
Computer-aided design (CAD), 409
  defined, 409
Computer-aided manufacturing (CAM), 409
  defined, 409
Computer-integrated manufacturing (CIM), 410–411, 410f
  defined, 410
Computerized Network Planning Report, example of, 397, 397f
Computerized operations management, 446
Computerized testing, in employee selection, 234–235, 235f
Concentration strategy, 117–118
  geographic expansion and, 117
  horizontal integration and, 117
  market penetration and, 117
  product development and, 117
Conceptual skills, 10
Concurrent (yes/no) control, defined, 368, 369f
Concurrent engineering, defined, 405
Conflict(s)
  interpersonal, management of, 214–217, 215f, 216f, 217t. See also Interpersonal conflict
  interunit, reduction of, organizing in, 184–185, 184f
  line-staff, defined, 184
Conglomerate diversification, defined, 118
Contingent reward, defined, 296
Contingent (or temporary) workers, defined, 229
Continuous production processes, 394
  defined, 394
Control
  boundary, 372, 372f
  command and, 259
  concurrent, 368, 369f
  defined, 366, 445–446
  diagnostic, 372, 372f, 373–379
  electronic performance monitoring and, 381

by entrepreneurs, 445–446
  feedback, 368–369
  interactive, 372, 372f, 380–381, 381f
  maintaining of, 370–373, 371f, 372f
  in management process, 366–367, 367f
  negative side of, 382
  personal/interactive, 372, 372f
  post-action, 368–369
  reactions to, 381–383
  span of, 154, 155f
  steering, 367
  unintended behavioral consequences of, 382–383
  yes/no, 368, 369f
Control process
  commitment-based, 372
  traditional, 371–372, 371f
Control systems
  basic management, 373–374, 374f
  commitment-based, uses of, 383–387, 386f
  effective, 366–370, 370f
  personal/interactive, 380–381, 381f
  traditional, 373–381. See also Traditional control systems
Controlling, in global environment, 467
Conversion system, 391
  defined, 391
Coordinating, 180–185, 181f, 182f, 184f. See also Coordination
Coordination, 180–185, 181f, 182f, 184f
  achievement of, methods for, 180–182, 181f
  chain of command in, 181
  committees in, 181
  defined, 180
  determinants of, 183
  direct supervision in, 181
  divisionalization in, 181
  independent integrators in, 181–182
  liaisons in, 181
  mutual adjustment in, 180
  procedures for, 180
  reduction of interunit conflict in, 184–185, 184f
  rules for, 180
  staff assistants in, 181
  standardization in, 180–181
Core competencies
  defined, 134
  strategic role of, 134–135
Corporate intrapreneurship, 425–426
Corporate social audit, 44–45, 44f
Corporate stakeholder, defined, 42, 42f
Corporate-level strategies, 117–120, 119f, 120f
  concentration, 117–118
  defined, 116
  diversification, 118–119
  investment reduction strategies, 119
  joint ventures, 119–120, 119f
  status quo strategies, 119
  strategic alliances, 119–120, 119f, 120f
  vertical integration, 118
Corporation(s), 433
  defined, 433
  horizontal, 159–161, 160f, 161f
  S, 433
  virtual, defined, 120
Cosmopolitan, defined, 462
Cost(s)
  acquisition, defined, 398
  fixed, defined, 76
  inventory-holding, defined, 399
  ordering, defined, 398
  stockout, defined, 399
  variable, defined, 76
Cost leadership, defined, 121

Dear Students:

For most people, the best way to learn how to do something is by actually doing it. The question is, how to build that kind of practical component into a textbook. What we've done in Management: Principles and Practices for Tomorrow's Leaders is create a portfolio of opportunities for you to use your newly acquired knowledge.

The Manager's Portfolio has three parts:

LEARN IT

Each chapter has 15 fill-in questions to help you review key concepts.

PRACTICE IT

A CD-ROM filled with realistic business scenarios challenges you to practice your new skills. You watch the scenario, read the discussion questions in this Manager's Portfolio, and then apply the principles and practices you learned in each chapter to solve the problems presented in the video.

Each video depicts a decision-making situation at CanGo, a startup company that sells a variety of products and services, ranging from books and videos to (eventually) providing online video games. Each of chapters 2-17 will have one video. Chapter 1 has two. The video segments are pretty much independent of one another. Therefore, you and your professor may decide to use only, say, the videos from chapters 5, 8, and 16 (or some others) without losing any continuity.

MORE PRACTICE

The CD-ROM also contains interactive exercises using tables and figures from the text. All are tied to the video situation, and you can use them to help solve the decision-making problem the video presents. You can also test yourself.

APPLY IT

Few decisions managers make involve just one management function (such as planning). Special Apply It Manager's Portfolio questions help you analyze selected CanGo scenarios in an integrated, multi-function way.

Gary Dessler

CHAPTER 1

MANAGING IN THE
21ST CENTURY

LEARN IT

Test Your Understanding

1. In our club we have people with formally assigned roles, all of whom must work together in order to achieve our goals. It is clear that our club meets the definition of a(n) _____.

2. Someone who plans, organizes, leads, and controls the people and the work of the organization in such a way that the organization reaches its goals is a(n)_____.

3. Sam is a top manager. He spends most of his time_____and setting goals.

4. When Lourdes spends time setting quality standards for her manufacturing team, she is _____.

5. Henrietta supervises the workers who actually produce the Christmas cookies for which her organization is known. She is a(n)_____.

6. Melanie is an ambitious and assertive manager who believes that she is a good public speaker and feels that she has the reputation of being able to deal with difficult people. She exhibits the _____personality orientation.

7. As a sales manager, George has always been competent at developing quarterly sales forecasts, setting realistic sales quotas for the team's commissioned sales reps and hiring exceptional sales people. He gets high marks for his_____skills.

8. Yet, George has been criticized by some of his sales reps as exhibiting favoritism towards his friends on the sales team and being overly harsh to new hires. For this reason he is attending workshop to improve his_____skills.

9. An executive at a top headhunting firm, Savanah is best known for her excellent _____skills, which enable her to cut through drawn out discussions on the details and present the big picture.

10. Toyota, a Japanese company, manufactures its Camry in Kentucky for sales in the United States, Canada and Mexico. It is part of a growing trend toward_____.

11. The huge increase in service jobs means that there is a growing emphasis on_____, the knowledge, education, training, skills and expertise of a firm's workers.

12. In the_____organization, employees reach across the company to interact with whomever they must to get the job done. This speeds decision-making immensely.

13. When Ritz-Carlton allows a front-line hotel employee to spend up to $2,000 to resolve a customer problem—all without consulting his or her supervisor—the company is exhibiting _____.

14. Many employees and supervisors have been affected by the change from a pyramid shaped organization with many levels to a(n)_____organization with subordinates who have more _____.

15. By training and coaching employees, sharing information with them and giving them the resources they need to do their jobs well, Erica is using a_____approach to management.

PRACTICE IT

Videos for The Environment and Foundations of Modern Management.

Video 1 The introductory video shows Elizabeth, CanGo's founder, as she introduces her management and employee team. Here's some background information on Elizabeth, and on each of the people you'll meet:

Elizabeth is CanGo's founder. She's a smart, enthusiastic, and driven CEO. She can be intimidating to some employees, but evokes a great deal of admiration from them as well. She's a visionary with a magnetic personality.

Andrew is director of marketing. He is enthusiastic and creative, and keeps his focus on what the competition is doing. He loves coming up with new ideas, and as far as CanGo is concerned, he's always thinking, "what are we going to do tomorrow?"

Ethel is director of accounting. She is a very detail oriented and meticulous person. Elizabeth and the company depend on her to consider the potential costs of all the new ideas managers and employees at CanGo are coming up with. You can count on her to raise important issues and to help shape profitable projects.

Warren is director of operations. He's been at CanGo since its inception. Warren is a realist, and his colleagues count on him to help make their new ideas become realities. He's also a sports buff: CanGo employees usually refer to him as "coach."

Maria is director of human resources. Like a good HR manager, she's a real "people person" who has to make many of the hard decisions regarding hiring and firing at CanGo. Many employees also turn to her to discuss personnel issues. Elizabeth leans heavily on her to provide advice and feedback.

Clark is director of finance. He's a realist, and whenever new ideas emerge within CanGo, you can count on him to ask, "Are we making our shareholders more money with this idea?" He adds an air of respectability to the young firm and is always the one to ask, "How does this new idea add value to the firm?"

Gail is a senior staff member. She's a perfectionist by nature and is very serious about her work at CanGo. She is quick to volunteer and is willing to work extra hours to get the job done. Her CanGo peers like and respect her.

Nick is also a senior staff member. He's a recent college graduate who is best known for his sense of humor. He is inexperienced, but anxious to please. The other staff members generally tolerate his good-natured antics.

Whitney, another staff member, is a single mother who enjoys her job at CanGo. She was attracted to the company by Elizabeth's concern for her employees and her desire to build an employee-friendly firm.

Debbie, another senior staff member, is a teacher by training. She likes the teamwork at CanGo and enjoys the fast-paced e-business environment CanGo operates within.

Video 2 In the second video clip, a difficult Christmas has just passed and CEO Elizabeth has called a meeting to compare last year's performance with this year's performance. Warren, director of operations, is obviously in the hot seat. He has asked Jack, a consulting operations system engineer, to accompany him to the meeting to offer suggestions on how to correct the problems the company experienced over the past 12 months. As you watch this video, pay particular attention to Elizabeth's management skills and to the techniques she uses to try to get to the bottom of problem, and to get her team started down the road toward a solution.

Watch the videos, and answer the following questions:

1. In terms of what we discussed in Chapter 1 about what managers do, list the specific management tasks Elizabeth seems to be demonstrating in this scenario. If you were watching this video and hadn't been told ahead of time who is in charge, how could you identify the person who is the head of the management team? Is there anyone else in the scenario who seems to be eligible to fill that role? Why?

2. While this and the preceding video in this chapter obviously don't give you a lot of detail about Elizabeth, do your best to answer the following question: Do you think she has the traits and competencies to be a manager? Why or why not?

3. Chapter 1 focuses on the four basic functions of management, namely, planning, organizing, leading, and controlling. This video provides you with realistic examples of what managing is really like in practice. (For example, Warren seems to be getting a little defensive when Elizabeth challenges him, a situation that will require Elizabeth to use her leadership and communication skills). Based on what you see in this video, list other specific examples of what managers do or should do, and categorize the examples under the topics planning, organizing or leading, or controlling.

LEARN IT

Test Your Understanding

1. Dana believes that any employee theft is wrong. This is a_____.

2. Josh is about to go for a job interview. In deciding whether to admit that he never completed his MBA or falsify his resume, Josh is making a(n)_____decision.

3. The pressure to meet unrealistic business expectations led Enron employees to fudge accounting figures and hide liabilities off the balance sheet. This is an example of how _____ _____influence(s) ethics.

4. By having flight attendants dress in costume, welcoming new hires with toys and balloons and teaching everyone company cheers, Southwest Airlines is using_____to create and sustain the company's fun culture.

5. Product managers at The Body Shop would purchase a cosmetic ingredient that has *not* been tested on animals over a less expensive one that has been tested on animals. The Body Shop is an example of a _____ _____company.

6. As a toy manufacturer, Tony's company is careful not to produce products that are potentially harmful for its customers, but also believes that profit maximization is a worthy goal. Apparently this company has adopted the_____view.

7. As part of their Moral Minimum approach to social responsibility, Lashawna's company encourages employees to report organizational wrongdoing. They are encouraging_____ _____ .

8. As the composition of our workforce changes dramatically, it is becoming increasingly important that we _____ _____, which means that we need to plan and implement systems and practices so that the potential advantages of diversity are maximized while its disadvantages are minimized.

9. Jim thinks that all women are poor drivers. This is a(n)_____. Jennifer is a woman, so Jim thinks that she is a bad driver. This is an example of_____.

10. _____is the tendency to view members of one's own group as the center of the universe and other social groups less favorably.

11. Maria is a Chicana woman who sued the company for_____when her boss repeatedly refused to promote her even though she brought in more sales than the white male managers in less senior positions.

12. We have 500 employees, and we recently hired three women vice-presidents even though we only have 100 women employees. This is an example of_____.

13. By admitting that the company hires too few women and African Americans, and by resolving to hire more minorities, the CEO of our company is using strong_____to manage diversity.

14. In the heavily male chemistry department, the University has assigned_____to all female scientists in order to provide them with the support, guidance and counseling that they do not get informally.

15. A written code of conduct or_____ _____will signal that top management is serious about ethics, but the organizational culture must support it and "walk the talk."

PRACTICE IT
Video for Managing in a Cultural and Ethical Environment

In this video, after some introductory small talk, the head of classicartwork.com suggests that Liz and CanGo sell his firm personal information about CanGo's customers. CanGo could make a tidy profit from the sale of this information, and it's not likely that CanGo's customers would find out where classicartwork.com.got its contact list. Furthermore, there is no privacy guarantee on CanGo's Web site. Liz is considering the offer, but she's obviously somewhat uncomfortable with it. Her CFO seems to be leaning toward accepting. As you watch this video, ask yourself, What is the right thing to do in this situation?

Watch the video, and answer the following questions:

1. Go to several popular Web sites, and read and compare their privacy statements. What kind of information about their users do these e-commerce companies gather? Will they sell your personal information?

2. Based upon what the three people in the video have done so far, identify actions or comments which are ethical and unethical.

3. Based on how this chapter defined the meaning of ethics, what do you think is the ethical thing for Liz to do in this case, and why?

CHAPTER 3

LEARN IT

Test Your Understanding

1. Charlie had established the monthly sales goal of $15,000. Last month his unit only sold $10,000. Charlie is looking at a(n)_____.

2. Melanie owns and manages a small, but growing, real estate firm. She is considering expanding her operations into two neighboring counties. This is a(n)_____decision.

3. Decisions that rely upon rules, are procedural in nature, and have well defined information and decision criteria are_____decisions

4. Colleen uses the rule of thumb "never give a perfect score" on a performance appraisal when making her decision as to what score to assign one of her employees. This decision-making shortcut is known as a(n)_____.

5. When choosing a location for the new manufacturing plant, Javier is concerned with several things: the distance from the company's major markets, the location of raw material, the quality and availability of the labor supply. Before making his decision, Javier needs to make his _____clear.

6. Marsha's department has an extremely high turnover rate. When asked by her boss what she is going to do about it, she simply said "Well, if they don't like working here, that is fine with me," instead of generating possible solutions. This rigid strategy or point of view is called Marsha's _____.

7. Our increased troop commitment in the Vietnam conflict is a good example of the _____trap in decision-making.

8. I wanted to eliminate tardiness in my department because it significantly impacts on customer service. After thinking about it I decided to implement attendance incentives. This has greatly reduced tardiness, but has not eliminated it. I guess that I will settle for that. I have decided to _____.

9. K.J. uses a trial-and-error approach to decision-making, bouncing from one alternative to another to get a feel for what works best. K.J. has a(n)_____decision-making style.

10. Lois is the leader of a very cohesive group. There is a strong need and desire among the group members to get along well with each other, and to present a unified front to non-group members. _____is a very real possibility in this situation.

11. When trying to think up a title for their new imprint, the editorial staff held a _____ session in which they all contributed their ideas with one condition: no comments or judgments until all their ideas had been aired.

12. Avram tends to take a logical, structured, step-by-step approach to solving problems. We can say that he has a (n)_____decision style.

13. The first candidate Kareem interviewed for the programmer position said that the job seemed to demand a lot of night and weekend time. He then found himself grilling subsequent applicants about whether they were comfortable working after hours—even though the position had never required it! Kareem has fallen into the_____trap.

14. You're want to resign from your job to start a new business, but before you make your decision you project yourself into the future and imagine what your days are like without your old colleagues, 9-5 hours and a steady source of income. You are analyzing the_____of your decision.

15. Dina gets paralyzed with fear whenever she has to make a decision, with the result that she misses deadlines and just got low marks on her performance review. Dina's mistake is that she overemphasizes the _____of each decision.

PRACTICE IT
Video for Decision Making

This video follows a decision made by Elizabeth (with some help from her employees and managers) to expand CanGo from a company that just offers books and related media over the Internet to one that also offers an opportunity for its users to play online games. After playing several video-type games—often with competing players in other countries—Liz came away very impressed with the prospects for offering opportunities for online games, and she and her team made the decision to get into this business. The video clip picks up at this point, and you see Andrew, Clark, and Warren discussing the pros and cons of this decision, which the company has already made. Andrew and Warren get into a heated discussion about whether or not CanGo's decision to enter the online gaming market is a good one. What sorts of things do you think are influencing them to take their positions?

Watch the video, and answer the following questions:

1. Based on what you read in Chapter 3, what would you suggest to improve the quality of Andrew's and Warren's evaluation of CanGo's decision to enter the on-line gaming market?

2. How valid is Clark's argument that since CanGo has sunk a "ton of money" into on-line gaming, the company is compelled to stick with this decision? Are there any decision-making biases underlying his view?

3. In making this decision, Elizabeth and her team defined the problem as "Should we get into on-line gaming, or not?" Name several other ways in which the team could have defined the problem. What you think actually triggered the problem in this situation?

LEARN IT

Test Your Understanding

1. Joni wants to graduate in two years with a degree in Journalism. This is a(n)_____.

2. At the recent management retreat we determined our firm's_____by answering the question, "What business are we in?" Then, we produced a(n)_____ _____ outlining what business we will be in during the next 3-5 years and the steps we must take to a accomplish this.

3. Our software company plans to shift its focus from technology to customer relationships, so now managers in the human resource department are developing _____ (or_____) plans that spell out how hiring, training, and other department activities can help accomplish this shift.

4. Shana's message to the sales force "Do your best and I'll be happy" is not an effective goal because it is neither_____nor_____.

5. A key characteristic of a(n)_____is that the plans and goals of each subordinate unit contributes to achieving the goals of the next higher unit's plans—and all contribute to the companywide plans and goals.

6. One of the best ways to ensure that employees are motivated to achieve goals is through their _____in setting them._____ ____ _____is a technique in which supervisor and subordinate jointly set goals for the latter and periodically assess progress toward those goals.

7. In order to best forecast sales of our new Robopuppy toy, our company is using _____ forecasting methods, such as gathering the opinion of our seasoned sales force, and _____forecasting methods, in which we use statistical methods to examine data and find underlying patterns.

8. Jeremy is responsible for inventory control at his store. He has decided that the best way to approach this responsibility is to take a series of biweekly observations of his inventory. He is using the _____forecasting method.

9. Katrina is certain that there is a relationship between sales in her department and the county-wide unemployment rate. As she tracks the unemployment rate, she makes her sales predictions. Katrina is doing_____forecasting.

10. While we were developing the Robomaster prototype, we went on the Internet to get sales reports from toy companies with similar products. After analyzing this_____data, we then gleaned_____data by observing 5-7 year old boys—our target market— playing with similar robotic toys.

11. We think that it is very important for our planning premises that we know and understand the competition. We "shop" their stores, hire their workers, and question their customers in order to gain information about them. These practices are known as_____ _____.

12. Even when thinking about your own career, a big first step in the planning process is defining your _____.

13. As most companies are moving away from having plans developed in large planning departments to having plans developed by product and divisional managers, we can say that planning is becoming more _____.

14. At our school we provide every student with a written plan of study that contains the courses that must be taken in order to graduate with a certain degree. This plan of study can be described as a(n) _____plan.

15. The economy was in a severe slump when Angus, a sales manager for a floundering computer company, told his department that they were to achieve a 50% increase in sales over the next two quarters. The sales reps were demoralized because this goal was not_____.

PRACTICE IT

Video for The Basic Planning Process

In this video, Warren, the company's operations manager, is telling one of his employees, Nick, that Nick has to develop a plan for the implementation of CanGo's new on-line gaming business, and that he has to do so as soon as possible. It seems obvious to Nick and his colleagues (but not to Warren) that Nick doesn't even know where to start regarding developing a plan for getting the new business off the ground. He and the team should use a number of planning tools. As you watch this video, consider what you'd tell Nick, and where you think Waren may have fallen down on his job.

Watch the video, and answer the following questions:

1. Explain what Warren did right and did wrong with respect to setting goals for Nick.

2. Create a Gantt chart for Nick that he can use as the basis for the plan he has to develop for Warren.

3. Are there any other types of plans that you think Nick should be using in order to provide Warren with the documentation that he wants, and if so what are they?

4. In this video, Nick's colleagues seem to be making the point that organizing and planning have something in common, since they say Nick won't be able to develop his plan until he gets organized. What do they mean by that? Can a company be organized without a plan? Can a company have a plan if the company is not organized?

APPLY IT

As is often the case, few decisions that managers have to make involve a single function only. In this video, you saw Warren giving an assignment to Nick. Based on what you know about management (from what you've read in chapters 1-4), how would you rate Warren's managerial skills in this video, with specific reference to his ability to plan, organize, lead, and control?

CHAPTER 5

STRATEGIC MANAGEMENT

LEARN IT

Test Your Understanding

1. The process of identifying and pursuing the organization's mission by aligning the organization's internal capabilities with the external demands of its environment is_____.

2. Tim Hortons, a Canadian restaurant chain, plans to boost sales in its existing United States units before opening more restaurants there. This growth strategy is called_____ _____.

3. Nestlè purchasing Hershey's would be an example of the growth strategy known as_____ _____, whereas when Levi's or Nike opened their own retail stores, they were pursuing the growth strategy of_____ _____ .

4. Many companies have downsized their operations in an attempt to remain competitive. This reduction in operations is also known as _____.

5. A temporary network of independent companies linked by information technology to share skills, costs, and access to one another's markets is a(n) _____ _____.

6. Network TV stations must now struggle to win their audiences' attention away from cable stations, DVDs, computer games and other forms of home entertainment. In order to establish a profitable and sustainable position in the industry, each network station needs a(n) _____ strategy.

7. A local electronic and small appliance chain advertises "We will NEVER be undersold." This competitive strategy is known as_____.

8. Cataloger Garnet Hill emphasizes the relationship between cost and quality. Its uniquely designed natural fiber clothes and linens may cost a bit more, but their quality is much higher. Garnet Hill has adopted the competitive strategy known as _____.

9. In SWOT analysis, strengths and weaknesses are _____while opportunities and threats are _____.

10. As a result of a recent SWOT analysis we know that one of our weaknesses is that we have extensive management turnover. We have identified a competitor who is the best in our industry at attracting, developing, and retaining management talent, and are carefully analyzing how he accomplishes this, so that we can improve our operations. This process is known as _____.

11. The pizza business in our region is saturated. Juan owns a small chain of pizza stores. He has low market share and the market is not growing. In terms of the BCG matrix, this business would be characterized as a(n) _____.

12. The collective learning and skills in the organization that often cut across departmental lines are known as _____.

13. Some companies do not utilize forecasting for their strategic planning. Instead, they develop "stories" about alternative possible futures. This approach to strategic planning is called _____planning.

14. Effective implementation of any strategic plan requires_____, which is developing functional plans so that all the firm's activities contribute in an orderly and coordinated way to what the company wants to achieve.

15. Hamel and Prahalad argue that rather than align the strategic plan with current resources, companies should supplement what they have and do more with what they have. In other words, they should_____ _____for future growth.

PRACTICE IT

Video for Strategic Management

One of the things this chapter stresses is the importance of having a clear-cut strategy and strategic plan. As the chapter notes, top managers need a strategy so that "they can know what mail to throw out in the morning." In other words, if you don't have a clear idea of what business you're in, you can't really evaluate proposals to enter new businesses (like the one that Ethel has brought to the management team in this video). The video actually illustrates something that's not uncommon in management: a proposal for forming a joint venture or entering a new business that just comes in unsolicited. In this case, Ethel gets a phone call from an old friend who's now the CEO of the new Radiojustforme.com. He wants to do business with CanGo. As you watch this video, ask yourself if this opportunity really fits with CanGo's strategy. Try to assess the extent to which the management team here is applying the principles and practices of strategic planning.

Watch the video, and answer the following questions:

1. Based on what you read in Chapter 5 and what you know about CanGo, what business is CanGo in now? What are its current corporate and business-level strategies?

2. Liz and the management team are thinking about spinning off the proposed venture with Radiojustforme.com (to offer jazz and swing MP3s), and to commit their own resources for Web page development, logistics, product distribution, and sales for doing so. That would seem to suggest CanGo would actually have to set up a separate subsidiary to run this spinoff. Does creating a separate business and division like this fit the way CanGo management has defined the business now? Why or why not?

3. Compare and contrast the strategy of (1) going into online games and (2) forming a joint venture with Radiojustforme.com. How well does each strategy fit with the business CanGo is in now (assuming it is not offering games at the moment)? Why do you say that, based on Chapter 5's discussions of corporate strategy?

4. Based upon what you know about CanGo's current definition of its business, develop a vision and mission statement for the company.

APPLY IT

As is often the case, few decisions that managers have to make involve a single function only. In this video, you saw CanGo presented with a business opportunity. Try to assess the extent to which the opportunity really fits with CanGo's strategy. To do this, you need to consider CanGo's business plan, as well as the opportunities and threats in its environment. Form teams of three or four students, and size up CanGo's opportunities and threats. Then use that information to explain whether or not CanGo should pursue the suggested new business.

LEARN IT

Test Your Understanding

1. If you want to see the structure of the organization, who is in charge of what area, and who is accountable to whom, you would look at a(n) _____ _____.

2. When Josh, who works in claims, wants to find out what is happening in the underwriting department, he calls Altagracia, who works in that department, instead of going through the chain of command. This is an example of the _____ organization.

3. In our automobile dealership we have a sales department, a finance department, and a service department. While this _____ departmentalization is logical and efficient, it also reduces our dealership's sensitivity to customers and produces fewer generalists.

4. Our publishing company realizes that colleges, high schools, and elementary schools are, in fact, different customers. We have separate divisions serving each of those different customers. We have adopted a _____ form of departmentalization.

5. Like IBM, our company has a(n) _____ structure in which employees are allocated permanently to one special functional department but simultaneously have ongoing assignments to project, custom, product or geographic unit heads.

6. Philippa is a market researcher on my software development team and complains that she often doesn't know whether to report to me or the company's marketing manager. Hence, a big drawback to our matrix organization structure is _____.

7. All product and operational decisions for our apparel company are made at the headquarters level. Don Li, who is the local manager of our Beijing plant, complains he lacks _____ to make decisions affecting his employees. This is one of the drawbacks of a _____ organizational structure.

8. Joe is one of the production managers at our plant, and since production is very essential to our business, he would be considered a _____ manager.

9. We have a very extensive legal department in our corporation. As the head of that department Mr. Nessing has the ability to tell his subordinates what to do, but no ability to order anyone in sales to do or not to do something. He can only advise sales personnel. Within his own department we can say that he has _____ _____.

10. One of my responsibilities is effective inventory control for my department. I have a very capable subordinate who is looking for new challenges, so I have decided to assign her the authority and the responsibility for effective inventory control. This is _____.

11. Advances in interactive communication technology have helped lead to the creation of _____ organizations, which link employees from different functions, departments, levels and geographic areas, so they can have free-flowing communication and get their jobs done more effectively.

12. Our biotech start-up is a _____ organization in which our 35 employees are all members of small, self-managing teams, and there's only one manager. We have no traditional organizational hierarchy or chain of command.

13. Judy only has three people reporting directly to her. This number of people reflects a relatively narrow _____ _____ _____.

14. Our company recently underwent some moderate downsizing. The resulting _____ organization gave the remaining managers a wider span of control, and it _____ workers to do their jobs without having to get managerial approval for every decision they need to make.

15. Most Human Resource Managers are considered _____ managers because they can only advise line managers, but cannot issue orders down the chain of command.

PRACTICE IT
Video for Fundamentals of Organizing

CanGo is at a crucial point, because it is preparing to go public. Issuing an IPO (an initial public offering of its stock) will bring a greater degree of outside scrutiny as potential investors try to assess the company's strengths, weaknesses, and future potential. Liz is obviously convinced that CanGo is not where it needs to be to issue an IPO, at least organizationally. CanGo's CEO seems to know the broad types of organizational changes she wants to make. However, she's obviously faced with the problem of convincing her managers that organizational change is required. In some sense, it's easy, watching the video, to understand her managers' concerns. After all, CanGo now seems to have just the sort of informal, network organization structure that encourages employees to freely "cross over." Things thus get done quickly. What could be wrong with that?

Watch the video, and answer the following questions:

1. Draw the company's current organization chart, as best you can, and list its pros and cons. Now, based on what you've seen in this video clip and what you've learned about CanGo from the previous five chapters, develop a new, preferred organization chart for the company. Include the specific recommendations in this video, such as Liz's desire to move customer service into Warren's department. Make sure it's clear what type of departmentalization you are proposing.

2. It's clear from the video that at least part of the managers' reluctance to reorganize seems to stem from their desire to avoid doing things more bureaucratically. Is it possible that her managers are correct, and that Liz might actually be doing more harm than good by formalizing things at CanGo? Why or why not?

3. What exactly are the pros and cons of hiring two new assistants, as suggested in this video. Might the idea backfire, and if so how?

APPLY IT

As is often the case, few decisions managers have to make involve a single function only. For example, to some extent, Liz's problem here is not just organizational; she has to motivate her managers to implement the change. Similarly, Warren's insistence that his own employees want to deal directly with him could raise the question of whether Warren is ready for broader managerial responsibilities. Watch this video clip, and list and briefly explain five specific examples from it that illustrate the fact that the problem Liz and her team face also involves planning, leading, and controlling.

CHAPTER 7

DESIGNING ORGANIZATIONAL STRUCTURES

LEARN IT

Test Your Understanding

1. Our former CEO was forever tinkering with the organizational chart, but, fortunately, our new CEO understands that_____drive the organization!

2. Last year our company let go of 325 of the company's 575 employees. The reduction in the workforce affected every level in the organization. This dramatic reduction in workforce is also known as_____.

3. When we shifted to purchasing supplies online, we also decentralized our purchasing department to allow lower level employees in all divisions to make quick purchasing decisions. Our company's ability to adapt quickly to new situations is one reason why we consider ourselves a _____organization.

4. One of the most important, but difficult, tasks in designing organizations to manage change is _____, the process of achieving unity of action among interdependent activities.

5. Every two months everyone in our whole company meets to go over the company values, mission statement, and strategic plan for the coming year. We're using_____to achieve coordination.

6. In order to streamline our bank and make every division more entrepreneurial, the president split the company up into_____.

7. Henry is working for a service organization in which he is encouraged to remain open to criticism, and be willing to accept "orders" from lower-ranking employees with expertise in certain areas. Henry is working for an organization that is attempting to pierce the_____ boundary.

8. If you look at our organization chart, it appears that responsibilities are separated into various "smokestacks." We have a production smokestack, a sales smokestack, and a finance smokestack. We are still operating in an environment with a_____boundary.

9. Our sales department is very cohesive. We all identify with "our" department, all the way from company athletic teams to issues with the production department. In terms of boundaries, we all have a(n)_____boundary.

10. At our magazine, the marketing and editorial employees are in constant conflict since marketing is trying to cut back on the space devoted to content. Then, our publisher had a brainstorm and decided that the marketing and editorial staff should switch places for one day. This really helped us reduce_____ _____.

11. A grantwriter for a nonprofit, Tanya was struggling with a grant proposal and couldn't finish it. She came into the development director's office and said, "Jonah, I just can't get the summary right." "Here, hand it to me and I'll finish it," sighed Jonah, who has just become a victim of _____ _____.

12. This morning our product manager handed me a two-inch thick stack of papers and said, "Here are the reviewers' comments on the alpha version of the software. Now run with it!" And, with that he left to go on a business trip. I feel lost. In order to delegate more effectively, our product manager needs to_____the assignment.

13. In practice, you can't decentralize everything. Decentralization must always represent a balance between delegated_____and_____ _____of essential functions.

14. Tanya works in a factory. Her job is very specialized, and she is expected to follow and use the chain of command to resolve issues. Her organization can probably be characterized as being _____.

15. An organic organization uses_____decision making with a(n) _____type of departmentalization.

PRACTICE IT

Video for Designing Organizational Structures

There is an ancient Chinese saying, "Be careful what you wish for, you are liable to get it." As you can see in this video, Elizabeth successfully imposed a much more formal organization structure on her company, and her company is now a long way from its days as a brash startup. The atmosphere is now more professional, more structured, and more formal. These developments were certainly necessary for CanGo to prepare for its planned IPO, which requires a more professional image and formal procedures. So, the changes had the intended benefits. However, as you'll see in this video, one unintended (but not entirely unexpected) outcome was that CanGo seems to be less fun. In other words, in changing its structure and procedures, Liz also changed CanGo's corporate culture, and in some respects not for the better. Watching the video, one has to wonder whether Liz didn't swing too far from an organic to a mechanistic type of organizational approach.

Watch the video, and answer the following questions:

1. Based on what you know about CanGo's industry and environment and its management team, explain (using what you learned in Chapter 7) what the situation calls for, in terms of organizing CanGo's lines of authority; departmentalization; degree of specialization of jobs; delegation and decentralization; and span of control. Do you think Elizabeth was right to impose a more formal organization on the company? Why or why not?

2. Based on what you know about the company, write a short (1/2 page) explanation of how you would reorganize CanGo from its current structure to that of a learning organization.

APPLY IT

As is often the case, few decisions that managers have to make involve a single function only. In this video, Elizabeth almost seems to be more concerned with non- organizational issues than with organizational ones; morale ("It used to be fun," as she puts in) is one example. Give several examples of planning, leading, or controlling issues she seems to be concerned about, and briefly explain how you would address them if you were Elizabeth.

CHAPTER 8

MANAGING ORGANIZATIONAL CHANGE

LEARN IT

Test Your Understanding

1. It is imperative that James implements a change in the work flow at his company as speedily as possible. Because speed is essential, he might consider using _____ as his primary method of overcoming resistance to change. However, the risk here is that influential employees will undermine the change.

2. In Paulette's company, everyone has heard rumors that the organization will soon be undergoing a "reorganization." In the past, this term has been a euphemism for downsizing. Paulette and her co-workers are afraid they will lose their jobs. They are experiencing _____ _____ resistance.

3. Benjamin has decided to distribute an attitude survey to all employees and then hold participatory informational meetings to discuss the results in order to get people to recognize the need for change. In Lewin's model, Benjamin is in the _____ step of the change process.

4. A key point to remember about business reengineering is that its purpose is to reengineer a business _____.

5. A local insurance company has recently decided to send every employee the latest customer satisfaction data, which shows the company ranking fourth out of five companies in customer satisfaction. Management is distributing this information in order to create a(n)_____ ____ _____.

6. The deregulation of the telecommunications industry and the subsequent increase in competition forced our telecom company to undergo a(n) _____ change.

7. While the business press is full of stories singing the praises of visionary change leaders such as IBM's former CEO Lou Gerstner, the truth is that most leaders effect change by creating a _____ _____.

8. We have decided to use action research to help our employees analyze and change various personnel practices such as our performance appraisal system and our reward system. These targets are evidence of the_____ _____management application or intervention.

9. A medical supply company that had recently been lambasted for the poor quality of its products decided to overhaul the entire company to focus on product quality. To keep employees motivated and give them feedback on the change process, the CEO decided to first use business process engineering on one easily fixed aspect of the production process. This company is creating

_____ _____.

10. Now that our company has reorganized into teams, Ellen has dug her heels in and absolutely refuses to take on her new responsibilities as team member. She continues to try to maintain control over her little marketing fiefdom. Yet, when other team members or I complain to Ryan, the team leader, he just shrugs our complaints off and says, "Ellen will come around. Give her time." In the meantime, we pick up her slack! Ryan's conflict resolution style is that of _____.

11. Marsha has discovered that even if both sides differ widely in their approaches, if they trust each other and can discuss their differences in a civil, problem-solving manner, the best conflict-resolution style is often _____.

12. Most labor-management contract negotiations are characterized by both sides giving up on certain issues in order to achieve gains in other areas. This conflict-resolution style is known as _____.

13. Our CEO and company vice presidents tried to make our organization more "open" by sharing information with all employees and even changing the layout of our offices so that everyone—even the CEO—sits in a cubicle. However, within a matter of months, the top managers were still holding meetings away from headquarters and sending out company newsletters with misleading information. This company is in danger of _____.

14. A special approach to organizational and cultural change in which the employees themselves formulate and implement changes that are required (sometimes with the assistance of a trained facilitator) is called_____ _____.

15. When we made the shift from a hierarchical organization to a team-based one, our progress was often halted by conflicts over our roles and responsibilities. Fortunately, our company used a human process application technique called _____ _____ in which data concerning the team's performance was collected and then fed back to the members of the group, to be examined, explained, and analyzed. Then specific action plans were recommended.

PRACTICE IT
Video for Managing Organizational Change

In this video, Liz and Warren have a discussion about the sorts of challenges Warren thinks he'll have in convincing his subordinates to go along with CanGo's new organizational structure (which, you may recall, includes bringing in two new assistants). It seems clear that CanGo's management team has now accepted the need for change, and is comfortable with the new structure and procedures. Managers are one thing, however, and employees are another. Warren is especially concerned about how the change will affect his team. He knows the change is necessary, and he knows that he has to get his team to accept the new way of doing things. The question is, how? Pay careful attention to Warren's concerns as you watch this video.

Watch the video, and answer the following questions:

1. Warren's point about his employees not "being focused on the big picture" is a good one. It's important that all of CanGo's employees have a clear idea of where the company is going and why their efforts matter if you want them to buy into the change. What would you do to show them the big picture?

2. We saw in Chapter 8 that changes in reporting relationships and work assignments which result from organizational restructuring are often a source of employee anxiety and concern. What approach should Warren use in explaining to his team that some of them will now be reporting to a different manager and will be performing new tasks?

3. Chapter 8 contains several useful tools, including a model for analyzing what needs to be changed, and a form for analyzing the need for (and how to) reorganizing. Use these two tools to size up the wisdom of the organizational changes CanGo has made to this point, and to make a recommendation to Elizabeth regarding what still needs to be changed at CanGo.

4. Based on the principles and practices in Chapter 8 and what you know about CanGo from this and the other videos, size up the company's organizational culture and make specific recommendations regarding how Elizabeth and her team can improve it.

APPLY IT

As is often the case, few decisions that managers have to make involve a single function only. In this video, Warren is concerned about getting his team to accept change. Give several examples of planning, leading, or controlling issues Warren should address in this attempt to manage change.

MP
19

STAFFING THE ORGANIZATION

LEARN IT

Test Your Understanding

1. If an organization has men and women performing the same or similar work, they must be paid equal pay according to the _____.

2. _____ _____ is now an important staffing tool for speeding the recruitment process, generating job descriptions, and facilitating training sessions.

3. Our employer feels that after the employee has been recruited and selected, the applicant should go through a(n) _____ program in which we cover such topics as safety rules, information about working conditions, and how to get on the payroll.

4. Yvonne must develop complete and accurate job descriptions for her organization. In order to do so she must first conduct a _____ _____.

5. Jennifer is trying to fill an opening in her department. She is looking for someone who is a college graduate, with at least three years' experience in the field, and with excellent computer skills. These requirements are _____ _____.

6. When Raymundo interviewed me for the Web designer job, he asked me, "If you could change the design of our current corporate Web site, how would you do it?" Fortunately, I was prepared to answer this _____ question, and I aced the interview!

7. Suzanne is very upset. The office where she works is not only male dominated but also prominently displays sexually suggestive posters and calendars that make her feel very uncomfortable. She is experiencing _____ _____.

8. Many companies use a variety of _____ _____ to screen for suitable job candidates, though they must pay attention to legal and ethical constraints. In addition, one can't use them to tell whether a prospective employee is likely to remain _____, an increasingly important consideration given today's uncertain economic climate.

9. Max owns a construction company that has several government contracts. He must make extra efforts to hire and promote women and minorities according to his _____ _____ plan.

10. As a first-line supervisor, Marika must evaluate the job performance of her 15 employees over the last year. Her company uses the _____ _____ method in which several job characteristics are listed, and she must rate each employee from poor to excellent on each of those characteristics.

11. Al, a project manager, hates using his company's performance appraisal method since he must give at least 10% of his employees a "poor" rating. This _____ _____ method places predetermined percentages of employees into performance categories. In recent years, Ford and other companies have come under fire for using it.

12. Helen's company has recently adopted a program by which an employee first gets an oral warning for breaking company rules, then a written warning, then a paid one-day "decision-making leave" for the next occurrence. This paid decision-making technique is known as_____ _____ _____.

13. Na'il feels that he has been discriminated against because of his race and color. If he chooses, he may file a complaint with the_____, which will investigate the charges.

14. Janis has a physical disability that prevents her from typing the reports required of her position. Her employer must make a(n)_____ for her in order to be compliant with the Americans with Disabilities Act of 1990.

15. Most fast-food organizations must ensure that they are paying their employees at least the minimum wage, and are not violating rules concerning the employment of minors. Both of these issues are regulated by the_____ _____ _____ Act.

PRACTICE IT
Video for Staffing the Organization

In this video, the CanGo management team gets a short presentation from Ethel, the company's accountant, regarding the results of the performance appraisals they did for each of their subordinates. As she explains it, the main problem seems to be that the managers are not discriminating very well among employees in terms of performance. Instead, they are rating all or most employees high, which means all are in line for merit raises and promotions. As you watch this video, consider the alternatives the management team proposes.

Watch the video, and answer the following questions:

1. Clark is clearly having a problem with the present system. What kind of error is he making? What can be done to lessen or eliminate this problem?

2. Evaluate Clark's suggestion that managers should rank, not rate, employees. Do you think that ranking generally works well? Will it work well at CanGo? Why or why not?

APPLY IT

As is often the case, few decisions managers have to make involve a single function only. In this video, for instance, you might ask whether Liz and her HR managers really did their jobs in terms of training the management team in how to use the performance appraisal form, and therefore avoid the problems Ethel is talking about now. Based on what you read in this chapter, what other staffing techniques might have helped Liz and the HR manager avoid the problems that are surfacing now? What could Liz have done in terms of planning, leading, or controlling that might have helped avoid these problems?

LEARN IT

Test Your Understanding

1. Jay is somewhat eccentric but he does a good job of influencing us to work willingly toward organizational objectives. This can also be called _____.

2. Natasha's leadership _____ include drive, integrity and self-confidence, but she also possesses important _____, such as her know-how and creativity, that spur us on to achieve our departmental goals.

3. Our team leader, Ranu, is modest, calm and always willing to take the blame when things go wrong, but, at the same time, he sets high standards and will settle for nothing less than the best—whatever gets the job done, he'll do. Ranu exhibits _____ _____ leadership.

4. As a recently hired manager, Oliver knows that power is important to leadership, and that a good degree of his power will stem from his _____ as manager.

5. Even though Ivan is not the manager of his department, he is recognized throughout the company when it comes to meeting ISO quality standards. Normally, if he says that something needs to happen in order to meet the latest quality standards, it happens. In this regard, Ivan is a(n) _____.

6. Martha always lets her subordinates know what she expects of them, gives them specific guidance as to what should be done, how it should be done and when it should be finished. According to the Ohio State University studies, Martha is exhibiting _____leadership.

7. Colleen is a very _____ leader in that when there is a need to make a decision, she makes the decision herself, rather than involving her subordinates.

8. My son works as a store manager for a retail hardware chain. His approach to leadership appears to be focusing upon accomplishing goals while maintaining good working relationships with his employees. He is a _____leader.

9. The educational environment is changing rapidly with the accessibility of the Internet and the move toward distance learning. Many of us at this college feel that we need a _____ leader, which is someone who can bring about change and innovation, and build employee commitment to those changes.

10. As a government agency that deals with people in extreme crisis, we feel that it is important that we choose a leader who will be a role model of patience, build effective relationships internally and externally, have a high degree of social sensitivity, and be a good communicator. The high scorers in these areas have mostly been _____.

11. David took an LPC test and, much to his surprise, found out that he had a very low LPC score. According to Fiedler, this means that he would be a _____ oriented leader.

12. I recently hired several young workers who seem to be willing to do the job but don't know how to do it. According to the Situational Leadership Theory, I should use the _____ style of leadership with these workers and a _____ style for those who are clearly able to do the job but are unwilling to do it.

13. Tamara is a supervisor with 10 highly skilled and highly educated subordinates. It is clear to even the most casual observer that she has an "in" group and an "out" group. According to the _____ _____ _____ theory, the "in" group members will be treated better and perform better than their "out" group counterparts.

14. Rebecca tends to give unreasonable work assignments and make the job difficult or unpleasant. She also frequently disciplines her staff for minor infractions and has even fired some of her employees. She speaks of these incidents as "setting an example." In terms of power, Rebecca appears to be exercising her _____ power.

15. Our new president is excellent! She shows me how to think about problems in new ways. In terms of being a transformational leader, she is providing _____.

PRACTICE IT

Video for Being a Leader

In this video scenario, CanGo CEO Elizabeth has decided to take her online book company into a new business-providing users with the ability to engage in real time online games like chess with people who may be thousands of miles away. As you'll see from the first scenario in this video, she's enormously enthusiastic about the business' potential. However, she knows she can't get this new business off the ground by herself. Her first order of business is to use her leadership skills to get her management team and employees to help her develop the plans CanGo needs to start this new business. As we saw in Chapter 10, the leader always has a variety of tools in his or her leadership toolbox. The video shows the leadership style Elizabeth uses, first with her management team (scenario one), and then with her employees (scenario two). The third scenario raises an interesting question: Since Liz is the same person in both scenarios, why is it she seems to have succeeded with the managers, but struck out with her employees?

Watch the video, and answer the following questions:

1. As a quick first approximation, why do you think she struck out with her employees? (Use what you learned in this chapter to answer, please).

2. If you had been in Liz' spot, what two leadership models that you learned how to use in this chapter would you use in these scenario situations, and why?

3. Apply those models in each scenario and explain where you think Elizabeth went wrong and what she should do about it now.

APPLY IT

As is often the case, few decisions that managers have to make involve a single function only. In the situations in this video, how will Liz's leadership style(s) influence her ability to get her plans for CanGo implemented? If her employees don't want to or can't do what she asks of them here, what tools do you think she will have to use to *control* their progress and final results?

CHAPTER 11

INFLUENCING INDIVIDUAL
BEHAVIOR AND
MOTIVATION

LEARN IT

Test Your Understanding

1. Many students enter college with doubts about their ability or capacity to do well in college. In other words their _____ _____ is low.

2. Jillian just won the lottery, so she doesn't have any money worries. She continues to work because she needs to be recognized and appreciated for what she does. In Maslow's terms, it appears that she is motivated to fulfill her _____ needs.

3. I agree with Herzberg: I think that in the workplace _____ factors such as salary and working conditions are dissatisfiers, in that if they are not present or not adequate they will produce dissatisfaction, but if they are adequate they will not motivate the employee.

4. According to McClelland, most teachers would have a strong need to influence or persuade others. He calls this need a need for _____.

5. Kristalee is a financial advisor for a new investment dot com. Her CEO believes that employees will be more motivated if they have a portion of their pay at risk, with the opportunity to earn additional pay. This year, Kristalee brought in so many new clients that she not only got back her 5% at risk but also earned an additional 10%. Kristalee's company is using a(n)_____ _____to motivate employees.

6. I am an assistant art director at the ad agency where I work now, and my boss, Lucy, knows I would really like to be an art director. She and I have worked together to outline specific, challenging goals I need to achieve before I can be moved up to the art director position. We could say that Lucy is using_____ _____ _____.

7. I feel that I am working harder than Dave and yet we are getting the same salary. I don't think that this is fair, so according to_____ theory I will be motivated to achieve a level of fairness.

8. Cyrus was happy to move into the project manager position and pleased that his boss, the vice president of research and development, had such confidence in his abilities. However, with no prior managerial experience and no training, Cyrus soon felt overwhelmed and unmotivated. According to Vroom's theory, Cyrus does not have the_____ that his effort will lead to performance.

9. I think that if you truly want to motivate someone to do something, then you need to apply contingent rewards or punishment to their behavior. This is the basis of _____ _____.

10. I know that many of our employees are bored. I have decided to change their jobs from being fairly specialized and only revolving around two or three tasks, to being responsible for doing four or five tasks on the same level. This horizontal loading of a job is called_____ _____.

11. Manny works for a company in which he changes jobs every nine months in order to increase worker flexibility and alleviate boredom. His company has adopted the practice of _____ _____.

12. Joyce has several customer service people working for her. She frequently observes them "doing something right," but she gives them positive reinforcement only at intervals because she knows that this is the most powerful method of sustaining behavior. She is using_____ _____ .

13. We always get prompt feedback on our work when we do it and praise for extraordinary performance at the monthly staff meetings. The leadership at our company knows that _____ is an inexpensive but extremely effective motivator.

14. If our department increases productivity over the next year, a portion of that gain in productivity will come back to us. This incentive plan is known as a _____ plan.

15. A grant writer for an environmental group, Beau was feeling increasingly bored with his work. After a discussion with his boss, the two realized that Beau needed more contact with the donors to whom the proposals were directed. The nonprofit redesigned Beau's job so that he would meet with major donors and solicit information directly from them. This is an example of using _____ _____to build motivators, such as opportunities for achievement and recognition, into a job.

PRACTICE IT

Video for Influencing Individual Behavior and Motivation

In this video, you'll see an uncomfortable meeting in which Liz is talking with Andrew about weaknesses in his department's performance. Andrew, in turn, is trying to get his subordinates to create a new logo quickly. Andrews says he's not clear why his staff is not producing the logo as he's told them to. As you watch this video, pay particular attention to how Andrew responds to Liz, and what you think he does wrong or what he fails to do in his attempts to motivate his staff to come up with the new logo.

Watch the video and answer the following questions:

1. Are you surprised that Andrew's group hasn't accomplished anything on the logo assignment? Why?

2. Whitney clearly feels that her work arrangement is unfair. She feels others in her group have less work to do than she does. How would you use Equity Theory to explain how this situation is leading to decreased motivation on her part?

3. Andrew seems to be under the impression that he is going to motivate his subordinates with a sort of pay for performance incentive plan ("I'll make you marketer of the month," or "We'll go to dinner"). However, judging from his subordinates' reactions, his approach seems to be not just ineffective, but counterproductive. Why you think they're reacting this way? If you were in Andrew's position, how would you handle his task now?

4. Do you think it would help if Andrew created a behavior management program for this particular project (developing a new logo)? Why or why not? Assuming you did decide to go ahead with a behavior management program, analyze the performance problem and recommend how to solve it, including a sample of the forms you might use.

APPLY IT

As is often the case, few decisions that managers have to make involve a single function only. In this video, watching Andrew might cause someone to question his managerial abilities in several areas. For example, watch very carefully how he responds to Liz (about how surprised he is that his employees haven't created the logo yet), and then how (in the video) he seems to be presenting them with the assignment for the first time. There seems to be a disconnect, one that might raise a question about Andrew's forthrightness. Beyond that, the whole situation — whether or not he set goals for completing the task, for instance, and how he controls progress and follows up — raises many questions about his management ability. Watch the video carefully and list the ways in which it raises questions about Andrew's managerial capabilities with respect to ethics, planning, organizing, leading, and controlling. Be specific.

LEARN IT

Test Your Understanding

1. Jennifer is preparing a sales presentation for tomorrow, and she wants to urge the sales reps to emphasize one particular feature of the new software package. This central idea is the _____ in the communication process. Jennifer's actual speech is the _____, and the face-to-face sales presentation is the communication _____.

2. In today's world of multi-tasking and information overload, one of the most important techniques to improve communication is actually one of the hardest to do: _____.

3. During my conversation with Lois over the sales projections, I noticed that she was standing with her arms crossed. This sign of defiance or defensiveness is a form of_____ communication.

4. Henry indicated that getting the Henderson account out was "Top Priority." Does this mean that I am supposed to drop the work I am doing for all my other customers and work on the Henderson account? This is an example of the interpersonal communication barrier of ambiguity of _____.

5. If I do drop everything else and work on the Henderson account, as the boss told me, what is going to happen when all the other customers start demanding their orders? This interpersonal communication barrier is known as ambiguity of _____.

6. When a manager argues, criticizes, or even gives advice to a subordinate, the manager is running the risk of triggering _____ mechanisms.

7. I am in the process of privately selling my car. I have three people who are very interested in purchasing it. I can use this competition to my advantage in negotiations. This knowledge is known as _____.

8. Anita is trying to persuade Shelly, the human resources manager, to support an initiative for a new on-site day care center. She knows Shelly has no children of her own but is very fond of her niece Keisha, who is in day care. Shelly says, "Just think how wonderful it would be for your sister if she could have Keisha near her during the day and could look in on her and know that she is safe!" Anita is trying to persuade Shelly by seeking _____ _____.

9. At monthly meetings our firm shares financial data, explains the numbers and rewards employees for performance improvements. In addition, sales data are posted weekly on company bulletin boards throughout headquarters. This method of fostering trust and commitment is called _____ _____ _____.

10. Social gatherings, attitude surveys, formal suggestion systems, and "open-door" policies are all mechanisms of encouraging _____ communication.

11. Toyota's top managers are often found on the shop floor, fielding questions, providing performance information, and ensuring that all employees are aware of their goals and direction. This practice is known as management by _____ _____.

12. In order to coordinate order processing for our company, which manufactures fleece tops, vests, and jackets, our catalog and retail sales managers have offices right on the factory floor. This is one way in which we seek to improve _____ communication.

13. As a manager, I would not send a memo or email in order to reprimand one of my staff members for poor performance because these forms of communication are too _____ in _____ _____.

14. In our company we use electronic questionnaires, electronic brainstorming tools, and tools for voting or setting priorities as part of an interactive computer-based system that facilitates the solution of unstructured problems by a team of decision makers. This technique is known as a _____ _____ _____ system.

15. We find that it is helpful to use a _____ _____ system that lets each group member put his or her own daily schedule into a shared database to identify the most suitable times for meetings.

PRACTICE IT

Video for Improving Communication Skills

This video raises further concerns about Andrew's managerial abilities. You'll see how Andrew's questionable communication skills confuse the situation with George, a new employee. It not only leaves George uncertain about what his work schedule is going to be, but actually triggers a round of rumors among other CanGo employees. As you watch the video, think about what Andrew could have done to avoid giving George a false impression.

Watch the video, and answer the following questions:

1. Based on what you read in Chapter 12, identify the communication barriers Andrew seems to be ignoring in this video. (Hint: on the CD, we've included a digital version of Figure 12.1, and you may want to use this figure to specify where exactly Andrew is going wrong).

2. If you were a consultant watching this interaction between Andrew and George, what exactly would you tell Andrew to do to improve his interpersonal communications, based on the principles and practices in Chapter 11?

3. What does this situation tell you about how rumors get started? Given that the rumor is now widespread around CanGo, what do you think Andrew (or some other manager) should do to clarify the situation?

APPLY IT

As is often the case, few decisions that managers have to make involve a single function only. In this video, Andrew seems to be exhibiting a number of traits and inadequacies that could raise further doubts about his abilities as a manager. Drawing on what you know to this point about individual behavior and motivation and about planning, organizing, leading, and controlling, how would you size up Andrew's managerial skills in this video? If you were advising Liz, what would you advise her to do about Andrew at this point?

LEARN IT

Test Your Understanding

1. I was surprised to learn that many managers rate _____ _____ programs as their biggest productivity boosters.

2. A _____ is distinguished by the fact that its members are committed to a common purpose or set of performance goals, while a _____ is two or more persons who are interacting with one another in such a manner that each person influences and is influenced by each other person.

3. Members of our work group always "cover" for each other when someone is having a bad day, but members of Chaz's group tend to stick to more rigidly defined roles. The behavior of either group could be labeled a group _____.

4. _____ competition, such as bowling tournaments between teams, tend to boost cohesiveness, whereas _____ competition among team members tends to undermine it.

5. Our work team has a lot of influence in the activities in our own work area, such as setting our own goals and scheduling our work, but we know that Tom is still the supervisor. We are a _____ _____ team.

6. Five of us have been assigned to the task of identifying workable alternatives for increasing productivity by 15 percent. We could be called a _____ team.

7. I wish that I were a member of Farah's team. They set their own work schedule, establish their own goals, hire and train team members, and deal with vendors on their own. They are obviously a _____ _____ team.

8. A semi-autonomous unit that is given the task of developing new and creative ideas and that has its own budget and leader, as well as the freedom to make decisions within broad guidelines, is a _____ team.

9. In today's world of global activities and demands, it is often very useful to utilize _____ teams whose members rarely, if ever, meet face-to-face. Instead, they rely upon information technology for their very existence.

10. Our team, which is spread out across several divisions, kicked off with a cocktail party at which we all introduced ourselves and spoke about our backgrounds and expectations for the team. I'm pleased that each team member has a specific task and role and is enthusiastic about our goal. All of these things contribute to creating a high level of _____.

11. It's a few weeks into our shift to self-managed teams, and members of our team are notably less enthusiastic. There is also considerable confusion about whom to report to on a daily basis. Yet our team leader says, "Not to worry, we're just in the _____ stage of team creation."

12. Bob has decided to avoid some of the possible disadvantages of group decision-making by soliciting experts' opinions via questionnaires. He is using the _____ _____.

13. One or two members of Lisa's group will inevitably try to dominate a group. Lisa has decided that in order to avoid this situation, she will appoint one person to defend the proposed group solution, and another person to argue against the proposed solution. Lisa is using the _____ _____ _____.

14. Our organization discovered the hard way that although social support is important, _____ _____ such as timely information, resources, and rewards that encourage group, rather than individual, performance are more important in ensuring cohesiveness.

15. Perhaps the most important determinant in producing cohesive and effective teams isn't demographic similarity, but creating teams whose members share _____ _____.

PRACTICE IT
Video for Managing Groups and Teams

CanGo is preparing for an IPO. If the IPO is successful, CanGo will have the funds it needs to expand. Before an IPO can happen, it is important that potential investors have a good understanding of what CanGo does and why it will be successful as a publicly owned company. The video revolves around an early stage in the process of taking CanGo public. It involves developing a presentation which makes the case that CanGo is ready for an IPO. Management needs to provide detailed information about all aspects of the business. This is a huge and immensely important task, because if the presentation fails, so may CanGo's IPO. It is not a project for just one person. The task is too big, the timing is too tight, and it requires integrating different areas of expertise. It calls for the work of a cohesive team. The video is focused on the formation of a work team to develop CanGo's presentation. As you watch, pay close attention to how the team is formed and to the directions and guidance the team gets.

Watch the video, and answer the following questions:

1. Based on what you learned in Chapter 13, analyze this team situation and discuss at least eight reasons why the team does or does not have the necessary building blocks to function effectively.

2. List at least six specific reasons why the team is not performing effectively.

3. List and discuss at least five reasons why you believe Nick (as usual, the funny man at CanGo) is or is not a team player.

4. Use the two checklists in Chapter 13, How To Build a Productive Team and How To Improve a Team's Performance, to suggest how you would improve the CanGo team's performance.

APPLY IT

As is often the case, few decisions that managers have to make involve a single function. The manager's actions in this video, for example, seem to reflect widespread inadequacies in how she plans, organizes, and gives orders. Pinpoint at least 4 non-teamwork-related managerial principles or practices she seems to be failing to apply effectively.

CHAPTER 14

CONTROLLING AND BUILDING COMMITMENT

LEARN IT

Test Your Understanding

1. In an effort to make his end-of-year performance results look better than they actually were in terms of expenses, Sam ran low on inventory even though he knew that the inventory would have to be purchased in January at a higher price. This is known as _____.

2. June has established a target of an A grade in her college course. The course has four exams, one paper, and a final exam. After each exam she checks her progress against her goal and takes whatever corrective action is required. June is using the various exams and papers in the course as _____ _____.

3. Our goal this year was to increase profits by 10 percent over last year. Our income statement shows that we increased profits by only 5 percent. In this case the income statement serves as a _____ _____.

4. Our company uses performance reviews as a method for establishing targets and goals for the coming year. They also serve as an excellent tool for identifying performance discrepancies. We use performance reviews as a _____ _____ system

5. Jean is so busy that she has stipulated to her employees that only exceptionally good or bad performance should be brought to her attention. Jean evidently believes in the _____ ___ _____.

6. _____ _____ ___ _____comprise the heart of the basic management control system.

7. _____ control systems involve setting standards and then monitoring performance through some kind of external monitoring process, whereas _____ control systems rely on getting employees to want to do things right—to exercise self-control.

8. One traditional way to monitor performance and maintain control is to use _____ ratios, such as return on investment (ROI), which compare one financial measure on a financial statement to another. Another way is to use _____ ratios, such as profit per customer or profit per customer visit, to sum up a strategy and monitor whether the company is on target in meeting its strategic goals.

9. When companies use computers to get data on the amount of orders an employee processes or other performance measures, they often _____ employees' feelings of personal control. For this reason _____ _____ _____ , while popular, is often controversial.

10. My law firm relies upon a reputation of trust and dependability that I have developed over the years. I am insistent upon every employee knowing and following our code of ethics. Our ethics code is a good example of a _____ control system.

11. Every Friday morning, I meet with all four department heads to discuss circulation numbers and revenues from advertising and to look at our strategies and the assumptions they are based upon. These face-to-face meetings could also be described as an_____ control system.

12. A large local restaurant has decided that one of its goals over the next three months is to increase the sale of desserts by 50 percent. Sales targets were established for the servers, and incentives for

reaching the targets were determined. After the end of the month we were surprised to find out that although dessert sales had increased by 75 percent, there had also been a 30 percent rise in customer complaints over the same period. Most of the complaints concerned "pushy" servers. This is an example of _____.

13. Company-wide integrated computer control systems, known now as _____ _____ _____ , aim to give managers real-time, instantaneous information regarding the costs and status of every activity and project in the business.

14. Shakim's organization desires to build employee commitment and reduce the need for strict written traditional controls. Building employee commitment usually starts with establishing a sound foundation of _____ _____ values.

15. At our Internet startup it's important that everyone—from the CEO to the administrative assistants—be happy to wear many hats and think in terms of "company first" rather than their own little areas. We also seek people who value creativity and risk-taking over security and playing it safe. Hence, when we interview job candidates, we use _____ _____ hiring practices.

PRACTICE IT
Video for Controlling and Building Commitment

Prior to the start of the scenario in this video, Elizabeth has gotten some very bad news from her CFO and her accountant. The bad news is that the CanGo financials look terrible. The company is running at a loss, revenues exceed expenses, and many of the important financial ratios suggest that, financially at least, the company is out of control. Elizabeth understandably does not want to take these results to the Board — or, to be more precise, she does not want to take these results to the Board unless she has a plan in place to correct the problem.

As the video opens, Liz's management team has obviously heard the bad news about the financial results, and they're concerned that one or more of them are liable to take the brunt of the blame. Instead, as you can see in the video, Liz comes in and takes the blame herself, saying that she should have kept her eye on the ball. Considering the gravity of the situation, Liz actually doesn't seem as concerned that you might expect her to be. As you watch the video, consider what you would do if you were in Liz's place and just received those horrendous financial results?

Watch the video, and answer the following questions:

1. In the video, Liz admits to the team that she had not used proper control techniques, particularly in dealing with the holiday rush. Exactly which control techniques should she have been using?

2. Liz says she wants a list of the managers' key success factors (KSFs) for their departments, including those for product quality, customer service, employee morale, and competition. Describe one measurable performance standard for each of the KSFs.

3. Based on what you've seen in this video and in the others, rate the adequacy of CanGo's control system, using the Checklist in chapter 14.

APPLY IT

As is often the case, few decisions managers have to make involve a single function only. This is particularly true when it comes to the control function. In this and the preceding 13 chapters, we've talked about the management process—namely, planning, organizing, leading, and controlling. Since this is a textbook, we necessarily cover the topic sequentially, one topic at a time. But as you can probably imagine, that's not the way managers really manage day-to-day. In other words, you generally won't have the luxury to spend Monday planning, Tuesday organizing, Wednesday and Thursday leading, and Friday controlling. Instead, you'll be doing all these tasks simultaneously. For example, as part of your planning function you'll be sitting with your subordinates trying to formulate goals and motivate them to accept them.

This integrative process is particularly evident when it comes to controlling and building commitment. For one thing, planning and controlling are merely two sides of the same coin: what you control and how you're doing depends entirely on where you want to go, so that deciding where planning leaves off and controlling begins is bound to be somewhat arbitrary. Form teams of three or four students and use Figure 14.1 to present at least five examples showing at what stages in the management process you think CanGo's current "control" problems got their start.

CHAPTER 15

MANAGING WORLD-CLASS
OPERATIONS

LEARN IT

Test Your Understanding

1. A & G Builders are construction contractors who work on their projects on a stop and start basis. In other words, they work on one building at a time, and the specifications for each are different. In terms of the basic types of production processes, they utilize the _____ production process.

2. Our chemical plant uses a _____ production process: it runs uninterrupted for long periods of time.

3. Bonnie has decided that she is going to open a new restaurant. Her target opening date is in four months. She has a good idea of the activities that need to be accomplished to keep to her planned opening date. She feels that the most appropriate scheduling would be a_____ _____.

4. Jim has the job of ensuring that his company has adequate numbers of all required parts and supplies while maximizing cost efficiency. Jim has a job in _____ _____.

5. Jill is the bar manager at a local restaurant. One of her important tasks is effective inventory management. She uses the _____ _____ _____system to determine the quantity of product that will minimize total inventory costs.

6. In a service business, such as a hospital, the _____ include the patients, doctors, nurses, beds, building, equipment and medicine and the _____ system consists of the technology used to heal the patients (diagnostic tests, medical procedures, effective use of medications, surgery, etc.). The _____ is healthier people or people who are experiencing less pain and other symptoms.

7. One of our long-time customers has notified us that they will not be doing any business with us in the future. The primary reason for this is that we ran out of raw materials and were not able to fill his order. The loss of his current order and future orders are _____costs.

8. With the current globalization trend continuing and growing, it is becoming imperative that we expand our operations into Europe. In order to do so we must be able to meet the_____ quality standards.

9. In order for our company to win the _____ _____ award, the entire company needs to be dedicated to _____ in its leadership, processes, human resources, product or services and customer interactions.

10. One of the tools that we utilize extensively to monitor quality problems is a _____ diagram, which outlines the four main categories of problems and helps us to analyze the problem and devise solutions.

11. You probably use _____ analysis without realizing it whenever you assume that a small portion of the defects accounts for a large portion of the problems or, to put it another way, when you assume that a small portion of customers accounts for a large portion of sales.

12. We are intent upon reducing or eliminating seven major waste areas: overproduction, waiting, transportation, processing, stock, motion, and making defective products. In order to do this we are implementing a _____ production control method, which ensures delivery of materials and assemblies just when they are to be used.

13. Whether a customer calls our business's main number, receives a letter from our customer service department, or talks to a sales associate at one of our stores, that instant of contact allows the customer to form an opinion about the quality of our service or product. We can learn a lot from each _____ ___ _____.

14. A logical extension of our current uses of automation combining JIT, flexible manufacturing, and CAD/CIM into one self-regulating process, or the total integration of all production-related business activities through the use of computer systems, is_____ _____ _____.

15. Our small chain of copy shops depends upon providing excellent customer service to give us a competitive advantage over the likes of Kinko's. In order to do this, we concentrate upon the _____ _____, which consists of a well-conceived service strategy, customer-oriented front-line people, and customer-friendly systems.

PRACTICE IT
Video for Managing World-Class Operations

In this video, Warren faces the task of implementing quality improvement in his department. This is particularly important now, given CanGo's prospective IPO. Quality is a subject that's especially relevant to Warren's area, since his group handles order fulfillment and information technology. Warren and his group therefore must be particularly concerned with eliminating errors in order fulfillment and downtime on CanGo servers. As you watch the video, observe the instructions Warren is giving his subordinates, and their reactions (such as, "let's do what?").

Watch the video, and answer the following questions:

1. What was Warren's first mistake?

2. In order to implement a quality improvement program, it is necessary to have a good understanding of the principles and practices of quality improvement. Warren clearly does not. What should he know that he does not seem to know now?

3. As you can see from the video, there is considerable confusion as to the cause of the "poor quality" problem. (For example, Warren's subordinates wonder whether he thinks there's an attitude problem, and some believe the problem is in the warehouse, not in order fulfillment). Form groups of three or four students, and develop a fishbone/cause and effect diagram to help Warren and his team analyze the quality problem. (You can use Figure 15.11 as a guide.)

4. Based on the quality control methods you read about in Chapter 15, how specifically would you suggest CanGo control quality when it comes to order fulfillment?

APPLY IT

As is often the case, few decisions that managers have to make involve a single function only. For example, this video raises important issues regarding Warren's and Liz's leadership, how they plan and set goals, and how they go about solving problems and making decisions. Based on what you see in this video, list two specific planning, organizing, leading, and controlling principles and practices that you think either Warren or Liz (or both) need to apply more effectively. Then choose one or two of these and explain exactly how you would suggest they apply this principle or practice in the situation Warren is facing in this video. For example, How would you go about forming a team, or teams, to improve quality at CanGo?

LEARN IT

Test Your Understanding

1. David turned his stint at teaching business English to Japanese businesspeople into a flourishing business. He formed a team of business English consultants who charge top dollar for their seminars and one-on-one sessions with businesspeople from a wide variety of countries. Because he created a valuable business from nothing, David is a classic example of a(n)_____.

2. David's brother Hank, who owns and runs the family deli, is considered a(n) _____ _____ _____. Yet both he and David, who started a business from scratch, must be well versed in _____ _____ _____, the art of planning, organizing, leading and controlling a small business.

3. _____ is not just for start-ups but for all companies that want to stimulate innovation and create new businesses. When corporations create radically new products or services using internal markets and relatively small autonomous or semi-autonomous business units, we call the process _____.

4. Entrepreneurship typically flourishes in regions where there is greater _____ _____ rather than in countries, like Cuba or North Korea, where there are governmental and bureaucratic obstacles to starting, financing and growing a business.

5. Deborah has struggled for years to get her line of silk-screened greeting cards on the shelves not only of local stationery stores but also of national venues like Barnes and Noble. She has trekked all over the country, showing her wares to buyers, some of who laughed in her face! Deborah certainly possesses _____, a common trait of entrepreneurs.

6. Wendys, McDonalds, and KFC are all examples of restaurant _____, firms that license other firms or individuals to use their business ideas and procedures and sell their goods in return for royalties or other payments.

7. Gabi had always liked being a(n) _____ _____ of her own publishing house because she owns all her business's profits (or losses) outright. However, she came up against a major disadvantage when she was sued by an author's estate over a copyright issue. Her _____ _____ meant that she was solely responsible for the claim against the firm and was forced to use her personal savings to settle the case.

8. Tad wants the freedom and adventure of starting a new business without taking on so much of the risk. He decided that a good option for him would be to open up a Dunkin Donuts store in his neighborhood. By becoming a _____, he gets much of the startup, preparatory work done by Dunkin Donuts and also gets a business that is based on a proven business model.

9. With a winning idea, Michelle was able to fund her Internet startup with _____ from wealthy private investors, known as _____, and also from _____ _____, professionals who specialize in evaluating new venture opportunities and funding those they deem worthy.

10. In 1994 two Cornell students came up with a business idea to create an online community— TheGlobe.com— where participants would go to find news, discussion forums and stuff to buy. They recruited employees in the student lounge, paid them with Dominoes pizza, drained bank accounts and lived off credit cards. Four years later TheGlobe.com sold stock to outsiders and netted $27 million in a(n) _____ _____ _____, and the former dorm buddies became joint CEOs.

11. The two Cornell students who started TheGlobe.com may have had a _____ _____, in which they were liable for the firm's debts only to the extent of their financial investment in the firm.

12. When Eileen finally quit United Airlines to start her own travel agency geared toward group tours for singles, her first step was to conduct a(n) _____ _____. She studied the market, customers, industry and competition to see whether her idea had a reasonable chance of success

13. The chances that Greg will get financing for his startup are practically nil without a solid _____ _____. I urged him to sit down today and outline what business he is in, where it is headed and how he plans to take it there!

14. General Motors, Eli Lilly, Dupont are examples of _____ . Each is a separate legal entity with shareholders that own a part interest in that entity. These shareholder owners also have _____ _____ _____ because the most a shareholder can lose is what he or she paid for the shares.

15. In addition to getting startup funding from their own bank accounts or from family and friends, entrepreneurs are likely to use borrowed capital, or _____, to finance their businesses.

PRACTICE IT
Video for Managing Entrepreneurial Organizations

In this video, Liz is in trouble with her Board of Directors' executive committee, and she knows it. By hiring a consultant, the executive committee has demonstrated their lack of faith in Liz's ability to lead CanGo and to make it a powerhouse in e-commerce. As you can see in the video, the consultant will identify areas of strength in the firm, and shortcomings in Elizabeth's management style. These representatives of the company's Board of Directors (who probably represent the financial companies that helped CanGo raise money through a sale of stock) understandably seem to be more concerned with Liz's shortcomings, insofar as they may prove fatal for the firm. All this is not unusual for a young, fast-growing entrepreneurial firm. As we saw in Chapter 16, entrepreneurs supply the spark that gets firms off the ground. Inevitably, though, they reach a point where everyone (including the entrepreneur) has to ask whether the capabilities and strengths of the company's founder are suitable for expanding the company's success as the firm matures. As you watch this video, listen to what the consultant has to say and to the board members' obvious concerns.

Watch the video, and answer the following questions:

1. From what you know about CanGo, list what you think Liz has done right and wrong with respect to starting CanGo.

2. Chapter 16 lists a number of activity areas for which a new business owner should establish controls. In teams of three or four students, review this list and use it to provide specific examples of controls you believe Liz should have but did not implement for CanGo.

3. Elizabeth is an entrepreneur, and yet the consultant says her main management flaw is that she micromanages too much. Based on what you've seen in the preceding videos, do you agree? Assuming for a moment that the consultant is right, do you think it's possible for a person to be both entrepreneurial and a micromanager? Do the two usually go together (based on what you learned in Chapter 16), or do they tend to be mutually exclusive?

APPLY IT

As is often the case, few decisions that managers have to make involve a single function only. This is particularly the case with respect to the situation Elizabeth finds herself in now with the Board of Directors. Chances are, she didn't just get into this situation by micromanaging. Instead, she exhibited definite shortcomings with respect to planning, organizing, leading, and controlling the people and resources at CanGo. Based on what you've seen in this and the preceding videos, form teams of three or four students and list five specific planning, organizing, leading, and controlling management principles and practices where Liz has fallen down on the job. Then (assuming the board is going to let her continue for now) develop a one-page summary telling her what you think she should do next in order to institute a more effective management system at CanGo.

LEARN IT

Test Your Understanding

1. After several successful years of retail carpet sales, Julie is planning to expand her chain of stores into Canada. If she does so, her business could be characterized as a(n) _____ business.

2. Shell is a giant petroleum company that basically sells the same things in the same ways everywhere. Shell, evidently, is a(n) _____.

3. NAFTA eliminated all barriers to trade among its member countries. In doing so it created a (n) _____ _____ _____ in which goods and services are freely traded among member nations.

4. Companies usually go global in order to expand _____, but they may also seek to reduce _____ _____.

5. We've just decided to sell our toys and games to markets in England, Australia and Canada. By _____ over the Internet, we may avoid _____, costly government taxes on imports.

6. Brun Corporation decided to start its international operations through _____by granting a Swedish firm the right to utilize one of its patents for three years in return for certain royalties.

7. Several Japanese auto manufacturer's have built manufacturing plants in the United States. For the Japanese firms, these efforts are examples of _____ _____ _____.

8. A large U.S. paper manufacturing company has decided to share the costs of developing very sophisticated lumbering technology with a Canadian company. It is in the interest of both companies to pursue this project. This strategic alliance is actually a(n) _____ _____.

9. Having a(n)_____ _____ is a relatively costly strategy for expanding into foreign markets in which the company makes the entire investment itself.

10. Philip, an expatriate manager in our China plant, made a drastic mistake when he assumed that the Chinese employees would be motivated by the same _____ as our American employees.

11. Our CEO is only comfortable internationalizing our operations into countries that are democratic in nature. He wants to limit our operations to a few individual foreign markets. It appears that he has a(n) _____ managerial philosophy.

12. The best global managers are flexible enough to accept that their own ways of doing things are not always the best, and they are willing to solve problems using the best solutions from different systems. We can say these managers have a(n) _____ _____.

13. By teaching local managers in foreign markets how to both use and adapt their sophisticated information technology, many American computer companies have achieved a successful _____ _____.

14. To take advantage of economies of scale, most automakers produce a standardized "world car" and then fine-tune it for subtle differences in national tastes. They are pursuing a _____ _____ strategy.

15. The institutionalization of inequality in India is very high. According to Hofstede, India would rank high in the area of _____.

PRACTICE IT

Video for Managing in a Global Environment

This video illustrates a common situation facing companies, and one, in fact, that's probably not dissimilar to the one that faced the Lincoln Electric Company (introduction to chapter 17). Before the video opened, Andrew suggested that CanGo should expand abroad and begin aggressively marketing its services in other countries. In the video, Liz is not entirely convinced of the wisdom of expanding abroad. After all, CanGo's stock and financial performance have not satisfied the Board of Directors, and Liz barely managed to avoid being booted. She rightfully points out that going global could involve more time, energy, and resources than CanGo can spare at the moment. Furthermore, as the consultant points out, international expansion might require expertise none of the CanGo team possesses. As in our discussion of the Lincoln Electric Company in Chapter 17, it looks like the management team at CanGo lacks strong experience and expertise in doing business abroad. As you watch this video, ask yourself whether you think this team at this juncture should be following up on Andrew's big opportunity and expanding abroad.

Watch the video, and answer the following questions:

1. In Chapter 17 we listed erroneous assumptions managers make in expanding abroad. Based on this video and what you know about CanGo, which of these erroneous assumptions seems to apply to its management team?

2. Before this video opened, Andrew has mentioned to Liz that the country he is particularly interested in expanding to is Japan. Using the principles and practices you learned in Chapter 17, explain to Liz's management team why CanGo is (or is not) a suitable candidate for expanding into Japan, based on the cultural, administrative, geographic, and economic "distance" between Japan and the United States.

APPLY IT

As is often the case, few decisions that managers have to make involve a single function. This is certainly the case when it comes to expanding your firm abroad. In fact, in the case of CanGo, some people might find it just a little mind-boggling that with the company's deteriorating financial situation and Elizabeth's precarious situation with the Board of Directors, CanGo is even considering expanding abroad at this time. In any case, assume for a minute that Liz has agreed to go to the Board of Directors and tell them that she wants to expand abroad. She knows that the Board is going to ask her many questions about how she plans to do this. One thing they're going to want to know are the five main tasks she thinks she and the company will have to address with respect to planning, organizing, leading, and controlling before CanGo can embark on international expansion. In teams of three or four students, put together those lists of tasks so that Elizabeth can take them to her board.

Management: Principle and Practices for Tomorrow's Leaders, Third Edition
PRENTICE-HALL, INC.
SINGLE PC LICENSE AGREEMENT AND LIMITED WARRANTY

READ THIS LICENSE CAREFULLY BEFORE OPENING THIS PACKAGE. BY OPENING THIS PACKAGE, YOU ARE AGREEING TO THE TERMS AND CONDITIONS OF THIS LICENSE. IF YOU DO NOT AGREE, DO NOT OPEN THE PACKAGE. PROMPTLY RETURN THE UNOPENED PACKAGE AND ALL ACCOMPANYING ITEMS TO THE PLACE YOU OBTAINED THEM [[FOR A FULL REFUND OF ANY SUMS YOU HAVE PAID FOR THE SOFTWARE]]. **THESE TERMS APPLY TO ALL LICENSED SOFTWARE ON THE DISK EXCEPT THAT THE TERMS FOR USE OF ANY SHAREWARE OR FREEWARE ON THE DISKETTES ARE AS SET FORTH IN THE ELECTRONIC LICENSE LOCATED ON THE DISK:**

1. GRANT OF LICENSE and OWNERSHIP: The enclosed computer programs and data ("Software") are licensed, not sold, to you by Pearson Education, Inc. publishing as Prentice-Hall, Inc. ("We" or the "Company") and in consideration of your purchase or adoption of the accompanying Company textbooks and/or other materials, and your agreement to these terms. We reserve any rights not granted to you. You own only the disk(s) but we and/or our licensors own the Software itself. This license allows you to use and display your copy of the Software on a single computer (i.e., with a single CPU) at a single location for academic use only, so long as you comply with the terms of this Agreement. You may make one copy for back up, or transfer your copy to another CPU, provided that the Software is usable on only one computer.

2. RESTRICTIONS: You may *not* transfer or distribute the Software or documentation to anyone else. Except for backup, you may *not* copy the documentation or the Software. You may *not* network the Software or otherwise use it on more than one computer or computer terminal at the same time. You may *not* reverse engineer, disassemble, decompile, modify, adapt, translate, or create derivative works based on the Software or the Documentation. You may be held legally responsible for any copying or copyright infringement that is caused by your failure to abide by the terms of these restrictions.

3. TERMINATION: This license is effective until terminated. This license will terminate automatically without notice from the Company if you fail to comply with any provisions or limitations of this license. Upon termination, you shall destroy the Documentation and all copies of the Software. All provisions of this Agreement as to limitation and disclaimer of warranties, limitation of liability, remedies or damages, and our ownership rights shall survive termination.

4. LIMITED WARRANTY AND DISCLAIMER OF WARRANTY: Company warrants that for a period of 60 days from the date you purchase this SOFTWARE (or purchase or adopt the accompanying textbook), the Software, when properly installed and used in accordance with the Documentation, will operate in substantial conformity with the description of the Software set forth in the Documentation, and that for a period of 30 days the disk(s) on which the Software is delivered shall be free from defects in materials and workmanship under normal use. The Company does not warrant that the Software will meet your requirements or that the operation of the Software will be uninterrupted or error-free. Your only remedy and the Company's only obligation under these limited warranties is, at the Company's

option, return of the disk for a refund of any amounts paid for it by you or replacement of the disk. THIS LIMITED WARRANTY IS THE ONLY WARRANTY PROVIDED BY THE COMPANY AND ITS LICENSORS, AND THE COMPANY AND ITS LICENSORS DISCLAIM ALL OTHER WARRANTIES, EXPRESS OR IMPLIED, INCLUDING WITHOUT LIMITATION, THE IMPLIED WARRANTIES OF MERCHANTABILITY AND FITNESS FOR A PARTICULAR PURPOSE. THE COMPANY DOES NOT WARRANT, GUARANTEE OR MAKE ANY REPRESENTATION REGARDING THE ACCURACY, RELIABILITY, CURRENTNESS, USE, OR RESULTS OF USE, OF THE SOFTWARE.

5. LIMITATION OF REMEDIES AND DAMAGES: IN NO EVENT, SHALL THE COMPANY OR ITS EMPLOYEES, AGENTS, LICENSORS, OR CONTRACTORS BE LIABLE FOR ANY INCIDENTAL, INDIRECT, SPECIAL, OR CONSEQUENTIAL DAMAGES ARISING OUT OF OR IN CONNECTION WITH THIS LICENSE OR THE SOFTWARE, INCLUDING FOR LOSS OF USE, LOSS OF DATA, LOSS OF INCOME OR PROFIT, OR OTHER LOSSES, SUSTAINED AS A RESULT OF INJURY TO ANY PERSON, OR LOSS OF OR DAMAGE TO PROPERTY, OR CLAIMS OF THIRD PARTIES, EVEN IF THE COMPANY OR AN AUTHORIZED REPRESENTATIVE OF THE COMPANY HAS BEEN ADVISED OF THE POSSIBILITY OF SUCH DAMAGES. IN NO EVENT SHALL THE LIABILITY OF THE COMPANY FOR DAMAGES WITH RESPECT TO THE SOFTWARE EXCEED THE AMOUNTS ACTUALLY PAID BY YOU, IF ANY, FOR THE SOFTWARE OR THE ACCOMPANYING TEXTBOOK. BECAUSE SOME JURISDICTIONS DO NOT ALLOW THE LIMITATION OF LIABILITY IN CERTAIN CIRCUMSTANCES, THE ABOVE LIMITATIONS MAY NOT ALWAYS APPLY TO YOU.

6. GENERAL: THIS AGREEMENT SHALL BE CONSTRUED IN ACCORDANCE WITH THE LAWS OF THE UNITED STATES OF AMERICA AND THE STATE OF NEW YORK, APPLICABLE TO CONTRACTS MADE IN NEW YORK, AND SHALL BENEFIT THE COMPANY, ITS AFFILIATES AND ASSIGNEES. HIS AGREEMENT IS THE COMPLETE AND EXCLUSIVE STATEMENT OF THE AGREEMENT BETWEEN YOU AND THE COMPANY AND SUPERSEDES ALL PROPOSALS OR PRIOR AGREEMENTS, ORAL, OR WRITTEN, AND ANY OTHER COMMUNICATIONS BETWEEN YOU AND THE COMPANY OR ANY REPRESENTATIVE OF THE COMPANY RELATING TO THE SUBJECT MATTER OF THIS AGREEMENT. If you are a U.S. Government user, this Software is licensed with "restricted rights" as set forth in subparagraphs (a)-(d) of the Commercial Computer-Restricted Rights clause at FAR 52.227-19 or in subparagraphs (c)(1)(ii) of the Rights in Technical Data and Computer Software clause at DFARS 252.227-7013, and similar clauses, as applicable.

Should you have any questions concerning this agreement or if you wish to contact the Company for any reason, please contact in writing:
Director of New Media
Higher Education Division
Prentice Hall, Inc.